A HISTORY
OF
ENGLAND

A HISTORY OF ENGLAND

SECOND EDITION

DAVID HARRIS WILLSON
University of Minnesota

THE DRYDEN PRESS INC.
Hinsdale, Illinois

Copyright © 1967, 1972 by Holt, Rinehart and Winston, Inc.
All rights reserved
Library of Congress Catalog Card Number: 74-182142
ISBN: 0-03-085315-X
Printed in the United States of America
2 3 4 5   071   9 8 7 6 5 4 3 2 1

Preface

The purpose of this book is to cover the whole span of English history in a single volume, to give form and meaning to the narrative, and to include the results of recent research. Although the story of events has been followed in an orthodox way, with chapters on political history interspersed with chapters on various other themes, the material of the book has been subjected to careful organization. The great amount of research that has been done during the last twenty-five years, both in England and America, has reshaped large sections of English history; and new interpretations have emerged with bewildering rapidity. Since English history is a rich and varied theme, I have tried, so far as I could, to preserve a touch of its fascination.

The book aims at a balance between political narrative and constitutional, religious, economic, and social history. Attention has been paid to the growth of the constitution, the changing position of kingship, the organs of administration, the common law courts, the evolution of Parliament, and the emergence of democracy, although these subjects have not been stressed as much as in some texts. The history of the church, both before and after the break with Rome, and the rise of nonconformity have been treated as matters of fundamental importance. A good deal of economic history has been included: agriculture, industry, and foreign trade, the expansion of England overseas, the Industrial Revolution, and the coming of the welfare state. Social history, now regarded as a field of serious study, is not without its dangers. It must not be antiquarian, or parochial, or loaded with banal generalizations. My method has been to treat social classes —their composition and manner of life, their economic condition and the basis of their wealth or poverty, their rise and decline, the way in which their interests and ambitions were translated into political action. A number of short character sketches have been included, partly because they help to make history come alive, partly because personalities reflect the society of which they are a part.

The appearance of a second edition has enabled me to add new material concerning cultural, literary, and social history. New sections—some of substantial length—deal with medieval architecture, with arts and letters in the age of Chaucer and in the age of Shakespeare, with aspects of economic history in the seventeenth century, with the romantic poets of the early nineteenth century and the principal literary men among the mid-Victorians, and finally with the profound social changes that have taken place in contemporary Britain. The last of these topics brings us to very recent times; a sense of relevance is perhaps increased but so are the dangers of over-simplification.

Two chapters in the first edition describing Anglo-Saxon England have been shortened and combined into one.

I wish to thank the Library of the University of Minnesota, where I have done the bulk of my reading, as well as the Library of the University of Texas, where, as a visitor in 1966–1967, I was shown every courtesy. My thanks are due also to those who have given me permission to have photographs made from books and manuscripts for use as illustrations or to reproduce photographs in their possession. Full acknowledgment of their kind permission is made in the text. Nor should I forget to express, though necessarily in a general way, my sense of indebtedness to the countless historians whose works I have studied over the years in preparing my book. I am grateful to those persons—unknown to me— who read and criticized my manuscript, as also to the efficient editorial staff of Holt, Rinehart and Winston—all of whom saved me from errors. The second edition has profited from the criticism of my former graduate students, now college and university professors. To thank such kindly critics is indeed a pleasure.

In addition I am indebted to Professor Josef L. Altholz of the University of Minnesota and to Professor Gerlof Homan of Illinois State University for reading portions of my book and for making helpful suggestions. I am indebted also to Professor Ralph A. Bellas of Illinois State University. To my wife—on whose sound judgment I have relied at many points—I record once more my grateful thanks.

D. H. W.

St. Paul, Minnesota
February 1972

Contents

CHURCH OF ENGLAND · THE STATE · HENRY'S LAST
YEARS

Genealogical Tables

Maps

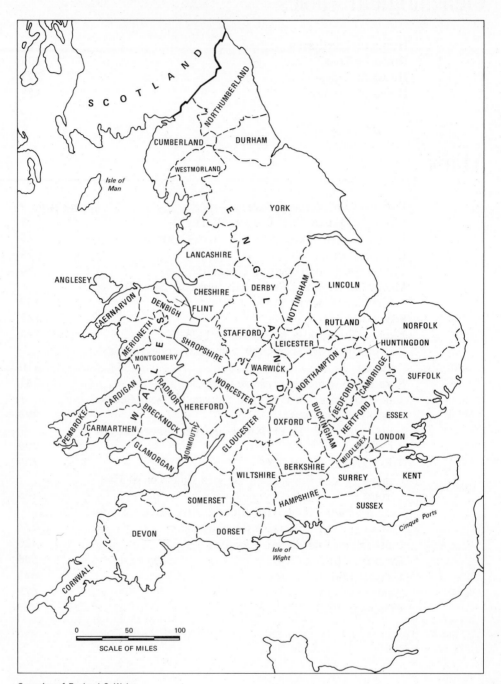

Counties of England & Wales

1

early peoples of Britain

MOUNTAIN AND PLAIN

The island of Britain is divided by nature into two parts, one an area of high hills and mountains, the other an area of rolling plain. The division may be marked by a line running from the southwestern to the northeastern part of the country. Beginning at the mouth of the Exe River in modern Devon, the line runs northward to the Bristol Channel, skirts the mountains of Wales, turns northeast around the southern edge of the Pennine Hills, and reaches the North Sea at the mouth of the river Tees, which separates the modern counties of York and Durham.

To the north and west of the Exe-Tees line there is a highland or mountainous zone which forms the remains of an ancient mountain chain and has three parts: the high moors of Devon, the mountains of Wales, and a very large area to the north which includes much of Scotland and northern England. Through the ages this mountain chain has been worn by erosion and battered by storms from the Atlantic, so that its western coast is ragged and irregular, with deep glens and valleys between the mountain masses. Where agriculture is possible, the soil is thin and stony and the rock formation beneath is very hard, so that water from the Atlantic rains does not sink easily into the ground but runs off in swift unnavigable streams or keeps the earth in a water-logged condition. The area is cold and windy, and although it is of great natural beauty, with the green of the hills running to the water's edge, it is, in general, unsuitable for agriculture and uninviting for permanent settlement.

The country to the south and east of the Exe-Tees line is a gently undulating plain with large expanses of almost level ground. Most of it is less than 500 feet above sea level, and although there are some hills they rarely reach a height of more than 1000 feet. The soil is normally fertile and productive, well suited either for pasture or for the cultivation of crops. There is a good deal of rain, but the climate is drier than in the highland zone, with more sunshine and less wind. Water sinks into the ground more easily. The temperature is moderate, without extremes of heat or cold. Life is easier and more comfortable than it is in the mountains. So long as Britain remained predominantly an agricultural country the lowland plain was the more prosperous, progressive, and thickly populated part of the island. But after the Industrial Revolution in the eighteenth century, population shifted to the areas near the coal fields which for the most part are north and west of the Exe-Tees line.

The water parting in Britain is far to the west. The western streams, flowing from the mountains toward the Atlantic or toward the Irish Sea, are swift and turbulent; but the eastern rivers flowing in the opposite direction are long, gentle, and slowly moving bodies of water on which small boats can travel for great distances. The Thames, of course, is the largest British river. It takes its rise far to the west and flows eastward through the southern part of the plain. To the north of the Thames Valley a number of smaller rivers, including the Ouse and the Welland, flow into the estuary known as the Wash; others, of which the longest is the Trent, join to form the Humber. Still farther to the north many streams —such as the Tees, the Tyne, and the Tweed—come down from the Pennine Hills in an easterly direction. The Severn River in the west is unique. Rising in the mountains of central Wales, it starts eastward, makes a half circle through western England, turns south, and enters the sea through the Bristol Channel. It is a natural and highly important waterway, navigable for long distances. Many cities have arisen upon its banks to form a thickly inhabited region in the western part of the country.

The lowland zone is broken by several chains of low hills. They appear to converge upon Salisbury Plain in the south-central portion of the country. One of these upland ridges, the South Downs, runs along the southern coast in Sussex and Hampshire. Another, the North Downs, follows a roughly parallel line farther to the east, skirting the southern edge of the Valley of the Thames. A third, the Chiltern Hills, stretches toward the southwest through the central portion of the plain; a fourth, known as the Cotswolds, is farther to the west near Wales. In prehistoric times, when most of Britain was covered by dense forest and there were large areas of marsh and fen, men walked on paths along the tops or sides of these chains of hills. One ancient path, known as the Icknield Way, began near the Wash and followed the Chilterns toward Salisbury Plain in the south. Another, the Harroway, running from Kent toward Salisbury, followed the North Downs for part of the distance. Invaders from the Continent, therefore, could quickly penetrate into the lowland zone. The Thames, the Ouse, and the Trent gave easy access to the interior, and the ancient pathways along the hills led directly into the heart of the country. As wave after wave of newcomers arrived in Britain, they took possession of the plain and drove the former inhabitants westward into the mountains. In the most important of these invasions, Anglo-Saxon tribes coming from Germany in the fifth and sixth centuries A.D. drove back the Celts into the mountains of Wales and Scotland and also into Ireland. Yet in truth the highland zone had already become a melting pot of earlier peoples.

Nor was it difficult for primitive men to cross the Channel. In modern times, of course, the Channel has become a protection against invasion; the sea has served England in the manner of a wall or as a moat defensive to a house. But the Channel only became a barrier when there were strong governments in England with armies and navies at their disposal to make invasion dangerous. In early times, when the coast was weakly defended or not defended at all, Britain

ABOVE 500 FEET
BELOW 500 FEET

SCOTLAND

Berwick
Tweed R.
CHEVIOT HILLS
Alnwick
ROMAN WALL
Newcastle
Tyne R.
Hexham
Solway Firth
Carlisle
Durham
LAKE DISTRICT
Tees R.
ENGLAND
York
PENNINE CHAIN
Humber
Mersey R.
Trent R.
Lincoln
Chester
Witham R.
Derby
Nottingham
The Wash
CAMBRIAN MTS.
Shrewsbury
Welland R.
Norwich
W
A
L
E
S
Severn R.
MALVERN HILLS
Worcester
Ouse R.
Wye R.
Stour R.
Gloucester
Colchester
COTSWOLDS
Oxford
CHILTERNS
London
Thames R.
Bath
Reading
Canterbury
Salisbury Plain
NORTH DOWNS
Dover
EXMOOR
MENDIP HILLS
Salisbury
Winchester
SOUTH DOWNS
THE WEALD
Exe R.
Tamar R.
DARTMOOR

0   50   100
SCALE OF MILES

Physical Map of England and Wales

was easy to invade. The passage by sea was short, and every little cove and inlet offered a safe landing place.

The inhabitants of the lowland and of the highland zones have differed from each other in medieval and modern times. This is largely a matter of race, since the plain has been occupied by Anglo-Saxons and the mountains by Celtic peoples. But it is possible that differences may be explained to some extent by geography. The mountaineers of Wales and Scotland have lived in poverty and isolation, cut off from contacts with the outside world. They have cherished their liberty and have resented interference from England. Conservative in temperament, they have been tenacious of old customs and old ways. New ideas and new movements coming into the highland zone of Britain have had to contend and compromise with ancient customs. The result has often been a blending of the two. In the lowland zone, where life is easier and more prosperous and where there are closer contacts with the Continent, changes have come about more readily. Yet in relation to the Continent the whole country possesses some of the characteristics of the highland area. Movements from the Continent, such as the Italian Renaissance or the Reformation or the spirit of the French Revolution, have tended to come to Britain rather late and to have penetrated rather slowly. They have usually been altered and modified and have blended and assimilated with older traditions.

EARLY PEOPLES IN BRITAIN

In a geological sense the Channel is a recent formation which may have come into existence as late as about 8000 B.C. Before that time Britain was connected with the Continent; the North Sea was a vast morass of marsh and fen through which the Rhine meandered toward the Arctic. The first human beings came to Britain by land perhaps half a million years ago. Geologists and archeologists have divided the almost endless eons of the stone age into periods of time and into types of culture, but such matters are beyond the scope of our study. We must think of the primitive men of the stone age as retreating and advancing before ice sheets and glaciers, digging for the precious flints—those pieces of very hard stone they chipped to a point or to a cutting edge—fighting bears and hyenas, stalking the reindeer or the woolly mammoth or the wild horse or the boar in the primeval forest. While the men hunted and fished, the women gathered fruits and vegetables, nuts, edible roots, and shellfish. The people continued to be hunters and gatherers of food, though their flints improved and some of their cultures displayed artistic impulses.

About 2500 B.C., in the Neolithic or late stone age, a more civilized race appeared in Britain. They were a Mediterranean people whose culture was derived originally from the Middle East. They migrated north through Spain and France and crossed the Channel to southern and southwestern Britain, to Wales, to Yorkshire and Lincolnshire, to lowland Scotland, and to northeastern Ireland. They were short, dark, and slightly built, with long heads and delicate features. Archeologists have given them the rather clumsy name of the Windmill Hill people because of an excavation of their remains at Windmill Hill in Wiltshire.

The great contribution of the Windmill Hill people was a primitive agriculture. They did no more than scratch the soil on the tops of the hills with stone hoes and grow a little wheat, but they introduced the fundamental change from a food-hunting to a food-producing society. They had domestic animals—cattle of a fair size, sheep, pigs, and dogs. The women were skillful in making pottery, and, though there is no evidence of weaving in Britain at this time, it is probable that weaving was carried on. Agriculture was supplemented by hunting deer and small game. The men used bows and arrows tipped with finely cut pygmy flints. Larger and heavier flints were used for axes and picks; in fact, the search for flints became a specialized industry in which pits were sunk to a depth of fifty feet and miners crawled through underground shafts carrying little lamps which were probably wicks floating in fat in small cups. The Windmill Hill people built encampments in which they and their animals could find protection, but there were also small villages and isolated houses.

The burial of the dead received much attention and was connected with magic and fertility cults and with worship of the earth as a life-giving mother. Bodies were placed in a crouching position in long pits or barrows and were covered with great piles of stones. Because of the leveling of time, these barrows today look like mere oblong mounds of rocks. But when they were constructed they were often highly elaborate, sometimes with a large wooden façade at one end, sometimes with underground passages and subterranean burial chambers in which new bodies could be placed from time to time. The impulse for these intricate tombs came in part from Iberian adventurers from Spain and Portugal who won easy domination over the simple peasants in Britain. These newcomers were perhaps as interested in trade and in metals—gold, copper, and tin—as they were in the magical cult of the burial barrows.

About the year 1900 B.C. Britain was invaded by a very warlike people who are known as the Beaker folk because of the distinctive shape of their drinking vessels. They belonged to the Alpine race which inhabited the mountainous area of Europe stretching from the Balkans to the Pyrenees. The Beaker folk appear to have come from Spain in two wings or divisions. One wing moved north along the Atlantic coast until it reached the Channel Islands, where it crossed to south-western Britain. A second and larger division expanded into eastern France and northern Italy, then turned north into central Europe, where it met and mingled to some extent with an even more warlike Nordic race to which archeologists have given the unprepossessing name of the Battle-Ax people. The Beaker folk then moved westward to the lower Rhine and from here crossed to many points along the eastern coast of Britain. Large numbers appear to have entered by the Wash and to have moved along the Icknield Way to Salisbury Plain. Their impact upon Britain was tremendous. Larger and more powerfully built than the Windmill Hill people, they quickly dispossessed the Windmill Hill people of their fields and cattle and also probably of their women. The native peoples were submerged, and although they were to reassert themselves at a later date, their civilization disappeared for the time being and the Beaker folk imposed a new type of culture.

We are now entering the early age of bronze. Bronze is an alloy of copper and tin, easily molded when hot but very hard after it cools; it led to the development of better tools and weapons. It is possible that the Beaker folk brought some bronze implements with them, but even before their coming there were smiths in Ireland and in the highland zone of Britain who were making copper axes, awls, and daggers. These copper instruments found a ready market among the Beaker folk, although they also used flints for daggers, knives, arrowheads, and polished axes, and employed a stone ax-hammer borrowed from the Battle-Ax peoples on the Continent. It was only very slowly that the stone age shaded into the age of bronze; stone tools and weapons continued to be used long after bronze ones came into existence.

The Beaker folk were a restless pastoral people who preferred to follow their flocks and herds rather than engage in the harder labor of tilling the soil. Cereal crops played only a small part in their economy. They had a keen interest in trade. Glass, gold, and amber ornaments found in their graves point to trade with the Mediterranean, Ireland, and the Baltic. They wore both linen and woolen clothes, which they held together with buttons. The women were skillful though not artistic potters. The Beaker folk did not build tombs but buried their dead singly in small round barrows in which were placed the weapons and ornaments of the deceased, together with a bowl presumably containing some kind of drink. The grave was then piled high with stones until it resembled an inverted saucer.

Though the Beaker folk did not lavish care upon their graves, they built majestic open-air temples. The most famous, though not the largest, is Stonehenge on Salisbury Plain. Here a space of level ground more than 300 feet across is surrounded by a circular ditch and bank. There is only one entrance which leads to the temple in the middle. This temple consists of two circles of huge stones fixed upright in the ground, one circle within the other. Inside these circles other stones form a kind of double horseshoe. The outer horseshoe is composed of five colossal trilithons, each a pair of huge rectangular stones standing upright with another stone resting upon them in the way a lintel rests over a doorway. The inner horseshoe is composed of "bluestones" known to have been brought from a place 200 miles away. At the center is a recumbent slab which forms an altar. As one stands before this slab looking toward the entrance, one faces the point at which the sun rises on the longest day of the year. Stonehenge and other stone circles show that the Beaker folk believed in a sky-god, connected in some way with the sun, whom they worshiped in the open air. It is possible that they worshiped the sun itself. Stonehenge is a monument to their religious zeal and to their patient labor. It implies a large population, an ability to transport huge stones for many miles (probably by sea), and some sort of political and social organization.

The force of the invasions by the Beaker folk gradually spent itself; their culture lost its distinct individuality; their blood and traditions merged with those of more ancient peoples whose civilization tended to reappear. A period of change and diversity was followed by one of more uniform culture throughout the island. During the later period (roughly from 1500 to 1000 B.C.) the population increased and pushed into Ireland and into areas of Britain formerly unoccupied. The people were largely pastoral, though they grew some barley as well as wheat. Archeologists call them the Urn people because they cremated their dead and buried the ashes either in coffins or in funereal urns. The period is known as the middle age of bronze. Better weapons were developed—archeologists have traced the evolution of a handsome bronze spearhead—clothing became more elaborate, and there were more objects of personal adornment. The civilization of this era displayed a more distinctive British quality.

Stonehenge. (Aerofilms Limited)

THE CELTS

A new series of invasions began about the year 1000 B.C. From about this date until the opening of the Christian Era much of western Europe north of the Alps was dominated by a race known as the Celts. They occupied a huge area which included modern France, Belgium, southern and western Germany, Switzerland, and the western Alps. The Celts did not belong exclusively to one of the three races of Europe (Nordic, Alpine, Mediterranean) but were a mixture of the first and second. They were descended in part from Battle-Ax peoples who came from the north of Europe and in part from Beaker folk who had been living in the upper Danube Valley and in the Alps. And they had in their veins a substratum of the blood of earlier peoples. Hence there was a strong family resemblance between them and the Beaker folk who had come to Britain almost a thousand years earlier and who in time had merged with older peoples to form what we have called the Urn societies of the middle age of bronze. The Celts in western Europe were under pressure from Teutonic tribes pressing down from the north and from Illyrian peoples invading Europe from the east. It is not surprising, therefore, that great numbers of Celts passed over to Britain in successive waves of invasion. They dominated the native peoples, merging with them but firmly establishing their own language and civilization.

It is thought that some Celtic refugees from the Continent may have come to Britain as early as the year 1000 B.C. But they were few in number, and they made little impression upon the Urn communities, whose pastoral life, supple-

mented by hunting, continued much as before. Celtic refugees may have stimulated the transition from the middle to the later age of bronze. New tools and
weapons were developed—an ax with a socket into which a handle could be
inserted, a bronze spearhead, a double-edged sword which provided for the first
time a slashing rather than a stabbing weapon. The Urn people quickly adopted
these implements.

About the middle of the eighth century, that is, about the year 750 B.C., the
Celts invaded Britain in far greater numbers. This invasion was probably begun
by Celts who had been living along the shores of the lakes in Switzerland.
Attacked by Germanic tribes, these lake dwellers migrated to the west and
crossed to Britain. In doing so they set other Celtic tribes in motion, so that the
number of Celts who invaded Britain at this time was very large. They brought a
renewed interest in agriculture. They had a light wooden plow drawn by two
oxen. The plowshare cut a shallow furrow in the soil though it did not turn the
furrow over. Wheat was grown in small enclosed fields, and cattle were bred in
small enclosed pastures. The Celts of this period had superior weapons, both
offensive and defensive, such as swords, spears, shields, and chest pieces for
horses; they also possessed improved tools for carpenters and workers in bronze
and silver, a well-designed sickle, and great bronze caldrons that were symbols
of wealth and power.

There were further Celtic invasions of Britain in the fifth, in the third, and
in the first century B.C. These invasions differed from each other, but they were
similar in that they brought to Britain the early age of iron. Coming into Europe
from the eastern Mediterranean, the use of iron became known to the tribes in
the central part of the Continent and gradually spread to the Celts living in the
west. The first iron-using civilization north of the Alps is known as the Hallstatt
culture. Hallstatt Celts invaded Britain in the sixth century, but the fifth century, when great numbers of Celts came to Britain, was the first true British iron
age. Early tools and weapons of iron were no better than those of bronze, but
iron was plentiful whereas bronze was scarce. Hence new implements of iron
could be readily and cheaply produced and soon passed into the hands of many
persons instead of only a few.

Meanwhile a new culture, the La Tène culture, was developing among
the Celts in eastern France and southern Germany. Its rise was stimulated
by Celtic trade with Italy and southern France. A principal import from
the south was wine, for which the Celts developed a strong liking. Wine was
brought north in bronze and pottery vessels decorated with Mediterranean
designs, and the decorations as well as the contents of these vessels inspired
Celtic craftsmen to develop patterns of their own. The Celts displayed a genius
for linear design and for abstract art. The wild, uninhibited, and flamboyant
tracery on Celtic pottery and weapons gave the La Tène culture a unique
distinction. Hence it may be said that La Tène art owed its existence partly to
Celtic thirst.

A table service of beautiful drinking vessels was the cherished possession of
a wealthy aristocrat or warrior chieftain. It was these Celtic lords of war who
invaded Britain in the third century B.C. They came from France around the
mouth of the Seine, bringing their swords and helmets, their horses and war
chariots, and their elaborate drinking flagons. They met with stiff resistance in
southern Britain, so that this area did not develop a wholly La Tène culture. The
invaders turned north into modern Norfolk and Suffolk, into Yorkshire and

Lancashire, and into Scotland. Their culture followed an aristocratic pattern, with wealth and power concentrated in the hands of a few warrior chieftains. They dressed in long cloaks or tartans fastened at the shoulder with safety-pin brooches. There was a love of personal adornments such as bracelets and necklaces. Society was sufficiently sophisticated for the women to use rouge and hand mirrors and for the men to possess not only dice but loaded dice. Weapons became more elaborate: daggers with bronze hilts and iron blades, iron swords sheathed in bronze scabbards, and oval wooden shields decorated with tracery in bronze. There were also two-wheeled war chariots which opened forward so that a warrior could dart along the shaft between the horses and rush out in front to attack his adversary. And yet, with all their martial prowess, their love of finery, and their artistic achievements, these warrior lords lived in squalor. Their houses were no more than huts without domestic comforts or amenities. It was this combination of rich adornment and squalid living which aroused the contempt of the Greeks and Romans for the barbarians.

The last Celtic invaders were the tribes of the Belgae who began coming to Britain about the year 75 B.C. They had been living in the area between the Rhine and the Seine rivers, under pressure from Germanic tribes to the north and from the Romans who were advancing into France from the Mediterranean. The Belgae—tall, fair-haired, and warlike—were Celts, but they contained a strong Germanic strain. They imposed themselves as a conquering aristocracy over the tribes of southeastern Britain, who hated them so bitterly that the cleavage between the Belgae and their neighbors was very sharp. The Belgae brought with them some features of the La Tène culture, but their distinction lay in their mastery of the arts of daily life. They were skillful in weaving bright-colored tartans; they made pottery on a true potter's wheel; they developed useful crafts such as those of the carpenter, the blacksmith, and the boat maker. Their most important innovation in Britain was a heavy wooden plow drawn by eight oxen. It was equipped not only with an iron plowshare but also with an iron colter to slit the furrow and a moldboard to turn the furrow over. A plow such as this made agriculture possible in the river valleys where the soil, though fertile, was heavy clay which had defied the lighter plow of earlier times. The advanced agriculture of the Belgae, their knowledge of arts and crafts, their military prowess, their trade with the Continent, their coinage, and their political organization under strong tribal chieftains made southeastern Britain the best grain-producing portion of the island, the channel of trade, and the seat of political power.

The religion of the Belgae was dark and superstitious. They believed in goblins, elves, and spirits who dwelt in springs, rocks, and sacred groves. Many of these spirits were malignant and had to be propitiated by sacrifices, even of human beings. There was a priestly caste, known as the Druids, who understood the mysteries of incantations and enchantments and who committed to memory vast quantities of sacred verse. They combined the functions of priests, teachers, and magistrates; they could condemn a man to complete isolation from his fellows.

The Belgae maintained close connections with their kinsmen in France—or Gaul—where Julius Caesar in eight years of brilliant campaigning (58 to 51 B.C.) was pushing the Roman frontier northward. In 55 and again in 54 B.C. he crossed the Channel in the first Roman invasions of Britain. He knew that the Celts in Gaul were receiving aid from the Celts in Britain, and his incursions were therefore in the nature of punitive expeditions. He may have hoped for an easy conquest. A Roman general who conquered a new province was received in triumph upon his return to Rome. By selling slaves and booty from the region he had won he made a fortune and added vastly to his political prestige and power. But Caesar's expeditions to Britain were failures. During his first invasion his fleet was damaged by a storm; the Celts, fighting in chariots, on horseback, and on foot, gave him some sharp encounters; and he returned to the Continent as soon as possible. In his second expedition he marched inland, stormed a Belgic hill fort near Canterbury, crossed the Thames near modern London, and after hard fighting obtained submission and a promise of tribute from the principal chieftains of southeastern Britain. But he returned to Gaul knowing that Britain was still to be conquered. Circumstances never permitted him to make a third attempt.

The Celts in Britain remained independent for almost another century. During that time the Belgic princes grew stronger and extended their territories westward. Their tribal centers, such as Winchester, Chichester, Verulamium (St. Albans), and Colchester, became small towns. Colchester was the capital of the greatest of the Belgic kings, Cunobelinus, the Cymbeline of Shakespeare's play, who ruled from about A.D. 10 to about 40. He possessed a mint and built docks for his extensive trade with Gaul, now a Roman province. Grain, tin, cattle, slaves, hunting dogs, and wild beasts for the shows in Rome were exported by the Celts in exchange for fine pottery, jewelry, and other luxuries. The Celts in eastern Britain were thus exposed to many Roman influences. But their civilization was very warlike, the Belgae fought among themselves, the hostility of other tribes toward them was implacable, and constant war caused hatreds and divisions among the inhabitants of Britain.[1]

ROMAN BRITAIN

In A.D. 43, almost a century after Caesar's invasions, Emperor Claudius dispatched a large army to make a thorough conquest of Britain. This invasion was a logical step in Roman imperial expansion and must be regarded as inevitable. The Romans, firmly established in Gaul, were well aware of conditions in Britain and may have hoped that a conquered Britain could export grain to Rome. They awaited only a fitting time and occasion for conquest. The Roman legions, fanning out from the southeastern corner of the country, subdued the lowland plain within five years. They began at once to lay down the great military roads which radiated from London as a center. A short and violent revolt by the Celts in the year 60, led by Queen Boudicca, was quickly and harshly suppressed.

To deal with the fierce Celtic tribes in the mountainous areas to the west and north, however, was a far more difficult undertaking. There was fighting in Wales for some thirty years. Eventually the country was subdued and was held in subjection through the use of a network of roads and fortresses. Indeed, the Romans found it possible to withdraw their garrisons some time in the second century. But the Celts in Wales were not Romanized; they were merely held

[1] See Jacquetta and Christopher Hawkes, *Prehistoric Britain* (London: Chatto & Windus, 1942).

down by superior force. A conquest of Scotland proved to be impossible, or at least not worth the cost. Agricola, who was Governor of Britain from 78 to 84, pushed north as far as modern Perthshire and inflicted a severe defeat upon the Celts, but the Scottish lowlands later were abandoned. The northern part of Roman Britain was made into a military zone defended by three legions, each of 30,000 to 40,000 men, one stationed at Chester to separate the Celts in Wales from those farther north, one at Carlisle to watch the tribes in southern Scotland, and one held in reserve at York. In 123, during the reign of the Emperor Hadrian, the Romans began the construction of a great wall, with forts and signal towers at fixed intervals, which ran for some seventy miles across the country from Solway Firth to the river Tyne. These arrangements were very expensive, but southern Britain, shielded by Hadrian's Wall and by an army of permanent occupation in the north, enjoyed a period of peace and prosperity, especially during the century from A.D. 200 to 300.

Britain was part of the Roman Empire for almost 400 years, but for a number of reasons the permanent effects of the Roman occupation were small.

In the first place, it was impossible to Romanize the northern military zone. Roman influences, coming into the north with the army, disappeared when the army was withdrawn. The atmosphere was always predominantly Celtic. There was some trade between the army and the native population, and eventually the Romans followed a policy of recruiting soldiers from Celtic farms and villages. These men must have adopted some Roman customs and taken them back to their homes when their period of service was over. Yet Romanization in the north was superficial.

The impact of Rome was far greater in the south. Roman civilization was essentially an urban civilization. The country produced the food and other raw materials requisite for sustaining life and was a pleasant retreat for a short time, but for a man to fulfill his potentialities he must live in a city. The Roman governors of Britain, therefore, set out to encourage urbanization, though they did so by example and not by force. They began by building four model Roman towns—Colchester, Lincoln, York, and Gloucester—with public buildings, amphitheaters, and baths, and filled them with Roman citizens, largely retired soldiers who had served their time in the legions. The government then encouraged the Celtic princes and aristocrats, who had ruled over tribes before the Roman conquest, to convert their tribal centers into cities. The Celtic nobles were soon imitating the model towns built by the Romans.

For various reasons these tribal cities never flourished. In the first place, they were very small. We hear of one which covered only a hundred acres and contained no more than eighty houses. These towns were centers of local government and to some extent of industry and commerce. Economically, however, they were a drain upon the countryside. The goods and services they offered were not an adequate return for the food they consumed. At some time in the third century they began to decline. Trade diminished, public buildings fell into decay, finances were disordered, public life was paralyzed, the citizens lived in squalid and wretched conditions. The Roman model towns did better because they were administrative centers, but they did not grow. In a word, the urban life introduced by the Romans was too costly and too ambitious; a luxury the British economy could not sustain, it was an artificial and not a spontaneous development. Moreover, the position of cities throughout the empire was tending to decline. The emperors, who had lost interest in supporting town life as an end in itself, drained away the wealth of the cities in order to maintain the army in a state of high efficiency. The towns in Britain, affected by these wider developments, suffered accordingly.

Country life, on the other hand, grew in popularity. The wealthy class of Romano-Britons, finding town life precarious, burdensome, and highly taxed, built houses in the country known as villas. These were isolated farmhouses, some quite simple, but some very elaborate. Roman in architecture and in their mode of life, they were surrounded by large open fields cultivated by slaves or semi-servile tenants. Here a British aristocrat could lead a leisurely and cultivated life and could at the same time become more prosperous by the businesslike management of his estate. The villas were self-sufficing units which produced the food that found an eager market in the cities. They also became centers of specialized industries. Because their growth was spontaneous, and because the Celt at heart preferred rural to urban living, the villas displayed a staying power which the towns did not. Old pre-Roman Britain was beginning to reappear.

The bulk of the population lived in native villages which were not a part of the system of villas but quite distinct from it. These villages were primitive collections of huts scattered about without streets. The peasants grew wheat in small fields and kept domestic animals in a common pasture. They displayed few indications of Romanization. Their lives were more peaceful and ordered than in the days before the Roman conquest, but they did not increase in prosperity nor were they greatly touched by Roman civilization.

During the first centuries of Roman rule there was a marked increase in British commerce and industry. The Romans made a determined attack upon the mineral resources of the country. Tin, copper, lead, iron, and coal were mined in large quantities. Except for coal, these items formed important articles of export. British woolen cloth found a ready market in the Mediterranean. Other exports remained much as before—grain, cattle, hides, slaves, and hunting dogs. Imports consisted of wine, olive oil, fine pottery, glassware, and other luxuries. The Romans also stimulated industry. Bricks, glass, pottery, and woolen cloth were manufactured; stone and slate were quarried for building; iron and bronze work of high quality continued from an earlier period. Roman coinage and Roman roads aided both commerce and industry, but as Roman power and affluence declined, exports reverted more and more to raw materials, and imports were largely confined to military stores.

During the fourth century there were increasing signs that the Roman Empire was in decay and that the Roman position in Britain was in grave danger. All along the frontier of the Rhine and the Danube barbarian peoples were pressing in upon Rome. As early as 275 there were raids against the eastern and southern shores of Britain by Saxon pirates from northwestern Germany. New defenses had to be constructed against an enemy who came by sea. A navy was built, fortresses were erected in important harbors, a special officer, known as the Count of the Saxon Shore, supervised the defenses of the coast. About the middle of the fourth century there were raids by the Picts from Scotland, who took to the sea and thus bypassed the Wall, and by Scots from Ireland. The military roads, used by marauders as well as by defenders, enabled Picts and Scots to penetrate to the southern parts of the island. In 367 there was a raid in which Picts, Scots, and Saxons descended simultaneously upon Britain. On more than one occasion, moreover, a Roman general or governor in Britain aspired to become the Emperor at Rome and led his troops across the Channel to fight on the Continent. These troops did not normally return to Britain. Finally, early in the fifth century, when the empire was crumbling at home and the barbarians were at the very gates of Rome, the Romans recalled the remaining soldiers and officials from Britain, leaving the British to fend for themselves. It is not surprising that the Romanized Celts found that the problems facing them were insoluble.

What, then, did the Romans leave that has had a lasting effect upon Britain? They left the roads which continued to be used for centuries and which marked out lines of communication that have not disappeared today. They left a tradition of urban life and a recognition of the favorable position of London as a center for commerce and administration. They also left Christianity, which had come to Britain along with various pagan cults and which was strong enough to survive the Roman collapse. Beyond these things the Romans left very little. Roman civilization, which was to have so profound an influence upon medieval England, was brought in later by the Christian church.

2

the anglo-saxons

The history of Britain during the century and a half lying roughly between the years 450 and 600 is very obscure. Yet these years are of the utmost importance, for during this time Britain was invaded by Germanic tribes of Angles, Saxons, and Jutes who took possession of the lowland plain and made it their own. Joining them in attacks upon Britain were other Teutonic tribesmen, such as Frisians and Swabians. The Celts, though they resisted fiercely, were defeated. Some remained among their conquerors, but for the most part they were driven westward into Devon and Cornwall, into Wales, or into a northwestern area known as Strathclyde. By the year 600 they were largely confined to the mountains of the west and north, leaving the plain in the hands of the invaders. Britain had become England, the land of the Angles; from that time forward the English have been predominantly of Anglo-Saxon blood, though tempered by Celtic and other races.

Written sources for the period of the invasions are extremely few. There is a tract composed during the 540s by a Celtic monk named Gildas. It is not a work of history, but rather a lamentation at the destruction wrought by the invaders and a call to the Celts to repent of their sins. The events described by Gildas are few, although he supplies hints that historians have found important. Two later works, Bede's *Ecclesiastical History of the English People,* completed in 731, and the *Anglo-Saxon Chronicle,* begun in the reign of King Alfred (871–899), contain materials drawn from earlier sources that were closer to the age of the invasions. These materials may have come from oral tradition or perhaps from some unknown written source. In addition, a few references to Britain are to be found in chronicles written on the Continent. These sources taken together are so few that historians have turned to archeology, which interprets the coins and weapons in Anglo-Saxon graves, and to a study of place names, which throws light upon the location and density of population of early Germanic settlements.

From these meager sources scholars in the last half century have constructed a picture of the Germanic invasions.

THE INVASION OF BRITAIN

The homeland of the Angles was Schleswig in southern Denmark; that of the Saxons was Holstein and the surrounding area in northern Germany. These peoples mingled and moved to the west until, just before their conquest of Britain, they occupied the coastal plain of northwest Germany between Denmark and the mouths of the Rhine. Under pressure from the Huns and the Avars, who were pushing into eastern Europe, the Anglo-Saxons turned toward Britain, partly from necessity, partly from desire. For over a century they had been conducting piratical raids against its shores. They knew that the protection of Rome had been withdrawn and that the Celts were left to defend themselves as best they could. The Anglo-Saxons, moreover, were maritime peoples for whom passage by sea in long, open boats presented few difficulties.

A tradition exists that about the year 450 a British ruler in Kent, to whom Gildas gives the name of Vortigern, invited Jutish warriors on the Continent to come to Britain to defend him from the Picts and Scots. According to this legend the Jutes arrived under their chieftains Hengist and Horsa. They served Vortigern for a few years, and then turned against him, slew many Britons, took possession of Kent, and opened the way for other Jutes to cross from the Continent. This story of the origin of the Jutish kingdom of Kent is not at all impossible, for it follows a pattern that can be found elsewhere. Historians have had some difficulty in identifying the Jutes. The easy theory that they came from Jutland has been discarded. Years later when the Kentish kingdom was well established, its social customs and its system of agriculture resembled those of the Franks in Gaul; hence the suggestion has been made that the Jutes were Frankish warriors from the lower Rhine. On the other hand, they may have been Saxons who found Frankish practices established in Kent and did not destroy them. Or the Jutes may have been miscellaneous tribesmen who achieved a sense of unity only after they had settled in Kent.

During the half century after 450 great numbers of Angles and Saxons swarmed into Britain, drove back the Celts, and laid the foundations for later Anglo-Saxon kingdoms. There was a settlement on the coast of Sussex, the land of the South Saxons, though it remained small and isolated. Other bands of invaders followed the river systems of the Thames, the Wash, and the Humber. Along the lower Thames they settled on both sides of the river and established a colony to the north, Essex (East Saxons), which later became of some importance. Farther up the river other Saxons (the West Saxons) first occupied the area of modern Berkshire. Some of them may have come up the river, some may have landed on the southern coast and made their way northward to the Thames Valley, some may have come in by the Wash and approached the river by following the Ouse and the Icknield Way. They then moved westward to establish the kingdom of Wessex in the regions now known as Wiltshire, Somerset, Dorset, and Devon. Other groups of Angles and Saxons, entering by the Wash, settled in East Anglia (the land of the East Angles) or moved far inland to the vicinity of modern Lichfield, Repton, and Tamworth, which became the heart of the later kingdom of Mercia. The Humber River also offered easy access to the interior. Here two settlements were made: Deira, which was colonized very early and extended from the Humber to the Tees; and Bernicia, settled somewhat later, which stretched north of the Tees to the Firth of Forth and thus included a portion of modern Scotland. These two provinces of Deira and Bernicia, though distinct in many ways, were later to form the kingdom of Northumbria. Thus the foundations were laid for the seven Anglo-Saxon kingdoms known as the heptarchy: Kent, Sussex, Essex, Wessex, Mercia, East Anglia, and Northumbria. Their fortunes, as we will find, constantly fluctuated, as did their frontiers.

About the year 500 the Anglo-Saxons suffered a severe defeat at the hands of a British general, Ambrosius Aurelianus, who stiffened the resistance of the Celts in western Britain and won an important victory at Mount Badon, which may have been on the upper Thames near modern Swindon. It has been suggested that he used cavalry effectively against the Saxons, who fought on foot. He forced them to settle down, consolidate their holdings, and abandon their course of easy plunder and destruction. It is on the basis of his achievements that there arose the legends of King Arthur, in which Ambrosius was made a King and his mounted soldiers converted into knights of the Round Table with all the glamour of medieval chivalry.

About the year 550 the Anglo-Saxon advance began once more. The West Saxons, pushing onward until they came to Bath and Gloucester, inflicted a severe defeat upon the Celts in the Battle of Dyrham in 577, a victory which carried the invaders to the Bristol Channel and separated the Celts in Wales from those in Cornwall and Devon. Somewhat later, between 613 and 616, the Angles defeated the Britons at Chester, thus dividing the Celts in Wales from those in Strathclyde. These battles marked the end of effective resistance by the Celts. They had fought bravely over a long span of years, but from the beginning they lacked skill in political and military organization, and their difficulties slowly overwhelmed them.

THE ANGLO-SAXONS

The Anglo-Saxons were barbarians when they invaded Britain. Living far to the north of Europe, they had missed the contacts with Rome which had moderated the savageness of the Germans along the Roman frontier. Their religion was that of Norse mythology; their political organization that of the tribal King or war leader surrounded by young warriors and older counselors. The Anglo-Saxon, tall, fair, red-haired, and blue-eyed, delighted in war. His poetry, sung by gleemen in the halls of the chieftains, recounted the deeds of mighty warriors and told of slaughter and bloodshed.[1] The Anglo-Saxon mother lulling her baby to sleep whispered in his ear that in time he would be a fighter who would redden the field with the blood of his victims. Gildas describes the fury of the Anglo-Saxon onslaught. He tells of the destruction of cities, the massacre of the inhabitants, and the devastation of the countryside. Those Britons who survived, says Gildas, became slaves or fled overseas or took refuge in the bleak western hills. The Roman civilization of Britain, decayed and enervated before the invaders arrived,

---

[1] *Beowulf*, the most famous of Anglo-Saxon poems, though of a much later date, recounts the deeds of a hero fighting monsters and dragons.

now disappeared; and the Romanized Celts who fled to the mountains sank per-force to the level of the cruder Celts with whom they lived.

The spearhead of the Anglo-Saxon invasion was the chieftain and his band of young warriors. It was known as the comitatus or group of companions. Barbaric and primitive as it was, it taught some important lessons. The chieftain must not be surpassed in bravery by his warriors, nor must they fall below the valor of their commander. To leave the battlefield alive after the chieftain had fallen was to earn lifelong shame and infamy. This ideal of mutual support and loyalty between the leader and his companions was a principal theme of Anglo-Saxon poetry. It was to be reflected in later times in the loyalty of a man to his feudal lord, in the loyalty of subjects to their King, in the loyalty of a man to his plighted word. The Anglo-Saxon warrior was not afraid of death; he believed that his fate would come at the appointed hour and that he could do nothing to avert his doom. He possessed a rough honesty, a kindliness toward his own people, and a crude sense of humor which expressed itself in practical jokes and in raucous horseplay. He loved to boast of his great deeds as he feasted in the timbered hall of his leader. The weapons of the chieftain consisted of a helmet, a shirt of ring mail, and a sword with fine decorations and inlaid jewels on the hilt. His men were not armed so well. They had spears and round wooden shields, but only a few had swords.

There was another aspect of the Anglo-Saxon invasions. After the war leader and his warriors had cleared the way, they were followed by the mass of the freemen, who were farmers. These freemen appropriated the arable fields of the Celts. Slowly and painfully over the centuries they brought new land under cultivation and established the villages of medieval England. Below the freemen was a class of slaves, largely captives in war. This threefold division of society into noble or warrior, churl or freeman farmer, and thrall or slave is found among all the early Germanic peoples.

CONVERSION OF THE ANGLO-SAXONS

The Christian Missions

Two themes of central importance in Anglo-Saxon history are the conversion of the heathen invaders to Christianity and the movement of the kingdoms toward political unification. The two themes flow together and are closely related. The church was able to construct an organization common to all England at a time when political unity was still far in the future. A united church pointed the way toward a united kingdom. But the church could not obliterate local patriotism; its greatest work was to bring the warming, uplifting, and civilizing influences of Christianity to a heathen and barbaric folk.

Christianity came to the Anglo-Saxons in two distinct missions: one from the Celtic church in Ireland and Scotland, the other from the church in Rome. The Romanized Celts who had fled into Wales had taken Christianity with them, but the church in Wales made no effort to convert the Anglo-Saxons who, in Celtic eyes, deserved nothing but damnation. Its influence upon England came in a roundabout way through Ireland and Scotland. Although Christianity had penetrated into Ireland in Roman times, the true founder of the Irish church was St. Patrick (c. 389–461). He was the son of a Romanized British official and was probably born near the modern city of Bristol. As a boy of fifteen he was kidnaped by Irish pirates who took him to Ulster. Some years later he escaped, visited Italy, and studied in southern France. Consecrated a bishop in 432, he returned to Ireland to work among the heathen Irish for almost thirty years. He preached from coast to coast, made Latin the language of the Irish church, and brought the country into contact with Rome. The organization he established was episcopal, with the diocese coinciding with the boundaries of the tribe.

After St. Patrick's death his organization disappeared, and the church in Ireland was controlled by monasteries. Founded by Kings or tribal chieftains and ruled by abbots who were normally members of the royal family, the monasteries, rather than the bishops' dioceses, became the units of ecclesiastical jurisdiction. The bishops were reduced to a minor position. The Irish church, cut off from Rome by the barbarian invasions, developed other peculiarities. It differed from Rome in ritual, in the method of consecrating bishops, in the tonsure of the monks, and in the way in which the date of Easter was determined. Lacking any central organization, the church could maintain only a loose discipline and monks were allowed to move from one monastery to another; even an abbot might abandon his charge to lead the life of a hermit. Irish Christianity inclined toward harsh asceticism. The monks lived in gaunt austerity in remote and desolate monasteries that were normally nothing more than groups of beehive huts surrounded by stockades for protection.

Nonetheless, Irish monasticism, especially in the century from 550 to 650, produced a most remarkable series of scholars, saints, and missionaries. Among them was St. Columba (c. 521–597), who on the small island of Iona off the western coast of Scotland founded a monastery which he used as a base for missionary work among the Celts on the mainland. It was from this monastery that Celtic Christianity later penetrated into the north of England and helped to convert the Anglo-Saxons.

In 597, which happened to be the year of St. Columba's death, a group of missionaries from Rome arrived in Kent. They had been sent by Pope Gregory the Great, who had entrusted the mission to Augustine, a Benedictine monk of the monastery of St. Andrew in Rome. Augustine and forty or so companions journeyed through Gaul, beset by fears of what might happen to them in England. However, they were kindly received by King Ethelbert of Kent (c. 560–616), who had always maintained close connections with Christian Gaul and who had married a Christian, the Frankish Princess Bertha. Her presence in Kent prepared the way for the conversion of her husband. A tradition recounts that Ethelbert, fearing that his visitors were magicians, insisted that their first interview be held in the open air. Nonetheless, he permitted them to preach and gave them an ancient British church near Canterbury. Somewhat later he accepted Christianity. In 601 Augustine became the first archbishop of Canterbury when Gregory sent him the pallium, or emblem of office, and empowered him to establish twelve bishoprics in southern England. He created only two, one at Rochester in western Kent, and one at London among the East Saxons, whose King was a nephew of Ethelbert. Another nephew, Redwald, the King of East Anglia, was persuaded by Ethelbert to accept baptism, though he did little more than erect a Christian altar in one of his heathen temples. Thus when Augustine died in 605 he had introduced Christianity into the three kingdoms of Kent, Essex, and East Anglia.

Augustine's accomplishments were rather limited. A narrow, pedantic, and rigid man, he lacked not only the strength and passion of the great missionary but also the tact to deal with delicate situations. He failed to reach an agreement with the Celtic bishops in Wales. Gregory had given him jurisdiction over them, which he asserted in arrogant terms. But the Celtic bishops, connecting Augustine with the Anglo-Saxons, refused to submit to his authority. A great opportunity was thus lost. Acceptance of Christianity by the Anglo-Saxons was at this time a formal matter which made little difference in the lives of the people. After Ethelbert's death in 616 there was a strong pagan reaction in Kent.

Christianity was brought into Northumbria during the reign of King Edwin (616–632). Again a woman played an important part. In 625 Edwin married a daughter of Ethelbert of Kent. It was agreed that the bride should continue to practice her Christian faith, and she brought with her as chaplain a Bishop Paulinus. Shortly thereafter Edwin was baptised. Then followed a rapid though superficial conversion of the Northumbrians. One of the famous passages in Bede's *History* is a description of Paulinus, tall and bent, with black hair, hooked nose, and emaciated face, baptising large numbers of converts in the river Trent.

In 632 Edwin was defeated and slain, Christianity was overwhelmed by a pagan reaction, and Paulinus narrowly escaped with his life as he fled to southern England. This disaster was more than retrieved during the reigns of two Northumbrian Kings, Oswald (633–641) and Oswy (641–670), brothers who had lived in exile at the Celtic monastery on Iona. As soon as Oswald was secure upon his throne he invited the monks at Iona to send missionaries to Northumbria. In 634 a group of monks under Aidan, a Scot, settled on the island of Lindisfarne off the Northumbrian coast. There followed a remarkable flowering of religious life in Northumbria. The Roman church of southern England also reappeared. One reason for the richness and depth of religious and scholarly achievement in Northumbria during the seventh and eighth centuries was the meeting and fusion of Celtic and Roman elements.

The two churches were not as hostile to each other as is often supposed, but since there were marked differences between them, the question arose which usage should predominate in Northumbria. The question was settled at the Council of Whitby in 663, when King Oswy decided to support the Roman forms. This was an important decision, for it meant that the church could be organized along Roman lines and would not be divided between Roman and Celtic practices. It is probable that even if the Council of Whitby had never met, the usages of Rome would have gradually prevailed. The Celtic church, magnificent as were its achievements, depended too much upon the devotion of the individual. The episcopal organization of the Roman church offered greater strength and durability. This was widely recognized. The future belonged to Rome. By the year 700 Christianity had been adopted by all the Anglo-Saxon kingdoms.

Organization of the Church

The Council of Whitby opened the way for the rapid organization of the Roman church in England and for the enforcement of its stronger discipline. This was the work of Theodore of Tarsus, an elderly Greek monk who was archbishop of Canterbury from 669 to 690. He and his close associate Hadrian, the abbot of Canterbury, worked together to give the church order, government, and unity. Theodore placed it firmly upon an episcopal basis, added to the number of bishops, and increased and defined their powers. Bishops formed the very life

St. Luke, Lindisfarne Gospels. The original is in vivid colors. (British Museum, Cottonian MS Nero D. iv, f. 137v.)

The opening words of the Gospel of St. Matthew, Lindisfarne Gospels. (British Museum, Cottonian MS Nero D. iv, f. 27)

of the early church. A bishop was required to travel incessantly, to baptise and confirm, to ordain deacons and priests, to preach, to teach, to visit monasteries. Theodore insisted that bishops regard the archbishop of Canterbury as their superior, that priests not leave their diocese without the consent of the bishop, nor monks their monasteries without the permission of the abbot. Theodore summoned ecclesiastical councils which legislated for the English church as a whole. He was called upon to rule on many points of morals and was celebrated for his system of penances and for his regulations concerning Christian marriage. He was formerly given credit for dividing the English dioceses into parishes, but it was only very slowly that the medieval parish—a village or a cluster of villages, with a resident priest—came into existence. In the age of Theodore the number of priests and the means for their support were quite inadequate for any such arrangement. Most of the early parishes were created by bishops to serve outlying portions of the diocese or by nobles and other wealthy persons who built churches on their lands and provided for the support of a priest. These nobles were apt to regard their churches as very much their own property. Hence there arose the right of advowson, the right of a founder (and his descendants) to appoint the priest for the parish, subject to the bishop's approval. Theodore's church was a united church, owing allegiance to the archbishop of Canterbury; its bishops met in councils to discuss the needs of the church for all England; and its example of unity and centralization offered an ideal to the Kings of the heptarchy.

Monasticism and Learning

The seventh and eighth centuries formed a brilliant period in English monastic life, especially in Northumbria. St. Hilda (614–680), a princess of the royal Northumbrian house, founded about 657 a famous monastery at Whitby of which she became abbess. This monastery was a school of literature and a training center for churchmen. A charming story in Bede's *History* tells how Caedmon, a laborer in the stables at Whitby, came to the abbess and recited to her a religious song which had come to him in a dream, the first English hymn. Benedict Biscop, a Northumbrian noble, devoted his life to the founding and adornment of two monasteries, Wearmouth (674) and Jarrow (681). He made the long journey to Rome five times, returning with relics, vestments, stained glass, and, above all, a magnificent collection of books for his monastic foundations. Another Northumbrian noble, Bishop Wilfrid (634–710), a proud and difficult but most energetic prelate, who deliberately emphasized the pomp of Rome as against the humility of the Irish monks, strengthened discipline in the monasteries and built churches at York, Ripon, and Hexham. There were Irish monks at Iona and Melrose in Scotland, at Lindisfarne in Northumbria, and at Malmesbury in southern England. Thus the monastic ideal, drawn both from Ireland and from Rome, caught the imagination of the Anglo-Saxon people.

Irish and Roman inspiration combined to give the monasteries and schools of England a high level of scholarship and culture. The Irish brought their learning to Lindisfarne, where the beautiful illuminated manuscript known as the Lindisfarne Gospels was written about the year 721. The Codex Amiatinus, a complete manuscript of the Vulgate Bible of St. Jerome, was copied at Wearmouth. Meanwhile, in the south, Theodore and Hadrian founded a school at Canterbury with a splendid library. Canterbury, Malmesbury, York, Wearmouth, and Jarrow were centers of learning and education at a time when the Continent was singularly devoid of culture.

The lovable and saintly Bede (c. 671–735), a scholar of European renown, was England's first historian. He was placed as a boy in the monastery of Jarrow in Northumbria and remained there all his life, "observing monastic discipline and always delighting in learning, teaching, and writing."[2] He knew the works of the early fathers of the church, wrote Latin with ease, and had some knowledge of Greek. His writings included commentaries on the Old and New Testaments, a life of St. Cuthbert, treatises on penmanship and chronology, and, above all, his *Ecclesiastical History of the English People.* It is a work of remarkable breadth. Bede conceives of all the English as belonging to one race, of the English church as part of the church universal, of events in England as a stage in world history. These themes are so skillfully fused that the book becomes not merely a history of the English church but of the formation of a people. Bede possesses the care and caution of the true historian, collecting and sifting his material conscientiously, telling where he obtained his information, and never filling the gaps with guesswork. He has a fine sense of chronology. It is he who introduced into England the practice of dating events from the year of the birth of Christ. This system of dating is not only simple and practical but places the central fact of Christianity at the heart of historical chronology. Bede wrote with simplicity, lucidity, and charm; his works abound in poetic figures and in vivid descriptions. His stories of saints and heroes are wonderfully fresh and natural. And all through his writings there shines his love of God and man.

THE ORIGINS OF POLITICAL UNITY

The Bretwaldas

The political unification of the Anglo-Saxon kingdoms was a slow development which was not complete until the descendants of King Alfred ruled over all of England in the late tenth century. Unification, when it came, meant more than the conquest of one kingdom by another: it meant that the English felt themselves to be one people who of their own good will gave obedience and submission to one single ruler. From early times there had usually been one King strong enough to impose some sort of subjection upon his neighbors. An overking of this kind might make or unmake lesser Kings, he might exact tribute from his dependencies, he might establish personal ties with subject princes on the honorable basis of master and man. The name given to an overking was Bretwalda (Britain-ruler). Bede mentions a number of them. Among the first were several who cannot have been more than mighty warriors against the Celts. King Ethelbert of Kent (c. 560–616), however, was a more important figure. His authority extended to Essex and to East Anglia, and Bede declares that it reached the Humber. During Ethelbert's reign Kent was the most civilized and probably the most populous of the kingdoms. He was the first Anglo-Saxon King to set down his laws in writing. As we have seen, he maintained close connections with the Franks and allowed Augustine to introduce Christianity.

At Ethelbert's death in 616, power passed to his warlike nephew, Redwald of

---

[2] These are Bede's words.

East Anglia, who for perhaps a decade was the most powerful of the south English Kings. Not many years ago a wonderful treasure was excavated at Sutton Hoo near one of his residences. It contained weapons—swords, shields, and spearheads—and other objects of iron and bronze, beautifully and elaborately decorated. There were also fine textile materials. English craftsmanship in weaving and in work in iron and bronze had obviously reached a high level. A purse with a gold frame was found to contain about forty gold Frankish coins. There was also a large number of silver objects—dishes, bowls, spoons, and ladles—which could hardly have been of Anglo-Saxon origin. Upon one bowl appears the monogram of a Roman emperor at Constantinople. The size and splendor of this collection are an indication that an East Anglian King in the seventh century was wealthier and more conversant with other parts of Europe than has been supposed. It is not certain that these treasures belonged to Redwald—they may be slightly later in time—but at least they attest to the wealth of Redwald's line. His authority disappeared with his death, and power passed in turn to the three kingdoms of Northumbria, Mercia, and Wessex.

During the greater part of the seventh century Northumbria was the strongest of the kingdoms. Bede gives King Edwin (616–632) the title of Bretwalda and describes him as the most powerful King that England had yet seen, overlord of most of the kingdoms south of the Humber, though Kent never submitted to him. He was followed by two Kings of outstanding ability, Oswald (633–641) and Oswy (641–670). They did not have great power south of the Humber, where Mercia was growing too strong for them, but they were vigorous Kings in Northumbria. Their reputation was so great that men in southern England looked to them for guidance and advice. "The nobility of all countries," says Bede, "frequented their courts and coveted to be received in their service." Here was the ideal of political unity, though Northumbria never fulfilled the promise it appeared to offer. After Oswy's death in 670 the country was torn by rival claimants to the throne and sank into anarchy.

Northumbria's position of political leadership was taken by Mercia in the eighth century. The tribes in central England had been forced into a confederacy and their territories had been greatly enlarged in the seventh century by an able and warlike King, Penda (632–654). He was followed in the eighth century by two eminent rulers, Ethelbald (716–757) and Offa (757–796), who were much more than local Kings. Ethelbald called himself King of the South English, and Offa used the style *Rex Anglorum*.

Offa incorporated Essex, Sussex, and probably East Anglia into Mercia in order to draw closer to the Continent and to bring London within his dominions. The first English King to have a foreign policy, he corresponded with Charlemagne and was interested in commerce and in the exportation of English woolen cloth. He built a great earthwork known as Offa's Dyke some 120 miles long to delineate his western frontier on the borders of Wales. His charters, written by professional clerks, indicate an efficient machinery of government and a systematic control over lesser Kings. A document of his reign, called the Tribal Hidage, shows that his officials collected tribute in an organized way over a wide area. His code of laws, now lost, was later referred to by King Alfred with respect. Offa exalted the church as a political ally, founded the abbey of St. Albans, and summoned important church councils. A papal mission was sent from Rome in 786 to incorporate England more fully into the church universal. In the next year Offa persuaded the Pope to create an archbishopric at Lichfield. But a third

PICTS

Iona

Firth of Forth

Edinburgh

Melrose   Lindisfarne

BERNICIA

STRATHCLYDE

Jarrow
Wearmouth

N
O
R
T
H
U
M
B
R
I
A

Carlisle

Whitby

Isle of
Man

DEIRA

York

Humber

Lincoln

Chester   LINDSEY

GWYNEDD

MERCIA   Repton

Lichfield   Tamworth   EAST ANGLIA

Sutton Hoo

Gloucester   ESSEX

St. Albans

London

Malmesbury

Dyrham   Rochester

KENT   Canterbury

WESSEX

Salisbury   SUSSEX

Sherborne

Exeter

0   50   100

SCALE OF MILES

England in the Seventh & Eighth Centuries

archbishopric was a step away from political unity, and it is fortunate that it lasted only until 803. Offa was followed by a series of incompetent Kings whose weakness opened the way for the rise of Wessex under King Egbert.

Egbert, King of Wessex from 802 to 839, greatly advanced the position of his kingdom. Having inflicted a defeat upon the Mercians in 825 which ended their supremacy, he was quickly acknowledged as Bretwalda by Sussex, Kent, Essex, and East Anglia. At the same time he thoroughly subdued the Celts in Cornwall. He thus brought all of southern England under the sway of a single kingdom.

England was now to face a new and terrible danger, the invasion of the Danes, Norse barbarians from Scandinavia, before whose onslaught the civilization of Anglo-Saxon England, and, indeed, the civilization of all western Europe, seemed likely to disappear. Most fortunately, Egbert was followed by a long line of brilliant and courageous Kings who slowly subdued the invaders and saved England from destruction.

The Danes

The Danish incursions into England were part of a larger movement of the Scandinavian peoples who, making piracy a business, hurled their destructive raids against all the coasts of Europe. Coming by sea in their long, narrow boats, swiftly propelled by both sail and oar, these Viking marauders could land armies of several thousand warriors at unexpected places, could penetrate far up the rivers of England, France, Spain, and Italy, and escape with their booty before resistance was organized. It was their practice to seize or build an armed camp near their ships, to round up the horses of the locality, and to make rapid inland raids until the terrified inhabitants paid them great sums to move away. The Northmen felt no compunction in sacking monasteries; around the year 800 they pillaged Lindisfarne, Jarrow, and Iona. They not only attacked western Europe but penetrated into modern Russia, connecting the Baltic and the Black seas. They dared to sail westward across the Atlantic until they discovered Iceland, Greenland, and North America.

It is not easy to explain the origins of this movement. In Norway it may have been due to overpopulation. Norse chieftains in the Atlantic fjords practiced polygamy until the coast was teeming with fierce young warriors who much preferred piracy to the slower labor of agriculture. In Denmark, as strong Kings consolidated their position, they drove out rebels and rival princes who led great bands of fighting men abroad. It has been argued that Charlemagne opened the way for the Danes by destroying the sea power of the Frisians. Even so, there is an element of mystery about the origins of the Viking explosion. The Northmen were similar to the Anglo-Saxons of the fifth century: fierce, heathen warriors with a lust for pillage and slaughter. They were very cruel. Human sacrifices were offered to their gods, widows were burned on the funeral pyres of their husbands, prisoners were mutilated. Tall, blond, and blue-eyed, the Danish warriors were dandies in their barbaric way, delighting in scarlet cloaks, in brooches and bracelets, in finely decorated swords and daggers. They combed their yellow hair to a nicety. Their first raids were plundering expeditions, but in 850 a Danish army wintered in Kent; in 865 a great host landed in East Anglia prepared to stay for years, to plunder systematically, and to seize land for Danish settlement. In the next few years the Danes destroyed the kingdoms of Northumbria and East Anglia and had to be bought off by Mercia. In 870 they turned upon Wessex, the last of the old kingdoms that now remained a political and fighting unit.

KING ALFRED, 871–899

Alfred and the Danes

The Danes attacked Wessex just as King Alfred came to the throne. Alfred was the supreme hero of the Anglo-Saxons, a man of many gifts and of great versatility, a statesman and a scholar as well as a splendid general. But his great task was to fight the Danes. He could turn his attention to government and to the arts of peace only in the intervals between his Danish wars. These wars may be divided into three major campaigns. The first was in 871 and 872. The Danes, pressing into Wessex from their base at Reading on the Thames, were met with stiff resistance. Alfred knew, however, that he could not hope to defeat them at this time, and in 872 he paid them tribute on condition that they leave his kingdom. This payment, though humiliating, gave him five precious years in which to build his defenses.

The campaign of 876–878 was much more dangerous. Guthrum, the Viking leader, marched through Wessex to the south coast at Exeter. From there in the winter of 878 he made a surprise attack to the north, seized the royal manor of Chippenham, forced Alfred to take refuge in a swampy region around Athelney, and overran much of the kingdom. Yet in the spring Alfred was able to reassemble his army and to inflict a severe defeat upon the Danes at Edington. This victory was a turning point in the war. Guthrum agreed to leave Wessex and to accept Christianity. The battle at Edington led to other important developments. In 886 Alfred was able to take possession of London, which became a symbol of resistance and a token of hope that the Danes could be overcome. In the same year he made a treaty with Guthrum which fixed a boundary between Wessex and the Danelaw, as the Danish portion of England was called. The line ran from near London to the area of Chester, giving Alfred control of the western portion of Mercia. The possession of London and the treaty with Guthrum added to Alfred's stature as a national leader. His lordship was recognized by all who were free to acknowledge it, not because of his military power but because he stood forth as a national hero who represented the common interests of the English race. He was converting the kingship of Wessex into the kingship of all England.

Alfred had to fight a third Danish war between 892 and 896. A Danish host landed in Kent and made three devastating raids across England as far as Wales and Chester. But Alfred's defenses, instead of collapsing, showed remarkable strength. The Danish army finally broke up and withdrew without a major battle. The campaign made clear that Alfred had organized his military forces along new and successful lines. One of his problems had been the reluctance of the peasant militia, known as the fyrd, to remain under arms when the work of sowing and harvesting demanded attention at home. Alfred met this difficulty in two ways. He divided the fyrd into two parts: one to work in the fields, the other to fight the Danes. By alternating these groups frequently, Alfred managed to keep a large force constantly ready for combat. Secondly, he encouraged the development of a military class, known as thegns, composed of nobles and wealthy landowners, who brought their retainers to battle and gave the army a

England, about 885

28

core of experienced fighting men. Alfred also devised a system of fortresses which served as centers of defense and as places of refuge for the people in time of danger. These fortresses were garrisoned and kept in repair by men from the villages of the surrounding districts. Although his attempt to build a navy met with only moderate success, he so improved the defenses of England that resistance to the invaders was now possible.

The Work of Civilization

Alfred believed that kingship was a sacred trust to protect and to uplift the people; it was his aim not merely to beat back the Danes but to restore the civilization they had nearly destroyed. His efforts to this end reveal his deep religious piety, his interest in scholarship, and his artistic appreciation of the use of words and of the beauties of nature. It is well to stress the practical aspects of his work. His object was to reconstruct society, and there was a utilitarian side to all that he did. To combat the lawlessness that comes with every war, he issued a code of laws, drawn partly from the laws of Wessex but also from those of Kent and Mercia. His code stressed the protection of the weak against the strong; the sacredness of oaths, which played a large part in legal decisions; and the duty owed by a man to his lord. These lords were the thegns whose armed retainers added such strength to the army. Alfred watched the operation of the legal system and did what he could to improve its effectiveness.

It was Alfred's faith in education that is most astonishing. His thegns, he believed, must be trained to take part in government. For this purpose he gathered around him a small group of learned men and founded a palace school to which the aristocracy might send their sons. He set himself the task of translating into Anglo-Saxon a number of Latin books of instruction. With the aid of his scholarly companions he translated five such books. One was the *Pastoral Care* of Gregory the Great, a guide to the clergy in the performance of their duties. Another was Bede's *Ecclesiastical History*. The purpose of this translation was to give the English a sense of their origin and traditions. A similar purpose may have lain behind the *Anglo-Saxon Chronicle,* which was begun in Alfred's reign. In its original form the *Chronicle* commenced with Caesar's invasion of Britain, sketched Roman history to about 450, and thereafter traced the history of Anglo-Saxon England. The original manuscript ended in 892. But it was copied and distributed to various monasteries, and continued by the monks, who included local as well as national history, so that the surviving manuscripts, though much the same for the period before 892, differ greatly thereafter. Alfred also translated a history of the ancient world by Orosius, to which he added much material of his own. His last two translations, the *Consolation of Philosophy* by Boethius and part of the *Soliloquies* of St. Augustine, dealt with religious ideas. Thus Alfred gave his people a remarkable literature in their own tongue.

Alfred's personality and character drew men to him. His lovable qualities, his breadth of interest, his understanding of humanity, his simplicity, idealism, and deep Christian piety—all won him affection. "England's darling," as he was called in the Middle Ages, he is the one ruler of his country who is known as "the Great."

THE RECONQUEST OF THE DANELAW

During the half century after Alfred's death his son and daughter and his grandsons reconquered the Danish portions of England. A number of factors made this achievement possible. For some eighty years there was no assault on a grand scale by armies invading from Denmark. It is true that northwestern England was attacked by Norse chieftains established in Ireland and that a Norse King of Dublin captured York in 919. But invasions from Scandinavia temporarily abated. Moreover, the Danes, now settled for a generation in East Anglia, in eastern Mercia, and in southern Northumbria, were changing somewhat in character. They were, of course, a different race from the Anglo-Saxons, and they were not easily assimilated; having a strong sense of independence they retained their own legal and social customs. But at least they were now farmers rather than warriors. In England, as in the rest of Europe, they turned easily from piracy to legitimate trade. They accepted Christianity; there was intermarriage between the two races; and some English thegns, doubtless at the instance of the King, purchased estates within Danish areas. Finally, the reconquest was made possible by Alfred's military reforms, by the popular support he had inspired for his dynasty, and by the valiant leadership of his descendants.

His son Edward (899–924) and his daughter Ethelfleda, the famous "Lady of Mercia" who ruled that area from 911 to 918, embarked together upon a systematic reconquest of the Danelaw. They built fortresses at strategic points along the border, advanced into one Danish district after another, defeated the Danes in battle, and built new fortresses which they garrisoned with English settlers. By the year 918 Edward had carried the English frontier to the Humber "in one of the best sustained and most decisive campaigns in the whole of the dark ages."[3] Edward's son Athelstan (924–939) captured York in 927. Ten years later he defeated a strong combination of Norsemen from Ireland and of Celts from Scotland and Strathclyde. Fighting continued in the north until 954, a date which marked the final conquest of Scandinavian England. On many counts Athelstan was a remarkable King. His importance in western Europe, his assemblies of the great men of his kingdom, his staff of clerks, his charters, his laws, his intellectual curiosity—all mark him as an outstanding ruler. "He is the one West Saxon King who will bear comparison with Alfred."[4]

THE HEIGHT AND THE DECLINE OF ENGLISH MONARCHY

To later generations the reign of Edgar the Peaceful (959–975) appeared to embody the highest achievement of Anglo-Saxon kingship. Edgar ruled without question over all England, he was accepted as overlord by the Celtic Kings of northern Britain, he kept the kingdom secure from foreign attack, and he maintained a high standard of internal order. He placed his full authority behind a notable religious revival led by Dunstan, whom he made archbishop of Canterbury. King and archbishop worked in close harmony, and the re-establishment of monasticism, only now recovering from the Danish invasions, was the

[3] Sir Frank Stenton, *Anglo-Saxon England* (Oxford: Clarendon Press, 1947), p. 331.
[4] *Ibid.*, p. 352.

greatest achievement of his reign. Edgar ruled with moderation. He ceded lands in northern Northumbria to Kenneth II, King of Scots. He permitted the men of the Danelaw to continue their own legal and social customs. He allowed very great authority to officials known as ealdormen who ruled over local districts. But though Edgar maintained peace, it was a peace made possible by his predecessors; his success was due in part to his own vigor and intelligence but much more to the earlier work of men like the great Alfred or the valiant Athelstan.

A grave weakness of Anglo-Saxon kingship was the lack of any fixed rule of succession. This weakness became obvious at Edgar's death. He left two sons, one by each of his two marriages: Edward, a very young man, and Ethelred, a boy about ten years old. For reasons not altogether clear, certain nobles supported Ethelred for King rather than his brother, and for some months England was close to civil war. Many nobles, moreover, resented the large grants of land made to monasteries in Edgar's reign and hoped to acquire these lands for themselves. The atmosphere was one of discontent and selfishness. It was darkened further in 978 by the murder of King Edward under circumstances of treachery by members of Ethelred's faction.

Ethelred did not participate in the crime, but he never escaped its ill repute. Throughout his reign (978–1016) a deep suspicion existed between him and his nobles. He acted like a man who knew that he had come to power through a crime so black that it could not be forgiven. This was the more unfortunate because at best he was a weak and incompetent ruler. Soft, luxury-loving, and unstable, he was completely ineffective in war. He floundered from one policy to another and constantly appeared to be acting on bad advice; his nickname of Ethelred Unread or Unready was an ironic play upon his name which meant "noble counsel." With a weak King and treachery and suspicion among the nobles, with many of the Danes in England only half loyal to the monarchy, and with oppression of the lower classes and a loss of morale among the people who had no confidence in their leaders, England fell an easy prey to renewed attacks by the Danes.

These attacks began, as they had begun a century and a half before, with isolated raids by small companies of Danes. Such raids were troublesome rather than dangerous, but they increased in size and daring until they involved the whole country. After ravaging wide areas in 991, the Danes obtained from Ethelred 22,000 pounds of gold and silver in return for their promise to depart. This was the first of many payments, known as Danegeld, by which Ethelred weakly bought peace. Danegeld, becoming a tax on land, imposed a crushing burden on the English peasantry. Between 997 and 1012 two large Danish armies remained in England for several years, draining away the wealth of the richest areas.

Then in 1013 the full strength of the Danish kingdom, directed by Swein, the King of Denmark, fell upon England in a fierce thrust at conquest. Advancing with precision and skill, Swein obtained the submission of one area after another. Ethelred took flight to Normandy. Swein died in the moment of his triumph, but the war continued with his son Cnut fighting against the brave Edmund Ironside, the son of Ethelred. There were fierce battles, but when Edmund died in 1016 Cnut was acknowledged as King of all England. A rich and ancient kingdom had fallen to the Vikings because it was wanting in competent leadership.

KING CNUT, 1016–1035

Cnut was a successful ruler. His reign, though humiliating to English pride, was about the best that could be hoped for under the circumstances. Controlling the country easily because of its exhaustion, he was wise enough to respect English institutions and to stress the continuity of his government with the English government of the past. A code of laws issued late in his reign was largely derived from the laws of earlier English Kings. The system of national administration, which had been developing in the tenth century, was also preserved. Royal charters and other documents of the type issued by Ethelred continued to be prepared by Cnut's writing staff.

Cnut saw the advantages of close alliance with the church. This alliance was based upon worldly wisdom as well as upon the veneration paid by a barbarian to the higher civilization the church represented. The church's sanction strengthened his hold upon the people; churchmen supplied him with his writing staff and recorded his reign with sympathy. He was the first Viking to be accepted by other rulers as a respectable Christian prince. The ordinary Englishman regarded him as a conqueror, but as a conqueror who brought peace and growing prosperity, who enforced the law, honored the church, opened new markets for traders, and offered careers to Englishmen.

The fact remained that Cnut was a foreign King with strong barbaric elements in his character. His accession was marked by a great deal of bloodshed, his enemies dying with convenient speed. At first he ruled England as a conquered province, dividing it arbitrarily into four large areas, each ruled by a Dane or by an Englishman with close Danish connections. It was only at the end of his reign that Englishmen became his chief advisers. Cnut surrounded himself with a body of picked fighting men, known as his housecarls, who formed the core of his army. Their position was one of honor, privilege, and wealth. For their support and for the support of a navy Cnut imposed heavy taxation. There is evidence that a good deal of land passed from the hands of Englishmen into the hands of Danes. Finally, his interest in Scandinavia remained strong, for he was King of Denmark and gained a temporary control of Norway and parts of Sweden.

At his death in 1035 he was succeeded as King of England by his two sons, Harold and Harthacnut, whose short and turbulent reigns were fortunately soon over. In 1042, Cnut's line having ended, the English turned back to the royal family of Wessex in the person of Edward, known as the Confessor because of his piety. The son of Ethelred and Emma of Normandy, he had grown up at the Norman court. He ruled until 1066, the date of the Norman Conquest.

SOCIAL CLASSES

In the first centuries of the Anglo-Saxon period there were three distinct ranks in society—nobles, freemen, and slaves—but as time went on and as society became more sophisticated, these ranks were modified in various ways. Rich and powerful Kings, who required an ever-increasing number of soldiers and officials, gave liberal rewards to men who served them well. As the number of nobles increased, a few became very wealthy and many acquired rights of various kinds over the classes below them. The freemen, on the other hand, suffered a gradual decline, so that by the end of the period large numbers had ceased to be completely free, in an economic if not in a personal sense, and were bound to give labor and produce to the great man of their locality. The position of the slave, though always miserable, sometimes improved. By the time of the Norman Conquest, there were four classes in England: nobles, freemen, and slaves, as before, but in addition there was a large intermediate class which was neither slave nor free but something in between.

The Nobles

The earliest Anglo-Saxon nobles were athelings and eorls. The athelings were members of the royal family, and the eorls were also nobles by birth. Both groups, however, were gradually superseded by men who became nobles through service to the King. The new nobles were known as gesiths and later as thegns. Gesith meant "companion," and thegn had once meant "servant." But the companions and servants of the King were his warriors, his chamberlains, his officials. They were members of his household and helped him govern the country. He rewarded them with gifts of land, with privileges and immunities, and with valuable rights over the lower classes. The wergeld of a noble—the fine imposed upon anyone who killed him—was very high (1200 shillings), six times as high as the wergeld of a freeman.[5] By the tenth century, nobility was based upon wealth as well as upon service. A rich freeman might become a thegn, as might also a merchant who crossed three times to the Continent in his own ship.[6]

A wealthy thegn owned large estates in various parts of the country, he and his family moving about from one estate to another. His house consisted of a timbered hall which served as a dining hall, as a center for the daily life of the household, and as the sleeping place of servants and retainers. The bedrooms of the noble and his family were separate from the hall and were sometimes in another building. The hall was furnished with tables and benches; mattresses and pillows lay on the floor to serve as beds; the walls were hung with curtains and tapestries. A noble and his guests feasted and drank in the hall, where the men boasted of their great deeds and listened to songs and to the music of the harp. A noble had many retainers—huntsmen, fowlers, messengers, domestic servants. He took pride in fine dogs and horses, in elaborate saddles and bridles, in handsomely decorated weapons, and in adornments of silver and gold. He dressed in trousers and in a long tunic falling to the knees, over which he might wear a silken mantle or a cloak of fur. His wife wore a tunic with a mantle over it, her tunic and mantle reaching to the ground and held in place by handsome brooches, often one on each shoulder. A noble had to serve the King in war and to spend time at court, where he probably held some official position. He had to control his servants and retainers, for he was responsible for their good behavior; and he had to attend the local courts and take part in the work of local government and justice.

The Ceorls or Freemen

The ceorl, the farmer of Anglo-Saxon England,[7] was a freeman, the independent master of a peasant household. He had a wergeld of 200 shillings

[5] See page 42.
[6] Dorothy Whitelock, *The Beginnings of English Society* (Harmondsworth, Middlesex: Penguin Books, 1952), pp. 83–114.
[7] There were various ranks among the ceorls. Leats and geburs were freemen of lower status than the ceorl. The cotsetlan, or cottage dweller, was lower still. Geneats, on the other hand, who rode about an estate on various errands, performed more elevated tasks than the ceorl.

and could obtain redress in court for any assault upon his property. He paid dues to the church and a food rent to the King. The food rent was a fairly large amount of food which was due from a group of peasants once a year and was sufficient to feed the King and his court for twenty-four hours. The freeman attended the local court, served in the fyrd or militia, and had the obligation of repairing roads, bridges, and fortresses. He also had miscellaneous duties, such as supplying carts to carry the King's luggage.

The Anglo-Saxon ceorls, drawn together for protection and companionship, lived for the most part in small, compact villages and cultivated the surrounding fields as a cooperative enterprise. Their houses were no more than primitive huts of wood or of lath and plaster and contained one large room which housed the peasant family and perhaps the livestock as well, for man and beast might sleep close together on a cold winter night. Smoke from the fire on an open hearth filled the hut (and at least kept down the fleas) before it escaped through a hole in the thatched roof. The village contained a mill and perhaps a church or the timbered hall of the great man of the area.

Beyond the village stretched large open fields without permanent fencing. There were normally two great fields, each cultivated in turn a year at a time, while the other lay fallow to regain its fertility. The fields were divided into long narrow strips, usually about 220 yards in length and about 16½ feet wide, stretching gracefully across the field in the shape of a huge elongated **S**. The strips were arranged in blocks, those in one block pointing in a different direction from those in another in order to obtain a natural drainage and to follow the contour of the land. There were shorter strips in queer-shaped blocks to fill out corners and irregularities in the open fields. A peasant's strips were scattered through the fields and interspersed with the strips of his neighbors. It was once thought that this scattering was due to a principle of equality by which each peasant secured some of the better and some of the poorer land in the open fields. The Anglo-Saxons, however, were practical farmers, not social theorists. Their problem was to wring a livelihood from the soil. They lived in fear of hunger, for a poor harvest might mean a famine. Faced with a common danger, they met it with a common effort. Very few peasants were rich enough to own the full team of eight oxen required to drag the heavy wooden plow. Cooperative farming was thus a practical method of agriculture, and cooperation presumably meant that the peasants had obtained their strips in rotation and not on the basis of any social theory.

The plow, with its colter to slit the soil, its iron share to cut the bottom of the furrow, and its moldboard to turn the furrow over, was in essence the plow we have today. But the ox team was difficult to turn, and hence the strips were as long as the oxen could go without a rest. The first furrow was cut down the middle of the strip and the next close beside it in the opposite direction, with the furrows turned toward each other. This method of plowing, with each furrow turned inward, created in time a slight elevation along the center of the strip and a slight depression on each side. The strips were separated by a small ditch which served for drainage. In addition to the arable fields, a village required a pasture; a meadow for hay, which was highly prized; and a wasteland on the border of the forest where fuel could be gathered and pigs and geese allowed to roam. To keep the farm animals alive through the winter was a constant problem. Bees were valued for their honey, which was used for sweetening and for making mead.

Although compact villages and open fields were the normal units of agriculture, they were by no means universal. From very early times the land in Kent had been divided into much smaller fields enclosed by hedges or fences as in modern farming. The land in Wales and in the north and west of England was too hilly and rugged for agriculture in open fields. These areas were better suited for pasturing sheep and cattle, and solitary homesteads or shepherds' lonely huts were scattered over the countryside. Some grain was grown, however, for the making of bread.

The Decline of the Ceorl. The position of the ceorl tended to decline. For this there were many reasons. One was his economic insecurity. An illness, a wound, a run of poor harvests, a murrain among his cattle, an attack by robbers, a war between rival kingdoms, an incursion by the Danes—any of these might bring ruin to the peasant. It is not surprising that many ceorls, left destitute by disaster, placed themselves under the protection of a lord. They could give their land to a lord (receiving back from him its possession and use) in return for his promise of protection. They could offer him their labor on certain days each week or they could offer produce from their lands. It was sometimes the lord who took the initiative. A noble or a monastery, requiring laborers, might give peasants the right to use their lands in return for produce and labor.

A peasant's act in placing himself or his land under a lord's protection was known as commendation. It did not necessarily imply servility, for a distinction was made between personal and economic dependence. But commendation normally meant that in the course of time the ceorl lost some part of his personal freedom. He was likely to become increasingly bound by the obligations he had undertaken.

In certain ways the actions of the King hastened the decline of the freemen. The King rewarded his thegns not only with grants of land but with grants of royal rights. A thegn might be given the food rents or other services owed to the King by the peasants of a village. If the villagers after some disaster could not pay the food rents, they might be compelled to offer the thegn their labor or a part of the produce from their strips of land. The King, moreover, might grant the thegn judicial rights, the right to retain that portion of the fines levied in a local court which had formerly gone to the King, or the right to establish a new court and keep the fines it imposed. Kings were always troubled by the difficulty of bringing lawless persons into court, and they tried to solve the problem by commanding that every man must have a lord who was responsible for his appearance when that was desired. These practices opened the way for a lord to strengthen his hold upon a village community. There were, then, many reasons why large numbers of ceorls sank into a semiservile status as time passed.

The Slaves. Slaves formed the lowest rank in society. Men became slaves in various ways. Some were captives taken in war, some were descendants of enslaved Celts, many were persons condemned to slavery as a punishment for crime or for inability to pay the fines levied upon them by the courts. The law gave them no protection. They had no wergeld. A man who killed a slave paid to the owner the slave's market value, which was roughly equivalent to that of eight oxen. Since slaves had no property in the eyes of the law, they could not be fined by the courts but were punished by flogging, by mutilation, or by death for serious crimes. The owner who maltreated or killed his slave was subject to the censures of the church but was not punished by public law.

In practice this harshness was somewhat mitigated. Custom and tradition gave certain rights to slaves. If they were laborers on the estates of their master, as most of them were, custom allowed them some share of the produce of the estate. The fact that they sometimes bought their freedom indicates that their right to acquire possessions was acknowledged. The church, frowning upon slavery, encouraged men to emancipate their slaves as an act of piety. Yet a freed slave was not fully free but remained subject in various ways to his former master. It was often to the owner's advantage to place strips of land at the slave's disposal in return for labor and produce; this practice meant that the position of the slave approached that of those former freemen who had sunk into the class of semiservile agricultural laborers.

The lot of the Anglo-Saxon slave was certainly hard. Slaves often ran away. During the Danish invasions they sometimes joined the Danish armies and found occasion to take vengeance on their former masters.

ANGLO-SAXON GOVERNMENT

A study of Anglo-Saxon government is by necessity a study of government during the later Anglo-Saxon period from about the year 900 to the Norman Conquest in 1066. The earlier centuries are obscure and many things can only be guessed at. But institutions developed rapidly, and new sources of information make them clearer, after Alfred's descendants came to rule all of England. It is possible to see that the Anglo-Saxons were building a system of government that was remarkably advanced. The central government contained the origins of later departments of state and employed ingenious devices of administration; the local government, with its many courts and officials, was to affect the whole course of English history.

Central Government: The King

The power and importance of the King, and the idea of what a King should be, constantly expanded during the Anglo-Saxon period. In the early days after the Germanic invasions England had contained many petty dynasties whose Kings had been merely the leaders of bands of warriors. In the years after 900, however, kingship was vastly more than this. The King was the powerful and accepted ruler of all England; he wielded great authority and possessed a machinery of government through which his power could be exercised. The meaning of kingship grew as the number of kingdoms diminished and as Kings ruled over wider areas. Alfred and his descendants, moreover, exalted kingship because they were national leaders against a common foe and because they inspired loyalty to the royal line of Wessex. They were sovereigns of international significance who were respected on the Continent.

English kingship also grew because of its close alliance with the church. Kings were taught that their first duty was to give the church honor and protection; in return for this protection churchmen cast about the King a halo of sanctity. Kingship acquired a religious significance. The King ruled by God's grace; he was the representative of God among a Christian folk. The church also gave Anglo-Saxon Kings a vision of the exalted position and high responsibilities of the emperors of Rome. Hence the Kings of the later Anglo-Saxon period regarded themselves as civil and religious rulers whose duty it was to protect the people and to promote the welfare of the country.

All public authority was derived from the King. He summoned and commanded the military forces of the kingdom in time of war. His favor gave men wealth and power. He appointed and removed officials. He also appointed leading churchmen—bishops, abbots, and priors. The choice of these prelates lay in theory with the monks of a monastic cathedral or of a monastery who, upon the death of a bishop or abbot, were empowered to elect a successor. But in practice the church, which owed so much to the King, accepted his candidates for high ecclesiastical office. The King summoned and dismissed the assembly of great men, known as the witan.

The King's authority may be illustrated by his laws and by the operation of the King's peace. His laws, which were issued after consultation with the witan, were national in scope and were aimed at the suppression of lawlessness and crime. The King's peace was based upon the notion that peace was attached to the house of every freeman. Fighting or violence by strangers in a man's house was a grievous offense which became infinitely more serious if the house was that of the King. But the King was mobile, constantly moving from one place to another, and hence his peace was brought temporarily to any area in which he happened to be. It extended itself gradually to places where he was present in theory, to the local courts, to roads and rivers, and to churches and monasteries. It was not until after the Norman Conquest, however, that the King's peace was thought to encompass the entire realm.

In the Anglo-Saxon period there was as yet no thought of a capital city. The central government was the household of the King and moved with him from place to place. It was essentially domestic, conducted by men who had once been the King's servants—his stewards, butlers, and chamberlains—and who were slowly developing into officers of the state.

Four divisions of the household were to become important administrative departments in later times. One was the chamber, the sleeping apartment of the King, his private retiring room, the heart of government and administration. A second was the wardrobe, an adjoining chamber, which contained not only the King's clothes but also his weapons, his jewels, his important documents, and his money. The money was kept in a treasure chest which traveled with him, though it is probable that at the end of the Anglo-Saxon period some treasure was left for safekeeping at the city of Winchester. Money came to the King from the profits of his estates; from rents; from fines levied in the local courts; from Danegeld, which developed into a tax on land; and from various miscellaneous sources. To handle these payments there must have been some kind of financial organization within the household, an organization which was to grow into the medieval treasury. Chamber, wardrobe, and treasury were in the hands of chamberlains who were acquiring administrative skills.

Then there was the chancery. This was the writing staff of the King, his secretarial department, where letters, charters, chirographs, and writs were prepared by a group of highly trained clerks. The first secretaries of the King had been the clergymen connected with the royal chapel. By the end of the Anglo-Saxon period they had developed into a body of skillful clerks; the chancery had become an ancient and sophisticated institution.

Charters were formal public documents by which the King made gifts of land or of privilege to monasteries or to nobles. Written in Latin, they were highly technical productions. The chirograph was a device to prevent the forgery of charters. A document was copied two or three times on the same piece of parchment; the copies were then cut apart in a saw-toothed line. Copies could later be authenticated by placing the irregular lines together and seeing whether they fitted properly. The writs were short informal letters of command or instruction from the King, written in English and addressed to local courts or magnates. An impression of the King's seal was attached to each writ, thus making it authentic. The writ, a most ingenious device, made efficient government possible and became the normal way in which medieval Kings issued commands to their subordinates. Surrounded by a group of chamberlains and clerks, the King must have consulted with them upon problems of law and government. Here was the faint foreshadowing of a royal council.

A serious weakness in Anglo-Saxon government was the lack of any fixed principle of royal succession. Germanic tradition contained an element of election, but Roman practice pointed to heredity. Both principles seem to have been in operation among the Anglo-Saxons. Kings came from the royal family, and normally a son succeeded his father. But in times of crisis, as happened when Alfred came to the throne in 871, the strongest member of the royal family became King and the children of the former King were passed over. Sometimes a King settled the succession by will or by associating his successor with him in the work of government. In any case, the new King could not feel secure until he had obtained acceptance by the great men of the kingdom who were normally members of the witan. The action of the witan was not an election; rather, it was a formal recognition of the person to whom heredity, or merit, or special circumstances, or even conquest pointed as the future leader. The vagueness surrounding the succession to the throne was at times a source of great danger.

An Anglo-Saxon King was limited in power by his coronation oath, a threefold promise given in the most solemn terms to defend the church, to punish crime and violence, and to temper his judgments with clemency and mercy. He was limited also by the ancient customs of the kingdom, which he could not violate with impunity. To some extent his power was restricted by the witan.

The Witan. The word "witan" or "witenagemot" meant an assembly of wise men and refers to meetings of the Anglo-Saxon King with the leading men of his kingdom. The witan was an ancient institution, for the early kingdoms had witans, but very little is known about it until the tenth century, when the successors of Alfred summoned witans composed of important persons from most of England. By that time the witan included members of the royal family and of the ancient nobility, bishops and abbots, the King's household officials, and his leading thegns. It reflected an aristocracy of birth, wisdom, and service.[8] Its membership was never fixed, nor were the times or places of its meetings. These were determined by the King.

There was considerable vagueness about the work and functions of the witan. It acted as a court to try cases in which the King or the great men of the kingdom were interested, but its judicial work was not large, and it was not a court of appeal. It played a part in legislation, for the King did not issue laws until he had placed them before the witan; yet it was the King and his household officials who drew up the laws, and the witan was merely asked to express its

[8] G. O. Sayles, *The Medieval Foundations of England* (London: Methuen, 1950), p. 176.

approval. In the same way it witnessed the King's charters, thus giving its sanction to royal gifts of land and privilege. It was asked to approve other acts of the King. "During the century before the Conquest its assent is recorded to the issue of laws and the imposition of taxes, to negotiations with foreign powers, and to measures undertaken for the defence of the land."[9]

The King was under no obligation to ask the consent or approval of the witan for his actions. Indeed, the witan never established its right to offer advice or to give its sanction. It never defined its position nor obtained a fixed place in the scheme of government. Yet in practice the King consulted it about most matters of importance. He would have been foolish not to have explained his policies to the leading men of his kingdom; hence the King and witan usually acted together in serious matters. There were times when a minority, a weak King, or a national crisis gave the witan considerable power. But its membership, its procedure, and its functions were so vague and ill-defined that a strong King could control it much as he pleased.

Local Government: The Shire

Most of England in the later Anglo-Saxon period was divided into administrative districts known as shires. They originated in various ways. Some of them, as Essex, Sussex, and Kent, were ancient kingdoms that had been reduced in size and finally absorbed into Wessex. Norfolk and Suffolk represented a tribal division in the old kingdom of East Anglia. The shires of Wessex seem to have originally been areas around towns. Later, as the Danelaw was subdued, it was divided arbitrarily into shires.

The earliest official of the King in the shire was the ealdorman. It is likely that he was often of royal blood and was always a trusted member of the King's household, appointed to represent the King's authority in the shire. He assembled and commanded the fyrd, or local militia. He and the bishop presided at the meetings of the shire court. It was his duty to enforce the decisions of the court. He compelled the nobles of the shire to keep the peace and to restrain their retainers from acts of violence. Royal writs containing the commands of the King were addressed jointly to the ealdorman and to the bishop. The wergeld upon the life of the ealdorman was very high, and valuable lands were set aside for his support. He held a position of great profit, dignity, and social prestige.

As the Danelaw was conquered in the tenth century, the ealdorman increased in power and importance and was often placed in charge of several shires. He received a part of the fines levied in the courts and part of the tolls and customs paid by the towns. He was so great a noble that lesser thegns and freemen attached themselves to him as to their lord. Under Cnut the office became even more influential. The ealdorman, to whom the Danish title of earl was now given, ruled over such wide areas that all of England was controlled by a few great men.

As the position of ealdormen and earls expanded and as they were drawn into national politics, they became detached from the details of local government. The need arose for a new official who would be closer to the people and more devoted to the administration of a single shire. Such an official was the shire-reeve, or sheriff, who appeared about the middle of the tenth century. By the time of the Norman Conquest he had become the King's principal executive officer in all branches of local government. As the name implies, he was the King's

[9] Sir Frank Stenton, *Anglo-Saxon England* (Oxford: Clarendon Press, 1947), p. 544.

reeve, that is, a royal servant charged with the protection of the Crown's financial interests. He collected money owed to the King. Royal estates were under his supervision. When a large assessment such as Danegeld was imposed, it was the sheriff's duty to assess and collect the money. In the absence of the ealdorman he presided over the shire court along with the bishop. He proclaimed the laws and commandments of the King, led in the pursuit of criminals, and enforced the decisions of the court. He also summoned the fyrd, thus becoming important in both local and national defense.

His significance in the late Anglo-Saxon period lies partly in the fact that he was the agent of the King, to whom he was directly responsible. The symbol of royal power, he kept the King's authority before the eyes of thegns and freemen. These men had few direct dealings with the earl, but their dealings with the sheriff were constant. He was thus a bridge between the central and the local government.

The shire court, which assembled twice a year, was the shire in action, capable of exercising all the functions of local government. It carried out the commands sent to it by the King. It was a court of law for all kinds of cases. An ancient court, it had once been attended by all the freemen of the area, but in the later Anglo-Saxon period many freemen had dropped out and the court was largely composed of the wealthier and more important persons of the shire. The duty of attendance became attached to certain pieces of land; men who held these lands owed service in the court. Although the court had grown more aristocratic and although the presiding officers were the ealdorman, the bishop, and the sheriff, it was, nonetheless, the assembled freemen who declared the law and who determined what the proof should be. The court was much used by the upper classes to confirm and publicize land titles.

The Hundred. In late Anglo-Saxon times the shires were divided into smaller judicial and administrative units known as hundreds. Although their origin is somewhat obscure, it is known that for a long time much of the work of local government had centered in the estates of the King. A royal estate served as the administrative core of the surrounding area and was under the supervision of a King's reeve or bailiff. These men did more and more work of a governmental nature, pursuing criminals, collecting money, keeping order in their localities. It is possible that this small unit of government came to be called a hundred in the tenth century.

Whatever its origin, the hundred was a very active unit of local government. It contained a court over which an official known as a hundred reeve presided. He was responsible to the sheriff, who occasionally visited the hundred court. The court, meeting every four weeks, was the place attended by the ordinary freeman for all kinds of judicial, police, and commercial business.

The Borough. A survey of Anglo-Saxon local government must include not only the shire and the hundred but also the town or borough. The boroughs differed widely from each other; yet they possessed common characteristics that marked them off sharply from the rest of the community. A borough, in the first place, was surrounded by a wall or by an earthen rampart which made it a fortress, a burgh, a defensible place. A borough also contained a market. It was thus a port, a place of trade; the King's official who governed it was the port-reeve, for Anglo-Saxon boroughs remained under royal control. The wealthier merchants who lived in the boroughs were allowed to form guilds for the protection of their business interests and to develop rules and customs for the regulation of trade. Sometimes these customs were enforced by a borough court. If the borough followed certain rules, it might also obtain the right to coin money.

Not all the inhabitants of a borough were burgesses, though all were freemen. A burgess held his plot of land in the town by burgage tenure, for which he paid rent to the King. Because he paid in money and not in labor or produce, his position differed sharply from that of a peasant in the country. Yet the connections between the borough and the surrounding countryside were very close. Outside the town lay open fields, meadows, and woodland, in which each townsman had his share.

The question arises why some towns and villages developed into boroughs whereas others did not. The explanation has been offered that the boroughs began in the fortresses built by Anglo-Saxons and Danes in the ninth and tenth centuries. But some of these fortresses grew into boroughs whereas others declined in prosperity. It was the economic factor that mattered: fortresses became boroughs only when their location, or their security, or some other advantage made them attractive as economic centers. Long before the boroughs of the ninth and tenth centuries, trade had developed between the Anglo-Saxons in southeastern England and the Franks in Gaul, a trade that stimulated such towns as London, Rochester, and Canterbury.

The Danish invasions, once their violence had subsided, brought a revival of commerce with the Low Countries, France, and even Italy. Some of the fortresses attracted merchants who were glad to obtain places of safe deposit for their goods and who made use of the portreeves or other responsible townsmen as witnesses in important business transactions. The King encouraged merchants to take up holdings in the boroughs. At the end of the Anglo-Saxon period London, Norwich, York, Lincoln, and Canterbury were important boroughs, and there were lesser ones in other places. London was by far the largest. It traded with most of the towns of western Europe and was the terminus of trade routes running across the Continent.

The Vill.   The smallest unit of local government was the vill, or village. We assume, although we have no direct evidence, that the men of a village met together to determine the calendar of the agricultural year in their cooperative enterprise of farming. The vill was also a small police unit. The difficulty Anglo-Saxon Kings encountered in bringing people to court led them to demand that every man, unless he was a member of the upper class, should find a surety, that is, someone who would guarantee to produce him if he were wanted. One method was to arrange the peasantry in groups of ten, known as tithing groups, each headed by a tithing man. If one of the ten was wanted, it was the duty of the other nine to find him and bring him to court; failure to do so was severely punished. The Normans continued this practice, calling it frankpledge. In Anglo-Saxon times the tithing sometimes merged with the vill, so that the entire village was responsible for producing any of its inhabitants.

Legal Procedure.   To modern eyes the law administered by the shire and the hundred courts may appear grossly barbaric. It must be remembered, however, that we are dealing with a primitive age in which law was only beginning to replace private vengeance and in which superstition mingled with a naïve belief that God would perform miracles to distinguish innocence from guilt. There was also an exaggerated reverence for oaths, based on the conviction that a man who swore falsely condemned his soul to eternal damnation.

A case in an Anglo-Saxon court proceeded somewhat as follows: The party who thought himself wronged appeared in court and made a formal accusation against his adversary. He then went to the house of the accused and, using a set formula of words, summoned him to come to court. Often the accused had no desire to comply. Various methods were devised to force his appearance, some of which have been mentioned. His kin, or his lord, or his tithing group was responsible for his coming. In extreme cases he might be outlawed, which meant that his enemies were free to slay him if they were able to do so. But if both parties were in court, each took a solemn oath, the plaintiff repeating his accusation and the defendant making his denial. At this medial point in the trial the assembled freemen gave their judgment by determining which party should give proof and what the proof should be.

One method of proof was by oath-helpers, or compurgators. The party making proof was told to find a set number of men who would swear that his oath was a good oath. If he produced the required number of oath-helpers he won his case. An oath was a very solemn thing, not to be made lightly, and a man of evil reputation might not be able to obtain oath-helpers. In cases of very serious crime the proof was sometimes by ordeal. This was an appeal to God to show by a miracle where guilt or innocence lay. The man undergoing the ordeal plunged his arm into boiling water or carried a piece of hot iron for several paces. If the wound healed quickly and well, he was considered innocent; if it did not, he was pronounced guilty. Or he might be bound and thrown into a body of water that had been blessed by a priest. It was thought that this water would not receive a guilty person. Hence if a man floated he was guilty; if he sank he was innocent and was rescued, we may hope, before he proved his innocence by drowning. Many a guilty person, believing that the ordeal would reveal his guilt, preferred to confess or to make some compensation rather than undergo the ordeal.

Disputes over property were often settled by the testimony of witnesses. A man accused of stealing cattle, for instance, might prove his innocence by producing witnesses who would testify that they had been present when the cattle were purchased. The custom arose of summoning witnesses at almost every commercial transaction; hence if a man accused of theft could not offer witnesses of this kind he all but confessed his guilt.

Almost any crime was punishable by a fine. The murderer paid a very heavy fine, the wergeld, to the family of his victim. For a lesser offense, such as cutting off a man's finger, the defendant paid a fine known as a bot to the injured party and also an additional fine, the wite, which went to the King. The collection of these fines, often a difficult matter, was the obligation of the victorious party. He was supported by public opinion and was sometimes aided by the sheriff or the ealdorman. A weakness of the law was its formality. Every summons, every word in a trial, must be spoken in the proper formula; one slip of the tongue lost the case. A saga from Iceland tells of a man who had committed a rare offense but could not be brought to court because he and he alone knew the words by which he must be summoned. The hero of this tale proved his ingenuity by tricking the culprit into revealing the precious formula.

THE ACHIEVEMENT OF THE ANGLO-SAXON KINGS

The Anglo-Saxon Kings, in the face of great difficulties, gave England territorial and political unity. For more than a century and a half before the Norman Conquest they labored to devise new methods of government. Basing local government upon the old institution of the folkmoot, they added vigor and authority to the shire and hundred courts and created officials through whom they could reach down to influence local affairs. Though it may have lagged behind local development, the central government contained the origins of various departments of state, ingenious devices of administration, and a strong tradition of monarchy. The Normans were to give these institutions new drive and energy, but they had little of their own either in political theory or in administrative practice that was as mature and sophisticated as the government of the Anglo-Saxons.

3

the norman conquest

The one date in English history that everybody knows is 1066; in that year William, Duke of Normandy, brought an army across the Channel, defeated the Anglo-Saxons at the Battle of Hastings, and was crowned as King of England in Westminster Abbey. The Norman Conquest was a turning point in English history. Sooner or later it affected every aspect of English life. A series of strong Norman Kings molded English institutions to exalt the power of monarchy. The old Anglo-Saxon nobility disappeared, and a foreign French-speaking nobility took its place. The introduction of Norman feudalism created new social, military, and legal patterns which were to have a permanent effect. England was drawn closer to the Continent. Yet there were things the Normans had no wish to do and could not have done had they wished. Posing as the lawful heir of Edward the Confessor, William claimed all the rights and privileges that Edward had enjoyed and thus continued the traditions of Anglo-Saxon government. The framework of the shire and hundred courts and many principles of Anglo-Saxon law remained much as before. The life of the peasants, as they labored in the open fields, was substantially unchanged. There was great continuity with the past, and the civilization which gradually emerged was essentially an English civilization though deeply marked by Norman influences.

NORMANDY

Normandy was a duchy in western France directly across the Channel from southern England. It centered in the broad valley of the lower Seine and extended westward to the border of Brittany. Its largest and most important city was Rouen. Other towns included Bec, the site of a famous monastery; Falaise, where William the Conqueror was born; and Caen, Bayeux, Coutances, and Avranches in the western portion of the duchy. Historians used to speak in glowing terms of Norman civilization and political genius. Normandy was called the most progressive and best-governed portion of France; the Conquest was said to have brought a higher culture to England. Historians today do not hold these views. The truth is that the materials for the history of pre-Conquest Normandy are very meager; our knowledge is slight; and what we know leaves the impression that the Normans were a fierce, violent, grasping, and warlike race, less literate and less civilized than the Anglo-Saxons whom they conquered.

Normandy may be regarded as a kind of French Danelaw. Pirates from Denmark had ravaged France in the ninth century in the same way that they had ravaged England. In 841 they sacked Rouen, and four years later they sacked Paris. In 885–886, when they reappeared at Paris with a force estimated by contemporaries at 700 ships and 40,000 warriors, the French King Charles the Fat saved the city by paying them 700 pounds of silver and by giving them permission to pillage the country farther up the Seine. Thus Charles the Fat attempted to buy peace as Ethelred the Unready attempted to buy it in England. But the Danes returned and began to make permanent settlements in Normandy.

In 911 another French King, Charles the Simple, concluded a treaty with a Danish chieftain named Rollo by which a line was drawn between Normandy and the rest of France in the same way that Alfred and Guthrum had drawn a line in England. The terms of the treaty between Charles and Rollo are not known. Rollo himself is a shadowy figure about whom there are many stories but few facts. One tale relates that when he was told to kiss·Charles's foot as an act of homage he refused and appointed one of his warriors to perform the rite. It was done so clumsily that the King was tumbled from his throne, to the amusement of the assembled Norsemen. This is doubtless a tall tale, but it is not unlikely that Rollo's creation as Duke of Normandy was somewhat rough and ready. It would appear that he was more at home in the role of pirate than in that of duke. He was baptised in 912, but his Christianity sat lightly upon him, and on his deathbed he decided not only to pray to the God of the Christians but also to propitiate the heathen gods of the north by human sacrifices.

During the century and a half between 911 and 1066 the Vikings in Normandy adopted the religion, the language, the methods of warfare, and the social customs of France, though we do not know much about how the transformation took place. By the time of the Conquest there was little to distinguish them from other Frenchmen. Their relations with the King at Paris brought the feudalism of northern France into Normandy. The duke held his duchy from the King in return for military service, that is, in return for supplying the King with a body of fully equipped knights when called upon to do so; and the Norman nobles held their lands from the duke upon similar terms. At this time a knight was no more than a soldier trained to fight on horseback. In the turbulent conditions of life in Normandy every noble of importance maintained a group of knights in his household. He could normally perform his duty to the duke by leading these knights to battle at the duke's command. By 1066 the feudal process had gone a step further: Norman nobles were granting estates to some of their knights in return for the military service the knights performed.

The military pre-eminence of the Normans rested on their skill as knights and as castle builders. They did not originate these methods of warfare; they merely borrowed them. But they became specialists in war, and they were able to employ their crude wooden castles as bases for extensive cavalry operations. Knights and castles, however, could be used to defy ducal authority. No duke before William had been able to prevent the nobles from building castles at their pleasure. Even William, although he inspired great dread, could not end private warfare among the Norman barons. The population of the duchy was increasing. There were large numbers of warriors—younger sons, unattached knights, knights dissatisfied with their small holdings—who were ready for warlike adventure. William was shrewd enough to use this potential power for his own advantage rather than allow it to turn against him or to slip away into enterprises which brought him no profit.

Although the Normans became great warriors, they were slow in developing a well-governed state. Prior to the Conquest there was no Norman system of administration which could function when the duke was weak or incompetent. The moment his authority faltered, the duchy sank into anarchy, and its history became a dreary tale of private war, murder, pillage, and revolt. The Normans had no written law to bring with them to England. There was a ducal household modeled upon that of France, but there was no chancery worthy of the name. Charters and writs, few and irregular, could not bear comparison with the impressive series of documents issued by the Anglo-Saxon Kings. The duke had a court composed in theory of his feudal barons. It met infrequently, however, and consisted largely of his household officials, his kinsmen, and his special friends. One of its members wrote that he had never known the court to differ from the duke. In comparison with the Anglo-Saxon witan it was rudimentary. There was a local official known as a vicomte not unlike the English sheriff, though large portions of the duchy were not entrusted to vicomtes but to William's kinsmen.

Both William and his greater barons founded monasteries and maintained them with rich gifts. Yet Norman enthusiasm for the church was rather recent; learned monks, such as Lanfranc and Anselm who made Norman monasteries famous, were importations from Italy. Over the church as a whole William exercised complete domination, appointing bishops and abbots, controlling church councils, and resisting the pretentions of the papacy to greater power. Normandy in 1066 was still a state in the making. The fact that William became duke despite his illegitimate birth was an indication that ordinary rules of church and of law could be defied.

Duke William

Historians have often overrated William and have endowed him with a political genius he probably did not possess. But he was certainly one of the strong men of history. Hard, grasping, masterful, and suspicious, he was as ruthless in imposing his will as he was unscrupulous in his methods. He was devout in a superstitious way, but he allowed religion to place no restraint upon his conduct. After the Conquest the English were chiefly impressed by his implacable severity against those who opposed his will. The *Anglo-Saxon Chronicle* spoke of him with bated breath:

> This King was a very wise and great man, and more honored and more powerful than any of his predecessors. He was mild to those good men who loved God, but severe beyond measure towards those who withstood his will. He founded a noble monastery on the spot where God permitted him to conquer England, and he established monks in it, and he made it very rich. . . . So also was he a very stern and wrathful man, so that none durst do anything against his will, and he kept in prison those earls who acted against his pleasure. He removed bishops from their sees and abbots from their offices, and he

imprisoned thegns, and at last he spared not his own brother Odo. . . . Truly there was much trouble in those times and very great distress. He caused castles to be built and he oppressed the poor. He took from his subjects many marks of gold and many hundred pounds of silver, and this either with or without right. He was given to avarice and greedily loved gain. He made large forests for his deer and enacted laws therein, so that whoever killed a hart or a hind should be blinded, and he loved the tall stags as if he were their father. . . . The rich complained and the poor murmured, but he was so sturdy that he recked naught of them. They must needs will all that the King willed if they would live.

William was born in 1027, the bastard son of Duke Robert the Magnificent by Arlette, a peasant girl, whom the duke had kidnaped and carried off to his castle at Falaise. In 1035, when William was eight years old, his father died on a pilgrimage to Jerusalem and William was proclaimed duke. But ducal authority was at a low ebb, and for the next twelve years William lived among disorders, revolts, and assassinations. He had four guardians in succession, all of whom met violent deaths. Disorder reached a climax in 1047, when most of western Normandy revolted. William was forced to make a perilous journey by night through the lands of his enemies. He was fortunate in retaining the allegiance of the eastern portion of his duchy and in having the support of his lord, King Henry I of France, who won for him the Battle of Val-ès-Dunes near Caen, where the rebel barons were crushed.

In the years that followed, William increased and consolidated his power by every means at his disposal. He effectively eliminated rebellious barons by cutting off their heads. He formed an alliance with the Count of Flanders, whose daughter Matilda he married in 1053, although the marriage brought him into conflict both with the church and with the King of France. The King invaded Normandy but was defeated in battles at Mortemer (1054) and Varaville (1058), battles which rendered William virtually independent of his lord. He waged war with the County of Anjou and seized the district of Maine, which lay between Anjou and Normandy. Reminded of his illegitimacy by the town of Alençon, William captured the town and cut off the hands and feet of thirty-two of the leading citizens. Thus by war, by diplomacy, trickery, and savage intimidation he increased his strength. In 1066 he was ready for fresh aggression.

THE LAST ENGLISH KINGS

It is natural to approach with the Norman Conquest in mind the reigns of the last two English Kings, Edward the Confessor (1042–1066) and Harold (January to September 1066). The death of Cnut was followed by the short and shameful reigns of his two sons. They were both dead by 1042, and the witan turned back to the descendants of Alfred, selecting Edward, the son of Ethelred the Unready by his second wife, Emma, who was a sister of the Norman Duke Richard II. Edward was thus half Norman, and he grew up in Normandy. Later known as the Confessor, he was a pious man, conscientious and well intentioned, but weak and incapable as a ruler. He had been educated by Norman monks, and at heart he remained a monk all his life. Although he did not entirely forfeit the powers or neglect the duties of kingship, he disliked affairs of state, preferring a life of contemplation dedicated to his private devotions, to his almsgiving, and to the building of Westminster Abbey. He surrounded himself with Normans, made

French the language of the court, and formed ties with Normandy which, in view of William's ambitions, were very dangerous to England. Edward complicated matters in another way: on the eve of his marriage he took a vow of chastity and hence produced no heir. The problem of the succession disturbed his reign and played into William's hands in 1066.

It often is said that England was endangered during Edward's reign by the excessive power of a few great earls. But Cnut had easily controlled the earls, and Edward could have done the same. It was his weakness which tempted them to take an unusually prominent part in national affairs. So colorless and incompetent a King was certain to cause dissensions unless a great noble became the power behind the throne. And if Edward invited strife and invasion by his refusal to beget an heir, why should not an English earl become his successor instead of a usurper from abroad? These circumstances more than justify the policies of Godwin, Earl of Wessex, and his son Harold. They were pushing and ambitious men, but they were not bent upon destroying monarchy. Their aim was to preserve it, to secure the throne for themselves at Edward's death, and thus to prevent foreign invasion.

From a simple thegn in Sussex, Godwin had risen to become the greatest and wealthiest noble in England. His advancement was due to the closeness of his connection with Cnut and to his marriage into the Danish royal house. Having supported Edward's succession in 1042, he naturally demanded his reward. His family grew ever richer and more important. His daughter became Edward's Queen, his son Swein secured an earldom in the Severn Valley, his son Harold became Earl of East Anglia, a nephew Beorn obtained an earldom north of London, while Godwin himself remained Earl of Wessex. Edward's reaction was to draw closer to his French and Norman friends, some of whom were most unworthy.

In 1051 a clash occurred between Edward and Godwin which proved to be a turning point in the reign. Anti-Norman sentiment was now strong in England, and Godwin showed his sympathy with it, first by an unsuccessful attempt to prevent the elevation of a Norman, Robert of Jumièges, to the archbishopric of Canterbury, and secondly by a quarrel with a visiting Norman, Eustace of Boulogne, the King's brother-in-law. Angered by this quarrel, Edward displayed unaccustomed energy, collected an army, and prepared to march against Godwin. Had Godwin been merely a rebel, he would have resisted. As it was, he submitted to a royal sentence of banishment and went into exile in Flanders. Edward employed his triumph to give Godwin's estates to greedy Normans and to welcome a visit from Duke William, whom he apparently named as his successor. In 1052 Godwin felt strong enough to return. He and his sons were welcomed by the people, Robert of Jumièges fled to Normandy, and the King perforce restored Godwin and his family to their former estates and dignities. Smarting under this humiliation, Edward lost what little interest he had in government and withdrew more completely than ever to his private devotions.

Godwin died in 1053 and his son Harold succeeded to his influence. The great fact in English history during the next twelve years was the steady rise of Harold to a position of pre-eminence. He was a remarkable man, valiant and expert in war, wise, cautious, and conciliatory in time of peace. He strengthened his popularity by a successful war against the Welsh and he increased the prosperity of the country. At the same time he advanced his family until he and his three brothers controlled all the earldoms except that of Mercia. "No subject of the English Crown had ever been at once so powerful in relation to other noble-men and so great a figure in the country at large."[1]

Harold's position was weakened in 1065 when Northumbria revolted from the harsh rule of his brother Tostig. Harold allowed the Northumbrians to expel Tostig, who fled abroad to become his brother's evil genius. Meanwhile Edward was dying, and the problem of the succession had to be solved. No one in Eng-land put forward a claim for William of Normandy, who was regarded as "essen-tially a Dane and a Dane of bastard origin."[2] The choice lay between Harold and a descendant of the old English line, Edgar the Atheling, a sickly boy who had grown up in exile. For twelve years Harold had been the protector and all but the ruler of the country. The witan selected him as a matter of course; for the next nine months he was the King of England.

THE NORMAN INVASION

William prepared for an invasion of England by propaganda and diplo-macy as well as by gathering an army. He insisted that Edward the Confessor had named him as his heir and that Harold, having fallen into his hands in 1064, had bound himself by an oath which concerned the succession. The terms of the oath are unknown, but presumably Harold broke them by accepting the crown of England. William also sought the support of the papacy. He posed in Rome as a true son of the church, desirous of freeing England from a perjured King and from an uncanonical archbishop. This archbishop, an Englishman named Stigand, had been appointed without papal approval after Robert of Jumièges had fled from the country. In the eyes of the papacy, hostile to lay interference in the affairs of the church, Stigand's elevation appeared highly reprehensible. Hence it was decided in Rome that William should be supported. The Pope sent him a consecrated banner, thus lending his sordid aggression an appearance of holiness. Papal approval was of advantage to William in raising an army. He had the support of the Norman barons, but their resources were insufficient for an enter-prise of this magnitude, and William had to attract adventurers from other parts of Europe. Some served for pay; some for hope of booty. It was a mark of Wil-liam's high quality as a commander that he gave his miscellaneous host some coherence and discipline.

William's army cannot have been larger than five or six thousand men. Per-haps half were knights; the remainder were infantrymen, archers, and crossbow-men. The leaders wore shirts of ring mail, such as Norse chieftains had worn for centuries, but now extended to the knee and divided in the middle to permit riding. Most of the knights, however, possessed only a leather garment of the same shape sewn over with metal rings. They wore helmets with a piece in front to protect the nose. Their shields were not round but were shaped like kites to protect the body and a portion of the leg of a man on horseback. They fought with sword and short spear. A horse, leather boots, bridle, saddle, stirrups, and spurs completed their equipment. They had passed through a long period of training in the household of a great baron, and they represented the most efficient fighting methods of the age.

The English forces, on the other hand, though large in number, or in poten-

[1] Sir Frank Stenton, *Anglo-Saxon England* (Oxford: Clarendon Press, 1947), p. 568.
[2] G. O. Sayles, *The Medieval Foundations of England* (London: Methuen, 1950), p. 162.

The Bayeux Tapestry. Norman soldiers attack a castle in Brittany. (From *The Bayeux Tapestry*, edited by Sir Frank Stenton, published by Phaidon Press Ltd., London, distributed in the USA by New York Graphic, Greenwich, Conn.)

tial number, were poorly organized, slow in mobilization, and almost impossible to keep in the field over an extended period. The English had neglected the new techniques of war which had developed on the Continent. Their army consisted of three elements—the housecarls of the King and other great lords; the thegns and their retainers; the militia of freemen known as the fyrd. The housecarls were professional soldiers, superb fighting men, trained, disciplined, and ready for instant combat, but they were too few to act unaided in extensive operations, and they had to be used as the core of larger armies. The thegns and their retainers were essential in any important campaign, but their mobilization might be a long-drawn-out affair. Finally, there was the fyrd. By 1066 the fyrd appears to have been less a national militia than a smaller body of selected men with some training and equipment for war. The thegns and housecarls wore shirts of ring mail but they fought on foot in a formation of massed infantry. Forming a wall with their round shields, they used the Danish battle-ax of their forefathers. They had done little to develop the art of archery. Although their methods were out of date and they lacked mobility and striking power, Harold was confident that he could prevent William from landing. He might well have done so had not circumstances combined to give William every advantage.

In the first place William was fortunate because for the moment he could leave Normandy without fear of its being attacked by its neighbors. He was also fortunate in that a favorable wind sprang up at the right time. Had it come earlier, Harold would have been ready on the English coast. Had it come later, William might not have been able to hold his motley host together. His greatest good fortune lay in the fact that Harold was suddenly caught in a cruel dilemma. His exiled brother Tostig had persuaded a famous warrior, Harold Hardrada, King of Norway, to try his fortunes in England. In September 1066 a Norwegian fleet of some 300 ships sailed up the Humber, defeated the local English levies, and captured York.

Harold of England, thus faced with the predicament of two simultaneous invasions, tried to meet them by a series of forced marches. Hastening northward, he fell upon the Norwegians at Stamford Bridge near York, defeated them soundly, and killed both Tostig and Harold Hardrada. Only a remnant of the Norwegian host made its escape. Stamford Bridge was a great English victory, but three days afterward William landed unopposed on the southern shore. Harold made a hasty pacification in the north and within two weeks was facing William at Hastings. But the English soldiers were tired, and Harold made the error of advancing against a dangerous foe before his forces had reached their full strength. He took his position on the crest of a low hill which fell off sharply on each side and was approached in front by a gentle slope. The hill was narrow and the English were crowded. Yet they withstood the charges of the Norman knights for many hours. It was only when the Normans pretended to take flight that some of the English broke their ranks and pursued, to be cut down by the Normans, who turned upon them. Between the charges of cavalry William used his archers to good effect. Slowly the pressure of mounted knight and unmounted archer wore down the English. By night the Normans had won, and Harold and his brave housecarls lay dead upon the field.

William advanced to London, devastating the country in a way to bring terror into men's hearts. Many Anglo-Saxons of wealth and position, accepting the inevitable, made their submission; William was soon recognized as King by most of England south of the Humber. Yet it was some five years before the English were completely subdued. There were revolts along the Welsh border, in Exeter, and in Northumbria. William determined to teach the north a lesson. He carried fire and sword through the northern shires, devastating an area of a

The Bayeux Tapestry. The Battle of Hastings showing Norman and Anglo-Saxon arms. (From *The Bayeux Tapestry*, edited by Sir Frank Stenton, published by Phaidon Press Ltd., London, distributed in the USA by New York Graphic, Greenwich, Conn.)

thousand square miles. He destroyed every inhabited place between York and Durham, burned farm implements and stores of food, and reduced the inhabitants to starvation. The destruction extended to Staffordshire, Derbyshire, and the vicinity of Chester. Thereafter there was little resistance save by the popular hero Hereward the Wake, who held out for some time in the fens around Ely.

Many dangers remained for William, who needed an army, not only to crush native revolts and to curb his restless followers, but also to prevent invasion from Scandinavia and to protect Normandy. He began a series of important arrangements to secure a permanent army of some size. He did so by introducing Norman feudalism.

FEUDALISM

Feudalism is a term used to describe certain institutions which emerged in western Europe in the seventh and eighth centuries and which developed rapidly in the two centuries that followed. These institutions appeared because rulers were so constantly engaged in war and so limited in their machinery of government that they could not protect the people at a time when Europe was under deadly attack by Saracens, Slavs, Magyars, and Norsemen. Feudalism was a means by which society placed itself on a permanent war footing and obtained some small amount of local government and local security.

As introduced into England by the Normans,[3] feudalism consisted of three basic elements. The first was personal. A baron who received English lands from William bound himself in the most sacred and solemn way to become William's man, his vassal, and to give him loyalty, service, and good counsel. The baron performed an act of homage and swore an oath of fealty, pledging himself to be William's faithful follower. William in turn promised protection to his vassal. This protection was not only military, but legal. William held a feudal court which the baron must attend and in which he could seek redress for any wrong done to him by another baron. This bond of lord and vassal, which we have seen foreshadowed in the comitatus, was made as sacred and as unbreakable as possible, for it held society together. And yet it was a contract. If the vassal failed to perform his duty and service, his lands were forfeited. If the King broke the contract by injustice or tyranny, the vassal could in extreme cases renounce his fealty in a declaration called a defiance. In practice the defiance was extremely rare, for it did the baron little good unless he could defend himself by successful revolt.

A second element of feudalism was the land granted by the King to a vassal in return for military service. The vassal was a tenant in chief because he received his land directly from the King; the land was held by feudal or military tenure and was called the fief. William had vast quantities of land, for he confiscated the estates not only of Harold and his brothers but of all the English who fought at Hastings or who later rose in rebellion. Indeed, there was the implicit claim that William was the proprietor of England and that all land belonged to him. He made arrangements with about 180 of his barons, lay and ecclesiastical, granting estates to each in return for the service of a stipulated number of knights, calculated for convenience in multiples of five. A few of the greatest barons owed

---

[3] It should be emphasized that feudalism differed in various parts of western Europe.

sixty or seventy knights, and in general the feudal burden was much heavier than it had been in Normandy for an equivalent amount of land. These knights equipped for battle must be brought to the feudal host and must serve for forty days a year, that is, for the summer campaign.

It was absolutely essential that a baron supply the knights he owed. So vital was this obligation that various safeguards, known as the feudal incidents, protected the King or feudal suzerain in case the knights were not forthcoming. The incidents, as they developed in Anglo-Norman feudalism, were somewhat as follows.

Relief. The estate held by a baron in military tenure was in practice hereditary. But in theory it was not, for death ended the contract, and when a baron died the King might legally take back the land. What happened was that the heir paid the King a sum of money known as relief and was then invested with his father's estates. The King demanded that the fief be held together and that one person be responsible for the knights due from it. Hence there arose the principle of primogeniture by which the fief descended to the eldest son and to him alone.[4] Primogeniture was a measure of the insistence with which the King demanded knights' service from a fief at the earliest possible moment.

Primer seizin. The King might seize and hold the property until relief was paid.

Wardship. If the heir was a child and thus unable to fulfill the military obligations of the fief, the King might take possession of the estate and manage it for his own profit until the heir came of age.

Marriage. Should the fief descend to a woman, the King was in danger of losing the military service owed him. The heiress might marry someone who could not perform this service, or she might marry an enemy of the King and transfer her wealth to him. Hence the King reserved the right to select a husband for an heiress, though the husband must not be her inferior in rank.

Escheat. If the vassal's family became extinct, or if the vassal suffered a long imprisonment for some grave offense, the fief reverted or escheated to the King, who regained complete control over it.

Fine on alienation. A vassal wishing to sell or alienate a portion of his fief could not do so without the King's consent and would normally pay a fine for the privilege of alienation.

Forfeiture. A vassal who failed to perform his military service, or who broke his agreement with the King in some other way, was tried in the King's feudal court and, if found guilty, forfeited his lands, which then reverted to the King.

These feudal incidents not only assured the King that knights' service would be forthcoming from a fief but also underscored the fact that the fief was not a gift but a conditional grant of land in which the King retained many rights. They provided occasional opportunities for the King to obtain revenue from the fief. In addition, the King could ask for the feudal aids, sums of money payable by a vassal when the King was in financial need. There was at first a good deal of uncertainty about the aids, but during the twelfth century they became payable

---

[4] The principle of primogeniture was not firmly established in England until about 1200.

on three occasions only: when the King knighted his eldest son, which might be an occasion of great splendor and expense; when he arranged the marriage of his eldest daughter and had to supply a dowry; and when he was captured in war and must be ransomed.

The third element of feudalism was private jurisdiction. The barons who obtained estates from William also obtained the right to hold courts for the men living on their lands. These courts were of various kinds. A court known as the manorial court existed for the unfree peasants on each estate. A feudal court was held for the vassals of a lord who had granted (or subinfeudated) a portion of his lands to his knights or to other persons in return for military service; and the private courts, the courts for the freemen of the area, which were usually the old hundred courts of the Anglo-Saxon period that the Norman barons took over either through a grant from the King or through quiet usurpation. It was this element of private jurisdiction that gave feudalism its governmental aspect. The enforcement of law was left in private hands in a way no modern state would permit.

These feudal principles will become clearer if we look more closely at what happened in the years following the Conquest. William granted fiefs, as we have seen, to about 180 of his barons, who were pledged to supply an army which contained at the least some 4000 knights and may have contained many more. This was a large army. The number of knights required from each fief was determined by the King, whose assessments seem very arbitrary, but he was often ignorant of the true value of the lands involved. Some of the fiefs were clustered around the sixty or so castles William built, and the knights served in rotation on garrison duty when they were not needed in the field. Such an arrangement was called a castellaria. In a few dangerous border districts—such as Chester, Shrewsbury, Hereford, Durham, and Kent—palatine earldoms were established in which an earl governed a compact block of territory with extraordinary powers.

Most of the great fiefs were composed of estates scattered throughout the kingdom. Henry de Ferrers, Earl of Derby, held lands in fourteen counties. This scattering of estates has sometimes been attributed to policy, but it was probably due to the piecemeal nature of the Conquest and to the way in which Anglo-Saxon nobles had held lands in various parts of the kingdom. The result was to lessen the military power of the Norman barons and to give them an interest in the country as a whole rather than in any one locality. The estates making up a great fief were known collectively as an honor, which was administered as a unit from the principal castle of the baron. It had its officials, its council, its feudal court, its exchequer; its organization and management were modeled upon the administration of the King. William held the greatest of honors, the honor of England.

Having obtained a fief, a Norman baron speedily took possession. The Anglo-Saxon nobles who survived the Conquest disappeared into poverty or exile; when William died in 1087 scarcely more than one percent of the land remained in the hands of those who had held it before 1066. William insisted that the Normans hold their lands with all the rights and obligations of the former owners. For this reason the Normans adopted the fiction that the Anglo-Saxon nobles had been their ancestors. Occasionally a Norman married the Anglo-Saxon heiress of the lands he had obtained from the King. To hold the people in subjection required military strength; the Norman baron, using the forced labor of the peasants, at once built a castle. This was done by digging a circular ditch and by throwing the earth into a great mound in the middle which was called the motte. On the top of the motte was built the castle, known as the keep or donjon, a crude timbered structure surrounded by a wooden stockade. The ditch was filled with water. Beyond it and below the castle was a courtyard or bailey which contained stables and outbuildings. It was protected like the castle with a stockade and was connected with the motte by a drawbridge that could be raised in time of danger. From these crude timbered castles, not replaced by stone for another century, the Norman barons and their knights rode forth to hold the countryside in subjection.

Every baron, lay and ecclesiastical, maintained a number of knights in his household. Knights were essential, not only to fulfill a baron's obligation to the King and to hold down the native population, but also to garrison castles and to escort the baron and his family as they traveled from one estate to another. The barons began very shortly to grant lands to some of their knights in return for military service. This process was known as subinfeudation, and the knight who obtained a fief became the King's subvassal. Knights were most anxious to be enfeoffed in this way. Without an estate they were apt to remain mere fighting men all their lives. They were rough and crude and brutalized by war. The Anglo-Saxons saw no reason to regard them with respect; in fact, the Anglo-Saxon word *cniht* meant servant or retainer. But if a knight could obtain a fief he might rise in the social scale. Some knights secured lands scattered through the honor of their lord, they attended his feudal court, they were perhaps his officials, they owed him the service of three or four knights. They held as much land as some of the smaller tenants in chief, and they were referred to as barons. They might receive fiefs from several lords, having one—their liege lord—to whom they owed loyalty above all others. This process, by which a great baron held land from the King and then subinfeudated part of it to knights or lesser barons (who might repeat the process to knights below them), created in time the elaborate hierarchy of the landed classes in medieval England.

In the reign of Henry I (1100–1135) there arose a practice of paying money to the King in lieu of military service. This payment, known as scutage or shield money, was often of advantage to both parties. A baron might be old or ill; and although there were warrior-bishops who loved to take part in battle—William's brother Bishop Odo swung a great club at the Battle of Hastings because canon law forbade him to shed blood by the sword—many churchmen preferred to pay scutage in place of knights' service. The King welcomed scutage because he had much fighting to do on the Continent, where he could easily hire knights. In the long run scutage had important results. The smaller barons became less warlike and more devoted to the management of their estates; men could assume the obligations of a fief although they did not intend to fight; and a baron could grant a fraction of a knight's fee, which was the amount of land necessary to support a knight.

A few general comments may be made at this point. In the first place, it is clear that feudal institutions concerned only the nobility. The mass of the people, peasants and townsmen and even merchants of some wealth, had no part in the feudal system. The obligations of the peasants as they worked in the fields were regulated by ancient custom; the land could change hands, from Anglo-Saxon to Norman, without altering the dues and services of the peasants. Secondly, feudalism under the strong Norman Kings was not disruptive. Rather, it strengthened the monarchy, held society together, and made possible the performance

Motte and bailey castle, Great Berkhamstead, Hertford. The motte is seen beyond the bailey. (Aerofilms Limited)

of public functions which otherwise would not have been carried out at all. The Norman nobles possessed a tightly knit cohesion and solidarity unknown before the Conquest. Yet, in the third place, the feudal structure was far more flexible than can be indicated in a short description. Every bargain between William and his tenants in chief, and between these tenants and their vassals, was a separate agreement which might differ from all others. Many of William's barons came from places other than Normandy and introduced feudal customs they had known in their homelands.

Finally, the question arises why feudalism had not developed in Anglo-Saxon England. Certainly feudal elements existed in Anglo-Saxon society. There was the personal loyalty of a man to his lord. There was the element of land, although royal grants were in the nature of gifts and were not conditional upon military service. A thegn fought for the King, not because he held land, but because the status of a thegn implied military activity. Private jurisdiction existed, but it was rare and was a delegation of royal authority, not a right which accompanied the holding of land. These elements were never fused into a system. They remained vague, casual, and haphazard until feudalism converted them into a precise and definite scheme. The feudal fief, land held directly for knights' service, did not exist; its introduction was perhaps the greatest innovation of the Conquest. There were other reasons why feudalism did not develop in pre-Conquest England. A line of strong Kings had led the nation to victory over the Danes. Monarchy acquired great prestige and won the loyal affection of the people.

Anglo-Saxon Kings did not have to bribe their nobles with lavish grants of land. The reconquest of the Danelaw made it possible for Kings to organize local government and to keep some control over it. Finally, because both Danes and Anglo-Saxons fought on foot, England was not called upon to meet the attack of mounted knights, and the cost of war could be kept comparatively low.

NORMAN MONARCHY

The King

William the Conqueror and his sons increased the strength of the monarchy and participated with drive and energy in the work of government. They had the advantage of ruling a kingdom in which the foundations of the state had been firmly laid. Anglo-Saxon Kings had given England a political and territorial unity quite unknown in France. The royal household contained the beginnings of various departments—chamber, wardrobe, treasury, and chancery. The Danegeld was a tax levied on a national scale, and in the King's chamber were officials experienced in the administration of finance. The chancery possessed its staff of skillful clerks, its charters, its writs, its royal seal. The local courts of the shire and of the hundred had vigorous traditions; the sheriff was a royal official connecting the local and central governments.

William wisely decided to accept the past, to rule as the heir of Edward the Confessor, and to preserve Anglo-Saxon law and institutions. In the first years after the Conquest he had the ideal of an Anglo-Norman state in which he would be served by men of both nations. This proved impossible, and in the end William made more changes than he intended. Yet his borrowings were numerous. It seems probable that the writing staff of the Confessor's chancery passed into the service of the Conqueror. William's first writs were in the English tradition and were in Anglo-Saxon. It was only after some years that their style became French and their language Latin. The Anglo-Saxon writ was quickly adopted. The Danegeld filled William with delight; he retained it, making it three times as heavy as before. Finding the sheriffs highly useful, he greatly increased their authority.

But while William assumed the rights and prerogatives of Anglo-Saxon Kings, he also acquired new rights as the supreme lord of many vassals. It was this combination of the sovereignty of the Anglo-Saxon monarch and the suzerainty of the feudal overlord which exalted the position of the Norman Kings. They claimed both the allegiance due from the people to an Anglo-Saxon King and the fealty due from feudal vassals to their lord. They retained the fyrd, though their military strength was based upon the feudal host. They continued Anglo-Saxon sources of revenue, making them more productive, and at the same time exacted the feudal aids and incidents from their barons. They preserved the popular justice of the shire and hundred courts, but also introduced the rules of feudal justice. They retained and strengthened the Anglo-Saxon doctrine that a King duly crowned and anointed ceased to be merely a layman and acquired a divine and holy character. He was God's vicar, deriving his authority from the Almighty; he possessed a miraculous power to heal the disease known as the scrofula. William did all that he could to exploit this sacrosanct position of kingship.

The Great Council

King William, says the *Anglo-Saxon Chronicle*, "wore his crown three times every year, as often as he was in England; at Easter he wore it at Winchester; at Whitsuntide at Westminster; at Midwinter at Gloucester; and then were with him all the rich men over all England, archbishops and suffragan bishops, abbots and earls, thegns and knights." These were the great social occasions of the year when the barons of the King met to do homage. There was solemn ritual and pageantry. High Mass was sung by one of the archbishops; the crown was placed upon William's head; liturgical laudes glorifying God, but also glorifying William by implication, were chanted before him. Pomp and circumstance were followed by feasting and revelry. And in conclusion William discussed matters of state with his barons.

This assembly, though known by different names, may be called the *Magnum Concilium* or the King's Great Council. It did not differ much in appearance from the Anglo-Saxon witan and it was sometimes called the witan by contemporaries. But there were fundamental differences between the two. The Great Council was a feudal body. It was the duty of a feudal suzerain to summon his tenants in chief to attend his court, and it was both the duty and the privilege of the tenants to be present. The basis of attendance was the possession of a fief held directly from the King. But William continued the prerogative of the Anglo-Saxon King to summon anyone he pleased. He included his household officials, his barons who held fiefs only in Normandy, foreign guests and envoys, and visiting dignitaries of the church. On one occasion in 1086 he summoned a very large assembly on Salisbury Plain, where all the barons, great and small, as well as their vassals, swore an oath of fealty to William as their paramount lord. Normally, however, the small tenants in chief did not attend, and the assembly consisted of fifty to seventy-five of the richest and greatest barons. A formal summons was not normally issued for the three great sessions of the year, but only for other meetings.

The principal function of the Great Council was to act as a court of feudal law. In 1075 it tried a baron for rebellion, found him guilty, and sentenced him to life imprisonment. Later in 1096 one baron in the council accused another of taking part in a revolt. The issue was decided by the Norman ordeal of battle. This ordeal, like those of the Anglo-Saxons, was an appeal to God to show which party was in the right. Plaintiff and defendant fought in mortal combat before the court, to the joy of the spectators; the victor was assumed to have won because his plea was just. When the unfortunate baron accused in 1096 was defeated, the King ordered that his eyes be put out and that he be castrated. The Great Council also tried cases of a nonfeudal nature, such as a dispute in 1070 between two bishops over certain lands, a case in which the council turned to the evidence of Anglo-Saxon charters.

Apart from its legal work, the functions of the Great Council were vague. It witnessed charters issued by the King and gave formal approval to many of his actions. It gave him advice on such matters as he chose to place before it. He sometimes turned to it for support in his relations with foreign powers or in his domestic policy. Opposition to his wishes, however, was extremely rare; he constantly acted without consulting the Great Council, and one must assume that it was no great check upon his power. Rather, it was a means of sounding out baronial opinion, for even the strong Norman Kings would have been foolish to have ignored entirely the wishes of their vassals.

The Small Council

The Great Council was only in occasional session, and the daily work of government was carried on by the King with the assistance of members of his household and of those barons who happened to be in attendance. Officers of the household supplied the professional skill required to carry on the work of central administration, and yet their duties were a strange mixture of official business and care for the domestic life of the King. A list of these officials dates from about 1135 and is headed by the chancellor, the chief of the royal chaplains, who presided over a staff of clerks and was responsible for the secretarial work of the government. Then comes the steward, who had charge of the hall and the arrangements for preparing and serving food; the chamberlain, who presided over the royal bedchamber and over the King's wardrobe; the treasurer; the butler, with his staff of cellarers and cupbearers; the constable, who managed the stables and outdoor activities; and the marshal, who maintained order in the court. Other members of the household were frequently away from court on various administrative tasks throughout the country. In addition a number of the greater barons seem to have been with William a good deal; and as he traveled around the kingdom he was attended by the barons of the area through which he was passing. Hence he always had officials and advisers with him. They formed what may be called the *Curia Regis,* or the King's small council.

The work of the small council should not be differentiated from that of the Great Council, for both bodies did much the same sort of business. When the Great Council met, the small council merged with it and became its heart and core. Questions of major importance were reserved for the larger body. But the members of the small council advised with the King, witnessed charters, corresponded with local officials, and frequently acted as a court of law.

We must picture William as constantly on the move, his court an armed camp, traveling from place to place, suppressing revolts, receiving oaths of fealty, deciding disputes, consuming the food collected against his coming, hunting in the forests, governing as he went. One scene on the Bayeux tapestry, a pictorial account of the Conquest in needlework, depicts an outdoor feast on the southern coast as the Normans celebrated their unopposed landing in 1066. Servants are cooking food in large pots; they place bowls of meat before William and his barons; they pour wine into shallow glasses. A servant offers William a basin of water and a towel so that he can wash his hands after eating. Many of his dinners must have been formal picnics of this kind. His household traveled with him. In the darkness before dawn, with a great clatter and commotion and doubtless with much violent language, the royal documents of state, the King's moneybags, his bed, his wardrobe, his arms and weapons, the pots and pans of the kitchen, the holy objects of the chapel, were all loaded on pack horses or placed in carts, as the royal cavalcade began its lumbering journey across the country.

Local Government

The Norman Conquest brought about important changes in local government. And yet old customs and old ways of doing things, the ancient folkright of the people, remained essentially unaltered. The courts of the shire and of the hundred continued to meet and to enforce Anglo-Saxon law. The peasant was still required to serve in the fyrd, to take part in the hue and cry, and to come to the hundred court to be assigned to a tithing group—a practice the Normans referred to as frankpledge. The Anglo-Saxon village retained its essential unity. The substructure of peasant society was not fundamentally altered.

The shire court was strengthened as a result of the Conquest. It became the means by which Norman Kings controlled local government and imposed their will upon all parts of the country. They thought it worth while to compel the people to attend the shire courts as in the past and thus to keep open a means by which the King and his subjects could have some contact with each other. William the Conqueror made great use of the sheriff, giving him large powers, so that the sheriff was more potent in the century following the Conquest than ever before or since. William's sheriffs were important barons holding large estates in their shires and were men whom William trusted. They presided in the shire courts and heard royal pleas or cases in which the King had an interest. Twice a year they visited the hundred courts in what was known as the sheriff's tourn. On these visits they checked attendance at the court, they saw that persons wanted by the court were present, and they supervised frankpledge. The sheriff helped with the hue and cry, apprehended criminals, enforced the decisions of the courts, and was responsible for law and order. He also called out the fyrd and acted as custodian of royal estates and castles. Highly important in finance, he collected all kinds of fines, taxes, and miscellaneous revenues from courts, lands, and boroughs. Much of this money he disbursed locally; the rest he sent to the King. He gave hospitality and protection to itinerant officials and to the royal court when it visited his shire. And in general he executed the commands of the King sent to him in royal writs.

So powerful did the sheriffs become that they posed problems for the government. There was danger that the office might become hereditary and that sheriffs might turn into great feudal magnates who could challenge the King's authority. But this was prevented. William II appointed a humbler type of sheriff who had no great standing in his locality or who had served as a minor official in the royal household. The sheriff was curbed by resident justices and later by the necessity of making semiannual reports of his finances to the exchequer.[5] Nonetheless he had many opportunities to oppress the people. Irregularities were winked at as long as he was loyal and brought in money. The problem of the unscrupulous sheriff continued for centuries.

The hundred courts were depressed by the Conquest. They lost business to the shire courts and to new courts which came in with feudalism. It was the right of a feudal lord to hold a court on each of his estates to which the peasants brought their disputes and in which they were punished for petty offenses. Lords, moreover, held feudal courts for their vassals. These feudal courts were important on the great fiefs, though jurisdiction of this type dwindled as time went on. But the Norman lords had exercised broad rights of justice on the Continent and expected to do the same in England. Many great fiefs contained several hundreds; and the Norman barons, sometimes with a royal charter and sometimes without, took over these hundred courts. Such courts lost their public character and became private courts. The men who attended them remained the same, but the lord's steward presided and the profits of justice went to the baron and not to the King. If the baron could also obtain the coveted right to supervise frankpledge, he might exclude the sheriff altogether from his private court. By the end of the thirteenth century, when Edward I tried to reverse this process, perhaps half of the hundred courts in England had passed into private hands.

[5] See pages 69–70.

THE PEASANT, THE VILLAGE, AND THE MANOR

The peasants were less affected by the Conquest than was the Anglo-Saxon nobility, but they were sharply depressed in prosperity and in legal status. They suffered in a material way from the destruction of property wrought by William the Conqueror in suppressing rebellions. They suffered from his policy of setting aside large tracts of land as royal forests. A village situated in these forest areas lived under a harsh and repressive code of forest regulations. Many an Anglo-Saxon freeman, moreover, his lands confiscated without compensation and given to a Norman, was compelled to become a laborer bound to the soil formerly his.

The peasants also suffered in legal status. The class of Anglo-Saxon peasants, as we know, was very heterogeneous: freemen at the top and slaves at the bottom, and in between great numbers of men economically dependent upon a lord and yet free in the eyes of the law. Thousands of peasants, though economically unfree, had some tincture of freedom about them. This combination of freedom and unfreedom in the same individual was incomprehensible to the Normans. Finding the legal status of such persons difficult to define, the Normans lumped them all together either as villeins (who had some rights in the land) or as cotters (who had not). Both were classed as unfree. In this crude way the Normans divided peasant society into two parts: a small number of freemen at the top; a huge mass of unfree serfs below. Slaves did not fit into feudal society. They were classed as the lowest rank of unfree serfs, though this slight rise in status brought them no material benefit.

The daily life of the majority of the peasants went on much as before. It had received a rude shock, but the traditions of the past remained unbroken. Agricultural prosperity slowly revived. The peasant was much more aware of the condition of the crops or of the weather than of the legal distinctions (or lack of them) imposed by his Norman conquerors.

In Anglo-Saxon times the unit of agriculture and the lowest unit of local government had been the village. The Normans introduced the manor. It may be defined as an estate under a single lord which was farmed and administered as an agricultural entity. A piece of property with an established value, it was thought of as consisting of two parts. The first was the lord's demesne, that is, his portion of the arable land, consisting either of strips scattered among the strips of the peasants or of a solid block of strips near the castle or manor house. In the economy of the manor the cultivation of the lord's demesne was paramount.

The second part of the manor comprised the arable strips of the peasants. The peasants held their land by servile tenure. They were bound to the soil and could be fetched back by force if they ran away. They owed the lord two or three days' labor each week upon the demesne, they owed him a portion of the produce of their own strips, they owed attendance at the manor court, and they owed a number of money payments such as the heriot, a death duty of their best farm animal payable when a peasant died and his son took over the holding, and the merchet, a fine imposed upon a peasant if his daughter married outside the manor and thus deprived the lord of a worker. In many ways the villein was at his lord's disposal.

Historians once thought that the village and the manor were identical in area and that all over England the Normans quickly molded the first into the second, but it is now known that the village and the manor were not two names for the same block of land and that the manor did not become universal after 1066. It was merely a part of the rural scene. The manor was a unit of property, a unit of tenure, a unit of feudal jurisdiction. The village, on the other hand, was a piece of land which could be splintered into a number of manors. In Norman England some villages were divided among several manors, and some manors contained more than one village. The two were rarely identical. There were lords who had surrendered parts of their demesne to other lords, freemen and even villeins who acquired land on more than one manor, villages of freemen who had no lord, manors without a lord's demesne, and manors without villeins or villein services. The manor, moreover, did not develop in the far north, nor along the Welsh border, nor in Kent. It was not the universal pattern in the northern Midlands nor in East Anglia. The area in which it occurred most frequently was the south and the southern Midlands. Thus the old picture of England as divided with neatness and precision into a great number of manors, each coinciding with an Anglo-Saxon village, is far too simple an interpretation. The rural organization of England was much more complex than has been supposed, and the manor was far from universal.

Men continued to think of the village as the essential unit of the countryside. The Kings did the same, for while they did not interfere with the internal affairs of the manor, they used the village as a unit of taxation, administration, and police. Deeply rooted in the traditions of the people, the village proved to be more permanent than the artificial division of the manor.

THE DOMESDAY BOOK

There is no clearer proof of William's power than the great survey of England he carried through in 1086. In that year he sent out officials to travel in four circuits through all of England south of the Tyne. They were instructed to visit each hundred and to summon the sheriff, the Norman barons and their vassals, the freemen who attended the hundred court, and the priest, the reeve, and six villeins from each village. These men, put under oath to tell the truth, were asked a long list of questions concerning every manor:

> how the manor is called, who held it in the time of King Edward, who holds it now, how many hides there are, how many ploughs in demesne, how many men, how many villeins, how many cotters, how many serfs, how many free-men, how many sokemen, how much woods, how much meadow, how many pastures, how many mills, how many fish-ponds, how much has been added or taken away, how much it was worth altogether and how much now, and how much each freeman or sokeman had or has there. All this information is given three times over: namely, in the time of King Edward, when King William gave it out, and how it is now—and whether more can be had from it than is being had.[6]

This mass of information was arranged in feudal groupings under the tenants in chief and the fiefs of each locality and was then compiled by the King's clerks in the various volumes of what is known as Domesday Book. Such a detailed inquiry exists for no other country during the Middle Ages. Historians

[6] Carl Stephenson and Frederick George Marcham, *Sources of English Constitutional History* (New York: Harper & Row, 1937), p. 40.

have wondered what prompted William to launch and carry it through. One theory is that Domesday Book was to form the basis for increased taxation. But it is possible that William may merely have wished to know in detail the extent and value of his great conquest. He may have planned to impose a more rigid feudal pattern upon what the Normans regarded as the chaos of Anglo-Saxon rights, jurisdictions, and social classes.

WILLIAM AND THE CHURCH

Norman monks, writing after the Conquest, spoke of the Anglo-Saxon church as in great need of reform. But if the church in England contained abuses, so did the church on the Continent. To understand William's policy we must take a broader look at the church throughout all Europe.

Three matters in particular worried men who had the interests of the church at heart: lay appointment to church office, simony, and the marriage of the clergy. For many centuries the church, seeking the protection of temporal rulers, had permitted them to exercise a large control over ecclesiastical appointments. Anglo-Saxon Kings had named bishops and abbots, as had the dukes in Normandy. But lay appointments were not without their dangers, and these dangers increased with the development of feudalism.

In a feudal society bishops and abbots played a double role. They were feudal tenants in chief holding large fiefs from the King; they were the King's advisers and administrators, often deeply involved in matters of state. But they were also high officials of the church upon whom its welfare depended. If the King appointed a bishop who could fulfill his obligations as a feudal vassal, there was no assurance that this bishop would serve the church in a spiritual way. And if the church appointed a bishop well qualified for holy office, there was no guarantee that such a bishop could perform his feudal duties to the satisfaction of the King. This dilemma caused bitter quarrels between church and state until in 1170 an archbishop of Canterbury lay murdered in his own cathedral. Although the combination of priest and warrior in the same person was not impossible in the eleventh century, this double role of the higher clergy could become grotesque and dangerous.

As feudalism developed, appointments to many offices in the church fell into the hands of nobles who sometimes regarded ecclesiastical office as a marketable commodity that could be sold to the highest bidder. Hence the abuse of simony —giving or receiving money in return for office in the church. Many churchmen were also disturbed by the large number of married clergy, for it was believed that only a celibate priesthood, which had renounced the world and the ties of family life, could devote its attention exclusively to the work of the church.

During the tenth and early eleventh centuries a movement for church reform began in various places—in the monastery of Cluny in Burgundy, in Lorraine, and in Italy. The papacy took no part, for it had fallen upon evil days. Then suddenly, about the year 1050, the papacy revived. A series of strong and aggressive popes asserted the independence of the church from lay control and proclaimed the revolutionary doctrine that the papacy was superior to Kings and Emperors. These claims reached their climax in the pontificate of Hildebrand, who became Pope Gregory VII (1073–1085). The principles of his program were somewhat as follows. (1) Papal authority must be supreme within the church; the clergy were to obey the commands of the pope without question. (2) The clergy must regard itself as a class apart from the rest of society. It must renounce all worldly ties; the symbol of this great denial was the celibacy of the priesthood. (3) The church must be independent of lay control. It should select its own officials and should not accept them from Kings or barons. (4) The pope, as the successor of St. Peter, must be superior to all lay rulers. He should dominate the world in order to bring it to salvation; temporal sovereigns must be subject to the church. Gregory's stand was certain to produce a crisis between church and state.

William was ready to reform the church in England, strengthen its administration, and endow it generously, but he had been master of the church in Normandy and he was determined to be its master in England. His ideal was strong and orderly government; an independent church would make strong monarchy impossible. He insisted, therefore, upon the older tradition of kingly control. He appointed bishops and abbots in the English church. When in 1080 Gregory demanded that he surrender England to the papacy and receive it back as a feudal fief, thus becoming the pope's vassal, William sent a prompt refusal. Indeed, going further, he laid down certain rules regarding his relations with Rome. No pope should be recognized in England without his consent. No papal letters should be received without his knowledge. No bishop should leave the country and no tenant in chief should be excommunicated without his permission. William also exercised a veto over the legislation of ecclesiastical councils meeting in England. He thus retained control of the English church despite the lofty claims now voiced in Rome. Gregory, preoccupied with affairs on the Continent and knowing that William was eager for reform, did not retaliate.

William's principal adviser in ecclesiastical affairs was Lanfranc, the archbishop of Canterbury, who worked closely with the King and supported his policy toward the papacy. Lanfranc was a remarkable man, an Italian who had studied and practiced law before he had turned to theology. He had been prior of the monastery at Bec in Normandy and later abbot at Caen. He brought to his work in England a broader experience and a wider knowledge of the world than was possessed by most churchmen there.

His aim was to make the church in England conform with continental practice. To clear the way for change, he and William gradually removed Anglo-Saxon bishops and abbots and replaced them with Normans. Lanfranc also established his supremacy over the archbishop of York. He then summoned a series of church councils which enacted important legislation. Bishops were instructed to strengthen their control over parish priests, to hold diocesan synods for the discipline of the lower clergy, to visit and investigate local churches. A priest could not leave his diocese without the permission of the bishop. Diocesan centers, often located in rural areas in Anglo-Saxon times, were transferred to large towns from which the bishop could govern more efficiently.

The number of married clergy in England was very large. Yet despite pressure from Rome, Lanfranc refrained from violent action. He obtained a decree providing that married clergymen need not put away their wives but that henceforth all candidates for the priesthood must take vows of celibacy. Lanfranc did no more than assert a principle, for marriage continued among the clergy. The evil of simony was forbidden. It had not been a serious abuse in Anglo-Saxon times, and it was certainly not ended by the Normans, who strengthened the organization and discipline of the church without greatly improving its morals.

Although William and Lanfranc resisted the pretentions of the papacy, each of them in turn took a step which would in the future strengthen papal power. About 1072 William decreed that ecclesiastical cases should not be heard in the hundred courts but should be reserved for church courts presided over by bishops. As a result, the bishops gradually ceased to attend the shire courts, and a sharp division arose between lay and ecclesiastical jurisdiction. In the twelfth century the church courts claimed many cases which William had not originally intended to give them. Throughout the Middle Ages the separate courts of the church formed a powerful means of extending Roman influence.

In preparing himself for his work as archbishop, Lanfranc made a thorough study of canon law. Later he drew up a summary of the law of the church. But canon law exalted the position of the papacy and encouraged churchmen to look to the pope rather than to the King as the source of ecclesiastical authority.

4

the sons of william i, stephen, and henry ii

William the Conqueror had three sons, among whom, as he lay on his death-bed, he divided his great possessions. To Robert, the eldest, he bequeathed the duchy of Normandy; to William, the kingdom of England; to Henry, the youngest, he left 5000 pounds of silver. Of these three sons, Robert was the least disagreeable. He was brave, generous, and good-natured, but he was also a man of weak character, soft and self-indulgent, without purpose or determination; under his wretched government Normandy sank rapidly into anarchy and chaos. William, King of England from 1087 to 1100, was short and stocky, with so fiery a face that he was nicknamed Rufus. He maintained the strong monarchy estab-lished by his father. An excellent soldier, he was generous and loyal to the men who helped him fight his wars. But that was about all that could be said for him. A monkish chronicler, who hated him as all churchmen did, wrote that every night he went to bed a worse man than he had been in the morning and every morning he arose a worse man than he had been the night before. Cynical, violent, cruel, avaricious, licentious, utterly untrustworthy, he was the Norman baron at his worst. His subjects fled at his approach, and his primary policy was to extract money from his people. Henry, who ruled England from 1100 to 1135, had many of the same qualities: he was stern and ruthless, cruel, licentious, and grasping, but he had his father's capacity for government. He liked order and efficiency. Patient and industrious, he was a prudent King who acted with caution and restraint. The machinery of government developed rapidly during his reign and was operating smoothly when he died.

In a confused series of wars the three brothers began at once to quarrel with each other over their inheritance. William led expeditions against Robert and obtained possession of the rich part of Normandy north and east of the river Seine. Joining forces, the two brothers then drove Henry from the western portion of the duchy, known as the Cotentin, which he had purchased from Robert for 3000 pounds of silver. In 1094 Robert secured the alliance of King Philip of France, who greatly feared William as a neighbor. But Philip was so lazy and self-indulgent—a chronicler wrote that he came hiccuping to the wars—

that he did Robert little good. Tiring perhaps of his own misgovernment, Robert took the Cross in 1096 and departed for the Holy Land on the First Crusade. Having no money with which to finance his enterprise, he pawned his duchy to William for three years for 10,000 marks of silver.[1] Thenceforth William ruled both England and Normandy until his death in 1100, when Robert, returning with an enhanced reputation acquired in the Holy Land and with a wealthy bride acquired in southern Italy, once more obtained possession of his duchy.

WILLIAM RUFUS, 1087–1100

In England William Rufus and his minister, Rannulf Flambard, had employed all the powers of the Crown to extract money from the people. The shire courts were encouraged to levy fines and confiscations. The feudal incidents were enforced with ruthless savagery. The relief demanded from heirs was so exorbitant that it equaled the value of the lands they were about to inherit. Heiresses and widows of tenants in chief were married to the men who would pay the highest price for them. Escheats and forfeitures were harshly extorted; new and heavy aids were demanded frequently. Thus the rules of law—both the law of the popular courts and the law of the feudal court of the King—were employed to obtain money. Similar methods were applied to the church. When high offices in the church fell vacant, William claimed a kind of ecclesiastical wardship and appropriated the revenues of a bishopric or monastery until a new appointment was made. It was thus to his advantage to keep the office vacant as long as possible; at the time of his death he was holding the lands of three vacant bishoprics and eleven monasteries. Newly appointed bishops and abbots had to pay great sums as relief; nonfeudal aids were demanded from the church. It is little wonder that the clergy looked to the papacy and not to the King for leadership in ecclesiastical affairs.

THE REIGN OF HENRY I, 1100–1135

On the afternoon of August 2, 1100, while hunting in the New Forest in Hampshire, William Rufus was struck by an arrow and killed. It is fairly well established that the arrow was shot by a Norman baron, Walter Tirel, but whether he killed the King by accident or by design remains a mystery. Though we cannot be sure, there are suggestions of a plot: Tirel at once fled abroad; no one was ever punished for the deed; the family into which Tirel had married was later treated with marked favor by Henry I. Henry's actions appear premeditated. On the day that William was killed, Henry galloped to Winchester and seized the royal treasure despite the protests of its keepers. On the day following he was approved as King by a mere handful of barons. And on August 5, three days after the shooting, he was crowned by the bishop of London, although the coronation was normally performed by one of the archbishops. Such hasty progress toward the throne was an indication that his position was precarious. He knew that Robert's claim was better than his, and unfortunately he had sworn fealty to Robert as his liege lord; thus his seizure of the throne exposed

---

[1] A mark was two thirds of a pound.

him to the charge of perjury. Moreover, the barons in England, smarting from the exactions of William Rufus, were in a discontented mood.

Henry therefore sought to win support not only from the barons but from the nation as a whole. He imprisoned Rannulf Flambard, William's instrument of extortion; he recalled Anselm, the archbishop of Canterbury, who had quarreled with William and was living in exile on the Continent. He also issued a coronation charter in which he made sweeping promises of better government. The charter contained the words: "I henceforth remove all the bad customs through which the kingdom of England has been unjustly oppressed." In the future, the charter declared, lands were not to be taken from the estates of bishoprics or monasteries during a vacancy. Heirs were not to buy back their fathers' lands but were to pay a "just and legitimate relief." The right to control the marriage of heiresses was to be exercised with moderation, and widows were not to be forced into marriage against their will. Oppressive exactions and other abuses were to be abolished.

Historians have sometimes made Henry's charter appear more important than it really was. It was not an admission by the Crown that there was an element of contract between King and barons in the feudal structure nor that this contract placed limitations upon the King. The charter was not an agreement with the barons. It was issued by the King alone and was addressed to all his subjects. There was no guarantee that its promises would be kept. As soon as he felt secure Henry disregarded them shamelessly. The charter was no more than a bid for general support. Nonetheless, its existence became generally known and was not forgotten a century later when the barons extracted Magna Carta from King John.

To ingratiate himself further with the native English, Henry married Edith, a descendant of the Anglo-Saxon Kings of Wessex. The marriage was a symbol that the age of Norman exploitation was drawing to an end and that Henry wished to obliterate the distinctions between Englishmen and Normans and to rule over a homogeneous people. "By intermarriage and by every other means in his power," wrote a chronicler, "he bound the two peoples into a firm union." In about 1170 it was said that one could not distinguish the one from the other.

In spite of Henry's conciliatory policy, there was a rebellion against him at the end of his first year as King. This revolt sprang from a group of unruly barons who held lands on both sides of the Channel and who believed that they had more to gain from the weak rule of Robert than from the strong rule of Henry. They persuaded Robert to invade England. Landing at Portsmouth in August 1101, he began to march toward London, but only a few barons joined him. He became alarmed, accepted Henry's offer of an annual subsidy of £2000 in return for a renunciation of the English throne, and returned rather tamely to Normandy. Thereupon Henry punished with great severity the barons who had revolted against him. He reached the conclusion that plotting would never cease until he was master of Normandy as well as of England. Laying his plans with care and finding allies on the borders of Normandy, he led three expeditions against his brother. Their culmination was the Battle of Tinchebrai, September 28, 1106, forty years to the day after the landing of William the Conqueror in 1066. Robert was defeated and spent the rest of his days as a prisoner. Transferred from castle to castle, he dragged out a miserable life for twenty-eight long years, dying at Cardiff in Wales in 1134, an old man of eighty, only a few months before the death of Henry. England and Normandy were thus united once more under one ruler.

As Duke of Normandy, Henry became deeply involved in wars and diplomacy on the Continent. His primary interests lay in continental affairs, and his experiments in English government and finance reflect this fact. The French King Louis VI (or Louis the Fat, 1108–1137) was beginning a policy which was to continue for centuries and by which the Kings of France slowly extended their authority over the great French fiefs until they were rulers of the entire country. On three occasions Louis began hostilities against Henry, only to be always baffled by diplomacy or war. At no time was Henry's hold on Normandy seriously threatened. Yet he spent almost half of his time on the Continent. He was forced to develop a system of government for England that would function when he was away and would help to carry the cost of his continental wars.

The Justiciar

To meet the need for a government without a resident sovereign, Henry devised a new official, the justiciar. The justiciar was the head of the administration, the King's most trusted minister, his viceroy or deputy with power to issue writs and to govern the country when the King was in Normandy. The first justiciar was Roger, bishop of Salisbury. This remarkable man had been an obscure priest in Normandy who had first attracted Henry's attention, it was said, by the rapidity with which he had conducted Mass one morning when Henry was eager to go hunting. He became Henry's steward, then his chancellor, and finally his justiciar. Roger expanded the functions of government and improved their procedure. He was the most important of a number of men whom Henry raised from obscurity to be his principal officials and whom he rewarded liberally with wealth and privilege. It was an indication of Henry's strength that he could thus dispense with feudal barons as ministers and develop an official aristocracy of service.

The King's small council was composed of these new bureaucrats, his household officials, and those barons who happened to be in attendance. When the King left the country he was apt to take his household officers with him, so that administration in England centered in the justiciar. The justiciar's court, sometimes called the King's court of the exchequer, handled every phase of government—financial, judicial, administrative—and formed the pivot of the entire administration.

The Early Exchequer

The early exchequer was famous in Henry's reign for its financial sessions. Twice a year, at Easter and at Michaelmas in the autumn, sheriffs and other officials who collected money appeared before it and rendered an account of their finances. There were two parts to the exchequer as Roger developed it. One was the lower exchequer or treasury, where the sheriffs paid the sums they had collected and where the coins were tested for weight and purity. The upper exchequer was the exchequer of account or of audit. Here a large table was covered with a black cloth on which squares (each about a foot in length and breadth) were marked as on a huge checker board. Each column of squares indicated a denomination of money: *d.* (pence), *s.* (shillings), £ (pounds), £20, £100, £1000, and £10,000; counters could be moved from square to square. At the head of the table sat the justiciar, flanked by the chancellor and other officials from the household. At the side of the table to the right of the justiciar sat the treasurer and clerks who entered the sums of money involved on long narrow strips of parchment known as the pipe rolls. On the opposite side of the table, to the left of the justiciar, was a calculator, who moved the counters, as well as a master of the writing office, who attended to any necessary correspondence.

Facing this formidable company, at the end of the table opposite the justiciar, appeared the sheriff. The sums of money for which he was responsible were read from the pipe roll, and counters were pushed into place to indicate the amounts he owed. The sums he had paid into the lower exchequer were then indicated by moving other counters; thus discrepancies and amounts still due were apparent to the penny. The exchequer was a most ingenious device. It must be remembered that the exchequer used roman, not arabic, numerals, and that with roman numerals the simplest calculations in arithmetic—such as addition—were all but impossible. The roman system had no symbol for zero; a blank square on the table represented it. The exchequer thus made accounting visual. After the accounting was complete, the sheriff received a stick on which were cut notches to indicate how much he had paid and how much was still due. The stick was then split into two parts, the sheriff retaining one and the exchequer the other.

The Sheriff

Appearance before the exchequer must have been a sobering experience for a sheriff. But the sheriffs of Henry's reign were in need of sobering. William the Conqueror, as we have seen, had appointed powerful barons as sheriffs and had allowed them great freedom. William Rufus, however, had sought to curb the sheriffs, and Henry continued this policy. Appointments were made from his trusted officials; sheriffs served for one year only and were required to render their accounts in the exchequer every six months. They were forbidden to summon meetings of the local courts in an arbitrary way. As in the reign of William Rufus, resident justices were appointed to curtail the sheriffs' power. Henry also continued a practice which had begun in Anglo-Saxon times. It was not uncommon for the King to send out special commissioners or justices to the local courts to preside over cases in which he had a special interest. These itinerant justices (or justices in eyre) were made a normal part of the machinery of government and law. When they presided in a local court, that court became a King's court; its authority was based not on Anglo-Saxon custom but on the King's writ. This development had great significance for the future.

The techniques of government steadily advanced during the reign of Henry I. Yet Henry's achievement had limitations. His rule was arbitrary and oppressive. Feudal fines and exactions were strained in favor of the Crown; government was based upon fear and severity; and Henry scarcely advanced beyond the limited concept of a feudal monarch whose principal concern was to hold the barons in subjection. A strong assertion of baronial independence was almost certain to come in the reign of Henry's successor.

Henry I and the Church

We have seen that during the pontificate of Hildebrand (Gregory VII, 1073–1085) the church had embarked on a program of reform, independence from lay control, and papal supremacy over Kings and Emperors. Of the many difficulties this program brought about between church and state, one of the chief concerned the appointment of bishops. The bishop played a double role. He was an official of the church, presiding over the administration of a diocese; he was also a feudal baron holding a great fief. It had been the practice in England and elsewhere for a bishop, having been elected by a cathedral chapter,[2] to do homage to the King for his lands and then to be invested by the King in his holy office through the formal presentation of a ring and staff as symbols of pastoral authority. This practice, known as lay investiture, gave the King control over the appointment of bishops. It was challenged by Anselm, the archbishop of Canterbury, who refused to do homage to Henry for his lands. Anselm, an Italian of good family, was a saint and a scholar, gentle and peace loving, but adamant in defense of principle. There was no compromise about him. He could be wholly unreasonable and obstinate. Without great experience or breadth of view, he did not recognize that the King might have a case in the clash of church and state. Henry stood his ground, demanding that Anselm do homage. This conflict, though conducted in a dignified way, continued for several years and became very awkward for both.

At length a compromise suggested by Ivo, bishop of Chartres, was reached. By it the King surrendered the right to invest bishops in their sacred office by the presentation of the ring and staff; on their part bishops continued to do homage for their lands. This was a triumph for the church in that the King lost all semblance of divine authority in appointing churchmen. Yet in a practical way it was the King who won. He could not be forced to accept the church's candidates, for he could refuse to receive their homage, and he was able to ensure in all cases that homage to him preceded consecration to holy office. Thus bishops and abbots continued to be men whom the King approved.

Two other issues between the church and the King arose in Henry's reign. One concerned appeals from the King's courts in England to the papal courts in Rome. So long as these appeals concerned disputes within the church there could be little objection to them. But if cases involving temporal matters were appealed from English to Roman courts, the King's position as the source of law might be severely damaged. There was no decision on this matter in Henry's reign and the problem was left for the future. A second dispute concerned papal legates, envoys sent out by the papacy to solve some local problem of the church. As such they had a long history. But Hildebrand had begun to arm them with such broad powers that they had full authority to act as though the pope himself were present. This was an obvious threat to royal power. After a long controversy it became the practice that the pope should have a permanent representative in England but that this representative should be the archbishop of Canterbury. Thus Henry controlled the church, though his control was not as complete as was that of his father.

The Succession

Henry was troubled for many years by the problem of the succession. William, his son and heir, had been drowned while crossing the Channel in 1120. The young noble and a group of gay companions, all more or less intoxicated, had set sail with an intoxicated crew, had struck a rock, and had perished. This tragedy left the King with only one legitimate child, his daughter Matilda. In 1114 she had been married to the German Emperor Henry V, but upon his death in 1125 she had returned to England. On two occasions her father obtained from the barons an oath, most reluctantly given, to accept her as their future Queen.

[2] See page 37.

In 1127 he arranged her marriage to Geoffrey, the heir to the county of Anjou. Although Norman hatred of Anjou was bitter, Henry hoped this marriage would prevent an attack from Anjou upon Normandy and would provide his daughter with a warlike and powerful husband. Nonetheless, when Henry died in 1135, most Englishmen were highly doubtful whether Matilda should be made their Queen. The mere notion of a woman ruler was novel and distasteful. If in some way the barons could be absolved from their oath to support Matilda, it was unlikely that she could command much backing in England. At the time of her marriage to Geoffrey in 1128 the bride and groom were an ill-assorted pair. Matilda's personality was against her. A woman of twenty-five, she was haughty and overbearing, ever mindful of the fact that she had once been an Empress. She was arrogant, tactless, obstinate, petulant, and grasping. Geoffrey, a boy of fourteen, had a temperament not unlike that of his wife. In 1133 she bore him a son, who was to become Henry II.

KING STEPHEN, 1135–1154

Since Matilda appeared so dubious a choice, it is not surprising that many men in England turned to another candidate who at first seemed more attractive. This was Count Stephen of Blois, whose mother, Adela, was a daughter of William the Conqueror. Stephen had many advantages. He had been a great favorite of his uncle, Henry I, who had enfeoffed him with large estates on both sides of the Channel. Stephen was well known and was very popular with the barons in England. He had, moreover, high connections in the English church. His brother, Henry of Blois, bishop of Winchester, persuaded other churchmen to support him and helped to induce the Pope to recognize him as King of England. The sanction of the papacy was a great advantage to Stephen, for it virtually absolved the barons from the oaths they had sworn to accept Matilda. High officials, such as Roger of Salisbury, eager to have the kingship settled, accepted Stephen as the candidate in possession, for upon Henry's death Stephen had hastily crossed to England, had been chosen King by the citizens of London in a highly doubtful manner, had seized the treasury at Winchester, and had been crowned, all, said a chronicler, "as in the twinkling of an eye."

Thus Stephen began his reign in a strong position. That he soon lost his prestige and allowed the country to sink into feudal anarchy was due to his weakness of character and to his limited concept of kingship. In some ways he was an attractive man. He was a great warrior who delighted in the wild and dangerous tournaments that were coming into fashion (in which knights rode about over a delimited area and fought anyone whom they happened to meet). He was chivalrous, kindly, and recklessly generous. But he was a simple-minded man with little plan or policy. Moreover, he was soft. Shortly after he became King two barons in different parts of the country each seized a royal castle. One can imagine how William I or his sons would have dealt with such temerity. But Stephen did nothing; unlawful seizure of property was soon occurring in many places. Thus Stephen failed to keep law and order; nor could he defend his frontiers. In 1137 he went to Normandy, which was under attack by Geoffrey of Anjou, but very shortly he concluded an unfavorable treaty with Geoffrey. An attack on England from Scotland was followed by the grant of a large area to the King of Scots. There were other flaws in Stephen's policy. He was almost entirely a feudal King who thought in terms of feudal custom and feudal law. The barons on their side were quick to think in similar terms. They debased allegiance to the King as a public duty to the mere fulfillment of their feudal obligations. Stephen also made the error of trying to win support by a policy of concession. Royal authority diminished quickly as lands and privileges were given away. The policy of concession, once begun, had to be continued, and in the end there arose an absurd situation in which the barons demanded more and more and then rebelled if they did not obtain what they asked.

Stephen's folly reached its height in dealing with the church, for he first made great concessions and then lost the church's support through a quarrel with Roger, bishop of Salisbury. He had allowed the church a large extension of its jurisdiction. In separating lay and ecclesiastical courts, William the Conqueror had intended no more than that the church should handle its own cases. A clergyman committing a lay offense was still to be tried in the lay courts. But under Stephen the church obtained the right to try all cases involving clergymen in any way and all cases involving ecclesiastical property. The church also secured jurisdiction over cases concerning marriage and the probate of wills. In addition it obtained the right to appoint bishops and abbots and to hold ecclesiastical councils without the royal consent. These concessions were so sweeping that never again in medieval times was the church in England controlled by the Crown as it had been in the past.

Having thus allowed the church to exalt itself, Stephen proceeded to quarrel with it. At the time of his accession, the administration of the government was in the hands of Roger of Salisbury and his rich and powerful relatives: three were bishops; among them they held many castles; with large bodies of retainers they moved about the country like great lords. Stephen became jealous of them, perhaps with some reason. In 1139 he arrested them on a trivial pretext, subjected them to needless humiliations, and seized their wealth. This foolish action disrupted the administration and deeply offended the church.

Matilda, watching events from the Continent, decided that the time had come to assert her rights. She landed in England in the autumn of 1139, accompanied by her half brother, Earl Robert of Gloucester, an able and resolute man who held great estates in western England.[3] He and Matilda soon dominated the west and awaited a time to strike at Stephen. Their opportunity came in 1141 when Stephen was facing a rebellion. Joining forces with the rebels, Robert defeated and captured Stephen in a battle at Lincoln. For the moment Stephen's government collapsed, and Matilda was recognized as Queen. Her triumph, however, was short-lived. Her tactlessness and arrogance were so offensive that she was expelled from London by the angry citizens. Stephen's forces rallied, defeated Matilda, and captured Earl Robert, who was exchanged for the King in 1141. Thenceforth the fighting diminished, though it dragged on until 1148, when Matilda departed for France, leaving Stephen in possession of England. In 1153 he made the Treaty of Wallingford with Henry, Matilda's son, who had come to England to battle for her rights. By this treaty Stephen was to remain on the throne until his death but was then to be succeeded by Henry. Stephen died, old and disillusioned, in the following year.

[3] Robert of Gloucester was an illegitimate son of Henry I.

The Extent of the Anarchy

Because Stephen's reign often is referred to as the anarchy, the question arises how far this name was justified and what lessons it taught. The period was certainly a time of widespread misery and suffering. Not only was there a civil war; there was also great lawlessness among the barons, who strengthened their castles, fought private wars, and played the tyrant in their own localities. A notorious baron, Geoffrey de Mandeville, retired to the fen country around Ely, from which base he ravaged the neighborhood in an orgy of blood, torture, and destruction. What he did on a great scale was done by lesser barons on a smaller one. Yet it is probable that conditions over the kingdom as a whole were not as dreadful as these. The civil war was fought largely in the west and did not touch many parts of the country. Plundering was local; the bloody careers of men like Geoffrey de Mandeville were usually short. Many barons, interested in their estates, had no desire for anarchy, which could only bring them loss. Some of them made mutual agreements not to molest one another. Moreover, there is evidence that the machinery of law and order was not entirely destroyed but continued to function in a halting way. It is significant that Stephen appears to have had a fair supply of money, an indication that he cultivated the towns, gave some protection to trade, and collected some revenues through the exchequer. Bad as conditions were, they were probably not as bad as the horrified chroniclers would have us believe. Perhaps the worst result was the tendency toward lawlessness and disregard for the rights of property.

The lessons of Stephen's reign were obvious. It was clear that strong and effective government bestowed inestimable benefits upon the nation, whereas the lack of such government brought chaos, misery, and war. It was equally clear that the only hope of good government lay in the monarchy. Only a King could govern well, but he must be more than a feudal suzerain. He must be a sovereign, using his prerogative power to protect the nation as a whole. He must be a strong personality. Government was still a personal institution which would not function without the guiding hand of a powerful ruler. An oppressive King was better than a weak one, and one great tyrant on the throne was less to be feared than hundreds of petty tyrants in every hill-top castle. Finally, the anarchy showed the danger of allowing a person to ascend the throne after some kind of dubious election. Stephen had stressed election, but Matilda had stood on hereditary right. Henceforth hereditary right was seldom set aside.

The same principle, moreover, came to be applied to the lands held by the barons. The Norman Kings had acted as though all the land of England belonged to them and as though the barons were mere tenants. This royal claim of ultimate ownership explains the arbitrary way in which the Kings had exacted the feudal aids and incidents. Indeed, much of the trouble of Stephen's reign arose from the insecurity of tenure felt by the barons. But now the doctrine that all land belonged to the King was abandoned; the new King, Henry II, fully recognized the right of a feudal heir to succeed to the lands held by his father.

HENRY II, 1154–1189, AND THE NEW MONARCHY

Whether England could recover from the anarchy depended upon the strength and character of the young man who became King at Stephen's death in 1154. It was England's supreme good fortune that Henry II was one of the greatest of her Kings. His wonderful sense of law and order, his interest in intellectual and cultural things, his boundless energy and keen intelligence enabled him to understand and to adopt the new theoretical and practical foundations of kingship that were being established in Europe in the twelfth century. The older, theocratic concept of a King as a holy and sacred ruler who derived his authority from God's grace was changing to the concept of a King as legislator. This idea was inspired by the revival of interest in Roman law which was part of the intellectual awakening of the twelfth century and was derived directly from the rediscovery and close study of the *Corpus Juris Civilis,* the compendium of Roman law compiled by Emperor Justinian in the second quarter of the sixth century. Kingship, of course, remained sacred, but the concept of a King as legislator brought a wealth of new meaning to his office.

Roman law, and the study of the principles that lay behind the law, exalted the role of kingship and taught the necessity of an organized legal system applied in a uniform way throughout the kingdom. Government was placed upon a higher plane than that of a crude suppression of the feudal barons.

Employing his prerogative freely, Henry improved and strengthened the law in England, devised new legal procedures, expanded the legal activity of the Crown, fought the lawlessness that was the heritage of Stephen's reign, and protected the rights of property.

We know a good deal about his appearance and character. He was a man of medium height, heavy and thick-set, with a bull neck, broad shoulders, powerful arms, and coarse, rough hands. His head was large, his hair red, his face freckled, his voice harsh and cracked. He possessed enormous physical strength and energy. He could hunt all day and then spend half the night solving some knotty problem of law or government among his clerks. A restless man, he arranged matters of business even in church, paced about his chamber while talking vivaciously with his courtiers, and roused his servants before dawn to begin a long day's journey. He was highly educated, a good linguist, though he never learned English, fond of literature and of the company of learned men. He had the mind of a lawyer and loved to wrestle with difficult points of law. A good soldier, he hated war, ever seeking to solve international problems by peaceful means. But there was a darker side to his character. He was subject to violent fits of anger in which his gray eyes darted fire, his mouth foamed, and he rolled on the ground in a paroxysm of violent rage.

Early Reforms

Henry's legal reforms were not begun during the first decade of his reign, for other matters required immediate attention. The first task was to impose order in place of anarchy and to restore the operation of the machinery of government. As soon as Henry was crowned on December 19, 1154, he ordered the mercenary troops—especially the "Flemish wolves"—of Stephen and Matilda out of the country. He resumed the royal castles and Crown lands Stephen had recklessly given away, he suppressed most of the earldoms Stephen had created, and he destroyed the strongholds of unruly barons. Most of Stephen's supporters yielded to him, some fled, and a few resisted. Indeed, the majority of the barons, weary of plunder and civil war, gladly cooperated with him. There was no rival candidate for the Crown around whom opposition could gather. Henry selected his ministers from both parties. Nigel, bishop of Ely, treasurer in the reign of Henry I, was restored to his former position; Thomas Becket became chancellor. These two men had supported the Angevin side. But Henry's justiciars, Robert, Earl of Leicester, and Richard de Lucy, had belonged to Stephen's party. The work of pacification was done so quickly and thoroughly that Henry was able to visit the Continent in 1156.

Henry seized an opportunity in 1166 to impose a new assessment of the feudal obligations of his tenants in chief. He asked them to declare the number of knights they were pledged to supply to him, and the number they had actually enfeoffed. The result of this inquiry, preserved in documents known as the *Cartae Baronum,* showed, as Henry was aware, that some tenants had enfeoffed fewer knights than they owed, whereas others had enfeoffed many more. He thereupon decreed that tenants with fewer enfeoffed knights than they were bound to supply must continue to send their ancient quota, and that those with more knights than were necessary must in future supply the full number they had enfeoffed. There was naturally much objection, but Henry carried his point. He also insisted that all subvassals do homage to him as to their liege lord, thus subordinating feudal homage to the older concept of universal allegiance to the King. In 1181 he breathed new life into the fyrd by regulations concerning the military equipment that each member must possess. He also made arrangements with certain ports on the southern coast, the Cinque Ports, to supply him with ships in time of war. By these measures Henry showed that he wished his military strength to rest not only upon the feudal host but also upon the whole body of freemen.

In 1170 Henry carried through a wide and ambitious investigation of local government. This inquiry, called the Inquest of Sheriffs, included a scrutiny of many other local officials—bailiffs and stewards of great nobles, royal foresters, and certain minor officials of the church. The King had been receiving complaints that the sheriffs were again becoming oppressive and that local officials were defrauding not only the people but also the central government. Dividing the country into circuits, Henry dispatched commissioners to collect information. The result was a salutary suppression of corrupt practices. Most of the sheriffs were dismissed, their places taken by royal officials. The new sheriffs were industrious and dependable bureaucrats, closely responsible to the King. They were gradually given a host of administrative duties and became the local agents of the Crown in the new legal reforms which now came into being.

THE LEGAL INNOVATIONS OF HENRY II

The legal reforms of Henry II, which constitute the glory of his reign, may be summarized as the development of a central court of administration and justice resident at Westminster; the reorganization and expansion of the system of itinerant justices to carry the King's law and administration into local areas; and the introduction of new principles and new methods of justice which greatly improved its quality.

Henry's problem, like that of his grandfather, was to create an administration which would continue to function while he was abroad. Hence it was not the Great Council of the tenants in chief which developed, nor even the small council of those who attended the King wherever he happened to be. It was the court of the justiciar—known as the exchequer—which grew and matured in Henry's reign. The exchequer contained highly trained clerks, skillful administrators, and judges or justices learned in the law. It was at once a financial bureau, a chancery with a busy staff of clerks, a place where decisions could be quickly made, and, above all, a court of law. As yet there was no great differentiation of function: administrators were judges and judges administrators. The business of government, however, was growing rapidly, and more and more legal work arose in which the King was interested. The problems of crime and violence inherited from Stephen's reign had to be faced. Moreover, many ancient Anglo-Saxon methods of justice were out of date.

The Common Law

Henry and his justices struck out in new directions, using some parts of Anglo-Saxon and Norman law, borrowing from Roman law and from the law of the church, devising new practices to meet new needs, until King and justices began to create a new law and to build a body of decisions from which precedents and legal principles could emerge. This was the origin of the English common law. The King's court was soon dispensing a type of justice that was superior to the justice of the local courts. Men wished to have their cases tried by the King's judges. They were willing to pay for this privilege by buying the proper writ, for the purchase of a writ—which was a command from the King—came to be the normal way in which a case was begun. So great was the demand for the King's justice that in 1178 Henry set aside five judges who were to remain at Westminster and to do nothing but hear pleas.

The Itinerant Justices

The court at Westminster normally tried cases involving important persons and large amounts of property. It did not handle smaller cases. But such cases were increasing rapidly, and Henry made the great decision to place his justice at the disposal of freemen and lesser barons by overhauling and improving the system of itinerant justices. Former Kings, as we know, had sent out officials to preside over cases in which the Crown had an interest. Henry developed the journeys or iters of the itinerant justices into a regular, smoothly operating, and indispensable organ of government. The kingdom was divided into circuits; and the highest officials of the Crown—justiciars, chancellors, archbishops of Canterbury—traveled through the counties, bringing the justice of the King to smaller litigants throughout the kingdom. A county court, when the justices were present, became for the moment a royal court; the same legal methods were employed as were used at Westminster. In this way the law became a common law—common to all England.

The itinerant justices also did a vast amount of work that was not judicial. They performed an ever-increasing number of administrative duties, inquiring into any matter in which the King might be interested, until half the county seemed to be attending to the business of the Crown and until a general iter, as it was called, was a dreaded experience for the people.

New Principles

Henry also introduced new principles and practices. One of the most important was the principle that a felony or a serious crime was an offense against the King because it broke the King's peace, and that its trial and punishment should not be left to the local courts but should be brought into the courts of the King and tried before the itinerant justices. The conception of felony, that is, of a crime that was particularly base and degrading, had come in with the Normans, as had the practice of escheating to the Crown the property of a convicted felon. Henry therefore had a number of inducements to transfer the trial of criminals from the local to the royal courts.

Another principle of no less importance was that the King, as the fountain of justice, was responsible for the protection of property and might intervene in the proceedings of the hundred or shire courts or the feudal or private courts of the nobles to ensure that cases concerning property were justly handled. Such intervention was carried out through royal writs. Henry issued what were known as writs of right, which were letters addressed to persons responsible for local justice, commanding them to see that justice was done and warning them that they would be called to account for any negligence. Henry also issued the writ *praecipe*, which had the effect of lifting a case from a local court and transferring it to the court of the King. Finally, Henry made use of the jury in both criminal and civil cases.[4]

The Criminal Jury. Let us look more closely at the way in which trials were conducted. At the beginning of Henry's reign a criminal trial was begun, as in Anglo-Saxon times, by an accusation. The injured party, or his relative, or his lord, must appear in court and make a formal charge against the accused. The court might order proof by the ancient methods of ordeal or compurgation. The Normans had introduced the duel or ordeal by battle. If the court permitted this method of proof, the accuser and the accused fought each other to the death. Should their weapons break, they must continue the fray with their hands, nails, and teeth, and if the vanquished party survived he was mutilated or hanged for his crime or heavily fined for his false accusation. These duels were not frequent, and usually were avoided in one way or another. But they were obviously barbaric, as was also the Anglo-Saxon ordeal. A new procedure was clearly needed.

It came in Henry's famous Assize (or decree) of Clarendon in 1166, which placed the responsibility for accusing criminals upon the local community. Twelve responsible men from every hundred and four from every vill had to appear before the sheriff and later before the justices in the county court and had to declare upon oath the names of persons in the neighborhood believed to be robbers, thieves, murderers, or the protectors of such persons. This was the jury of accusation, the ancestor of the modern grand jury. When the justices arrived it was the duty of the sheriff to produce the persons suspected.

The normal method of proof employed by the justices was the Anglo-Saxon ordeal of cold water. The accused was bound and lowered into a body of water which had been sanctified by a priest. It was thought that water sanctified in this way would not receive a guilty person, and hence if a man floated he was guilty, if he sank he was innocent. Punishment was swift and terrible: a man found guilty at the ordeal had his right foot cut off and must abjure the realm. In 1178 Henry added forgery and arson to the list of felonies and decreed that if a man failed at the ordeal he should lose his right hand as well as his right foot. Mutilation was not the only method of punishment. After the iter of 1166, when the justices tried cases in London and Middlesex, the sheriffs reported in the exchequer the cost of thirty-four ordeals, five duels, fourteen mutilations, and fourteen hangings. The trials of men suspected of felonies were known as the pleas of the Crown.

The origin of the accusing jury is a matter of dispute among historians. The usual opinion is that the jury was of continental origin. It is known that in the

---

[4] A civil case was a dispute over property, usually over land, in which no crime had been committed. In Henry's reign, however, disputes over land often involved violence, such as the seizure of property without a court judgment.

later Roman Empire men were put on oath to tell the truth and then were asked to assess the value of land. This use of the jury, it is thought, passed from Rome to the Franks, to the Normans, and so was brought to England at the time of the Conquest. In the Domesday survey of 1086 William's commissioners employed juries to assess the value of property. A jury of this type has no connection with a trial; it is thought that Henry's innovation was to bring the jury into court and use it in the accusation of criminals.

Some historians, however, believe that the accusing jury was of Anglo-Saxon origin. They point to a decree by Ethelred the Unready about 997 in which it was ordered that twelve leading thegns in the courts of the Danelaw should be sworn to tell the truth and should then give information about criminals. After this single decree, no more is heard of such juries, but historians who support an Anglo-Saxon origin of the jury believe they continued. In the hundred and shire courts, it is held, men were constantly employed in the apprehension and punishment of criminals, and many persons must have been tried without an accusation by an injured party. It is likely that "small groups, as groups, were being compelled to voice suspicions, tell tales, inform against the criminal."[5] According to this interpretation Henry's innovation was to bring the accusing jury, or something like it, from the obscurity of local procedure and to employ it in courts where it appeared at once in the public records.

Henry clearly did not like the ordeal of cold water as a method of proof. Nonetheless, it continued until a council of the church decreed in 1215 that priests should take no part in ordeals. This decree deprived the ordeal of its justification as a judgment of God. It straightway disappeared, and a second jury, known as the petty jury, was used to determine the question of innocence or guilt.

The Civil Jury. In civil cases, which involved disputes over land or other property, Henry opened the royal courts to all freemen and again made use of the jury. His reforms began with what are known as the petty assizes, court actions which offered a temporary rather than a permanent settlement but which had the enormous advantage of prompt redress of wrong. The most important was the assize of *novel disseisin*, that is, recent dispossession. The assize offered speedy justice for the man who had been ejected from his property without a judgment in court. Such a person could buy a writ of *novel disseisin*, which ordered the sheriff to bring a jury before the itinerant justices. The jury was asked a simple question: had the purchaser of the writ been dispossessed of property without a court judgment? If the answer was yes, he was placed once more in possession. A random case will illustrate the speed and effectiveness of this procedure:

> An assize comes to declare whether Richard with the beard unjustly and without judgment disseised Geoffrey with the beard of his free tenement in Northborough after the king's coronation at Canterbury. The jurors say that he so dispossessed him. Judgment, Richard is in mercy and let Geoffrey have his seisin. Damages, nothing. Amercement half a mark.[6]

There were other petty assizes, though for the most part they were variations of the same theme and were very popular. But they were preliminary in nature

---

[5] G. O. Sayles, *The Medieval Foundations of England* (London: Methuen, 1950), p. 335.
[6] Quoted in Austin Lane Poole, *From Domesday Book to Magna Carta 1087–1216* (Oxford: Clarendon Press, 1955), p. 407. A man in mercy was punished as the King saw fit. If he was fined, as was usually the case, the fine was known as an amercement.

and did not settle the question of ownership or best right. Disputes over the best right to property were normally tried in the feudal courts of the barons and were determined by the ordeal of battle. Henry began to intervene in various ways until, by a procedure known as the grand assize, of which the probable date is 1179, he laid down certain principles: that anyone who wished to challenge a freeman's title to his land must open the case by the purchase of a writ; that a freeman so challenged could, if he wished, transfer the case from a feudal court (where it would be tried by the ordeal of battle) to the court of the King; and that after such transfer the freeman, by the purchase of the proper writ, could have the case tried by a jury. The grand assize was not swift like the petty assizes. It was a solemn affair tried before the court at Westminster. All the parties to the suit and the jury as well might have to travel a long distance. But the grand assize was hailed as a measure of the highest equity, for it enabled a freeman to avoid the hazards of combat and to have his case tried by a jury. By these wise and salutary measures Henry protected the possession of property, offered jury trial in cases of best right, extended the scope of royal justice, and decreased the number of cases that came before the feudal courts.

HENRY II AND THE CHURCH

A clash of some kind between the King and the church was inevitable in Henry's reign. Under Stephen, as we have seen, the church had obtained new privileges and independence. A strong King like Henry II was certain to resist the pretensions of the clergy and to seek to regain the control exercised by his predecessors. He saw, moreover, that the church sheltered abuses which hindered his program of legal reform. The unnecessary violence of his clash with the church was due to the arrogant and uncompromising stand of Thomas Becket, the archbishop of Canterbury.

Becket's character is not easy to analyze. He was born into a middle-class family in London, was given a sound education, and became attached to the household of Archbishop Theobald. His exceptional ability as a diplomat and man of business brought him rapid promotion. At Henry's accession he obtained the high office of chancellor; and as chancellor from 1154 to 1162 he threw himself ardently into the administrative work of the government, supporting the interests of the King against those of the church. He appeared the worldly courtier, gay, handsomely dressed, fond of hunting, the jovial companion of the King. Then suddenly, upon his appointment as archbishop in 1162, he became the unbending churchman, ostentatiously ascetic, the upholder of the most extreme claims of clerical independence and of papal supremacy. It is difficult to explain this sudden change. Sobered by the significance of his new office, he may perhaps have experienced a religious conversion. Or there may have been some psychological twist to his character. A vain and self-important man, he may have been an actor who played to the full every role he undertook. In any case, as archbishop he quarreled with the King at once, opposing him on matters in which no principle appeared to be involved. At the same time Henry heard of a number of ugly crimes committed by clerks in minor orders who were able to escape with light sentences in the church courts.

Angered by these events Henry issued the Constitutions of Clarendon in 1164. This document was a careful and accurate statement of the "ancient cus-

The murder of Archbishop Thomas Becket, as shown in a twelfth century manuscript. (British Museum, Harleian MS 5102, f. 32)

toms," that is, of the rules and practices which had governed the relations of the church and the state under William the Conqueror and his sons. According to those rules, as the document pointed out, cases concerning advowson and debt, and disputes as to whether lands were held by ecclesiastical or lay tenure, should be tried in the lay courts. Clerks convicted of a crime should be punished in the same way as laymen who had committed the same offense. Laymen should not be prosecuted in the church courts on the basis of rumor but only upon accusation by an individual or by a jury. Other clauses repeated rules laid down by William the Conqueror: without the King's consent no clergyman should leave the country, no cases could be appealed to Rome, and no official or tenant in chief could be excommunicated. The compromise of the reign of Henry I concerning investiture should stand.

Although the Constitutions of Clarendon were moderate in tone, they proved to be a cardinal error. The position of the church had altered since the days of William I. The papacy had been exalted, papal government highly organized, canon law expanded and matured. The church could not ignore these developments. Hence both the Pope and the English bishops, although they disapproved of Becket's conduct, were forced to oppose the "ancient customs." Henry had acted too quickly and had played into Becket's hands.

Becket eventually rejected all the "ancient customs." The clash between him and Henry, however, centered upon the trial and punishment of criminous clerks. It should be remembered that an enormous number of persons had some slight connection with the church and that below the ranks of respectable and beneficed clergymen were many clerks in minor orders, some without occupation and a few disreputable. The church courts did not shed blood. They might unfrock a clerk, that is, deprive him of the right to exercise his office in the church, or they might fine or imprison him; even for serious crimes the church courts often did no more than impose a sentence of fine and penance. They failed to inflict the harsh punishments that were needed to maintain order in a violent age. Henry did not claim the right to try criminous clerks. He asked that the accusation be made and the offense be proved in a lay court, that the culprit then be tried in the church court in the presence of a royal representative, and that if found guilty he be unfrocked and returned to the lay court for punishment. Becket refused these arrangements. The entire trial of clerks, he held, must lie in the church courts.

Thenceforth the quarrel of King and archbishop became more bitter and acrimonious. Henry tried to ruin his adversary. In 1164 Becket fled to the Continent, where he kept the quarrel alive through a voluminous correspondence. Six years later in 1170 Henry offered Becket a hollow reconciliation and permitted his return to England. But Becket immediately excommunicated certain bishops who had crowned the King's son, an act normally reserved for the archbishop. It was at this new affront that Henry uttered the fatal words, "Will no one rid me of this troublesome priest?" A few days later four of his knights murdered the archbishop in the cathedral at Canterbury.

Few events in the Middle Ages shocked Europe as profoundly as did the murder of Becket. The head of the church in England had been struck down by the King. Here was a tragedy made to order for all who supported the pretensions of Rome. The people at large were also deeply affected. The cult of St. Thomas Becket flourished mightily; visits to the shrine of the holy blissful martyr at Canterbury became the most popular of English pilgrimages.

After the initial outcry of indignation had subsided, Henry was able to make his peace with Rome. He conceded two important points. Surrendering his claim to try clerks for felonies, he allowed the church courts full jurisdiction over them. For the many offenses below the rank of felony, however, the clergy were to be tried in the lay courts, where they had no special privilege. A second concession made by Henry was a promise not to obstruct appeals to Rome, a point in which the Pope felt much more interest than in the trial of criminous clerks. Appeals to Rome of all sorts of cases had been growing steadily, and the number now continued to increase. In other respects Henry was able to stand his ground. He continued to control the appointment of bishops and abbots. He continued to enjoy the revenues of vacant sees; no excommunication of his tenants in chief or his high officials and no visits to England by papal legates were to be permitted without his approval. The church courts tried cases concerning wills and marriages, ecclesiastical property, and offenses against morality. But the lay courts retained jurisdiction over advowson, over debts and contracts, and over misdeeds of the clergy below the rank of felony.

THE ANGEVIN EMPIRE

One must think of Henry as a great French noble whose primary interests lay in his continental possessions. For every year that he spent in England he spent two abroad. He was already an international figure in 1154, when he obtained the English throne at the age of twenty-one. He had inherited Anjou, Maine, and Touraine from Geoffrey, his father, who had died in 1151. From his mother, Matilda, he had inherited Normandy. In 1152 by a sudden turn of fortune he had acquired the right to rule over vast new territories. This had come about through his marriage to Eleanor, the heiress of Aquitaine, the greatest fief of southern France. Eleanor had formerly been the wife of the French King Louis VII. But Louis and Eleanor were far from congenial. Louis was a pious man, obsequious toward the church, rigid in his conduct, rather clumsy and simple-minded in policy. Eleanor was young and beautiful, a vivid personality, proud and high-spirited, representing the full-blooded and vivacious temper of the south. She scorned a husband indifferent to love, and the two were divorced in March 1152.

In May of the same year she married Henry, thus transferring to him her enormous possessions of Aquitaine, Poitou, and Auvergne. Before he became King of England Henry controlled half of France. Thereafter he was master of an empire which extended from Scotland to the Pyrenees, far more extensive than the shorn lands of his overlord, the King of France. But Henry's possessions did not form a unit in any way. They differed in interests, in laws, and in language; allegiance to him was the one strong bond of union. Henry was constantly on the move, often traveling at great speed; his peoples saw more of him than might be supposed and his enemies were constantly confounded by his sudden appearances.

During the first years of his reign his object was to consolidate his empire. He made several expeditions against the Welsh; he forced the Scots to cede territory they held in northern England and later he obtained the homage of William, the Scottish King; he visited Ireland and received the submission of most of the Irish Kings. It is a pity that he did not use his strength to unify the British Isles once and for all, but his mind was on his continental possessions.

By diplomacy and by the marriages of his children (some of whom were wed while they were infants), he obtained the Vexin, an area on the Seine, and gained control of Brittany. The possession of Aquitaine brought him wider contacts—with Spain, with the German Emperor Frederick Barbarossa, and more distantly with Italy. He forced the Count of Toulouse to do him homage. But his dream of power in Italy, and perhaps in the empire also, never materialized, for he was drawn from his ambitions by the serious rebellion of 1173–1174.

The French Dominions of Henry II

Henry, it was said, could rule every household but his own. His four sons grew up discontented and hostile toward him, without respect or loyalty, and in the end they ruined his policy. Henry was partly to blame. As a parent he was indulgent and yet masterful, he gave his sons titles but little money or power, he sent them to represent him in various parts of his dominions but expected them to be as obedient as paid officials. Henry, the eldest, was a handsome and attractive young man, but sinful and treacherous. Richard, the second son, grew to be a mighty warrior but without a sense of government and with a morbid hatred of his father. Geoffrey, the third, was a brainless plunderer. The career of John, the fourth son, speaks for itself, as we shall see. The three older brothers were eager to revolt against their father. In this they were encouraged by their mother, Eleanor, who no longer lived with the King. She held her court at Poitiers in her own lands in France, where she presided over a motley society of knights and troubadours who exalted knightly love, war, and the cult of chivalry. Eleanor's fame as an attractive woman was expressed in a German student song:

> Were the world all mine
> From the sea to the Rhine
> I'd give it all
> If so be the Queen of England
> Lay in my arms.[7]

Henry's sons also were encouraged in revolt by Louis VII of France. The great rebellion of 1173–1174, which included risings in England, Normandy, Brittany, and Aquitaine, was managed—or, rather, mismanaged—by Louis. It was the far-flung nature of the revolt that made it dangerous. But Henry was supported by the church, by his great officials, by the smaller tenants in the country, and by the towns. His sons were too young to lead so extensive an enterprise, Louis was inept, there was little over-all planning. Hence the revolt was put down, as it had arisen, in piecemeal fashion. Louis was driven back to Paris, an invasion of England from Flanders was defeated, Eleanor was captured while masquerading in male attire. The King of Scots, while invading from the north, also was captured. Henry forgave his sons and increased their revenues. But he destroyed the castles of the barons who had revolted against him and he kept his wife under restraint for the rest of his life. His sons revolted again in 1183, a rebellion in which the young Henry died while fighting both his father and his brother Richard. Another uprising was planned for 1186; and in 1189 Richard and John joined the French King Philip Augustus in war against their father. This was Henry's last campaign. When he heard that John, his favorite son, had joined the rebels, he lost heart. Turning his face to the wall and "muttering 'Shame, shame on a conquered king,' he passed sullenly away."[8]

[7] Poole, p. 333.
[8] John Richard Green, *A Short History of the English People* (New York: The Colonial Press, 1900), I, p. 138.

5

kings and barons

The splendid machinery of government developed by Henry II was so firmly and soundly established that it continued to function during the reigns of his irresponsible sons. It survived the absence of Richard and the avarice of John. Indeed, during these reigns the authority of the Crown increased, and the Angevin monarchy, immensely powerful under Henry II, became more powerful than ever. It was obviously freeing itself from old restraints imposed in the past by custom, feudal law, and the influence of the church. How far was royal authority to go? Was the King to become an irresponsible despot? Should powers and prerogatives—beneficial in the hands of a good King—be left at the disposal of an evil one? And if a bad King was to be curbed, how was it to be done? The reign of Richard illustrated the growth of royal power; the reign of John drove home the lesson that disastrous things might happen if that power fell into the hands of a tyrant. Hence the small number of people who thought in terms of politics—that is, some of the barons and a few members of the upper clergy—began to consider carefully what should be the proper relation of the Crown to the baronage and to the law and what should be the proper relation of the barons to the growing machinery of government. It is in the light of these problems that we must study Magna Carta, the first major check upon the growth of royal absolutism.

RICHARD I, 1189–1199

Richard was more highly regarded by his contemporaries than he is by posterity. Although he neglected England, he played a great part in continental affairs. Everywhere he went, in Europe or in the Holy Land, he was always a power. He was reverenced as a crusader who had done brave deeds beyond the seas, and he was feared by his enemies as a man of strength and shrewdness. Above all else he was a soldier. Of great physical strength and with great skill in arms, he was a superb general with a fine eye for tactics in battle and for the strategy of a campaign. He was chivalrous, impulsive, and extravagant, with something of the dash and sense of grandeur of his mother. Fond of music and poetry, he was a patron of the troubadours of southern France. Although he was false to his father, he respected those who had fought faithfully on his father's side. He was born in England but has been called the least English of her Kings. He might have been a successful ruler, but he despised the arts of peace and did not take the trouble to understand the problems of English government. He spent only five months of his reign in England, regarding that country merely as a source of financial support for his many wars.

When he ascended the throne in 1189 he was pledged to take part in the Third Crusade; he devoted himself to the task of raising money for his great enterprise. In addition to tapping the usual sources of revenue, he sold places in the government to the highest bidder. "Everything was for sale," wrote a contemporary, "powers, lordships, earldoms, shrievalties, castles, towns, and manors." "I would sell London," Richard remarked, "if I could find a suitable purchaser." His provisions for the government of England during his absence showed little wisdom. He divided authority between two justiciars: Hugh de Puiset, the princely bishop of Durham, and William Longchamp, a faithful servant but a foreigner of humble origin who was inclined to be tactless and highhanded. Longchamp first drove Hugh de Puiset from office and then was superseded by a new justiciar, Walter of Coutances, archbishop of Rouen. There was thus much friction in England. John, the King's younger brother, caused endless trouble. Richard had given him large estates, a rich wife—Isabel of Gloucester—and a dominion of six counties over which he ruled as an independent prince. Nonetheless, John plotted and intrigued against his brother. When Richard was captured on his way home from the Holy Land, John at once claimed the English throne. Rebuffed at home, he crossed to France and was recognized as King of England by the French King, Philip Augustus, who was Richard's enemy. But the appointment in 1193 of a new and able justiciar, Hubert Walter, and Richard's release in 1194 exposed John as a traitor and retrieved an ugly situation.

The Third Crusade

The Third Crusade took place because of the disasters which had befallen Christian arms in the Holy Land. It was now a century since Pope Urban II had first appealed to the military aristocracy of Europe to reconquer Jerusalem from the hands of the Muslims. His appeal had met with tremendous enthusiasm. A number of crusading armies had converged upon Constantinople in 1097, to the dismay of Emperor Alexius Comnenus, who had hurried the crusaders forward on the long and dangerous march across Asia Minor to the Holy Land. Ignorant of local conditions, the crusaders had been parched with thirst because they neglected to take water bottles and had suffered from dysentery because they were careless about their diet. Nevertheless, by sheer bravery, brute force, and a sublime assurance of victory, they defeated the Turks at Antioch; marched southward to Jerusalem, which they captured in 1099; and set up a Latin kingdom with Jerusalem as its center. Most of the crusaders then returned to Europe.

Those who remained in the Holy Land were compelled to govern and to defend their conquests with very limited resources. They treated the Muslim peasants with leniency and they built huge, impregnable castles at strategic points. But their position was precarious. The Second Crusade (1147–1149), which proved a total failure, was undertaken when the fall of Edessa weakened the northern flank of the Christians. By the last quarter of the twelfth century, moreover, the Muslims, who had formerly been divided among themselves, were united under Saladin, a remarkable man who was King of both Egypt and Syria. Partly to hold his people together, he preached a war against the Christians, overran much of the Holy Land, and captured the cities of Acre and Jerusalem in 1187. These disasters furnished the impulse for the Third Crusade.

Richard left England in December 1189 but remained in France until the following summer. He then embarked on the Mediterranean and coasted leisurely along the Italian shore until he came to Sicily, where he was soon involved in local politics. There he had to face the animosity of Philip Augustus of France, who had also taken the Cross. The two Kings, having spent the winter of 1190–1191 in constant bickering, sailed for the Holy Land with deep bitterness toward one another. Richard stopped on his way to conquer Cyprus and arrived before the walls of Acre in June 1191. Within a few months the crusaders captured that city; and later took Jaffa. Upon two occasions Richard brought his troops within sight of Jerusalem, but Jerusalem never was captured. In July 1191 Philip returned to France, where he continued his former intrigues against the Angevin empire. Richard remained in the Holy Land for another year, but he knew that he could accomplish little without large reinforcements and he sailed for home in October 1192.

Fearing that Philip was plotting to prevent his return, he made his way up the Adriatic Sea and came to Vienna, where he was captured by Leopold, Duke of Austria, and then handed over to the German Emperor Henry VI as a prisoner. Such treatment of a crusader was an indication that the religious zeal of the crusading movement had degenerated badly. Henry demanded an enormous ransom of £100,000, a sum equal to five years' revenue in England. It is a tribute to the efficiency of the exchequer and to the prosperity of the country that a substantial portion was raised and sent to Germany. Richard returned to England in 1194, only to demand more money for a war against Philip in France. To this war he devoted the last five years of his life. In alliance with his former captor, Henry VI, he pressed Philip very hard. Philip might have lost his kingdom had he not been relieved by Henry's death in 1197 and by Richard's in 1199. Richard died from a wound received in a skirmish with one of his own vassals.

Meanwhile in England, despite the King's absence and the enormous drain upon finance, the government in Hubert Walter's hands continued to function normally. A distinguished lawyer and skillful administrator, Hubert Walter was perhaps the ablest of the long line of able justiciars; he was also archbishop of Canterbury and papal legate. He thus combined authority in lay and clerical affairs. To ensure that the King's financial rights were fully exploited, he sent out itinerant justices in 1194 to make a strict and searching inquiry into the whole fabric of local government. The records of this inquiry reveal the existence of a new official, the coroner, who investigated crimes as soon as they were committed and brought suspected persons before the justices from London. In 1198 Hubert Walter attempted to introduce a new land tax known as a carucage, but the scheme was not fully developed. In the same year there was a proposal that the tenants in chief, instead of performing their normal military service, should supply funds sufficient to maintain a force of 300 knights under constant arms on the Continent. When the barons became suspicious, the plan was dropped.

KING JOHN, 1199–1216

Richard was succeeded by his brother, John, traditionally pictured as a monster of iniquity who deliberately chose the path of evil and took pleasure in following it. In recent years, however, historians have regarded him more favorably. They have stressed his ability and nimble wit, his industry, and his interest in government and administration. The truth is that this fat little man was a highly complicated person of many contradictions. His private morals were admittedly bad: he was cruel, vindictive, revengeful, and treacherous. His sense of fun was ghoulish[1] and sadistic. He was, or could be, most extortionate, twisting the rights of the Crown for his own advantage until he provoked the rebellion that resulted in Magna Carta. He was regarded with deep suspicion by his contemporaries. So profound and constant was this mistrust that it was never allayed; it goes far to explain the hostility between John and most of his barons. Yet as a public official John had much to his credit. He was energetic and active, constantly moving about the country to supervise its government. He was genuinely interested in the administration of justice. If a case touched his own interests, he was apt to be partial and extortionate; but if it did not, he could act with fairness and honesty. He struck hard at those who broke the peace. He also was interested in the functioning of the exchequer, which he sometimes attended in person, and he was not entirely unsympathetic toward the work of the church. As a diplomat he was shrewd and clever.[2] On the other hand, he displayed great instability. He would follow a policy for a time with great energy; yet he seemed incapable of prolonged and sustained effort. His apologists have pointed out that he faced very strong opponents: Philip Augustus, the wily King of France; Innocent III, the most potent of medieval popes; and the English barons just as they were becoming politically self-conscious. In each of these struggles John was defeated. As he sustained one frustration after another he became more bitter and more suspicious.

Fastidious about his personal appearance, and something of a dandy, he wore fine clothes and jewelry. He liked royal splendor and enjoyed a good table.

The Loss of Normandy, 1199–1206

The first years of John's reign were occupied in a struggle with Philip of France, in which the Angevin empire collapsed and Normandy was lost to England. Philip easily found pretexts for war. Richard's death had been followed by a disputed succession. England and Normandy readily accepted John, but the nobles of Aquitaine did homage, not to John, but to his mother, Eleanor; whereas Brittany, Anjou, Maine, and Touraine acknowledged Arthur, the son of John's deceased brother Geoffrey and Constance of Brittany. Arthur was a boy of twelve. His mother sought the protection of Philip, who thus was able to champion Arthur against John. But the war did not begin at once. In the year 1200 John recognized Philip as his overlord for the Angevin lands in France, made certain territorial concessions, and paid the large relief of 20,000 marks.

[1] The word is that of Christopher Brooke, *From Alfred to Henry III 871–1272* (Edinburgh: T. Nelson, 1961), p. 216.
[2] During the reigns of John and his son, Henry III, there was an advance in the keeping of public records. Historians are able to examine the government in this period in far greater depth than can be done for any other European monarchy.

In return he was recognized as Richard's heir and did homage for his French lands. Arthur became his vassal as Duke of Brittany.

John, however, quickly gave Philip a new pretext for beginning hostilities. A dispute had arisen between the families of Angoulême and Lusignan in Poitou over an area known as La Marche. Then the families made peace; Hugh de Lusignan was betrothed to Isabel of Angoulême, a handsome young girl of fourteen. At this point John intervened. He allied himself with Angoulême, married Isabel,[3] and seized certain lands of the house of Lusignan. Hugh appealed to Philip as his supreme lord, and John was summoned to Philip's feudal court in Paris. Failing to appear, John eventually was sentenced to the loss of all his French possessions, and war began in earnest in 1202. In August, John achieved one of his few triumphs by capturing Arthur and a number of prominent persons of Poitou. This was a victory which might have aided John greatly, but he turned his gain to loss. Arthur disappeared. His fate is unknown, but it is assumed that he was done to death at John's order. Rebellion broke out against John in Brittany and indignation against him swept through France.

A general debacle followed in which John's possessions in northern France quickly slipped from his grasp. Normandy was lost by 1204; by 1206, Anjou, Touraine, and Brittany were also lost. Aquitaine, including Poitou, remained in English hands, for Eleanor made over her rights to her son. But Philip was far stronger than before, whereas John suffered an enormous loss of prestige. Suspicion deepened between him and his English barons, each party blaming the other for the defeat in France. Moreover, those barons who elected to retain their English estates and to forfeit their French ones, for they had to make a choice, now thought solely in terms of their English possessions.

John and Innocent III

John refused to believe that his continental possessions were irretrievably lost. But for some years—from 1206 to 1213—he was so preoccupied by a quarrel with Pope Innocent III that he could do little in France. This quarrel, the most violent clash of church and state in England during the whole of the Middle Ages, began in a disputed election to the archbishopric of Canterbury, left vacant at the death of Hubert Walter in 1205. By canon law the right of election lay with the monks of the cathedral chapter at Canterbury. But John was determined to replace Walter with another royal official; the bishops of the province, wishing to share in the election, sided with the King. Fearing to lose their privilege, some of the monks secretly elected one of their own number and sent him to Rome to obtain the Pope's approval. When John heard of this move he came to Canterbury in great wrath and induced the monks to elect his candidate, who also journeyed to Rome. Confronted by these rivals, Innocent determined to take matters into his own hands. He was a most aggressive prelate, determined to exalt the papacy above all temporal rulers. He therefore quashed both elections, ruled that the right of election lay solely in the hands of the monks, and induced those at Rome to select Stephen Langton, a learned and able Englishman recently appointed a cardinal.

Innocent was asserting new and unprecedented powers. Had John acquiesced he might well have lost all control of episcopal elections in England; hence it is not surprising that he refused to accept Stephen Langton. In reply Innocent

---

[3] John had secured an annulment of his marriage to his childless first wife, Isabel of Gloucester.

placed England under an interdict. This papal weapon closed all the churches in the kingdom and withheld from the people the normal services of the clergy. Only baptism and confession for the dying were allowed. In 1209 John was excommunicated. In great bitterness he began a systematic spoliation of the church, appropriating large amounts of church property and diverting ecclesiastical revenues to the sum of £100,000. Many bishops and abbots fled from the country; the monks in some monasteries were dispersed. Yet England remained quiet. But in 1212 there were indications that the barons might revolt; Philip was preparing an invasion of England. In 1213 John suddenly submitted to Rome. He agreed to receive Stephen Langton as archbishop, to recall the exiled clergy, and to recompense the church for the losses it had suffered. He further consented to hold England as a feudal fief from Innocent, to whom he agreed to pay an annual tribute of 1000 marks. Thus John was thoroughly worsted in his quarrel with the papacy. Yet his submission was eminently wise, for the Pope now became his protector. Philip could not invade England without quarreling with Rome, and a new alliance against France became possible.

John's Defeat in France, 1214

For some time John had been building an alliance against France. It consisted of England, Germany under Otto IV, Flanders, and lesser principalities in the Low Countries. Otto and the Count of Flanders were to attack France from the northeast; John was to operate from Poitou and to push northward toward Paris. The plan was sound, and Philip was in great danger. John landed at La Rochelle in 1214 and had some initial success. But he was checked on the Loire because the nobles of Poitou under his command refused to fight against Philip, their supreme lord; John fled back to La Rochelle. This disaster enabled Philip to operate in the north without fear for his southern flank. He met the armies of Otto and of the Count of Flanders at the village of Bouvines on a hot afternoon in July. Philip was completely victorious, the leaders of the coalition against him being either captured or dispersed in flight. Bouvines was one of the few medieval battles which decided great issues: it left Philip supreme in France and in Flanders, it ended Otto's rule in Germany, and it forced John to return dismally to England, defeated once again.

Magna Carta

John's wars, though unsuccessful, were extremely expensive. The age was one of inflation, especially in soldiers' wages. Partly because the English barons were reluctant to fight overseas, John relied heavily on mercenaries—knights; men-at-arms, both mounted and unmounted; foreign crossbowmen; and other foreign mercenaries who were sometimes mere gangs of freebooters. They were all expensive, as were the construction and the repair of castles. Richard had spent thousands of pounds on his beloved Château Gaillard on the Seine. Siege engines, such as stone throwers, were now so improved that the stoutest castle was certain to be badly mauled in a siege and to require frequent repair. John also poured out money in building his alliances against France. He lived in a costly fashion. In the exchequer he had an effective means of extorting money, and he wrung the last penny from his subjects. It was the frequency and size of John's demands that infuriated the barons. There were, of course, other abuses in his government: he distorted his feudal rights to his own advantage, his justice could be highly arbitrary, he employed dishonest persons as sheriffs and as other local officials; he used the law of the forests to increase his revenues; and he demanded hostages from the barons and sometimes treated these hostages with great cruelty. Not only was there suspicion between him and the nobles; there was deep and bitter hate.

Even before John's disastrous expedition to Poitou in 1214, a number of barons had met at St. Paul's Cathedral in London to discuss means of curbing the King's bad government. It was recalled that Henry I had issued a charter renouncing abuses, and it was proposed that some kind of charter might be extracted from John. Hence, when John returned from the Continent, defeated and shattered in prestige, and demanded further taxes, there was an explosion. A number of barons formed a coalition, pledged themselves to act together, renounced their allegiance in a formal defiance, occupied London, and compelled the King to set his seal to Magna Carta in the summer of 1215. It should not be assumed that all the barons thought or acted alike. Some were moved only by personal grievances. Others believed that all would be well if the King abided by feudal law. Only the more enlightened barons saw that the problem went beyond feudalism, that the issue was the preservation of good government under an evil King. Many of the older barons feared a civil war, whereas those demanding the charter were young and impetuous. Stephen Langton, the new archbishop, strove for peace, but revolt took place against his advice.

In later centuries Magna Carta was to become a guarantee of good government and a symbol of English liberty. It was to be praised and glorified and appealed to again and again. But men in succeeding ages, as they looked back at Magna Carta, usually found the things in it they wished to find. They gave it interpretations the document cannot bear. The barons of 1215 would have been bewildered indeed if they had been told that they were the founders of Parliament or of democracy or were advocates of the principle of no taxation without representation or of the right of all men to be tried by jury. These points were not in the charter. Our problem is to see what the barons did in Magna Carta and the contemporary significance of the document.

Magna Carta was drawn up by feudal barons, whose interests naturally predominated in it. A large part of the charter, therefore, was devoted to the detailed workings of feudalism with the object of preventing the King from abusing his feudal rights. Many of these rights were dangerously vague and the barons wished to define them more exactly. Hence there were many articles dealing with the incidents of relief, wardship, and marriage. The sums of money the King could ask for relief were set down in precise terms. He was not to have relief if he had already enjoyed the incident of wardship. The lands of a ward were not to be spoiled or wasted, but must be returned to him when he came of age in as good condition as they had been when the wardship began. A ward was not to be married to a person whose rank was inferior to his. A widow was to be allowed her dower (the lands she had brought to her husband) and was not to be compelled to remarry against her will.

Other articles protected the rights of inheritance of a deceased baron's heirs and prohibited the arbitrary seizure of his chattels to pay debts he owed to the Crown. There were also other articles about debts, for even a great lord might be forced to borrow money in order to meet his obligations to the exchequer. A famous article declared that the King might levy the three ordinary aids allowed by feudal custom but could not collect other aids without the consent of the barons. This consent must be obtained in the feudal council of the tenants in chief. It is possible that this arrangement was inserted by the King's negoti-ators, for the barons would hardly erect machinery by which they could be taxed. The barons suppressed the writ *praecipe*, which transferred cases from feudal to royal courts. The charter was thus a statement of feudal custom with safe-guards against royal abuse.

If Magna Carta had dealt only with the details of feudalism it would have lost significance as feudalism passed away. But it also laid emphasis upon the principle of a feudal contract between the King and his tenants in chief. This principle—that the barons could resist if the King broke his part of the agreement —was one that could be applied in the future long after feudalism had dis-appeared. Moreover, the charter went beyond feudalism in a number of ways.

In the first place, the charter was a protest against the arbitrary use of the system of law and government which had arisen during the twelfth century, especially during the reign of Henry II. The barons accepted this system and wished to preserve it, but they understood its strength and efficiency and they feared what its machinery could do in the hands of an evil King: it could itself become a tyranny. John had refused to issue certain writs, he had suspended courts and withheld justice, he had seized property arbitrarily, and he had inflicted punishment without trial. The charter declared that these abuses were not to continue. There were to be frequent visits of the itinerant justices to try the petty assizes. The writ *de odio et atia*, which protected a man from false accusation, was to be issued free of charge. Justice was not to be sold, refused, nor delayed. Common pleas were to be held in some fixed place, so that litigants would know where their cases could be tried. Article 39 declared: "No free man may be arrested or imprisoned or disseised or outlawed or exiled, or in any way brought to ruin, nor shall we go against him nor send others in pursuit of him, save by the legal judgment of his peers or by the law of the land." This article meant that a man must be tried by due process of law before he could be pun-ished. He must be tried by his social equals. He was not guaranteed trial by jury, for the law of the land did not always provide jury trial. The charter did not define the law of the land, but it stated that there was a law, that there were recognized legal procedures, and that these must be followed.

In demanding that the King not misuse the machinery of government, the barons were standing upon the feudal contract, for they were saying that the King could not alter the law, punish his vassals, nor take their money without consulting his tenants in chief. Another principle arose from the thinking of the church. Many of the higher clergy believed that the duty of the King was to establish a government of law and morality which upheld as far as possible the moral law ordained by God and revealed in the Scriptures. If the King failed in his moral duty he became a tyrant; he forfeited his authority and should be removed from power. The idea of the feudal contract, the protest against arbi-trary government, and the thinking of the church all pointed to the fundamental principle that even the King must obey the law.

The charter also transcended feudalism by granting benefits to classes other than the nobility. The first article declared that the English Church should be free, that is, free from the control of the King and free to obey the papacy. The privileges of London and of other boroughs were confirmed. Foreign merchants should enter England freely and be exempt from arbitrary tolls. Justice was to be done to Welshmen who had lost their property or were held as hostages. Tenants in chief should pass on to their vassals the benefits they had received from the King. Even the peasants profited from an article declaring that they must not be amerced so heavily as to lose their means of livelihood. There were also articles of a general nature which benefited the nation as a whole: dishonest officials should be dismissed, arbitrary exactions ended, and the forest areas curtailed. The legal reforms of Henry II, including many uses of the jury, were confirmed. We must not read too much into these concessions, most of which profited the barons indirectly. Yet the fact that other classes besides the barons gained advantage indicates that the charter was more than a feudal document.

The charter also passed beyond feudalism in its attempt to devise machinery by which the King could be forced to keep his promises. A representative council of twenty-five barons was established to watch John's government and to bring to his attention any infringement of the charter. If the infringement was not corrected, the twenty-five barons should organize and lead an armed revolt against the King. This provision was crude because it legalized civil war, but it is difficult to see what else the barons could have done. The attempt to control the King, which was a step toward limited monarchy, was of great significance for the future. Moreover, it gave opposition a lawful place in the scheme of government. Basing their actions upon the feudal contract, the barons could now resist the Crown without incurring the stigma of treason.

The agreement between John and the barons embodied in the Great Charter lasted only about two months. John had no difficulty in persuading Innocent III to denounce the charter and to free him from his promises. He summoned mercenary troops from the Continent and prepared for war. The barons on their side invoked the article legalizing rebellion and invited Louis, the son of Philip Augustus, to come to England and be their King. Louis soon held London and the southeastern portion of the country while John held the north and west. Then, in October 1216, after a meal of peaches and new cider, John suddenly died. It can at least be said of him that he was not a nonentity: few monarchs have left so strong a mark on England. His vices were the vices of the Angevins in exaggerated form; his virtues were also their virtues, though in him they appeared in pale reflection.

HENRY III, 1216–1272

The Early Years of the Reign, 1216–1232

Friction between the King and the barons continued throughout the long reign of Henry III. The problem was different, for the barons had to deal, not with a King who was a tyrant, but with one who wished to rule in a personal way but lacked the capacity to do so. Yet the fundamental issue of forcing the King to meet his responsibilities remained.

John's son, Henry III, was only nine years old when he came to the throne. His position was very weak. For the first time since the Conquest the King was a minor. The country was divided by civil war; a foreign invader, Louis of France, was in possession of important sections of the kingdom. But the young King, who at his coronation made a pretty little knight, was a disarming figure. His adherents wisely selected a regent, William Marshal, Earl of Pembroke, to rule in his place. Marshal was a fine type of warrior-statesman, a man of great strength of character, of blunt, rough honesty, and of long experience in government. He was able to end the civil war and to begin the task of bringing order out of chaos. Defeated by a rather lucky chance, Louis agreed to leave the country, though he obtained excellent terms. John's death removed the greatest cause of conflict, and with both John and Louis out of the way, the rebel barons returned to their allegiance. The King's party was surprisingly successful.

After Marshal's death in 1219, Hubert de Burgh, the justiciar, was able to make himself supreme. He was the last of the justiciars to rule as though they were Kings. There was much less need for such an office now that Normandy had been lost and the King was not apt to spend long periods abroad. Nor was De Burgh a man of the high quality of his predecessors. He did good work in restoring order, but he was self-seeking and rather arbitrary, and he might well have been driven from office had he not had the constant support of Archbishop Stephen Langton. Eventually Henry tired of him, and he lost his position in 1232 after a long period of power.

Henry's Personal Rule, 1232–1258

In 1232 the King was twenty-five years old. He had been kept in tutelage much longer than was normal, but once he obtained control of affairs he showed himself determined to rule and to continue the autocratic power of his predecessors. He began to gather the reins of authority into his own hands. This was not difficult to do. During the minority a few great barons had worked along with high officials in the daily tasks of administration. Although the Great Council of all the tenants in chief did not meet frequently, the barons could feel that they were being consulted and that barons were joined with professional administrators in what may be called a government by council. But there was no tradition for such a government. The tradition was that of a strong King who could seek advice where he pleased. Henry acted without consulting the barons, insisting upon freedom in selecting his officials.

Unfortunately, he was thoroughly incompetent as a ruler. He was a religious man, chaste and pious in his private life. He was also artistic, a person of finely cultivated taste, with a passion for building and decorating churches and for the collecting of beautiful objects, such as images, jewels, and pictures. Like Edward the Confessor, whom he greatly admired, he devoted much attention to the building of Westminster Abbey. But in affairs of state he was weak, foolish, extravagant, and thoroughly exasperating. Like many weaklings, he could be petty and obstinate, and he was quite ready to deceive when he found himself in a tight corner.

Henry longed to regain the provinces in France lost by his father. In two expeditions against France he displayed complete incompetence, and in 1259 he concluded a treaty with Louis IX in which he acknowledged the loss of English possessions in northern France and did homage for Aquitaine and Gascony in the south. He also made the mistake of showing favor to large numbers of Frenchmen and Italians who came flocking to the English court. Their refined manners and obsequious flattery pleased the King greatly; he gave them money, lands, and offices. A number of Frenchmen from Poitou were introduced into the government by Peter des Roches, the bishop of Winchester, who became important after the fall of Hubert de Burgh. Moreover, Henry's wife, Eleanor of Provence, and his mother, Isabel of Angoulême, had many kinsmen. They crowded into England and were rewarded by the King. Although some were able men, the majority were mere adventurers.

Henry's close relations with the papacy also brought in Italians. The King displayed a surprising subservience to Rome. He believed that he had owed his throne to the support of the papacy during his minority, and he was humbly grateful. Unfortunately his reign coincided with a period in which the pope was in great need of money, for if the papacy was to become a universal ecclesiastical state, a monarchy on a European scale, its financial requirements were necessarily enormous. Means must be found to support a host of officials at Rome and a network of legates, diplomats, and tax collectors throughout Christendom. Demands for money from the church in England became constant and merciless. Not only were the clergy heavily taxed; there were unprecedented applications for such things as a year's income from vacant churches, a monk's share from every monastery, and two prebends (stipends of members of cathedral chapters) from each diocese. There were also appointments by Rome to offices and livings in the church in England; English bishops were instructed to find parishes for Italians who often continued to live abroad. There was naturally a storm of protest. Lay patrons lost their rights of advowson; clergymen, their opportunities of advancement. Henry, however, was sympathetic toward the papal policy, and his remonstrances against it were halfhearted. His unsuccessful expeditions to France, his welcome to aliens who came to England, his acquiescence in the exorbitant financial demands of Rome—all gave the impression that he was weak and incompetent.

A program of reform gradually took shape among the baronial leaders. They asked, in the first place, that Magna Carta be reissued again, as it had been on various occasions. They also asked that they should be consulted about the problems of government. This was sound feudal doctrine, for a feudal suzerain was supposed to summon his tenants in chief in meetings of the Great Council and to talk with them concerning affairs of state. Thus the barons, regarding themselves as the natural counselors of the King, refused to be ignored. Further, they sought to obtain some control over the machinery of government, especially over the appointment of the great ministers of state, the Treasurer, the Chancellor, and sometimes the Justiciar. The Exchequer and the Chancery were now distinct departments separate from the rest of the government. Their officials were powerful and, the barons thought, too independent. If they could be brought under baronial surveillance, the power of the Crown to rule irresponsibly would be much diminished.

It was only in times of great crisis that the barons attempted to control the royal household. This also had grown in importance because Henry II, finding the exchequer and the chancery too cumbersome to transact quickly the personal affairs of the King, had developed a miniature exchequer and secretariat in the chamber, that is, in the King's sleeping apartment. Under Henry III a similar development took place in the wardrobe, the apartment where the King kept his clothes and armor. Certain revenues were paid into the wardrobe, which was not under the control of the Exchequer.

It should not be thought that the barons were seeking to build a new constitution. They were protecting what they considered to be their ancient rights. As amateurs in government they suspected the expert and disliked the trained official. And yet in opposing the King they easily assumed that they were speaking for the nation and that they represented a community of the realm with which the King should cooperate.

The Provisions of Oxford, 1258

Henry's financial difficulties came to a head in 1258. In prolonged negotiations with the papacy in 1254–1255 he had foolishly accepted the crown of Sicily for Edmund, his second son. The Pope was at war with Sicily at the time and did not control that territory. Yet Henry agreed to pay all past and future expenses of the papal campaign and thus made himself responsible for financing a distant war over which he had no control. The papal forces made little headway, the venture was hopeless by 1257, and Henry was responsible for the huge debts incurred by Rome. At the same time he was overwhelmed by other expenses. A campaign in France and a war in Wales had to be paid for, Westminster Abbey was unfinished, and a hard winter in 1257–1258 rendered extraordinary taxation impossible. When the barons, exasperated by the folly of the Sicilian adventure, demanded sweeping reforms in 1258, the King had no alternative but surrender.

The demands of the barons were incorporated in a famous memorandum, known as the Provisions of Oxford. A council of fifteen persons, almost entirely barons, some selected from supporters of the King and some from his opponents, was placed in virtual control of the government. The council was to advise the King on all matters of policy, so that he could make no important decision without its knowledge and consent. It was to appoint the Treasurer, the Chancellor, and the Justiciar, who were made responsible to it. The provisions also included administrative reforms and gave the council control over local officials.

It is interesting to compare this document with Magna Carta, which was concerned with feudalism. The Provisions of Oxford, however, show that the barons were less interested in the details of feudalism than in the machinery of government and that they accepted that machinery as a matter of course. They wished to capture it but they also wished to continue its operation. Distrusting the King, they put the kingship in commission by transferring royal authority to the council of fifteen. But the work of government was done by a larger group. The Justiciar, though not one of the council, almost certainly sat with it. Prominent judges and heads of departments worked with it in close cooperation. Thus the council relied upon the experience of ministers of state, employing their technical skill and their close acquaintance with the details of government.

The Provisions of Oxford remained in force until 1262. At first the important magnates who had created the new government displayed remarkable unanimity, introducing reforms and allowing local knights to draw up lists of grievances. But government by council was a novel idea, and the barons, looking at events from the standpoint of their own class, resented demands that they reform the management of their own estates. They began to quarrel among themselves. In 1259 the Lord Edward, Henry's son, emerged as a person of importance and formed a small royal party. He allied for a moment with Simon de Montfort, a more radical leader; but Henry broke up the combination, reasserted himself, and began to undermine the Provisions of Oxford. Civil war broke out in 1264. Edward commanded the King's forces; Simon de Montfort led the opposition. At the Battle of Lewes, in Sussex, Simon defeated Edward, captured the King, and found himself in control of the government.

Simon de Montfort, 1264–1265

Historians have often glorified Simon de Montfort as though he were an apostle of liberty and one of the great architects of Parliament. As a matter of fact, he was neither. He was a French feudal baron who looked upon the world from the point of view of his class. But he was an unusually able, clear-headed, and confident man, an advocate of reform, and one of the first statesmen to see that a middle element, below the baronage but above the peasants, was beginning to emerge in English society. In great need of support, he courted this middle element.

He was not considered a foreigner by the English nobility. When he had come to England in 1231, Henry had welcomed him warmly, had given him lands which had been held by Simon's father, had made him an earl, and had bestowed upon him the King's sister in marriage. For a time Henry had sent him to rule Gascony. When Henry became dissatisfied with Simon's administration, however, he recalled him and forced him to submit to a trial in which the King himself attacked Simon bitterly. There could be no friendship between the two men after this. The discontented nobles gathered around Simon as much because he was the King's brother-in-law as because he was a strong man and an advocate of reform. After the Battle of Lewes he held dictatorial power, but he did not wish to be a dictator. He thought it possible to return to the Provisions of Oxford, for he was quite aware that government of the ordinary kind was out of the question. A magnate in his position, with the King in captivity and the barons divided, could hardly hope to remain in power long. Simon, with two close associates, ruled in the King's name. They selected a council of nine members whose functions were somewhat similar to those of the earlier council of fifteen.

To strengthen this highly precarious experiment in government, Simon turned for support to the middle elements of English society. During the thirteenth century the meetings of the Great Council of the barons were beginning to be known as Parliaments. The early history of the English Parliament will be considered in a later chapter,[4] but it may be said in a word that the King, for his own convenience, sometimes summoned groups of smaller landowners (who were called knights of the shire) to meet with him at the same time as his tenants in chief in the Great Council. Simon de Montfort continued and extended this practice. To a Parliament in 1264 he summoned not only the barons and high churchmen who were his adherents but also knights from each shire. And in 1265 he summoned not only knights from the shires but also burgesses from a selected number of towns. He was not trying to construct a new institution. He merely saw that the support of smaller landowners and of prosperous townsmen was worth obtaining and that a Parliament in which they were present was a place where important business could be transacted.

Simon's position was weakened in 1265. He lost the support of one of his most powerful adherents, the Earl of Gloucester, who turned against his government. At about the same time the Lord Edward escaped, joined Gloucester, and gathered an army. Together they defeated Simon at the Battle of Evesham, Worcestershire, in which Simon was slain. The King was released from captivity and resumed control of the government, though actual power was exercised not by Henry but by his son, the Lord Edward.

To all appearances the barons had accomplished very little by their attempts to control the King. The full force of monarchy was quickly reestablished after Simon's death, and Edward was to prove a King who asserted the full authority

[4] See pages 147–151.

of kingship. The oligarchical rule of a small group of barons was not the answer to the problem of an irresponsible sovereign. Certain things, however, had been accomplished. A number of the reforms desired by the barons were continued and became a permanent part of the administration. There was now an established principle that affairs of state should be discussed in meetings of the Great Council or of Parliament. Indeed, a broader concept emerged that the King should consult his subjects when their rights were involved and that he should seek cooperation with all the groups and interests among the ruling classes. Finally, the barons had set a precedent of great importance when they attempted to curb the power of the King without destroying the fabric of the machinery of government.

6

society in the twelfth
and thirteenth centuries

THE CHURCH

It is probable that the Christian Church had a greater hold upon the minds of men in the Middle Ages than it has ever had before or since. Its primary function was to lead them to salvation. There were certain acts and ceremonies, known as the sacraments—baptism, confirmation, penance, the Holy Eucharist or Mass, extreme unction, marriage, ordination of the priesthood—through which God's grace was imparted by the church to men. These rites and holy mysteries, with their hope of salvation, exerted an incalculable influence over the people. But the church touched men's lives in countless other ways. The parish church in a small village was a social as well as a religious center, the village market might be held in the churchyard, and social life revolved around the festivals of the Christian year. The painting of religious scenes on the inner walls of the parish church were vivid works of art. Cathedrals in the cities embodied the majesty of the church. The church courts dealt not only with heresy, but with perjury, moral offenses and matrimonial cases, and the probate of wills and settlements of property. And while Christianity thus touched the people on every hand, it was itself growing more humane. The mercy, the love, the tender compassion of Christ, His life on earth, and His sufferings upon the Cross received new emphasis. There was an increase in the cult of the Virgin Mary, who represented the human aspect of Christ and who could intercede with her Son in behalf of frail humanity.

The church was highly complex, containing great varieties of wealth, function, and social division. It contained men in minor orders, such as deacons and subdeacons, who knew only enough to conduct the services, and sophisticated philosophers of great breadth and subtlety of learning. The parish priest often farmed the glebe belonging to his church whereas the upper clergy were wealthy aristocrats who controlled great estates and held high office in the service of the Crown. Great numbers of men and women had retired from the world to lead religious lives in monasteries and nunneries. In the thirteenth century the Franciscan and Dominican friars appeared in England and were eagerly supported. Men sometimes lived in solitude, as hermits and anchorites, devoting themselves to religious contemplation.

The Organization of the Church

Archbishops, bishops, and parish priests formed the three principal ranks of the secular clergy. The bishop ruled over an area known as a diocese. Some of his duties have already been mentioned.[1] He alone could perform the sacrament of confirmation and ordain men to the priesthood. Although lay patrons nominated priests to livings, the bishop held a veto; it was his duty to prevent unsuitable appointments and to secure an adequate stipend for a newly installed priest. The bishop dedicated altars and consecrated churches, disciplined the clergy of the diocese, and either in person or by deputy visited (that is, inspected) the parishes within his diocese and corrected irregularities. We know, for example, that late in the thirteenth century Archbishop Pecham made very searching visitations. The bishop visited monasteries in the same way. It was his duty to summon annual synods of the principal clergy of the diocese.

The administrative center of a diocese was normally the most important town of the area. Here the bishop had his palace and his cathedral. A formal body of disciplined clergy connected with each cathedral was known as the cathedral chapter. By a system peculiar to England, a number of the cathedrals, such as Canterbury and Durham, were the churches of Benedictine abbeys, their chapters being composed of monks who conducted the daily services. Other cathedral chapters were made up of canons, who were secular priests. The head of the chapter was the dean. He was assisted by the precentor, who was responsible for the daily liturgy; the chancellor, who might also be the master of the cathedral school; the treasurer; and the resident and nonresident canons. Some canonries in the secular cathedrals had prebends, or incomes without duties attached to them; these places were sought by the King as rewards for his servants and by the pope for officials at Rome, who might never come to England. During the twelfth century cathedral chapters became invested with the right to elect the bishop (though not without advice from the King) and with the administration of the diocese during a vacancy. The chapter, managing its own endowments, generally acquired considerable independence from the bishop. Thus situations arose in which a bishop might have little jurisdiction over his cathedral or over the chapter attached to it.

The bishop therefore developed his own household of clerks and officials quite apart from the dean and chapter. For a long time the bishop worked informally, assisted by a small, though sometimes brilliant, group of clerks. A change took place early in the thirteenth century when the administrative and legal activities of a bishopric greatly expanded. Episcopal registers appeared, containing a record of all the bishop's activities, and a group of officials emerged who did much of his formal work. The most important officials were the registrar, who presided in the bishop's court, and the vicar-general, who was the bishop's deputy in administration. These offices were sometimes combined in one person, known as the chancellor. Certain functions, however, could only be performed by a person with the rank of bishop. Hence a suffragan bishop was sometimes appointed. He was no more than a temporary assistant to the bishop,

[1] See page 22.

Anglo-Norman Romanesque Architecture. Durham Cathedral. Note the round arches, the alternating round pillars and clustered columns, the triforium, and the clerestory. (Marburg-Art Reference Bureau)

Anglo-Norman Romanesque Architecture. Side aisle, Durham Cathedral, showing round arches and detail of designs on round pillars. (Marburg-Art Reference Bureau)

Anglo-Norman Romanesque Architecture. South door, Ely Cathedral, showing intricate carving on round arch. (A. F. Kersting)

holding a title without a see or being given an inaccessible see in Ireland. Below these officials were archdeacons and rural deans. The archdeacon, who held an ecclesiastical court in a subdivision of the diocese, made visitations in the parishes under his jurisdiction, summoned offenders to his court, and imposed fines for moral and ecclesiastical offenses. He was a highly unpopular official.

Medieval Dioceses, with Monasteries and Towns Mentioned in the Text

The rural dean or archpriest exercised similar, though very restricted, powers over small areas. The archdeacon, like the cathedral chapter, acquired some independence from the authority of the bishop. A bishopric contained a good many islands, such as exempt monasteries and churches belonging to other dioceses, in which the bishop could not exert authority.

Dioceses differed greatly in size and endowments. The dioceses of York and Lincoln were enormous, whereas those of Ely and Rochester were very small. Canterbury, York, Winchester, Ely, and Durham possessed princely endowments; others, such as the Welsh bishoprics, were poverty-stricken. Like other magnates, the bishops were expected to live in a lavish way, with large staffs of officials and household servants. A few men of humble origin attained bishoprics, but the bishops were normally drawn from the monasteries, the universities, or the officials of the Crown. Many of them were men of distinction in scholarship or in royal administration. The thirteenth century was fortunate in having a number of outstanding bishops, such as St. Edmund of Abingdon, St. Richard Wych, and Robert Grosseteste, bishop of Lincoln and the first chancellor of Oxford University. The provinces of Canterbury and York were unequal in size. The archbishop of Canterbury presided over eighteen bishoprics, including four in Wales; the archbishop of York, over only three. The archbishop acted as bishop in his own diocese and exercised jurisdiction over the other bishops of his province. Under an aggressive archbishop this jurisdiction could be very real, but normally an archbishop did not attempt a close control over his bishops. The archbishop of Canterbury was so occupied with business at the court of the King that he paid little attention to the affairs of Canterbury, much less to those of other bishoprics.

A rural parish usually covered the area of a small village of perhaps three hundred to four hundred people. The priest was often of peasant origin and lived much like other peasants. Certain things, of course, marked him off from his parishioners. He had been educated at a monastic school or in the household of a bishop, although he had not been educated very well. He probably lived in a better house than the other peasants and held more land in the open fields. And his sacred duties must have exalted his position. But on weekdays he was often a farmer who tilled the glebe of the parish, and he is known to have occasionally performed villein services for the lord of the manor. He derived his income from the glebe and from tithes paid in agricultural produce by his parishioners. But an ecclesiastical living was regarded as a piece of property; hence the right to appoint a priest (advowson) and to dispose of the income of a parish might pass from the lord of the manor to a monastery or to a cathedral or perhaps to the King. When this happened, or when the rector of a parish was permitted to be nonresident, part of the parish income was normally used to supply a vicar, who performed the necessary duties of the parish church. These arrangements could lead to serious abuses. At the time of the Norman Conquest many parish priests were married, and even in the thirteenth century the celibacy of the clergy was far from universal, despite the insistence of the church.

The Monasteries

During the century following the Norman Conquest there was a remarkable revival of monasticism in England. William the Conqueror and his barons founded many monasteries; Stephen's reign, despite the anarchy, was a time of many new foundations. At the time of Stephen's death in 1154 the number of monastic houses had risen to nearly 300.[2] An impulse of reform came first from a famous monastery founded at Cluny in French Burgundy in 910 and later from new orders which established themselves in England. Many of the leading churchmen of the time, including both Lanfranc and Anselm, were monks. The psychology of the founders was sometimes curious. The rough barons of Stephen's reign first plundered the countryside and then established religious houses with the proceeds, but the movement could not have received such universal support had it not made a strong appeal to men of the twelfth century. The monastic ideal of rejection of the world, of devotion to religion in the regu-

[2] Christopher Brooke, *From Alfred to Henry III 871–1272* (Edinburgh: T. Nelson, 1961), p. 143.

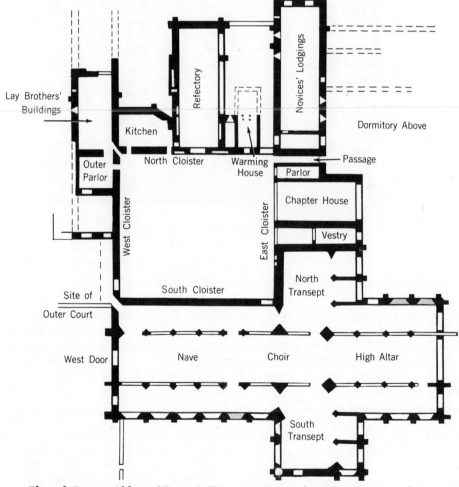

Plan of Tintern Abbey. (From *A History of Britain* by E. H. Carter and R. A. F. Mears, published by Clarendon Press, Oxford)

Monks singing the daily services, fifteenth century. (British Museum, *King Henry VI's Psalter*, Cottonian MS Domitian A. xvii, f. 122v.)

lated life of the cloister, caught the imagination of the people. To say that a man was converted to religion did not mean that he had become a Christian but that he had become a monk. And Kings and nobles continued to come forward with rich gifts. The movement declined somewhat in the thirteenth century, for it was almost impossible to maintain the high ideals of monastic life after a monastery had become wealthy. Nevertheless, the monks continued to be important in the life of the nation, quite apart from their wealth and prestige.

Monastic life rested primarily upon the teachings of St. Benedict (c. 480–c. 544). This Italian monk, disliking the fanaticism of early monks and hermits in Egypt and Syria, devised a famous rule by which religious men could live a communal life together in austerity and self-restraint without undue excesses. Upon entering a Benedictine abbey a novice took the usual vows of poverty, chastity, and obedience. He also took a vow of stability, that is, he swore to remain in the monastery until his death. There were both common sense and humanity in St. Benedict's rule. It gave great authority to the abbot and left many details to his discretion. The vow of stability brought permanence to monastic life. The rule also provided that monks should spend several hours each day in manual labor. This gave their lives variety and made the monastery self-supporting at least to the extent that it could refuse corrupting gifts.

Though it remained the basis of monastic regulations, the rule of St. Benedict had been revised and modified in various ways by the twelfth century. The ritual of the daily services became more elaborate so that the monks spent a larger part of their time in church. There was greater attention to scholarship, in which St. Benedict had had little interest. The monks became the custodians of learning. Copying and illuminating manuscripts, they also kept chronicles, and taught in monastic schools. St. Benedict's injunction to labor in the fields was abandoned; it became the practice for a monastery to add a number of lay brothers who cultivated the monastic lands. They were peasants of a religious cast of mind who took vows of poverty, chastity, and obedience but were too ignorant to sing the services.

The best way to understand monastic life is to study the buildings of a monastic foundation. Let us look at Tintern Abbey, a Cistercian monastery in the lovely valley of the Wye River. The southern portion of the monastic buildings was a large church. St. Benedict set down detailed instructions for the services, or offices, to be performed each day. These services, known as the *Opus Dei,* "the Work of God," formed the center of monastic life, and nothing was allowed to interfere with them. They consisted of singing psalms, saying responses, and reading lessons from the Scriptures. The first, Matins, was performed at two in the morning and was followed immediately by a second, Lauds. The monks then retired to their dormitory, to which the church was accessible by a stairway, and slept until six, when they arose for a series of services and Masses which continued until about half past eight. There followed a meeting in the chapter house, where the business affairs of the abbey were discussed. The monks then read and worked in the fields until the midday meal. In the afternoon they read and worked again (for the Cistercians did not follow other orders in abandoning manual labor). Supper was followed by two more services, Vespers and Compline, before the monks retired.

Apart from the church, the life of a monastery centered in and around the cloisters. A cloister was an enclosed walk or arcade, perhaps twenty feet wide, forming a square around an open lawn or garden. The cloisters gave access to almost every part of the monastery. It was in the cloisters that the monks spent their hours of reading and teaching. A building at the northwest corner of Tintern Abbey was reserved for the lay brothers. Beside it was the kitchen, then the refectory or dining hall, then the warming room, probably the only warm room in the abbey. To the east of the cloisters, below the dormitory of the monks, were quarters for novices (young men and boys preparing to be monks) and a chapter house. To the west an open court contained the abbot's house, an almoner's lodge, where alms were given to the poor, and the hospitium, where guests and travelers could spend the night.

Most of the monastic foundations in England were Benedictine houses. They included some very large and prominent houses, such as St. Albans, Bury St. Edmunds, Glastonbury, and St. Mary's, York. Of the new orders, the most influential was the order of Cistercians, which originated in 1098 at the monastery of Cîteaux in the desolate forest area of Burgundy near Dijon. It was one of the frequent attempts to regain the simplicity envisaged by St. Benedict. The monks lived in great austerity, following the rule to the letter: without "coats, capes, worsted cloth, hoods, pants, combs, counterpanes, and bedclothes," without fine food in the refectory or anything else contrary to the rule. Their first foundation in England was at Waverley in Surrey in 1129, but their most famous houses were in the desolate north, at Rievaulx, Fountains, and Kirkstall in the solitary dales of Yorkshire. They founded so many daughter houses that their monasteries can be arranged in a kind of family tree. They owned huge flocks of sheep and became wealthy through the sale of wool. An even stricter order was that of the Carthusians, who followed a very early and pre-Benedictine form of monasticism in which the monks lived alone in cells, each monk preparing his own food and saying the daily offices to himself. The first Carthusian house in England was Witham Abbey in Somerset, founded in 1179. Its first prior was Hugh of Avalon, a Burgundian who became bishop of Lincoln and was a personal friend of Henry II. But the order was too severe to be popular and only a handful of Carthusian monasteries existed in England. The Gilbertines were an English order of pious women, founded about 1131.

So strong was the monastic ideal that groups of priests serving large churches or forming cathedral chapters felt the urge to live according to a rule. These priests, known as regular canons, followed the rule of St. Augustine (354–430), which was more elastic than the rule of St. Benedict. During the twelfth century more than a hundred houses of Augustinian, or Austin, canons were established in England.

In the thirteenth century there was a decline in the idealism and influence of the monasteries, which no longer supplied the religious and intellectual leadership they had in the past. Although some new houses were established, the great age of founding monasteries was over, and although they continued to be supported reasonably well by gifts and endowments, many benefactions of the upper classes were going elsewhere. It is true that a baron or other wealthy person often inherited an interest in a particular house and was ready to assist it as occasion offered. Some of the larger Benedictine and Cistercian abbeys profited greatly from the high farming of the thirteenth century. The Benedictine houses were inspected by their own order as well as by the bishops. They also sent representatives to central assemblies known as chapters, which acquired powers of government over the order.

But the monasteries were by now wealthy and well-established institutions, and it was not easy to maintain the spirit of the Benedictine rule. Monastic life became more comfortable. Glass windows, clocks, and softer beds were introduced. The monks became more interested in good living; they ate meat, which was forbidden by the rule. They also paid greater attention to the management of their property. It was only to be expected that a vigorous abbot would watch over the monastic estates and manage them in a businesslike way. A worldly spirit was creeping into monastic life, though this is a matter difficult to judge, and every monastery differed to some extent from every other. Nonetheless, it seems clear that the monasteries, though a stable and traditional element in society, had lost much of their early religious fervor.

The Friars

The friars, who represented the last great movement of reform in the medieval church, were perhaps the most vital element in English religious life during the thirteenth century. They first appeared in 1221, when a body of Dominicans, or Friars of the Order of Preachers, arrived in England. The order had been founded by St. Dominic (1170–1221), a Spanish priest who had been combating the heresy that had arisen in northern Spain and in southern France. Reflecting on the needs of the church, he conceived of an order of well-educated and skillful preachers who, living in poverty, could move among the people, correcting the deficiencies of the lower clergy in teaching and preaching and strengthening the orthodoxy of the church by attacking heretical doctrines. The Dominicans therefore laid great stress on the education of their members. They established at once a convent at Oxford for the training of young friars.

Friar preaching out of doors, fourteenth century. (Bodleian Library, Oxford, Bodleian MS 264, f. 79, Historical Pictures Service, Chicago)

They were fortunate in obtaining the assistance of Robert Grosseteste, later bishop of Lincoln, who became deeply interested in the order.

A second group of friars, the Order of the Friars Minor, the Franciscans, came to England three years later. Their founder was St. Francis of Assisi (1181–1226), one of the most attractive figures of the Middle Ages. The son of a prosperous Italian merchant, he experienced a conversion as a young man, renounced his inheritance, and lived in complete poverty, begging for his daily bread as he traveled about preaching and doing good works among the poor. His message to his followers was the message of Jesus to His disciples—to renounce the world and to live among the destitute. In 1210 St. Francis obtained from Innocent III a somewhat hesitant approval of his band as a new order in the church. Later, under the supervision of the papacy, the order was given a necessary organization, much to the sorrow of its founder.

The Dominicans and the Franciscans, though differing in purpose, had much in common and tended to grow very much alike. Their members took the usual vows of poverty, chastity, and obedience. They lived by a rule, though not a monastic rule, for the friars mingled with the people. By the end of the century each of the orders had established about fifty houses in England. Almost from the first, the Franciscans recognized the importance of education and scholarship, though St. Francis had not done so. Like the Dominicans, they established a convent at Oxford which attracted a group of eminent scholars. Robert Grosseteste, although he was not a friar, agreed to lecture on theology. Other distinguished thinkers at the Franciscan convent were Adam Marsh, John Pecham, who was later archbishop of Canterbury, and Roger Bacon.

The friars made a great appeal to the men of the time. They were the evangelists of the Middle Ages, living among the poor in the towns, attending the sick and destitute, and preaching to classes neglected by the church. They were far better educated than the parish priests, and they spiced their sermons with wit and humor as well as eloquence.

In the fourteenth century the orders declined, not because of their wealth, for they had comparatively little, but because of the excessive privileges and immunities given to them by the papacy. They could use the parish churches, celebrate Mass, hear confession, and impose penance, and they were greatly sought after by the laity to perform the normal functions of the clergy. Yet they were responsible only to their own superiors, who in turn were responsible only to the pope. In competition with the priests for the attention of the public and with the monks for gifts and endowments, they were normally on very bad terms with both. Their begging became a nuisance; at the end of the fourteenth century Geoffrey Chaucer had little good to say of them.

ARCHITECTURE

The Normans began a great age of English architecture. Their architectural style—the Norman or the Anglo-Norman Romanesque—appeared about 1090 and continued to be used until about 1175. During that period cathedrals and large monastic churches were built or rebuilt at Durham, Tewkesbury, Winchester, Canterbury, Old Sarum, Chichester, Ely, Norwich, Bath, and elsewhere. Despite rebuilding in later centuries, many fine examples of Norman architecture may still be seen; they illustrate the distinctive features of this style. These cathedrals were of enormous size, twice the length of the Saxon cathedral at North Elmham in Norfolk, which measured 140 feet. As a matter of fact, the tendency to build large churches existed all over Europe, chiefly because of the increasing pomp and ceremony of the liturgy. But English cathedrals were large even for the era of their construction. In addition to size, they gave the impression of strength and solidity, ideas conveyed by their massive piers or pillars carrying heavy rounded arches, their large lantern towers above the middle of the church, and their thick and heavy walls.

Cathedrals were built in the shape of a cross, with the upper portion of the cross pointing toward the east. The lower portion was represented by the nave, which was the main body of the church. The fine proportions, great impressiveness, and massive strength of these Norman naves are still evident today. The transepts, large projections built to the north and south, represented the arms of the cross. It was above the intersection of nave and transepts that the central tower was erected. To the east of the transepts was the choir, which formed the upper portion of the cross and was the place where the clergy assembled to sing the daily services. Smaller than the nave, the choir contained stalls or carved wooden seats for the clergy; at the eastern end was the high altar. Along both sides of the nave and choir ran a wide aisle separated from the central part of the church by an arcade of piers or pillars. At Durham, where some of the best Norman work has survived, the arcade consisted of alternating round piers and clustered columns; the piers were ornamented with bold spiral or zig-zag patterns and the rounded arches with running motifs of various designs. Above the piers was the triforium, a small gallery close to the wall, decorated with arches and small columns. Above this was the clerestory, a portion of the wall pierced by narrow windows. Sometimes the aisles ended at the east of the church in small rounded apses which were used as chapels; sometimes they were continued and joined together in a semicircle behind the choir. In later ages the apses often disappeared and were replaced by a square east end. A notable feature at Durham was the stone vaulting carried by cross-ribs to form the interior of the roof. This style of vaulting made the clerestory possible; the weight of a stone barrel-vault required solid walls.

Late in the twelfth century Romanesque architecture gave way to the Gothic or Early English style. Gothic architecture, as it had been developing in France, was first brought to England by the Cistercian monks who came from Burgundy and built their English abbeys in the style they had known at home. About the same time, the monks at Canterbury engaged a Frenchman, William of Sens, to rebuild the choir. Like the Cistercians he employed the Gothic style he had known in his own country. The style at Canterbury was soon followed in other English cathedrals, as at Wells and Lincoln, which were being built in the last decade of the twelfth century and were almost entirely Gothic. These churches, together with Salisbury and Westminster Abbey, formed the greatest monuments of Early English architecture. Salisbury was completed within thirty or forty years after it was begun in 1220 and thus possessed great unity of design and purity of style. Westminster Abbey, upon which Henry III lavished care and money, was more elaborate than the others. A happy blending of French and English influences, with a beautifully proportioned nave and with handsomely sculptured stone, it brought new richness and splendor to architecture in England.

An obvious feature of Early English architecture was the pointed arch, which appeared in many shapes and sizes and culminated in the lofty arches of the vaulting supported by columns rising from the floor. These columns, massive at first, became in time more slender and graceful and often were adorned by clusters of Purbeck marble shafts. Strengthened by buttresses on the outside of the building, the columns supported the roof, relieving the walls of much dead weight and making larger windows possible. Stained glass and tracery in geometrical patterns were used in the windows; and their larger size increased the amount of light, which combined with pointed arches and slender columns to give the cathedral an airy grace and chaste aesthetic beauty. Simple, austere, restrained, these cathedrals were finely built though not extravagant. They relied upon symbolism rather than upon exact copies of natural objects, and they achieved a synthesis of the arts by subordinating them to religious purposes and to structural needs.[3]

[3] See pages 175–182 for a discussion of architecture in the later Middle Ages.

Gothic or Early English Architecture. Lincoln Cathedral. Note the many pointed arches. (A. F. Kersting)

Gothic or Early English Architecture. Salisbury Cathedral. (A. F. Kersting)

THE INTELLECTUAL RENAISSANCE

In the twelfth and thirteenth centuries a remarkable awakening of intellectual life took place in Europe. It was cosmopolitan in nature. Learned men among the upper clergy moved easily from one to another of the schools of western Europe; students gathered around a famous teacher and followed him from place to place; there was, of course, a universal language of scholarship: Latin. In the opening years of the twelfth century Archbishop Anselm was the most eminent scholar in England. As priors of the monastery of Bec in Normandy, both he and Lanfranc had made that monastery a center of learning. Later in England Anselm gathered a group of pupils around him at Canterbury. But the group was small, and Anselm was the last of the great monastic teachers. The monastic schools, whose primary purpose was the training of monks to take part in the daily services, produced great scholars only as a kind of by-product. By the middle of the twelfth century these schools had fallen into eclipse; educational leadership had moved from the regular to the secular clergy, from the monastic schools to those connected with cathedrals. But although the cathedral schools in England were advancing in reputation, it was the fashion for English students to complete their education by attending the more famous schools on the Continent.

The Classics

The intellectual awakening that began in the eleventh century centered in the cathedral schools of northern France at Laon, Paris, Chartres, Tours, and Orléans. Its first expression was an intense interest in the classical literature of Rome. Most of the Latin authors known today were known in the eleventh century. They were eagerly studied, not merely as models of literary grace, but as a means of understanding the thought and culture of Roman antiquity. This classical education produced excellent results: students trained in the French schools became men of letters with wide cultural interests and great literary skill.

The most distinguished Englishman among them was John of Salisbury. For some twelve years he continued his education, studying first under the famous Abelard at Paris and then at Chartres, the home of classical scholarship. The breadth of his reading in Roman literature was amazing; it is said that he wrote in the purest Latin style to be found throughout the Middle Ages. Among the distinguished men he met at Paris was Abbot Peter of Celle, with whom he continued a long and intimate correspondence, one of the few that has survived from medieval times. Between 1154 and 1161 John of Salisbury was a member of the household of Archbishop Theobald at Canterbury, acting as his secretary and writing many of his letters. Theobald sent him to Rome on various missions of which John has left lively descriptions. At Rome he was a friend of Nicholas Breakspear, an English cardinal who, as Adrian IV, became the only English pope. While John was living at Canterbury he wrote a long treatise on political theory and a shorter one on logic, both dedicated to Thomas Becket. After Theobald's death John entered Becket's household, defended him in his quarrel with Henry II, and later wrote his biography. John ended his life as bishop of Chartres.

Another scholar connected with the household of Archbishop Theobald was Peter of Blois, the author of numerous letters. Literary men often found employment at the court of Henry II. Walter Map, a Welshman who had studied at

The Gloucester Candlestick, c. 1104–1113. Gilded bronze, twenty-three inches in height. (Victoria and Albert Museum)

Paris, was highly regarded by Henry and served him as ambassador and itinerant justice. Map wrote a witty and penetrating account of Henry's court. Gerald of Wales, also a former student at Paris and a friend of the King, wrote books on Wales and Ireland and a treatise on the education of princes in which he made some caustic comments on Henry and his sons. An author of a very different type was Geoffrey of Monmouth, whose history of the early Kings of Britain was a collection of Celtic tales which supplied later writers with material for legends of King Arthur. These men illustrate the breadth of twelfth-century culture, its love of belles-lettres, and also Henry's appreciation of literary talent.

Philosophy and Theology

About the middle of the twelfth century, interest in classical literature was overwhelmed by a greater interest in philosophy and theology. John of Salisbury and other literary men complained that young students neglected the classics to hurry on to the study of theology and law, the utilitarian subjects of the day. The new interest in philosophy and theology developed into a type of learning known as scholasticism, an attempt to apply reason and deductive logic to the study of theology and to seek the solution of theological questions through logical argumentation. The most famous exponent of this method in the twelfth century was Abelard (d. 1142), a brilliant thinker and teacher who attracted hundreds of students to Paris. In his book *Sic et Non (Yes and No)* Abelard showed that the Bible and the writings of the early church fathers contained many contradictions, and he sought the truth through the application of reason. He aroused the hostility of conservative churchmen, who feared that he was placing reason above faith and dogma and whose view was well expressed by Anselm's famous aphorism, "Believe that you may understand." Faith must be placed before reason, dogma before knowledge. Abelard, on the other hand, would have said, "Understand that you may believe." The difference was fundamental. Abelard fascinated the younger generation of churchmen as much as he horrified the old. But he had no thought of challenging faith, and the controversy developed into efforts to reconcile faith and reason and to achieve a synthesis that would satisfy the demands of both.

Behind these arguments and largely responsible for them was the gradual recovery of the works of Aristotle (384–322 B.C.), the Greek philosopher who held that knowledge must begin with the collection of facts and that only after facts had been assembled and assimilated could a philosophy of life or an understanding of truth be constructed. Before the twelfth century only a small portion of Aristotle's works was known in western Europe. The rest of his writings, however, were recovered during the twelfth century and were available to scholars in the thirteenth.

Eastern Science

A knowledge of Greek was almost unknown among the scholars of western Europe. Hence the writings of Aristotle and other Greek philosophers and scientists had to be translated into Latin before they were generally accessible. There was some translation directly into Latin from Greek, but a much larger portion of the writings of the Greeks made their way into western Europe through the Arabs who had studied Greek civilization, had translated Greek texts into Arabic, and, especially in mathematics and medicine, had developed Greek thought. It was by contact with Arab sources in Spain, in Sicily and southern Italy, and in Asia Minor that Western scholars learned of Eastern science and brought back a knowledge of it. In this diffusion of Arabic learning Englishmen played an important part.

One of the first was Adelard of Bath (c.1099–c.1150). The details of his life are obscure, but it is known that he studied at Tours in northern France and taught at Laon. He traveled widely, in Greece, in Asia Minor, in Sicily and southern Italy, and perhaps in Spain, and translated into Latin a number of Arab texts on philosophic and scientific subjects, of which the most important was Euclid's work on geometry. A translation of Ptolemy's *Almagest,* the standard work on ancient astronomy, also is attributed to Adelard. It is probable that he was employed in England by Henry I as an official in the Exchequer and that his knowledge of Greek and Arabic mathematics helped to develop its technique. To catch the attention of young Henry Plantagenet, later Henry II, Adelard wrote a treatise on falconry, the first of its kind in western Europe. He is a remarkable link between Christian and Muslim learning and between the scientist and the man of letters.

His contemporary, Robert of Chester, an even more elusive figure, studied in northern Spain and was commissioned by the abbot of Cluny to make a translation of the Koran. His chief interests were mathematical. He translated an Arabic work on algebra which introduced that subject to western Europe; it may have been due to him that Arabic numerals became known in the West, though centuries passed before their use became general. Daniel of Morley, another Englishman, interested in astrology, studied in Toledo in the last quarter of the twelfth century. In the thirteenth century Michael the Scot also worked at Toledo, made a translation of Aristotle's treatise on animals, and became a famous astrologer. Two other Englishmen interested in science should be mentioned. One was Robert Grosseteste, bishop of Lincoln, a theologian, a lecturer at Oxford, and a busy man of the world who nonetheless found time to study mathematics and to experiment with lenses. His student Roger Bacon was also a scientist. An independent and original thinker, though something of an intellectual snob, Bacon criticized scholastic dependence upon argument and called, instead, for experimentation.

Law

Interest in Roman antiquity in the twelfth century included a study of the Roman law, which in turn produced a notable advance in the development of the canon law of the church. The two systems were somewhat alike, for the church had borrowed freely from Roman law. During the twelfth century, Italian scholars made a thorough investigation of the code of Roman law compiled by Emperor Justinian; they wrote elaborate commentaries or glosses upon it. The canon law, which had been in a state of great confusion, was drawn into systematic form in a famous work, the *Decretum,* written by the monk Gratian about the year 1140. This textbook of canon law was arranged by subject and easy to use; it greatly promoted knowledge of the canon law and increased the activity of the ecclesiastical courts.

The development of canon and Roman law naturally had its effect on England. Archbishop Theobald, seeing the increase of litigation in the church courts, made every effort to promote legal studies. The clerks of his household, including Thomas Becket, discussed and argued points of law; Becket himself went abroad to study law at Bologna and at Auxerre. One can see in this activity at Canterbury the background of Becket's clash with Henry II. To obtain professional assistance and to train the clergy, Theobald brought to England an Italian jurist, Vacarius, who taught Roman law at Canterbury and may have taught it later at Oxford. The study of Roman law, although it led to no profitable profession in England and came to be frowned upon by the church, was very popular at Oxford, where a thriving school of law developed.

But England had a law of its own, the common law. This law was affected by the spirit and logic of the Roman law, not by its substance. A famous legal work of the twelfth century, *Treatise on the Laws and Customs of England,* normally attributed to the lay justiciar Rannulf Glanville, confined itself to the law administered in the King's courts. Glanville had a smattering of Roman law, but this did no more than lead him to arrange his book in a logical and systematic form. The greatest book of law produced in England during the Middle Ages was Henry de Bracton's treatise, *Concerning the Laws and Customs of England,* written largely between 1250 and 1258. Bracton, a justice of the King's Bench, spent his life in the royal courts. He compiled a notebook containing digests of some two thousand cases; his treatise was based upon them and upon his long experience as a justice. He was familiar with Roman and canon law. He drew from them an understanding of what a law book should be, how it should be organized, and how the principles of law should be set forth. He understood the rules of Roman and canon law as they applied to English law, but his book, like Glanville's, was a description of English common law as it was administered in the royal courts.

History

The intellectual revival affected the writing of history. Historical writing now contained far greater detail than in the past and exhibited a broader view, a more critical judgment of the value of evidence, and a higher literary quality. Two monastic chroniclers of the twelfth century—William of Malmesbury and William of Newburgh—were men who may be termed historians. Not all historians were monks. Henry of Huntingdon was an archdeacon, Ralph de Diceto was dean of St. Paul's, and Roger of Hoveden was an itinerant justice in the reign of Henry II. In the thirteenth century there were two monks at St. Albans who carried the writing of history to a high level of achievement. Roger of Wendover expanded the range and detail of the monastery's chronicle and wrote in a lively style. Matthew Paris, who continued the chronicle from 1235 to 1259, was a man of wide knowledge, keen intelligence, and perfect truthfulness. Since he was a person of some eminence who knew many important people, including King Henry III, he was well informed about public events. He told a story admirably. He was courageous, outspoken, and quite independent in his judgments.

The Rise of Universities

The rise of universities in the twelfth and thirteenth centuries was the result of the new learning that was coming into western Europe, for there was now much more to teach and many more men who were eager to acquire knowledge. Universities grew slowly and imperceptibly. The earliest in time was the university at Salerno in southern Italy, where a school of medicine existed in the eleventh century. But Salerno remained a medical university and contributed little to the growth of university institutions, which grew more fully at

Bologna. Though Bologna was chiefly famous as a school of law, it had become a many-sided institution by the middle of the twelfth century, with a charter of privileges from the Emperor and a student body of several hundred from many parts of Europe. The students formed a guild as a protection against exorbitant landlords and against teachers who accepted student fees but did not perform their duties properly. At Paris the university sprang from the cathedral school of Notre Dame. Paris was an excellent geographical location and possessed a brilliant teacher in Abelard, who made it a center for philosophic and theological studies. The professors formed a guild in order to exclude teachers who did not have the M.A. degree. This degree was only conferred after difficult examinations and was in effect a license to teach. The university at Paris clashed with the bishop, who wished to retain his ancient right to grant such licenses. But the Pope sided with the university and decreed in 1231 that if the faculty granted the license it could not be vetoed by the bishop.

In the thirteenth century a university had distinct characteristics. It contained a cosmopolitan student body drawn from a number of countries; it was a *studium generale*, a general resort of students. This was the term generally employed, for the word *universitas* meant the total membership of any guild and might apply equally to guilds of carpenters or to guilds of students. The faculty of a university was of some size and distinction. Its members held the degree of M.A. Furthermore, a university contained at least one of the higher faculties of law, medicine, or theology. The masters or students, or both, had formed a guild. And finally, the university had obtained from kings or from the papacy a charter conferring upon it various immunities and privileges of self-government.

The first universities were merely groups of teachers and students without university buildings. The students found lodgings where they could; the lectures were given in rented halls. In an age without printing, textbooks were impossibly expensive, and the normal method of instruction was for students to attend lectures, take careful notes, and memorize them. At the end of three or four years a student qualified for the A.B. degree by taking examinations or by engaging in public disputations. There was almost no discipline in the early universities; and the students, who matriculated at an early age (thirteen to sixteen), indulged in a good deal of drinking, brawling, and bad company. They were constantly short of money. They probably did not come from noble families or from the peasantry, but from the middle classes of gentry and townspeople.

A number of schools of distinction existed in England in the second half of the twelfth century. Northampton, Exeter, Lincoln, and Winchester possessed schools that might have grown into universities, but for one reason or another they did not do so, and the first English university developed at Oxford. A number of learned men, such as Robert Pullen, who later became a cardinal and papal chancellor, Geoffrey of Monmouth, and Robert of Cricklade, were lecturing at Oxford or were resident in the town before the middle of the century. Some new stimulus might easily turn the Oxford schools into a *studium generale*. Such a stimulus occurred about the year 1167 when Henry II, engaged in his quarrel with Becket, ordered that all the English students at Paris should return to England. A number of them presumably came to Oxford, for from about this time the Oxford schools developed steadily. In 1209, however, a serious incident occurred when one of the students killed a woman. The townspeople arrested several of his fellow lodgers and hanged two of them. Lectures were at once suspended, and students and faculties dispersed, not to reassemble for some five years. In 1214 the citizens were forced to accept humiliating terms which provided, among other things, that the students were subject to the jurisdiction of the bishop of Lincoln or his representative, the chancellor of the university. Power gradually passed into the hands of the chancellor who held a court in which cases involving students were tried. By the end of the thirteenth century Oxford was one of the leading centers of learning in Europe. The body of masters and students numbered about 1500. Cambridge, which was smaller, grew more slowly. A unique feature of English universities was the system of colleges which developed in both institutions. Originally the colleges were hostels where students could lodge under some supervision. But the colleges became so important in themselves that they went far toward overshadowing the university.

SOCIAL AND ECONOMIC LIFE

Population and Wealth

During the twelfth and thirteenth centuries England became populous and wealthy. In very round numbers, which can be no more than estimates, the population rose from about 1.5 million to about 3 million persons. This was a startling increase, for which the explanation is not entirely clear. Life in the Middle Ages was hazardous and insecure at best. Population, however, has a tendency to rise unless it is cut down by plague or famine. There was no plague in England during this period; and the rise of a money economy lessened the danger of famine, for if a man possessed a little money he was not entirely dependent upon the food that he himself had grown. Increasing wealth enabled the upper classes to improve their conditions of living and thus to raise larger families, but the standard of life among the poor remained low and primitive. The wealth of the kingdom greatly increased. A growing population required greater amounts of food, the price of agricultural products mounted steadily, men farmed their lands intensively and brought new land under cultivation. Fens were drained, forests cleared, wastelands brought under the plow. Old villages expanded and subdivided and new ones appeared. The prudent management of estates in a businesslike way was a skill that was carefully fostered. Small boroughs and towns, and with them the number of fairs and markets, grew larger. There was also a notable increase in foreign trade with the Baltic, with Flanders, with Gascony, and with the Mediterranean.

The Magnates and High Farming

A large part of the new wealth was in the hands of a few men at the top of society—twelve to fifteen earls, twenty to thirty baronial families of considerable means, bishops, and abbots of large monasteries. These were the magnates, the great men of the kingdom. Below them a much larger number of knights and country gentlemen also shared in the rising prosperity.

The pressure of a large population upon the soil placed the great landowner in a highly advantageous position. He was an agricultural millionaire who could lease his land at a high rent or farm it himself at a good profit. He probably used the manors surrounding his castle to supply his table, while his more distant manors produced grain, meat, or wool that could be sold. The greatest magnates held vast amounts of land. Their manors were sometimes divided into geographical groups. Gilbert de Clare, Earl of Gloucester, held at the end of the thirteenth century one group of manors in South Wales, another in Dorset, and a third in East Anglia.

An estate of this size required an elaborate system of management. Accounts must be kept, rents collected, the unpaid labor of the villeins exploited, and the dishonesty of the reeves, who were skillful at cheating their masters, guarded against. One method of protection was to estimate in advance the revenues that might be expected from every source, and then to watch closely how income agreed with these estimates. A magnate normally had a steward who was responsible for the whole of the estate, in addition to a bailiff in charge of each manor. A reeve, who was a kind of foreman for the peasants, was elected by them once a year and supervised their labor on the demesne. Receivers collected money and auditors checked accounts. To supplement the work of villeins and casual hired laborers, some estates maintained a permanent staff of workers, such as plowmen and shepherds. A constant effort was made to enlarge the size of the estate by purchase or reclamation. Landowners specialized in a single crop, or in cattle for meat or milk, or, more often, in raising sheep. Some lords and monasteries owned flocks that numbered ten or twelve thousand. Attempts were made to discover the type of grain best suited for cultivation in various kinds of soil, cattle were moved from one pasture to another as grasses matured, small fields were enclosed by hedges to promote better farming. Marl and loam served as fertilizers. The use of horses in place of oxen increased the efficiency of agriculture. A system of three instead of two open fields was sometimes adopted, so that only a third of the land lay fallow each year. High farming of this kind could only be conducted on large estates, of which there were many in the thirteenth century. Castles, manor houses, abbeys, and cathedrals dominated the countryside, each drawing support from the agriculture of a large surrounding area.

A baron drew revenue not only from his estates but also from the offices he held at the court of the King and from royal gifts of land and money. He could hardly hope to prosper unless he enjoyed the good will of the monarch. When an heir inherited an estate, for example, he was required to pay relief. The sums demanded were very large, but a favored noble might hope to have his payments reduced or perhaps forgiven entirely. The idea arose that the King should provide his barons with an amount of wealth commensurate with their social position. Thus the barons looked to the court as a source of wealth.

A baron might have a large income, but he also had heavy expenses. He maintained a castle and an elaborate household. The wooden castles of the eleventh century had been superseded in the twelfth by large stone keeps. These were strong high towers, circular or rectangular in shape, dark, crowded, and uncomfortable. In the thirteenth century a baron built a more sumptuous house that centered in a great hall, with the private apartments of the baron at one end and the kitchen at the other. The house was surrounded by a strong wall, known as a curtain wall, with battlements and towers upon it. These battlements became very elaborate, the space enclosed by the wall contained a number of buildings, and the whole attained a considerable magnificence. The household of a baron included a steward to supervise the establishment, a clerk to keep accounts, a chaplain, and many domestic servants. The baron had a council of his important adherents—his relatives, friends, lawyers, and officials—to advise him on matters of business.

Open Fields at Laxton, Nottinghamshire. (Aerofilms Limited)

He was expected to dispense a lavish hospitality and to be generous in gifts and favors. He had to have a large and extravagant retinue of knights and followers to escort him when he traveled about the country and to enhance his prestige when he went to court. The cost of armor had so increased that a knight was a lesser aristocrat, and yet retinues grew more and more elaborate. This magnificence reached its height in the fourteenth century. The best entertainment that a baron could devise was a tournament. These costly shows consisted of jousts or encounters between pairs of knights who fought according to set rules. Prizes were given to the victors and hospitality was provided for all who came to see the show.

Feudal relations remained important between the King and his tenants in chief, but below this level feudal bonds had loosened or ended, especially after subinfeudation was prohibited in the reign of Edward I. A wealthy magnate, wishing to increase the number of his followers, sometimes made contracts or indentures with knights or country gentlemen or lawyers or chaplains, or even minstrels or cooks, to become his retainers in return for lands or money. These contracts were business arrangements quite outside the feudal structure. The services to be rendered were specified and might be of any kind; the contracts might run for life or for a limited period. The principal purpose of such contracts was obviously for display, but they offered a magnate opportunity to aid his friends and kinsmen. Though very costly, they enabled a baron to raise a small army quickly, and they added to his prestige in politics and society.

Knights and country gentlemen formed a lesser nobility, later known as gentry. Holding small estates of one or two manors, they were far below the great barons in wealth and power. Their primary interest was the management of their property. Knights, however, were still warriors trained to fight on horseback. They had received knighthood through an elaborate and costly ceremony, and they were surprisingly few in number. In war they served as retainers in the retinue of the King or of a great magnate or commanded bodies of mercenary troops.

The Peasants

The life of the peasants altered less during the twelfth and thirteenth centuries than did the life of the upper classes. A peasant's status and obligations remained much the same as they had been in the years following the Norman Conquest. Such changes as occurred were due to the value of labor services in a time of agricultural prosperity and to the increase in the quantity and use of money, which deeply affected rural life. These forces, however, did not always move in the same direction.

The village was likely to be larger than it had been in the past. The houses stretched along a single street or were arranged around a village green. Some cottages had a framework of wooden crucks, that is, of curved timbers which stood upright in the ground but bent together and met at the apex of the roof, where they were fastened to a pole that ran from one set of crucks to the next. A house of this type could be lengthened to form several rooms, though there were rarely more than two. The walls between the crucks were made of hardened mud or sometimes of timber. Beyond the village stretched the open fields, the meadow, the pasture, and the waste.

The basic division among the peasants was that between the freeman and the villein. The freeman was the virtual owner of his land. There was a feudal touch about his tenure, for he performed an act of homage to the lord of the manor and paid relief when he entered upon his holding. But the rents and services he owed were small and were far below the annual value of the land, so that they were not rents in the modern sense of the word. By paying a fee he could obtain permission to sell his land, and in general he was much less at the lord's disposal than was the unfree villein. As the use of money increased, a class of leaseholders appeared who normally paid a good rent which approached the true value of the land.

By far the largest number of peasants were unfree villeins who held land by servile tenure. They were bound to the soil and could not marry or leave the manor without the lord's consent. They owed him week work, that is, two or three days' work each week upon the demesne without compensation; and boon work, which meant extra labor at the busy times of plowing and harvesting. In addition the villein owed substantial payments in kind, in animals and produce, at stated dates during the year. There were also other fees, and the villein was much at the lord's disposal. The villein must also attend the manorial court, which tried petty criminal offenses and any civil suits in which the peasant became involved. For serious crime he was tried in the courts of the King, but he could not bring civil suits into those courts. The normal holding of a villein was called a virgate and amounted roughly to thirty acres. The lowest class of villeins, known as cotters, held much less, perhaps five or ten acres, and performed much lighter services. The cotters were close to the subsistence level.

The lot of the villein was certainly hard. He lived in poverty, performed backbreaking labor, and was subject to galling restrictions. Because of the high price of agricultural products the lords wanted as much labor as possible, and there was a tendency for labor services to be carefully defined and strictly enforced. In a quarrel with his lord the villein was at a great disadvantage in the manorial court, though there were peasants who stood up for their rights, as the many lawsuits of the time make clear. Yet there is reason to believe that the villein's lot was not as hard as the laws of villeinage might suggest. Week work was not as burdensome as it sounds. A villein with several sons need only send one to work on the demesne, and presumably that son was not the most efficient worker in the family. The villein's rights were protected by the custom of the manor and by the fact that a lord, dependent upon the labor of his villeins, could not afford to treat them harshly. Moreover, the rise of a money economy enabled a thrifty peasant to purchase land and to buy relief from some of the services he owed his lord. This process is known as commutation. Such relief did not make the villein a freeman, but it was a step in that direction. Commutation, which had begun in the twelfth century, diminished in the thirteenth because the lord required labor. Nonetheless, lords might find that hired labor was more efficient than grudging unpaid services, and commutation continued in the thirteenth century, though on a reduced scale.

Commerce

Commerce developed to a remarkable degree in medieval England. On the local level, weekly or monthly markets were held in towns and many villages when the country people came in to sell their produce and to buy manufactured goods. The right to hold a market was acquired by a town or village from a local lord or sometimes from the King. It was a prized possession, for tolls were levied upon all who sold at the markets. Far more elaborate were the annual

Agricultural scenes, fourteenth century. (British Museum, *The Luttrell Psalter*. Additional MS 42,130, Historical Pictures Service, Chicago)

fairs held by a lord or a high churchman under a royal grant. These fairs attracted merchants from all over the country and sometimes from abroad. At the largest fairs a good deal of wholesale as well as retail business was carried on. Famous fairs were held at St. Ives (Huntingdonshire), Northampton, Stamford, and Boston. St. Giles's Fair at Winchester and Stourbridge Fair near Cambridge were international in scope. Many such fairs were held in western Europe. The dates for holding them were staggered so that merchants could travel from one to another. Courts, known in England as courts of piepoudre,[4] settled disputes on the spot according to the law merchant, a code of rules that had grown up among traders. But in the thirteenth century a growing amount of business was done outside the fairs by English merchants settled in the larger towns and seaports. The number of these merchants had greatly increased, and they played a large role in foreign trade. Many foreign merchants came to England. It is evident that foreign commerce existed on a large scale, that commodities traveled over long distances, and that trade was concerned not merely with the import of luxuries but with the exchange of basic goods.

The largest single article of import was wine from Gascony in southern France. Most of this trade was carried in French ships, for the amount of English shipping was small. In exchange for wine the French bought English grain, fish, and coarsely woven woolen cloth. The economies of England and Gascony complemented each other very nicely, and the trade was highly important to both areas.

Except for woolen cloth, English exports consisted almost entirely of raw materials: tin, lead, a little coal, grain, fish, salted meats, sheepskins (with the fleece on them), leather, and, above all, wool. Wool, the basic article of English foreign commerce, was produced in enormous quantities. The poorest peasants possessed a few sheep, but the monasteries of Yorkshire and Lincolnshire, such as the Cistercian abbeys of Fountains and Rievaulx, owned huge flocks and acted as agents to collect wool from smaller producers to sell directly to Italian merchants. At the end of the thirteenth century England was exporting about 32,000 sacks of wool a year, which amounted to nearly 6000 tons.

This extraordinary expansion of trade was due to the foreign merchants, who bought about two thirds of the wool exported from the country. The merchants of the Hanseatic League, a commercial alliance of north German cities which dominated the trade of the Baltic Sea, had secured many privileges in England. They had their own guildhall in London and were exempt from paying duty on cloth. They exported wool, cloth, and tin, and brought in timber and furs from the Baltic and fine cloth from Flanders. Flemish merchants exported English wool, which came back in the form of cloth from Flanders. But the Italians were the most important. They represented large firms in northern Italy, where not only industry and commerce but also finance and banking were more advanced than anywhere else in Europe. They had come to England originally as papal tax collectors. These taxes were paid in produce as well as in money, and the Italians became accustomed to handling English wool. They had large cash balances in the country and formed connections with English religious houses. They not only bought great quantities of wool, but served as bankers, supplying capital and credit and teaching Englishmen the techniques of finance and inter-

[4] From the French *pied poudre,* meaning that men came into the court informally with dusty shoes.

national trade. They imported wines, fruit, raisins and currants, as well as the luxuries of the East—Oriental rugs, silks, muslins and other fine cloth, spices, and precious stones. The Italian merchants were held in high regard by the King, who protected them, granted them many privileges, borrowed heavily from them, and eventually ruined their position in England because he did not repay his loans.

Industry

In the twelfth and thirteenth centuries England was essentially a producer of raw materials. Industry, lagging behind commerce, was primitive in comparison with industrial development in Flanders or Italy. Some industries were carried on in rural areas. Coal, tin, and iron were mined in considerable quantity; some weaving of woolen cloth was done in the country, for a good deal of the manufacture could be performed in a peasant's cottage; the making of iron had to be carried on near forests which supplied charcoal for fuel. But the towns, of course, were the industrial centers. An established artisan who owned a house manufactured articles of common use—shoes or candles or clothing—in a back room or shed and displayed them for sale in another room opening onto the street.

Merchants or craftsmen formed themselves into guilds to protect their interests and monopolize particular trades. In many towns an organization known as the guild merchant was composed of all those who offered goods for sale. Its purpose was to control the trade of the town. Merchants from other towns were subjected to many restrictions. They must pay tolls, they were forbidden to deal in certain articles, they must carry on wholesale business only with members of the guild merchant. The guilds settled disputes among their members and attempted to protect them in other towns. They were also fraternal and charitable societies. Their meetings, held for conducting business, were social occasions with much feasting and drinking; to "drink the guild merchant" was to attend an assembly of the fraternity. The guilds assumed responsibility for members in sickness and old age, attended their funerals, and supported the widows and orphans of those who died in poverty. But their principal purpose was always to protect their economic interests in a highly exclusive and monopolistic spirit.

As industry became more complex in the larger towns, guilds known as craft guilds were formed of artisans engaged in a single craft or mystery. In the middle of the fourteenth century the more important guilds in London were listed as the "grocers, mercers, fishmongers, drapers, goldsmiths, woolmongers, vintners, saddlers, tailors, cordwainers, butchers, and ironmongers."[5] These guilds were similar in many ways to the guilds merchant but were more exclusively interested in industry. They set standards for the quality of the goods produced, regulated holidays and hours of work, and fixed prices and wages to some extent.

The desire to ensure high standards of competence in trade and industry led to a system of apprenticeship. A boy or a young man was apprenticed to a master, usually for seven years. In return for a sum of money from the parents of the apprentice, the master agreed to support him and to teach him the mysteries of the craft. The apprentice worked without wages. When his apprenticeship was

[5] George Holmes, *The Later Middle Ages 1272–1485* (Edinburgh: T. Nelson, 1962), p. 35n.

over, he was eligible to become a master and to open a shop of his own. Before the end of the thirteenth century, however, many apprentices discovered that they could not set themselves up in business. The capital required for such a venture had increased, the trade could support only a limited number of masters, and the masters had no wish to admit new members. Many apprentices, unable to become masters, remained as employees working for wages. They were known as journeymen, and in the fourteenth century they formed guilds of their own. Like the guild merchant, the craft guilds were fraternal and charitable societies. It was the masters who ran the guilds. As time went on, the guilds became more aristocratic, dominated by the richer masters who were almost always the men in control of the government of the town.

The Towns

By the end of the thirteenth century there were more than 100 towns or boroughs in England.[6] The towns differed greatly in size, importance, and the amount of their independence from their lords or from the King. London, with a population of between 25,000 and 40,000, was by far the largest. The population of Bristol was about 17,000, that of Norwich about 13,000, that of York about 10,000. Many towns were little places of perhaps 2000 or 3000 inhabitants. They were small struggling communities in an alien world of barons, castles, and monasteries. Nonetheless, the towns were becoming an important element in medieval society. A village became a borough when the lord permitted its inhabitants to hold their land by burgage tenure, which allowed them to pay rent in place of the normal obligations of the manor. As the towns grew in size and importance they became self-conscious communities with a corporate spirit, and their increased wealth permitted them to bargain with their lord or with the King for charters granting them varying degrees of self-government and independence.

These charters began in the eleventh century, and eventually most towns of any consequence held charters from the King. They never became free cities, as did some of the towns in Germany and Italy, for the government of the King was too strong and all-pervasive, but they obtained various rights, somewhat as follows. A town wished to collect the rents, tolls, taxes, and court fines it owed the Crown and to pay the King in a lump sum in order to free it from interference by the sheriff in its internal affairs. For the same reason, a town wished to receive and execute the King's writs. A town desired the right to hold a court. Towns sought freedom from tolls imposed by other towns and districts. They wanted to hold a market or a fair and to levy tolls on merchandise sold within their borders. Finally, they wished to establish guilds and to elect their own officials. Only the more important and wealthy towns could hope to obtain all or most of these privileges, and there was great diversity.

The government of the towns differed widely. In a simple form of government the burgesses met in the borough court and elected a mayor. Burgesses paid taxes and owned property and were not identical with the inhabitants of the borough. They were apt to be about the same as the members of the guild merchant. In larger boroughs the mayor was assisted by a council, the councilors being known as aldermen. By the close of the thirteenth century many towns

---

[6] A town was called a city only when it contained a cathedral and was thus the administrative center of a diocese.

had lost their democratic features and were governed by oligarchies over which the burgesses had little control. The aldermen held office for long periods, even for life; they chose new aldermen as vacancies occurred in their membership; they elected one of their own number as mayor. The city of Oxford, for example, was governed by a mayor and twelve councilors, four of whom were elected for life, the rest probably chosen by the other councilors.[7]

[7] George Holmes, *The Later Middle Ages 1272–1485*, p. 40.

7

EDWARD I AND EDWARD II

EDWARD I, 1272–1307

Edward I, who came to the throne in 1272, was an aggressive ruler determined to assert his rights as sovereign and to exercise fully his powers of kingship. When the archbishop of Canterbury reproached him for his wars in Scotland, he is said to have retorted: "By God's blood Syon shall not silence me nor shall Jerusalem keep me from defending my right as long as I have strength of body and breath of life." But although he was aggressive and sometimes acted without scruple, he was dominated by a concept of the community of the realm and of the common good. This concept assumed that the kingdom was a corporate society, that there was a body politic, that government should be conducted for the general welfare, and that this welfare transcended the advantage of individuals or of social classes. The King, Edward believed, should be the judge of what was best for the community, should be a legislator, and should exert the full powers of kingship to promote the public good. Yet his subjects had rights he could not invade, and he should consult with the great men of the kingdom when those rights were in question.

Edward was not an innovator like Henry II; rather, he was an organizer and administrator who desired order, efficiency, and a smoothly running government. An untidy situation annoyed him, and he wished to set it to rights. During the first half of his reign he made prolonged and careful inquiries into many aspects of government. These inquiries formed the most thorough process of stocktaking since the days of William the Conqueror. On the basis of his findings Edward reconstructed the administration of the government and of the law, partly by statutes, partly by informal instructions to his ministers. His reign was a period of legal definition. He did not aim to make new law but to restate the old with gaps, errors, and inconsistencies removed. His statutes concerned a wide variety of subjects: the duties and powers of officials, the feudal rights of the magnates, the militia and the police, the merchants, the land law, the civil and criminal law, legal procedure, and the reform of organs of government. At the same time he pursued a spirited foreign policy in defense of his rights in Wales, Scotland, and France; he hoped to unite the nations of Europe in a new crusade.

For many years he ruled successfully and well. Unfortunately after 1293 he became entangled in protracted wars which proved to be more costly than the resources of the Crown could support. He looked about desperately for money and took it where he could. As a result he aroused the discontent of the magnates and left the Crown hopelessly in debt. His need for money in his later years led to rapid development in methods of taxation and in the growth of Parliament.

Edward's character is not easy to understand. He was an active man, both physically and mentally, who responded quickly to every situation and acted with vigor and determination. He fulfilled the medieval ideal of what a King should be. He was a majestic figure, tall, erect, lithe, and athletic. He was also a crusader and a warrior who loved tournaments and hunting; he defended his frontiers and made foreign conquests. He spoke with firmness and clarity. Industrious in government, he lavished care upon his statutes and administration. And yet there was a cold and unsympathetic quality about him which was perhaps due to the legal cast of his mind. If the law was on his side, he was apt to exact his pound of flesh. He endangered his conquest of Wales and destroyed his hopes of success in Scotland by the rigidity with which he stood upon what he considered his legal rights. He was easily moved to anger and hated to be crossed. A conventional man, he lacked imagination and humanity, and a slothful strain in his character suggests that his resolution and energy were not entirely natural but sprang from a sense of duty and obligation.[1]

THE GOVERNMENT OF EDWARD I

Edward governed in close collaboration with his principal advisers. They were his great officials, such as the Chancellor and the Treasurer, the heads of lesser departments, the judges, the "King's clerks" who saw him daily and wrote his letters, and a few knights and magnates who took part in the central administration. Most of them, drawn from the middle class, were bureaucrats who spent their lives as royal officials and grew old in the King's service. Some who rose to high positions were recruited from the lower ranks of the King's service, from the households of barons and churchmen, or were recommended to the King by patrons. A closely knit society of clerics and laymen, a self-conscious elite in the personnel of royal administration, they moved from department to department doing all kinds of business.

The barons did not relish the growth of this bureaucracy, but Edward selected his officials as he pleased. His best-loved servant for the first sixteen years of his reign was the Chancellor, Robert Burnell, who became a major figure in the government and a clearinghouse for all kinds of public affairs. A shrewd and competent man of business with a fine mind but with probably no great education, he had entered Edward's household in 1254 and had served him in many capacities. He rose to be Chancellor, bishop of Bath and Wells, and the King's closest adviser. He and others like him served Edward well.

There were four principal parts of the administrative side of the govern-

[1] Sir Maurice Powicke, *The Thirteenth Century 1216–1307* (Oxford: Clarendon Press, 1962), pp. 227–230.

ment: the Chancery, the Exchequer, the Household, and the Council. The first two are familiar to us. The Chancery was the secretarial department where charters, writs, and formal letters were prepared by a staff of skillful clerks. The Chancellor was the keeper of the Great Seal used to authenticate documents. He was usually a churchman, sometimes the archbishop of Canterbury, though the pope denied that office to Burnell, who was more businessman than cleric. The Exchequer received and issued money, scrutinized the semiannual accounts of sheriffs and other local officials, and kept the pipe rolls. It was presided over by the Treasurer, its important officials were known as the Barons of the Exchequer, and it was staffed by a large number of clerks. Both departments were now old and venerable, and they had gone out of court, that is, they were separate departments distinct from the Household and the Council. They were stationary at Westminster. It would be a mistake to think that they were removed from the central administration. The Chancellor and the Treasurer were important councilors and familiar figures in the Household. Burnell was no less a trusted servant of the King because he did much of his work in his own department.

Nonetheless, the procedures of the Chancery and the Exchequer had become somewhat formal, routine, and cumbersome. Edward felt a loss of efficiency when he was on a journey or a campaign while the Chancellor or the Treasurer remained in London. He therefore followed the practice of earlier Kings in developing the Household, which normally traveled with him. Its staff was large, perhaps some fifty officials. Within the Household wherever he went he had his private apartments or chamber, the inner sanctum of government. In the chamber, protected by ushers who guarded the doors, Edward talked in private with his intimate friends and advisers and made those countless decisions which did not require consultation with the whole Council. The principal steward of the Household was a layman, usually a knight of high social position, who was close to the King and was an important figure at court.

The portion of the Household which developed most fully in Edward's reign was the wardrobe. It had its treasurer or keeper, its controller, its cofferer, and many clerks. There was a privy seal in the wardrobe, a small royal seal the King kept with him. It was employed to authenticate letters dispatched from the Household and to send instructions to the Chancellor concerning the use of the Great Seal at Westminster. Various revenues, diverted from the Exchequer, were brought directly to the wardrobe, which became the organ of government Edward used to finance his wars. Thus miniature secretarial and financial departments were created within the wardrobe independent of the Chancery and the Exchequer. The barons did not like this development, for they thought it made the King too independent, and in the reign of Edward II they found occasion to end the wardrobe's expansion.

The most vital organ of administration was the King's Council.[2] It consisted of his principal ministers, his judges, his most trusted clerks, and a select few of the magnates. The Council dealt with all kinds of business. Here the King consulted with his advisers in a more formal way than in the chamber, and here he made important decisions. His close association with his councilors, including

[2] In discussing the century following the Norman Conquest, the term "small council" has been used to refer to the group of officials in constant attendance upon the king, and the term "Great Council" to refer to a meeting of the tenants in chief. See pp. 58–59. In the thirteenth century the smaller group was called the Council and the larger group was coming to be known as Parliament.

his judges, gave firmness and confidence to his policy, for he felt that he was not acting alone. The Council did a great deal of administrative work. It dealt with matters that were unusual or extraordinary or did not fall within the competence of established departments, which often referred difficult points to the Council.

Above all, the Council was a court. It tried cases that fell outside the jurisdiction of other courts, or that other courts could not determine, or that the King referred to the Council because his interests were involved. The Council reviewed cases from the lower courts on writs of error, though the notion of appeal played little part in medieval common law. There was an element of equity in the Council's legal decisions, for the Council was close to the King and felt no obligation to adhere strictly to the common law. It framed new writs and interpreted the meaning of royal charters. Cases of unusual importance or difficulty were brought before it, for it was regarded as higher than other courts. And sometimes, when a case was of a public nature and affected the whole community, it was taken to the assembly of the King's tenants in chief of which the Council was a part. This assembly, the Great Council, was now called Parliament and was the highest court of all.

The Law

Edward and his judges were influenced by a famous book, *Concerning the Laws and Customs of England,* which had been written about the middle of the thirteenth century by Henry de Bracton, the greatest of English medieval jurists. Bracton had been a judge under Henry III, and his book was a description of the daily operation of the law in the King's courts. He showed how the common law had grown from the accumulation of decisions in the royal courts and how principles of law could be deduced from particular cases. Bracton set forth the doctrine that the King must not govern by caprice but by the rules of the law. The King, said Bracton, was not under man but under God and under the law, for it was the law that made him King. The King was the fountain of justice. All jurisdiction in private or local hands, though protected by charters or by long usage, was derived ultimately from the Crown.

The growth of the common law during the thirteenth century had steadily strengthened the principles set forth by Bracton. As the itinerant justices had carried the common law throughout the kingdom they had undermined the ancient jurisdiction of the hundred and the shire courts and had reduced the scope of the private courts of barons and great churchmen. Royal justice was on its way to supremacy. Yet when Edward came to the throne there were many areas, known as franchises or liberties, in which jurisdiction was in private hands, especially in the north and west. The most conspicuous example was the county palatine of the bishop of Durham, where the bishop had his own justices, sheriffs, and chancery, and where he exercised a jurisdiction within his liberty similar to that of the King in other parts of the realm. Franchises were held by many lords in the Welsh marches, by the church of Ely, by the abbot of Bury St. Edmunds, while lesser lords had restricted rights over what had once been hundred courts.

In the reign of Henry III the government had occasionally issued writs of quo warranto, demanding to know by what warrant a lord exercised his rights of private jurisdiction. The principle of these writs was carried much further in the Statute of Gloucester (1278) in which Edward declared that all holders of private jurisdiction must prove their warrant before the King's justices. A few of the barons possessed royal charters which justified their rights, but most of them did not. They strongly resented the King's action. Edward therefore offered a compromise by which he confirmed jurisdictions that had been exercised without interruption since the accession of Richard I in 1189. As a result of the quo warranto proceedings Edward did not annul many franchises, but he curbed their expansion and established the principles that private jurisdictions were delegations from the Crown and that the Crown could interfere in them if it saw reason. Franchises grew less and less important as time went on.

Edward also attempted to adjust the law relating to land held by feudal tenure. Feudal relations remained important as a set of fiscal rights, but as land was subinfeudated again and again over the years, the arrangements concerning it grew highly complicated, and the tenants in chief had difficulty in obtaining the feudal incidents due them. They complained to the King that they were losing their rights, and Edward knew that he was losing in the same way. His legislation was an effort to protect himself and his tenants in chief in this respect.

The Statute of Mortmain (1279) prohibited a vassal from giving land to the church without his lord's consent. The difficulty here was that a gift of land by a vassal to the church deprived the lord of most of the feudal incidents because the church never married, had children, or died; hence the land was held by a dead hand (mortmain) so far as the grantor's lord was concerned. As a matter of fact, grants to the church continued, for Edward was soon selling the right to break the statute.

In 1285 Edward issued the Second Statute of Westminster which, among other provisions, regulated the rights of both parties when a lord sought to recover land from a tenant who was not fulfilling his feudal obligations. The most important clause in the statute, the clause beginning with the words *De Donis Conditionalibus*, established the principle of entailed estates. An entailed estate was one which could descend from one generation to the next only under the conditions set forth in the original grant. The grant normally required that the entire estate should pass as a whole from father to eldest son. The effect was to hold the estate together, to make it heritable as an undivided unit, and to strengthen the principle of primogeniture.

In the Statute of Quia Emptores (1290) Edward prohibited further subinfeudation. Henceforth, if A granted (or sold) land to B, B did not become the vassal of A but of A's lord. Only the King could now make a man his feudal vassal. The unforeseen result of this statute was that feudal relations declined in importance. Land became an article of commerce to be bought and sold at the pleasure of the owner. These statutes indicate that although feudalism was passing away it left a deep and permanent stamp upon the land law of England.

The Machinery of Justice

Edward improved the machinery of justice in the courts at Westminster and in the work of the itinerant justices. At Westminster, as we have seen, the highest tribunals of justice were the King in Council and those solemn assemblies known as Parliaments. Below them were three central courts of common law which had developed during the thirteenth century. By Edward's reign these courts had separated or were separating from the rest of the government. One was the Court of Exchequer. From an early date the Exchequer had found that collection of money from the King's debtors had involved some legal business. So swift and efficient had been the methods of the Exchequer in collecting these debts that private creditors had wished to have their debts collected by the same tribunal. Thus the Exchequer began to try cases between private litigants involving debts and the collection of damages. During the thirteenth century the Court of Exchequer separated from the financial Exchequer. It had its own roll and its own judges, who were known as Barons of the Exchequer.

A second court was the Court of Common Pleas. The faint foreshadowings of this court may be seen in 1178, when Henry II had set aside five justices to remain at Westminster to hear pleas. Magna Carta (Article 17) had decreed that common pleas were to be held in some fixed place. During the thirteenth century this court also separated from the Council and acquired a roll and judges of its own. It dealt with civil cases, that is, disputes over property. The third court of common law was the Court of the King's Bench. It may be discerned in Edward's reign though it had not yet separated from the Council. It was closer to the King than the other two courts because it tried criminal cases (the pleas of the Crown) in which the King as guardian of the peace had a special interest.

Edward increased the efficiency of the central law courts by designating certain periods of time each year, known as the law terms, when the courts were all to be in session. Four law terms were established: Hilary term, which lasted for a month or six weeks early in the year; Easter term, later in the spring; Trinity term, in the summer; and Michaelmas term, which was the longest of the four and might continue for some ten weeks in the course of the autumn. The itinerant justices were normally sent out on circuit during the intervals between the terms. Circuits were arranged so that the justices visited each locality once a year. In the past the justices had been burdened with very heavy commissions and had been required to do all sorts of administrative and judicial work; hence their stay in each locality had been prolonged and tedious. A whole village had once taken to the woods at their approach. In place of these general iters in which many kinds of business were transacted, Edward sent out the justices with limited commissions. They normally tried one class of cases only. This made their circuits more rapid and efficient, and the general iter came to an end. Lawyers were attached to the courts visited by the itinerant justices, so that litigants could obtain legal counsel if they so desired. Thus the whole machinery of justice was made to function with more order and precision.

The reign of Edward I marked a definite break in the history of the common law. During the century from about 1150 to about 1250 the law had been flexible and had been growing rapidly. New law developed from the decisions of the justices and from new writs issued by the Chancellor. The result was rapid legal development but also some confusion. It was Edward's achievement, by his statutes, to give the law order and organization, but he also made it more rigid. Judge-made law is flexible; statute law is fixed and timeless. Statutes blocked the growth of unenacted law. This process of ending the law's flexibility had begun under Henry III. The barons, suspicious of the King, had opposed the issue of new writs by the Chancellor, because new writs made new law. The Provisions of Oxford stated that new writs were to be issued only with the consent of both King and Council (which was to be baronial). Under Edward I the principle was growing that new law could be made only with the consent of Parliament. Rigidity also was increased by a new type of judge and by the rise of a legal profession. Both judges and lawyers were specialists. They knew the common law but they cared little about other forms of knowledge and the study of Roman law was neglected. Hence the common law ceased to grow. In fact,

Beaumaris Castle, Anglesey, built by Edward I. Note the double wall and flanking towers. (Aerofilms Limited)

there was a general feeling that it was about complete. The way was opened for the rise in later centuries of a system of equity and of the court of chancery.

EDWARD AND THE CELTIC PEOPLES

As England grew stronger and more wealthy in the thirteenth century she was certain to extend her influence into the Celtic lands of Wales, Scotland, and Ireland. It is not surprising that during the Middle Ages this process reached its height in the reign of an aggressive King like Edward I, who subdued the Welsh, fought the Scots in futile wars that altered the whole course of Anglo-Scottish history, and increased royal power in Ireland.

Wales

In the thirteenth century the Welsh were still a pastoral people living in a very primitive state. Matters of marriage and legitimacy were taken rather lightly. They had no towns. The peasants did not even have houses but built huts of the boughs of trees for temporary shelters as they followed their cattle from one pasture ground to another. The only area where grain was grown in any quantity was the island of Anglesey. The people were divided into tribes ruled by chieftains, who lived high in the mountains and counted their wealth in terms of cattle. Bards and minstrels, with vivid imaginations and great musical skill, sang in a rather doleful strain of the glories and wealth of ancient warriors and kings. There was constant war between the tribes, who fought by rushing down the mountainside in a wild, disordered charge to the sound of war horns and flinging themselves upon their foes. If the first savage rush was repulsed, they turned and fled.

Shortly after the Norman Conquest, a number of Norman barons had pushed into central Wales, where they built castles, carved out baronies, and imposed servile obligations upon the peasants. Many of the Welsh had fled to their tribal chieftains in the hills and from their mountain fastnesses they raided and fought the Norman intruders. The barons in the marches of Wales were feudal vassals of England. But the King's writ did not run in their lands; they ruled as though they were little kings. They represented Norman expansion rather than the spreading influence of English monarchy.

In the thirteenth century there was a Welsh revival under the Llywelyn princes of Gwynedd, an area in North Wales centering upon the mountainous district of Snowdon. Llywelyn ap Gruffydd, Prince of Wales, had conquered a large principality in the northern and central parts of the country, some of it taken from the marcher lords. Recognized by Henry III in 1267, it was independent in all but name, though nominally held as a feudal fief from the King of England. Llywelyn might have kept it had he not acted with great arrogance and indiscretion toward Edward. He refused to do homage when Edward came to the throne, making the excuse that his brother David, an exile in England, was plotting against him. In 1275 he arranged a marriage with Eleanor, a daughter of Simon de Montfort, but she was captured by the English as she sailed from France to Wales. This episode brought about war in 1277. In a masterly campaign assisted by many marcher lords, Edward invaded Wales with a large army, closed in upon Llywelyn as he hid in the fastnesses of Snowdon, and starved him into submission. By the Treaty of Conway late in 1277 Llywelyn surrendered the lands he had taken from the marcher barons. Paying a large indemnity, he did homage as Edward demanded. He then was permitted to marry Eleanor and to retain the title of Prince of Wales.

The Treaty of Conway lasted for a little more than four years, but there was bitter litigation over the lands to be returned to the marcher lords. Llywelyn accused Edward and his judges of bad faith, and in 1282 a revolt broke out in Wales. It was begun by David, Llywelyn's brother, but Llywelyn quickly joined it. Once more Edward invaded the country. At first the Welsh met with some success, but very shortly they were discouraged by the death of Llywelyn, who was killed almost by chance, and by the capture of David. The revolt was over in 1283. The Statute of Rhuddlan in the following year annexed Llywelyn's principality to the Crown of England. The principality was divided into shires, English criminal law was introduced, and the country was administered by the justices of North and South Wales. Edward built a series of magnificent castles to ensure his conquest. These castles—the majestic ruins of which are still standing—were constructed at a time when the art of castle building had reached its height. They were elaborate, strong, and very expensive. The most important were Conway, Harlech, Rhuddlan, Beaumaris, and Caernarvon. The portions of Wales outside the principality remained in the hands of the marcher lords, whose semi-independent status Edward dared not disturb. So they remained through the rest of the Middle Ages. The Welsh were conquered, though their assimilation with England was only beginning.

Scotland

In contrast to the success of Edward's wars in Wales, his wars against the Scots formed the greatest blunder of his reign. Not only did he fail to conquer Scotland; he aroused among the Scots a hatred of England that was to last for centuries.

The kingdom of Scotland had been created by the gradual union of four distinct peoples: Picts, Scots, Britons, and Angles. The Picts were the original Celtic inhabitants; the Scots came from Ireland, largely in the fifth century, and occupied the area of modern Argyllshire; a little later the Angles in Northumbria extended that kingdom northward to the Firth of Forth, thus including a portion of what is now modern Scotland; the final element, the Britons, were Celts who had been pushed westward into Strathclyde by the Angles of Northumbria. The process of unification began in the year 843, when Kenneth MacAlpin King of Scots subdued the Picts and added Pict-land to Scot-land. Scotland was deeply affected by the Viking invasions. Settling first in the Shetland and Orkney Islands, the Norsemen moved down the western coast of Scotland, separating the Scots from their old connections with Ireland. Meanwhile Danish invaders destroyed the Anglo-Saxon kingdom of Northumbria; eventually the northern portion of Northumbria was united with Scotland. This all-important part of Scotland, extending from the Cheviot Hills to the Firth of Forth and centering upon the rock-fortress of Edinburgh, was inhabited by Angles, who added a Germanic element to the Scottish race. After the Norman Conquest other Anglo-Saxons fled northward to escape the fury of William the Conqueror. Meanwhile the Kings of Scotland acquired domination over the Britons in northern Strathclyde.

In the centuries between the Norman Conquest and the reign of Edward I, English and Norman influences penetrated into the Lowlands of Scotland, while Celtic and tribal life shrank back into the Highlands. This process began in the

Herstmonceux Castle, Sussex, fifteenth century. Built for comfort as well as defense. (Copyright Country Life)

reign of King Malcolm III (1058–1093), who had spent his boyhood at the court of Edward the Confessor. His second wife, the saintly and strong-minded Margaret, was a Saxon princess. She strengthened the use of the Anglo-Saxon tongue in Scotland and introduced reforms in the Scottish church, bringing it in line with the church in England and on the Continent. Her son, David I (1124–1153), transformed Scotland into a feudal kingdom. He too had lived in England. He saw the vast superiority of the Norman knight fighting on horseback over the wild rush of the Celts as they flung themselves with spear and claymore upon their foes. He therefore invited English and Norman barons, including the families of Balliol and Bruce, to come to Scotland and to accept fiefs from him as his feudal vassals. The Normans built castles in Scotland and enforced servile obligations upon the peasantry, but as they had done in England they also built churches and monasteries. David introduced into Scotland many English and Norman institutions of law and government. Thus in the twelfth and thirteenth centuries a feudal kingdom, though not a very strong one, arose in the Scottish Lowlands. Turning its back on the Celtic Highlands, it looked to England and maintained fairly cordial relations with that country.

This era of Anglo-Scottish amity came to an end in the reign of Edward I. In 1286 the Scottish King, Alexander III, was killed when his horse fell over a sea cliff. His only heir was his little granddaughter, Margaret, a child of about three who was living in Norway. Her mother, Alexander's daughter, had married the King of Norway but was now dead. In 1290 the Scots and Edward I arranged a treaty by which the "Fair Maid of Norway" was to be brought home to be married to Edward's son, the future Edward II. The Scots inserted clauses in the treaty guaranteeing their independence. Had the treaty taken effect the two countries, each with its own institutions, would have remained separate kingdoms but would soon have had the same person as King.

Unhappily the little Maid of Norway died on the voyage to Scotland, leaving the Scottish throne in dispute. Nine claimants arose, including John Balliol and Robert Bruce; the number soon swelled to thirteen. Fearing a prolonged civil war, some of the Scots suggested that Edward be asked for aid and counsel. Seeing an opportunity to advance his interests, Edward summoned the Scottish barons to meet him at Norham on the English side of the Border, where he declared that he would do justice among the many claimants to the Scottish throne but that he would do so as the feudal lord of the Kings of Scotland. This claim was highly doubtful. It was true that some Scottish Kings had been vassals of the Norman Kings of England, but in 1189 Richard I, willing to turn any right into cash, had freed the Kings of Scotland from this obligation; henceforth they had done homage only for lands they held in England. Nine of the Scottish claimants, however, accepted Edward's terms, each hoping to ingratiate himself with the King and thus obtain the Scottish throne.

Edward's decision, which was quite justifiable, went in favor of John Balliol, who was crowned in 1292 and did homage to Edward as his lord. Edward soon showed his determination to exercise fully his rights as feudal suzerain. He accepted appeals from Scottish courts, summoned Balliol to England as a feudal vassal, and demanded military service for a campaign in Gascony. Such opposition arose in Scotland that Balliol was forced to refuse Edward's demands. The Scots allied themselves with the French, with whom Edward went to war in 1294. In 1296 he marched north to punish the Scots. Their army was defeated, Balliol was forced to abdicate and was thrust aside. Making a triumphal progress as far north as Elgin, Edward brought back to England the Stone of Scone and sacred relics from the abbey at Holyrood. He held a Parliament at Berwick, where the Scottish barons did homage to him as their King. English garrisons occupied the principal fortresses of Scotland.

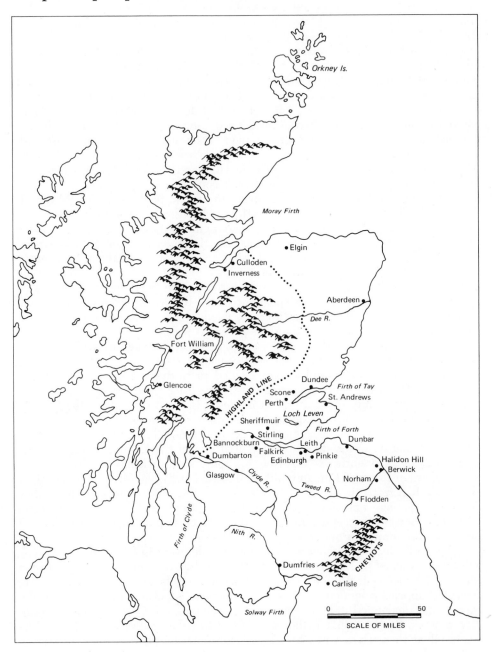

Scotland

Alnwick Castle, Northumberland. Parts of the castle were built in the twelfth century. There has been much restoration in modern times. (Copyright Country Life)

But this conquest of Scotland was too easy to endure. Edward had aroused in Scotland a spirit not often found in the Middle Ages—a spirit of democratic patriotism. The revolt that broke out in 1297 was not led by the nobility, many of whom held lands in England and had no wish to quarrel with the English King. The leader was William Wallace, a member of the gentry, under whose inspiration scattered risings swelled into a national revolt. Defeating an English force at Stirling, Wallace began to harry the northern counties of England. Edward came north again in 1298 and defeated Wallace at the Battle of Falkirk, which ended Wallace's effective career. As resistance continued English armies entered Scotland almost yearly. In 1303–1304 Edward subdued the country for a second time; captured Wallace, who died a traitor's death; and took up the reins of government once more. Another revolt took place in 1306 under a new leader, Robert Bruce, the grandson of the claimant of 1290. Defeated in his first encounters, Bruce resorted to guerrilla tactics in which he was making progress when Edward died in 1307 as he led an army northward for the last time.

His death left the struggle more equal, for Edward II was a man of small capacity. With the aid of Sir James Douglas, Bruce established himself as King Robert I, destroyed his personal enemies, raided into England, and gradually captured the Scottish castles in English hands. Edward II, occupied at home quarreling with the magnates, in 1314 made a supreme effort to relieve Stirling Castle. Invading Scotland with a large army, he pushed on to Stirling. Not far from its walls, on the field of Bannockburn, he allowed his army to be caught on a narrow space of ground flanked on both sides by marshes. His cavalry could not maneuver and his archers could not fan out to harass the Scots. The homely Scottish sheltrons, bodies of massed spearsmen, thrust the English back upon themselves. The battle became a rout, the rout a disaster, the worst defeat for English arms in all the Middle Ages.

Bannockburn gave the Scots their independence. During the rest of the Middle Ages English Kings became too involved in France to return to the conquest of Scotland. But the Scots paid a heavy price for their freedom. Warfare along the Border exposed the wealthiest part of Scotland to devastating raids. The French alliance brought far more harm than benefit. Scotland remained a lawless, backward, and poverty-stricken land, its nobles quarrelsome, its church corrupt, its economy primitive, its government weak and inefficient.

Ireland

At the beginning of Edward's reign, Ireland, like Wales, was a half-conquered country. There were really three Irelands. One was the English Pale, a narrow coastal strip behind Dublin and Drogheda, settled by Englishmen in the twelfth century. Here was to be found the English law and the English language. The Pale was governed from Dublin, where there was a justiciar who represented English authority, with an exchequer and a chancery on the English model. But the Pale was small. The western and northern half of the island was almost purely Celtic. There were tribal chieftains as in Wales, a pastoral people who counted their wealth in cattle, constant intertribal wars, cattle rustling as a national preoccupation, minstrelsy, and a little primitive agriculture.

Between the Pale and this Celtic world was a middle zone which shaded into the frontiers and into the characteristics of both the others. It had been conquered, or partially conquered, in the twelfth century by Norman barons, much like those who had pressed into central Wales. Indeed, many of these barons came from the Welsh marches and were partly Welsh in blood. Led by Richard de Clare, Earl of Pembroke, known as "Strongbow," they had defeated the Irish in various areas, had erected baronies, and had built castles according to Norman custom. Their descendants in Edward's reign owed allegiance to the King of England, but he was far away. In fact, the Anglo-Irish barons did about as they pleased. Surrounded by a Celtic atmosphere and isolated from England, they came in time to resemble Irish chieftains rather than the barons of England.

Edward made efforts to increase his influence in Ireland, but he never visited that country, and he accomplished little. He tried to extend the Pale, he introduced a Parliament at Dublin on the English model, and he increased the commerce of a few coastal towns such as Dublin, Cork, and Waterford. Unfortunately, after Bannockburn, Edward Bruce, the brother of the Scottish King, invaded Ireland through Ulster, rousing the Celtic Irish and some of the Anglo-Irish barons against English rule, and carrying fire and sword to the very walls of Dublin. English power in Ireland suffered greatly from this incursion and declined during the fourteenth century. The Pale became a little island of English life in an alien Celtic world. The only King of England who visited Ireland during the rest of the Middle Ages was Richard II, but his authority crumbled at home and his Irish policy collapsed. The English conquest of Ireland began again in modern times.

EDWARD I AND FRANCE

The first twenty years of Edward's reign were remarkably successful. His reorganization of government and law, his famous statutes, his conquest of Wales, his early successes in Scotland, his able diplomacy on the Continent—all belong to this period. About the year 1293, however, there was a change for the worse. Revolts occurred in Wales in 1294 and 1295 that required immediate attention. The war with Scotland, begun in 1296, continued intermittently for the rest of the reign. And above all, Edward became involved in war with France. Military operations on the Continent against such a powerful kingdom as France were more costly and difficult than were the wars in Britain. Edward's expenses soared far beyond the resources at his disposal. His constant demands for taxation aroused bitter opposition at home.

From the Norman Conquest to the middle of the fifteenth century—a span of almost 400 years—the Kings of England held large possessions in France. This fact was the fundamental cause of the many wars between the two countries. As the Kings of France extended their power over the great French fiefs and as France developed a sense of nationality, the constant ambition of French rulers was to drive out the English. And yet no English King could relinquish his holdings on the Continent without incurring unpopularity and disgrace at home. An important step in Anglo-French relations had been taken in a treaty between Henry III and Louis IX in 1259. Henry abandoned all claim to Normandy, Maine, Anjou, and Poitou. In return he was confirmed in his title of Duke of Aquitaine and in his lordship of Gascony as a fief from the King of France. In addition Henry was promised certain territories to the north and east of Gascony which had once belonged to Henry II and Eleanor of Aquitaine but had later been lost to France. He never obtained possession of these territories, and in a later treaty in 1279 Edward wisely agreed to accept part of them and to relinquish his claim to the rest. For many years his relations with France were not unfriendly.

Then in 1293 the French King, Philip IV (1285–1314), determined to undermine the English position in Gascony by asserting his authority as supreme lord of that area. Acting much as Edward was doing in Scotland, Philip encouraged appeals to his feudal court from Edward's vassals in Gascony and summoned Edward to appear in Paris. Edward refused the summons and made grandiose plans for an attack upon France in 1294. A large army was collected in England; and alliances were concluded with Philip's enemies, the Count of Flanders, the Duke of Brabant, and Adolf of Nassau, the King of Germany. Simultaneous assaults were to be made upon France from Gascony, Flanders, and the Rhine. But then came troubles in Wales and Scotland. Edward did not leave England for Flanders until 1297. By that time Adolf had made peace with Philip, and Edward was having great difficulty in raising money in England. His expedition to Flanders, on which he had spent vast sums, ended tamely in a truce with Philip after a brief campaign. After years of negotiations a peace was made in 1303 on the basis of the *status quo* before the war. Edward had successfully defended his rights in France, though at a high price.

TAXATION

For the campaigns in Britain and abroad the King required armies and the money to pay for them. Edward could summon the feudal host of his tenants in chief, but they were growing less effective as a fighting force. They expected to be paid after the first forty days of a campaign and they displayed great reluctance to fight on the Continent. Although Edward could also call upon the militia to serve as infantry, he did not summon the militia as a whole but perfected a system of commissions of array addressed to the local gentry, requiring them to raise a limited number of men on the basis of a quota from each shire and borough. At first the militia served without pay, though by the end of the reign the custom of wages was coming in. But since the King required a much larger army than these methods could supply, he began to raise troops by making contracts with nobles or with military leaders to supply him with soldiers of various kinds at set wages. These mercenary troops were efficient but costly.

The old feudal forms of royal income were falling into decay, and new methods of taxation were obviously necessary. One innovation of the thirteenth century was a tax on income and movable goods, levied upon clergymen as well as laymen. Cathedrals, monasteries, and rectors of parishes, for example, might be asked to pay a tenth of the assessed value of their annual incomes. The assessments were low, but through them the King obtained large sums of money. Landowners in the shires and burgesses in the towns paid a percentage (a sixth, a tenth, a fifteenth, or a thirtieth) of their movable property and income. Assessments were made by local juries under the supervision of sheriffs and royal officials, and the standard tax of the later Middle Ages became a fifteenth of personal property in the shires and a tenth in the towns.

Because in theory this tax was a voluntary feudal aid it was necessary to obtain the consent of the classes to be taxed. This could be done in various ways. During much of the thirteenth century the clergy consented to taxation in diocesan synods. In Edward's reign, however, the clergy developed a body known as convocation, a kind of ecclesiastical parliament, one for each archbishopric, and it was in convocation that churchmen granted taxes. It was customary for the clergy not to consent to taxation without the approval of the pope; this gave them a certain protection. For some time laymen granted taxes in various bodies. In 1283 consent was given in provincial assemblies of knights and clergy. In 1297 the barons and the knights consented to the levy of an eighth. By the end of the century the normal place where laymen granted taxes was Parliament.

There were also customs duties upon exports and imports. These levies had begun in the twelfth century, but they remained unorganized until Edward's reign. In 1275 he obtained from Parliament an export duty of 6s. 8d. upon every sack of wool, which became a standard levy and was termed the Ancient Custom. During the financial pinch of the 1290s Edward made arrangements with the merchants to impose a much heavier duty of £2 on every sack, and although this duty was abolished in 1297, the King later arranged with foreign merchants to levy heavy duties, known as the New Custom, upon wool and other articles. Customs duties became the largest single source of income of the later medieval Kings.

EDWARD'S LAST YEARS

Edward's last years were ones of strain and conflict. He felt that he had been betrayed by the Scots and defrauded by the French. As his mood hardened into a grim determination to maintain his rights as he understood them, he became grasping and extortionate. The result was trouble in Parliament and suspicion on the part of the barons. Between 1294 and 1297 every effort was made to raise money: the New Custom on wool; the high taxes obtained from Parliament in 1294, 1295, and 1296; the heavy contributions required of the church. A crisis arose when even more money was demanded in 1297. Robert Winchelsea, the archbishop of Canterbury, was determined to protect the interests of the church. When Pope Boniface VIII issued the bull *Clericis Laicos* in 1296, which stated firmly that no ruler should tax the clergy without papal consent, Winchelsea led the clergy in refusing further payments. It was only when Boniface modified the bull to say that churchmen could grant money to the King in emergencies and could judge for themselves when emergencies existed that Winchelsea withdrew his opposition to a clerical grant in 1297.

There was also trouble with the barons, who were irritated by the constant demands for money, by an attempt of Edward to enforce knighthood upon all landowners whose estates were worth £20 a year, and by a command that some of them should fight in Gascony while the King was in Flanders. The barons prevented the collection of a tax Edward had obtained from a small assembly of accommodating nobles. Edward was driven to summon a full assembly of barons and knights, to annul the grant already made, and to obtain a new one by making a solemn confirmation of Magna Carta and the Charter of the Forest. An important clause was added to the effect that no tax should be levied in the future without the consent of the whole community of the realm and for the common benefit of the kingdom.

The controversy between King and barons continued after 1297. Magna Carta and the Charter of the Forest were again confirmed in 1299; twenty new articles were added in the Parliament of 1300. These articles declared that the King's rights in the forests should be investigated, that purveyance should be restricted, and that legal actions should be begun by writs under the Great Seal and not under the privy seal.[3] Again in 1301 the charters were confirmed. The barons made an unsuccessful attempt to force the resignation of the Treasurer, Walter Langton, bishop of Lichfield. Thus Edward's reign, which began with an increase in royal power and prerogative, ended with their curtailment.

PARLIAMENT

The origin of Parliament is to be found in the Great Council, the feudal court of the King, which was attended by his tenants in chief—archbishops, bishops, abbots, priors, earls, and greater barons. Attendance was part of their feudal duty: the King could summon them whenever he pleased. The Great Council was not a large body of all the tenants in chief great and small; it was a small select assembly of wealthy and powerful persons, great magnates, lay and

---

[3] Purveyance was the right of the King to live off the country as he traveled about. For a discussion of the privy seal, see page 134.

ecclesiastical. In theory the obligation of attendance fell equally upon all tenants in chief, but in practice the lesser tenants of the King did not come to the meetings of his court and were not expected to do so. They did not receive individual summons, as did the great barons, but were summoned in general terms through the sheriff. This they regarded as permission to stay away. By the thirteenth century they had become small landowners—knights or gentry—interested in the management of their estates and in local affairs. They had dropped out of the baronial class. The greater barons, however, had not yet hardened into a fixed caste. Among them were men whose status was not yet established. Sometimes they were summoned to the Great Council and sometimes not, and the King's choice of members could be capricious.

About the middle of the thirteenth century the meetings of the Great Council began to be called parliaments. The word "parliament" at this time meant merely a parley, a talking together, a meeting at which there was conference or debate. It was an occasion, not an institution, and there were other meetings of entirely different kinds which also were referred to as parliaments. Meetings of the Great Council, of a parliament, were occasions when the King met with the great men of the kingdom to talk about matters of high importance and to transact various kinds of business. These meetings were encouraged by the thirteenth-century concept of the community of the realm. A good King, it was held, should seek the cooperation of his magnates; and the noblest type of government was to be found in a harmony of King and barons ruling together. The barons who attended these meetings thought of themselves as representing the nation as a whole, as speaking for the community of the realm, and they sometimes referred to themselves as though they were that community. Their decisions were binding upon the community as a whole.

The heart and center of medieval parliaments were the King and his small council of judges and administrators. Parliament, which, as the Great Council, had always been a court, was thus well equipped for judicial work. It was the high court of Parliament, the supreme court of the kingdom, where cases of great importance or cases which touched the public interest were brought for trial. Grievances were aired and wrongs righted in Parliament. Great numbers of petitions from persons high and low begging for legal action were submitted to Parliament; as early as 1278 a procedure arose by which these petitions were sorted and cases of small importance assigned to the ordinary courts.

Parliament had many other uses. Edward I promulgated his statutes there. Although these statutes were drawn by the King's officials, they often were inspired by complaints made in Parliament or they sought to rectify defects in the law that had become apparent as a result of Parliament's deliberations. Parliament discussed political problems, gave approval to royal policy, and supplied information upon which better government could be based. It consented to taxation. The King, it was held, could not alter the law or levy extraordinary taxes without the consent of the magnates.

During the course of the thirteenth century the King began to summon representatives from the middle classes to meet with him and with the barons in Parliament. The growth of this practice was slow and intermittent; one must not think that it happened quickly or that the King was doing more than acting for his own convenience. The middle classes in the counties were the knights and country gentlemen whose ancestors had obtained their lands as small tenants in chief or as vassals of the greater barons. By the thirteenth century these knights and gentry had become less warlike and more interested in the management of their property. They were substantial people who were constantly used by the Crown in the work of local government, as sheriffs and coroners, as men who supplied information to royal agents sent out to make inquiries, and in these capacities they frequently represented the local community. The idea of representation was far older than Parliament. The middle class also included the wealthier burgesses in the towns, men who controlled the guilds, who governed the boroughs as mayors and aldermen, and who in the thirteenth century were acquiring moderate riches. They often represented their towns in negotiations with royal officials and in many other ways. The middle classes thus were experienced in government and were familiar with the idea of representation.

When the King wished to investigate local conditions, he normally sent out his itinerant justices to travel from place to place and to make inquiries. But he sometimes found it more convenient to summon representatives of various localities to meet with his officials at some central place. One of the first examples of a meeting of this kind occurred in 1204 when King John ordered that twelve men from each of the Cinque Ports assemble at a central point to discuss matters of commerce with royal officials. Again in 1213 John summoned the reeve and four men from each of certain villages to meet at St. Albans in order to report the damage done to local churches during the King's quarrel with the papacy. These meetings in essence were concentrations of juries. The King, however, might find it more convenient to summon representatives from localities to assemble before him and before his officials or magnates and to give the information there. In 1213 John instructed the sheriffs to cause four knights from each shire to come before the King and the Great Council at Oxford.[4] Again in 1227 the sheriffs were directed to obtain the election of four knights in every county court to meet with the King and the Great Council. These knights were to report complaints against the sheriffs. Two knights were elected in each county in 1254 to meet with the Great Council at Westminster and to determine upon an aid to be sent to the King in Gascony. In both 1264 and 1265, as we have seen, Simon de Montfort summoned knights from the shires to meet with the barons in Parliament, and to the second of these assemblies he also summoned burgesses from certain towns. His Parliaments, it is true, were revolutionary assemblies, for the King was under restraint and Simon was trying to rally support for his dubious government.

During the next thirty years there were concentrations of many kinds. Most of them were meetings of the magnates alone. One, at least, contained representatives of the lower clergy but neither knights nor burgesses. On another occasion some knights and burgesses were instructed to meet at York while others met at Northampton. In 1283 a Parliament at Shrewsbury did certain business and then divided—the barons remained where they were to pass judgment upon Prince David of Wales, while the burgesses went to Acton Burnell to discuss matters of trade. It is obvious that Edward occasionally summoned knights and burgesses merely because their presence helped him to get things done. In 1295, however, under pressing need for money, he summoned a Parliament which contained many elements—bishops, abbots, heads of religious orders, knights, burgesses, and representatives of the lower clergy. This was the largest of medieval Parliaments.[5]

[4] It is doubtful whether these two assemblies summoned by King John in 1213 ever met.
[5] It is often called the Model Parliament, though there was nothing model about it except that it contained all the classes found in later medieval Parliaments.

In these early assemblies, in which the role of the representative element was very slight, knights and burgesses were not an essential part. They stood deferentially at the rear of the chamber, sometimes as mere observers. They might be asked to grant taxes but were then dismissed, while the barons remained in session to transact other business. In 1297, however, in the Confirmation of the Charters, an additional clause laid down the principle that taxes should be granted by the whole community of the realm and not merely by the class to be taxed. Thus representative elements were emerging as normal members of Parliament, though they had not been so regarded through the thirteenth century.

EDWARD II, 1307–1327

The reign of Edward II was an unhappy interlude of strife, bitter personal hatreds, and occasional civil wars, with constant quarrels between King and magnates. We may pity Edward II for the almost insoluble problems left to him by his father and for his tragic and humiliating fate. But he was altogether lacking in the dignity and high dedication required of a King. Weak and unambitious, he was ignorant of the business of government and incapable as a leader in war. He liked unkingly amusements, such as amateur theatricals, rowing, driving, digging, and thatching houses. He fell easily under the influence of young men. This fondness for favorites was an ill omen, for it meant that he turned to "evil counselors" instead of working with the barons who in their own estimation were the natural and legitimate advisers of the Crown.[6] There was deep suspicion between him and the magnates from the very beginning of the reign. This suspicion has been explained as a baronial reaction against the strong rule of Edward I, but it was certainly increased by the new King's character. The magnates probably knew enough about him as Prince of Wales to suspect his inadequacy and constantly sought to check his power as King. They introduced an unusual clause into his coronation oath by which he pledged himself to observe such laws as should be determined by the communality of the realm.

Edward quickly justified these apprehensions. He recalled to England a young Gascon knight, Peter de Gaveston, who had been exiled earlier because of his questionable influence over Edward as Prince of Wales. Gaveston was an able man, but tactless and insolent toward the barons, who disliked him cordially. The leader of the opposition was the King's cousin Thomas, Earl of Lancaster, the holder of five earldoms, a magnate of enormous wealth and influence, with a vast retinue that could be swelled into an army at a moment's notice. As early as 1310 Lancaster and other magnates forced the King to appoint a committee of twenty-one barons to prepare a series of ordinances for the better government of the realm. These ordinances of 1311 were reminiscent of the Provisions of Oxford of 1258. They stipulated that Gaveston and an unpopular Italian banker be banished, that the chief officials of the royal Household be appointed only with the consent of the magnates in Parliament, that the King not go to war without baronial approval, that heavy duties laid by Edward I upon exported wool be abolished, and that money not be brought to the wardrobe without

---

[6] "Evil counselors" was a conventional term used by antiroyalist magnates whenever they disapproved of the men close to the King.

passing through the Exchequer. But though these ordinances were a vigorous statement of baronial grievances, there was no provision for their enforcement, and they remained an expression of opinion rather than a frame of government. Gaveston went into exile but returned before the end of the year. In 1312 the barons were in open revolt. Gaveston was seized by one of his many enemies and beheaded. A war was avoided only when Edward submitted to further restrictions. For some years Lancaster shared royal power with him, but never won the King's friendship or his confidence and was lacking in energy and constructive talent. In 1318 a middle party arose at court. Its aim was to protect the King from dependence on favorites as well as to protect him from an over-powerful subject such as Lancaster, whose influence began to diminish.

It was not long before one of the middle party, Hugh Despenser, began to dominate the King as Gaveston had done and to build a personal ascendancy at court. Even more objectionable, he soon had many enemies among the marcher lords of Wales, where he was increasing his possessions, and among the northern lords who followed Thomas of Lancaster. In 1322 the King displayed unusual energy, collected an army, and defeated Lancaster at the Battle of Borough-bridge in Yorkshire. Lancaster was executed, and the ordinances of 1311 were formally revoked in Parliament. For some years Edward and Despenser controlled the government. The favorite established a number of reforms in the royal Household, but more arrogant and grasping than before, he aroused a host of enemies, two of whom were very dangerous. One was Roger Mortimer of Wigmore, a marcher lord, who was imprisoned but escaped and fled to France. The other was Edward's Queen, Isabella, a sister of the French King, Charles IV. In 1325 Isabella was sent to France to negotiate with her brother concerning the affairs of Gascony. She did not return, but joined forces with Roger Mortimer in Paris and became his mistress. She persuaded her husband to send their son, the young Prince Edward, a boy of twelve, to France to do homage to Charles IV for Gascony. With the prince in her hands, she and Mortimer arranged a marriage for him with Philippa, a daughter of the Count of Hainault. Using the dowry to buy arms, they invaded England in 1326. Edward, defeated, was forced to abdicate in 1327 and was murdered shortly thereafter. So ended his tragic career.

Parliament in the Reign of Edward II

Although limitations upon Edward's power were imposed in meetings of Parliament, it is clear that the magnates formed the driving force and that the role of the knights and burgesses was largely passive. When the barons in 1311 asked for frequent Parliaments, they were thinking of aristocratic assemblies of their own class. Yet knights and burgesses were present in Parliament in almost every year of Edward's reign; they were present in Parliament at moments of crisis in 1311, 1322, and 1327. When Edward's deposition was determined upon, a deputation representing various elements in Parliament waited upon him at Kenilworth and extorted some kind of abdication. Moreover, knights and burgesses consented to every tax that was levied during the reign; and a statement made by Edward in 1322 declared that matters of importance should be treated in Parliament with the assent not only of the magnates but also of the community of the realm. Knights and burgesses were now recognized as normal members of Parliament.

8

EDWARD III
and RICHARD II

The fourteenth century had characteristics of its own which differentiated it from earlier and later periods. It was, in the first place, a very warlike century. Although feudalism had subsided, the upper classes still were organized for war, in which they eagerly engaged, seeking financial profit as well as honor and renown. They gladly followed Edward III in a great war with France, the first part of the Hundred Years' War. A modern spirit of nationalism arose and England found unity and strength in the brutal game of plundering the French, but later in the century military success was followed by military failure. Richard II, an unwarlike King, was faced by the opposition of powerful and discontented barons, critical Parliaments, and a disillusioned people.

The fourteenth century was profoundly influenced by the plague. This dread disease, which greatly reduced the population, created an atmosphere of alarm and a sense of crisis. Social and economic conflict arose as a reduced labor force demanded better wages and freedom from the bonds of serfdom. Commerce and industry appeared to suffer less than agriculture, for it was during this period that England ceased to be merely a producer of raw wool and became a manufacturer of woolen cloth. Some merchants prospered greatly. There was a gradual rise in the standard of living. And thus, although the nobles were still very grand and powerful, and some attained great wealth, the gulf between them and the middle classes was less than it had been in earlier centuries. For many reasons the influence of the clergy declined in the fourteenth century, and a strong anticlerical sentiment arose. Finally, it was in this period that English emerged as a literary language, although the nobility continued to speak and write in French, and Latin remained the language of the church.

EDWARD III, 1327–1377

The Minority
The deposition and murder of Edward II in 1327 was followed by a few

years in which his widow, Queen Isabella, the she-wolf of France, and her paramour, Roger Mortimer, dominated the government. They were an avaricious and disreputable pair; Mortimer, who was made the Earl of March, increased his estates until he became a great landed magnate; the court was torn by quarrels and hatreds as in the days before Edward's deposition. In October 1330, the young King, Edward III, who was just under eighteen years of age, carried through a palace revolution in which Mortimer was seized and later condemned in Parliament. The Queen was placed in honorable confinement. Assuming control of the government, Edward ruled for almost half a century.

Edward's Character

The chroniclers of Edward's reign lavished praise on him, but modern historians, until very recently, have tended to judge him rather harshly. A soldier, his lifework was the war in France. To promote the war, he allowed the magnates unprecedented influence in the government, he made concessions to Parliament, and he sacrificed the interests of the church, of sound administration, and of the trading classes. He squandered the resources of the Crown, leaving an empty exchequer and many problems to his successor. Historians have accused him of sacrificing the future for the present, of waging an aggressive war which was doomed to ultimate failure, and of neglecting the problems arising from social and economic change.

A recent writer, however, has drawn a more favorable picture of Edward.[1] According to this author, he was keenly aware that his father's reign had ended in tragedy because of quarrels with the barons. Determined to avoid that error, he cultivated the good will of the magnates and sought to remove old feuds and hostilities. The earldom of March was restored to the grandson of Roger Mortimer, the definition of treason was modified, the King was generous with titles, honors, and gifts of land. By waging a successful foreign war he kept the magnates occupied abroad and offered them the opportunity to gain renown and riches. These policies succeeded admirably. Edward surrounded himself with a group of young and warlike barons who sympathized with him, admired him, and remained loyal to him even in his declining years. The same may be said of his five sons. Edward's relations with his nobles were closer and happier than were those of any other medieval King in England. He may not have been a man of intellectual power, but he fitted perfectly into the temper of the times. He won the loyalty of his people and the affection of his magnates, he raised his dynasty from the degradation of Edward II's reign, and he ruled in a moderate and conciliatory way, carefully avoiding clashes with the church, Parliament, or the nobility.

CHIVALRY AND WAR

Edward was a majestic figure as he sat in state surrounded by his noble Queen and his five tall sons. An extravagant and cheerful man, he loved the pomp and pageantry of war and chivalry. He delighted in palaces, costly feasts, and elaborate tournaments, which were now jousts or encounters between two knights, fought according to rules, still very dangerous, though not as deadly as

---

[1] May McKisack, "Edward III and the Historians," *History,* XLV (1960), 1–15.

the old tournaments of Norman times. They were held in an open field called the lists, not unlike a modern football field, surrounded by galleries for spectators. The ladies of the court, who attended the tournaments, added a note of romance and helped to civilize jousting by turning it into a means of winning honor for one's lady.

Chivalry—a social and moral code of knightly behavior—laid stress on disinterested bravery; on honor, virtue, and courtesy; and on devotion to the service of a lady as her attendant and champion. It was set forth in romances about King Arthur and his Round Table or in tales taken from the classics and given a medieval setting. These stories often related the adventures of a lonely knight who wandered about seeking to do noble deeds that might bring honor to his lady.

Edward added to the cult of chivalry and used it to his own advantage by creating the famous Order of the Garter about 1348. Inspired by the ideals of King Arthur and his Round Table, the order was an exclusive society of twenty-six knights, including the sovereign. Its members were bound to fidelity and friendship toward each other in a lasting brotherhood of honor. The order had its chapel, herald, feasts, and tournaments; membership in it was a mark of high distinction.

As a matter of fact, however, this code of chivalry had little relation to daily life, for the position of women was low and they often were beaten and maltreated. The marriage of an heiress was a matter of business and diplomacy. A great noble regarded his sisters and daughters as so many pawns in the game of marriage alliances with other noble houses; even the King sought marriages for his sons with the great heiresses of the kingdom. This had the unfortunate result in later years that almost any revolt against the Crown could find leaders who were related to the royal family, but in Edward's reign there was no such danger; concentration of wealth in the hands of the King's sons supported their dignity and added strength to their father's regime. Heiresses often were married as children. We hear of a little girl who had three husbands before she reached eleven, and although the church frowned upon child marriages, it took no effective steps to prevent them. Courtly love, moreover, with its devotion to the service of a lady, often meant that a knight fought for the honor of one lady but happened to be married to another. Hence courtly love could easily lead to immorality.

Careful marriages, the generosity of the King, and the profits of the wars in France sometimes combined to bring enormous estates into the hands of a few magnates. As in the thirteenth century, these men lived in great ostentation, maintaining sumptuous households, dispensing a lavish hospitality, and adding to their dignity and power by an ever-increasing number of dependents and retainers. And yet, as we shall see, the income from agriculture was declining. Hence the magnates were greatly interested in the profits that could be derived from war. Not only was a successful commander rewarded by the King; he also might obtain rich plunder during a campaign in France. The capture of Calais in 1347 yielded tremendous spoils, so that, as a contemporary wrote, a new sun seemed to have arisen in England and almost every woman in the land appeared to be dressed in gowns, furs, and ornaments brought from France. But the most lucrative form of plunder was the ransom demanded by the English from prisoners of war, for every captured Frenchman had his price and noble captives yielded enormous sums. Holding both the King of France and the King of Scotland as prisoners, Edward obtained a ransom of half a million pounds from the first and a hundred thousand marks from the second. It is small wonder that the war was popular. The common soldier drew excellent wages, and commanders might make a fortune.

The English armies that fought in France were raised in various ways. We have seen that the old feudal host was falling into decay, and it was fully understood in Edward's time that the only way to build an efficient and disciplined army was to pay for it. Even the greatest commanders—the Black Prince, for example—drew wages at a daily rate. The King made contracts or indentures with nobles or with celebrated captains to supply him with fixed numbers of fighting men. Indentures were of various kinds. Those made with lesser commanders were fairly simple. Edward Montagu, for instance, agreed to serve in Brittany in 1341 for forty days and to supply six knights, twenty men-at-arms (who may have been light horsemen), twelve armed men, and twelve archers.

But agreements with great nobles were much more elaborate, covering such details as the cost of transportation, wages, length of service, compensation for lost horses, and the division of ransom money. A noble might make up his quota of soldiers from his own household, from his retainers, or from subcontracts. Edward I, as we have seen, had organized a system of commissioners of array in order to obtain soldiers from the militia. The commissioners were local gentry who surveyed the men available for duty and selected the best to serve for wages with the King. There was no need to exert pressure: a peasant could obtain better wages as a soldier than as an agricultural laborer. More volunteers came forward than could be used.

The commanders were drawn from the aristocracy and from the class of nonnoble knights. Great nobles sat in council with the King to determine general strategy. A select rank of knights, known as bannerets, who were skillful captains and men of some wealth, commanded troops, garrisoned castles, and conducted other operations in the field. Below them were the knights bachelors, less wealthy than bannerets but men of standing and experience. Knights wore costly and elaborate armor made of plate, now so heavy that shields disappeared. They were armed with sword, lance, and dagger. Each knight was supplied with three or four warhorses, for although the knight fought on foot, horses were essential in the raids in France and were used to pursue the enemy.

Below the knights were various kinds of men-at-arms: lightly armored horsemen who carried the same weapons as the knights, foot soldiers and foot archers armed with short swords, knives, and bows and arrows. The foot archer soon was replaced by the mounted archer, who combined mobility with great firepower. He used a six-foot bow, a Welsh weapon developed in England, where archery had become the great national sport. Drawn with the whole strength of the archer's body, it could send an arrow through chain mail; a good bowman could shoot ten or twelve arrows a minute. The longbow was a magnificent defensive weapon against the charge of French feudal knights, for it sent a deadly shower of arrows among them and maddened the horses. The archer fought on foot. Normally, the English formed a line, with groups of various types of soldiers interspersed with each other, to resist advancing cavalry, and so long as the French were foolish enough to charge in the old disorderly fashion, as they did at Crécy, Poitiers, and much later at Agincourt, they went down to defeat before the English defense.

One other part of the English army should be mentioned. Among the foot soldiers were many Welshmen, armed only with long knives and daggers. When the French knights were thrown from their horses, these Welsh troopers darted forward to slit the throats of the fallen Frenchmen, for a knife could be thrust between the plates of armor. This was not fighting according to the rules of chivalry: it was the deadly business of slaughtering the foe.[2]

Edward's First Campaigns

Edward's first campaigns were fought against the Scots. But although he defeated them at the Battle of Halidon Hill near Berwick in 1333 and led expeditions into Scotland in 1335 and 1336, he soon discovered that campaigning in Scotland offered hard blows with little hope of plunder; his mind turned to the more profitable field of fighting in France. In 1337 excuses for fighting France were not hard to find: the French had been assisting the Scots; the English were intriguing with the cloth-manufacturing towns of Flanders against the French; the French King, Philip VI, announced the annexation of Gascony; Edward laid claim to the French crown through his mother, Isabella, a daughter of King Philip IV. These causes of conflict might well have led to hostilities. But one suspects that Edward and his magnates, inspired by high spirits and material greed, were ready to employ any excuse that served their turn.

Edward's first campaigns against France were planned upon a magnificent scale. Alliances were concluded with various rulers in the Low Countries and along the Rhine, including the German Emperor, Lewis IV; the wool trade was manipulated to increase royal revenue and to force the Count of Flanders to turn against the French; plans were made to invade France through the Netherlands. Edward crossed to Flanders in 1338 but found that his allies were far from eager for war; meanwhile he was spending great sums of money. Throughout the years 1339 and 1340 he was able to do no more than conduct two small campaigns which ended tamely in a truce. His principal success was a naval victory over a French fleet at Sluys. In 1340 he returned to England, angry and disillusioned. His strategy had failed because it was conceived on too grandiose and lavish a scale. His money was gone before he and his expensive allies had struck a serious blow at the enemy.

The Hundred Years' War, 1337–1361

Thenceforth Edward turned to a new pattern of warfare which proved to be highly successful: to cross directly to France and to make raids into the interior. These inexpensive raids did not need costly allies and the mobile English armies could live on the country and plunder as they moved about. The raids began in 1341 in the duchy of Brittany, where a disputed succession enabled the English to support one candidate while the French supported another. In 1342 Edward overran much of Brittany, which became an important base for English operations. In 1345 raids were made into France from Brittany and Gascony.

The next few years brought brilliant victories. In 1346 Edward crossed to Normandy with an army of some 10,000 men, of whom 7000 were archers. Sacking the city of Caen, he moved northward to the area of Ponthieu and the river Somme. On August 26, at the village of Crécy, he was met by a large French

[2] May McKisack, *The Fourteenth Century 1307–1399* (Oxford: Clarendon Press, 1959), Chap. IX.

army. The French knights charged the English line, riding over their own cross-bowmen in their eagerness, but fell in bloody defeat under a hail of English arrows. Crécy pointed to the passing of the feudal knight, who could thus be conquered by the fire of plebeian archers and the knives of Welsh peasants. Other victories followed. In the same year, 1346, the Scots were defeated at the Battle of Neville's Cross near Durham, and the Scottish King, David II, was taken prisoner. In 1347 the English defeated the French in Brittany and after a long siege captured the city of Calais which remained an English outpost in France for more than two centuries. A long pause in the Hundred Years' War was due to the Black Death, which devastated both England and France, disrupting trade and the collection of taxes.

War began once more in 1355, when two large English expeditions crossed to the Continent. One of them, commanded by the King, operated from Calais but accomplished nothing of moment. The other, led by the Black Prince,[3] penetrated from Bordeaux into Gascony and Toulouse. In 1356, as the Black Prince was marching toward the city of Tours, he was met at Poitiers by a huge French army commanded by John, the chivalrous but inept King of France. Again the French knights charged the English line and again they were completely defeated. Large numbers of the French nobility, including the French King, were taken prisoners and were brought to England to be held for ransom.

But Edward's resources were exhausted and he was ready to make peace. Conditions in France were miserable. The Black Death raged without mercy, the government was disrupted by the absence of the King, great stretches of the countryside lay waste, the wretched peasants rose in revolt, free companies of English soldiers roamed about the country plundering as they went. In 1359 the Black Prince led an army in a great circle around Paris. Negotiations for peace, opened in 1360, led to the Treaty of Bretigny in the following year. Gascony and large adjacent areas including Poitou and, in the north, Ponthieu and Calais passed to Edward in full sovereignty. King John's ransom was fixed at £500,000. In return Edward renounced his claim to the French throne and restored certain lands and fortresses outside the area covered by the treaty. In 1362, however, the treaty was modified at Calais. Edward's renunciation was to become effective only under certain conditions which were not likely to be fulfilled, and the way was left open for future claims by English sovereigns. The French honored the terms of the treaty, making English influence in France greater than it had been since the days of Henry II.

PARLIAMENT IN THE REIGN OF EDWARD III

The magnates might like war with France, but the knights and burgesses assembled in Parliament often did not, for their part was the unromantic one of paying the bill. Yet the King's constant need for money gave Parliament, and especially the Commons, an opportunity to develop rapidly. It was in this reign that Parliament assumed its historic structure of Lords and Commons and began, though in a tentative way, to acquire some of its basic powers.

---

[3] Edward, the Black Prince, was the eldest son of Edward III. Duke of Cornwall and Prince of Wales, he developed into one of the finest soldiers of the age. He was never King, for he died a few months before his father.

Forty-eight Parliaments met during Edward's reign of fifty years, and to every one of them he summoned the classes which had composed the Model Parliament of 1295: the upper clergy, the magnates and greater barons, proctors representing the lower clergy, knights from the shires, and burgesses from the towns. He also summoned a few of his great officers, councilors, and judges; these men still formed the heart and core of Parliament, guiding its activities and guarding the interests of the Crown. Some Parliaments continued to sit after the knights and burgesses had been dismissed, but none of them met without the presence of the Commons, whose members were fully accepted as an essential part of Parliament.

Parliament was composed of various classes. The upper clergy, or spiritual lords, consisted of twenty-one bishops and archbishops and a group of abbots and priors. The number of abbots and priors differed from time to time. Edward I had summoned seventy in 1295, but the number declined during the fourteenth century until it became established at twenty-seven in 1364. The magnates and greater barons, or temporal lords, consisted of dukes, marquises, earls, and barons.[4] In the thirteenth century the only duke had been the King (who was Duke of Aquitaine), but Edward III conferred dukedoms on four of his five sons; later in the century six other dukes were created. The title of marquis first was conferred in 1385 by Richard II. At the end of Edward's reign there were about fourteen earls. These nobles were summoned as a matter of course. The number of barons called to Parliament, however, varied greatly— from ninety in 1321 to thirty in 1346. Sometimes both a father and his son were summoned together, sometimes a son in place of his father, sometimes a man in the right of his wife. Occasionally a knight banneret was summoned. A clearly delimited nobility, with an exclusive right to be summoned to Parliament, did not exist in the fourteenth century. But the tendency was in this direction, for the lords now considered themselves a class apart and above all others. They were the peers of the realm, a unique and superior caste. After Richard II began to create peers by letters patent in 1387, the list of nobles summoned to Parliament gradually hardened into a fixed class of peers. Only then can one speak of a House of Lords.

All the persons mentioned above received individual summons to Parliament. But the representatives of the lower clergy were summoned indirectly through the bishops, and the knights and burgesses through the sheriffs. The lower clergy gradually ceased to attend. When a Parliament was called, the sheriff of each of thirty-seven counties (Chester and Durham were not represented) received a writ directing him to cause two knights to be elected in the shire court, two citizens in every city, and two burgesses in every borough. Some cities and boroughs, however, hoping to escape expense, managed to evade the command of the sheriff and did not return members.

We do not know much about these elections, but we know that they were neither popular nor democratic. Often the sheriff or some local magnate, or the two working together, proposed names in the shire court; these names were accepted by acclamation, and the election was over. Undoubtedly the sheriff exercised great influence, and a local lord with a body of retainers might easily sway the electors. The writ called for knights as members, but the number of

---

[4] The title of viscount, a rank between that of earl and baron, was not introduced until the fifteenth century.

knights was insufficient,[5] and members were of various kinds. They might be the sons of nobles, or knights or country gentlemen, or well-to-do farmers below the rank of gentry. They were often retainers of local magnates or men interested in trade. Very likely they had served in some local office, and they combined wealth with experience in government and knowledge of local conditions.

The elections in the boroughs are even more difficult to describe, for practices differed from town to town. But the elections normally were controlled by the wealthy merchants and industrialists who dominated the guilds and the town governments. Members from the boroughs were lawyers, capitalists, merchants, or smaller business men; but even in the Middle Ages members of the gentry class were sometimes returned by neighboring towns. The number of towns that sent members varied somewhat, averaging between seventy and eighty-three in the reigns of Edward III and Richard II.

The most important developments of the fourteenth century were the division of Parliament into two parts, the Lords and the Commons; and the union of the knights and burgesses to form the second of these divisions. The lords spiritual and temporal naturally acted together as an aristocracy, receiving individual summons and holding land directly from the King; the lower clergy dropped out; and the vital question remained whether the knights would join with the lords or whether they would unite with the burgesses. In some early Parliaments the knights met with the lords to decide upon taxation, but as the aristocracy hardened into the peerage the knights found themselves excluded. Knights and burgesses bore the heaviest burden of taxation and had a common interest in resisting demands for money. They also discovered that the grievances and abuses they wished redressed were of the same general nature. By 1339 knights and burgesses were acting together, and henceforth they formed a single body. This union was of the utmost importance. Without it the burgesses would have remained in a position of permanent subordination, but knight and burgess acting together had some hope of defending their interests against King and aristocracy.

Sessions of Parliament were short, lasting normally only two or three weeks. Lords and Commons met together in the Parliament chamber at the opening of a Parliament, as they do today, and heard an oration from one of the councilors explaining the reasons for the meeting. Petitions, addressed to the King and his Council, not to Parliament, were then presented. The Parliament divided for deliberation, the Lords remaining in the Parliament chamber while the Commons met elsewhere, normally in the chapter house or the refectory of Westminster Abbey.

The work of Parliament may be divided into deliberation, action on taxation, judicial work, and legislation. Edward III used Parliament as a clearinghouse for discussion, laying important questions before the Lords and the Commons. The Lords gave advice, which might or might not be followed. The Commons, however, were hesitant in offering opinions. Apparently they feared that advice might commit them to paying the cost of royal policy. Hence unless their interests were directly affected, they were rather noncommittal. Their great victory was in the field of taxation. By 1340 the principle was established that taxes could be levied only with the consent of Lords and Commons; by the end of the century it was

---

[5] A sheriff once reported that there was only one knight in his shire and that he was "languidus et impotens ad laborandum." May McKisack, *The Fourteenth Century 1307–1399*, p. 188n.

recognized that proposals for grants of money must originate in the Commons. Control of taxation gave the Commons power to bargain with the King for the redress of grievances, which normally preceded the voting of supply.

Judicial work was largely the function of the Lords, who continued, as in the thirteenth century, to form the high court of Parliament, the highest court in the land. But the judicial work of the Lords was declining. Many cases could be settled in the three central law courts, and in the fourteenth century a new court, the court of chancery, arose which based its decisions upon equity rather than upon the strict letter of the law. The court of chancery could handle many of the unusual cases formerly brought to the Lords. Moreover, the legal work in the Lords was done largely by the judges who were summoned to Parliament, but as the Lords made the peerage more rigid and exclusive, they resented the presence of these judges, who were normally not peers. This attitude naturally tended to discourage the legal work of the judges in Parliament. In one aspect of judicial work the Commons played an important part. In 1376 we find the first case of impeachment. In this procedure the Commons, acting as a body, placed accusations against corrupt officials before the Lords. The Lords then acted as a court to try the ministers in question. Impeachment gave the Commons power, not to control the selection of ministers, but to attack those who broke the law.

The Commons also gained some share in legislation, though their achievements were limited. As soon as Parliament met, as we have seen, it received petitions of various kinds; these were addressed to the King and his Council with a request for action or redress. Such petitions might be sponsored by individual members, but it shortly occurred to the Commons that there would be advantage in pooling their petitions and their pressures upon the Crown. Thus arose the common petition backed by the whole body of the Commons. If the Lords assented and if the King accepted the petition, it could be thrown into the form of a statute and become the law of the land. "The common petition is thus the root of the house of commons as a separate legislative assembly."[6] The King however, possessed various methods of rendering these petitions ineffective, even though he had accepted them. The wording of the statute might be quite different from the wording of the petition, with vital matters altered or omitted. The statute might remain a dead letter for lack of provision for its enforcement or because the King blocked its execution. He might issue a decree or ordinance which invalidated the force of a statute. In 1341 Edward attempted to annul a statute as contrary to his prerogative. But the next Parliament formally repealed the statute in question, and there was no other attempt to void a statute by royal pronouncement. In the fourteenth century the Commons never wholly succeeded in preventing evasions and omissions in the form of statutes.

It is obvious, nonetheless, that the Commons made great gains in the fourteenth century: they debated matters laid before them by the Crown, they gained the great victory of control of taxation, they devised the procedure of impeachment, and they obtained some share in legislation. A Speaker of the Commons appears in 1376. It is true that the early Speakers were the agents of the King and of the magnates rather than of the Commons, and that the Commons often opposed the Crown only because they were assured of the backing of some of the magnates. The influence of the Commons must not be exaggerated, but their progress in the fourteenth century was impressive.

[6] A. F. Pollard, *The Evolution of Parliament* (New York: McKay, 1926), p. 120.

THE LAST YEARS OF EDWARD III

During the 1360s Edward enjoyed the rewards of successful war. He did not have to ask Parliament for large supplies because he was collecting the huge ransom of the French King John. English politics were tranquil. After the war was renewed in 1369, however, the situation altered radically, and the years between 1369 and 1382 were filled with stress and turmoil both at home and abroad. The war went steadily against the English, for there was a remarkable revival of royal power in France. Charles V (1364–1380) and his brother, Philip the Bold, Duke of Burgundy, were able and vigorous leaders. In Bertrand Du Guesclin they possessed an excellent general whose tactics against the English were effective. He avoided pitched battles and the stupid old charge of the feudal knights. Instead he employed guerrilla methods, harassing the English and wearing them down until they were forced to turn homeward, leaving France damaged but unconquered.

The war began when the French nobles in Gascony revolted from English rule and were assisted by Charles V. English countermoves were feeble. Edward, too old to fight, was sinking into his dotage. The Black Prince was ill. An English expedition based upon Calais in 1370 was a failure, and a march by John of Gaunt, the King's third son, from Calais to Bordeaux, was spectacular rather than important. Moreover, the English had to fight Castile as well as France. In 1367 Castile had been invaded by the Black Prince in support of King Pedro the Cruel, who had been driven from the Castilian throne by a French candidate. Pedro was restored, but only for a short time. Thereafter Castile allied with France, and the English in Gascony had an enemy on both flanks. The Castilian navy, joining that of France, defeated an English fleet in 1372, won control of the Channel, and helped to raid the English coast. English conquests in France were quickly lost, so that when Edward III died in 1377 the English held no more than the city of Calais, a narrow strip around Bordeaux, and scattered harbors along the coast of Brittany. Events in England must be seen against this background of defeat.

There was also a decline in morale at the English court. After the death of Queen Philippa in 1369 Edward fell under the influence of an unscrupulous mistress, Alice Perrers. She and William Latimer, the chamberlain, dominated the court and used their position to fill their own pockets. They were protected by John of Gaunt, Duke of Lancaster and the most influential son of the King. The corruption at court and the mismanagement of the war caused an explosion in the Good Parliament of 1376. Sir Peter de la Mare, the Speaker of the Commons, with the secret support of certain magnates, attacked the court party and brought charges before the Lords. This was the first use of impeachment. Latimer and Richard Lyons, a financier, were condemned; Alice Perrers was driven from court.

The Good Parliament inaugurated a period of political crisis which lasted for some years, but in itself it accomplished very little. Alice Perrers and Latimer were soon back at court once more. Edward III died in 1377. Despite the military glory of his prime, his reign ended on a note of gloom, defeat, and corruption. A general sense of frustration, fear, and discontent existed among the people. The causes of this tension will become clear as we look at social and economic conditions.

SOCIAL AND ECONOMIC LIFE

The Black Death

In August 1348 the bubonic plague, or Black Death, suddenly appeared in England. Its germs were carried by the fleas on black rats that came into the country on ships from abroad. The first outbreak of the plague was of intense ferocity, for the people had no immunity and persons living close to the margin of subsistence fell victims to the disease. Returning in 1361, the plague caused high mortality among children born since 1348; there were other visitations in 1368 and 1375. Thereafter the plague subsided in the rural areas but remained endemic in London and other towns, where it could become active at any time and could spread along lines of communication into the country. It remained in England for more than 300 years.

The plague caused a sharp and sudden drop in population. The best estimates place the population of England (exclusive of Wales, Scotland, and Ireland) at about 1.1 million in 1086, about 3.7 million in 1348, about 2.2 million in 1377, and not much more than that by 1450. The startling fact about these figures is the amazing drop between 1348 and 1377. It may be that the number of people in overcrowded England already was beginning to decline before the coming of the Black Death. There were floods and famines in the years between 1315 and 1317. Certainly the plague caused a high mortality. In some monasteries the monks all but disappeared (it is thought that half the clergy in England fell victims to the pestilence); there were deserted villages and many unoccupied peasant holdings. After the first visitation widows and widowers remarried quickly and produced as many children as before; but because of the high mortality among young people this population increase was not maintained later in the century.

Agriculture

The Black Death had its most striking effect on the rural economy. The balance between the number of laborers and the amount of land under cultivation and the relations between lord and peasant were quickly altered. High farming in the thirteenth century had been based on a scarcity of land, a large population, and a great demand for food—conditions that had forced the peasants to remain on their holdings and to accept the burdens of serfdom. But in an age of declining population, when the demand for food was less, the profits of agriculture shrank. High farming, which had already been slipping before 1348, came to an end. The immediate result of the Black Death was a scarcity of labor. The work of the manor could not be performed by the villeins who had survived the plague; the lord had to employ casual labor at wages that doubled within a decade. Moreover, a villein, once tied to his holding by economic necessity, could easily run away to another manor where employment would be offered to him with no questions asked.

Landowners complained bitterly of the labor shortage and of the wages they had to pay. In 1351 they obtained the Statute of Laborers, which fixed wages at the rates before the plague, declared that all landless men must accept work when it was offered to them, and prohibited peasants from moving from one manor to another. For a time the statute had some effect, but in the long run it was useless, for wages continued to rise and employers had to pay them. There was also a scarcity of tenants. Few manors were without vacant holdings; hence the yield was less and income from the land declined. Agricultural products no longer fetched high prices. Yet the cost of luxuries and of manufactured goods was rising.

Faced with these difficulties, the lord of a manor might take one of several courses. He might treat his villeins with severity, holding them to their old obligations, denying them concessions, even forcing them to take up land they did not want. But the villeins were very restless under such treatment and were keenly aware of their value in a labor shortage. They saw opportunities to enrich themselves in the new conditions of rural life. Chafing bitterly at the restraints of serfdom, they conspired to refuse their former services. The tempo of resistance quickened until it exploded in the Peasants' Revolt in 1381.

A second course open to the lord was to abandon cultivation of the demesne and to lease it to peasant farmers. This process went on rapidly during the second half of the fourteenth century. The new leaseholders might be freemen or villeins or adventurers from outside the manor. They were the more efficient and more energetic peasants who saw their opportunity to prosper and to rise in the world. Some of them became big farmers with large estates. Within a few generations they sometimes were inheriting the position of the manorial lords and were pushing their way into the gentry. Great differences in wealth soon developed between the prosperous peasant who acquired land and the landless agricultural laborer who worked for a daily wage. Yet the laborer's wage was high in the later Middles Ages.

A third course open to the lord was to turn the demesne into a sheep pasture and sell the wool, which fetched a good price. This was done extensively in the fifteenth and sixteenth centuries. Or the demesne could be made into a deer park, which added to the dignity of the lord and provided his table with venison. In any case his income from his lands declined. He became a landlord living on rents rather than a country gentleman cultivating his own estates.

The Peasants' Revolt

In 1381 the peasants rose in revolt. The immediate cause of the rising was a series of poll taxes imposed by Parliament between 1377 and 1381. These taxes—attempts to shift part of the burden of taxation on the peasantry—were clumsily drafted and harshly collected. They caused great resentment, but it was soon apparent that the rising had other and more fundamental causes. The rebels were not desperate or starving men; they were peasants who held land, who were getting on in the world, and who found the burdens and irritations of villeinage intolerable. What they wanted was an end to villeinage and a low rent for land. But there was also an element of social revolt against the class distinctions of the time. John Ball, a priest who played a large part in the rising, preached radical sermons declaring that all men should be equal, that lordship should be abolished, and that land should be taken away from the aristocracy and upper clergy and distributed among the poor. Ball used a text that became famous:

> When Adam delf, and Eve span,
> Wo was thenne a gentilman?

Thus the desire for material gain combined with radical theories of social equality.

Rising in Essex and Kent, the peasants moved toward London. On their way they burned manor houses, destroyed manorial records which contained

On the left Richard II meets Wat Tyler. The picture shows the slaying of Tyler. On the right Richard addresses the mob. (British Museum, Royal MS 18 E. i, f. 175)

evidence of their villeinage, and murdered unpopular landlords. The government, fearing to make preparations because the peasants had so many friends in the city, seemed helpless. The rebels entered London without opposition. They sacked and burned a number of buildings and killed unpopular officials, including the archbishop of Canterbury. They demanded an interview with the King. With great bravery Richard II granted this request, and two astonishing meetings took place between him and the peasants: one at Mile End to the east of the city, the other at Smithfield just north of the city wall. At Mile End the peasants demanded the abolition of villeinage and an annual rent for land of not more than 4d. an acre. The King promised to grant all they asked, and many of the men from Essex returned homeward, naïvely believing that their new rights would be permanent.

The next day there was a much more dangerous meeting at Smithfield between the King, attended by a few councilors, and the peasants from Kent led by Wat Tyler, a man of vigor and determination who repeated the demands of the previous day but added new ones. There was to be no law save the police regulations of Edward I—this was a protest against the Statute of Laborers. There was to be no lordship save that of the King, no bishopric save one, all other men should be equal, and the lands of lords and clergy should be divided among the peasantry. Richard declared that all should be as the rebels asked. At this point a dispute arose between Tyler and the mayor of London, who was with the King. Tyler was suddenly pulled from his horse and slain. A great cry arose from the peasants, who might well have attacked the King. But with great presence of mind Richard rode forward and shouted that he would be their captain. He led them away from the city and ordered them to disperse. Strangely enough, they obeyed, perhaps believing they had accomplished their purpose. There were risings in other parts of the country. But within a month the peasants were suppressed, the promises of the King were withdrawn, and the revolt was over.

The revolt accomplished nothing. The economic forces of the time continued to operate as before. Landowners were faced with low prices for agricultural products, low rents, rising wages, declining villein services, and vacant tenements. Since the peasants would not accept land on the old terms, a new type of land tenure appeared, known as copyhold, by which the tenant was free from villein services and paid rent for his holdings. The agreement between lord and peasant was inscribed on the manor roll, and the peasant was given a copy. Land held in this way passed from father to son upon the payment of a fee. Thus the new tenant was a freeman holding his land by what was virtually a perpetual lease.

It once was believed that the villeins became freemen largely by commuting their obligations into money payments. This undoubtedly took place in many cases, but villeinage often disappeared in other ways. The rise of tenure by copyhold, as we have seen, replaced villeins with free tenants. Moreover, when a villein family died out it could not be replaced by other villeins. Many villeins ran away to the towns or to other manors, where their villeinage was forgotten. When a lord rented his demesne he could dispense with villein services. Thus villeinage practically disappeared by 1485.

The Towns

The clash of interest between lord and peasant was paralleled to some extent by conflicts in the towns. A shortage of labor existed in industry as well as in agriculture, and workers saw the opportunity to improve their position. Journeymen formed guilds of their own to bargain with employers; artisans founded organizations which, under the guise of religious guilds, were aimed at economic objectives. Conflicts could take various forms. They might be struggles between the masters of the guilds and their employees. Or, since the masters controlled the government of the towns, they might be quarrels between the town corporation and the citizens. In some cases the larger merchants defended their position by opposing both the citizens and the industrial guilds. Ill will might also develop between the larger and the smaller masters. On the whole, the wealthy classes held their own more successfully in the towns than in the country because commerce was less affected than was agriculture by the Black Death. Troublesome guilds and troublesome individuals were suppressed. In fact, this suppression was one reason why many workers in the early fifteenth century left the towns and carried weaving and other industries into the rural districts.

Commerce and Industry

Changes in commerce and industry were as remarkable in the fourteenth century as were the changes in agriculture. When the century opened, England was essentially an exporter of raw materials, of which wool continued to be by far the most important. The English could well understand the legend written on the house of a fifteenth-century wool merchant:

> I thank God and ever shall,
> It is the sheep hath paid for all.

The wool trade prospered when the government interfered least with the natural forces of commercial enterprise, but both the King and the big exporters wanted control. The King was interested, not merely because the wool trade brought revenue in customs and loans, but because it was a diplomatic weapon against foreign countries. The larger exporters wished a system by which they could monopolize the trade. Hence there arose the idea of a staple. A staple was a town, usually on the Continent, which was decreed by the King as a special center of English trade. English exporters took their goods to the staple, where the King secured privileges for them from local rulers and where a continuous trade was carried on with foreign buyers as though a fair were in constant progress. The first compulsory staple, to which exporters were required to take their merchandise, was set up at St.-Omer in Flanders in 1314. At the beginning of the Hundred Years' War Edward III established staples at Antwerp and later at Bruges. The plan pleased the large exporters but was disliked by the growers and the smaller merchants, who thought that the staple was used to hold down the price of wool in England. In 1353 the Commons obtained a statute which set up staples in various English towns, but this arrangement broke down, and in 1363 the staple was established at Calais, where it remained, except for brief intervals, for almost 200 years.

Supervision at Calais was entrusted to a company of twenty-six English merchants, known as the merchants of the staple. They monopolized the export of English wool[7] and laid down rules for its sale in Calais and for the behavior of English and foreign merchants. The company itself did not trade. It established conditions and standards under which the members of the company could buy and sell, each merchant taking his own profit or loss. Though the export of wool remained an essential part of the economy, the volume of trade declined after the establishment of the staple at Calais. Strict control did not foster expansion.

The principal reason for this decline of trade, however, was the great increase in the manufacture of woolen cloth in England during the second half of the fourteenth century. By a remarkable industrial development England became the exporter of a manufactured article as well as of raw wool. It is not easy to explain this fundamental change. Edward III induced some foreign weavers to migrate to England, but their coming can hardly explain so great a development. More vital was the fact that while the King laid heavy duties on the export of wool, he imposed very light ones on exported woolen cloth. Weavers in Flanders complained that they paid as much for raw wool at Calais as other merchants paid for manufactured cloth. Thus the English manufacturer had a great advantage.

The industry in England, moreover, was freer from regulation by guilds and municipalities than was the older weaving industry on the Continent. The decline in agriculture may well have turned peasants as well as landowners to the

---

[7] Italian merchants were permitted to buy wool in England and to export it directly to Italy.

opportunities offered by the manufacture of cloth. And finally, in the last quarter of the fourteenth century, English merchants were aggressive in seeking markets for English cloth in western Germany, the Baltic, the Netherlands, and the Mediterranean countries. By the end of the century the value of wool exports through Calais and the value of exported woolen cloth were about the same. And though in the fifteenth century the English were driven from the Baltic by the Hanseatic League and though they never made much progress in the Mediterranean, where the trade was in the hands of Italians, the market for English cloth in the Netherlands steadily increased, whereas the export of wool continued to decline.

Meanwhile another important economic trend was becoming apparent. The clothing industry had first developed in the towns. York, Norwich, and Coventry became large weaving centers, but in the late fourteenth and early fifteenth centuries the industry began to move into the rural areas. Again the reasons are not entirely clear. There had always been some workers who were outside the organization of the guilds, and as the guilds became more aristocratic many journeymen and small masters believed that they did not derive much benefit from them. These men were ready to move into the country if they could find employment. Conditions in rural areas favored the small wool grower and manufacturer, who found a labor force among peasants ready to turn from agriculture to weaving.

Probably the principal reason for this industrial development was that the process of fulling or cleaning the cloth became mechanized so that it could be done by water power. Fulling mills required swift streams of pure water, which were to be found in hilly districts away from the towns. Important cloth-making areas developed in the southern Cotswolds in Gloucestershire, in western Wiltshire, in the valley of the Stour River in Suffolk and Essex, and in the western part of Yorkshire. As the industry grew the merchant clothier became important. He was a capitalist who bought wool from the grower and distributed it among spinners, weavers, fullers, and so on, until the cloth was finished and ready for market. The merchant clothiers were sometimes wealthy men who gave employment to hundreds of workers. During the fifteenth century the rural industry continued to expand at the expense of both the clothing towns and the export of raw wool through Calais.

THE CHURCH

In the second half of the fourteenth century three famous writers—John Wycliffe the philosopher, Geoffrey Chaucer the poet, and William Langland the moralist—were all highly critical of the clergy. Wycliffe challenged the whole position of the church. Chaucer exposed its weaknesses with courtly satire. Langland's puritanical piety was shocked by the worldliness of the upper clergy. At the same time a strong anticlerical sentiment in Parliament prompted the Commons to insist that the church pay its full share of taxation and to suggest that the lands of the monasteries be confiscated by the Crown. A fable was told about an owl (the church) whose feathers (endowments) had been given to it by other birds (lay patrons), but in time of need the feathers should be returned to their former owners.

Parliament was also critical of appointments, known as provisions, made by

Pilgrims leaving Canterbury. The walls of the city are seen in the background. (British Museum, Royal MS 18 D. ii, f. 148)

the papacy to places in the English church. The church had been endowed, it was held, for the spiritual benefit of Englishmen, and its patronage should not be used for the convenience of the papacy. In 1343 Edward III sent the pope a strong letter of protest. Aliens appointed to benefices in England, he said, did not know their congregations, did not speak the English tongue, and often did not live in England. The result was a decline in devotion.[8] From 1309 to 1377 the popes were not in Rome but in Avignon in southern France.[9] During these years, when most of the popes and cardinals were Frenchmen, it was believed in England that money going to Avignon gave support to the Kings of France, with whom England was at war.

Some famous antipapal statutes were passed at this time. Two Statutes of Provisors (1351, 1390) dealt with Roman appointments to places in the church in England. By the first act the King could expel a person so appointed and fill the vacancy himself. The second imposed heavy penalties upon those who accepted benefices at papal hands or helped others to obtain them; no sentence imposed by Rome in retaliation was to be brought into England. Three Statutes of Praemunire (1353, 1365, and 1393), which forbade appeals from English courts to foreign ones, were obviously aimed at cases concerning provisions. The first act was not directed against all appeals abroad but only against those which attempted to reverse decisions made in the King's courts. The statute of 1393 went much further, declaring that no citations to Rome, no letters of excommunication, and no bulls concerning provisions should be brought into England. The Roman curia was forbidden to deal with cases concerning English benefices. Yet, as we shall see, these statutes remained largely a dead letter, used by the Kings as diplomatic weapons, but not enforced in any systematic way.

Despite the anticlericalism of the fourteenth century, the English were a religious people. Traditional Catholicism retained its hold, and the normal apparatus of the church was taken as a matter of course. It should not be thought that the church was in decay or that abuses were more prevalent than in earlier centuries. If many of the bishops were in the service of the King and were thus absent from their dioceses, this was nothing new. And if the individual monk was criticized, monasticism as a holy way of life was not questioned. The friars, it is true, were unpopular. They suffered in prestige because they were beggars and because their begging had been systematized until it was merely an additional payment in support of the church. The fourteenth-century friar was contrasted unfavorably with St. Francis, who was still a living memory. Yet the number of religious guilds, chantries, and pilgrimages testified to the strength of orthodox Catholicism. The heresies of Wycliffe were repudiated.

Why, then, was there such an eruption of anticlerical sentiment, especially in the years from 1371 to 1384? The answer is not entirely clear. It should be said, in the first place, that denunciations of the pope and the clergy during these years cannot be taken at their face value. Attacks upon the church often sprang from motives that were not disinterested and were not prompted by indignation at abuses or desire for reform. Modern research has tended to vindicate the character of the popes at Avignon and to regard papal provisions as no worse than appointments by the King or by cathedral chapters in England. The truth was that both the King and the pope wished to exploit the English church. The

[8] May McKisack, *The Fourteenth Century 1307–1399*, p. 273.
[9] See pages 171, 235–236.

King wished to obtain clerical offices for his servants so that they would draw their incomes from the church and not from the royal exchequer. The pope tried to increase the income of cardinals and other important churchmen by providing them with cathedral offices—canonries, prebends, and archdeaconries. It was here and not at the parish level, that the pope made appointments, for he seldom interfered with private rights of advowson. Both King and pope wished to tax the English clergy. The King had the advantage, for he could exert pressure upon the English church, and the attitude of the Commons was such that they would not tolerate papal taxation of the clergy. In the quarrels of King and pope the English Parliament sided wholeheartedly with the Crown.

But these quarrels never amounted to an open break. Rivalry remained on the level of bickerings and reproaches. The popes did not wish to lose the friendship of the English Kings, and the Kings found the popes and the cardinals useful in their diplomacy. Hence King and pope often worked together, with compromises and adjustments. When the pope was asked to pay part of the ransom for the French King John, some of the money was raised from the English clergy with the assistance of the King of England. Although both King and pope had rights in the selection of English bishops, it was normally the former who got his way; and in return he was inclined to allow the papacy to make provisions for lesser places. There was a remarkable agreement of this kind between Richard II and the pope in 1398. Hence royal denunciations of papal provisions often were made for effect; but Parliament opposed papal taxation in order to make the clergy's money available for the King and thus lighten the burden on the laity.

There were other reasons for the anticlericalism of the time. The church in the fourteenth century was not animated by great religious zeal. There was no movement of reform, such as the monastic revival in the eleventh and twelfth centuries or the rise of the friars in the thirteenth, to sharpen religious enthusiasm. The spiritual leadership of former ages was lacking. A parish church or a cathedral office was regarded as a piece of property to be sought and exploited rather than as a means of serving God. The churchmen portrayed in Chaucer's *Canterbury Tales* were not people to inspire deep veneration or devout respect. There was, it is true, the poor parson of the town who taught Christ's word but first followed it himself. But Chaucer's description of the prioress, Madame Eglentyne, shows how petty worldliness, snobbery, love of fashion, and attention to dress and refined manners had made their way into the nunneries. Chaucer's monk loves hunting and good cheer, his friar feels the lure of money, his summoner and pardoner are low and despicable. The fervor of an earlier age seems to have departed.

The church was not as wealthy as it appeared. In the twelfth and thirteenth centuries it had been the master of such vast wealth that it could hold its own with kings and magnates, but it had lost heavily as land values sank in the fourteenth century and the income from agriculture declined. The church could not recoup its fortunes, as did the nobility, by going to war. Although the greater monasteries recovered from the shock of the Black Death, many smaller ones and many nunneries were in financial difficulties. If a monastery leased its demesne, it lost control of its own lands; monks living on rents appeared less useful than those who actively managed their property. Monasteries, which were heavily taxed, had other financial burdens. Their hospitality offered to travelers imposed a heavy drain. A visit of Richard II to Bury St. Edmunds was said to have cost the abbey 800 marks. The monastery at Gloucester once entertained the whole Parliament. Richard's Queen left her little dogs to be kept by the monks at Canterbury. Nobles and patrons were constantly asking monasteries to provide for old retainers and servants. Considerable expense was involved when an abbot attended Parliament or when a new abbot had to be chosen.

Many parish priests lived in poverty. John Ball, the priest who was prominent in the Peasants' Revolt, was a poor man who would gladly have seen the upper clergy turned out of their comfortable livings. In the long run this decline in the wealth of the church was certain to bring a decline in influence. Yet the clergy often were regarded with jealousy because of their landed property and because of the wealth of a few great churchmen.

The prestige of the pope as the head of the universal church also declined during this period. Very early in the century a conflict arose between Philip IV of France and Boniface VIII, an arrogant and lofty pope who was so badly defeated in the quarrel that he died of chagrin in 1303. Two years later Philip persuaded the cardinals to elect a French pope, Clement V, who eventually established a new papal capital at Avignon in Provence just on the frontier of France. For almost seventy years the popes remained at Avignon and were closely associated with the French monarchy. This association damaged their position as international leaders, and in 1378 another scandal befell the papacy when a disputed election led one pope to live in Rome and another at Avignon. The Great Schism, as it was called, continued until 1417 and did much harm to the unity of the church.

Meanwhile in England anticlericalism was given a theological justification by a group of writers and thinkers at Oxford. Of these writers the most important, though perhaps not the ablest, was John Wycliffe. A man of intellectual power but of rather narrow sympathies, he dominated thought at Oxford in his own generation. He entered the royal service early in the 1370s and was prominent in politics for some years, especially in 1376, when he acted as the agent of John of Gaunt, who was quarreling with the bishops over taxation.

With a strong bias against ecclesiastical authority, he set forth views which became increasingly heretical. He held that no lordship, lay or clerical, was justified unless the lord was a good man in a state of grace. A sinful person had no right to authority or property, and if a churchman abused his property the secular power might deprive him of it. This doctrine, which was subversive of all ecclesiastical authority, was condemned by the pope in 1377. Wycliffe also developed the concept that the true church was the community of believers and not the hierarchy of ecclesiastical dignitaries. Though not heretical in itself, this view led to assertions by Wycliffe that popes and cardinals could err, that they were not necessary for the government of the church, and that a worldly pope was a heretic who ought to be deposed. Finally, Wycliffe struck at the heart of Catholic orthodoxy by denying the doctrine of transubstantiation, the belief that in the Mass the bread and wine became Christ's body and blood. Wycliffe stressed the Scriptures as the source of truth, sufficient in themselves both as a revelation of Christ and as a guide to conduct.

These views gave strength to John of Gaunt's anticlerical policy; hence he protected Wycliffe for some years, but the English bishops were thoroughly alarmed. Wycliffe's doctrines were condemned in 1381; in the next year the church's machinery for punishing heretics again was strengthened, and a persecution was begun. In 1401 a statute provided that heretics be burned at the stake.

Nevertheless, Wycliffe's views, adopted by a number of persons known as Lollards, continued to exist for many years. A few Lollards were to be found at Oxford and even among the gentry, but most of them were obscure, unlicensed preachers. It is difficult to know whether these preachers were merely critical of the church or whether they represented a serious heretical movement. Wycliffe's connection with them also is uncertain, but he contributed to the movement in two ways. He collected a group of followers at Oxford, though they were largely dispersed by pressure from the church. He also did some of his writing in English and sponsored an English translation of the Latin Vulgate Bible, a project completed by the Lollards in the 1390s. Whether Lollardry continued as a conscious movement into the sixteenth century is doubtful. England remained orthodox during the later Middle Ages, although the prestige of the church was shaken somewhat.

RICHARD II, 1377–1399

Edward III died in 1377 and the throne passed to his grandson, Richard II, a boy of ten and the son of the Black Prince. One of the problems of the time was the tremendous power of a few great magnates who had grown rich in the French war and to whom Edward, as we have seen, had given unusual influence in the government. Chief among the magnates were the young King's uncles. Edward, the Black Prince, and Lionel, Duke of Clarence, were dead, but three other sons of Edward III remained: John of Gaunt, Duke of Lancaster; Edmund Langley, Duke of York; and Thomas of Woodstock, soon to be Duke of Gloucester. Other magnates were the powerful earls of Arundel, Warwick, and Nottingham. The war with France was going badly. If it was to be continued, it would have to be financed by the Commons, who showed themselves reluctant to give money for unsuccessful expeditions. Behind the problem of finance loomed social and economic questions and a restless sense of impending crisis. The Peasants' Revolt took place in 1381.

A council of regency was established to rule during the King's minority. It was composed of various parties, but the most influential councilor was John of Gaunt. He had great prestige and power as the eldest living son of Edward III and as the owner of the estates of the duchy of Lancaster. He was not all powerful, however, for he was opposed by Archbishop Courtenay, that formidable champion of the church, and was regarded with jealousy by Thomas of Woodstock and by the Earl of Arundel. The King's mother, Joan of Kent, was also influential at court until her death in 1385. As the young King grew to manhood his character became increasingly important.

Richard has been a favorite theme of dramatists, who have sometimes portrayed him as half-mad. This is far from the truth, for he was a highly intelligent person, but emotional, unstable, and unpredictable. Many of his policies—such as his desire to make peace with France, his interest in Ireland, and his belief that the Crown should be superior to the magnates—were essentially good policies that have been praised when followed by later Kings. But in Richard's day they were ahead of the times and were certain to cause trouble between the King and the magnates. Richard was a refined and sensitive person who regarded the nobles as crude and brutal. He excluded them from his friendship and built his own circle of friends and favorites. The magnates, however, regarding themselves as the natural advisers of the Crown, resented Richard's favorites and thought that his innovations in manners—such as the use of pocket handkerchiefs —were effeminate. The King's emotional nature led him to act in an impulsive, violent, and high-handed way. Given to melancholy and introspection, he brooded over any injury done him, awaiting the hour for revenge. He could be vindictive in turning upon his foes. He resented his uncles, who sought to dominate the government, and he disliked any interference with his actions, either from the magnates or from Parliament. In a word, he displayed a lack of political judgment and an obstinate determination to have his own way which proved fatal to his success as a ruler.

Richard's reign may be divided into three parts, though the same themes run through them all. As he grew to early manhood, he surrounded himself with a group of courtiers and officials who shared his tastes and opinions. The most important were Michael de la Pole, the son of a famous merchant, who became Chancellor and Earl of Suffolk, and Robert de Vere, Earl of Oxford, whom Richard created a marquis and later a duke. The magnates regarded these promotions with aversion, but Richard kept his friends and quarreled with John of Gaunt and with other nobles. As a result there were two explosions. One took place in 1386, when Parliament, inspired by the magnates, demanded and obtained the removal of Suffolk from the chancellorship, impeached him, and condemned him to prison. A council was set up to advise the King. It included Thomas of Woodstock, Richard's most hated uncle, and Arundel, his most bitter foe. In 1387 Richard restored Suffolk to favor and prepared for civil war. In the next year, however, he agreed to the summons of Parliament, the so-called Merciless Parliament, which produced a second explosion. It struck down most of the King's friends. Suffolk and Oxford were driven into exile, others were imprisoned, and a few were executed. The magnates did not employ the procedure of impeachment: they merely accused or appealed Richard's party of treason before the Lords in Parliament. Hence the leading magnates were known as the Lords Appellant. They included Woodstock, Henry Bolingbroke (the son of John of Gaunt), Arundel, Warwick, and Nottingham. Threatened with deposition, Richard could only give way.

The second portion of the reign extended from 1388 to 1397. It was a relatively quiet time in which Richard appeared to accept the domination of the Lords Appellant. He remained on good terms with John of Gaunt and with Henry Bolingbroke, but there were indications of the King's deep resentment. In 1389 he declared himself of age and announced that he was free to rule as he pleased. He showed his hatred of Arundel by striking him when Arundel insultingly arrived late at the funeral of Richard's beloved Queen, Anne of Bohemia. And he quietly built a party at court, more moderate and less objectionable than the court circle of the first years of the reign. Suddenly in 1397 Richard lashed out at his foes. Woodstock, Arundel, and Warwick were arrested and were appealed in Parliament just as they had appealed the King's friends in 1388. Arundel was executed, Warwick was banished, Woodstock was already dead, having been murdered shortly after his arrest. Archbishop Courtenay also was banished; in the next year both Bolingbroke and Nottingham followed him into exile. Thus Richard took vengeance upon the Lords Appellant: he had struck down the most important men of the kingdom.

His success seems to have gone to his head. In the third period of the reign, from 1397 to 1399, he committed many high-handed actions. He sought to free himself from the control of Parliament. In 1399, at the death of John of Gaunt, Richard seized the estates of the duchy of Lancaster, which should have descended to Gaunt's son, Henry Bolingbroke. It was this act which brought about Richard's downfall. Within a year Bolingbroke invaded England. Finding himself without support, Richard was forced to surrender. Some form of abdication was extorted from him and was presented to Parliament. Bolingbroke then arose and claimed the vacant throne. Since he had a large army behind him, no one objected, and he became King. In a word, one of the magnates, who happened to be the King's first cousin, had seized the throne. Shortly afterward there was a plot by Richard's friends to restore him to power, but the plot failed. At this Richard disappeared, miserably done to death in prison. The distance between the prisons and the graves of princes, as a chronicler remarked, usually was short.

LITERATURE AND THE ARTS

Richard II had made his court a center of artistic achievement; hence it is fitting to conclude an account of his reign with a word about literature and the arts in the second half of the fourteenth century. The most important literary development was the replacing of French by English as the language of the upper classes. Henceforth, except for the Latin of the clergy, English was the spoken tongue of all the people. Writing in English had never entirely disappeared during the centuries since the Norman Conquest. This writing had dealt with religious and devotional themes, with denunciations of sin, and with legends and Bible stories. It had often taken the form of translations from French or Latin works. It continued into the early fourteenth century; but it was crude and parochial in comparison with the many works in Latin or with the brilliant literary achievements of the French in the twelfth and thirteenth centuries.

In the years following 1350, however, writing in English greatly increased, partly in revulsion against all things French. Wycliffe, as we have seen, did some of his writing in English and sponsored an English translation of the Latin Vulgate Bible, a project completed in the 1390s. This was the first translation of the entire Bible into the vernacular. John of Trevisa, a scholar at Oxford, translated books on history and science. A more cheerful work, *The Travels of Sir John Mandeville*, a translation from the French, recounted the fabulous and exotic adventures of a fictitious English knight on a pilgrimage to Jerusalem. Also written in English were the miracle plays. These dramatic representations of episodes from the Scriptures were performed by members of the craft guilds in the principal towns. Of four famous cycles of miracle plays—those of Chester, York, Coventry, and Wakefield—the first three were developed at this time. Moreover, some English poetry appeared in the north of England. Three of these poems, *Pearl, Patience*, and *Purity*, contained the usual medieval moralizing. A fourth, *Sir Gawayne and the Grene Knight*, was an Arthurian romance of great imaginative power. Thus writing in the vernacular was increasing rapidly.

The three most important writers of the time were William Langland, John Gower, and—by far the greatest—Geoffrey Chaucer. Langland, the author of *Piers Plowman*, was a poor cleric in minor orders but a man of genius and of some learning. Much of his poem was a satire upon the weakness of the church. His tone was somber and fervent. He was the simple seeker after truth, bitterly disillusioned with the theologians, the friars, and the wealthy prelates at the top of the hierarchy. The unrhymed alliterative verse of the poem seems archaic, but there are passages of strength and beauty.

John Gower, a very different kind of person, was a cultivated gentleman of wealth and leisure. A stylist interested in the correctness of his verses, he wrote with clarity and ease in French, Latin, and English. His first long poem, in French, was a denunciation of sin. But though a moralist, he had no sympathy with the poor. In a second poem, in Latin, he expressed the horror and detestation aroused in the minds of the upper classes by the Peasants' Revolt. In the same poem he criticized King Richard II with some severity, urging him to emulate his noble father, the Black Prince. Nonetheless, he tells us, the King was kind to him and urged him to compose something more palatable to royalty. It is possible that the King advised him to write in English, which he did in his *Confessio Amantis*, a collection of about a hundred tales intended to entertain as well as to instruct the reader.

Few poets have led such an active life in the world of men and of business as did Geoffrey Chaucer. The son of a wine merchant, he became comptroller of the petty customs at the port of London. Through his position as page in a noble household and as valet and esquire to Edward III, as well as through his marriage to a lady of the court, he was connected with fashionable society. He served as a soldier in two campaigns in France, in one of which he was captured and had to be ransomed; he was sent on embassies to France and Italy. He was a justice of the peace and a member of Parliament. Later he held two important posts: clerk of the King's works (buildings belonging to the Crown) and deputyforester in a royal forest. These activities would have filled the life of an ordinary man. But Chaucer was also a tremendous reader, who came home from a long day's work to spend the evening with his books. Besides all this, he was one of England's greatest poets.

He gave his country what had been lacking since Anglo-Saxon times— creative writing in the vernacular that could bear comparison with anything produced on the Continent. He did so, not by returning to archaic verse forms, but by studying continental models and learning from them. In his early poems— *The Boke of the Duchesse, The Hous of Fame,* and *The Parlement of Foules*— there was too much French influence. But the genius of the poet was maturing. In his *Troilus and Criseyde* he transformed Boccaccio's sensuous tale into a series of subtle character studies. Chaucer's masterpiece was the *Canterbury Tales,* written between 1387 and his death in 1400. This was a collection of stories told by members of a company of pilgrims as they journeyed from London to Canterbury; the storytellers were described in the famous *Prologue,* one of the finest bits of social history in English literature.

Chaucer's greatness lay in his sympathetic understanding of all humanity, in his tolerance, humor, and gentle satire, in his poetic gifts, and his powers of description and of vivid imagery. Above all, he made his characters live for all time, though their speech and his are from a world that is gone.

In architecture two principal developments took place during the fourteenth century. First, the Early English style, which was simple, austere, and restrained, with great reliance upon symbolism,[10] developed into the more elaborate and luxuriant Decorated Gothic. This new style was dominant from about 1275 to

[10] See pages 113–115.

The Tomb of King Edward II, Gloucester Cathedral. An example of ornate decoration. (A. F. Kersting)

The head of the effigy of King Edward II in Gloucester Cathedral. Notice the elaborate carving and the figure of an angel in the foreground. (A. F. Kersting)

about 1350. It was made possible by greater technical skill in engineering and building and in carving in stone and alabaster. A greater interest in the world of nature called for more realism and exactness in copying natural forms.

Columns became stronger and more slender, walls and roofs lighter in weight though more firmly constructed. Hence it was possible to enlarge the windows and to place them in the aisles rather than in the clerestory. Huge windows often were constructed in the east or west end of the church. The tracery in the windows ceased to be geometrical and became flowing, flamboyant, and curvilinear, with freedom for the play of colored glass and intricate design. Artistic sculpture produced fine carvings of leaves, flowers, animals, and human figures and also of small arches, pinnacles, and canopies surrounding a tomb. Sometimes the result was such a riot of exuberant decoration, as in the tomb of Edward II at Gloucester, that the tomb itself was all but hidden. There was a fondness for the ogival arch, which, curving outward and then inward and rising to a point, was sophisticated and decorative, though structurally weak. Brightly colored paint was used freely on tombs, effigies, and pictured walls. The vaulting also became more elaborate. Cross-ribs of stone had always been used to help support the roof, but now other ribs were introduced to cover the vault with complicated designs. Finally, architectural devices were employed to soften the divisions between parts of the cathedral and to make them flow together with greater unity.

Many of the embellishments of the Decorated style were works of art. And yet, over all, something was lost. The restraint of the thirteenth century degenerated into ostentation, into prettyness, and into decoration for its own sake quite apart from any religious purpose.

A second development in architecture was the emergence about the middle of the fourteenth century of the Perpendicular style. This style, which was to dominate English architecture during the rest of the Middle Ages, was almost entirely confined to England. The reasons for its appearance are not wholly clear. It may have resulted from a desire, as in literature, to repudiate French influence. While the Decorated Gothic became ever more ornate in France, English Perpendicular architecture conveyed an impression of somber and pious austerity symbolic of English thought in the later Middle Ages. Moreover, building in the Perpendicular style was comparatively cheap. Parts could be prepared in standardized units before they were set in place. And since contracts were made with master masons at prearranged prices, it was to the mason's interest to build as cheaply as he could within the terms of the contract.

An early example of the Perpendicular style may be found in the choir at Gloucester Cathedral built between 1330 and 1340. Here the impression was created of an open hall, brightly lighted by an enormous east window and by other windows high in the north and south walls. Much of the space below the windows was covered by unadorned rectilinear stone paneling; vertical lines in the columns and in the tracery of the east window conveyed a sense of height and somber grandeur. Slender piers built into the walls carried the eye to the vaulting where cross-ribs formed an intricate pattern.

Distinctive features of the Perpendicular style included splendid fan vaulting as in the Ante-chapel at King's College, Cambridge, or in St. George's Chapel at Windsor; enormous windows as at York Minster; increased height of the columns and of the clerestory in the nave, with the triforium shrinking to a

An early example of the Perpendicular Style of Architecture. The choir and east window of Gloucester Cathedral. (National Monuments Record. Crown Copyright)

The Perpendicular Style of Architecture. The Ante-chapel, looking west, King's College Chapel, Cambridge. (Royal Commission on Historical Monuments, Crown Copyright)

The Perpendicular Style of Architecture. Fan vaulting in the nave, King's College Chapel, Cambridge. (A. F. Kersting)

strip of paneling; and constant emphasis upon vertical lines which carried the eye ever upward.

Art took many other forms in the second half of the fourteenth century. Fine halls, such as Westminster Hall, were constructed with elaborate wooden roofs. English embroidery, used to decorate ceremonial robes, was famous for its designs and bright colors; it was made by nuns and by professional embroiderers in London. In the same way the illumination of manuscripts with elegant initial letters and with drawings of leaves, animals (especially rabbits), and human figures, was brought to a high state of perfection in the monasteries and in the shops of professionals. Sculpture in stone and alabaster, wall paintings in churches and in manor houses, stained glass, effigies in stone or cast in bronze— all indicated that Richard's reign attained a high level of artistic achievement.

9

kingship in the
fifteenth century

At first glance the fifteenth century appears to be a time of confusion, of battles, murders, and sudden deaths, of wars between kites and crows, as Milton put it. But there is at least one central theme that draws the period together and gives it meaning. This is the story of kingship. The power of the Crown was diminished greatly by the revolution in 1399, when Henry of Lancaster seized the throne, and about the middle of the century kingship sank to a very low ebb. There was degeneration in government and civil war among the nobles. Certain aspects of medieval monarchy disappeared forever. But toward the end of the century kingship began to revive and foundations were laid for a strong government. The new monarchy differed from the old, and although its development was only begun in the fifteenth century, it looked toward modern times and is of great interest to the historian.

HENRY IV, 1399–1413

Henry Bolingbroke was the first Lancastrian King. He was the son of John of Gaunt, Duke of Lancaster, and, as we have seen, he brought about the deposition of Richard II in 1399 and secured the Crown as Henry IV. Like his father, Henry was a regal figure, accustomed to riches and magnificence, with the lofty and impressive bearing of a prince. He was an able and energetic man of much independence of character. Although he could be both impulsive and obstinate, the harsh experiences of his youth and exile had taught him caution, determination, and self-restraint. He longed for military glory, and as a youth had shown great skill in jousting, but he was troubled all his life by poor health. Mental strain was apt to prostrate him physically. At one time he looked so pale and white that it was whispered at court that he had contracted leprosy. He was a studious man, passionately fond of music.

Under more happy conditions he might have proved a highly successful sovereign, but he was faced with many difficulties, and as King he was not so fortunate as he had been in the great coup by which he obtained the throne. He never escaped the fact that he was a usurper. Richard II, being childless, had named as his heirs the descendants of his uncle Lionel, Duke of Clarence. These descendants belonged to the family of Mortimer, headed by the Earl of March. They had a better claim to the throne than Henry because the Duke of Clarence was the second son of Edward III whereas John of Gaunt was the third. Hence the circumstances of Henry's accession offered a standing excuse for rebellion against him. Although he was cautious and conciliatory, quite ready to make concessions and to placate opposition, his reign was troubled and his position insecure. Unable to rule effectively, he was constantly harassed on all sides.

His first difficulties arose in Wales, where much sympathy was felt for Richard II and where discontent was widespread among the Welsh, who believed that they were being exploited both by the English government and by the marcher lords. This discontent was fanned into rebellion by Owen Glendower,[1] a Welsh landowner. The revolt, spreading throughout all Wales so that in large areas the English held only a few castles, proved very difficult to extinguish. It became much more dangerous in 1402, when Glendower was joined by discontented factions in England. He had captured Sir Edmund Mortimer, the uncle of the Earl of March, and Mortimer expected that Henry would ransom him. When Henry declined to do so Mortimer joined Glendower.

Meanwhile the King found that he had irritated the Percy family, who held large territories in the north of England. The head of the family was Henry Percy, Earl of Northumberland, whose son Henry, nicknamed Hotspur, has been made famous by Shakespeare. Although members of the Percy family had been among the King's most valuable supporters in the revolt of 1399, they were now rebellious. Perhaps they thought that having helped to make one King they could make another more to their liking. They were irritated because Henry owed them money for their services as wardens of the marches facing Scotland, and because, when Harry Hotspur defeated the Scots at Homildon Hill in 1402, the King demanded that the Scottish prisoners be surrendered to him for ransom. Hotspur, moreover, was Mortimer's brother-in-law. The Percys suddenly joined Glendower. Acting with promptness and vigor, the King gathered an army and defeated and killed Hotspur at the Battle of Shrewsbury in 1403. Glendower, however, continued to receive aid from Northumberland and obtained some assistance from France. His rebellion was over by 1410, and he himself disappeared into the mountains. For many years there was a legend in Wales that he would return. He had caused Henry great anxiety but he had left his own country shattered.

Throughout the time of the Welsh revolt Henry was greatly troubled by France. These difficulties began because Richard II's widow, Isabella, was the daughter of the French King, Charles VI, and the revolution in 1399 had thus involved the deposition of a French princess. Naturally, the French were angry. Henry wished to keep Isabella in England and to arrange a marriage between her and his eldest son, thus continuing the peace with Paris. But the French demanded a return of Isabella's dowry, and in the end Henry sent her back to her family in great state and at great expense.

He hoped that the return of Isabella would end the matter but discovered that he had merely lost a trump card, for relations with France grew worse.

[1] The Welsh name was Owain Glyn Dwr.

Taking the initiative, the French harried the southern coast of England, burning Plymouth in 1403 and landing on the Isle of Wight in the following year. They also sent aid to Glendower and it was even feared that they might attack Calais. Such aggressions disrupted trade in the Channel and annoyed the English merchants. The magnates, wishing for plundering expeditions against France in the old manner, regarded the King's policy as tame, but Henry had no thought of war. He had no money for such a large undertaking and no wish to push the French into greater hostility. Danger from France subsided after 1407, when a bitter feud developed between two branches of the French royal family, the Orleanists and the Burgundians.

Henry had been accustomed to great private riches, but as King he found that his finances were difficult and that demands of all kinds kept him very short of funds. His poverty put him at the mercy of the Commons, who tightened their hold on taxation, criticized his defense of the southern coast, and demanded that he curtail his expenses. They appointed councils to supervise his administration, so that he "was constitutionally unable to control any part of the machinery of government without the consent of a council whose nomination had been imposed upon him."[2] It was in Henry's time that the Commons reached the height of their influence during the Middle Ages. Historians used to speak of a "Lancastrian constitution," as though the Commons were attempting to build a system of parliamentary control. But this myth has been discarded. We have nothing more than a period in which the monarchy was weak and in which the Commons naturally took advantage of that weakness.

Toward the end of the reign Henry also had difficulties with members of the royal family, especially with his son Henry, Prince of Wales. Though still very young, the prince was masterful and ambitious and appeared eager to take his father's place. He quarreled with his father over policy, resisted the King's efforts to inquire into Lollardry at Oxford University, opposed his father's Chancellor, and supported one faction in France while his father favored another. It is possible that the prince's differences with the King may have sprung from an honest clash of policy and that there was a campaign of slander against the younger Henry, but he was certainly pushing and impatient. Twice he came to London with troops as though he meant to take over the government by force.

Another branch of the royal family was becoming prominent. John, Henry, and Thomas Beaufort—the King's half brothers—were the sons of John of Gaunt and Katherine Swynford, who had been Gaunt's mistress before she became his third wife. The sons had been legitimized by Parliament in 1397. John, Earl of Somerset, became chamberlain and captain of Calais but died in 1410. Henry, bishop of Winchester and later a cardinal, was a brilliant though scheming man who was to play a great part in politics for many years. Thomas, Earl of Dorset, who served for a time as Chancellor, was a noble of fine character, willing to occupy high office without using it for his own advantage. The Beauforts appear to have allied with the prince, though the details are obscure.

Henry IV died in 1413, a disillusioned man broken in health and spirit. In his last years he was a neurotic, constantly fearful about his physical condition. His ability and strength of character had been overwhelmed by the many cares of his position as King.

---

[2] George Holmes, *The Later Middle Ages 1272–1485* (Edinburgh: T. Nelson, 1962), p. 245.

HENRY V (1413–1422) AND THE WAR WITH FRANCE

Henry V, the warlike King who renewed the long conflict with France, was highly praised by his contemporaries as the leader who brought glory to English arms after the tame and humiliating inaction of Henry IV. For Shakespeare he was the happy warrior; and Winston Churchill's literary style grows more Churchillian as he recounts the triumphs of Henry's French campaigns. Henry was a tough young soldier with a gift for leadership and a sense of discipline. He had grown up in the Welsh wars against Owen Glendower, and although he was only twenty-five at the time of his accession in 1413, he had

Battle scene, fifteenth century. (British Museum, Cottonian MS Julius E. iv, Art 6, f. 20v.)

Siege of a coastal town, fifteenth century. (British Museum, Royal MS 14 E. iv, f.23)

been commanding troops in the field for more than a decade. He was a formidable person, domineering, severe, highly ambitious, supremely self-confident. He could demolish the arguments of his opponents with a keen and passionate logic. He was very self-righteous, certain that God would give him justice against the wicked Frenchmen who had deprived him of his rights by conquering the areas ceded to England at Bretigny in 1361. He treated the French with great severity, as though he were God's avenging angel. He was quite ready to coerce. But although his character was not attractive, his achievements should not be underestimated. Like Edward III, he won the confidence of the aristocratic classes; all the great English magnates followed him to the French wars. Once more the nation was united in patriotic endeavor against a foreign foe. His victories were spectacular, for he made England the first power in Europe. He would have been King of France if his short life had been a few months longer.

Henry's ambition to conquer France once and for all, to create a dual monarchy in which the same King ruled in London and in Paris, was an impossible one. It gravely miscalculated the temper of France, it placed an unbearable strain on the monarchy in England, and it condemned both countries to war and suffering. And thus, although Henry's hold on his kingdom was stronger than his father's had been, he cannot be said to have ruled effectively or to have added stability and permanence to the kingship. His triumphs were ephemeral. During the long rule of his weak son (Henry VI) the whole structure of English domination in France and English monarchy at home was to come crashing down. In a word, Henry was not a statesman. He was an adventurer ready to undertake projects so risky and so uncertain that they should never have been attempted. His best excuse is that in the later Middle Ages the inducement of immediate gain by aggressive war was more potent than the sober consideration of consequences.

Henry was very fortunate in attacking France just when he did. The revival of French power begun in the 1360s was now at an end, and France was highly vulnerable. Elderly King Charles VI was subject to fits of insanity. Moreover, there was a bitter feud between two factions of the royal family. One was led by John the Fearless, Duke of Burgundy and son of Philip the Bold, who had made Burgundy into a powerful duchy, including large districts in the Netherlands. His strength lay to the east and north of France. The other faction, the Orleanists or Armagnacs, were the followers of the Duke of Orleans, a brother of the King. In 1407 Orleans had been murdered by the Burgundians, and this crime so deepened the feud that the two sides were at daggers' points. Both had appealed to England for help in the later years of Henry IV, who had sympathized with the Orleanists, but Henry V, then Prince of Wales, had pursued his own policy of friendship with the Burgundians. As soon as he became King he put forward a claim to the French throne and to the territories ceded to England at Bretigny. The Orleanists at Paris tried to restrain him by various concessions, but he quickly prepared for war.

In 1415 he landed with a well-equipped army at Harfleur in Normandy, took the town after a month's siege, and began a long march through Normandy to Calais. Not far from Calais he was met by a large French army at Agincourt. The French knights counted upon overwhelming the English line of defense by sheer numbers, but they allowed themselves to be caught on a narrow front with English archers on both flanks, and they were slaughtered like sheep in a terrible and damaging defeat. The battle brought Henry great prestige and large sums of money from ransoms but no great political advantage. Changing his strategy, he invaded Normandy again in 1417 and began a systematic conquest of the principal towns in order to obtain a permanent hold on some portion of France. This action was possible because the Burgundians were attacking Paris, which they captured in 1418 and with it the French King. France now was divided among three parties: the Burgundians in the north, the Orleanists in the area south of the Loire River, and Henry in Normandy.

For a moment it seemed possible that Orleanists and Burgundians might join forces, but in 1419 an Orleanist murdered the Duke of Burgundy, and the rift between the factions widened hopelessly. The new Duke of Burgundy, Philip the Good, quickly allied with Henry, making possible the Treaty of Troyes, which was concluded in 1420. This famous treaty provided that Henry should become the King of France upon the death of Charles VI and that meanwhile he should be regent and should marry Charles's daughter Catherine. Charles's son, the Dauphin, was disinherited. But southern France remained loyal to him and refused to accept the treaty. Determined to crush the Dauphin's party, Henry continued the struggle. He contracted dysentery in a campaign in 1422 and died at thirty-five.

HENRY VI, 1422–1461

The Minority

The sudden removal of the dominant personality of Henry V was one of the decisive facts in the history of the Lancastrian dynasty. Henry left as his heir an infant nine months old. England was faced with a long minority in which there would be a vacuum in the supreme place of monarchy. There was great danger of faction and conflict among councilors and nobles; moreover, England was saddled with the task of governing large areas of France. Most unfortunately the vacuum continued after Henry VI came of age. He proved to be a pious, gentle, well-intentioned recluse, utterly incapable in war and politics. He was always managed by somebody, either his councilors, or his uncles, or his wife; in his last years he was subject to fits of insanity. He lived to see his great inheritance crumble, his finances decay, his crown tossed about among usurpers, his magnates engaged in civil war. His reign represents the nadir of medieval kingship.

For many years the government was dominated by three uncles of the King, ruling with the support and guidance of a council nominated in Parliament. The most respected of these three men was John, Duke of Bedford, a brother of Henry V. He was a man of high character, a skillful soldier and an able administrator. His task was the government of France under the Treaty of Troyes. For some years he maintained English power and was able to extend it, but he was constantly abroad and hence could not play a dominant role in English politics. A second brother of Henry V was Humphrey, Duke of Gloucester. Gloucester was a glamorous kind of man, a great patron of the arts, who occasionally won a following among the merchants and among the people at large. But he was rash and unstable as a politician and pursued policies at variance with those of Bedford and other councilors. He was mistrusted by almost everyone in authority. Henry V had intended that he should have a large share in governing England, and in 1422 Gloucester wanted to be named as regent. The magnates in Parliament refused to give him such power. Instead, he was made protector and defender of the realm but was to hold this title only when Bedford was in France. Parliament, moreover, established a nominated council. Gloucester became "chief of the King's Council," but he was not to act without its consent. Dissatisfied with this arrangement, he proved to be very troublesome.

Gloucester was also constantly at odds with the King's great-uncle, Henry Beaufort, bishop of Winchester. Beaufort was important in politics for an unusually long period—from 1404, when for a time he held the office of Chancellor, to his death in 1447. He was extremely wealthy, drawing riches not only from his bishopric but also from his position as a trustee of the duchy of Lancaster. He loaned large sums of money to the government, saving it at times from financial collapse. His control of money and his astuteness as a politician were more than a match for Gloucester, who was always worsted in their encounters. On more than one occasion Bedford was summoned home to settle their disputes. Beaufort's faction gradually became supreme, dominating the King and the Council. It included John and Edmund, Dukes of Somerset, William de la Pole, Earl of Suffolk, and Queen Margaret of Anjou, whom the King married in 1445. These persons controlled the government during the 1440s.

The War in France, 1422–1453

English success in the Hundred Years' War continued for some years after the death of Henry V. Henry VI succeeded Charles VI as King of France, and most of the northern part of France was ruled from Rouen by the English Duke of Bedford acting as regent. Bedford maintained a close alliance with Duke Philip of Burgundy, whose sister he married, though the alliance was strained by the antics of Humphrey, Duke of Gloucester, who indulged in a personal feud against Burgundy. English possessions were consolidated and extended, Bedford won an important victory at Verneuil in 1424, and many English magnates and lesser captains gained renown in France. This was a time of success and enrichment for the English nobility, at the expense of the people of northern France, who were subjected to many hardships.

The period of English triumph, however, came to an end in 1429 with the

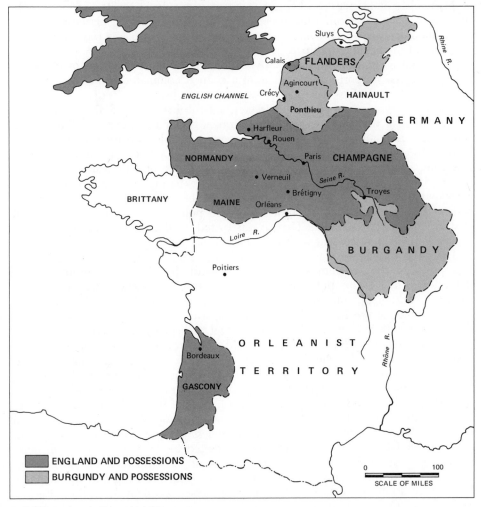

English Possessions in France in 1428

appearance of Joan of Arc. In one of the miraculous stories of history this saintly peasant girl persuaded the Dauphin that victory was within his reach and gave him new hope and determination. She was permitted to accompany the army and to share in planning its strategy. Riding with the vanguard in full armor, accompanied by a body of priests, she inspired the troops with religious and patriotic fervor. The English were besieging the city of Orléans, the door to southern France. They were quickly driven north, and the Dauphin was consecrated as King Charles VII. Although Joan was captured by the Burgundians, sold to the English, and burned at the stake for heresy in 1431 and although the young Henry VI was brought to Paris and crowned in the same year, success in the war was now with the French. The death of Bedford in 1435 was a blow to the English cause. The Burgundian alliance died with him, for the duke saw the way in which events were moving; he thereupon made peace with Charles VII and recognized him as King of France.

The new English commander, Richard, Duke of York, made little headway against the French, who took the initiative both in Normandy and in Gascony in the south. It was felt in England that the war must end. A truce was arranged in 1444, largely through the Earl of Suffolk; in the next year the marriage of Henry with Margaret of Anjou opened the way to peace. But Charles began the war again in 1449 and expelled the English from Gascony in 1453. Calais was now the only French territory in English hands. The dream of conquering France was at an end. The victory of the French was due in part to an improvement in military tactics—French artillery was the answer to the longbow—and to the centralized government established by Charles VII. It was also due to a decline in English morale and efficiency and to degeneration in English monarchy.

The Wars of the Roses, 1455–1471

The degeneration in the English monarchy led to a period of civil wars in England known as the Wars of the Roses. Henry's government weakened steadily under the impact of military defeat, corruption, poverty, and increasing disorder throughout the country. An impossible King who simply retired from the scene and let affairs take their course, he permitted dangerous rivalries and animosities among the nobles. Such a rivalry arose between the Beauforts, who were members of the House of Lancaster, and the Yorkists, another branch of the royal family. There was no great issue at stake between them. The Yorkists were discontented magnates who felt themselves excluded from power in a weak and corrupt court. There was, however, a cause for personal dislike. After Bedford's death in 1435, Richard, Duke of York, had been appointed supreme commander in France but later had been superseded by the Beaufort Dukes of Somerset and had been forced to yield his authority to them. Smarting under this humiliation, he was naturally critical of their failure to stem the tide of French victory. He also became critical of their administration at home.

It was this rivalry that erupted into the Wars of the Roses. The wars occurred at a time when the nobles were no longer expending their energies in France and were apt to cause trouble in England. Moreover, all through the fifteenth century there was uncertainty about the succession to the throne. This uncertainty went back to the revolution in 1399, when the Lancastrians had seized power. Richard of York's claim was a very good one. On his mother's side, through the line of the Mortimers, he was descended from Lionel, Duke of Clarence, the second son of Edward III. His father was the son of Edmund

Langley, Duke of York, Edward's fourth son.[3] Richard was the wealthiest magnate in the kingdom. Hence, when Henry VI proved a failure, there was an alternate claimant about whom discontent could rally.

The period of the Wars of the Roses was a time of trouble and disorder, not one of constant war. The wars were no more than occasional battles between rival magnates, and there were long intervals of peace. The life of the nation was not disrupted as much as one might suppose. However, because the wars came at a time when the government was close to collapse they made that collapse more complete. Their name is misleading, for although the white rose was the emblem of the Yorkists, the red rose was not a badge of the Lancastrians but of the Tudors, who did not come to the throne until 1485.

Widespread hostility arose against the Beauforts in 1450. In that year the Earl of Suffolk, a member of the Beaufort faction, who had arranged the King's marriage by making concessions to France, was impeached in Parliament, exiled, and murdered as he was crossing the Channel. In the same year there was a rising in Kent known as Jack Cade's Rebellion. It differed greatly from the Peasants' Revolt of 1381, for it was joined by small landowners and respectable members of the middle classes. Its aims were political rather than economic. Actually, it was a protest against corrupt officials, against the lack of justice, against supposed treachery in the loss of France, against the interference of great lords in parliamentary elections, and against the Statute of Laborers. The rebels wished to drive the Beaufort faction from power and to introduce reforms. Their sympathy was Yorkist. They entered London and murdered several courtiers but soon were suppressed.

The importance of the revolt lay in its disclosure of deep and widespread dissatisfaction with the government. In two Parliaments between 1450 and 1454 Edmund Beaufort, Duke of Somerset, was hotly denounced by the Yorkists. The two parties were now so hostile that they fought a battle at St. Albans in 1455 in which Somerset was killed. For a time the Lancastrians retained control of the government, but in 1460 the Earl of Warwick invaded England from Calais with a Yorkist army, occupied London, and defeated the Lancastrians at Northampton. Richard now claimed the throne. However, he was killed in a battle at Wakefield in Yorkshire; it was his son Edward who obtained the crown in 1461. The Lancastrians were defeated once more at Towton near York. Margaret and Henry VI fled to Scotland.

THE COLLAPSE OF GOVERNMENT UNDER HENRY VI

The reign of Henry VI was more than a time of weak government and of civil war between factions of the nobles; it was a period in which the whole structure of medieval government collapsed. In the first place, the old system of taxation fell to pieces. Taxes, as they had developed in the thirteenth and fourteenth centuries, consisted of lay subsidies and customs duties voted in Parliament and of clerical subsidies voted in Convocation. These taxes continued through the reign of Henry V. Henry's victories in France stirred the patriotism of Englishmen, and he was able to obtain large grants from the Commons. But Henry VI was not so fortunate, for in his reign the Commons strongly resisted taxation.

[3] See the genealogical table on page 204.

The Tower of London with London Bridge in the background, fifteenth century. Charles, Duke of Orleans, captured at Agincourt, is seen looking out of the window, writing a letter, and in the courtyard sending a letter. (British Museum, *Poems of Charles, Duke of Orleans*, Royal MS 16 F. ii, f. 73)

A number of reasons account for the lack of generosity of the Commons. It was discouraging to vote money for a war that was being lost. During the 1420s the cost of war and government in France had been met to a considerable extent by plunder and by levies on the French, especially in Normandy, but as these sources dried up the full burden was thrown upon the English Exchequer. The Commons suspected that affairs in France were being mishandled and that courtiers obtained the funds intended for military operations. It was known that Cardinal Beaufort and other creditors of the King were enjoying large profits and that Suffolk and the Queen were making gifts in order to build their faction. Hence the government was not in a position to be persuasive in asking the Commons for money.

Even more important was the fact that the fifteenth century was not a period of economic growth but one of recession, arrested development, and declining national income. There was also a shrinkage in agriculture. Many towns declined, but London and Southampton were exceptions, and Bristol remained prosperous; Norwich, Nottingham, Northampton, Leicester, and other places were losing ground. It is probable that the clothing industry, having grown rapidly in the second half of the fourteenth century, tended to level off in the fifteenth and may even have declined. Many districts, therefore, could not maintain the old level of taxation. Poverty was both a cause and a standing excuse for refusal to grant taxes.

Grants of money by convocation also grew less. Part of the difficulty in the time of Wycliffe and John of Gaunt had been that the church was fighting against the principle that its subsidies should parallel the subsidies of the Commons. By the reign of Henry VI the church had won, and its contributions were on a lower scale than those of a century before. The Crown, of course, had other sources of revenue, the most important of which was the duty on exported wool, the steadiest and most reliable support of the dynasty. But it, too, was declining and was burdened with exemptions and assignments that greatly reduced its yield. The Crown owned estates in Wales, Cornwall, Cheshire, Yorkshire, and elsewhere, though they were not managed as well as they should have been. There were also miscellaneous revenues, often coming from old feudal rights. Had there been no war, the monarchy might have paid its way. But, as things stood, the Crown resorted to constant borrowing, anticipation of income, and dubious devices to make ends meet. The government has been described as a pauper government ruling with the consent of its wealthier subjects, who were given economic favors and inducements to lend the King their money. Before the Wars of the Roses the Crown's finances had fallen into a state of pitiful dilapidation.

In the second place, the medieval conception of the community of the realm in which there was close consultation between the King and the ruling classes in Parliament now came to an end. Parliament, especially the Commons, having developed greatly in the time of Edward III, had come to occupy a place of surprising importance in the reigns of Richard II and Henry IV. There is, of course, the suspicion that the Commons frequently were prompted to action by the magnates. Occasionally they were overawed by the King. But there were many occasions when they were intent on their own interests and took a stand on them. Somewhere about 1430 a change came. Parliaments were summoned occasionally, though not as frequently as in the past, but they no longer held a central place in the government. This decline took place partly because no section of the government was functioning properly and later because the issues involved in the Wars of the Roses were concerned almost completely with the relations of King and nobles. Sometimes Parliament was caught up in the struggle and became no more than the agent of the faction in power, but a principal reason why Parliament declined was that the King saw little hope of obtaining funds.

The time of greatest influence of the medieval Parliament in the late fourteenth and early fifteenth centuries was also a time when there was much government by council. During the reigns of Richard II and Henry IV councils were nominated in Parliament to remain with the King and to control his actions. The Good Parliament of 1376, having impeached several royal ministers, set up a council in the vain hope of preventing a recurrence of old evils. A council established in 1386 was an attempt by the magnates to check the actions of Richard II. This development reached its climax in the reign of Henry IV, when in 1404 and again in 1406 continual councils were named in Parliament to supervise the government. Such councils disappeared in the reign of Henry V, but the minority of Henry VI necessitated a council of regency, and this council continued to be important until, in the 1440s, power fell into the hands of the Beaufort faction. The effectiveness of these nominated councils varied greatly as circumstances altered, but there were periods in which they exercised considerable authority. They came to an end in the upheavals of the mid-fifteenth century.

A third way in which government degenerated in the reign of Henry VI was the increasing amount of corruption among officials. Corruption was nothing new, but it was new for great men to regard their offices merely as a means of increasing their own wealth and power and of obtaining places for their friends and retainers. Government was becoming a spoils system in which the interests of the Crown were forgotten. The rivalry of York and Lancaster increased these tendencies. The Earl of Warwick, for example, was captain of Calais in the last years of Henry VI, from whom he held his commission. He refused to surrender his position at the command of the King, made Calais a Yorkist center, and in 1460, using Calais as a base, he invaded England.

Finally, the Crown could not maintain law and order. Apart from the battles of Lancaster and York, there was much disorder and violence throughout the country. This violence could erupt into petty wars between great landed families, as when members of the Percy and the Neville families fought each other at Stamford Bridge in 1453. Many lords not only had retainers who could supply them with troops but maintained small armies of men-at-arms who wore the distinctive badge or livery of their master. This practice was known as livery and maintenance. Maintenance meant more than physical support. It meant that a lord attempted to obtain places in the government for his followers and defended them if they fell afoul of the law. It was not uncommon for a lord to come to court with a body of armed men when one of his dependents was on trial. Such action was disruptive of all impartial justice. Sheriffs and justices of the peace[4] were intimidated, jurors were bribed, and even the itinerant justices from London were defied. The men-at-arms who followed a magnate were often ruffians, terrorizing their localities, committing violent crimes, and engaging

---

[4] Justices of the peace were country gentlemen who at first were appointed to assist the itinerant justices. In time they were commissioned to try many kinds of cases. See pages 215, 326–328.

A walled garden in a town, late fifteenth century. (British Museum, Additional MS 19,720, f. 214)

in brawls and riots that could become small battles. It was impossible for a poor man to obtain justice against the rich and powerful, and it might be dangerous to make the attempt. Thus the machinery of justice was paralyzed by the weakness of the Crown.

EDWARD IV, 1461–1483

The First Decade of the Reign

The first ten years of the reign of Edward IV were largely a continuation of wars and troubles. The Lancastrians were strong in the northern part of the country, and Queen Margaret was seeking aid from her kinsman, Louis XI of France. In 1464 a break occurred between Edward and his strongest supporter, Richard Neville, Earl of Warwick, known as the Kingmaker. For some years they had been so occupied in suppressing Lancastrian centers of opposition that they had not thought much about their relations with each other. Warwick held great authority in military affairs, was given a general supervision of the north, and led a number of expeditions against castles still in Lancastrian hands. The rift began when Edward secretly married Elizabeth Woodville, a beautiful widow whose connections were Lancastrian. Warwick considered the marriage unsuitable and was angered because he had been left in the dark about it while he was negotiating for the King's marriage abroad. He discovered that the Woodvilles, who were very numerous, were obtaining offices and places at court.

There was also a disagreement over foreign policy. France and Burgundy were hostile toward each other and both hoped for alliance with England. Warwick favored an agreement with Louis XI, who had dropped his early support of Queen Margaret. But Edward turned to Burgundy. He wished to protect the market for English cloth in the Netherlands, which was controlled by Burgundy. In 1467 he concluded an alliance with Burgundy and arranged for the marriage of his sister, Margaret, with Duke Charles the Bold. Hostility between Edward and Warwick increased.

In 1470 Warwick changed sides, joined the Lancastrians, and began a revolt. Edward, caught off guard without an army, fled to the Netherlands. For a moment Warwick was master of the kingdom. The poor old mad King, Henry VI, was brought from the Tower (he had been captured by Edward in 1465), and Warwick ruled in his name. Edward struck back quickly. Gathering forces in Burgundy and the Netherlands, he returned to England in 1471, defeated and slew Warwick at the Battle of Barnet, and captured Henry VI, who was put to death in the Tower a few months later. At the Battle of Tewkesbury in western England Edward defeated and captured Queen Margaret and killed her son Edward, the Prince of Wales. The direct line of the Lancastrian dynasty was now extinct; Warwick the Kingmaker was no more. For the remainder of his reign Edward occupied the throne in relative security.

He is described as a tall, fine-looking man, large but well proportioned, with a quick wit, high spirits, and a retentive memory. He was quite unconventional, with little sense of class distinctions, genial and affable to everyone with an easy familiarity. He became interested in people quickly, sometimes too quickly, and his proneness to sexual indulgence led him to connections that were below his dignity. Behind these traits of good fellowship and dissipation, however, were other qualities that made him a successful King. He was a good soldier with a facility for determined action and with the ability to extricate himself from danger. He was an excellent man of business and was keenly interested in economic questions. In fact, he paid such careful attention to the management of his finances that he died a wealthy man. An able administrator who improved the efficiency and honesty of the government, he restored law and order to the best of his ability. It was during his reign that the power of the monarchy began to revive.

The Government of Edward IV

Edward's achievement in creating a strong monarchy and a peaceful countryside was remarkable, and, though he left much to be done by his successors, the Tudor Kings, he laid foundations upon which they were able to build. Certain developments were in his favor. About the middle of the fifteenth century the population began to increase once more, though very slowly. Land resumed its former value and the profits of agriculture revived. Commerce also became more prosperous before Edward's reign was over, thus increasing his revenues from customs duties. The people, moreover, were tired of strife and welcomed a King who would promote law and order.

His principal success was improving the finances of the Crown. This was done largely in two ways, both basically quite simple. The first was the abandonment of the war in France. This in itself transformed the whole financial picture, for it had always been the cost of the war that had drained the King's coffers. Edward escaped from the vicious old circle in which the King had first wrung money from a reluctant House of Commons and then spent it on a war that enriched the nobles but impoverished the Crown and drove the King back to the Commons for further funds. On one occasion Edward did secure from the Commons a grant for a campaign in France. Having done so, he allowed himself to be bought off by the French King, who offered him a pension in return for peace. Edward never fought a battle in France.

The second foundation of his finances was his steady accumulation of land. In the fourteenth century the amount of land in the hands of the King had been relatively small, and estates coming to the Crown through escheats and forfeitures had been freely granted to courtiers and to the nobility. But the Commons became critical of the King's liberality and in 1404 suggested that he examine the grants made over the last forty years with a view toward resuming the lands that had been given away. To resume lands once they had been granted was an impossible procedure that would have alienated half the aristocracy; yet the Commons continued to insist that it be attempted.

Edward acquired lands in various ways. Some old Crown lands came into his possession when he became King. To these he added three of the largest inheritances of the later Middle Ages. One was the property of the Yorkists, which came to him from his father. Another was the duchy of Lancaster. This had been added to the lands of the Crown, though it was administered separately, when Henry Bolingbroke, Duke of Lancaster, became Henry IV. The duchy was seized by Edward after his defeat of the Lancastrians. A third group of estates, the very extensive property of Warwick the Kingmaker, was confiscated following Warwick's revolt. There were additional confiscations from the King's brother George, Duke of Clarence, and from other rebel lords.

Edward's policy toward the lands of the Crown was very different from that of earlier rulers. The lands were now retained, increased at every opportunity, and managed with great care. A magnate, as we know, employed a number of officials who were experts in the management of landed property, but the King's lands had not been handled in this way. The Exchequer was a department of receipt, not of supervision. It audited the money that was brought to it but did not go into the country to see that the King was obtaining all that was his due. Edward, however, placed his lands in the custody of professionals who applied the careful scrutiny given to private estates. These officials were usually members of the royal household; the money they collected was brought to the chamber, which again became a financial department as it had been some centuries before; and the Exchequer was by-passed. The vast estates of the Crown, scattered throughout the country, now represented the King's capital, his endowment, his accumulated wealth, which brought him substantial revenues and made him independent of Parliament.

There were other sources of income: customs duties, the pension from France, fines levied in the courts, occasional grants from Parliament and from convocation, forced loans and benevolences. A forced loan was what the name implies: a loan to the King made under some pressure. It was normally repaid. A benevolence, however, was a gift. The King became skillful in extracting benevolences from wealthy men. A foreigner wrote:

> I have frequently seen our neighbors here who were summoned before the king, and when they went they looked as if they were going to the gallows; when they returned they were joyful, saying that they had spoken to the king and he had spoken to them so benignly that they did not regret the money they had paid. From what I have heard, the king adopted this method: when anyone

Little Sodbury, Gloucestershire. A fifteenth-century manor house. (Copyright Country Life)

went before him he gave him a welcome as if he had known him always; after some time he asked him what he could pay of his free will towards this expedition; if the man offered something proper, he had his notary ready, who took down the name and the amount; if the king thought otherwise, he told him "such a one who is poorer than you, has paid so much; you, who are richer, can easily pay more," and thus by fair words he brought him up to the mark.[5]

Edward lived in some state and magnificence, for he rightly believed that a show of wealth and power added to the authority of the Crown.

Edward made his government more effective by centralizing power in the hands of his trusted councilors and household officials. His council was no nominated council. It was composed of men who were royal servants, selected by the King because they were industrious, efficient, loyal, and reasonably honest. They could be dismissed at any time. The King's agents, they drew their authority from him and were completely at his command. Edward was free from conciliar as well as from parliamentary control.

Edward attempted to make his authority felt in all parts of the realm. He showed an interest in local affairs and selected household officials who had had a share in local government and who maintained their former connections with local officers. On two occasions Edward accompanied his itinerant justices as they made their circuits. To enforce the law in disturbed districts he gave judicial authority to magnates and local councils. There was a small council to administer the royal principality in Wales, and to this council Edward issued a commission to supervise the four English counties of Shropshire, Hereford, Worcester, and Gloucester. He entrusted judicial power in the north to his brother Richard, Duke of Gloucester, and to the Earl of Northumberland. Later, when he became King, Richard continued this experiment by establishing a Council in the North Parts.[6]

RICHARD III, 1483–1485

That Edward had only made a beginning in the suppression of lawlessness is evident from the short and bloody reign of his brother Richard, Duke of Gloucester, who became Richard III. This King was not the complete villain that legend and Shakespeare have made him. An intense, reserved, and silent man, Richard had a serious, even puritanical, side to his character. He had always been completely loyal to his brother, though he might well have sided with Warwick the Kingmaker, who was his tutor. He had taken a prominent part in the Wars of the Roses and had commanded the right wing of Edward's army at the crucial Battle of Barnet. Edward had trusted him with great authority in the north of England. He fully intended to continue and improve the government established by his brother. At Edward's death, however, he was suddenly faced with a choice either of seizing power (which he could justly claim as his) or of allowing it to slip away. He not only seized it but did so with great violence; and having started upon the course of removing his adversaries by killing them he could not turn back. He created fear and terror. In 1485, in one of the rebellions against him he lost his life.

[5] Quoted in Cora Louise Scofield, *Life and Reign of Edward IV* (New York: McKay, 1923), II, p. 105.
[6] George Holmes, *The Later Middle Ages 1272–1485,* Chap. XII.

Royaulte me Lie

The true Portraiture of Richard Plantagenest, of England and of France King Lord of Ireland the third King Richard

Richard III. (From Sir George Buck, *The History of the Life and Reigne of Richard the Third*, London, 1647. Department of Special Collections, Walter Library, University of Minnesota)

The heir to the throne at the death of Edward IV in 1483 was his young son, a boy of twelve, who figures in English history as Edward V although he never ruled. His mother, the Queen, was Elizabeth Woodville, whose relatives filled many of the highest offices, sharing power with a handful of other intimate associates of the late King. The Woodvilles naturally wished to remain in control. Apparently they planned to have Edward crowned at once, to establish a regency with the Queen Mother as regent, and to rule through a council composed of their faction. Richard was in the northern part of the kingdom where his power lay. He was the strongest man in the country, and if he could win a few allies among the older nobility he could easily drive the Woodvilles from court. He discovered, moreover, that his brother had made a will naming him as protector of the King and kingdom. Thus the issue was clearly drawn between the two factions. Richard came down from the north and struck quickly. Acting with Henry Stafford, Duke of Buckingham, he seized the King and his escort of Woodvilles as they were on their way to London for the coronation. This violent deed caused consternation among the Woodvilles at court. Some of them fled abroad; the Queen entered sanctuary at Westminster. Coming to London, Richard easily persuaded the Council to accept him as protector.

Here the matter might have ended. Richard might well have remained protector for some years and the Woodvilles might have sunk into obscurity. But the atmosphere was filled with whisperings of plots and intrigues, and Richard became suspicious of certain councilors, especially William Lord Hastings, the former chamberlain of Edward IV. At a meeting of the Council Richard suddenly accused Hastings of treason and hurried him off to immediate execution. This fatal crime led directly to Richard's seizure of the throne. Summoning Parliament, Richard declared that the marriage of Edward IV and Elizabeth Woodville had been illegal, that Edward V was therefore illegitimate, and that he, Richard, was the rightful successor to his brother. No one was powerful enough to object, and Richard assumed the crown at once. All these events took place within three months of the death of Edward IV. A number of Woodvilles were now executed, and Edward V and his younger brother, a boy of ten, were imprisoned in the Tower. Shortly thereafter they disappeared. There is no evidence of their fate and nothing can be proved. One can only say that they disappeared while Richard was on the throne and that he never answered the rumors that they had been murdered.

Richard's reign was very short. A revolt in 1483 by the Duke of Buckingham in favor of Henry Tudor, a Lancastrian, was suppressed, but a second attempt by Henry in 1485 succeeded and Richard was slain at the Battle of Bosworth Field. The Yorkist attempt to reconstruct the government on a basis of law and order failed in Richard's reign. Yet the Yorkist monarchy, at least under Edward IV, foreshadowed and helped make possible the success of the Tudors.

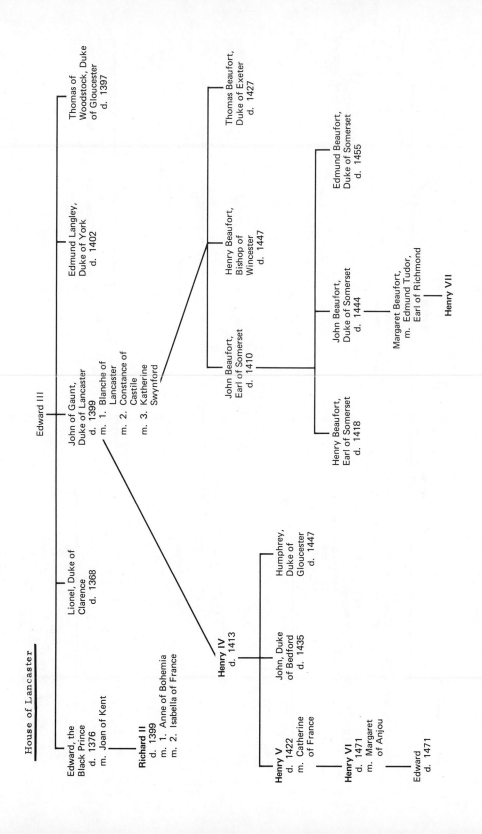

Edward III

Edward, the
Black Prince
d. 1376
m. Joan of Kent

Richard II
d. 1399
m. 1. Anne of Bohemia
m. 2. Isabella of France

Lionel, Duke of
Clarence
d. 1368

John of Gaunt,
Duke of Lancaster
d. 1399
m. 1. Blanche of
Lancaster
m. 2. Constance of
Castile
m. 3. Katherine
Swynford

Edmund Langley,
Duke of York
d. 1402

Thomas of
Woodstock, Duke
of Gloucester
d. 1397

Henry Beaufort,
Bishop of
Wincester
d. 1447

Thomas Beaufort,
Duke of Exeter
d. 1427

John Beaufort,
Earl of Somerset
d. 1410

Henry Beaufort,
Earl of Somerset
d. 1418

John Beaufort,
Duke of Somerset
d. 1444

Edmund Beaufort,
Duke of Somerset
d. 1455

Margaret Beaufort,
m. Edmund Tudor,
Earl of Richmond

Henry VII

Henry IV
d. 1413

Henry V
d. 1422
m. Catherine
of France

John, Duke
of Bedford
d. 1435

Humphrey,
Duke of
Gloucester
d. 1447

Henry VI
d. 1471
m. Margaret
of Anjou

Edward
d. 1471

House of York

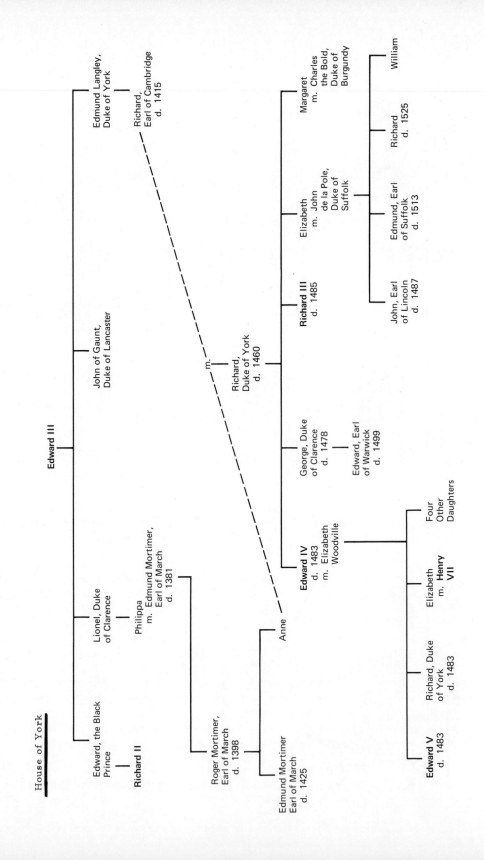

10

henry vii:
the strengthening
of kingship

During the century in which England was ruled by the Tudor sovereigns (1485–1603) the country passed from late medieval to early modern times. In the course of this wonderful century England felt the healthful impulse of strong and able rulers, the machinery of government was modernized and a new concept of the state emerged, intellectual life was stirred by the Italian Renaissance, the English Church became independent of Rome, nationalism intensified, wealth increased and economic life assumed new forms, and a beginning was made in the great epic of English expansion overseas. In a word, England emerged from the doubts and stagnation of the fifteenth century into an era of action, success, and supreme self-confidence. These developments, however, unfolded slowly. Henry VII, the first of the Tudors, was a conservative man, essentially medieval in his point of view. He did not make many innovations. Rather, he brought new strength and vigor to the institutions of government already in existence and made them forceful and effective.

The key to his reign is to be found in the power and dignity he gave to kingship. The Crown, as we know, had been very strong in England from the time of the Norman Conquest to the end of the thirteenth century, and to this fact can be traced the rapid development of government and law. During the fourteenth and fifteenth centuries, however, the strength of the Crown declined, reaching its lowest level in the disastrous reign of Henry VI and in the chaos of the Wars of the Roses. Then, under Edward IV, monarchy began to revive. Much of the achievement of Henry VII, as we shall see, was a continuation and development of policies that Edward had begun. The task of reconstruction was enormous; Edward had made only a beginning. His work was damaged and partly undone by the violence of Richard III.

Henry VII, coming to the throne in 1485, faced many of the old problems. His position on the throne was most insecure. The nobles were far too powerful. Their private armies remained intact despite statutes against livery and maintenance. The system of indentures or contracts by which they recruited their military retainers expanded to other forms of service until a great noble was surrounded by a large household of clerks, lawyers, land agents, and other servants. The collapse of local government continued. Great lords interfered with the course of justice, crime and lawlessness were commonplace, brawls and riots swelled into small battles. Henry VII made kingship powerful once more and restored conditions under which ordinary life could be carried on in peace and safety. He was most fortunate in that he came to the throne when the worst was over. The nobles, who had been slaughtering each other in the Wars of the Roses, were less powerful than they had been; the plague was receding and population was once again on the increase; the people longed for peace and tranquillity; the recession of the fifteenth century in trade and farming was beginning to lift.

HENRY VII, 1485–1509

Henry was only twenty-eight when he came to the throne, but he had already shown himself to be a good soldier and a man of action who could strike hard blows at his enemies. "His dealing in times of perils and dangers," wrote a contemporary, "was cold and sober with great hardiness." Yet he was far removed from the medieval warrior, such as Richard I or Edward III. He was essentially a man of peace and business, practical, shrewd, calculating, and successful. He saw that England required an end to the civil wars once and for all. For this reason, after he was secure upon the throne, his policy was one of mercy in order to heal the wounds of the past. But his was the cold-blooded mercy of a man whose emotions were under firm control. To self-restraint he added high intelligence, inflexible resolution, and hard common sense. He was most industrious. He labored long at the tasks of government, with an infinite capacity for detail, as is apparent from his careful scrutiny of expenditure. He was "incomparably the best business man to sit upon the English throne, . . . the most uniformly successful of English kings, and a millionaire into the bargain."[1] He was determined to be a King. "He was of an high mind, and loved his own will and his own way, as one that revered himself and would reign indeed . . . not admitting any near or full approach either to his power or to his secrets. He was a prince sad [grave], serious, and full of thoughts and secret observations; and full of notes and memorials of his own hand, especially touching persons; as whom to employ, whom to reward, whom to inquire of, whom to beware of; keeping as it were a journal of his thoughts."[2] This hard, industrious, self-contained, and prudent statesman was the founder of the Tudor character.

SECURING THE DYNASTY

Henry's Claim to the Throne

Henry won the Battle of Bosworth by hard fighting and slew his enemy, Richard III. Richard's naked corpse was carelessly flung over a horse's back and taken to an obscure grave. The crown, which Richard had worn into battle, was found under a hawthorn bush and placed on Henry's head while his soldiers shouted their acclamation. But Henry was only a King by conquest. During the

---

[1] S. T. Bindoff, *Tudor England* (Harmondsworth, Middlesex: Penguin Books, 1950), pp. 65–66.
[2] A contemporary description quoted in J. R. Tanner, *Tudor Constitutional Documents* (Cambridge: Cambridge University Press, 1930), p. 3.

Henry VII, by an unknown Flemish artist. (National Portrait Gallery, London)

quarter century ending in 1485 the Crown had been lost and won by violence on several occasions; and to the people of the time Bosworth must have appeared nothing more than another turn of fortune in the endless Wars of the Roses. No one could know that Henry was to prove one of the wisest and most successful of English rulers and was to establish a dynasty which would last more than a hundred years.

His claim to the throne by inheritance was weak indeed. Through his father he had no claim at all. His grandfather, Owen Tudor, was a gentleman from

Wales, clerk of the wardrobe in the household of Catherine of France, the widow of Henry V. But Owen Tudor, with the audacity characteristic of his family, commended himself so successfully to Catherine that she accepted him as her husband. When this presumptuous marriage became known, Owen Tudor was summoned before the Council, was twice imprisoned and twice escaped. Later he fought on the side of the Lancastrians, was captured by the Yorkists, and executed. He had two sons by Catherine, Edmund and Jasper Tudor, who were thus half brothers to Henry VI. Henry treated them kindly, and in return for their loyal support he created Edmund Earl of Richmond and Jasper Earl of Pembroke. This good fortune, however, gave Edmund, the father of Henry VII, no royal claim to pass on to his son. What claim Henry possessed came through his mother, Margaret Beaufort, daughter of John Beaufort, Duke of Somerset, a descendant of John of Gaunt. This descent came through John of Gaunt's third wife, Katherine Swynford. She had been Gaunt's mistress before she became his wife, and her children had been born out of wedlock. Parliament legitimized them in 1397, but in 1407 Henry IV declared them debarred from the succession.[3]

These were the obvious weaknesses in Henry's title, quite apart from the fact that in 1485 members of the Yorkist royal family were still alive. Indeed, Henry had been important solely because his claim was the best the Lancastrians could put forward and because he had long been the hope of that party. His youth had been spent in adversity. Born in Wales in 1457, he was a posthumous child, his father, Edmund, having died at the age of twenty-six before his son's birth; his mother at the time was but fourteen. Jasper Tudor, Henry's uncle, gave protection to mother and child. In 1471, when the Yorkists appeared triumphant, Jasper took Henry to Brittany, where he lived for many years, an exile and sometimes a semiprisoner. Later Henry went to Paris and was befriended by the French King, Charles VIII. In Paris Lancastrians and Yorkist dissentients gathered around him. But he might well have been assassinated by Richard's agents (fear of whom doubtless prompted him to make a bid for the Crown). Or he might well have remained an exile for life had not Richard's bloody rule in England produced the far-flung conspiracy which brought Henry to the throne.

The Elimination of Rivals

Henry was well aware that though he had won the throne with comparative ease he could keep it only with difficulty. Yorkist claimants were still alive, their followers embittered by the confiscation of lands and by the loss of office which followed Bosworth; Ireland was Yorkist in sympathy; and Henry had enemies on the Continent eager to support Yorkist plots. For twelve years he had to face dangerous conspiracies. During those years he showed his capacity for kingship merely by remaining King.

His first task was to eliminate his Yorkist rivals. Richard III, very fortunately, was childless and had smoothed Henry's way by the crime of which he was probably guilty—the murder in the Tower of the two young sons of Edward IV. But Edward left five daughters and five nephews. The daughters were disposed of easily. The eldest, Elizabeth, became Henry's Queen. Their marriage had formed part of the agreement between Lancastrian and Yorkist plotters before Henry's invasion of England, and Henry fully intended to carry it through. But he did not marry Elizabeth at once: undue haste would imply that he owed his

---

[3] See genealogical tables on pages 203 and 223.

crown to his wife. He waited until his first Parliament, which, having been carefully coached, requested him to marry the Princess Elizabeth. This he graciously consented to do. The marriage took place in January 1486; in September of the same year Elizabeth gave birth to a son who received the Welsh name of Arthur. Thus the houses of York and Lancaster were united. The fact that Henry's son combined the claims of both greatly strengthened his dynasty. Three of the Queen's sisters were married to men whom Henry believed he could trust, though one of them, Lord William Courtenay, later fell under suspicion and was imprisoned in the Tower. The fifth sister became a nun.

The nephews of Edward IV remained to be dealt with. One was Edward, Earl of Warwick, a lad of ten who in 1485 was placed in the Tower, where he remained—the innocent center of Yorkist plots—until he was executed in 1499. Another was a restless young noble, John de la Pole, Earl of Lincoln, whom Richard III had designated as his heir. It was inevitable that Lincoln would plot against Henry. He was probably implicated in a minor conspiracy in 1486 and certainly in a major one in the following year.

The second of these conspiracies originated in the mind of a priest of Yorkist sympathies who taught one of his pupils—a gentle boy named Lambert Simnel—to impersonate Edward, the young Earl of Warwick, the prisoner in the Tower. It was easy for the Yorkists to spread false rumors that Warwick had escaped, which persisted even though Henry brought the Earl from the Tower and paraded him through the streets of London. Lincoln and other Yorkists took up Simnel's cause. They knew he was an impostor and would doubtless have pushed him aside once he had served their turn. They took him to Ireland, where he was well received. Lincoln raised an army of 6000 Irish troops and obtained 2000 German mercenaries from the Netherlands, sent by that archenemy of the Tudors, Margaret, the Dowager Duchess of Burgundy and sister of Edward IV. Lincoln and Simnel landed in Lancashire in 1487. But the English, sick of civil war, showed them little sympathy, and at the grimly contested Battle of Stoke in Yorkshire Henry defeated the rebels. Lincoln was slain and Simnel captured. Pretending to hold the revolt in derision, Henry made Simnel a scullion in the royal kitchen and had him wait at table on other Yorkist prisoners. The rising, however, was no jest; it was dangerous while it lasted.

Some years later Henry was threatened by another pretender, Perkin Warbeck, who proved to be far more troublesome than Lambert Simnel. Warbeck, a native of Flanders, was first heard of in Ireland in 1491. He pretended to be Richard, son of Edward IV, the younger of the two little princes murdered in the Tower. Actually, he was the servant of a Breton merchant. A youth of charm and intelligence, he played his impudent part with some skill, but he lacked the toughness of character needed to achieve success. He was dangerous because he was supported by the Yorkists, by Henry's enemies abroad, and by some of the King's officials at home. From Ireland, where he was backed by the Earls of Desmond and Kildare, Warbeck went to France and was well received by Charles VIII, then at war with Henry. But the treaty which ended the war in 1492 contained a clause expelling Warbeck from France, and he made his way to the Netherlands. There he was supported by the Dowager Duchess of Burgundy, Emperor Maximilian, and Philip, Maximilian's son. Yorkists came to him from England. There were arrests and executions at home when Henry discovered a cell of the conspiracy in his own household.

In 1495 Warbeck led an expedition against England, but his men were driven back when they landed in Kent (Warbeck himself remained prudently on his ship), and the little fleet sailed on to Ireland and then to Scotland. King James IV of Scotland received him kindly and arranged a marriage for him with the daughter of a Scottish earl. Warbeck stayed in Scotland until 1497, but he accomplished nothing beyond a few border raids. The savagery of these raids, it was said, rather sickened his unwarlike nature. In 1497, when an uprising occurred in Cornwall, Warbeck thought his opportunity had come. He sailed from Scotland, only to arrive in Cornwall after the revolt had been crushed; an invasion of England from Scotland was turned back; no aid came from the Continent, where Henry's diplomacy had robbed Warbeck of support. The impostor was captured, placed at first in easy custody, then imprisoned in the Tower, and executed in 1499. At this time the Earl of Warwick also was executed. The circumstances are obscure, but it was obviously thought that conspiracies were apt to be woven around him.

Thus ended two of Edward's nephews: Warwick and John de la Pole, Earl of Lincoln, who had fallen in the Simnel rising. Lincoln had three younger brothers. Two of them, after further intrigues, died in the Tower. The third entered the French army and was killed at the Battle of Pavia in Italy in 1525. So ended the De la Poles, and the danger of Yorkist revolt died with them.

Foreign Relations

It might be supposed that Henry, faced with grave problems at home, would have little share in the diplomacy and wars of Europe. Yet as long as Yorkist pretenders received aid from abroad, Henry was forced in his own defense to take part in the complicated affairs of the Continent. He was eager, moreover, to gain recognition for his dynasty and to form an alliance with a strong continental power. Such an alliance would aid him against his enemies, would increase his prestige, and would benefit English merchants trading abroad.

The dominant powers of western Europe were France and Spain, both now emerging as strong national states. The history of France in the Middle Ages had been the story of the slow and painful extension of royal control over the country as a whole. By alliances, wars, and marriages, the kings had added new territories to the royal domain. The process was almost complete by 1500. That crafty monarch, Louis XI (1461–1483), had acquired parts of Burgundy, Anjou, and Provence. He had strengthened the monarchy by increasing its authority throughout the kingdom, improving its army and its finances, and fostering industry and commerce.

Spain also was becoming a great power. In the eighth century the country had been invaded by Moors from North Africa, who had rudely pushed the frontiers of Christendom northward. But small Christian kingdoms had continued to exist in the mountainous areas of the Pyrenees. Slowly in the later Middle Ages these kingdoms inched southward and at the same time united with each other. This twofold process of conquest and unification was completed during the last quarter of the fifteenth century. Granada, the last Moorish stronghold in the south, was conquered in 1492; the famous marriage in 1469 of Ferdinand of Aragon (1479–1516) and Isabella of Castile (1474–1504) enabled these rulers to govern Spain as a unit and to lay the foundations for Spanish greatness in the sixteenth century. Isabella was all that a Queen should be—pious, benevolent, and wise; Ferdinand was famous for his shrewdness and cunning as well as for his success. Other powers played only subordinate roles. Feudal disintegration had broken the Holy Roman Empire into a mass of small principalities, ecclesiastical states, and free cities; Maximilian, King of the Romans and later Emperor (1493–1519), was a slightly ridiculous figure who turned from one project to another and failed in most of them. The pope had lost his ancient authority. France and Spain, the strong powers, were also bitter rivals in western Europe.

Henry VII was bound to France by ties of gratitude, for he had lived in Paris before his invasion of England and had been aided in that enterprise by the French King, Charles VIII (1483–1498), but circumstances induced him to look toward Spain as an ally. He found that hostility to France was very strong in England and that English possession of Calais was a constant irritant to the French. Charles VIII, moreover, was attempting to absorb the independent duchy of Brittany, an attempt England opposed. When Francis II, Duke of Brittany, died in 1488, leaving only a daughter, Anne, twelve years old, Charles claimed her wardship. When this was refused he sent an army against her. In the same year a band of volunteers sailed from England to the defense of Brittany, but they were slain almost to a man, and feeling against France ran high in England.

Thus drawn into hostility toward France, Henry in 1489 concluded the Treaty of Medina del Campo with Spain. In some respects Henry obtained what he wanted. His son Arthur was to be married to Catherine, daughter of Ferdinand and Isabella, when the children should reach marriageable age. The dowry was to be large; Catherine was to be sent to England with jewels and other furnishings befitting a princess. Neither Spain nor England was to harbor the rebels of the other. English merchants were to enjoy valuable concessions in Spain. But other clauses in the treaty indicated that Henry was the weaker party and was paying a high price for the alliance. The treaty bound him to go to war with France. Spain desired two French provinces in the Pyrenees—Roussillon and Cerdagne. If Spain secured them, she could, by the terms of the treaty, withdraw from the war, but Henry could withdraw only if France ceded Normandy and Aquitaine to him, which was quite impossible. Henry, in other words, had to fight until Spain got what she wanted.

Meanwhile the situation in France altered rapidly in 1491 and 1492. Although Henry was sending aid to Brittany, the French were winning the war, but suddenly in 1491 the young duchess agreed to marry her adversary and to become the Queen of France. The absorption of Brittany into France could not be prevented. Yet Henry was pledged to war. In 1492, having obtained funds from Parliament, he crossed to France with an army. Again the situation altered. Charles VIII cherished ambitions to conquer Italy, where he had a claim to Milan and where internal rivalries invited French aggression, but he could not begin an Italian campaign while Spain threatened his southern frontier and while an English army remained in northern France. He therefore made a hasty peace with Spain, ceding to her the coveted provinces in the Pyrenees. With Henry he concluded the Treaty of Étaples, in which he excluded the pretender Perkin Warbeck from France and paid Henry a handsome sum of money to return to England. Henry accepted these terms most gladly. He was indeed fortunate. He had fulfilled the terms of his agreement with Spain, and he could now make an honorable peace with France. He had obtained funds from Parliament to begin the war, and he now obtained funds from France to end it. If his sudden return to England after a very short campaign appeared disappointingly tame to his soldiers, no one could doubt the wisdom of his action.

In 1502 a heavy blow fell on him. His son Arthur had married Catherine in

1501, but within six months the young prince was dead and Catherine was a widow. The patient diplomacy of many years appeared to be shattered. Beginning once more, Henry concluded an agreement with Spain in 1503 by which Catherine should remain in England (along with her dowry) and should in due course marry Henry's second son, the future Henry VIII. This marriage, which did not take place until 1509, was to alter the course of English history. In 1503 Henry VII became a widower. There had been affection and fidelity between him and his Queen, but he began at once to seek another wife. Secure upon his throne, he apparently wished to play a greater role on the Continent, and he regarded his unmarried state as a diplomatic advantage not to be lost. He alarmed the Spaniards by suggesting that he marry Catherine, his son's widow. He considered other ladies, among them Joanna, another daughter of Ferdinand and Isabella. This pathetic princess had lost her reason, a minor point Henry was ready to ignore. These unsavory negotiations came to nothing. The King, now old and toothless, remained unwed.

Scotland and Ireland

Scotland and Ireland were connected with the King's foreign policy. Since the Battle of Bannockburn in 1314 the Scots had been independent; yet they were convinced that England would attempt to conquer them if that were ever possible. They therefore continued their alliance with France, though it brought them little good; there was constant raiding and fighting along the Border; James IV, as we have seen, invaded England in support of Perkin Warbeck. But Henry was too wise to be swayed by a blind hatred of the Scots. In 1499 he proposed a marriage between his daughter Margaret and James IV. The marriage, which took place in 1503, produced only a temporary improvement in Anglo-Scottish relations.

By the beginning of the Tudor period the English Pale in Ireland had shrunk to a small coastal area around Dublin and Drogheda. Its nobility and gentry were largely of English or Norman descent. Some of them maintained English traditions, but others were as Irish as the Irish themselves. Beyond the Pale the country was controlled by tribal chieftains, either pure Irish like the O'Neills in Ulster or Norman-Irish like the Burkes of Connaught. These chieftains ignored the English government altogether.

The Pale was ruled by a Lord Deputy appointed in England, usually from the Anglo-Irish nobility. The Earl of Kildare, Lord Deputy at the beginning of Henry's reign, was of this class. Like most of the nobility in the Pale, he was Yorkist in sympathy and supported Lambert Simnel. Henry thereupon removed him and in 1494 sent over an Englishman, Sir Edward Poynings, as deputy. Poynings summoned a Parliament at Drogheda and secured a number of famous acts. One of them declared that henceforth no Parliament could meet in Ireland until its proposed agenda had been approved by the English King and Council. Another act provided that all English statutes existing in 1494 should apply in Ireland and England alike. Other acts attempted to strengthen the government of the Pale and to make it more efficient. These attempts to model the government of Ireland upon that of England were only partially successful, for after the departure of Poynings the new administration broke down. Satisfied that danger from Yorkist plots was over, Henry reinstated Kildare as a man who could at least keep order. Henry obtained peace in Ireland during his reign but left the larger problems of Ireland to his successors.

THE STRENGTHENING OF KINGSHIP

Bad government and the decay of law and order in the fifteenth century had been due to the weakness of the Kings and not to any fundamental defect in the constitution or in the people. A ruler, such as Henry VII, determined to restore the ancient strength of the monarchy, could find the basic materials with which to build. Yet it is easier to observe and to admire the results of his reign than to understand how they were achieved. Henry certainly did not grow strong through military force. He had no standing army; the armed guard with which he surrounded himself was more for display than for any military purpose. It might protect him from assassination but it could not repress disorder on a large scale. Henry relied upon the ancient duty of every male citizen to serve in the militia when need arose. The leaders of the militia were the nobility and the more prominent gentry; Henry's problem was to preserve the military value of the militia, led as it was by nobles, without allowing the nobles' power to get out of hand. His method was to punish unlawful recruiting of retainers, but in emergencies to issue commissions of array to nobles and gentry whom he could trust. A commission of array was a command to raise troops to meet a specific danger and to lead them to the area where trouble threatened. Conspiracies and invasions were met in this way. Henry could thus raise small armies to fend off local dangers without permitting the nobility to retain armed men on a permanent basis.

In essence Henry relied upon the good will of the people. The middle classes —gentry, merchants, and craftsmen, those below the peerage but above the peasantry—were ready and eager to support a King who could repress disorder and preserve the peace. It was the gentry who counted most and whom Henry knew he must cultivate. The class of merchants, whose support was also sought by the King, was still small and its importance can easily be exaggerated. It would be an error to think that Henry wooed any class or classes above all others. His method was to exalt the monarchy as something to be reverenced by all. Kingship had been cheapened in various ways, and it was his policy to place it on a new plane of eminence. His court was brilliant, and he spent large sums on ceremonial occasions to increase the splendor and magnificence of monarchy. He built a beautiful chapel in Westminster Abbey and made it the home of the Order of the Bath.

The King, the symbol of the state, was exalted far above the greatest of his subjects. This could be done more easily because the older nobility had been weakened by the wars and disasters of the fifteenth century. Nobles too closely related to the royal family gradually were liquidated. Henry did not oppose the nobles as such. He opposed lawless and troublesome persons of any class. His followers were ambitious to enter the ranks of the peerage, and he gradually created a class of new nobles who owed their promotion to him and who were well aware that they must be loyal. They were despised by the older nobility; hence their protection lay in the exalted position of an all-powerful King, the sole fountain of honor, who could ennoble anyone he pleased.

The same principle may be seen in Henry's Council. Historians have stressed the fact that many of his councilors were from the gentry or were men of humbler origin.[4] This is both true and important, but the Council also contained nobles

---

[4] G. R. Elton, *England under the Tudors* (London: Methuen, 1955), pp. 17, 44.

and bishops as it had done in the past. The point is that Henry selected his councilors as he pleased and expected loyal service from them all. He made Tudor kingship strong in itself without dependence on anyone. He created loyalty by removing rivals to the throne who might be magnets for treason, he ruled with moderation and drove no class to despair, and he added to his powers. He exalted the royal prerogative, that reservoir of undefined rights and powers inherent in the Crown by which the King could act in emergencies and rule for the public good. His policies were national and he expected support from all classes. If the middle classes derived the greatest benefit from his rule they did so because they stood to gain the most from the kind of government he provided.

Law and Order

Henry knew that law and order must be restored and maintained and that for this purpose the government must be strengthened at all levels. The central core of administration consisted of the King and his Council. The Council was large and somewhat nebulous—about 150 men took the councilor's oath during his reign. They were the King's civil servants, his bureaucrats and administrators. Henry did a good deal of governing in informal interviews, and he could summon any councilors whom he wished to consult. There was some differentiation of function. We hear of a legal council to advise the King in matters of law. There was a court of requests, to which poor men might bring petitions, and also the Council in the Star Chamber. An inner circle of some twenty to thirty councilors were close to the King and were the most important in government. They were his principal administrators, controlling and supervising the details of government throughout the entire kingdom. Selected because of their ability, loyalty, and efficiency, they rose in the King's service by merit and hard work. Henry gave them great power because they were wholly dependent on him and because they represented his will in action. We begin to understand why the Tudor period is sometimes called the age of government by council.

Henry's Council did a large amount of judicial work. For this purpose it met in the Star Chamber, a room in the council building decorated with stars in the ceiling. The Star Chamber in Henry's reign was not separate from the rest of the Council. It was merely the place where councilors met to transact judicial business, work chiefly connected with the problem of law and order. Any man could bring complaints to the King and Council; persons who had suffered wrong through local disturbances were encouraged to petition the Council for redress. Cases could also be begun with an accusation by the King's attorney general. The Council heard complaints of riot, which meant almost any breach of the peace; of brawls and bloody affrays; of illegal assemblies, which were the normal precursors of violence; of bribery and intimidation of jurors and sheriffs; and of corruption and misconduct by local officials. In a word, the Council heard complaints of those offenses which had undermined local justice during the fifteenth century. The Council also heard cases of the poor against the rich—cases which were likely to go wrong in the local courts because of the "great might" of one party and the "great unmight" of the other.

The Council in the Star Chamber developed a swift and effective procedure. It did not use the jury, which had failed so often to do justice in the local courts. It put men under oath and forced them to answer questions that might incriminate them. Procedure consisted of an accusation, an answer by the accused, the collection of evidence, and the hearing of witnesses. This material was written down, and on the basis of these written documents the councilors reached their decision. Punishments consisted of fines, confiscation of property, and imprisonment. The Council in the Star Chamber did not deal with treason and never inflicted the death penalty. It did not have a law of its own. It enforced the common law and made it work. The councilors in the Star Chamber were powerful because they represented the King. They could not be intimidated, bribed, or defied, and they could act impartially in dealing with powerful offenders.

An act of Parliament in 1487 dealt with the Star Chamber. This act has puzzled historians, but too much has been made of it. It was no more than an attempt to increase the efficiency of the Council's judicial work by providing that the holders of certain offices should serve as judges in the Star Chamber and should hear petitions of certain kinds. The Star Chamber did its work well. It was a boon to the people in the early Tudor period and remained a popular and busy court for more than a century.

Henry also strengthened local government. The Council in the Star Chamber might curb the overmighty subject, but numbers of lesser offenders disturbed the peace and had to be dealt with locally. The wars of the fifteenth century had created a spirit of violence. Men were quick to challenge their adversaries, to draw their daggers, and to come to blows. Henry enacted a number of laws dealing with local law and order. It became illegal to hunt in disguise, for this practice led to murders and assaults. Women could not be taken from their homes without their own consent. No man could have retainers who were tenants of the King. Other laws struck at the perjury and corruption so frequent among fifteenth-century jurors. A sheriff might be punished for empaneling a juror who was obviously unfit for his task. In general, the duties of local officials were defined more clearly. In 1504 the laws concerning livery and maintenance were drawn into a code.

It was enforcement, not new law, that was required. Henry did not restore the sheriff to his ancient importance, for the sheriff had acquired a bad name in the fifteenth century. Instead, Henry made increasing use of the justices of the peace. These justices of the peace were country gentlemen who, as we have seen, had been employed in the later Middle Ages to assist the itinerant justices and to try minor cases in the local courts. The judicial work of the justices of the peace had expanded in the fifteenth century and continued to increase under the Tudors until the justices could deal with a large number of offenses. Henry watched the justices carefully. He took a personal interest in their selection, appointed them for one year at a time, and usually included some of his councilors in the commission. Justices were quickly reproved for any neglect of duty. To be dropped from the commission of the peace was a sharp setback for a country gentleman, the more so because Henry regarded service in the capacity of justice as a kind of apprenticeship to be completed successfully before a man could hope for higher office. The justices, on the whole, did their work well; the problem of local law and order was being solved.

Finance

Henry further strengthened his government by improving his finances. He has been called a miser, but this is unfair, for he did not hesitate to spend money on things he deemed essential. A vital aspect of kingship was involved. Many English Kings in the later Middle Ages had been weak because they had grown poor. They had allowed the resources of the Crown to be drained away by war and by other causes which had enriched a few great nobles but had impoverished the Crown. It was the Yorkist Edward IV who first reversed this trend and set about the necessary task of making the Crown independent by making it wealthy. In the sixteenth century money was more essential than ever because an increasing number of services had to be paid for in cash; a poverty-stricken King was in a hopeless position. For Henry, therefore, the accumulation of wealth was absolutely necessary if he wished to be strong and independent. Doubtless he enjoyed the process, but he had no choice. In 1485 he was poor, owing money to his backers in France and Brittany.

The kingship, once gained, had many financial resources. Henry exploited them to the full, husbanded his wealth, and left a handsome treasure to his son. The revenues of the Crown were derived from what may be called ordinary and extraordinary sources. Ordinary sources—Crown lands, the customs, feudal rights, the profits of justice—provided income which belonged to the King by law. They were his by legal right. Extraordinary sources consisted of grants by Parliament and of such things as loans and benevolences. It was the theory of the time that under normal conditions the King should live of his own, that is, from his ordinary revenues. Only some great crisis or emergency, such as a war, entitled him to seek funds in extraordinary ways. Henry accepted this theory. He did not wish to incur the unpopularity that was certain to arise if he demanded large grants of money from Parliament. He asked Parliament for taxes in time of war, but as his financial position improved he held fewer Parliaments, preferring to enlarge and cultivate his ordinary sources of income. Other Tudors followed the same policy. Throughout the Tudor period, although it was a time of inflation, the Crown did not demand large money grants from Parliament. The people were obtaining better government than they were paying for in taxation. It was a situation that could not endure forever, as the unfortunate Stuart Kings found to their cost.

Of the four principal sources of ordinary revenue, Crown lands were the most important in Henry's reign. Like Edward IV, he systematically increased the landed property of the Crown. He naturally took possession of the estates belonging to the Yorkist Kings; and his first Parliament allowed him to resume all the lands held by the Lancastrian King Henry VI in 1455. He was thus the inheritor of both Yorkist and Lancastrian estates. By dating the commencement of his reign on the day before the Battle of Bosworth, he was able to confiscate the lands of all who had fought against him in that battle; later conspiracies and revolts were followed by further confiscations. The lands acquired in these ways were managed with business skill and produced an ever-increasing revenue.

The customs duties formed a second source of income. The amounts that could legally be collected had hardened into a fixed schedule, known as tonnage and poundage, which Parliament gave to the King for life. Henry could increase his income slightly by placing a higher valuation on goods which were taxed at rates proportionate to their estimated value. But there were only two ways in which the customs could be made to produce substantially larger sums: to increase the volume of foreign trade, in which Henry had some success; or to reduce smuggling, in which he made little progress. Indeed, the customs never produced the revenue they should have done at this time.

Income also came from the profits of justice. Some money was obtained from the sale of writs and from miscellaneous fees charged by the courts. A far more lucrative source of income consisted of fines and amercements levied by the courts as punishment for many kinds of offenses. The Star Chamber, as we have seen, inflicted heavy fines. Revolts and conspiracies also were punished by fines; fines, large and small, were imposed for all sorts of misdemeanors. From the great noble who paid heavily for keeping too many retainers to the petty merchant who smuggled a few woolen cloths out of the kingdom, fines formed the normal punishment. Many fines were so heavy that the offender could pay them only over a number of years. Toward the end of the reign, when Henry felt secure, he was not above accepting money in return for promises of royal favor to litigants in the courts.

Henry further increased his revenues through a systematic enforcement of his feudal rights. In the confusion of the fifteenth century these rights had often been lost to the Crown, but Henry revived them and made them highly valuable. In 1504 he obtained money from Parliament in lieu of a feudal aid for knighting Arthur, his eldest son, though Arthur was dead; and for marrying Margaret, his eldest daughter, though her marriage had taken place some time before. Such feudal incidents as wardship, relief, and escheat, if carefully exacted, could bring in large sums of money. It was to the interest of tenants to conceal the occurrence of these incidents where they could; hence Henry set up commissions of inquiry to establish his claims. These commissions were deeply resented. There was, indeed, a pitiless quality about Henry's financial policy, and his agents, such as the notorious Richard Empson and Edmund Dudley, were cordially hated. Henry became impatient with the antiquated methods of the Exchequer. Reviving a practice of medieval Kings, he formed an office of finance in his household. Income was diverted from the Exchequer to the Chamber; and his treasurers of the Chamber, Sir Thomas Lovell and later Sir John Heron, became the principal financial officers of the Crown. Henry himself checked and initialed most of their accounts.

COMMERCIAL POLICY

As good a businessman as Henry VII was certain to have great interest in foreign commerce. To enrich the merchants was to enrich himself through increased customs duties and at the same time to win the gratitude of the business classes. Henry's efforts to increase England's foreign commerce, however, must not be erected into a system. He did what he could as circumstances permitted, but he was always the opportunist; he discovered that there were many things he could not do and he often was forced to subordinate trade to the necessities of foreign policy. The great bulk of English exports still consisted of wool and woolen cloth. The export of raw wool, however, had declined until, in 1485, the amount sent abroad was only about 10,000 sacks a year, scarcely a third of the figure for the 1340s. This trade, as we know, was monopolized by the merchants of the staple, who took their wool to Calais. Though still important in Henry's reign, the staplers were losing ground. They found it difficult to fulfill their obligation of supporting the English garrison in Calais, and when Calais was lost to the French in 1557 the staplers ceased to exist.

On the other hand, woolen cloth was exported in very large quantities (perhaps 50,000 cloths a year) at the beginning of the Tudor period. Until about 1450 this cloth had been shipped from a number of English ports to various towns along the Atlantic seaboard of Europe. English merchants had pushed aggressively into the Baltic Sea and into western Germany. But they met the bitter hostility of the Hanseatic League of North German trading towns. There followed almost a century of strife, a war in 1468, and a treaty in 1474 by which the English were largely excluded from the Baltic. Meanwhile merchants trading to Gascony and Spain found their business ruined by the Hundred Years' War and other disturbances. Exporters of English cloth therefore tended to crowd into the Netherlands, the one great market that remained, and to confine their trade to Antwerp, where they had acquired privileges during the fifteenth century.

The merchants of London, who had opened the trade to Antwerp, resisted the intrusion of merchants from other parts of the kingdom. The Londoners drew together, at first in a loose organization of traders who belonged to various London companies. In 1486 they became the Fellowship of the Merchant Adventurers of London and set out to monopolize the cloth trade to Antwerp by making the entrance fees to their society so high that merchants from the rest of the country could not afford to enter. A bitter wrangle ensued. In 1497 an act of Parliament forced a settlement on the London Adventurers by which they were compelled to reduce their entrance fees and to admit other English merchants into their society. This may appear as a sharp defeat but actually the arrangement of 1497 implied the right of the Londoners to control admission to the trade to Antwerp and to impose conditions on those who wished to engage in it. Gradually the Merchant Adventurers developed into a powerful corporation, intimately connected with the state and enjoying the monopoly of a highly desirable trade.

They benefited greatly from a treaty made by Henry with the Netherlands in 1496. For some years he had been at odds with the government in Flanders over its support of Perkin Warbeck. In 1493 he had forbidden all trade between England and the Netherlands and had moved the staple of the Merchant Adventurers to Calais. This had been a heavy blow to merchants on both sides of the Channel, but the Flemings had felt it more keenly than the English. In 1496 they yielded, withdrew their support from Perkin Warbeck, and agreed to a commercial treaty known as the *Intercursus Magnus*. This treaty accepted the principle of freedom of trade between England and the Netherlands, established a schedule of customs duties, granted mutual fishing rights, and proposed joint action against pirates. The Merchant Adventurers returned to Antwerp under favorable conditions.

Ten years later in 1506 Henry employed a devious trick to obtain even better terms. While voyaging to Spain, Archduke Philip, ruler of the Netherlands, was shipwrecked on the English coast in heavy weather. Henry brought him to London and treated him with great courtesy, but before he left England Philip was induced to sign a new commercial treaty. The name given this treaty in the Netherlands, the *Intercursus Malus*, is an indication of its one-sided character. English merchants, paying only the customs established in 1496, were to be free from all local tolls in Flanders and were permitted to engage in retail trade throughout the country. This placed them in a more favorable position than that of native Flemish merchants. It is no wonder that as soon as he was out of England Philip repudiated the treaty; Henry consented to its modification in 1507.

The Merchant Adventurers prospered in Henry's reign. Their prosperity increased the demand for wool in England and encouraged the expansion of the cloth-making industry, with important economic results.[5] In addition to the staplers and the Merchant Adventurers there were unincorporated English merchants trading to Spain, southern France, and Ireland. Although their principal objective was political alliance, Henry's treaties with Spain improved conditions for English merchants doing business with that country. The trade with southern France, consisting of imports of wine from Bordeaux and of woad (used in dyeing) from Toulouse, was conducted largely in French ships. Henry attempted to transfer this commerce to English shipping and offered bounties for ships built in England. He secured a Navigation Act declaring that the trade to southern France must be carried on in English bottoms. He found, however, that the act could not be enforced. The volume of English shipping was too small to meet the needs of foreign trade, and a large portion of English commerce still had to be carried in vessels belonging to foreigners.

Two important branches of English trade were almost entirely in foreign hands. The Hanseatic League of German trading towns along the coasts of the Baltic Sea and in northwestern Germany was perhaps the most influential mercantile organization of the Middle Ages. It was a power in international affairs and controlled large quantities of shipping. The merchants of the Hansa were in a strong position in England. Although they had a large establishment in London known as the Steelyard, where merchants from dozens of Baltic towns displayed and sold their wares and bought in exchange large quantities of wool and woolen cloth, they excluded English merchants from the Baltic and monopolized trade to that important area. Henry would gladly have curtailed the excessive privileges of the Hanseatic League in England. He punished the Hansa merchants severely when he caught them abusing their rights, he obtained their permission for Englishmen to trade to Iceland, and he made a treaty with the King of Denmark in 1490 by which he hoped to obtain access to the Baltic for English shipping, though the Hansa was able to prevent the fulfillment of the treaty. Yet Henry was cautious in dealing with the Hanseatic League. Its sea power could be dangerous to him, especially after important Yorkists fled to Germany in 1501. The Hansa merchants flourished in England during his reign, and it was only in the middle of the century that their privileges were drastically curtailed.

Henry was more successful in dealing with the Venetians. At the beginning of the reign the Venetians monopolized trade between England and the Mediterranean. Once every year a fleet of their galleys came through the Strait of Gibraltar and made its way to Antwerp, trading at various points along the route. Stopping at Southampton and at London the Venetians did a large volume of business. Despite the Venetian monopoly some English merchants were beginning to find their way into the Mediterranean, trading in Crete and in Chios, where choice wines could be obtained. Irritated by this traffic, the Venetians, in control in Crete, imposed new and larger customs upon English goods. In retaliation Henry increased the customs to be paid by the Venetians trading in England. He also concluded a treaty with Florence that made Pisa, its seaport, the sole distributing center for English wool in the Mediterranean. The staple at Pisa was short-lived, but it served its turn. The Venetians gave way, and English voyages to Crete and Chios continued.

[5] See pages 261–262.

THE EXPANSION OF EUROPE OVERSEAS

The success of Henry's commercial policy lessened his interest in the wonderful voyages of oceanic discovery that were taking place during his reign. These voyages, one of the epics of history, are a mark of cleavage between medieval and modern times. They sprang directly from Europe's interest in Oriental trade. For centuries the merchants of Italy had traded in the Near East, bringing to Europe the spices, dyes, and fragrant woods, the jewels, silks, tapestries, and rugs of Asia. But European merchants could go no farther than the eastern shores of the Mediterranean, for there they met the hostile world of Arabs and Turks through which they could not penetrate. For a moment in the late thirteenth and early fourteenth centuries the road to the Far East appeared to be opening. This was due to the sudden extension of Mongol conquest into northern China and throughout all central Asia. The first conquests of the Mongols or Tartars under Ghengis Khan, who died in 1227, were conducted with ferocity, but contact with the gentler civilization of China moderated the temper of the later Khans. They displayed a condescending curiosity about Europe, and for a time they welcomed European travelers within their dominions.

The most famous of these travelers was the Venetian Marco Polo, who journeyed to Peking in 1271 and spent twenty years at the court of Kublai Khan. For three years he was the governor of a Chinese city. Kublai Khan sent him on embassies to many parts of Asia, where it was his duty to observe and report on what he saw. Trained to remember details, he acquired an astonishing knowledge of Asia. A lucky chance enabled him to return to Europe, and in 1298 he wrote an account of his adventures, the best travel book of all time. It contained, of course, a good deal of fiction, but modern research has shown that there was also a great residue of solid truth. What Marco Polo saw he described accurately and well, he visited places so remote that they were not seen again by Europeans until the nineteenth century, and he may be pardoned if he spoke of the wealth of China in extravagant terms. He dwelt upon the vast quantities of gold, silver, and precious stones belonging to the Khan; he told of China's populous cities and great rivers, her temples, palaces, and gardens, her peaceful, industrious, and skillful artisans. In comparison with China, he implied, Europe was sunk in abject poverty. Here was a story to stir the imagination. The European might be poor and his commerce primitive, but he was an excellent fighter, and the wealthy and peaceful cities of Cathay offered alluring prospects if only they could be reached. The dream soon faded. In the fourteenth century the Mongol empire fell into chaos, the Turks advanced toward Europe, and Mohammedanism of a fanatical type spread over the Middle East.

The path to the Orient was closed, and if Europeans were to reach the East they must do so by sea. The first European nation to accomplish this feat was Portugal. Led by the vision of Prince Henry the Navigator (1394–1460), Portuguese seamen began to work their way south along the western coast of Africa. In 1487 Bartholomew Diaz reached the Cape of Good Hope; ten years later Vasco da Gama sailed around the Cape and up the eastern coast of Africa until he found pilots who took him to India. The Portuguese quickly established themselves along the western coast of India with their capital at Goa, broke Muslim sea power in the Indian Ocean, seized Ormuz at the mouth of the Persian Gulf, and pushed farther east to the Malay Archipelago—Java, Sumatra, and the smaller islands where the best spices were found. The trade from Asia to Europe was diverted from the old routes and began to flow around Africa. Lisbon grew rich while the Italian cities declined, and Portugal enjoyed a brief period of wealth and greatness.

Meanwhile another voyage was made, not so difficult as that of Vasco da Gama, yet bulking larger in men's minds because it was a great act of faith. Christopher Columbus believed he could reach Cathay by sailing west. In 1492 he made his famous voyage across the unknown Atlantic, discovered the West Indies, and sent to the naked Indians a formal letter from Ferdinand and Isabella addressed to the Great Khan. The Spanish soon established themselves in the larger islands. From Cuba as a base Cortez conquered Mexico between 1519 and 1522; and in 1535 Pizarro sailed from the western side of the Isthmus of Panama to the conquest of Peru. This era of oceanic discoverey reached its climax when Magellan, a Portuguese sailing in the service of Spain, passed through the strait that bears his name and crossed the Pacific in a heroic voyage lasting a hundred days. In the Philippines he was killed by the natives, but one of his ships continued through the Malay Archipelago, rounded Africa, and completed the circumnavigation of the world. Its commander was given a coat of arms containing a globe with the sublime legend, *Primus Circumdedisti Me.* Magellan's voyage was perhaps the greatest achievement of mankind upon the ocean.

The Voyages of John Cabot

Englishmen were slow to take part in this movement of world expansion. During the fifteenth century they had consumed their blood and treasure in futile wars in France and in even more futile wars at home. They had been cut off from the Mediterranean, that center of scientific geography and navigation, and the old trades with France and the Netherlands had been so profitable as to discourage adventure in new directions. But a memorable voyage from England in Henry's reign resulted in the discovery of North America. The English city most interested in the Atlantic was Bristol. Bristol seamen, voyaging to Iceland for whales, must have heard of the Norse discoveries in America about the year 1000. Bristol merchants traded to Portugal and knew of the Portuguese voyages along the African coast. There were some voyages from Bristol into the Atlantic during the fifteenth century, though the evidence is vague, and there was a tradition that an unknown island existed in the Atlantic somewhere to the west of Ireland.

About 1490 an Italian seaman named John Cabot came to Bristol. Not much is known about him, for his name seldom appears in the records of the time and in later years his son, Sebastian Cabot, claimed credit for the voyages made by his father. Yet John Cabot may have been a greater man than Columbus, with a more lucid mind and a sounder concept of geography. A native of Genoa, he became a citizen of Venice and traded in Egypt as a Venetian merchant. He read Marco Polo and was a student of geography, skilled in maps and globes as well as in practical seamanship. Like Columbus he hoped to reach China by sailing across the Atlantic. He came to Bristol after he had been refused support in Spain and Portugal. But why did he select Bristol? He may have known of Bristol's interest in the Atlantic. He wished to make his westward voyage in northern latitudes because the distance from Europe to Asia would be shorter than if he sailed farther to the south. He believed that the coast of Asia sloped in a southwesterly direction, so that it was closest to Europe in the north. Cabot's arrival in Bristol brought together a number of maritime traditions: the Norse discoveries, the voyages of Bristol seamen, the science of Italy, Italian trade in the Near East, and the Portuguese voyages along West Africa.

Henry VII showed an interest in the project, giving Cabot a monopoly of trade with any lands he might discover and naming Bristol as the only port through which that trade should pass. But he gave Cabot no ships. Bristol supplied him with only one, a tiny craft, the *Mathew*, and a crew of eighteen men. In this little vessel Cabot crossed the Atlantic in the summer of 1497, reaching the coast of America at an unknown point, more probably on the mainland than on Newfoundland. The season was advanced, however, and he returned to England without attempting to sail south along the American coast. He believed that he had reached Asia and announced that he had done so. Great excitement prevailed in both London and Bristol. Cabot secured five ships for a second voyage in 1498. But here his story fades into anticlimax, for he never returned from his second voyage. Perhaps some of his ships came back. If they did, they brought no lading from the Orient, and the merchants who had financed the voyage must have lost both their money and their enthusiasm. Henceforth for three quarters of a century there were few English voyages to the mainland of North America. If the old trades brought profit and the new ones loss, a man of business need not puzzle long as to where to put his money. Gradually it became evident that Cabot had not reached Asia but had discovered a new continent which barred the way to the East. At that time it could be exploited in only one way. Cabot had noticed the great quantities of fish in the waters south of Newfoundland, and fishermen of many nations soon came to this area. Such is the honorable story of John Cabot. It was he who discovered North America at the close of the fifteenth century, and he had done so in an English ship.

Henry VII died in 1509 and was buried in the beautiful chapel he had added to Westminster Abbey. He was not a spectacular or showy King, but he established his dynasty on a firm foundation, he gave England peace, prosperity, and good government, he left rich funds in his treasury, and he won the loyalty though perhaps not the love of his people.

House of Tudor

Owen Tudor
d. 1461
m. Catherine of France,
Widow of Henry V

Jasper Tudor,
Earl of Pembroke
d. 1495

Edmund Tudor,
Earl of Richmond
d. 1456
m. Margaret Beaufort

Henry VII
d. 1509
m. Elizabeth of York

Arthur
d. 1502
m. Catherine
of Aragon

Margaret
d. 1539
m. 1. James IV
m. 2. Archibald
Douglas, Earl
of Angus

Henry VIII

Mary
m. 1. Louis XII
m. 2. Charles Brandon,
Duke of Suffolk

Edward VI

Mary

Elizabeth

Frances
m. Henry Grey,
Duke of Suffolk

Lady Catherine Grey
m. Edward Seymour,
Earl of Hertford
d. 1621

Lady Jane Grey
d. 1554

James V
d. 1542
m. Mary of
Guise

Margaret
m. Matthew Stuart,
Earl of Lennox

Charles Stuart,
Earl of Lennox
m. Elizabeth
Cavendish

Edward Seymour,
Lord Beauchamp
d. 1612

Mary Queen
of Scots
d. 1587

m.

Henry Stuart,
Lord Darnley

Arabella Stuart

m.

William Seymour,
Lord Beauchamp

James VI and I

11

henry viii: the break with rome

HENRY VIII, 1509–1547: THE YOUNG KING

The death of Henry VII was not greatly lamented. The unpleasant side of his character—his cold, suspicious, and grasping nature—had grown more obvious in his old age; hence England turned gladly to the colorful and attractive young prince who now ascended the throne. Henry VIII, not quite eighteen at the time of his father's death, appeared to contemporaries as a prince from a fairy tale: handsome, gay, intelligent, rich, with great endowments of nature and every courtly grace. He was also a fine athlete, a skillful rider and huntsman, an excellent archer and tennis player. "It is the prettiest thing in the world to see him play," wrote a foreign ambassador, "his fair skin glowing through a shirt of the finest texture." He enjoyed the company of learned men and had been carefully educated in the new learning of the Renaissance; he spoke Latin, French, and Spanish. A student of theology, he wrote *Assertio Septem Sacramentorum,* an attack on Martin Luther, for which the Pope conferred on him the title of Defender of the Faith. He was something of a musician and wrote songs he set to music and sang to his own accompaniment. Their sentiments are amusing in the light of later events:

> As the holly groweth green
> And never changeth hue,
> So I am, and ever hath been
> Unto my lady true.
> Now unto my lady
> Promise to her I make;
> From all other only
> To her I me betake.

It was natural enough that in the first flush of youth Henry should devote himself largely to pleasure, to music, to hunting, to endless pageants and tournaments, and to the easy task of spending his father's money. His gaiety, glamour, and openhanded expenditures captured the imagination of the people and brought him a popularity he never lost, but his time of youthful pleasure lasted too long. During the first twenty years of his reign one looks in vain for any noble purpose or notable achievement. Henry spurned the drudgery of close application to business and left the details of government to his minister, Cardinal Wolsey. Instead of building the state, as his father had done, the young Henry turned to the empty honor and glory of diplomacy and war (that sport of kings) and to the excitement of struggle for power on the Continent.

He soon displayed those darker traits for which he is best known: he was both unscrupulous and cruel. In a desire to win popularity he brought fictitious charges of treason against two of his father's ministers—Empson and Dudley— and hustled them off to execution. These men had been extortionate, but they had been loyal servants of the old King. Henry combined supreme self-confidence with supreme selfishness. He had, of course, been born to the purple and had not had to struggle as Henry VII had done. The father clawed his way to achievement; the son was flattered and lionized from the cradle until he believed that his own will and his own way were the will and way of heaven. The father had sacrificed lives to clear the succession; the son continued to sacrifice lives but clouded the succession by his interest in mistresses, though it was prophetic that these connections produced only one son, the illegitimate Duke of Richmond. In a word, Henry was quite ready to sacrifice others but had no intention of sacrificing himself.

Henry's Early Wars

Henry's reign fell within a period of intense rivalry between the Valois Kings of France and the Hapsburg rulers of Spain and Austria, much of whose fighting was done in Italy. These wars, confused and endless, have little meaning for English history. They began when the French King, Charles VIII, attracted by the wealth and disunity of Italy, invaded that country in 1494 in the vain hope of adding it to the dominions of France. Despite his failure, his example was followed by other French Kings—Louis XII (1498–1515) and Francis I (1515–1547). In 1515 Francis was young, vigorous, mildly artistic, and highly ambitious, though his character was essentially shallow and frivolous. His wars in Italy merged with other causes to bring about a long conflict between France and Spain.

Almost at the same time Ferdinand of Spain was succeeded by his grandson, Charles V (1516–1556), Archduke of the Netherlands. Through a remarkable series of marriages, Charles inherited the Netherlands and other portions of the old Burgundian duchy, the Hapsburg lands in and around Austria, together with Spain and the Spanish possessions of Naples, Sicily, and Sardinia, as well as all the Spanish colonies in the New World. In 1519 he became Holy Roman Emperor. He was not a brilliant man, but he possessed common sense, industry, patience, and determination. He was sovereign of vaster territories than Europe had seen in the hands of one person for many centuries, and though his possessions were scattered and diverse, almost incapable of united action, they were bound together by a common loyalty to him.

Between these two rulers stood Henry VIII, the weakest of the three, yet hopeful of using their rivalry to give England a dominant place in the affairs of the Continent.

During the first twenty years of his reign Henry fought two wars with

France (1512–1514 and 1522–1526) and one with Spain (1528–1529). In 1511 the papacy, Spain, and Venice formed what they termed the Holy League to drive the French from northern Italy. Invited to join the league, Henry made war on France. The war was based on no true English interest and was confused and meaningless from beginning to end. In 1512 Henry sent an army under the Marquis of Dorset to cooperate with Ferdinand in southern France, but it soon became evident that Ferdinand was using the English to facilitate his conquest of a part of Navarre, which was shortly in his hands. Thereupon he withdrew from the war. The English troops, in miserable condition from neglect and dysentery, ignored their commander and came home without permission. A more complete fiasco could hardly be imagined. Boiling with rage against both France and Spain, Henry collected an army and crossed to Calais in 1513. Defeating the French in a brilliant cavalry action known as the Battle of the Spurs, Henry captured the French town of Thérouanne and the fortress of Tournai and returned to England in a blaze of empty glory.

A much more important victory had been won during Henry's absence. The Scots, very hostile to England, maintained the "Auld Alliance" with France, and Henry had to assume that there would be fighting in the north while he was abroad. The defense of England was placed in the hands of the Earl of Surrey, an able general who led an army northward just in time to meet the Scottish King, James IV, as he crossed the Border in August 1513. The Scots at first occupied a strong defensive position on Flodden Hill, a spur of the Cheviots, but James IV allowed himself to be enticed onto more level ground. Both wings of his army were defeated, and the English closed upon the Scottish center, where the King, surrounded by the flower of the Scottish nobility, fought fiercely against a solid ring of foes. As Scott wrote in *Marmion*:

> The stubborn spearsmen still made good
> Their dark impenetrable wood,
> Each stepping where his comrade stood,
>   The instant that he fell.

At length the King was slain, and the broken remnant of his defenders escaped under cover of darkness. Flodden was no disgrace for Scotland, for it was bravely fought. But it was a national disaster. Thirteen earls, fourteen lords, an archbishop, a bishop, two abbots, and scores of knights and gentlemen fell with their King. For the moment Scotland was crushed. The new King, James V, was a child. The Regent, Queen Margaret, was Henry's sister.

Deserted by Spain, Henry determined to make terms with France. With Wolsey's aid he concluded a peace in 1514 which allowed him to retain Tournai and provided for the marriage of his younger sister, Mary, to Louis XII. The marriage was short-lived. It took place in July 1514; but Louis, an old man at fifty-two, was unequal to the social whirl demanded by his lively Queen and was dead within a year. Henry wished his sister to marry her husband's successor, Francis I, but the lady had other views and secretly married Henry's Ambassador to France, Charles Brandon, Duke of Suffolk, on whom she had looked with favor before her marriage to Louis. Timidly the couple returned to England. Wolsey, meeting them at Dover, assured them dolefully that they would both be executed. But Henry, having extracted a fine from Suffolk, pardoned his favorite sister and allowed the pair to live quietly in the country.

France and Spain were again at war in 1520, each seeking the alliance of

England. In the course of these negotiations there was a friendly meeting between Henry and Francis on French soil near Calais at the so-called Field of the Cloth of Gold, where each King sought to outdo the other in manly sports and royal magnificence. Nevertheless, in the next year Henry allied with Spain and in 1522 began a second war with France. This war brought him no showy triumphs, for two large and very costly expeditions against France accomplished nothing. The inevitable war against the Scots amounted to no more than some fierce Border raids: Surrey, the son of the victor of Flodden, burned the Scottish town of Jedburgh but was so harassed by Scottish guerrillas, who caused a stampede of 800 English horses, that he retired to England. It was Emperor Charles who startled Europe by inflicting a crushing defeat on Francis at Pavia in Italy in 1525.

So abject was Francis' plight that Henry shifted his policy and attempted to restore the balance of power by joining France in a war against Spain in 1528–1529. This war was disastrous for Henry in a number of ways. To England's great economic loss it disturbed the cloth trade at Antwerp. The fighting, chiefly in Italy, resulted only in additional defeats for France. The Battle of Pavia and the astonishing sack of Rome in 1527 by Charles's mutinous troops left the Pope a prisoner in Charles's hands. It was at this unfortunate juncture that Henry sought a divorce from Catherine of Aragon, who was Charles's aunt. Only the Pope could decide upon the divorce, but he was now in the power of Charles, the enemy of the King of England.

Meanwhile Henry was gravely embarrassed financially. The first war with France had exhausted the treasure of Henry VII. The second was financed in part by a benevolence, or forced gift, imposed on the well-to-do in 1522, and in part by a parliamentary grant in 1523 which was obtained only after a sharp struggle. When a demand was made for a second benevolence—while Wolsey's agents still were collecting the first—and when the second benevolence was applied to the poor as well as to the rich, murmurs of discontent broke into an uproar. The money could not be collected; indeed, the peasants of Kent, East Anglia, and Lincolnshire were on the verge of revolt. The government was forced to withdraw its demand and to abandon a projected campaign in France. The wars of the 1520s brought Henry close to bankruptcy. So soon had Henry VII's treasure been exhausted and his fiscal prudence thrown to the winds.

THE GREAT CARDINAL

The first French war had shown Henry the great administrative talents of his minister, Thomas Wolsey. This remarkable man, under the King, was the ruler of England for almost twenty years. He sprang from humble origins, for his father was a butcher and cattle dealer of Ipswich in Suffolk. Displaying great promise as a youth, Wolsey took his B.A. at Oxford when he was fifteen and entered the church as the normal road to a career. In 1507 he became a chaplain to Henry VII, who employed him as a diplomat and rewarded him with the deanery of Lincoln. Under Henry VIII he rose rapidly. A member of the Council in 1509, he became successively bishop of Tournai in France, bishop of Lincoln, and archbishop of York in 1514. In the next year he induced the Pope to create him a cardinal. It was also in 1515 that he became Lord Chancellor. Thenceforth he was the King's principal minister—dominant in government, law, and diplomacy. He owed his advancement to his splendid intellectual gifts, to his tremendous industry and drive, and to his devotion to the interests of the King. So long as he retained Henry's favor he held the reality of power.

Wolsey was a vain, arrogant, and showy man. Perhaps because he had risen from obscurity to prominence, he held the most lofty views of his own importance and gloried in extravagant display of wealth and luxury: in magnificent houses, of which the grandest was his palace at Hampton Court, and in the sumptuous banquets, at which he ate and drank immoderately. He paid great attention to his dress and personal adornment. When he came from his private chambers to hear cases at Westminster Hall, he was "apparelled all in red, in the habit of a cardinal." The Great Seal of England and his cardinal's hat were borne before him by a noble or a gentleman. He was surrounded by footmen who carried gilded battle axes or crosses of silver; and his mule was trapped in crimson velvet with silver stirrups. There was policy in this display, for authority was increased by a show of pomp and circumstance, but there was also great vulgarity. The rotund cardinal, basking in self-glorification and reveling in the good things of the world, was gross and fleshy.

His manner of life was so extravagant that he was constantly seeking means of increasing his revenues. A shameless pluralist, he always held at least one bishopric in addition to the archbishopric of York; he was abbot of the monastery of St. Albans, which was quite improper for a secular priest; and he was not above accepting bribes and extorting money by threats of his displeasure. His fees from the many courts he headed, his revenues from sees to which foreigners had been appointed as bishops, his gifts from continental rulers and from people at home who sought his favor—all taken together may have swelled his income to perhaps £50,000 a year at a time when one fifth of that sum would have made him the richest man in England aside from the King.

Wolsey as an Administrator

As an administrator Wolsey was arrogant and highhanded, unable to translate his ability and drive into any great accomplishment. He did not have to make many changes in the details of administration, for Henry VII had left them running in orderly efficiency. Finance continued to be conducted through the Chamber; the one important innovation was the appointment of two general surveyors to audit the accounts and to administer revenues from Crown lands. Henry VII had done this work himself, but his son could not be bothered. Wolsey destroyed the inner group of councilors who had surrounded the old King and quickly stood forth as the one all-important minister of state. Through his offices and his dependents he controlled the Great Seal, the privy seal, and the signet,[1] thus dominating a large portion of the administration. His policy in general was a continuation of the work of Henry VII—to strengthen the Crown, to centralize its power, to exalt the sovereign—and thereby to exalt himself. But although he was the effective ruler of the country, so that contemporaries overestimated his power, he was always the servant and the King the master. He held his vast authority because it was Henry's pleasure that he do so.

As a financial minister Wolsey was weak. He did not understand the importance of trade, and he was surprisingly blind to the economic forces of the

---

[1] The signet was a small royal seal, often inserted in a ring, which the King kept with him in the custody of his secretary.

time, as he showed by his efforts to stop the enclosing of land. He destroyed some illegal enclosures, but he did not relieve the agrarian problem from which enclosing arose[2] and he antagonized the landed classes, which were the natural supporters of the Crown. He was unable to create new sources of revenue, merely looking about rather desperately for money, getting it where and how he could. His efforts in the 1520s were, as we have seen, unsuccessful. His methods increased the exasperation of the aristocracy and gentry, which were the classes represented in Parliament. Wolsey never learned to manage the House of Commons. He approached it with arrogance and contempt, giving it to understand that its role was merely to grant money. Hence he infuriated members and reduced the government's chances of obtaining funds. His numerous enemies increased in the 1520s when he enforced economies at court which reduced the pensions and perquisites of many courtiers.

Wolsey and the Courts

Wolsey's best work was done in the field of justice, where again he carried forward the policy of Henry VII. The country was far more law-abiding than in the fifteenth century, but the old spirit of violence and personal revenge had not disappeared. Wolsey was determined that the overmighty subject should be taught to obey the law, that the royal courts should be respected, and that there should be one course of justice for rich and poor alike. His determination may have been more resolute because the upper classes never accepted him as one of themselves. The chancellorship gave Wolsey power over the whole system of justice, and he employed this power to the full. He made great use of the Star Chamber, of which the Chancellor was the presiding judge. The Star Chamber had been rather inactive during the early years of Henry VIII, but Wolsey revived it, lent it his great authority, and used it freely to punish riots, brawls, and disorders of every kind. He once wrote Henry that, though the kingdom as a whole was tranquil, he had heard of a bloody affray between the followers of two wealthy men who were quarreling over a ward. "I trust at the next term to learn them the law of the Star Chamber, that they shall ware how from thenceforth they shall redress their matter with their own hands." Thus Wolsey used the Star Chamber to enforce the law and to make it effective. He took cases of perjury, forgery, and libel away from the courts of the church and transferred them to the Star Chamber. Above all, he transformed the Star Chamber from a court used primarily by the Crown into a popular tribunal to which large numbers of people brought their cases. The Star Chamber, with its dignity enhanced and its jurisdiction broadened, became a normal part of the judicial system.

Wolsey also strengthened the court of chancery and increased its business. The court of chancery was a court of equity for civil suits, for such matters as trusts, wills, contracts, and disputes over property; it had developed in the fourteenth and fifteenth centuries because the common law was too rigid. It decided cases on their merits rather than on the technicalities of the common law. Wolsey made the court more efficient, more expeditious, and better able to enforce its decisions. He transformed it, as he had done the Star Chamber, into a normal part of the legal structure of the kingdom. He also revived the court of requests, which was a kind of poor man's court of chancery, where

[2] See pages 262–265.

wrongs against the weak and needy could be heard upon petition. He drew other cases within his jurisdiction by appointing commissioners to hear individual cases and by assigning cases in the northern parts of the country and in Wales to the local councils in those areas.[3] Many cases were thus taken from the common-law courts and brought within the jurisdiction of courts connected with the Council.

It used to be said that the very existence of the common law was in danger during the Tudor period because of the rival courts set up by the Crown. The danger was never great, but if ever it existed, it existed in the period of Wolsey's power. Wolsey discovered, however, that the volume of business thus brought to the conciliar courts was greater than they could handle. He had invited the people to bring their cases to him, and the response was more than he had expected. In 1528 he transferred a mass of minor cases from the Star Chamber to the courts of common law, thus admitting the necessity of these courts. Nonetheless, his encroachments upon the jurisdiction of the common-law courts were sufficient to enrage the common lawyers, who saw their business decline before the highhanded aggressiveness of the Chancellor. Wolsey thus added the lawyers to the ranks of his enemies.

Wolsey and the Church

Wolsey ruled the church as autocratically as he ruled the state. His policy was twofold. He wished to dominate the church, for his temper was domineering. At the same time he wished to introduce reforms. He talked of reforming the monastic orders, of tightening discipline among the secular clergy, of improving their education, of creating new bishoprics, and of making war on many abuses. But he spent more time and energy in acquiring the powers necessary to inaugurate a policy of reform than on the reforms themselves. He was peculiarly unsuited to play the role of reformer, for he was guilty of almost every abuse from which the church was suffering. How could the greatest of all pluralists, the greediest of all money grabbers, the priest who obtained livings for his illegitimate (and very youthful) son tell other clerics to mend their ways? His reforms, therefore, amounted to very little. He investigated and dissolved a few small monasteries. He established a number of new lectureships at Oxford and founded an Oxford college (which survives as Christ Church) for the training of priests. The school he set up in his native Ipswich to feed the college at Oxford disappeared when he fell from power. But this was about all; domination over the church was closer to his heart than its reform.

The two provinces of York and Canterbury were independent of each other; hence as archbishop of York Wolsey had no authority over the church in England as a whole. His hope of becoming archbishop of Canterbury was thwarted by the perverse longevity of Archbishop Warham. Wolsey therefore induced the Pope to appoint him *legatus a latere,* an office which made him papal viceroy in England. During their visitations *legati* superseded all local ecclesiastical authorities. This appointment enabled Wolsey to override Warham and to control the province of Canterbury as well as that of York. Thereupon he subjected the church in England to a despotism such as it had never known before. Papal supremacy, which in the past had been mild and far distant, was now severe and close at hand. Wolsey allowed long vacancies to occur between

---

[3] See pages 200, 247.

the death of one bishop and the appointment of the next, so that in the interim he might appropriate their revenues. He encouraged the appointment of foreigners as bishops on condition that he receive a part of their income and he even forced some English bishops to hold their bishoprics on similar terms. Convocations met less frequently and the scope of their work was curtailed. Drawing cases from episcopal courts into his court as legate, Wolsey extracted larger fees than customary. He frequently interfered with the ordinary administration of abbots and bishops. The church in England had never been so impotent in managing its own affairs.

Wolsey's domination was disastrous for the church in England. His greatly augmented power over the church was based on papal power; hence the English upper clergy, united in hatred of him, came to look askance upon the source from which his authority was derived. If papal supremacy meant what Wolsey was making it, then papal supremacy was evil. Supremacy of the King could hardly be worse. Thus the bishops did not oppose Henry's later encroachments as ardently as they might have done had Wolsey never existed. Wolsey, moreover, had so weakened and undermined the position and influence of the bishops that they could not hope to withstand the King in the struggle that was to come.

BACKGROUND OF THE BREAK WITH ROME

The King's Matter

Early in 1527 the King became concerned about the validity of his marriage to Catherine of Aragon, who had been his brother's widow. A union of this kind was prohibited by canon law; and a verse in the Scriptures (Leviticus 20:21) declared that a man who married his brother's widow should be childless. At the time of the marriage, however, the Pope granted a dispensation and all appeared to be well. The marriage at first was a happy one. Henry was eighteen, his bride twenty-four; for many years, despite an occasional peccadillo, the King treated his wife with respect and affection. But a curse seemed to lie on Henry's children. One after another they died at birth or in early infancy; the one normal and healthy child who survived was a daughter, the Princess Mary. The sad death of his children turned the King's mind to the ominous verse in Leviticus. Perhaps he was being punished by God for his uncanonical marriage. Perhaps the Pope had exceeded his powers in granting the dispensation. Henry became convinced that his marriage was a sin, these whisperings of conscience being strongly fortified by other considerations.

Henry was, in the first place, greatly worried about the succession, which rested on the life of one young girl. Without the assurance of a strong and lasting dynasty there could be no permanent peace; the anarchy and civil wars of the fifteenth century could easily return. Henry had complicated the succession by an irresponsible affair with one of the Queen's ladies in waiting, Elizabeth Blount, who became the mother of his illegitimate son, Henry Fitzroy, Duke of Richmond. Henry showered honors and offices upon this boy, obviously with the possibility in mind of making him his heir, but Catherine was certain to fight like a lioness for the rights of her daughter. If this daughter succeeded to the throne, there would be grave dangers ahead. There had only been one ruling Queen of England—Matilda in the twelfth century—an unhappy precedent. It

Henry VIII, after Hans Holbein. (National Portrait Gallery, London)

Catherine of Aragon, artist unknown. (National Portrait Gallery, London)

was not at all certain that a female ruler could inspire the awe and exact the obedience a male sovereign could command. Her marriage would raise grave difficulties. If she married a foreigner (as Mary was to do), the door would be open for undue influence on English affairs by a foreign power. If she married an Englishman, she would arouse the jealousy of others. Henry's longing for a legitimate male heir was shared by the people, although most of them were shocked and angered by Henry's sordid efforts to discard Catherine and to obtain a wife who could bear him children; nevertheless, they acquiesced in Henry's actions because they understood the importance of a male heir to the throne.

There was also another consideration. Some time between 1525 and 1527 the King fell in love with a lady at court, Anne Boleyn, the daughter of a diplomat, Sir Thomas Boleyn. Catherine at forty was no longer attractive physically; it is not surprising that Henry in his middle thirties became infatuated (as his love letters show) with a lively young woman of twenty or a little less. Thus as Henry questioned the validity of his marriage the need for a male heir grew more insistent; Anne Boleyn offered a tempting solution to the problem if Catherine could be eliminated.

It was soon apparent, however, that to obtain a divorce would be extremely difficult. One obstacle was Catherine's righteous indignation at the wrong to which she was subjected; innocent, proud, queenly—the object of universal sympathy and respect—she stood her ground against her husband. The question could be settled only by the Pope. What Henry wanted was a papal pronouncement that the dispensation of 1509 was in error, that the marriage to Catherine had been invalid from the beginning, and that the King was therefore in an unmarried state, free to take a wife whenever he chose. Clement VII, though he naturally disliked his role, would probably have found a solution, but he was completely in the power of Charles of Spain, who was Catherine's nephew and who supported her against her husband. Clement dared not offend Charles in order to please Henry.

Henry, if left to himself, might conceivably have made a deal with Charles, recognizing Spanish supremacy in Italy in return for the divorce, but such a solution was impossible for Wolsey, for it meant the abandonment of the papacy to Spanish influence. Wolsey tried to free the Pope by making war on Spain in alliance with France (1528–1529). In this he failed. Clement turned this way and that, hoping for some unforeseen escape from his dilemma. Meanwhile, as Wolsey's failure became obvious, an angry King took affairs into his own hands, stripped the cardinal of his offices and allowed him to die in disgrace, and, within the space of seven stormy years (1529–1536), severed the ancient bonds between the church in England and the church in Rome. Within these seven years an enormous amount of history was concentrated. The revolution thus effected in church and state has shaped the course of English history from that day to this.

Condition of the Church

To understand how Henry was able to bring about these momentous changes we must look at the church in the early sixteenth century and at the way in which it was regarded by the people. There is little doubt that in the later Middle Ages the church had been drawn away from its ideals, that it contained many weaknesses, and that reform was overdue. Clergymen in the early

Tudor period were no longer accorded the respect and affection that had been given to them in the past. The church as an institution still was venerated and the English were quite orthodox, but anticlericalism was widespread. The besetting sin of the upper clergy, as often before, was worldliness. Bishops, archdeacons, abbots, holders of rich livings, often born, like Wolsey, in the middle class and advanced because of their drive and ability, were apt to be sophisticated men of business rather than spiritual leaders. Many were taken from the service of the church and employed by the Crown as lawyers, administrators, councilors, and diplomats; hence they were immersed constantly in the secular work of government. Drawn into the world, they tended to accept its standards. They accumulated offices and livings in the church; they practiced nonresidence, nepotism, and simony; their wealth and ostentation were resented by the lower clergy and by the people at large.

Great numbers of clerks in minor orders engaged in all sorts of secular occupations while claiming the immunities of the clergy. The parish priest, normally of peasant stock, was often a small farmer, cultivating the glebe of the parish church. His poverty tempted him to exact his tithes and perquisites with unbecoming zeal; moreover, he often lacked the education, the material means, and the social standing to command respect.

Monasticism, which had never recovered from the Black Death, was in decay in the early sixteenth century. Although there were notable exceptions, the bulk of the monasteries had lost their early fervor. They differed greatly from each other in wealth, population, and spiritual life. Some maintained the high ideals and traditions of the past, but many—chiefly small houses—had degenerated hopelessly and had little justification for existence. Between these extremes were many large and medium-sized houses, sometimes with more than adequate incomes in relation to the number of inmates, where there was much worldliness as well as a decline in devotion and, occasionally, graver abuses. These monasteries, on the whole, were harmless and might have been tolerated. Yet they had ceased to be of any value to the community. Their hospitality had declined, and so had their spiritual life and their intellectual vigor. They no longer evoked the devotion of the people or appeared to justify the wealth with which they had been endowed by the piety of a more zealous age.[4]

The church was a very expensive institution. Clerics serving the Crown were rewarded by appointments to ecclesiastical office and thus drew their incomes from the church, so that actually their money came from the people. The high fees charged by the clergy for baptisms, marriages, and burials, the fines and charges levied by the ecclesiastical courts, even the normal collection of tithes for the support of the parish priest—all were beginning to arouse a growing resentment. The church, it appeared, was wealthy; yet it must forever be taking money from ordinary folk. Resentment increased when the money went to Rome, for Rome was regarded as a corrupt and luxurious city, draining away the wealth of poorer and more wholesome communities. Men wondered whether the services of the church were being paid for at too dear a rate.

The history of the papacy in the later Middle Ages tended to lower it in popular estimation. For almost seventy years (1309–1377) the popes resided in the city of Avignon on the southern frontier of France, a period during which

[4] See the conclusions of Dom David Knowles, *The Religious Orders in England. The Tudor Age* (Cambridge: Cambridge University Press, 1959), III, pp. 464–466.

most of the popes and cardinals were Frenchmen and the papacy was virtually subordinate to the French government. There followed the Great Schism (1378–1417) when, to the scandal of western Christendom, there was one pope in Rome and another in Avignon.[5] The schism was ended only with great difficulty. A council of the church held at Pisa in 1409 resulted in the election of a third pope; the schism was healed only in 1417 when the Council of Constance (1414–1418) deposed two popes and obtained the abdication of the third. In the subsequent long struggle for supremacy between the popes and a series of church councils the popes were triumphant, but meanwhile, fearful lest they lose control of the papal lands in Italy, they became deeply involved in Italian politics. They had many reasons for doing so, but the loss was greater than the gain. By the end of the fifteenth century the popes were regarded by many Englishmen as Italian princes rather than as the spiritual leaders of Christendom.

The King and the Church

We have seen how often in the Middle Ages the double allegiance of the clergy—to the pope and to the King—had caused trouble between the church and the English government. Disputes of a serious nature had arisen in the reigns of many Kings—William II, Henry I, Henry II, John, and Edward I. For a moment in the fourteenth century it seemed as though these quarrels were coming to a climax. But a break was avoided, largely for two reasons. In the first place, the English were orthodox. Their criticism of the papacy was political, not religious. The heretical views of Wycliffe were repudiated and the Lollards were suppressed. It is a mistake to think, as some historians have done, that Lollardry had any influence on the break with Rome in the reign of Henry VIII. Secondly, a new harmony arose at the end of the fourteenth century between the popes and the English Kings. The Lancastrian rulers were in need of papal support, and the popes of the time of the Great Schism lacked the authority to combat antipapal legislation in England. The Kings, wishing to reward their servants with bishoprics, found that the popes were willing to concur in the necessary appointments. Papal provisions to lesser benefices in England tended to diminish. Hence there were few quarrels in the century preceding Henry's divorce.

But Tudor despotism, with its exaltation of kingship and its emphasis on the power of the Crown, was likely to revive old disputes with the church. The King tended to regard the church as a barrier to good government. Anyone connected with the church, even when the connection was tenuous, could claim benefit of clergy, that is, the right to be tried by the courts of the church. The culprit did not fall afoul of the King's courts until he had committed a second crime. As a matter of fact, benefit of clergy was being curtailed before Henry's break with Rome. By an act of 1491 clerks convicted in the church courts were to be burned in the hand, so that, if they later came before the King's courts, the judges would know they had already been convicted. An act of 1512 deprived clerks of benefit of clergy unless they had taken major orders. The right of sanctuary by which a criminal fleeing from justice could claim asylum in a church or a churchyard or in an ecclesiastical liberty was another hindrance to royal justice. It, too, was being whittled away and was to disappear in the 1530s.

Sanctuary and benefit of clergy were illustrations of the dual allegiance of churchmen. Archbishop Cranmer later remarked that the clergy were loyal to the pope "to the intent that they may have as it were a kingdom and laws within themselves, distinct from the laws of the Crown, and wherewith the Crown may not meddle; and so being exempt from the laws of the realm, might live in this realm like lords and kings without danger or fear of any man, so that they please their high and sovereign head at Rome." Henry told the Commons in 1532: "We thought that the clergy of our realm had been our subjects wholly; but now we have well perceived that they be but half our subjects—yea, and scarce our subjects. For all the prelates at their consecration make an oath to the Pope clean contrary to the oath they make to us, so that they seem his subjects and not ours." Tudor despotism demanded that every person in the realm should owe the King an undivided allegiance and that the clash of jurisdictions should end in the complete victory of the Crown. This was Henry's view, and on the whole the people agreed with him.

In summary it may be said that Henry quarreled with the Pope at a time when the church was weakened by abuses, when its cost bore heavily on the people, when the papacy had fallen into scandals which lowered its prestige, and when the new monarchy of the Tudors would brook no rival to its authority in England.

The English Humanists

The early Tudor period was a time of great intellectual activity. New colleges were founded at Oxford and Cambridge, the old curriculum of the universities was called into question, such aristocrats as Lady Margaret Beaufort, the mother of Henry VII, and William Blount, Lord Mountjoy, the friend of Henry VIII, became patrons of learning. A group of brilliant scholars at the universities and at court, known as the English humanists, represented the impact upon England of both the literary and artistic Renaissance that originated in Italy and the more religious humanism that developed in Germany and the Netherlands. The Renaissance, which began in Italy in the fourteenth century as a renewed interest in the literature and culture of ancient Greece and Rome, was a reaction against scholasticism. Italian scholars, or humanists, did not break with the idea of authority but found their authority in pre-Christian pagan authors. The classics opened new fields of study and provided a bolder and freer spirit of criticism and inquiry than could be found in the medieval school-men. The humanists thought of the world, not as a dreary desert in which men sought painfully to save their own souls, but as an interesting and beautiful place, to be studied, understood, and enjoyed for its own sake. Gradually the Renaissance flowered into new activity in every form of intellectual, artistic, and practical life—in literature, scholarship, science, painting and sculpture, political thought, geographical discovery, and business and finance. Here was the beginning of the modern world.

Secular in tone, the Italian Renaissance sought the satisfaction of esthetic tastes and intellectual curiosity and absorbed the pagan philosophy inherent in classical literature. But as the Renaissance passed into northern Europe it changed somewhat in character. In the north there was a deeper piety and greater preoccupation with religion. The northern humanists remained Christian. They turned with zest to the study of classical authors, but they were also concerned with Christian antiquity, that is, with the Bible and with the writings of the fathers of the church in the first centuries of the Christian Era. They wished to study these Christian sources in the original texts, and for this they had to know Greek and Hebrew as well as Latin.

The humanists in England were of the northern Christian type, combining a devotion to classical studies with a deep religious feeling. They were critical of the abuses they saw in the church but had no thought of breaking away. The new learning, they believed, was to reform and refresh the church, not to destroy it. The English humanists were a most attractive group of men. Their idealism and high character contrasted vividly with the baseness of the rascal politicians who were to tear down the ancient church.

Sir Thomas More, after Hans Holbein. (National Portrait Gallery, London)

An early humanist was William Grocyn, a famous Greek scholar who studied in Italy, was intimate with many learned men, and lectured in Greek at Oxford. Another was William Linacre, who combined the study of Greek with the practice of medicine. Like Grocyn he visited Italy and taught for a time at Oxford. He then came to court as the tutor of the King's children and as one of the physicians of Henry VIII. He helped found the College of Physicians in 1518. His fame among his contemporaries, however, rested on his Grecian studies and on his translations from Greek into Latin. John Colet, another humanist, was dean of St. Paul's Cathedral in London and the founder of St. Paul's school for boys (where the Greek scholar William Lily was the first headmaster). Colet was a more ardent reformer than Grocyn or Linacre. So sharply did he denounce abuses in the church that on one occasion he was cited for heresy before the church courts. Like later reformers, he preached a return to the purity and simplicity of early Christianity.

The most inspiring of the English humanists was Sir Thomas More. As a student at Oxford under Grocyn and Linacre he became so absorbed in the new learning that his father, a barrister, took him out of the university and set him to reading law in London. More studied law with avidity, built up an excellent practice, and was later drawn into the service of Henry VIII, who made him Lord Chancellor after the fall of Wolsey. More devoted his leisure to humanistic studies and made his household famous for its cultured atmosphere and learned guests. Beneath his love of letters and his brilliant wit lay a deep religious feeling, a devotion to principle, and an unshakable courage. As the King moved toward separation from Rome, More did not conceal his disapproval and retired to private life. But he was too important to be let alone. When he refused the oaths required by Henry's legislation, he was imprisoned and executed, a martyr to the older faith. His most famous work was his *Utopia* in which, under the guise of describing an imaginary community, he criticized the abuses of his day. All the English humanists paid deep respect to Erasmus, the greatest scholar of the age, who made long visits to England and lectured for a time at Cambridge.

Did the humanists prepare the way for the break with Rome? Historians in the past have held they did. A recent authority,[6] however, has denied this, saying that the humanists were loyal to the papacy and that they did nothing to cause or lead to the English Reformation. They were, of course, a small group of intellectuals confined to the universities and to the court. Henry's break with Rome was political in nature, not religious, and it could not have come when it did had not the Crown taken the lead. Nonetheless, the humanists were critical of the church, they wrote books to that effect, and these books, in an age when books were few, must have had some impact. It can at least be said that the humanists swelled the chorus of criticism and supplied arguments for those who wished a break. Hence it would seem that they had some influence, though that influence should not be exaggerated.

THE REFORMATION PARLIAMENT, 1529–1536

The famous Parliament which Henry summoned in 1529 passed a large amount of complicated and highly important legislation. This legislation can be

[6] G. R. Elton, *England under the Tudors* (London: Methuen, 1955), pp. 111–114.

divided for convenience into four groups of acts. Such a division will help to explain the course of events, for at the beginning of the Parliament neither its members nor the King himself had any notion how far they were to travel. The first group of acts was initiated by the Commons and not by the Crown. Allowing anticlericalism to take its course, Henry permitted the Commons to debate what the members pleased, and they passed at once a number of bills against abuses in the church. A Probate Act and a Mortuaries Act in 1529 reduced and regulated the fees that could be charged by the church courts for probating wills and by the clergy for conducting burials. A Pluralities Act of the same year declared that a clergyman who held a living worth £8 a year must resign it if he accepted a second benefice. Benefit of clergy, already restricted, was further curtailed in 1531, as was also the right of sanctuary. Henry hoped to frighten the Pope by these statutes, but the Pope, more afraid of the King of Spain than of the King of England, stood firm.

A second group of acts deprived the English clergy of independence and forced them into complete subordination to the Crown. Henry knew that if he were to make headway against Rome he had to control his own clergy and must silence Convocation, which had displayed some opposition to his policies. He therefore took the astonishing course of accusing the entire body of the English clergy of having broken the Statute of Praemunire. This statute, as we have seen,[7] dealt with appeals from English courts to the papal curia, but its language was so vague that almost any business with Rome could be brought within its compass. The accusation was clearly absurd.

Yet public opinion was all against the church; the clergy were thoroughly frightened. The Convocations of Canterbury and York obtained a pardon only by paying fines of £100,000 and £18,000, respectively, and by making a submission to the King. This submission, Henry asked, should recognize him as "sole protector and supreme head of the Church and clergy in England"; but Convocation managed to substitute the words "singular protector, only and supreme lord, and, as far as the law of Christ allows, even supreme head." In 1532 Henry obtained an even humbler surrender. Convocation granted him the right to review all its past canons or ordinances and to abrogate those he disliked, and it was further agreed that all future canons must receive his approval before they became effective. These concessions were embodied in an Act for the Submission of the Clergy in 1534. Henry did not bother to review the canons. His victory was achieved: he had been accepted by the church as its supreme legislator in place of the pope; the independence of the clergy was ended.

To understand a third group of statutes we must look for a moment at a new minister who was becoming important. This was Thomas Cromwell. Of humble birth—his father having been a blacksmith and a fuller in London—for some years Cromwell knocked about on the Continent as soldier, lawyer, land agent, and merchant. During the 1520s he was in Wolsey's service. Then, after Wolsey's fall, he caught the King's attention by his skill in managing the House of Commons in the interest of the Crown. He was soon on his way to high office, becoming Secretary by 1534.

Cromwell has often been denounced as the King's evil genius, the cunning and unscrupulous agent of royalty in destroying the ancient church. Cold and ruthless he certainly was, but he had great ability; he possessed a remarkable

---

[7] See page 169.

gift for penetrating to the heart of a problem, seeing his objective clearly, and driving at it with remorseless and single-minded purpose. He knew where he was going when other councilors floundered. His mind was secular, and he was strongly anticlerical. His great purpose was to increase the power and wealth of the King and at the same time to hold his position as the King's chief minister. He saw that the way to achieve these ends was to exclude the papacy completely from England and to seize the wealth of the church for his royal master. During the crucial years of the Reformation Parliament the King was usually following his counsel.

A series of statutes now aimed directly at the powers of the pope in England. In 1532 an Act in Conditional Restraint of Annates declared that annates and other fees due Rome from the English clergy might be withheld at the discretion of the King. Here was the most obvious pressure to obtain the divorce, but the Pope remained adamant. Hence the payments were withheld; and in 1534, when a break with Rome had become inevitable, an Act in Absolute Restraint of Annates ended these payments altogether. The act of 1532 had withheld them on the ground that they were extortionate, but another statute in 1534 explained a little lamely that they were still to be paid, though henceforth the money should go to the King. These acts also provided for the selection of bishops and archbishops in England by the King alone. Cathedral chapters in the past, when about to make an election, had received advice from both King and pope. Henceforth the law required that only the King should give advice and that his nominee should be elected automatically.

Late in 1532, Anne Boleyn, timing her surrender nicely, ceased to resist the King's advances. Catherine was removed from Whitehall, Anne was installed in her place, and she and Henry were secretly married in January 1533. Anne was soon pregnant, and fast action was required if her child was to be legitimate. There followed the most crucial act of the Reformation Parliament: a statute forbidding appeals from English courts to any courts abroad in spiritual suits. The act provided that the final court of appeal in ecclesiastical cases should be the court of the archbishop of Canterbury, or, in cases which concerned the King, the upper house of Convocation. Shortly thereafter the archbishop's court declared that the marriage to Catherine was null and void. Anne Boleyn's child, born in September, was legitimate in English common law. To the King's chagrin it proved to be a girl, the future Queen Elizabeth. In 1534 the Act of Appeals was amended. The King, if he wished, could appeal a case to a new court, the Court of Delegates, which was to consist of commissioners appointed by the Crown in Chancery. The outcome of an appeal taken to the Court of Delegates could be prophesied with some assurance.

A fourth and final series of statutes was designed to construct a new ecclesiastical framework in place of that which had been demolished. The Act for the Submission of the Clergy, already mentioned, gave Henry the right to control the clergy and thereby to build the church anew. An Act of Supremacy in 1534 acknowledged the King as the supreme head of the English Church on earth, with all the titles, honors, jurisdiction, and powers inherent in that position. He was to be accepted as supreme head by the people, who could be required to take an oath supporting the principles of the act. The royal power to reform errors and heresies within the church also was acknowledged. An Act of Succession declared that the succession to the throne lay in the children of Henry and Anne Boleyn. Their marriage was not to be criticized, and again there was an oath accepting the principle of the act. It was the refusal of this oath which brought about the executions of Sir Thomas More and Bishop Fisher of Rochester. The Ten Articles (1536) and the Six Articles (1539) were attempts to define the doctrines of the church.

THE DISSOLUTION OF THE MONASTERIES

Kings had often cast envious eyes at the wealth of the monasteries. It is not surprising that Cromwell, wishing to make his master rich, should have advised the spoliation of the church over which Henry was gaining mastery. The methods employed in the great dissolution were crass and hypocritical. Appointed vicar-general in 1535, Cromwell was given power to visit and investigate the religious foundations in England; during the next six months his agents, an unscrupulous crew, dashed from one monastery to another, paying far greater attention to cataloguing the wealth of the monks than to inquiring into their morals. This was a visitation to end, not to mend, the monasteries. It was decided to begin with the smaller houses. An act of 1536 dissolved all monasteries with an income of less than £200 a year. Some 300 small monasteries, nunneries, and convents were dissolved, their lands and other possessions passing into the hands of the King. The larger foundations soon discovered that their turn would come. Within the next three years many of them, hoping to secure favorable terms, made voluntary surrenders by which they placed themselves at the King's mercy. They were thereupon dissolved. The end came in 1539, when an act of that year dissolved those that remained. All told, some 800 houses, including friaries, disappeared.

The dissolution of the monasteries leads us to the social and economic results of the Reformation, which will be discussed in the next chapter. Here only a few points need be mentioned. An important form of religious life ceased to exist. Monks and nuns became unknown in England for many centuries. The transition to Protestantism was simplified and made more abrupt, for the monks had been a bulwark of the Roman Catholic Church and might have retarded changes. There was great destruction of buildings and churches as well as loss of objects of medieval art and of books and manuscripts, for Henry allowed the monastic libraries to be scattered. The monks who had belonged to the richer monasteries did not fare badly. They were given pensions or were provided with livings in parish churches. The nuns and friars whose houses were less prosperous were not treated so well, and some of them received nothing. A few royal ministers, including Cromwell, a few court favorites, and some local supporters of the King, were given large estates. But as long as Cromwell lived the great bulk of the monastic lands was retained by the Crown. After his death in 1540 perhaps two thirds of these lands were sold, often in a very unbusinesslike way. For the most part they passed into the hands of the nobility and gentry, often laying the foundation for the rise of new families.

It has been argued that Henry should have kept the land as a permanent endowment for the Crown, but there was shrewdness in allowing it to enrich the upper classes. The new owners, bound to the Tudor dynasty by the closest of bonds, would never tolerate a return to the ancient church. The permanence of the new dispensation was guarded in another way. During the Middle Ages there had always been an ecclesiastical majority in the House of Lords. Abbots,

The Abbot's Parlor, Thame Park, Oxfordshire. (Copyright Country Life)

The Vyne, Hampshire. A manor house of patterned brick built in the reign of Henry VIII. (Copyright Country Life)

priors, and bishops could outvote the temporal peers. But now the abbots and priors were gone, and, though the bishops remained, the lay peers in that chamber formed a majority they have retained ever since. Henry did little to redeem his pledge that he would put the wealth of the monasteries to better uses than in the past. It is true that he created six new bishoprics, which were badly needed. But next to nothing was done to relieve the poverty of the lower clergy, or to found schools or colleges, or to assist the poor. Most of the money from the monastic lands went into a very costly war which Henry waged against France in the last years of his reign.

THE CHURCH OF ENGLAND

The significance of the changes made in the church may be gathered from the preamble to the Act of Appeals in 1533. This preamble contained a ringing declaration that England was an empire, that is, a free and sovereign state, owing no allegiance whatever to any foreign prince. The empire of England, the preamble continued, was governed by a ruler who was supreme head in matters spiritual and King in matters temporal, possessing "plenary, whole, and entire power, preeminence, authority, prerogative, and jurisdiction" over the people of his realm; and the people, both clergy and laity, owed him a natural and humble obedience. These powers came to him, not from any earthly source, but from "the goodness and sufferance of Almighty God."

The pope thus was excluded, and Henry assumed all the powers which the papacy had formerly exercised in England. He could administer the church, he could discipline its clergy, he could control its laws through Convocation, he could tax it and dip into its revenues, he could appoint its officers and dignitaries, and he could supervise its courts. Holding that his supremacy came directly from God, Henry returned in theory to the position of the Anglo-Saxon Kings, who combined temporal authority with spiritual attributes. The King was not a priest and did not perform priestly functions. Nonetheless, he possessed a sacred quality, he was both *rex* and *sacerdos*, and he could determine doctrine and regulate ritual. This definition of the King's supremacy broke sharply with the doctrine of the pope as supreme pontiff. Henry was establishing a new church. The church *in* England was becoming the Church *of* England.[8]

The people as a whole accepted these changes with surprising tranquillity. A few brave men, such as More and Fisher, resisted them to the death; and a rebellion in the north in 1536 known as the Pilgrimage of Grace looked danger-ous for a moment but in the end amounted to little. Henry's alterations in the church were accepted probably for two reasons. One was the genuine hostility to Rome and the willingness to support the King. Secondly, the dogma and ritual of the church remained virtually unchanged. The Mass was performed as it always had been, ancient creeds and ceremonies remained, and the ordinary man attending the parish church as he had done from childhood saw only minor changes from the past. Pilgrimages and prayers to saints were suppressed, shrines were demolished, but when Parliament defined dogma in the Six Articles in 1539 the faith of the church remained Catholic. Transubstantiation was con-firmed, communion in one kind remained, the Mass and auricular confession continued, private Masses were justified, clerical marriage remained illegal. But if Henry thought that the church would continue in this condition, without the intrusion of Protestant doctrine, he was quite wrong, for such doctrines came in rapidly after his death. Indeed, he himself paved the way. In 1539 a Bible translated into English was placed in every church. And thus the Scriptures became available in English to the nation as a whole.

THE STATE

The preamble of the Act of Appeals acknowledged that the temporal power of the King was as ample as his supremacy over the church. Henry stood high above his subjects: he inspired confidence in his capacity to govern; he was able to cast his plans into forms which were acceptable to the people; and he embodied national aspirations. The new sovereign state, over which he ruled and of which he was the symbol, was thought of as total and all-powerful. Its interests transcended the interests of individuals, corporations, and ancient institutions. Hence the King's power was very real, and his mastery and leader-ship were acknowledged. Yet while Henry built his absolutism, he also supplied the limitation to that absolutism. He had revolutionized the church through parliamentary statute; and he had shown that he was most potent when he was King-in-Parliament, that is, when King, Lords, and Commons united in making law. He thus acknowledged that the House of Commons was an integral part of the state, a partner of the Crown in legislation. If he had not been able to control the Commons, his views might have been less enlightened.

He and Cromwell may be said to have invented the art of parliamentary management. The task was not difficult, for Parliament was still a primitive

[8] G. R. Elton, *England under the Tudors,* pp. 160–165.

institution: the Lords were largely Tudor creations; the Commons were far more deferential and compliant than they became later in the century. The Commons contained a number of royal officials, including those members of the King's Council who were not peers and who now sought election to Parliament. These men could speak in favor of royal measures and could carry with them something of royal authority. The Speaker in a house still without rigid procedure could help greatly in parliamentary management. Cromwell used his influence with county magnates and town corporations to return members favorable to royal policy. Above all, he carefully drafted the great statutes which brought about the break with Rome. Thus the Commons were given a program to debate and were not left to their own devices.

It is the paradox of Tudor history that under this treatment the Commons made rapid advance. They were given a thorough schooling in the art of legislation, for the statutes of Henry's reign equaled in bulk the statutes of all the medieval Kings. The self-respect and self-confidence of the Commons were increased by Henry's attitude. Ready to persuade rather than coerce, he tolerated occasional criticism of his policy. The Commons obtained some control over their own members and something of the aspect of a court in punishing offenders against their privileges. We must not, of course, be too charmed by Henry's methods. He was an awesome figure, inspiring some terror, and much of Cromwell's manipulation was very crude. But at least the Commons knew that they were worth manipulating.

A number of administrative reforms strengthened the government. One was the development of the Privy Council. In the large and loosely organized Council of Henry VII there had been an inner ring of councilors close to the ruler. This group had disappeared during Wolsey's ascendancy, for Wolsey, brooking no rivals, had preferred to make the Star Chamber the center of the Council. After his fall, however, the Star Chamber was less prominent, and an inner ring of councilors reappeared. Cromwell developed this group and used it, though he kept it well under control. It became known as the Privy Council. The distinction between it and the Star Chamber was clearly visible by 1540. The Star Chamber was judicial; the Privy Council was political, advisory, and administrative.

Composed of fifteen to twenty of the King's principal ministers, most of them holding high office, the Privy Council watched over the entire administration of the kingdom. It kept in close touch with local officials, whom it directed and controlled by constant correspondence about roads and bridges, religious laws, disturbances of the peace, inns and alehouses, the care of the poor, and economic conditions and economic quarrels. It concerned itself with naval and military administration, with the royal household, with English ambassadors abroad, and Ireland, Wales, and the Channel Islands. It took a paternal interest in the nobility, settling disputes and dividing estates among heirs. The Privy Council was the King in action, ubiquitous in its watchfulness, flexible in its capacity to deal with any problem which affected the interest of the state. Much of its work had a judicial implication, for the Tudors did not distinguish sharply between the administrative and the judicial functions of its servants.

The dissolution of the monasteries involved a great deal of financial administration for which the Chamber, as developed by Henry VII, proved inadequate. Cromwell therefore took revenue away from the Chamber and set up six separate institutions which acted both as courts and as financial departments. The Exchequer administered revenues coming from the customs and from parliamentary grants. The duchy of Lancaster handled the lands belonging to it. A court of general surveyors dealt with the land acquired by Henry VII, while a body known as the court of augmentations controlled the lands taken from the monasteries. A court of first fruits and tenths collected revenues coming from the church; a court of wards and liveries handled the feudal revenues of the Crown.

Cromwell held the office of the King's principal Secretary, and in his hands this office became the most important in the state. The Secretary was developed into the chief executive minister of the Crown, responsible for the direction of both foreign and domestic policy. Much of later administrative history was merely the growth of this office and the subdivision of its work among a number of secretaries.

During the Middle Ages numerous bits of territory scattered through the kingdom were known as franchises or liberties, which in one way or another retained semi-independent rights. There had been many such franchises in the north, in Wales, and in the Welsh marches which had been the source of great trouble during the fifteenth century. A statute of 1536 swept them away, so that the King's government became supreme for the first time throughout the entire kingdom. It was this statute which ended the county palatine of Durham; a natural sequel was the establishment in 1537 of a permanent Council of the North. This Council, composed of royal officials with both judicial and administrative powers, governed the five northern counties as a branch office of the Council in London. There had been temporary councils in the north since the reign of Edward IV, but now a strong and permanent one was set up to quiet those "peccant parts." Cromwell gave new strength and vigor to the council in Wales established by Edward IV. Moreover, a famous statute in 1536 (expanded in 1543) incorporated the whole of Wales with England. The old lordships of the Welsh marches were dissolved, some annexed to existing shires, the others divided into five new counties. Justices of the peace were appointed, and the Welsh counties and boroughs were to return twenty-four members to the House of Commons. Thus the law and administration of England were extended to Wales in this first act of union.

HENRY'S LAST YEARS

In his last years Henry was a most unpleasant figure, bloated and sickly in body—so corpulent that a little derrick had to be arranged to lift him from bed—cynical, suspicious, and cruel, though still vigorous in mind. The charming young prince was gone; a sour, coarse, and bad-tempered old man had taken his place. The problem of the succession continued to haunt him. His matrimonial vicissitudes became so complicated that they give a touch of the ridiculous to the story of a most regal figure. In 1536 Anne Boleyn, having failed to produce a male heir and having disillusioned the King in other ways, was condemned to death and executed. The next day Henry married his third wife, Jane Seymour, a pale and gentle lady, who died in 1537 a few days after she gave birth to a son, the future Edward VI. Henry at length had a male heir, though the heir was likely to be under age at the time of his father's death. In 1540 Henry married Anne of Cleves. This marriage was a move in the game of diplomacy, for Cromwell was seeking an alliance with the Protestant states of Germany. Anne, however, was not the most beautiful of princesses. Henry married her with a sigh and then, resolving there were things he could not do for England, arranged a separation which enabled her to live in quiet affluence—intent on her needle-work—until her death is 1557. Cromwell paid the price for his error, fell from power, and was executed under a bill of attainder. Catherine Howard, the King's fifth wife, was married to him in 1540 and was executed for her youthful indiscretions in 1542; Catherine Parr, whom Henry married in 1543, proved an excellent nurse for her irascible old husband and managed to survive him. The reign ended in gloom and degeneration. One should think of Henry, not in his old age, but in the vigor of his prime when he showed himself a ruler of ability, a fine parliamentarian, a King who carried his people with him through revolutionary change.

12

εδWARδ VI aηδ maRy: RελIGIOUS aηδ εcoηomIc chaηGε

EDWARD VI, 1547–1553, AND THE RETURN OF FACTION

The paramount political fact of Edward's reign was that the King was a child. Edward was nine years old when he ascended the throne and only fifteen when he died of tuberculosis. From the moment of his birth he was surrounded by an elaborate household with all the trappings of royalty, he knew himself to be a King, and he was inclined to assume a cold and rather imperious attitude toward his councilors. With little interest in sports, he was much more inclined to his books and to questions of theology. His sympathies were Protestant. He was an intelligent boy who seemed to grasp the significance of religious and political problems, but he was so young that he had no will of his own and was controlled by the men around him.

This situation struck at the essence of Tudor government. Henry VIII had vastly increased the powers of the King, he had been a most regal figure before whom his councilors trembled, and he had fashioned a state which depended upon the presence of a strong ruler at the helm. Now suddenly that strength was gone; power at the center was followed by a vacuum. The result was a return to faction, to quarrels and intrigues among ambitious councilors, and to instability, weakness, and corruption in government. Yet England escaped a return to the chaos of the fifteenth century because Tudor government had been built so well that it could not be overthrown in a day; it survived the dangerous crisis of Edward's minority.

The Lord Protector Somerset, 1547–1549

Henry had attempted to devise a government that would function after his death. His will provided, not for a regent, but for a council of regency. A council of this kind, however, could be effective only if it acted as a unit, which was found to be impossible; and only if it provided leadership, a function for which Henry had given it no training. His Council had existed merely to do his bidding. His plan for Edward's reign collapsed at once. The clique in power, composed of nobles and politicians who hoped for the spoils of office, carried out a *coup d'état* by which Henry's will was set aside. Edward Seymour, Earl of Hertford, became Duke of Somerset and assumed the office of Lord Protector and Governor of the young King. Somerset was a logical person to step into pre-eminence, for he was a soldier, he had been a favorite of Henry, he was the brother of Henry's third wife, Jane Seymour, and hence the uncle of Edward VI. But there was another councilor, John Dudley, Viscount Lisle and later Duke of Northumberland, who might have been made Protector. Failing in this, he became a bitter rival of Somerset; the struggle of these two men fills much of the annals of the reign.

Somerset, who was much the more attractive, was something of a liberal and an idealist, though he was ambitious, rather arrogant in manner, and ready to enrich himself as he saw opportunity. His good intentions could never express themselves in practical policy. Believing that leniency was better than terror, he relaxed the restraints of Henry's rule, but as a result he opened the way for unscrupulous politicians to turn liberty into license. With a generous sympathy for the poor, he attempted to relieve their sufferings, thus incurring the hostility of the prosperous middle classes. Like Henry, he hoped to eliminate French influence in Scotland and to draw the two countries together by a marriage between Edward and Mary, Queen of Scots, then a child about four years old. But Henry, unable to come to terms with the Scots, had made war upon them. Somerset did the same when he invaded Scotland and won the useless Battle of Pinkie Clough near Edinburgh in 1547. His actions drove the Scots closer to France. Within a few years they sent their little Queen to Paris to be educated as the future wife of the Dauphin, later King Francis II. French influence in Scotland increased and remained a problem for years to come. Nor did Somerset's Protestant reforms win him popularity. Like many another liberal, he inspired discontent rather than gratitude. As a statesman he must be considered a failure.

Northumberland in Power, 1549–1553

Somerset's followers became restive, and it was not difficult for Northumberland to intrigue against him. Following a revolt in 1549, known as Kett's Rebellion,[1] which was thought to have been caused by Somerset's sympathies for the lower classes, a cabal of councilors led by Northumberland forced the Protector out of office and sent him to the Tower. He was released in the following year. For a short time there was some cooperation between him and Northumberland, but soon their rivalry became more deadly than ever. In December 1551 Somerset, accused of plotting against Northumberland and the King, was tried for treason and executed early in 1552. Northumberland secured the first place in the Council though he was never Lord Protector. He returned to Henry's policy of force and ruthlessness, but he did not make the government popular or strong. He was an unscrupulous adventurer, the new statesman at its worst, without pity or moral restraint, a gambler playing for high stakes in the dangerous game of politics.

His fall came suddenly. For some time he had strengthened his position by cultivating the good will of the King, but he discovered in 1553 that the young King was dying. If Edward was succeeded by his sister Mary, the Catholic

[1] See page 265.

daughter of Catherine of Aragon, Northumberland knew his ruin would follow. He devised a daring plot by which he proposed to alter the succession. He arranged a marriage between his fourth son, Guildford Dudley, and Lady Jane Grey, a granddaughter of Mary Tudor, the sister of Henry VIII. Mary Tudor had married Charles Brandon, Duke of Suffolk; her daughter Frances was the mother of Lady Jane Grey. Other marriages were arranged to win supporters; councilors and judges were browbeaten into acquiescence. But the plot failed, for at Edward's death the country stood for Mary, the rightful Queen. She displayed her courage by escaping from Northumberland's power into the county of Suffolk, where supporters quickly gathered round her. The plot collapsed and Northumberland was executed. The pathetic victim of his machinations was Lady Jane Grey, an attractive, learned, and completely innocent young lady, imprisoned with her husband at the time of the plot and executed in 1554 when Mary was faced with a dangerous rebellion.

Radical Protestantism

It was in the reign of Edward that the Church of England became definitely Protestant. Henry's alterations had been political and constitutional, and he had not made radical changes in the doctrine or ceremonies of the medieval church. In Edward's reign there was a sudden turn to the left; the Church of England became more radically Protestant than at any other time in its history. The abruptness of this shift comes as something of a shock. How can it be explained?

Henry's break with Rome had been the first step toward Protestantism, but his heavy hand had prevented the introduction of Protestant doctrine. Somerset, however, permitted much more freedom of debate. There followed a period of intense theological discussion and of rapid entry into England of religious ideas from the Continent. Henry himself had paved the way for new ideas by placing an English translation of the Bible in every parish church.

A surprising number of continental reformers came to England at this time. Some were exiles from persecution, some were invited by Somerset or by Archbishop Cranmer. The learned Italian Peter Martyr, a former Augustinian monk, arrived in 1547 and became a professor of divinity at Oxford in 1549. In that year Cranmer invited another famous reformer, Martin Bucer, an Alsatian, made professor of divinity at Cambridge, who brought with him Paul Fagius, a Hebrew scholar. Others included John à Lasco, or Laski, a Pole; Vallerandus Pollamus, a former minister at Strasbourg; and Francisco de Enzinas, a Spaniard.

These men and others brought many variations of continental Protestant thought. Essentially, however, their doctrines were those of Martin Luther: justification by faith (the belief that man obtained salvation through faith that God would save him); reliance on the Bible as the sole source of religious truth; sanctity of conscience as the supreme guide to moral conduct. Discussion in England centered upon the Eucharist, the sacrament of the Lord's Supper. Transubstantiation, the Catholic doctrine that the elements of bread and wine became the body and blood of Christ, was rejected by the Protestants, but they could not agree upon what to put in its place. Peter Martyr wrote from Oxford that there was contention about the Eucharist in every corner of the land and that even in the Council there was great disputing among the bishops and other members.

Thomas Cranmer, archbishop of Canterbury, was of great importance in

Thomas Cranmer, Archbishop of Canterbury, by G. Fliccius. (National Portrait Gallery, London)

these discussions. He was a scholar, not a man of action, and in the reign of Henry VIII he had appeared to follow rather too tamely the dictates of his master. His theological views developed slowly, but they steadily became more Protestant. He was in close touch with the reformers on the Continent and with the continental visitors in England, though his beliefs were less extreme than theirs and he constantly sought a compromise which would be accepted by most of his countrymen. Somerset and Northumberland accepted a policy of reform out of political rather than religious motives. Somerset appears to have had some sympathy with Protestantism, but he hoped to win popularity by a Protestant policy and he feared that Catholics might plot in favor of the Princess Mary, the King's sister. He knew that his followers hoped to enrich themselves by the continued spoliation of the church, which could be done in the name of reform. Northumberland was without religious interest or scruple. He feared the Princess Mary even more than Somerset had done, he planned to pillage the church, and he found it expedient in politics to throw in his lot with the reformers.

Alterations in religion, then, came rapidly in Edward's reign for a number of reasons: restraints imposed by Henry were removed; an English Bible opened the way for individual interpretation; radical ideas came crowding in from the Continent; Cranmer's beliefs moved toward the left; there were "hot-gospelers," such as Nicholas Ridley, John Hooper, and John Knox; greedy courtiers sought the pillage of the church; and, finally, Somerset and Northumberland saw political advantage in a Protestant policy.

Shortly after Somerset became Protector the government issued a set of injunctions addressed to both clergy and laity. The clergy were urged to attack the Roman Catholic Church from the pulpit, while the laity were warned against such Roman things as images, candlesticks, and religious paintings on the walls of churches. Both clergy and laity responded with zeal, and mobs destroyed sacred objects in churches and desecrated shrines. Stressing the Scriptures as the only source of religious truth, the injunctions commanded the clergy to study the Bible and teach it to the people. Parts of the service were to be said or sung in English: the Epistles and Gospels and Cranmer's beautiful translation of the Litany. His book of homilies or short sermons, which taught justification by faith, was recommended.

A Parliament summoned in 1547 passed a number of important acts. Laws concerning heresy and Henry's act of Six Articles were repealed. Another act provided that bishops be appointed by letters patent, as were other officers of state. This was followed by an act dissolving the chantries and confiscating the religious endowments of guilds, fraternities, and colleges on the plea that they encouraged "vain opinion of purgatory," for the chantry priests sang Masses for the souls of the founders. The avowed purpose of the act was to provide endowments for education, but in reality the money went largely to unworthy courtiers; education suffered greatly from the weakening or destruction of schools and colleges, though some of the old foundations were spared and a few new grammar schools were begun. The act was sheer spoliation, and little can be said in its defense.

Another Parliament, meeting in 1548 and 1549, passed the first Act of Uniformity. Freedom of religious expression had degenerated into chaos, so that it became necessary to bring order and uniformity into divine worship. For some time a commission had been at work on a prayer book which could be made common throughout the kingdom. The new Prayer Book was largely the work of Cranmer, who headed the commission. Its tone was conservative, since it was for the most part a translation of the Latin service of the Catholic Church, but the fact that it was in English, so that the congregation could understand what was being said, was a step away from Rome. This Prayer Book—one of the most lovely expressions of devotion in the English language—displayed Cranmer's power of writing beautiful prose. It was imposed upon all churches. Priests who made use of any other service were subject to severe penalties, but the laity were not compelled to attend divine service. Finally, an act of this Parliament permitted priests to marry. Such were the more important religious changes during Somerset's regime. They represented cautious and moderate reform.

Northumberland's legislation was more drastic. An act of 1550 required that service books not authorized by the Act of Uniformity be destroyed. Another act appointed a commission to reform the canon law; a new commission was appointed to revise the Prayer Book. A second Prayer Book, again the work of Cranmer, and more radical than the first, was embodied in a second Act of Uniformity in 1552. The act swept away much Catholic ritual, eliminated minor officials of the ancient church, and referred to the priest as a minister and to the altar as a table. Transubstantiation was denied. The people were to receive the Communion (both bread and wine) in a kneeling position, but the Prayer Book made clear that this did not imply an adoration of the elements. A general confession, spoken by the congregation, took the place of private confession to a priest; the sacrament of baptism and the vestments worn by the clergy were made more simple; attendance at church on Sundays and Holy Days was now required of the laity. Meanwhile Catholics were removed from the Council and from the bench of bishops. Cranmer listed the doctrines of the church in Forty-two Articles which he naïvely hoped would be accepted by everyone. The new Prayer Book was in force only about eight months and may never have penetrated to some parts of the country.

Protestant beliefs and practices which came into the church during this period included justification by faith and the appeal to conscience, denial of transubstantiation, communion in both kinds, simplification of ritual, the service in English, the acceptance of the Bible as the sole repository of religious truth, the dissolution of the chantries, and the marriage of the priesthood.

MARY TUDOR (1553–1558) AND THE CATHOLIC REACTION

The reign of Mary was a sterile period that seems strangely out of place in Tudor history, although the same problems arose as in other reigns: religion, the marriage of the ruler, the succession, the machinery of government. There is no doubt that Mary exercised a profound influence on the course of English history. She checked the headlong rush toward radical Protestantism and drove England in the opposite direction, thus preparing the way for the religious compromise of the reign of Queen Elizabeth. Nevertheless, the results of Mary's policies were the opposite of what she hoped. Her militant Catholicism implanted in her people a hatred and suspicion of Rome which was to last for centuries. Her marriage to Philip of Spain resulted in English hostility to all things Spanish. Finally, her reign tested the machinery of government set up by her father. Events were to show what that machinery could do when it was directed by a vigorous personality—and what it could not.

Mary had many Tudor traits—pride, courage, ability, fixity of purpose, ruthlessness, and strength of will—but in her the Tudor character went wrong. Until she was about fifteen she had been a favorite of her father and the heiress presumptive to his throne. Then came divorce and disgrace for her mother, the taint of illegitimacy for herself, and the slurring attacks on the church she loved. Close to her mother, she shared her Spanish sympathies and had her

Mary Tudor, by Antonio Moro. (Museo del Prado, Madrid)

stern Spanish piety; hence she felt very deeply her mother's shame. Mary became warped and bitter. She hated the Reformation which had brought such humiliations on her. The Catholic religion was her one solace and she became a religious fanatic. Loving her people, she was determined, if ever it was within her power, to save their souls by bringing them back to the Church of Rome. According to her lights, her policy was noble. It was self-sacrificing, for she was ready to risk her throne in its behalf; it was honest, for she acted with complete sincerity. Yet she lacked patriotism and the ability to identify herself with her country. She could be gentle and forgiving in dealing with political offenders, but her determination in matters of religion was implacable; it brought tragedy on herself and grief to her kingdom.

Mary was in a strong position during the first months of her reign. The support accorded to her against Northumberland had been spontaneous and widespread. It was natural that Northumberland's followers be turned out of office, as they were. She was then able to appoint Catholic ministers and to liberate and restore the Catholic bishops who had been imprisoned in Edward's reign. Stephen Gardiner, bishop of Winchester, became Lord Chancellor and the Queen's principal adviser until the arrival of Cardinal Pole from Rome in 1554. Declaring herself a Roman Catholic, Mary encouraged priests to celebrate the Mass, which now reappeared throughout the country. The continental reformers, so influential under Edward, were told to leave the country. They were followed by a considerable number of Englishmen who preferred exile to life under a Catholic Queen. These Marian exiles, as they were called, were to be of great importance. Settling in various Protestant centers in Germany and Switzerland, where they grew more radical with the years, they were to bring their doctrines back to England in the first years of Queen Elizabeth.

Mary's first Parliament carried through part of her program with surprising alacrity. It annulled the divorce of Henry and Catherine of Aragon, thus removing all question of the legitimacy of Catherine's daughter. Proceeding further, Parliament swept away the statutes of Edward VI concerning religion. The church was brought back to where it had been at the death of Henry VIII. On the other hand, there were things this Parliament would not do. It refused to touch the royal supremacy over the church or to revive papal power. The Erastian nature of the English Reformation—that is, the subordination of the church to the control of the state—was too firmly fixed to be easily altered. Parliament also refused to restore the monastic lands which had passed into the hands of the laity. It declined to impose any penalty upon those who did not attend the Mass. Moreover, Parliament was giving the Queen a lesson regarding its position and power under the constitution. It knew very well what she wanted, but it decided what should be granted and what should be denied. Mary might well have heeded this warning. She might have seen that public opinion, as displayed in Parliament, was ready to return to the church of Henry VIII and to the Mass as practiced in the last years of his reign, but that it was unwilling to restore papal supremacy, or to force people to attend church, or to touch the monastic lands. Finally, Parliament showed itself suspicious of a Spanish marriage by petitioning the Queen to marry one of her own subjects.

The Spanish Marriage

The warnings were disregarded. Within a year Mary married Philip of Spain, son of Emperor Charles V, and brought England once more within the fold of the Roman Catholic Church. The marriage of a Queen, in an age when women were subject to their husbands, was a difficult matter; but Mary, like her father, felt a compelling necessity for an heir. If she had none, the throne would go to her sister, Elizabeth, the daughter of the hated Anne Boleyn. Catholics regarded Elizabeth as illegitimate; if she became Queen, the future of Catholicism looked dim. It was natural for Mary to turn to Spain for a husband. She was half Spanish by blood and more than half by sympathy. An alliance with the Hapsburgs, the most powerful rulers in Europe, appealed to her pride; their devotion to the Catholic Church appealed to her religious sympathies. Philip, when he arrived, seemed more than satisfactory, and Mary fell in love with him. He was twenty-seven; she was thirty-eight, austere, strait-laced, and very plain. Her love was not returned, so that a new sorrow soon entered her life. The marriage took place at Winchester in July 1554.

The terms of the marriage treaty were quite favorable to England. Philip and Mary were named as joint sovereigns and Philip was to have the title of King, but Mary was to appoint her ministers of state, who were to be English. England's foreign commitments remained as before and the country was not to be drawn into Spain's many wars on the Continent. A child born of the marriage should be Philip's heir in the Netherlands and in Burgundy as well as Mary's heir in England; Philip, if Mary died without children, should have no claim upon the English throne.

Despite these favorable terms the English were violently opposed to the marriage. The Spanish ruler, Charles V, aimed at the domination of the Continent. It could hardly be expected that Philip would abandon his father's ambition; hence England, despite the treaty, might well be used to advance the march of Spanish imperialism. England might become a dependency of Spain, ruled by a foreigner, and exploited for Spanish purposes. Thus the work of Henry VIII might be undone. The marriage not only posed a formidable threat to English independence but aroused the Englishman's traditional dislike and suspicion of foreigners. Although nationalism in England in the sixteenth century was very strong, it was still crude and unreasonable, and it was deeply offended by the prospect of a foreign King. The possibility that an English ruler might one day control the Netherlands was rendered less attractive by the decline of Antwerp as a market for English cloth.

More than one violent protest was made when the marriage treaty was concluded in January 1554. In Devonshire Sir Peter Carew plotted revolt, and a much more serious rebellion broke out in Kent under Sir Thomas Wyatt. Wyatt's Rebellion was highly dangerous because Kent was so close to the capital and because there was much sympathy for it in London. As Wyatt advanced from Rochester with a small army, troops were sent against him, but they changed sides and joined his cause. The Privy Council was in panic, but Mary, showing her courage by remaining in London, was able to rally the citizens in her defense. Wyatt found London Bridge so strongly held against him that he could not cross the Thames at that point. He moved upsteam to Kingston, crossed the river, and came toward London from the west. He was stopped at Ludgate, found himself hemmed in from the rear, and surrendered. His rebellion collapsed, but it was a clear indication that England wished to have no Spanish King.

The Return to Rome

The marriage in July 1554 was followed by the return to Rome in November. Mary succeeded in obtaining a House of Commons which was more amenable to her will than its predecessor. It petitioned her to restore papal supremacy by returning the Church of England to the Catholic fold. This was done on the arrival in England of Reginald Pole, a cardinal and *legatus a latere* from Rome. He was an aristocratic Englishman, a descendant of the Yorkist Kings, whose devotion to the Catholic Church had forced him into exile in the reign of Henry VIII. A power in Rome, he was almost elected Pope in 1549. On November 25, 1554, upon the intercession of King and Queen, he absolved England from the sin of schism and received her into the Roman Church. But he and Mary had to pay a price. Before Parliament sanctioned Pole's coming, it passed an act which safeguarded, carefully and completely, the retention of the monastic lands by those holding them, who were to continue to enjoy them "without scruple of conscience, . . . without impeachment or trouble by pretence of any General Council, canons, or ecclesiastical law, and clear from all dangers of the canons of the Church." The church lands remained in the hands of the nobility and gentry, and neither Queen nor cardinal could touch them. A complete return to the old order was thus impossible.

The Parliament of 1554, however, passed other legislation which Mary desired. It repealed in a great sweep all the ecclesiastical statutes of Henry's reign after 1528, thus undoing the English Reformation, at least on paper; it restored old laws against heresy and re-established the former jurisdiction of the church courts. This opened the way for the persecution which now began. Mary and Cardinal Pole believed that a few executions would terrify the people into universal acceptance of Catholicism, but they were wrong. The blood of martyrs is the life of the church; and the dauntless men and women who suffered the torture of being burned at the stake gave strength and inspiration to other Protestants to remain true to their religion.

Before the close of Mary's reign some 300 persons had been put to death. About a third of them were clergymen, some sixty were women. Neither the upper classes nor the peasantry provided many martyrs. It was the common folk of the industrial towns, especially in the southeastern portion of the country, the artisans and small tradesmen, who suffered steadfastly for their faith. Among the clerics were some famous victims: Cranmer, the archbishop; Hooper, "the father of nonconformity"; Ridley, the radical bishop of London; Latimer, the fearless preacher. "Be of good comfort," said Latimer to Ridley, as they died together, "we shall this day light a candle, by God's grace, in England, as I trust shall never be put out." This was a true prophecy. The burnings of Mary's reign, though insignificant in comparison with those on the Continent, were unparalleled in English history. They sank deeply into the minds of the people and created a fierce hatred of Roman Catholicism as well as the Protestant spirit which Mary had sought to extinguish.

In politics, as in religion, Mary's misguided actions produced much evil. Despite the safeguards of the marriage treaty, it was only to be expected that Philip would attempt to align England with Spain in her constant wars against France. When new hostilities broke out in 1557, he persuaded Mary to bring England into the conflict as Spain's ally. This was bad enough, but there was worse behind, for Spanish imperialism in Italy aroused the hostility of Pope Paul IV, who allied with France and excommunicated Philip. Mary was thus in a cruel dilemma: her two great loyalties, to the Pope and to her husband, were in open conflict. The war went very badly. The English people did not support it financially, nor did the English soldiers display much fighting spirit.

As a result the French captured Calais in January 1558. Its loss did England little harm; in fact, the kingdom was relieved of a burden, but Calais was a symbol of achievement and of the victories of the Hundred Years' War. The supine way in which it was surrendered was a national disgrace and Mary felt the shame keenly. At her death, she said, the word "Calais" would be found written on her heart. The Queen was in a tragic plight. Deserted by her husband, who spent his time in Spain, deprived of the hope of motherhood, faced by the animosity of her people, tainted with bloody persecution, oppressed by a terrible sense of failure, she sank into a state of melancholia which all but deranged her mind. On November 17, 1558, this broken, misguided, and melancholy figure passed away, leaving her country impoverished, torn, and defeated.

ECONOMIC TENSION

Although the Tudor period was an age of vigorous economic growth and increasing wealth and prosperity, the middle years of the century were years of economic crisis which, as it swelled to a climax and then slowly receded, affected a large part of the century and pointed the way to economic and social change. It caused great suffering among the lower classes. Preachers and reformers protested loudly that the times were out of joint, for economic forces had the effect of adding to the wealth of those who were already wealthy and of depressing those who were already depressed.

INFLATION

A fundamental cause of economic dislocation in the Tudor period was the constant inflationary rise in prices. For perhaps a century and a half in the later Middle Ages the level of prices had been steady or declining. Between 1500 and 1540, however, prices increased by some fifty percent; during the next twenty years they more than doubled; after 1560 they were perhaps five times what they had been when the Tudor period began. Contemporaries were bewildered by this phenomenon. They continued to think, as people had done in the Middle Ages, that every commodity had a just price determined by natural law. In the same way money had a just value, which was equal to the worth of the bullion it contained. If, then, goods had a just price and money a just value, the price level should remain constant unless wicked persons tampered with it for their own ends. Men could understand that in a time of dearth or famine, when goods were scarce while the amount of money remained the same, prices would rise. But it was only late in the century that they grasped the fact that prices would also rise if the amount of goods remained relatively steady while the amount of money increased. This is what was happening in the Tudor period. Inflation did not come from the greed of particular men, or from shortages of goods, for the age in general was a time of abundance; it sprang from a sharp increase in the amount of minted bullion.

The serious lack of bullion in the later Middle Ages had produced a determined effort to extract more silver from old mines in Germany and Bohemia. The amount of silver coin on the Continent increased, and it is there, perhaps, that the rise in prices began. The impact was quickly felt in England because of

Thomas Paycocke's House, Great Coggeshall, Essex. Paycocke was a wealthy
merchant clothier. (Copyright Country Life)

the cloth trade with the Netherlands. The rapidity with which Henry VIII squandered his father's treasure may have added to the amount of money in circulation. Gold and silver objects taken from the monasteries were turned into coin; moreover, the increased tempo of business activity resulting from the dissolution had an effect similar to an increase in money, for if money circulates rapidly it adds to the effective amount of coin.

The fantastic rise in prices during the last years of Henry VIII and the first years of Edward VI, however, was the result of a reckless debasement of the coinage. There had been a minor debasement in 1526, but the worst ones came between 1544 and 1551, when Henry found himself close to bankruptcy because of his wars with France and when Somerset, Lord Protector under Edward VI, debased the coinage still further. English money was lowered in both weight and quality until the amount of silver in it was only about a sixth of what it had been in 1485. The Crown made a large profit, perhaps half a million pounds, though the advantage soon disappeared because of the rise in the cost of everything the government bought. The people suffered cruelly. Retailers would not accept the new coins as the equivalent of the old, and prices shot up in an appalling way.

In 1551 the government, seeing its error, began to stabilize the coinage. In that year Northumberland, having followed Somerset in power, devaluated the "little shilling" to half its face value and began to issue new shillings containing a larger amount of silver. The coinage improved, and by 1560, in the reign of Elizabeth, money had regained its old proportion of bullion. Prices, however, continued to rise. Europe was now feeling the impact of the vast quantities of bullion brought by Spain from the mines of Mexico and Peru. One need only read the story of Potosí, a mountain discovered in Bolivia in 1545, which contained a fabulous amount of silver. This silver went to Spain but did not stay there. It bounced in and out of Spain, wrote a contemporary, like a ball in a tennis court. Spain had commitments throughout Europe, and the new coin spread far and wide. And so the rise in prices continued.

THE CLOTH TRADE

In the first half of the century the manufacture and export of woolen cloth was greatly stimulated by inflation. The export trade, as we have seen, was largely in the hands of the Merchant Adventurers,[2] who channeled the cloth through London to the great market at Antwerp. Fine English broadcloth sold well on the Continent, but the demand for coarse cheap cloth, known as kersey, seemed insatiable. English merchants had the advantage of selling in a market where the rise of prices was even greater than at home, and the export trade to Antwerp, which grew rapidly, received a fresh and violent impetus from Henry's debasement of the coinage. A pound sterling which was exchanged for 32 Flemish shillings in 1522 brought only 13 shillings 4 pence in 1551. Foreign buyers could thus obtain English cloth at a cheap rate, and the trade at Antwerp rose to such enormous heights that the whole English economy became distorted. A contemporary estimated that half the population of England was engaged in one way or another in supplying the demand for English cloth

[2] See pages 217–219.

abroad. Although this was a great exaggeration, it was true that English industry and agriculture, as well as foreign trade, received an enormous stimulus and that economic life became dangerously dependent upon the Antwerp market.

Industry

The manufacture of woolen cloth experienced a rapid and continual expansion. It was carried on both in the towns and in the country. The urban workers, trained by apprenticeship and controlled by the regulations of the guilds, were superior craftsmen who produced the finest cloth. But the industry in the towns was closely organized and restricted along medieval lines, was not elastic, and could not easily expand. The rural industry, on the other hand, was free from tradition, was younger and more pliable, and could be altered and expanded to meet the requirements of the market. Moreover, it produced the cheaper cloths, the kerseys, which sold so well in Antwerp. Hence it was the rural branch of the industry which developed in the early Tudor period. Spinners, weavers, and fullers multiplied in clothmaking areas; many villages became semi-industrial centers.

This rapid expansion seems to have resulted in some decline in the quality of the cloth produced. On the other hand, the industry became better organized and the flow of production more efficient. One difficulty in the domestic system of manufacture in the rural areas was a lack of coordination among its many units. The weaver might have to wait for his yarn and the fuller for his cloth; there was much carrying of goods from one worker to another. The industry in the country was only made possible by the merchant clothier, who bought the raw wool, put it out to be spun, woven, and finished by his workmen, paid them wages, collected the finished product, and sent it on to a larger merchant or exporter. In the expanding economy of the early Tudor period the clothier developed greatly and he sometimes became a very wealthy man. By skillful planning he controlled the flow of materials from one group of workers to the next, adjusted the volume of cloth produced to the demand of the market, and made the domestic system a more efficient method of manufacture.

AGRICULTURE

Agriculture as well as industry felt the effects of inflation and of increased demand for English cloth abroad. The medieval manor, with its lord and peasants, its open fields divided into age-old strips, its lord's demesne, its common pasture, common meadow, and common waste or woodland, was still the unit of agriculture in the grain-producing portions of England. The peasant had obtained his freedom in various ways, but by whatever tenure he held his land, whether by free socage or by copyhold or customary tenure or by a shorter lease, he paid some sort of rent to the lord of the manor. The owner of an estate was thus a landlord, deriving his income from rents, from fines paid by the peasants upon entry to their lands, from the profits of the manorial court. These payments were determined by custom and were relatively fixed, but the man with a fixed income in a time of inflation found himself in difficulties. His costs went up, his visits to London became more expensive, his standard of living was undermined. He might easily be dragged from riches to poverty. In order to escape ruin he must in some way extract a larger income from his land.

What did landlords do? It is obvious that many lords did nothing, either from conservative pride in the old way of life, or from kindly sympathy for their peasants, or from sheer inertia; in the majority of manors there was no change. But other landlords, desperate for cash, broke away from the restrictions of custom and seized upon any measures which offered hope of larger incomes. Such a lord might raise rents whenever opportunity served—when leases expired or when a peasant entered upon the land held by his father; if a peasant could not pay he was evicted and another peasant was found who could. There appears to have been a general rise in rents about the middle of the century. Or a landlord might rent his demesne to a big farmer, who thus obtained control over a considerable portion of the estate. The big farmer, paying a good rent, was also under pressure to increase his income from the land.

Finally, an enterprising owner might take the management of his estate into his own hands and share directly in the profits to be derived from selling agricultural products in a rising market. Such a landlord might improve old methods of husbandry. If he could manage his transportation problem he might join in the national industry of supplying London with food. He might dig for coal or other minerals on his property or take part in some local industrial enterprise. Or, more frequently, he might raise sheep and thus profit from the incessant and rising demand for wool. The number of sheep in England had been rising steadily since the middle of the fifteenth century. In Professor Bindoff's witty phrase, England was a place where the meek had inherited the earth. The sheep is not difficult to please. It will graze on the rough grass of the waste or village common as well as on lush pastures. One shepherd with his boy and his dog can care for a large flock. The amount of land under pasture steadily increased, reaching a peak between 1540 and 1555. But at the end of the fifteenth century the human population of the country also began to rise. There were more mouths to feed, and a contest ensued between the amount of land to be devoted to pasture and the amount to be kept in crops. The landlord who profited from the high price of wool was apt to clash with the peasant who derived his living from crops raised on the arable fields.

Enclosures

The extension of pasturage for sheep led to enclosures. An enclosure was a solid block of land carved out from some portion of the manor and surrounded by a hedge or fence so that domestic animals could not leave or enter. There had been some enclosing in the later Middle Ages by the peasants. An upper class of peasants had emerged, more prosperous than their neighbors, who had acquired land and had sometimes surrounded their holdings by a hedge. One happy aspect of the Tudor period was that these peasants often throve, became yeomen, and sometimes made their way into the lower ranks of the gentry.

Most Tudor enclosures, however, were carried out by bigger men than peasants. The process often began with the enclosure of the demesne, sometimes for raising food for the manor house, sometimes for ostentation in making a deer park, more frequently for raising sheep. The peasant might lose heavily by the enclosing of the demesne. The interests of the manor were cut in two, the lord wishing to raise sheep; the peasant, crops. The peasant could no longer graze his animals on the demesne after the harvest had been gathered. And if the lord departed for London, the peasant and his family lost casual employment as servants in the great house of the village. A second step was to enclose the village waste or pasture or meadow. This type of enclosing was bitterly resented, for it left the peasant without pasture for his animals. And finally the lord or big farmer might rid himself of the peasants altogether and turn the open fields of the village into great sheep runs. The results were deserted villages, evicted peasants, and increased vagabondage.

One must not exaggerate the amount of enclosing that took place. Only a small fraction of the open fields was enclosed during the Tudor period; even in counties where the movement was strong it is probable that less than a third of the arable land was enclosed. There was some enclosing for improved cultivation of the soil and some was carried out by the peasants themselves. It is true that peasants were evicted at times in a highhanded way, and that some of them, being simple folk, suffered wrong without asserting their rights. But most peasants fought for what was theirs, and for the most part found that the courts would defend them.

A peasant owning his land could not be deprived of it against his will. Customary tenants and copyholders held land by a kind of perpetual lease renewable by one generation after another upon the payment of a fine. The agreement between lord and peasant was enscribed on the manor roll. Copyholders possessed a copy of this enrollment whereas the customary tenant did not. What really mattered was less the possession of the copy than the exact terms on which the land was held. If these terms were clear and precise and if a peasant could pass his lands to his son upon payment of a fixed amount, he was relatively safe. If the terms were vague, if the peasant held only a life interest in the land, or if the sum payable by his son could be arbitrarily increased, the peasant was in a dangerous position. He was better off, however, than the tenant at will, who held land merely at the lord's pleasure and could be evicted at any moment. A peasant who lost his holding was in a pitiable condition. He and his family drifted away to the towns, or swelled the ranks of vagabonds and beggars, or settled as unwelcome squatters on the wastelands of unenclosed manors. A small amount of enclosing could inflict a very great amount of suffering upon the poor.

Into this millstream of inflation, debasement, enclosures, and artificially stimulated foreign trade, Henry VIII flung the lands he had taken from the monasteries. To meet the cost of the French war, great quantities of these lands were unloaded on the market for what they would fetch. There were about a thousand buyers, some of whom purchased land as a long-term investment, some of whom were London speculators who sold as soon as they could make a profit. Often the land changed hands a number of times; indeed, a brisk land market existed for many years. This process probably stimulated enclosing. A new owner, perhaps a businessman, regarding his purchase partly as an investment and lacking the kindly sympathies of a man who had known a locality from childhood, was doubtless inclined to reap a profit where he could. In the long run, however, most of the monastic lands made their way into the hands of the nobility and even more into the hands of the gentry, who probably dealt with their new tenants much as they had dealt with the old. The land hunger of the age did not always arise from a desire for profit. Many a wealthy merchant, lawyer, or official was ambitious to found a county family (and if he was not, his wife and daughters were). The first step was the acquisition of an estate. The urge to own property in the country, to break into the magic circle of the gentry, to display one's wealth by building a fine country house, to enjoy the pleasures of rural life made land attractive and raised its price.

Kett's Rebellion, 1549

The Protector Somerset permitted more freedom of speech and of the press than had been allowed in Henry's reign; hence a sudden outburst of indignation at the economic ills of the time and a bitter denunciation of enclosing were to be expected. Writers such as Henry Brinkelow and Robert Crowley (who printed an edition of *Piers Ploughman*), preachers such as Hugh Latimer and Thomas Lever, and politicians such as John Hales lashed at the greed and materialism of the age and depicted the sufferings of the lower classes in vivid colors. These reformers declared that men must have consideration for the general welfare—for the commonweal—and must not be allowed to do as they pleased, even with their own, if they brought distress upon other people.

In 1548 John Hales, who had the support of Somerset, obtained two measures which might have brought some relief to the poor. One was a subsidy bill by which the government was to surrender purveyance—the right of the King to live off the country as he traveled about—and in exchange should levy a small tax on sheep and on wool used in manufacturing cloth, and a heavier tax on each broadcloth exported from the kingdom. The object of the act was to discourage concentration of the economy on the manufacture and export of cloth. Hales's second measure was the appointment of a commission to investigate the extent of enclosures, both as a warning to landlords that their actions were being watched and as a promise to the poor that some relief from their sufferings was at hand. But the commission found its work obstructed by the upper classes, who would not give the information asked; and the peasants, excited by the hope the measure offered, broke into a series of revolts.

For some years there had been local riots against enclosing. In 1548 these riots swelled into an uprising of the peasants through much of southern England. In Cornwall and Devon the rebellion was partly a protest against the religious radicalism of Edward's reign. This part of the revolt, as it moved eastward, was stopped at Exeter and was crushed by government troops. More serious was a remarkable rebellion in Norfolk led by Robert Kett in 1549. It has been called a sitdown strike, for the peasants of Norfolk gathered in a great host outside the city of Norwich and simply stayed there, setting up a kind of communistic state with governors, councils, and law courts. They were surprisingly orderly and religious, and they used the new Prayer Book recently issued by the government. It is difficult to explain their inertia. It may be that Kett, knowing that Somerset had much sympathy with the poor, believed he would support the uprising. Or Kett may have considered himself an unofficial agent of the state who had assumed unbidden the task of teaching a lesson to the gentry of East Anglia. If Kett had such thoughts he was in error. The peasants were slaughtered by royal troops, the rebellion was made an excuse to turn Somerset out of power; and under Northumberland a reaction took place against Somerset's liberal policy.

THE END OF THE BOOM

In 1551 Northumberland called down the shilling to half its face value. This action had an immediate effect on the English market for cloth at Antwerp. Devaluation of the English shilling meant that foreign buyers must pay twice as much for English cloth as before. The Antwerp market came crashing down and the great boom ended forever. In the 1560s the Netherlands revolted against

Spain; in these wars Antwerp was so thoroughly devastated that it never recovered its old position. In England the results were depression in the cloth industry and much suffering among the craftsmen. The clothier fell upon evil days. It is in the glut of unsold cloth and in the decline of the market at Antwerp that we find the origin of a new and determined effort to open new trades and markets overseas for the sale of English goods. Enclosing subsided, though it did not disappear, and some land used for pasture was again put in crops.

The Merchant Adventurers, having lost their staple at Antwerp, sought some other city on the Continent to make the headquarters of their trade. They moved from place to place. Finally, toward the end of the century, they settled at Middelburg in Zeeland. Seeing their trade decline, they sought a tighter monopoly of what remained to them. They obtained government action against the merchants of the Hansa who, though much less powerful than they had been earlier in the century, still did business in England. The privileged position of the Hansa was revoked in 1552, partially restored in 1554, but revoked once more in 1558. The Merchant Adventurers also turned against those members of their society who were not Londoners and drove them from the association. In 1564 the Merchant Adventurers obtained a new charter which gave them a virtual monopoly of the export of cloth to the Continent. Thenceforth they merely attempted to keep what they had. They suffered greatly from interlopers who invaded their monopoly and disturbed their closely regulated commerce. Their great days were also over.

THE DECLINE OF THE GUILDS

A few additional points may be made concerning the economic history of the time. Of these the most crucial was the rapid decline of the guilds. The guilds in the later Middle Ages, as we have seen,[3] had lost the unity of their membership. It had become impossible for most apprentices to become masters. Instead, they became journeymen who worked for wages; and the journeymen, finding that they had little to gain from the old guilds, had formed guilds of their own or had migrated into rural areas in search of freer conditions. The old conception of master and apprentice had been transformed into the modern relationship of employer and employee. A division between the richer and the poorer masters also appeared. The wealthier ones, usually those engaged in selling, had obtained control of the guild organization as well as control of the government of the towns in which they resided.

Similar forces operated in the Tudor period. The exodus to the country continued. New industries, such as the refining of sugar and the manufacture of glass, grew up in rural areas away from guild restrictions, and many industries using wood or coal as fuel migrated to regions where those fuels could be obtained. There was a great deal of mining, not only of coal, lead, iron, and copper, but of zinc (for brass cannon), saltpeter (for gunpowder), and alum (for dyeing).

The gulf between richer and poorer masters widened. In the fifteenth century livery companies began to appear. These were guilds in which a small group of masters secured for themselves a status superior to the others. To be

[3] See pages 129–130.

"of the livery," a master must pay a heavy fee and purchase an expensive livery to be worn on state occasions. In 1483 at the coronation of Richard III, 406 members of the London livery companies rode in mulberry-colored coats. These liverymen were capitalists inside the guilds who controlled the guild organization and who monopolized—or tried to monopolize—the sale of the articles the guild produced. Their development may be illustrated by the tailors' guild in London. The tailors had long held a monopoly of their trade in the capital. In 1502 they secured a new charter which permitted them to call themselves Merchant Tailors, since they sold throughout the kingdom, and to control admission to their number. In other words, liverymen were becoming merchants who sold the goods made by craftsmen of the guilds. Because the livery controlled its own membership, it could require that only men with capital be admitted. Smaller masters, though they employed apprentices and journeymen, sold their goods to liverymen and lost contact with the customer.

Other companies appeared, composed of merchants who had nothing to do with manufacture. Although they took their name from some trade—they were grocers, or mercers, or vintners, or haberdashers—these companies were composed of merchants who secured charters allowing them to sell a particular article. They claimed the sole right of selling at retail and tried to exclude the smaller masters from retail business. There was little left of the old guild organization.

The guilds also suffered from an ever-increasing regulation of economic life by the state. It is true that some statutes and other actions of the government at times protected the guilds, but the general tendency was in the opposite direction. The Privy Council devoted an enormous amount of time to the regulation of industry; and many statutes dealt with the true making of this or that manufacture. Two acts of 1504 undermined the position of the guilds: they could not make new rules concerning industry without obtaining the consent of the government and they could not forbid their members from appealing to the national courts in trades disputes. In 1547 Parliament dissolved the chantries, which were small endowed churches or chapels, but the act was so worded that it also swept away other religious foundations, including endowments held by the guilds for religious and social purposes. Some guilds never recovered from this heavy financial loss. The Statute of Artificers of 1563, which was a great industrial code, gave power to the justices of the peace to control local prices, wages, and hours of labor, thus superseding much guild regulation. By the end of the century the guilds no longer staged their mystery plays, partly because of their poverty, partly because professional actors in London were beginning to make tours into the provinces. In some towns the guilds kept alive only by combining into a single organization.

THE LONDON MONEY MARKET

An important money market developed in London. It can be illustrated by the career of Lionel Cranfield, about whom a fascinating book has been written.[4] He was a successful young merchant in London in the last decade of

---

[4] R. H. Tawney, *Business and Politics under James I. Lionel Cranfield as Merchant and Minister* (Cambridge: Cambridge University Press, 1958).

Elizabeth's reign. A member of the Mercers Company and of the Merchant Adventurers, he exported fine English cloth to Holland and coarser kerseys to Stade in northern Germany. His imports consisted largely of expensive Italian fabrics and other luxuries to be sold to the fashionable world at court. With the money accumulated in trade, Cranfield moved into the position of a capitalist with wealthy associates in the City and with influential friends at court. He speculated in the collection of the customs, in Crown lands, and in the exploitation of economic privileges bestowed by the Queen on her courtiers. With other moneyed men in the City he helped raise loans for the government. He also acted as a banker, accepting private funds on deposit and paying them out on demand; he was entrusted with money to be put out at interest; and he made loans to needy aristocrats on the security of their estates (which sometimes fell into his hands). He was the hard, shrewd, moneyed man of the City, with a hand in countless deals.

13

ELIZABETH I: THE FIRST TEN YEARS OF THE REIGN

THE QUEEN

Queen Elizabeth I is famous for her political genius, for the brilliant success of her reign, and for the loyalty she evoked in the hearts of her people. She shaped her country's destiny. She came to the throne at twenty-five, an attractive young woman, tall, well-built, vigorous in mind and body, with an olive complexion and reddish-gold hair. Her traits of character were not the feminine qualities of sweetness and gentleness but the masculine ones of pride, strength, aggressiveness, self-confidence, and courage. There was an imperious quality about her that made men think of her father. Like him she was determined to rule. She held lofty views of her royal prerogatives, and she could stand her ground against councilors, Parliament, and people.

She was an excellent conversationalist, alternating gracious affability with tart reproof, kindly approbation with biting criticism; she could win, she could baffle, she could deceive. A story is told of an audience with an ambassador from Poland who boastfully advised her that for her own good she should ally with his master. The ambassador spoke in Latin. In reply, Elizabeth poured forth a torrent of Latin invective which amazed the court and deflated the ambassador. Elizabeth was highly educated; besides Latin, she spoke French and Italian. Even after she was Queen she read Latin and Greek with her old tutor, Roger Ascham. It was her practice after a stormy interview to retire to her chamber and regain her serenity by reading Latin verse. As an administrator she possessed a grasp of reality. She was industrious, willing to spend time on the details of government, very careful of her money, and a fine judge of character. Her boldness was tempered by prudence, and she hated to make decisions which could not later be revoked. As a diplomat she was shrewd, deceitful, and wily, quite able to hold her own with other sovereigns.

Like her father, she was vain, with a keen awareness of physical appearance both in herself and in others. She once forced the Scottish Ambassador, Robert Melville, to compare her with Mary, Queen of Scots. Who was fairer, who was

Queen Elizabeth I, painted c. 1575, artist unknown. (National Portrait Gallery, London)

taller, who played more skillfully on the lute and the virginals, who danced better? The hard-pressed ambassador answered as best he could, but admitted that Elizabeth danced "higher and more composedly." She enjoyed the company and admiration of handsome men. Her courtiers had to pretend they were smitten by her charms long after those charms had withered. During the first months of her reign, when the popularity of the Tudor dynasty was at a low ebb, she set out to win the hearts of the people. By every grace and art of an attractive young woman, mingling mildness with majesty, she sought popular support by courting her subjects, a courtship she continued throughout her reign. Nor was it mere acting. She possessed a broad and genuine humanity, a lively sympathy with the joys and sorrows, the hopes and prejudices of her people. She loved England, she identified herself with her country, she gloried in being "mere English."

Her youth had taught her that intelligence, not emotion, must guide her conduct. When she was only fifteen she had had a short love affair, unsavory but harmless, with Thomas Seymour, brother of the Lord Protector Somerset. Seymour had sought to advance himself by intriguing to marry her. Suddenly he had been arrested and executed for his folly and some discredit had been thrown upon Elizabeth. The episode was a lesson in the dangers that scandal could bring. During the reign of Mary Tudor, Elizabeth had been the unwitting pawn in every conspiracy against the throne; she had been sent to the Tower under suspicion of complicity in Wyatt's Rebellion; a false step might have cost her her life. From these experiences she emerged self-reliant, cautious, and self-controlled, but hard, suspicious, and rather lacking in magnanimity.

INITIAL PROBLEMS

Relations with Foreign States

At the accession of Elizabeth the country was faced by problems of the most serious kind. Conditions abroad were very dangerous. England was still at war with France, though the fighting was over and Calais was lost. France, the national enemy, possessed a great advantage in the Franco-Scottish alliance. In 1548 the Scots had sent their little Queen, Mary, who was only five, to France, where she was educated to marry Francis, the eldest son of the French King, Henry II. The marriage took place in 1558. Mary was a descendant of Henry VII;[1] in Catholic eyes she was the rightful Queen of England, for Catholics regarded Elizabeth as illegitimate. As soon as Elizabeth ascended the throne, the French proclaimed Mary the Queen of England. Her mother, Mary of Guise, who was Regent in Scotland, ruled that country in the French interest. Hence a French army aimed at the invasion of England could easily land in Scotland. The French King, said an Englishman, "bestrides the realm, having one foot in Calais and the other in Scotland." England was almost defenseless—its forts decayed, its finances disordered, its army demoralized, its navy worthless. One hope lay in the fact that Philip of Spain, in his hostility to France, would not allow that country to conquer England. Elizabeth judged rightly that should France try to invade England Philip would defend her in order to protect himself. So sure of this was she that when Philip made her a condescending offer of marriage she

[1] See genealogical table, page 223.

had the fortitude to decline. Yet there must have been a fear gnawing at her heart. When Spain and England on the one hand and France on the other made peace at Le Cateau-Cambrésis in 1559, one section of the treaty provided for Philip's marriage to a daughter of the King of France. If Catholic Spain and Catholic France became allies, the prospects of a Protestant England were dim indeed.

William Cecil, Lord Burghley, probably by Marcus Gheeraerts. (National Portrait Gallery, London)

A Woman Ruler

At home many problems centered in the person of the Queen. That a woman could rule successfully was a novel idea; that an unmarried woman could do so was unthinkable. Just before Elizabeth ascended the throne, John Knox in Scotland had written a denunciation of female rulers, *The First Blast of the Trumpet against the Monstrous Regiment of Women.* "It is more than a monster in nature," he wrote, "that a woman should reign and bear empire above men." This war whoop had been directed against Mary of Guise; and Knox was abashed, though he would not apologize, when Elizabeth became Queen. He merely expressed the view of his contemporaries, who wondered whether Elizabeth could obtain the obedience of her councilors and courtiers.

She had reconstructed her Privy Council, retaining eleven of Mary's ministers and adding seven new ones, thus wisely reducing the Council to about half its former size. Her most important appointment was that of her Secretary, Sir William Cecil, later Lord Burghley. Cecil's lucid mind and grasp of realities, his sagacity, his industry and attention to detail, his utter loyalty made him a perfect minister. The trust between him and the Queen was to grow with time, and he was to remain her principal adviser for forty years. Yet even Cecil was at first inclined to think that young women should follow the counsel of their masculine elders. Elizabeth rarely attended the meetings of her Council. She feared that in the give-and-take of discussion she might be overruled; her practice was to have problems debated in the Council and its advice brought to her, so that she could accept or reject that advice as she saw fit. Much of her governing was done in private interviews with one or two of her ministers, but she soon established her authority. Shortly after her accession the Spanish Ambassador wrote that she was "incomparably more feared than her sister, and gives her orders and has her way as absolutely as her father did." This was no small achievement for a young woman of twenty-five.

Then there was the court, a giant household of some 1500 persons, including all ranks of society from nobles and statesmen to the servants in the kitchen. The court was the center both of government and of fashion; it was the symbol of royalty, the place to which all men looked who hoped for a career in the service of the state. Elizabeth must maintain its splendor and high spirits to attract men to it, to keep the nobility amused, and to impress the envoys of foreign lands. She must win the loyalty of her courtiers, since from them she selected officials and ministers. She must pacify the quarrels of proud nobles and jealous bureaucrats and must restrain her many servants within the bounds of decency and decorum. And all had to be done at a reasonable charge. Elizabeth controlled the court through her masterful personality as well as her unique ability to create the atmosphere of a fairy idyll in which all men pretended to be in love with her and to serve her as the mistress of their hearts. The comedy was artificial and tended to false flattery, but it served its turn.

Other problems concerned the Queen's marriage and the succession. Elizabeth was the last of the children of Henry VIII; if she died without issue the throne would go to a collateral line. The Scottish claim was represented by Mary of Scotland. But Mary's succession, which would have been backed by France and by the Catholic north of England, would almost certainly have provoked a civil war. In his will Henry VIII had passed over the Scottish line and had vested the succession, in case his children died without issue, in the descendants of his younger sister Mary, who had married Charles Brandon, Duke of Suffolk. The

Suffolk claim was represented in Elizabeth's reign by Lady Catherine Grey and later by her son, Edward Seymour, Lord Beauchamp. But Catherine's secret marriage, of dubious legality, enraged Elizabeth and all but excluded both Lady Catherine and her son from the succession.

It was assumed by everyone that Elizabeth would marry. Her protestations that she was content to remain a virgin produced at first polite approval and then downright annoyance. She had many suitors, most of them foreigners who never came to England. But she was determined not to marry without seeing what she was getting; and she feared that a husband who was a foreigner might influence policy in behalf of his own country, as Philip of Spain had done in the reign of Mary Tudor. Hence her many negotiations for marriage were no more than moves in the game of diplomacy.

Early in the reign she was fascinated by one of her courtiers, Robert Dudley, son of the Duke of Northumberland who had ruled England in Edward's reign. Dudley was a handsome and dashing soldier, an accomplished courtier, and a good conversationalist, though actually a man of no great ability. The court was filled with rumors of an impending match. But the thought of Dudley as the Queen's husband horrified councilors and courtiers. Moreover, he was already married; and when his wife, Amy Robsart, at her lonely house in the country, fell downstairs and broke her neck, there were ugly suspicions of murder. Had Elizabeth married Dudley under these circumstances she would have risked her throne. Her intelligence fought with her emotions, and her intelligence won. Dudley remained the Master of the Horse and became Earl of Leicester, a friend and favorite of the Queen, but nothing more. It is not unlikely that in rejecting him she rejected marriage. For thirty years the English lived in dread that her sudden death would be followed by chaos.

The Settlement of Religion

Religion was another vital problem. Within a few years the country had experienced three ecclesiastical settlements: the Anglo-Catholicism of Henry, who had repudiated the Pope but had retained the Mass; the radical Protestantism of Edward; the return to Rome under Mary. Elizabeth was not a religious person. She had none of Mary's fanatical zeal and had no wish to make windows into men's souls. Like the *politiques* in France, she regarded peace as more important than a solution of the religious quarrel. What she wanted was unity— a settlement which the bulk of the people would accept and which would diminish the danger of internal strife. Her approach was conservative. She believed that the Crown had the right to impose a religious settlement; she liked decorum, form, and order in the church as well as in everything else; she would have preferred a return to conditions as her father had left them. But such a return was impossible; her choice lay between Catholicism and the Protestantism of Edward.

Without a doubt she weighed the advantages of retaining a moderate Catholic Church purged of Mary's fanatical fury. Such a solution not only would have eased her relations with continental states but would have enabled her to keep the church much as it was without the turmoil of a new upheaval. But the adoption of Catholicism would have been an appeasement of Catholic Europe. Elizabeth's courage—her faith in herself and in her people—dictated a bolder course. Her pride revolted at the thought of acknowledging papal supremacy. She knew that large numbers of her subjects were bitterly opposed to Rome and that this opposition would be strengthened by the return of the 500 or so English Protestants who had gone into exile in Mary's reign. Many were gentry and many were clergymen; they would be leaders of English religious thought for years to come. On the Continent they had been deeply influenced by the doctrines of John Calvin; they returned to England more radically Protestant than when they had left. Moreover, the Protestants at home who had supported Elizabeth during Mary's reign and who hailed her now as their hope and deliverer were strongly anti-Catholic. Should she reward their loyalty by deserting them? Elizabeth chose to be Protestant. But she wished to move in that direction slowly, so as not to alienate Philip of Spain before she was well seated on her throne.

Her religious settlement was made in her first Parliament in 1559. This Parliament was thoroughly Protestant. A dozen of the Marian exiles were influential members, and at least a fourth of the Commons were eager for radical change. Slowly Elizabeth was coerced into a more Protestant settlement than she desired. Her wish seems to have been that Parliament should pass an act of supremacy restoring the legislation of Henry VIII, but that the Mass should be retained, at least for the present. The Commons, on the other hand, desired not only an act of supremacy but also a Protestant form of worship, to be embodied in a new act of uniformity by which the Mass should be abolished. There was a struggle, but Elizabeth eventually accepted both supremacy and uniformity. Thus the settlement was one dictated in part by the lay politicians in the House of Commons.

The Act of Supremacy of 1559 restored the laws of Henry VIII separating the English Church from Rome. There were certain alterations. The Queen assumed the title of Supreme Governor of the Church, not that of Supreme Head. This change of title, although meaningless in practice, was a concession to Catholics, who regarded the pope as the only head of the church and also a concession to those radical Protestants who held that the church had no earthly head but only Christ. The new act, like that of Henry, contained an oath; a person taking the oath swore that he believed in the principles of the act. Henry's oath, however, could be forced upon anyone; refusal had often meant death. Elizabeth's oath could be required only of officeholders, and the penalty for refusal was no more than loss of office.

The Act of Uniformity provided for a new Prayer Book to be used by the clergy in divine worship throughout the kingdom. Although it was based on the second and more Protestant Prayer Book of Edward VI, modifications rendered it more conservative than Edward's. Certain words in the service of Holy Communion implied a belief in the doctrine of transubstantiation, whereas other words appeared to reject that doctrine. Thus more than one interpretation was possible. Attendance of the people at church on Sundays and holy days was compulsory, but the penalty for absence was merely a fine of one shilling. These acts were followed by royal injunctions which permitted clergymen to marry, prescribed the clerical vestments to be worn in church, decided the position of the altar, and governed the conduct of the people during divine worship.

Although the church was in Catholic hands at Elizabeth's accession, the transfer to Protestantism was accomplished with surprising ease. Cardinal Pole, by a strange oversight, had left five bishoprics vacant at the end of Mary's reign; his death added a sixth. Four more Catholic bishops died within a year. There were thus ten vacancies in an episcopal bench of twenty-six; and these ten bishoprics, as the Spanish Ambassador wrote gloomily, "would now be given to as many ministers of Lucifer." The remaining Catholic bishops, with one exception, refused the Oath of Supremacy and were deprived of office. Their opposition was only to be expected. What is surprising is that the majority of parish priests accepted Elizabeth's church and remained within it. There were, of course, some who refused. The number is not known; guesses have ranged from a figure of 200 up to 1000. Whatever the truth, it is clear that Elizabeth's church began its existence with a serious shortage of parish priests—a source of just criticism for years to come.

The Elizabethan settlement was mild, wise, and generous. For some years it appeared to be working well. Later in the reign Elizabeth found herself under attack from the Catholic Church on the one hand and from Puritan extremists on the other and was compelled to deal more harshly with her opponents.

The Treaty of Edinburgh

A crisis arose in 1559 as a result of the Scottish Reformation. The Reformation in Scotland differed entirely from that in England. It was not a movement led from above by an autocratic ruler such as Henry VIII; it was a revolt from below against a Catholic government. Hence from the first it contained an antimonarchical and republican element; it was more violent than in England, more uncompromising, and more complete. Its tone was set by John Knox, that thundering Scottish Elijah who dreaded one Mass more than 10,000 foreign foes and who filled his followers with a horror of all things Roman. There had been some Protestantism in Scotland for a number of years. A reformer, George Wishart, had been executed in 1546; in the same year there had been a small uprising in which Cardinal Beaton, a hated Catholic prelate, had been assassinated. This uprising, however, was easily put down.

In the 1550s the reforming movement became more formidable. It was led by a group of nobles, the Lords of the Congregation, but it drew its strength from the towns, from the lairds or gentry, and from a handful of clergymen, of whom John Knox was the most important. Though not involved in the murder of Beaton, Knox had joined the insurgents, had been captured, and had been sent to France, where for a time he was a galley slave. Later he had been in England. His return to Scotland in 1559 caused an explosion. A sermon at Perth was followed by a riot in which the church was demolished. Knox was not a pleasant man. He was narrow, hard, rough, and uncompromising, but he was a great leader, a fighter, and a powerful preacher. Of boundless energy and courage, he "neither flattered nor feared any flesh."

Scottish Protestantism was strengthened by Scottish national feeling. Since 1554 the country had been ruled by Mary of Guise, a Frenchwoman and mother of Mary, Queen of Scots. With French advisers and French troops, Mary of Guise had been making Scotland a mere dependency of France. Opposition was bitter. The Scots, having fought for centuries to remain independent of England, had no mind to become a French satellite. Their old ally was becoming their tyrant. Mary of Guise, moreover, had conducted a vigorous campaign against Protestantism. Hence patriotism merged with religious zeal in hostility to her regime. A rebellion broke out in 1559. But it became obvious that the Scottish Protestants could not defeat the government without assistance. Mary of Guise, backed by French troops, was too strong for them. Before the summer of 1559 was over they appealed to Elizabeth for aid.

Elizabeth was faced with a difficult decision. She hated rebels and she disliked religious radicals; yet the Scottish Protestants were both. As for Knox, who had blown the trumpet against female rulers, no one dared to mention him in her presence. The French court was very anti-English. Henry II died in July and was succeeded by his son, Francis II, a boy of fifteen whose wife, Mary, Queen of Scots, was now Queen of France. Her ambitious uncles, the Duke of Guise and the cardinal of Lorraine, dominated the court. If Elizabeth sent assistance to the Scots she threw down a challenge to France that might result in a general war. If she did nothing she tightened French control in Scotland and increased the Franco-Scottish-Catholic threat at her northern border. If, on the other hand, the Scottish Protestants with her assistance could drive out the French, her position would be vastly improved. A friendly Protestant government could perhaps be set up in Scotland in place of a hostile Catholic one. The bold course of intervention was thus supported by strong arguments, and Elizabeth followed it.

At first she sent aid secretly and shamelessly denied what she was doing. Money and arms were dispatched to the north in the summer of 1559. In January 1560, an English fleet under Admiral William Winter entered the Firth of Forth, destroyed French shipping, and prevented the landing of war supplies from France. Winter blandly told Mary of Guise that he was acting solely on his own responsibility. Within a few months, however, the mask was thrown aside. An English army entered Scotland and advanced against the French fortress at Leith. The response from France was surprisingly weak. The Guises, who had just crushed a conspiracy against them, had their hands full at home. Two French fleets dispatched to Scotland were driven back by heavy weather with great loss. And in Scotland Mary of Guise was at the point of death. The French, therefore, instead of fighting further, sent a delegation to treat for peace.

The important Treaty of Edinburgh, which followed in 1560, provided that both French and English troops be withdrawn from Scotland; that Scotland be governed by twelve Scottish nobles, six to be named by Mary and six by the Scots themselves; that France recognize Elizabeth as the rightful Queen of England. Francis and Mary, refusing to yield this final point, declined to ratify the treaty. Their refusal made comparatively little difference. The French troops left for home, and the Protestant Scottish nobles took over the government. The Scottish Reformation proceeded apace. Papal jurisdiction was renounced, the Mass forbidden, and a reformed church set up, though its organization was left for the future. The Treaty of Edinburgh was a notable triumph for Elizabeth, who had adopted a daring and courageous policy and had carried it through to success. Unaided by Spain she had driven the French from Scotland. Her prestige abroad was vastly enhanced, and foundations were laid for an era of cooperation between England and Scotland based upon a common Protestantism and a common hostility to interference from the Continent.

SCOTLAND AND MARY, QUEEN OF SCOTS

Scotland continued to occupy Elizabeth's attention. Francis II of France died in December 1560, a blow that shattered Mary's high position as Queen of France. Her uncles of Guise lost their influence at court, and her wish to marry the new King Charles IX, a boy of about eleven, was thwarted by the malice of her mother-in-law, Catherine de Médicis. There was no course open but a return to Scotland. On a dreary day in August 1561, in the midst of storm and fog, Mary landed at Leith. How dour and barren Scotland must have seemed to this young widow of nineteen who had lived for thirteen years in sunny France.

Scotland was a lawless, backward, and poverty-stricken country, torn by feuds of rival clans and by constant deeds of violence. The power of the Crown was small in the Highlands and in the Cheviot Hills along the Border; it scarcely existed in the primitive Western Isles. And even in the Lowlands, centering in the area around Glasgow, Stirling, St. Andrews, and Edinburgh, royal authority was diminished greatly by the exorbitant power of the nobles. There was not much hope that Mary could rule Scotland with success. Her beauty, her bewitching charms and graces, her love of music and dancing, her high spirits and reckless daring, her fondness for war and manly sports, her ambition, and the intensity of her loves and hates—these things made her a fascinating woman to whom men were strongly attracted. Her diplomacy and plottings were bold and clever, but they were also brittle and unrealistic. She was lacking in judgment, in maturity, in the capacity to control her emotions. In short, she was not really intelligent. She had little interest in government. Indeed, she had little interest in Scotland save as a steppingstone for her ambitions. She did not love Scotland as Elizabeth loved England.

Mary's first years in Scotland were not unsuccessful. She came with a desire to please and she did not question the authority of the Protestant lords whom she found in control of the government; in her half brother, the Earl of Moray, an illegitimate son of James V, and even more in her able Secretary, William Maitland of Lethington, she possessed sound advisers. She could not get on with Knox. He thundered against her because she attended Mass; he denounced her gaiety and dancing—the skipping at court, as he called it, not very comely for honest women. Mary tried to win him, first by her charms and then by her tears, which the crabbed preacher referred to as so much "owling." Nonetheless, conditions in Scotland were better than might have been expected. Had Mary been able to satisfy her ambitions by a brilliant marriage or by the recognition of her right to succeed Elizabeth, she might have remained content. But Elizabeth, for reasons of sound policy, blocked Mary's moves toward marriage and refused recognition of her title to the English succession.

As the two Queens drifted into hostility Mary began to chafe. She grew weary of Maitland's tutelage, of Knox's rantings, and of Elizabeth's condescension. When a match with Don Carlos of Spain grew cold, Mary cast her eye upon a young noble at the English court, Henry Stewart, Lord Darnley, a descendant of Margaret Tudor by her second husband, Archibald Douglas, Earl of Angus. Darnley was close to the Scottish throne and was also a possible heir to that of England. Having tricked Elizabeth into allowing Darnley to come to Scotland, Mary proceeded to fall in love with him. He was a pretty boy of nineteen, tall and slender, with a pleasant face and yellow hair, and with the outward graces of the courtier. When Mary married him in July 1565 she did so in defiance of her Protestant councilors, of Knox, and of Elizabeth. Darnley's background was Catholic. The marriage placed Mary at the head of the Catholic party in both kingdoms. At first she was successful. The Protestant lords revolted, but she drove them into England in an exciting campaign in which she rode in armor with her troops and forded a river on horseback during a violent storm.

The marriage with Darnley was Mary's undoing. He proved to be an impos-

Mary, Queen of Scots, by Peter Oudry. (National Galleries of Scotland, Edinburgh)

sible raw youth, not only stupid but vain, insolent, treacherous, and debauched. The court was full of quarrels, and Mary soon regarded her husband with a kind of nausea. She turned for consolation and counsel to a young Italian at her court, David Rizzio, who became her favorite. The folly of her affection for him can hardly be exaggerated. Italians with their dandified ways were not popular; the Scots were grieved "to see their sovereign guided by such a fellow." Darnley, growing jealous, plotted with the exiled Protestant lords; together on March 9, 1566, they entered Mary's chamber during her dinner, seized Rizzio, and murdered him almost in her presence. Mary was a captive. Yet with great presence of mind she persuaded Darnley to desert his fellow conspirators and to escape with her to Dunbar. Her friends rallied round her and once more she was able to drive the Protestant lords into England and recover her position in Scotland. Three months later she enjoyed another triumph, the birth of a son, James, who was to become King of both Scotland and England.

But Mary hated her husband. She was now infatuated with a Scottish noble, James Hepburn, the Earl of Bothwell, a reckless and proud young man of about thirty. She could scarcely have chosen a more dangerous love. In February 1567 Darnley was murdered at Kirk o' Field just beyond the walls of Edinburgh. That Bothwell was in touch with the murderers is clear; that Mary approved the deed seems certain. She made no effort to bring him to justice. In April, doubtless by prearrangement, he seized her person and carried her to his castle at Dunbar. A month later they were married. These events were too much for the godly Scots, who now rebelled. Mary's forces and those of her enemies met at Carberry Hill in June. There was no battle, but Bothwell fled from Scotland and Mary was imprisoned in Lochleven Castle. She was forced to abdicate in favor of her infant son. In May of the following year, 1568, she escaped from her prison, raised an army, was defeated at Langside near Glasgow, and fled to England.

Mary went to England of her own will, not at the invitation of Elizabeth. Elizabeth had been foolishly berating the Scottish lords for treating their sovereign so roughly, and Mary hoped that Elizabeth would restore her to the Scottish throne by force. This was a vain hope: Elizabeth might believe that Queens should stand together, but to make war on the Protestant Scots in Mary's behalf would have been a complete reversal of England's Scottish policy. Elizabeth could not hand Mary back to her subjects, for they would most certainly have killed her. Nor could Elizabeth allow Mary her freedom. With her winning ways, her Catholicism, and her claim to the English throne Mary was too dangerous a magnet for those who were discontented with Elizabeth's rule. Hence Mary was kept in honorable confinement, lodged as a guest in various country houses, allowed to hunt and, at first, to correspond with her friends. But her intrigues and plottings were endless; as a result she was guarded more strictly. Her confinement became a lifelong imprisonment that ended on the executioner's block in Fotheringay on February 8, 1587.

ECONOMIC REFORM

Mary's arrival in England in 1568 combined with other events to mark the close of one period in Elizabeth's reign and the opening of another. Hence we may pause in the narrative to consider other developments. When Elizabeth came to the throne the economic prospect was clouded. The finances of the government were in disorder, the currency still was debased, the wool trade was depressed, the marketing of food was disorganized, there was a dangerous amount of unemployment, poverty, and vagabondage. Improvement in government finance was essential for any economic progress. Most fortunately Elizabeth resembled her grandfather, Henry VII, in her thrift, and in her sense of the value of money. She has been accused of meanness; but in truth her parsimony was one of the secrets of her success, for she kept England solvent while other nations were going bankrupt. From her sister Mary she inherited a debt of £250,000; her annual revenue in the first years of her reign was not above £200,000. Yet from this small sum she paid the ordinary peacetime expenses of government and began to reduce the debt.

To finance her wars she had to find additional income. Knowing that heavy taxation would impair her popularity, she did not ask Parliament for large sums. Income from parliamentary taxation averaged only some £50,000 a year throughout her reign. To pay for war she was driven to diminish her capital by selling Crown lands in times of emergency. There were three periods in which Crown lands were sold in large quantities. The first came in 1559–1560, when she was assisting the Scottish Protestants; the second at the time of the Spanish Armada; the third in the 1590s, when she had to quell a revolt in Ireland. Her sale of lands averaged some £20,000 a year. This was a diminution of capital, but it was wiser politically than high taxation. And her credit was so good that she could borrow in the Netherlands at a lower rate of interest than could Philip of Spain, with all the wealth of the Indies behind him.

In 1560–1561 the English government completed the reform of the coinage begun by Northumberland about a decade earlier. To restore confidence in the coinage debased and mutilated coins were recalled and new ones issued in which the silver content equaled the face value. The Parliament of 1563 passed a number of laws to stabilize the economy: old statutes against enclosures were re-enacted; the poor law was revised and a new principle was added: contributions from the richer persons in the parish for the support of the poor—formerly on a voluntary basis—were made compulsory; the people were required to eat fish on Wednesdays and Fridays, not as a matter of religion but as an encouragement to the fishing industry from which the navy drew its seamen. The importation of luxuries, such as jewelry and fine cloth, was restricted, and middlemen were licensed in the grain and cattle trades in order to stabilize the food market.

Parliament also passed the Statute of Artificers, which was a great industrial code. The statute encouraged agriculture and to a lesser degree the cloth trade by making entrance into other occupations more difficult. Anyone wishing to learn some other trade must serve an apprenticeship of seven years. The statute also attempted to stabilize employment and to prevent the lower classes from wandering about. In hiring workmen an employer had to agree to retain them in his service for a certain time, usually a year; and workmen seeking employment had to present a certificate showing that they were entitled to offer their services. At the same time the justices of the peace were empowered to establish the wages that should be paid in various occupations; wages thus determined were to remain in force for a year. The government also encouraged merchants to seek new trades and overseas markets in order to diminish the excessive dependence of English foreign trade upon the city of Antwerp. These measures stabilized the economy and helped to lift the country from the depression of the middle of the century.

THE CATHOLICS

In her religious settlement Elizabeth had aimed at establishing a church which would be accepted by the bulk of the people. In a broad way she was successful, but she was never able to satisfy the ardent Catholics on the one hand nor the radical Protestants on the other.

For some time after 1559 the English Catholics were apathetic and leaderless. Then in the 1570s their strength and spirit were revived by a movement known as the Counter Reformation, a prolonged, intense, and often successful effort by the Catholic Church on the Continent to set its own house in order, to halt the spread of Protestantism, and to recover the ground that had been lost. The Counter Reformation had many aspects. One was a series of zealous popes dedicated to the task of combating Protestantism. Another was the Jesuit order, or the Society of Jesus founded in 1540 by a Spaniard, Ignatius Loyola. The Jesuits were priests, selected and educated with great care, who formed the church's spearhead against Protestantism. Famous as teachers and as missionaries, they accepted the dangerous assignment of propagating the faith among Protestant peoples. Loyola, who had been a soldier until a cannon ball had left him a cripple, instilled into the Jesuit order the militant spirit of a crusade. Obedience, selflessness, and complete devotion to the interests of the church were fundamental principles of the Jesuits, who worked more often among the upper classes than among the poor, and who were selected in part for their ability to deal with aristocrats and with chiefs of state. Hence in many Catholic courts they became political advisers and exerted a profound influence upon policy.

Another part of the Counter Reformation was a church council, the Council of Trent, which met intermittently between 1545 and 1563. It defined and sharpened Catholic doctrine, denounced Protestantism, inaugurated reforms, and inspired Catholics with a new intensity—even ferocity—in fighting the battle of the church. The Inquisition, an ecclesiastical court for the suppression of heresy, was active in Spain and Italy but not in northern Europe. The strongest of Catholic rulers, Philip of Spain, became the temporal head of the Counter Reformation and had a deep sense of mission in promoting its success.

The first overt attack of the Catholic Church upon Elizabeth was the papal bull *Regnans in Excelsis,* published against her in 1570 by Pope Pius V. The bull excommunicated Elizabeth, declared her deposed, absolved her subjects from their allegiance (thereby encouraging them to revolt), and called on Catholic princes to enforce its decrees. In many ways it was an ill-timed and inept document: it came too late to assist a Catholic revolt in 1569, to which we will turn later; it accused Elizabeth of things she had not done; and it offended Philip, the only ruler who could enforce it, because he had not been consulted in advance. The English nation as a whole turned fiercely against Rome as an enemy ready to sow seeds of subtle treason among English subjects.

The bull placed English Catholics in a cruel dilemma, for it ended the dual allegiance by which they had hoped to remain loyal to Elizabeth and at the same time true to their church. They must now make a choice: adherence to the Queen meant denial of papal authority; obedience to the pope meant treason to England. Many Catholics followed the urge of patriotism and became members of the Church of England; others clung to Rome with a new devotion and politically became more dangerous. Elizabeth and her councilors naturally considered the bull an ultimatum. Henceforth they regarded Catholics as suspected persons ready to plot against the state. Parliament made it treason to bring papal bulls into England, or to deny that Elizabeth was the lawful Queen, or to call her a heretic or a schismatic; the property of Englishmen who had fled abroad was to be confiscated unless they returned within a year.

The government became more suspicious because, beginning in 1575, a stream of priests and later of Jesuits came to England from the Continent to work among English Catholics. For some time there had been groups of self-exiled English Catholics on the Continent; in 1568 William Allen, one of the refugees, founded a college at Douai in Flanders to form a center for these groups and to educate the young men among them. Many of these were trained as priests who then returned to England to work among the English Catholics. Allen, a gifted teacher, inspired his students with a zealous devotion and with a willingness—even a longing—to suffer martyrdom for the ancient faith. Other colleges or seminaries were founded at Rome, at Valladolid, and at Seville; by 1580 there were 100 priests secretly at work in England.

Their mission was a spiritual one; they had been commanded to let politics alone. But it was impossible for the English government to regard their activities as purely religious, for religion and politics could not be separated: the patrons of the seminaries were the pope and the King of Spain; the papal bull of 1570 invited English Catholics to be traitors. The English government believed that under the guise of saving souls the priests had come to carry out the bull. An act of Parliament declared it treason to convert an English subject to Catholicism. Hence the priests walked into a trap, for they were hunted down and executed with growing ferocity.

This situation—heroic zeal on one side and the stark necessity of suppressing treason on the other—became more deadly with the arrival of a Jesuit mission in 1580. The Jesuits, like the seminary priests, came to propagate their faith, but circumstances increased the government's suspicions. Gregory XIII, who became Pope in 1572, was Elizabeth's sworn enemy. He was zealous, optimistic, and resourceful; but he was impetuous and his plans did not fit together. He was the principal sponsor of the Jesuit mission; yet in 1578, shortly before the Jesuits arrived in England, he sent an Italian force, led by the English renegade Sir Thomas Stukeley, to stir up trouble in Ireland. He constantly advocated a Catholic invasion of England—the "Enterprise of England" as it was called. Thus the Jesuits arrived at a moment when the struggle between Rome and Protestant England was becoming a fight to the death.

Two famous Jesuits came to England in 1580. One was Edmund Campion, a man of saintliness, heroism, and ability, who represented the noblest qualities of the Counter Reformation and who brought to English Catholics a new fervor and determination. His object was purely religious. "We are dead men to the world," he cried on the scaffold (for he was so indifferent to danger that he was soon captured). "We travelled only for souls; we touched neither state nor policy; we had no such commission." The other Jesuit was Robert Parsons, a subtle and complex character, who abstained from political intrigue only with great reluctance. In 1581 he fled to the Continent to become a famous pamphleteer and the adviser of Philip, of the pope, and of the Guisian faction on English affairs. A skillful writer, politician, and organizer of intrigue, the man of action rather than the priest, he had as his object the overthrow of Elizabeth.

The appearance of the Jesuits resulted in a new code of anti-Catholic legislation. The fine of 1s. a Sunday for nonattendance at church was increased to £20 a month; presence at Mass was punishable by a fine of 100 marks and a year's imprisonment. If a Catholic did not pay the fines levied upon him the government could seize his property and retain two thirds of its income. An earlier law had imposed the death penalty for converting an English subject to Rome; a new law inflicted the same penalty on the convert. Thus, while being a Catholic was punishable by fine and imprisonment, the act of becoming a Catholic could be punished by death. All priests and Jesuits were banished on pain of high treason; their very presence in England made them liable to the death sentence. Young Englishmen in foreign seminaries were summoned home on pain of treason. This code was not enforced to the letter; it was used more often as a threat to keep the Catholics quiet. But there was persecution enough. During the next twenty years some 250 Catholics or persons suspected of Catholicism died on the scaffold or in prison. Although the number is small in comparison with those executed on the Continent, it indicates the ferocity of the religious conflict.

THE PURITANS

Elizabeth's church was also assailed by the Puritans. Puritanism had many roots in the past, but its immediate origin is found in the English Protestants who fled from the country in Mary's reign. Living in exile on the Continent, they were strongly influenced by the teachings of John Calvin. They returned to England as soon as Elizabeth ascended the throne, and they became the religious radicals of her reign. They were members of her church, attending its services and conforming for the most part to its regulations, but they were deeply dissatisfied with it. They wished to carry the Reformation to its logical conclusion by destroying every trace of Roman Catholicism and by making a fresh start.

The Puritans represented many shades of opinion and should not be regarded as a compact sect unified in theory and practice. Nevertheless, the teachings of John Calvin lay behind all Puritan thought. Calvin stressed the majesty and omnipotence of God rather than His gentleness and mercy. God was the austere and jealous Jehovah of the Old Testament, demanding a strict obedience from all believers. Man's function on earth was to glorify God and to carry out His will. God had a program: to wage a stern and constant battle against evil wherever evil was to be found, in the church, in the state, or in the world at large. The Calvinist was thus God's agent, God's warrior, in an endless conflict. Man discovered God's will by a study of the Scriptures. And having thus learned the will of God, the Calvinist sought to carry it out with great courage and with small regard for the wishes of earthly Kings.

Calvin taught further that if God was omnipotent He must also be omniscient, that is, He must know all things, including the course of future events. Hence Calvin was led to his doctrine of predestination. According to this doctrine God knew, even before a man was born, whether or not that man was to be saved. If he was to be saved he was one of the elect, that small and chosen company who did God's will on earth. If not, he belonged to the majority of mankind, the reprobate, all on the primrose path to the everlasting bonfire. It might be thought that such a doctrine, imposing upon man God's unalterable decree, would have rendered the Calvinist indifferent about his conduct; it was not so. Except in rare moments of doubt, the Calvinist was thoroughly convinced he was one of the elect; and from this conviction he derived a sense of exaltation and moral rectitude. But assurance made him rigid, for he believed that he knew the truth whereas other men did not. Nor was he content to go his own way and let the reprobate go his. He wished to persuade or, if need be, coerce his fellow mortals into leading godly lives. Nothing in daily life was too trivial for him to examine and condemn and he was quite ready to tell others of their faults. In Scotland the clergyman in the pulpit would select a wretched member of the congregation and denounce his transgressions openly before the whole assembly.

The Puritans, accepting Calvin's theology, challenged the assumptions which underlay Elizabeth's religious settlement and were highly critical of her church. They resented the Tudor doctrine that every member of the state was automatically a member of the state church. This made the church a political body. In the minds of the Puritans the church was not political; it was a voluntary association of believers, a holy society of the elect, quite independent of the state. The state had no right to establish a church, which was the domain of the clergy. The church had no earthly head; spiritual power flowed from God the Father through Christ the Mediator directly to His Church, by-passing Queen and Parliament.

Elizabeth assumed that the Roman Catholic Church, if reformed and purged of evil as she and her father had reformed and purged it, could be made acceptable. But the Puritan, hating Rome, saw nothing but error in the medieval church. The Puritan also disliked the element of compromise in Elizabeth's church. It seemed to him a makeshift: Protestant in dogma but Catholic in ritual, and established merely to solve the political problem of the diversity of religious belief. As he looked at Elizabeth's church the Puritan saw many things to criticize. He did not like its ritual. He did not like its bishops, who were officials appointed by the Crown to serve the interests of the state. Unfortunately some Elizabethan bishops displayed a spirit of worldliness and greed which justified sharp criticism. The Crown itself set a bad example, for newly appointed bishops were often coerced into bargains by which a portion of the see's endowment passed into royal hands. Pluralities and nonresidence continued; the lower clergy were often ill-trained and ignorant; the church courts contained abuses. Thus the Puritan had grounds for his complaint.

Puritan hostility to the church took many forms. Early in the reign a controversy arose concerning the vestments worn by the clergy. The Puritans considered these vestments too much like those of the Roman priesthood, and they thought that ministers should be permitted to wear whatever vestments they saw fit. This rather trivial matter became important because the Puritans made it a point of conscience, whereas Elizabeth, as governor of the church, made it a point of obedience. The dispute spread to other matters of form and ritual: to the practice of kneeling at Communion, to the sign of the cross in baptism, to the ring in marriage, to organs and choral singing in churches. As a result of these disputes there were many divergent practices in the church. In 1563 Elizabeth ordered Archbishop Parker to enforce "an exact order and uniformity in all external rites and ceremonies." The archbishop was poorly obeyed.

The controversy then moved to more dangerous ground, for the Puritans began to challenge the authority of the bishops to rule the church. Calvinism stressed the equality or the parity of all clergymen; it rejected bishops as symbols of Roman error and of royal tyranny. The doctrine of parity was given great impetus by Thomas Cartwright, a professor of divinity at Cambridge. From his studies of the New Testament Cartwright drew the conclusion that the Scriptures contained no justification for the government of the church by bishops. The early bishops, he believed, had been preachers and teachers. He insisted that bishops be confined to these ancient functions and that the church be governed by presbyteries, that is, by disciplinary courts composed of local clergy such as were arising in Scotland. Congregations, he believed, should select their own ministers. Such doctrines were undiluted Calvinism. Cartwright gave the Puritans a battle cry: "The bishops must be unlorded." He broadened the conflict from a quarrel over minor points to a clash over fundamentals, for to question the authority of bishops was to question the authority of the Queen, who appointed bishops and gave them power. In 1570 Cartwright was deprived of his professorship, and four years later he fled to the Continent.

Puritan hostility to the bishops continued. It reached a raucous climax in the Martin Marprelate libels published between 1587 and 1589. These were anonymous tracts attacking the bishops with great violence but with a ribald humor that made the tracts good reading. They "swept away in a tide of unrestrained jocularity all the traditional reverence for the episcopate."[2] The secret press from which the tracts emanated was discovered by the government, a number of people were punished, and at least one was executed.

Puritan attempts to alter the Church of England took other forms. One was a campaign by Puritan members in the House of Commons. In 1566 the Commons sent Elizabeth a petition asking for reform of certain abuses in the church. In 1571 a Puritan, Walter Strickland, introduced a bill to modify the Prayer Book. Elizabeth acted quickly. Strickland was summoned before the Council and suspended from the House, to the indignation of the Commons. In the following year the Queen commanded that no bills concerning religion should be introduced in Parliament "unless the same be first considered and liked of by the clergy." This prohibition impelled a Puritan firebrand, Peter Wentworth, to make a bold defense of the right of free speech in the Commons. He pleaded eloquently for the liberties of Parliament, though he would have used those liberties to Puritanize the church through legislation. The campaign in Parliament failed, and the Puritans turned to other methods.

They held meetings known as "prophesyings" or "exercises," public assemblies of the clergymen of a locality who gathered to study the Scriptures, to discuss the improvement of morals, and at times to denounce notorious offenders. Laymen were permitted to attend, though they took no part in the discussions. Such meetings might do good, but they had a Presbyterian flavor and their discussions could easily degenerate into criticism of the church. Elizabeth insisted that they be discontinued. There was also the "classis" movement. A classis was a secret meeting of clergymen with Presbyterian tendencies. These meetings were modeled on the Scottish presbyteries; their purpose was to find subtle ways in which the Anglican service could be given a Presbyterian tone without open challenge of the law.

In 1580 a group of extreme Puritans led by Robert Browne and Henry Barrow broke away from the church altogether and began to preach a new form

[2] J. B. Black, *The Reign of Elizabeth 1558–1603* (Oxford: Clarendon Press, 1959), p. 202.

of religious organization. Church and state, they argued, should have no connection with each other. The congregation, the voluntary association of believers, should be the only ecclesiastical unit and should manage its affairs without supervision or control by any higher authority. These separatists or Congregationalists, as they were called later, worshiped in gatherings known as conventicles in which the forms of the church were not used. The separatists made religion emotional; they rejected the necessity of a learned ministry and relied upon inspiration. They were violently anti-Catholic and violently anti-Anglican. Hence they clashed at once with the government, and Barrow later was executed for seditious words.

Elizabeth was highly irritated by the Puritans, for in rejecting her authority to govern the church they were striking at her authority to govern the state. "There is risen both in your realm and mine," she wrote to the King of Scotland, "a sect of perilous consequence, such as would have no kings but a presbytery and would take our place while they enjoy our privilege. Yea, look we well unto them." Elizabeth's first archbishop, Matthew Parker (1559–1575), a wise and moderate man, found the suppression of Puritanism a difficult matter, partly because he was not given sufficient power. His successor, Edmund Grindal (1576–1583), displayed sympathy with the Puritans. Refusing to obey the Queen's command to suppress prophesyings, he was suspended from office.

At his death in 1583 Elizabeth determined to find a sterner archbishop. She selected John Whitgift, a disciplinarian and an enemy of Puritans. He demanded at once that the clergy acknowledge complete acceptance of the principal tenets of the church; some 200 ministers refused and were suspended. Whitgift developed a new weapon, the Court of High Commission, an ecclesiastical court authorized by the Act of Supremacy. This court, which did not follow the practices of the common law, had no jury and it forced suspects to swear that they would answer all questions truthfully. If a man refused, he was punished by the Star Chamber. If he consented, his answers were used against him and he might be fined or imprisoned without appeal. After the Martin Marprelate libels the government struck hard blows. Puritan leaders were imprisoned, and a few were executed. An act of 1593 inflicted the death penalty upon persons who stubbornly refused to attend the services of the church or who repeatedly worshiped in conventicles. Puritanism declined in the last fifteen years of the reign, Puritans in high office had died, and the religious leaders of the movement had been thinned and silenced by persecution.

14

ELizaBeth I:
the spanish armada

CHANGES IN THE ALIGNMENT OF POWERS

For more than half a century before Elizabeth came to the throne the international politics of western Europe had been dominated by the wars and rivalries of France and Spain. During this half century France had been strong, nationalistic, and aggressive under her active rulers Francis I (1515–1547) and Henry II (1547–1559), allied with Scotland, hostile to England, at almost constant war with Spain. France had been opposed by Spain under Emperor Charles V (1516–1556), whose vast possessions in the Netherlands, Germany, and Italy were of great potential strength but were weakened by geographical separation and national diversities. Spain had been allied with England. Hence Elizabeth in her first years as Queen thought of Spain as an ally (though not perhaps as a friend) and of France as an obvious enemy.

With the abdication of Charles V, the accession of Elizabeth, and the death of Henry II—all falling within the space of a few years—the old system of international politics dissolved. The new one that replaced it was based on the division between Protestants and Catholics. Although religious differences cut across national frontiers, England emerged as the leading Protestant state and Spain as the leading Catholic one. Under a series of weak Kings, France sank into chaos and civil war. The French religious wars between Catholics and Calvinist Huguenots continued almost until the end of the century, so that France played a surprisingly minor role in the impending struggle between England and Spain. The Franco-Scottish alliance ended with the Scottish Reformation.

Changes also occurred in Spain and England. Charles V left Austria and Bohemia to his brother Ferdinand, but the rest of his possessions went to his son, Philip II, the former husband of Mary Tudor. Philip was a man of austere sense of duty, of stoical calm in victory or defeat, of Machiavellian policy, of tremendous though plodding industry, and of the deepest devotion to the Catholic faith. He made up his mind slowly and painfully but adhered to his resolve with great perseverance. He was building for himself that strangest of royal residences, the Escurial, partly monastery, partly cathedral, partly palace, partly mausoleum; in the inner depths of this building he was constructing a small, monkish set of rooms from which in later years he ruled his empire. The Escurial was in the mountains where the King could be alone, some thirty miles from Madrid.[1] More and more as the reign progressed, Philip made the advancement of Catholicism his primary goal. He became the temporal head of the Counter Reformation, the patron of the Jesuits, the ruler who sent the Armada of 1588 against England. Horrified to discover that Calvinism was making progress in the Netherlands, he determined to crush it even at the cost of ruining his richest province. There was thus religious division in Spanish lands as well as in France.

England was the strongest Protestant state in Europe. The Queen had none of Philip's religious zeal but she could not ignore the Spanish menace. And quite naturally she allied, though at first in a clandestine way, with the Calvinists in the Netherlands and with the Huguenots in France. But England also had her religious divisions. What might be called a constant conspiracy was formed between Philip and certain Catholic elements in England and Scotland; the Irish, among whom the Jesuits achieved one of their greatest triumphs, gladly allied with Spain against their English oppressors.

THE BEGINNING OF CONFLICT

The Break with Spain

The first break between England and Spain occurred about 1568. It is worth while to examine the causes, though some points will have to be repeated later. Ten years before, when Elizabeth ascended the throne, Philip had offered her a condescending friendship. But when she established a Protestant church (which he refused to regard as permanent), when she aided Protestants in Scotland and in France, when she made Mary, Queen of Scots, her prisoner, and when France grew weak and divided, Philip altered his policy. In 1568 he dismissed Elizabeth's Ambassador in Spain, Dr. John Man, a married churchman and a strong Protestant who had given offense; as his Ambassador in London Philip sent a fiery and zealous Catholic, Don Guerau de Spes. De Spes proved to be more indiscreet than Philip had intended. He conducted himself as though he were leading a crusade against the English government. He plotted with Mary Stuart, he taught the English Catholics to be disloyal, he intrigued with Irish rebels, he urged Madrid to be hostile.

Meanwhile another development underscored the clash of religions. The initial phase of the Calvinist revolt in the Netherlands took place in 1566 with riots and the destruction of Catholic churches. Elizabeth, who encouraged these actions by propaganda and secret assistance, had no thought of overthrowing Philip's government. She merely wished to cause him a little trouble, as he was causing her, and to prevent him from making the Netherlands a springboard for an attack on England.

Economic friction also appeared between England and Spain. In the 1560s a famous English merchant and seaman, John Hawkins, made a number of voyages to Spanish America. His purpose was peaceful trade, but the Spanish were furious at his intrusion; and his third voyage ended in disaster when he

[1] Garrett Mattingly, *The Armada* (Boston: Houghton Mifflin, 1959), pp. 69–75.

was treacherously attacked by a Spanish fleet. The episode caused deep resentment in both countries. Anglo-Spanish quarrels, moreover, were disturbing English trade to Antwerp: rather aggressively the English had placed restrictions on Flemish merchants trading in London; Spanish countermeasures at Antwerp had dislocated the delicate balance of trade. As a result some English merchants had moved their staple to the German port of Emden.

In December 1568, after Hawkins' third voyage, there came a greater shock. A Spanish fleet sailing up the Channel with 800,000 ducats (£85,000) for the Spanish army in the Netherlands was driven into English ports by Huguenot pirates. Elizabeth discovered that the money was a loan to Philip from Genoese bankers and that by contract it remained the property of the bankers until it was delivered in Flanders. She thereupon seized it as a loan to herself. The Spanish at once laid an embargo on English property in the Netherlands, the English seized Spanish property in England, and trade with the Netherlands ended. So vital was this trade to both England and Antwerp, however, that it was reopened in 1573. Thus a number of factors were driving Spain and England apart. The principal cause of their quarrel was religion, and here Philip was certainly the aggressor. But there were also economic and political rivalries in which England, rather than Spain, took the initiative.[2]

Plots in England

Anglo-Spanish tension was increased greatly by a series of plots in England. They began, significantly, with the arrival of Mary, Queen of Scots. The first of them had its origin in aristocratic discontent which drifted into treason. A group of conservative English peers, resentful of the influence of Cecil and other nonnoble councilors and led in the south by the Duke of Norfolk and in the north by the Earls of Northumberland and Westmorland, were critical of Elizabeth's policy. They were sympathetic to Mary, believing that she should be recognized as Elizabeth's successor and restored to the Scottish throne. Moreover, they disliked the growing tension with Spain. Some, though not all, were Catholics and desired to restore the ancient faith. Such sentiments could easily degenerate into treason. The Duke of Norfolk began to plot with Mary and with De Spes, who hoped for a Catholic rising aided by Spanish troops. But Norfolk was not a brave or resolute man. And when in October 1569 Elizabeth summoned him peremptorily to court, he hesitated, obeyed, and tamely allowed himself to be imprisoned in the Tower. Plotting among the southern lords collapsed.

But the north, more valiant and more combustible, differed greatly from the south; it obeyed its own great lords—Percy, Neville, and Dacre; its society was feudal, its religion Catholic. When the Earls of Northumberland (Percy) and Westmorland (Neville) also were summoned to court they broke into rebellion. Their followers entered Durham Cathedral, destroyed Protestant Bibles, and set up the Mass. For a moment the rebels controlled the north. They made a southern lunge toward Tutbury, where Mary was confined, but she was spirited away and the rebels retreated. The troops of the government closed in upon them, their army broke up, Northumberland and Westmorland fled to Scotland, Leonard Dacre was defeated near Carlisle, and the rebellion was at an end. It had been a dangerous affair.

The rebellion was scarcely over when a new plot, the Ridolfi or second

---

[2] J. B. Black, *The Reign of Elizabeth* (Oxford: Clarendon Press, 1959), pp. 119–130.

Norfolk plot, developed in 1570–1571. Roberto di Ridolfi was an Italian banker resident in England, an exuberant and oversanguine schemer who believed, like De Spes, that many English Catholics were ready to rise against Elizabeth. He plotted with De Spes, with Mary, and with Norfolk, who weakly allowed himself to be drawn into new treasons. The plot called for a Catholic insurrection, a Spanish invasion from the Netherlands, a marriage between Mary and Norfolk, who were to be placed on the English throne, the disappearance of Elizabeth, and the restoration of Catholicism. But Alva, Governor of the Spanish Netherlands, regarded the plot as fantastic, Norfolk as a coward, and Ridolfi as a windbag. He refused to act until a revolt in England was well under way and until Elizabeth was assassinated. Meanwhile Cecil discovered the essentials of the plot. De Spes was dismissed in disgrace. Norfolk was convicted of treason and executed in 1572. Parliament clamored for the execution of Mary, that "bosom serpent," as an English statesman called her, but Elizabeth would not consent. These plots made a profound impression upon the English people. Their anger against Mary, their suspicion of Spain, their hatred of Catholicism, their devotion to Elizabeth, who appeared to be their sole protection, were all assuming a deep and passionate character.

France

These events, underscoring the hostility of Spain, caused Elizabeth to review her relations with France. These had been hostile; in 1562 she had committed the blunder of an open alliance with the Huguenots against the French King, hoping to aid them as she had aided the Protestants in Scotland, perhaps even regaining Calais in the process. The Huguenots permitted her to occupy the port of Le Havre, but the venture ended in failure: the Huguenots and the French Crown made peace and joined forces against England; the plague broke out among the English troops in Le Havre; and in July 1563 the place had to be abandoned, Elizabeth withdrawing from her luckless enterprise with what grace she could.

Her failure showed her that France, more complicated than Scotland, was not divided in a simple way between Catholics and Protestants. There was also a middle party, the *politiques*, who regarded peace and political reform as more urgent than deciding the religious quarrel by force of arms. They were Catholic but moderate in religious zeal, nationalist and royalist in character, eager to promote the interests of France, and very hostile to Spain. They resisted the domination of the Huguenots as well as of the ultra-Catholic party of the Duke of Guise. Catherine de Médicis, who controlled her weak sons Charles IX (1560–1574) and Henry III (1574–1589), supported the *politiques*. Her policy was one Elizabeth could understand, for it had certain similarities to her own policy in England, though in England the middle party was moderately Protestant whereas in France it was moderately Catholic.

With great need of support on the Continent, Elizabeth in 1570 began negotiations for a marriage alliance between England and France. Charles IX was married, but he had two younger brothers, Henry, Duke of Anjou (later Henry III), a young man not quite nineteen, and Francis, Duke of Alençon, three years younger. Elizabeth was thirty-seven. Negotiations for her marriage with Anjou were wrecked by his refusal to abandon Catholicism; those with Alençon dragged on for a time and then ended, though they were to be renewed at a later date. But Elizabeth achieved her purpose: the improvement of relations with France.

In 1572 the two countries concluded the Treaty of Blois by which each promised to assist the other in case of attack.

Increased cordiality with France was endangered by the Massacre of St. Bartholomew in 1572. Catherine de Médicis had feared that the Huguenot leader, Admiral Coligny, would induce Charles IX to aid the rebels in the Netherlands, thus causing war between France and Spain. Catherine and the party of Guise plotted to assassinate Coligny. Their opportunity came when the Protestant nobles assembled in Paris in August 1572 to celebrate the marriage of the young Huguenot prince, Henry of Navarre, with the King's sister, Marguerite of Valois. Coligny was shot in the streets of Paris but was only wounded. The Protestant nobles there were in a dangerous mood, and Catherine persuaded Charles to sanction their slaughter while they were in his power. The result was a general massacre of Protestants by Catholics which spread from Paris to other cities until the number of victims may have reached seven or eight thousand.

This massacre stirred Protestants throughout Europe to bitter anger. In England there was an outcry for stricter laws against Catholics, for the execution of Mary, and for new measures to ensure Elizabeth's safety. When the French Ambassador requested an audience in which to offer explanations, Elizabeth kept him waiting for three days and received him in stony silence. In France the massacre renewed the religious wars. Large numbers of Huguenots took refuge in the city of La Rochelle on the Bay of Biscay, already a kind of Huguenot capital, from which privateers preyed on Catholic commerce. Their loot financed the war on land. Although Elizabeth could not aid the Huguenots openly without breaking the recent treaty with France, she considered it imperative that the French be kept busy within their own borders and so she connived at assistance to La Rochelle from Protestants in England. At the same time she did not break with the legitimate French government, and normal relations between the two courts gradually were resumed. France was not England's ally, but not her enemy. Thus the wars of religion prevented France from taking an active part in international affairs.

The Revolt of the Netherlands

An important cause of the war between England and Spain was the assistance Elizabeth gave to the Netherlands in their revolt against Spanish rule. The seventeen rich and populous provinces of the Netherlands, comprising both modern Holland and modern Belgium, had fallen under control of the Dukes of Burgundy during the later Middle Ages and had eventually become possessions of Spain. Splendidly located at the mouths of the Rhine and Scheldt rivers, their cities were wealthy centers of commerce and manufacturing. During the first half of the sixteenth century Antwerp was the greatest commercial center of western Europe. The Netherlands had been ruled by Charles V with sympathy and understanding, but Philip's arbitrary and dictatorial government ignored their ancient rights and liberties. Their very prosperity irritated Philip. Far too much of the treasure from America, he thought, found its way into the pockets of Dutch and Flemish merchants. His remedy was the imposition of heavy taxation upon his richest province. Moreover, his rigid orthodoxy was outraged by the growth of Protestantism; he would bring the Netherlands back to the church, he said, or else "so waste the land that neither the natives could live there nor any should thereafter desire the place for habitation."

Resentment against his policy broke into revolt in 1566. In the following year he sent the Duke of Alva to restore order. Alva, though a good soldier and a hard-headed statesman, was harsh and cruel. He began a reign of terror with bloodshed and confiscation of property which cowed the people and inspired a deep hatred of Spain. On land Alva crushed the revolt; the first campaigns of the national hero, William, Prince of Orange, who invaded the Netherlands from Germany, were failures.

At sea the rebels were more successful. In 1569 the Prince of Orange, following the tactics of the Huguenots, issued commissions to Dutch privateers to prey upon Catholic commerce. These Dutch Sea Beggars, as they were called, levied a heavy toll on the shipping of Spain as well as that of their own Catholic countrymen. For some time Elizabeth allowed them to dispose of their booty in England and English merchants picked up fine cargoes at bargain rates. But the Sea Beggars, a rough lot, caused disturbances in English ports; in 1572 their visits were prohibited. The result was unexpected. The Dutch privateers turned to the port of Brille in Holland as a new base of operations. This was the signal for a more determined revolt against Spain, and other coastal towns joined forces with the men at Brille. As the war at sea expanded, the defiant spirit of the seaports spread to the interior and created a new revolutionary zeal there. The revolt of the Netherlands had begun in earnest.

In the early years of the war Elizabeth aided the rebels in secret and underhand ways, but she would not be pushed into an open break with Spain or into a Protestant crusade. Her object was not so much to aid the Dutch, though she wanted to keep them fighting, as to guard the welfare and safety of England. She did not wish to drive Philip from the Netherlands but to keep him busy there; moreover, she dreaded intervention by France, for she believed that French domination of the Netherlands would be as dangerous to England as domination by Spain. After 1578, however, the position of the rebels degenerated. In the preceding year Philip had sent a new governor, Alexander Farnese, Duke of Parma, a very able man and the first soldier of the age, who combined the qualities of a great general with those of a diplomat. By causing dissension between the Dutch in the north and the Flemings in the south, and by constant military pressure, he gradually broke the resistance of the ten southern provinces and brought them once more under Spanish control. The seven northern provinces, forming the Union of Utrecht in 1579, fought on, though they were hard pressed.

They had hopes of a new champion in Francis, Duke of Alençon, the younger brother of the French King, who campaigned off and on for a number of years in their behalf. The reappearance of French intervention at first alarmed Elizabeth but in 1578 she altered her policy and revived marriage negotiations with Alençon. If he was to drive Spain from the Netherlands he should do so as England's friend. He responded gallantly to Elizabeth's overtures. Paying two visits to England, he was duly smitten by her charms (she was now in her middle forties), and courted her with great fervor and diligence. It was all a bit ridiculous. He was a little man, with a face badly marked by smallpox and with a nose somewhat bulbous in contour. Elizabeth called him her frog. He had an agent in England, one Jean de Simier, whom the Queen, with her love for nicknames, referred to as her monkey. "Be assured on the faith of a monkey," Simier once wrote her, "that your frog lives in hope." But Alençon failed on the field of battle and died in 1584, leaving the Dutch in worse plight than before. In the same year William of Orange was assassinated. And the Duke of Guise made a treaty with Philip to stamp out Protestantism in France. French aid to the Dutch thus became impossible.

Elizabeth was faced with the fact that if she did not give greater assistance to the Dutch they would surely be conquered. As usual she hesitated. By 1585, however, relations with Spain had reached the breaking point; there was every indication that a Spanish victory over Holland would be followed by a Spanish invasion of England. The Dutch formed Elizabeth's one line of defense abroad: their ruin might well be followed by her own. In 1585 she made a treaty with the Dutch by which she promised to send an army to their assistance at her own charge. She had already loaned them large sums of money, and as a guarantee for repayment the treaty allowed her to occupy the Dutch towns of Brille, Flushing, and Rammekens. In December 1585 the Earl of Leicester sailed to Holland with a powerful force of 7600 men. But Leicester showed himself to be a poor general and a poorer statesman. He exceeded and disobeyed his instructions, he quarreled with the Dutch and with his own subordinates, he spent money freely, and he complained groundlessly of parsimony at home, for Elizabeth had not spared in equipping the army. His forces melted away without substantial achievement, and he returned to England in 1586 with great loss of credit. Sent back to his post in the year following, he was more incompetent than ever. The English campaigns on land during these years brought little but failure and dishonor. Happily the war at sea had more fortunate consequences.

ENGLISH MARITIME ENTERPRISE

It was in Elizabeth's reign that England first became a great sea power with a navy capable of striking heavy blows in waters far from Britain. The background of the Elizabethan navy is to be found, in the first place, in a gradual revolution in naval warfare, the construction and use of warships, and the development of naval gunnery. These changes began in the reign of Henry VIII and were expanded greatly under Elizabeth. We will examine them presently. But naval strength could be created only among a people with a maritime tradition and with some genius for the sea. Hence the background of Elizabeth's naval power lies also in many scattered voyages of discovery and of commercial expansion overseas throughout the Tudor period. From these voyages English seamen learned how ships should be built and sailed and fought.

The way in which Englishmen thought of the ocean is also important. An extensive literature arose in the Tudor period dealing with maritime affairs: with maps, mathematics, and navigation; with descriptions of distant lands and of the bizarre adventures of explorers; with propaganda for discovery, the extension of trade, and the planting of colonies. Educated people added these books to their libraries, and there arose that alliance of merchants, seamen, scholars, and gentry which produced the age of Drake and of the Armada. The English were proud of their seamen. Sailors replaced soldiers as the national heroes. In 1589 Richard Hakluyt published the first edition of his famous work, *The Principal Navigations, Voyages, and Discoveries of the English Nation*, in which he told the epic story of English enterprise at sea. Finally, there was a dawning realization that the Atlantic had superseded the Mediterranean as the chief area of European commerce. This shift gave England a splendid geographical location for leadership in Atlantic enterprise.

Englishmen, as we know, had taken little part in the first age of oceanic discovery. John Cabot's voyages from Bristol caused excited interest when it was thought he had reached Asia, and disillusionment when it became evident he had not. The old trade with Antwerp in woolen cloth, which was then doing well, stifled interest in new worlds beyond the seas. But in the depression in the middle of the century trade with Antwerp slackened and the danger of over-dependence on that market became painfully clear. English merchants, under great pressure to open new trades, turned again to maritime enterprise.

Voyages of Commercial Expansion

The first venture of which we hear was a voyage to the Atlantic coast of Morocco in 1551 when a group of London merchants sent out two ships under Captain Thomas Wyndham to trade at Agadir. In 1552 he made a second voyage, trading a "good quantity of linen and woollen cloth, coral, amber, jet, and divers other things well accepted by the Moors" in return for "sugar, dates, almonds, and molasses or sugar syrup."[3] This trade became permanent; a Barbary Company was chartered in 1585. Meanwhile Wyndham embarked upon a much more dangerous venture. Accompanied by a Portuguese renegade, Antonio Pinteado, who served as pilot, Wyndham sailed in 1553 to the Gold Coast in tropical West Africa, where he obtained a good quantity of gold. He then went on to the Niger River in search of pepper. In the Niger Delta a fever broke out among his crew; Wyndham, Pinteado, and many others died; only a third of the party ever returned to England. Nevertheless, the cargo of gold, ivory, and pepper made the voyage a financial success. In the next year Captain John Lok brought home from the Gold Coast 400 pounds of gold, a very large amount.

The Portuguese lodged a formal complaint with the English government. The entire coast of West Africa, they said, was theirs, and no other Europeans should trespass upon it. The English merchants, called before the Privy Council, answered by asserting a principle to which England adhered for generations: only effective occupation of an overseas territory by a European power could confer exclusive rights upon that power. They denied that mere discovery gave perpetual monopoly over vast unoccupied areas. Philip, at that time King of England, prohibited the voyages, but they continued nonetheless. When Elizabeth came to the throne, the Portuguese protested again, but received the same answer.

Another venture, born of the depression, began as an attempt to find a northeast passage to the Orient in the waters north of Scandinavia, Russia, and Siberia. In 1553 a group of merchants and courtiers sent out three vessels upon this hopeless quest. Sir Hugh Willoughby, who commanded the expedition, rounded the North Cape of Norway, sailed eastward to the island of Novaya Zemlya, attempted to winter on the Siberian coast, and, with his men, was frozen to death. But one of his ships commanded by Richard Chancellor entered the White Sea and thus came in contact with the Russians. Landing at Archangel, Chancellor made his way to Moscow. He was well received by Czar Ivan the Terrible, who readily granted English merchants the right to trade in Russia; at Chancellor's return to England in 1554 the merchants who had sent him out transformed themselves into the Muscovy Company and began a precarious trade with that country. The company took out cloth and hardware and brought back wax, amber, train oil, tallow, furs, cordage, and timber for masts and spars. Here was a new market won by the daring and enterprise of English seamen.

Chancellor served the company well; another outstanding explorer and adventurer, Anthony Jenkinson, went out to Russia in 1557. Jenkinson not only saved the position of the company as Ivan grew more difficult, but also made

---

[3] Quoted in T. S. Willan, *Studies in Elizabethan Foreign Trade* (Manchester: Manchester University Press, 1959), p. 99.

some remarkable journeys in the hope of opening trade to the Orient. In 1558 he followed the Volga River down to the Caspian Sea and thence traveled eastward to Bukhara in Turkistan. In medieval times Bukhara had been an important point on the trade route to China, but Jenkinson found central Asia in anarchy, inhabited by wild nomadic tribes without settled government. Trade was impossible. Later he traveled again to the southern shore of the Caspian in an attempt to open trade with Persia. For a moment this trade was successful, though it soon flickered out; Jenkinson's endeavor to tap the trade of the Orient by way of Russia was unavailing.

Attempts were also made to find a northwest passage. Early in Elizabeth's reign a friendly controversy arose between Anthony Jenkinson, who favored search for a passage in the northeast, and Sir Humphrey Gilbert, soldier and courtier, who favored the northwest. In 1566 Gilbert set forth his views in *A Discourse for a Discovery for a new Passage to Cataia,* a work which circulated in manuscript for a decade before it was published. Although Gilbert's arguments to prove the existence of a passage were superficial and even childish, he aroused great interest and was widely read. Another propagandist for a northern passage was Dr. John Dee, a mathematician and geographer who invented instruments and devised map projections for determining a ship's location in high latitudes. He also collected much information about the northern seas.

There were two series of Elizabethan voyages to the northwest. The first was connected with Michael Lok and Martin Frobisher. Lok was a merchant and traveler whose "ream of notes" convinced him of the existence of a northwest passage. In 1574 he renewed an old acquaintance with Martin Frobisher, a courageous seaman of enormous physical strength, rough, blustering, but an unscrupulous man whose past was somewhat questionable. He too believed in a northwest passage, and the two men worked together to raise funds for a voyage. Frobisher sailed in the summer of 1576. Reaching the coast of Baffin Land, he entered a gulf now known as Frobisher Bay. He convinced himself that this was a northwest passage and so announced on his return to England. There was a wave of excited interest, money was subscribed freely, and the Queen gave the adventurers a charter as the Company of Cathay. But a new twist was given to the enterprise when a piece of black ore brought home by Frobisher was declared to contain traces of gold. Sent out on a second voyage in 1577, Frobisher was instructed to bring back a lading of ore; this he did, though not from the site where he had found his original sample. A fever of speculation ensued in London; Frobisher sailed a third time in 1578 with a fleet of fifteen ships. He encountered foul weather. The sailors, eager to be home from a dangerous coast, collected as ore the first rocks they could find. Frobisher discovered upon his return that his former shipment was under grave suspicion and that the Company of Cathay had ended in bankruptcy and disgrace. His cargo of rock, brought all the way from Canada, was used to fill holes in a road near Deptford.

Despite this fiasco, the search for a northwest passage was renewed a decade later by Captain John Davis, a far more scientific explorer, who made three voyages (1585–1587) into the waters between Greenland and Baffin Land. Sailing much farther north than Frobisher and carefully charting the coasts he visited, he added greatly to geographical knowledge. He was a competent seaman and an intelligent explorer who was not deceived into thinking that every inlet was a northwest passage.

The usual organization of merchants and adventurers for enterprise overseas in the Tudor period was the chartered company. Three of these companies—the Barbary Company, the Muscovy Company, and the Company of Cathay—have been mentioned, but there were many more. The charters, obtained from the Crown, conferred exclusive rights of exploration, trade, or settlement in a given area. Monopoly was justified by the high degree of risk involved in these ventures and by the large amount of capital required. No individual merchant could afford such danger of loss or provide such sums of ready cash. These companies were of a new type known as joint-stock companies. The investor did not trade in person, as in the regulated companies, but bought shares, as in a modern corporation, letting the company conduct the enterprise and divide the profit or loss among the shareholders. The chartered companies illustrate the free enterprise of the people functioning with the approval of the state; they contrast sharply with the close control of all mercantile ventures exercised by the Crown in Spain and Portugal.

An Eastland Company for trade in the Baltic Sea was chartered in 1579. English merchants had traded in this area in the fifteenth century, but they had been driven back by the Hanseatic League; in the early Tudor period there was only a trickle of English commerce to the Baltic. Now, as the Hansa sank in power, the time was ripe for a new venture. The Eastland Company brought home pitch, canvas, cables, and cordage, and timber for masts and spars. Its establishment was an excellent preparation for the naval struggle with Spain.

Another company was chartered in 1581 to trade in the Mediterranean. English commerce in the Mediterranean, begun under Henry VII, had come to an end in the middle of the century. It had ended partly because the Turks, established in Constantinople and the Levant, were difficult to deal with. They were warriors who regarded merchants as inferior beings sent by Allah to be fleeced. Moreover, piracy was the national occupation of the little Moorish states along the north coast of Africa. Finally, Spain was hostile to English penetration in the Mediterranean. English merchantmen literally fought their way through the Straits of Gibraltar. Nonetheless, in 1578 two London merchants, Edward Osborne and Richard Stapler, sent out an agent to negotiate with the Sultan at Constantinople for trading privileges. A Turkey Company was chartered in 1581 and a Venice Company in 1583. In 1592 the two companies merged as the Levant Company which, with many ups and downs in fortune, continued for more than two centuries. Young Englishmen went out to the Levant, learned the native tongues, and traded English broadcloth, kerseys, rabbit skins, tin, and mercury for spices, drugs, indigo, silk, cotton cloth, and linens. This was the modest beginning of England's role as a Mediterranean power. The English East India Company, the greatest of them all, will be discussed later.

Attempts at Colonization

The Elizabethans never established a permanent colony in the New World. But despite their failure, they were the founders of the movement which was to people the Atlantic Coast of North America with men of English blood. The Elizabethans thought and wrote concerning the advantages of planting colonies in America; in 1584 Richard Hakluyt tried to interest the Queen by presenting her with his pamphlet, *Discourse of Western Planting*. Attempts at colonization in Elizabeth's reign were connected with three famous men—Sir Humphrey Gilbert, Sir Walter Ralegh, and Sir Richard Grenville. They were not of sailor or merchant stock but were members of the gentry. In 1578 Gilbert

Sir Walter Ralegh, artist unknown. (National Portrait Gallery, London)

obtained a patent permitting him in very general terms to colonize barbarous lands unoccupied by any friendly power. He collected a fleet at once and set sail. What happened on the voyage remains a mystery, but he was soon back in port in a somewhat battered condition. The Spanish accused him of piracy. Raising funds with difficulty, he tried again in 1583. He crossed the Atlantic and landed on Newfoundland of which he took formal possession in the name of Queen Elizabeth. He then sailed to the mainland to select a site for his colony. But the expedition was failing. Gilbert had little notion of the tremendous difficulties of his undertaking, and he lacked that iron control of his men essential for desperate ventures. His largest ship had deserted shortly after he left England. He lost his supplies and most of his colonists when another of his vessels was wrecked on the coast of modern Nova Scotia. There was nothing to do but turn homeward. Gilbert was drowned on the voyage to England when his tiny ship, the *Squirrel,* of only ten tons, foundered in a gale off the Azores.

The task of planting a colony in America was carried on by Sir Walter Ralegh, Gilbert's half brother. Obtaining a patent in 1584, Ralegh wisely sent an expedition to find a good location. His captains, Philip Amadas and Arthur Barlow, followed the coast northward from the West Indies to Roanoke Island off the shore of the present state of North Carolina. Roanoke appeared an ideal location. In 1585 Ralegh sent out 100 colonists. Sir Richard Grenville, who commanded the fleet, landed the colonists at Roanoke, placed Ralph Lane, a soldier, in charge, and departed, promising to return in a year's time. By the following summer the colonists, having neglected to plant crops and having quarreled with the Indians, were in desperate straits. In June a large fleet appeared. It was commanded by Francis Drake, who offered the colonists a passage to England. The temptation was too strong to be resisted; the settlers abandoned the colony and came home bag and baggage. Two weeks later a fleet under Sir Richard Grenville arrived at Roanoke with fresh supplies. Thus Ralegh's first colony failed partly through sheer bad luck. He was courageous enough to try again. In 1587 he sent out some 150 colonists, with John White as governor, who reoccupied the former settlement on Roanoke Island. Bad luck again dogged Ralegh's enterprise. During the next few years the war with Spain absorbed all the shipping available in England, and it was not until 1590 that Ralegh was able to dispatch a relief fleet to Roanoke. Its commander found the settlement deserted. The colonists had disappeared, and their fate is still unknown. This failure ended Elizabethan attempts to plant a settlement in America.

The English Attack on Spanish America

English colonization in North America was resented by Spain, but the appearance of English seamen in the closely guarded area of the Caribbean was resented much more. The English intrusion into Spanish America may be divided into two parts: first, an attempt at peaceful trade; secondly, a series of plundering expeditions which amounted to undeclared war. The earlier period is connected with the name of Sir John Hawkins, one of the great men of the age. We hear of him first as a prosperous west country merchant trading out of Plymouth to Spain and to the Canary Islands. From his friends in the Canaries he learned that French privateers were raiding in the West Indies, that Spain gave her subjects there little protection, and that the rigid commercial system of one fleet of merchant vessels a year between Spain and the Indies forced the colonists to pay outrageous prices for European goods. Hawkins also learned that the colonists were in great need of slaves from Africa. He believed that by using the good offices of his friends and by combining tact with an occasional show of force, he could trade with the Spanish colonists without arousing the wrath of their government. He may also have hoped to secure a privileged position in that trade by defending Spanish shipping from French attack.

In 1562 he sailed from Plymouth with four ships, secured a pilot in the Canaries, obtained 400 Negroes on the coast of West Africa, and crossed the Atlantic to the island of Santo Domingo. The colonists were eager to buy the

Habes Lector candide fortiß.ac inuictiß.Ducis Draeck ad Vinon Jmaginem qui toto terrarum orbe, duorum annorum, et menfium decem fpatio, Zephiris fauentibus circumducto, Angliam fedes proprias. 4. Cal Octobr: anno á partu Virginis 1520 reuifit cum antea portu foluißet Jd. Decem: anni 1577

Sir Francis Drake. A contemporary engraving. (British Museum) slaves, and the authorities seemed willing to wink at the traffic. Hawkins brought home a valuable cargo of hides, sugar, pearls, and a little gold. Two years later he sailed again. This voyage was on a larger scale than the first. Elizabeth invested in it, not with money, but by lending a ship from the navy, the *Jesus of Lübeck,* a large but cranky vessel that almost foundered on more than one occasion. Having obtained his Negroes—partly by taking them from Portuguese ships—Hawkins sailed to the Spanish Main, that is, to the northern coast of South America between Panama and the mouth of the Orinoco River. The colonists there had been commanded not to trade with him but were eager to do so. Hence a little comedy was enacted: upon the colonists' refusal to trade, Hawkins fired a cannon ball or two at the shore; whereupon the colonists capitulated (having a story for the authorities) and permitted trade to begin. Again Hawkins came home with a valuable cargo.

But his third voyage ended in disaster. Determined to maintain their monopoly, the Spanish punished the colonial governors who had not molested Hawkins, and armed their American fleet more heavily. Hawkins sailed in 1567 with six vessels. With great difficulty he obtained a small number of Negroes. After trading along the Spanish Main, he was about to sail homeward when his fleet was struck by a gale which badly damaged the *Jesus.* In order to make repairs Hawkins entered the harbor of San Juan de Ulúa, the port for the Mexican city of Vera Cruz. Hardly had he secured the harbor when a large Spanish fleet appeared. He could have excluded it, but that would have been an act of war, so he permitted the two fleets to anchor side by side. Suddenly the Spanish attacked him, all but destroying his little flotilla. Only two of his ships escaped to make their way home with great suffering. Thus ended the hope of peaceful English trade in the Indies.

Hawkins' disaster at San Juan de Ulúa, which caused great bitterness in England, was followed by English raids that made no pretense at commerce but aimed solely at plunder. By far the most famous of the raiders was Francis Drake. He had been born in Devon, but his father, a zealous Protestant, migrated to Kent, where the family lived in poverty. Drake, who had had little education, was wholly the man of action, supremely self-confident, with a gift for leadership, a genius for naval war both in tactics and in grand strategy, and an itch for plunder. He was serving under Hawkins when the Spanish attacked at San Juan de Ulúa. Thenceforth he devoted himself to a one-man war against Spain, completely assured that he represented the forces of light against the forces of darkness. In an expedition in 1571 he lurked in a secret harbor on the Isthmus of Panama while he studied the route by which the Spaniards shipped their treasure. It came largely from Peru, was brought up the west coast by sea to Panama, was carried by mule train across the isthmus to the town of Nombre de Dios on the Atlantic side, where it was stored until a fleet arrived from Spain. Drake saw that Nombre de Dios was the crucial point. In 1572 he entered the town in a surprise attack before dawn, broke into the treasure house, where he saw great quantities of silver. Unfortunately he was wounded and collapsed, and his men carried him to the boats, leaving the treasure behind. But before he sailed for England he captured a mule train within sight of Nombre de Dios, and brought home so much plunder that Elizabeth, fearing a break with Spain, dared not receive him openly but sent him to Ireland for a year or two.

In 1577 Drake sailed on his most famous exploit. Attacks on the Isthmus of Panama had now been rather overdone, and Drake devised a new plan. This was to pass through the Strait of Magellan into the Pacific and to raid the west coast of South America, where the Spaniards considered themselves quite safe. Such a plan was bolder and more original than might appear today. It was believed at the time that the Strait of Magellan separated South America from a great antarctic continent; hence there was no choice but to pass through it. The strait was highly dangerous: between Magellan's voyage and Drake's only two captains had managed to penetrate to the Pacific. For a generation before Drake no one had even attempted the passage. Drake sailed in December 1577 with five ships and about 160 men and boys, including Thomas Doughty, a dangerous and disloyal person who attempted to create a mutiny. He was tried and executed, for Drake knew that he must have absolute control over his men. The passage through the strait was fortunately swift, but in the Pacific the fleet encountered foul weather which lasted an entire month. One ship went down with all hands; another was blown back into the strait and then taken to England by the crew, much against the will of John Winter, the commander. Two other ships, mere victualers, had been broken up before entering the strait. Thus Drake was alone in his famous vessel, the *Golden Hind.* He sailed up the west coast of South America, plundering as he went but apparently not taking the life of a single Spaniard. He then went north to California and thence across the Pacific, through the Malay Archipelago, around Africa, and so home, with treasure valued by contemporaries at one and a half million pounds. The second captain to circumnavigate the earth, his voyage brought the war with Spain much closer.

Other English seamen attempted to imitate his exploits, but few succeeded. In 1575 John Oxenham sailed to Panama, marched his men across to the Pacific, where he constructed two small vessels and obtained some treasure, but was captured and hanged as a pirate. In the next year Andrew Barker of Bristol sailed to the Spanish Main but also was killed by the Spaniards. Between 1586 and 1588 Thomas Cavendish followed Drake's route through the Strait of Magellan, plundered the west coast of South America, and made his way home to England by sailing around the world. His success was due in part to sheer good luck, for he was far inferior to Drake as a commander, and in a second attempt in 1591 he failed to penetrate the strait. Another seaman, John Chidley, failed in 1589. Sir Richard Hawkins, son of John Hawkins, entered the Pacific in 1593, only to be captured and slain. It was thus most dangerous for Englishmen to venture into Spanish-American waters. Failure was more frequent than success, for the Spaniards were learning to defend themselves more adequately.

The English Navy

The voyages we have been describing taught English sailors many things about their ships. Long voyages to America or north to the Arctic or south to West Africa meant that ships must be able to remain at sea in all weather for extended periods of time. A merchantman trading to the Levant must be large and heavily armed whereas a sea rover in Spanish America must be fast and nimble. Conditions at sea in the sixteenth century almost always approximated conditions of war; and the lessons learned in peaceful trade could be applied directly to battle. A large merchant vessel was a formidable fighting unit that could take its place in combat by the side of the Royal Navy; its sailors felt quite at home in ships built only for war. Finally, from these voyages of maritime enterprise there emerged a generation of famous captains eager to transfer their skills from more or less peaceful trade to open war with Spain.

Henry VIII had been greatly interested in the navy, had left a fleet of some fifty vessels great and small, and had introduced changes which were to revolutionize naval warfare although he was only half aware of their implications. Mindful of the possibility of invasion by Catholic powers, he had created a fighting navy, built with the purpose of stopping invasion in mid-Channel and of destroying the army of the enemy at sea. He had given the navy a new role, the defense of the kingdom.

But Henry's ships were not very formidable. They were large ships of a type known as carracks, wide in proportion to their length, built high above the water with towering castles fore and aft from which soldiers could shoot down upon the decks of the enemy. These ships, designed for grappling, carried soldiers who boarded the enemy after the opposing ships had been lashed together and who fought hand to hand with the foe. Although Henry's ships were awe-inspiring, they were poor sailors. Top-heavy and cranky at sea, they rolled and tossed until they developed leaks. Nor could they remain at sea for any length of time without revictualing.

But before the end of the reign, Henry made important innovations. Becoming interested in some cannon of unusual size and power, he conceived the idea of placing them in his ships. Because the cannon were too heavy for the flimsy superstructure they were arranged along the sides of the ships on the cargo deck, ports having been cut in the hull through which they could fire broadsides. Here was the beginning of modern naval warfare, for the broadside, when properly developed, could batter and sink the enemy without boarding. Henry also strengthened the navy by building dockyards up the Thames, where ships were safe from enemy action, and by establishing a government board for naval administration.[4]

After Henry's death the fleet so degenerated that Elizabeth inherited only a shadow of her father's naval strength. Her navy remained weak for many years because she had little money to spend on it, and that little was wasted by the dishonesty of the navy board. It was John Hawkins who rebuilt the navy along more modern lines. Having convinced Burghley that the navy board was corrupt, and having become a member of the board in 1578, he began to improve administration, remodel old ships, and build new ones. The normal warship of northern Europe in Elizabeth's reign was the galleon, a heavy fighting ship, more slender, longer, and lower in the water than the carrack, without so much superstructure and with her guns arranged to fire broadsides.

Hawkins entertained advanced ideas concerning naval gunnery and architecture. He increased the length of the ships still further so that they could mount more artillery; he built a gun deck, reserved solely for guns, over the cargo deck; he cut down drastically the old-fashioned castles fore and aft, making the ships faster, steadier, more nimble at sea, able to sail closer to the wind. The guns were improved in size and quality. Hawkins' ships did not require soldiers but naval gunners and captains who could sail their ships with dexterity. Smaller crews diminished the danger of epidemics and increased the time a ship could remain at sea without revictualing. By 1587, when Hawkins retired from office, he had provided the Queen with eighteen large galleons and seven smaller ones, most of them of the latest design and all in readiness for battle. The captains were in love with their ships. "I protest it before God," wrote Lord Admiral

[4] Michael Lewis, *The History of the British Navy* (Harmondsworth, Middlesex: Penguin Books, 1957), pp. 34–45.

Howard, "that I had rather live in the company of these noble ships than in any place.... There is not one but I durst go to the Rio de la Plata in her." A recent historian has observed that when the Spanish Armada sailed in 1588 "Elizabeth I was the mistress of the most powerful navy Europe had ever seen."[5]

THE SPANISH ARMADA

The enterprise of invading England is first heard of early in Elizabeth's reign among the English Catholic exiles, who wandered about like ghosts on the Continent. Then for a time the project was sponsored by the Duke of Guise, who hoped to rescue Mary Stuart. After 1580 it became more and more a Spanish affair. Philip's preparations at first were very slow. They increased in tempo when Elizabeth sent open aid to the Dutch and when Drake made a devastating raid on Spanish America in 1585–1586. Sailing first to Vigo Bay in Spain, then to the Canaries and to the Cape Verde Islands, Drake crossed the Atlantic in eighteen days, captured Santo Domingo, the capital of the West Indies, and Cartagena, the capital of the Spanish Main, leaving a path of destruction behind him. In 1587 he struck again, descending upon the coasts of Spain and Portugal, burning ships in Cadiz Harbor and throwing Spanish plans into chaos.

In reply Philip pushed his preparations with increased ardor. He had become the religious crusader, determined to send forth his fleet at all costs, refusing to weigh dispassionately the enormous difficulties of the enterprise, relying upon God, as it seemed, to perform a miracle in giving victory to Spanish arms. The leading admiral of Spain was the Marquis of Santa Cruz, a veteran of many battles, but by then an old man. Philip pushed him hard. In a kind of senile frenzy Santa Cruz gathered ships at Lisbon and threw guns and provisions into them in hurly-burly fashion. In the midst of this senseless rush he died. Philip then appointed the Duke of Medina-Sidonia, an aristocratic administrator and a brave and conscientious leader but not an experienced seaman. Medina-Sidonia brought order into the chaos at Lisbon and strengthened the fleet in many ways.

When it sailed against England in the summer of 1588, the Spanish fleet was a powerful fighting force, although events were to reveal its many defects. For one thing, it was less homogeneous than the English fleet. The backbone of its fighting strength consisted, as in England, of some twenty galleons. About half were ships of Castile, whose normal duty was to convoy the treasure fleets from America. About half were Portuguese, a fleet with a great fighting tradition though now in some decay. One galleon belonged to the Grand Duke of Tuscany, whose beautiful ship had been commandeered by the Spaniards despite his agonized protests. The Armada also contained four galleasses from Naples, light, maneuverable ships which could be heavily armed and which cruised under sail but in combat were propelled by oars. These ships, supplemented by four large merchantmen, made up the first battle line of the Armada. A second line comprised some forty merchant vessels, some very large though without many guns. In addition to these were light, fast ships for scouting, and a large number of victualers and other hulks, slow, cumbersome, and quite helpless in battle. The total was some 130 ships. But the Spaniards had fewer large guns

[5] Garrett Mattingly, *The Armada*, p. 195.

Ark Royal, Lord Admiral Howard's flagship in the battle against the Spanish Armada. Woodcut. (British Museum)

than the English, fewer naval gunners, and insufficient amounts of ammunition. Provisions proved defective. The sailing qualities of the Spanish ships were far below those of England. Of these deficiencies the Spaniards were painfully aware.

There was, moreover, a fatal defect in the planning of the Spanish campaign. The primary purpose of the Armada, in Philip's mind, was to escort Parma's army from the Netherlands to England. Where was the all-important rendezvous between the fleet and the army to take place? The Flemish coast was so shallow that the large Spanish ships could not approach the shore. It would be necessary for Parma to set sail without the Armada's assistance and to rendezvous with the Spanish fleet at sea. This was obviously Philip's plan, for he commanded Medina-Sidonia to meet Parma "off the cape of Margate." Such a meeting at sea, in the face of the English fleet, was the most dangerous operation imaginable. It entirely overlooked the Dutch flyboats, which could sail in shallow water and intercept Parma before he reached the Armada. Parma's naval position was extremely weak. Aside from a few light warships that could not repulse the Dutch, he had nothing but crude canal barges in which he must herd his precious soldiers like cattle. In a word, he could not meet the Armada at sea, and the Armada could not come close to the shore. Parma had explained this situation to Philip but not, apparently, to Medina-Sidonia, who greatly exaggerated Parma's naval strength. The blame for these fatal errors must be laid at Philip's door. He was indeed sending forth his fleet on a mission which only a miracle could render successful.

The Armada sailed from the port of Lisbon on May 20, 1588. As it worked its slow way northward it was buffeted by foul weather, and there was alarming spoilage in the provisions as well as sickness among the men. The duke put in at Corunna in northern Spain to refit. From Corunna he wrote a surprising letter to Philip, suggesting that the entire enterprise be abandoned. But Philip was adamant, and the Armada set sail again on July 12. Carried by a fair wind, it entered the English Channel. The Spanish ships sailed line abreast in a tight formation which gave the impression of a vast crescent whose wings inclined backward. The victualers sailed safely within the protecting arc of warships. The bulk of the English fleet, commanded by Lord Admiral Howard, with such famous captains as Hawkins, Drake, and Frobisher, was stationed at Plymouth. The English quickly obtained the weather gauge of the Spanish, that is, they fell behind the Armada with the wind at their back, so that they could engage or not at will. Day after day they harried the wings of the Armada in heavy fighting. Their ships sailed line ahead and poured in broadsides, but avoided grappling or fighting in a melee as the Spanish desired.

Undoubtedly the English inflicted more damage than they received. Yet these battles in the Channel were frustrating to both sides. The Spanish crescent was a defensive formation which could do no great harm to the English ships. The English, on their side, found that their gunnery, though better than the Spanish, was less effective than they had hoped. They could not break up the Spanish formation. As Medina-Sidonia approached the strait between Calais and Dover his worries increased. He had no harbor in which to take refuge, he had no firm word from Parma, he could not drive off the English fleet, he was running out of cannon balls. On the night of July 27 he anchored off the coast at Calais and sent desperate messages to Parma to send him ammunition and naval assistance. The next night the English sent in fire ships. As these blazing hulks descended upon the Armada, the Spanish captains cut their cables and drifted about in helpless fashion. The formation of the crescent was broken at last.

The English, reinforced by ships which had been blockading the Flemish coast, attacked next morning in what is known as the Battle of Gravelines. The Spanish fought with great bravery and gradually resumed their old formation, or at least part of it, but now for the first time they were severely beaten. The English could outflank and worry them at will, the English broadsides fired at closer range were more deadly than before, and the Spanish, fleeing for home, sailed into the North Sea a battered and broken fleet. The English followed as far as the Firth of Forth and then turned back. As the Spanish sailed north of Scotland, west of Ireland, and so south to Spain, they were tormented by bad weather, by leaking and shattered ships, by rotten provisions and lack of drinking water, and by fevers among the crews. Some ships made for the coast of Ireland. Without maps or pilots, most of these ships were wrecked, and most of the men were slaughtered, not by the Irish, as is often stated, but by the English, determined to show no mercy. Yet thanks to the fortitude and courage of Medina-Sidonia almost two thirds of the Armada reached Spain.

England's victory did not end the war, which dragged on for the rest of Elizabeth's reign. It did not produce the sudden eclipse of Spain as a great power. It did not even give England control of the sea, for Spain at once began to build a new and better navy. In the sixteenth century the forces of destruction which one nation could hurl upon another were still puny. Yet a victory such as that of England was certain to have wide repercussions. It added vastly to England's prestige and lowered that of Spain. All Europe had been watching intently. Protestants in Holland, France, and Germany took new heart; the Dutch became independent in fact if not in international law. The greatest result of the defeat of the Armada was a check to the advance of the Counter Reformation. It was now obvious that Protestantism was not to be swept away. The great Catholic champion had suffered a body blow. "From that time forward, though Spain's preponderance was to last for more than another generation, the peak of her prestige had passed."[6]

England's victory gave her people self-confidence and aggressiveness. The fear of invasion receded, the sense of a great future on the ocean increased. "England in the nineties was a different place from what it had been in the eighties. Elizabeth herself was different. She turned quickly from a defensive to an aggressive policy and with her, as with her councillors, the old fears gave place to a new confidence in England's strength and in England's destiny."[7]

[6] Mattingly, pp. 400–401.
[7] Conyers Read in *American Historical Review*, LXV (April 1960), 588.

15

eLizaBethan enGLanD

THE SPANISH WAR, 1588–1603

The War at Sea

After its early climax in the defeat of the Armada, the war with Spain dragged on through the rest of Elizabeth's reign. When neither side could knock out the other the war became one of attrition, fought on several fronts, of which the most important was the sea. Early in 1589 the English dispatched a large fleet of about 100 vessels commanded by Drake, with 20,000 troops under Sir John Norris, a famous soldier. This voyage, known as the Portugal expedition, was a failure, partly because of divided counsels. Elizabeth had urged an attack on the ships of the Armada, which still lay scattered and helpless in the ports of northern Spain, but Drake had conceived the notion of starting a revolt in Portugal, then under Spanish control. An exiled claimant to the Portuguese throne, Don Antonio, happened to be in England and accompanied the fleet. After touching uselessly at Corunna, where only one Spanish galleon was found, the fleet sailed for Lisbon. But an attack on the city was repulsed, the Portuguese displayed no interest in Don Antonio, disease played havoc among the troops, victuals ran low. The fleet came straggling home with a loss of 8000 men at a cost of £60,000. It was the failure of the Armada in reverse.

During the next few years an attempt was made to blockade the Spanish coast in hope of intercepting the treasure fleets from America. But the blockade was intermittent and failed in its purpose. Philip slowly rebuilt and improved his navy. In 1591, hearing that an English squadron was in the Azores, he sent out his new ships in overwhelming force. Most of the English fleet escaped, but one ship, the *Revenge,* commanded by Sir Richard Grenville, was cut off and surrounded. Either in desperation or out of bravado, Grenville fought the entire Spanish fleet, doing great damage before he was mortally wounded and his ship taken.

In 1595 an attempt was made to capture the city of Panama and thus cut off the flow of American treasure. Drake and Hawkins were in command. But times were changing, the Spanish defense was far stronger than in the past, Drake and Hawkins quarreled, and both died on the voyage, which proved a failure. The older generation of English seamen was passing away. An expedition in 1596, which succeeded in destroying a Spanish fleet at Cadiz, was commanded by new men, Lord Thomas Howard, Sir Walter Ralegh, and the young Earl of Essex. A third large expedition in 1597 aimed at the Azores produced little except quarrels between the commanders, Ralegh and Essex. The war at sea then declined, and English energies were devoted to warfare in Ireland.

Ireland

When Elizabeth ascended the throne English power in Ireland had sunk to a very low ebb. A lord deputy in Dublin ruled the Pale, and English influence existed in some of the coastal towns. The rest of the country, under its tribal chieftains, was still a Celtic world of feuds, raids, and murders, and of primitive social and economic structure. For a moment around 1540 Henry VIII had taken an interest in Ireland. He had assumed the title of King of Ireland and had followed a policy of persuading the chiefs to surrender their lands to the English Crown and to receive them back again as grants from the King. Under Mary Tudor the Pale was enlarged, though the new territories were not securely held. Elizabeth, having broken with Spain and with the papacy, could not allow Ireland to remain in this unsettled condition. It offered too tempting a base for enemy action against her. Her policy was to establish English control, which could only be done by conquering the Irish chiefs. The conquest of Ireland occupied her entire reign; at her death it was complete. During these wars the Irish became for the first time ardently Roman Catholic. Catholicism was strengthened because it was a symbol of resistance, because Spain and the papacy were potential allies, and because there was a highly successful mission of the Jesuits. "At the beginning of the reign Ireland was virtually ungoverned and heathen; by the end it was firmly under English control and Roman Catholic."[1]

For many years Elizabeth attempted to conquer Ireland without spending much money, but in the 1590s she was faced with a serious war in Ulster. Ulster lay to the north, the most backward part of Ireland, and had many connections with the Western Isles of Scotland. Its most potent chieftain was Hugh O'Neill, Earl of Tyrone. He had been educated at the English court, but when he returned to Ulster in 1585 he was determined to make himself an independent prince. He was a man of ability, a subtle diplomat who constantly outwitted the English, a soldier who for the first time converted the Irish warriors into half-disciplined troops. Tyrone was also patient, ready to bide his time, but apt to hesitate in a crisis. He and Hugh Roe O'Donnell, Lord of Tyrconnel, led a revolt in Ulster in 1595. Three years later, in a battle on the Blackwater River, Tyrone inflicted a disastrous defeat on the English. He might have marched to Dublin, but he waited for help from Spain. On two occasions, in 1596 and 1597, Philip had dispatched fleets to Ireland, but both expeditions had been ruined by foul weather.

Then in 1599 Elizabeth sent over her favorite, Robert Devereux, Earl of Essex, with a large and well-equipped army. But Essex wasted his opportunities, concluded a shameful truce with Tyrone, and suddenly, conscious of his failure,

---

[1] G. R. Elton, *England under the Tudors* (London: Methuen, 1955), p. 387.

abandoned his command and rushed back to England. This ended his career, as we shall see. He was succeeded by Charles Blount, Lord Mountjoy, an excellent general who gradually broke the power of Tyrone. When the war was all but over, the Spanish finally arrived. A Spanish force of 4000 men landed at Kinsale on the southern coast in 1601. Tyrone came down from Ulster. But by great skill and dash and against greatly superior numbers Mountjoy defeated both Irish and Spanish forces. Tyrone fled north with his shattered army, Tyrconnel became an exile in Spain, the Spanish in Ireland surrendered; the country lay defeated and prostrate.

One feature of Elizabeth's reign was the planting of English colonies in Ireland. Confiscated lands were granted to English gentlemen, who took out

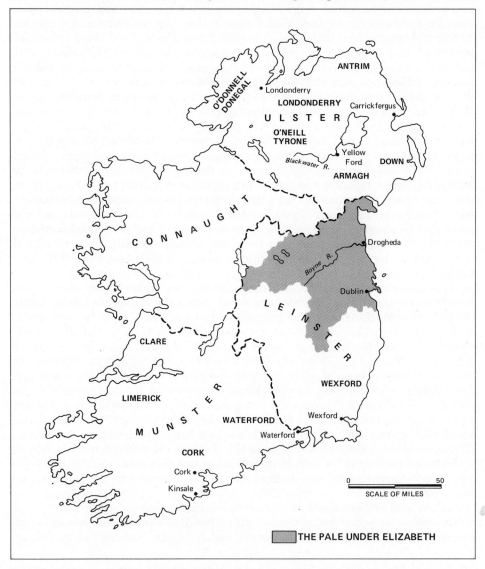

Ireland in the Sixteenth and Seventeenth Centuries

English farmers and artisans in much the same way as they later took them to Virginia. Most of these settlements, however, disappeared in the Irish wars.

In addition to the war in Ireland and to the war at sea, England also was fighting in the Netherlands and in France. English volunteers served in the Dutch armies, and Elizabeth maintained a separate force in the Netherlands, never less than about 6000 men. When the Huguenot leader, Henry of Navarre, became King Henry IV of France in 1589, he was at war both with Spain and with the French Catholic family of Guise. Elizabeth sent five expeditions to his assistance.

The Cost of War

Operations on such a vast and far-flung scale were extremely expensive, imposing an almost intolerable strain on the nation. Between 1588 and 1603 the government spent the unprecedented sum of more than £4 million on the war. About half this amount was provided by parliamentary taxation, the remainder coming from increased customs duties (at a time when trade was declining), from the spoils of war, and from the extensive sale of Crown lands.

The nation was not in a position to carry this heavy burden easily. About one in twenty men were in the armed services, the plague broke out in London and other cities, there was a run of bad harvests, and trade and industry were depressed by the loss and confusion of war. Markets in lands controlled by Spain or in areas whose approach was dominated by Spain were shut to English goods. Moreover, though the exploits of Drake and other raiders stirred the imagination, they were injurious to legitimate commerce, diverting large sums from normal business ventures, undermining international credit, and encouraging a tendency toward monopoly in business ventures. "The unsafety of the high seas raised freights, hindered small enterprise, necessitated governmental protection, justified a system of licenses, and so led on to restriction and monopoly."[2] English trading companies, seeing that the volume of commerce was declining, sought to control and monopolize what remained. The Merchant Adventurers, for example, were forced to abandon Antwerp as their staple, were later excluded from the German Empire, and finally settled at Middelburg in Zeeland. Although they struggled fiercely to maintain some portion of their old monopoly, they suffered heavy losses from these moves and were troubled greatly by interlopers who intruded into their preserves.

THE EAST INDIA COMPANY

If most trading companies became more interested in the control than in the expansion of commerce, the East India Company was a brilliant exception. All through the sixteenth century the English had longed to sail around Africa to the Spice Islands of the Malay Archipelago, but they had hesitated because they lacked the necessary knowledge of geography, because they considered their ships too small for such a lengthy passage, and because the Portuguese were already in possession. These obstacles gradually were removed.

In 1591 a group of London merchants sent out an expedition commanded by George Raymond and James Lancaster, both of whom had fought against the

[2] Quoted in S. T. Bindoff, *Tudor England* (Harmondsworth, Middlesex: Penguin Books, 1950), p. 286.

Spanish Armada. The voyage was an armed reconnaissance, not for trade but for the discovery of trading possibilities; it was to pay its way by the plunder of Portuguese shipping. After rounding Africa the little fleet was struck by a storm which sent Raymond's ship down with all hands. Lancaster continued alone, reached Sumatra and the western coast of the Malay Peninsula, and took some Portuguese prizes. He lost so many of his men through disease, however, that he could scarcely work his way homeward. Once more in the Atlantic, he made for the West Indies, but while he was on shore in search of provisions, his ship drifted away and was captured by the Spaniards. After many hardships Lancaster was rescued by a French vessel and brought home to Europe. Another voyage sent out in 1596 under the command of Benjamin Wood was even more disastrous, for only one survivor ever returned. Wood reached the west coast of the Malay Peninsula, where he was shipwrecked. A few survivors trusted themselves on the Indian Ocean in a canoe and were lost. One member of the ship's company was later picked up by a Dutch vessel.

The loss and sufferings of these voyages might well have discouraged further effort, but the English were now urged forward by the appearance of the Dutch as competitors for the trade of the East, for Holland had grown into a maritime power. The Dutch were given a description of the East in a book by Jan Huygen van Linschoten, who had lived six years in India. In 1595 a Dutch company sent out a fleet which reached the pepper depot of Bantam in Java. The Dutch now threw themselves into the Eastern trade with the greatest energy and determination. Twenty-two ships sailed from Holland in 1598. By 1602 there were so many competing Dutch companies that the government forced a consolidation by creating a Dutch East India Company. This company, which was little less than a department of state, was backed by abundant capital and by the nation as a whole.

It would be ironic if English voyages had merely paved the way for Dutch success. Hence, after many delays, an English East India Company was formed in 1600, consisting of 218 merchants and other adventurers who elected a governor and a directing committee of 24. Happily the first voyage was a brilliant success. Five ships under the command of James Lancaster left England in 1601. Lancaster reached the city of Achin in northern Sumatra, where he obtained permission to buy pepper. He then sailed through the Sunda Strait to Bantam, again obtaining the right to buy pepper and also to establish a factory. These factories, or trading posts, were essential because the sudden arrival of a ship from Europe shot up the price of local products and depressed the price of European goods. Hence it was necessary to leave a group of merchants in a factory to buy and sell over an extended period. For many years Bantam remained the principal station of the English in the Malay Archipelago. Lancaster returned to England with a million pounds of pepper, together with small quantities of cloves, cinnamon, and nutmeg. Before he reach England Elizabeth had died.

GRATUITIES AND FACTION

Decline in Political Morality

The long war with Spain, as we have seen, brought unhappy economic results, as most wars do. It also produced a decline in public morals. For thirty years before the Armada the English had been living under the triple threat of invasion, civil war, and an uncertain succession to the throne. Year by year the tension had mounted. This sense of fear and common danger had produced a high level of national unity, patriotic zeal, and self-sacrifice in the service of the state. Then suddenly the tension eased. The fear of invasion receded. Although the execution of Mary, Queen of Scots, in 1587 may have spurred Philip to greater effort, it removed the danger of a Catholic heir, for Mary's son, King James VI of Scotland, was a Protestant. Safety no longer depended on the single thread of Elizabeth's life. Puritanism, as a political irritant, subsided. It is small wonder that the morale of public men declined, that the new generation of politicians, though aggressive and confident, were less stable, less restrained, less careful in distinguishing between integrity and corruption.

The salaries of high officials were very small, often standing at the same figure as in the Middle Ages. Elizabeth could not pay salaries in any sense commensurate with the value of the services she received. Officials were expected to live by obtaining payments from everyone—suitors, tradesmen, office seekers—with whom they dealt in the ordinary work of government. There were fees for various services, and these fees had hardened into a tariff. But there were other payments—gifts, gratuities, sometimes bribes—that were given in secret.

The Crown was the fountain of patronage. Hundreds of offices and places were at the Queen's disposal; she could give lands and leases on easy terms and many kinds of economic privilege; a word from her could influence patronage in places where she had no direct control. The suitors who thronged the court could not hope for private interviews with her. Hence they turned to officials, to courtiers, to great ladies, to anyone who could enter the Queen's privy chamber and bring suits to her attention. In a word, courtiers and officials sold their influence with the Queen and accepted money from all who desired royal favors. "I ever took it," wrote an official, "that a man may with honesty accept a gratuity given." Offices were bought and sold, not directly by the Crown, but by bargains between the man who relinquished an office and the man who obtained it. The household of a high official or courtier, such as that of Burghley or of Essex, was a little court in itself. It was filled with followers and clients for whom the great man was expected to obtain favors. If he was successful he attracted new followers, he was offered gratuities, he added to his influence by surrounding the Queen with his adherents.

This was at best a dangerous system and was tolerable only because Elizabeth distributed patronage widely. Quite aware of what was going on, she did not make appointments without private information about those to whom she gave office. But in the last fifteen years of her reign the atmosphere at court degenerated. Burghley's son, Robert Cecil, though a man of ability and character, was not as scrupulous as his father. The new generation was out of touch with the old Queen and her ways. She sensed the difference. "Now the wit of the fox is everywhere on foot," she said, "so as hardly a faithful or virtuous man may be found."[3]

The Earl of Essex
The last years of Elizabeth's reign were marked by faction at court as well as by declining honesty. Rivalry arose between the Cecils—Lord Burghley and his son Robert—and Robert Devereux, Earl of Essex. Essex was a cousin of

[3] J. E. Neale, "The Elizabethan Political Scene," *Proceedings of the British Academy,* XXXIV (1948), 1–23.

Elizabeth through the Boleyn family; his stepfather was the Earl of Leicester, who first introduced him at court in 1584 when he was a youth of seventeen. A handsome young man with a dignified bearing and with great dash and spirit, he at once attracted the Queen's attention. His domineering egotism, his impulsive, ill-disciplined, and jealous nature, and his unreasonable ambitions were as yet concealed. He soon won a reputation as a soldier. He accompanied Leicester to the Netherlands in 1585, sailed with the Portugal expedition in 1589, and commanded Elizabeth's first venture to assist Henry IV in France. In the early 1590s a brilliant prospect opened before him. Leicester, the Queen's favorite, was now dead, and Burghley, her principal adviser, was growing old. Why should he not fill the place of both and dominate the court?

But he found himself opposed by the Cecils. Burghley's ambition in his old age was to obtain high office for his son Robert. He groomed him for the secretaryship, which fell vacant in 1590; a contest over this office was the first trial of strength between the Cecils and Essex. Elizabeth compromised by leaving the place vacant, though she gave it to Robert Cecil in 1596. Meanwhile the rivalry of the two factions became general. For every vacant office Essex had a candidate whom he urged upon the Queen with pressing importunity. There were stormy scenes between them; once Elizabeth boxed his ears. In 1599, on his own urging, he was sent as Lord Deputy to Ireland. Failing against Tyrone, as we have seen, he conceived the treasonable idea of using the young gallants in his train to force Elizabeth to ruin the Cecils and to give him predominance at court. He returned against orders, only to be arrested and later condemned to the loss of all his offices.

Brooding over his wrongs, insanely jealous of the Cecils, and using violent language against the Queen, he allowed his house in London to become the resort of "swordsmen, bold confident fellows, discontented persons, and such as saucily used their tongues in railing against all men." In February 1601 he tried the desperate venture of seizing the court. But the government was forewarned, the city of London did not rise at Essex's urging, and he was quickly confined to his house and forced to surrender. Within ten days he was condemned for treason and within another week he was beheaded. There was great sympathy for him, but the people knew he deserved his fate. The Cecils were left supreme.

THE SPIRIT OF THE AGE

It is a mistake to emphasize unduly the dislocations caused by the long war with Spain. A broad and general view of society in the age of Queen Elizabeth reveals a brighter and more hopeful picture. What we see is a young and vigorous people emerging from the Middle Ages into the warmer and more intense life of the Renaissance. The Elizabethans were very much alive, alert to the world around them, not merely to grasp the main chance in a material way and to rise in the social scale, but to respond to intellectual and artistic impulses. It was an age of superb writing in prose and verse, of fine achievements in music and architecture. The upper classes were better educated than they had ever been before. Oxford and Cambridge were well attended in the Tudor period, especially by the gentry. The printing press, first introduced in the late fifteenth century by William Caxton, had vastly increased the reading matter available to the public.

Along with alertness went enthusiasm. The Elizabethans were not afraid to throw themselves with vigor into their many undertakings. They were natural and uninhibited, sometimes naïve, sometimes bizarre, but satisfied to be themselves. Self-centered, proud, and self-confident they had a sense of success and achievement arising from good government, increasing wealth, and patriotic pride in the defeat of Spain. They were sure they could succeed at whatever they attempted. Some men of the time were astonishingly versatile. Sir Walter Ralegh, for example, was a courtier and royal favorite, soldier, sailor, discoverer, colonizer, poet, and writer of prose. When in the reign of James I he fell from favor, was cast into prison and decided to write a book, he selected for his topic a history of the world! Interested in chemistry and medicine, he compounded a famous pill which he sent his friends upon request and which doubtless made them much more ill than they had been before.

The Elizabethan Age was a secular age. Despite the Puritans, the Elizabethans were more interested in this world than in the next, in new forms of wealth, in industry, and in overseas expansion. It was not an honest age: people got what they could, marriage was a business arrangement, great officers of state did not hesitate to accept gratuities. London was full of sharpers out to fleece the unwary. The underworld had a vocabulary of its own. The "cony-catcher" "cozened" the "gull," which meant that the trickster cheated the gullible out of his money. The same spirit is found in the monopolies the government permitted. A monopoly might be a legitimate protection for a new invention (as is a patent today) but more normally it was some economic privilege obtained from the Queen and shrewdly exploited at the expense of the public. In some ways this was a childish age. There was a love of finery and trinkets, of bright colors, and bizarre costumes, of shows, and parades, and of the wonders and monstrosities of nature. In Fleet Street in London one could see trained bears and monkeys, Indians, dwarfs, large fish, and other marvels. There were pleasures of a simple kind such as singing and dancing around maypoles, though maypoles were not as innocent as they appeared and some sports involved great cruelty to animals.

How can this vitality and exuberance be explained? One can hazard a few guesses. It was in Elizabeth's reign that England felt the full impact of the Italian Renaissance, which came streaming in from many parts of the Continent. During the first half of the century the new learning had been largely devoted to theological debate, but now it broadened into a humanism that was wider, fuller, and more urbane. Although the break with Rome had unpleasant aspects, it was bold and adventurous and freed religious discussion from the trammels of authority. It gave a boost to the national economy. There were also advances in scientific thought, as in the revolutionary concept of Copernicus that the earth revolved about the sun and not the sun about the earth. Equally important were geographical discoveries which opened men's minds to a knowledge of the world as it really was. One must add to these things an outburst of intellectual and aesthetic experience. The Elizabethan scene, moreover, was filled with vivid personalities and bold adventures that stirred the imagination and prompted men to action.

Illustrations from a song-book. The Month of May. (From Thomas Fella, *A Book of Divers Devices,* London, 1622. Folger Shakespeare Library)

LITERATURE

Elizabethan writers caught up the exuberance of the age and translated it into a great literature. Writing was stimulated in many ways. The Englishman's pride in his family, in the history of his country, in its language, geography, and antiquities, in its great deeds on sea and land, provided new and abundant themes on which to write. The improved education of the upper classes created the ideal of the cultured gentleman, who combined patriotism with courtesy, learning, and a love of poetry. A flood of translations from the classics and from contemporary works in French, Spanish, and Italian offered literary forms and subject matter from which Englishmen could borrow. In addition, the Elizabethans were ready to experiment. And hence the English language as an instrument of literary expression developed wonderfully from the stiffness of the early sixteenth century to the lively flexibility of the later Elizabethans. This period of literary flowering, beginning about 1580, continued into the seventeenth century at least until the death of Shakespeare in 1616.

Much Elizabethan prose, of course, was good without rising to the level of literature. This was true of the many books concerning local geography and antiquities, such as the *Perambulation of Kent* by William Lambarde and the *Britannia* by William Camden, who traveled laboriously from county to county examining local records and antiquarian lore. Historical writing included collections of medieval tales and chronicles by Richard Grafton, John Stow, and Raphael Holinshed; Samuel Daniel's *History of England;* Francis Bacon's *History of Henry VII;* and John Foxe's *Book of Martyrs,* which dealt with the persecutions of Mary's reign. In his *Annales . . . Regnante Elizabetha* William Camden traced the history of his own time. Though lacking in form and polish, this work showed Camden's industry and critical judgment and his knowledge of domestic and foreign affairs. Lord Burghley had supplied him with a mass of documents, "in the rigging and searching whereof," Camden wrote, "I labored till I sweat, being covered over with dust." A work of similar dedication was William Hakluyt's prose epic of English expansion overseas, *The Principal Navigations . . . of the English Nation, made by Sea or over Land.*

When John Lyly published his *Euphues* (1579) and his *Euphues His England* (1580), he did a distinct disservice to English prose. Describing the tiresome adventures of a young Athenian named Euphues, Lyly attempted to give his prose the poetic tone and ornaments of verse. The result, however, was artificial and pedantic, for he introduced such contrivances as farfetched similes, alliteration, and strained antithesis. His sentence structure was dull and monotonous. Yet euphuism became a literary cult; its baneful affectations were copied widely. Only slowly did the realization dawn that prose should not attempt to imitate verse but should describe real things with accuracy and precision. A more spontaneous and realistic style appeared in the tracts of Robert Greene and Thomas Dekker depicting the life of the London underworld. The pamphleteer and satirist Thomas Nash, who attacked the absurdities of euphuism, also carried forward the movement toward realistic and natural writing. Translators of books in foreign languages were forced to be accurate rather than ornate. Moreover, controversy, which aimed to convince the reader, produced straightforward and unadorned prose. The best writing on religion was the treatise, *Of the Laws of Ecclesiastical Politie,* by Richard Hooker, a defense of the Church of England. This work in its melodious flow of well-phrased argumentation, often rose to the plane of great literature. Perhaps the ultimate in compact phrasing and tightly woven form was to be found in the Latinized style of Bacon's *Essays.*

It was in poetry, however, that the Elizabethans excelled. The ode, the madrigal, the song, the eclogue, the ballad, the sonnet—indeed all kinds of lyrics expressing the feelings of the poet—were brought to a high level of excellence. Blank verse became the characteristic form of the drama.

A name famous in poetry was that of Sir Philip Sidney. His high social position, noble spirit, and reputation as the perfect gentleman, together with his early death in the war against Spain, tempted contemporaries to be overlavish in their praise. But Sidney, endowed with high poetic gifts, caught the imagination of his countrymen. Almost three centuries later Shelley wrote of Sidney,

> Sublimely mild, a spirit without spot.

His first work of any length was his *Arcadia,* a prose romance of love and chivalry in which battles and tournaments, plots and counterplots alternated with eclogues or pastoral poems contrasting rural life with the life of a court. The *Arcadia* reflected Sidney's wide reading in the literature of Spain and Italy, but the style betrayed the influence of euphuism. His *Astrophel and Stella* was a collection of 108 love sonnets and 11 songs addressed to Lady Penelope Devereux, the vivacious sister of Elizabeth's favorite, the Earl of Essex. Although the first sonnets were rather cold, later ones portrayed a passionate attachment. Their fine phrasing and energetic sentiment place them among the best of their kind. Sidney's *Apologie for Poetrie,* an early attempt at literary criticism, was a prose essay containing advice which poets have fortunately ignored.

Aside from Shakespeare, the finest poet of the age was Edmund Spenser. A learned poet, he was well acquainted with Greek and Latin literature as well as with French and Italian. In 1580 he accepted a post as secretary to the Lord Deputy of Ireland and lived in that country until his death in 1599, holding various offices in the English administration. He found Ireland a most uncongenial and depressing place. His lack of sympathy with his surroundings and his sense of exile engendered in him a somber melancholy and despair of the world as he saw it. Hence he retired into a fairyland of his own imagination where virtue triumphed over vice and where a man's duty and desires pointed in the same direction. Of his writings the most important were: *The Shepheards Calender,* a series of twelve eclogues; three satires on English society and life at court; a number of splendid lyrics; *The Faerie Queene;* and a prose pamphlet on the state of Ireland.

The Faerie Queene is a long narrative poem placed in a setting of medieval romance in which knights representing virtues such as holiness, temperance, chastity, and justice do battle against opposing vices and appetites. The greatness of the poem is derived from Spenser's high poetic spirit, vivid imagination, and superb mastery of words. He bestows upon his narrative a lush pictorial imagery, a play of fancy, and a flowing melody which waft the reader gently into a fairy world of languorous music and exotic romance.

The drama, of prime importance in Elizabethan literature, was exactly suited to the temper of the age. It satisfied the Elizabethan love of action, of pageantry, and of amusement, as well as the love of songs and poetry. At the beginning of the reign the drama was still in a primitive state. Private theatricals were performed on special occasions at court and at the universities, but there were no public theaters; actors were regarded by the authorities as so many rogues and vagabonds. However, the drama developed with amazing rapidity. Plays became increasingly popular at court. The first company of actors was formed under the patronage of the Earl of Leicester in 1574; theaters began to be built, not in London itself but across the river in Southwark.

The tremendous possibilities of the drama for public amusement first were demonstrated by the plays of Thomas Kyd and Christopher Marlowe. Kyd's *Spanish Tragedy* (1586), a roaring drama of blood and thunder, possessed plot and stagecraft but was devoid of poetry. The plays of Marlowe were much more important. His fine blank verse brought excellent poetry to the stage for the first time. If his plays were somewhat lacking in plot and characterization, they had a concentration of purpose as their heroes struggled for power in one form or another. Although Marlowe was killed in a tavern brawl in 1592 at the age of twenty-nine, he had already written four great plays: *Tamburlaine, Doctor Faustus, The Jew of Malta,* and *Edward II.*

Dramatists were normally men of education; they thought of themselves as superior to a young playwright, William Shakespeare, who had attended no university but sprang from the despised community of actors. Yet Shakespeare, of course, far surpassed them all. He was especially skillful where most of them failed, in characterization; his plays were filled with characters that have become immortal. When he turned to drama dealing with the history of England, some of his figures, such as Richard III, were so vivid that they have remained what he made them in defiance of modern research. His unique genius enabled him to write all kinds of plays—fairy plays, romantic and serious comedies, lyrical dramas, histories, profound tragedies, fanciful plays—all with greatness and success. It was his universal appeal and understanding of all mankind and his excellence in all forms of poetry that made him one of the greatest of writers.

Sir Philip Sidney, artist unknown. (National Portrait Gallery, London)

His work may be divided into three periods. The first, from about 1592 to about 1600, a time in which by a curious chance his rivals disappeared and he had the stage to himself, was the period of most of the histories, of *A Midsummer-Night's Dream, Romeo and Juliet,* and the romantic comedies. Then came a more somber era (1601–1608) in which he wrote his great tragedies, *Hamlet, Othello, King Lear,* and *Macbeth,* his Roman plays, and a few rather gloomy comedies. In a final period, from 1608 until his death in 1616, his mood became tranquil and gently disillusioned. The plays of this time were *Pericles, Cymbeline, The Winter's Tale,* and *The Tempest.* A great dramatist, he was one of the greatest of poets, whose marvelous imagery and inventiveness, enormous vocabulary, and superb felicity of diction have molded English literature and language from his day to this.

THE UPPER CLASSES

The Nobility

The nobility of Elizabeth's reign was a subdued and diluted version of the medieval aristocracy. In the fifteenth century, as we know, the nobles had been powerful, troublesome, and numerous. Seventy-three temporal peers had attended the Parliament of 1453–1454. But those nobles who survived the Wars of the Roses were disciplined by the early Tudor Kings. At the same time, Henry VII and his son were under pressure to ennoble their supporters. Henry VII created eleven peers; Henry VIII, thirty-eight; Edward, seven; and Mary, nine. The new nobility was loyal to the dynasty that had brought it into being, and the Tudor peerage, on the whole, was submissive and obedient. The bloody baron had become the sophisticated courtier. But noble families have a way of dying out. In 1547 there were only fifty-four temporal peers. Elizabeth, very conservative in her creations, ennobled only fourteen new peers during the course of her long reign. At her death there were fifty-nine lay nobles.

The conception of a noble in the reign of Elizabeth was that of an exalted, eminent, and wealthy person who sprang from an ancient lineage or who had performed great public service, or, better yet, who combined the two. He should be a man of action, not of contemplation. He could be called upon to perform high public functions without remuneration. He might be asked to lead an embassy abroad, a most costly duty. When the Earl of Derby took an embassy to France in 1584, his train consisted of 130 gentlemen, each with a gold chain and two costly liveries. Or he might be asked to entertain a continental grandee or keep in custody a political prisoner such as Mary, Queen of Scots. To entertain Queen Elizabeth on her summer progress was an expensive honor, as Leicester found when her visit cost him £6000 in 1575. And she visited Burghley twelve times! Nobles were placed in command of military expeditions. They were made lords lieutenants,[4] lord deputies of Ireland, or presidents of the Council of the North. The greatest of them owned town houses in London and were expected to add to the splendor of the court. Thus, though they had lost their medieval power and importance, they performed a number of useful functions.

Nobles lived in the grand manner with elaborate households, rural palaces, fine furniture, and costly clothes. They offered liberal hospitality and spent money

---

[4] See page 325.

freely as they moved about the country. At death, after elaborate funerals they were laid in expensive tombs. Some of them lived so extravagantly that they ended in financial ruin. Historians have wondered whether as a class they were declining, but this is to be doubted. Land was more stable than other forms of wealth. In an age of inflation, increasing land values, and higher rents, a noble might prosper through the careful management of his estates. It is interesting that the Crown, which suppressed the nobles in the early part of the century, later became solicitous for their welfare, regarding them as a class to be preserved and protected.

The Gentry

The gentry were more important than the nobles in the Elizabethan period. Country gentlemen as a class were becoming the most wealthy and powerful in the kingdom. Having acquired much of the land of the monasteries, they continued to increase their possessions at the expense both of the nobility and of the Crown, and, engaging in a hundred local activities, controlled the administration of rural England as justices of the peace. They were the great men of the countryside, accustomed to power, authority, and respect. Country gentlemen had many connections with well-to-do lawyers and merchants in the towns. They crowded into the House of Commons and filled many offices in the central as well as in the local government. They set the patterns of social behavior and of humane manners.

Although some gentry families had held their lands since the Middle Ages, there was great fluidity in the class of country gentlemen in the Tudor period. Some yeomen were wealthy enough to push into the lower ranks of the gentry. Rich merchants and businessmen in London, successful lawyers like Sir Edward Coke, officials who had climbed to the top, such as Sir Nicholas Bacon and Sir William Petre, bought estates in the country and established country families. Perhaps the most spectacular ascent was that of the Cecils. The first Cecil of whom we hear in England was a man-at-arms under Henry VII. In the second generation a Cecil was a knight; in the third, a baron; in the fourth there were two branches of the family, each headed by an earl. Younger sons of the nobility also belonged to the gentry class, sometimes holding lands from their fathers or brothers. There were, of course, gentry who fell upon evil days and sold their property, but the trend was upward. The country gentleman was not what we call a dirt farmer. He was a landlord who lived upon rents, but he often retained a home farm which he managed himself, and he knew something about agriculture, and about soils, crops, and orchards.

There were various types of country gentlemen. A few were very rich and were closely associated with the nobility. Sir Philip Sidney, the perfect courtier and gentleman, was related to several members of the peerage and mingled freely with this class. Such men lived as lavishly as the nobles, though they could ruin themselves in the process. On the other end of the scale was the rustic type, the homespun squire who probably lived remote from London and was glad to be home after his brief visits to the capital. He was on intimate terms with his tenant farmers, whom he met at the village alehouse and with whom he talked about crops and cattle. He was fond of hunting and decorated his hall with the skins of foxes and polecats and other trophies of the chase. But there was also the more intellectual type of country gentleman who had a library of the classics as well as books on history and government. He was interested

Hardwick Hall, Derbyshire. Note the large glass windows. (Copyright Country Life)

in the law because he was a justice of the peace and because he was apt to be involved in lawsuits with his neighbors. He was a university man; perhaps he had taken a grand tour which brought him in touch with French or Italian art and letters. He had an interest in architecture and music. The commonest type of country gentleman, however, was not extremely rich, or boorish, or intellectual. He was a business type who wished to make a profit from his estates, to stand well with his neighbors, and to perform his duties in local government.

Technically a man was a member of the gentry if the Heralds' College had granted him a coat of arms and the right to gentility. This college consisted of the Earl Marshal, who kept order at the royal court, and kings, heralds, and pursuivants with goodly titles, such as Garter King-of-Arms, Clarenceux King-of-Arms, York Herald, Rouge Dragon, Rouge Croix, Blue Mantle, and Portcullis. The duties of the college were to construct coats of arms, to record pedigrees of gentle families, and to supervise funerals. During the Tudor period they granted hundreds of coats of arms, undoubtedly making up many out of whole cloth when the ancestry of a petitioner was too humble to bear investigation. The college made visitations through the counties, investigated the local gentry, and excluded some from the ranks of gentility, a bitter humiliation to an aspiring yeoman. Shields and coats of arms became so elaborate that they were ridiculous, and some families demanded a return to medieval simplicity.

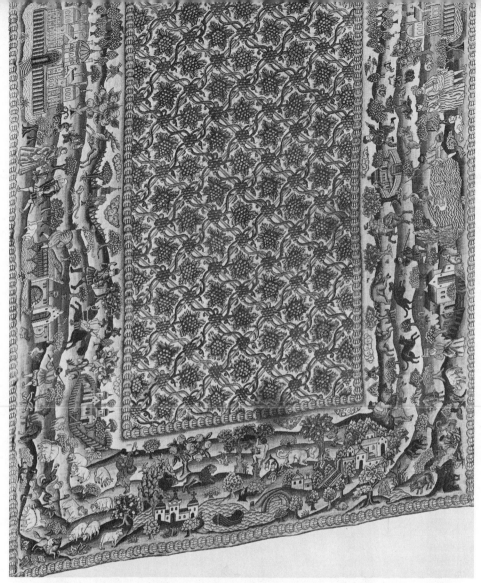

Elizabethan table carpet, worked in silk on a linen canvas. (Victoria and Albert Museum, London)

A country gentleman took great pride in his estate. With a deep sense of continuity, he regarded himself as the trustee of his property in which he held only a life interest and which he must pass on to his heir, enlarged if possible but certainly not diminished. The Tudor gentry were great builders. There are many fine Tudor houses still in existence, such as Hardwick Hall, more glass than wall, built by that acquisitive old termagant, Bess of Hardwick, or Hatfield House built by Robert Cecil. Tudor houses combined English medieval tradition with the new influence of the Renaissance. The result was not a pure architectural style but one that was virile, pleasing, and often artistic. The medieval house, as we know, centered in a great hall with apartments at one end for the lord and his family and rooms at the other for the kitchen and its accessories.

These apartments increased in number, but they were built in a hodgepodge without planning. Later in the Middle Ages houses often were built in a rectangular form around an open court with the windows facing on the courtyard and with a strong gatehouse at the entrance.

The Renaissance brought attention to balance and symmetry and to decorative columns and porticoes. Great houses continued to be built around courts, sometimes in the shape of the capital letter H. Such a house would have two open courts with an entrance at each end, with the great hall as the crosspiece, and with the private apartments of the owner forming one side of the H and those of the kitchen and servants forming the other. A house might be built in the shape of the letter E. Here the great hall was placed in the middle of the long side of the E, thus separating private rooms from the servants' quarters.[5] Other rooms might be a parlor, a long gallery for family portraits, a kitchen of enormous size, and a winter parlor near the kitchen. There were many fireplaces, chimneys, and bay windows. Furniture, though ponderous, was becoming more comfortable and better looking. Even the poor had pewter bowls and spoons. Guests brought their own knives, which were carried in sheaths. Forks were not

[5] An added attraction of a house shaped like an E was that this is the first letter of Elizabeth's name.

The Great Bed of Ware. (Victoria and Albert Museum, London)

in common use, and people still ate with their fingers, washing them in bowls after meals. A Tudor house had a flower garden and perhaps a deer park, but there was little or no landscaping.

Below the gentry was the class of yeomen who were substantial farmers owning their land. Then came tenants of all kinds, large and small, copyholders who held a permanent lease and tenants at will who could be dismissed at any time. At the bottom was a large class of cotters or landless agricultural laborers.

Local Government

The Tudors achieved a revolution in local government. Broken and debased in the fifteenth century, the government of rural England was reconstructed and developed in a remarkable way. There was a great extension of the administrative activities of local officers and an increased control and supervision from the central government. Country gentlemen served without pay. They were willing to do so because they had a strong feeling for their counties and because their rewards came in the form of enhanced prestige among their neighbors. The most important officers of local government were the lords lieutenants, the sheriffs, and the justices of the peace.

The lord lieutenant was almost always a noble, often a member of the Privy Council and an important figure at court. He was placed at the apex of the system of local government. A Tudor creation, he was first appointed by Henry VIII to organize local military precautions in times of emergency and to act as a connecting link between the Crown and the provinces. He received instructions from above and exercised authority on the spot. But since he was often away from his county, country gentlemen were appointed as deputy lieutenants. They were the cream of the local gentry; by the end of Elizabeth's reign there were some 200 of them. The principal duty of the lord lieutenant was the training of the militia in gatherings known as musters. Here the best men were selected for the trained bands, their armor and weapons were inspected, and they were drilled by professional soldiers called mustermasters. The gentry provided a quota of light horsemen. The system was rather amateurish, for the periods of training were too brief. The militia was not expected to function outside its own county and was not used for expeditions overseas.

The lord lieutenant had many other functions. When the government issued privy seals, that is, letters requesting loans, the requests were distributed by the deputy lieutenants and justices of the peace—a most unpleasant duty. A lord lieutenant might be asked to enforce the laws about religion, to administer relief in times of famine, to regulate markets, and to prevent the export of wheat. The lord lieutenant often held the office of *Custos Rotulorum*, the keeper of the shire records, though the actual work was done by a clerk of the peace.

The sheriff was still important, though he had lost most of his medieval power. Sheriffs were nominated by the privy councilors and judges, who met once a year and prepared lists of three names for each shire. Of these the Queen selected one. This was an office that men so wished to avoid that they offered bribes to escape from it. The sheriff was now the executive officer of the county court. He made arrests, kept suspects in jail, brought prisoners into court, impaneled juries, and carried out the sentences imposed. He did not make decisions; he performed the unpleasant functions of local justice.

He had many miscellaneous duties, some of which involved great expense, and although he served for one year only, he was usually much the poorer when his term of office ended. He must collect debts owing to the Crown and might be held responsible for the payment of any money he could not extract from others. The dignity of his office must be maintained. He traveled about with thirty or forty men in his train, he entertained judges and ambassadors, he met the Queen with a large escort when she came into his county. He had charge of the Crown lands in his shire. One of his most important duties was to summon the county court for the election of the knights of the shire. He had a bad name for trickery in parliamentary elections. He must also help keep the peace, must suppress riots, must bring to London persons wanted by the Council, and in general must assist in the work of local justice. In all this he was aided by undersheriffs and bailiffs.

The Justices of the Peace

The persons on whom local government depended most were the justices of the peace, who formed a group unique to England, for they were unpaid local magistrates drawn from the upper strata of the gentry. They worked hard at their judicial and administrative tasks, which constantly grew heavier during the Tudor period. "It is sessions with me every day all the day long, and I have no time for my own occasions," wrote a justice of the peace. "There were yesterday fourteen brought before me that are so fit for no place as the house of correction."[6] Justices of the peace were either ordinary justices or justices of the "quorum." Those of the "quorum" had legal training and experience and one of them had to be present when certain judicial work was being done. But all the justices of the peace knew a little law. Of numerous guidebooks to tell them of their duties, the best known was William Lambarde's *Eirenarcha: Or the Office of the Justices of Peace.* The justices were selected by the Lord Chancellor with the help of privy councilors and judges. In a large county such as Devon there might be fifty or sixty justices; in other counties, less than half that number. To be a justice brought local honor and distinction; to be excluded was an affront that was deeply resented. The plays of the time made fun of the justices, and Shakespeare left a famous caricature in his picture of Justice Shallow. But the standard was normally high.

We first hear of them in the fourteenth century, when they were appointed to assist the itinerant justices and to help keep the peace. A statute of 1361 permitted them to try cases themselves. In the Tudor period one justice acting alone could punish petty offenses brought to his attention by an accuser or by the petty constable, the policeman of the village. He could punish drunkenness, or card playing on the Sabbath, or the refusal to work at harvest time. He could order that a vagabond be whipped. He could force suspected persons to give bond to keep the peace or to appear in court. Or he could hold them in jail until they were tried. It was his duty to stop a riot before it became dangerous, though he himself could not punish the rioters. Two justices acting together in what were known as petty sessions could ask the sheriff to impanel a jury to determine minor cases. Four times a year the justices of the county met at the Quarter Sessions. All the legal officials of the county were present: justices, sheriff, high constables (there were usually two for each hundred), petty constables, jailors, jurors, the clerk of the peace. For three days the justices of the peace tried cases. An account

---

[6] Quoted in Wallace Notestein, *The English People on the Eve of Colonization 1603–1630* (New York: Harper & Row, 1954), p. 211.

Old London Bridge. Detail of an engraving by Claes Jansz Visscher, imprinted 1885. (Folger Shakespeare Library)

of each case was then sent up to London. The trial of serious crimes, such as felonies, was left to the itinerant justices, who visited each locality once a year.

Aside from judicial work, the justices of the peace engaged in an enormous amount of administrative activity. They helped conduct the musters, they apprenticed pauper children to a trade, they levied small rates for the support of maimed soldiers, they met yearly to fix wages and prices for their locality, they licensed inns and alehouses and closed places that became disorderly, and they looked to footpaths, roads, ferries, and bridges. They spent an enormous amount of time administering the poor law. The care of the poor was a heavy burden, for the country swarmed with vagrants of all kinds—some poor impotent wretches broken by age or disease, some sturdy beggars apt to be in all kinds of mischief. At the beginning of the Tudor period the government had no solution but harsh repression. Gradually it was recognized that poverty was not always the result of idleness or vice. Various statutes concerning the poor were made into a code in the Parliaments of 1597 and 1601. The law provided that each parish was responsible for its own poor, that is, for persons who had been born in the parish. Vagabonds were whipped and told to return to the parish of their birth. There they were supported in a workhouse, a place where work was provided but where the impotent poor also were lodged. The workhouse was financed by a parish rate. Officials known as overseers of the poor acted under the direction of the justices of the peace. Thus although an effort was made to cope with this serious problem, harshness and injustice remained. Each parish tried to shift as much of the burden as possible upon neighboring parishes, and justices of the peace constantly had vagrants thrust upon them for whom they did not know how to provide.

LONDON

Not knowing where to go, many of the poor drifted to the towns, especially to London, which grew so rapidly that by the end of the reign it may have numbered 250,000 persons. The government disliked this growth, for it added to the danger of the plague and to the possibility that some fanatic might attempt the life of the Queen. There were proclamations against the erection of new houses and the crowding of poor people into tenements and slums. The worst slums were just outside the city walls, which formed a rough half circle on the north bank of the Thames. Within the walls the houses were tall, narrow, half-timbered buildings inhabited for the most part by respectable merchants, manufacturers, and tradesmen. The city was expanding in various directions: eastward down the Thames, along the main roads leading from the city, and into the area toward Westminster, that is, into Holborn and the district north of the Strand. There were many buildings in Southwark across London Bridge. Here were the Tabbard and the White Hart, inns from which travelers rode to Canterbury and Dover; theaters, the Globe and the Swan; Paris Garden, where there were bull- and bearbaitings; and for the rest a rather disreputable area.

The Thames was the heart of the city. The Queen, the lord mayor, and some of the livery companies had barges that were used on state occasions; there were innumerable small boats; and thousands of watermen rowed passengers up and down the river. London Bridge, with its heavy piers and narrow arches, was an obstacle made dangerous by the rushing of the tide, and a wary traveler alighted from his boat and took another beyond the bridge. The river was used for pageants and processions for which there might be fireworks and music. It made London and Westminster one town. The finest houses lined its northern bank. At the eastern corner was the Tower of London, used not only as a state prison but as a mint, an arsenal, a repository for government documents, and a zoo. Along the city front were docks and markets, the Steelyard of the Hanseatic League, the Customs House, several towers and old priories converted into fashionable apartments, the gardens of the Inns of Court. West of the city the houses of the aristocracy followed the river, their gardens running down to the water's edge. At Westminster one found the royal Palace of Whitehall, government buildings, the Parliament house, and Westminster Abbey. In the center of the city was St. Paul's, an ancient Gothic cathedral later destroyed in the great fire in 1666. Famous streets in London were Fleet, Cheapside, Cornhill, Lombard, and Leadenhall, where prosperous merchants had their shops. The streets of London were narrow, dirty, and noisy with carts, coaches, and the cries of hucksters shouting their wares. There were famous inns: the Mitre, the Mermaid, the Dagger, the Boar's Head, and the Devil at Temple Bar, with a sign showing St. Dunstan pulling the Devil by the nose.

THE COURT

At Whitehall Palace we enter the world of the court. Elizabeth shared to the full her people's fondness for fine clothes, jewels, and costly trinkets, for music and dancing, and for riding and the chase. Even in the early years of the reign, when frugality was a necessity, foreigners were impressed with the gaiety of the court, its banquets, plays, and masques, and its water parties on the Thames. Elizabeth's suitors added to the glitter with their expensive costumes, elaborate retinues, and quaint devices, such as the bleeding hearts one admirer embroidered on the coats of all his train. Tournaments were reduced to spectacular foolery. On one occasion a fortress of perfect beauty was constructed in the tiltyard in which Elizabeth was besieged by four courtiers who called themselves the four foster children of desire. They challenged all comers to combat and tilted with a group of defenders, among whom were Adam and Eve.

For the government of the court three principal officers were responsible. One was the Lord Chamberlain, a dignified major domo who was responsible for the section of the palace in which the Queen lived. Under his supervision were special departments, such as the beds, the wardrobe, the jewel house, the sergeants at arms, the chapel, the revels, the Queen's barge, and many others. He was in charge of entertainments and of ceremonial occasions. A second official was the Lord Steward, who supervised the purchase of provisions and the preparation of food. It is probable that two of his subordinates, the treasurer and the comptroller of the household, together with the cofferer (who was responsible for purveyance), did most of the work. They formed a little court called the court of the Green Cloth, which settled disputes with tradesmen. Below these officials were the kitchen, the bakehouse, the pastry, the cellar, the buttery, the spicery, the chandlery, the confectionery, the laundry, the boiling house, the scullery, and many more. A third important official, the Master of the Horse, who was always a favorite of the Queen and in constant attendance upon her, was in charge of the stables, hunting, picnics, and other outdoor activities.

The life of the court revolved around the presence chamber, the privy chamber, and the Queen's withdrawing rooms. The presence chamber was open to anyone in proper attire who was entitled to appear at court. It contained a throne. Here Elizabeth received ambassadors and distinguished guests in formal interviews, and here young courtiers and country gentlemen might be presented to her. Admission to the privy chamber, on the other hand, was very difficult. Gentlemen ushers stood guard at the door. Elizabeth sat in the privy chamber with her ladies and intimate friends. Nobles and their wives normally were admitted, and great councilors came to consult with the Queen. Behind the privy chamber were the Queen's withdrawing rooms, where she ate and slept, surrounded by the ladies of her bedchamber and her famous maids of honor, a group of girls of good family who attended her, read to her, and entertained her with music and dancing in which she herself took part even in her later years.

The Queen always desired to be seen and loved by the people. Every year she made a progress through some part of the kingdom and was received with

Queen Elizabeth in Parliament. The scene is in the House of Lords. The Commons are standing in the foreground. (From Sir Simonds D'Ewes, *The Journals of All the Parliaments during the Reign of Queen Elizabeth*, London, 1682. Copy in the possession of the author)

elaborate ceremonies by towns and by members of the nobility and gentry with whom she visited. A progress was a complicated affair which required long preparation. Hundreds of carts carried the royal wardrobe and household furnishings, for the Queen brought her own things with her, so that a gentleman whom she visited often need do no more than offer her his house. But this was thought to be niggardly, and usually the Queen was received in sumptuous style. There were pageants, plays, and all kinds of curious devices such as ships, goddesses, nymphs, and fairies who welcomed her with songs and dances. It was all highly artificial yet pleasing and glamorous.

THE PRIVY COUNCIL

Alongside the frivolity of the court was the serious business of government. Although the Queen made decisions with the advice of a few great councilors, the Privy Council as a body did an enormous amount of administrative and judicial work. It was composed of some twelve to twenty high officials, normally including the archbishop of Canterbury, the Lord Chancellor, the Secretary (there were sometimes two), the Lord Treasurer, the Chancellor of the Exchequer, the Lord Privy Seal, the Lord Admiral, the Lord Chamberlain, the Master of the Horse, the Chancellor of the Duchy of Lancaster, the Lord Warden of the Cinque Ports, and perhaps a few nobles whose judgment the Queen respected. The councilors, of course, held office at the pleasure of the Queen. They debated questions of high policy only when she asked them to do so, and most of their work was concerned with detail. As in the latter years of the reign of Henry VIII,[7] the Council watched the operation of local government, corresponded at length with lords lieutenants, sheriffs, justices of the peace, and local councils, instructed English ambassadors abroad, supervised the royal household. Increasingly it dealt with economic questions, with the enforcement of religious laws, with military and naval operations, with London, with Ireland, and with the poor law—no matter was too small for the Council's attention. It also heard petitions and acted as a court. All councilors, moreover, now sat as judges in the Star Chamber. The Council did not keep a record of its debates but merely of its decisions and of the enormous number of letters which it wrote in the course of business. The Council was the Crown in action, the administrative machine that controlled the work of government.

PARLIAMENT

The House of Commons in Queen Elizabeth's time grew steadily in strength and influence. The reign of Henry VIII, as we have seen, had been for the Commons a time of training in the art of legislation and a period of growing self-confidence. In the reign of Elizabeth they became far more aggressive and independent. They assumed that they had a recognized place in the counsels of the nation, they were developing parliamentary procedures and making their privileges realities, and they were much more in the public eye. Resenting manipulation by the Crown, they criticized royal policy with surprising freedom.

[7] See pages 246–247.

There was not one session in Elizabeth's long reign in which some dispute did not arise between her and the Commons.

The Tudor conception of the role of the Commons was very conservative. Henry had believed that the Commons should do three things: vote taxes as the need arose; pass or reject the legislation proposed by the Crown; and give advice to the sovereign, though only when he asked for it. Elizabeth held similar views. Members were told in 1593 that they might "say yes or no to bills; but they were not to speak of all causes as they listed or to frame a form of religion or a state of government as to their idle brains seemed meetest. No king fit for his state would suffer such absurdities."[8] The Commons were thus to play a negative and advisory role; they were not to initiate policy; and there were high matters of state—religion, the Queen's marriage, the succession—with which they should not meddle.

Henry had manipulated Parliament, and so did Elizabeth, though she acted with more finesse than her father had shown. Much of this manipulation was justified. The Commons met only occasionally[9] and possessed little organization. Because members were apt to wrangle and to criticize the government in an irresponsible way some leadership was necessary. It was supplied by the privy councilors who were members of the Commons. Clustered in a group close to the Speaker, these men formed a kind of ministerial bench and were, in fact, the leaders of the Commons. They introduced the most important laws, they guided the course of debate, they made clear the need for subsidies, they answered criticism of the government, they were members of almost all committees, and they formed a breakwater against the demands of the Commons for more liberty in the house and for less autocratic rule in church and state. The councilors were supported by a group of lesser officials who held some place in the government or in the royal household.

The Speaker was important. Elected in theory by the Commons, he was in reality a nominee of the Queen from whom he received his fees and other rewards. He was not the impartial moderator of modern times but a servant of the Crown, eager to promote the business desired by the ruler. The primitive state of parliamentary procedure gave him great power: he could determine the order of business; he worded the questions on which the Commons voted; and since most votes were decided by a shout of "Aye" or "No," it was the Speaker who declared whether a question had been carried. He and the privy councilors could hold whispered consultations, he could take part in naming the members of committees, he could give the floor, he could stop a debate, he could adjourn the house for the day. Elizabeth preferred to remain in the background, leaving the details of parliamentary management to her ministers, but when she did intervene she did so with skill and vigor in speeches that were models of persuasion and eloquence. Her regal bearing and tactful management, her alternation of gracious affability and tart reproof created in her subjects a loyalty tinged with awe. Her success in dealing with the Commons was due in no small part to her unique and masterful personality.

Elizabeth was not unopposed in her manipulation of the Commons. A principal source of opposition was the growing strength of the country gentlemen who, as a class, were becoming the most influential in the kingdom. They found

[8] This is a slight modification of a document quoted in J. E. Neale, *Elizabeth I and Her Parliaments 1584–1601* (London: J. Cape, 1957), p. 249.
[9] There were ten Parliaments in Elizabeth's reign, meeting in thirteen sessions.

a seat in Parliament most attractive as a symbol of local as well as national importance. As they crowded into the House of Commons they added greatly to its wealth, its talent, and its social standing. They were the elite of the nation, "the flower and choice of the realm." An astonishing number of the important people of Elizabethan England sat in the House of Commons. Such a body—so self-assured, so aggressive, so talkative, so sophisticated—could not be excluded from a larger part in shaping the national destiny.

As in the Middle Ages, the Commons were divided into knights of the shire and burgesses of the towns. The number of knights remained constant at 90 during the reign of Elizabeth. But the number of burgesses steadily grew larger throughout the Tudor period. There were 224 borough members in the first Parliament of Henry VIII; 308 in the first Parliament of Elizabeth; 372 in her last (when knights and burgesses together totaled 462).[10] It was the prerogative of the Crown to grant a city or a borough the right to return members, and the Tudors were lavish with such grants. In fact, historians once believed that the Tudors were attempting to pack the House of Commons, but it is now thought that the pressure to create new parliamentary boroughs came from the gentry, who were eager to obtain representation for places in which they had influence. If the boroughs, new and old, had always returned their own citizens, there would have been about four burgesses in the Commons to every country gentleman representing a shire. Actually, the proportion was reversed; there were about four members of the gentry to every burgess. Members did not have to reside in the constituencies they represented. As a result the gentry pushed into the seats of towns and cities. It has been estimated that in the Parliament of 1584, to take an example, there were about 240 country gentlemen, about 75 officials, about 53 practicing lawyers, and about the same number of townsmen.[11]

Another source of opposition to Elizabeth in the Commons was the rise of Puritanism. The Puritans, as we have seen, attempted to modify the Church of England through legislative action. Their campaign deeply annoyed Elizabeth, who did not hesitate to strike back. Her methods raised questions of parliamentary privilege. The violence of the Puritan attack and the way in which it led to quarrels over privilege are illustrated by the career of Peter Wentworth, a man of property who had nothing to gain by opposing the Queen in Parliament. He was impelled solely by conscience. In 1576 he made a bitter attack on Elizabeth's practice of forbidding the introduction of bills on religion. By the Queen's prohibition, he said, "God was the last session shut out of doors." Moreover, the Commons' privilege of free speech had been violated. In an eloquent oration he declared that voting had been influenced by rumors started in the Commons: "Take heed what you do, the Queen's Majesty liketh not of such a matter, whosoever preferreth it she will be offended with him." He told of a member, Robert Bell, who for a bold speech had been summoned before the Council and severely reprimanded. He pointed out that some members waited until they saw how the privy councilors voted and then voted with them. There is none without fault, cried Wentworth, no, not our noble Queen.

The Commons were astonished at such language. Knowing that Elizabeth would punish Wentworth, they decided to act themselves and sent him to the Tower, where he remained for a month. Ten years later he was again in trouble.

[10] S. T. Bindoff, *Tudor England*, p. 215.
[11] J. E. Neale, *The Elizabethan House of Commons* (London: J. Cape, 1949), p. 302.

Elizabeth had stopped a Puritan move in the Commons, and Wentworth there-upon compiled a list of questions he wished the Speaker to read to the house. These questions would have opened a debate upon the right of the Crown, and of the Speaker as the Crown's agent, to interfere with the deliberations in the Commons. The Speaker showed the questions to the Council, and Wentworth was sent to the Tower once again. His final collision with Elizabeth came in 1593, when he was imprisoned—this time for the rest of his life—because he had planned action in Parliament upon the forbidden subject of the succession. His place in history is that of a martyr for free speech (which was yet to be won), but his prime purpose was to advance the Puritan cause.

Despite these differences and tensions there was an essential harmony between Elizabeth and the House of Commons. Both Queen and Parliament had the common purpose of promoting England's safety and welfare. The Commons' veneration for their heroic sovereign grew with the years. They loved her for the dangers she had passed. That she also loved them was clear throughout her reign and showed brightly in the words with which she bade them a last farewell in 1601: "Though God hath raised me high, yet this I count the glory of my crown, that I have reigned with your loves. . . . It is not my desire to live or reign longer than my life and reign shall be for your good. And though you have had, and may have, many mightier and wiser princes sitting in this seat, yet you never had, nor shall have, any that will love you better."

16

james i: the prerogative challenged

For over a century the Tudors had taught their subjects that loyalty to the Crown was the greatest of virtues and disloyalty the blackest of crimes. Yet forty years after Elizabeth's death a large proportion of the people took up arms against the King in the English Civil War. What were the causes of this astounding explosion? Historians have often assumed in an uncritical way that the fault lay entirely with the luckless Stuart sovereigns, James I (1603–1625) and his son, Charles I (1625–1649). The Stuarts, it must be admitted, were inept rulers. But it should be remembered that Elizabeth, despite the glories of her reign, left problems of the most serious kind to her successors. Her religious settlement, wise as it was, satisfied neither Roman Catholics nor Puritans. Parliament, grown more aggressive, more loquacious, and more difficult to manage, was reaching for control of policy. If that control were obtained, the Commons and not the King would be supreme. Elizabeth left public finance in an unstable condition. With all her parsimony she had done no more than make ends meet; the growing cost of government in a time of inflation was certain to be a thorny question. Public virtue, as we have seen, had declined; corruption in the government was on the increase. Even relations with foreign states were not as satisfactory as they appeared. It is true that Spain was a defeated power in 1603, but Catholicism was regaining strength throughout Europe. If Spain improved her international position, the outlook for England might darken. And meanwhile, as the war with Spain had dragged on, Elizabeth's relations with the Dutch and with Henry IV of France had grown cooler. It is not surprising that James I was unable to deal with these problems successfully.

THE BRITISH SOLOMON

James's character contained so many contradictions that it is not easy to describe him in a few words. He was highly intelligent. His councilors admired the ease and rapidity with which he comprehended business and made his decisions. He had a good memory and more than a touch of the native shrewdness of the Scot. He talked rapidly and well. "His speech is swift and cursory, in the full dialect of his country," wrote Francis Bacon, "in point of business short, in point of discourse large." James was a learned man, fond of study, especially of theology. There was no more familiar sight at court than the King at dinner with a group of the upper clergy standing behind his chair debating with him the meaning of some passage in the Scriptures. Hating war and violence, James hoped to keep England at peace; indeed, to bring peace to all of Europe. His desire was to rule well and to be good to the Church of England. An affectionate man, he wanted to be on terms of friendly intimacy with those about him. He could be jovial, witty, kindly, and good-natured.

After his death certain scandalous writers, hoping to please the Puritans, described him as a ridiculous person, a buffoon in purple, an impossible pedant without dignity or judgment. Such an interpretation was superficial; yet it is true that his many good qualities were rendered all but useless by grave defects in his character. He was astonishingly vain. No flattery was too gross, no praise too extreme for his taste. He held a lofty opinion of his own wisdom, delighting in being compared with Solomon. In his more exalted moments he felt a celestial proximity to Heaven, as though he and the Deity had much in common. He was lazy and self-indulgent, lacking in control of his emotions and given to bursts of temper. Although he was determined to dictate policy, the drudgery of daily attention to the details of government was repugnant to him, and he left it to his councilors.

Disliking London, he much preferred a country life, partly to escape the press of business, partly to indulge his love of hunting, partly to retire with his boon companions to some distant palace or country house where he could be jovial, intimate, careless, idle, and debauched. He lingered in the country for weeks at a time, at his "paradise of pleasure," when his presence was urgently needed in London. His boldness in hunting contrasted with his normal timidity, for he was very apprehensive, constantly fearful of danger and of assassination. He wore heavy padded clothes which would resist the sudden thrust of a dagger. He was very extravagant. Any money that came into his hands was regarded as a windfall to be squandered at once. He had none of Elizabeth's ability to scrutinize at all times the whole fabric of public finance. He also lacked her power to command. "When he wishes to speak like a king," wrote Tillières, the French Ambassador, "he rails like a tyrant and when he wishes to yield he does so with indecency."[1]

James's Scottish Background

James's training and experience as a Scottish King did not fit him to solve the difficulties left by Elizabeth. Placed on the Scottish throne as an infant, he was for many years a helpless pawn in the hands of the Scottish nobility. He lived in constant danger of capture by rival bands of nobles who wished to control the government, and especially by the wild young Earl of Bothwell. Bothwell's constant misbehavior had gradually reduced him to the life of an outlaw, but he had the notion that he could recoup his fortunes if only he could obtain possession of the King. James awoke more than once in the middle of the night to find Bothwell attacking the gates of his palace or even hammering at the door of his bed-

---

[1] David Harris Willson, *King James VI and I* (London: J. Cape, 1956), Chap. X.

James VI & I, artist unknown. (National Galleries of Scotland, Edinburgh)

chamber. At the same time a group of northern earls, Catholic in religion and pro-Spanish in politics, plotted and rebelled against him. The Scottish nobles did not regard the King as a sovereign lord but rather as a feudal suzerain against whom revolt was no great crime. They were themselves little kings in their own districts, combining the authority of feudal chieftains, landlords, magistrates, and heads of clans. They could raise the whole countryside against the government. In trying to suppress them James had little assistance from the weak middle class. He had to build his own power, as Henry VII had done in England. Scotland could only be ruled by tyranny—but tyranny was an evil heritage for a future King of England.

James also had to contend with the strident claims of the Scottish Kirk. John Knox, the leader of the Scottish Reformation, proclaimed that the laws of God should rule the state. Kings who fought against God, that is, Kings who opposed the Kirk, should be brushed aside. Andrew Melville, who led the Kirk in James's reign, molded the theocracy of Knox into the famous doctrine of the two kingdoms. Melville made a distinction between the civil power of the King, to be exercised in temporal affairs, and the spiritual power of the Kirk, to have jurisdiction in matters of religion. The spiritual power, Melville contended, flowed directly from God to His Kirk; thus the ministers ruled the Kirk by divine right of the most immediate kind. The King was to have no share in ecclesiastical affairs. But although the independence of the Kirk was inviolable, the independence of the state was not. God spoke through His clergy, and to God's word the King should render obedience. As a matter of fact, the ministers interfered constantly in the temporal affairs of the state. Had they had their way, they would have dictated to James on all occasions. They denounced and bullied him brutally; in return he hated and loathed them. This was poor training for a King who would have to deal with the English Puritans.

In combating the pretensions of the ministers and the lawlessness of the nobility, James adopted a theory of government known as the divine right of Kings. He did not originate it, but he became its ardent advocate, dwelling upon it constantly in his speeches and writing a concise and lucid description of it in 1598, *The Trew Law of Free Monarchies.* According to this theory, Kings were placed on their thrones by God. Many passages in the Scriptures could be cited in support of this belief, especially those in the Old Testament in which the Israelites begged God to send them a King. God made Kings, and only God could unmake them. It was God's decree that subjects obey their King, offer no resistance, and refrain from criticism, even in secret thought. Evil Kings as well as good ones came from God; the only recourse of the people lay in prayers and sobs to Heaven.

James also employed history to reinforce his argument. King Fergus I, coming out of Ireland, had conquered Scotland (according to the version of Scottish history held in James's reign), and William I had conquered England. These rulers, James argued, had acquired rights in their kingdoms which amounted to absolute ownership. Absolute ownership brought absolute power. As the King was overlord of the whole land, "so was he master over every person that inhabiteth the same, having power over the life and death of every one of them." James drew an analogy from feudalism, giving the King as lord of the kingdom all the rights a feudal baron held over his fief. In a word, the King was above the law, above the church, above the Parliament. Such views were not likely to commend themselves to the English House of Commons.

During James's last years in Scotland he made surprising progress in translating his theory into fact. He dealt the nobility shrewd blows. He drove Bothwell into exile and forced the northern earls to take temporary refuge on the Continent. He imposed bishops upon the Kirk. With the aid of his able adviser, John Maitland of Thirlestane, he created a strong and loyal bureaucracy which could be trusted to govern the country in his interest. The Scottish Parliament was subject to his will. "This I must say for Scotland," he boasted in England in 1607, "here I sit and govern it with my pen, I write and it is done, and by a clerk of the Council I govern Scotland now, which others could not do by the sword." His methods, however, were those of a despot.

There were other ways in which his rule in Scotland was an unfortunate preparation for his rule in England. Early in life, under the guidance of bad advisers, he learned to intrigue with every foreign power from which he thought he might derive some benefit. He gave Elizabeth protestations of friendship but at the same time courted the good will of her enemies. In his desire to obtain the English succession he sent secret envoys to Catholic rulers, hoping to win their approval or at least to blunt their hostility. He gave them the impression that he was not unfriendly to Catholicism and, indeed, that his conversion was not to be despaired of. He conveyed the same impression to the Pope. Thus he offered a secret hand of friendship to the Catholic world and was in touch with Elizabeth's foes. At the same time he secretly courted the English Puritans; yet he posed in public as the champion of the Church of England. Such scattered insinuations and contradictory half promises were certain to cause future trouble. Finally, his training in finance was very bad. A starveling prince, his poverty in Scotland was excruciating. He learned to try any dodge, however low, which offered hope of a little cash. He borrowed from his councilors and asked them to employ their private credit in his behalf. He was careless about money, in part because he never had any to be careful of.

THE RELIGIOUS SETTLEMENT

The Puritans

In Scotland James had been content with the simple ritual of the Presbyterian Kirk, but in England he became an ardent supporter of Elizabeth's church. He liked its ceremonies, partly no doubt for themselves, partly because they stressed the divinity of Kings. He liked the upper clergy, many of whom were his personal friends. Above all, he liked a church which was under the firm control of bishops and of which he was the acknowledged head.

He sympathized with a movement which may be referred to as Anglican, though described in his day as anti-Calvinist, anti-predestination, or Arminian.[2] Refusing to consider the church as a political compromise, a convenient halfway house between Rome and Geneva, the Anglicans sought a more convincing foundation. Turning to the primitive church during the first five centuries of the Christian Era before the rise of the medieval papacy, they studied early creeds and councils and the writings of the early fathers and reached the conclusion that the Church of England, as reformed in the sixteenth century, was the true descendant of primitive Christianity. They regarded the church of Rome as one

[2] Arminius was a Dutch professor of theology who rejected the doctrine of predestination.

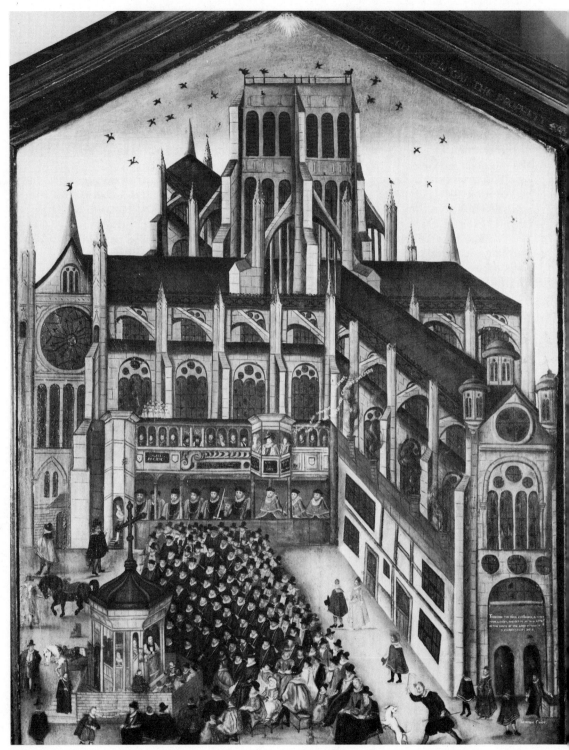

James I attending a sermon at St. Paul's Cross. Sixteenth-century panel painting.
(Society of Antiquaries)

which had fallen into error but which nonetheless had preserved in medieval times the primitive truths and godly ceremonies of the early church. Anglicanism was a conservative reaction against the rigidity of the Puritans. Its outlook was broader, more moderate, and more humane. Unfortunately its theoretical advantage was lessened by its practice. Closely allied with the King, it did not criticize the vice and corruption of the court. It was ready to strike at humble folk who were Puritans but was strangely complacent about the errors and wickedness of the great.

While James was on his journey from Scotland, he was presented with the Millenary Petition, signed, it was said, by 1000 Puritan clergymen. The petitioners asked for discontinuance of the use of the sign of the cross in baptism, of the ring in marriage, of the terms "priest" and "absolution." They wished the rite of confirmation abolished, the wearing of the surplice made optional, and the length of the service and the amount of choral singing curtailed. They asked also for a more learned ministry, for an end to pluralities and nonresidence, for reform of the ecclesiastical courts, and for stricter observance of the Sabbath. The King reserved judgment, but he agreed to hold a conference between Puritans and Anglicans. In January 1604 this conference took place at Hampton Court. Surrounded by his bishops and councilors, James admitted a delegation of four leading Puritans and asked them what alterations they desired in the church. In addition to the points of the Millenary Petition, they asked that the doctrine of predestination be more fully recognized, that the clergy be permitted to administer the Communion without subscribing to the full doctrine of the church concerning it, that there be a new translation of the Bible,[3] and that the Apocryphal books should not be read in church. As these points were made they were interrupted and scoffed at by the bishops, and James grew irritable.

It was then that Dr. Rainolds, the principal Puritan spokesman, used the unfortunate word "presbytery," which made the King believe that the Puritans were Presbyterians. He turned upon them in fury. A Scottish presbytery, he cried, "as well agreeth with a monarchy as God and the Devil. . . . Stay, I pray you, for one seven years before you demand that of me; and if you find me pursy and fat and my windpipes stuffed I will perhaps hearken unto you. For let that government be once up . . . we shall all have work enough, both our hands full. But, Dr. Rainolds, till you find I grow lazy, let that alone. . . . No bishop, no king. When I mean to live under a presbytery I will go into Scotland again, but while I am in England I will have bishops to govern the Church." As for the Puritans, "I will make them conform themselves or I will harry them out of this land." And so the abashed Puritans in their black gowns hastened from the court of Solomon.

James was much pleased with his part in the conference. "We have kept such a revel with the Puritans here these two days as was never heard the like, where I peppered them soundly." In truth, he had done great harm. He had first encouraged the Puritans, called them to argue a case that was already decided against them, and then treated them with scorn and contumely. Clergymen who would not conform to the regulations of the church now were deprived of their livings or suspended from them. The Puritans claimed that some 300 ministers were thus removed, but the church placed those deprived at 50. Recent research has raised that number to about 90. There was no further attack on the Puritans

---

[3] The new translation, the King James Bible, was published in 1611.

during the reign, though James's Declaration of Sports in 1618, permitting games and dancing after church on Sundays, was highly offensive to them. Drawing together into a hard core of opposition, they found much to criticize in James's government, and they were strongly supported by the House of Commons. A few refused to conform at all. A little congregation in the town of Scrooby in Nottinghamshire fled with their ejected ministers to Holland; from there in 1620 they sailed in the *Mayflower* to America. It was thus that the Pilgrim Fathers came to New England.[4]

The Catholics

James was more enlightened and more tolerant in dealing with the English Roman Catholics than with the Puritans. He feared and distrusted Roman priests, especially Jesuits, but he distinguished between them and the laity for whom he had much sympathy and to whom he hoped to give a restricted toleration. He was, he said, opposed to persecution; on the other hand, he could not permit the number of Catholics to increase. He therefore asked two things of them: first, that they be loyal subjects, and, second, that as a token of outward conformity and obedience they attend the services of the Church of England. In return he would allow the savage penal code of Elizabeth, with its heavy fines, to remain in abeyance. For about a year and a half the fines were not levied, and the King was on his way to toleration.

James found his policy of toleration difficult. It was strongly opposed by the Anglican bishops, his councilors, and his judges. Queen Anne, who was a Catholic, favored her coreligionists in an irritating way. Pope Clement VIII, deceived by James's hints before 1603, believed he was about to become a Catholic. There was a suspicion that Sir Walter Ralegh and his follower Lord Cobham were plotting with the Ambassador from the Spanish Netherlands to place James's cousin Arabella Stuart on the throne. As a result of these pinpricks and irritations, James turned back to the Elizabethan code in February 1605.

The Gunpowder Plot of November 1605 was the result of James's broken promises to the Catholic world. It seems to have originated in the mind of Robert Catesby as early as 1603. Catesby was a Roman Catholic gentleman who had been active in many Catholic enterprises. By May 1604 he had confided his plan to four men, including his friend Thomas Percy, a relative of the Earl of Northumberland, and Guy Fawkes, a soldier of great toughness of character brought over from the Spanish Netherlands. The plot was to place barrels of gunpowder under the Parliament house and, at the opening of the next session of Parliament, to blow up the King, the Queen, and Prince Henry, bishops, nobles, councilors, judges, knights, and burgesses—all in one thunderclap. The conspirators rented a house which had a cellar running under the Parliament building. Into this cellar Guy Fawkes carried some twenty barrels of gunpowder, placed iron bars upon them to increase the impact of the explosion, and laid over all a covering of faggots. The conspirators, however, ran out of funds and were forced to confide their secret to a number of other people. One of these was Francis Tresham, who betrayed the plot. He wrote his brother-in-law, Lord Monteagle, to stay away from Parliament on the appointed day, and Monteagle took the letter to the government. It was not until late at night, on the eve of the meeting of Parliament, that Guy Fawkes was discovered keeping watch over the gunpowder.

[4] Godfrey Davies, *The Early Stuarts 1603–1660* (Oxford: Clarendon Press, 1959), Chap. III.

The Gunpowder Plot made a tremendous impression on the men of the time. The wicked Roman Emperors Nero and Caligula, wrote a courtier, were but fly swatters compared with these horrible plotters. Parliament passed stricter laws against Catholics. Although James was thoroughly terrified he tried to salvage something of his program of toleration. He devised a new oath, the Oath of Allegiance, which could be offered to Catholics. It was thought that loyal ones would take this oath, whereas those who were disloyal would not. The oath, in fact, made this distinction rather neatly. James soon returned to a policy of remitting the penal fines for Catholics who were willing to take the oath. After 1614, as we shall see, his diplomacy drew him closer to Spain, and Spain demanded that the English Catholics be treated well. Hence in the later years of the reign they were better off than might have been expected.

THE PARLIAMENT OF 1604-1610

The great constitutional issue of the Stuart period was the clash of King and Parliament; in fact, the entire history of the seventeenth century was to revolve about this theme. The quarrel began with surprising suddenness after James's accession. A ruler who paraded the divine right of Kings and a Parliament intent upon increasing its control of policy were certain to come to blows. James's government brought evils the Commons were not slow to point out. Redress of grievances became their constant cry, but grievances meant more than new abuses. Under a ruler for whom the Commons felt no affection, as they had felt affection for Elizabeth, many aspects of government that had been tolerated before 1603 now seemed outmoded and insufferable. The time had come for reform. But reforms often involved a lessening of royal authority or royal revenue. The Commons were demanding a fundamental change that would shift power from the King to themselves: they were grasping at control of the executive. Naturally the King fought back, and thus the question of sovereignty became all-important. Where did ultimate authority lie? And where should disputes be settled if neither King nor Parliament would yield?

James knew little about the English Parliament. He knew only the Parliament of Scotland which, for all its age, was a weak and primitive body that could easily be manipulated. In dealing with the English House of Commons James committed many blunders. He made too many speeches, sent too many messages, often couched in a scolding and didactic tone, and was much too quick to interfere in parliamentary business. This interference not only irritated the Commons but disturbed those avenues of influence still open to the Crown. James's principal minister, Robert Cecil, soon to be Earl of Salisbury, had managed the parliamentary business of the Crown during Elizabeth's last years. He continued to do so in the new reign, though he worked under disadvantages. Now a member of the House of Lords, he could speak to the Commons only when committees from both houses met in conference. He could make use of the Speaker as well as a group of officials and courtiers in the Commons, of whom the most able was Sir Francis Bacon. But Bacon was not a councilor; in fact, the number of councilors in the Commons was very small, and hence the Crown was not as well represented in the lower house as it had been under Elizabeth. Rather strangely, Salisbury had not attempted to influence elections in 1604; he could compensate for his error only by managing by-elections as the Parliament progressed. Above all, he was frustrated by the constant meddling of the King, who followed events in Parliament closely, day by day and even hour by hour, in order to send his principal minister detailed—and misguided and disturbing—instructions.

A quarrel arose as soon as Parliament met in 1604. Two men, Sir Francis Goodwin and Sir John Fortescue, claimed to have been elected to the same seat in the Commons. Where was this question to be settled? James announced that since the writs summoning Parliament had been issued by the Chancery, the Chancery had the right, if it suspected irregularity, to issue a writ for a new election. This had been the Tudor practice. But the Commons demanded the right to settle election disputes, and they promptly declared that Goodwin had won the seat in question. James asked them to confer with the Lords. The Commons refused, saying that the Lords had nothing to do with the question. Somewhat taken aback, the King told the Commons to confer with the judges and then to report their findings to the Privy Council. Again the Commons refused.

James then sent them a peremptory message, commanding "as an absolute king that there might be a conference between the House and the judges," he and his councilors to be present. The Commons were astonished but decided to give way. "The Prince's command is like a thunderbolt," said a member, "his command upon our allegiance like the roaring of a lion. To his command there is no contradiction." Fortunately the conference went well. James suggested a compromise: that the election of both Goodwin and Fortescue be voided, that neither stand again for the seat in question, and that a new election be held. The Commons agreed. James was delighted with his own graciousness and wisdom. But the Commons had won, for henceforth they settled election disputes without challenge. James had lost much and gained nothing.

The Commons turned to grievances. They debated purveyance, the right of the monarch to live off the country as he traveled about. The difficulty was that James traveled a great deal and allowed his purveyors to exceed their rights. The Commons also objected to the court of wards, a court set up by Henry VIII that administered the estates of minors who were wards of the King. Wardship was undoubtedly the source of great abuse. The Commons further showed much sympathy for the Puritans, especially for the "silenced brethren" who had been ejected from their churches. When James wished to assume the style of King of Great Britain, the Commons refused their consent. They also declined to vote new taxes, since payments still were due from taxes voted to Elizabeth. At the end of the session the Commons drew up a famous document, the Apology of 1604. It was a bold declaration of right, a lecture to a foreign King upon the constitution of his new kingdom. An important point concerned the origin of parliamentary privilege. In the case of Goodwin *v.* Fortescue James had declared that the Commons "derived all matters of privilege from him and by his grant," but the Apology asserted that parliamentary privileges were the right and inheritance of the Commons—no less than their lands and goods—and did not spring from royal grace. Surveying the events of the session, the Commons justified their actions at every turn, and added a statement that the King could not alter laws on religion without their consent. James replied in a scolding speech, and so the session ended.

The parliamentary session of 1606–1607 was devoted largely to the question of closer union between England and Scotland. The two kingdoms, of course, now had the same ruler but otherwise were distinct and independent. It was

James's noble ambition to draw them together into a perfect union. He would have one kingdom with one King, one faith, one language, one people alike in manners and allegiance. The names of England and Scotland should disappear in the name of Britain, the Border should be erased and become the middle shires, the Englishman and the Scot should love one another as brothers. But James was in too much of a hurry. He forgot the long and mutual hostility of the two nations. Unfortunately he had brought with him to England a large number of Scots to whom he had been excessively generous, thus arousing the jealousy of the English courtiers. It is not surprising that his proposals were coldly received by the English House of Commons.

In 1606 James proposed four preliminary steps to union: the repeal of hostile laws, that is, laws of each country aimed at the other; mutual naturalization; a commercial treaty looking toward free trade; and improvement of justice along the Border. The hostile laws were repealed without question, but the rest of the program met with intense opposition. A commercial treaty was completely refused, and the measures for Border justice were whittled down to very little. Debates on naturalization were long and interesting, but the Commons declined to naturalize the Scots unless English law was imposed on Scotland. The King grew angry, and the session ended with little accomplished. In the next year, 1608, James obtained from the English judges a decision that Scots born after the union of the Crowns were citizens of both kingdoms.

A major crisis developed in the parliamentary sessions of 1610. Debate revolved about the fundamental questions of the royal prerogative and the royal finance. The prerogative—that sovereign power inherent in the King to act on his own authority—had been brought to the fore by a number of issues. There had been a feud between the courts of the church, especially the Court of High Commission, supported by the combative archbishop of Canterbury, Richard Bancroft, and the courts of common law, supported by the famous judge, Sir Edward Coke, who loved the common law and became its champion against the church courts and against the royal theory of divine right. In defense of the common law Coke could be the most obstinate and difficult of men. On more than one occasion, when the King stormed at him, he fell upon his knees; yet even in that position he clung to his opinions.

A dispute arose about an ancient writ, the writ of prohibition, through which the common-law judges exercised considerable control over the courts of the church. This writ halted proceedings in any ecclesiastical court until the judges were satisfied that the matter in dispute fell properly within the jurisdiction of that court. In 1605 Archbishop Bancroft appealed to the King against the writ of prohibition. All judicial authority, he argued, began in the Crown and flowed thence in two streams, the temporal jurisdiction to the courts of common law, the spiritual to the courts of the church. Hence the two systems were on an equality, the writ of prohibition should be ended, and the King should decide disputes between the two jurisdictions. But Coke answered sharply that the writ of prohibition was a part of the law, and the law could be altered only by Parliament.

Two years later Bancroft asserted that the King, as supreme judge, should hear and decide doubtful cases. "To which it was answered by me," wrote Coke, "that the king in his own person cannot adjudge any case, but this ought to be determined and adjudged in some court of justice . . . and that the law was the golden metwand and measure to try the causes of the subjects and which protected his Majesty in safety and peace. With which the King was greatly offended and said that then he should be under the law, which was treason to affirm; to which I said that Bracton saith that the king should not be under man but under God and the law."[5]

In 1607 a book appeared which underscored the prerogative in another way. This was *The Interpreter*, a law dictionary written by John Cowell, a professor of the civil law at Cambridge and a protégé of Bancroft. *The Interpreter* exalted the prerogative beyond all measure, asserting that the King was absolute, above the Parliament, and above the law.

The prerogative was connected closely with the question of finance. James had been living far beyond his means and had run deeply into debt. In 1608 he appointed Salisbury Lord Treasurer. Salisbury found that he could not lessen expenditure; he could only increase the revenue, as he did substantially. Among other expedients he levied impositions, that is, customs duties over and above the normal schedule of tonnage and poundage authorized by Parliament. It was a dangerous experiment, for the Commons were certain to object. But Salisbury had a legal decision in his favor. In 1606 a merchant named Bate, who imported currants from the Levant, had refused to pay impositions and had been tried in the Court of Exchequer. The decision was that, since the prerogative included the regulation of commerce and since impositions formed part of that regulation, the duties were legal though they had not been voted by Parliament.

The sessions of 1610 were stormy ones. The Commons insisted on discussing grievances. In a long and important debate on impositions the Commons asserted firmly that these levies were illegal unless they were granted by Parliament. Other aspects of the prerogative came under attack: the Court of High Commission, the use of proclamations to modify law, the jurisdiction of the council of Wales over certain English shires. In July a petition of grievances was presented to the King. It was so long, said James, that he thought he might use it for a tapestry.

Meanwhile Salisbury, who was striving to extract money from the Commons, proposed that in addition to a grant of the customary kind, though of unusual size, the Commons should vote the King a permanent revenue. In return Salisbury offered that the King would abandon purveyance and most of his feudal rights, including wardship. This bargain known as the Great Contract was tentatively approved in July, but in the autumn neither side wished to continue it and so it was dropped, to Salisbury's infinite sorrow. James was growing more and more angry with the Commons. A member compared him to King Joram, a wicked king of the Jews. There was also evidence of strong hostility in the Commons against the Scots. James wrote Salisbury that in seven years he had received nothing from Parliament but disgraces, censures, and indignities. He had shown great patience, but he could not show "asinine patience." He dissolved his first Parliament in anger early in 1611.

THE PARLIAMENT OF 1614

James's first Parliament had lasted for seven years; his second, for two months. Impelled by his abject poverty, he very reluctantly summoned Parlia-

[5] J. R. Tanner, *Constitutional Documents of the Reign of James I* (Cambridge: Cambridge University Press, 1952), p. 187. For Bracton, see pages 135–136.

SERO SED SERIO

Robert Cecil, Earl of Salisbury, artist unknown. (National Portrait Gallery, London)

ment again in 1614. The debt was high, bills were unpaid, future revenues were anticipated. The decay in public finance had turned to dead rot. When James faced the Commons he tried to be conciliatory. This Parliament, he said, was to be a Parliament of love in which he and the Commons would aid each other in a spirit of mutual affection, and he offered a number of small concessions. Brushing aside these concessions rather impolitely, the Commons turned to more fundamental grievances. They began by a searching inquiry into the recent elections, for they had heard that a group of courtiers had plotted to influence elections on a large scale in return for promises of office. This rumor was false, and the Commons found little to complain of, but their scrutiny prompted them to expel a privy councilor, Sir Thomas Parry, for corrupt electioneering practices, and to question the right of the Attorney General, Bacon, to sit in the Commons.

It was clear that the Commons would debate grievances thoroughly before they turned to supply. When they took up the delicate matter of impositions, the debate grew heated. They asked the House of Lords for a conference on impositions, but the Lords refused. One bishop in the Lords made such a violent attack on the lower house that the Commons resolved to conduct no business until they received satisfaction. This sullen resolve annoyed the King, who told them if they did not vote supply he would dissolve the Parliament. The Commons stood their ground; so did James. The Parliament was dissolved after a session of two months without passing a single bill. The King was very angry: the Commons had rejected his proffered love, had assailed his prerogative, and had spoken irreverently of Kings. Perhaps they sought his life. One member, foolishly using words suggested to him by an outsider, spoke as though there might be a massacre of the Scots in London. James was through with Parliaments. If he had had his way, there would have been no more Parliaments in England.

DEGENERATION IN GOVERNMENT

For the next seven years, from 1614 to 1621, James ruled without a Parliament. Unfortunately these were years of failure, of scandal, and of increasing difficulties both at home and abroad. The efficiency and the standards of government degenerated. During the first decade of the reign the King's chief minister had been Robert Cecil, Earl of Salisbury, who, as Principal Secretary, master of the court of wards, and Lord Treasurer, had been the pivot about which the entire administration revolved. If he was not a great man, he at least came close to greatness. His solid judgment and steady nerve, his prudence, sagacity, and self-control, and his tremendous industry kept affairs on an even keel and continued Tudor ideals of government in the first years of the Stuart period. Amid endless routine he did not lose sight of larger objectives. He was a man of wit and liveliness, a spirited writer and speaker, a cultured gentleman who could be warm and generous in friendship. But after his death in 1612, government fell into weaker hands.

The Howards

Several members of the Howard family became important. Henry Howard, Earl of Northampton, a man greatly trusted by James, was a worthless, self-seeking, and crafty courtier. His intense jealousy led him to dislike his colleagues. His Catholicism was only half-concealed, and he stood constantly for leniency to Catholics, severity to Puritans, alliance with Spain, and an end to Parliaments. He died in 1614. His nephew Thomas Howard, Earl of Suffolk, later Lord Treasurer, was a brave sailor and a loyal subject, but he was lax and easygoing, and had small strength of character. A distant cousin, Charles Howard, Earl of Nottingham, had commanded the English fleet against the Armada. He continued to be Lord Admiral in James's reign, but as he grew old he permitted the navy

Inigo Jones, the architect. Portrait sketch by Anthony Van Dyck. (Trustees of the Chatsworth Settlement)

The Banqueting Hall, Westminster, designed by Inigo Jones. Completed in 1622. (Royal Commission on Historical Monuments)

to fall into decay. Against the Howards there arose a party of opposition: Lord Chancellor Ellesmere, very Protestant and anti-Spanish; Archbishop Abbot; and William Herbert, Earl of Pembroke, the richest peer in England. The rivalries of these two factions dominated politics for many years.

The Howards soon won a great advantage. In 1607 the King fell under the influence of a young Scot, Robert Carr, whom he made his intimate friend. Carr was a shallow person, of small ability or judgment, but he was handsome and companionable and had the graces of the courtier. After Salisbury's death, James allowed suits and requests for patronage to pass through Carr's hands. Carr soon became rich, for everyone who had business to transact with the Crown was ready to give him gifts in return for his favor. Courted by both the Howard and the anti-Howard factions, he held aloof for some time. But he fell in love with Lady Frances Howard, the daughter of the Earl of Suffolk, who drew him irresistibly toward the Howard camp. Unfortunately she was married to someone else, and she could only marry Carr (now Earl of Somerset) in 1613 after a scandalous divorce. For several years following the marriage Somerset and his father-in-law, Suffolk, dominated the government. Then suddenly in 1616 Somerset fell from power. It was discovered that the divorce of Lady Frances had involved not only scandal but crime: the lady was accused of having administered poison to a courtier (Sir Thomas Overbury), who was a friend of Somerset and who had opposed the marriage. In 1616 she was accused of this murder and her husband was suspected, though he was probably innocent. They were tried, found guilty, and sent to live in the Tower. One can imagine what the Puritans thought of such scandals.

George Villiers, Later Duke of Buckingham

Even before the fall of Somerset, a new favorite was rising at court. This was George Villiers, a handsome young man who caught the fancy of the King in 1614. Villiers was to have a remarkable career. By 1617, when he was only twenty-five, he had become the Master of the Horse, a knight of the Garter, Earl of Buckingham, and a member of the Privy Council. His position at first was somewhat similar to that which Somerset had held. He was private secretary and boon companion of the King, the channel through which suits and requests for patronage came to the ruler. He did not at first aspire to dominate policy. Rather, he gloried in his control of patronage, for this was the highest ambition of the courtier. Great men and small paid homage to him, the King foremost among his worshipers. It is small wonder that his head was turned, that he became vain, willful and arrogant, easily offended by opposition and determined to have his way.

His rise to power brought many evils. He and his extortionate mother, Lady Compton, developed a system of spoliation and blackmail; they used Buckingham's influence with the King to extract money from all aspirants to office. But in his pride and egotism, Buckingham went further. Those who attained a place in the government must do more than pay for it: they must acknowledge their subservience to him. The ministers of state must be his creatures, swelling the crowd of his hangers-on and making the world aware of their dependence. Deviation from his wishes meant loss of office, and his path became strewn with men whom he first advanced and later ruined. His ascendancy increased the debauchery at court, where the King often was intoxicated at his jovial suppers.

In 1618 Buckingham was able to drive from office the Howards, who had always been hostile to him as an upstart whose fortune stemmed from the fall of Somerset. The year 1618 was one of great financial difficulty. The fiscal picture became so dark and the means of raising money so shameful—such as the sale of peerages—that even James knew something must be done. A movement for reform began. Joining this movement, Buckingham found in Lionel Cranfield a man willing to do the required work. Cranfield, a successful merchant and capitalist, had become a financial adviser of the government and was later to attain high office. In 1618, with Buckingham's backing, he investigated many departments—including the Treasury over which Suffolk presided—and showed many ways in which the King could save money. His investigations produced a struggle between Buckingham and the Howards. It was easy to show that Suffolk had mismanaged money and was probably corrupt. He was tried for embezzlement of funds, found guilty, and dismissed from office. Nottingham, the ancient Lord Admiral, was induced to resign without a trial, and his office was given to Buckingham. As other Howards fell in rapid succession Buckingham was left supreme. Although a few great personages at court owed him nothing, the majority of officials now received their places from him and were dependent on his good will. His appointments were not all bad. He tended to give office to devoted and efficient bureaucrats who would do as they were told; and he developed skill in obtaining work from these officials. But he and the King made all the important decisions.

The King and the Judges

Early in the reign, as we have seen, the King had clashed with the great lawyer, Sir Edward Coke. The points at issue had been fundamental: the rivalry of the courts of common law with the extralegal or prerogative courts; and the relation of the Crown to the common law. Several important cases between 1610 and 1616 underscored these issues and pointed to new ones: in 1610, in one such case, Coke delivered a clear and important opinion concerning royal proclamations, which had been increasing during James's reign. The King, said Coke, could not add to existing law or create new offenses by proclamation. He could issue proclamations only to admonish his subjects that certain laws existed and must be obeyed. In another, the Bonham Case, Coke made an unsuccessful effort to introduce the principle of judicial review. He held that "when an act of Parliament is against common right and reason or repugnant or impossible to be performed, the common law will control it and adjudge such act to be void." He would thus have allowed the judges to decide whether an act of Parliament was or was not to be enforced. This principle, so important in American history, was never established in England.

In Courtney *v.* Glanvil (1615) Coke made a crude attack upon the court of chancery, arguing that once a case had been decided in the common-law courts that case could not be reopened in the chancery. James, who regarded it as a court under his special protection, was highly irritated, and his anger was increased by two other cases which involved another principle—the independence of the bench. The Peacham Case (1615) concerned a soured and broken clergyman, Edmund Peacham, who secretly wrote notes for a sermon predicting the death of the King. James, intent on severity, decided to consult the judges before the trial, not an unusual procedure. The novelty was that James, fearing that Coke might prove difficult, hit on the plan of consulting the judges one by one and not as a group. Coke objected, declaring that "this auricular taking of opinions, single and apart, was new and dangerous." Finally, in the case of Commendams (1616), James asked the judges to postpone their decision until he had consulted with them. Coke persuaded them to reply that they could not delay justice at the King's command. In a great rage James called the judges before him; they fell upon their knees. The King then asked them whether in the future they would be willing to delay a case involving the interests of the Crown until they had spoken to him. All agreed, save Coke, who merely said that he would do what it was fitting for a judge to do. Later that year he was dismissed from the bench. By this drastic action James freed himself from the opposition of the judges, but he struck a heavy blow at the moral weight of their decisions. Coke's shortcomings were forgotten; he became a martyr of the commonwealth, a symbol of the widely held conviction that the liberties provided by the common law should be left as they were.

Foreign Affairs

England's international position, as well as her government, declined alarmingly during the interparliamentary period between 1614 and 1621. To understand this decline we must return for a moment to the first part of the reign. When James ascended the English throne in 1603 he was in a strong position relative to foreign powers. He was King of the most powerful Protestant state, strengthened by union with Scotland. His prestige was high in Scandinavia, northern Germany, and Holland. He was on good terms with certain Catholic states opposed to Spain: France, Venice, and Tuscany. To English friendship with France he could add the ancient tradition of Franco-Scottish alliance. Thus when he stepped into Elizabeth's place as a leader of Protestant and anti-Spanish Europe, he inherited her strength but added some of his own.

James's great departure from Elizabeth's policy was his belief that he could lead Protestant Europe and at the same time be a friend of Spain. In the past he had feared Spain greatly, but he now considered himself sufficiently powerful and well established to offer Spain his friendship and thus to make complete the circle of his amity. He was, as we know, a man who loved peace, whose ambition was not merely to keep England out of war, but to make peace universal throughout Europe. Friendly with all nations, allied with Protestant states, on peaceful terms with Spanish lands: this was his noble vision of bringing peace and concord to Europe as a whole.

This vision, of course, was an empty one, and his failure in foreign policy was to prove the most shameful failure of his reign. The reasons are clear. His cardinal error was to believe that he could be a Protestant champion and at the same time a friend of Spain. This basic contradiction involved him in countless difficulties. His policy, moreover, was a personal policy he never explained to his people, who regarded him as more pro-Spanish than he was. They allowed him to be without funds, and Parliament was tempted to make for the first time a serious demand for a voice in shaping foreign policy. James was not merely averse to war; he regarded it with terror. He could not bear the sight of a naked sword or of men drilling for combat. The story was told that once when a soldier was about to kiss his hand, the King suddenly drew it back, saying he was afraid it would be bitten. His fear of assassination played an important part in his diplomacy. Hence he gave the impression that he wanted peace at any price and his enemies came to count on his inaction. Since he had no money he could neither fulfill his commitments nor make good his threats. Thus he became a defender who could defend no one, a champion who could do nothing but talk.

For the first decade of his reign he was much closer to Protestant Europe than to Spain. Although he made peace with Spain in 1604, thus ending the long war, the peace was no surrender. James promised not to assist the Dutch, but he allowed them to raise money and volunteers in England, whereas a similar concession to Spain meant nothing. He did not accept the Spanish claim of monopoly in the New World; in the end the treaty said nothing about Englishmen in the Spanish Indies (where they continued to go at their own risk). England and Scotland benefited by the peace. They could trade in Spain and in the Netherlands; Ireland could be pacified without fear of Spanish intervention; and Spain was left fighting the Dutch and in constant danger of war with France.

Nevertheless, the peace was an uneasy one. James quarreled with Spain over one issue after another, and as a consequence drew closer to Protestant and anti-Spanish Europe. When he looked for a bride for Prince Henry, he turned to anti-Spanish lands—France, Savoy, and Tuscany. In 1613 his daughter Elizabeth was married to Frederick V of the Palatinate, the leading Calvinist ruler in Germany. This marriage brought James into close contact with the Protestant princes of southern Germany, who in 1608 had formed a defensive alliance known as the Protestant Union. James in effect became a member. His position as Protestant champion was enhanced, and his relations with Spain became so strained that many Englishmen thought, and hoped, that the Elizabethan war with Spain would be renewed.

Then, about 1614, a shift occurred. James's international position weakened while that of Spain improved. The deaths of Henry IV of France in 1610, of Salisbury and Prince Henry in 1612, were, each in its own way, a grievous blow to England. Unfortunate quarrels separated James from the Dutch, from Savoy, and from France. The efficiency of English government declined and the breach with Parliament widened. Meanwhile Spain had grown stronger, at least in her relations with other powers. She had concluded a truce in 1609 with the Dutch; her relations with France had greatly improved; she had in England a most astute ambassador, Sarmiento, later Count Gondomar.

As a result, James became more conciliatory; treating with Spain as with an equal or even a superior power, he drifted into a policy of appeasement. Left without funds by Parliament in 1614, he began negotiations to arrange a marriage between his second son, Prince Charles, and a Spanish infanta (princess) who would, he assumed, bring him a large dowry. Sarmiento eagerly advocated the marriage, but the Spanish government did not. Nonetheless, in 1615 the Spanish drew up articles to serve as a basis for negotiations. They stipulated that English Catholics be permitted the exercise of their religion through non-enforcement of the penal laws. The infanta must control the education of her children, who must be baptized according to the Roman Catholic use. They must be free to choose their own religion and, if they selected Catholicism, they must not be debarred thereby from the English succession. The infanta's household must be Catholic, her chapel must be large and open to the public, her priests must wear their normal habits. James's first reaction to these articles amounted to a refusal, but in the end he accepted them as a basis for negotiation. In 1617 the Spanish raised their terms. The English penal laws must be repealed altogether, and until this was done the infanta was to remain in Spain and not a penny of the dowry was to be paid. The prince must come to Madrid for his bride, the implication being that his visit would result in his conversion. James knew that he could not repeal the penal laws; only Parliament could repeal them and such action by the Puritan Commons was unthinkable. Hence the negotiations were deadlocked. Yet James still hoped for a Spanish dowry, and the Spanish continued to negotiate with him, if only to separate him from his old friends.

It was at this unfortunate moment in 1618 that Sir Walter Ralegh returned from his last voyage to the Spanish Indies. A prisoner in the Tower since 1603, he had been released in 1616 in order to seek a gold mine which he believed to exist on the Orinoco River in modern Venezuela. Delighted at the thought of gold, James seems to have convinced himself that Ralegh's voyage would make the Spanish more eager for the marriage treaty. Ralegh had given the most solemn pledges that he would not molest the Spaniards. But this had proved to be impossible, and he returned to England not only without gold but guilty of an attack upon a Spanish settlement. Under sharp pressure from Spain, James weakly sent Ralegh to the block, to the bitter indignation of the people.[6]

The Thirty Years' War

In 1618 a great war broke out between Protestants and Catholics in Germany. It began as a revolt in the kingdom of Bohemia. The aged and childless Emperor Matthias, seeking to establish his cousin, Ferdinand of Styria, as the successor to his dominions, had demanded in 1617 that the Bohemians accept

[6] David Harris Willson, *King James VI and I*, Chaps. XV and XIX.

Ferdinand as their future King. The Bohemian nobles, who were largely Protestant, refused. They rose in rebellion, broke into the palace at Prague, seized the Emperor's agents, and flung them out of the window. The rebels, soon in possession of Bohemia, appealed to James for assistance, while the Emperor appealed to Spain. But James's mind was taking a turn of its own. A suggestion had come to him from Spain that he, as a virtuous prince, should mediate between the Emperor and the Bohemians. He eagerly accepted this proposal, not seeing that it was a trick; for while he vainly attempted to mediate, Spain was left free to aid the Emperor. Meanwhile great events took place. Matthias died and Ferdinand was elected Emperor. Thereupon that Bohemians deposed him as their King and elected in his stead James's son-in-law, Frederick of the Palatinate. Frederick hesitated, as well he might, then accepted, and traveled to Prague in October 1618.

These events caused a surge of anti-Catholic and anti-Spanish sentiment in England. James, under heavy pressure to drop his friendship with Spain and to assist his son-in-law, was in great perplexity. He sharply criticized Frederick's rashness in accepting the Bohemian crown. James hated all war; but from a war to support revolt and usurpation he shrank as from the plague. He loathed the vexation of action. He had no army, and he could obtain one only by summoning Parliament. To send assistance to Frederick would ruin his reputation as the peacemaker of Europe and would end all hope of the Spanish match. The Spaniards would foster plots among the English Catholics, and his life would be in danger. Yet Frederick was his son-in-law, and Frederick's wife was his daughter. Should he desert his own flesh and blood? Torn this way and that, he sank into irresolution. To the exasperation of his people, month after month slipped by without his taking action.

Meanwhile the Catholic powers made their plans. A secret agreement between Ferdinand and Philip III of Spain provided that Ferdinand should move against Prague while Philip created a diversion by attacking the Palatinate from the Spanish Netherlands. There is no doubt that Philip was most reluctant; his decision might have been different if James had shown clearly that he would defend the Palatinate. For although the Bohemian adventure was an act of aggression, a Spanish attack on the Palatinate would be equally aggressive. The Palatinate was Frederick's rightful possession. A Catholic conquest of it would dissolve the Protestant Union and would threaten every Protestant interest in southern Germany.

In August 1620 the blow fell. A Spanish army flung itself upon the Palatinate. The Emperor moved into Bohemia, defeated Frederick, and sent him flying northward for his very life. The Bohemian venture was over; and the Palatinate was in grave danger. It was under these circumstances that James summoned the Parliament of 1621.

THE PARLIAMENT OF 1621

The Parliament of 1621 was the most important one of James's reign. If the King obtained supplies, he could defend the Palatinate and perhaps could stem the tide of Catholic victory. Without money he was helpless. In view of these sobering considerations both King and Commons acted for some months with marked restraint. Yet the Commons were in a grim mood. A mistaken foreign policy, they believed, was exposing their country and their religion to untold dangers. For one thing, they regarded the Spanish match with deep alarm. For another, they were keenly aware that at home grave abuses had crept into the government. An economic depression which they did not understand rendered them even more irritable. Hence they were determined, not only to improve foreign policy where they could, but also to begin a broad and searching investigation of domestic conditions.

Warned away from criticism of the King's foreign policy, the Commons turned to grievances at home. They made a thorough inquiry into patents and monopolies. These patents brought little money to the Crown but were highly profitable to certain courtiers, including a number of Buckingham's relatives. So alarmed was Buckingham that he posed as a reformer and allowed his relatives to be punished. The Commons also wished to investigate the so-called referees, that is, the councilors to whom patents had been referred for appraisal before they had been granted. Had the Commons brought formal charges against the referees, they would in effect have revived the medieval practice of impeachment. James managed to stop this attack upon his ministers, but hostility to the referees continued, and when sudden and dramatic charges of bribery were brought against Bacon, now Lord Chancellor, the Commons pushed the accusations and forced Bacon out of office. Meanwhile the foreign situation deteriorated, and Frederick's cause was near collapse.

In the autumn session of the Parliament the Commons could be restrained no longer. They entered upon a long debate on foreign policy in which member after member pointed to Spain as the great enemy. Let the war be against Spain, not by pottering in the Palatinate, but by attacking Spain and the Spanish Indies on land and sea in true Elizabethan fashion. Let measures be taken against the Roman Catholics at home. The debate reached its crescendo in a violent speech by Sir Edward Coke, who poured forth vituperation upon Spain and Catholicism. The Commons voted one subsidy to aid the Palatinate over the winter. Then they prepared a petition asking for the enforcement of the anti-Catholic laws, for a war with Spain, and for a Protestant marriage for the prince.

Upon hearing of the petition James dashed off an angry letter to the Commons. They were, he said, debating matters far above their reach and capacity. He commanded them not to meddle with his government nor "deal with our dearest son's match with the daughter of Spain, nor touch the honor of that King." He added "that we think ourselves very free and able to punish any man's misdemeanors in Parliament as well during their sitting as after; which we mean not to spare henceforth." In reply the Commons drew up a protestation. It declared that their privileges were their undoubted birthright and inheritance, that weighty affairs of the kingdom should be debated in Parliament, and that every member had freedom of speech and freedom from arrest. James then dissolved the Parliament in bitter anger. Coming to the Council chamber, he called for the Journal of the Commons and with his own hands tore out the page containing the protestation.

JAMES'S LAST YEARS

The dissolution of Parliament marked the eclipse of James as a potent and respected ruler. A feeble old man sinking into his dotage, cut off from the sympathy of his people, he found his position hopeless in both domestic and foreign affairs. At home his finances fell once more into disorder. Prince Charles and Buckingham, impatient with his fumbling timidity, were eager to take control of policy. He lacked the power to intervene in continental affairs. He could not send assistance to Frederick in the Palatinate. He could only ask Spain to be kind. But he had to ask for a great deal: that the Spaniards withdraw their victorious forces from the Palatinate, that they persuade the Emperor to do the same, and that, if the Emperor refused, they make war upon their Catholic kinsman to please the Protestant King of England. To expect this of Spain was fatuous.

Yet James thought it might be done through the Spanish match, and negotiations to this end continued through 1622. They reached their climax in 1623, when Charles and Buckingham, with romantic folly, determined to go to Spain in person, to conclude a marriage treaty quickly, and to "bring back that angel," the infanta, with whom Charles imagined himself to be in love. Luckily the two young men reached Spain in safety. But the Spanish, with the prince in their possession, naturally raised their terms. James must now proclaim that the penal laws were suspended, must swear that they would never be reimposed, and must obtain the consent of Parliament for his action. Until these things were done, the infanta was to remain in Spain even after her marriage. Charles foolishly agreed to these impossible terms; and James, terrified lest his dear son was a hostage, sadly swore the required oaths.

The Spanish marriage never took place, for Charles was at last awakened from his romantic dream. Anger and resentment against Spain extinguished his infatuation for the infanta, and when he and Buckingham returned to England, they demanded a complete reversal of policy. They wished to make war on Spain, to build a great European alliance against her, and to restore Frederick to the Palatinate by force. The old King was horrified. But his son and his favorite, treating him with some brutality, hurried him into policies he detested. A Parliament in 1624 was easily persuaded to demand an end to the Spanish treaties and the beginning of a war. The Commons voted a small supply, promising to give more when war was declared. English diplomats were dispatched in all directions to form an anti-Spanish front.

In this search for allies Charles and Buckingham turned to France, proposing a marriage between the prince and Henrietta Maria, sister of the French King. Unfortunately, and largely out of pride, the French demanded that the English Catholics be given terms as favorable as those in the abortive treaties with Spain. This condition was accepted. James died in March 1625, leaving his son a discontented kingdom, an empty treasury, a war with Spain, and a marriage treaty with France that could not possibly be fulfilled.

the REIGN OF CHARLES I to 1642

THE NEW KING, 1625–1649

King Charles I, born in Scotland in 1600 and brought to England in 1604, was very delicate as a child. "He was so weak in his joints," wrote a courtier, "and especially his ankles, that many feared they were out of joint." Slow in learning to talk, he retained for years a slight impediment in speaking. His father suggested that he wear iron boots and that the string under his tongue be cut; but Lady Carey, to whom he was entrusted in England, resisted such drastic remedies. Charles gradually outgrew his physical defects. As a young man at court he was healthy, though not robust, fond of theatricals and sports, an excellent horseman who delighted in hunting and in running at the ring. His early contacts with his father and Buckingham were not happy. He resented the glamorous favorite whom all must worship. James made matters worse by showing that he was fonder of Buckingham than of his son. Quarrels between the two young men became so numerous that the King called them before him in 1618 and commanded them on their allegiance to become more friendly. Henceforth their relations improved.

Although Charles was frequently embarrassed by his father's lack of dignity, he was at the same time overawed and silenced by James's rapid conversation, quick intelligence, and choleric temper. Charles was slow and halting in thought and speech and so it is probable that he felt himself inferior. If we assume that he did and that he struggled to overcome this feeling, his character becomes clearer. He schooled himself to be a brave and courageous person. With a natural love of propriety, he perhaps took refuge in laying emphasis upon what was decorous and orderly. His first act as King was to cleanse the court of the bawds and drunkards whom his father had tolerated. His family life was always dignified and correct. Perhaps to counteract any feeling of inferiority he developed a lofty and majestic deportment toward all with whom he dealt. He accepted fully the theory of the divine right of Kings. James had stressed the divine origin of kingship; Charles dwelt upon the duty and obedience owed to a ruler by his subjects. He believed that opposition to the royal will was sin; and this became the constant theme of sermons by the Anglican clergy. It followed that if the people were wicked enough to force concessions from the King, the King need not keep his word to them but could revoke his promises when opportunity served. Charles thus acquired an unpleasant reputation for deceit and unreliability. There was a cold, unsympathetic rigidity about the man, who lived in a world of his own in which the feelings and ambitions of others played no part. He could not understand the moral force of Puritanism or the aspirations of the Commons. In his mind the Church of England was the only possible church, and monarchy by divine right the only possible government. Such a King was certain to turn to dictatorial and arbitrary rule.

Charles, however, did not possess the vigorous personality necessary for an absolute sovereign. Left to himself he could not make incisive decisions or take strong action, and so he leaned on others more resolute than he. He relied at first on Buckingham, whose complete self-confidence and lavish extravagance symbolized the magnificence and glory of kingship. Later he was influenced by his wife who, reflecting the absolutism of France, urged her husband to play a kingly and decisive role. Later in the reign Charles relied on Archbishop Laud and on Thomas Wentworth, Earl of Strafford, both advocates of authority, discipline, and coercion. When these props were gone, Charles was left with courage and tenacity, but little more.

THE CLASH WITH THE COMMONS

Diplomacy, War, and Parliament

When Charles ascended the throne in 1625 he did not understand that he was already in an awkward position. He was the unhappy heir of all the grievances and discontents that had arisen in the reign of his father. There were additional difficulties of his own making. Since he could not fulfill the terms of the marriage treaty with France, he was very likely to have difficulties with that country. He was committed to war with Spain; he and Buckingham, hoping to build a great anti-Spanish front, had promised large sums to King Christian of Denmark, the Dutch, and Count Mansfeld, Frederick's freebooting general. Money must also be spent on the English fleet. Unless Parliament came to Charles's assistance, he could not hope to honor these huge commitments. His one military venture had been Mansfeld's expedition in 1624, which had proved a shameful fiasco. The plan had called for Mansfeld to lead an English army directly across France to the relief of the Palatinate. To this the French objected; and after great uncertainty and change of plan, the English soldiers had been landed at Flushing in Holland. Unpaid, starving, stricken with fever, they had dwindled in a few months from an army of 12,000 men to some 3000 wretches who were of no use to anyone.

Charles was also in difficulty at home. The terms of the French treaty were unknown, but it was suspected that they favored the Roman Catholics. Henrietta Maria, the pretty little French princess who was to be Charles's wife, was regarded as a missionary of her Catholic faith. Moreover, it soon became evident that Charles favored the High Anglican or Laudian school of churchmen. Laud's views were Arminian, not popish. But the reliance of the Arminians on the primitive church rather than on the Scriptures alone, their insistence on the continuity

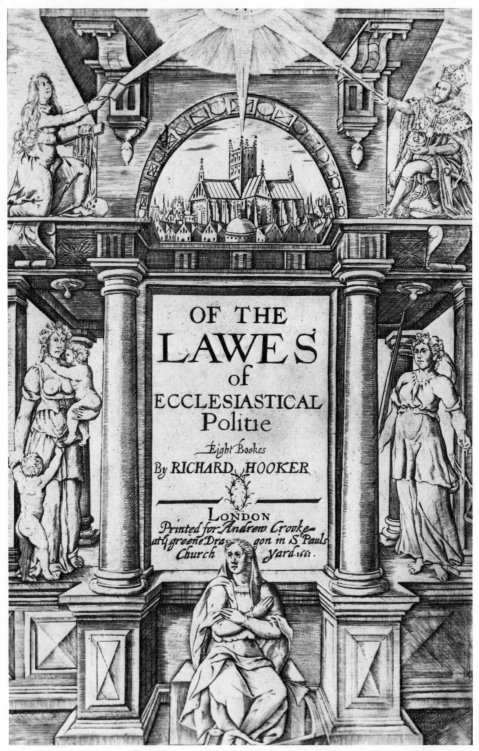

OF THE
LAWES
of
ECCLESIASTICAL
Politie

Eight Bookes

By RICHARD HOOKER

LONDON
Printed for Andrew Crooke
at ↄ greene Dragon in St. Pauls
Church yard. 1661.

Title page of Richard Hooker, *Of the Lawes of Ecclesiastical Politie*, 1661.
(Department of Special Collections, Walter Library, University of Minnesota)

of the Church of England with the Roman Catholic Church before the Reformation, and their revival of medieval ritual appeared to presage a return to Roman Catholicism. The lofty position of the Anglican bishops in Charles's reign gave great offense. Their claim that episcopacy was divine in origin, their persecution of the Puritans in the Court of High Commission, their increasing pomp and dignity, their employment by the King in high offices of state aroused the strong antagonism of many people. The courtiers were jealous of Buckingham's monopoly of power and of royal favor. And, finally, the economic depression of the 1620s had not yet lifted. It deepened momentarily in 1625 because of the plague which settled upon London and disturbed every phase of social and economic life.

Amid these difficulties Charles and Buckingham should have approached their first Parliament with care. But they acted with blind self-confidence, assuming that their success in 1624 would repeat itself. The Commons, summoned for May 17, 1625, were kept waiting in plague-stricken London for a month before Parliament began. The departure of Henrietta Maria from France had been delayed, and Charles did not wish to meet Parliament until she arrived. His opening speech was vague. He had been advised by Parliament to break with Spain, he said, and he now needed money to conduct the war, but he did not say how much was required or where the war was to be fought. This last point was important, for the Commons wanted a war at sea in the Elizabethan tradition, not a costly war in Germany. Charles's councilors in the House of Commons, having no instructions, were equally noncommittal. Taking advantage of this uncertainty, the opposition moved and carried a vote for a small supply of two subsidies. This action contained an element of trickery, which was unfortunate, but the government had invited some such move by its laxness in stating its case. About a week later Charles attempted a similar device. His councilors gave the Commons for the first time an account of the situation abroad and asked for a large amount of money. But members had been slipping away from London and the plague. Attendance was thin and those who remained refused to commit their fellow members to heavy taxation.

Charles then adjourned Parliament to Oxford, where the Commons reassembled in a rather sullen mood. At Oxford Charles and Buckingham committed new tactical blunders. Buckingham offended the Commons by summoning them before him and speaking to them as though he himself were King. The Commons criticized him sharply, attacked an Arminian divine, Richard Montague, and refused to increase their former grant. The Parliament then was dissolved. It had set a pattern of mismanagement by the Crown, of distrust between King and Parliament, and of refusal by the Commons to grant adequate supply.[1]

Meanwhile the King and Buckingham had been gathering a great fleet at Plymouth for an attack on Spain. They hoped to assault Cadiz as Drake had done in 1587. But everything went wrong. The expedition contained only nine ships of the Royal Navy; the rest were merchant vessels pressed into unwilling service. Ten thousand soldiers and five thousand sailors were also pressed, but the former were largely vagabonds who could not be turned into an effective army. The commander, Edward Cecil, Viscount Wimbledon, was a soldier without experience at sea. The expedition did not sail until October 1625, when the

[1] David Harris Willson, *The Privy Councillors in the House of Commons 1604–1629* (Minneapolis: University of Minnesota Press, 1940), pp. 167–183.

fair weather of the summer months had ended. And the provisions were so miserable, an officer wrote, that a stray dog in London would not have touched them. Upon arrival at the harbor of Cadiz, Cecil was able to capture an outlying fort and to land his men, but Cadiz itself was some miles away. After a long march without food in the heat of the Spanish sun, the soldiers discovered a quantity of wine and promptly became intoxicated. They could have been slaughtered by a determined attack. There was nothing for it but to send them back to the ships and to abandon the assault upon Cadiz, which had been strongly reinforced. The homeward voyage became a tragedy of pestilence and starvation. Provisions were now completely rotten, the fleet was buffeted by storms, and hundreds of men died of disease and malnutrition; as the ships straggled back to Plymouth the poor wretches from the expedition continued to die in the very streets of the town. Buckingham's great enterprise had ended in disgraceful disaster.

The Parliament of 1626

It was under the shadow of this failure that Charles's second Parliament met early in 1626. The King had no choice but to summon it because of his many commitments and his lack of money. Knowing that Parliament would be difficult, he made what preparations he could. He ordered a strict enforcement of the penal laws against the Roman Catholics, thus breaking the pledges of the marriage treaty with France. He excluded certain leaders of opposition in the Commons by appointing them sheriffs. He attempted also to exclude the Earl of Bristol from the House of Lords because he feared that Bristol might attack Buckingham there. Bristol had been ambassador in Spain in 1623 when Charles and Buckingham had visited Madrid. Later they blamed him for their failure and removed him from office.

But these scurvy devices did not succeed. Bristol appeared in the Lords, where he made damaging revelations concerning the conduct of Buckingham in Madrid. In the Commons a new leader appeared, Sir John Eliot, a man of high ideals and patriotism, but of less ability and prudence than were possessed by the men whom Charles had excluded. Eliot's fiery oratory was apt to lead the Commons into rash and violent action. He had seen men dying in the streets of Plymouth, and he boldly called attention to recent disasters. "Our honor is ruined," he cried, "our ships are sunk, our men perished; not by the sword, not by the enemy, not by chance, but . . . by those we trust."

The Commons, determined to have a strict accounting for what had happened, began to investigate the responsibility for Mansfeld's disaster and soon launched into a broad attack on Buckingham. They tried to impeach him, but they did so with more violence than skill. Eliot and Sir Dudley Digges, laying the charges of the Commons before the Lords, used language for which Charles sent them to the Tower. The impeachment failed, largely because the King withheld evidence and thus prevented the Commons from proving their case. In a tantalizing way the Commons had passed a resolution to give the King three subsidies but had not put the resolution in the form of a bill. After the attack on Buckingham failed, the resolution was allowed to lapse, and Charles received no money from this Parliament, which was shortly dissolved.

Charles's allies on the Continent were ruined because he could not send them the money he had promised. Mansfeld, ordered to assist the Dutch, was defeated; Christian of Denmark was badly beaten, largely because his troops would not fight without pay. Charles made matters worse by drifting into a war with France. The French alliance had been formed in the hope of drawing Louis XIII into war against Spain, but it was soon apparent that Louis was not to be rushed. Charles and Buckingham were offended at the coyness of their ally, and Buckingham took an unstatesmanlike revenge by making love to the French Queen.

There were other causes of friction. Louis was angered when Charles enforced the penal laws despite the marriage treaty. A coolness arose between Charles and Henrietta Maria, whose French attendants were disliked in London. Eventually Charles sent them back to France, thus breaking the treaty once more. Moreover, James and Buckingham had promised to lend the French eight English ships to be sent against the Huguenots at La Rochelle who were defying the French government. But the use of English ships to repress Protestants caused such a furor in England that Buckingham tried to prevent the delivery of the ships to France. Charles now posed as the protector of the Huguenots against Louis, each nation seized the merchant vessels of the other, and war soon followed. In June 1627, a large English expedition sent to the relief of La Rochelle made a landing nearby on the Île de Ré. But a French fort on the island could not be captured, an English army was cut to pieces, and the expedition, another dismal failure, returned to England.

The Forced Loan of 1627

Meanwhile Charles, in trying to raise money, determined in 1627 to levy a forced loan. The money was to be collected as though it had been voted by Parliament and was to amount to five subsidies. But the widespread opposition was increased rather than lessened by the sermons of Arminian clergymen, who preached the religious duty of obedience. Sir Randolph Crew, Chief Justice of the King's Bench, was dismissed for refusing to declare that the loan was legal. So many men declined payment that pressures of various kinds were applied; a number of the gentry were imprisoned. Five of them brought matters to a head by applying for writs of habeas corpus, which enabled them to ask why they had been put in prison; their purpose was to force the courts to declare whether or not a refusal to contribute to the recent loan was a legal cause for imprisonment. The judges were placed in a difficult position, for it was obvious that a man could not be imprisoned merely because he would not lend his money. The judges therefore returned the knights to jail without giving any reason. But the nation believed that the judges endorsed the view that imprisonment for refusal to lend money was legal and that the King could keep men in jail indefinitely without showing cause. The episode was regarded as a dangerous attack upon personal liberty and on the rights of property.

Discontent was increased by two other grievances. Without means to feed or house his troops, Charles began to billet them in private homes. A householder was informed that he must give board and lodging to two or three soldiers, who might well be lawless rogues, and it was suspected that persons who had refused to lend their money were the first to have soldiers billeted on them. In order to deal with the many quarrels between the soldiers and their reluctant hosts and to maintain discipline in the rabble that Charles called his army, martial law was proclaimed in certain areas. These four points—forced loans, imprisonment without cause shown, billeting, and martial law—formed the basis for debate and action in Charles's third Parliament, which met in 1628.

The Petition of Right

The Parliament of 1628 differed from its predecessors. The Crown was desperate, for government simply could not be carried further without funds. The Commons, on their side, were in deadly earnest. Goaded by the nation's military defeat and by the Crown's attacks on personal liberty, they displayed a new hardness and determination.

Before the Parliament met, Buckingham had talked of a standing army, obviously to beat down opposition, and the government had considered highly dubious expedients for raising money. These wild plans were dropped. The Crown concentrated on winning support in the coming session. Key men in the opposition were offered office and other rewards if they would side with the King. The slender ranks of royal officials in the Commons were given better instructions. An attempt was made to influence elections. "The Duke stays in London," wrote the Venetian Ambassador, "negotiating and working with all his might, so that members returned for the Lower House may be on his side." This interference failed completely. Men who had been imprisoned because they had refused to lend money were everywhere returned. "It is feared . . . because such patriots are chosen, the Parliament will not last above eight days."

The members of this House of Commons were men of position and wealth, able, it was said, to buy out the House of Lords thrice over. The opposition leaders were in complete control and had by now developed procedures—such as the committee of the whole house—by which they could obtain quick action in the Commons. They decided to drop the impeachment of Buckingham and to concentrate on the defense of personal liberties. They began by passing resolutions against unparliamentary taxation and against imprisonment without cause shown. When these resolutions were modified by the Lords, the Commons attempted to frame a bill that would guarantee the liberties of the subject. But it proved difficult to turn the wording of their resolutions into the wording of a bill. If a bill required the King to confirm old statutes and ancient liberties, the implication was that those liberties no longer existed. A member remarked that if "we tell our constituents we have confirmed old statutes, they will ask us when those statutes had been repealed." Hence the Commons adopted the happy idea of Sir Edward Coke that they employ the device of a Petition of Right to the King to redress specific wrongs. Such petitions were used in the law courts in cases in which petitioners, claiming that the King had overridden the law, asked merely that they be given the law's protection. The form of a petition enabled the Commons to assert that the laws had been broken and to demand that the King not break them again. Charles endeavored to answer in vague terms, but in the end, in return for a substantial grant, he gave a firm assent.

The Petition of Right contained four points: no man thereafter should be compelled to make any gift, loan, benevolence, tax, or such like charge without common consent by act of Parliament; no man should be imprisoned or detained without cause shown; soldiers and sailors should not be billeted on private individuals against the will of these individuals; and commissions for martial law should not be issued in the future. The Petition of Right, regarded as one of the great documents of English liberty, had its weaknesses: it was not a statute, it contained loopholes, it had to be modified by later generations because it deprived the King of powers a government trusted by the people could be allowed to possess. Nonetheless, it set a limit to the arbitrary power of the Crown and was the first great check upon Stuart absolutism.

Those who hoped it would bring peace between King and Commons were shortly disappointed. Largely because of Eliot's impetuous and unreasonable tactics, the Commons drew up a remonstrance which complained of other grievances and attacked both Laud and Buckingham. A second remonstrance declared that the collection of tonnage and poundage without consent of Parliament was a breach of liberty. The duties of tonnage and poundage formed the normal schedule of the customs. For generations they had been granted to every King for life upon his accession. In 1625, however, they had been given for one year only, but the Commons' bill to this effect had never become law. Without the customs the King was all but penniless. Eliot's audacious move was beyond the wishes of moderate men. In reply the King prorogued Parliament, which did not meet again until early in 1629.

Charles and Buckingham learned little from their failures. Laud and other Arminian churchmen now were advanced to important posts. A new expedition was prepared for the relief of La Rochelle. Ships, ordnance, and provisions of all kinds were assembled at Portsmouth in the summer of 1628. Soldiers and sailors were rounded up in the usual way. But, as before, things went wrong. The sailors were so mutinous for lack of pay that Charles himself went down to Portsmouth to pacify them. The movement of soldiers through the country revived the problem of billeting. Localities were assured in solemn terms that the King would pay for the support of his troops. But the presence of the soldiers was deeply resented, people would do nothing for them, and some Irish troopers were found to be pawning their arms in order to obtain money for food. Meanwhile merchants were refusing to pay customs duties not authorized by Parliament.

Everywhere murmurs arose against the hated Duke of Buckingham. One John Felton, an unpaid and unpromoted lieutenant in the navy, bought a butcher's knife, made his way on foot to Portsmouth, and stabbed Buckingham to death as he stood amid his followers. The people rejoiced, and Felton was a popular hero. But Buckingham's blood separated Charles from his subjects in a new and bitter way. The fleet set sail for La Rochelle in September despite the Lord Admiral's death. But La Rochelle, where the hard-pressed garrison had been subsisting on a diet of boiled leather, surrendered to the French King in October, and the English fleet returned without glory.

Parliament met in a short and stormy session in 1629. The Commons turned at once to the collection of tonnage and poundage without their consent. They attacked the Arminian clergy, who were represented as undermining sound religion. Charles determined to end the debate. He sent a message to the Speaker to adjourn the house. There followed a famous scene on March 2, 1629, when the Speaker sought to leave the chair but was held down by force while the Commons passed three resolutions: that whoever should introduce innovations in religion by bringing in popery or Arminianism should be accounted a capital enemy of the King and kingdom; that whoever should advise the levying of tonnage and poundage without consent of Parliament should be accounted the same; and that whoever should pay tonnage and poundage levied without the consent of Parliament should be held a betrayer of the liberty of the subject and a capital enemy of the King and kingdom. Meanwhile the King's messengers were hammering at the locked doors of the lower house. Once the resolutions were passed, the doors were opened and a royal message announced the adjournment of the Commons. A week later Charles dissolved Parliament. He imprisoned a number of the opposition leaders. Some were soon liberated but some stayed in prison for years; one, Sir John Eliot, died of tuberculosis in the Tower. Charles was through with Parliaments for eleven years.

The breach between King and Commons was regarded by thinking men with infinite sadness, "the most gloomy, sad, and dismal day for England that happened in five hundred years last past."

CHARLES'S PERSONAL RULE

Charles was now able to rule England according to his own conception of government. He was not without idealism. He wished to be a conscientious and patriarchal King who, with the aid of his councilors, would protect his subjects in all walks of life from suffering wrong. He thought of himself as the guardian, not only of the people, but of the church and the ancient constitution against irreligious and seditious persons—those "vipers" among the Commons who had "cast this mist of undutifulness over the eyes" of their fellow members. The difficulty was that Charles reserved to himself, as King, all power to decide what the church should be, what rights should be protected, and what laws should be obeyed. The people were not to share in determining these matters: their duty was to obey. Charles thought in terms of the complete unity of church and state. To attack the one was to attack the other. Men who criticized the church could not be loyal subjects. Charles was prone, moreover, to determine in his own mind what the laws should mean and then to dismiss any judge who disagreed with him.

A number of reasons can be suggested to explain why Charles was able to rule for eleven years without summoning a Parliament. It is probable that the views of members of the House of Commons were more radical than those of the nation as a whole, for the English were a conservative people trained to obey their Kings. Charles did not look like a tyrant. His decorous court, his habit of doing things in the traditional way, and his mediocre councilors—all made his government appear normal and innocuous. England was accustomed, when Parliament was not in session, to be ruled by the King, the Council, the law courts, and the justices of the peace. All these organs of government continued to function. Moreover, the period of personal rule was a time of economic prosperity. England was at peace, and the economy had recovered from the depression of the 1620s. Charles did not demand large sums of money. Had they been willing, the English could easily have paid what he asked.

Charles was able to withdraw rather easily from the wars in which he had become involved. In April 1629 he made peace with France without difficulty. The fall of La Rochelle showed that he could not defend the Huguenots; the terms offered them by Louis made it clear that Charles need not make the attempt. About the same time Christian IV of Denmark withdrew from the war in Germany. He had been defeated, but his enemies, afraid of Sweden, gave him favorable terms. His withdrawal relieved Charles of an embarrassing ally and enabled him to make peace with Spain more easily in 1630. Nonetheless, the treaty with Spain was a rather shameful conclusion to the long years of English intervention on the Continent since the beginning of the Thirty Years' War. The net result of English efforts was the loss of the Palatinate, the desertion of the Dutch, the fall of La Rochelle, and the defeat of Christian IV—a dismal record.

Title page of John Stow, *Annales, or A Generall Chronicle of England*, 1631.
(Department of Special Collections, Walter Library, University of Minnesota)

But Charles was now at peace, free from the impossible problem of waging war without the support of Parliament.

The great war in Germany was entering a new phase. Sweden under her famous King Gustavus Adolphus invaded northern Germany on the Protestant side. Allied with France, she faced the Hapsburgs of Spain and Austria. The two alliances were not unevenly matched. Hence Charles could evade the burden of defending Protestantism on the Continent and could decide with which camp he wished to ally. He hoped to employ this advantage to regain the Palatinate by diplomacy. But his weak and vacillating policy, his bargaining with one side and then with the other as the fortunes of war swayed back and forth, rendered him despicable. No one wanted as an ally a King who had no military power and who might desert his friends at a moment's notice.

Finance

Blessed with peace abroad and with tranquillity at home, Charles seemed secure. In love with his Queen, happy with his collection of art treasures, he believed himself to be the most fortunate King in Christendom.[2] But by a long series of highhanded actions he gradually alienated his people and prepared the way for the sea of troubles which overwhelmed him in the 1640s. Charles's revenues from extraparliamentary sources during his years of personal rule were large but not large enough for his needs. To make ends meet he was forced to ignore the debt, to curtail expenses, and to find new sources of income. In 1629 the debt from the war years stood at something like £1 million. Most of it never was repaid, the loudest creditors being soothed by favors and privileges of various kinds. Expenditure at court and in the administration was decreased. Ship money, to which we will turn presently, was a means by which Charles hoped to be relieved of the cost of the navy.

New income was raised by several devices. One was distraint of knighthood. In the late thirteenth century Henry III and Edward I, finding that landowners attempted to evade the duties of knighthood, decreed that every man who held land worth £20 a year should become a knight. Raising the sum to £40 a year, Charles enforced this ancient rule and collected fines and compositions from persons who had neglected to be knighted. More than £100,000 were raised by this means within two years. The payments, however, were extracted from the landed classes, which were Charles's natural supporters. The value of the fines was not worth the irritation they aroused. Charles also revived the ancient laws and boundaries of the medieval forests. These forests, it will be remembered, had been extensive areas set aside for the royal sport of hunting. Redefining the forest boundaries, Charles imposed fines for the disregard of obsolete rules everyone had forgotten. For example, almost the entire county of Essex was found to be a forest, and forest law was enforced upon land which had been in private hands for centuries. As a matter of fact, very little money came to the Treasury by this means; although the fines could not be collected they aroused strong animosity among the upper classes. Wealthy families also were incensed by the increased revenues Charles obtained from the vexatious court of wards.

Moreover, Charles offended industrialists and merchants. He imposed a fine of £70,000 on certain London companies because they had not fulfilled their promises in the colonization of Ulster. Of this huge fine, he obtained only £12,000

---

[2] C. V. Wedgwood, *The King's Peace 1637–1641* (London: Collins, 1955), pp. 19–24.

after a long dispute. He irritated the people at large by granting monopolies to certain retailers of soap, bricks, coal, and salt. Monopolies had been declared illegal by the Parliament of 1624, but Charles evaded the letter of the law by giving monopolies to corporations rather than to individuals.

His most famous expedient was ship money. The Crown possessed an unchallenged right to impress ships from the port towns in times of emergency. Hence the first levy of ship money in 1634 for an expedition against pirates did not arouse resistance. In the following year, however, ship money was demanded once more, this time from the inland counties as well as from the ports. Opposition increased, but the money was collected. But a third levy, in 1636, met widespread hostility, for it was evident that ship money was becoming a permanent form of extraparliamentary taxation. John Hampden, a wealthy gentleman of Buckinghamshire, refused to pay. His case, watched intently by all England, came before the Exchequer Chamber in 1637, when the judges decided, though only by a vote of 7 to 5, that ship money was legal in time of danger and that only the King could decide when danger existed. Ship money continued to be levied, though its collection grew more difficult. But the Hampden Case dramatized the arbitrary nature of Charles's government. Disaffection was widespread against a system of rule and taxation in which Parliament had no share.

Persecution of Puritanism

An even deeper hostility was aroused by Charles's ecclesiastical policy. Favoring the Arminian or High Anglican churchmen, he promoted them to places of trust both in the church and in the state and defended them vigorously against the attacks of the House of Commons. To the Puritans and to many moderate Anglicans, the Arminians seemed to be heading toward Rome. This impression was confirmed by the pro-Spanish policy of James and at times that of Charles, by the presence of Henrietta Maria and many Roman Catholics at Charles's court, by his failure to strike a blow on behalf of continental Protestantism, and by the fact that the anti-Catholic laws were unenforced whereas the full force of the law was used to persecute Puritans. It was this partiality, this basic unfairness of Charles's policy, that caused dislike.

We can understand it better if we look at Archbishop Laud, who was hated with a violence difficult to grasp. A jest of the court fool, Archie Armstrong, "All praise to God and little Laud to the devil," became the theme of a popular song. Modern historians have called attention to Laud's good points: he was a scholar, a patron of his Oxford college, a brave and resolute man, a skillful administrator who improved the organization of the church. But although tolerant in theory, he was utterly intolerant in practice; he was a disciplinarian, an advocate of authority and of obedience. Harsh and uncompromising, he took an almost savage pleasure in punishing his opponents. Moreover, he was a meddlesome person, as zealous in matters of petty detail as in the enforcement of broad policy. And he was unfair. The Arminian clergy were to enjoy every facility for expressing their opinions, but the Puritans were to be silenced; Arminians were encouraged to defend their church, but the slightest criticism of it was to be suppressed. Laud's partiality was driven home because he was important in the state as well as in the church. A member of the Privy Council, of the Court of High Commission, and of the Star Chamber, he was also on commissions for the Treasury and for foreign affairs. He freely employed the power of the state to enforce his ecclesiastical policy. Sitting on the bench in cases involving Puritans, he was both a judge and a party to the suit. His lack of a sense of fair play, his great power, his ostentatious manner of life aroused resentment, a resentment which spread to the bishops as a whole.

Laud's aim was to suppress all religious services except those of the Arminians, to hold the clergy to strict obedience and conformity, and to stifle criticism of his church. Let us glance at these three points.

In some towns the practice had arisen of hiring a clergyman, known as a lecturer, to preach a sermon each Sunday after the service of the church had been read. Wealthy gentlemen also employed lecturers as private chaplains. These lecturers were Puritan clergymen who had no living of their own. Normally they did not use the Prayer Book, and thus at least approached nonconformity. Laud saw to it that lecturers were suppressed and that private chaplains were permitted only in exceptional cases. Laud also dispersed a group of well-to-do London Puritans, known as the feoffees for impropriations, who had bought up advowsons and impropriated tithes in order to place Puritan clergymen in parishes or to support them as lecturers. Conventicles, secret gatherings for worship in which the Prayer Book was not used, were harshly suppressed. Those who attended these conventicles were normally drawn from the lower classes, and their trials and punishment by the Court of High Commission often were pitiful.

To enforce conformity on the clergy Laud employed the metropolitan visitation, an ancient right of the archbishop to visit in person or by deputy not only parishes within the diocese of Canterbury but those throughout the province. By searching inquiry and by disciplinary action Laud ensured that every parish priest followed the ritual he prescribed and was orthodox in both religion and politics. In 1633 he found an opportunity to test the obedience of the clergy and at the same time to strike at Puritanism. In that year Charles reissued his father's Declaration of Sports, which permitted games and dancing on Sunday after congregations had attended divine worship. Laud required that the King's decree be read in every parish church, and he ejected those ministers who refused. Clergymen willing to accept such strict control were either sincere ritualists or else timeservers, those "blind mouths" of Milton's *Lycidas* whose

> . . . lean and flashy songs
> Grate on their scrannel pipes of wretched straw.

Laud's ceremonial was forced on congregations who were not permitted to worship elsewhere.

Criticism of the church was brutally suppressed. No book or pamphlet could legally be printed or sold without a license, and Puritans who wrote secret pamphlets attacking the church were punished harshly. In 1630 Alexander Leighton was whipped, pilloried, and mutilated for printing abroad *An Appeal to Parliament; or Sion's Plea against Prelacy*, in which he challenged the doctrine that episcopacy was divine in origin. Four years later William Prynne, a rather obnoxious Puritan lawyer, was sentenced to life imprisonment, to a fine of £5,000, to disbarment, to mutilation, and to the pillory because of his *Histrio-Mastix: A Scourge of Stage Players*, an attack on the drama which was interpreted as a reflection on the Queen. In 1637 Prynne was tried again for further pamphlet writing; Henry Burton, a clergyman, for his sermons; and John Bastwick, a doctor, for writings against the bishops. All three were sentenced to the pillory and to mutilation; and Prynne, having lost his ears in 1634, had the stubs scraped and was branded on the cheek with the letters "S. L." (Seditious Libeler). When execution was done upon these men an unusual event occurred. The mob, which usually assembled to deride and torment such victims, was full of sympathy for them and howled its angry resentment at the government. It is small wonder that by 1640 the Puritans were wholly estranged from the church.

The Explosion in Scotland

The year 1637 may be considered the first year of open opposition. It was the year of the Hampden Case, resisting ship money, and of the trial of Prynne, Burton, and Bastwick. It was also in 1637 that serious trouble arose in Scotland.

After James had become King of England in 1603 he had ruled Scotland firmly through the Scottish Privy Council, which contained some very able men. In 1606 an act of the Scottish Parliament declared that the royal prerogative was superior to all estates, powers, and causes in the kingdom. The wilder portions of the country were beaten into submission. It is not surprising, therefore, to find the King, exulting in his new strength, determined to break the power of the Kirk and to assimilate it to the Church of England. For several years he prevented a meeting of the Kirk's General Assembly, and when a handful of ministers defiantly assembled at Aberdeen in 1605 James had them tried for treason. Other leaders of the Kirk were summoned to England, some never to return. Deprived of their more zealous members, General Assemblies became amenable to the King's will. Meanwhile James was exalting the bishops whom he had superimposed on the Presbyterian system of the Kirk. They received once more, at least on paper, the lands their predecessors had possessed; they were restored to their legal jurisdiction, augmented in 1610 by two Courts of High Commission for Scotland; and they were installed as the constant moderators of synods. By 1612 episcopacy was an established fact in Scotland.

James was successful largely because he had deprived the Kirk of the support of the Scottish nobility and because he had not disturbed old forms of worship to which the people were attached. Congregations remained seated as they received the Communion, the observance of holy days was rare, the clergy preached in their black Geneva gowns and followed the simple ritual of Knox's Book of Common Order. To most of the people these forms of worship were of greater importance than the resurgence of episcopacy. After some years James began the dangerous experiment of forcing Anglican ceremonies upon the Scots. When he visited Scotland in 1617 he proposed five innovations: that Communion be received in a kneeling position, that private Communion be permitted in cases of necessity, that the same be true of private baptism, that the festivals of the church be properly observed, and that confirmation be administered by bishops. In spite of strong popular objection a General Assembly at Perth in 1618 (subjected to great pressure) accepted the King's Five Articles, which were confirmed by Parliament in 1621. But James was sufficiently well acquainted with the Scots not to demand a strict conformity. The new rules were widely disobeyed, and the churches in which they were observed were notoriously empty. This was the situation at James's death.

Charles handled his Scottish subjects in so highhanded a manner that he slowly drove them into rebellion. He began with an Act of Revocation in 1625 by which he recalled all grants of land (including church lands and tithes) made by the Crown since 1540. Such acts of revocation were not uncommon in Scotland, but Charles's act was so sweeping and covered so long a period of time that it affected almost every substantial landowner in the country. In 1627 he permitted the Scots to redeem their estates by money payments, but he had thoroughly alienated the upper classes. He forgot that James, as a matter of policy, had increased the loyalty of the Scottish nobility and gentry by grants from the possessions of the ancient church.

When Charles visited Scotland in 1633 he added new irritations. He introduced English innovations into the Scottish coronation service and permitted Laud to flaunt Arminian ritual before the eyes of the horrified Scots. When he attended the Scottish Parliament he noted the names of those who opposed his wishes. Upon his return to England he decided that changes should be made in the government and in the Kirk of Scotland. Very unwisely he excluded the Lords of Session, that is, the judges of Scotland's high court for civil cases, from membership in the Privy Council. The power of the Scottish bishops on the Council was thus increased, and in 1635 Charles named Archbishop Spottiswoode as Chancellor of Scotland.

More dangerously he decided that the liturgy of the Kirk should be based on the English Book of Common Prayer. The Prayer Book prepared for Scotland used to be called "Laud's Liturgy," but a recent study has shown that it was largely the work of the Scottish bishops.[3] Their modifications of the English Prayer Book, to make it more palatable for the Scots, were carefully supervised by the King. "The principal author and inspirer of the book, outside of Scotland, was King Charles himself."[4] Laud had little part in it. When it was used for the first (and last) time in St. Giles's Cathedral in Edinburgh in 1637 it provoked a famous riot. Tradition has it that Jenny Geddes, a "she-zealot," shouted, "The Mass is entered among us!" and threw her stool at the minister. The story is probably untrue, but stools certainly were thrown. All Scotland was in an uproar. "The whole people," wrote a Presbyterian, "thinks popery at the doors." The Scots appointed a body of commissioners, often called the Tables, who formed a sort of opposition government. To consolidate public opinion, they issued a famous document known as the National Covenant. It contained a pledge to resist the recent innovations in religion and to support the authority of the Crown. These two points were obviously inconsistent, but they united Scotland for the moment, and thousands of persons eagerly subscribed to the Covenant. Scotland was in revolt. If Charles were to enforce his Prayer Book he would have to do so by military might.

THE BISHOPS' WARS AND THE SHORT PARLIAMENT

For a moment Charles bowed before the storm in Scotland. He promised that a General Assembly would meet in 1638 and a Scottish Parliament in 1639. As soon as the Assembly convened it summoned the Scottish bishops to appear before it; on their refusal, the Assembly abolished episcopacy. It proceeded to do away with the Prayer Book of 1637, with the canons by which the book was to have been enforced, and with the Five Articles of Perth. It then re-established the presbyterian form of church government and decreed that nonpresbyterian clergymen should be expelled from their pulpits.

[3] Gordon Donaldson, *The Making of the Scottish Prayer Book of 1637* (Edinburgh: University of Edinburgh Press, 1954).
[4] Donaldson, p. 80.

When Charles refused to recognize the actions of this Assembly both sides prepared for war. The Scots soon had a disciplined army under Alexander Leslie, a veteran of the Thirty Years' War and an able administrator, who brought back from Germany a number of other Scottish officers. The whole country was busy "preaching, praying, and drilling." Without funds, Charles summoned the English nobility to serve at their own charge and called out the militia of the northern counties. But the men were untrained, their equipment was defective, and they were unpaid. A troop of the King's horse pushed into Scotland, saw the Scots army, turned without fighting, and fled south across the Border. An invasion of Scotland became an impossibility. Charles concluded the Pacification of Berwick with the Scots in June 1639, by which both sides agreed to disband their forces. A new General Assembly and a Scottish Parliament were to determine the future government of Scotland.

This pacification was short-lived. The General Assembly confirmed all that its predecessor had done, the Parliament repealed laws in favor of episcopacy and increased its own powers, the Scottish army remained in existence. A second Bishops' War was inevitable. But Charles's resources were so limited that the momentous decision was taken to summon a Parliament in England. Charles's councilors argued that a Parliament would show the people that the King wished to obtain funds in the old accustomed way. If Parliament did not vote him supplies in his great emergency he would be free to use any means at his disposal to raise money for war. Councilors hoped that anti-Scottish feeling in England would bring support for the King; Wentworth, now summoned back from Ireland, thought that the Commons could be managed.

The result was the Short Parliament, which met from April 13 to May 5, 1640. Many of the popular leaders were returned. The Commons were told in an arrogant way that they should vote money at once and that the King would then listen to any grievances they might have. The answer of the Commons is to be found in a speech by John Pym, who presented in a moderate but devastating way the long list of grievances which had accumulated since 1629. Beginning with Charles's attacks on parliamentary privilege, Pym traced the innovations in religion and the assaults on the rights of property. He called for reform and when he sat down there were cries of "A good oration!" Under his leadership, the Commons began a systematic collection and examination of popular complaints. Grievances were to precede supply. The King, angry at a rumor that the leaders of the Commons were in secret communication with the Scots, dissolved the Parliament.

Charles was left with the old problem of fighting a war without money. His principal adviser at this crisis was Thomas Wentworth, now Earl of Strafford, known to the people as "Black Tom the Tyrant." Strafford, one of the popular leaders in the 1620s, had been imprisoned in 1627 for refusing to lend money to the King. But after the Petition of Right he had come over to the side of the Crown and for this has been accused of apostasy. He was a masterful man whose temper was autocratic. He had no interest in free institutions and no sympathy with Puritanism. Skillful and resolute as an administrator, he believed in authority, demanded unquestioning obedience, and was prone to drive at what he desired without too nice an attention to legality. It was natural for such a man to take his place with the King. From 1628 to 1632 he was president of the Council in the North; from 1632 to 1640, Lord Deputy in Ireland. It was only toward the end of Charles's personal rule that this hard, bold, and determined man was summoned from Ireland to become one of the King's principal counselors. After the dissolution of the Short Parliament he advised Charles to prosecute the war against the Scots with vigor, to consider himself free from all normal rules of government, and to do anything "that power might admit." "You have an army in Ireland you may employ here to reduce this kingdom." Was "this kingdom" Scotland, or was it England?

It was easier to speak boldly than to raise an army. Loans could not be obtained either from London or from sources overseas. Charles called out the militia from the southern part of the country, but the men were not only half trained but half mutinous. Many of them deserted; others broke into disorders which often were demonstrations against the Laudian church. England's heart was not in the war, and the arbitrary methods of the government only increased the general discontent. The Scots, therefore, took the initiative. Crossing the Tweed unopposed on August 20, 1640, they occupied the two northern counties of Northumberland and Durham, upon which they levied £850 a day for their support. "Never came any man to so lost a business," wrote Strafford as he moved northward. The Scots, however, had no intention of pushing farther south. With two counties and with the coal fields around Newcastle in their possession, they held hostages enough. On all sides in England the demand arose for a meeting of Parliament. Charles, not yet convinced, summoned instead a Great Council consisting only of peers, such as had not met in England for at least two centuries. The peers arranged a treaty with the Scots that left things as they were until a more lasting settlement could be made. Thus a meeting of Parliament became absolutely necessary. Charles summoned one for November 3, 1640.

THE FIRST YEARS OF THE LONG PARLIAMENT

The members of the House of Commons who assembled in November 1640 were in a determined mood. Estranged from the Crown by years of arbitrary government, they believed that the time had come for the removal of abuses and for curtailment of the royal prerogative. The King, defeated and bankrupt, was in their power. And yet it is probable that most members thought in the traditional fashion of redressing wrongs and driving out "evil counselors." They had no thought of revolution or of removing the King from office. But a group of leaders—men such as John Pym and John Hampden in the Commons and a handful of Puritan peers—wanted something more than did ordinary members. Not that these leaders thought in terms of physical revolt. What they wanted was a transference of power from the King to the House of Commons. It seemed intolerable to them that a wrong-headed King, whose government was really bad, should continue to formulate policy (which he could not carry into effect), while members of the gentry (upon whom the execution of government rested) should have no share in making decisions. These leaders believed that sovereignty should pass from the King to Parliament. During the next few years a majority of members came to agree with them.

The Commons began by striking at the ministers of the King. It was resolved at once to impeach the Earl of Strafford. In this the Commons were prompted as much by fear as by determination to punish evil deeds; they secured Strafford's imprisonment even before the charges against him were formulated. Laud also was imprisoned, but he was not thought dangerous; his trial and execution did not take place until 1644–1645. Other ministers—Windebank, the Secretary who was believed to have favored Catholics, and Finch, the judge who had supported ship money—fled abroad. Charles's administration collapsed.

Strafford's trial before the House of Lords began in March 1641 and ended three weeks later without a verdict. He was accused of treason for attempting to subvert the fundamental laws of the realm and for advising the King to substitute an arbitrary and tyrannical government, but it soon became evident that the Commons' case was weak. The basic definition of treason was an offense against the King, of which Strafford was not guilty. He was accused, in fact, of treason against the nation, a new concept in law. His words to the King, "You have an army in Ireland you may employ here to reduce this kingdom," might well have referred to Scotland, as he claimed they did; in any case they rested on the oath of only one witness. The impeachment seemed likely to fail.

When the Commons discovered that certain courtiers were plotting to bring down the army from the north in order to dissolve the Parliament, they dropped the impeachment in a panic and substituted a bill of attainder, which required no proof, but which must pass the Lords and be signed by the King. There was now a great deal of tumult. Mobs from the city, sometimes composed of well-dressed persons and sometimes of mere rabble, milled around Westminster. Danger arose that the mob might attack the palace; cries were heard demanding the life of the Queen. Threatened with violence, the Lords passed the bill in a very thin house, and the King, after days of agony, signed it, to his great loss both in strength and in honor. Strafford was executed next morning.

To secure their position the Commons passed the Triennial Act, which provided that no more than three years should elapse between the dissolution of one Parliament and the meeting of the next; and an act declaring that the Parliament now assembled should not be dissolved without its own consent. When Charles signed the second of these bills, he lost his last shred of power over the Commons. The most basic control of Parliament by the Crown had been its right to summon and dissolve at will; with the curtailment of this power the Crown was indeed laid low. Charles had decreed a perpetual Parliament.

A series of important acts followed. Ship money, forest laws, and distraint of knighthood were swept away. Tonnage and poundage, though granted for a short time, was declared illegal without the consent of Parliament. Another measure abolished the Star Chamber, the High Commission, the Council in the North, the power of the Privy Council to deal with the property rights of the people, and the jurisdiction of the Council of Wales in so far as it resembled that of the Star Chamber. The courts of common law remained supreme, victorious in their long contest with the prerogative courts.

The early work of the Long Parliament, which we have been describing, was done with surprising unanimity, but when the Commons turned to religious issues their unanimity disappeared. They could agree that the penal laws against Catholics should be enforced, that the church should not be Laudian, that Parliament should exercise some control over it, but here agreement ended. As differences multiplied, a royalist party began to take shape in the Commons. It was composed of moderate Anglicans, men loyal to the Church of England and to its Prayer Book and who desired to retain episcopacy with the excessive power of the bishops curtailed. But a majority of the Commons wished to over-throw the church, to end it root and branch, and to set up some form of Puritanism in its place. What form was that to be? Presbyterianism, although strong in London and in other parts of the country, did not as yet command much support in the Commons. The same was true of Independency, or Congregationalism, though the few members who supported it were men of considerable influence. Pym, followed by a majority of the Commons, thought in terms of a Puritan state church controlled by lay commissioners who in turn would be controlled by Parliament. This solution in effect would transfer to Parliament the ecclesiastical supremacy the Crown had exercised since the Reformation. As these Puritan groups emerged, the Anglicans drew together, not only in defense of the Prayer Book and a reformed episcopacy, but in defense of the King, whose powers, it was thought, should not be reduced any further.

Division between Puritans and Anglicans was increased greatly in the autumn of 1641, when news arrived of a rebellion in Ireland. With Strafford, who had ruled Ireland with a heavy hand, now gone, the Irish Catholics saw an opportunity to turn on their oppressors. They had hoped for a general insurrection, though what took place was a rising in Ulster, where there were many English and Scottish landowners. The stories that reached England were greatly exaggerated, but it is certain that some thousands of Protestants were murdered and that thousands more died of exposure and privation. The Commons, determined on revenge, voted money at once for an efficient army. This raised a fundamental issue, for the Commons dared not entrust the new army to the King, and the King could not entrust it to the Parliament. In this crisis Pym and other Puritan leaders drew up the Grand Remonstrance, a long document of 204 clauses which reviewed past grievances over many years, set forth the remedies advocated by Parliament, and demanded that the King employ officers and ministers of state whom the Commons could trust. The Grand Remonstrance was an appeal to the people by the Puritan party in the Commons. As such it was opposed by the royalists, who now formed a compact party. The debates on the Grand Remonstrance became so heated that there was danger of a scuffle on the floor of the Commons. In the end the Remonstrance passed by the slim majority of 159 to 148.

Events now moved rapidly to the outbreak of war. Tumults and mobs at Westminster became common. The bishops, fearing attack, ceased to attend the House of Lords. Men drew their swords in the streets; the names of Cavalier and Roundhead came into use. Charles had a party in each house, but in a wild and foolish move he ordered his attorney general to prepare impeachment proceedings against five of the leading Puritans in the Commons. When that house would not surrender them, Charles took the fatal step of coming in person to the Commons in an attempt to arrest the five members. This was regarded as a monstrous breach of privilege—as it was—though no worse a violation of constitutional principles than the Commons' use of the mob to terrorize Westminster. The five members had slipped away to London. Four thousand men came up from Buckinghamshire to defend their hero Hampden. The Commons sent one of their number, Sir John Hotham, to secure the arsenal at Hull and passed an ordinance which placed their nominees in control of the militia. Charles withdrew to Hampton Court and sent the Queen to France. In March 1642 he went to York, in April he was refused admission to Hull, in August he raised his standard at Nottingham. The Civil War had begun.

THE CAUSES OF THE CIVIL WAR

Historians in recent years have been much concerned with the causes of the English Civil War. They have modified the Whig interpretation of the nineteenth century that the war was simply a clash over religious and constitutional principles. This view made the early Stuarts too evil and the parliamentary leaders too virtuous. The present tendency is to regard James and Charles in a more favorable light, not as tyrants, but as conservative monarchs defending, with justice but without much skill, the ancient rights of the Crown against the aggressive onslaught of the Commons. But why were the Commons so aggressive? A great scholar, R. H. Tawney, has set forth the view that the gentry class, after advancing in wealth for a century at the expense of the aristocracy and the Crown, discovered that its economic strength was far greater than its political power. It demanded a larger voice in shaping the national destiny, and this demand produced the clash with the Crown. The Commons, in other words, made war upon the King to bring their political position into line with their economic wealth.

This view has been criticized on various grounds. It has been argued that not all the gentry were rising in the economic scale; that some were declining; that great wealth did not normally come from land alone, but from trade, from the law, and from high office; and that the declining gentry, jealous of the officeholders about the King, were ripe for revolt when the opportunity served. A third interpretation is that the prosperous gentry in control of the House of Commons had many interconnections with other classes, such as the merchants in the towns, and should not be considered as a class distinct from all others. For a long time the gentry sought to regulate, not to overthrow, the Crown, and acted more from religious and constitutional motives than from a desire to improve their economic position. We may perhaps say that the gentry's wealth and influence made an advance to political power inevitable, but that the quarrel with the King was over religious and constitutional issues.[5]

Nonetheless, economic issues played a part in bringing about the Civil War. During the early Stuart period the aggressive country gentleman, as well as the pushing merchant and industrialist, saw many ways in which economic profit could be made. What these men wanted was greater freedom, especially in dealing with labor, and a relaxation of Tudor control of economic life. The early Stuarts, however, believed that the regulation of the economy was a royal prerogative to be employed for the protection of the Crown and for the advancement of the general good. Desiring stability rather than progress, James and Charles were suspicious of private enterprise; they resisted economic change which, they feared, might cause unemployment and social unrest. They stood for the *status quo*. Moreover, they regarded themselves as patriarchal rulers who protected the poor against the wealthy. But their efforts in this direction were so feeble, their economic policies so inconsistent and contradictory, so full of exceptions imposed by poverty, that they irritated the landed and business classes without bringing noticeable relief to the poor.

Inflation kept up the price of agricultural products. The country gentleman who could engage in the national industry of feeding London or who owned property rich in minerals or timber could make a good thing of his estates. The

[5] See page 793.

agricultural frontier was moving westward into Wales and northward toward the Border. Wishing to bring more land under cultivation, landowners enclosed their estates, drained marshes, and encroached upon the waste land between villages. The government resisted these moves, partly because they injured the poor, partly because they offered opportunity to levy fines upon the rich. Yet wealthy men who loaned money to the King were allowed to act about as they pleased.

The same tendencies may be seen in commerce and industry. In James's first Parliament a demand arose for freer trading conditions, that is, for a curtailment of the monopolies enjoyed by the London trading companies. But the Crown defended the rights of the London companies. Moreover, many merchants resented the government's weakness in opposing the Dutch and in allowing the navy to decay, so that it gave little protection to English seaborne trade. Industry had expanded steadily in the century before the Civil War. To a considerable extent this expansion was based upon a greater use of coal in heating houses and in new industrial techniques. A remarkable growth had taken place in the amount of capital invested in business enterprises. London grew steadily as an economic center; the population slowly increased. Yet capitalists found that they were commanded to do uneconomical things such as keeping their workpeople employed when trade was slack, that the Star Chamber was used when the common law courts would not support the Crown, that the middleman was disliked, that economic regulation became complex and rigid, that the government broke its own rules, that monopolies increased, that interference by the Crown in economic life did more harm than good.

As for the poor, they obtained little benefit either from the expansion of the economy or from the policy of the state. The population, though not large, was greater than the economy of the time could absorb. Hence there was underemployment and extremely low wages, no protection against disaster, and a bad system of poor relief. The poor, it may be noted, did not support the King during the Civil War. The business classes, with some exceptions, were alienated; the landed aristocracy was at least divided in sympathy.[6]

[6] Christopher Hill, *The Century of Revolution 1603–1714* (Edinburgh: T. Nelson, 1966), pp. 15–42.

18

the CIVIL WARS
and the RULE of the saints

The Civil Wars were fought with spirit and resolution. The fighting began in a rather amateurish way, but both sides soon acquired professional technique from veterans returning from the wars on the Continent. Friends and relatives found themselves on opposite sides. Two nobles who charged with the King's forces at the Battle of Edgehill knew that their sons were in the parliamentary camp. The parliamentary general, Sir William Waller, wrote to his opponent, Sir Ralph Hopton:

> My affections to you are so unchangeable that hostility itself cannot violate my friendship to your person. . . . The great God, who is the searcher of my heart, knows with what reluctance I go upon this service and with what perfect hatred I look upon a war without an enemy. . . . We must act the parts that are assigned us in this tragedy. Let us do it in a way of honor, and without personal animosities.

Both sides, seeking the support of noncombatants, treated them with respect. A fiercer spirit prevailed when Englishmen fought Scots or Irishmen; yet the war in England generally was conducted with honor and humanity.

HOW THE COUNTRY DIVIDED

Some eighty of the nobility sided with the King, some thirty against him. The nobles felt instinctively that their greatness was bound up with that of the Crown; they feared the mob and the chaos of revolution. Some had a sense of personal gratitude to Charles. "Had I a million crowns or scores of sons," wrote Lord Goring, "the King and his cause should have them all. . . . I had all from the King, and he hath all again." Of the nobles supporting Parliament, a few were Puritan, a few hoped to be on the winning side. The gentry were divided, the majority for the King, a large minority for Parliament. They were influenced by the same considerations as were the nobles, though Puritanism was stronger among them than among the peers. Accustomed to riding, they had the makings of excellent cavalry officers, and they often brought a body of horsemen with them for the King's service. "The honest country gentlemen," wrote a Royalist, "raises the troop at his own charge, then gets a Low Country lieutenant to fight his troop for him, and sends for his son from school to be cornet." The yeomen tended to side with the gentry of their areas; the peasants were indifferent. Although a few London merchants were Royalists, the business classes of the towns sided with Parliament; London, which was strongly Presbyterian, supplied the Commons with an inexhaustible source of men and money.

To some extent every locality was divided; the war began with a great number of small clashes as each side attempted to capture military stores and to control the militia. There was, however, a rough geographical division. The north and the west of the kingdom sided with the King, the south and the east with Parliament, while much of the Midlands formed a no man's land between. The King's territory was excellent recruiting ground, though his soldiers were difficult to discipline, prone to plunder, and apt to disappear if they did not receive their pay. The shires under Parliament's control were more amenable to discipline and to taxation, the London trained bands were the best infantry in the kingdom at the beginning of the war, and Parliament secured the three principal arsenals of London, Hull, and Portsmouth.

Parliament held two great advantages. One was sea power. The adherence of the navy permitted Parliament to control and to continue foreign trade, to collect customs, to hinder the King in importing munitions, and to maintain coastal towns behind his lines. Parliament's second advantage lay in money. Controlling the richer and more populous portions of the country, it could levy assessments on prosperous farming counties, sequester Royalists' estates, and raise loans in London. Although the pay of its soldiers was often in arrears,

Seventeenth-century woodcut satirizing Cavaliers and Roundheads. (Illustration Research Service)

Parliament could always find new recruits. The King, on the other hand, depended almost entirely on the generosity of his followers; great nobles, such as the Earls of Worcester and Newcastle, gave him huge sums. But the most lavish private gifts run out at last and are a poor substitute for taxation. As the King's finances became more and more desperate, recruiting fell off, and munitions were difficult to come by. The fact that the royal troops lived on the countryside made the peasants hostile.

England in the Seventeenth Century

THE CIVIL WAR, 1642–1646

Nonetheless, the King held an initial advantage, partly because the parliamentary general, the Earl of Essex, was so dilatory that he allowed the King to grow strong. Charles moved west from Nottingham to Shrewsbury, seeking recruits and weapons. By October 1642 he was able to march toward London, hoping to end the war at a blow. Essex met him at Edgehill in Warwickshire in the first battle of the war. Charles's cavalry, commanded by his impetuous nephew, Prince Rupert of the Palatinate, drove Essex's horsemen from the field, but most of the parliamentary foot stood firm and the King's infantry was badly mauled. The fruits of victory fell to Charles, who entered Oxford and continued his march toward London. But though Rupert stormed Brentford a dozen miles from the city, the London trained bands supported Essex. Charles withdrew to Oxford, which became his headquarters for the remainder of the war. He had shown more skill and daring than Essex, but he had failed to win the war in a single decisive campaign.

There was one parliamentary officer who studied these events to advantage. Oliver Cromwell, watching the battle at Edgehill, saw clearly that the parliamentary forces could never be victorious until their cavalry was equal to that of the King. He said to his cousin, John Hampden, "Your troops are most of them old decayed serving-men, tapsters, and such kind of fellows; do you think that the spirits of such base, mean fellows will ever be able to encounter gentlemen that have honor, and courage, and resolution in them? You must get men of a spirit that is likely to go as far as gentlemen will go, or you will be beaten still." Cromwell was a member of the gentry, owning estates around Huntingdon, and he obtained leave to go home to raise a troop of cavalry.

This famous troop, expanding gradually from 80 to 1100 men, was to give its spirit to the whole parliamentary army. Most of its soldiers were farmers, many owning their land and their horses. They were very religious, "having the fear of God before them and making some conscience of what they did." Cromwell was proud of his troop. "I have," he wrote, "a lovely company." Enforcing rigid discipline, he trained his men carefully. He taught them to look after and groom their horses and to keep their weapons bright and ready for use. Each trooper was armed with a pair of pistols and a sword and was protected by a light helmet called a pot and by two pieces of armor, known as back and breast, which fitted over the upper part of the body and were laced together at the sides. Cromwell trained his men to charge "at a good round trot," firing their pistols as they met the enemy and then relying upon the sharpness of their swords.

Cromwell had a natural aptitude for war. An introvert in his religious life, forever seeking flaws in his soul, he was an extrovert in battle, with a capacity for instant decision and a wonderful alertness and vitality. He was "naturally of such a vivacity, hilarity, and alacrity as another man hath when he hath drunken a cup too much." He created his own troop and selected his own officers; he saw that his men received their pay and their supplies. At first he was merely a dashing cavalry officer, but he grew with astonishing rapidity, developing into a superb general by whom all the arts and techniques of war—military, logistic, psychological—were employed with masterly success.

Following the Battle of Edgehill Parliament increased the efficiency of the war effort by dividing its territory into groups of counties known as associations. Of these the Eastern Association, consisting of East Anglia and the counties from

Sir Thomas Fairfax. (From Joshua Sprigg, *Anglia Rediviva; England's Recovery*, London, 1647. Department of Special Collections, Walter Library, University of Minnesota)

Lincolnshire down to Hertford, was the most important. An army raised in this area was commanded by the Presbyterian Earl of Manchester. Cromwell's regiment formed part of this army.

The fortunes of the King in the Civil War reached their height in 1643. In addition to the army at Oxford, there was a royal army in the north under the Earl of Newcastle, who in the previous year had moved from Durham into Yorkshire, pushing back the parliamentary forces under Lord Fairfax and his son Sir Thomas. In 1643 Newcastle entered Lincolnshire, and though his vanguard was roughly handled by Cromwell at Gainsborough, he soon occupied the entire county. In the southwest a third army under Sir Ralph Hopton and Sir Bevil Grenville overran Cornwall and Devon except for the walled towns. With the capture of Bristol in July the King's hold on the west seemed secure. Thus he occupied a central position at Oxford, with supporting forces on each flank, and there was scope for a broader strategy. Essex opened the campaign with a lunge toward Oxford, but he was checked and withdrew, allowing the Queen, who had landed in the north, to enter Oxford with a large convoy of reinforcements and supplies. Encouraged by these successes, Charles planned a three-pronged assault on London by a converging movement of all his armies. But Newcastle hesitated to push south while Hull remained uncaptured in his rear; a similar dread haunted the Royalists in the west, for they had not taken Plymouth. Charles therefore turned west to besiege the fortified city of Gloucester. Parliament was in difficulty, but it rose to the occasion, imposed new taxes, and sent Essex to Gloucester's relief. Charles abandoned the siege and met Essex at the Battle of Newbury, which was called a draw, though the King's losses were greater than those of Essex.

A crisis in the war was approaching, and both sides sought allies. The King turned to Ireland, where his Lord Deputy, Ormonde, held Dublin with a small Royalist force. Arranging a truce with the Irish Catholics, Ormonde sent troops to England, though they were not numerous enough to make any great difference. Charles was soon hoping for aid from the Irish Catholic rebels; a secret treaty was arranged which made them large concessions in return for assistance. Unfortunately a copy of the treaty was captured by Parliament, and great discredit was brought upon the King, for the use of Irish troops in England was abhorrent to all parties.

Meanwhile Parliament approached the Scots, asking for a political alliance for the resolute prosecution of the war. But the Scots wanted a religious covenant. They knew that the Presbyterian party held a strong position in the House of Commons and that Parliament was in great need of assistance. They demanded and secured the Solemn League and Covenant, a treaty containing an implied promise that Parliament would establish Presbyterianism as the state religion in both England and Ireland. This treaty had far-reaching results. It divided the Commons between the Presbyterians and another party, the Independents, to whom we will turn presently. Eventually, when the Independents came to power, the treaty brought war between England and Scotland but meanwhile it helped enormously in defeating the King.

In January 1644 a well-equipped Scottish army of 21,000 men crossed the Border into England. The military picture suddenly was altered. Newcastle, the King's general, turned to face the Scots and was thrown on the defensive. He was driven into York, where he was besieged by the Scots, by the Fairfaxes, and by Manchester's forces. Prince Rupert, coming to the rescue from the west, broke up the siege but made the mistake of following the parliamentary armies as they retreated and of forcing a battle at Marston Moor. This was in July 1644. As the battle was joined, Goring swept back the cavalry of Fairfax, and part of the parliamentary foot gave way. But some of the foot stood firm, and Cromwell, having defeated the cavalry of Rupert, closed in on the Royalist center. The result was a Royalist disaster. Rupert retreated with his cavalry, having lost his infantry, his guns, and his baggage. The King's hold on the north of England was crushed.

Elsewhere Charles did not fare badly. Essex was defeated in Cornwall, and a second Battle of Newbury ended in a draw, though the King should have been routed. Meanwhile the great adventurer, James Graham, Marquis of Montrose, was raising the Scottish Highlands for the King, to the consternation of the Lowland Scots. Nevertheless, Charles was in a precarious position. He was almost without money and without a resolute plan.

Meanwhile Parliament reconstructed and improved its army. There had been a quarrel between Cromwell and the Earl of Manchester in which, with his usual force and bluntness, Cromwell had accused the earl of inefficiency and of wishing to make peace with the King. As a result Parliament passed the Self-denying Ordinance, which forced the resignation of persons holding commands, civil or military, who were members of that Parliament. Essex, Manchester, and Waller were eliminated; Fairfax became general, Skippon, major general; the office of lieutenant general, left open for a time, was given to Cromwell. By the Self-denying Ordinance he should have been passed over, but he had a great following in the army and his services were too valuable to lose. His appointment was an indication that in a crisis the army could force its will upon the Commons. The New Model Army, as it was called, was better led and better organized; the soldiers were paid regularly by a monthly assessment levied on all the counties under Parliament's control. It was this army that speedily brought the war to a close. Charles, with no firm plan, foolishly marched into enemy territory and was crushed at Naseby in June 1645, another battle in which Cromwell played a distinguished part. Thereafter the King was a fugitive and the war subsided into sieges and small operations. In May 1646 Charles surrendered himself to the Scots.

PRESBYTERIANS AND INDEPENDENTS

To defeat the King was far easier than to construct a new government. The King could not be restored as if nothing had happened; nor could the House of Commons, which had fought a war and governed the country for five years, be set once more in its old position. King and Parliament would have to cooperate in a new government, and many wounds would have to be healed. These problems proved too difficult for solution. There were bitter quarrels— between Presbyterians and Independents, between Parliament and the army, between England and the Scots—until chaos threatened and the Second Civil War was fought. Then the army, bitter against the King, seized control of Parliament and brought Charles to his tragic death.

When Royalist members left Parliament at the beginning of the Civil Wars, the party that remained was the Root and Branch party, determined to destroy the Anglican Church. In 1642 it summoned a meeting of clergymen, known as the Westminster Assembly, to suggest reforms. The Solemn League and Covenant gave power to the Presbyterians in the Commons, and the church gradually assumed a Presbyterian tone. A Directory took the place of the Prayer Book, the hierarchy of the Church of England was abolished, there was a new Confession of Faith as well as a new Catechism. The new church, when fully constructed, would be a Presbyterian Church, though it would be subject to Parliament and not free and sovereign as in Scotland.

A new form of ecclesiastical government—that of the Independents—was emerging in England. The Independents had begun in the reign of Elizabeth when a group of religious radicals, the Brownists or Separatists, broke from the church and set up their own congregations. The churches in New England and some English churches in Holland were of this type. They rejected any kind of ecclesiastical hierarchy, whether Anglican or Presbyterian. Each congregation, they believed, should be complete, autonomous, and sovereign in itself. Uncontrolled from above, it should select its own minister and should determine its own beliefs and ritual. The Independents laid great stress on individual interpretation of the Scriptures and believed that man could discover God's will as well as find a guide to conduct in the Bible. "If thou wilt seek to know the mind of God in all that chain of Providence," wrote Cromwell, "seek of the Lord to teach thee what that is; and He will do it." Hence the Independents believed in new revelations, new directives, to be found in God's written word. The result was great diversity of doctrine and a great variety of sects—Congregationalists, Anabaptists, Antinomians, Fifth Monarchy Men, Seekers, Quakers, and, to the far left, the Diggers, who rejected church buildings and all ritual and made religion a silent communion of the spirit between God and man. The Independents were weak in the House of Commons. They could number only fifty or sixty votes. But their leaders, such as Sir Henry Vane the Younger and Oliver St. John, were so able that they exerted an influence out of proportion to their numbers.

Presbyterians and Independents represented not only two churches but two philosophies of government. The Presbyterians proclaimed the sovereignty of Parliament. Like the members of the General Assembly in Scotland, they believed that God had given them the right to rule the state. The Independents, on the other hand, found sovereignty in the people. Democracy in the Independent churches led to democracy in politics. Just as a congregation selected its pastor, so the people should select their governors; Parliament should be kept close to the sovereign people by frequent elections. Just as the church was a voluntary association of believers held together by a covenant, so the state was an association of freemen held together by a contract. The government should not interfere in matters of the spirit. There should be liberty of conscience for every individual to believe and worship as he wished. Thus the ideas of modern political democracy were foreshadowed by the Independents.

If weak in the House of Commons, the Independents were strong in the army. All sorts of sects were to be found among the soldiers. Trusting in new revelations, they believed that God, by the victories He had given them, had marked them as the protectors of religion with a mission to control the state. The soldiers were hostile to the King. He had been their enemy, and they could not trust themselves under his power in any form of restored monarchy.

The army looked to Cromwell as its leader in politics as well as in war. He was very popular with the soldiers, jovial and familiar with them, and did not stand on his dignity; and if a fiery temper underlay his joviality, this did not make him less popular. He represented their views much better in religion than he did in politics. He has been called the great Independent. Though he did not associate himself with any one sect, he sympathized with the spirit of all of them and embodied their religious ideals. As a young man of about twenty-eight he had experienced a conversion through which, after great mental and spiritual agony, he became convinced that he was one of God's elect, chosen by the Almighty to fulfill His plans on earth. Thenceforth it was Cromwell's primary aim to discover what God's will was, and for this purpose he devoted long periods to prayer and meditation. He was a strong advocate of liberty of conscience, and he defended the sectaries in the army against the intolerance of the Presbyterians. After the Battle of Naseby he wrote to the Speaker of the House of Commons:

> Honest men served you faithfully in this action. They are trusty; I beseech you in the name of God not to discourage them. He that ventures his life for the liberty of his country, I wish he trust God for the liberty of his conscience, and you for the liberty he fights for.[1]

In politics Cromwell did not represent the soldiers so well: his political views were those of the landowning classes. Because of his strong sense of property and his dread of chaos he labored to make the soldiers obedient to Parliament and to restrain them from using force in politics. He thus exposed himself to the suspicion of the radicals and to the charge of hypocrisy.

Parliament and the Army

Shortly after the war came to an end, the relations between Parliament and the army became very tense. There was no hope that Parliament, with its intolerant Presbyterian majority, would accept the Independent and democratic ideas of the soldiers. The Presbyterian leaders acted very foolishly. They planned at once to disband the army, not only without indemnity for acts committed in war but also without arrears of pay. They hoped to persuade the disbanded soldiers to enlist for service in Ireland. Discontent in the army became alarming; the soldiers organized themselves politically by electing representatives, called Agitators or Agents, to present their views to Parliament. The army refused to disband. Thereupon in the spring of 1647 the Presbyterian leaders determined to disperse it by force. The plan was to bring the Scottish army into England and to employ it against the men who had won the war. At this point the army mutinied. It began by arresting the King.

Charles had been a prisoner of the Scots for eight months. He had been negotiating both with them and with Parliament, but he had refused Presbyterianism; in January 1647 the Scots in disgust handed him over to the English and crossed the Border into their own country. In June he was seized by the English army; in August the army occupied London; the radicals, or Levelers, drew up a famous document, the Agreement of the People, to be laid before the House of Commons. It demanded that the Parliament then in session be dissolved, that there be an election every two years, that electoral districts be made equal, and that there be universal manhood suffrage. The King and the House of Lords were not mentioned and presumably would disappear. An assertion of

[1] For Cromwell's religious life, see Maurice Ashley, *The Greatness of Oliver Cromwell* (New York: Macmillan, 1958), Chap. III.

Carolus Rex Angliæ
Scotiæ franciæ et Hiberniæ &

Charles I. (From *Bibliotheca Regia*, . . . *containing a Collection of such of the papers of His Late Majesty . . . as have escaped the Wrack and Ruines of these times*, London, 1659. Department of Special Collections, Walter Library, University of Minnesota) natural rights followed: all Englishmen should enjoy freedom of conscience, freedom from impressment, and equality before the law. Cromwell and many officers would have been satisfied with a limited monarchy, but in the Agreement of the People the soldiers were demanding a democratic republic based on a written constitution, both novel ideas in English history. At Cromwell's urging, the Agreement was modified and presented to Parliament in the form of proposals.[2]

Events suddenly took a dramatic turn, for on the night of November 11, 1647, the King escaped from Hampton Court and made his way to the Isle of Wight off the southern coast. He had concluded a secret agreement with the Scots that he would establish Presbyterianism throughout his dominions for three years if they would restore him to his throne. There followed the Second Civil War in 1648. It consisted of scattered risings by Cavaliers, the desertion of part of the fleet, and an invasion from Scotland, but these sporadic moves were not directed by any master mind. The people as a whole were apathetic. Local risings were quelled without great difficulty, and in a lightning campaign Cromwell overwhelmed the Scots at Preston, Wigan, and Warrington in the northwest of England.

The Death of the King

After these victories the English army assumed control. Its mood was one of harsh severity against the King, whose intrigues with all parties, and especially his last treaty with the Scots, which resulted in the Second Civil War, hardened the hearts of the soldiers against him. "We came to a very clear resolution," wrote one of them, "that it was our duty, if ever the Lord brought us back again in peace, to call Charles Stuart, that man of blood, to account for the blood he had shed, and mischief he had done to the utmost against the Lord's cause and people in these poor nations." London was occupied once more in December 1648. Parliament was dealt with in a simple way. Colonel Pride, placing his musketeers at the door of the House of Commons, excluded about 140 Presbyterian members (arresting 45 of them) and admitted only the Independents, some 50 or 60 strong.

A court was then set up to try the King. Charles refused to recognize its jurisdiction, but it condemned him to death for treason against the nation. Charles met his fate with fortitude and courage. Steadfast in his opinions, he said on the scaffold,

> For the people I desire their liberty and freedom as much as anybody whomsoever; but I must tell you that their liberty and freedom consists in having government, in those laws by which their life and goods may be most their own. It is not their having a share in government; that is nothing pertaining to them.

He then prayed for a moment, laid his comely head on the block, and signaled the executioner to strike. At one blow his head was severed from his body. A groan broke from the people—"such a groan," wrote a spectator, "as I never heard before, and desire I may never hear again."

[2] This document in modified form appeared again in 1649. See Charles Firth, *Oliver Cromwell and the Rule of the Puritans in England* (London: Putnam, 1901), pp. 177, 183, 236–237.

THE COMMONWEALTH, 1649–1653

Shortly after the King's execution Parliament abolished the office of King as dangerous and unnecessary. It also abolished the House of Lords. "England," it declared, "shall henceforth be governed as a Commonwealth, or a Free State, by the supreme authority of this nation, the representatives of the people in Parliament." On another occasion the Commons affirmed that the people were, under God, the origin of all just power. But despite these democratic sentiments, the members of the House of Commons, now about ninety Independents, clung to power with the utmost tenacity. The army strongly desired an election, but no election was held. The Commonwealth was in reality a continuation of the rule of the Long Parliament under a new name. Parliament was more powerful than ever, for there was neither a King nor a House of Lords to impose restraint.

The Commons appointed a Council of State to which administrative power was entrusted; the Council, however, was to be elected annually by the Commons, and thirty-one of its forty-one members were also members of Parliament. It was no more than the Commons in administrative session. Nor could Parliament claim to represent the nation. Large areas of the country had no members in the Commons. Parliament represented only the Independents, who were a handful of sectaries, a fraction of the whole people. Parliament, moreover, did not meet occasionally as in the past. It remained in session the year round; there seemed no hope of ending it, for it could not legally be dissolved without its own consent. The Commons contained energetic and dedicated men, some of them very able, but it is not surprising that their government was highly unpopular. The army, taking its stand on the principles of the Agreement of the People, was deeply dissatisfied; it tolerated the new government only because there were enemies on every side.

At home the Commonwealth faced the hatred of Royalists and Presbyterians. These groups, and many persons outside them, could never forgive the Puritans for killing the King. The Independents had thought of Charles's death as just retribution, but it proved to be their most egregious blunder. To lay violent hands upon the King, to touch the Lord's anointed, to shed his blood as though he were a common criminal was to shock and horrify a large proportion of the people. Charles haunted the Independents from his grave. The reaction in his favor that had begun before his death was greatly intensified by the appearance of *Eikon Basilike,* a touching book about his last days of suffering. It was written by a clergyman, Dr. Gauden, who drew largely on his own imagination, but Royalists were certain that it had been written by Charles himself and that its noble thoughts were those of the King. This book kept green among Cavaliers the memory of their martyred ruler.

The popular image of the King now altered. Charles, the friend of Laud, the imposer of ship money, the shady trickster, and the man of blood disappeared; Charles the Martyr took his place. John Milton hoped to shatter this image in a learned pamphlet, *Eikonoklastes,* but no one read it. The death of the King was remembered, his weakness forgotten. For the moment the Commonwealth had little to fear from Royalists or Presbyterians. The Royalists were battered and impoverished, their estates sequestered and redeemable only by the payment of large fines. The Presbyterians, though strong among the business classes in the towns, went no further than a sullen passive resistance.

The Commonwealth was also under attack from the political radicals, known as the Levelers. Their leader, John Lilburne, a restless and unreasonable man, was an energetic pamphleteer. He denounced the Commons for refusing to grant annual elections, manhood suffrage, and complete religious liberty. He said bitter things about Cromwell, whom he regarded as a traitor to democratic principles. Cromwell believed that Lilburne was politically dangerous and ought to be suppressed. "I tell you," he said in the Council, "you have no other way to deal with these men but to break them, or they will break you." Lilburne was sent to the Tower.

Cromwell was wise enough to ignore a small and harmless group who called themselves True Levelers and were known as Diggers. Their leader, Gerrard Winstanley, was a religious mystic who applied the principle of equality not only to politics but to social and economic life. He envisaged a kind of communist utopia. Believing that the poor had been excluded from their birthright, the land of England, he wished the people to take over the land and to hold it in common. His desire was to eliminate landlords, clergymen, and lawyers. But Winstanley, a gentle rebel, began his revolution by leading a group of poor men to a village near London, where they squatted on the common, dug up the ground, and planted beans. They were shortly dispersed by the landowners of the village.

Charles's death produced a violent reaction abroad. In Russia the Czar imprisoned English merchants. In Holland the Stadtholder, William II, who had married Charles's daughter Mary, allowed Royalist privateers to refit in Dutch ports. An English ambassador at The Hague and another in Madrid were murdered by Royalists almost with impunity. France was openly hostile; Spain was a little more friendly only because she was at war with France. The Puritans were regarded on the Continent as barbarians, revolutionists, and blood-stained villains.

Surrounded by enemies, the Commonwealth perforce became a military state. It maintained an army of 44,000 men, of whom 12,000 were to be sent to Ireland. This army, the finest in Europe, was commanded by officers who made it their career. The men were well paid. The famous redcoat of the British soldier was now introduced and made universal. The navy was reorganized, and some forty warships were built within three years. There was much for these forces to do. The navy hunted down royalist privateers, for some of Charles's followers, desperate in poverty, had taken to the sea and preyed upon English commerce. Small nests of Royalists were cleared from the Channel Islands, from the Scilly Isles off the coast of Cornwall, and from the Isle of Man. The North American and West Indian colonies were forced to submit to the Commonwealth. From 1652 to 1654 there was an important and fiercely fought naval war with the Dutch, to which we will return presently. Meanwhile the army had rough work to do in Ireland and Scotland.

Ireland and Scotland

Ireland was very dangerous for the Commonwealth in 1649. For some years she had been left to her own devices, but the Second Civil War and the execution of the King produced an alliance of Protestant Royalists and Irish Roman Catholics. Ireland, if left alone, would not only be independent; she would become a base for an invasion of England. Parliament therefore turned to its best general, and in the summer of 1649 Cromwell landed in Dublin with a well-equipped army of some 12,000 men. There was no Irish army that could meet him in the field; instead, the Irish relied on fortresses and walled towns to delay his progress. Cromwell at once struck north at Drogheda. When the town refused to surrender, Cromwell took it by storm and put the entire garrison of 2800 men to the sword. This massacre was justified by the rules of war, but it would not have happened in England and it was done in a spirit of revenge. Cromwell believed that he had come to Ireland not only as a conqueror but as a judge. He termed the slaughter at Drogheda a "righteous judgment of God upon these barbarous wretches." Another massacre took place at Wexford, though Cromwell did not order it. The terror inspired by these incidents induced other towns to capitulate; by the end of 1649 all the southern and eastern coast, with the exception of Waterford, was in English hands. Early in 1650 Cromwell struck inland into Munster and captured Kilkenny, the seat of the Roman Catholic alliance.

Cromwell left Ireland in the summer of 1650. The conquest, completed by his lieutenants, was over by 1652, when the country was utterly devastated, a third of the population had perished, and a traveler could journey for miles in some areas without seeing a living creature. The settlement of Ireland after the war was very harsh. The lands of all Roman Catholics who had taken part in the rebellion were confiscated and allotted either to Englishmen who had advanced money for the campaign or to Cromwell's soldiers as arrears of pay. Some Catholics received inferior land in Connaught as compensation, but many received nothing. It is said that two thirds of the land in Ireland changed hands, and a large part of the Irish upper classes were ordered to move into Connaught or county Clare. Ireland became a country in which the great landowners were Protestant. Cromwell's soldiers, however, who were small farmers, often married Irish women, though they were forbidden to do so. In a few generations their descendants were Catholic in religion and Irish in sympathy. The Irish peasants remained as landless laborers on the estates of the new owners. Cromwell's settlement in Ireland included a number of other points. Anti-Catholic laws were enforced, and an attempt was made to strengthen Protestant congregations. There was impartial justice in the courts, Ireland obtained thirty members in the English Parliament, and free trade was established between the two countries. But these measures benefited the English in Ireland rather than the Irish themselves. Irish hatred of England grew to white heat.

In Scotland the Presbyterians, deeply offended by the triumph of the Independents in England and by Charles's execution, at once proclaimed Charles II as their King. They sent envoys to England who demanded that he also be recognized there and that the terms of the Solemn League and Covenant be honored. In reply the English expelled the envoys and prepared for another war. This was a national war, for Scotland, like Ireland, was attempting to dictate to England how she should be governed; the struggle became one for supremacy in Britain. The Scots turned to Charles II, an exile in the Netherlands, then about twenty years old. He was told that they would place him upon the English throne on condition that he accept the Covenant and establish Presbyterianism in both England and Ireland. He resisted these terms until Cromwell's victories in Ireland ended all hope of aid from that country. Then Charles came reluctantly to Scotland. His acceptance of the Covenant was hypocritical, and the Scots knew it was hypocritical; yet they insisted upon it. Charles found himself a semiprisoner of the Kirk. He was forced to deplore in public the episcopacy of his father and the Catholicism of his mother; many years later he remarked that he would rather be hanged than return to the accursed land of Scotland.

His reign at that time was brief. Cromwell crossed the Border in July 1650. At first he made little headway and retired from the vicinity of Edinburgh to Dunbar. There, on September 3, he caught the Scots in an awkward position and inflicted a crushing defeat on them. Three thousand Scots fell in the battle and ten thousand were taken prisoner. The effect in Scotland was overwhelming, for the ministers had been confident of victory. Charles was able to gain some control of policy. In the next year he led an army into England, hoping for an uprising in his favor, but his army was annihilated at the Battle of Worcester. In this battle Cromwell did not defeat the enemy; he wiped it out. Scarcely a Scot reached home after that ordeal. Charles wandered as a fugitive for some six weeks before he found a boat to take him to France. The English conquest of Scotland followed shortly. Annexed to England, she lost her Parliament and General Assembly, though local churches were let alone. English rule in Scotland was impartial, efficient, and deeply resented.

The End of the Commonwealth

Despite these victories, there was strong sentiment in the army that the Commonwealth was a provisional government which should be superseded by something more stable and lasting. Cromwell urged the Commons to fix a date for their dissolution, but the date they determined upon was 1654, three years in the future. Meanwhile the management of constant war occupied their energies, and they had no time for much-needed reforms. A law was finally passed granting amnesty to the defeated Royalists, but it was clogged with many exceptions. There was also need for legal and social reform, for the normal relations of debtor and creditor and of landlord and tenant had been disturbed. The prisons were full of debtors; the country swarmed with beggars. Parliament appointed a commission to review the law, but few of its suggestions were adopted. A reorganization of the church was also necessary. Presbyterianism had been established in London and in a few other places, but in large portions of the country each congregation went its own way. A group of clergymen, headed by John Owen, who had been Cromwell's chaplain in Ireland, presented Parliament with a comprehensive scheme for the settlement of the church. But the result was nil.

The irritation of the army with Parliament increased. When a bill was finally introduced for a new election, the Commons changed it into a plan for their continuance in power, suggesting that they should remain members of all future Parliaments, and that elections should merely add to their number. Cromwell and the army officers objected and believed that the bill would not be pushed. Then suddenly in April 1653, Cromwell learned that the bill was about to be passed. He came down to the Commons, berated the members soundly, and called in his musketeers. The members then filed out of the chamber and the door was locked behind them.

This action was at first very popular. A ballad ran thus:

> Brave Oliver came to the House like a sprite,
>   His fiery face struck the Speaker dumb,
> "Begone," said he, "you have sate long enough;
>   Do you mean to sit here until Doomsday come?"

Like the execution of the King, the dissolution of Parliament by force proved to be a political blunder. The House of Commons had been the one last shred of legality covering the actions of government. Now it was flung away, and with it the only link with the old constitution. Military might was revealed as the sole source of power. Cromwell spent the rest of his life trying to give the rule of the sword some sort of constitutional form.

THE BAREBONES PARLIAMENT AND THE INSTRUMENT OF GOVERNMENT

At the dissolution of the Long Parliament, some people wished Cromwell to be King. His picture was hung up in London with the inscription:

> Ascend three thrones, great captain and divine,
> I' th' will of God, old Lion, they are thine.

But Cromwell had no wish to become either a King or a military dictator. As commander in chief he considered himself in authority for the moment, but he desired to lay that authority down and to divest the army of governmental power. He and the army officers determined to summon a new assembly and to place power in its hands. This assembly, however, was not elected by the old franchise. Independent churches were asked to make nominations, and from this list Cromwell and the officers selected 140 persons. They were all Puritan notables—preachers, idealists, reformers—but they had no experience in government. They were strongly influenced by the Fifth Monarchy Men, who believed that Christ would soon come to rule the world and that, until His coming, "His saints should take the kingdom and possess it." This assembly was nicknamed the Little or Barebones Parliament, since one of its members was an Anabaptist preacher named Praise-God Barbon or Barebones, who seems to have contributed nothing but his name. The Parliament entered upon a reckless course of hasty and unwise reform. It abolished the court of chancery after one day's debate. It appointed a committee to codify the law, which was to be so reduced that a man could carry it in a little book in his pocket. Some members wished to abolish the law entirely and to substitute the laws of Moses. Tithes were to be abolished before any other way was found for the support of the church. Cromwell and the army officers were disgusted and alarmed, and so were the more moderate members of the Parliament. These moderates met early one morning, marched from the Parliament building to Whitehall, and returned to Cromwell the powers he had given them. The rule of the Barebone saints was over. It had lasted from July to December 1653.

Cromwell then accepted a plan advanced by certain army officers that the government should consist of a Lord Protector, a Council of State, and a Parliament. The plan was in the form of a written constitution, the only written constitution ever to be in effect in England. This Instrument of Government, as it was called, was written because its authors wanted something permanent, fundamental, and unchangeable. In religion they thought of a covenant between God and man, and so in politics they were led to think of a contract between man and his governors. The army officers were more conservative than they had been in 1649: the franchise was limited to men of property; Parliament was to meet only once in three years and then for only five months; it could not vote away the constitution; there was a portion of the revenue it could not control. On the other hand, the Protector had no veto; he must consult the council or Parlia-

Oliver Cromwell. (From Gregorio Leti, *Historia, e memorie recondite sopra alla vita di Oliviero Cromvele*, Amsterdam, 1692. Department of Special Collections, Walter Library, University of Minnesota)

ment or both. The councilors held office for life and could name the Protector's successor. Thus the army officers built checks and balances into their constitution. The document is also interesting because in it one can see the old constitution creeping back. Finally, it guaranteed religious liberty to all Christians except to Catholics and to members of the Church of England.

THE PROTECTORATE, 1653–1659

There is irony in the fact that Cromwell, having defeated the King in the name of Parliament, discovered as Protector that he could not manage the House of Commons any more than could Charles I. Cromwell wished to rule with Parliament's consent and cooperation and not by military force, but he feared a Parliament which claimed to be all-powerful, as the Long Parliament had done, and he was determined to maintain a large measure of religious toleration. He therefore took his stand on the Instrument of Government.

His Parliaments, on the other hand, were so hostile to military rule that they disliked the Instrument of Government because it was the work of the army. They assumed the lofty tone of the Long Parliament in claiming to be the supreme power in the state. "The government," they declared, "should be in the Parliament and in a single person limited or restricted as the Parliament should think fit." Cromwell's first Parliament (1654–1655) began at once to amend the constitution, making elective the office of Protector, bringing the council more under Parliament's control, seeking to limit religious toleration, and trying to reduce the size of the army as well as to subject it to parliamentary authority. Cromwell protested and offered compromises. He dismissed the Parliament at the earliest possible moment.

In 1655 he made a serious blunder. There had been rumors of Cavalier plots. He therefore divided the country into twelve districts and placed a major general in charge of each. This was effective as a police measure, but it brought the power of the army to every man's doorstep and intensified the hatred of military rule. The elections to Cromwell's second Parliament in 1656 went against the government. Although about a hundred members were excluded as dangerous, the Commons showed little interest in toleration and great hostility to the major generals. But they had a strong desire to return to the old constitution.

This desire took the startling form of asking Cromwell to assume the title of King. One of his Secretaries wrote:

> Parliament will not be persuaded that there can be a settlement any other way. The title is not the question, but it's the office, which is known to the laws and to the people. They know their duty to a king and his to them. Whatever else there is will be wholly new, and upon the next occasion will be changed again. Besides they say the name Protector came in with the sword, . . . nor will there be a free Parliament so long as that continues, and as it savors of the sword now, so it will at last bring all things to be military.

The proposal, known as the Humble Petition and Advice, was made to Cromwell by Parliament in March 1657. He rejected it. He saw the advantage of a settlement that would bring a sense of permanence, but he knew that most of his old fellow soldiers would be deeply offended. In May the Humble Petition and Advice was presented to him again, with the word "Protector" substituted for "King." And this time he accepted. He was now hereditary Protector, a King in all but name. There was also to be a second chamber of Parliament to which he could appoint members for life. He was given a more ample revenue. Parliament asked and obtained the right to control its own election disputes; the power of the Protector to exclude members was dropped. But in a second session of this Parliament a quarrel arose between the two houses; moreover, the hard core of republicans in the Commons was violently opposed to the new arrangements. Before another Parliament met, Cromwell was dead (September 3, 1658).

Cromwell's contemporaries judged him with the utmost severity. To Clarendon, the Royalist historian of the Great Rebellion, he was "a brave bad man," possessing "all the wickedness against which damnation is pronounced and for which hell fire is prepared." Clarendon, though he condemned, could not refrain from admiration, but most Royalists saw nothing to palliate the blackness of Cromwell's character. He also was assailed from the left by radicals who believed that he had betrayed the cause for which he had fought and had been led by ambition to grasp the sovereign power in the state. "In all his changes," wrote the republican Ludlow, "he designed nothing but to advance himself." These views reflect the fact that he was the leader of a party and not of the nation.

A more sympathetic estimate by his steward, John Maidston, described Cromwell the man—his fiery temper, his marvelous courage, his unselfishness and devotion to a cause, his promptness and vigor in action, his deeply religious nature, his strength and depth of character, his compassion for persons in distress. "A larger soul," wrote Maidston, "hath seldom dwelt in house of clay." Much of his work was destroyed by the Restoration; yet his great achievements stand out clearly. His superb ability as a soldier broke the absolutism of the Stuarts and changed the course of English history. He held the British Isles together when they threatened to fly apart. He saved England from anarchy and gave her a strong executive at a time when she might easily have sunk into chaos. He advanced the cause of religious toleration. He raised English prestige abroad. He added to England's possessions overseas and gave her for the first time a colonial and imperial policy.[3] To this last point we must now turn our attention.

OVERSEAS EXPANSION

The Rise of the Dutch

English expansion overseas in the Stuart period developed naturally from the achievements of the Elizabethans. Brilliant as those achievements had been, they were for the most part experimental; when Elizabeth died in 1603 England did not possess a single colony. It was in the seventeenth century that Englishmen founded and developed an empire. Building on Tudor experience, they intensified their efforts and learned the difficult lesson that colonies must be built slowly through toil and patience and not through bold adventure alone.

Conditions of international rivalry had altered. The Elizabethans had

[3] See the estimate of Cromwell in the last chapter of Charles Firth, *Oliver Cromwell and the Rule of the Puritans in England.*

thought of Spain as their great opponent, a belief which persisted in the reign of James I, though Spain was falling rapidly into decay. For the first three quarters of the seventeenth century it was the Dutch and not the Spanish who were England's commercial rivals. While fighting their fierce wars of independence against Spain, the Dutch had become a great maritime power. Their East India Company was far stronger and more wealthy than its English rival. During the early seventeenth century Dutch fleets swept through the Caribbean, driving the Spanish from the sea; and in 1628 Piet Hein—a Dutch Sir Francis Drake—captured the whole of the Spanish treasure fleet. By 1626 Holland had planted a settlement on the island of Manhattan; in the 1620s a Dutch West India Company established itself in northern Brazil. All over the world—in the East, in the West, in the Levant, in Russia, in the Baltic, in the herring fisheries of the North Sea, and in the whaling areas of the arctic—wherever the English went to trade, or to fish, or to colonize, there were the hardheaded Dutch eager to drive them out. Holland possessed a great merchant marine and hoped to monopolize the carrying trade of the world.

The English were slow to recognize the challenge of the Dutch, though there were warning voices. Sir Walter Ralegh wrote a pamphlet declaring that Holland "possessed already as many ships as eleven kingdoms, England being one of them." In 1614 Tobias Gentleman warned that the English neglected fishing: "Look but on these fellows that we call the plump Hollanders, behold their diligence in fishing and our own careless negligence." Another author contrasted the smallness of England's foreign trade with that of "our neighbors the new Sea-Herrs." These warnings fell upon deaf ears. King James, intent on the Spanish match, would do nothing; and King Charles, without resources, could do nothing if he would. It was left for the Puritans to beat back the Dutch.

The Carribean Sea in the Sixteenth & Seventeenth Centuries

English Colonies in America

Between the old war with Spain and the new ones with Holland there was an interval in which the English sought to expand overseas through the arts of peace. During the first half of the seventeenth century Englishmen swarmed to North America and even more to the West Indies. A mass migration such as England had never seen before, it consisted of two waves. One planted Virginia, Maryland, and the English West Indies. In 1606 two companies were founded, the Plymouth and the London, to establish colonies in North America under the supervision of a royal council. The Plymouth Company accomplished nothing permanent, but the London Company in 1607 planted a colony at Jamestown in Virginia. After a period of intense suffering, the colonists found a staple crop in tobacco, much to King James's disgust, for he had conceived a strong aversion to that expensive luxury, that "precious stink." The affairs of the company became involved in English politics, and in 1624 the King dissolved the company and took Virginia under his control, making it the first Crown colony. In 1632 George Calvert, Lord Baltimore, a Roman Catholic who had been one of James's Secretaries, obtained permission to establish a colony in the northern part of Chesapeake Bay. This project, carried out by his son, resulted in the founding of Maryland in 1634.

Tiny English settlements were also attempted in Guiana—an unoccupied area between the Spanish in modern Venezuela and the Portuguese in Brazil—and on the Amazon and Orinoco rivers. These settlements were failures, but they led to colonies in the West Indies. The Spanish had ignored the smaller islands, for they contained no gold, were densely wooded, and were inhabited by savage Carib tribes who had the unpleasant habit of eating Europeans. In 1624 Captain Thomas Warner, having failed on the mainland, made a settlement on the island of St. Christopher (St. Kitts), whence the English spread to nearby Nevis (1628) and to Antigua and Montserrat (1632). In 1627, a settlement was made on the beautiful island of Barbados from a ship belonging to Sir William Courteen, an English merchant.

A number of motives lay behind this wave of colonization. The first was economic, the desire for products unobtainable at home—the precious metals, naval stores, cotton, tobacco, sugar, and rare woods. There was also a social motive. England teemed with beggars, and it was thought that the country was overcrowded; hence the idea that colonies might drain off surplus population. Moreover, an English base in the New World was regarded as a great advantage in any future war with Spain. Propaganda in favor of colonization often spoke of the mission of converting the Indians, although, as a matter of fact, little was done in this direction; England did not become a missionary nation until the nineteenth century. And finally, colonial trade would help to build the merchant marine.

Another wave of expansion sprang from religious motives and produced the colonies in New England. Groups of Separatists emigrated to Holland in the early seventeenth century; in 1620 the Pilgrim Fathers crossed the Atlantic in the *Mayflower* and founded a colony at Plymouth. About ten years later a larger group of Puritan malcontents, led by men of more wealth and social standing than the Pilgrims, formed the Massachusetts Bay Company. They set-tled in the area of Boston and were soon the largest colony in North America, for Laud's persecution drove thousands across the Atlantic. Colonization in New England was not a normal phenomenon of overseas expansion. Rather, it was a secession of a part of the English race from the religion and government of the homeland. The Pilgrims felt a hostility toward England which became a part of the American tradition.

In 1631 a group of Puritan leaders in England, combining religious zeal with Elizabethan ideas of plunder, established a short-lived colony on Santa Catalina Island in the Caribbean. Renamed Providence Island, it lay directly in the path of Spanish commerce between the Isthmus of Panama and Havana; the colony was to form a model Puritan town and at the same time to prey upon Spanish shipping. It quickly degenerated into a center of buccaneering, frequented by most unpuritanical cutthroats, until the Spanish, in an unusual burst of energy, destroyed it in 1641 as an intolerable nuisance.

The Navigation Acts of 1650 and 1651

After the Commonwealth was established in 1649 its attention was focused on the West Indies, where strange things had been taking place. The early days of colonization on St. Kitts and Barbados had been very difficult. The islands were overcrowded, the plantations were small, the planters were quarrelsome and shiftless, and their thousands of miserable indentured servants raised crops of inferior tobacco and cotton. About 1640, at the suggestion of Dutch traders, the English began to cultivate sugar. The result was astonishing. Concentrating upon sugar, the West Indies sprang suddenly into wealth and importance. Small holdings were thrown together into large plantations, the landless whites were left to shift for themselves as best they could, and Negro slaves were imported to work the fields of sugar cane. From these changes the Dutch profited greatly. They extended credit to the planters, sold them slaves, and bought their sugar, taking it to Holland. The West Indies might be English colonies, but all the advantages were going to the Dutch. Moreover, at the end of the Civil Wars, many Royalists went to the islands. Barbados and Antigua, as well as Virginia and Maryland, recognized Charles II as King after the death of his father.

In 1650 Parliament passed an ordinance forbidding all trade with the colonies as long as they remained in rebellion. This was by way of punishment. But the ordinance also contained a clause prohibiting trade by foreign vessels with any English colonies at any time, a provision thereafter enforced. A naval expedition in 1651 reduced the colonies to submission, though some clandestine trade with the Dutch continued. There followed the famous Navigation Act of 1651, which was the basis of English trade for almost 200 years. It declared that products from Asia, Africa, and America could be brought to England or to her colonies only in English or colonial ships of which the master and a majority of the crew were English. Products from Europe, the ordinance continued, might come to England only in English ships or in the ships of the country producing the goods. Thus foreign traders were excluded from English colonies, colonial goods must come to England in English ships, and European goods must come either in English ships or in ships of the nation in which the goods were produced. The colonists might take their products to foreign ports if they could gain access, but the bulk of their trade would be with England; the carrying trade of the Dutch was thus dealt a heavy blow. The English Parliament was legislating for the empire as a whole and was drawing the mother country and the colonies closer together.

The First Dutch War, 1652–1654

The Navigation Act of 1651, the culmination of a long period of friction, brought war between England and Holland. "The English are about to attack a mountain of gold," groaned a Dutchman; "we a mountain of iron." The mountain of gold was the vast merchant marine of Holland. During the war it sailed in convoys protected by warships, for the Dutch had to continue their trade in order to live. The mountain of iron was the English battle fleet built by the Commonwealth. Its warships were large, solid, and heavily armed; its administration was excellent; its movements were directed by the state. Three of Cromwell's soldiers—Blake, Monck, and Deane—took to the sea and gave to the navy the martial spirit of the New Model Army. The fighting was hard, close, and deadly. Both fleets sailed in line ahead formation, but the lines were often broken, and battles developed into furious melees in which new techniques developed rapidly. At first the Dutch won some advantage, but a battle in June 1653 damaged their fleet and permitted the English to blockade their coast, halting commerce and ruining hundreds of Dutch merchants. After nine pitched battles in two years, both sides were glad to make peace in 1654. The Dutch accepted the Navigation Act of 1651, agreed to salute English ships in the Channel, and paid damages for injuries inflicted upon the English East India Company. The peace, however, was a truce, and Anglo-Dutch rivalry continued.

Cromwell's Western Design

Cromwell, the first English ruler systematically to employ his power to win new colonial possessions, conceived the idea of uniting English colonies in North America with those in the West Indies, at the same time extending English possessions in both areas to form a great dominion in the West. During the Dutch war he encouraged the colonists in New England to attack the Dutch "in the Manhattoes," and, when this project was ended by peace in Europe, to attack the French in Canada. The whole area from the Penobscot River in modern Maine to the mouth of the St. Lawrence fell into English hands, though it was restored to France in 1668. When the Dutch war was over, Cromwell turned to the Spanish West Indies. Friction between Spanish and English colonists justified an attack; and Cromwell, with his Elizabethan ideas, believed he could capture the Spanish islands without causing a war in Europe. He was encouraged by some of his advisers—especially by Thomas Gage, a renegade friar who had lived for many years in Guatemala—to underestimate the difficulties of the enterprise.

In 1655 Cromwell sent an expedition against the Spanish Islands, but it was not prepared with his usual care. The sailors were of good quality, but the troops consisted of men rejected by the army in England or pressed from the London slums; 3000 recruits picked up in Barbados were human derelicts, "the most profane debauched persons that we ever saw." It is small wonder that an assault on Santo Domingo was a total failure. The commanders of the expedition, Admiral Penn (whose son was the founder of Pennsylvania) and General Venables, fearing the wrath of Cromwell, determined to attack Jamaica, which was weakly held by a few hundred Spanish planters. The English army, some 10,000 strong, gallantly captured this island. Cromwell was deeply chagrined, the more so because he found himself at war with Spain in Europe, but he determined to retain Jamaica, which became in time an important sugar island.

His grandiose dream of a western dominion faded away, but it was the beginning of England's age-long effort to build an empire overseas.

The English East India Company

The English East India Company, as we have seen, had made an excellent beginning. Its first voyage under James Lancaster had obtained the right to buy pepper at Achin in Sumatra and at Bantam in Java and to establish a trading post at the latter port. The second voyage, commanded by Henry Middleton, had sailed east of Java to the smaller Spice Islands and had traded in Ceram and Amboina, in the Banda Islands, and in Ternate and Tidore. But Middleton experienced great difficulties with the Dutch, who were steadily increasing their hold upon this area. Their policy was one of open hostility to the English, hostility which reached a climax in a massacre on Amboina in 1623 when eighteen English merchants were seized and tortured, ten of them murdered. It was this deed that brought home to England the true meaning of Dutch commercial rivalry. After 1623 the English abandoned the smaller islands, though they continued to trade at Achin and Bantam.

Even before the friction with the Dutch had become so acute, the English had begun to turn to India. Here the Portuguese were established along the western coast, though their hold was weak. In 1612 Captain Best, after driving away a Portuguese fleet, secured from the local Mogul Governor the right to establish a factory at Surat. In 1622 the English drove the Portuguese from Ormuz at the mouth of the Persian Gulf and obtained a factory there. In 1635 a treaty was made with the Portuguese by which the English were permitted to trade in Portuguese ports. Surat remained the principal English trading area until Bombay was secured in the reign of Charles II. On the eastern coast of India the English established themselves first at Masulipatam in 1611 and later at Madras in 1639. It was not until later in the century that a firm foothold was secured in the area of Bengal. The English brought home muslins and other cotton fabrics, saltpeter, and indigo (a blue dye).

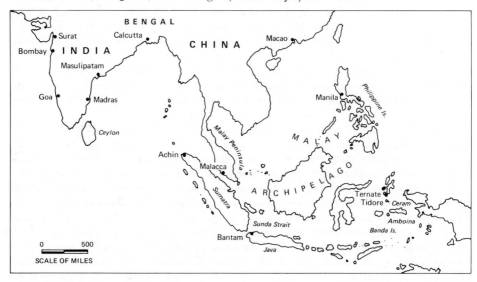

India and the East Indies in the Seventeenth Century

In the East the company was making headway, but difficulties arose at home. The company's system of bookkeeping was cumbersome, for each voyage was handled as a separate venture. It was accused of taking coin out of England and bringing back luxuries. Parliament was hostile because the company was a monopoly. Worst of all, it could not rely on the King, from whom it held its charter. Both James and Charles permitted interlopers to go to India, where they acted more like pirates than merchants, doing the company great harm. The company also suffered from the dislocations of the Civil Wars; for a time it ceased to trade as a corporation, though it licensed private merchants to trade as individuals. Cromwell restored the fortunes of the company and set it trading once more with a new charter in 1657.

ECONOMIC CHANGE

Historians now regard the two decades between 1640 and 1660 as highly important in the economic history of England. It was during this time that the capitalist classes—agricultural, industrial, and commercial alike—freed themselves from the control over economic life formerly exercised by the Crown. "The fall of the absolute monarchy was the turning point in the evolution of capitalism." Henceforth wealthy people were at liberty to do as they pleased with their property and to manage their affairs for their own economic advantage.

A tremendous amount of land was bought and sold during this period. The government sold quantities of Crown lands—so that there was little left by 1660 —and also much property belonging to the Church of England. Estates of well-to-do Royalists were sequestered and could be recovered only by the payment of heavy fines, while other estates were confiscated and sold. Moreover, many Royalists, under pressures of all kinds, sold their lands privately. These men, after the Restoration of 1660, could usually recover confiscated estates through legal action; but for lands sold privately there was no redress. Yet the majority of Royalists survived. Much land was purchased during this period by men who had made money in trade or were connected in some way with the government. Thus the landowners after 1660 were both Cavaliers and Roundheads.

The emancipation of the landed classes may be said to have taken place in three distinct phases. In the first place, there was obvious freedom from the restrictions and burdens imposed by the government of Charles I. Indeed, the government now did everything it could to encourage agricultural productivity. Opposition to enclosing disappeared; acts were passed for the draining of the fens; improved farming methods, such as the use of clover in a better rotation of crops, were supported by the government, which also felt a new responsibility for transportation and for a postal service. In the second place, the landowning classes profited enormously from the abolition of feudal or military tenure and an end to the court of wards. Feudal tenure was now converted into freehold or common socage. So great was the desire of landowners for this relief that feudal tenure was abolished thrice over, in 1646, in 1656, and in 1660. The change has been called "possibly the most important single event in the history of English landholding." It deprived the Crown of a vital means of controlling the upper classes and it gave landowners the absolute right to do as they pleased with their estates. Knowing that their titles were secure, they were much more inclined to invest money in long-term improvements. Finally, the landed classes were able to defeat efforts by the Levelers and by other radical groups to obtain permanent rights in the land for copyholders and small tenants. Indeed, the man who bought land as an investment and the Royalist who recovered his estates after a costly struggle were apt to regard the poor with little sympathy. The temporary assertiveness of the lower classes was something to be suppressed. Hence the new developments in agriculture, although they caused productivity to leap forward, brought small benefit to the poor. There was a grave problem of rural poverty at the end of the century.

A similar story may be told of industry. The government no longer attempted to regulate prices or wages or hours and conditions of labor, or to supervise the quality of workmanship. Industrial monopolies came to an end; economic favors were no longer available to parasitic courtiers. Employers were free to conduct business enterprises along economic lines. Moreover, the common law courts, which protected the rights of the individual, were now supreme. As to the merchants, we have seen that the state was willing to use diplomacy, and even armed force, to advance their interests in overseas expansion.[4]

THE END OF THE PROTECTORATE

After Cromwell's death the Protectorate crumbled, and events moved quickly to the restoration of the Stuarts. Richard, Oliver's son, lacked the character and experience to remain in power. His first move was correct, for he refused a demand of the army to be allowed to select its own commander in chief. In January 1659 he summoned a Parliament which on the whole was ready to support him; but under pressure from the army he dissolved it in April. This action ended his short rule as Protector. The army, left in control, recalled the Long Parliament, quarreled with it, and dismissed it. But army opinion was divided; at this point General Monck, the commander in Scotland, determined that the nation, not the army, should decide what it wished to do. Monck marched down from Scotland, outwitted the army leaders in London, recalled the Long Parliament once again, obtained a majority by adding the Presbyterian members expelled in 1648, and forced it to dissolve itself and to issue writs for a free Parliament elected under the old historic franchise. This Parliament met in April 1660 and invited Charles II to return to England. He required little urging.

[4] Christopher Hill, *The Century of Revolution 1603–1714* (Edinburgh: T. Nelson, 1966), pp. 145–161.

19

restoration
and revolution

THE RESTORATION

The Restoration of 1660 was a rejection of the constitutional experiments of the Puritans and a return to the ancient form of government by King, Lords, and Commons. But neither kingship nor Parliament was what it had been before the Civil Wars. The Crown had lost many powers. Charles II and his minister, Edward Hyde, Earl of Clarendon, wisely retained the early legislation of the Long Parliament which had been accepted by Charles I. This meant that many of the old devices for raising money and for exalting the prerogative were now gone. The King was left entirely dependent upon Parliament for money; the prerogative courts disappeared. The Crown, however, retained control of the executive branch of government. Charles II appointed his ministers, bishops, and judges. He directed foreign affairs, controlled the army and navy, and supervised the daily administration and the expenditure of funds. He summoned and dissolved Parliament. A new Triennial Act in 1664 declared that there ought to be a session of Parliament every three years but provided no machinery to make a session obligatory. Charles retained the veto and an undefined prerogative of suspending and dispensing with statutes in times of emergency.

Parliament in 1660, however, was in a far stronger position than it had held before the Civil Wars. Neither Parliament nor the King could forget that for twenty years the Commons had controlled administration, had raised armies, had built a navy, had fought wars, had eliminated monarchy and the House of Lords, had declared itself the supreme power in the state, and, above all, had brought a King to the block. Parliament after 1660 possessed an indisputable sovereignty in taxation and legislation; moreover, its competence had become all-embracing. There was no sphere in which it could not act. It assumed at once the right to arrange a settlement of the church. Parliamentary privilege was now sacred; older methods of royal influence, such as the control of the Speaker, became impossible. Charles met a storm of protest when he attempted to create a new parliamentary borough. The Commons audited his accounts

Charles II, a copy after Lely. (National Portrait Gallery, London)

and impeached his ministers. Thus Parliament entered upon the heritage of the Puritan revolution. The great problem of the future was to devise a means by which the Commons could control the executive without precipitating a crisis over every detail.

Charles II

When Charles II landed at Dover in May 1660 and made his way through shouting throngs to London, the kingdom was wild with joy. Maidens strewed flowers in his path, loyal healths were drunk in endless numbers, may-poles were set up again, and Cromwell's corpse was exhumed from Westminster

Abbey and hanged at Tyburn. England was England once more. The people had a King. They knew what they wanted—but they did not know what they were getting.

Charles II, born in May 1630 (the planet Venus being in the ascendant), was a dark and ugly baby and became a dark and ugly man. He was tall and athletic and always enjoyed excellent health. His education was interrupted by the Civil War. As a youth he knocked about on the Continent, in poverty, idleness, hopelessness, and debauchery. He grew up to be lazy and irresolute, prone to follow the course of least resistance, untrustworthy, ungrateful, and irreligious. Having few principles of any kind, he saw virtue only in dissimulation and compromise; he believed that every man and woman could be bought at a price. Because he was kept very short of money by Parliament, he used his control of foreign affairs to obtain subsidies from the King of France for which he was ready to betray the religion of his country. His sympathies were French and Roman Catholic. Confident that God would not damn a man for a little pleasure, he drank heavily and kept a harem of mistresses. Whitehall became a licentious and wicked place. Charles's good qualities should not be forgotten. He made no pretense at being anything but what he was. Witty, charming, and amusing, he possessed a keen intelligence and was a good judge of character. He could be affable and familiar with his subordinates without a loss of dignity. He was loyal to his family. He was interested in commerce, he loved the sea and the navy, he dabbled in chemistry, and he was a patron of science. Wishing to go his own way and to let others go theirs, he was ready for a policy of religious toleration. Yet his dark dealings with France and his sympathy with a religion hated by his people introduced into political life an explosive violence which poisoned the atmosphere at Westminster.

The Convention Parliament

While Charles was still on the Continent he had issued the Declaration of Breda, in which he promised to abide by Parliament's decision on the principal issues requiring immediate settlement. The Convention Parliament, which sat until December 1660, took action on three of these issues. An act of indemnity pardoned all those who had fought against Charles I or had taken part in the governments of the interregnum, except for some fifty persons whom the act listed by name. Of these, thirteen were executed, twelve being regicides; the thirteenth, Sir Henry Vane, was considered too dangerous to live. In an age as cruel as the seventeenth century, these thirteen lives were but a mild revenge for a Civil War and the death of a King.

Closely connected with indemnity was the question of a land settlement. Any solution was certain to cause injustice and bitterness. It was decided that Royalists whose estates had been confiscated by the Puritans should be allowed to recover their lands through the courts, but that those who had sold their estates should receive no compensation. This decision was important for the pattern of landownership in the following century. It meant that many Puritans who had purchased estates during the interregnum were able to retain them after 1660. The future landowners of the kingdom were to be the descendants of Roundheads as well as of Cavaliers. The great families who had sided with Charles I were more successful in recovering their former property than were the smaller Royalists; and these great families often added to their holdings after 1660 by purchases from Royalists who were in need. There was thus a tendency for more and more land to accumulate in a few hands. The large landowners turned against James II in 1688 and often profited from the revolution in that year. Hence there emerged two classes that will become familiar in the eighteenth century: the great Whig magnate owning vast estates, and the small Tory squire, sullen, resentful, and dissatisfied.

The Convention Parliament had also to provide the King with money. The system of taxation and of government finance was antiquated, but there was no time for reform. Money was required at once to pay off the army, and hence Parliament quickly raised the necessary funds by levying direct assessments upon local areas. To meet the ordinary expenses of government, it granted to Charles II the customs duties and an excise on beer, ale, tea, and coffee. This revenue was expected to amount to £1,200,000 a year, but unfortunately it never reached that amount. In return for this grant Charles surrendered the right to wardship and to other survivals of the age of feudalism. Feudal tenures were abolished; the great landowners now held their estates in common socage. They benefited greatly from the change, for they were relieved of heavy payments and became more independent of the Crown.

The Clarendon Code

There remained the question of a religious settlement—a most difficult question, for the country was thoroughly divided. Of England's 9000 parish churches, some 2000 were held by Presbyterian clergymen and perhaps 400 by Independents. There was also a large number of sectaries, comprising perhaps a tenth of the population, who went their own way, as did the Quakers, in various forms of unregulated religious life. But the Anglican clergymen, who now returned from exile or emerged from hiding, naturally expected to be restored to their former livings. So long as the Convention Parliament remained in session there was a possibility of compromise. This Parliament contained many Presbyterians who hoped that their opinions would carry weight and who were willing to accept bishops associated in some way with synods. The King was ready for toleration, and Clarendon was disposed to be moderate. A few Presbyterians were offered preferment in the church, but the moment of possible compromise quickly passed. A conference between Anglican and Presbyterian leaders broke down completely and Anglican bigotry hardened against all nonconformists. The Cavalier Parliament, elected early in 1661, contained a majority of Royalist Anglicans determined to restore the church as it had been before the Civil Wars, to drive out the Puritans, and to exclude them from political life.

Hating and fearing all forms of nonconformity, the Cavaliers passed a number of acts known collectively as the Clarendon Code, though Clarendon was only partially responsible for them. The Corporation Act of 1661 excluded from the governing bodies of the towns all persons who refused to swear to the unlawfulness of resistance to the King and who declined to receive the Communion according to the rites of the Church of England. The Act of Uniformity in 1662 issued a new Prayer Book and provided that clergymen must either accept it or resign their livings. Some 1200 clergymen refused, vacating their churches. Their number is an indication of the strength of nonconformity. The Conventicle Act of 1664 imposed harsh penalties on those who attended religious services in which the forms of the Anglican church were not used. A number of events gave rise to this drastic measure. A rising in London by a Quaker fanatic,

Edward, Earl of Clarendon. (From Edward, Earl of Clarendon, *The History of the Rebellion and Civil Wars in England*, Oxford, 1702. Department of Special Collections, Walter Library, University of Minnesota)

Thomas Venner, resulted in the Quakers' Act, which prohibited their meetings. The government was afraid that conspiracies might be plotted in nonconformist gatherings. And an attempt by the King to modify the Act of Uniformity by dispensing with it in individual cases was stopped. An ever harsher Conventicle Act became law in 1670. In 1665 the Five Mile Act prohibited clergymen from coming within five miles of a parish from which they had been ejected. A licensing act permitted the archbishop of Canterbury and the bishop of London to control the press and the printing of books.

The Clarendon Code brought about great social changes. It divided religious life in England into two parts: the church and nonconformity. The church, purged of Puritans and fanatics, was to hold the position of power: it regained its church buildings and other property, it could levy tithes, it controlled education on all levels. Nonconformists were excluded from the universities, from many professions, from municipal government, from all offices under the Crown (by the Test Act of 1673), and from membership in the House of Commons. A social stigma became attached to nonconformity. Persons outside the church were considered fanatic, ignorant, and low class. Indeed, in the eighteenth century the church was sometimes spoken of as though it were synonymous with Christianity.

These disabilities undoubtedly weakened the nonconformists greatly. Men of ambition, finding the sacrifices too heavy, moved into the church; and in the eighteenth century there were few persons of importance who were not Anglicans. Nonconformity, on the other hand, was now lawful. The Tudor doctrine that everyone must belong to the state church was abandoned. Nonconformity was strong enough to remain a permanent element in English life. It had struck deep roots among the lower middle classes, among shopkeepers, artisans, and small farmers. Deprived of many of the opportunities of their fellow citizens, nonconformists entered trade and business. Their industry, thrift, and sobriety brought them material success: they became merchants, bankers, and manufacturers. They were strengthened by the rise of Methodism in the eighteenth century. And as they gradually emerged from their disabilities, they formed a group apart, with a culture and a morality of their own.

THE FALL OF CLARENDON

For seven years the Earl of Clarendon remained Charles's principal minister. His position seemed secure, not only because of his great services during the interregnum but because his daughter Anne Hyde had become first the mistress and then the wife of James, Duke of York, the heir presumptive to the throne. But although Clarendon possessed ability and noble character, he was proud, austere, and rigid. He returned to England in 1660 to find himself old-fashioned and out of touch with the times. He was hated by the buffoons and loose women around the King, whom he irritated by lectures on morality. He was suspicious of Parliament, to which he assigned a subordinate role it resented. With many enemies, he was apt to be blamed when anything went wrong. He fell from power in 1667, largely because of mischances in foreign affairs for which he was only partially responsible.

The first was the choice of a Portuguese princess, Catherine of Braganza, as Charles's wife. Portugal, having been subject to Spain from 1580 to 1640, was struggling in 1660 to maintain a precarious independence. She offered England generous terms for a marriage alliance. The dowry was to be £800,000 in cash, along with the town of Bombay in India and the fortress of Tangier in North Africa near Gibraltar. The English, moreover, were to be permitted to trade throughout her empire. The marriage was pleasing to France, for Louis XIV welcomed an alliance that weakened Spain. The Dutch, however, were furious: they wanted the Portuguese empire for themselves. The marriage alliance was accepted in London, but the results proved disappointing. The short and dumpy figure of the bride, her prominent teeth, and her stolid manner contrasted sadly with the allurements of Lady Castlemaine, that voluptuous goddess who presided at Charles's court. Moreover, Catherine was childless. Bombay was a fever-ridden and profitless possession in 1661, though it became valuable later. Tangier's value as a Mediterranean base was not appreciated, and because it proved very costly Tangier was abandoned in 1683. Portugal appeared to have had the better of the bargain, for she gained a strong ally.

In 1662 Charles sold Dunkirk to the French. The cost of its garrison was heavy and it was difficult to defend from an attack by land. Dunkirk, conquered from Spain by Cromwell's redcoats, was highly prized in England; hence its sale was most unpopular. To England's great cost it was to be used later by Louis XIV as a base for privateering.

Then came a second naval war with Holland (1665–1667), which has been called the clearest case in English history of a purely commercial war. Rivalry between the two countries was again at fever pitch; even before war was declared, there had been fighting over slaving stations in West Africa, and an English squadron had seized the New Netherlands in America. This war, like the first, was a war of fierce naval engagements between large and powerful fleets. It was fought for the most part in the seas between Britain and the Continent. By 1666 both sides were feeling the strain. The Dutch, having raised enormous loans, were at the end of their financial resources; England had suffered two calamities which for the moment quelled her fighting spirit.

In the spring of 1665 the plague appeared in London, killing some 68,000 persons before it subsided late in 1666. Everyone fled London who could, leaving a desert of closed houses, of houses with a red cross painted on the door which meant that the plague was within, of panic and misery which paralyzed economic life. This was the final visitation of the bubonic plague, endemic in England since the fourteenth century and carried by the fleas on black rats; one explanation for its failure to return is that black rats were then driven out by brown. In September 1666 occurred the Great Fire of London. The summer had been very dry. Starting accidentally near London Bridge and driven by a high wind, the fire swept through the old city and destroyed the greater part of it. The people, more intent on flight and on saving their household goods than on putting out the flames, fled through the suburbs to the countryside beyond. The fire lasted four days, destroying some 13,000 houses, 84 churches including St. Paul's, and many public buildings, none of them covered by insurance. The people stumbled back over hot ashes to begin building London anew. The new houses were usually made of brick instead of wood and plaster.

Bankrupt and without allies, England now sought peace. Negotiations began, and much of the fleet was laid up. But the war was not over, and the Dutch determined upon a daring exploit. Following a carefully laid plan, they sailed up the estuary of the Thames and attacked the dockyards at Chatham. Fire

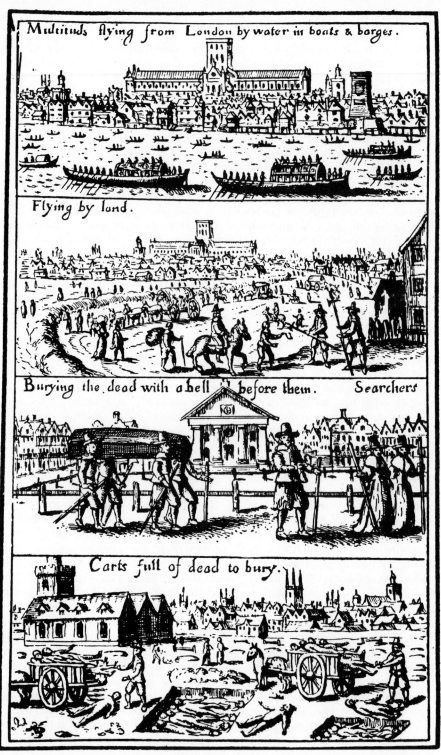

Seventeenth-century woodcut narrating aspects of the plague in London, 1665–1666. (World Health Organization)

ships destroyed many English vessels, and the Dutch guns could be heard in London. The bold Hollanders towed away as prize the *Royal Charles,* the flagship of the English fleet. Peace was made at Breda in July 1667. The English retained New York and New Jersey; the Dutch, most of the places in dispute along the African Coast and in the East Indies. The Navigation Act was modified slightly in Holland's favor, and the English flag need be saluted only in the Channel. The war had been far from glorious. Clarendon, as so often, received the blame. Yielding to his minister's enemies, Charles dismissed him from office. Clarendon then was impeached by the Commons, fled abroad, and spent his exile in writing his famous *History of the Great Rebellion.* There were some who pushed responsibility for recent disasters closer to the King. "It is strange," wrote a contemporary, "how everybody do now reflect upon Oliver, and commend him, what brave things he did, and made all the neighbor princes fear him; while here a prince, come in with all the love and prayers and good liking of his people . . . hath lost all so soon that it is a miracle what way a man could devise to lose so much in so little time."

THE CABAL AND THE SECRET TREATY OF DOVER

For some time after the fall of Clarendon there was no chief minister. Charles attempted a more personal rule and a more personal direction of foreign policy. Five of his ministers, whose names began with letters which formed the word "cabal," were of more importance than the rest. One was Sir Thomas Clifford, later Lord Treasurer. His patron, Lord Arlington, principal Secretary of State, was an experienced and industrious diplomat whose policy in general was anti-French. Both men died Roman Catholics. A third member of the Cabal, George Villiers, second Duke of Buckingham, the son of the favorite of James I, was a despicable person, said to be "without principles either of religion, virtue, or friendship," and stupid to boot. He later drifted into opposition. Lord Ashley, afterward Earl of Shaftesbury, was more important. A man of great courage and resourcefulness, though given to violent action, he was a strong Protestant and an opponent of arbitrary government. Like Buckingham, he was to turn against the Crown. The last of the five, Lauderdale, advised the King on Scottish affairs.

European politics in the second half of the seventeenth century centered upon two great facts: the decay of Spain and the aggressiveness of Louis XIV. Spain's sun had set in 1659 at the conclusion of a long war with France. With the death of the Spanish King Philip IV in 1665 and the accession of his sickly and half-witted son, Charles II, the Spanish empire seemed ready for dismemberment. It was still a splendid empire, including large portions of Italy and scattered footholds throughout the Mediterranean, the Spanish Netherlands, Mexico, Central and South America except Brazil, most of the larger West Indian islands, the Philippines, Morocco, and the Canary Islands. Louis XIV cast a covetous eye on these valuable territories. He had married a Spanish princess, Maria Theresa, a daughter of Philip IV; and in 1667 he put forward a claim to the Spanish Netherlands based in part on the nonpayment of his wife's dowry and in part on the law of "devolution" which governed the inheritance of property in the Netherlands. Attacking this area forthwith, he was soon in possession of a number of fortresses within Spanish territory.

Charles's diplomacy during these years was unsettled, with many shifts and little purpose. His basic principle was friendship with France. Louis was the grand monarch of Europe, wealthy, powerful, magnificent, the symbol of absolutism and Catholicism, the model of etiquette and manners, the observed of all observers, with rich merchants, splendid diplomats, and superb armies. Charles regarded him with envy, with admiration, and with the hope of obtaining money, but his first move was to form a Triple Alliance with Holland and Sweden in 1668 to prevent Louis from absorbing the whole of the Spanish Netherlands and also, perhaps, to raise the price of English friendship. Meanwhile Louis made a secret treaty with Emperor Leopold of Austria for the division of the Spanish empire if the Spanish King died while still young, as everybody assumed he would. Hoping for greater things to come, Louis called off the war in the Netherlands in 1668; the Triple Alliance had little to do with his decision.

Louis was angry with the Dutch. They had dared to oppose his ambitions, they were France's commerical rivals, they must not be in a position to cause trouble when the Spanish empire was divided. To isolate the Dutch, Louis sought an agreement with England. The result was the Treaty of Dover in 1670. Charles's motives in making this treaty are still debatable. Perhaps he was misled by his need for money or by his love for his sister Henrietta, who had married the brother of the French King. At any rate, the treaty was a shameful one. In it Charles declared that he was convinced of the truth of the Catholic religion and that he would announce his conversion when his affairs permitted. He had every reason to believe, the treaty stated, that his people would accept his decision, but, if they did not, Louis agreed to provide 6000 French troops to assist in its enforcement. Meanwhile, as a token of friendship, Louis was to send Charles £166,000. (By later agreements during the next eight years Charles obtained additional subsidies. He received in all some £742,000.) The treaty also provided that England and France join in a war against the Dutch and that the English might annex certain parts of Holland, which, however, they must conquer for themselves. A public treaty contained the clauses concerning the Dutch war; the other clauses remained secret.[1] Just before the war began in 1672, Charles issued a sweeping Declaration of Indulgence by which he suspended the penal laws against both Catholics and nonconformists.

Parliament met in an unpleasant mood in January 1673, deeply suspicious of the King. The Commons did not know the secret terms of the Treaty of Dover, but they made some shrewd guesses. "The public articles are ill enough," said a member. "What are then the private articles?" The war with Holland began abruptly with no immediate cause. The Commons were anti-Catholic and anti-French. Commercial rivalry with Holland was beginning to abate, and there was a dawning realization that France, not Holland, was the great enemy.

The Declaration of Indulgence was a bold use of the suspending power. A new apprehension was appearing—the dread of arbitrary government at home. Popery, France, and despotic power were emerging as the things to be feared. The Commons voted money for the Dutch war, but not until Charles withdrew the Declaration of Indulgence. Parliament then passed the Test Act, which prohibited anyone from holding office under the Crown, either civil or

---

[1] G. N. Clark, *The Later Stuarts* (Oxford: Clarendon Press, 1956), pp. 72–75.

military, until he had taken the Anglican Sacrament and had made a declaration against transubstantiation which no Roman Catholic would accept. All Catholic officials, including the Duke of York, were driven from office.

The war did not go well. It differed from the first two wars because the Dutch, regarding France as their principal enemy, stood on the defensive at sea. One large naval battle, off the Texel in 1673, demonstrated that the English could not hope to invade Holland and that they must lift their blockade of the Dutch coast. Parliament was so insistent that Charles withdraw from the war that he did so in 1674. He had gained nothing from his crafty dealings: his Declaration of Indulgence had failed, and the Dutch war had sacrificed men and money to little purpose. Ashley and Buckingham were soon to join the opposition. Thus the year 1674 may be taken as a dividing date in the reign. Charles's attempt at personal government had broken down, leaving a legacy of fear and confusion.

DANBY, POLITICAL PARTIES, AND LOUIS XIV

The Cabal broke up after the third Dutch war. Charles's principal minister from 1674 to 1678 was the Lord Treasurer, Thomas Osborne, soon to be Earl of Danby, a robust and vigorous man with a policy of his own. Pro-Dutch, anti-French, and anti-Catholic, he hoped, on the one hand, to draw Charles away from his unpopular policies and, on the other, to rekindle in the Commons their former loyalty to the Crown. He offered Parliament strong support of the Church of England and sound administration of public finance.

Danby paid great attention to the management of the Commons. The Commons were divided, as they had been in the first part of the century, into a Court party, which normally supported the King, and a Country party, which normally opposed him. These groups now were organized into political parties, though they lacked the discipline and clear-cut division of parties today. Danby cultivated the members of the Court party, not only by offering them policies which he hoped they would like, but by judicious distribution of offices, pensions, and even payment in cash. His efforts called forth a corresponding organization of the opposition. This was the work of Shaftesbury, who drew the Country party together, established a party headquarters in London known as the Green Ribbon Club, and gradually developed an organization throughout the kingdom. He was in close contact with the political thinker John Locke,[2] whose theories of limited monarchy were to exert great influence. Later in the reign the terms "Whig" and "Tory" came into use. The Tories, led by Danby, supported the church and the prerogatives of the Crown. The Whigs, following Shaftesbury, stood for limitation of royal power and for increased toleration for Protestants though not for Catholics.

Thus Danby organized the Court party but failed to conciliate Parliament as a whole. The Commons were tense and nervous. Their nervousness was increased by the policy of Charles and Louis as well as by a panic that resulted from a supposed Popish Plot.

After 1674 England was officially neutral in the war between Holland and France, which continued until 1678. Louis had found the war unexpectedly

[2] See page 422.

difficult, for the Dutch had discovered a leader in their young Stadtholder, William III, who succeeded in building a coalition of powers against France. Both sides sought English support. The Dutch won favor in the House of Commons, whereas Louis succeeded with the King, who continued to make secret agreements in return for French money. In 1675 Charles promised that if Parliament offered him subsidies for a war against France he would refuse them. Later he agreed not to make treaties with continental states without Louis' consent; at one point he promised not to summon Parliament for a certain length of time. The Commons became more and more anti-French. In 1677–1678 Charles was induced to take a step away from France by consenting to a marriage between Mary, the elder daughter of James, Duke of York, and William III. By the Treaty of Nimwegen in 1678 Louis made peace with the Dutch, who lost no territory in Europe, but, battered and broken, ceased to be a great power.

THE POPISH PLOT

The English, who by now had been living for years in an atmosphere of tension, were thrown into panic in 1678 by the false disclosures of two informers, Titus Oates and Israel Tonge. Oates was a rascal whose vices had caused him to be ejected from school, from an Anglican living, and from a Jesuit seminary. Coming forward with astonishing effrontery, he declared that he knew of a Jesuit plot to assassinate the King and to place James, his Catholic brother, on the throne. This central lie was surrounded by many lesser ones and by accusations against innocent persons. Oates had stumbled on a few facts which gave a superficial appearance of truth to his stories. It was discovered that a group of Jesuits had held a secret meeting in London and that Edward Coleman, a secretary of James's second wife, Mary of Modena, had been in dangerous correspondence with Catholics in France. Israel Tonge, the other informer, was a half-crazed clergyman, a D.D. from Oxford, who probably believed he was telling the truth.

He and Oates had first made their revelations before a London justice of the peace, Sir Edmund Berry Godfrey, who, disappearing suddenly, was found dead with a sword thrust through his back. His death is a mystery, but it was followed by a furious wave of false accusations against Catholics. Many were put to death, even though persons in authority, including the King, were convinced of their innocence. For almost two years the panic continued, Oates living like a king, with no one daring to contradict his lies. The Commons listened gravely to evidence brought before them by ratcatchers, they impeached Catholic peers, and they passed a bill strengthening the terms of the Test Act. They turned on Danby, who, at Charles's command, had written one of the King's letters to Louis. Shaftesbury wildly accused the Queen of treason. To save his minister from impeachment, to save his Queen, and perhaps even to save the powers of the Crown, Charles dissolved the Cavalier Parliament in January 1679.

THE EXCLUSION STRUGGLE

The Catholic episode gave a new turn to English politics. Led by Shaftesbury, the Whigs embarked on a campaign to exclude the Catholic Duke of York from the succession to the throne. This policy first appeared in Charles's second Parliament, elected in February of 1679, a violent Parliament in which the opposition was in full control of the Commons. It imprisoned Danby, brushed aside a compromise advanced by Charles to limit his brother's powers as King, and introduced a bill excluding James from the throne. Charles's answer was to send his brother into temporary exile and to prorogue Parliament, which he dissolved in the summer.

The question of exclusion continued to be the storm center of politics, but Shaftesbury and other Whigs encountered difficulty in selecting a candidate to take James's place. The most obvious choice was Mary, James's elder daughter, a Protestant who had married William III. But the time had not yet come when England would accept a Dutchman as King, and Shaftesbury was anti-Dutch. He made the error of championing Charles's illegitimate son, James Scott, Duke of Monmouth, whose mother, Lucy Walter, had been a mistress of the King during his exile. Monmouth was a soldier, quite romantic in his way, but brainless, vain, and irresponsible. The story was put about that Charles had married Lucy Walter, but the King, although he was fond of Monmouth, never spoke of him as legitimate. The Whigs were divided; some favored the succession of James with limited powers, some favored Monmouth, some Mary, some a republic. Charles called two more Parliaments, in 1680 and in 1681. The first introduced another exclusion bill which was stopped in the Lords. The second was a wild affair to which the Whigs came armed as though to begin an insurrection. The members from London had the motto "No Popery, No Slavery" woven into their hats. This Parliament lasted for only one week and was the last to be summoned by Charles II.

Royalist Reaction

The violence of the Whigs, which appeared to be leading the nation into another civil war, caused a reaction in favor of both the King and the Duke of York. Charles regained much of his early popularity. Emboldened by the support of the Tories, he ventured to arrest Shaftesbury for treason, though Shaftesbury was acquitted by a London jury. Thereupon Charles secured the appointment of Tory sheriffs who could be trusted to pack the juries of the capital. He also challenged the London charter. The charters of many other towns were examined and remodeled so as to exclude Whigs from the municipal corporations.

At first the Whigs turned from opposition to conspiracy. Some of the Whig leaders—Shaftesbury, Lord Russell, the Earl of Essex, and Algernon Sidney—held secret meetings in which they talked of revolt, although their plans never reached a very advanced state. Meanwhile Monmouth was plotting in an irresponsible way with more questionable characters, and a plot known as the Rye House Plot was devised to assassinate the King and his brother. When this was betrayed to the government, the Whig leaders, whether they were connected with it or not, knew that their cause was lost. Shaftesbury fled to the Continent, followed by Monmouth. Essex committed suicide. Russell and Sidney were convicted, not for a part in the Rye House Plot, but for their opinion that resistance to the King was lawful. Both were executed, though they were men of character and principle. Meanwhile the Tories rallied about James, displaying an extraordinary loyalty to him and proclaiming the doctrines of divine right and of nonresistance. It was their practice to fall upon their knees and drink his health as they shouted a loud "Huzzah!" They assumed that he would be a Tory

King who would keep the Whigs under control, would uphold the Church of England, and would regard his Catholicism as a private affair.

In February 1685 King Charles suffered a sudden stroke and died within a few days. As the King was dying, a Catholic priest who had helped him to escape from Cromwell's forces after the Battle of Worcester was admitted to his bedchamber and received him into the Roman Church.

JAMES II, 1685–1688

King James II was fifty-one when he ascended the throne. As a young man he had served in the armies of France and Spain and was accounted a good officer. In Charles's reign he had become Lord Admiral, had been a successful naval administrator, and had seen action as the commander of an English fleet against the Dutch. But as King he was impossible—dull, obstinate, rigid, brusque, suspicious, blind to public opinion, determined to have his way whatever the consequences. It is possible that he suffered a mental decline about the time he secured the throne. His soldiering left him with an inflated confidence in military power and with a callousness toward human suffering. He practiced his Catholicism openly, and should at least be given credit for his honesty, but he was bigoted in religion and was determined to force Catholicism on England. For this object he was quite ready to play the tyrant, brushing law and custom aside. In less than four years he drove his people to revolution and lost his throne.

He began his reign in a strong position. The Whigs were crushed, the Tories blindly loyal. Tory town corporations could be trusted to return Tory members to the House of Commons. Thus fortified, James summoned Parliament in May 1685. It was a packed assembly, strongly Tory. The King promised "to preserve the government in Church and State as it is now by law established," and demanded money. The Commons obligingly granted him the customs for life, so that he had an ample revenue; the Revolution, when it came, was not caused by quarrels over finance.

Meanwhile an event took place which appeared to add to his power. This was a rebellion in the southwest of England led by the Duke of Monmouth. Fleeing from England in the last years of Charles's reign, Monmouth traveled to Holland, where William III advised him politely to go and fight the Turks. Instead, he obtained a ship and some ammunition in Amsterdam and landed at Lyme Regis in Dorset in June 1685. Here he proclaimed himself the rightful King. The gentry did not join him, but some 6000 of the peasants, armed chiefly with scythes and other farming implements, flocked to his standard. The area was a clothmaking district in which much poverty and unemployment existed. There was not the slightest hope of success. The local militia retreated at first but soon was stiffened by regular troops, and at the night Battle of Sedgemoor Monmouth's men blundered into an impassable ditch, where they were slaughtered without mercy. This pathetic rising, the last peasants' revolt in England, was savagely punished. Some 300 peasants were executed and some 800 more were sold as slaves in the West Indies. The country was shocked by the butchery of these poor simple folk. Moreover, James used the rebellion as an excuse to increase the size of the army.

In November James summoned Parliament into its second and final session. He demanded a large sum of money for the support of the army, which contained many Roman Catholic officers who had not complied with the requirements of the Test Act. The Commons, pointing to these officers, offered a considerable grant if the Test Act were enforced. But the King declined, and Parliament was prorogued after a session of about ten days. It never met again in James's reign. The King in effect had asked the Commons to repeal or modify the Test Act, and the Commons had refused to do so.

These developments startled the Tories, who had made themselves champions of hereditary succession and nonresistance. But they were also champions of the Church of England and of a constitution which might allow the King high prerogatives but debarred him from despotic power. They regarded the Test Act as the bulwark of Anglican supremacy; moreover, they loathed the thought of rule by the sword, for they had suffered more from Cromwell's army than had any other section of the people. If their loyalty had blinded them to reality, it had also blinded the King. James seems to have imagined that the Anglicans were so close to Rome, and the Tories so committed to nonresistance, that he could obtain the repeal of the Test Act and could then place Roman Catholics in positions of authority. He should have been warned by the parliamentary session of November 1685 that he was in error.

Nevertheless, he pressed forward, and the nation saw one triumph after another for his Romanizing and despotic policies. About half the army was encamped on Hounslow Heath outside London with the obvious intention of overawing the city. Roman Catholic recruits were brought over from Ireland. A famous case in the courts established a means of retaining Catholic officers. A collusive suit was brought against Sir Edward Hales, who was a Roman Catholic officer in the army, but Hales pleaded that he held a dispensation from the King to retain his place despite the Test Act, and the judges agreed that the dispensation was legal. A Catholic commanded the army in Ireland, another the fleet in England. The Earl of Sunderland, a vigorous but reckless man, Judge Jeffreys, the cruel judge who had dealt so harshly with the Monmouth rebels, and a Jesuit, Father Edward Petre, zealous but unwise, became the King's closest advisers.

In 1686 James attempted to bend the Church of England to his will by creating a court of Ecclesiastical Commission with large powers over the clergy. This court was illegal, for the old High Commission had been abolished in 1641 and the creation of similar courts had been forbidden. The Ecclesiastical Commission began by suspending Henry Compton, bishop of London, from office. It then turned upon the University of Oxford, where three colleges— Christ Church, University, and Magdalen—were placed under Roman Catholic rule; the fellows or faculty of Magdalen College were expelled because they would not elect the King's candidate as their president. Oxford was an Anglican and Tory stronghold; hence the King was attacking his own supporters. Moreover, the fellows of an Oxford college, like parish priests, held their livings as freehold property, from which they could be ejected only through due process of law. The tyranny of the King placed the living of every clergyman in jeopardy.

Having thus alienated the church, James sought the support of the nonconformists. In April 1687 he issued a Declaration of Indulgence which suspended all the penal laws, leaving both Catholics and nonconformists free to worship in public and to hold office. This was a bold move. From dispensing with a single statute, as in the case of Sir Edward Hales, the King now moved to the suspension by prerogative of a long list of statutes. It was, said a member of Parliament, "to dispense with laws in a lump." Had it succeeded, the King would have been free from all legal restraints.

Knowing that he could not maintain his position without the approval of Parliament, James began a campaign to pack the Commons. The town charters again were remodeled, Tories were expelled from town corporations, and Roman Catholics were introduced in their places. Naming Catholics as lords lieutenants of counties, he instructed them to ask the justices of the peace whether, if they were returned to Parliament, they would vote for the repeal of the Test Act. The answer was so universally negative that James did not summon Parliament again.

Meanwhile the great question was whether the nonconformists would accept the toleration offered to them by the King and ally with him against the Church of England. Some few of them did, although they knew that in the long run they could expect but short shrift from a Catholic government. The Church of England promised that if ever it came to power once more it would grant them toleration. William III also issued a declaration that he supported religious toleration for nonconformists, though not their admission to office. More and more through 1687 the dissenting bodies came round to the support of the church against the Crown. His opponents were uniting against James.

Two events in 1688 produced the Revolution. One was the trial of seven bishops. In May James had reissued the Declaration of Indulgence with the command that it be read on two successive Sundays in every parish church. Sancroft, the archbishop, and six other bishops petitioned the King to withdraw this command. They printed and distributed their petition, which was a technical breach of the law; the King prosecuted them for publishing a seditious libel against his government. The nation waited breathlessly as the seven bishops, men of high character and unquestioned loyalty, were tried by a London jury. The verdict "Not guilty" set the whole people rejoicing; the soldiers cheered on Hounslow Heath.

The second event which precipitated the Revolution was the birth of a son to James and his Queen, Mary of Modena, on June 10, 1688. They had been married for fifteen years, their other children had died, and it had been assumed that they would have no more. As long as James was childless by his second wife, the throne at his death would go to one of his grown Protestant daughters, Mary or Anne. But the birth of a son altered this picture. The little prince, known in history as the Old Pretender, would take precedence over his older sisters. The fact that he would certainly be brought up in the Catholic faith opened the prospect of an endless line of Roman Catholic Kings. So surprising was his birth that Catholics pronounced the event a miracle, but Protestants spread the story that the child was not of royal parentage but had been brought into the palace in a warming pan. His birth changed the course of history. A group of Whig and Tory leaders, acting together, extended an invitation to William III to invade England with a military force around which the country could rally in revolt against its present King.

THE ENGLISH REVOLUTION

William viewed the possibility of intervention in England from the standpoint of a continental statesman. The great object of his life was opposition to Louis XIV; if he came to England he would come in order to strengthen his position against France. But developments on the Continent and in England seemed to be converging. A new war against Louis was about to begin. James, as Louis' ally, might perhaps bring England in on the French side. Resentment against James in England seemed to be about as strong as it was likely to become. By the beginning of 1688, William, who was in touch with Whig and Tory leaders, appears to have made up his mind to intervene if he could, but he acted cautiously. He refused to come, as Monmouth had done, without an invitation, and he refused to come without an army, although the presence of Dutch troops in England would certainly cause irritation.

Events played into William's hands. The Dutch naturally feared that Louis would attack them while their army was away, but the Grand Monarch, less interested in England than in the Rhine, sent his armies eastward against the Palatinate, opening the way for William's enterprise. Louis offered James the aid of the French fleet, but in a stupid pique James declined this assistance; as a matter of fact, Louis had few ships to send, for his fleet was largely in the Mediterranean. Not without reason Louis believed that William's invasion would lead to a civil war which would neutralize both England and Holland while the French would be free to conquer parts of Germany. Hence William sailed unopposed. A fresh "Protestant" wind from the east carried him through the Channel. On November 5, the anniversary of the Gunpowder Plot, William and his army landed safely at Torbay in Devon.

James in a panic made many concessions, but it was too late. He advanced with his army to Salisbury, returned to London, then did the one thing that was certain to overthrow his government: he ran away. Leaving London late at night, he took ship near Chatham, but was captured by some English fishermen and brought back to England. William wanted no royal martyr. The King was left unguarded and obligingly escaped once more, this time making his way to France. The English were left with little choice but to accept William as their King.

William assumed temporary control of the government and summoned a free Parliament, which met in February 1689. Whigs and Tories, sobered by a sense of crisis, met in a conciliatory spirit, though party differences soon appeared. The Whigs wanted a declaration that the throne was vacant: such a statement would break hereditary succession and give the next King a parliamentary title. The Tories, half ashamed of their opposition to James II, wished to soften the Revolution by asserting that the King had abdicated, thus absolving themselves from the sin of having deposed him. Some Tories hoped that he might be brought back with limited powers, or that William might be regent, or that Mary might be Queen with William as Prince Consort. These suggestions were swept away by the course of events. James had no intention of returning without a French army to re-establish his former powers; William refused to be anything but King; and Mary declined to be Queen unless her husband shared the royal title with her. The Commons therefore drew up an illogical statement declaring that James, having broken the fundamental laws and having withdrawn himself out of the kingdom, had abdicated the government and that the throne was thereby vacant. William and Mary were then made joint sovereigns, with the administration vested in William.

The Revolutionary Settlement

Within the next few years Parliament passed a number of acts which, taken together, formed the revolutionary settlement. Although they sprang largely from the deposition of James II, they were remarkable for their broad conception of liberty, a theme inherent in the Puritan revolt against Charles I but made acceptable to the upper classes after 1660 by a group of political thinkers—Algernon Sidney; Henry Neville; George Savile, Marquis of Halifax; and, above all, John Locke. These men rejected the egalitarian democracy of the Independents and placed political power in the hands of the property-owning classes, but insisted that all men possessed inalienable rights to personal liberty and to religious equality (though there was to be no religious toleration for Catholics).

Of these thinkers the most important was John Locke, a man of common sense who believed that philosophical principles must be founded on human experience. In its simplest terms, his political theory was that of a social contract between governors and governed. Rejecting all notions of divine right, hereditary succession, nonresistance, and the all-powerful state, he held that governments could be justly overthrown when they ceased to fulfill the functions for which they had been established. Locke argued further that man had certain inalienable rights, such as religious liberty and equality before the law, with which the state could not interfere. Before governments had come into existence, he argued (very mistakenly), men were free and equal and bound only by moral law. The great end for which they had placed themselves under governments was the protection of their property. The preservation of life, liberty, and property was the solemn trust placed in the hands of the state. Governments must be limited in power to prevent them from degenerating into tyranny; this should be done by introducing checks and balances, of which the most important was the division into executive, legislative, and judicial branches which imposed restraints upon each other. Locke's reasonable, utilitarian, and liberal approach made a strong appeal to the men of his time, deeply affected government throughout the eighteenth century, and appeared in the American Constitution.

The Bill of Rights (1689), the greatest constitutional document since Magna Carta, began by asserting that James II, abetted by evil advisers, had sought the destruction of the Protestant religion and the laws and liberties of the country. Certain things therefore were named as illegal: the use of the suspending power without parliamentary consent; the dispensing power, first "as it hath been exercised of late," and secondly altogether; the court of Ecclesiastical Commission; the levying of money in any way other than that in which it had been granted; a standing army in time of peace without the consent of Parliament. It was further declared that elections to Parliament should be free; that free speech in Parliament should not be questioned except by Parliament itself; that Parliaments should be summoned frequently; that subjects might petition the King; that excessive bail and cruel and unusual punishments were prohibited; that jurors in treason trials should be freeholders; and finally that no Roman Catholic, nor anyone marrying a Roman Catholic, should succeed to the throne and that all future Kings should subscribe to the Test Act as revised in 1678.

The Bill of Rights has been criticized because it did not deprive the King of power more completely. He remained the hereditary head of the administrative part of the government. But the Bill of Rights, a practical document seeking to end abuses, did not attempt to provide for all contingencies. Rather it asserted a number of principles which established England as a limited monarchy. It affirmed the ancient doctrine that the King was under the law, it implied the existence of a contract between the King and the nation, it asserted the sovereignty of Parliament, and it set forth the elementary legal rights of the subject.

The Bill of Rights should be connected with the Coronation Oath (1689) prepared for the new sovereigns. This oath pledged William and Mary to rule according to "the statutes in Parliament agreed upon, and the laws and customs of the same." Former oaths had merely referred to the laws and customs of earlier Kings; but now the words "statutes in Parliament" were introduced for the first time. The new rulers also swore to uphold "the Protestant Reformed Religion established by law," as well as the Church of England and Ireland "as by law established." The words appear redundant. But many people believed that the Church of England was too close to Roman Catholicism; hence Parliament included the words "Protestant" and "Reformed," words which referred to the changes brought about in the Church of England under Henry VIII and Elizabeth.[3]

The Toleration Act (1689)[4] granted the right of public worship to Protestant nonconformists but debarred them from office in the central or local government. The Test Act and the Corporation Act remained in operation; the rest of the Clarendon Code was not enforced. The Toleration Act did not extend liberty of worship to Catholics or to Unitarians, but thenceforth they were normally let alone.

A Mutiny Act of 1689, which had to be renewed annually and thus necessitated a meeting of Parliament every year, authorized the maintenance of military discipline in the army by courts-martial. Although annual sessions of Parliament had now begun, a Triennial Act in 1694 provided that Parliament should meet at least once every three years and should not be longer than three years in duration. A Trials for Treason Act (1696) stated that a person on trial for treason should be shown the accusations against him, should have advice of counsel, and should not be convicted except upon the testimony of two independent witnesses. Censorship of the press was allowed to lapse in the same year, though laws against libel remained very strict.

The House of Commons consolidated its control over finance. It assumed full responsibility for military and naval expenditures which were met—after a consideration of the estimates—by appropriations and not by grants to the King. The use of appropriations greatly assisted the government in negotiating loans, which were facilitated further by the establishment of the Bank of England in 1694. The Commons, moreover, appointed certain members as commissioners for public accounts, though the commission did not at first work closely with the Treasury. A grant known as the civil list was voted to the King to cover the expenses of civil government. It became the custom to vote this money for the reign of the sovereign.

The Act of Settlement in 1701 provided that if William or Anne should die without children (Queen Mary had died in 1694), the throne should descend, not to the exiled Stuarts, but to Sophia, Electress Dowager of Hanover, a granddaughter of King James I, or to her heirs.[5] The opportunity was taken to impose new restrictions upon the King: he must in future be a member of the Church of

[3] David Ogg, *England in the Reigns of James II and William III* (Oxford: Clarendon Press, 1963), pp. 235–245.
[4] The exact title was "An Act for exempting their Majesties' Protestant Subjects, differing from the Church of England, from the Penalties of certain Laws."
[5] See genealogical table on page 428.

England; should he be a foreigner, he must not involve England in war in defense of his foreign possessions; he must not leave the British Isles without the consent of Parliament; a royal pardon could not be pleaded in bar of impeachment; judges should hold office during good behavior and could be dismissed only upon a joint address of both houses of Parliament. The final point was perhaps the most important. The judges were now independent of the Crown and were becoming the cold and impartial deities of modern times.[6]

Thus England declared herself to be a limited monarchy and a Protestant state. The ancient belief that Kings governed by some divine dispensation and were supported by sacred prerogatives was dead: for all practical purposes sovereignty resided in the nation.

SCIENCE AND THE ARTS

The age of the later Stuarts contained more than plots, intrigues, and revolutions. It was an age of great activity in overseas expansion, as will be explained briefly in the next chapter. It was also an age of intellectual and literary endeavor. Its achievements in science were remarkable. A growing interest in science earlier in the century, inspired by Francis Bacon and by the French philosopher Descartes, flowered in the reign of Charles II. The King himself, his cousin Rupert, and his favorite, the Duke of Buckingham, had their private laboratories. These dilettante experiments by prominent persons constituted a danger to the spirit of pure scientific inquiry, which nevertheless made great progress. The Royal Society was founded in 1662 to promote experiments in physics and mathematics. For some time the society included talented men from various walks of life: John Aubrey, who wrote brief lives of his contemporaries; Sir Christopher Wren, the architect; John Evelyn, the botanist and numismatist; Samuel Pepys, the naval administrator and diarist; John Locke, the philosopher; and Sir William Petty, the statistician. There were also scientists: Robert Boyle, physicist and chemist, who formulated the law concerning the elasticity of gases; Isaac Barrow, a mathematician; Robert Hooke, mathematician and physicist; and Jonathan Goddard, who made telescopes. After 1684, influenced by the discoveries of Isaac Newton, the society became more purely scientific. Professor of Mathematics at Cambridge at twenty-seven, Newton was one of the great mathematicians of all time. His many discoveries concerning gravitation, calculus, optics, dynamics, and the theory of equations showed his genius. He was president of the society for twenty-four years.

There was as yet no thought of a clash between science and religion. Boyle and Newton were both religious men; the first historian of the Royal Society, a clergyman, praised its endeavors "to increase the powers of all mankind and to free them from the bondage of errors." Yet these scientists were finding paths to truth which were entirely outside theology. They were creating a mode of thought which regarded the age of miracles as past, rejected the new revelations of the Puritans, and believed that the universe was governed by natural law. One excellent result was the decline of superstition. There was, for instance, less

---

[6] Two other provisions of the act—that business normally transacted in the Privy Council should not be transacted elsewhere and that officeholders under the Crown should not be eligible for membership in the House of Commons—never became operative.

Church of St. Mary-le-Bow, Cheapside, London, built by Sir Christopher Wren between 1671 and 1677. It is surmounted by a dragon. (National Monuments Record. Royal Commission on Historical Monuments. Crown Copyright)

St. Paul's Cathedral, London, designed by Sir Christopher Wren. Begun in 1675, it was opened for services in 1697 and was said to be complete in 1716, though much remained to be done. (British Tourist Authority)

belief in witchcraft. The peasant long continued to believe in witches, as evidenced by Burns's rollicking poem, "Tam o' Shanter," but educated men grew skeptical. When a witch was brought before a certain judge in the reign of Queen Anne and accused of flying from London to Oxford on a broomstick, the judge remarked that he knew of no law against this, and so dismissed the case.

The great name in music in this age was that of Henry Purcell, a man of genius, who "wrote masterpieces in every department of music practiced in his time."[7] Before the Civil Wars English music for the most part had been either church music or madrigals. It now broadened into many other forms. Purcell wrote operas, incidental music for plays, and sonatas for strings and harpsichord. The violin was introduced into England in the reign of Charles II, when the first public concerts were given. In architecture the outstanding figure was Sir Christopher Wren, who built the modern St. Paul's Cathedral after the Great Fire. The great dome of the new cathedral, which is of the Renaissance style of architecture, still dominates the financial center of the City.

English drama had ceased for a time when the Puritans closed the London theaters, and there were only two theaters open in the early years of Charles II. The theaters of the Restoration, depending largely upon the patronage of the royal court, reflected the degenerate taste of Charles's courtiers. Plays were either heroic tragedies, melodramas of knightly love, or comedies of manners, witty but coarse and cynical. The technique of play acting was improved. Scenery now was used, and female parts were performed by actresses and not by boys, as in Shakespeare's time.

[7] Quoted in Maurice Ashley, *England in the Seventeenth Century* (Baltimore: Penguin Books, 1962), pp. 160–161.

House of Stuart

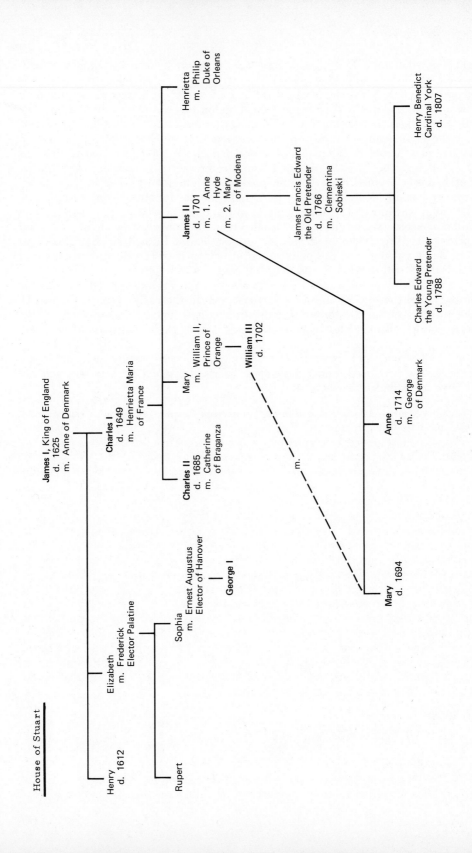

20

WILLIAM III AND ANNE

WILLIAM III, 1689–1702

In the difficult years after the Revolution England was fortunate in having as great a King as William III. He was not a popular ruler. His thoughts were forever on his beloved Holland, his intimates were mostly Dutchmen, he never gave his confidence to English generals or statesmen. Small, slightly deformed, a sufferer from asthma and from a tubercular lung, he was not impressive physically. Since the smoke of London gave him a cough, he spent his time in the country as much as possible. Hence there was no court to bring him into contact with the people, as there had been under Queen Elizabeth or Charles II. He was a cold man, without social arts or graces, an exacting taskmaster, liked by the army but by few persons outside it.

William's virtues were those of the soldier—bravery in mortal danger, stoic calm in adversity, the highest sense of duty. His life was dominated by a hatred of Louis XIV. In governing England William was somewhat highhanded, for he was an autocrat who despised the quarrels of Whigs and Tories, but he displayed both patience and magnanimity toward them. He knew that he was surrounded by treachery, that many Tories and some Whigs were in touch with James II. Yet with great forbearance, he ignored this double-dealing and employed false men if he thought they could be useful. He was happiest when on the battlefield. But his gifts as a soldier were far less than his powers as a diplomat and statesman. Aside from ruling England and Holland, he held together an alliance against France, fought a long war from 1689 to 1697, and prepared for a greater war which came under his successor, Queen Anne.

WAR WITH FRANCE

Ireland

William was forced at once to turn his attention to Ireland. James II had been good to the Irish Catholics, and when he called on them for help they rose in his behalf. In March 1689 James arrived in Dublin with French officers and French money. The island was soon in Catholic hands. Protestants fled to England or went into hiding or crowded into Londonderry, which withstood a siege lasting 105 days. A Catholic Parliament re-established the Roman Catholic Church and began to restore the land to its former Catholic owners. Early in 1690 some 7000 troops arrived from France, creating a dangerous threat to England. But James's cause did not prosper. The closer he associated himself with Irish Catholicism, the less was his hope of regaining England. Moreover, his counsels were divided: he thought in terms of the English throne, but the Irish aimed at independence, and the French at a long war that would cause William a maximum amount of harm. William landed in Ireland in June 1690 with an army of 36,000 men. On July 1 he fought the Battle of the Boyne, completely defeating James, who immediately fled to France. Within a year the Irish rebellion was crushed.

The Irish received condign punishment. They were hated and feared both as Catholics and as rebels, and England began a policy of ruthless repression and of impregnable Protestant ascendancy. Henceforth no Catholic could hold office, sit in the Irish Parliament, or vote for its members. He could enter no learned profession save medicine. He was subject to unjust and discriminatory taxation; he suffered legal disabilities which made it difficult for him to go to law against a Protestant; and he was excluded from almost every means of acquiring wealth, knowledge, or influence. He could not purchase land or hold long leases. If he was a landowner, his land was divided at his death among his sons, unless the eldest turned Protestant, in which case he got it all. Catholic worship was not forbidden, but it was hedged with severe restrictions.

There was also a repressive economic code. The Irish were excluded from trade with the colonies, nor could colonial products come to Ireland except by way of England. Thus Ireland's shipping was all but destroyed; her many fine harbors brought her little profit. A prosperous trade in exporting cattle and sheep to England was ended, though the Irish exported cattle to other parts of Europe. They developed the manufacture of woolen cloth, but this was restricted, and in 1699 the export of woolen cloth was forbidden. Nor could raw wool be sent to England. The manufacture of linen was encouraged, but the industry was retarded by lack of capital.

The mass of the population thus was compelled to wring a precarious subsistence from the soil. It is small wonder that the Irish peasant became idle, shiftless, and indifferent to the squalor of his surroundings. He learned to hate the law and to regard it as his enemy. But his religion gave him depth and earnestness and a love of ancient custom. It taught him conjugal fidelity; the Irish became a chaste people with a delicate sense of female honor. The peasant was affectionate toward his family, sympathetic toward the sufferings of others, grateful for kindness, polite, tactful, and hospitable to strangers. His character displayed contradictions. His Celtic temperament was gay and cheerful, but his sufferings produced a strain of religious and poetic melancholy. He could be patient and submissive under great provocation, yet brood over ancient wrongs and await the hour of sudden revenge.

Anglo-French Colonial and Commercial Rivalry

The support given by Louis to James's enterprise in Ireland brought war between England and France. Parliament voted supplies at once to meet the

French and Irish danger; war was declared against France in May 1689. The English, however, were thinking of the security of their new regime and of the defense of their country from invasion. It is conceivable that once Ireland had been subdued, England would not have joined in the European war against France. Her entry was due in no small measure to colonial and commercial rivalry.

Both Charles II and his brother gave great encouragement to commerce and colonization, courtiers and politicians followed their example, and the amount of capital available for investment increased. The result was a burst of activity in overseas expansion unequaled since the reign of Elizabeth. The older trading companies, which had suffered heavily during the Civil Wars, entered a period of prosperity. The East India Company under a new charter of 1661 did exceptionally well. Bombay, surviving initial difficulties, became a fine town, superseding Surat as the chief English factory on the western coast. Madras also expanded; the English at last obtained a foothold in Bengal. On an average, the company paid dividends of twenty-five percent; at the height of its prosperity in 1683 the price of its stock had risen fivefold.

Several new companies were established. The Royal Adventurers of England Trading to Africa, chartered by Charles in 1662 with James as governor, brought slaves from West Africa to the New World. It was ruined by the second Dutch war and its stock was taken over in 1672 by a new body, the Royal African Company. James again was governor. The new company prospered for about twenty years but then fell into difficulties, partly because it could not maintain its monopoly. The Hudson's Bay Company, the only one of these early companies still in existence, was begun when Prince Rupert, the Royalist general of the Civil War, became interested in the possibilities of the fur trade in the area of Hudson Bay. He obtained a charter in 1670. The company, always very conservative, operated on a modest scale and prospered in spite of French attacks.

Meanwhile the colonies in the New World were expanding. New York and New Jersey were acquired from the Dutch; the Carolinas and Pennsylvania were founded. The population of the English settlements in North America had risen by 1688 to perhaps 200,000 persons. In the British West Indies the large island of Jamaica developed slowly, and the administration of the settlements was tightened and improved.

A famous code of laws, the Acts of Trade, was devised to control colonial commerce. An act of 1660, based on the Navigation Act of 1651, provided that the trade of the English colonies, both export and import, must be conducted in English ships, and that certain enumerated articles, such as sugar, tobacco, cotton, ginger, indigo (the list grew longer in later years), must be shipped only to England or to other English colonies. From the non-English parts of Asia, Africa, and America, goods could be brought to England only in English or colonial ships directly from the place of origin. But since English vessels normally were excluded from the possessions of other powers, the practical effect of this provision was to confine the colonial trade of England to her own colonies. Colonial products other than the enumerated articles could still be taken to foreign ports. Of these products the most important were fish from the Newfoundland Banks, which were shipped to southern Europe and sold for cash, thus helping to create a favorable balance of trade. The Staples Act of 1663 provided that manufactured goods from the Continent could enter the English colonies only if the goods had been brought to England before they were shipped across the

Atlantic. Finally, the Plantations Act of 1673 concerned the enumerated articles, about which there was difficulty from the first. New England skippers took sugar and tobacco to continental ports in defiance of the act of 1660. To end this illegal traffic, the Plantations Act imposed new duties on exporters of enumerated articles at the port of lading unless the exporters gave security that the goods in question were bound for England.

Although the Acts of Trade have been condemned by modern historians as crude and selfish, they were not so regarded in the seventeenth century. Since the colonies had been founded by English enterprise, it was considered only just that their trade be channeled to England. The mercantile theory of the time embodied the ideal of a self-sufficing empire in which merchandise need not be purchased from foreign countries. Tropical products from the West Indies, it was thought, added directly to the wealth of England since they could not be produced at home and were often re-exported for sale on the Continent. It was argued further that the colonies were defended by the English navy and were heavily protected in the English market. The colonists made little or no objection to the exclusion of foreigners from colonial ports. What they disliked was the necessity of taking the enumerated articles to England. The Acts of Trade were not as oppressive in the seventeeth century as they became in the eighteenth. Devised by men well versed in colonial trade, they prevented the Dutch from exploiting English colonies; the English merchant marine throve under their operation. English tonnage doubled in the first decade after 1660 and continued to increase rapidly. American trade, which in 1670 amounted to one tenth of all English foreign commerce, rose to one seventh in 1700.

Important as it was, it was only a fraction of England's foreign trade. The Merchant Adventurers and the Eastland, Muscovy, and Levant companies carried English commodities, especially woolen cloth, throughout central and northern Europe and into the Near East. The tendency at the end of the seventeenth century was to throw open these trades to a larger number of English merchants; the great trading companies became less exclusive than their structure implied. There were also unincorporated merchants who traded with Spain and Portugal. Commerce was becoming the very lifeblood of the nation. The age was one in which the techniques of manufacturing were still primitive, but in which there was no lack of capital or of business skill; hence the mercantile instincts of the nation turned to commerce rather than to industry. The growing community of merchants and capitalists was acquiring greater influence at Westminster than it had possessed in the past and was becoming one of the most powerful forces in the kingdom. Thus the rise of France as a colonial and commercial rival was a matter of grave concern.

In a general way the history of French expansion overseas parallels that of England, though the French moved more slowly and founded fewer colonies. In the sixteenth century there were desultory French voyages to North America. The first permanent colony was founded in 1608 at Quebec; about the same time a colony was planted at Port Royal in Acadia (Nova Scotia). The number of French colonists in Canada in 1689 was probably less than 15,000, but they ranged over an enormous area from the St. Lawrence Valley westward through the Great Lakes and down the Mississippi. The French islands in the West Indies were equal or even superior to the English ones. Martinique, Guadeloupe, western Santo Domingo (Haiti), and the French portion of St. Kitts were excellent sugar islands whose soil was less depleted by constant cropping than was the soil of the English West Indies. The French held slaving stations around St.-Louis on the Senegal River in West Africa. Although they had made a number of false starts in founding an East India company, a permanent organization was established by Colbert in 1664. Its early factories in India were located at Surat (1668), at Pondicherry (1674), which grew into its best town; and at Chandarnagar (1690) on the Hooghly River in Bengal. These colonies were supported by the French state, by a fine navy, and by a growing mercantile marine. It is not surprising that English merchants regarded this French expansion with apprehension.

England's entry into the war against Louis in 1689 constituted a change of policy. The ancient hostility of the two countries in the later Middle Ages had subsided in the reign of Queen Elizabeth, and for almost a century, except for brief periods of hostility, England and France had been at peace. This amity was now broken. There began a century of conflict, a new Hundred Years' War, which was concluded only when Napoleon was defeated at Waterloo in 1815. This struggle, although it centered in commerce, colonies, and sea power, affected English policy in many ways. England must have an army as well as a navy, Ireland and Scotland could not be permitted to interfere with the war effort, and the fact that taxation must be increased underscored the dominant position of the House of Commons. The moneyed classes who made loans to the government had to be cultivated and allowed an increasingly strong position.

The War of the League of Augsburg, 1689–1697

The aggressions of Louis XIV against his neighbors gradually surrounded France with a ring of hostile states that formed the League of Augsburg in 1686 for their mutual protection. Just as the Revolution was taking place in England, a war broke out in 1688 when Louis attacked the Palatinate. Aligned against him were the members of the so-called Grand Alliance of England, Holland, Austria, Spain, a number of the German states, of which Brandenburg, Saxony, Hanover, and Bavaria were the most important, and later Savoy and the papacy. Sweden had joined the league in 1686 but took no part in the war. Such an alliance might appear invincible. But France had the advantage of inner lines, whereas the allied powers, scattered around the circumference, were divided by jealousies and conflicting ambitions. Decisive action depended upon what England and Holland could accomplish at sea and in the Spanish Netherlands.

The French navy, which was able at first to challenge the fleets of both England and Holland, secured temporary control of the Channel at the time of James's expedition to Ireland and defeated the English and Dutch at the Battle of Beachy Head off the coast of Sussex in 1690. But the French fleet could not control both the Channel and the Mediterranean. It was defeated by the English in 1692 at La Hogue in the Channel near Normandy; when Louis began operations against Spain and Savoy in 1694, an English squadron entered the Mediterranean, blockaded the French in Toulon, and disrupted the assault on Spain.

On the other hand, Louis had the better of the fighting in the Spanish Netherlands. He possessed every advantage of veteran troops, excellent generals, and strategic positions. He captured Mons in 1691 and Namur in 1692 and defeated William in the Battle of Steenkerke in the latter year. William again was defeated in 1693. Although William retook Namur in 1695, Louis was winning the war on land and was dividing the allies by his diplomacy. Nevertheless, Louis was ready for peace in 1697 and so were his opponents. The Peace of Ryswick in that year provided that France restore all her conquests since 1678 except Strasbourg, allow the Dutch to garrison a line of fortresses in the Spanish Netherlands along the French frontier, and acknowledge William as King of England. This peace was merely a breathing space before the opening of another war.

WILLIAM AND ENGLISH POLITICS

Meanwhile William was contending with political factions in England. Politics at this time are difficult to understand because although we hear of Whigs and Tories they were not like modern parties. Of the many reasons for this perhaps the most important was the position of the King. William kept power in his own hands as far as possible. He insisted on having complete control over the army and over foreign affairs, he did not allow Parliament to meet when he was abroad, and he rarely took an English minister with him when he went to the Continent. Acting as his own prime minister, he controlled policy and made appointments as he saw fit. He used all the powers of the Crown which had not been taken away and resisted any encroachment on those powers. With so strong and energetic a ruler, modern political parties which today control policy and distribute patronage were impossible.

Modern political parties were also impossible because of the aristocratic nature of society. Country gentlemen with wealth and local influence could obtain election to the House of Commons through their own efforts and were completely independent of any party organization, speaking and voting as they pleased in Parliament. There were also family groups of members. A great noble holding large estates could secure the return of his relatives, employees, and other connections; this group looked to him and not to a party for leadership. Political parties in the modern sense were also out of the question because there was no connection between a change of ministers and an election to the House of Commons. William did not appoint ministers because their party had won a majority. Indeed, it was the other way round, for the King's ministers could build a Court party in Parliament. At least a hundred members were placemen who held some office in the gift of the Crown, and this patronage could be used to influence elections and to obtain votes after Parliament assembled. Members might storm at ministers but could not turn them out except by the clumsy method of impeachment.

Both parties were affected by the Revolution. The Tories lost their political philosophy. Some of them were Jacobite, but the majority accepted Locke's utilitarian view of kingship. Yet they could not pay William the respect they had accorded the Stuarts; they thought of him as the enemy of their church. The Tories represented the interests of the landowning gentry who had no inclination to pay high taxes for the support of a war on behalf of commerce. The Whigs had attacked the prerogatives of the Stuart Kings but now found themselves with a ruler who used his prerogatives with vigor. Hence they were goaded into seeking further reduction in the powers of the Crown and further increases in the powers of Parliament. They stood for religious toleration, for the commercial interests of merchants and bankers, and for a vigorous prosecution of the war against a commercial rival. Finally, because both parties contained moderates and extremists their condition was confused and fluid.

Under these circumstances both the ministers of the King and the opposition to him in the Commons were apt to be coalitions of both parties; the best descriptive terms are a Country party in the Commons which criticized the government and a Court party which defended it. In the first part of the reign the Whigs had a majority in the Commons. Irritated by the King's appointment of both Whigs and Tories to the ministry, the Whigs set themselves to annoy the government. They voted money for only short periods, they made inquiries into military and naval mishaps, they set up committees to audit the accounts, they forced William to cancel grants made to his favorites, and they dealt with the affairs of the East India Company, which had previously been the province of the Crown. William naturally was irritated, but he discovered that the Tories also opposed him. They lacked enthusiasm for the war, they sought to reduce the size of the army, and some of them were in correspondence with James II.

To William the prosecution of the war was all-important; hence he brought more Whigs into the government until, between 1694 and 1698, the ministry was largely Whig, although a moderate Tory, Sidney Godolphin, an official in the Treasury who was a kind of indispensable civil servant, remained in office. The leading Whigs were known as the Junto. Lord Keeper Somers was the most attractive and probably the most able. A statesman-lawyer, with remarkable breadth of view, he had helped to solve the legal problems which had arisen at the time of the Revolution. Charles Montagu, later Lord Halifax, was an able financier of an original turn of mind. Thomas Lord Wharton, though violent and irreligious, organized the Court party with skill. Another Whig, Edward Russell, Lord Orford, was a sea captain and naval administrator, able but bad-tempered and vindictive. The best work of the Whigs was the founding of the Bank of England in 1694. The subscribers to a government loan of £1,200,000 were incorporated by Parliament as a joint-stock bank with the right to issue notes and discount bills. This was a modest beginning, but the bank helped to finance the war, and since the government was not required to repay the loan so long as it paid interest, the arrangement was the origin of the national debt.

After the Peace of Ryswick in 1697, the country eagerly turned away from war. A new leader appeared in the Commons, Robert Harley, who won much popular approval but greatly angered the King by demanding a reduction in the cost of government, a smaller army than William advised, and an end to royal gifts to favorites. The Whigs were discredited by this attack and by revelations that some of them were in secret correspondence with James II. The King gradually replaced them with Tory ministers, of whom Godolphin and John Churchill, Earl of Marlborough, were the most important. This was the situation at the end of the reign.

THE PARTITION TREATIES

The problem of the fate of the Spanish empire was growing more pressing in the last years of the century. The Spanish King, Charles II, though taking an unconscionable time in dying, would certainly do so soon. The two strongest claimants to the inheritance of Spain were Louis of France and Emperor Leopold of Austria, both of whom had married sisters of the Spanish King. A third possible heir was Leopold's grandson. Prince Joseph Ferdinand of Bavaria, who was still a child. William's great fear was that the Spanish Netherlands would fall to France, and he devoted his last years to the completion of two partition treaties with Louis by which he hoped to divide the Spanish possessions without a war and without France's obtaining the Netherlands. But neither Spain nor Austria was consulted about these treaties. The Spanish, resentful at the proposed dismemberment of their empire, believed that France could keep their possessions united better than could Austria; hence Charles II, now really on his deathbed, was induced to sign a will which left the Spanish empire to Philip, Duke of Anjou, a grandson of Louis XIV, on condition that it not be divided. Louis had before him the prospect of enormous new possessions but also the sobering thought that they would have to be fought for. His decision was to accept the will.

It appeared at first that no general war would follow. Holland recognized Philip as King of Spain, and the English seemed willing to do the same, for the will provided that if Philip accepted the crown of Spain he should forfeit that of France. Louis, however, made a number of miscalculations. Hoping to prevent a war by frightening his opponents, he seized a number of strategic points in the Spanish Netherlands, in Cologne, and in Milan. These moves showed clearly that, though Philip might become the King of Spain, his policy would be dominated by France. Nor did Louis give any indication that Philip, if King of Spain, would renounce his claim to the French crown. Moreover, it became evident that French merchants would be permitted to exploit the Spanish empire: a French company was given the right to supply the Spanish colonies with African slaves. Above all, at the death of James II, Louis recognized James's son, James Edward, the Old Pretender, as King of England, a gratuitous insult which united the English against France. Tories as well as Whigs, determined to preserve the revolutionary settlement, agreed that the country must prepare for war. Preparations were under way when William died in March 1702. He was thrown heavily from his horse as it stumbled over a molehill, and his weary body could not rally from the shock. The cruel toast of the High Tories to "the little gentleman in black velvet," who had caused the accident, testified to their satisfaction at William's departure.

QUEEN ANNE, 1702–1714

The reign of Queen Anne, as described in a textbook, may seem to be dominated by the great war with France. And in a sense it was. But behind the war clouds the reign was studded with brilliant names and could boast notable achievements: Marlborough in war and diplomacy; Newton in science; Wren in architecture; Godolphin, Somers, Halifax, Harley, and Bolingbroke in politics; Pope, Swift, Defoe, Congreve, Addison, and Steele in literature—all added luster to what is often called the Augustan Age. English wealth and commerce increased while Louis' power was beaten down, the empire was enlarged, and a lasting union with Scotland was effected.

These achievements cannot be attributed to Queen Anne, a semi-invalid who suffered from gout and who had borne some sixteen children, only to see them die. A woman of very mediocre abilities, she was slow-witted, obstinate, opinionated—and rather dowdy in appearance. She disliked both the memory of William and the thought that the Hanoverians would succeed her. She was pious and devout, a strong supporter of the Church of England and of the Tory party, fond of female favorites, though devoted to her sponge of a husband, Prince George of Denmark, of whom Charles II had said, "I have tried him drunk and tried him sober, and there is nothing in him." Anne's one hobby, it has been remarked, was eating.[1] Yet she had both courage and a sense of duty. She tried to play her part and to maintain her prerogatives. Disliking political parties, she once burst out, "Why for God's sake must I, who have no thought but for the good of my country, be made so miserable as to be brought into the power of one set of men?" Yet she could not avoid dependence on her ministers. A small inner group of advisers supplied the leadership which William had exercised personally, and thus the practice of limited monarchy was advanced during her reign.

The Marlborough-Godolphin Coalition

Anne began her reign by selecting a coalition ministry consisting of both Whigs and Tories. The most important members were the Earl of Marlborough, who was captain general (that is, supreme commander of the army), and Sidney Godolphin, the Lord Treasurer. Marlborough, one of England's greatest generals, was a man of extraordinary gifts both as a soldier and as a diplomat. He had spent all his life at war or at court. He had fought at Tangier, in Flanders, in Alsace, in Ireland, and in Flanders again before he became commander in chief. He was a splendid tactician. Armies were still small enough for a single mind to direct their movements during battle, and one must imagine Marlborough deploying troops, placing artillery, at times leading a charge in person. He taught his cavalry to charge home (as Cromwell had done), and his infantry to fire in a single volley by platoons. The grenade and the bayonet were new weapons that made close fighting more deadly. Marlborough was equally successful in planning grand strategy and in viewing campaigns as a whole. At the same time he was an excellent diplomat. Year after year he traveled from one capital to another, holding together an alliance of nations with diverse and selfish aims. His strong position at home made it possible for him to coordinate war and politics. A contemporary called him "the greatest general and the greatest minister that our country, or perhaps any country, has produced." There were serious flaws in his character. He was much too fond of money. As a young man he did not scruple to obtain advancement by becoming one of the lovers of Lady Castlemaine, the mistress of Charles II. A servant of James II, he deserted him, though only when his cause was hopeless; a servant of William, he corresponded secretly with James.

His wife, Sarah, was an avaricious, violent, and overbearing woman who for many years was a favorite of Queen Anne. To place themselves on a basis of complete equality, Anne and Sarah called each other Mrs. Morley and Mrs. Freeman. This connection aided Marlborough greatly, though his wife was so partisan and vehement a Whig that she made it difficult for him to work with the Tories. Godolphin, as we have seen, was a very able administrator, sound and steady, a moderate Tory with a touch of the Jacobite. At the beginning of the reign Anne wrote to Sarah, "We four must never part till death mows us down with his impartial hand." Other members of the coalition were Somers and Halifax from the Whig Junto, Robert Harley, a moderate Tory, and a number of High Tories.

The High Tories of the coalition proved to be difficult. They raised the cry that the church was in danger, and twice attempted to pass occasional conformity

---

[1] This phrase is taken from Maurice Ashley, *England in the Seventeenth Century* (Baltimore: Penguin Books, 1962), p. 197.

bills which would have prevented nonconformists from qualifying for office by occasionally taking the Anglican sacrament. Their view of England's role in the war differed from that of Godolphin and Marlborough. Marlborough's strategy was to drive the French from the Netherlands, defeat them in a pitched battle, and so open the way for a march on Paris. But the High Tories, less interested in the war, wished England to rely on sea power and to play only an auxiliary part in the war on land. Marlborough and Godolphin broke with the High Tories, several of whom were dismissed in 1703. Robert Harley became Secretary of State in 1704. Henceforth the three principal ministers, known as the Triumvirate, were Marlborough, Godolphin, and Harley. At the same time a brilliant young member of the Commons, Henry St. John, later Viscount Bolingbroke, was made Secretary at War. This moderately Tory ministry was displeasing to the extremists of both parties and would not have survived for long had not Marlborough won the victory of Blenheim in 1704.

The War of the Spanish Succession, 1702–1713

The first years of the War of the Spanish Succession did not go well. Allied with Spain, Savoy, Bavaria, and Cologne, Louis was in a strong position, he had placed French troops in a number of strategic places, his fleet at Toulon dominated the western Mediterranean. Arrayed against him was the Grand Alliance of England, Holland, and Austria as well as Denmark, Prussia, Hanover, and lesser German states. But it was difficult, as before, for the allies to work together. Austria in particular had her own interests in Italy, was slow in any cooperative venture, and was dangerously threatened in 1703 by a French penetration into southern Germany. Success depended largely on good relations between England and Holland, which for the most part were maintained, though the Dutch, who undoubtedly were making great sacrifices, were fearful of the pitched battles desired by Marlborough. Hence for two years Marlborough's campaigns in the Netherlands and along the lower Rhine accomplished little, and English operations at sea were not much better. Admiral Benbow won some successes in the Caribbean (and had innumerable alehouses named after him in England), but an attack on Cadiz was a failure, and though Admiral Sir George Rooke destroyed a Spanish fleet at Vigo Bay, there was more good fortune than good management in that victory.

Successes in these years were diplomatic rather than military. In 1703 both Savoy and Portugal joined the allies. The adherence of Savoy was helpful in northern Italy and on the upper Danube against Bavaria, while the port of Lisbon supplied a naval base close to the Mediterranean. The Portuguese, however, came in only on conditions. They asked that the Emperor's son, the Archduke Charles, be declared King of Spain instead of Philip, Louis' grandson; that Charles come in person to Lisbon; and that the war continue until Spain had been won for Austria. These conditions were accepted, though they forced the allies to fight in Spain under disadvantages which in the long run proved insurmountable. There was also a commercial treaty between England and Portugal, the Methuen Treaty, by which English cloth entered Portugal and Portuguese port wine entered England at low custom rates: hence the English taste for port during the eighteenth century.

In 1704 the fortunes of the allies rose greatly. To assist the Austrians, who were pleading for help, Marlborough conceived the bold design of taking his army up the Rhine and into Bavaria to knock out the Bavarians before they and the French could attack Vienna. With masterly precision he marched 600 miles to Coblenz, to Frankfort on the Main, and so to Ulm, where he joined the Austrian commander, Prince Eugene, and the Margrave of Baden. They defeated the Bavarians at the Battle of the Schellenberg, and on August 13, 1704, met and overwhelmed a combined French and Bavarian army at Blenheim. Blenheim was

The Netherlands in 1700

a decisive battle. For the first time in two generations a large French army suffered a crushing defeat. Austria was saved, its future aggrandizement was assured, and Louis lost all hope of extending his territories beyond the Rhine. The Godolphin-Marlborough coalition was strengthened in England and remained in power for four more years. Almost at the same moment Admiral Rooke captured Gibraltar and beat off a French fleet at nearby Málaga. Gibraltar remained in English hands despite counterattacks by the French and Spanish.

In the years following Blenheim the war went steadily against Louis except in Spain. Marlborough won the important victory of Ramillies in 1706, with the result that the French were cleared from the Spanish Netherlands; after another victory, Audenaarde, in 1708, he might have pushed on to Paris but was restrained by the fears of his allies. In 1709 Louis attempted to make peace, but was offered such hard terms that he determined to continue the war. Making a supreme effort, he raised new armies and inspired France to heroic exertion. Marlborough's costly victory in the Battle of Malplaquet, also in the Netherlands, was really a strategic victory for Louis, for it stopped an advance to Paris and retrieved the reputation of French arms. In Spain, on the other hand, the allies were unsuccessful. At first they made easy gains and occupied Madrid in 1706, but the Spanish people did not want the Archduke Charles as their King. They wanted Philip of France, and they rallied so effectively to his cause that the allies abandoned Madrid and were badly defeated at Almanza in 1707. The Austrian cause in Spain was hopeless.

English Politics, 1705–1710

Two alterations, both gradual, took place in the relative position of parties during these years. The first came as a result of the elections in 1705 and 1708, when the Whigs increased their strength in the House of Commons. The old Whig Junto of William's reign was loud in demanding office, and since the Whigs favored the vigorous prosecution of the war, the government gradually yielded. Sunderland, Marlborough's son-in-law and Sarah's favorite, became Ambassador to Vienna in 1705; in the next year he was made Secretary of State, a colleague for whom Harley had little liking. Somers and Wharton were brought into the government in 1708, Orford in 1709. These men forced Harley to resign. Thus the ministry of Marlborough and Godolphin gradually was shifted from one that was moderately Tory to one containing many Whigs. The Queen was most reluctant to make these changes. She thought of the Whigs as the opponents of her church and of the prerogatives of the Crown, both of which she was determined to defend. It was only with the greatest difficulty that she was persuaded to admit Whigs to office.

After 1708, however, the Marlborough-Godolphin-Whig coalition began to go to pieces. The basic cause was war-weariness among the people. The war was very costly, and although Marlborough's victories were most satisfying, they did not appear to be bringing the war to a conclusion. It was remembered that Louis had offered to make peace in 1709. The government also was weakened because Anne was at last growing tired of the domineering Sarah and was turning to a new favorite, Mrs. Abigail Masham, red-nosed but ingratiating.[2] Mrs. Masham, a cousin of Robert Harley, was a Tory who favored a purely Tory ministry.

A famous trial in 1710 which further undermined the position of the coali-

---

[2] The phrase is Ashley's, p. 206.

tion was that of Dr. Sacheverell, a Tory clergyman who attacked the Whigs in his sermons, declared that the church was in danger, and denounced the principles of the Revolution by defending divine right and passive obedience to Kings. He was really a windy seeker after notoriety, but he gained a great following. There was no doubt that his utterances were treasonous. The government decided to impeach him and succeeded in doing so. But then, knowing that severity would be unpopular, the ministers gave him so light a sentence that they made themselves ridiculous. Sensing that the country was turning against the Whigs, Anne began to break up the ministry. She dismissed Sarah after a stormy scene. She then dropped Sunderland, whom she thoroughly disliked, and finally Godolphin, along with the Whigs of the Junto. Tories were brought in, of whom the chief was Robert Harley, Lord Treasurer, later the Earl of Oxford, and St. John, Secretary of State, later Lord Bolingbroke. Though he had won the war, Marlborough was dismissed in 1711.

The Treaty of Utrecht, 1713

The Tory ministers at once set about making peace with France. Their methods were dishonorable, for they made secret preliminary agreements with Louis safeguarding English interests before they consulted their allies. Yet the settlement was not unjust and brought England many benefits. Louis recognized Anne and the future sovereigns from Hanover as the rightful rulers of England; he banished the Old Pretender from France. The fortifications of Dunkirk, a center for French privateers, were destroyed under the supervision of English troops. England obtained important colonial concessions. The area of Hudson Bay, Acadia (Nova Scotia), and the island of Newfoundland were ceded to her by France, as was also the French portion of St. Kitts in the West Indies. From Spain England secured Gibraltar, the island of Minorca in the Mediterranean, a monopoly of supplying Spanish America with Negro slaves, and the right to send one ship a year to the fairs at Vera Cruz or at Cartagena.

The settlement on the Continent recognized Philip as King of Spain but provided that he renounce his claims to the French throne and that the crowns of France and Spain never be united. The Austrians received the Spanish Netherlands, Milan, and Naples. The Dutch obtained the right to garrison the border fortresses against France, but they did not secure, as they wished, a share in the commercial concessions given to England. In fact, they were treated rather shabbily. The French gave up their conquests beyond the Rhine but retained Strasbourg and Landau.

The Treaty of Utrecht left France in an exhausted and bankrupt condition from which she recovered only slowly. Her colonial and commercial development also received a serious reversal, though they resumed their progress much more rapidly than did France as a whole. The Dutch sank into the position of a second-rate power—secure, wealthy, but unimportant. England emerged from the war with the most lively and busy colonial empire in the world and the largest navy. It is an indication of the prime importance of commerce to England that the Tory ministers who made this treaty were no less intent on colonial and commercial advantage than the Whigs would have been.

The Hanoverian Succession

Having dismissed her Whig ministers and appointed Tory ones in 1710, Anne dissolved Parliament. The result was a Tory victory, for she had gauged the temper of the electorate correctly. The Tories appeared to be firmly entrenched, with a Tory Queen, Tory ministers, and a Tory House of Commons. Yet within four years their party was fragmented and ruined, never to be revived in its early eighteenth-century form. The cause of this debacle was the entanglement of the Tories with Jacobitism. The story has sometimes been written as though they engaged in a deep and sinister plot, but in truth they were drawn into Jacobite dealings by the necessities of their position.

Their task was to make peace after the Whigs had won the war. Though their policy was correct, their methods, as we have seen, were questionable, for they safeguarded English interests by deserting their allies. As this came to light, the allies were deeply incensed—none more so than George, the Elector of Hanover. For various reasons he had wished to fight France to a finish, and he was furious over the Tory policy. So were the Whigs. Indeed, so vehement was Whig hostility that Anne was forced to create twelve Tory peers to pass the treaties through the House of Lords. Thus George of Hanover and the Whigs were drawn together. The Tories, fearful of the future, believed that if George became King they would be impeached for treason. Like many statesmen of both parties, they had occasionally flirted with Jacobitism in the past. Now they began to go further in their messages to the exiled Stuarts.

James II, of course, was dead. His son, James Edward, the Old Pretender, a young man in his early twenties, was not a promising candidate for the throne. He was a devout Catholic, his health was poor, and though he was always dignified and correct, there was a settled melancholy about him, as though he knew himself to be a man doomed to futility. His principal disadvantages as a possible King of England were his Catholicism and his dependence on France. Early in 1714, after a serious illness of the Queen, Oxford, acting through the French Ambassador, inquired of the Pretender whether he was prepared to alter his religion if called to the English throne. When he replied in most definite terms that he was not he ended all chances of a Stuart restoration.

The Tories had made no secret of their approach to the Pretender, and a debate in Parliament, in which the Whigs charged that the Protestant succession was in danger, caused a quarrel between Oxford and Bolingbroke. Oxford, though an able administrator, had grown irresolute and dilatory and was intoxicated frequently. Bolingbroke, a vehement man who hated half measures, was no more Jacobite than Oxford, but he loathed a policy of drift and believed that the Tories should obtain a position of power so that they could bargain with George when the crisis arrived. He asked Anne to dismiss Oxford, which she did in July 1714. Then suddenly the crisis came. Anne was on her deathbed, but Oxford's successor as Lord Treasurer had not been appointed. The Privy Council, which met without the Queen, was dominated by men who did not wish a Roman Catholic sovereign. They determined to suggest the Duke of Shrewsbury as Treasurer, and Anne accepted the appointment, perhaps without knowing what she was doing, for she died two days later. Shrewsbury, like his fellow councilors, was resolved to promote the Hanoverian succession. Bolingbroke was helpless, and all hope of a Stuart restoration disappeared.

The Scottish Union, 1707

The most important achievement of the Whigs in domestic affairs during the middle years of Anne's reign was the completion of a union between England and Scotland. At the time of the Restoration in 1660 the Cromwellian union had been dissolved. Scotland had reverted to its former position under the early

Stuarts, becoming once more a separate country with its own Privy Council and Parliament. But its King remained the King of England. Charles II governed Scotland harshly through a Secretary in London and an amenable Privy Council in Edinburgh. Episcopacy was re-established; the Lords of the Articles again dominated the Scottish Parliament.

It is not surprising, therefore, that the Revolution in 1688 appeared to the Scots as an opportunity to strike for greater freedom. They wished not only to be rid of a Catholic sovereign, but also to overthrow a despotic government, to reassert Presbyterianism, and to obtain a free Parliament. Hence a Scottish Convention Parliament summoned by William used stronger language than was used in England, declaring that James II had "forfeited" the Scottish throne, which was thereupon offered to William and Mary. But this offer was accompanied by an urgent request for parliamentary liberty and by a complaint that episcopacy was an intolerable grievance. Before William answered, a revolt took place in the Highlands, where the Royalist John Graham of Claverhouse (Viscount Dundee) roused the clans on behalf of James. In July 1689 Dundee defeated General Mackay at the Battle of Killiecrankie. But Dundee was slain, the Highlanders stopped to plunder, and were later beaten off at Dunkeld. They soon dispersed.

William decided, however, that he could keep his throne in Scotland only by making concessions. He permitted the re-establishment of Presbyterianism and allowed the Lords of the Articles to be abolished, so that the Scottish Parliament was at liberty to conduct business as it chose. There was danger in this concession: the Parliaments in the two kingdoms could now go separate ways, for there was nothing to hold them together except the royal veto.

The settlement in Scotland was marred by a brutal crime. The Highland chiefs had been ordered to come in and swear allegiance to William before the first of January 1692. All came but Macdonald of Glencoe, who, waiting until the last moment and then delayed by bad weather, did not make his submission until January 6. He might well have been forgiven, but his enemies sent a troop of Campbells to Glencoe, who first fraternized with the Macdonalds and then slaughtered them.

Despite William's concessions, Scotland never was reconciled to his rule, and bitterness against England was increased greatly by a commercial failure in 1699. The Scots, debarred as aliens from trade with the English plantations (though they engaged in a good deal of smuggling), founded in 1695 a Scottish company to trade with Asia, Africa, and America. It was hoped at first that some capital could be secured from England, but the English Parliament opposed the plan, and in the end capital came only from Scots. Persons of every rank subscribed to the venture. The plan to trade in Asia and Africa was abandoned because of English opposition, and the company decided to plant a colony on the Isthmus of Panama. Ignoring local conditions and strangely discounting the certain hostility of Spain, the company sent out three ships with colonists and with goods (including periwigs) to be sold to the Indians. But the climate in Panama was unhealthy, the Spanish attacked the colony, and William, allied with Spain against France, would send no help. The venture ended in failure, with hundreds of Scots losing their savings in this hapless enterprise.

Smarting under this debacle, for which they blamed the English, the Scots were incensed further by the English Act of Settlement in 1701, which arranged for the Hanoverian succession without prior consultation with Scotland, and by the English declaration of war against France in 1702. In 1703 the Scottish Parliament passed an act which forbade the King to involve Scotland in war without its consent. Parliament also passed the famous Act of Security—a kind of declaration of independence—providing that unless Scotland received broad securities, she would not accept the same ruler as England after the death of Queen Anne. Fearing that Scotland might ally with France, English statesmen resolved on a closer union between the two parts of Britain. Commissioners were appointed to prepare a union with Scotland, and the threat was made that if this union were not completed quickly Scottish trade to England would be sharply curtailed.

The Scots were in a cruel dilemma. An alliance with France while England and France were at war would be disastrous. A restoration of the Catholic Stuarts would spell the ruin of the Kirk. Moreover, the only remedy for Scotland's economic plight lay in trade with England and her colonies. Scotland, in a word, faced disaster unless she accepted union. And therefore, despite its anger, the Scottish Parliament appointed commissioners to meet with those of England. A union of the two countries was accepted in 1707. The Scots gave up their Parliament. Thenceforth they were to send forty-five members to the English House of Commons and sixteen representative peers to the English House of Lords. As the Scottish Chancellor recorded the act, he is said to have exclaimed, "Now, there's ane end of ane auld song."

In return the Scots received freedom of trade with England and with the English colonies. They retained Presbyterianism as their national church; they also retained their law, their local government, and their banking system. Customs duties and taxation in the two countries were amalgamated. Since Scotland would now be partially responsible for the combined national debt, she was given a considerable sum of money, about £398,000 known as the Equivalent. This made the union a little more acceptable; much of the Equivalent was used to compensate investors in the disastrous attempt to plant a colony in Panama.

The union gave economic opportunity to Scotland and relieved England from the danger of a Franco-Scottish alliance. In the long run it brought lasting benefits to both countries, but for at least half a century it was resented bitterly in Scotland. When it came into force on May 1, 1707, the bells rang out in St. Giles's Cathedral in Edinburgh, but their first tune was a popular air, "Why should I be sad on my wedding day?"

21

walpole

THE EIGHTEENTH CENTURY

Every age, as it develops its own character and genius, is to some extent in revolt against the age that preceded it. The contrast between the seventeenth and eighteenth centuries was very marked. The religious fervor and political violence of the seventeenth century were regarded with abhorrence by the century that followed; the ideals of the eighteenth century were restraint, moderation, stability, correctness, balance, and proportion. Although a strong sense of personal religion by no means disappeared, as evidenced by the influence of William Law's *Serious Call to a Devout and Holy Life* and by the rise of Methodism, a good deal of indifference and skepticism existed among the upper classes. Divine worship in the Church of England was cold and formal and conducted without intensity. Political life grew more urbane and moderate, party hatreds subsided, the prevailing tone was one of compromise and expediency. Rejecting the florid and involved style of seventeenth-century writing, literary taste demanded correctness, polish, and purity of diction. Englishmen in the eighteenth century had a strong desire for social stability, for an ordered and tranquil society in which each class knew its duties and remained in its place. The tone of politics was aristocratic; it was assumed that political power should rest in the hands of the wealthy and influential. The ruling class was very small. It consisted of the nobles and their connections, of the landed gentry, of rich merchants who controlled the larger trading companies and the Bank of England, and of a small number of wealthy lawyers and ministers of state.

The eighteenth century was an age of art and elegance, when good taste and aesthetic feeling were fairly widespread among the upper classes. The search for excellence may be seen in the polished verses of Alexander Pope, in the artistic chinaware of Wedgwood and Spode and the furniture of Chippendale and Sheraton, and in the brilliance and poised self-confidence of fashionable society.

Yet ideals were often lost in practice. There was little moderation in the

445

drinking and gambling which debauched society. Elegance of manners could be accompanied by coarseness and vulgarity of thought and expression. In contrast to the lavish expenditure of the aristocracy, the lower classes often were sunk in squalor, ignorance, and brutality. The constitution was idealized as a beautifully balanced threefold structure of executive, legislative, and judiciary bodies, each with its allotted functions. Yet in truth the constitution often worked very badly in the eighteenth century, a chaos of ancient offices that had lost their meaning required reform, and there was much nepotism and jobbery in political life.

Eighteenth-century society was secular, practical, and materialistic. Weary of religious and political controversy, men turned their thoughts to ways in which they could increase their wealth. Nobles and gentry invested time and money in improving their estates. Young men on the grand tour studied continental methods of farming and introduced new flowers, crops, and vegetables at home, sometimes with an eye to the exotic, often with the thought of agricultural improvement. Great interest arose in mechanical inventions, for an improved technology in industry was greatly needed; inventions swelled during the century until we begin to talk of an industrial revolution. Although commerce, colonies, and sea power continued to be cherished, industry was taking its place beside them. The new materialism had its unlovely side. The lower classes were exploited and ignored, wealth and influence were worshiped shamelessly, there was much display and ostentation. Wars of commercial aggression were fought against other countries. Yet material wealth increased enormously and with it the general well-being of the nation.

England continued to be essentially rural. Of a population of some 5,500,000 in England and Wales in 1700, the great majority lived in tiny hamlets and small country towns. London, with a population of about 675,000, was the one great city; after London there came a tremendous drop to Bristol and Norwich, with some 50,000 each. Other places—Manchester, Liverpool, Leeds, Sheffield, Birmingham, Coventry—had ceased to be sprawling villages and were growing into unsightly industrial towns. They were still small in 1700. Nonetheless, they were most unhealthy places, without sanitation of any kind, and with high death rates, especially among children. These towns increased in population only because of a steady migration from the countryside. The total population of the kingdom rose to about seven million in 1760 and to about nine million in 1801.

THE HANOVERIAN KINGS

Although the characteristics of eighteenth-century England may be seen emerging in the reign of Queen Anne, the accession of the Hanoverians marks a break in English history. George I (1714–1727) and George II (1727–1760) were thoroughly German, foreigners in the land which had made them Kings. They had little sympathy with English ways or with English parliamentary institutions. Their domestic lives were grim and unattractive, and their courts were shunned by fashionable society. Their greatest asset lay in the fact that they stood for the Protestant succession against the exiled Stuarts. Hence the utilitarian view of kingship, the belief that England had a King because a King was useful, was greatly strengthened.

The Revolution in 1688–1689, despite its liberal character, left very considerable powers in the hands of the King. He was hereditary head of the executive branch of a parliamentary state. Neither a figurehead nor an abstract idea, he was the supreme magistrate whose duty it was to see that the government was carried on. For this purpose he was at liberty to select his ministers. He was thus the fountain of power. His control of patronage extended far beyond his principal ministers to a host of minor places in the administration and in the royal household. The Georges snubbed and kept at a distance those politicians whom they disliked. George II was able for many years to exclude the elder Pitt from the Cabinet and on one occasion in 1746 he attempted the experiment of appointing ministers disliked by the House of Commons. But Pitt eventually was admitted to power; the experiment of 1746 ended in a few days. The Georges learned the necessity of appointing ministers who could win the confidence of Parliament, for government was impossible unless ministers and Commons acted in essential harmony. The Georges possessed the wisdom and good judgment to accept this situation and to take things in England as they found them. They made no attempt to be absolute. Though they were irascible and narrow and of only mediocre ability, and though they could and did make themselves disagreeable, they were essentially honest and sensible men, loyal to those ministers in whom they placed their confidence.

The Georges could exert some influence through the civil list, the money granted by Parliament to the Crown for the purposes of civil government.[1] The civil list included pensions and the salaries of ambassadors and of many ministers. Once it was granted, it was the King's for life. In two other phases of government the Georges believed they could rightfully exercise some influence. One was the army. Clinging to the tradition that the King was supreme over the armed forces, George I and George II watched the details of military administration. The second area was the realm of foreign affairs. The Georges were deeply interested in the politics of Germany, they wished to defend and benefit Hanover, and they felt with some justice that they understood the issues involved. These issues were of growing importance because of the rise of Russia and Prussia as European powers.

GEORGE I

George I did not bother to come to England for seven weeks after the death of Queen Anne, and never took the trouble to learn English. He brought with him a large German entourage, German advisers, and three German mistresses, one of them so stout as to be nicknamed the elephant by the London mob, another so thin as to be called the hop pole. After the virtuous court of Queen Anne, George's amours seemed gross and indecent. The English found him cold, awkward, silent, and aloof, preferring German to English associates, and Hanover to England. He was fifty-four years old, set in the stiff mold of a German soldier, a crude, unpleasant, grim little man, a disciplinarian toward his subordinates and a tyrant in his family circle. Yet he possessed sufficient common sense to know that England was not Hanover; and although he chafed at what he considered the absurdities of the British constitution and roundly cursed the House of Commons, he made no attempt to be absolute in England. But he was not popular with his new subjects.

It was a foregone conclusion that he would regard the Whigs as his friends and the Tories as his enemies, for the Whigs had supported the Hanoverian

---

[1] The civil list was sharply separated from the military and naval estimates.

succession with constancy whereas the Tories, as we have seen, had toyed with the idea of recalling the Stuarts at Anne's death. Even before his arrival in England, George ordered that Henry St. John, Viscount Bolingbroke, a Tory Secretary of State, be dismissed from office and that his papers be retained for investigation. The Duke of Ormonde, the Tory captain general, also was dismissed.

The new ministers were almost entirely Whigs. Three were of special importance. One was General James Stanhope, later Earl Stanhope, a soldier and diplomat. He was an energetic, resolute, and enterprising man whose diplomacy was, on the whole, highly successful, though some of his colleagues thought it too aggressive and too likely to lead to war. He was Secretary of State for the Southern Department.[2] The other Secretary was Lord Townshend, a solid Whig, whose temperament, active and warmhearted though bordering on rashness, was somewhat akin to Stanhope's. Townshend was the brother-in-law of Robert Walpole, the ablest and most promising of the new ministers. Walpole at first held the lesser but highly lucrative post of paymaster of the forces; in 1715 he became the First Lord of the Treasury and Chancellor of the Exchequer. The great office of Lord Treasurer was suppressed, never, as it turned out, to be revived, and the Treasury was placed in commission, the first commissioner being called the First Lord. Walpole displayed great skill in public finance. He consolidated the national debt at a uniform and lower rate of interest, and he established a sinking fund to which certain taxes were allotted and which, it was hoped, could some day be used to pay off the national debt.

When an election in 1715 returned a Whig majority in the House of Commons, the government turned to the congenial task of dismissing all Tories from local as well as from central offices. Impeachment proceedings were begun against the former Tory ministers, including Bolingbroke, Ormonde, and Robert Harley, Earl of Oxford, who had been Lord Treasurer. Bolingbroke and Ormonde foolishly fled to France and joined the Old Pretender. As Ormonde was about to go, Oxford said to him, "Farewell, Duke without a dukedom"; to which Ormonde replied, "Farewell, Earl without a head." But Oxford did not lose his head; he merely served a short term in the Tower. Bolingbroke and Ormonde, on the other hand, not only ruined themselves by joining the Pretender but gave the Whigs an opportunity to brand all Tories as Jacobites and traitors.

The Fifteen

Bolingbroke and Ormonde found the Old Pretender and his little court of exiles hopeful that an uprising in Britain would shortly drive George from the throne. It was known that George was unpopular, that the recent purge of Tories had caused bitterness, and that there was some economic dislocation due to the transition from war to peace. Jacobite riots had become so frequent in London and in the marches of Wales that Parliament had passed a riot act by which individuals who gathered in an assembly of twelve persons to the dis-

---

[2] The medieval secretary had been the private secretary of the king. It was Thomas Cromwell in the reign of Henry VIII who raised the secretaryship to a great office of state with general supervision over both foreign and domestic policy. A second Secretary was added in 1540. In the later Tudor period one Secretary was normally much more important than the other, but James I placed the two Secretaries on a more equal basis. One was a Protestant who dealt with the countries of northern Europe; the other a man with Catholic sympathies who was concerned with southern Europe. This division was formalized in the reign of Charles II into a Secretary for the Northern Department and another for the Southern Department. In addition to continental affairs, the first dealt with Ireland; the other, with the colonies.

turbance of the peace and who refused to disperse at the command of a magistrate were guilty of felony. Misjudging these events, the Pretender and his advisers convinced themselves that England was ready for revolt. But the Pretender, now a young man of twenty-seven, had no gift for leadership. Dignified but rather melancholy, he acted as though he knew he would justify his later sobriquet of "Old Mr. Misfortunate." Refusing to take advice, he showed himself incompetent and narrow. He was surrounded by foolish courtiers and chattering women who did his cause great harm: "those busy flies," wrote Bolingbroke, "that buzz all day about me." With the arrival of Bolingbroke came a flash of intelligence in the counsels of the exiled court. Bolingbroke advised that the principal rising must take place in England, that James must seek the support of the common people, and that the principles of the Revolution, now thoroughly established in English thought, must be accepted. Such advice was beyond the Pretender's imagination. He turned rather to Ormonde, who suggested a rising in Scotland and an adherence to the Stuart tradition of divine right.

From the beginning everything went wrong. The English government, with an excellent intelligence service in France, was well informed, and its preparations were vigorous and adequate. The sudden death of Louis XIV deprived the Pretender of essential aid. Moreover, the risings were not coordinated. On two occasions Ormonde set sail from France to make a landing in southwestern England but found no support and returned to the Continent with nothing accomplished. A small group of Jacobites rose near Newcastle, wandered into Scotland, and returned to England, where they were crushed easily in Lancashire. Only in Scotland was revolt dangerous. In September 1715 a Scottish noble, the Earl of Mar—"Bobbing John," as he was called because he changed sides so often—raised the Pretender's standard at Perth. With an army of 10,000 Highlanders he advanced against a small government force under the Duke of Argyll, who managed to avoid defeat at the Battle of Sheriffmuir. Mar thereupon retired to Perth, where he remained inactive and where the Pretender, landing in Scotland in December, found him. The revolt was now hopeless, for by then Argyll was strongly reinforced. Mar and the Pretender fled to France; the Highlanders, dispersing as best they could, were hunted down by government troops. The rising was over.

The failure of the Fifteen, as it was called from the year in which it took place, was a shattering blow to the Pretender and to the Tories in England. An English treaty with France forced the Pretender to leave French territory. He traveled first to Avignon and then to Italy, where he was much farther from England and so much less a threat. The Whigs continued their purge of Tories, whom they could now call traitors with some justification. Mixed ministries of Whigs and Tories were out of the question, and the Tory party of this period was ruined. The government, not wishing to face an election in such troubled times, passed the Septennial Act in 1716, which extended the life of the existing Parliament and subsequent ones from three to seven years. This act remained in force for the next two centuries.

A Rift among the Whigs

Although the future belonged to the Whigs, the leadership of the party was uncertain, and a rift appeared in which Stanhope and the Earl of Sunderland[3] on the one hand were opposed to Townshend and Walpole on the other.

---

[3] A Whig politician who had married Marlborough's daughter.

This division was caused in part by personal animosities, for Stanhope was a great favorite of George I, and Sunderland had carefully cultivated the good will of the King's mistresses, whereas Townshend and Walpole thought themselves neglected. The quarrel was also over policy, both foreign and domestic. Stanhope's management of foreign affairs was brilliant but bold and even rash. He succeeded admirably in wooing Holland and Austria into renewed alliance with England. These countries had been alienated in 1713 when the English, in negotiating the Treaty of Utrecht with France, had shamefully ignored their interests. Stanhope was also successful in improving relations with France. The French King, Louis XV, was a sickly child. If he should die without an heir, and if the Peace of Utrecht which separated the Crowns of France and Spain should be honored, the throne of France would pass to the Duke of Orleans, the French Regent, who was Louis' uncle. But if, on Louis' death without issue, the settlement of Utrecht were cast aside, the heir to France would then be Philip V, the King of Spain, who did not conceal his ambition to become ruler of both kingdoms. Hence the Duke of Orleans gladly allied with Stanhope to preserve the Utrecht treaties.

All this was excellent. Stanhope, however, had to deal with serious problems in Italy and Scandinavia. In Italy, as in France, it was Philip of Spain who was causing trouble. The Treaty of Utrecht had taken Naples and Sicily from Spain, giving the first to Austria and the second to Savoy. Philip regarded these losses as intolerable; his ambitious wife, Elizabeth Farnese, was eager to obtain the Italian provinces of Parma and Tuscany for her son. In 1717 England and France together proposed a compromise by which Parma and Tuscany should revert to the son of Elizabeth Farnese, Austria obtaining Sicily through a treaty with Savoy. The policy of these powers was to persuade Spain to accept this arrangement. Stanhope's persuasions became so strenuous that in 1718 an English fleet sank a Spanish one at Passero off the southern coast of Sicily. After a short war between Spain and England Spain yielded in 1720.

Meanwhile the Baltic was disturbed by a long war between Sweden under Charles XII, her fighting cock of a King, and all the other Baltic powers including Russia. This war was harmful to English commerce in the Baltic, threatened to cut off her supplies of naval stores, and involved the interests of Hanover. Stanhope sent British fleets to the Baltic, often running the risk of war. His policy was to restore peace between Sweden and her enemies and to repress the rising power of Russia. In the first of these objectives he was successful, in the second he failed. On the whole his diplomacy was excellent, but it was too aggressive for Townshend and Walpole, who disliked all dangerous adventures and who also opposed Stanhope's policies at home.

To strengthen the position of the Whigs, Stanhope was willing to allow Protestant nonconformists to hold office; and he was also willing to make concessions to Roman Catholics. Townshend and Walpole supported him in repealing two minor acts passed by the Tories against nonconformists in the last days of Queen Anne's reign, but they would go no further. In 1717 Townshend was dismissed and Walpole resigned. They strongly opposed a bill concerning the peerage which Stanhope introduced in 1719 and which was aimed at maintaining the Whig majority in the House of Lords. It proposed that the Crown be forbidden to create more than six new peerages, except for princes of the royal blood and for the replacement of noble houses which had become extinct. Had the Crown lost the right to create new nobles and hence the power to alter the composition of the House of Lords, that house would have become a closed and impregnable corporation able to impose its will on the nation. Walpole fought the measure with skill and success. Stanhope was forced to withdraw the bill and to admit defeat by bringing Townshend and Walpole back into the Cabinet in 1720.[4]

This division among ministers, though it might appear to weaken the Whigs, in fact strengthened them greatly. There were now Whigs in opposition as well as in the government, and if one group of Whig politicians fell from power, another group was ready and eager to take its place. Though the Whigs might quarrel among themselves, all of them supported the Hanoverian dynasty; any hope of the Tories that they might return to power, tainted as they were by the suspicion of treason, was even further removed. Indeed, a situation slowly developed during the first half of the century in which the Tory party so disintegrated that everyone who hoped for office called himself a Whig. The advantage of the division among the Whigs quickly made itself apparent.

The South Sea Bubble

Stanhope, Sunderland, and other ministers were suddenly engulfed in 1720 in the scandal of the South Sea Bubble. The national debt, which stood at some £51 million, was thought to be excessive and dangerous, and the government was intent on its reduction. Early in 1720 the South Sea Company, founded in 1711 to trade with Spanish America, came forward with a proposal to administer the debt by incorporating it into the company's finances. The company offered to pay off £7 million at once and to accept from the government a reduced rate of interest for the remainder. The company, on its side, hoped for more business and for more capital. It proposed to call in the government certificates or bonds held by the investing public and to issue instead new shares of company stock. The Cabinet found the plan attractive and accepted it, but the result was a wave of speculation in the shares of the South Sea Company. Shares that had been selling for £150 soon sold at £1000. And all sorts of unlikely projects suddenly made their appearance. There were schemes to salvage wrecks off the Irish coast, to import Spanish asses, to make salt water fresh, to invent a wheel of perpetual motion. One rascal sold shares for "an undertaking of great profit in due time to be revealed" and promptly absconded with the proceeds.

In September 1720 came the inevitable crash, the people lost large sums, and a great outcry arose against the government. The dominant faction of the Whigs suffered severely. Stanhope, though not responsible for the scandal, was placed under heavy strain, suffered a stroke, and died. Another minister committed suicide, Sunderland pushed Walpole forward as the man who could save the situation, doubtless in the hope that Walpole would fail. But he succeeded. He had not been in office when the South Sea scheme was begun, and he could not be accused of malpractice. He now persuaded the East India Company and the Bank of England to take over £18 million of South Sea Company stock. This helped to restore public credit and saved for the stockholders a fraction of their original investment. Walpole was the man of the hour. In April

---

[4] The word "Cabinet," in general use at this time, meant the small, inner group of the King's principal ministers. It did not refer to the modern Cabinet system of government, which had not yet come into existence.

1721 he became First Lord of the Treasury and Chancellor of the Exchequer. He remained in supreme control of the government for the next twenty-one years, England's first Prime Minister in fact if not in name.

SIR ROBERT WALPOLE

Walpole's career illustrates the great length of time that many modern English statesmen have spent in public life, for although in 1721 he was but forty-five years old, he had already served in Parliament for twenty-one years and was to remain in office for twenty-one years more. He sprang from a line of Norfolk country gentlemen. The third son in a family of nineteen children, he had at first been destined for the church and had been sent to Eton and to King's College, Cambridge. But upon the death of his two elder brothers he was brought home by his father to learn to manage the estate and to take part in the affairs of the county. He became thoroughly acquainted with the class of hardheaded and masterful country gentlemen whom he was to meet in the House of Commons. He was a man's man. He drank heavily, as did many politicians of the age, filled his conversation with bawdy jests because, as he said, women formed a topic in which all could join, and although he rebuilt his country seat at Houghton in lavish style and filled it with statues and paintings he had little interest in art or literature. He was a domineering man who loved power, running the government as though it were a business which could have but one head, and ridding himself systematically of rivals to his supremacy. Yet he had remarkable gifts and was remarkably successful. With great energy, industry, and capacity for work, he possessed a clear head, a quick and solid judgment, and a keen insight into human character. Because he threw the whole force of his personality into the business at hand, he could usually enforce his will. The work of government was still on a small scale, so that he knew its details and could encompass in his own mind the whole fabric of the administration. He was intimately acquainted with his subordinates and gave them a warmhearted loyalty, though he was ruthless in dealing with his adversaries. He was a great financial minister and a great House of Commons man.

For some years after 1721 he was favored by fortune in his rise to supreme power. The way was cleared by the death of Stanhope in 1721 and that of Sunderland in 1722; and when the brilliant but arrogant Lord Carteret assumed Sunderland's role as a rival leader of the Whigs, Walpole skillfully maneuvered him into temporary obscurity and gave his place as Secretary of State to the Duke of Newcastle. In these early years Walpole was able to devote himself to domestic issues, of which he was master, and did not have to venture into the realm of foreign affairs, which were managed by Townshend. His fear of Jacobite plots appeared to be justified by a small rising in Scotland in 1719 and by a larger conspiracy in England in 1722, of which he took advantage to drive into exile the most influential Jacobite in England, Francis Atterbury, the learned and popular bishop of Rochester. Thereafter there was small danger from the Jacobites, though Walpole kept the issue alive as an excellent slogan at election time. When George II came to the throne in 1727 it was thought that Walpole's day was done, for George had quarreled with his father and hence with his father's minister. The new King tried the experiment of dropping Walpole, only to find that he was indispensable; Walpole quickly was recalled. He found an unexpected ally in Queen Caroline, George's remarkably clever wife. After dis-

Sir Robert Walpole, by Jean Baptiste Van Loo. (National Portrait Gallery, London)

cussing measures with Walpole, Caroline would persuade the King that they had originated in the royal mind and thus were worthy of adoption. During the 1720s Walpole and Townshend were supreme, and Walpole accomplished his best work.

Fiscal Policy

It was in financial and economic policy that Walpole excelled. He believed that the best protection against Jacobitism was a prosperous and contented people, and he set about making England loyal to the Hanoverians by making it rich. In public finance he at once began to save interest by repaying short-term government borrowings, not at stated intervals, but as money came into the Exchequer. He continued his former policy of assigning certain taxes to a sinking fund which he used to pay off portions of the national debt. By 1727 he had discharged £8.5 million of a debt of some £54 million and had reduced the interest on the balance to a uniform four percent. Had payments continued at this rate the entire debt might have been liquidated in a comparatively short time. But Walpole was determined to reduce the tax on land, a tax which fell heavily upon the country squires, who formed a majority of the House of Commons. Many squires were discontented Tories whose good will Walpole was anxious to obtain. In his first budget he lowered the land tax from 3s. to 2s. on each pound of assessed value. At one point he reduced the tax further to 1s., though this figure could not be maintained, and in time of war the tax rose to 4s. But he kept it as low as possible by an occasional raid on the sinking fund to meet sudden and unexpected emergencies. He has been criticized for using the sinking fund in this way. But the national debt was not large in proportion to the wealth of the nation, and Walpole was probably wise to conciliate the landed classes rather than to repay a larger portion of the debt.

He was aware that taxation should be used, not merely to produce revenue, but to stimulate commerce and industry. Aside from the tax on land and from an unpopular tax on every house (with mounting assessments according to the number of windows), the principal taxes were excises, levied internally on necessities, such as malt, candles, leather, soap, and salt; and the customs duties on imported and exported articles. The excises were more certain of collection and produced a greater yield, but they savored of oppression because the excise men descended on retailers and even entered private houses to ensure that the excises were paid. The customs, on the other hand, were a hodgepodge of illogical and complicated duties. They were out of date, for the book of rates had not been revised since 1660; they left evaluation to the guesswork of officials; some articles, such as pepper, were subject to a number of different levies. The result was an enormous amount of smuggling, especially in such luxuries as tea, wine, and brandy. The public felt no compunction about buying articles that had not paid duty. Rev. James Woodforde relates quite casually in his diary how he obtained wines from smugglers who brought them to his parsonage.

To correct these evils Walpole issued a new and simplified book of rates. He lowered or abolished the import duties on various raw materials used in English industry, such as dyes, undressed flax, raw silk, salt for curing fish, old rags and rope for making paper, and beaver skins for hats. Duties were abolished on exported agricultural produce and on many manufactured articles, and bounties were offered for the exportation of grain, silk, sailcloths, spirits, and refined sugar. Walpole also sought to maintain high quality in goods manufactured for export. By more dubious legislation he held down the wages of artisans, since low wages were considered necessary for a successful export trade. To combat smuggling he increased the penalties for evading customs regulations and enlarged the number and powers of customs officials. His measures against smuggling, however, were not effective.

It is not to be thought that Walpole was in any way a free trader. He believed in high protective duties and in the Acts of Trade. English industries were heavily protected against Irish and American competition. The Molasses Act of 1733 was passed to force the American colonists to buy molasses in the

British West Indies and not in the French or Dutch islands. But though Walpole was a mercantilist, he was an enlightened one who saw that the regulation of economic life must be directed by practical common sense. His object, he told Parliament, was "to make the exportation of our own manufactures, and the importation of the commodities used in the manufacturing of them, as practicable and as easy as may be; by this means, the balance of trade may be preserved in our favor, our navigation increased, and the greater number of our poor employed."[5]

In 1723 Walpole introduced a plan of bonded warehouses. Certain imported articles—tea, coffee, chocolate, and coconuts—were not to be subject to immediate duty upon being landed in England, but were to be placed in government warehouses. If these articles were then re-exported, they might be taken from the warehouses without payment of any duty at all. The arrangement brought great advantage to merchants who had formerly paid duties on all imported articles and then, in case of re-export, had recovered the duties from the government, a long and tedious process. If the goods were taken from the warehouses for retail sale in England they were subject to an excise. The plan worked so well that Walpole was able to reduce the excise tax on these articles and at the same time increase the sums paid to the government. In 1733, therefore, he proposed to handle tobacco in the same way, and wines were to follow.

A fierce opposition arose. The hated excise men, it was said, were to be increased in number and authority and would soon curtail the ancient liberties of the nation. The patronage at the disposal of the government would be extended, thus increasing the jobbery in public life. Here was an issue on which all of Walpole's opponents could unite although something could be said on both sides. The plan was economically wise, but the dislike of excises had some foundation in an age when the people were often at the mercy of minor government agents. As opposition grew, Walpole's majority in the Commons dwindled, and when London threatened violent measures, he yielded. He withdrew his bill from the Commons but proceeded to purge the administration of all office-holders who had not supported him. It was only at the end of the century that the younger Pitt revived the plan, with highly beneficial results.

Walpole's Decline

The failure of Walpole's excise plan in 1733 was something of a turning point in his fortunes. Thenceforth he began to lose ground, for he hesitated to take any action that might arouse opposition, and fiscal reform came to an end. The death of Queen Caroline in 1737 was a severe loss which increased his difficulty in managing the King. As Walpole grew older the opposition, which was composed of many elements, took new heart. There was still a large body of Tories in the Commons. Their opposition was at its height during Walpole's regime; their number at the time of his fall from power has been estimated at 136.[6] Old Jacobites like Bolingbroke, though they had abandoned the cause of the Pretender, carried on a constant campaign against Walpole. Drawing the literary talent of the nation to their side, they published an ably written newspaper, the *Craftsman*, which was read by Tories and by many who called themselves Whigs. Moreover, a number of Whig politicians had been dismissed by

[5] Quoted in Basil Williams, *The Whig Supremacy 1714–1760* (Oxford: Clarendon Press, 1939), p. 183.
[6] John B. Owen, *The Rise of the Pelhams* (London: Methuen, 1957), p. 66.

Walpole at one time or another and were his personal enemies. This group, which included Lord Carteret and William and Daniel Pulteney, was joined later by the Duke of Argyll, who exercised great influence over the Scottish members. Meanwhile in 1730 Townshend, having quarreled with Walpole, retired from politics to conduct agricultural experiments on his estates. Frederick, the Prince of Wales, followed Hanoverian practice by quarreling with his father. His London residence, Leicester House, became a center of opposition to the Cabinet, though Frederick was not an effective person and many Whigs in opposition had little to do with him.

Meanwhile, a new figure was rising in the Commons—William Pitt, who was to be one of the great statesmen of the century. Closely allied with the merchants in London, he voiced their conviction that Walpole was too timid and unaggressive in foreign affairs. The commerce and sea power of France, he declared, were growing so formidable that they threatened those of England; moreover, France and Spain were drawing together and France would soon dominate the trade of Spanish America. The remedy, said Pitt, was a war of aggression before it was too late. There was a brutal quality about Pitt's aggressiveness, but he opened vistas of expansion for England's colonial trade and inspired a sense of British destiny overseas. Walpole sneered at him as the "Boy Patriot" but nonetheless feared him.

To an opposition which demanded an expanding foreign trade for Britain, Walpole's policy seemed tame and not without danger. Both Russia and Prussia were emerging as powers on the Continent; yet England had won the friendship of neither. The alliance formed after Utrecht with Austria, Holland, and France was breaking down. English relations with Spain continued to deteriorate.

There were many causes of friction between England and Austria. To the alarm of English merchants, an East India company, known as the Ostend Company, had been formed in the Austrian Netherlands to trade with India and China. Only after prolonged and irritating negotiations was the company suppressed in 1731. Two years later a war broke out between Austria and France, the War of the Polish Succession, in which Walpole offended Austria by keeping England neutral. France emerged from the war with increased prestige and improved relations with Spain. After Utrecht, as we have seen, Philip of Spain still hoped that he might some day be King of France. This had placed him in opposition to the French government. But Louis XV had married early and had a son; Philip's chances of inheriting the French throne were now so small that he gave up his old ambition, altered his policy, and drew closer to France. The two nations agreed to cooperate in the Family Compact of 1733, which was renewed ten years later. The fear of the commercial classes in England that France might be the heir of Spain in Latin America was not without justification.

The War of Jenkins's Ear, 1739

In 1739 the opposition in Parliament clamored for a war against Spain. Friction between the two countries had been increasing for a long time. Spain never ceased to resent the concessions—especially the surrender of Gibraltar and Minorca—made to England by the Treaty of Utrecht in 1713. Further difficulty arose over English trade in Spanish America. In the first place, the treaty gave England the right to supply the Spanish colonists with Negro slaves and to send one ship each year with English goods for sale at the fairs at Vera Cruz or at

Cartagena. The English also were permitted by the treaty to buy land in Spanish America to use as slave pens where Negroes were brought back to health after the voyage from Africa before they were sold. And English ships in need of repair might call at Spanish American ports. The British employed these rights to cover a large amount of smuggling. The annual English ship at the fairs was replenished at night from other vessels; the slave pens and the visits of British ships were used to carry on a large illicit trade.

The Spanish, on their side, established a system of coast guards who intercepted and searched British ships, took them to Spanish ports where the cargoes were confiscated on flimsy pretexts, or took off the goods at sea and set the ships adrift. The coast guards maltreated English sailors. A notorious case was that of Captain Jenkins in 1731, who later testified before a committee of the Commons that he had been bound to his own mast and had had one of his ears torn off. The legend runs that when Jenkins testified he carried a box which, he alleged, contained his ear.

In 1739 Walpole faced a Cabinet crisis in which some of his colleagues sided with the opposition. He reluctantly agreed to war. "It is your war," he said to Newcastle, "and I wish you joy of it."

The fighting in Spanish America did not amount to much. Admiral Vernon, after whom Mount Vernon in Virginia was named, burned the town of Puerto Bello, but as he was about to descend upon Cartagena his men were smitten by fever and he was forced to withdraw. Admiral Anson, ordered to attack the Spanish in the Pacific, completed a remarkable voyage. In the years of peace since 1713 English naval and military strength had been allowed to decay. Anson, to his astonishment, was allotted 500 men from Chelsea Hospital, an old soldiers' home. Those with the strength to run away promptly did so, leaving Anson with invalids and men in their sixties and seventies. Nonetheless he completed his mission and sailed around the world, returning with one man and one ship for every five with which he had embarked. The war merged into a larger conflict on the Continent to which we will turn in the next chapter.

Walpole remained in office until 1742, but his influence was greatly diminished. His world had been one in which England had remained at peace and had increased the wealth of the upper classes, who benefited from security and low taxation and from keeping things as they were. A new and more turbulent era was at hand, when the country, hoping for an expansion of trade and possessing the power to seize it, was eager for aggressive wars against her commercial rivals. In 1742 Walpole was defeated in the Commons and resigned.

WALPOLE AND THE STRUCTURE OF POLITICS

An inquiry into the structure of politics during Walpole's administration helps to explain his long success and his ultimate failure in the Commons. The simplest explanation of his defeat in 1742 is that the opposition in Parliament became too strong for him. He was opposed by the Tories and by many discontented Whigs whose numbers increased as he excluded from power all those who threatened his supremacy. Hence, when the war with Spain went badly, when there were tensions within the Cabinet, when some of the lesser officeholders deliberately abstained from voting in his support, and when his opponents won over many independent members, he could no longer carry on the King's business in so hostile a House of Commons. He did not resign because of any constitutional scruple that a minister defeated in Parliament must at once leave office. He had already lost a number of divisions. He resigned because it became evident that no Cabinet of which he was the head could secure the general approbation of Parliament. Thus his resignation demonstrates the fact that in the eighteenth century a minister could not survive, even though he enjoyed the confidence of the King, unless he was also acceptable to the Commons. The Commons were not telling the King whom he should employ as his minister; they were telling him whom he could not employ.

But this explanation is rather negative, and Walpole's resignation may be given a broader interpretation. The Revolution in 1688 had left the problem of how the King, who headed the administration, and the Commons, who controlled taxation and legislation, were to function together without friction. The ultimate solution was to be the Cabinet system of government. But this system is dependent upon well-organized political parties, and parties of this kind did not exist in the eighteenth century. It was necessary to find some other means to ensure the smooth cooperation of King and Commons.

It is often supposed that this cooperation was achieved through influence, that is, through the use of royal patronage to build a following in the Commons strong enough to give the King's ministers a majority. It is certainly true that patronage existed and that Walpole made use of it. Creations and promotions in the peerage, the appointment and advancement of bishops, the bestowal of office and of pensions from the civil list were made with an eye toward obtaining support in Parliament. Men who were friendly to the administration and who controlled seats in the Commons which they were ready to place at the disposal of ministers were carefully cultivated. The Treasury used small offices and perquisites in the dockyards and in the excise and customs service, livings in the church, and secret service money to influence elections in small boroughs. In this way a Court and Treasury party was constructed upon which the Cabinet could depend for support in Parliament.

Upon careful analysis, however, it becomes evident that this system was not nearly so corrupt or so effective as is often supposed. Patronage is only a part of the picture and is inadequate as an explanation of Walpole's long tenure of power. The Cabinet could not hope to influence everybody, for there was not enough patronage to go around. Of 558 members of the Commons, scarcely a fourth held places of profit under the Crown, and the great majority were independent of any control by the government. Some of these independent members accepted small bits of patronage for themselves or for their constituencies. They might ask for a concession for a relative or for a person from their locality or might even receive financial assistance in fighting an election. But these small favors did not bind them to constant support of the government. Patronage of a minor kind was considered a natural recompense for the time and money expended by a member in seeking election and in serving in the Commons, where he received no wages. A sharp distinction should be made between the members of the Court and Treasury party whose incomes were supplemented by the Crown and the much larger number of independent members who accepted small and temporary favors.

Thus the fundamental fact emerges that most of the members of the Commons were independent. They were men of wealth and of property. Candidates in the counties usually were selected by leading families before they presented themselves to the voters. Compromises were arranged between families, so that contested elections, which were very costly, were relatively few. When they did take place, they revolved around local rivalries and local issues of which Parliament was frequently the arbiter. Country gentlemen sought election to advance the interests of their families or to heighten their local prestige. Their roots were in the country, not in London. They resided in the capital for about half the year and enjoyed its political life, but they were not part of that life and were not necessarily politicians. Indeed, they often left London before the session was over. They responded to family loyalties, to personal ties and friendships, and to local issues. The prestige of Parliament was high. It attracted talented and wealthy men. And it is absurd to think that the country gentlemen of England, having subordinated the Crown in the Revolution in 1688, would barter away their freedom of action for a little petty cash.

In addition to the Court and Treasury party and to the much larger number of independent members, there was a group of men who may be called politicians, who made politics their profession. They were divided between those who were in the government and those who were out. The "ins," merging with the Court and Treasury party, often held very good posts. They were the "men of business," the civil servants, active administrators who did much of the detailed work of government. They were often skilled debaters who defended the Cabinet in the Commons and sought the support of independent members. They defended the government, not from venal motives, but because they were a part of it. The government had to have them, for they represented the administrative talent and debating strength necessary for any successful administration. Seats had to be found for them in the Commons, and the Cabinet had to give seats under its control to persons already pledged to support the administration, a fact which in itself restricted the wide distribution of patronage. The "outs" were in opposition. They hoped, by exploiting the weaknesses of the Cabinet and by winning the adherence of independent members, to force their own admission to office. Thus two groups of politicans were trying to influence independent members. But it would be quite wrong to think of this situation as representing the functioning of a two-party system.

Walpole's supporters consisted of three general classes. The first was a group of about 50 politicians or civil servants who represented the core of the Cabinet's administrative and debating talent and who seldom voted against the government. The second consisted of about 100 other members of the Court and Treasury party. They were judicial officers, members of the royal household, army and navy officers, holders of minor posts and sinecures, and government contractors. They were loyal to Walpole while he dominated the government but were undependable as his power declined, for they wanted to retain their places and had to consider who might be Walpole's successor. Family groups did not play as great a part during Walpole's regime as they came to play later in the century. There were only two of any consequence and they were small. Walpole controlled five seats, in which he placed friends and relatives. Through his family connections the Duke of Newcastle controlled nine seats and managed a few boroughs dominated by the Treasury. In all he could influence about fifteen seats. He did not manage elections on a national scale until he became First Lord of the Treasury in 1754. In addition, Walpole was supported by well over 100 independent members—country gentlemen, merchants, and professional men, such as lawyers, who owed nothing to the government but were inclined to give it support.

All these groups were more independent than might be imagined. The third group was the most independent, though some of its members doubtless hoped for favors from the administration. Of the politicians and members of the Court and Treasury party, some were so well placed that they could afford to vote against the Cabinet if they disagreed with it sharply. They were entrenched in Treasury boroughs or held posts or sinecures for life. It is a mistake to think that Walpole could buy support as he pleased. The patronage of the Cabinet should be regarded as jobbery to keep a limited number of people in good humor, to support what might be termed the civil service, even at times to provide a kind of charity, and not as an attempt at universal corruption.

No organized opposition existed. It has been suggested that its absence was due to the feeling that formal opposition smacked of disloyalty and that therefore it gathered around Frederick, the Prince of Wales, who opposed his father. But in fact people went into opposition despite its ill repute; and Frederick had little to offer either as a leader or as a distributor of patronage. Two other reasons appear more plausible. In the first place, members were too independent to be controlled; it was impossible for the leaders of the opposition to exert party discipline. Secondly, the Tories kept to themselves and did not cooperate with those Whigs who were in opposition.

The Tories were in a strange position. The Hanoverian dynasty was now fully accepted and they no longer had any thought of supporting the Pretender. They had no cause to defend the church, for its position was firmly established. In fact, there was no great issue to divide a very stable society. The Tories had outlived their reason for existence and yet they refused to die. They were a party of tradition. Almost all of them came from Tory stock and were Tories because their ancestors had been Tories. They were instinctively suspicious of the Whig government; they opposed patronage, largely because they never got any; they disliked the Septennial Act; they opposed standing armies and continental wars; they wanted the land tax reduced; and they strongly desired influence over local government. As their numbers declined some of them became Whigs. They could do this by merely ceasing to be Tories and by giving the government a general support. The term "Whig" was coming to mean little or nothing. The Whiggism of 1688 was now old-fashioned; the principles of the Revolution were fully accepted. Everyone who hoped for office was a Whig. Everyone was a Whig unless he was distinctly a Tory.

The Office of Prime Minister

Something more than influence was needed to secure harmony between King and Commons. It was here that Walpole showed his greatness and built a unique place for himself in politics. He saw that when the King headed the administration and when the Commons controlled the purse and the making of statutes, a minister must have the confidence of both sources of power. Walpole's achievement was to gain this double confidence. He made himself indispensable to both and for many years was the link between them.

He usually is portrayed as a great Parliament man, as he certainly was. An excellent speaker, direct and forceful, whose practical arguments appealed to the squires in the Commons, he sensed their moods and prejudices, he knew their limitations as well as their good qualities, he could judge what could and what could not be done in Parliament. He paid members the compliment of giving them clear and complete explanations of what his policies were; he taught them that their function was not merely to criticize but to cooperate with ministers in conducting the King's government and to think of themselves as a senate debating with responsible gravity the problems of the state. He looked upon the Commons, not the Lords, as the proper sphere of activity of the King's principal minister. "I have lived long enough in the world, Sir," he once said in the Commons, "to know that the safety of a minister lies in his having the approbation of this House. Former ministers, Sir, neglected this, and therefore they fell; I have always made it my first study to obtain it, and therefore I hope to stand." His ascendancy depended upon clear judgment, forceful exposition, and the magnetism of a masterful personality.

But he was also a great King's man. He was the trusted Minister of the King in the House of Commons as well as the trusted Minister of the Commons in the King's Closet. It was this combination of function which gave him his pre-eminence and made him the first Prime Minister of England. For much of his time in office he was the only member of the Cabinet who was also a member of the Commons, where he defended the whole administration, of which, as we have seen, he had a firsthand knowledge. Thus he rose far above his colleagues, who were mostly peers, becoming much more than the head of a single department. His achievement was the creation of the office of Prime Minister, bringing King and Commons together.

But when he yielded to the demand for war with Spain, of which he disapproved, he forfeited his dominant position as Prime Minister. He could no longer form an effective link between the King and the Commons when both strongly supported a war he did not want. The basis of his former power was destroyed. The Commons turned against him, though George II did not. Accepting the fact that a minister must have the approbation of the Commons, he resigned, though only after a struggle, when he knew that that approbation had ended.

The office of Prime Minister was not understood at the time and was allowed to fall into temporary abeyance after Walpole's resignation. But it reappeared in 1746 when Henry Pelham achieved a position essentially the same as that which Walpole had occupied.[7]

[7] This analysis of the structure of politics is based upon the opening chapters of John B. Owen, *The Rise of the Pelhams.*

22

the pelhams, pitt, and the seven years' war

THE RISE OF THE PELHAMS

The office of Prime Minister, which Walpole had created, was not understood by the politicians of the time. Indeed, the concept of a "sole" or "overgrown" minister was thoroughly disliked and was indignantly repudiated by those in power. This hostility arose because a minister who possessed the confidence of both the King and the House of Commons was apt to remain in office for a long time. Having the patronage of the Crown at his disposal, he confined it to his followers and permanently excluded a large section of the men in public life. The "outs," who were out until the death of the King or of the Prime Minister, increasingly resented their subordinate position. Nevertheless, a Prime Minister was coming to be a necessity. Hence Walpole's fall was followed by a period of strife and confusion in politics until Henry Pelham early in 1746 achieved a position somewhat akin to that which Walpole had held. Stability then returned to political life.

The new administration formed in 1742 consisted of Walpole's followers with the addition of some new Whigs brought in from the opposition. George II wished to make as few changes as possible. His aim, in which he succeeded very well, was to give office to just enough of the opposition to secure a majority without disturbing the loyalty of the old corps of Whigs who had supported Walpole. Of these 200 or so Whigs about half were politicians, civil servants, placemen, or pensioners, plus those who sat either for Treasury boroughs or for places which they owed to patrons who were friends of the government. The other half were independent members who had normally supported Walpole. Both groups had been larger in the heyday of his power, but had diminished as his position weakened; now that he was gone they could be expected to increase. The two groups were accustomed to act together, but would have to be strengthened by additional support in the Commons. Like the King, they wished as few changes in the administration as possible.

Of the old ministers the King retained the Duke of Newcastle, his brother

Henry Pelham, Lord Chancellor Hardwicke, the Earl of Harrington, and the Duke of Devonshire. Overtures were made to Lord Carteret and to William Pulteney, Whigs whom Walpole had edged out of power. These men entered the administration, though the office of First Lord of the Treasury, which was normally held by the most important member of the Cabinet, was given to a nonentity, Lord Wilmington, and was thus kept out of their hands. Carteret as Secretary of State, an office in which he shared responsibility for foreign affairs with Newcastle, stepped into a position of great power. But Pulteney lost his influence in the Commons by accepting a peerage as Earl of Bath. The opposition, which had expected great things at Walpole's fall, was disappointed with these arrangements and was angry at Carteret and Pulteney.

Since Pulteney was now in the Lords, the Cabinet required a spokesman in the Commons. The duty fell on Henry Pelham, who became indispensable as the one commoner in the Cabinet and as the minister for the House of Commons. He was made First Lord of the Treasury in 1743. A rather timid man, diffident about his own powers, he was not a person from whom heroic measures were to be hoped for, but he was respected in Parliament for his integrity, moderation, and reasonableness. He possessed industry, common sense, sound judgment, knowledge of business, and long parliamentary experience. The old corps of Whigs accepted him as Walpole's successor. Thus he was able to regain the confidence Walpole had lost and to act as intermediary between Cabinet and Commons.

Henry Pelham, however, did not have the confidence of the King, who much preferred Lord Carteret. Carteret, a brilliant man, an able diplomat, and a fine linguist, pleased the King by his knowledge of German politics and of the German language, as well as by his willingness to support the interests of Hanover. Unfortunately he did not make a good minister. Egotistical and overconfident, he believed that if he had the favor of the King he had everything. He treated his colleagues with contempt and arrogance, insulting them gratuitously, as when he refused to dine with them at the Feathers Tavern because, he said, he never dined in taverns. Even foreign princes complained that he regarded them with a certain disdain. After some initial success, he made commitments on the Continent in 1743 which his colleagues, who had not been properly informed, refused to sanction. The result was a rupture between him and the Pelhams. Supported by most of the Cabinet, the Pelhams informed the King in November 1744 that they would resign unless Carteret, now the Earl of Granville, was dismissed. With great reluctance George asked Granville to resign.

Since Granville had not been defeated in the House of Commons, his dismissal has sometimes been portrayed as the result of an intrigue by the Pelham brothers. But Granville would certainly have been defeated in the next session of Parliament. Hence the situation of 1742 was being repeated. No one could tell the King whom to employ as his minister, but if the affairs of the kingdom were mismanaged, as the Commons believed they were, the King could be told whom not to employ. The Pelhams merely were anticipating events. They were taking the precaution of having Granville removed before a defeat in the Commons which might well have ruined their position as well as his.

The Pelhams then reconstructed the ministry with the aim of forming a kind of coalition government, known as the Broad-bottom administration, to which many groups were admitted. The support of the old Whigs was retained by treating them well, but some of the followers of Granville and Bath were removed to make way for new appointments from the opposition. Some of Pitt's friends were admitted to office, though the King refused to have Pitt himself, for Pitt had done much to bring about the fall of Granville and had opposed English support for Hanover. Yet others almost equally obnoxious to the King were brought in; one Tory was given office.

George accepted these changes with great reluctance. He continued to show great confidence in Granville and Bath, especially in Granville, who remained a dominant figure in the government. On the other hand, the King treated the Pelhams with studied hostility. They considered resignation, for their position was most unpleasant and the King's lack of confidence was affecting their influence in the Commons. But for some time they remained in office because of a war on the Continent and a rising in Scotland in 1745. Late in that year a crisis arose over foreign policy and over the wish of the Pelhams to bring Pitt into the Cabinet as Secretary at War. George violently opposed them and began arrangements to dismiss the Pelhams and to form a new administration under Granville and Bath. Thereupon, early in 1746, the Pelhams and some forty-five other members of the administration resigned. For a few days the King persisted in his plan but then gave up the attempt and indicated that he wished the Pelhams to return. Naturally they returned on their own terms. The King's hostility to them was to end and he was to withdraw his confidence from Granville and Bath. Pitt was to be brought into the ministry, although out of deference to the King, he was to have the office of paymaster of the forces, not that of Secretary at War. George was to give other indications that he placed his trust in the Pelhams. From this time forward, Henry Pelham, as the undisputed head of the Cabinet, enjoying the confidence of both the King and the Commons, was England's second Prime Minister.[1]

The events in politics between 1744 and 1746 look more like the working of the modern Cabinet system than they actually were. The historian Sir Lewis Namier calls the whole series of crises an accident arising from what would be considered today an essentially unconstitutional situation.[2] The Pelhams did not come to the King with a strong majority in the Commons and demand changes in the name of that majority. Rather it was the King who was the head of the state and who, through royal patronage, gave to the Pelhams their position of strength in the Commons. It is obvious that both in the government and in Parliament there was much less loyalty to the Pelhams than there was hostility to Granville and Bath. The King's power to select his ministers was challenged only in a negative way. He was told whom he should not employ. Granville and Bath being debarred, George's limitation of choice was the result of his own dislikes and prejudices. He detested the Tories, he detested his son, Prince Frederick, who might have brought him some new support, he detested the opposition Whigs and even some who were allies of the government, and he detested the Pelhams. On the whole, he disliked the Pelhams less than the others and chose them as the least objectionable. He had to have ministers, but the initiative in selecting them was always in his hands.

[1] John B. Owen, *The Rise of the Pelhams* (London: Methuen, 1957), Chaps. VI–VIII.
[2] L. B. Namier, *England in the Age of the American Revolution* (London: Macmillan, 1930), pp. 51–60.

THE WAR OF THE AUSTRIAN SUCCESSION, 1740–1748

It was unfortunate that these crises came at a time when England was at war on the Continent. The colonial war against Spain begun in 1739 had merged into a larger conflict known as the War of the Austrian Succession. A confusing war, more significant for the Continent than for England, it is important largely because it shaped the future alignment of European powers. When Emperor Charles VI of Austria died in 1740 he left his dominions to his daughter Maria Theresa. For many years he had sought guarantees from other countries that his daughter would be allowed to succeed him peacefully, a policy known as the Pragmatic Sanction. But Charles's death precipitated a general assault on Austria and her new ruler. Frederick of Prussia seized the opportunity to weaken Austria's position in Germany, to teach the other German princes to look

Europe in the First Half of the Eighteenth Century

Charles Edward Stuart, the Young Pretender, by A. David. (National Portrait Gallery, London)

to him as their leader, and to secure the Austrian possession of Silesia, which he promptly invaded. To the French the time appeared ripe for a final reckoning with the Austrian Hapsburgs, their traditional foes. They allied with various German princes to partition the German possessions of Austria and to obtain the election of Charles Albert of Bavaria as the next Emperor. The Spanish hoped to secure additional territory in northern Italy at Austria's expense. Lesser states watched for an opportunity to obtain some of the spoils.

Maria Theresa called for assistance from Holland, Russia, Savoy, and England, all of whom had accepted the Pragmatic Sanction. But in the early part of the war, only Britain responded. Regarding Maria Theresa with much sympathy, the English were bound by a treaty of 1731 to come to her assistance. They were already at war with Spain, the close ally of France; they feared a French attack on the Austrian Netherlands; and George II, as Elector of Hanover, was angered by Frederick's aggression in Silesia. Rather unwillingly, Walpole supplied Maria Theresa with a subsidy of £300,000 in 1741 and also agreed to pay for Danish and Hessian troops in her service. But when the French sent an army into Germany, George became alarmed. He declared the neutrality of Hanover and offered to cast his vote for Charles Albert of Bavaria as Emperor, who was duly elected in 1742. Meanwhile Walpole had persuaded Maria Theresa to cede Silesia to Frederick, thus eliminating for the moment her most dangerous foe.

When Carteret became Secretary of State in 1742 he threw himself energetically into European affairs. Maria Theresa was now in great danger: the French had occupied Bohemia, Frederick had entered the war a second time to safeguard his conquest of Silesia, the Spanish had sent an army to northern Italy. Carteret obtained new subsidies for Maria Theresa, persuaded George to end the neutrality of Hanover, took Hanoverian and Hessian troops into English pay, secured Frederick's second withdrawal from the war, and employed the navy against the Spanish in Italy. Moreover, he dispatched an army to the Austrian Netherlands. A rather motley host, it contained English, Hanoverian, Hessian, and later Dutch and Austrian troops. In 1743 this army, commanded by George II in person, was set in motion against the French, whom it defeated in the Battle of Dettingen. Dettingen marked the height of Carteret's influence. He now attempted to detach the enemies of Maria Theresa one by one, to unite German princes in an anti-French alliance, and to keep the slippery Charles Emmanuel of Savoy on the side of Austria. But Carteret achieved only temporary success. He was so lavish with promises of English subsidies that his colleagues refused to sanction his commitments. He offended Frederick, who disliked English interference in German affairs. He soon was dismissed from office.

The war went badly for England during the years 1744 and 1745. An English fleet in the Mediterranean failed to stop a French and Spanish squadron bound for northern Italy. In the Netherlands the English army was defeated at Fontenoy by Marshal Saxe, France's best general. By the end of 1745 most of the British forces had been withdrawn from the Continent to meet a sudden rising in Scotland on behalf of the Young Pretender.

The Forty-Five

For a moment early in 1744 the French played with the idea of invading England. They collected transports at Dunkirk, to be convoyed across the Channel by a large fleet, and they proposed to bring with them a representative of the exiled Stuart Kings. Since the Old Pretender was now a broken and gloomy man of fifty-seven, the French summoned to Paris his son, Charles Edward, the Young Pretender, known in Scottish history as Bonnie Prince Charlie. Then in his middle twenties, Charles was tall, handsome, athletic, gay and vivacious, ambitious, spirited, and adventurous. But he was rash to the point of folly, supremely confident of his own opinions, and childishly hostile toward those who disagreed with him. When stormy weather scattered the transports at Dunkirk the French abandoned any thought of invasion and turned to a campaign in the Netherlands. Left to his own devices, Charles Edward conceived the mad notion of going to Scotland without French aid. Borrowing a little money, he obtained two ships and boldly set forth to conquer an empire.

On July 23, 1745, he landed in the Hebrides and was soon on the mainland. The youthful glamour of his personality won him the backing of a number of the Highland chiefs. He was idolized by his men, for he was ready to endure the hardships of the common soldier. As he marched on foot at the head of his little column, clad in the bravery of a royal Highland chief, he cast a spell on his followers, infusing them with his confidence and love of high adventure. He had but 3000 men when he reached Perth. Thanks to the blunders of his adversary, General Cope, he was able to take the city of Edinburgh, though not the castle, and to defeat the English at the Battle of Prestonpans. He then invaded England. But Lowland Scotland had not risen, nor did northern England. Charles Edward marched south as far as Derby, causing great alarm. But at Derby his officers, knowing that English armies overwhelming in size were not far distant, refused to follow him further. There was nothing to do but retreat, which he did in great dejection. Having lost his former hold on Edinburgh, he pushed north to Inverness. At nearby Culloden, in April 1746, he was completely defeated. Five months later after many adventures he escaped to France. Thereafter he degenerated in character, drank heavily, and died in Rome in 1788. The rebellion was followed by severe punishment. There were many executions, and large portions of the Highlands were laid waste. An attempt was made to extinguish the ancient customs of the Highland clans. Land tenure by military service and the jurisdiction of the chieftains as magistrates were abolished, the people were disarmed, the Highland garb of kilt and tartan was forbidden.

The Peace of Aix-la-Chapelle, 1748

The war on the Continent, which continued until 1748, went badly for the English in the Netherlands but much better for Maria Theresa in central Europe. In 1746 the French Marshal Saxe occupied the whole of the Austrian Netherlands; in the next year he invaded Holland, defeating an English and allied army of more than 100,000 men in the Battle of Lauffeld. These reverses were partially offset by a success in North America. A force of New Englanders, assisted by the royal navy, captured the French fortress of Louisbourg on Cape Breton Island in 1745. In the following year, however, the French took the English town of Madras in India.

Meanwhile Maria Theresa's fortunes were improving. At the death of Charles Albert of Bavaria in 1745, she was able to make peace with his son and to secure the election of her husband, Francis of Lorraine, as Emperor. She drove Frederick from Bohemia when he entered the war for the third time. The Spanish were defeated in northern Italy.

In 1747 the English navy, which grew stronger as the war progressed, intercepted two large French convoys on their way to the French colonies. These English victories at sea made the French eager for peace. Their national finances were close to collapse and their colonial trade and their Newfoundland fisheries at a standstill. England also was tired of the war. Her trade had increased, but the financial strain of fighting in the Netherlands and of subsidizing allies in various parts of Europe had become very heavy. Peace was concluded at Aix-la-Chapelle in 1748.

By this treaty England restored to France the Canadian fortress of Louis-bourg in exchange for Madras in India. France relinquished her conquests in Holland and in the Austrian Netherlands, recognized the Hanoverian dynasty, and repudiated the exiled Stuarts. But the two countries made no settlement concerning their many colonial disputes in the West Indies, North America, and India. Nor did the treaty mention the Spanish coast guards whose rough treatment of smugglers had been a major cause of the war with Spain. England's monopoly of the slave trade in Spanish America and her right to send one trading ship a year to the Caribbean were renewed for four years only (and then were relinquished by another treaty). Thus colonial rivalries were left unsettled.

Spain obtained Parma and Piacenza in northern Italy, acquisitions England had fought to prevent. Holland was content with the restitution of her territories, but Maria Theresa was deeply dissatisfied. She was forced to yield Silesia to Frederick, to permit the Dutch to garrison a line of fortresses in the Netherlands facing France, and to make concessions in northern Italy.

The significance of the war is obscure because it was fought over dynastic issues, because the belligerents moved in and out, and because their war aims were not clear even to themselves. Frederick knew what he wanted and so did Charles Emmanuel of Savoy, who strengthened his position in northern Italy. But France was very shortsighted. She followed tradition in fighting Austria, whereas her interest lay in preparing for the colonial struggle that was certain to come with England. Even in Great Britain the true issues were not clearly understood. Carteret recognized France as the great enemy, but he attempted to defeat her on land, ignoring colonial rivalries. He also failed to see that the rise of Prussia introduced a new element in international affairs and that Maria Theresa regarded Prussia, not France, as her primary foe. Thus the war emphasized the growing importance of Prussia, the deep animosity between Prussia and Austria, and the rivalry of England and France. The Anglo-French struggle for commerce and colonies was still to be decided.

POLITICS, 1748–1754

During the years between the Peace of Aix-la-Chapelle and the death of Pelham in 1754 English politics were surprisingly tranquil. A bird might build her nest in the Speaker's chair or in his wig, said a member, and not be disturbed by the debates. Henry Pelham, as First Lord of the Treasury and Chancellor of the Exchequer, managed financial policy, which he did very well, making a number of improvements, while Newcastle, as Secretary, was responsible for foreign affairs. Pelham's position was secure. Gradually the King became reconciled to him, praised his care and parsimony in handling public money, and lamented his death with sincere sorrow. Pelham met with little opposition in

Parliament, partly because of his conciliatory manner and partly because he drew most of the talent of the Commons to the support of the government. William Pitt, who might have been dangerous, devoted his time to the reform of his office of paymaster of the forces and gave Pelham a general support. Opposition was weakened by the death in 1751 of Frederick, Prince of Wales, around whom discontented members had rallied. Patronage, of course, played its part in maintaining a majority, but there was less need for it than in the past. The gradual disintegration of parties continued. The number of Tories was diminishing. Some became Whigs, for they could do so merely by ceasing to be Tories. The term "Whig" had less and less meaning: almost everyone was a Whig.

Pelham was succeeded as First Lord of the Treasury by his brother Thomas, Duke of Newcastle, a man of strange eccentricities which made him appear ridiculous to his contemporaries and to later historians. He was consumed by neurotic fears and jealousies, he often imagined that he was about to be impeached, and he would fling himself, as he admitted, upon his friends for their support and advice in his many supposed difficulties. He loved to distribute the patronage of the Crown, to dole out the financial advantages the government could offer, to manage elections, and to maintain the government's influence in Treasury boroughs. After he became the First Lord in 1754 he had ample opportunity to indulge these tastes, for the number of Whigs was constantly growing and the administration had to "find pasture for the beasts that they must feed." A man who wasted his time on trifles, Newcastle looked decidedly foolish. But it is probable, as a contemporary said, that "public opinion put him below his level." He possessed a wide knowledge of foreign affairs, a fund of intelligence and common sense, much warm human kindness and sincere good will, and a desire to serve his country without mean or sordid motives. Yet he must be counted as a mediocre statesman, beyond his depth in the colonial war with France that began during his ministry.

Since he was a peer, the problem arose of finding a minister for the House of Commons. Newcastle wanted someone who would not dominate the Cabinet and yet would bring it additional strength in Parliament. The outstanding man in the Commons, William Pitt, was disliked by the King and had no great following; hence Newcastle selected a mediocrity, Sir Thomas Robinson, who proved to be incompetent. Thus, although Newcastle acquired a reputation as the "overgrown" minister who monopolized power and managed the House of Commons, he was not a Prime Minister as Walpole and Henry Pelham had been. Little remained of that position when Newcastle left office: he had reduced it to his own dimensions.[3]

THE CLASH OF EMPIRES

The British Empire about 1750

One should think of all the lands bordering on the North Atlantic as belonging to one great trading area. Winds and currents carried trade in a great circle. From Europe south to West Africa the prevailing winds in the autumn came from the north, while the easterly trade winds north of the equator carried vessels

---

[3] L. B. Namier, *England in the Age of the American Revolution*, pp. 75–94. For a more favorable estimate see John B. Owen, *The Rise of the Pelhams*, pp. 127–129.

The Old Custom House, 1753. From a colored engraving by T. Bowles. (Historical Pictures Service, Chicago)

with ease from Africa to the Caribbean. Thence a current swept north along the eastern coast of Florida. Farther north, from New England and Canada, the prevailing winds were from the west and brought the trader back to Europe.

Trade followed this circle in a general way, though there were endless variations. Cheap manufactured goods were taken to Africa to lure the Arab slave drivers, luxuries went to the wealthy West Indian planters, less costly manufactures to the colonists along the Atlantic seaboard. Slaves were brought from Africa to the Caribbean and to the southern colonies, whence sugar was carried to refineries in Europe or to New England to be made into rum; from North America came tobacco, rice, cotton, lumber, and naval stores, with furs from Hudson Bay and fish from the Newfoundland Banks. Fish were taken to southern Europe or to the West Indies to feed the slaves; salt was picked up in Portugal, Venezuela, and St. Kitts. "All this enterprise, in its thousands of little sailing ships, seldom over 200 tons in burden, began and ended in a few home ports. Bristol and Boston were opposite numbers, New York and others were on a lower scale, but London by far transcended them all."[4] It was for control of this great area of trade that England, France, and Spain contended in the wars of the eighteenth century.

Although there were small English colonies on Newfoundland and in Nova Scotia by the middle of the eighteenth century, the great growth in the empire was taking place to the south in the English colonies along the Atlantic seaboard. Twelve of these colonies had been planted in the seventeenth century. The

[4] J. A. Williamson, *The Ocean in English History* (Oxford: Clarendon Press, 1941), p. 55.

thirteenth was Georgia, founded in 1733 through the efforts of General James Oglethorpe, a philanthropist who hoped to make Georgia a haven for debtors who had been imprisoned in England. The American colonies had advanced from primitive and rather squalid settlements to large and flourishing communities of solid wealth and considerable culture. By 1760 their population reached the figure of almost 2 million at a time when the population of England and Wales was scarcely more than 7 million.

In the Caribbean the most valuable English possessions were Jamaica, St. Kitts, and Barbados, but there were many lesser English islands: the Bermudas, the Bahamas, Antigua, Nevis, Barbuda, Montserrat, and some of the Virgin Islands, although these last were of no importance save as hiding places for pirates. The population of the English islands in 1750 amounted to some 320,000, of whom 230,000 were Negro slaves. In West Africa the English were established on the Gambia River and held a number of forts and depots on the Gold Coast, where they obtained most of their slaves. There was also solid progress in India, to which we will turn presently.

The French Empire in 1750

The history of French colonial expansion at this time is one of defeat and difficulty during the wars of Louis XIV but of rapid, even striking, recovery after 1720, so that by the middle of the eighteenth century the French possessed a highly valuable empire.

Louis' minister Colbert had laid great stress on colonial expansion, but after his death in 1683 a reaction set in against his policy. Thenceforth the French government, though supporting overseas expansion in time of peace, was inclined to neglect and even sacrifice it in time of war. The French possessed an energetic governor in Canada, the Comte de Frontenac, who served from 1672 to 1682 and again from 1688 to his death in 1698. He kept the western frontier of New England and New York in a state of alarm and harassed the English in Newfoundland and in the area of Hudson Bay. During the war from 1701 to 1713, however, the French were unable to send much aid to their colonies. By the Treaty of Utrecht they ceded the fringes of New France: Newfoundland, Nova Scotia, and the Hudson Bay Territory. Louis' wars also harmed the French East India Company. Its servants continued to make progress in India, but at home their affairs fell into confusion. For almost eight years after 1712 the company as such sent no ships to the East, although private traders were licensed to carry on the trade.

Between 1717 and 1720 French expansion was dominated by the schemes of John Law, a Scottish financier who proposed to combine all the French trading companies into one huge organization which would also administer the national debt and work in close association with the government. His plan, which bore some resemblance to the South Sea Bubble in England, ended in a similar crash. Yet despite the confusion that he created, he at least set French expansion in motion once again. One of his achievements was to send out 5000 colonists who founded New Orleans in 1717.

French colonies and French trade overseas expanded rapidly between 1720 and 1750. The population of Canada increased from about 20,000 in 1713 to about 54,000 in 1744. It was a population of high military efficiency. The service of every man was required in the militia, in which he was well trained and well led. The French obviously intended not only to defend Canada but to regain the territories they had lost by the Treaty of Utrecht. They settled their disbanded soldiers along the banks of the Richelieu River, which flows north from Lake Champlain into the St. Lawrence and forms a natural approach to the Hudson and so to New York. In 1720 the French began to build the fortress of Louisbourg which, as we have seen, was captured by the New England colonists in 1745 but returned to France in 1748. Fortified posts along the Mississippi River were constructed in order to connect Canada with New Orleans.

The French West Indian islands were making remarkable progress. By the middle of the eighteenth century French Santo Domingo, Martinique, and Guadeloupe produced much more sugar than the English islands and had largely captured the European market. Along the coast of West Africa the French held the important fortress of St.-Louis on the Senegal River and the slaving station of Gorée slightly to the south. In India their towns were increasing in wealth under energetic governors. The largest was Pondicherry, but there were smaller stations at Surat, Chandarnagar, Mahé, and Karikal. At home French merchants studied economic conditions and developed docks and shipping facilities, especially at Marseilles, a port from which they acquired much of Europe's trade with Turkey. The merchant marine of France increased sixfold between 1715 and 1735—from 300 to 1800 vessels. It was this rapid recovery and progress during the years of peace that alarmed William Pitt and the merchants of London.

The Coming of War

In the years following the Peace of Aix-la-Chapelle colonial rivalry between France and England moved from the stage of commercial competition to that of armed conflict. Difficulties between the two companies in India became more acute, there were disputes in the West Indies, and when the French strengthened Louisbourg the English fortified the town of Halifax in Nova Scotia. Nova Scotia was the source of many quarrels. Since its boundaries had never been exactly determined, each side made large claims against the other. The arrival in 1749 of 3000 disbanded English soldiers and their families, sent out by Lord Halifax, the President of the Board of Trade, caused serious trouble with the French colonists. Incited by secret agents from Quebec, the French inhabitants and the Indians of the area turned on the English settlers. In 1755 the government in London took the drastic step of collecting the French colonists of Nova Scotia and shipping them to various points along the Atlantic seaboard to the south.

During the years 1753 and 1754 the French, pushing into the Ohio Valley, built Fort Presque Isle on the present site of the city of Erie, Fort Le Boeuf slightly to the south, and Fort Duquesne at the junction of the Allegheny and Monongahela rivers. Meanwhile in the English colonies a number of companies had been formed to settle the Ohio region and to trade with the Indians. In 1754 Governor Dinwiddie of Virginia sent young Colonel Washington to expel the French from the vicinity of Fort Duquesne, but Washington was driven back by a superior force. His expedition, which resulted in some bloodshed, may be said to have begun the war for North America.

Although England and France were still at peace in Europe, both countries dispatched small armies to America in 1755. The English were commanded by General Braddock, who was instructed to raise additional troops in the colonies, to capture Fort Duquesne, and to move against the French forts along the southern shores of the Great Lakes. Obtaining a few colonial troops, whom he regarded with contempt, he marched through the wilderness to Fort Duquesne, where his expedition was destroyed by an ambush of French and Indians. At about the same time a body of New Englanders was repulsed near Lake George. Meanwhile a French army set sail for Canada. The English Admiral Boscawen, sent to intercept it at sea, captured two French frigates and thus committed an act of war. But the other French ships reached Quebec in safety. For the moment Canada was impregnable.

The year 1756 was also a time of disaster. The western frontier of the American colonies was swept by Indian raids. The French captured Oswego on the southern shore of Lake Ontario. In England there was fear of a French invasion. This threat soon faded, but the French sent an expedition from Toulon against the British naval base on the island of Minorca. Admiral Byng, the British commander, dispatched with an inadequate fleet to defend the island, fought an indecisive action, and then, believing that Minorca could not be held, sailed away and left it to its fate. An outcry arose against him in England, to which Newcastle weakly submitted. Byng was tried by court-martial and shot on the deck of his flagship. In England, said Voltaire, they shoot some of their admirals in order to encourage the others.

Meanwhile, Newcastle, in attempting to build a European coalition against France, discovered that the Dutch would not be drawn into new entanglements and that Maria Theresa, though eager for revenge on Prussia, had no interest in fighting France. Newcastle's proposed coalition dwindled into a series of agreements with German states and with Russia, all backed by English subsidies,

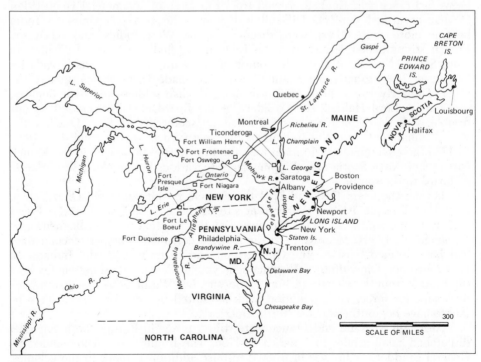

The American Colonies during the Seven Years' War and the American Revolution

which appeared to be more concerned with the safety of Hanover than with war against the French. The arrangement with Russia produced an unexpected result. It so alarmed Frederick of Prussia that early in 1756 he concluded a treaty with England by which each country guaranteed the dominions of the other and promised to resist the entry of foreign armies into Germany. This treaty in turn induced the French to make an alliance with Austria, much to the satisfaction of Maria Theresa and her minister Kaunitz. Thus the alliances of the War of the Austrian Succession were reversed: England was now allied with Prussia; France with Austria. But the two great enmities of Europe—Austria against Prussia and England against France—remained as before.

Ministerial Changes

Newcastle's fumbling policy naturally brought sharp criticism in the House of Commons, especially from Pitt and Henry Fox. As early as December 1754 Newcastle silenced Fox by bringing him into the Cabinet and by giving him the office of Secretary a year later. But Pitt became more outspoken and was joined by other leaders. He refused to enter Newcastle's Cabinet when a place was offered to him. Thereupon Fox resigned; Newcastle, admitting defeat, also resigned. A long period of confused negotiations followed, until finally in June 1757 Newcastle and Pitt formed a new ministry in which Newcastle as First Lord of the Treasury managed the patronage of the government while Pitt as Secretary obtained the power to manage the war effort as he saw fit. Pitt was now a national figure. In addition to the Court party of civil servants, placemen, and pensioners under Newcastle's control, Pitt secured the wide and spontaneous support of many independent members of the Commons, much as Winston Churchill was given almost universal backing in 1940.

Pitt's Character

Pitt's genius lay in his energy, his commanding personality, his gift for leadership, and his confidence in himself and in his country. He did not belong to the aristocracy but sprang from a family of aggressive merchants. His grandfather, "Diamond Pitt," had begun his career as an interloper in India. Eventually he became governor of Madras and brought home a diamond worth £135,000. He was rough, brutal, choleric, and quarrelsome. He believed that England should be aggressive, should seize the trade of the world, and should fight the wars that such a policy made necessary. His grandson, William Pitt, thought the same. For years he had demanded an attack upon the empires of France and Spain, but he was more interested in trade than in the acquisition of territory. To him Canada meant furs, fish, and naval stores; the West Indies, sugar; Africa, gum and slaves; India, cotton fabrics, indigo, and saltpeter. He worked in close harmony with the merchants of London, to whom he offered hopes of expanding commerce and increased wealth.

Pitt acquired a commanding position in the House of Commons. Tall, majestic, and dramatic, he had a fine voice and used effective gestures in speaking; he had great oratorical power. He spoke without notes in a rapid, easy, and conversational style; yet his speeches abounded in poetic conceptions and in light touches of fancy and imagination. He gave a moral grandeur to the theme of empire, as though Britain's destiny spoke through him. One of his principal weapons was a blasting invective which frightened members into silence. He did not bother to build a party; his power extended beyond the Commons to the

William Pitt, Earl of Chatham, after Richard Brompton. (National Portrait Gallery, London)

nation as a whole. His weaknesses were glaring. There was much that was bombastic about him; he was petulant, intractable, and difficult to get on with; he exasperated his colleagues by his haughty manners; and he had illusions of grandeur. Often ill, both physically and mentally, his fierce aggressiveness sprang in part from his sufferings.

The Progress of the War, 1756–1763

Pitt from the first took the people into his confidence. Telling them of difficulties and of failures as well as of successes, and explaining clearly the sacrifices he expected them to make, he was able to call forth their patriotic cooperation. One of his early steps was to send away the Hessian and Hanoverian troops whom Newcastle had brought to England during the invasion scare of 1756. By strengthening the militia he gave the nation a means of self-defense and at the same time made it possible to send more of the regular army overseas. He recruited Highland regiments, though the Highlands had been in revolt in 1745. The American colonists were encouraged to raise troops and were made to believe that their interests would be safeguarded. Knowing that Americans resented the arrogance of British officers, Pitt reduced friction by placing colonial officers on an equality with regulars of the same rank. He constantly sought talent among the younger men in the armed forces, often advancing them over older officers who had proved incompetent. In planning colonial campaigns, which he did with great care, he obtained detailed information concerning geography and other local conditions. But once he had placed this information before his officers, he gave them freedom to manage operations as they judged best.

Pitt's strategy was to keep the French preoccupied in Europe while he destroyed their empire and captured their trade. For this purpose he supported Frederick the Great with generous subsidies. In the past he had denounced commitments and subsidies on the Continent because they had seemed to benefit Hanover rather than England. But the situation had now altered. England already was bound by treaty to come to Frederick's assistance; and Frederick, opposed not only by France but also by Austria and Russia, might well be overwhelmed, leaving the French at liberty to concentrate on the war with England. Pitt therefore organized an army of Hanoverians and Hessians, commanded by the Duke of Cumberland, the King's son, to defend Hanover and to protect Frederick's western flank against the French. He also sent commando raids against the French coast. These raids struck at St.-Malo, Cherbourg, and elsewhere. Some of them were costly failures, which brought sharp criticism at home, but they immobilized large bodies of French troops, disturbed the plans of the French command, and made it dissipate its forces.

Pitt had a firm grasp of the strategic importance of sea power. If the French fleets could be destroyed at sea or blockaded at Brest and Toulon, the link between France and her colonies would be severed and French forces overseas would wither for lack of supplies from home. Thus an English blockade of Brest and Toulon became an essential feature of the war. It achieved much more than keeping the French inactive. A blockaded fleet suffers a sharp decline in morale and efficiency, whereas the blockading squadron remains in a state of preparedness and keenness for battle. Pitt also employed the navy skillfully to cooperate with land forces in Canada and India and to meet the French in purely naval engagements.

For some time after taking office in June 1757 he had few successes. On the very day he came to power he learned that Frederick had suffered a defeat at the Battle of Kolin in an attempt to invade Bohemia. Shortly afterward news arrived in England that the town of Calcutta in Bengal had been captured by a hostile native prince. And later in the year the Duke of Cumberland, defeated by the French, signed the disastrous Convention of Kloster-Zeven, which left Hanover unprotected and exposed Frederick to French attack. The first of Pitt's commando raids ended in failure. Meanwhile in America an English attempt against Louisbourg was abandoned, and the French General Montcalm captured Fort William Henry on Lake George.

Late in 1757 the tide began to turn. Frederick defeated the French at Rossbach and the Austrians at Leuthen. Pitt reconstructed the Hanoverian army, stiffened it with British troops, and found a new commander in Prince Ferdinand of Brunswick. Successes continued in 1758. When two French fleets with reinforcements and supplies for the war in America were turned back, English strength in the colonies became much greater than that of France. Amherst and Wolfe, two of the younger officers selected by Pitt, finally captured the fortress of Louisbourg, thus opening the St. Lawrence to British penetration. It was Pitt's plan that, while the French were occupied at Louisbourg, an attack should be made on Quebec by a force moving up the Hudson and down the Richelieu rivers; but this army, led by the dilatory Abercromby, was stopped with considerable loss at Fort Ticonderoga on Lake Champlain. On the other hand, Colonel Bradstreet captured Forts Frontenac and Oswego, thus separating the St. Lawrence Valley from the Great Lakes; an expedition across Pennsylvania against Fort Duquesne ended in anticlimax, for the French, believing that they needed all their strength for the defense of Canada, had abandoned Duquesne and the whole of the Ohio Valley. In the same year a British force expelled the French from Emden in Germany; three raids did much damage on the French coast; a carefully planned and executed campaign resulted in the capture of the French slaving stations of St.-Louis and Gorée in West Africa.

The next year, 1759, brought fresh triumphs. In Germany Frederick was hard-pressed and badly defeated at the Battle of Kunersdorf, but Prince Ferdinand's victory at Minden pushed back the French and probably saved Frederick from destruction. Meanwhile, an English expedition captured the French West Indian island of Guadeloupe. Pitt was now intent on the conquest of Canada, to be accomplished by a two-pronged attack. Amherst, who was to strike north by way of Lake Champlain and the Richelieu River, failed in his purpose, but Wolfe, instructed to ascend the St. Lawrence and to capture Quebec, was successful. Ably supported by Saunders, who brought a fleet up the St. Lawrence in spite of great dangers, Wolfe landed on the Île d'Orléans in the river below Quebec. For more than two months he feigned attacks from various points along the river, then finally discovered an ill-guarded path up the steep bank to the Heights of Abraham above. Both he and Montcalm fell in the engagement that followed, but the French were defeated; part of their army surrendered and the remainder withdrew to Montreal. Montreal, and with it the last French army in North America, surrendered in 1760.

Meanwhile, in 1759, the management of affairs in France passed into the able hands of the Duc de Choiseul, who once more threatened England with invasion. For such an enterprise he required sea power, but the French fleet at Toulon, escaping from that port in an attempt to reach Brest, was defeated at Lagos Bay off the coast of Portugal; in September the fleet at Brest, which came out to carry French troops to England, was crippled at Quiberon Bay by Admiral Hawke. The danger of invasion passed away, and the French seemed beaten everywhere.

In March 1761 the French indicated their desire to treat for peace. The Cabinet agreed to negotiate, though at the same time Pitt continued hostilities, for he had plans to capture the rest of the French West Indies and he wished to be in a position to obtain concessions for Frederick of Prussia. The Cabinet rejected a number of Choiseul's proposals, which tended to stiffen as time went on. Pitt then discovered that France and Spain had concluded a secret treaty by which the latter agreed to enter the war. Convinced that England would soon be fighting Spain, he favored an immediate attack on her, but the Cabinet was against him. Newcastle, alarmed at the mounting cost of the war, did not wish to see it extended. England, he felt, had already captured many colonies and could not afford to fight for more. Lord Bute, whom the young King George III had brought into the Cabinet, was of much the same opinion. Thereupon, in October 1761, Pitt resigned. He was not dismissed by the King. Unable to endure contradiction, he resigned because of disagreement with his colleagues over policy.

As he had predicted, Spain entered the war in 1762, but speedily showed herself so devoid of strength that instead of helping France she lost her own possessions—Havana in Cuba and Manila in the Philippines.

Negotiations for peace were continued by Lord Bute. A curious mood had developed in England. If France were treated too harshly, it was thought, she would soon seek a war of revenge in which she would be supported by the rest of Europe. It might be wiser to return to her some portion of her former possessions. Such a policy left Pitt cold. He later declared in Parliament: "France is chiefly, if not solely, to be dreaded by us in the light of a maritime and commercial power; and therefore by restoring to her all the valuable West India Islands, and by our concessions in the Newfoundland fishery, we have given her the means of recovering her prodigious losses and of becoming once more formidable to us at sea."

The Peace of Paris, 1763

Nonetheless the Peace of Paris was highly advantageous to England. Great Britain retained her conquests of Canada and Cape Breton Island; St. Vincent, Tobago, Dominica, and Grenada in the West Indies; and Senegal in West Africa. Minorca passed again into English hands. On the other hand, England restored to France the West Indian islands of Guadeloupe, Martinique, Marie Galante, and St. Lucia; the post of Gorée in Africa; and fishing rights in Newfoundland with two small islands, St. Pierre and Miquelon, on which the fish could be dried. In India the French were given back their towns, but these were not to be fortified; they could be occupied by British forces whenever the British so desired. Hence the French hope of hegemony in India was gone. England restored to Spain both Havana and Manila, but received all of Florida and a recognition of the right to cut logwood in Honduras. France then completed her departure from North America by ceding Louisiana to Spain in compensation for Spanish losses. In making peace England almost entirely ignored Frederick's interests.

These treaties marked the culmination of Britain's first colonial empire and the old mercantile system. Spain, Holland, France, and England had struggled to control the trade of the North Atlantic, and now England had emerged victorious. Yet the fear that the very completeness of her victory contained dangers for the future was well founded. Within twenty years she was to see her empire shattered and Europe combined against her.

The Seven Years' War in India

The Seven Years' War determined two points of supreme importance in India. The first was the obvious one that France was defeated and that the dominant European power in India was to be England. In addition, the English emerged from the war not merely as merchants trading at various points along

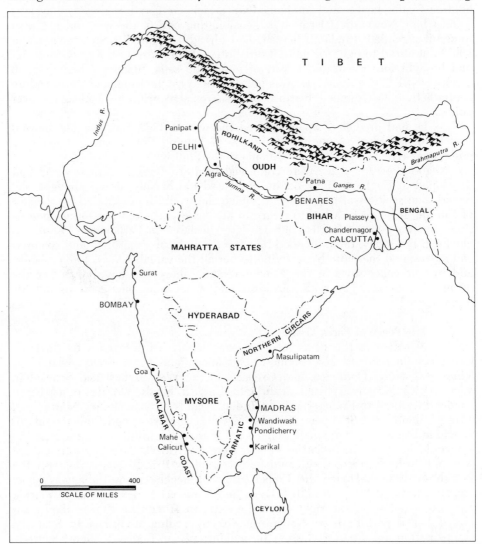

India in the Eighteenth Century

The Old East India House before it was rebuilt between 1726 and 1729. (From *Gentleman's Magazine*, July 1784. Walter Library, University of Minnesota)

the coast but as the masters and governors of large and valuable Indian territories. This second development quickly altered the position of the East India Company in England and the role of its servants in the East.

Although the French East India Company made striking progress in India during the first half of the eighteenth century, the English company was much more firmly established and enjoyed a much larger and more profitable trade. The English had been in India for a longer period; their towns—Madras, Bombay, and Calcutta—were prosperous and flourishing communities. It was only in the area of Madras, where the French possessed the fine town of Pondicherry, that the rivalry of the two companies had spectacular results.

In England the East India Company was a sound, respectable, and wealthy corporation, the largest trading organization in the kingdom, and of great importance as a part of the London money market. Its directors were men of influence in the City and were often members of the House of Commons. In close touch with the government, they were normally its allies in London politics. They possessed a certain amount of patronage both in England and in India. Of much greater importance was the fact that the Cabinet looked to the company, as it looked to the South Sea Company and to the Bank of England, for assistance in raising loans. When the government wished to borrow, it summoned representatives of the large public companies and other monied men of the City to a meeting at which amounts and terms were arranged. After a meeting of this kind in 1759–1760, when the large sum of £8,000,000 was to be borrowed, the government noted: "Mr. Burrell for the Bank of England £466,000, Mr. Bristow for the South Sea Company £330,000, Mr. Godfrey for the East India Company £200,000."[5] Thus the company was one of the corporations on which national credit depended. It issued its own instruments, known as India bonds. By 1732 the sale of its imports amounted to some £2,000,000 a year. The company, which rested on private enterprise, had as its directors sound and experienced administrators who were guided by long tradition and were well versed in foreign trade.

The French company, on the other hand, was connected closely with the state. It owed its origin to royal policy. Its stockholders were courtiers, nobles, bureaucrats, and churchmen, for the business classes held aloof. Its directors were appointed by the King; and since it obtained loans and grants from the government, to which it was usually in debt, it could not avoid control by the Crown.

Meanwhile a fundamental change had taken place in the political structure of India. Since the middle of the sixteenth century the Mogul Empire, centering in the cities of Delhi and Agra, had given political stability to northern India and had imposed varying degrees of subjection on the principalities in the south. For about a century and a half the Mogul Empire continued to be strong and vigorous. But Emperor Aurangzeb (1658–1707), the last of the great Moguls, brought disaster on his dominions. He has been compared with Louis XIV. His elaborate court was a heavy drain on his revenues. A bigoted Mohammedan, he reversed the more tolerant policy of earlier emperors and persecuted his Hindu subjects. Moreover, he was a warlike prince, who spent his strength in conquering southern India and in extending his frontier to the northwest.

Aurangzeb's campaigns brought him weakness rather than power, for in the later years of his reign he was faced with constant revolts. In the northwest his border fortresses, which protected India from invasion, were captured by Persians and by Afghan rebels. In central India he was unable to subdue the Marathas, a Hindu people who inhabited the mountains east of Bombay. They had risen to power as bands of robbers who raided through central India but

[5] Quoted in Lucy S. Sutherland, *The East India Company in Eighteenth-Century Politics* (Oxford: Clarendon Press, 1952), p. 26.

were welded into a nation by their leader Sivaji (1627–1680). They represented a resurgence of Hinduism against Muslim rule. Weakened by extravagance, persecution, and war, the Mogul Empire rapidly went to pieces after Aurangzeb's death, when provincial governors became independent princes and robber chiefs and military adventurers carved out dominions. An invader from Persia sacked Delhi in 1737; another from Afghanistan seized the Punjab and defeated the Marathas at Panipat in 1761. Thus India was reduced to political chaos.

This situation in India tempted the French to play a greater part in native politics. During the War of the Spanish Succession early in the century the two companies in India had arranged an unofficial truce and did not molest each other. But in the 1740s the French adopted a more warlike policy, which was largely the work of François Dupleix, governor first of Chandarnagar in Bengal (1730–1741) and then of Pondicherry (1741–1754). Ambitious and daring, though rather oversanguine, he captured the English town of Madras in 1746, thus greatly impressing the native chiefs. To his chagrin Madras was restored to the English by the Treaty of Aix-la-Chapelle.

But the war had shown Dupleix the possibility of attracting the native princes and of forming alliances with them which could be directed against the English. His prestige among the chiefs was high, for they recognized that European troops, with their arms and discipline, were far superior to the unwieldy and poorly trained armies of India. Dupleix began to lend his troops to his allies and adherents among the native rulers. The English followed a similar policy, giving military support to chieftains who were fighting the allies of the French. Thus, although England and France were at peace in Europe, their two companies were at war in India, not as principals but as allies of rival native princes. There arose a long series of intrigues and skirmishes, known as the War of the Carnatic, in which the English and the French supported opposing candidates for the thrones of Hyderabad and of the Carnatic, a district along the southeastern coast. The English gradually gained the upper hand. In 1754 the French company recalled Dupleix, his plans collapsed, and the English candidates were successful.

Why did Dupleix fail? He contended that he had not been properly supported from home, and this was true. But he had made a number of miscalculations. His native allies proved fickle, eager to follow him in victory but quick to desert him in defeat. In his preoccupation with the war, he had allowed the commerce of the French company to decline and suffer a loss. He was not himself a soldier, and he had no captains to match the ability of two English commanders, Stringer Lawrence and Robert Clive, a young clerk in the company's service in Madras who quickly displayed an aptitude for war. Finally, Dupleix ignored the significance of sea power. He could not hope to build a lasting empire in India without regard for the control of the sea between that country and France. The wars in India were fought on a very small scale; the arrival of a fleet from Europe could alter entirely the balance of power between the two contestants.

When the Seven Years' War broke out in Europe hostilities began once more in India. The French sent out the Comte de Lally, a soldier of Irish extraction, who arrived in India in 1758. Though a brave and determined officer, he was headstrong and quarrelsome, and was so hated by his subordinates that some of them refused to obey him. He at once laid siege to Madras, but he had to withdraw in 1759 at the arrival of a British fleet. In 1760 he was defeated at the

Battle of Wandiwash and was besieged in Pondicherry, which surrendered in the
year following. This ended the Seven Years' War in India.

It was in Bengal that the English first became masters of large Indian territories; this came about because they clashed with the native ruler. Bengal, the
wealthiest portion of India, was conquered with surprising ease. Its people were
peaceful merchants, artisans, and peasants; the province was easily accessible
from the sea through the many mouths of the Ganges. Moreover, it was divided
against itself. Its rulers for many years had been foreigners, nominally officials
of the Mogul Empire but in fact independent princes. The Nabob, Ali Vardi
Khan, who ruled from 1741 to 1756, was an Afghan, a shrewd and able man who
governed with justice though with severity. His rule was resented by the Hindu
merchants, who looked upon him as a tyrant and as a Muslim foreigner. Hence
the events then about to take place in Bengal were in part a revolution of the
Hindus against a foreign dynasty.

Ali Vardi Khan died in 1756 and was succeeded by Siraj-ud-daula, a weak,
vicious, and headstrong young man who quarreled with the English at once. They
had been forbidden to fortify Calcutta but, fearing the French, had disobeyed
and strengthened the town. The English had also abused their trading privileges.
Suddenly in the summer of 1756 Siraj-ud-daula marched on them with an army
of 50,000 men. The English, apparently taken by surprise, were overwhelmed in
a few days. Calcutta and some upcountry agencies fell into the Nabob's hands,
and for the moment the English were driven from Bengal.[6]

In Madras, after anxious counsels, it was decided to send an army to Bengal,
though there were fears of a French attack in the south. The command was given
to Robert Clive, who sailed from Madras with about 2500 men. In January 1757
he recaptured Calcutta, fought an inconclusive action with the Nabob, and
obtained a treaty restoring their former privileges to the English. Because he was
in a difficult position he joined a conspiracy of discontented nobles to overthrow
Siraj-ud-daula by a palace revolution and to set up the Nabob's relative Mir Jafar.
Having made his bargain with Mir Jafar, Clive quarreled openly with Siraj-ud-
daula, advanced against him with a small army of 3000 men, and on June 23,
1757, defeated him at the Battle of Plassey. It was a rout rather than a battle.
Siraj-ud-daula's huge army fled in disorder, he himself was hunted down and
slain, and Mir Jafar, who had held aloof until he saw which side would be victorious, was hailed as the new Nabob. But though he had that title and was
responsible for the government of Bengal, Mir Jafar was a mere puppet of the
English, who were the true masters of the province. This achievement was the
direct result of Clive's boldness, energy, and skill.

It cannot be denied, however, that Clive's rapacity menaced the permanence
of his work. His agreement with Mir Jafar, made in the name of the East India
Company, provided for gifts to himself and to other English officers. Clive mentioned these gifts in the report he sent to England, but he gave no figures. His
share alone amounted to £234,000; other Englishmen received from £50,000 to
£80,000 each. Many years later, when Clive was questioned by the House of
Commons, he answered that he could only wonder at his own moderation. But
in truth he had taken all there was. He might have known, moreover, that one
palace revolution could be followed by another. Within the next few years a

---

[6] The incident of the Black Hole of Calcutta occurred at this time when a number of English
prisoners, placed in a small guard room, suffocated during a hot tropical night.

number of native rulers followed each other in Bengal, and every transfer of power was accompanied by large presents of money to British officials. Clive engendered a spirit of plunder that was not eradicated for a number of years.

The acquisition of Bengal altered at once the role of Englishmen in India, the problems faced by the directors at home, and the attitude of the government toward the East India Company.

society in the eighteenth century

SOCIAL CLASSES IN THE COUNTRY

The Nobles

Society in the eighteenth century was dominated by the nobles, who would have been called princes on the Continent. They formed a small, privileged, and wealthy caste which tended to harden as the century advanced. Custom demanded that a noble or a wealthy country gentleman seek marriages for his daughters that would give them the highest possible rank and social position; this close intermarriage among aristocrats built up enormous estates in the hands of a few men. Estates were held together by the creation of strict entails. Thus the English peers formed a tightly knit group of about 160 persons; their number increased in the reign of George III but was well below 200 at the end of the century. The nobility, though keenly aware of its unique position and very difficult to enter, was saved from complete rigidity by two factors: the younger sons of peers remained commoners who were willing to enter the professions or even engage in trade, though this became less frequent as the century advanced; and nobles were willing to marry the daughters of wealthy businessmen. A City heiress could find her way into the aristocracy more easily than could her brother. Two of the granddaughters of Sir Josiah Child, a great merchant and banker, became duchesses.

Some of the nobles were enormously wealthy. The Duke of Newcastle owned estates in twelve counties and is said to have enjoyed a rent-roll approaching £40,000 a year. The Duke of Bedford owned most of Bedfordshire as well as land in London. In almost every county there were one or two noble families with large and valuable estates. Land was not the only source of a nobleman's wealth. In an age of rapid economic growth, a rich man who could secure good advice found many opportunities for profitable investment. The Duke of Chandos invested large sums in building projects; in clay, coal, copper, and alum mines; in land speculations in America; in the manufacture of glass, soap, and spirits; and in diamonds and silver. He illustrates another source of income, for he had become a wealthy man by holding the lucrative post of paymaster of the forces. It was said in 1726 that a quarter of the nobility occupied some office at court or in the government. In addition to his income from land, a noble might derive wealth from office and from business enterprises.

These rural millionaires lived on a lavish scale. They built large country mansions, filled them with fine pictures, furniture, statuary, and beautifully bound books, and surrounded them with elaborate gardens. A few of these country palaces, such as Blenheim Palace and Castle Howard, both designed by Sir John Vanbrugh, were massive and grandiose, so that a wit gave Vanbrugh the epitaph:

> Lie heavy on him, earth, for he,
> Laid many a heavy weight on thee.

A reaction set in against this pretentiousness; most country houses though imposing in design and classical in inspiration, often of the Palladian school of Italian Renaissance architecture, were smaller, quieter, and in better taste. The rooms in these houses were beautifully proportioned and handsomely decorated with oval and elliptical designs on the ceilings, lovely mantelpieces and side-boards, and small columns and fanlights in the doorways. The owner of a great house was much concerned about his grounds. Early in the century gardens were formal, with straight walks and with flower beds arranged in symmetrical patterns. Later it became the fashion to give gardens a look of natural and unkempt wildness. The result, however, was frequently an increased artificiality. Contrived waterfalls and planned wildernesses were far from what nature would have produced. Gothic ruins, built to lend an atmosphere of antiquity, were merely grotesque. The landscape gardener Lancelot Brown was fond of these novelties and was so extravagant in his ideas that some men ruined themselves in making over their grounds. When Brown was called upon for advice he would begin by saying, "I see great capability for improvement here." Hence his nickname "Capability Brown."

The country palace of a noble was more than a means of satisfying his desire for ostentatious display. The administrative center for his estates and for investments, it was a symbol of his power and influence. An eighteenth-century nobleman was honored not only because he was wealthy but because he was a leader of the landed interest, which was the greatest interest in the country. Wealth in land gave greater prestige than wealth in any other form. A noble was the great man of his locality who drove about the country in a coach and four, distributed local patronage, arranged local elections, and played a large part in local government. His influence extended to national politics, for which he was trained from childhood. He was a member of the House of Lords and sometimes a member of the Cabinet. Around him gathered a group of relatives, secretaries, lawyers, and hangers-on. Having placed some of these men in the Commons, he could bargain with the government to give them offices and sinecures in return for their support. The nobility also dominated high society; their London houses were centers of fashionable life. The artists of the age painted their portraits, the architects built their houses, the writers wrote to please them. "Perhaps no set of men and women since the world began enjoyed so many different sides of life, with so much zest, as the English upper class of this period. The literary, the sporting, the fashionable, and the political 'sets' were one and the same."[1]

[1] G. M. Trevelyan, *English Social History* (London: Longmans, 1942), p. 404.

The Gentry

The country gentry, or the squires, varied greatly in wealth, culture, and influence. A few were rich enough to imitate the elegance and extravagance of the nobility, to be "in mortar," as the phrase went, meaning that they were building a new country house or were remodeling the old; a few could afford to come to London for the season, send their sons on the grand tour, or arrange rich marriages for their daughters. But for the most part the gentry were not able to do this; those who tried were apt to end in ruin. Sir Thomas Cave of Stanford Hall in Leicestershire is an example of one who tried to live in the grand manner. He was fond of horse racing and hunting, he practiced an open-handed hospitality, and he stood for Parliament at great expense. Then suddenly he died, leaving his lands so encumbered with debt that his widow held them together only by the harshest frugality. It was the burden of debt that dragged men down: many ancient families first mortgaged and then sold their estates. The gentry were in a dilemma. If they tried to ape the nobles, they lived beyond their means; if they went their own way, ignoring the peerage, they themselves were apt to be ignored while other men turned to the nobles as more promising

The anteroom in Syon House near London. A room of great magnificence designed by Robert Adam. (Copyright Country Life)

A staircase in Tythrop House, Oxfordshire. (Copyright Country Life)

patrons. This accounts for the sullen Tory politics of the smaller gentry, as opposed to the Whiggism of the great lords.,

If, on the other hand, a country gentleman was willing to live modestly, he could enjoy rustic comfort and even abundance. We hear of a certain Squire Hastings, a younger brother of the Earl of Huntingdon. The squire's house stood in a large timbered park which supplied him with firewood and venison. Fishponds and rabbit warrens on the estate also provided the squire with food. His manor house contained a great hall in which hounds and spaniels dozed before the fire or nosed among the marrowbones that littered the floor. Cats slept in the armchairs. The squire dined in the hall among his dogs and cats; he would throw the dogs pieces of meat but kept a little stick beside his plate with which he would beat them down if they became too eager. The walls of the hall were hung with the skins of foxes and polecats, the deep window ledges contained bows and arrows, on one table might be seen a bowl of oysters, on another the Bible and Foxe's *Book of Martyrs*. Scattered about in various receptacles were tobacco pipes, pheasants' eggs, and dice and cards. The hall led into a chapel which was no longer used, but the pulpit, being out of reach of the dogs, was filled with cold venison, beef, and apple pie.[2]

Squires of this homespun variety enjoyed a few luxuries, such as tea, or wine,

[2] R. B. Mowat, *England in the Eighteenth Century* (New York: McBride, n.d.), pp. 52–53.

Interior of a house at Blanford, Dorset, mid-eighteenth century. (Copyright Country Life)

or oysters, but otherwise their table was much the same as that of a prosperous tenant farmer. Such squires possessed coats of arms and could pride themselves on their gentle blood; they maintained sporting establishments of dogs and horses. But their journeys beyond their own counties were rare; and their normal associates were the well-to-do yeomen and tenant farmers and the local merchants and lawyers who were their neighbors. And yet, in an age of unquestioned class distinctions, the squire regarded himself as belonging to an entirely different social order from those associates with whom he did business. The lesser squire has sometimes been depicted as a country lout who thought of nothing beyond his dogs and horses, who damned his servants, drank with his huntsmen, and caroused every night with men of his own kind. This picture must be regarded as a myth.

The squire was apt to be a shrewd, successful, and hardheaded manager of his estates; acquisitive, masterful, with a gift for leadership; intent on his account books and on the careers of his sons and the marriages of his daughters; or involved in local government as a justice of the peace. His position as a justice gave him power, independence, and self-confidence. A single justice or two or three acting together in petty sessions could deal summarily with a large number of minor offenses and administrative matters. At quarter sessions he and other justices heard important cases. The justices sometimes supervised local manufactures; they bound boys as apprentices, they supervised the entire operation of the poor law; they levied rates for the repair of bridges and roads, they controlled the constables and licensed fairs and alehouses. Supervision of their activities by the central government was almost nil. They were the government of the county and they desired no assistance from higher authorities.

The dominance of a squire over a village in which he owned much of the land was even more marked. The village lived very much to itself. The local tradesmen and artisans regarded the squire as their best customer; the tenant farmers knew they could not offend him. It was he and his wife who brought back new ideas and new fashions from London. If agricultural improvements were to be made it was the squire who must lead the way. Indeed, these improvements often made the laborer more dependent on him than ever as the principal employer in the village.

The squire was not without education or interest in intellectual things. The manor house often contained a library. The squire read history and law. He was interested in architecture, liked music, and perhaps knew a little about painting. He was normally content to educate his sons in the local grammar school, though some boys were sent to Eton, or Winchester, or the fashionable school at Harrow. The sons of the gentry were less likely to attend the universities than had been those in the seventeenth century. They went into politics, into the law, into the church, into the army, and often into trade. There was little education for the squire's daughters unless they were taught by tutors brought in for the sons of the family. Most girls learned from their mothers to manage the domestic side of the manor house. Marriage was still a matter of business to be arranged by the parents of young people.[3]

The Lower Classes

Below the nobility and the gentry the rural population may be divided roughly into yeomen who owned their land; tenant farmers, a few with large holdings but most of them with small; copyholders who held perpetual leases on a few strips in the open fields; and cottagers, or landless laborers, dependent on casual employment and on trivial rights in the common land of the village. These classes did not fare alike, but speaking generally they did not prosper. A great amount of poverty and distress existed among the rural poor. The yeomen, who had flourished during the Tudor and Stuart periods and who constituted a substantial and independent middle class, were still prosperous at the beginning of the eighteenth century, but their fortunes declined as the century went on. Although this was a time of great advance in scientific agriculture, the new techniques could be exploited only by the rich who farmed on a large scale and had the capital to improve their lands. The yeoman could not afford these improvements. The price of wheat and of other agricultural products was low in the early part of the century; yet the yeoman must pay his laborers and make up his taxes. He knew, however, that he could sell his holding at a good figure, for the big farmer always wanted land and the city merchant was eager to acquire a country estate. Thus the yeoman was tempted to sell. If he did so, he might perhaps become a land agent or manager on a large estate, or he might obtain a new farm as a tenant. But he was more likely to sink in the scale of rural life.

The tenant farmer, if he rented a farm of some size, and if he had an improving landlord, might benefit from the new techniques of agriculture, but

[3] See the first chapter in J. H. Plumb, *Sir Robert Walpole. The Making of a Statesman* (London: Cresset, 1960).

most tenants and copyholders held only small farms. Where a few men paid a rent of £70 or £80 a year, many paid only £10 or even £5. These small farmers, trying to wrest a living from a section of the open fields, were poor and insecure. A contemporary wrote that they were really not as well off as their own laborers. The laborers "know their work and wages and are troubled with no cares for paying rents, or making good markets, or for the loss of corn or cattle, the rotting of sheep or the unfavorable weather, nor for providing for wife and children and paying laborers' and servants' wages." It was a fortunate tenant who could afford a piece of fresh meat once a week; he must be content with bacon or hanged beef, "enough to try the stomach of an ostrich." He must sell his little pigs or small chickens, his eggs, his apples or his pears in order to find the money for his rent. "All the best of his butter and cheese he must sell, and feed himself and children and servants with skimmed cheese and skimmed milk and whey curds."[4]

The small farmer was not as well off as the small shopkeeper or artisan in the town. But he was well above the large class of landless laborers who lived in a state of misery and degradation. These cottagers, as Sir Francis Bacon had written a century before, were "but housed beggars." The cottage was a shack, built on the village waste or common, to which no land was attached. The cottager might own a few pigs or geese, he might be allowed to gather faggots from the village woodland, he might work casually for a neighboring farmer, but he was never far from destitution. He had a bad name for poaching, and he was almost certain to end his days as a pauper. If men of this type drifted to the towns to work in factories they might feel a loss of liberty but their lot was no worse than before. In fact, it was probably better.

The end of the century was a bad time for all the smaller people in the countryside. The movement toward enclosure disrupted their lives, and the Napoleonic wars inflated prices, bringing misery and starvation to the agricultural poor. We will deal with this subject in a later chapter.

THE GROWTH OF LONDON

Most English cities still gave the impression of overgrown country towns; but London, as in the reign of Elizabeth, was unique. Its life was thoroughly urban and distinct from the rest of the kingdom. Even in the clothing of its people it differed from other places, so that the rustic visitor, gazing in wonder at its crowded thoroughfares, its street lamps, its fashionable shops and handsome buildings, could easily be spotted—and often as easily fleeced. The greatest port in the country, London sucked into itself a large proportion of the kingdom's trade; it was the center of political life; the center of fashion and society, of arts and letters, of drama and music. Its population of about 675,000 in 1700 did not grow greatly until the second half of the century, but in 1801, the date of the first census, population had reached almost 900,000 and ten years later was over a million.

In the eighteenth century London spread far beyond its ancient bounds.[5] It

[4] Quoted in M. Dorothy George, *England in Transition: Life and Work in the Eighteenth Century* (Baltimore: Penguin Books, 1962), p. 12.
[5] The growth of London in the eighteenth century may be studied by examining two maps at the back of G. M. Trevelyan, *English Social History*, pp. 592–595. The first of these maps shows London under George I, the second, during the Napoleonic wars.

expanded eastward along Ratcliffe Highway on the north bank of the Thames, to the northeast along Whitechapel Road and Shoreditch to Bethnal Green and Hackney, and far to the north until it reached the new road from Paddington to Islington. The area of Southwark across the river was also filling up rapidly, especially after Westminster Bridge was completed in 1750. But the most remarkable growth was toward the west. In earlier times wealthy men had occupied houses within the walls or along the Strand between the City and Westminster, but now the fashionable world was moving westward to escape the "fumes, steams, and stinks" of old London, the prevailing winds being from the west. Lincoln's Inn Fields, Bloomsbury Square, and Soho Square were fashionable in the reign of Queen Anne; under George I the eastern end of Piccadilly was built up, houses extended along the southern side of the Oxford Road, New Bond Street and Hanover Square were completed, Cavendish Square was under construction. But open fields still existed in Mayfair east of Hyde Park and south of Westminster and Buckingham House. By the end of the century Mayfair was filled with houses and many new squares—Manchester, Portman, Grosvenor, and Berkeley—had been built. These squares consisted of handsome houses, three or four stories high, built in a solid row around an open square or oval. Most of them were erected as speculative ventures. But one at least had a different origin. When Southampton House (later Bedford House) was built by a great noble, he

Covent Garden in the eighteenth century. (From *Gentleman's Magazine*, April 1749. Walter Library, University of Minnesota)

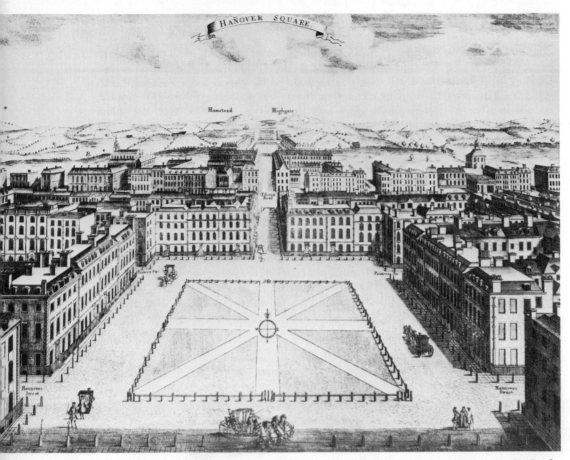

Hanover Square, early eighteenth century. Note the open country in the background. (Historical Pictures Service, Chicago)

kept the land in front of it vacant in order to obtain a vista; persons dependent upon him in various capacities gradually erected smaller houses around the edges of this open space, thus forming Bloomsbury Square. Once a fashionable square was built, it was shortly surrounded by small streets, alleys, and mews until housing covered an extensive area.

THE WORLD OF FASHION

The London season began in October and lasted until May. Fashionable life no longer centered in the royal court. Whitehall Palace, which had burned down in 1698, was not rebuilt; King William III and Queen Anne lived very quietly; the domestic life of the first two Georges was forbidding; George III, setting his face against the vices of the day, found amusement in simple domestic festivities which did not attract society. Fashionable life moved to the houses of the nobility, to public places of amusement, to clubs and gambling houses, to the theater and opera.

494

The Mall above St. James's Park was a fashionable promenade where ladies and gentlemen sauntered up and down or were carried in sedan chairs, while a few rode grandly in a coach drawn by six horses. Ranelagh and Vauxhall Gardens were famous resorts. The first, in Chelsea, consisted of gardens and a large pavilion or rotunda, where visitors could walk about or dine at side tables to the music of an orchestra. Vauxhall, across the river south of Lambeth, was more elaborate. Extensive gardens were laid out with walks and with replicas of Greek temples and statuary, trees were festooned with colored lights, suppers were served in shaded alcoves, a central promenade called the Grove contained a pavilion or concert hall. The paths beneath the trees included a dark Lovers' Walk, not so much frequented by lovers as by young men seeking amorous adventure. Less fashionable and certainly less respectable were Cupid's Gardens, across the Thames from the Strand. The Thames was still a great thoroughfare, and the manners of the rivermen had not improved.

Later in the century the aristocracy was drawn away to other places of amusement. In the 1760s a certain Madame Cornelys, a foreign singer, presided over subscription balls, concerts, and masquerades at her "Society" in Soho

The Mall, 1751, from a contemporary engraving by H. Roberts. St. James Palace is seen on the left and the west towers of Westminster Abbey on the extreme right. (Historical Pictures Service, Chicago)

The interior of the Rotunda at Ranelagh Gardens. (British Museum)

Square. Almack's Club was opened in St. James's Street about the same time. Though it began as a place for balls and suppers, its principal interest soon became gambling. Here and at other clubs nearby, such as White's and Boodle's, there was nightly play for high stakes. Men sat at the card tables for twenty-four hours at a stretch. Thousands of pounds changed hands at a single sitting, estates were won and lost, and foolish young men encumbered their lands with debt. Ladies played as recklessly as men, though they did not play at clubs but in their own drawing rooms. The passion for gambling was seen also in wagers of all kinds, often on the most trivial matters and on those governed wholly by chance.

There was a great deal of drinking. The Methuen Treaty with Portugal in 1703 allowed port wine to be brought into England at a low duty, and port superseded French claret as the drink of the upper classes. Port, a heady wine, was consumed in great quantities. Many of the statesmen of the eighteenth century—even such an austere person as the younger Pitt—were heavy drinkers. The face of his friend Dundas was a convivial purple. George III once said to Lord Chancellor Northington, "My lord, they tell me that you love a glass of wine." "Those who have informed your Majesty have done me great injustice," the Lord Chancellor replied. "They should have said a bottle." Some drivers of hackney coaches roamed about the West End of London late at night to pick up drunken gentlemen. If these gentlemen could supply their addresses, they were taken home. If not, they were deposited at certain inns till morning, when the drivers reappeared and took them to their houses. The oaths and vulgarities of intoxicated persons, their quarrels and disorderly conduct, and the frenzied excitement of the gaming table made society coarse and brutal despite its courtly manners. Drinking affected the health of the upper classes, enlarging their girths and shortening their lives. Suffering from gout and other disorders connected with

Vauxhall Gardens. (From *Gentleman's Magazine*, August 1765. Walter Library, University of Minnesota)

Plan of Vauxhall Gardens about 1751. From a contemporary drawing by Samuel Wale. (Historical Pictures Service, Chicago)

An eighteenth century coffeehouse, from an engraving of the early nineteenth century. (New York Public Library, Print Division)

drinking, they became old and decrepit before they reached middle age.

One cure for gout, it was thought, was to visit a spa or mineral spring and drink the waters or bathe in them. Inland spas were very popular in the eighteenth century. Charles II had patronized Epsom and Tunbridge Wells; these and similar places—Bath, Cheltenham, the Hotwells near Bristol—were visited both by high society and by the middle classes. Bath was the most interesting. A visit by Queen Anne in 1702 had called attention to the hot mineral springs and the old Roman baths there, but at that time Bath was a rather dirty little town without the buildings or atmosphere essential for a fashionable resort. It owed its later fame to Richard Nash, a charming adventurer with genuine social gifts. A professional gambler, he first came to Bath in 1705 to fleece the populace at cards. When he saw the possibility of making Bath a pleasure city he persuaded the town council to build a new pump room, an assembly room, and a theater; he engaged a good orchestra, raised money to improve the road from London, and forced landlords to lower their prices and chairmen to improve their manners.

As master of ceremonies, Nash imposed a code of dress, manners, and etiquette. A daily program was devised for visitors. The early hours of the day were spent at the baths, which were not overly clean, were approached through unpleasant passages, and were provided with hot and steamy dressing rooms. Ladies and gentlemen, dressed in elaborate bathing costumes, walked about solemnly in the baths, the water coming to their waists. Ladies were provided with little floating trays on which to carry their cosmetics. After bathing they drank the waters in the pump room to the accompaniment of music. Then came breakfast, then the morning service in Bath Abbey, then riding or driving until dinner at three in the afternoon. After dinner the guests promenaded in their fine clothes till teatime and in the evening played cards, attended the theater, or danced in the assembly room. Nash did much to improve the manners of the middle classes and even those of the aristocracy.

The vogue for sea bathing also accounted for the popularity of Weymouth, Scarborough, and Harrogate. The novelist Fanny Burney tells how she bathed at Brighton in late November at six o'clock in the morning "by the pale blink of the moon" and found the water cold. "We then returned home and dressed by candle light."

ARTS AND LETTERS

Until the end of the eighteenth century there were few writers and artists and almost all of these were in London; they knew each other well because they met in coffeehouses and taverns. It was a great age for clubs, which were formed by men with common interests or professions who agreed to dine together each week or fortnight at a certain tavern or coffeehouse. Each man ordered what he pleased and paid his own score; the bond was simply their enjoyment of each other's company and conversation. A club might have a guiding spirit, perhaps a literary figure, whose praise or condemnation of new books reached far beyond the club's membership and might make or unmake reputations. Joseph Addison, the writer of charming essays, was a kind of literary dictator for the first two decades of the century. Surrounded by his friends at Button's Coffee House in Russell Street, he loved to talk about literature, from Virgil to the latest book in the London bookstalls. At his death in 1719 the role of literary oracle passed to Alexander Pope. He was unexcelled in the type of verse he employed—the heroic couplet—and brought it to a high state of perfection. But he spoke to the mind rather than to the heart, and a gradual revolt took place against his formal and unsentimental writing, a revolt which paved the way for the romantic movement at the end of the century. Pope's delicate health did not permit him to sit up half the night in a tavern; he lived at Twickenham, near Richmond, a few miles from London. Horace Walpole, famous for his letters and memoirs, also lived at Twickenham, where he bought a small estate called Strawberry Hill. He converted the house into a strange combination of cottage and Gothic castle and filled it with pictures, statues, miniatures, and all sorts of curios, chiefly of Italian origin. Here he entertained his friends with spicy anecdotes of the great world of London. He was a connoisseur and scandalmonger, not a great writer, but he has described most vividly the eighteenth-century social scene.

The literary world of the middle of the century was dominated by the bulky figure of Dr. Samuel Johnson, who came to London from Lichfield in 1737 to earn a precarious living by his pen. The appearance of his *Dictionary* in 1755 established his reputation, and he gradually won a dominant position in English letters. His influence was exercised in part through the Literary Club founded in 1763 or 1764. This club included at one time or another an astonishing number of well-known men: Dr. Johnson, his biographer James Boswell, the painter Sir Joshua Reynolds, the orator Edmund Burke, the economist Adam Smith, the liberal statesman Charles James Fox, the playwright Richard Brinsley Sheridan, and such writers as Oliver Goldsmith, Edward Gibbon, and Sir Walter Scott. In the discussions of the Literary Club Johnson's ponderous word was law; he was highly venerated by the reading public, and newcomers to the literary world sought his approval. He was a gifted conversationalist but as a writer he was more the critic than the creative artist. A man of many prejudices and eccentricities, he did not welcome new trends in literature. Yet his literary judgments usually were sound, and his standards of writing and conduct were high.

Perhaps the most important development in literature at the time was the rise of the novel. It owed much to that gifted writer Daniel Defoe, whose narratives were vivid, realistic, and entirely natural. The novels of Samuel Richardson, on the other hand, almost discarded adventure. They were written in the form of letters, emphasized the portrayal and analysis of character, and made love and society their central themes. Henry Fielding, whose humor was broad, reverted to Defoe's novel of incident and adventure; his novels, *Joseph Andrews*, *Tom Jones*, and *Amelia*, pictured life in England: the innkeepers, the justices of the peace, the clergymen, the people of fashion, the footmen, and the ladies' maids. Fielding, who was cheerful and optimistic, hated shams and selfishness; he was a social reformer. Tobias Smollett, once a ship's surgeon, wrote stories of the sea. He could depict character with great skill, but he was coarse and his satire was savage. A fantastic clergyman, Laurence Sterne, wrote novels, as he said, "on the design of shocking people and amusing myself." Fanny Burney was the attractive and sprightly daughter of a famous music teacher, Charles Burney. Her first and best novel, *Evelina*, portrayed the thoughts and feelings of a young girl as she first entered London society. Miss Burney accepted a position as second keeper of the robes to Queen Charlotte, the wife of George III. But she found that her duties were those of a lady's maid. She managed with difficulty to

Dr. Samuel Johnson, by Sir Joshua Reynolds. (National Portrait Gallery, London)

resign her office, married a French refugee, General d'Arblay, and was living in Brussels when the Battle of Waterloo was fought nearby.

To judge from the novels of the time, men in the eighteenth century liked their women to be stupid. Heroines are frail and insipid; they faint easily and are the prey of the opposite sex. Yet there were many brilliant women in the eighteenth century. Lady Mary Wortley Montagu was a famous writer of letters. The daughter of a duke, she eloped on the night before her marriage rather than accept the person whom her father had selected. Her husband was the English Ambassador to Turkey, where she lived for many years. Another lady of the same name, Mrs. Elizabeth Montagu, created a *salon* in emulation of the *salons* of Paris. Her conversational powers, her essay on Shakespeare, and her lavish hospitality enabled her to attract to her assemblies politicians, writers, and artists, no small accomplishment in a city of masculine clubs and coffeehouses. These and other ladies who combined a high position in society with an interest in letters were known as the Bluestockings.

Portrait painting had a long tradition in England, but the artists had been largely foreign. Now there arose a school of English portrait painters. Sir Joshua Reynolds settled in London in 1752, was at once successful, and remained for almost forty years a kind of national celebrity. A master of color, he was able to give each portrait a character of its own, and thus avoid the pitfall of creating a type. His name is connected with the establishment in 1768 of the Royal Academy, where paintings were exhibited for sale. Yet the very success of the academy made portrait painting somewhat stereotyped and the art was soon on its way to vulgarization. Thomas Gainsborough was both a portrait and a landscape painter. A man of real genius, he did not have Reynolds' social ambitions and was quite happy in the obscurity of his early life in Ipswich. Thence he went to Bath and finally to London in 1774. The third member of this trio was George Romney, who painted portraits of much freshness and charm. Richard Wilson was a splendid landscape painter, though he was never recognized by his contemporaries.

Every age in art contains its rebels. Early in the century, William Hogarth, famous as an engraver though also a fine painter, revolted from the Italian influence on English art and struck a purely native note. In a well-known series of engravings he depicted with great realism, humor, and detail the seamy side of English life and the evils of hard living. William Blake was an entirely different kind of artist, a mystic, a poet, and a painter who introduced a strange, ethereal otherworldliness into his paintings. He detested Reynolds and the comfortable, materialistic, and compromising approach to art which Reynolds represented.

The London stage was at a low ebb during the first half of the century. Plays were coarse and indecent, with illicit love their invariable theme; ladies, if they came to the theater at all, came wearing masks until the practice was forbidden in 1704. Audiences were vulgar and rowdy. An apron stage extended from the principal stage into the pit, thus bringing the performers close to the audience; some patrons, by paying an extra charge, were allowed to sit on the stage itself. These evils were reformed only slowly. Led by the clergyman Jeremy Collier, protests against the immorality of the stage grew so strong that dramatists attempted to make their plays seem moral by introducing banal lines in praise of virtue. Inevitably such plays were likely to be dull. Some managers turned from the drama to variety shows in which elaborate scenery, dancing, and costumes, gods and goddesses, shepherdesses and milkmaids, at least made a pretty picture. The best feature of this development was the use of pantomime by the manager John Rich.

During the second half of the century the theater improved. Oliver Goldsmith and Richard Sheridan wrote excellent comedies which brought liveliness and wit to the stage without being indelicate. The greatest actor of the age was David Garrick, who took London by storm in 1741 with his performance of *Richard III*. He helped to bring about a revival of Shakespeare, though the plays often were mutilated. Even Garrick made unfortunate changes to please the supposed taste of his audiences. As an actor he was natural and realistic, skilled in conveying emotion through facial expression. He was also a person of refinement and intellect; Dr. Johnson called him "the first man in the world for sprightly conversation." Mrs. Siddons (Sarah Kemble) was an excellent tragedienne, famous as Lady Macbeth and as Queen Catherine in *Henry VIII*. Peg Woffington was popular not only for her versatile acting but for her somewhat boisterous good humor. She and Mrs. Siddons, both handsome women, were favorites of the portrait painters.

Two types of opera were to be found in eighteenth-century England. One was light opera, of which John Gay's *Beggar's Opera*, first produced in 1728, with its songs, comedy, and political allusions, proved to be the most successful. The second type was Italian opera, of rather poor quality and written largely to give the singers an opportunity to display their talents. In 1710 G. F. Handel arrived in England. Although a German he was well versed in Italian music and wrote as well as produced many Italian operas, which, however, were not much better than the others. Later he turned to the writing of oratorios, for which he became famous. An oratorio at this time was not necessarily religious music but might be almost any kind of choral singing. Handel wrote them because he found that they were more popular—and were cheaper to produce—than operas. Although his reputation was—and is—very great, his music was, after all, foreign and may have hindered the development of a native school of composers. Handel normally enjoyed the patronage of the Hanoverian rulers. Once when Lord Chesterfield found the King and Queen listening to an oratorio in a very thin house, Chesterfield withdrew, saying he did not wish to intrude upon the privacy of his sovereign.

LONDON: THE EAST END

A handful of merchants, bankers, and capitalists in the City were extremely rich and lived on a scale as lavish as that of the nobility. "Some merchants are certainly far wealthier than many sovereign princes of Germany and Italy," wrote a foreign observer; "they live in great state, their houses are richly furnished, their tables spread with delicacies." Sir John Barnard, William Beckford, and Sir Francis Baring, the founder of a famous banking house, were men of this kind, national figures who were consulted by the government in matters of commerce and finance. Below them were hundreds of lesser merchants of varying degrees of prosperity who formed an upper middle class in the economic scale. They normally lived near their shops or countinghouses, though some were moving into the new parts of London. Others, as in former times, lived over their places of business, with the first floor devoted to trade or manufacturing, the second to the living quarters of the family, the garret and the cellar to servants and apprentices.

Below these groups were the working people, the mass of the London population. Distinctions and gradations among classes were sharply drawn, and one must differentiate between the artisan and the unskilled laborer, between the master and his apprentices, between the man who occupied a house and the mere lodger. An amusing contemporary list of trades descended from the "genteel" through the "dirty genteel," the "genteelish," the "ordinary," the "mean," to the "mean, nasty and stinking."[6] Most manufacturing was done under the domestic

---

[6] M. Dorothy George, *London Life in the Eighteenth Century* (London: Routledge, 1925), p. 163. The following pages depend largely on Mrs. George's excellent book.

system; boys and young men were apprenticed, though there was a great difference between the apprentice of a great London company, who might be the son
of a gentleman and who looked forward to a partnership in a prosperous business, and the orphan apprenticed by the parish to a chimney sweep.

The principal distinction was between the artisan who had served an apprenticeship and the unskilled laborer whose physical strength was all he had to offer.
Many artisans produced beautiful and intricate articles. Of this class were the
makers of fine furniture, of watches, clocks, and nautical instruments; locksmiths
and workers in metals; the painter of signs (to hang over shops); and interior
decorators of all kinds. Artisans working at home produced goods on order from
a master of the trade. Some artisans had shops and sold directly to the public,
thus merging with the class of storekeepers. But many shopkeepers (chandlers,
sellers of milk, vegetables, tripe, and gin) operated on so small a scale, perhaps
in a cellar, that they must be classed as unskilled workers. The artisan, if he
possessed industry and thrift, could live well above the subsistence level, though
a depression in trade could easily reduce him to want.

The numbers of unskilled workers were enormous: porters, chairmen, coal
heavers, dock workers, drivers of carts and drovers of cattle, watermen,
scavengers, butchers and slaughterers, sailors, fishermen, and hundreds of domestic servants of all kinds. Some trades, such as weaving and silk throwing,
required skill but were so badly organized that they paid poorly and offered only
irregular employment. Lower still were hawkers selling milk, fish, vegetables,
matches, and so on, who merged with the class of beggars. And below them all
was a large and seething underworld of footpads, murderers, prostitutes, and all
manner of rogues and sharpers. It was easy for the poor to slip into this class, for
they were never much above the subsistence level, and a slight depression could
reduce them to want. Late in the century the public was shocked at the discovery
of a number of women who had crept into an abandoned house and had there
starved to death.

The London poor lived under dreadful conditions of overcrowding in old
tumble-down tenements which had either seen better days or had been built in
a cheap and shoddy way. In the sixteenth and seventeenth centuries the government had prohibited the building of new houses in the hope of keeping down
the population. The results had been unfortunate. People could not build new
houses; hence they patched up crumbling old ones, adding rooms in garrets and
cellars and in projections fastened to the house by iron bars. Tenements sometimes collapsed through sheer dilapidation. In the eighteenth century new houses
—or more often shacks—were built very cheaply in courts and alleys or on bits of
wasteland until areas were covered completely with a labyrinth of dwellings to
which access could be obtained only through dark and noisome passages or
even through other houses. When the building was on land leased only for a
short term of years, the builder, by a nice calculation, aimed at constructing
houses that would be worthless about the time the lease expired.

In many of these tenements an entire family occupied a single room, which
often contained nothing but a bed, a fireplace, and a few broken cooking utensils.
Such rooms lacked running water and all sanitary arrangements. Filth was thrown
out of the window or into a vault or cesspool at the back of the house, or
allowed to accumulate in piles in open courts and alleys. In the early part of
the century sewers were open ditches through which water moved sluggishly
toward the Thames. The very poorest families lived in garrets under leaking

roofs or in wet cellars where ventilation was impossible and even the light was dim. In such rooms many a man not only kept his family but carried on his trade, bringing the dirt and confusion of manufacture into what served him for a home. The poorest buildings were lodginghouses in which space, perhaps a part of a bed, was let for one night at a time.

The worst areas were not in the old City but in a semicircle around it, in Southwark, in Spitalfields, Bethnal Green, and Shoreditch, and around Tyburn, where there were colonies of Irish. A number of foreign Jews had settled in London. They often were molested in the streets until by chance one of them (Mendoza) became a successful and famous boxer and taught the art to his fellows. It was then wiser to let the Jews alone.

Temptations of Low London Life

The poor in London were surrounded by temptations and dangers, of which the greatest was heavy drinking. Social life centered in the tavern or ale-house. A workingman, living with his family in one room, had no place to go in the evening or during weekends except to the nearest tavern. Many things combined to tempt him to drink. There was the yearning for excitement after long hours at monotonous labor. The week's wages sometimes were paid in a tavern on a Saturday night, and the money was withheld until a late hour so that drinking could go on in anticipation. Taverns were employment agencies, headquarters for benefit societies and for clubs of workingmen, places where doubtful young men met doubtful young women in what were known as cock and hen clubs to drink and sing songs. Taverns like the Blue Lion (called the Blue Cat), the Bull and Pond, the Shepherd and Shepherdess, the Temple of Flora, and the Dog and Duck became notorious for riot and debauchery.

Conditions were worse between 1720 and 1750 when the poor learned to drink gin instead of beer or ale. The abundance and cheapness of grain in the early eighteenth century led to the distilling of spirits, which increased twenty-fold between 1688 and 1750. Gin shops multiplied in the poorer parts of London, for gin could be sold without a license, and every little chandler offered it for sale. A few large distillers manufactured the raw gin, but smaller people mixed it with fruit juices and distilled it again. The beverage thus produced was fiery, adulterated, poisonous, and highly intoxicating. It was primarily a drink for the poor: it was cheap, it warmed the body, and it quickly brought forgetfulness of want and misery. But it also brought a decline in the birth rate and an increase in the death rate, and contributed to the degeneration of the poor and the alarming increase in the number of criminals. Gradually the government awoke to the harm that gin was doing; an act of 1751 prohibited distillers from selling it retail, required all retailers to have a license, and sharply increased the tax on spirits. Thereafter gin drinking gradually declined.

Other hazards endangered the poor in London: no protection against unemployment existed, trades were badly organized, and the system of apprenticeship produced many evils. When the parents of a boy apprenticed him to the master of a trade, they paid the master a fee for which he agreed to teach his trade to the apprentice and to feed and clothe him for seven years. During the first part of an apprentice's time he was of little use to the master; but in the last years he would be keenly aware that he was doing valuable work without any pay. Such a relationship could easily degenerate into neglect, brutality, and exploitation by the master and dishonesty and hatred on the part of the apprentice.

London apprentices were traditionally rowdy and dissolute, but if the master spent his evenings at the tavern, the apprentice quite naturally followed his example.

The debtors' prison was a constant menace. A man could be arrested for a small debt; once in prison he was unable to earn money either to satisfy his creditors or to support his family. Another evil arose from the lax laws concerning marriage. Some taverns and tenements around the Fleet and other prisons began a base traffic in performing the marriage ceremony for all who applied. A man would be tempted by the invitation, "Sir, will you be pleased to walk in and be married?" Inside the shop or tavern a clergyman who had fallen into evil ways was ready to marry any couple for a small fee. This abuse was ended by Lord Hardwicke's Marriage Act of 1753, which provided that marriages were illegal unless they were performed in a parish church of the Church of England after the banns had been properly asked on three successive Sundays. Though a grievance to nonconformists, the act was highly beneficial.

During the first half of the century a great amount of crime existed in London. Purses, hats, and wigs were snatched from people in the streets; robberies were accompanied by violence in which the victims were beaten or even killed. A turn for the better took place in 1749, when Henry Fielding, the lawyer and novelist, was appointed principal magistrate for Westminster and established a police station in Bow Street. He and his remarkable brother, Sir John Fielding, who was blind from birth, began an improved police force known as the Bow Street Runners. London was a difficult place in which to catch criminals. The mazes of little lanes and alleys and the many doors and subdivisions in old houses gave the criminal a good chance to escape. Parliament made one offense after another punishable by death until the law was so cruel that juries would not convict for petty crimes which carried the death penalty. Hence the law was capricious in its operation, sometimes too lenient and sometimes enforced with harshness. One of the pastimes of the mob was to watch public executions at Tyburn (where those who met death with swaggering nonchalance were applauded by the rabble).

These evil conditions began to be reformed about the middle of the century. In 1829, a Londoner could write: "The people are better dressed, better fed, cleanlier, better educated, in every class respectively, much more frugal, and much happier. Money which would have been spent at the tavern, the brothel, the tea garden, the skittle-ground, the bull-bait, and in numerous other low-lived and degrading pursuits, is now expended in comfort and conveniences, or saved for some useful purpose."[7] A good many causes combined to produce this improvement. About the middle of the century, as we have seen, Fleet marriages became illegal, the traffic in gin came under some control, and the Fielding brothers introduced an improved police force, though a thorough reform of the London police did not come until the 1820s. More fundamental causes of improved conditions were the agrarian and industrial revolutions that took place in the eighteenth century[8] and that made more food and better clothing available to the lower classes. Cheap cotton underwear improved their health, especially the health of women, who could now discard the leather stays they had formerly worn. Cotton dresses enabled young women of the lower classes to look dainty and feminine.

[7] Quoted in George, p. 4.
[8] See Chapter 25.

Moreover, London never became a factory city of the type that was growing in the north. It grew less industrial as the century advanced. Some industries migrated in search of cheaper fuel and cheaper labor; instead of being a manufacturing center, London grew as a commercial and financial center. The port of London developed tremendously, as did banking and the stock exchange. The number of schools, hospitals, and charitable institutions multiplied. As a result, the tremendous number of unskilled laborers gradually declined, their place taken by a growing population of clerks, officials, caretakers, contractors, stockbrokers, merchants, administrators, doctors, and schoolmasters.

A gradual improvement occurred in the government of the city. Early in the century, dishonest justices of the peace had regarded the offenses and quarrels of the poor as so many opportunities to collect small fees. But the justice of the peace was becoming a police magistrate at a fixed salary. Keenly aware of the evils around him, he was sometimes a social reformer. Henry Fielding tried to inform the public of the condition of the London poor. His brother, Sir John, called attention to the number of deserted boys and girls from whom the criminal classes were recruited. Working with the philanthropist Jonas Hanway, he established in 1756 the Marine Society to send boys to sea, not as stray waifs but on a respectable basis. Two years later he helped to found an orphanage for deserted girls.

Some of the worst conditions were partially corrected when parish officials became more active in covering open drains and sewers, in lighting and paving the streets, and in providing more running water. It is probable that the London poor also benefited, at least to some extent, from the advance of medicine in the eighteenth century. The number of hospitals, dispensaries, and clinics and the number of physicians and surgeons increased. Two Scottish doctors, John and William Hunter, placed surgery on more scientific foundations; Sir John Pringle improved the hygiene of the army; William Smellie revolutionized the art of midwifery. Partly owing to his work, a number of lying-in hospitals were opened in London during the second half of the century; charities were developed to assist women in their homes during childbirth.

These beginnings of modern medicine appeared so impressive to historians about half a century ago that they laid great stress on them and attributed to them the rise in population that was taking place throughout Britain at the time. But today historians are not so sure. The segregation of patients with infectious diseases into separate wards and hospitals was only beginning in the eighteenth century, so that a patient might go to a hospital for one ailment and soon contract another. The training of nurses was still primitive. Although surgery might be skillful, it was surgery without anesthetics; hence a patient might die of shock; and because surgery was performed without antiseptic precautions, the patient might die from infection. The mortality rate in some of the lying-in hospitals was very high. And some practices, such as bleeding, could do great harm. Hence historians no longer believe that the advance of medicine in the eighteenth century contributed much to the increase in the size of the population. Even so, it is probably safe to assume that the lower classes in London received better medical attention in 1800 than they had received half a century earlier.

Certainly the lower classes profited from an increase in philanthropic work. Early in the century Captain Thomas Coram, a retired sailor, was horrified at the way in which unwanted babies were left in the streets to die. For seventeen years he labored to establish Foundling Hospital, which opened in 1745. A number of wealthy and prominent persons, including Handel and Hogarth, became interested in this project. George II presented the hospital with his portrait. The hospital admitted infants and small children and cared for them until they could be apprenticed to a trade. In the present century the hospital was moved into the country; its former site is now a playground for children, appropriately named Coram's Fields. So many children born in London poorhouses died there that a plan was devised to send them to be nursed in the country, where they lived and throve. Many men did philanthropic work: the Fielding brothers, Jonas Hanway, Thomas Coram, James Oglethorpe, and John Howard—the last two were especially interested in prison reform. Greater humanitarianism and greater wisdom in dispensing charity were paving the way for the reforms of the nineteenth century.

THE CHURCH AND METHODISM

During the eighteenth century the rural population attended the parish churches much as it had done in the past, and religious feelings were strong among the nonconformist bodies. But a good deal of skepticism existed among the upper classes, while thousands of the slum dwellers in the cities, sunk in heathen ignorance, did not go to church at all.

A number of factors combined to weaken the spiritual leadership of the church in the first half of the eighteenth century. Like society as a whole, the church recoiled from the fanaticism of the century before. Regarding religious zeal with distaste, it taught restraint, sobriety, and common sense. It stressed the rational and reasonable aspects of Christianity, did not dwell on dogma, and played down miracles and the sacerdotal quality of the priesthood. The essence of its teaching was a cold, unemotional morality which left the heart untouched. Sermons became literary essays, logical and polished, but rather languid and quite devoid of inspiration. They were normally read. Voltaire noted the difference between a sermon in France and one in England. In France, he said, a sermon was a long declamation delivered with enthusiasm; in England it was a solid but dry dissertation read without gestures or modulation of the voice. In the reign of William and Mary preaching of this kind had been introduced by Archbishop Tillotson, who employed a simple, straightforward style, certainly an improvement on the elaborate subtleties of the past, but who taught little more than a sense of duty and a prudential morality based on reason and appealing to common sense.

The church had lost much of its thunder. Its two great themes before 1688 had been the wickedness of the nonconformists and the divinity of kings, dead issues in the eighteenth century. The Revolution had placed the church, as it had placed the Tory party, in an awkward dilemma. A few of the clergy had refused to swear allegiance to William and Mary and had forfeited their places in the church, but most churchmen had accepted positions under the new government. This was inevitable; yet it was a reproach to the church and clergymen were a little ashamed of the part they were playing. William attempted to counteract this frame of mind by appointing Low-Church and liberal bishops who were sympathetic toward the new position of the monarchy. But the rank and file of the clergy remained sullenly Jacobite and Tory. It was not until the middle of the century that the church was thoroughly reconciled to the Hanoverian dynasty. Meanwhile Convocation was prorogued in 1717, met in 1741 only to be prorogued again, and did not reassemble until 1855.

The growth of science weakened the church. The Puritan had believed that God constantly intervened in the daily life of man, but this conception faded as science showed how the universe was controlled by natural laws. The church made no effort to combat scientific discoveries, for science was thought to prove that God governed the universe on rational and understandable principles. Yet in truth the progress of scientific thought tended to undermine the mysticism of orthodox religion, diminish the authority of the church, and enthrone reason in its stead. Religion of a cold and rational kind led easily to deism and Unitarianism. The deist acknowledged the existence of God on the testimony of reason but rejected all revealed religion. He believed in God because he recognized that the universe must have had some creator or prime cause, but once the world had come into being, God receded into remoteness and uncertainty. The Unitarians, affirming the unipersonality of the Godhead, denied the divinity of Christ. In the eighteenth century many English Presbyterians became Unitarians.

The structure of the Church of England did not make matters easier. The higher clergy were drawn from the aristocratic classes. Bishops usually were selected from the heads of colleges in the universities, from royal chaplains, from tutors to great nobles, or from popular preachers in fashionable London churches. Worldly men with large incomes and with high positions in society, they lived in palaces and moved about the country in state. They were appointed by the government and hence knew that they were expected to attend the House of Lords regularly and to vote with those who had selected them. The wonder is that eighteenth-century bishops were as learned, as conscientious, and as mindful of the church's welfare as they were.

The lower clergy, recruited from clerical families or from the middle classes, were almost always university men with some learning and culture. A few stayed in the universities all their lives. Most college fellowships required that their incumbents be in holy orders, but these men were scholars first and clerics only in a secondary way, and though they performed religious duties they did so in a somewhat perfunctory fashion. A second group of clergymen were chaplains in noble houses. They have been called the failures of the university world. They usually were easygoing men who liked hunting and country life. But since they had to retain the good will of their employer, they could not reprove his shortcomings with firmness. Their position must have been galling to men of independence.

The parish clergy, far more numerous than the scholars or the private chaplains, obtained their churches through advowsons belonging to their colleges or to lay patrons. Having secured a living with a good income, a country parson in the eighteenth century could enjoy a pleasant and leisurely life. The diary of Rev. James Woodforde shows that he lived comfortably in a good house with a number of servants; he entertained frequently and often dined with the squire. As improvements in agriculture increased the value of clerical livings, members of the gentry began to think it worth while to bestow churches on their younger sons or on their sons-in-law. The clergyman in such a parish would be a social equal of the squire and would keep the life of the parish on a plane of decent order and aristocratic dignity. The eighteenth-century parish priest usually attended to his spiritual duties and was kindly, sensible, and charitable in his relations with his parishioners, but he had no great spiritual earnestness and was not consumed with holy zeal. The historian Lecky has described these clergymen as "small country gentry, slightly superior to their neighbors in education and moral conduct, discharging their official duties of religion, but mixing, without

John Wesley, by Nathaniel Hone. (National Portrait Gallery, London)

scruple and without question, in country business and in country sports. Their
standard was low. Their zeal was very languid, but their influence, such as it
was, was chiefly for good."[9]

Unfortunately large numbers of the parish clergy never attained this comfortable condition but lived as vicars or perpetual curates on a much simpler

[9] William Edward Hartpole Lecky, *History of England in the Eighteenth Century* (London:
Longmans, 1879–1890, 8 vols.), II, 545.

scale. The Rev. Dr. Primrose in Goldsmith's *Vicar of Wakefield,* a good, charitable man with an income of £15 per annum, lived like a small yeoman. Queen Anne, who was deeply interested in the church, had taken funds coming to the Crown from annates and first fruits and had employed them to supplement the incomes of poor clergymen. This was known as Queen Anne's Bounty.

Perhaps the greatest omission of the church in the eighteenth century was its disregard of the industrial poor. It was to these neglected souls that Methodism brought its message. John Wesley, one of the greatest men of the age, was born in 1703. His father, Samuel Wesley, was an Anglican clergyman, poetic, emotional, vivid, but a futile man in practical affairs. His mother, Susannah, was a woman of deep personal religion and of inflexible will, determined to implant her convictions in her children and to make them like herself. She taught them industry and prayer, and once a week they carefully examined the state of their souls. But Susannah had little love or tenderness for her children. John Wesley inherited his mother's powerful intellect, imperious will, unflagging energy, and hard determination. For all his greatness he was a rigid, domineering man, hostile to intellectual and artistic things, so uncompromising that he did not believe in play even for children. Yet he also had his father's yearning for life and for love. It was to his marvelous organizing ability that the success of his movement was due. His brother Charles, the author of many famous hymns, was gentler and more poetic. The Wesleys were joined by George Whitefield, the popular preacher and revivalist.

In his youth Wesley was a stern High-churchman. While at Oxford he formed a Holy Club of theological students who practiced such severe asceticism that one member died. Wesley went as a missionary to Georgia, where he failed in his attempt to impose High-Church observances on the rough colonists. Moreover, he fell in love and behaved very badly when the lady married someone else. Eventually he was hounded from the colony. On his return to England he was deeply influenced by a group of German Moravians whose personal religion and calm assurance impressed him. Then, in 1738, he experienced a conversion. "I felt my heart strangely warmed," he wrote. "I felt that I did trust in Christ, Christ alone for salvation; and an assurance was given me that He had taken *my* sins, even *mine,* and saved me from the law of sin and death."[10]

It is important to understand what Wesley meant by conversion. Man, he believed, was in a state of sin and infamy, and in order to escape man must pass through a conversion in which he realized that Christ by His death upon the Cross had expiated human sins and had made salvation possible. This revelation brought a sense of pardon for past sin, a conviction that sin could be overcome, an assurance of salvation, and a lofty feeling of constant and eternal peace. Wesley determined to carry this message to the world. In the next fifty years he traveled some 224,000 miles and preached some 40,000 sermons, an average of 15 a week. At first he spoke in Anglican churches but soon was excluded from them. He and Whitefield preached with intense fervor and earnestness to congregations which often were convulsed by sobs and such hysterical paroxysms of devotion and remorse that they howled and rolled on the floor. Whitefield, it was said, could cause his hearers to burst into tears by the way in which he pronounced the word "Mesopotamia." It is small wonder that the Wesleys were

---

[10] Quoted in J. H. Plumb, *England in the Eighteenth Century* (Baltimore: Penguin Books, 1964), p. 92.

soon shut out from the parish churches by the horrified clergy. In 1739 Wesley began the field preaching that took him to the industrial areas of the towns and to savage mining villages. He kindled a living piety among many who heard him.

Wesley created such a tightly knit organization over which his will was law that his enemies called him Pope John. The largest local unit was the society, which was subdivided carefully into small classes and bands. These smaller groups of perhaps a dozen persons met for weekly prayer, exhortation, and mutual confession. Representatives from the societies gathered in an annual conference to receive the commands of their leader. Methodism taught an active, selfless, Christian life characterized by thrift, toil, abstinence, and discipline. It was a purely religious movement, for Wesley, a rigid Tory, permitted no political overtones to creep into his society. In fact, one of the strengths of Methodism was its abhorrence of political radicalism of every kind. Although rather hostile to the upper classes, it ignored them and went its own way. Methodism not only brought an emotional release to its members but gave many of them an opportunity for social leadership. Wesley always regarded himself as a member of the Anglican Church, and it was only toward the end of his life in 1784 that he began to ordain his own ministers since the church would not ordain them.

Methodism in the eighteenth century had many weaknesses. It was anti-intellectual; it had no interest in education; it tolerated child labor in the factories; it was fundamentalist, believing in a literal interpretation of the Scriptures; it was hostile to Jews and Catholics; and it reflected many of the prejudices of the uneducated classes, such as a belief in witches and in quack medicines. Yet it altered the religious history of England and was the greatest single element in producing the piety and religious revival of the Victorian Age.

24

GEORGE III and the
American Revolution

Whig historians, writing in the reign of Queen Victoria, set forth a distorted and erroneous picture of George III. They believed that when he came to the throne in 1760 as a young man of twenty-two, he was determined to increase the powers of the Crown, to "be a King" as his mother urged him to do, to govern and not merely to reign. With this purpose in mind, he was supposed to have moved from one tyrannical act to another until he lost the American colonies and brought England to disaster in 1783. Then, according to this view, the people, with prophetic vision, demanded that the younger Pitt be placed in power to restore the fortunes of the nation.

It is true that the first twenty years of the reign were disastrous and the King made a number of political mistakes; otherwise this summary is inaccurate.

GEORGE III, 1760–1820

George had no wish to be absolute or tyrannical. On the contrary, he regarded the English system of government as perfect. As a young man he spoke of "the beauty, excellence, and perfection of the British constitution as by law established"; he never aimed at being more than the constitution made him, the hereditary head of the executive branch of a parliamentary state. He assumed that he could select his own ministers, as did everyone else, but he recognized fully that he could not retain them unless they were supported by the House of Commons: "George III never left the safe ground of parliamentary government, and merely acted the *primus inter pares,* the first among the borough-mongering, electioneering gentlemen of England. While the Stuarts tried to browbeat the House and circumscribe the range of its actions, George III fully accepted its constitution and recognized its powers, and merely tried to work it in accordance with the customs of the time."[1]

Unhappily, George's mind was rather disturbed. He became excited under

[1] L. B. Namier, *England in the Age of the American Revolution* (London: Macmillan, 1930), p. 4.

pressure and later in life was subject to fits of insanity. Both his father, Frederick, the Prince of Wales (who died in 1751), and his mother, the Princess Augusta, from Saxe-Gotha in Germany, hated George II; and George as a child learned to hate before he learned to think. "The neurotic boy, bitter in soul and mentally underdeveloped, concentrated on the King the hostility of the heir and rival, while his love went out to Lord Bute [his tutor], to him the incarnation of a tutelary paternal spirit."[2] In his youth he spoke of Bute as the only honest man, sent by God to aid him in his future task of ruling England; he besought Bute never to desert him. George had heard his father talk, as men out of power always talked, of the corruption of those in office. Believing what he heard, he was sure that his grandfather's ministers were "ungrateful, faithless, and corrupt." When he became King he would make them smart. Thus he grew up prejudiced and narrow, lacking in sympathy and breadth of view.

As a young man he vacillated between moments of self-abasement, when he felt himself sinful and unfit for his future position, and moments of exaltation when he fancied himself in partnership with God. In the first of these moods he was apt to become melancholy. But he was a man of pluck and courage, as he showed many times in later life. Determined to overcome his weaknesses by resolution and strength of will, he was constantly making a great effort, which placed him under heavy strain. His effort also made him obstinate, and obstinacy became his defense mechanism, his method of facing the world. And when he found himself opposed by forces his obstinacy could not overcome, he was apt to go to pieces. In his moods of exaltation he aspired to purge political life of its jobbery and corruption, for he was a pious and virtuous young man who set his face against the vicious social customs of the day. He enjoyed simple pleasures. Interested in agriculture, he wrote articles on farming and was nicknamed "Farmer George." He was loyal to those ministers whom he trusted and he was honest in politics. But he was too innocent and unsophisticated, too idealistic, and too inflexible to cope with the problems of political life.

SHIFTING MINISTRIES

The Resignations of Pitt and Newcastle

During the first ten years of the reign George found that his problem was not to purify government but to have any government at all. The quarrels and jealousies of ambitious politicians broke up one Cabinet after another and prevented the formation of a strong stable ministry; moreover, the unfortunate side of Pitt's character—his petulance and desire to dominate—was very marked. Seven different Cabinets held office for brief periods between 1760 and 1770. Thus the young King was in constant trouble.

The administration seemed stable enough when George came to the throne. It was dominated by Pitt, at the height of his fame as a war minister, and by Newcastle, the manager of patronage and elections and the manipulator of personal allegiance. A third person of some importance in the Cabinet was Henry Fox, who was occupied in becoming wealthy as paymaster of the forces. But the Cabinet was not as united as it appeared. Pitt conducted the war on a heroic plane with little thought of expense, while Newcastle had the mundane

[2] Namier, p. 96.

George III as a young man, by Allan Ramsay. (National Portrait Gallery, London)

task of finding money to meet its enormous cost. Moreover, Pitt regarded Newcastle with a contempt he did not bother to conceal. As a patriot who wished to win the war, George made no immediate change in the Cabinet, though he regarded both Pitt and Newcastle with suspicion.

The clash of personalities was increased when, after a few months, George added Bute to the Cabinet, a perfectly natural move which everyone accepted and which should not be given a sinister interpretation. Bute was of sufficient importance to be placed in high office quite apart from his friendship with the King. A connection of the influential Duke of Argyll, Bute had sat in the House of Lords as a Scottish representative peer. After Argyll's death in 1761, he succeeded to the management of the Scottish members of both houses. This alone made him important. In addition, his wife brought him great wealth; and his daughter married Sir James Lowther, who controlled a number of English parliamentary boroughs. Thus Bute possessed the riches to maintain a great position and enjoyed an electoral interest in both countries. He had been associated in politics with Frederick, the King's father. After Frederick's death, Bute had become the friend and adviser of Frederick's widow and the tutor of the young Prince George. Few politicians in the eighteenth century held so many trump cards and few played them so badly.

Unfortunately, within two years of George's accession, both Pitt and Newcastle resigned. Pitt left the Cabinet in 1761 when, as we have seen, he could not persuade his colleagues to declare war on Spain. Newcastle resigned in the following year because he was jealous of Bute and because he had been defeated in the Cabinet over the size of the subsidy to be given to Frederick of Prussia. Thus both Pitt and Newcastle resigned because they disagreed with their colleagues, and not because they were dismissed by the King. Yet George was glad to see them go. He was now rid of both the tyrannical and corrupting ministers of his grandfather. But if he had been more experienced and sophisticated he would have known that it was dangerous to lose these men, the twin pillars of the administration. Pitt, with his prestige and eloquence, would be a most formidable opponent. And although Newcastle's management of patronage may have appeared low and grubbing to the idealistic young King, it was a part of political life that could not be ignored. George should have done his utmost to prevent these resignations. Instead, he appointed Bute as First Lord of the Treasury and George Grenville, a brother-in-law but no friend of Pitt, as Secretary.

Lord Bute

Newcastle's resignation was followed by the collapse of his political empire. He did not at first understand what was happening, for he assumed that the many persons who owed their places to him would continue to follow his lead. He expected them to remain in office but to show their displeasure at his dismissal and to work for his recall. Bute, however, would not permit the placemen and pensioners of the Court party to remain half-loyal to Newcastle. In October 1762 he forced them to declare themselves either for or against the preliminaries of peace that were being arranged in Paris. Later in the same year he informed them that they must either vote with the Cabinet or lose their places. Newcastle, meanwhile, had asked his friends to resign. Some few did so, very grudgingly; but most of them did not. Holding good positions under the Crown, they refused to sacrifice them at Newcastle's bidding. They had followed him as the First Lord of the Treasury, but not as a personal friend or as a leading statesman, and they were ready to shift their loyalty to the government of the day. Bute's purge of the "Pelhamite Innocents" was not perhaps as important as it appeared. The old duke was left disconsolate as he saw his influence vanish, but the change would have come in any case, for it was the Crown, not Newcastle, that was the source of patronage. Bute further strengthened his position by appointing Henry Fox as leader of the Court party in the Commons.

Although Bute appeared to be successful, he was growing weary of political wrangling. A series of unpleasant episodes exposed his lack of nerve and fortitude. Peace having been made with France, the country expected a reduction in taxation. But Bute, knowing this to be impossible, introduced a tax on cider. A great outcry arose against it. Like Walpole's scheme in 1733, the tax was an excise and was quickly opposed as tyrannical. The government, however, did not draw back, as Walpole had done, but forced the tax through Parliament. Bute naturally suffered some scurrilous abuse. He was attacked as a Scot, as the advocate of arbitrary government, as the favorite and paramour of the King's mother. He was too thin-skinned to endure such slander. Moreover, there was an awkward quarrel with Henry Fox, who wanted a peerage. Negotiations took place between George and Bute on one hand and Fox on the other. But a misunderstanding arose. The King and Bute understood that Fox, upon becoming Lord Holland, would resign his office of paymaster of the forces; but Fox believed that he was to be permitted to keep it. A compromise finally was arranged by which Fox retained the office for two years. This episode, as it was told in public, created an impression of chicanery in the politics of the court. In April 1763 Bute resigned.

George Grenville, 1763–1765

The King was left with the problem of finding someone to whom he could give his confidence and who could also perform the difficult task of managing the House of Commons. To bring back Pitt or Newcastle would be to admit that his attempt to run the government on simple and honest lines had been a failure. He could not turn to Bute or Fox. He therefore appointed George Grenville, the Secretary, as the head of a new administration. At least Grenville was not one of the old gang of George II, and he posed as an authority on the procedure of the Commons, to which he expressed great devotion.

Grenville was First Lord of the Treasury from 1763 to 1765. He was a domineering man with considerable strength of will, methodical, businesslike, and careful about details, but he was quite devoid of imagination, he had little depth of character, and he lacked both eloquence and finesse. He tried to strengthen his position by rules and regulations. In order to control his colleagues and to attract the support of the Commons, he sought to show them that he enjoyed the complete confidence of the monarch. No one was to consult the King without Grenville's permission. George soon found himself, as he said, "too much restrained, and that when anything was proposed to him, it was no longer counsel, but what he was to obey."[3] In the same spirit Grenville ruled that all the patronage of the Crown must be in his hands; he would have no rival in the loyalty of the Court party. It is small wonder that this pedantic disciplinarian lasted for only two years.

John Wilkes. Grenville had to deal with a political firebrand, John Wilkes,

[3] J. Steven Watson, *The Reign of George III 1760–1815* (Oxford: Clarendon Press, 1960), p. 109.

who had a flair for publicity and a knack of making ministers look ridiculous. His early career was not unlike that of other men who were rising in the world. The son of a wealthy distiller, he was well educated. He married a rich wife, bought a seat in Parliament, and secured the office of colonel in the militia. But then, separating from his wife, he entered a fast set in London, and became reckless and extreme in his politics. For a time he was supported by Pitt and other leaders of the opposition because he criticized the government. In 1763, having established a newspaper, the *North Briton,* he wrote a slashing attack upon the Cabinet, and by implication upon the King, because of a speech from the throne defending the peace with France.

The Cabinet decided to punish him. It issued a general warrant, that is, a warrant which contained no names, directing the arrest of all persons connected with the offensive number of the *North Briton,* on a charge of seditious libel. Wilkes fought back fiercely. Appearing in court, he claimed that general warrants were illegal, that a Secretary of State was not a magistrate who could issue a warrant, and that he (Wilkes) had freedom from arrest as a Member of Parliament. The judge, Sir John Pratt, ruled that the Secretary had acted within his rights but that Wilkes was covered by parliamentary privilege. Later, in another case concerning Wilkes, he ruled that general warrants were illegal. Meanwhile Wilkes was seeking the support of the London mob and was portraying the action of the Cabinet as an attack on the liberties of the people.

As Wilkes became more violent and disreputable he was deserted by his political allies, who refused to defend him in the Commons, where angry members unwisely voted that parliamentary privilege did not protect him from arrest. At this point, being involved in new legal difficulties and having been wounded in a duel, Wilkes fled to France, to all appearances a ruined man, though he was to return later to trouble the government once more. He should not be regarded as an apostle of liberty contending against an arbitrary government. The Cabinet had not intended to be arbitrary, but the legality of general warrants was certainly questionable; in fact, the Commons later supported Pratt by declaring them illegal. Thus the Cabinet had acted in a crude and blundering way which Wilkes could easily exploit.

Grenville also blundered in trying to tax the American colonies, a point to which we will turn presently.

Rockingham, 1765–1766

The King tolerated Grenville for two years, largely because he could find no alternative as the head of the government. "I see I must yield," he said in all sincerity. "I do it for the good of my people." In 1765, however, he commissioned his uncle, the Duke of Cumberland, to negotiate for a new Cabinet. Cumberland thought in terms of the old alliance of Pitt and Newcastle. But negotiations with Pitt came to nothing. Pitt merely showed that the political confusion of the period was due in no small part to him. He must have everything his own way; he would enter no Cabinet in which he did not dominate. Newcastle was now an old man. The few adherents who were still loyal to him were led by the Marquis of Rockingham.

Rockingham might well have hesitated to accept office, for he would have powerful opponents and many problems. Nonetheless, in July 1765, he agreed to form an administration. He was a wealthy landowner with important connections in the House of Lords. A reasonable, sensible man, though rather colorless and with no great force or talent, he hoped to end the quarrels and jealousies of public life by forming a broad-bottom administration somewhat as Pelham had done in the middle of the century. He was ready to admit other groups to office if they would accept his leadership and work with him in friendly cooperation. He continued to negotiate with Pitt, though to no avail. But his friendly policy toward the American colonies split his Cabinet, Pitt played upon these differences, and after about a year the Rockingham Cabinet broke up. The King was still in search of a stable administration.

The State of Parties, 1766

The problem of instability in government, which worried many members of Parliament, was discussed at an interesting meeting of politicians in January 1766. They believed that the King should play a more active role in politics, that he should select his ministers as he saw fit and not place himself in the hands of a single group or party. The members who attended this meeting, declaring that they had always acted upon the sole principle of attachment to the Crown, were ready to support any ministry which offered hope of permanence and stability. Prominent among them was a group of minor officials who were beginning to develop into the modern civil service. They wanted continuity in administration, partly for the sake of efficiency and partly because they wished to remain in office, for they were exposed to dismissal by every ephemeral Cabinet wanting to find places for its followers. They looked to the Crown for support, which George attempted to give them; he had learned to appreciate these industrious and loyal officials who did much of the real work of government while the party leaders wrangled. These minor officials merged into a larger group of members. Some, lacking office, wanted to obtain it, but many were ready to support the Crown in an unofficial, independent, and patriotic way without hope of gain. They were called the King's Friends. Never organized into a political party, they represented a frame of mind rather than a party. They believed themselves numerous enough to form an administration, but they lacked one essential—a leader of national stature who could become the center of a Cabinet.

The parties or factions clustering around prominent persons at this time have been carefully analyzed.[4] One such party followed Pitt, now Earl of Chatham. However, it was very small. Chatham always claimed to despise parties and to be above them, and certainly he never tried to build one. After the peace with France he lost the spontaneous support which independent members had given him during the war, retaining only a handful of hero-worshipers, such as the Duke of Grafton, and a few friends with whom he had personal connections. A second faction, the Bedford party, was a family group of three or four peers connected by marriage with that great magnate, the Duke of Bedford. Each of them could place a few members in the Commons where, all told, the party controlled about twenty votes. Too small to form an administration by itself, the Bedford faction was compact, ably led, and a valuable ally for any cabinet in power. A third party followed George Grenville. This was not a family group but rather a number of men whom Grenville had attracted while he was in office and who remained loyal to him afterward. He could sometimes muster as many as twenty-five votes in the Commons, though he could never be sure that

[4] John Brooke, *The Chatham Administration 1766–1768* (London: Macmillan, 1956), Chaps. VI and VII.

his followers would stay with him. The Marquis of Rockingham, like Bedford, was the leader of a number of peers who were connected with each other by blood, marriage, or personal friendship.[5] Each was followed by a handful of members in the lower house, although these members had little in common save that their patrons worked together.

It is clear that no one noble controlled more than a few votes in the Commons. The great magnates, after all, were far from dominant. And there remained a large segment of independent country gentlemen, normally inclined to follow the government, but quite at liberty to take an independent line whenever they chose.

Chatham and Grafton, 1766–1770

When Rockingham's Cabinet broke up in 1766, the King decided to ask Chatham to return as the head of a new administration. Chatham at last obtained what he wanted—power on his own terms. He was to select his Cabinet and follow his own policy. He appeared to have every advantage—the confidence of the King, the patronage of the Crown, the good will of the King's Friends, the support of many independent members, the prestige of his success as a war minister. And yet he threw them all away, so that stability in government was soon as far distant as before.

Chatham set out to destroy party groups and to select from the ruins those ministers he desired. The Duke of Grafton, detached somewhat earlier from the Rockingham faction, became the First Lord of the Treasury; Henry Conway, Secretary under Rockingham, was induced to remain, thus deserting his former friends; Lord Shelburne, formerly attached to Bute, accepted office as the other Secretary. The Cabinet included Charles Townshend as Chancellor of the Exchequer and Pratt, the judge in Wilkes's case, as Lord Chancellor. Chatham took the minor office of Lord Privy Seal in order to obtain the leisure to direct the whole.

But Chatham met with a number of rebuffs. He did not destroy existing parties; he detached a few individuals and left the rest more compact and hostile than before. He hoped to end Britain's isolation in Europe by renewing his old alliance with Frederick of Prussia, but Frederick declined to alter his policy at Chatham's bidding. He wooed the Americans, but they found new grievances. He lost his audience in the Commons, for he was now a peer. Neglecting to organize his Cabinet, he found that members went their separate ways.

Defeated on so many fronts, Chatham simply retired from politics. For more than two years, though holding office, he absented himself from the court and from Parliament. He suffered from some kind of mental illness, sitting for days in a darkened room, cut off from all contact with the world. It is possible, though one can only guess, that his imperious will could not tolerate a world it did not dominate. His colleagues acted without supervision, adopting policies of which he would not have approved. Charles Townshend, for instance, renewed Grenville's attempts to tax the American colonists. This policy divided the Cabinet, for Grafton and Shelburne were sympathetic toward America. But the Bedford group, which was brought into the administration in 1768 after prolonged negotiations, was anti-American. In the same year Chatham emerged from his retirement, though only to resign.

---

[5] One of these peers was Newcastle. He suffered a stroke in 1767 and died in 1768.

His follower, the Duke of Grafton, continued to head the Cabinet for two more years. He remained in office partly out of loyalty to the King and partly because he became involved in another encounter with Wilkes and did not wish to retire in the midst of it. But he was an incompetent person, more the grandee than the statesman; his Cabinet was weak and disorderly.

The Return of Wilkes. A general election in 1768 gave Wilkes an opportunity to return to England and to strike again at the government. He stood for election to the Commons first in London, where he was defeated, and then in Middlesex, the county adjacent to the city. A small county, Middlesex was already half urbanized as London outgrew its ancient borders; it contained a turbulent and radical industrial population that welcomed a candidate posing as the victim of oppression. Wilkes, who was returned in a disorderly election, then insisted upon being arrested on old charges, thus adding to his role as a martyr. In a scuffle outside his prison between his followers and a body of troops —who unfortunately were Scots—a man was killed. Of this episode Wilkes made the most, inciting the mob against the Cabinet. Although he had no program for the benefit of the poor, he was a symbol of revolt for industrial workers in some economic distress.

The Cabinet decided that Wilkes should be ejected from Parliament. It was not difficult to persuade the Commons to expel him, but he flourished on grievances, stood for re-election, and was promptly returned. Expelled again, he was quickly re-elected. This happened three times. The Commons then declared him ineligible for membership and gave the contested seat to his opponent. This action, a blunder, made the King and the Cabinet appear tyrannical. To many people, both inside and outside Parliament, the rights of the electorate appeared to have been violated. At last Wilkes had a constitutional grievance, which he exploited to form a radical party in London. Yet to other persons, including the liberal-minded Charles James Fox, the Commons had acted entirely within their rights. It was held that the Commons must maintain their freedom, not only against the court from above, but against the rabble from below. It was the right of the Commons to settle election disputes and to discipline their own members. But Wilkes, refusing to accept their decision, had employed violence and unacceptable means to force their hand. In 1770 the Duke of Grafton resigned.

LORD NORTH'S ADMINISTRATION, 1770–1782

A change came over British politics when Lord North succeeded Grafton as First Lord of the Treasury in 1770. The period of ministerial instability ended, and North established a firm and settled administration which lasted for twelve years. It bore many resemblances to the government of Henry Pelham.

Lord North, a son of the Earl of Guilford, had received a classical education, spoke a number of modern languages, and had served an apprenticeship as a junior official in the Treasury. He became Chancellor of the Exchequer in 1767 after the death of Charles Townshend. Three years later, at the age of thirty-seven, he took over Grafton's ministry. He had first been brought into office by Newcastle, but he had no close party ties and was without a personal following in the Commons. His talent lay in his ability to operate the delicate balance of political forces and to maintain a smoothly running administration.

He was shrewd but relaxed, an easygoing man of business who met problems as they arose and was not committed to a long-term program. Many of the crises of recent years had arisen because ministers had espoused causes or adopted policies that were unpopular in the Commons. But North did not wish to force the Commons along any particular line of action; his interest was in government. He sought moderate and general policies which would be approved by the majority of members. He had the advantage of being in the Commons, where his easy and natural manner, his disarming humor, his good sense, good temper, and affability helped to calm the storms of political life. Honest, reliable, and steady, if not very exciting, he won the approbation of both King and Commons as a minister worthy of trust.

So far as possible North avoided controversial issues. He refused to clash with Wilkes, who was allowed to take his seat in the Commons after the election of 1774. The problems of discontent in America and improvement in the government of British India[6] were both approached in a moderate and conciliatory way. The Rockingham group, which was the principal party of opposition, could find no popular issue on which to fight him. And he won general applause by his skill and care in handling financial business.

Like Pelham he was not greedy for personal power but sought to broaden his administration by seeking talented debaters and admitting former opponents to office. The Bedford faction, which had joined the government in 1768, was retained as a political ally. The Grenville party, which did not survive its leader's death in 1770, was brought back to the support of the government. The Duke of Grafton was offered and accepted office. In this way North constructed a broad coalition of various groups and opinions. The stability of his administration was especially acceptable to the civil servants and to others in the group known as the King's Friends.

North's position appeared unshakable by 1774. After that date, however, he became involved in difficulties with the American colonists and was less successful as a war than as a peace minister.

THE REVOLT OF THE AMERICAN COLONIES

Causes of the Revolt

While British politicians quarreled and refused to cooperate during the first decade of George's reign, discontent of a serious nature arose among the American colonists. Having grown into prosperous and stable communities with a sense of constitutional and economic freedom, the colonies refused to be taxed by a Parliament in which they were not represented. Their refusal led to lawlessness and defiance; in fact, they developed a frame of mind in which any act of the British government was regarded with suspicion. They began to question and then to repudiate Parliament's right to legislate for them as well as to tax them, and ultimately they rejected the King himself.

The English, on their side, had no wish to dominate the political life of America, toward which they felt a somewhat contemptuous indifference. Their principal aim was to regulate commerce, for they were still traders, not imperialists. It was taken for granted in England that Parliament was supreme; hence the American challenge to Parliament's authority was resented. The

[6] See pages 561–564.

Americans, it was felt, must be put in their place. This in turn led to unwise and provocative attempts at punishment which, far from cowing the colonists, increased their truculence. Exasperation mounted on both sides of the Atlantic until fighting began in 1775. The British had no wish to be tyrannical, but they lacked sufficient knowledge of conditions and opinions in America, they acted in anger, and they assumed a moral superiority, as though they knew how to manage America better than the Americans did themselves. The British also suffered from a lack of continuous and consistent policy: they were paying the price for the instability of politics at home.

There was a strong tradition of liberty in America. In a distorted though useful view of English history the colonists pictured the Anglo-Saxon period as a golden age of freedom. This freedom, it was thought, had been lost at the time of the Norman Conquest and had then been slowly and painfully regained, especially by the Civil War in the 1640s and by the Revolution in 1688. Freedom had been won because Parliament had subdued the King and had established the principle that the King could not take an Englishman's property without his consent expressed through a representative body. The colonists exulted in this victory, which they compared with the victory of their elected assemblies over the royal governors. Consequently, they thought, the people, in America as in England, levied their own taxes, made their own laws, and ran their own affairs.

This tradition of liberty was strengthened in several ways. Except for the regulation of trade, the English government had left the colonies pretty much to themselves. An American might live his entire life without seeing an imperial official. Indeed, there were very few such officials in America except for the governors and for those entrusted with the enforcement of the Navigation Laws. The governors, of course, were appointed in England (except for the popularly elected governors of Connecticut and Rhode Island), but every colony possessed an assembly which controlled finance. The assembly, representing local and popular interests, and the governor, representing imperial and royal interests, were often at odds. It was the governor who usually gave way, for his salary came from the assembly and he was not certain of the support of the home authorities in any quarrel with the colonists. Serving for a short term, he tended to take the line of least resistance, to ease his relations with the colonists by concessions, and to allow basic differences to drift. The assemblies pushed their fiscal advantage against the governors in an aggressive and self-righteous way, much as Parliament in the seventeenth century had pushed its advantage against the poverty-stricken Stuarts.

The home authorities did not appear to be disturbed by these developments. The administration of the colonies was part of the executive jurisdiction of the King, who left it in the hands of the Secretary of State for the Southern Department. The Secretary relied heavily upon a Board of Trade and Plantations created in 1696 which considered colonial business and advised him what to do. The Secretary then made his decision, which was passed on to the royal governors. But the colonists normally did what they pleased and were accustomed to a very loose control. What control there was came from the King and his ministers. The colonists failed to realize that a command from the King was really a command from Parliament also. They had never considered, nor had it been considered in England, just what would happen if a contest arose, not between the assemblies and the weak colonial governors, but between the assemblies and the supreme authority in England, namely, the Parliament.

A sense of liberty was increased by the fact that most Americans lived on the soil. It is now believed probable that most of them owned the land they cultivated. Their land was their property. It gave them economic independence, for by industry they could make it yield a fair return and could thus be free from control by other men. Moreover, it gave them political independence, for ownership of land conferred the right to vote. Hence they had a very strong sense of property. Property was not merely a possession, to be cherished and increased: it was the fountain of life and liberty. Property and liberty went together. But a man had no security for his property if it could be taken from him without his consent.

Historians of a generation ago laid great stress upon the Acts of Trade as a cause of the American Revolution. These acts, it will be remembered,[7] required that many colonial raw products, if they were exported, could be taken only to England or to other English colonies, and that imported manufactured articles from Europe must come from England, having been either produced there or brought to England from the Continent. All colonial trade, export and import, was confined to English and colonial shipping; high duties were placed on certain imports of non-British origin; and the colonists were forbidden to engage in many forms of manufacture. Looking at these acts, historians developed an economic interpretation of the American revolt. The colonists, it was asserted, believed themselves the victims of economic restrictions imposed upon them for the benefit of the mother country.

At the present time, however, the Acts of Trade are not considered a primary cause of the Revolution for two reasons. In the first place, the acts permitted trade to flow in its natural channels. Trade would have followed much the same course had there been no acts at all. Great Britain was the natural market for America's raw products and the natural source of her manufactured imports. Secondly, the acts were not strictly enforced, at least not in New England. The Molasses Act of 1733, for example, was one that might have imposed hardship. The New Englanders had built a large industry upon molasses. It was brought from the West Indies and made into rum, which was sold throughout the colonies or taken to Africa to exchange for slaves. So extensive had this industry become that the British West Indies could not supply molasses in sufficient quantities, and New England skippers bought it in the French and Dutch islands. To protect the British planters, the Molasses Act imposed a prohibitive duty of 6d. a gallon upon molasses imported into the colonies from non-British sources. Had the act been enforced, an important segment of colonial trade and industry would have been crippled. But a standard bribe of 1d. to 1½d. a gallon was arranged between New England traders and the venal customs officials in America, and the trade went on as before.[8]

A New Imperial Policy

After the close of the Seven Years' War in 1763 the British government felt compelled to pay greater attention to colonial problems. The vast territories acquired from the French in Canada and in the area west of the Appalachian Mountains would have to be pacified and defended. It was thought that for this purpose an army of 10,000 men was necessary at a cost of some £350,000 a year.

[7] See pages 400, 431–432.
[8] Edmund S. Morgan, *The Birth of the Republic* (Chicago: University of Chicago Press, 1956), pp. 8–13.

Moreover, the lax enforcement of the Acts of Trade had been underlined during the war when, to the exasperation of the British, Americans had continued to trade with the French West Indies.

It was George Grenville who first moved to meet these problems during his administration between 1763 and 1765. He began by placing the trans-Appalachian West under direct imperial control. The plan was to keep this territory roughly as it was. A line was drawn along the mountains, and "for the present" the colonists were not to expand beyond it. Grenville, who feared that a sudden rush across the mountains would cause Indian wars, wished to make treaties with the Indians, to foster the fur trade, and to divert American migration to Nova Scotia and to Florida. In due time he would release the western lands for settlement in an orderly and gradual way. On paper this scheme seemed excellent, but the so-called Proclamation Line ignored a number of factors. Colonial settlements already existed west of the mountains. Several of the colonies claimed that their western boundaries extended to the Mississippi. During the recent war volunteers had been recruited in America by the promise of western lands, and land companies had been formed to exploit the West. To many groups in the colonies the Proclamation Line was a great disappointment.

Grenville also began the policy of taxing the American colonists. The Acts of Trade, which hitherto had been employed to regulate commerce, were now to be made to produce revenue. Customs officials could no longer remain in England and employ deputies to perform their duties in America; they must go to America in person. American skippers must prepare elaborate papers for every voyage. The navy was to hunt down smugglers, who were to be tried by Admiralty courts and not by colonial juries. In 1764 Grenville passed the Sugar Act, which superseded the Molasses Act and cut the duty from 6*d.* to 3*d.* a gallon, but he warned that the new duty would be collected. In 1765 he passed the Stamp Act. Stamped paper, on which a tax had been paid, must be used for all legal documents, deeds, bonds, ships' papers, as well as for almanacs, newspapers, and advertisements.

To British statesmen these taxes seemed fair and just. The Seven Years' War had brought great benefit to the colonies, freeing them from the threat of the French in Canada and opening lands to the West (though these lands might be withheld for the moment); but the war had doubled the British national debt and had been followed by an economic depression in Britain. Hence it was felt that though the colonies could never pay for the cost of defeating the French, they should at least meet the bill for the 10,000 troops sent to guard the lands west of the mountains. Most of the cost of defending the colonies, including all the charges of the navy, would still be borne by the British taxpayer.

The colonists, on the other hand, viewed these taxes very differently. They had learned the importance of the taxing power from their struggles with the colonial governors; they regarded a tax to which they had not consented as an attack upon their property. They raised the fundamental question whether Parliament could levy taxes on them and claimed that it could not. Parliament in England, they held, was a representative body which protected the British citizen from arbitrary taxation. But since the colonists were not represented, Parliament gave them no protection. On the contrary, when it asked them to pay ungranted taxes over which they had no control, it became a threat. The colonists made no distinction between indirect taxes levied through customs duties and direct taxes, such as that imposed by the Stamp Act.

In England, at the instance of Grenville, one of his subordinates, Thomas Whateley, wrote a pamphlet[9] to answer the Americans. Largely a defense of the Sugar Act, it also made the claim that although the colonists were not members of Parliament and could not vote for members, they were represented nonetheless. Many Englishmen, the pamphlet argued, did not vote and yet enjoyed virtual representation because their interests were the same as the interests of Englishmen who possessed the franchise. The colonists, then, were as fully represented as those Englishmen who could not vote. Moreover, members of the Commons represented the whole empire and not merely their own constituencies. These arguments fell flat in the colonies, as they deserved to do, and were demolished in an answer[10] by Daniel Dulany, a lawyer in Maryland. A nonvoting Englishman, said Dulany, might have the same interests as the Englishman who voted, but an American did not. American interests, far from being identical with those of England, were frequently the complete opposite. Members of the Commons might in theory represent the empire, but in fact their interests normally were confined to their own localities. Nor would the presence in Parliament of a few American representatives be any solution, for such members would have no influence on Parliament's decisions.

Meanwhile the Stamp Act could not be enforced. Rioters burned the stamps and intimidated the distributers of the stamped paper, radicals formed societies known as "Sons of Liberty," merchants refused to import British manufactures, resolutions were passed denouncing taxation by Parliament, a Stamp Act Congress met in New York to which nine colonies sent representatives. This assembly, after acknowledging the King as supreme head, made a distinction between Parliament's right to legislate for America, which was accepted, and Parliament's right to tax, which was denied.

These events came as a shock to England. Many members of Parliament believed that concessions should not be made to rioters and that weakness in Britain would spell the end of all control over the colonies. But Rockingham, who succeeded Grenville as head of the Cabinet in 1765, had opposed the Stamp Act and was under pressure from English merchants injured by the disruption of American trade. He therefore repealed the Stamp Act in March 1766. But he found the Commons reluctant to make concessions; hence the repeal was accompanied by a Declaratory Act which asserted the right of Parliament to make statutes binding the colonies "in all cases whatsoever." Unfortunately Rockingham allowed members to receive the impression that the colonists objected only to direct taxation and not to indirect taxes through customs duties, although no such distinction existed in America. Rockingham recognized that the Sugar Act was a burden on the economy of New England, and so the duty on non-British molasses imported into the colonies was reduced to 1d. a gallon.

William Pitt, now Earl of Chatham, whose administration began in July 1766, was even more friendly toward the colonists than was Rockingham. But when he attempted to persuade them to tax themselves in order to supply food and shelter for the soldiers stationed in America, his request was resisted; after his physical collapse American affairs fell into the hands of Charles Townshend, the Chancellor of the Exchequer, a clever but shallow man. Grasping in a sharp

[9] *The Regulations Lately Made concerning the Colonies and the Taxes Imposed upon them, considered* (London, 1765).
[10] *Considerations on the Propriety of imposing Taxes in the British Colonies, for the Purpose of raising a Revenue, by Act of Parliament* (Annapolis, Md., 1765).

legalistic way at the supposed distinction between direct and indirect taxes, he devised a plan to impose new customs duties on glass, lead, paper, paints, and tea imported from Britain into the colonies. He also established a board of customs commissioners in Boston to manage the customs service along the whole American coast. The proceeds from the customs would be used, first, to support the army in America and, then, to pay the salaries of British officials in the colonies, thus freeing them from dependence on the assemblies.

The Townshend duties proved disastrous. Their yield, which was estimated at only £40,000, was quite inadequate for the ends Townshend suggested. His talk of paying officials from the proceeds of the customs aroused suspicion in America; his new duties made possible a sinister interpretation of what the Declaratory Act really meant. Agitation and disorder began again in the colonies, with nonimportation agreements and vigorous denials of Parliament's right to tax. One part of Townshend's legislation, which suspended the assembly in New York for its refusal to billet soldiers, was regarded in America as an attack on all the colonial assemblies. Moreover, the customs commissioners established in Boston proved to be corrupt men who used their powers to enrich themselves at the expense of American traders. The Sugar Act, as passed in 1764, gave the commissioners authority to seize the ships and goods of violators, a power they used to the full. Soon cordially hated in Boston, they called on the authorities in England to send troops for their support.

Persuaded that Boston was in the hands of smugglers and rowdies, Lord Hillsborough, who held the newly created post of Secretary for America, sent troops in September 1768. Their presence aroused hostility not only in Boston but in the other colonies. Here was proof that Parliament's power to legislate was fully as dangerous as its power to tax. Nonetheless, an uneasy calm existed in Boston for many months. In March 1770, however, in a collision between the soldiers and the mob five Bostonians were killed.

This explosion had a sobering effect on both sides. Many Americans thought that Boston had gone too far and that mobbing was becoming dangerous. At almost the same time Lord North became head of the Cabinet at home. In a move toward conciliation, he repealed all the Townshend duties except that on tea and informed the colonies that no further taxes would be imposed on them for the purpose of raising revenue. There followed a period of almost three years in which relations between England and America improved. Nonimportation agreements ceased to operate. Some of the old good will between the two countries returned. The colonies were prosperous, constitutional issues receded, and it was hoped in England that North's conciliation had solved the American question.

But beginning in 1772 new causes of friction arose which quickly brought matters to a head. One such cause was the rapacity of the customs commissioners in Boston, who continued to confiscate colonial shipping. When in June 1772 a British revenue vessel, the *Gaspée*, pursuing a suspected smuggler, ran aground near Providence, a group of colonists boarded it at night and burned it to the water's edge. Late in the same year Benjamin Franklin obtained possession in England of a number of letters by British officials in America who urged the home government to take strong measures against the colonists. The publication of these letters aroused strong resentment. The colonists were therefore in a state of alarm and excitement when in May 1773 Lord North passed a Tea Act which permitted the East India Company to carry tea directly to America, where it would be distributed to retailers, thus bypassing the wholesale merchants in both countries. North's purpose was to assist the East India Company, but the wholesale merchants in America denounced the act as a subtle scheme to raise new revenues in America. The people took alarm. In most ports the captains bringing the tea were persuaded to take it away without unloading it, but in Boston the colonists dumped it into the harbor.

Lord North's answer was to pass the Coercive Acts to punish Boston. The port was closed, the Governor's council was to be appointed by the King, town meetings were forbidden except for the election of officials, trials might be transferred to England if the Governor saw fit, troops were again stationed in the town, and General Gage, their commander, became Governor of Massachusetts. Unfortunately at the same time Parliament passed the Quebec Act, which established a new government in Canada and extended the province of Quebec southward to the Ohio River. This act was misinterpreted in America as another indication of British hostility. The First Continental Congress, which met in Philadelphia in September 1774, declared that the colonies had the right to legislate for themselves in their provincial assemblies, subject only to the veto of the British Crown. This claim placed the assemblies upon an equality with Parliament, for it meant that the King should govern the colonies through the assemblies just as he governed England through the Parliament. Yet the resolution adopted by the Congress contained a somewhat contradictory statement that Parliament should continue to regulate the commerce of the empire as a whole.

The assembly of the First Continental Congress appeared to the British as nothing short of treason. Other acts were passed restricting the commerce of New England. Meanwhile the colonists in Massachusetts had collected arms and ammunition at Concord. An attempt of the British to seize these arms led to the skirmish at Lexington in April 1775 and the attack on the British troops as they returned from Concord to Boston. The Second Continental Congress, which met in May 1775, found itself conducting a war and selected Washington as commander in chief. Before he reached Boston, the Battle of Bunker Hill had taken place in June. Although the Congress was preparing for war, it sent a petition to George III urging him to withstand the efforts of Parliament to deprive the Americans of their liberty. But no one in England was more eager than the King to uphold the sovereignty of Parliament over the colonies. As the Americans hesitated, they were influenced strongly by a pamphlet, *Common Sense*, written by Thomas Paine, a radical Englishman who happened to be in Philadelphia. The logical conclusion of the colonists' course, said Paine, was independence. Any trust in the King was a delusion, for George was worse than his ministers.

In May 1776 the Congress adopted a resolution advising each colonial assembly to assume the powers of government in its own locality. In June a resolution declaring independence was moved in the Congress. It was adopted on July 2. Two days later a more famous declaration of independence, the work of Thomas Jefferson, was also formally adopted.

The War with the Colonies

As the colonists moved from discontent to open war, British opinion hardened against them. The opposition in Parliament led by Rockingham, still friendly to the Americans, appeared factious and unpatriotic. Independent members, rallying behind the throne and its ministers, gave North a large majority in the Commons and greatly strengthened his political position, but a good deal of discord existed in the Cabinet. Lord George Sackville Germain, who became the American Secretary in November 1775, was anxious to push the war with vigor and to end it by a series of quick decisive blows. He criticized North for hoping that a reconciliation might still be effected. Barrington, the Secretary at War, was gloomy, contending that British land forces were insufficient to subdue America. He advocated instead a naval war. But Lord Sandwich, the head of the Admiralty, feared an attack from France and did not want to send many ships to America.

North, who did not control the Cabinet properly, tried to soothe differences of opinion by compromise rather than by leadership. His reputation rested upon his economies in finance and upon his wish, like Walpole's, to avoid controversial issues. Yet he was committed to a policy of teaching the Americans a lesson. He faced the dilemma that if he spent freely he would be accused of extravagance; and if he did not, he would be attacked by those who wanted quick and total victory. In the end he was criticized on both accounts. He allowed several policies to be pursued at once, tried to keep down costs, and soon showed that he was a poor war minister. From the first the Cabinet lacked a strong, long-range planner, as Pitt had been in the Seven Years' War.

The military problem in America was really very difficult although the colonists rarely possessed an army that could face the British in the field. The British could capture almost any point they wished but they could not occupy the whole country. Once they left an area behind, their control over it was likely to disappear. When they ventured inland they were harassed and ambushed by irregulars who gathered quickly from farms and small towns. These irregulars knew how to use firearms, and though they were undependable in pitched battles, they could turn a British victory parade into a hasty retreat. In a word, this was a people's war. The American armies could count on local support. The loyalists, from whom the British hoped so much, made a poor showing. The British had to bring their supplies all the way from England; moreover, their commanders were often dilatory and failed to make the most of their opportunities. Such a war might well have ended in stalemate had not foreign aid given the Americans an opportunity to win.

In the early days of the war the American cause looked bleak. General William Howe, who had succeeded General Gage as commander in Boston, was forced to evacuate that city and to withdraw to Halifax in Nova Scotia. But in July 1776, just as the Americans were declaring their independence, he landed unopposed on Staten Island with a considerable force. He was shortly joined by his brother, Admiral Lord Howe, who brought a fleet and reinforcements from England. The army on Staten Island soon numbered more than 30,000 men, and at the Battle of Long Island in August 1776 Washington was badly beaten. General Howe thereupon occupied New York and pushed Washington in a southwesterly direction across New Jersey to the Delaware. For the time this seemed sufficient, and Howe went into winter quarters. But on the night of December 25, 1776, Washington recrossed the Delaware and made a surprise attack on the British at Trenton, capturing about 1000 Hessians and British cavalry. This victory, though not of great military importance, revived the hopes of the colonists and showed that their cause need not collapse.

The British made a more determined effort in 1777. France and Spain were sending aid to the colonists, British finances already were strained, and it was felt that the war must be ended quickly. In 1775 the Americans had invaded Canada. Although this invasion was both a military and a political failure, it had alarmed the British, who had sent an army of some size to Quebec. In planning the campaign for 1777, General John Burgoyne, working with Lord George Germain, devised a plan to bring this army down from Montreal by way of the Richelieu River and Lake Champlain to the Hudson and so to Albany, where it could be met by General Howe coming up from New York. The British forces would thus be united and New England would be severed from the rest of the colonies. This plan has usually been considered sound strategy, though it failed in execution. But, as a matter of fact, it was not good strategy. Since New York was already in English hands, and since communications between New England and the rest of the colonies were largely by sea, the plan, if successful, would not have been very effective. And it involved a long march through rough country inhabited by the enemy. Nonetheless, Burgoyne was on Lake Champlain in June with 7000 men; in July he took Ticonderoga.

At this point, however, General Howe moved the bulk of his forces to Philadelphia. His reasons for doing so are not entirely clear. He had been thinking about an attack on Philadelphia for some time, and had obtained Lord George Germain's consent to this change of plan. Howe believed that Burgoyne was doing well. It has been argued that he did not want to go to Albany too soon and so give Washington freedom of action along the seaboard. Whatever Howe's motive, the result was disastrous. After a difficult voyage along the Jersey coast, he entered Chesapeake Bay, defeated Washington at Brandywine Creek, and entered Philadelphia. But once in the city he could not go north to meet Burgoyne, who was in serious difficulty. With his communications very extended, Burgoyne found himself in a hilly and roadless wilderness some forty miles north of Albany, hemmed in and harassed by large numbers of American troops and irregulars. General Clinton in New York was unable to send adequate reinforcements. In October 1777, at Saratoga, Burgoyne surrendered his army, now shrunk to 5000 men.

This defeat altered the entire character of the war. Ever since 1763 the French had been hoping for a war of revenge. They had strengthened their navy and had sought a close alliance with Spain. Their plan was to secure their position in the Mediterranean and to obtain compensation for the loss of Canada by acquiring new possessions in the Caribbean. But the American revolt opened new prospects. Even before the colonists asked for assistance, the French Foreign Minister, Vergennes, had persuaded Louis XVI to grant them a million livres for the purchase of arms. Vergennes persuaded Spain to do the same. Other credits followed.

The French would not commit themselves to military and naval assistance until they were sure that the American war would be a long and difficult struggle for Britain. Saratoga convinced them that this would be so. In February 1778 they concluded two treaties with Benjamin Franklin, whom the colonists had sent to Paris. One was a treaty of amity which recognized the United States and dealt largely with commerce. The other was a treaty of military alliance in case a war should follow between France and England, as it did in June of the same year. The French agreed not to make peace until the independence of the United States was secured. They disclaimed any ambition to acquire territory in North America, though French conquests in the West Indies were to be recognized by the United States. These highly advantageous treaties gave the colonists a firm foundation for success.

In 1779 Spain entered the war against England. She did not conclude an alliance with the Americans, however, for their independence would be a bad example for the Spanish colonies in the New World. The Spanish objective was to regain the possessions Spain had lost to Britain since the beginning of the century. The English also faced the hostility of neutral nations whose ships were stopped by the British navy and searched for contraband of war. When Holland refused to tolerate this practice, England declared war on her in 1780. The same grievance brought Russia and the Scandinavian powers together in a League of Armed Neutrality. With an inefficient and unwarlike government, England faced a hostile world. She also had to meet serious difficulties in India and Ireland.

Recognizing his own inadequacy, Lord North begged to be allowed to resign. But he remained in office at the earnest solicitation of the King, who could find no one to replace him. No other member of the Cabinet would do. Nor did the opposition offer better prospects. The Rockingham group advocated the independence of America, which was anathema to the King. Chatham and his follower, Lord Shelburne, who were also in opposition, were ready to conciliate the colonists though not to capitulate to them.

The war effort in America necessarily slackened. Sir Henry Clinton, who succeeded General Howe as commander, was given new instructions. If he could not bring Washington to a decisive battle, he was to confine himself to raids against the coastal towns and to the destruction of American shipping. He was to send part of his army to the West Indies to cooperate with the navy in an attack on the French island of St. Lucia. Meanwhile he should evacuate Philadelphia and return to New York, which was exposed to an assault by sea. Shortly after his arrival a strong French fleet under the Count d'Estaing approached New York. But thanks to the energy and daring of Admiral Howe, D'Estaing moved on to Newport, Rhode Island, where he disappointed the colonists by not attacking the town, then to Boston to refit, and finally to the West Indies.

In 1779 Clinton continued a policy of raids along the coast, especially in the South, where he was so successful that the Cabinet allowed him to open an offensive on land. Late in 1778 a British force captured Savannah in Georgia and quickly brought the entire colony under royal control. A more important triumph followed. Clinton attacked the city of Charleston in South Carolina, which surrendered in May 1780 with some 7000 American troops. He then returned to New York, for D'Estaing was again in American waters.

The general left in charge of southern operations was Lord Cornwallis. At first he was very successful. In August 1780 he defeated the Americans severely at Camden, South Carolina. But as he moved through the interior he felt the pressure of a hostile population. Constantly harassed by an able American commander, General Nathanael Greene, Cornwallis marched north rather quickly into Virginia and established himself at Yorktown, expecting reinforcements from Clinton in New York.

Disaster now came quickly upon Cornwallis. A powerful French fleet under command of the Count de Grasse won temporary control of the sea off the coast of Virginia and blockaded Cornwallis at Yorktown. Washington, after feigning an attack on New York, marched south, strengthened by a French army under the Count de Rochambeau. Cornwallis was besieged by sea and land, many of his men were ill, the French and American guns swept his camp. His surrender in October 1781 virtually ended the war in America.

The War in Europe

England continued the war against France and Spain for another year, winning an important naval action in the West Indies which helped her greatly in the negotiations for peace, but in general the war was disastrous for her. Constantly on the defensive, without an ally in the world, and governed by a minister who recognized his own incompetence in war, she was fortunate to fend off the attacks of the Bourbon powers as well as she did. The French army, since it did not have to fight on the Continent, was kept close to the Channel, a potential threat of invasion. The combined navies of France and Spain were superior in fighting strength to that of England. They numbered about 140 ships of the line; of these the French ships were highly efficient, the Spanish well built but poorly handled. On paper the British could muster about 150 ships of the line, but some were so old and decayed that they never went to sea. Hence the British could not always control the Channel. There was a moment of great danger in the summer of 1779, when a French and Spanish fleet of 60 to 70 ships entered the Channel and hovered off Plymouth. A much smaller British force could only watch at a respectful distance. Why the enemy did not attempt a landing is something of a mystery. There would have been no great resistance at Plymouth, where the cannon balls did not fit the guns in the harbor. But sickness broke out in the Spanish ships, a gale dispersed the fleet, and the threat of invasion passed away.

Meanwhile large French and British naval units were operating in the West Indies. For some years they captured each other's islands without fighting a general action. When De Grasse returned to the West Indies in 1781 after the surrender of Cornwallis, the English islands appeared to be gravely menaced. But in the following year Admiral George Rodney, the most enterprising admiral of the war, inflicted a severe defeat on De Grasse which ended the French threat in the Caribbean.

The Spanish displayed unusual vigor. They were strong enough to besiege both Gibraltar and Minorca and at the same time send an army to West Florida. The French were active in India, intriguing with native princes against the English; for a time a French squadron operated in Indian waters. The British navy, faced with so many foes and fighting in so many theaters, was under enormous strain. It had to guard the Channel, fight in the West Indies, supply the forces in America, run provisions through the Spanish blockade at Gibraltar, remain in touch with India, and watch the fleets of the enemy as best it could. Toward the end of the war Lord North could raise money in Britain only at ruinous rates of interest. His majority in the Commons having melted away, he resigned in the spring of 1782.

The Peace of Paris, 1783

The ministers who followed North and who made the peace of 1783 were members of a coalition of the Rockingham and Shelburne groups who had recently been in opposition. Shelburne was Secretary for Home and Colonial Affairs, while the Secretary for Foreign Affairs was Charles James Fox. Peace with America fell within Shelburne's jurisdiction; peace with France within that of Fox. Unfortunately, the two men disliked each other and did not work together. A difference arose over policy in making peace with America. Fox wished to recognize the independence of the United States at the beginning of negotiations, thus taking America out of the war and making possible a firmer tone with France. Questions of American boundaries and trade could be dealt with later. Shelburne, on the other hand, wished to postpone the granting of independence until independence was defined clearly. He still hoped that the Americans would be satisfied with freedom to manage their domestic affairs and could be persuaded to cooperate with Britain in commerce and foreign policy. He wanted the two countries to be partners in the trade of the Atlantic, and he hoped that the King and his ministers might still be allowed to control the foreign policy of both. He was willing to grant to the United States the lands between the Appalachian Mountains and the Mississippi.

American negotiators in Paris were shrewd enough to take advantage of these differences. When France and Spain opposed the extension of American territory west of the mountains, the Americans made what amounted to a separate peace with England despite the treaty of alliance with France. By the terms of the peace (September 1783) the United States became independent. Her territory, with a northern frontier not very different from what it is today, was extended westward to the Mississippi, and south to the thirty-first parallel, leaving Florida in the hands of Spain. The treaty recognized that debts owed by Americans to Englishmen were valid debts. The Americans received no commercial privileges in Britain, but they secured the right to fish off the Newfoundland Banks and gave no guarantee that the loyalists would escape persecution.

The settlement between England and France was largely based upon a mutual restoration of conquests in the West Indies. The French regained their fishing rights off Newfoundland and received both Senegal and Gorée in West Africa. Spain kept her conquests of Minorca and Florida.

RADICALS AND CONSERVATIVES

Under the impact of the American war, politics in Britain took a new turn. The radicalism associated with John Wilkes in the 1760s was renewed, though not by Wilkes himself, and a demand arose for reform in political life and for drastic changes in the constitution. But these proposals were disliked by the independent country gentlemen in the Commons, whose instincts were basically conservative. Suspicious of radical reformers, independent members resisted change, preferring to support Lord North as a minister who represented long-established methods of government. Thus a revived radicalism was opposed by a new conservative impulse.

At the beginning of the war Lord North enjoyed a large majority in the Commons, but by 1778, as disasters mounted, his political strength had greatly diminished. His very manner betrayed indecision and lack of energy. As a result of his weakness, the opposition in the Commons began to take new hope. This opposition consisted largely of the followers of Rockingham and those of Lord Shelburne, Chatham's political heir. Both groups were sympathetic toward America and both contained men who were to be important: Charles James Fox, Rockingham's close friend, Edmund Burke, who was Rockingham's private secretary, and, somewhat later, William Pitt the Younger, Chatham's son, who entered political life as a follower of Shelburne.

The weakness of the opposition lay in the fact that its criticism of the Cabinet during a war appeared unpatriotic. But the leaders claimed they were justified in opposing a war which was badly managed and that England would not have suffered such disasters if they had been in power. They also asserted that they were kept from office by the excessive influence of the Crown, which employed its patronage to build Lord North's majority. Too strong an executive, they argued, had corrupted the self-righting forces of the constitution and kept them out of power.

In 1779 two movements for reform began outside Parliament, both quite separate from the politics of parliamentary life. Their fundamental cause was the general disappointment and chagrin at the failures of the American war. The blame had to be placed somewhere, and it was easy to place it upon the parliamentary system of the day. One part of this reforming movement arose among the old associates of Wilkes in the county of Middlesex. The people, it was argued, should have greater power to influence events in Parliament. There should be more organization among voters and a larger number of constituencies —such as Middlesex and the city of Westminster—in which a large and articulate electorate gave force and vigor to parliamentary elections. A second movement for reform began in the north. A meeting in Yorkshire expressed the view held by many persons that the counties—where an electorate of some size chose country gentlemen as knights of the shire—were the soundest and purest part of the constitution. Country gentlemen of means and standing in their localities would shun corrupting influences and would take an independent line in politics. Again reformers stressed the excessive power of the Crown. They wanted more independent members who, it was assumed, would not tolerate bungling ministers like North. The Yorkshire leaders sent petitions to the House of Commons. Their program was a demand for rigorous economy (which North was practicing already), for the addition of 100 new county members to the total membership of the Commons, and for annual elections.

The members of the opposition pressed forward to take part in these movements and if possible to lead them. William Pitt, Charles James Fox, John Wilkes, and a number of the nobility all were interested. In the Commons Edmund Burke introduced several bills calling for radical reform. He wished to abolish sinecures, to investigate and prune the civil list, and to end the Board of Trade. Other members of the opposition called on the government to publish the list of pensioners. This rather petulant demand for reform reached its climax in a motion by John Dunning "that the influence of the Crown has increased, is increasing, and ought to be diminished," which was adopted by the Commons in April 1780. The truth of this famous resolution was highly doubtful. George III had not kept Lord North in power against the will of the nation. For a long time North's policies had had general support. It was only when his government ran into difficulties that the country, less loyal than the King, turned upon him as a scapegoat for the failure of the war. He himself had created a false impression by his frequent assertions that he would like to resign.

Dunning was able to carry two other motions: that the Cabinet should disclose the amount of money given to members from the civil list, and that subordinate members of the King's household should be debarred from Parliament. But a bill to disfranchise revenue officers was defeated; and a radical proposal that Parliament should continue until a better balanced constitution had been obtained was soundly defeated.

A reaction set in against the reformers and in favor of North. If North resigned, his place would be taken by an opposition that was showing itself to be wild, oppressive, and factious. The violence of Charles James Fox, for example, was already making men doubt the soundness of his judgment, however much they liked him personally. And it presently became evident that independent country gentlemen much preferred the broadly based and relaxed administration of North, who represented moderation and tradition, to the intense fury and unpredictable policy of the radical reformers. This feeling was strengthened immensely by the Lord George Gordon riots in June 1780. Beginning in a foolish demonstration against an act that allowed Roman Catholics to enlist in the army without taking old-fashioned oaths against their religion, the rioting in London got completely out of hand and raged for a week before order was restored. This famous riot was a sharp reminder of the danger of exciting the mob over political issues. Horrified country gentlemen turned against reformers who made themselves responsible in any way for agitation among the people. The strength of North was revealed to be far deeper than mere support of the Crown. He remained in power until his majority disappeared as a result of Yorktown.

Thus Parliament was divided between the radical reforming zeal of Fox and Rockingham and the conservative instincts of independent country gentlemen.

25

the industrial revolution

The economic changes that took place in the eighteenth century laid the foundations of our modern industrial world. The invention of heavy machines propelled by water power or by steam, in place of light ones turned by the human arm, and the advance of technology on every side began to undermine the domestic system of manufacturing and to substitute the industrial plant or factory as we know it today. This development, as it gathered momentum, vastly increased the volume of production, altered the working conditions of the laboring classes, created a new type of industrial capitalist, and deeply affected the daily life of the entire population.

The change was so sharp and fundamental that it is called the Industrial Revolution. That term, however, has fallen into some disrepute among historians. The reason is that the writers of the late nineteenth century, who first talked about the Industrial Revolution, came to conclusions concerning it which were frequently erroneous. They imagined that the revolution began quite abruptly about 1760 with a group of great inventors who suddenly appeared from nowhere, that factories came in with a rush, and that by 1820 the domestic system had all but disappeared. These writers idealized the domestic system, dwelling upon the happy state of the domestic worker who combined a little agriculture with manufacturing in the contented atmosphere of the home. Furthermore, these writers, influenced by the rise of modern sociology, tended to overemphasize the evils of the new factories and of the new factory towns, with their dirt, smoke, drabness, and lack of sanitation. In short, it was held that the Industrial Revolution destroyed happiness, produced misery, and on the whole was unfortunate.

These notions have now been modified. It is realized, in the first place, that technological progress did not begin in 1760 but had been gradually evolving for centuries. There was, of course, a tremendous increase in the number of inventions between 1770 and 1800, but they had their roots in the past. "The developments which took place in the reign of George III must therefore be regarded as the quickening of an age-long evolutionary process, rather than as a violent break with the past and a fresh beginning."[1] Secondly, it is understood now that industry as a whole changed very slowly. To be sure, some industries, such as the making of cotton thread, shot forward. But cotton was not typical, and other industries lagged far behind it. The manufacture of woolen goods, for example, remained largely in the hands of domestic workers after most of the cotton industry had passed into factories. Some processes in an industry might become mechanized whereas others might not; and the invention of a machine was no guarantee that it would pass at once into general use. In short, every industry had its own problems which might hasten or retard its entrance into the factory system of manufacture. Thus the domestic system continued side by side with the new factories. It is believed that even in 1830 no single industry was completely mechanized and more than half of the industrial workers were still outside the factories.

Thirdly, despite the obvious evils of the factories and the factory towns, it is now held that on the whole the workpeople derived more benefit than misfortune from the changes that were taking place. Here, of course, we are partly in the realm of the intangible. A peasant coming to the city doubtless longed for the peace and quiet of the countryside, and his wife yearned for her flower garden. But both of them were probably better fed and better clothed and received better medical attention. The workers hated the discipline of the factories and gave them a bad reputation. But at least some of the evils for which the factories have been blamed were also to be found in the domestic system, which had its own shortcomings. Not all historians agree that factories brought more benefits than miseries, though those who take an optimistic view appear to be in the majority. Finally, industrial change cannot be studied in a vacuum. It must be connected with an increase in population, with improvements in agriculture, with better methods of transport, as well as with inventions and the factory system.

INDUSTRY IN THE FIRST HALF OF THE CENTURY

Industry under the domestic system was found in the cities but also was scattered through many rural areas and small towns. There were independent domestic artisans in the country who were self-employed, who carried on manufacture in their houses, who owned their tools, bought their raw materials, perhaps employed a few helpers in a shed, and sold their products at the local market. But most of the domestic workers were employees of some wealthy merchant manufacturer. This was particularly true in the large textile and metal industries. The master clothier, employing a network of agents and middlemen, sent out his wool over a wide area to be manufactured into cloth. "The Norwich draper, the Leeds clothier, the Manchester warehouseman, and the Nottingham hosier, each, like a spider at the center of a vast web, gave out material and drew in finished or semifinished goods from hundreds, or even thousands, of spinners and weavers."[2] Very few of the later factories employed as many persons as this. The iron and brass made into cutlery, nails, swords, buckles, spurs, and

[1] Arthur Redford, *The Economic History of England 1760–1860* (New York: Longmans, 1931), p. 4.
[2] T. S. Ashton, *An Economic History of England. The Eighteenth Century* (New York: Barnes & Noble, 1955), p. 99.

Domestic industry. The women are spinning; the man is at a frame for knitting stockings. (From *The Universal Magazine*, August 1750. Historical Pictures Service, Chicago)

bits for horses by the domestic workers in the metal trades were given out by capitalists who owned the foundries, forges, and slitting mills. Not only was the domestic system highly capitalized, with large funds in the hands of wealthy men; there was also a great deal of specialization and division of labor among workmen who performed one process only. Both developments had gone about as far as they could profitably go. The great need was for a more advanced technology.

The domestic system should not be idealized. The notion of the happy domestic worker at his loom, surrounded by his wife and children carding and spinning—all contented and busy, with a vegetable garden and perhaps a cow on his little plot of land—is a fallacious notion. It is based in part on a famous description by Defoe of the woolen industry near Halifax in Yorkshire. Defoe found the district populous with many villages "and at every considerable house a manufactury." The hills supplied coal and pure running water. Each master clothier kept a horse or two to take his cloth to market. His workers lived in "an infinite number of cottages," in which women and children were carding and spinning. There were no beggars. "If we knock'd at the door of any of the master manufacturers, we presently saw a house full of lusty fellows, some at the dye-vat, some dressing the cloths, some in the loom, some one thing, and some another, all hard at work and full employment upon the manufacture, and all seeming to have sufficient business." The master clothier's house was surrounded by a plot of ground on which he kept a cow, but the cottagers had no land.[3] This pleasant picture perhaps owed something to Defoe's love of honest work and productive activity; it applied only to a restricted area and was not, strictly speaking, a description of the domestic system at all. It was rather a picture of a small factory, for the men came to work at the house of the master.

The normal domestic worker was in quite a different position. He brought into his home the dirt and confusion of manufacturing as well as the nervous strain of sweated industry. He did not combine agriculture with manufacturing, for the weaver was a weaver, the farmer a farmer. The chasm between the domestic worker and the wealthy clothier was as wide as that between the factory worker and factory owner in later times. The clothier was tempted to squeeze his workmen and to pay them in truck, that is, in provisions, often of poor quality, instead of in cash. He could easily shift the burden of a depression onto the shoulders of his employees. He merely stopped giving out work; he could do so with much smaller loss than that suffered by a factory owner who shut down his factory. In Nottingham and Leicester the clothier owned the stocking-frames used by the hosiery workers who paid him rent whether he supplied them with work or not. There was great irregularity of employment. Periods of demand were followed by periods of depression; some industries were so dependent on the weather that exports and imports could be delayed for weeks by contrary winds.

The domestic worker lost time between the completion of one assignment of work and the beginning of the next. He must often carry his finished goods to the employer, perhaps trudging for an entire day in each direction. "A great part of their time," wrote a contemporary, "is spent in fetching home their materials, or carrying home their work, or in seeking after their money."[4] Such irregularities bred bad habits. The domestic worker was tempted to produce shoddy goods. Since he could determine his own hours, he also was tempted to spend the first days of the week at the alehouse, celebrating Saint Monday and even Saint Tuesday, and then to rush through the week's work in three or four days of very long hours. Sedentary workers, like weavers, felt the deadly monotony of repeating the same mechanical processes for hours on end; even the most reliable sought occasional solace in drink. Hence employers came to believe that higher wages would merely result in greater debauchery. And to what could the domestic worker look forward in his old age except the poor house?

The cities which grew most rapidly in the eighteenth century were those in which new industries were established or in which old ones employed new techniques. London was unique, displaying conflicting tendencies. It contained a vast amount of domestic manufacture—trades connected with navigation, luxury trades to cater to the world of fashion, new trades growing from the

[3] Quoted in M. Dorothy George, *England in Transition: Life and Work in the Eighteenth Century* (Baltimore: Penguin Books, 1962), pp. 45–47.
[4] George, p. 57.

grain and cattle brought to feed the metropolis (flour mills, breweries, the manufacture of soap, glue, and candles, and the processing of leather). Yet London did not grow as a factory city but as a commercial and distributing center. Goods came from every quarter of the kingdom to be finished, to be exported, to be distributed throughout the country. London's future could be seen in the development in the early eighteenth century of the fashionable shop, in which as much money went into elegant decorations and furnishings as into the stock itself. Defoe disliked the fashionable shop as luxurious and wasteful, but it had come to stay. As a manufacturing city London lost ground in the eighteenth century. Bristol, England's second city in 1700, grew as a port and as a center for the manufacture of iron and other metals, but it declined in textiles and by 1800 was surpassed by Liverpool in commerce. Norwich, the third city in 1700, sank rapidly into a provincial town. At the time of the census of 1801 "the eight greatest towns of Britain were London with 864,000, Manchester 84,000, Edinburgh 82,500, Glasgow 77,300, Liverpool 77,000, Birmingham 73,000, Bristol 68,000 and Leeds 53,000."[5] Not far behind were Sheffield, making knives, swords, and razors; Nottingham and Leicester, hosiery; and Newcastle upon Tyne, articles connected with mining and navigation.

A number of important inventions were made in the first half of the century. The steam pump of Savery and Newcomen, constructed in 1712, was used to lift water from coal mines. A huge unwieldy contrivance with many imperfections and very wasteful of fuel, it acted on the principle that condensing steam created a vacuum which sucked water from the coal pits. This engine helped to solve the problem created by water that seeped into the mines as they grew deeper. Another invention saved the iron industry. In the past the foundries where iron ore was smelted had used wood in the form of charcoal as a fuel, but in the eighteenth century the forests of Britain were all but gone and the lack of charcoal seemed destined to kill the iron industry. The solution was found by the two Abraham Darbys, father and son, of Coalbrookdale in Shropshire, who discovered a means of smelting by coal in the form of coke. This method was used by the elder Darby in about 1709 and later was improved by his son. But for years they kept it a trade secret; it did not pass into general use until about 1750. After that date, the iron industry recovered lost ground and expanded enormously.

A third invention was John Kay's flying shuttle, patented in 1733. This ingenious device could be attached to a hand loom and enabled one man to weave a broader piece of cloth than before. Formerly, if a broad piece of cloth was being made, two men were needed to throw the shuttle back and forth. But the use of Kay's flying shuttle did not spread rapidly. Its immediate effect was small because it was an improvement in weaving, whereas the great need of the time was for a faster method of spinning thread. Another important contrivance of the early eighteenth century was the use of the overshot water wheel in place of one that was undershot. By this substitution a small flow of water could be made to produce as much power as a larger flow had formerly done. At Coalbrookdale one of Newcomen's engines was used to throw back water from below the mill run so that it passed over the water wheel again and again.

<hr/>

[5] J. Steven Watson, *The Reign of George III 1760–1815* (Oxford: Clarendon Press, 1960), p. 517.

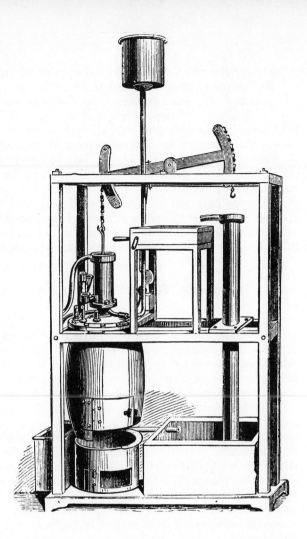

The Savery and Newcomen engine, early eighteenth century. (Historical Pictures Service, Chicago)

As industry grew there was a tendency toward larger units of production in which many workers were gathered in a single building or factory. The state fostered this tendency both by example and by government contracts. In the early years of the century the naval dockyards and arsenals at Chatham formed the largest single unit of production in the kingdom. "The building-yards, docks, timber-yard, deal-yard, mast-yard, gun-yard, rope-walks," wrote Defoe, "and all the other yards and places, set apart for the works belonging to the navy, are like a well-ordered city."[6] Government contracts for cannon, shoes, uniforms, and blankets were naturally given to firms with sufficient facilities and with sufficient control of labor to ensure high quality and rapid production. On a much smaller scale, the parish workhouses in which paupers were assembled to perform simple industrial tasks may have served as examples to later owners of factories. The rise of industrial towns increased the tendency toward larger units. When a new industry settled in a town the workers had to be trained and supervised; hence the work was done in buildings provided by the firm. This was also true of silversmiths and manufacturers of costly imported wool, for

[6] Quoted in T. S. Ashton, *An Economic History of England. The Eighteenth Century*, p. 113.

these materials were too valuable to be scattered among workers in their homes.

The greatest pressure toward larger units, however, was the need for power, which at first was water power. Power was responsible for the first large factory built in England, the famous silk mill of John and Thomas Lombe at Derby. In 1716 John Lombe had gone to Italy and had obtained, by not very scrupulous means, the secret of an Italian process of making silk thread by machinery. Between 1717 and 1721 the Lombe brothers built a large factory 400 feet long and 5 stories high, with 26,000 wheels, in which they employed over 300 women and children. John Lombe died shortly after, and stories were at once afoot that he had been poisoned by a vengeful Italian, but Thomas continued the works and made a fortune. There was thus a full-fledged factory in England by 1721. The pressure toward factories increased as machines grew heavier and as, toward the end of the century, Watt's steam engine began to be used in industry.

CAUSES OF THE QUICKENING OF INDUSTRY

Population
Of the many factors that converged to quicken industry in the last thirty years of the eighteenth century one was an increase in population. The causes of this increase are not entirely clear, but the best opinion seems to be that it was primarily due to a larger number of early marriages.[7] It was a rural and not an urban phenomenon. As the old pattern of village life was disrupted in the eighteenth century, restrictions on marriage imposed by custom or by parental authority were weakened, and young people tended to marry earlier. Thus the span of childbearing years for a married woman was increased, with a cumulative effect over a number of generations. The growth of population provided a larger market for the sale of manufactures and swelled the labor force. In the eighteenth century the employment of children in industry was not regarded as an evil but as a boon to the poor and a benefit to society. Children of five and six years of age worked in factories. The labor force was augmented further by a more systematic employment of paupers and by a steady stream of Irish immigration.

An increase also took place in the numbers of the lower middle classes from which many of the new industrial leaders arose. They were men of ability and of some education, with habits of thrift and hard work, drive, and a tough determination to make their way in the world. Many of them were nonconformists. Discussions in the Methodist chapel or in the Quaker meetinghouse sharpened their wits, and in the schools and academies founded by dissenting bodies they learned languages, bookkeeping, and elementary science. The expansion of industry brought them opportunity.

Agriculture
A movement toward improved methods of agriculture begun in the later seventeenth century and continued into the eighteenth was largely the work of well-to-do country gentlemen who could afford to experiment and who combined the pleasure of creating model farms with the practical aim of obtaining increased profits. One of the first was Jethro Tull, who owned estates in Oxford-

[7] See pages 611–612.

shire and Berkshire. Although something of a crank and often wrong in his opinions, he had a keen eye for improvements in agriculture. He invented an important device known as a drill, a little horse-drawn contrivance by which it was possible to plant seeds in rows instead of scattering them broadcast over the ground. He advocated the cultivation or pulverization of the soil between rows of crops; for this purpose he invented a horse-drawn hoe. By using these methods he grew wheat on one field for thirteen consecutive years without the addition of fertilizer. His experiments continued through the first decades of the century, though it was only in the last ten years of his life (1731–1741) that he published accounts of what he had been doing.

Another name famous in agriculture was that of Lord Townshend, a landowner in Norfolk. When Turnip Townshend, as he was called, was driven from office in 1730 by his brother-in-law Sir Robert Walpole, he abandoned politics and experimented on his estates with grasses and root crops. He publicized a rotation of crops—wheat, turnips, barley or oats, and clover or rye—by which he eliminated the wasteful practice of leaving one field fallow every year. Turnips and clover could be fed to sheep and cattle during the winter, thus making unnecessary the slaughter of the weaker animals that was customary in the autumn.

Experiments in stock breeding also took place. By intense inbreeding, Robert Bakewell, a Leicestershire farmer, greatly increased the weight of his sheep and cattle. He also developed a breed of strong black horses, much used by the army. He treated his animals with tender care, keeping his rams as clean as race horses. By the end of the century an astonishing transformation in English livestock had taken place. Sheep ceased to be the small, stunted animals of the past—looking like a cross between a dog and a goat[8]—and became valuable for meat as well as for wool. Cattle grew sleek and fat; the roast beef of old England was the pride of Englishmen, though few could afford to eat it. The weights of sheep and oxen more than doubled between 1710 and 1795, while that of calves increased threefold. Bakewell was visited by celebrities whom he entertained so lavishly in his farm kitchen that eventually he went bankrupt.

A number of improvers revolutionized the agriculture of East Anglia. Of these the best known was Thomas Coke of Holkham, later the Earl of Leicester, who enriched the light soil of his estates in Norfolk by marling. Marl was a fertilizer, a clay containing carbonate of lime. Although its value had been known in the Middle Ages, the practice was lost, then resumed in the eighteenth century. Giving his tenants long leases, Coke required them to employ the latest methods of agriculture. The success of these experiments created a wave of enthusiasm for agricultural improvement and it became fashionable for gentlemen to improve their lands. There were farmers' societies, cattle shows, and medals for superior crops. In 1793 the government established a Board of Agriculture, of which the secretary was Arthur Young, perhaps the greatest of all English writers on agriculture. His accounts of his tours through Britain and on the Continent, written with singular enthusiasm and charm, combined sprightly anecdotes with sober descriptions of agricultural improvements. He published a journal, the *Annals of Agriculture*, to which George III contributed under the name of Ralph Robinson, his shepherd at Windsor.

[8] The phrase is that of J. H. Plumb, *England in the Eighteenth Century* (Baltimore: Penguin Books, 1964), p. 83. See his table of the weights of animals on p. 82.

Improvements were impossible unless the old open fields were enclosed and broken into smaller units, each surrounded by its fence or hedgerow. We have often heard of enclosing in English history. It was done to some extent in the medieval period and it became important under the Tudors as fields were converted into sheep runs, but it is surprising that so much of England remained unenclosed in the early eighteenth century. During the first half of the century the number of enclosures was small. After 1750 the movement picked up speed and continued at a faster and faster tempo until, by about 1830, the countryside had acquired its present appearance and an unenclosed field was a relic of an age that had passed.

The reasons for this rapid increase in enclosing are fairly clear. Agricultural writers, looking with strong disapproval on open-field farming, preached the necessity of enclosures with the fervor of missionaries. The growth of population was both a cause and a result of improved agriculture. Better roads enabled farmers to take their produce to market, and the great coaching days at the end of the century meant an increase in the number of horses which had to be fed. Moreover, wars brought large government orders of foodstuffs for armies and navies. Thus pressure on the land to produce more food grew ever stronger so that by 1773 or thereabouts England ceased to export grain in any quantity. An increasing population brought about enclosures, and enclosures made possible the growth of population. That enclosures produced more food than the open fields is certain, but unfortunately they were carried through in a way which benefited the large landowners at the expense of the small ones and imposed new hardships on the poor.

In order to enclose the lands of a village in the eighteenth century it was necessary to obtain a private act of Parliament. A number of the wealthier landowners of a village might petition Parliament for such an act. If they obtained it, the land was surveyed, then reapportioned in compact blocks, each owner receiving an amount proportionate to the size of his former holding. In this process the open fields, the pasture, the commons, and the waste all disappeared by being thrown together, and a new pattern of small fields emerged. The large owners, who profited greatly, possessed the capital to pay their share of the costs of the act, to drain and level their fields by filling in the depressions between the strips, and to plant hedges. But the little man often suffered: perhaps he received an allotment of land too small for profitable farming or perhaps he lacked the capital for the necessary improvements. If he sold his land he might rent a farm from a larger owner, but he was more likely to sink to the position of a landless laborer. The cottagers also suffered, for they lost their rights in the commons and in the waste. These rights had so little value that the cottager could not be given land but received a sum of money, which was soon spent. Moreover, he lost the possibility of improving his status, for he could no longer hope to obtain a little land and thus rise in the social scale. The gulf between the rich and the poor grew wider, and though the population of the villages did not decline, the number of small farms grew less. Wages rose with the advance of agriculture, but prices rose even faster. An agricultural laborer could attain a modest prosperity only if his wife and children found some employment. Toward the end of the century disaster fell upon the rural poor. We will return to this point at the end of the present chapter.

Transportation

The increasing tempo of industrial production was connected closely with improvement in transport. Good roads came only slowly; throughout the eighteenth century England depended to a large extent on the sea. Hundreds of small vessels plied from town to town along the eastern coast of Britain between London and the Scottish ports. It was said in 1774 that some 1800 ships were engaged in the coal trade alone, and that about 900 more carried other commodities. Shipping along the western coast was not so great, but it was considerable, amounting perhaps to 400 or 500 vessels. Cargoes for the most part consisted of the heavier and bulkier goods which could be transported by land only at prohibitive prices—coal, slate, stone, clay, and grain. These goods were carried long distances by sea rather than very short ones by land. But this coastwise traffic had disadvantages. Sailing ships were dependent on the weather and could be held up for days and weeks on end by contrary winds. They stayed in port during the dead of winter. In time of war they were exposed to capture or destruction by enemy action, and their crews might be pressed into the navy. Goods paid considerable duties as they reentered the country; moreover, thievery from ships at anchor in the Thames was a major problem. Manufacturers and farmers looked first to inland waterways and then to improvement in the roads.

The possibility of improving the rivers was limited. Of English streams, the Severn was best suited to navigation, for it could be traversed without the use of locks and floodgates. Barges traveled from Bristol to Gloucester, Worcester, Kidderminster, Shrewsbury, and even into Wales, and could ascend a number of the river's tributaries. The Thames was navigable as far as Oxford, though above the reaches of the tide it was not as satisfactory as one might suppose. Smaller streams presented many difficulties, some of them man-made, for mills and fishweirs formed obstructions to river traffic. Nonetheless, considerable work was done in the late seventeenth and early eighteenth centuries to improve the rivers. Weirs were removed, banks strengthened, river beds dredged, and locks constructed. By 1725 more than a thousand miles of river were open for navigation.

An age of canal building began about 1760. The Sankey Navigation, started in 1755, was constructed to carry coal from a nearby mine to Liverpool. A more famous canal was built between 1759 and 1761 by the Duke of Bridgewater, with the aid of the engineer James Brindley, to bring coal to Manchester from the ducal mines at Worsley. The canal was only eleven miles in length, but it presented some difficult problems of engineering and caught the imagination of the public. At Worsley a portion of the canal ran underground to the very site of the mine; at Barton an aqueduct carried the canal over the Irwell River, so that barges above and below passed each other at right angles. This intersection illustrated the way in which a canal substituted capital for labor. Half a dozen of the duke's barges coupled together moved easily along the canal, drawn by a horse or by two men, while below eight or ten lusty fellows pulled and hauled to move a small boat up the Irwell River. The moment the canal was opened the price of coal in Manchester was cut in half.

Many other canals were built in the years that followed. At first they were constructed to bring a raw material such as coal to an industrial area or to

The Worsley-Manchester Canal. A tunnel carries the canal underground to the mine. Outside the tunnel men are working in a quarry and are lifting large blocks of stone onto a barge by means of a crane. (From Arthur Young, *Six Months' Tour through the North of England*, London, 1770. Walter Library, University of Minnesota)

The Worsley-Manchester Canal. The canal is carried across the Irwell River at Barton Bridge by aqueduct. (From Arthur Young, *Six Months' Tour through the North of England*, London, 1770. Walter Library, University of Minnesota)

connect that area with the sea. Ultimately engineers conceived the bolder plan of linking the major ports of the kingdom by a network of canals. This was carried well to completion, though for technical reasons it was some time before London became part of the system. By 1830 over 4000 miles of canals in England and some 500 miles in Scotland and Wales were in operation. After that date the building of railways caused the abandonment of canal construction. The building of a canal required both engineering and organizing skill. Large amounts of stone and other materials must be assembled at out-of-the-way places; great numbers of laborers, many of them Irish, must be gathered together, housed, and controlled.

Tudor legislation had made each parish responsible for the maintenance of the roads within its boundaries. Parishioners were summoned each year to work for a few days on the roads without compensation. But under this arrangement the roads were neglected and tended to degenerate. It is probable that in the eighteenth century most country roads, which were nothing but dirt lanes, sufficed for the limited needs of the locality; but the main highways, especially those leading to London, now subjected to heavy traffic, were cut by the narrow wheels of carriages and churned into a sea of mud by herds of cattle driven to the London market. These roads were impassable for wagons during the winter months, when goods could be carried only by pack horses. The Great North Road from London to Edinburgh fell into such a state of disrepair that men and horses were known to have drowned in its great holes. Parliament attempted improvement without much success, regulating the loads to be carried by large wagons, the number of horses to each, and the width of the wagon wheels. A broad wheel was thought to do less damage to the road (though more to the vehicle) than a narrow one. Tolls were arranged so that wagons with broad wheels, sometimes sixteen inches wide, were given preferential treatment.

It soon became evident that less attention should be paid to the traffic and more to the surface of the roads. The task of improving the highways was entrusted more and more to corporate bodies, known as turnpike trusts, which were authorized to charge tolls on sections of road in return for keeping them in repair. These companies employed engineers who introduced new techniques in building roads. John Metcalf, the blind engineer of Knaresborough, constructed roads by digging out the soft dirt, placing heather on the ground, covering the heather with stone, and the stone with gravel. At the end of the century Macadam and Telford were building good highways by topping them with small crushed stones which the traffic ground together into a hard surface. These roads were slightly convex so that water ran off to the sides.

With the development of hard-surfaced roads, stagecoaches traveled at a faster pace. Express coaches carrying mail and passengers, who had to be persons of some fortitude, were introduced in 1784. By changing horses frequently, the coach from Liverpool to Manchester raced along the road at fourteen miles an hour. Such speed for a lumbering coach, though picturesque, was highly dangerous: coaches could easily overturn. Travelers who could afford the cost hired chaises and post horses. For fear of highwaymen coaches often carried a red-coated guard armed with a blunderbuss. In 1775, when a coach was waylaid in Epping Forest, the guard shot three of the highwaymen before he himself was slain. By the end of the century coaches were running on advertised schedules between the more important towns of the country. These great coaching days continued until the coming of the railways.

Inventions

By the middle of the eighteenth century the impulse to invent was widespread, and an ever-increasing number of discoveries, inventions, and improvements enabled industry to exploit new sources of energy, to reduce the cost of labor, to conserve materials, to liberate capital, and to produce in greater volume. A contemporary wrote that "at Birmingham, Wolverhampton, Sheffield, and other manufacturing places, almost every manufacturer hath a new invention of his own, and is daily improving on those of others."[9] This quotation is a reminder that one should not stress unduly the inventions of a few famous men but should think also of the countless small contrivances and tiny improvements which gradually produced a new technology.

The spinning of cotton thread was the fastest-growing industry of the 1770s and 1780s. Fine cotton fabrics had been imported for centuries from Italy and later from India, but they had been very costly. Early in the seventeenth century a small cotton industry had developed in Lancashire, where cotton from the Levant and linen yarn from Ireland had been woven into a cloth known as fustian. Cotton was later available from America, but the industry remained small until after 1750. In 1738 Lewis Paul patented a machine to produce cotton thread by passing the raw cotton through rollers; ten years later he invented a carding machine to brush the cotton into long stringy fibers before it was spun. These devices, however, were not successful; the most important invention, Kay's flying shuttle,[10] was an improvement in weaving, whereas the great need was for new techniques in spinning. Weavers could use more thread than the spinners could produce; hence the shortage of yarn was chronic.

The problem was solved by three famous inventions. In the 1760s a poor weaver, James Hargreaves, who lived near Blackburn in Lancashire, invented the spinning jenny, a multiple spinning wheel, turned on its side, with spindles in place of wheels. It could spin eight threads at a time, and soon, as it was improved and enlarged, it could spin a hundred. A simple machine that could be set up in a cottage and driven by hand, it was patented in 1770. A year earlier Richard Arkwright had invented the water frame. Arkwright was a self-made man who became wealthy and famous. Beginning life as a barber, he had traveled from village to village collecting human hair to be made into wigs. It is probable that his water frame owed something to Lewis Paul, for it was a machine which produced cotton thread by passing the raw cotton between a series of rollers. As the thread emerged from the last set of rollers it was given a twist to make it tough and strong. The water frame was a heavy machine which required artificial power and could not be placed in a cottage. Hence Arkwright built factories. His first machines were powered by horses, who walked round and round in a circle, but he soon turned to water power. He displayed great ability, not only as an inventor, but also as a man of business who could promote his enterprises, organize his factories, and use his employees to the best advantage. Eventually he was conducting under one roof all the processes required to make raw cotton into finished cotton thread. More than anyone else he made the spinning of cotton thread a factory industry.

In 1779 Samuel Crompton, a Lancashire spinner, invented a machine, known as the mule, which combined features of the jenny and the water frame. By 1800

[9] Quoted in T. S. Ashton, *An Economic History of England. The Eighteenth Century*, p. 104.
[10] See page 540.

this beautiful and fairly intricate machine could spin 400 threads of the finest yarn. The industry forged ahead because its problems could be solved by machines that were not difficult to construct, its supply of raw material from America was unlimited, and it enjoyed a highly flexible market. The weaving of cotton cloth still continued to be done by domestic workers. In 1785 Edmund Cartwright, a clergyman, invented a mechanical loom run by water power, but it was not a success; and it was not until the 1820s that a power loom brought the weaving of cotton fabrics into factories, condemning the hand weavers to a bitter and hopeless struggle for existence.

The mechanization of spinning and weaving woolen goods was much slower, for wool was a fragile material which required gentle handling. The spinning of woolen yarn was not a factory industry until the early nineteenth century; the weaving of high-grade woolen cloth remained a domestic industry until the 1870s and 1880s.

The iron industry expanded rapidly in the second half of the eighteenth century. It was aided, as we have seen,[11] by the discovery of the Abraham Darbys that coke could be used in smelting in place of charcoal, a discovery which became generally known about the middle of the century. Iron thus produced was pig or cast iron. The ironmasters greatly increased the variety of cast-iron products and created a wide market for them. But cast iron contained carbon and other impurities which made it brittle and apt to break under stress or heavy blows. Malleable or wrought iron, which would bend rather than break and which could be hammered into various shapes, was obtained by removing these impurities. An advance to this end was made in 1760 when John Smeaton perfected a blowing engine which forced a constant blast of air into burning coke and thus produced the high temperatures necessary to refine iron properly. In 1766 Thomas and George Cranage patented a reverberatory furnace in which flames played upon the molten iron and hot gases passed over it to burn out the carbon content. A better process, known as puddling, was patented independently in 1784 by Peter Onions and Henry Cort. In this process a long puddling rod stirred and turned the molten iron as the carbon escaped in the form of sulfureous gases. Cleaner and tougher wrought iron was thus obtained. Cort also improved the slitting and rolling of iron by which it was cut into small pieces for the manufacture of nails, bolts, locks, and the like, or passed between rollers to form plates or rails.

These improvements made possible the production of good wrought iron at comparatively cheap rates, so that England was soon manufacturing the cheapest iron bars in Europe. In 1825 the cost at Cardiff was £10 a ton, whereas in France the cost was £26; by 1830 almost three fourths of the British product was wrought iron. The uses to which iron could be put were expanded enormously. An imaginative ironmaster, John Wilkinson, believed that iron could be used for every purpose for which wood or stone was commonly employed. "He produced railroads for mines (1767), built the first iron bridge in the world over the Severn (1779), built an iron chapel for the Wesleyans, saw the first iron boat afloat (1787), and finally was buried suitably in an iron coffin (1805)."[12] The industry was most efficient when concentrated in a few great plants, such as the Carron works in Scotland and the Dowlais works in Wales, where all the proc-

[11] See page 540.
[12] J. H. Plumb, *England in the Eighteenth Century*, p. 79.

esses of manufacture were performed together under one management. They were located in areas producing both coal and iron; some firms owned and operated their own mines. Thus the industry was highly capitalized. Yet the metal trades in which iron was made into a great variety of small objects continued to be carried on by domestic workers until well into the nineteenth century.

A word should be added concerning other industries. The demand for coal steadily increased, though not as rapidly as might be supposed, because of the frequent use of water power. Perhaps four times as much coal was mined in 1800 as had been mined a century earlier. As the miners worked farther and farther away from the bottom of the mine shaft, iron rails were installed underground on which carts, drawn by horses or by human beings, carried the coal to the bottom of the shaft, where it was raised to the surface by new hoisting machinery. There was great need for an industry to manufacture machines according to exact specifications. Such an industry did not appear until the nineteenth century, but a step toward it was made in 1794 when Henry Maudsley invented a side rest for the lathe. The side rest held a cutting tool against the article turning in the lathe, greatly increasing the accuracy with which work could be done.

The making of china, porcelain, and other potteries became an important industry in the eighteenth century. Josiah Wedgwood displayed great skill in every department of this manufacture. He not only developed a high quality of chinaware but created artistic shapes and designs. An enterprising and aggressive businessman who extended the market for his wares throughout Europe and America, he became one of the great industrialists of the century. Another manufacturer of chinaware was Josiah Spode, whose willowware design, a modification of a Chinese pattern, is still used extensively today. Pottery works also produced less expensive china which the lower classes could afford to buy. Much easier to clean than pewter, chinaware was a factor in improving the health of the nation.

The development of the steam engine, of prime importance in the Industrial Revolution, is connected with the name of James Watt, an inventor of genius. He was at first a maker of scientific instruments at the University of Glasgow, where he prepared apparatus for experiments in astronomy and physics. In 1763 he began a study of the principles of the Savery and Newcomen engine. Over a period of many years, handicapped because he could not obtain parts cut to exact specifications, he gradually constructed a vastly improved engine and adapted it for use in industry. His engine, a true steam engine in that steam was fed into each end of a closed cylinder and pushed the piston up and down, was patented in 1769. Between 1782 and 1784 Watt perfected a device by which his engine could turn a wheel. The invention of an engine using coal and turning the wheels of a factory made industry independent of water power and opened a new phase of the Industrial Revolution. About 300 of Watt's engines were in use in industry by 1800.

FIRST RESULTS OF THE INDUSTRIAL REVOLUTION

Of the more immediate effects of these changes the most striking was the enormously increased volume of production at greatly reduced costs. The imports of raw cotton into England rose from 4 million pounds in 1761 to 56

A coal wagon on rails. (From *The London Magazine*, 1764. Historical Pictures Service, Chicago)

million in 1800 and to 100 million in 1815. The cost of production of cotton thread declined between 1779 and 1812 in the ratio of 100 to 7; between 1779 and 1882 in the ratio of 100 to 2. In 1796 there were 21 million yards of cotton cloth manufactured; in 1830 the figure had risen to 347 million. A machine tended by a young girl who mended broken threads could weave as much cotton cloth as could ten weavers working by hand. The same astonishing acceleration may be seen in the iron industry. In 1740 England produced 17,000 tons of pig iron; in 1796, 125,000 tons; in 1806, 256,000 tons. There was a corresponding increase in British shipping. The tonnage of ships that cleared from British ports rose from 289,000 in 1709 to 2,130,000 in 1800. At the height of the struggle with Napoleon, between 1800 and 1810, the English constructed thirty acres of new iron docks in London, making it by far the greatest port in the world.

The inventions of the age made a deep impression on the people. As they saw the new canals and factories, the speeding coaches, and the new machines, as they breathlessly watched the first daredevil ascend in a balloon (from a spot, as was noted, near Bedlam), they were filled with wonder and astonishment. The newspapers of the time were constantly using such words as "amazing," "unprecedented," and "astounding." The agricultural writer Arthur Young, in attempting to prove that population was rising (which some people doubted), wrote as follows: "View the navigation, the roads, harbors, and all other public works. Take notice of the spirit with which manufactures are carried on. . . . Move your eyes which side you will, you behold nothing but great riches and yet greater resources. It is vain to talk of tables of births and lists of houses and windows, as proofs of our loss of people; the flourishing state of our agriculture, our manufactures and commerce, with our general wealth prove the contrary."[13] Here was born that belief in progress which in the nineteenth century became almost a religion. Such wonder at the achievement of machines and such faith in the idea of progress may seem naïve, but to men living in 1800 mechanical gadgets appeared the symbols of a brave new world.

There was at the same time a change in economic thought. The mercantile views which, as we know, had dominated the thinking of the early modern period laid emphasis on trade rather than on production, assumed that a nation increased its commerce by seizing the commerce of some other power, and set up a favorable balance of trade as the great goal of the nation. Gold and silver were believed to constitute wealth. To attain these objectives it was the duty of government to regulate minutely the economic life of the nation, not with the individual merchant in mind but for the corporate economic good of the com- monwealth. These theories were demolished by a famous book, Adam Smith's *Wealth of Nations,* published in 1776. It was a declaration of independence no less than the one in America. It held that wealth did not consist of the precious metals but of consumable goods—of buildings, canals, machines, and industrial plants; of the useful articles being produced. Adam Smith laid emphasis on production rather than on commerce. The way to increase production, he believed, was to allow the individual manufacturer the greatest possible freedom, for his self-interest would lead him to produce the goods that society wanted. The state should not interfere, but should permit the private enterprise of the manufacturer to come into gradual alignment with the needs of society. Artificial barriers to trade should be removed. This was the doctrine of laissez faire (to let alone) which led England eventually to adopt free trade. For some time the effect of this thinking was merely negative. The government stopped making new regulations but did not repeal old ones. Later, in the 1820s, regulatory laws began to be removed from the statute book. Meanwhile the younger Pitt became a disciple of Adam Smith, with important results.

The first scientific census, carried through by John Rickman in 1801, showed that the population of England and Wales had risen to about 9 million, whereas it had stood at about 5½ million in 1700. Also because of the census, an important shift of population, dimly perceptible throughout the century, was now made clear. Population was leaving the south and east of the country and was moving to the north and west, to Lancashire and to the West Riding of Yorkshire, to Newcastle, to Birmingham and Coventry, to cities in the Severn Valley, and to South Wales—in a word, to the coal fields and the manufacturing towns. This shift of population was slow, quiet, subtle, almost unobservable, a kind of caterpillar crawl, by which the people living near a town moved into it and the places they left vacant gradually were filled by other people living farther away. The south and east of England, except for the area of London, lost its old pre- eminence in the national life and subsided into a quiet land of large estates. The future of England lay in the industrial north. From time out of mind the southern counties had returned more than their share of members to the House of Com- mons, and the movement of population to the north made ever sharper and more glaring the inequities of the electoral system.

The growth of industry produced a type of capitalist who was a newcomer to the English scene. He was likely to have risen from humble origins. It was

13 Quoted in Plumb, p. 143.

said that as a middle-aged man Richard Arkwright devoted an hour a day to the improvement of his English and his penmanship. The new capitalist was a businessman, tough and rugged in temperament, with drive and determination, who had clawed his way up the ladder of success from poverty to riches. He had many admirable qualities, but he was not a gentleman. The aristocracy looked upon him with hostility. He found himself excluded from the social circle of the country gentry and from that preserve of English gentlemen, the life of politics. Occasionally a millionaire like the elder Sir Robert Peel, a magnate of the cotton industry, could secure, at least for his children, a place in society and politics. But most of the industrialists could not. Many of the smaller factories were in the country, the squalid cottages of the workers clustering about the manufactury. The owner was in close proximity to the local gentry. The result was a mutual dislike and bitterness which in time produced its political repercussions.

The new wealth was distributed badly, and the poor got little of it. Their condition was rendered much worse at the end of the century by the long war with France which began in 1793 and continued, with one short intermission, until 1815. War brought inflation and high prices for food; wages, though they rose, did not keep pace with this increase. The fortunes of war and the opening and closing of markets on the Continent made business conditions unstable and employment uncertain. Factory hours were very long. The slums of the industrial towns showed little improvement. It is not surprising that there were frequent riots, sometimes for food and sometimes because the human animal revolted against the burden of poverty and overwork thrust upon him. Yet the factory worker was better off than the landless agricultural laborer who was dependent upon low wages and who could not afford to buy the food he himself had helped to raise. Rural slums could be almost as horrid as urban ones.

The lower classes, in both town and country, suffered from the bad administration of the Poor Law. The Elizabethan Poor Law of 1601 was still in force, though it often was modified in practice. The parish remained the unit of poor relief: it must support its own poor in the parish workhouse, and many were the dodges of local officials to shift the burden of the poor, whenever possible, to some other parish. Employers living in one parish favored laborers living in another so that if work became slack the support of the unemployed would fall upon the parish where the laborers resided. The diseased and the infirm, even persons at the point of death, were hustled out of a parish when some excuse could be made for their support by another. The workhouse was often a place of filth and misery into which were crowded, without thought of segregation, the young and the old, the diseased and the healthy, the vagabond and the honest laborer, supported—or, rather, kept from starvation—by rates levied on their grudging fellow parishioners. As the condition of the poor grew worse, the justices of the peace of Berkshire, meeting at Speenhamland in 1795, adopted the policy of outdoor relief, that is, the practice of taking money from the poor rates to supplement the wages of laborers who were not living in the workhouse. This local measure designed to meet a local emergency soon spread to other parts of the country and the results were disastrous: wages sank below the level of subsistence, for employers need not pay a living wage when the parish would make up the difference; the independent laborer who wished to support himself could not compete with laborers subsidized by the poor rates; the poor rates rose alarmingly and threw an intolerable burden on the middle class. Thus the century ended darkly for the poor, especially for the poor in the rural areas.

26

the younger pitt
and the great war
with france

The peace with America in 1783 was followed first by a short period of political crisis and then by a decade of reconstruction and recovery under the premiership of William Pitt the Younger, a statesman of remarkable ability and dedication. Pitt steadily improved the efficiency of government in a quiet and unobtrusive way. It was well for England that he did his work so effectively. In 1789 came the shock of the French Revolution, which greatly alarmed the English upper classes. In 1793 England and France went to war. From then until the final defeat of Napoleon in 1815 the energies of the nation were absorbed by the struggle with France, and domestic reform of any kind became almost impossible.

POLITICAL INSTABILITY, 1782–1784

The fall of Lord North's administration in March 1782 was followed by two years of political instability. A demand for peace with America compelled the King to find a minister who had not been closely associated with the war; hence he was forced to turn to the opposition. The new ministry was a coalition of the group led by Rockingham, which included Charles James Fox and Edmund Burke, and the group led by Shelburne, the political heir of Chatham. Rockingham became the First Lord of the Treasury; Shelburne and Fox, Secretaries; and Burke, paymaster of the forces.

The new Cabinet did not promise to last long. The Rockingham group did not like Shelburne, a man of ability, knowledge, and breadth of view. Even his opponents admired his clearness of thought and his ruthless sense of purpose, but he was considered too close to the King, too secretive in his methods, and too masterful in action. Fox began to talk as though Shelburne represented a royal faction within the new ministry and declared that he planned to give the influence of the Crown a stout blow. As a matter of fact, the Crown's influence was at a low ebb. George had wished to continue the war because he believed that France was on the verge of collapse, he feared that an American victory would spell the end of the empire, and he felt that radical and dangerous forces were abroad which ought to be suppressed. He now saw all his policies reversed. He regarded Fox as his enemy, partly because of Fox's offensive speeches and partly because Fox was a friend of the Prince of Wales, whom he was leading into gambling and debauchery.

Both groups in the Cabinet desired reform, but their approach and their objectives differed. Shelburne wished to reform the Commons by increasing the number of independent country members. He also suggested reforms of administrative methods. He began an inquiry into abuses in raising loans during the American war, he advocated the payment of officials by salaries and not by fees, and he proposed clearer divisions between the work of administrative departments. At the same time he hoped to raise the standing of the Crown and to preserve its position in politics.

Burke and Fox, on the other hand, obsessed with the idea of the King's excessive power, aimed directly at reducing the possibility of royal influence over the Commons. They passed an act which disfranchised the revenue officers of the Crown as persons open to direct pressure from the government. Another act disqualified men who held government contracts from sitting in the Commons. Burke also obtained a measure which compelled the paymaster of the forces to separate his private funds from funds belonging to the state and to keep the latter in an official account at the Bank of England. He further devised an act concerning the civil list which was to be so arranged that ministers' salaries were to be paid only after other items charged to the civil list had been provided for. The purpose was to make ministers economical, but they soon disregarded the act as a dead letter.

The Rockingham-Shelburne coalition ended in the summer of 1782, when Fox resigned after a quarrel with Shelburne over the peace negotiations in Paris. Rockingham died in July. His followers hoped that the King would appoint the Duke of Portland as head of a Cabinet dominated by Fox but the King offered the first place to Shelburne, who accepted.

It was estimated that at this time three main groups existed in the Commons. Shelburne, who commanded about 140 votes, was followed by those who thought of him as a disciple of Chatham, as the true reformer of the day, and as the head of the government who could bestow political favors. Fox headed a party of about 90 members. The leader of the Rockingham group, he had added followers of his own who felt the charm of his personality and thought that he would soon be in power. The third group was North's, numbering some 120 members. It consisted of men who had attached themselves to North during his long period of office and who now felt some awkwardness in breaking away, though desertions were taking place as his position weakened. Beyond these factions, more than 100 members maintained complete independence.

Although no one group could control the Commons, Shelburne made the attempt. Disliking party government, he did not negotiate with party leaders. He hoped that as his administration became stable it would attract individuals from other groups and would gain the support of independent country gentlemen. But his career was ended by the peace settlement negotiated in Paris. The country accepted the peace but repudiated the man who made it; Shelburne fell in February 1783.

An alliance of two of the three groups in the Commons was now essential. The one which emerged was a coalition of Fox and North, a coalition which held office only from April to December 1783 and which has often been portrayed as unnatural and almost wicked. It was certainly an alliance of convenience, but it was not as strange as it appeared. Although the two men had opposed each other during the American war, that war was over and differences of opinion about it could be forgotten. Both North and Fox believed that they were better off with each other than either of them would have been with Shelburne. It was true that North was conservative whereas Fox stood for radical reform. But Fox, thinking perhaps that reform had gone far enough for the present, agreed not to push it further in the immediate future. Thus the alliance could be justified in a number of ways, although it made a painful impression in the country: Fox appeared to be abandoning his principles in order to obtain power. The King was so deeply incensed that for over a month he did not summon his new ministers to take office.

The short life of the coalition revolved around Fox's India bill, which was an attempt to take control of Indian affairs away from the East India Company without placing that control in the hands of the King. Seven commissioners, assisted by nine others expert in commerce, were to govern British India. Unfortunately, the commissioners named in the bill were all members of the parties of Fox and North. The country came to the conclusion that Fox was seeking to place the patronage of India in the hands of his friends. For this reason the bill alienated public opinion.

To the King, who was ready to believe the worst, the bill appeared a monstrous abuse of power. Duty compelled him, he thought, to stop the bill if possible and to remove ministers who advocated such legislation. He was within his constitutional rights to make the attempt, though if the country did not support him, the result might be disastrous. He discovered that North was being deserted by some of his followers. The possibility arose that young William Pitt, who was free from any connection with the American war, might be able to attract these deserters and thus form a stable administration. In December 1783, therefore, George took the unusual step of using his personal influence to bring about the defeat of the bill in the House of Lords. He then dismissed Fox and North and appointed Pitt as First Lord of the Treasury. The King was taking the chance that in the long run the Commons would approve this action. And in the long run they did.

WILLIAM PITT

Pitt came forward as the opponent of faction and of party government. He hoped to succeed where Shelburne had failed in building a nonparty administration upon a broad basis of general support. It was Fox who embodied party, but he had made party government appear unscrupulous and clannish. Pitt hoped to become what the Commons and the country wanted—an able, sensible, incorruptible, and patriotic leader who symbolized national unity and offered calm and practical administration as opposed to the heated imaginations of Burke and Fox. Pitt stood for a reconciliation of King and Commons; he was both a friend of the King and a minister pledged to reform.

If Pitt was to pacify the quarrels and conflicts of party politics, he must stand well with both King and Commons. He could count upon the support of the King because George lived in dread of Fox's return to power. But Pitt could not abuse this strong position: the King must not be coerced. If King and minister were symbols of patriotic unity, they must work together. Nor could Pitt coerce the Commons. As a nonparty statesman seeking general support, he could bring his plans for reform before the House, but the Commons could accept or reject them as they saw fit. They could not be compelled to follow his lead, and, as we shall see, a number of his reforms were defeated. Yet as he consolidated his power, as he drew men to him from the followers of North and even of Fox, as the King's health grew precarious, and as Pitt's colleagues regarded him with growing deference, he became increasingly the cornerstone of government upon whom the country depended. "I have long looked on him," wrote a noble in 1801, "as the Atlas of our reeling globe."[1] He stood alone, for a long time the only member of the House of Commons who was in the Cabinet, the laborious and heroic statesman, with great strength of character and the highest sense of duty.

He had many qualities of leadership. From his father, the Earl of Chatham, he drew his ambition, his dedication to public service, and his command of majestic English. Though not the orator that his father had been, he always spoke well and could rise to heights of eloquence. His speeches were based on exact information; his arguments were clear, detailed, and enlightening. In temperament he resembled his mother, a Grenville, who passed to her son the solidity and good judgment of her family. Pitt was always the practical statesman, approaching problems with calm and wise detachment.

His genius blossomed early. A member of the Commons at twenty-two, he was Chancellor of the Exchequer at twenty-three and First Lord of the Treasury at twenty-four. As a young man he was most unusual—cautious, dignified, formidable, industrious, and wise. Though his best work was done in detailed administration, he was a shrewd politician and a parliamentarian who understood the ways and moods of the House of Commons. In middle age he was not as remarkable as in his youth. A delicate constitution, overwork, and the responsibilities of office exhausted his energies and reduced him to a kind of subdued mechanical competence.

From the Grenvilles Pitt inherited a formal stiffness and cold reserve. There was a freezing quality about his oratory which his opponents interpreted as haughty disdain. His friend Wilberforce once remarked that Pitt's "great natural shyness and even awkwardness often produced effects for which pride was falsely charged on him." The tendency of a shy person to seek protection in a lofty manner was intensified because Pitt became the head of the Cabinet at an extremely early age and was forced to control colleagues much older than he. Only among intimate friends could Pitt unbend; with them he could be witty and genial.

CHARLES JAMES FOX

Pitt's lifelong opponent in politics was Charles James Fox. Fox was a man of ability and charm. Warmhearted and generous, with humor, vitality, and attractive manners, he possessed far more personal magnetism than did the austere Pitt. A true liberal, he espoused the causes of the American colonists,

[1] Quoted in J. Holland Rose, *A Short Life of William Pitt* (London: G. Bell, 1925), p. 176.

William Pitt the Younger, by John Hoppner. (National Portrait Gallery, London)

Charles James Fox, by Karl Anton Hickel. (National Portrait Gallery, London)

Ireland, and the French revolutionists; he was a strong opponent of the slave trade. Fox was an excellent debater, very skillful in reply, able to grasp the significance of each argument in debate, develop it logically, and present it to the Commons with remarkable clarity. His excellent memory supplied him with apt quotations. He was thus a formidable figure in the Commons.

But his private life told heavily against him. The son of Henry Fox, Lord Holland, he was accustomed to have everything he wanted. His father gave him a good education but no moral guidance; he had grown up among the young aristocrats who drank and gambled in London's fashionable clubs. In fact, gambling was his great vice. When Charles James Fox was twenty-five years old, his father paid his debts of £140,000. These excesses left him little coolness or balance as a politician. He was rash and violent, his speeches were often heated and overcharged, he could display great lack of judgment. His alliance with North, his India bill, his disregard for the feelings of the King, and his bitter attacks on Pitt when Pitt first came to power were serious political blunders. He was scarcely ever in office. This was more than chance. The nation regarded Pitt as the safer and saner man, though in sheer ability he was probably Fox's inferior.

PITT'S RISE TO POWER

Pitt's first months as Prime Minister were difficult ones. He did not have a majority in the Commons, and the way in which he had come to power by a kind of palace intrigue embittered Fox and his followers. But Fox made the mistake of being too violent, using his majority to hold up supplies and to postpone the normal passage of the Mutiny Act. He persuaded the Commons to send a representation to the King asking him to dismiss his present ministers. The fact that he also denounced the possibility of a general election showed that Fox feared its consequence. Such vindictive measures told against him, for he appeared to be denying the King's right to dissolve Parliament and to select his ministers.

Pitt, on the other hand, played his cards with coolness and judgment. He carefully cultivated the business community in London and the friendship of reformers like Wilberforce. He brought in an excellent India bill, which was defeated by only eight votes. He showed that he was making a serious attempt at sound government, and many people believed that he represented the last possibility of decent administration. Thus, when the election was held in April 1784, Pitt won a surprising victory and Fox went down to ignominious defeat. It is true that Pitt had the support of government patronage, which was used freely in his behalf. He also received financial backing from a number of wealthy men, such as those in the East India Company, who had been terrified by Fox's proposed solution of the Indian problem. Some of Fox's followers, seeing little hope of election, decided not to stand for Parliament. But there was more than this. Public opinion, aroused in an unusual way, supported Pitt. One hundred and sixty of Fox's followers either did not run or were defeated. George's calculation in dismissing Fox and North was justified by the result.

PITT AS A PEACE MINISTER

Administration and Finance

Pitt's greatest achievement, upon which his reputation justly rests, was his thorough investigation and steady reform of administration and finance. He did not concentrate on the civil list, as Fox and Burke had done, but looked at the work of every clerk in the employment of the state and at every item of receipt and expenditure. It was this constant scrutiny of details that slowly improved the machinery of government. It is truer to think of Pitt as a patient reformer of the details of government all his life than to call him a reformer in his youth and a reactionary in middle age. He worked quietly and slowly, avoiding strife and publicity so far as possible. Thus he preferred to end sinecures, not by a sweep of the pen, as Burke would have done, but by waiting until the holder of a sinecure died and then refusing to appoint a successor. On the whole this was cheaper than to abolish the sinecure and compensate the incumbent. In substituting salaries for fees he was also slow, and for much the same reason. But civil servants discovered that the volume of their work steadily increased. Much more application was now expected of them, so that the government received value for its money.

Pitt improved financial arrangements in the customs service by having all customs duties paid into one consolidated fund instead of into a number of funds as in the past. He thus eliminated many offices and also simplified bookkeeping. Loans secured by the customs duties as a whole were more easily handled than those secured by individual duties. The civil list, formerly the preserve of the Crown, was now reviewed by Parliament, and a beginning was made in appropriations for separate items, leaving to the King only such money as was required for his private necessities. In raising loans for the government Pitt obtained better terms by asking that competitive bids be offered in sealed letters.

It was necessary to obtain new sources of revenue. Pitt's early budgets imposed taxes on luxuries in a rather haphazard way. Thus a tax on windows in houses, which he made an important part of the tax structure, proved to be less a levy on the rich than a discouragement to the building of windows in lower class housing and in factories, where windows were badly needed. Pitt's taxes, however, became more scientific as time went on. Finding that high duties on tea, wines, and tobacco increased smuggling, he reduced the duties, extended the excise to these articles (as Walpole had vainly attempted to do), and struck fiercely at the smugglers. A disciple of Adam Smith, Pitt sought to remove impediments to the growth of industry and to promote freer trade. In 1785 he attempted to establish free trade with Ireland, though the opposition of business interests in England forced him to drop the measure. He succeeded in concluding a commercial treaty with France by which both countries lowered their tariffs. English cloth entered France more cheaply than before, and French wines came into England at lowered prices.

To reduce the national debt, which stood at £238 million in 1783 and consumed half the government's income in interest charges, Pitt revived the sinking fund set up by Walpole. According to Pitt's plan, half a million pounds a year were placed in the sinking fund for the gradual reduction of the debt. Ridicule has often been thrown upon this measure because, after the war with France began, money was borrowed to be placed in the fund. Pitt's defense was that he had imposed rigid rules so that the fund would not be raided as had happened in Walpole's time.

In ten years Pitt raised the government's revenue by a third and paid off £11 million of the debt. He was able to balance the budget, though only by reduction of military and naval expenditure. His financial success depended on the maintenance of peace and ended under the strain of the war with France. Nonetheless, a rapid revival of the English economy took place between 1783 and 1793. The resilience and buoyancy of the new industrialism came as a gratifying surprise.

India

Shortly after the election in 1784 Pitt reintroduced his bill on India, which became law in the same year. To understand this important bill it is necessary to glance back at the history of the East India Company since Clive's conquest of Bengal in 1757.

The history of the company was highly complicated during this period. The company was basically a trading corporation which enjoyed a monopoly of commerce between England and India, but it was much more. In Bengal it was gradually assuming the powers of government. This in itself raised serious problems because the commercial interests of the company might easily conflict with its duty in governing a large native population. At home the company not only conducted eastern trade but was also a financial and banking house to which the government turned when it wished to borrow money. The company itself raised funds by issuing bonds. It possessed a good deal of patronage, which was highly valuable because even a minor clerkship in the East offered a young Englishman an opportunity to grow wealthy. Moreover, the directors of the company were important men in London who could influence city politics and help return members to Parliament. In fact, they were courted by the government. This history of the company was further complicated by the existence of feuds and factions within the group of directors.

The impression prevailed in England during the 1760s that the profits of the company would be enormous. Its stock rose rapidly in price. Fearing that the Cabinet might interfere in its affairs, the company agreed to pay the government the large annual sum of £400,000 in order to be let alone. But profits did not materialize. Wars on the frontiers of Bengal, a severe famine in that province, the corruption of Englishmen in the East, and divided policies at home combined to diminish the company's profits until, in 1772, it was forced to confess that it was in serious financial straits. Yet some of its servants were coming home with enormous fortunes. These "nabobs," as they were called, with their Orientalized manners and vulgar display of wealth, became familiar figures in the English social scene. The opportunity for illegal gains in Bengal was fostered by Clive's dual system of government, through which the company drew revenue not only from trade but also from the native treasury, though responsibility for law and order was left in the feeble hands of the native ruler.

Lord North, as usual, wished to find a peaceful compromise. He gave the company a loan to carry it over its current difficulties, but he could not prevent Parliament from investigating the company and from asking Clive questions so awkward that he committed suicide. In 1773 North passed a Regulating Act, the first blundering attempt of the executive at home to improve and control the government of British India.

Meanwhile, in 1772, two years before the act went into operation, Warren Hastings became the Governor General in Bengal. A great administrator with a firm grasp of the essentials of Indian government, he combined boldness in decision with grim determination to fight to the finish against his many foes. He was not a reformer. Having grown up in the service of the company during its worst period of corruption, he merely tried to keep irregularities within tolerable bounds. He was suspicious of doctrinaire schemes for improving Indian government, preferring to use his personal influence with Indian rulers and with subordinates in the company. His attitude was somewhat similar to that of a benevolent native prince. He was sincerely interested in Indian culture and in the people of Bengal and he felt very keenly the conflict of interest between his position as the manager of a commercial enterprise and his role as the ruler of an Indian province. During his first two years in office he laid the foundations for a greatly improved system of finance and administration. Following orders from home, he abolished Clive's dual system and assumed full control of the government of Bengal. The taxes were collected by native officials supervised by Englishmen drawn from the senior ranks of the service. These in turn reported to a central revenue board. They also tried civil cases, though criminal cases were left in the hands of native judges using Hindu and Muslim law. Two courts of appeal, one civil, the other criminal, also were established. Here was the beginning of an administrative system which fused English and native elements and which could be understood by the Indians.

In foreign affairs Hastings wished to surround Bengal with a ring of friendly native powers to serve as buffers against hostile states beyond. In pursuing this policy Hastings loaned English troops to his ally, the ruler of Oudh, to suppress a number of Afghan chieftains known as the Rohillas. Hastings later was criticized for thus taking part in a war against the Rohillas, with whom he had no direct quarrel, though they were thought to be intriguing with enemies of both Oudh and Bengal.

Good progress in these directions was being made when Lord North's act came into effect. What was needed in Bengal was a strong and incorruptible executive with authority to act quickly. But North's Regulating Act, inspired by suspicion of a strong executive in general and of the servants of the company in particular, set up a council of four men without whose consent Hastings could not act. His authority was reduced further by the establishment of a new supreme court in Bengal, with a very vaguely defined jurisdiction, and by a limitation of his power over the towns of Madras and Bombay.

The new council may have intended to cooperate with Hastings, but almost at once it began to quarrel with him. Led by the malicious Philip Francis, who wanted to have Hastings' place, the council opposed him on almost every issue. A weaker man would have been hounded from office, but Hastings fought back fiercely. Eventually two of the councilors died and Hastings wounded Francis in a duel. By 1776 he had regained control. It was well that he did so, for the period of the American Revolution was a time of great danger for the British in India. Partly because of French intrigue and partly because of the blunders of the English in Madras and Bombay, Hastings was drawn into war with an alliance of the three most powerful native states in India—the Marathas, Mysore, and Hyderabad. He could hope for little aid from home but he fought the war with great energy and determination. By his able diplomacy he split the alliance and was able to make peace with his enemies one by one.

During this struggle Hastings did some things that could not bear examination. He levied an enormous fine on Chait Singh, the Raja of Benares, an ally of the company, and pressed for payment until Chait Singh rose in wild revolt and had to be dethroned. When the Nabob of Oudh claimed that he could not make certain payments to the English because he was owed money by his great-aunts, the Begums, or princesses, of Oudh, Hastings sent soldiers to seize the treasure of the elderly Begums. These episodes and the Rohilla war formed three of the counts against Hastings when he was later impeached in England.

The failure of Lord North's India Act soon became evident. But North had little time to devote to Indian affairs. New legislation was obviously necessary. In 1783, when he was in office, Fox brought forward an India bill which would have transferred all power over British India to a group of commissioners in London. As we have seen, however, Fox made the mistake of appointing his friends and followers as commissioners. The company attacked his bill, and King George took advantage of it to dismiss Fox from office.

The Indian problem was still to be solved when Pitt came to power. He profited from the consternation which Fox's bill had created among the directors of the company, who were now much more reasonable. Pitt's bill separated the government of Bengal, which was to be controlled by the Cabinet, from the management of commerce and from patronage, both of which were left to the company. Officials sent to India continued to be named by the company, though the Cabinet influenced major appointments. But when these officials reached the East, they received their instructions in civil and military matters from the government at home. A board of control was established in London; its president was a member of the Cabinet; it was he who governed British India so far as it could be governed from London. By a supplementary act in 1786 the powers of the Governor General were increased. His council was reduced from four members to three, he could override its decisions if he took full responsibility, and his control over Bombay and Madras was made complete.

Hastings came home in 1785. Led by Fox and Burke, who acted in a kind of partisan frenzy, the opposition in the Commons insisted that Hastings be impeached. The impeachment dragged on for seven years; and Hastings, though acquitted at last, was ruined by the huge expenses of the trial. It was a poor return for saving India.

The next Governor General, sent out in 1786, was Lord Cornwallis. Despite his defeat at Yorktown, he continued to enjoy the confidence of his countrymen. He went to India with great power and prestige. He was not a servant of the company, but an officer of the Crown, a noble lord, the friend of Pitt and Dundas. Answerable only to the board of control, he could defy the company. Under his wise administration, the honesty and efficiency of English officials in India steadily improved.

Other Attempts at Reform

Although the Commons accepted Pitt's financial reforms and his bill on India, they did not hesitate to defeat some of his other proposals. In 1785 he introduced a bill to eliminate thirty-six pocket boroughs (with generous compensation to borough owners), to transfer the seats to London and to large counties, and to extend the franchise by giving the vote to copyholders whose lands were worth forty shillings a year. The measure was defeated by a large majority. Accepting this verdict, Pitt made no further move to alter the electoral system. Indeed, he conferred peerages on owners of pocket boroughs, so that his friend Wilberforce lamented that he governed through influence rather than through principle.

Pitt also wished to abolish the slave trade. This traffic, which had been accepted as a matter of course until the middle of the century, was now under attack by the Quakers, by the Methodists, and by an evangelical movement within the church. In 1772 Judge Mansfield ruled that a slave became free if he set foot in Britain. An Abolitionist Society was founded in 1787. Pitt brought the question before the Commons in 1788 and on subsequent occasions, but the opposition of vested interests was so strong that the matter dragged on until it was lost in the conservatism resulting from the French Revolution. Pitt accepted the tacit understanding that the Commons might defeat his measures although members had no intention of driving him from office.

Foreign Affairs

During the ten years of peace between 1783 and 1793 Pitt conducted the foreign affairs of England with considerable success. His aims, apart from temporary crises, were to end the isolation in which Britain found herself after the American war, to frustrate the designs of France on Belgium and Holland, and to resist the advance of Russia into eastern Europe. In 1784 the Austrian Emperor Joseph II proposed to exchange the Austrian Netherlands for the electorate of Bavaria. This exchange would have strengthened Austria's position in Germany, for which Prussia had no inclination, and would have opened the way for French encroachment on the Netherlands, which England was certain to oppose. Hence Prussian and English policy coincided, and the proposal came to nothing.

A more serious crisis developed in Holland, where conflict arose between the Stadtholder and an aristocratic party which desired to overthrow him. France allied with the Dutch insurgents; England and Prussia supported the Stadtholder. In 1787, using a somewhat thin excuse, Prussia sent troops into Holland and firmly established the Stadtholder in power, a course which England approved. Faced with bankruptcy at home, France made no move to intervene. This was a diplomatic victory for Pitt. In the year following he was able to construct alliances of England with both Prussia and Holland, thus ending British isolation.

In another episode in a quite different part of the world, French financial decay again played its part. English fishermen had established a settlement on Vancouver Island on the Pacific coast of North America. But the Spanish, claiming a monopoly of the entire Pacific shore, seized an English ship in Nootka Sound off Vancouver. Pitt protested while Spain prepared for war. Then finding that no help would be forthcoming from France, Spain gave way and the crisis passed.

Pitt was less successful in opposing Russia. In a war between Russia and Sweden, England, acting with Holland and Prussia, assisted the Swedes by forcing Denmark to remain at peace. But in 1791, when Pitt wished to fight the Russians, who were about to seize certain Turkish territories in the vicinity of Oczakov on the Black Sea, he was unable to obtain support in England for a war in defense of Turkey. He was forced to accept this extension of Russian possessions.

THE FRENCH REVOLUTION

Meanwhile events were taking place in France which were to reshape the political and social structure of Europe and to have a profound effect upon England. We are apt to think of Britain in the eighteenth century as aristocratic and oligarchical; yet England was democratic in comparison with France. In France, without the principle of primogeniture, there were some 110,000 nobles who enjoyed a disproportionate amount of wealth and privilege at the expense of the rest of the nation. They owned almost half the land, monopolized the higher offices in the church and in the government, and were enriched further by frequent gifts from the King. They paid practically no taxes. The wealthier nobles lived at Versailles; the others remained in the provincial cities or on their estates. Yet the nobles as a whole were dissatisfied, feeling that they had lost their ancient rights. Their discontent helped to prepare the way for the Revolution.

Below the nobility were the bourgeoisie, a middle class of lawyers, doctors, and bureaucrats, of merchants, manufacturers, and heads of guilds, many of them prosperous, intelligent, and educated. The most modern and progressive part of the nation, they were irritated by the privileges of the nobility and by the rigid class distinctions dividing society. Yet, speaking very broadly, the middle class was not dissatisfied; it could normally obtain what it wanted. But when ordinances went forth summoning the Estates General to meet in 1789, the middle class discovered that voting was to be by estate, of which there were three: the church, the nobility, and the third estate representing everybody else, though its delegates were drawn from the middle class. The middle class believed that it was being cheated; its self-respect was deeply wounded. Hence it was goaded into beginning its own revolution.

At the bottom of French society were the peasants, who formed the mass of the population. They were for the most part freemen and were probably better off than the peasants in other parts of the Continent, but their lot was hard enough. They lived in poverty; yet they paid most of the taxes. They owed labor and produce to the seigneur, tithes to the church, oppressive payments to the state. The old three-field system of agriculture still prevailed, so that the peasant received no great return for his labor, and of that small return he could keep only a fraction for himself.

These conditions might have been borne had the government been efficient and successful. It was not. The King claimed to rule by divine right and to be the embodiment of the state, but he was merely the captive of an evil system of government which brought extravagance at court and confusion in every department of administration. Although the kingdom was bankrupt, vested interests defied attempts at reform. The conviction arose that the existing state of affairs was unnecessary and absurd. Clever writers like Voltaire scoffed at weaknesses in the government and in the church, scholars like Montesquieu and Diderot pointed to the necessity for change, democrats like Rousseau proclaimed the natural rights of the common man. The American Revolution supplied a stirring example of what a determined people could do.

We cannot do more than outline the course of the Revolution. Once the Estates General was assembled in 1789, the third estate declared itself a National Assembly and assumed control. It was protected by the Paris mob. The early work of the Assembly was of fundamental importance: the abolition of feudalism, serfdom, and all feudal dues; the abrogation of special privilege; the declaration that all classes should be taxed on a basis of equality; and the ending of tithes. In some ways these declarations only confirmed what had taken place, for the peasants had risen in many parts of the country, had expelled the nobles, and had taken the land for themselves. The National Assembly meanwhile declared that men were born free and equal, with rights to "liberty, property, security, and resistance to oppression." Religious toleration, freedom of the press, and free speech were guaranteed, as was the right of every citizen to have a voice in the selection of officials.

The work of the Assembly was marred by certain errors. It buttressed the sinking credit of the state by seizing the property of the church, an act which alienated the clergy and was to cause great trouble. The Assembly also decreed a constitution in 1791 which was idealistic and impractical. It made the King responsible for good government but denied him the power to achieve it. As a result he was constantly at odds with the Assembly. Meanwhile the country was faced with invasion and other dangers, and a break occurred between the bourgeoisie, who had controlled the Revolution so far, and the lower classes, who felt they were being excluded from its benefits. In August 1792 the mob in Paris rose in revolt, and the more radical elements seized power. France was declared a republic, the King and Queen were executed, nobles and bourgeoisie alike were sent to the guillotine. This Reign of Terror lasted about a year in 1793 and 1794. Then, following the fall of Robespierre in 1794, more moderate groups among the revolutionaries regained control and set up a government known as the Directory in 1795. But it was weak and corrupt and in 1799 was overthrown by its most brilliant general, Napoleon Bonaparte, who made himself the head of the state as First Consul and became the Emperor of the French in 1804.

ENGLAND AND THE FRENCH REVOLUTION

The first events of the Revolution were well received in England. When Fox heard of the fall of the Bastille, he exclaimed, "How much the greatest event that has happened in the world and how much the best." English reformers rejoiced to see a progressive spirit in France. Political societies, formed to celebrate the centenary of 1688, remained in existence to acclaim the French. Poets found it "bliss to be alive." Even conservative Englishmen were glad to see constitutional monarchy replacing absolutism, and if France chose to weaken herself by internal strife, so much the better.

But as the Revolution grew more violent and radical, as the lower classes obtained control, as monarchy ended in bloody butchery, as the intervention of Austria and Prussia was repulsed, English opinion altered and the English upper classes first became disgusted, then alarmed, then panic stricken. Seeing the awesome power of the mob, they were convinced that the principles of the French Revolution, if applied in England, would bring about their destruction. It was Burke who first sounded a note of terror in his *Reflections on the Revolution in France*, published in October 1790. With his belief in the sanctity of ancient institutions and his veneration for the aristocracy, he regarded the Revolution as a catastrophe. Unless it was crushed it would spread to other countries, ruin the civilization of Europe, and lead to an orgy in which cutthroats persuaded the mob to guillotine Kings, despoil churches, and confiscate the property of the well-to-do. Burke made a profound impression, giving a strong conservative bias to English society and politics. He was answered by Tom Paine's book, *The Rights of Man*, which only increased the terror of the upper classes. Paine, though of Quaker origin, was a firebrand in politics. In America he had urged the colonists to revolt. Now in England he declared that government was derived from the people, that the monarchy and the House of Lords should be abolished, and that a democratically elected House of Commons should take control. His book was revolutionary propaganda, displaying little patriotism and little self-restraint.

A number of radical societies sprang up in England. Their leadership did not come from Fox or from the poorest class of industrial workers, but from lower middle-class persons, such as John Telwall, a tailor and attorney's clerk, and Thomas Hardy, a shoemaker, backed by "artisans, shopkeepers, dissenting ministers, and schoolmasters."[2] They were men of some ability, very conscious of their lack of privilege. The societies talked the jargon of the Revolution, cor-

[2] Quoted in J. Steven Watson, *The Reign of George III 1760–1815* (Oxford: Clarendon Press, 1960), p. 357.

responded with clubs and societies in France, rejoiced in French victories, and passed resolutions assuring the French that English arms would never be used against them. The London Corresponding Society, founded by Thomas Hardy in 1792, aimed at a national organization based on local committees. It held a convention in Edinburgh in 1793 which challenged authority by acting as though it would substitute itself for Parliament. After England and France went to war in 1793, the radicals talked as though they sympathized with the enemy; the high price of food led to riots in the industrial towns; a stone was thrown at the glass carriage in which George III was riding to open Parliament; and Ireland was close to rebellion.

Yet there was really no danger of revolution in England. The clubs, for the most part, were frothy and clamorous rather than violent. Even the Corresponding Society, basing its radicalism on John Locke (with a spice of Rousseau) did not talk of revolution but of manhood suffrage, annual Parliaments, less expensive government, and a simplified legal system. Nonetheless, the country gentlemen in the Commons may perhaps be forgiven if they became alarmed. They were acquiring a philosophy. Following Burke, they reverenced ancient institutions, but they went further. Fiercely on the defensive, they were determined to preserve the position of the upper classes. Maintenance of the *status quo* was all important; fear of radical upheaval became hysterical. Pitt assumed a new significance: he was valued above all as the resolute opponent of French ideas.

The difference of opinion between Burke, who continued to denounce the French Revolution, and Fox, who continued to praise it, led eventually to a split in the opposition. The two men quarreled openly in the Commons in 1791. The Duke of Portland, the leader of the more conservative wing of the opposition, was urged to come to terms with Pitt. Negotiations in 1792 for a more broadly based Cabinet came to nothing. For some time Portland remained loyal to Fox, not wishing to break the party. But early in 1793 his followers began to join Pitt as individuals, and in 1794 Portland formally moved into support of the government. Pitt's majority became overwhelming, for Fox was left in hopeless opposition with some ninety followers. His quarrel with Fox ended Burke's political career. For a time Burke took his place on the ministerial side, then dropped out of public life.

A long series of repressive measures followed. A proclamation in 1793 against seditious writings warned that a conspiracy was under way against the state. An Aliens Act placed foreigners under strict surveillance; habeas corpus was suspended; a Treasonable Practices Act extended treason to the writing or speaking of words inciting to treason; and a Seditious Meetings Act prohibited gatherings of more than fifty persons without prior notice to a local magistrate, who might stop the meeting at any time. The press was controlled; clubs and societies were forbidden; trials and convictions were savage. But when Hardy and others were tried for treason in 1794, with death as the penalty demanded by the state, they were acquitted, and Pitt received a warning that repression must not be carried too far. Gradually the fire went out of the clubs, partly because of Pitt's measures, partly because of disillusion over the course of events in France. An agitation among the lower classes in 1798 was not revolutionary; it was industrial, inspired by hard times and high prices. It was answered by the Combination Acts (1799–1800), which prohibited any combination or union of workingmen for any purpose whatever. This legislation sprang from fear of the new industrial proletariat and formed a prelude to the class struggles of the nineteenth century.

PITT AS A WAR MINISTER

The French War, 1793–1797

In February 1793 France declared war on England, Holland, and Spain. In the summer of 1792 Austria and Prussia had invaded France, intent on crushing the Revolution. But the French, keyed to a high pitch of patriotic zeal, had checked the invaders at Valmy in September and had forced them to retreat. The ardor of the French made them aggressive and they pushed into the Rhineland and into Savoy. Promising assistance to any people who sought to overthrow their rulers, the French invaded the Austrian Netherlands, won the Battle of Jemappes, threatened Holland, and declared that the Scheldt River, closed to commerce by international agreements, should now be opened. To open the Scheldt, which connected Antwerp with the North Sea, was to overthrow the commercial balance of the area. It was a fixed principle of English policy to prevent France from dominating the Austrian Netherlands and Holland. Hence Pitt reluctantly accepted the challenge of war in 1793.

Although Pitt was to guide the war for many years, he was not a good war minister. "He had neither Chatham's eye for a campaign, his power of sifting the primary from the secondary aim, nor his magical faculty of selecting and inspiring the right commanders."[3] England's strategic objective in 1793 should have been a direct thrust at the heart of France, but Pitt entered the war with very limited aims. He believed that there were certain areas of Europe—the Austrian Netherlands, the Mediterranean, the Baltic—which were vital to British interests, and these must be defended. But he did not plan to fight on the Continent as a principal. The fighting there should be left to Britain's allies, to whom Pitt was ready to give handsome subsidies. England's true interests, he believed, lay outside Europe: his aim was to capture French trade and French colonies, especially in the West Indies.

This, in a general way, had been Chatham's policy, but times had changed. Chatham had fought the effete France of Louis XV and Madame de Pompadour; Pitt fought a France with a new spirit, a nation in arms, with patriotic troops and ruthless commanders, soon to be reinforced by the genius of Napoleon Bonaparte. Chatham's ally on the Continent had been Frederick the Great; Pitt was allied with the reactionary and hesitant powers of Austria, Prussia, and Russia, all more intent on the partition of Poland than on the war with France. England had been more warlike in 1756 than she was in 1793. In a word, Pitt's task was so much more difficult than that of his father that comparisons are perhaps unfair; if Pitt had fought the Seven Years' War he might well have won it.

Nonetheless, his blunders are obvious. He expanded the army in an unfortunate way which allowed some men to buy exemptions from service and took others into the militia when they should have gone into the regular army. For many years there was no commander in chief; and Dundas, who became Secretary for War, was no better strategist than Pitt. Pitt placed too much confidence

---

[3] J. Holland Rose, *A Short Life of William Pitt*, p. 114.

in English gold. He constantly underrated the strength of France and overrated the power of his allies. He could not understand how France, without money or prestige, could withstand the nations allied against her. These nations—Austria, Prussia, Sardinia, Spain, Naples, and Portugal, with a promise of help from Russia which never came—Pitt formed into the First Coalition. The word "coalition" implies a closer alliance than really existed. The one point on which the allies were united was their common desire to secure British funds. Above all, Pitt made the error of scattering his energies in many small expeditions, none of them strong enough to achieve its objectives.

As a result there were years of dismal failure. A British army sent to aid the Austrians in the Netherlands in 1793 met at first with some success but lacked both strength and leadership. The Austrians wasted time in reducing fortresses when they should have invaded France. Eventually the British retreated into Holland, then into Hanover, and finally were evacuated at Bremen in 1795. The French secured both Flanders and Holland, obtaining possession of the Dutch fleet. British expeditions to cooperate with French peasants revolting against the government in Paris were also failures because the peasants could not obtain a foothold on the coast. For a few months in 1793 an English fleet, sent to protect Sardinia and Naples from French invasion, occupied the naval base of Toulon, but abandoned it later in the year.

Britain met with some success at sea and in the West Indies. On June 1, 1794, Admiral Howe mauled a French fleet some 400 miles off the coast of Brittany and Pitt carried forward his plan of capturing the French and Dutch colonies. His principal effort was against the French West Indies. A number of islands were taken, but the cost in human life was high. By 1796 the British had lost 40,000 dead; as many more were made unfit for military service. For Pitt and Dundas to pour half the army into the West Indies to fight rebellious Negroes and to die of yellow fever was, to say the least, a grave error in judgment.

After two years of war the French army had not been defeated and the French navy had not been destroyed; even their seaborne trade, though greatly diminished, had not disappeared. Worse was to follow.

Between 1795 and 1797 the First Coalition broke up. Prussia, having spent Pitt's money in Poland, made peace with France and lapsed into spineless neutrality. Spain and the small Italian state of Tuscany abandoned the struggle in 1795. The French were thus free to concentrate against Austria. Led by their brilliant young general, Napoleon Bonaparte, they defeated one Austrian army after another and imposed the Peace of Campo Formio in 1797. Austria ceded the Netherlands, accepted the Rhine as France's eastern frontier, and agreed to abandon Italy except for Venice. The first half of 1797 was a bad time for England, now fighting alone against France. Taxation was extremely heavy, food was scarce, prices were cruelly high. So much gold had been sent to Austria in a vain attempt to keep her in the war that a financial crisis developed in London. Ireland was restive. A mutiny in the fleets off Portsmouth and off the mouth of the Thames was due to bad conditions, niggardly pay, and the low character of some seamen. A demand for peace arose in England; talks were held with the French at Lille, but they came to nothing.

Revival of British Sea Power

The mutiny in the fleets was only a passing episode. The last quarter of the eighteenth century was notable for a marked revival of British sea power.

A generation of famous admirals—Rodney, Howe, Keppel, Hood—steadily improved the fighting quality of the navy and gave it a new spirit. In 1795 Admiral John Jervis, sent to command the fleet in the Mediterranean, raised its morale by combining rigid discipline with greater attention to the welfare of the crews and to the details of naval administration. He trained some fine captains, of whom Horatio Nelson was to become the most famous. Nelson's fighting genius and his chieftain's experience and professional competence formed an excellent combination. British sea power revived only just in time, for late in 1796 the French tried to invade Ireland. But their fleet was scattered by a month of storms and they failed to accomplish their goal. Although the French had acquired the navies of both Spain and Holland, these fleets had been destroyed by the end of 1797. Early in that year Jervis won a decisive victory over the Spanish fleet off Cape St. Vincent near Cadiz, a battle in which a bold maneuver by Nelson added to the impact of the British assault. In October Admiral Duncan destroyed a large portion of the Dutch fleet off the coast of Holland. These victories ended for the time any threat of French invasion.

The navy played a great part in the fighting in 1798, the year in which Napoleon conceived his plan for an expedition to Egypt as a step toward French control of the Mediterranean and toward the ultimate conquest of India. After capturing Malta, Napoleon was soon established in Egypt. The British sent Nelson after him. Nelson was the supreme embodiment of fighting spirit at sea, as Napolean was on land. But there was much more to the "Nelson touch" than desperate courage and joy in combat. He had the power of instant decision and he was a master of naval tactics, which he planned and discussed with his captains, his "band of brothers," until each captain knew what was expected of him in almost any circumstance. Nelson's patriotism, his devotion to duty, and his confidence of victory made him a spiritual force. His object was not the defeat but the annihilation of the enemy. Entering the Mediterranean, he at first had some difficulty in locating Napoleon's squadron. At sundown on August 1, 1798, he found it in an exposed anchorage in Aboukir Bay at the Rosetta Mouth of the Nile. He attacked instantly, the forward ships of his line coming in on both sides of the enemy's van, so that the concentration of numbers was 8 to 5. The French, caught unaware, received a crippling bombardment. Of thirteen French warships only two escaped destruction or capture in one of the most overwhelming defeats in naval history. Control of the Mediterranean was won at a blow; Napoleon was left a hopeless adventurer cut off from France.

This victory enabled Pitt to form the Second Coalition of Great Britain, Austria, Russia, and a number of smaller powers. At first it met with success. In southern Germany the French were driven back to the Rhine. Suvorov, the able general of Czar Paul of Russia, commanding a Russo-Austrian army in northern Italy, for some time carried all before him. The Bourbon ruler of Naples was emboldened to attack the French, though he was quickly defeated. These successes soon melted away, and the Second Coalition dissolved in 1799 and 1800 for much the same reasons that had ruined the first. The Austrians acted selfishly, leaving Suvorov to fight alone while they tried to enlarge their territories. Nelson displayed personal weakness by falling under the influence of Lady Hamilton, a blonde of easy morals who was living in Naples. Pitt sent no troops to Italy, but dispatched an expedition against Holland which was a failure. In August 1799, Napoleon, deserting his army in Egypt, slipped back to France. Within a year he defeated Austria, forcing upon her a peace which left him master of western Europe. Russia had withdrawn from the coalition, and England was once more alone.

Sea power, however, enabled England to defeat the French in Egypt and to capture Malta. When it appeared that the Danish fleet would fall into French hands, an English squadron was sent to the Baltic. Its admiral was the rather cautious Sir Hyde Parker, but Nelson was second in command, and at the Battle of Copenhagen he destroyed much of the Danish fleet. From this engagement emerges the most famous of Nelson stories. At a critical moment Parker signaled to discontinue action, but Nelson, putting his telescope to his blind eye (lost in fighting in Corsica), disregarded the signal. The war was becoming one in which France appeared invincible on land and England invincible at sea.

The Union with Ireland, 1800

In March 1801 England was stunned by the news that Pitt had resigned. He resigned over Ireland, and we must turn for a moment to Irish affairs. Until the middle of the eighteenth century Ireland had lain prostrate under the religious and economic code imposed upon her after 1688. Then conditions began slowly to improve, bitterness between Catholics and Protestants diminished, and many of the penal laws were laxly enforced. Ireland achieved a modest prosperity. A society of some wealth, culture, and learning arose in Dublin. The Irish House of Commons began to agitate against the restrictions by which it was bound.

Despite these stirrings, the institutions of the country were firmly in the hands of the Protestant minority and were controlled from England. The upper clergy and the senior officials in Ireland were appointed by the Cabinet in London as part of its normal patronage; scarcely an Irishman was to be found in the higher ranks. The Irish establishment in both church and state was far more elaborate and costly than the country required. Even by English standards the Irish Parliament was narrow and corrupt: no Catholic could vote in an election or be a member, Presbyterians were excluded in practice because various tests debarred them from the town corporations which controlled the majority of elections, and Poynings' law,[4] restricting the Irish Parliament, was still in force. By an act of 1719 the English Parliament possessed the right to make laws that were binding in Ireland.

The American and French revolutions gave Ireland an opportunity to strike for freer government and freer trade. As troops were withdrawn from Ireland to be sent to America and as the danger of French invasion mounted, both Protestant and Catholic Irishmen enrolled in a national militia known as the United Volunteers which eventually had 80,000 members. At the same time a group of reformers appeared in the Irish Parliament, led by Henry Grattan and Henry Flood, who used the threat of Irish revolt to obtain concessions from Britain. In the years between 1778 and 1783 England yielded a number of important points: Roman Catholics were permitted to inherit property and to hold long leases; the Acts of Trade were modified; Irishmen were allowed to trade with the British colonies; and the Irish Parliament was given its independence. Poynings' law, enacted under Henry VII, and the Act of 1719 were repealed; the Irish Parliament could legislate as it wished, though the English Crown retained a veto; and the English Parliament ceased to pass laws concerning Ireland. The Irish, however, had not obtained self-government. Their Parliament was elected on so

---

[4] See page 212.

narrow a franchise that it could be controlled through patronage and the manipulation of pocket boroughs. It possessed no power over the executive officials in Dublin Castle, who were appointed in England. Religious disabilities and a wretched agrarian system continued.

The French Revolution brought wilder hopes and passions. Irish radicals, looking to France for aid, dreamed of complete independence—the goal of the Society of United Irishmen, founded in 1791 by Wolfe Tone, though its nominal purpose was to press for parliamentary reform. The society at first included both Catholics and Protestants, but animosities arose between the two religious groups. Catholics clamored for admission to Parliament but, though they obtained the vote in 1793, they still were excluded from membership. Fear of French radicalism and French invasion rallied the Protestants to the support of the government, but many Catholics were ready to cooperate with France. Secret societies were formed along religious lines—Protestant "Peep-o'-Day Boys" against Catholic "Defenders." The government caught the spirit of panic which prevailed in England. It permitted Protestant magistrates and militiamen to suppress the Catholics; the irregular troops, in the name of law and order, committed outrages—torturing, flogging, and shooting in cold blood. The result, a Catholic revolt in 1798, was never formidable and was easily suppressed.

Watching these developments, Pitt became convinced that in such dangerous times the Irish Parliament could not be allowed freedom of action. As was true of England and Scotland before the union of 1707, independent Parliaments in England and Ireland could and did take conflicting action on very important issues. Pitt came to believe that there must be a legislative union by which the Irish Parliament would cease to exist and Irish members would be added to the Parliament in London. He planned to couple union with far-reaching reforms. In particular he wished to grant Catholic emancipation, that is, the admission of Catholics to the English House of Commons; he also wished to modify the tithes paid by Irish peasants to the Anglican Church, to provide salaries for the Irish Catholic priesthood, and to establish free trade between the two countries.

Unfortunately he passed the union without the reforms. By the distribution of bribes and pensions, by promotions in the Irish peerage, and by promises that Catholic relief would follow, the Irish Parliament was induced to vote itself out of existence in 1800. One hundred Irish members were added to the English House of Commons; four Irish bishops, sitting according to a scheme of rotation, and twenty-eight lay peers, elected by all the Irish nobles from their own number, were to sit in the English House of Lords. The seats in the Commons were not reserved for Irishmen. On the other hand, since the twenty-eight Irish peers in the Lords were elected for life, other Irish nobles might seek election to the English House of Commons. But when Pitt turned to Catholic emancipation, he met the implacable opposition of the King. George was again on the verge of insanity, and since the very mention of Catholic emancipation disturbed him greatly, Pitt felt that he could not press the issue. He therefore resigned. It is strange that he had not come to an understanding with George earlier, for the King's views were well known. Union without emancipation embittered the Irish Catholics, who felt with some justice that they had been deceived.

Pitt and Cabinet Government

Although the modern system of Cabinet government was still in its infancy, some aspects of it may be seen during Pitt's long tenure of power. In the first place, the King receded from the important role he had played in managing the details of government. This statement may appear to be contradicted by George's successful opposition to Catholic emancipation. Nevertheless, during the second half of his long reign of sixty years, he was relatively passive, due to his fits of insanity. The importance of the Prime Minister therefore was enhanced. Moreover, Pitt did so much of the work himself and towered so completely over his colleagues, that his policy became the policy of the Cabinet. Hence the unity of the Cabinet was increased, as was also the idea of a Cabinet policy which all ministers must support. Finally, Pitt was upheld by a large majority in the Commons, from which he derived his strength. This strength came to him spontaneously and not as the result of corruption. Indeed, the cruder and more blatant forms of corruption gradually were disappearing. These developments looked toward modern practice, though the Cabinet system as we know it today was far in the future.

THE PEACE OF AMIENS, 1802

Pitt was succeeded as Prime Minister by his friend Henry Addington, who had been Speaker of the House of Commons for many years. An extremely conservative and cautious man, Addington possessed common sense and reliability but no great talent. He represented the war weariness of many Englishmen. Although he regarded the war with France as just, he was ready to end it in a draw because of its great expense. In opposing any kind of domestic reform as dangerous experimentation he seems to have personified the mood of the moment. With only a small following of his own in the Commons, he received that general support which many members had grown accustomed to give to the government of the day. He had very few friends among the leading politicians. But with the support of the King, Pitt, and a majority in the Commons, his administration seemed likely to last for some time.

Addington stood for peace and retrenchment. He opened negotiations for peace with France. Napoleon, on his side, welcomed a breathing space but drove a hard bargain. Except for Ceylon (captured from the Dutch) and Trinidad (captured from Spain), England restored all the colonies taken from France and her dependencies, whereas Napoleon promised little more than to evacuate Egypt and to withdraw from southern Italy. This one-sided peace was possible only because the English assumed that Napoleon, in the Treaty of Lunéville with Austria in 1801, had guaranteed the independence of Switzerland, Holland, and northern Italy. Addington then began to cut down the size of the army and navy and to concentrate on financial reform. At first the peace was popular in England. Fox and other liberals visited Paris to wonder at the military pomp of Napoleon's court and to admire the works of art he had stolen from the rest of Europe. It soon became clear, however, that Napoleon had no thought of enduring peace. He continued his aggressive policies: armed peace was to carry on the work of war. Hostilities with England began again in May 1803 after a cessation of fourteen months.

Addington thought in terms of a defensive war, but his military preparations for even this limited objective were so bungled and his prospects as a war minister appeared so dim that opposition mounted in the Commons and he resigned in May 1804. Pitt then returned to office. He wished to form a Cabinet of complete national unity in preparation for a great struggle, but quarrels and bickerings had developed among politicians. The Commons were now divided into four main groups. Pitt could muster about 58 followers; Fox, about 70; Lord Grenville, formerly allied with Pitt but now separated from him by a quarrel, also about 70. Before his resignation Addington was supported by some 230 members, though this number declined after he left office. Thus Pitt was compelled to form a narrow ministry from his own followers and from those of Addington, though the two groups disliked each other. It was not a strong Cabinet. It consisted, said the wits, of William and Pitt. Henceforth Pitt had to devote time and energy to political maneuvers merely to remain in office.

THE WAR, 1803–1815

Napoleon at the Height of His Power

"Make us master of the Channel for three days," Napoleon had once said in his grand way, "and we are masters of the world." Addington's concentration on defense gave Napoleon the opportunity to bring his army to the Channel ports of France. Fortunately the French plans were mismanaged Napoleon hoped at first to rely on surprise and to take his army across the Channel on a dark night in small boats armed only to resist light attack. Then he concluded that a French fleet must have temporary control of the Channel. In 1805 there were French squadrons at the naval bases of Brest, Rochefort, and Toulon, and Spanish ships at Cadiz, and El Ferrol. They were blockaded by English units, but the English could not watch all of them all the time. The French units at Rochefort and Toulon evaded the blockade and sailed for the West Indies. This was intended at first merely as a diversion, but Napoleon conceived the idea that if his fleets could rendezvous in the West Indies, they might return to Europe together, pick up the Spanish units, and hold the Channel long enough for a French army to cross to England. The plan miscarried, partly because fleets could not be moved on an exact timetable, partly because the Toulon fleet, which Nelson followed to the West Indies, failed to effect its junction with the main French fleet, but chiefly because Austria reentered the war against France in August 1805.

Pitt's countermove against the threat of invasion had been to construct a Third Coalition of Britain, Russia, and Austria. Its existence was brief. Abandoning the plan of invasion, Napoleon quickly turned his armies eastward. On October 20, 1805, he defeated the Austrian vanguard at Ulm. On December 2 he crushed the combined Austrian and Russian armies at Austerlitz, perhaps the greatest of his victories. When Pitt heard the news, his face assumed what was called the "Austerlitz look," his frail health gave way, and in January 1806 he died.

England, too, won a great victory. On October 21, 1805, the day after the Battle of Ulm, the French Admiral Villeneuve sailed from Cadiz with a French and Spanish fleet in a dash for the Mediterranean. Off Cape Trafalgar he was met by Nelson. The French and Spanish line extended in a great half-moon. Dividing the bulk of his fleet into two attacking columns, Nelson dared to approach the enemy almost at right angles. His forward ships were badly mauled, but he broke the enemy line and inflicted an overwhelming defeat in which eighteen ships were captured or destroyed. Nelson was killed in this action. The effects of Trafalgar were far reaching. Napoleon's naval power was ended for the time being, though it was later to revive; a French invasion of England became impossible. Each side looked for new ways to attack the other. To the English, Trafalgar suggested the possibility of a land front which could be sustained from the sea.

On land Napoleon continued his victories. King Frederick William III, the foolish ruler of Prussia, after leaning toward alliance with Napoleon, suddenly declared war against him in 1806. At the Battle of Jena in October Prussia was totally defeated. Her military power collapsed, Napoleon entered Berlin in triumph, and Prussia was shorn of large portions of her dominions. In the following year, after defeating Russia at the Battle of Friedland, Napoleon made an alliance at Tilsit with the impressionable young Czar, Alexander I. Napoleon's power had reached its height. His supremacy in Europe appeared impregnable. French ideas in government, in law, and in education, as well as in war, were accepted and admired throughout the Continent.

English Politics, 1806–1815

Pitt's Cabinet broke up after his death in 1806. The King accepted a coalition drawn from the opposition. It was known as the Ministry of All the Talents because it included Fox, Lord Grenville, and Addington (now Lord Sidmouth). In reality the new Cabinet was narrowly Foxite. Fox proved to be a good man in office, both as a leader and as a colleague, though he accomplished little against Napoleon either in war or in diplomacy. Having opposed Pitt's coalitions with continental powers, Fox tried again to make peace only to discover that an honorable peace with Napoleon was impossible. He might have held office for a long time, but he died in 1806. The one important domestic measure of the ministry was the abolition of the slave trade throughout the empire. On another liberal issue, a proposal to admit Roman Catholics to high office in the armed forces, the Cabinet encountered the opposition both of the King and of many members of the Commons. Thereupon the Cabinet broke up.

It is possible, in speaking of the Ministry of All the Talents, to use the terms "Whig" and "Tory" without confusion. Fox's heirs were Whigs. Pitt, who had never ceased to call himself a Whig, was now dead; and George Canning, one of his disciples now coming into prominence, adopted the word "Tory" to denote his conservative principles.

Yet in 1807 the groups in the Commons again were broken and divided. A Tory Cabinet was patched up under the Duke of Portland (1807–1809), an elderly and rather slow-witted man. Its interest lies largely in his younger colleagues, who were to give the country Tory government for many years to come. One was Lord Eldon, not young at fifty-six, but destined to remain in politics for a long time. He was an ultraconservative lawyer who opposed change of any kind. Another lawyer, Spencer Perceval, who succeeded Portland as Prime Minister in 1809, was also very conservative, especially on the Catholic question, but he possessed a good mind and great courage; he was a "gallant fighter," both as a speaker in the Commons and as an enemy of Napoleon.

This Cabinet also contained Lord Castlereagh, the eldest son of the Irish Marquis of Londonderry. A brilliant diplomat and man of action, Castlereagh was calm and unruffled in demeanor, with a simple and massive dignity, though with no great skill in debate. Cautious and sound, with solidity of character and judgment, he acquired an extensive experience in foreign affairs. More than any other man, he held the foes of Napoleon together until victory was won and a settlement of Europe achieved. Portland's Cabinet included George Canning, the son of an Irishman of good family but of straitened circumstances who had come to London to live by his pen, had failed, and had died in despair. Canning's mother was an actress, a woman of great beauty. Young Canning was well educated by an uncle, entered politics, and became a follower of Pitt. An able administrator, a shrewd and daring diplomat, a brilliant speaker, he was, unfortunately, egotistical, difficult, and ambitious, with a sharp tongue that earned him enemies. Disliking Castlereagh, he intrigued against him. The two men fought a duel in 1809 and both resigned from the Cabinet. Castlereagh came back as Foreign Secretary in 1812, a position he retained for a decade. Canning was out for a longer period, holding only minor office until 1822, when he succeeded his rival as Foreign Secretary. Another member of this Cabinet was Lord Liverpool, who was to be Prime Minister for an extraordinary length of time, from 1812 to 1827. His principal talent was his ability to keep difficult colleagues working together as a team. These men pushed the war with new vigor and with more strategic insight than had prevailed in the days of Pitt.

The Decline of Napoleon

After 1808 the nature of the war began to change. Although Napoleon was older and naturally more inclined to take his ease, he retained more authority than any one man, however brilliant, could hope to employ properly. The character of his army also altered. When he had first led it to victory, it had been inspired by patriotism and by the ideals of the Revolution. But these ideas were fading: the army was now selfish and materialistic—a host of mercenaries who followed a plundering tyrant for their own advantage. Napoleon quartered his troops outside France, forcing other nations to support them. Because of this heavy burden France began to be considered, not as a liberator, but as a despot which squeezed the lifeblood from its victims. Resentment fostered a sense of nationality among the exploited peoples. The ideals of liberty, equality, and fraternity, taking root in Germany, Spain, and elsewhere, worked against Napoleon and not for him. Because of England's resistance, his rule meant constant war: he brought neither peace, nor prosperity, nor permanence.

Napoleon's Continental System angered Europe and prepared the way for his downfall. Knowing that he could not defeat England by invasion, he attempted to ruin her economy by excluding her goods from Europe. By a series of decrees between 1806 and 1810 he commanded that every country under his control or in alliance with him refuse to admit British manufactures or raw materials from British colonies. The English answered by a number of orders in council which declared Europe to be in a state of blockade, cut off from trade with the rest of the world. England suffered from the Continental System, especially between 1810 and 1812, and became involved in quarrels with neutral countries who wished to trade with the Continent. These difficulties were the principal cause of a short war with the United States (1812–1814). But it became evident that the Continent suffered more from the blockade than England did from lack of markets. Italy and Holland saw their commerce throttled; Germany and Russia could obtain neither manufactured articles nor tropical products. Moreover, if the Continental System were to be effective, it must be universal. Napoleon was drawn into new ventures, into control of Scandinavia, into attacks on Portugal and Spain, and finally into war with Russia. His empire became over-extended because every corner of the Continent must be sealed away from trade with England.

In 1808 the English sent an army to the Continent once more. In the preceding year Napoleon had attacked Portugal in order to tighten the Continental System. In 1808, having an army in Spain, he deposed the Spanish ruling house, though he was in alliance with it, and installed his brother Joseph as King of that country. The result was a Spanish uprising. For the first time Napoleon found himself at war with a continental people fired by the spirit of nationalism. Although the Spanish could not face his armies in the field, they were excellent guerrillas and their constant attacks and ambushes forced him to keep large garrisons in Spain. In July 1808 Sir Arthur Wellesley, later the Duke of Wellington, was sent with a small army to drive the French from Portugal. This he succeeded in doing but he was then superseded by other English generals. One of them, Sir John Moore, after a daring raid into Spain, was forced to retreat over desolate country in winter weather and evacuate his shattered army at Corunna. The English were discouraged. Nonetheless, the government persevered, and Wellesley (now Lord Wellington) returned to Portugal in 1809. Thenceforth there was always a British front in Spain and Portugal. Sometimes Wellington could move into Spain, sometimes he could merely hold his position in Portugal. Eventually he defeated the French at Salamanca (1812) and at Vitoria (1813), fought his way through the Pyrenees, and invaded southern France late in 1813.

Meanwhile, Napoleon was in grave trouble. Nationalism spread to Austria, and though that country again was defeated in 1809 at the Battle of Wagram, the Austrians remained thoroughly hostile. A national revival took place in Prussia, where the people turned fiercely against the French despot. Finally a rupture took place between Napoleon and Alexander of Russia. Alexander had many reasons for resentment, but the principal cause of the war was his partial abandonment of the Continental System. Napoleon must either fight Russia or give up his one great weapon against Great Britain. His invasion of Russia and his retreat from Moscow during the winter of 1812 were disastrous. All Europe turned against him. In the three-day Battle of Leipzig he was driven from Germany. His empire beyond France quickly collapsed. During the first months of 1814 he fought in France with great skill against a number of invading armies, but their pressure made resistance hopeless. In April Napoleon abdicated as Emperor and was sent to the island of Elba, off the west coast of Italy. In May the allies signed the Treaty of Paris with Louis XVIII of the Bourbon line of Kings, now restored in France. But many questions remained to be settled by a congress of powers which met in Vienna in September. While the victors were negotiating and quarreling in Vienna, Napoleon suddenly reappeared in France on March 1, 1815, and was soon at the head of a large army. His return united the allies against him. At the Battle of Waterloo in Belgium in June 1815 he was thoroughly defeated by Wellington and by the Prussians under General Blücher. He then was exiled to the island of St. Helena, far away in the South Atlantic Ocean, where he died in 1821.

THE SETTLEMENT OF EUROPE

Castlereagh and Wellington, who represented England at the Congress of Vienna, believed that Europe would be more peaceful and stable if France were treated well. The Treaty of Paris had restored her frontiers as of 1792 and had returned the bulk of her colonies, but this settlement was made more severe at Vienna. France now received her frontiers of 1790, was forced to pay a large indemnity, to support an army of occupation until the money was paid, and to return the works of art which Napoleon had looted from the capitals of Europe. Yet even this was generous treatment.

In order to restrain France from aggression in the future, Castlereagh sought to strengthen the states along her borders. Belgium was placed under the King of Holland, Prussia was given lands along the Rhine, the Kingdom of Sardinia was enlarged, Austria dominated the rest of northern Italy. In central Europe Castlereagh hoped to strengthen Prussia and Austria as a counterpoise to Russia in the east and France in the west. Here he was less successful. Although all three of the eastern powers obtained increased territories, Russia received the lion's share—Finland in the north, most of Poland in the center, and Bessarabia from Turkey in the south.

England's gains were colonial. During the war she had swept up not only the French possessions overseas but also the whole of the Dutch empire in the Malay Archipelago. These colonies now were returned except for Ceylon, ceded by Holland in 1802, and the French West Indian islands of Tobago and St. Lucia. In the Caribbean area England also acquired Trinidad from Spain and a portion of Dutch Guiana from Holland. In the east she kept French Mauritius and the Seychelle Islands. She also retained the Cape of Good Hope, for which she paid Holland a compensation of £2 million, to be used in building fortifications against France. In European waters England obtained Heligoland in the North Sea, Malta in the Mediterranean, and the Ionian Islands in the Aegean.

These possessions made her the greatest imperial power in the world and gave her a firm hold on the principal sea lanes of the world's commerce. Her supremacy at sea was undisputed until the end of the nineteenth century.

transition from war
to peace

ENGLAND IN 1815

Englishmen hailed the peace of 1815 with great joy. They had much to be proud of. Of all the nations of Europe they alone had never bowed to Napoleon; rather, they had continued the struggle against him after their allies had collapsed. Their navy had prevented invasion, had broken the sea power of the French, and had made possible the expansion of trade and empire. Their armies had played a great part in defeating Napoleon as had their statesmen in making the peace. The English constitution had weathered the stress of a generation of war. Manufacturers, merchants, and landlords, on the whole, had prospered. Industrial development had made steady progress. As Englishmen considered all this, they drew a sharp distinction between themselves and the peoples on the Continent, whom they regarded with condescension and with a sense of moral superiority.

This was the brighter side of the picture, but there was also a darker side. For many reasons, as we shall see, the transition from war to peace was to be extremely difficult, for other and more fundamental problems existed. England was entering a new age. The old world of the eighteenth century had been shattered by the growth of population, the rise of the northern industrial towns, the American and French revolutions, and the Napoleonic wars. The new world of the early nineteenth century was a harsh world, with sharp distinctions between classes as well as bitter class antagonisms. At the top of society were the nobility and gentry, in the heyday of their power and influence, with their monopoly of political life, their landed estates, their church, their pocket boroughs, their privileged universities. The middle classes included a larger and larger variety of many kinds of people, from rich merchants and bankers to small shopkeepers. But though they were growing in wealth and numbers, they were largely excluded from political power. Below them were the depressed agricultural laborers, the seething mass of industrial workers in the towns, and many special groups, such as miners, sailors, and domestic servants.

The poor were often in desperate straits. Scientific agriculture and high prices for agricultural products had enriched the landowners and tenant farmers but had often inflicted hardship on the rural laborer, who found himself deprived of ancient rights and almost wholly dependent on his wages. A bad harvest, a stretch of unemployment, or a rise in the cost of living could easily reduce him and his family to the verge of starvation. The increase of mills and factories had brought a steady stream of laborers into the towns. These grimy workpeople, living a squalid life in slums and factories, were uneducated, brutal, even savage, totally unorganized and totally unprotected against exploitation and sudden unemployment. Unless the English harvest was abundant, they paid high prices for food, for there had been little opportunity to import grain during the French wars. A bad system of poor relief increased the number of paupers, demoralized the lower classes, and imposed a heavy financial burden on the nation.

England thus was faced with new and difficult problems. Most of her institutions, devised in an earlier and simpler age, were inadequate for the complex problems of the nineteenth century: the poor law was Elizabethan; so was the church which, with its many abuses, its badly distributed revenues, and its neglect of the urban poor, had not been overhauled since the Tudor period; the Acts of Trade, a product of the seventeenth century, were still in force; the universities and the Inns of Court were just awakening from their eighteenth-century slumbers; the law was in great need of reform; there was an exaggerated respect for the rights of property and of vested interest. England might boast of her constitution, but in truth she was inefficiently governed by a small landed aristocracy whose standard of conduct, both in public service and in private morals, was not high. Although the power of the Crown in politics had diminished, it could still influence the composition and actions of the government. The Cabinet system had advanced, yet Cabinet coherence and discipline were still in their infancy, and most ministers thought of themselves as the servants of the King. Above all, Parliament was unreformed: the franchise in the counties was governed by a law of 1430, new boroughs had not been added since 1688, the industrial north was grossly underrepresented. Old Sarum, which was uninhabited, continued to send members to the Commons; Birmingham and Manchester, which were nearing populations of 100,000 each early in the century and doubled in size during the next thirty years, sent none. Reform in a broad sense could hardly be achieved until the House of Commons was reformed.

The French Revolution and the Napoleonic wars came at a most unfortunate time for England. There had been hope of reform after the American war. But the French Revolution frightened the upper classes, ended all possibility of immediate change, and poisoned the relations of rich and poor. Proposals for mild and needed reform were branded as dangerous and radical. Men do not stop to repair their houses, said a member of Parliament, while a hurricane is raging.

There was a deep and unreasoning fear of the mob. A phrase such as the "swinish multitude," heard in the Commons in the early nineteenth century, would not have been used before the Revolution. Any demonstration of discontent on the part of the poor inspired terror as though it was the prelude to insurrection, and men believed that at any time they might be compelled to take up arms against the violence of the lower classes. The word "democracy" was a nasty word, recalling the guillotine and the French Reign of Terror. The years since 1789 had been years of profound economic and social change, but the government, intent on the war, had done nothing to guide the forces of industrial development and rapid urbanization. Employers had managed their factories as they pleased; the new towns had grown up raw and hideous. With reform deferred, with antiquated institutions, with a vast national debt, with inflationary prices and depreciated currency, with suffering among the poor and apprehension among the rich, and with a difficult transition from war to peace, it is no wonder that the years after 1815 were years of stress and conflict.

HARD TIMES, RADICALISM, AND REPRESSION

Agriculture had enjoyed a boom during the war. Landlords who had received good rents and tenant farmers who had enjoyed good incomes were tempted to speculate by growing grain on marginal land which could be farmed profitably only when the price of grain was high. Conditions suddenly altered at the end of the war: grain could be imported from abroad, the government ceased to buy for the armed forces, there was a bumper crop in 1813. The price of grain sank rapidly. Bankrupt farmers laid off their laborers until rural unemployment became a tragedy rendered more acute as demobilized soldiers returned to their villages. The poor rates became so onerous that they dragged down the small yeoman farmers.

Meanwhile, the landowning members of Parliament attempted to raise the price of wheat by legislation. The Corn Law of 1815 prohibited the importation of foreign wheat until the price in England had risen to 80s. a quarter (8 bushels). The act was a failure, for it did not hold the price at 80s., nor did it save the landowning classes from a long period of agricultural depression, but it did arouse the bitter hostility of the poor, who blamed it for the high price of bread. This hostility was shared by the factory owners, who believed that cheaper wheat would mean lower wages. As a matter of fact, however, the price was determined far more by the abundance of the English harvest than by the availability of foreign wheat, and the effect of the Corn Law was exaggerated on both sides. Certainly the Corn Law did not stabilize the price of wheat, which fluctuated violently and fell in 1822 as low as 38s. 10d. The law was so inadequate that in 1828 the government experimented with a sliding scale. Foreign wheat could be imported duty-free when the price was 74s. or above in England; there was a duty of 1s. when the price was 73s.; thereafter the duty rose sharply as the English price declined. This measure, however, led to speculation and was not satisfactory. The price of wheat and the distress of the laborer continued to rise and fall with good or bad harvests. Bad harvests between 1828 and 1831 reduced the rural poor in the south to such abject misery that the starving laborers sought vengeance by burning the hayricks of wealthy landlords. Agriculture remained generally depressed for many years. In fact, it was not until the middle 1830s that conditions improved and a more even prosperity returned to the countryside.

Like agriculture, industry had prospered during the war, but it had been even more speculative. One manufacturer might make enormous profits whereas another, his market suddenly closed by the fortunes of war, might be ruined. The management of a factory posed new problems to which businessmen were as yet unaccustomed. They could not borrow money easily, and once their private capital had been exhausted they could only shut down and discharge their workpeople. They made mistakes in calculating future demand. They were certainly wrong in 1815. Assuming that Europe was eager to buy their goods, they laid in large supplies, only to discover that the Continent was too impoverished to purchase English manufactures and that war orders from the government at home came abruptly to an end.

In these unhappy years trade was badly depressed, wages were cut, factories were closed, and the poor suffered greatly through unemployment. "The Tyneside colliers, the Preston cotton-weavers, the Wiltshire cloth-workers, the jute-workers of Dundee,—all were alike in ferment, demanding more employment, higher wages, and cheaper food."[1] Angry mobs destroyed the machines they thought were robbing them of employment and sacked bakers' and butchers' shops in their search for food. Rioting and arson occurred in Norfolk and Suffolk. A great mob, meeting at Spa Fields in London in 1816 with a notion of sending a petition to the Regent, got out of hand and broke into nearby shops. In 1817 a band of poor weavers in Manchester, desperate at their pitiful wages, determined to march on London. They set out, each carrying a blanket for protection at night, from which their journey was called the March of the Blanketeers, but they soon were dispersed by force.

Although the cause of these disturbances was simply the misery of the poor, popular radicalism was increased by irresponsible demagogues, of whom "Orator" Hunt and William Cobbett were the most famous. Hunt, a rascal but a good public speaker, was violent and thoroughly disreputable. Cobbett was more interesting and more personable. The son of a small farmer and innkeeper, he looked back to the village life of his youth with nostalgia and hated the new industrialism with all his heart. Completely ignorant of economics, he turned easily to abuse and rash statements that excited the passions of the mob. He was not a revolutionist but a kind of John Bull incarnate, and his racy writings were the vigorous protests of the bluff and hearty countryman against the evils of the time. He taught the people to agitate for the reform of Parliament. Other reforms were impossible, he argued, until the electoral system had been widened. It was Parliament which caused bad government and economic distress. But if, by its reform, the poor could obtain a voice in the House of Commons, then by some miracle, which Cobbett did not explain, enlightened legislation could restore the old England that was being destroyed by machines. Cobbett began a radical journal, the *Political Register*, reduced its price from a shilling to twopence, and for a time sold thousands of copies a week. Societies were formed, mass meetings were held, and petitions in favor of reform were sent to the House of Commons. This campaign for a democratic suffrage, however, was a working-class movement from which the middle classes held aloof.

The government offered nothing but repression. Tory ministers, with their fear of the mob, believed that a conspiracy existed to overthrow the government and to despoil the rich. In 1817 the Cabinet suspended habeas corpus, passed harsher measures against seditious meetings, and urged local magistrates to enroll special constables and to make prompt arrests. The number of government spies and informers was increased. Public meetings came to an end. Agitation among the lower classes subsided, partly because of a good harvest in 1817, but rose again in 1819, when another cruel depression in trade brought lowered wages and much unemployment. The bitterness and discontent of the poor

[1] J. A. R. Marriott, *England Since Waterloo* (London: Methuen, 1916), p. 26.

Cartoon of soldiers attacking a gathering at St. Peter's Field in Manchester in 1819, by "Phiz." (The Mansell Collection)

reached alarming proportions and monster meetings of protest were held in many cities. An assembly in Birmingham went through the form of electing a representative to Parliament which was, of course, quite illegal. A meeting in St. Peter's Field in Manchester ended in tragedy. A throng of 50,000 to 60,000 persons, many marching in ranks carrying banners with such slogans as "Annual Parliaments" and "Universal Suffrage," met in orderly fashion to hear a speech by "Orator" Hunt. The magistrates permitted the crowd to assemble; then, losing their nerve, they attempted to arrest Hunt as soon as he appeared. A body of mounted yeomanry was sent to make the arrest. Jostled and pushed about by the crowd, the yeomanry drew their sabers but had to be rescued by a troop of soldiers. In the following panic many persons were trodden under foot, some were sabered, 11 were killed, and some 400 were injured. The government congratulated the magistrates on their conduct, but to the poor the events in St. Peter's Field, renamed Peterloo in mocking comparison with the Battle of Waterloo, became a symbol of harsh tyranny that was long remembered.

The Cabinet then passed six acts to suppress disorder. Three of them, which hastened trials for offenders, prohibited drilling, and authorized search for hidden arms, were reasonable, but the others were very reactionary: they restricted public assemblies, authorized seizure of seditious literature, and increased duties on pamphlets and newspapers. The hostility between rich and poor was growing dangerous.

Two events in 1820 provided the lower classes with an opportunity to express their feelings. One, a wild plot known as the Cato Street Conspiracy, aimed at nothing less than the assassination of the entire Cabinet. It was discovered and crushed, but the lower classes were plainly disappointed that the plot had not succeeded. In the same year a scandal in the royal family permitted the people to display their dislike of and contempt for their rulers. King George III had finally passed away and was succeeded by his disreputable son, George IV (1820-1830). The matrimonial affairs of the new ruler were somewhat unconventional. As a young man in 1785 he had married a Roman Catholic, Mrs. Fitzherbert, a marriage that might have cost him the throne because the King of England could not marry a Catholic. He was saved by another law which provided that the Prince of Wales could not marry legally without his father's consent. Ten years later he married a German princess, Caroline of Brunswick-Wolfenbüttel. He did not like his wife and he treated her with brutality. Some years later Caroline left England and spent her time in Italy, where her conduct was rather indiscreet. When George IV became King he asked the Cabinet to obtain a divorce for him by special act of Parliament. Meanwhile Caroline returned to England and demanded her rights as Queen. The lower classes took up her cause with enthusiasm, pulled her carriage through the streets when she appeared in public, and demonstrated wildly in her favor. The bill for divorce passed the House of Lords, but its prospects in the Commons were so doubtful that it was withdrawn. The Queen died shortly thereafter. This episode, sordid as it was, provided a safety valve for the emotions of the poor and eased the tension between classes. An improvement in trade after 1820 also helped to relieve the crisis.

The Tories who held office in the terrible years following Waterloo should not be regarded as cruel or evil men. Liverpool, the tactful Prime Minister; Eldon, the ultraconservative Lord Chancellor; Wellington, with his great prestige and high sense of duty; Sidmouth, the timid Home Secretary; Castlereagh, the brilliant diplomat—these were men of intelligence and common sense, but they were narrow and unimaginative, without much hope of improving things. Determined to preserve the position of the upper classes, they feared that any change might be for the worse. And it must be remembered that most of the Whigs supported the repressive measures of the Tories and that even though the Cabinet had attempted to give relief to the poor the administrative machinery at its disposal was quite inadequate.

THE BEGINNING OF A MORE LIBERAL ERA

The suicide of Castlereagh in 1822 was followed by a reconstruction of the Cabinet. Liverpool remained as Prime Minister; George Canning became Foreign Secretary and leader of the Tories in the House of Commons; Sir Robert Peel became Home Secretary; and William Huskisson, President of the Board of Trade. It has sometimes been said that these men brought a new liberal tone to the Cabinet. This is not quite correct, for they maintained Tory principles and opposed the reform of Parliament. The change after 1822 was, rather, a change in the temper of the times. The French Revolution was now far in the past, the aftermath of the great war with France had lost its bitterness, and economic conditions were somewhat easier; hence the ultraconservatism of the war generation was softened into a more moderate kind of Tory policy. Canning, Peel, and Huskisson were Tories, but they were not reactionaries; they were conservative but open-minded men. Some of the older type of Tories remained in the Cabinet, however, and this division was to split the party after Liverpool's resignation in 1827. But for a time, from 1822 to 1827, he presided over a strong and able Cabinet.

Canning's Foreign Policy

Canning followed the principles of foreign policy laid down by Castlereagh, but he employed bolder methods and he explained his actions to the British public, which Castlereagh had never done. Hence the change after 1822 appeared more fundamental than it actually was. Both Castlereagh and Canning had to deal with the autocratic states of Austria, Russia, and Prussia, with whom England had formed a Quadruple Alliance, first to defeat Napoleon and later to preserve the peace settlement of 1815. Castlereagh hoped for close cooperation among the great powers, and it was at his suggestion that they agreed to hold periodic conferences to discuss the problems of Europe. But from the first there arose a difference between England and her allies. Austria, Russia, and Prussia were eager to suppress revolutionary movements. Alexander of Russia, in particular, desired the allies to guarantee not only the frontiers but also the existing governments of Europe. To this Castlereagh objected. He was willing to put down any Bonapartist rising in France, but he refused to commit England to a general policy of suppressing revolts or of guaranteeing borders. The test came in 1820, when there were revolts in Spain, Naples, and Portugal against the despotic governments set up in 1815. When the eastern autocracies wished to intervene, Castlereagh refused to meddle in the domestic concerns of small independent states. Thus Castlereagh broke with the Quadruple Alliance before his death, but he regretted the necessity of doing so.

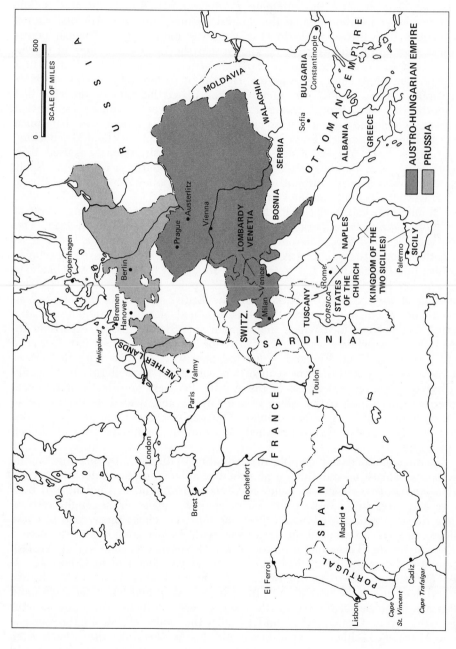

SCALE OF MILES

500

0

RUSSIA

Copenhagen

MOLDAVIA

WALACHIA

BULGARIA

Constantinople

SERBIA

Sofia

BOSNIA

O T T O M A N   E M P I R E

Austerlitz

Vienna

Prague

Berlin

Bremen

Hanover

Heligoland

NETHERLANDS

Valmy

Paris

London

Rochefort

Brest

El Ferrol

Madrid

SPAIN

PORTUGAL

Lisbon

Cape St. Vincent

Cadiz

Cape Trafalgar

ALBANIA

GREECE

LOMBARDY
VENETIA

SWITZ.

Milan

Venice

Rome

TUSCANY

CORSICA

STATES
OF THE
CHURCH

NAPLES

(KINGDOM OF THE
TWO SICILIES)

Palermo

SICILY

S A R D I N I A

Toulon

F R A N C E

AUSTRO-HUNGARIAN EMPIRE

PRUSSIA

Europe in 1815

Canning, on the other hand, welcomed the break, emphasized it in every way he could, and sought to destroy the alliance of the autocratic powers, whom he could not prevent from suppressing the Spanish insurgents and from restoring the former Spanish King, the villainous Ferdinand VII. But it was at this time that revolt was spreading among the Spanish colonies in Latin America, and it was obvious that British trade in that area was increasing as Spanish power declined. Canning therefore let it be known that the European system of repression was not to be extended to the Spanish colonies and that the British fleet would prevent intervention in America. He sought to interest the United States in a similar policy. In 1823 President Monroe issued his famous doctrine that henceforth the New World was not to be considered a sphere for further European colonization. This was somewhat more than Canning had bargained for, especially as Monroe's brave words were rather empty without the backing of the British fleet. Yet the result was that the Spanish colonies secured their independence, and Canning could boast that if the Bourbons ruled over Spain once more it was a Spain without the Indies. British policy stood forth as liberal in contrast to the tyranny on the Continent.

Canning also had to deal with the Near East, where a smoldering revolt of the Greeks against their Turkish rulers burst into open rebellion in 1821. This revolt was regarded very differently by the various powers. Austria and Prussia saw nothing more than another rebellion which should be suppressed as soon as possible. But Russia, with her great desire for Turkish territory, was likely to intervene on the side of the Greeks. British policy was opposed to Russian expansion at the expense of Turkey, for the British feared, as they feared all through the nineteenth century, that Russia aimed at Constantinople and at a position in the Near East which might open a path for Russian expansion toward India. Meanwhile a wave of sympathy for the cause of Greek independence swept over France and England. Educated men were familiar with the glories of Greek antiquity and did not realize that conditions in modern Greece could hardly be compared with those in the Age of Pericles. The death of the poet Byron, who championed the cause of the Greeks and who died in Greece in 1824, profoundly affected public opinion. The war was going against the Greeks; moreover, the Turkish Sultan obtained aid from his nominal vassal, Mehemet Ali of Egypt.

Canning handled this complicated situation with skill. By playing on the differences of Austria and Russia, he split the alliance of the autocrats beyond repair. He had two choices of policy in Greece. He might, as England did both before and after him, support the Turks against Russia; or he might restrain Russia by cooperating with her in the Near East. He chose the second of these policies. In 1827 he secured an agreement with France and Russia to force a settlement on the Turks on the basis of Greek self-government under Turkish suzerainty. A combined British, French, and Russian fleet sent to Greece blockaded Turkish and Egyptian squadrons in Navarino Bay. Codrington, the British admiral, had been told he could use force if necessary, and when the Turks and Egyptians sailed out of the harbor their ships were blown to bits. A few months before this event Canning died and in 1828 the Duke of Wellington became Prime Minister. Disliking cooperation with Russia, the duke drew back from Canning's policy. There followed a short war between Russia and Turkey, and Russia received most of the credit for the peace in 1829 which gave the Greeks their independence.

Peel at the Home Office

Sir Robert Peel, who became Home Secretary in 1822, was to be one of the leading Tory statesmen for the next quarter of a century. He did not spring from the aristocracy. His father, the first Sir Robert, had made a huge fortune in the cotton industry and was determined that his son should have a great career in politics. In fact, the younger Peel was trained for parliamentary life. He was educated at Harrow and at Christ Church, Oxford; his father then found him a seat in the Commons, gave him a fine house in London, and provided him with an ample income. Peel soon made his mark in the Commons; within a few years he was Secretary for Ireland. Although he was brought up in Tory principles, he was a man open to conviction, ready to examine facts, and honest enough to alter his opinions in the light of what he saw. Thoughtful and cautious, with a high sense of dedication, he possessed great ability in handling public business. His manner was cold and reserved. The Irish statesman O'Connell, who disliked him, said that Peel's smile resembled the silver plate on the top of a coffin.

Despite this exterior, Peel felt a very real sympathy for the sufferings of the poor. As Home Secretary he cleared out the gang of government spies and informers who had done so much to exasperate the lower classes. He also made important reforms in the criminal law, which contained many barbarities, for Parliament in the eighteenth century had imposed the death penalty upon one offense after another until men could be hanged for any one of some 200 petty crimes. The death penalty, for example, could be inflicted for stealing a fish from a fish stand, for taking 40 shillings or more from a dwelling, or for appearing on the road with a blackened face, a disguise used by highwaymen. These savage punishments did not deter the criminal. The police were so inadequate that there was always a good chance of escape, and juries frequently refused to convict when a minor offense might bring the death penalty. Yet punishment could fall with terrible severity on unlucky persons, and the poet Shelley could write of "sanguine laws which tempt and slay."[2] For some years rather fruitless efforts had been made to modify the criminal code. In 1808 a member of Parliament, Sir Samuel Romilly, had obtained an act which removed the death penalty for the offense of picking a pocket of goods worth more than twelve pence. Later Sir James Mackintosh continued the agitation, but not much was accomplished until Peel took up the task. Within a few years he cut in half the number of offenses punishable by death. Peel also was interested in prison reform. Here again there had been a long agitation, led in the eighteenth century by John Howard and in the early nineteenth by Elizabeth Fry, a Quaker who worked for more humane treatment of female prisoners. Peel began the inspection of prisons and provided salaries for turnkeys in place of fees, but his work was limited and did not affect debtors' prisons, which continued until the middle of the century.

Peel recognized that crime would decline only when detection and punishment became more certain, but he also knew that surer detection could be obtained only through a better police force. No adequate police force existed. The fumbling old constables in most country towns were hopeless. In London the Bow Street Runners and the Thames police were more efficient, but the magis-

---

[2] The need for reform of the criminal law was dramatized in 1818 when, in the celebrated case of *Ashford v. Thornton*, a man on trial for murder suddenly demanded the medieval right of trial by battle against his accuser. Parliament abolished trial by battle in 1819.

trates in various parishes did not cooperate properly; hence there was much room for improvement. One reason why the upper classes were so fearful of the mob was that there was no way of controlling a disorderly crowd except to call in soldiers and begin to shoot. Peel established a new metropolitan police force which was soon extended to all of London. Its headquarters was in Scotland Yard and it was responsible to the Home Office. The men were drawn from retired noncommissioned officers in the army, wore top hats and blue, belted coats, and were armed with clubs but not with firearms. The "bobbies" or "peelers" were regarded at first with some derision but soon won general respect. They learned to establish contact with disorder very quickly, to prevent the formation of dangerous mobs, and to make the apprehension of criminals far more certain. They also developed such a tradition of politeness that the modern British bobby, combining firmness with good manners, has become a model for the world. The London police was gradually copied throughout the country. Peel established mounted patrols to deal with highwaymen and took action against innkeepers who protected criminals. The picturesque but barbarous figure of the highwayman disappeared from English life.

Huskisson and the Board of Trade

William Huskisson, President of the Board of Trade, reformed the customs duties. A man of humble origin, "tall, slovenly, and ignoble-looking," he nonetheless possessed great ability and was in closer touch with the new world of business than his predecessors had been. As a disciple of Adam Smith he agreed with merchants and manufacturers that the way to promote foreign trade was to remove restrictions on the free enterprise of the commercial classes. He found, however, a host of government regulations of many kinds, some dating back to the old colonial system, others passed more recently as war measures.

Huskisson could not hope to introduce complete free trade, for a large proportion of the government's revenue was derived from customs and excises, and his aim was to substitute protective for prohibitive duties. He lowered import duties on silk, wool, and rum, on cotton, linen, and woolen goods, and on glass, paper, porcelain, coffee, copper, zinc, lead, and iron. A general duty on imported manufactured articles was lowered from about fifty to about twenty percent. The Navigation Acts, which had already been modified in 1822 to allow freer trade with South America and to permit British colonial products to be sent directly to the Continent, were relaxed further in 1823 by ending the extra duties levied on goods imported into England in foreign ships. Thus Huskisson lowered duties, allowed freer colonial trade, and modified the Navigation Laws.

TORY DIVISION

Canning, Peel, and Huskisson, who had dominated the Cabinet since 1822, had not been able to pass their enlightened measures without opposition from the ultraconservative members of the Tory party led by Wellington and Eldon. It had only been Liverpool's tact and skill in handling difficult colleagues that had kept the party together; when he resigned in February 1827, after a paralytic stroke, the rift among the Tories became an open one. Neither Canning nor Wellington would serve under each other. Canning became the new Prime

Minister, forming a coalition of his followers with a few Whigs who accepted minor positions in the Cabinet. This coalition was important because it showed a tendency, obvious by 1830, for the liberal elements in both parties to draw together. Wellington, Eldon, and Peel refused to join Canning's Cabinet. Canning's term in office was brief and troubled, and in August 1827 he died. For a few months his friend, Viscount Goderich, known as Goodie Goderich, stumbled along as Prime Minister and then tendered his resignation amid a flood of tears.

The King turned to the Duke of Wellington. Wellington's Cabinet was composed at first of High Tories and Canning's followers, but dissensions between the two groups continued, and Wellington complained that he spent his time in "assuaging what gentlemen called their feelings." In May 1828 he found an opportunity to dismiss the Canningites and seized it with soldierly brusqueness. For almost three years, until late in 1830, the country was ruled by the High Tories alone. It did not enjoy the experience, and it became increasingly impatient with what one Whig called "the stupid old Tory party." On almost every issue Wellington failed to satisfy the nation: his policy in the Near East after the Battle of Navarino was considered weak and pro-Turkish, his sliding scale of duties on imported wheat was unsatisfactory, his attitude toward parliamentary reform became clear when he refused to give to Manchester two seats from a small borough disfranchised for corruption. Wellington possessed sound judgment and solidity of character but he lacked the skill and finesse of the successful politician.

Nevertheless, much against his will, Wellington passed one reform of first-rate importance: the Catholic Emancipation Act, which permitted the admission of Roman Catholics to membership in Parliament. The measure was significant, not only because it advanced religious toleration, but because it involved Ireland.

Ireland in the 1820s

The Irish question was to appear in many forms during the nineteenth century. Essentially, however, there were three principal Irish grievances. One was religious. The Church of England was the established church in Ireland, though it served only a small minority of the population. Although it was more than amply endowed, the Roman Catholic peasants were required to pay tithes for its support. The harsh penal code imposed on Irish Catholics in an earlier age was now largely relaxed, they could hold land on equal terms with Protestants, they could vote for members of the English House of Commons, but they could not hold civil or judicial office, nor could they sit in the English Parliament.

The second grievance was political. The Irish had lost their Parliament in 1800, and they longed to have it back again. Home Rule, as it came to be called, meant the restoration of the Parliament in Dublin. The Irish believed that the first step toward such a restoration was the admission of Irish Roman Catholics to membership in the English Commons; hence the importance of Catholic emancipation.

The third great grievance was agrarian. As in the eighteenth century, many landlords were absentees, renting their estates on long leases to middlemen who sublet them to the peasants in small parcels. The peasants often subdivided and sublet the land even further, until an estate might be teeming with people, all dependent on the potato to keep them from starvation. The population was growing rapidly, the land was used unscientifically, and the quality of the potatoes was declining. From June to September, when the crop of the preceding year had been eaten and the new crop had not yet been harvested, many a poor peasant family was without means of subsistence; wife and children went on the road to beg while the husband sought casual employment, often in Britain. Neither landlords nor peasants felt any incentive to improve their methods of agriculture. A peasant who attempted more scientific farming might find that he had merely raised the rent by his pains. A landlord who wished to improve his estate could do so only by clearing out some of the peasants and by throwing together small parcels of land into larger fields. This process meant evictions and more suffering for the poor, who cordially hated the improving landlord. Yet the number of evictions was high. The landlord was permitted by law to seize the crops and cattle of a peasant in arrears with his rent; a peasant who thus lost his means of livelihood was almost certain to be evicted in the long run.

Believing that the law was loaded against him the peasant sought to protect himself and to enforce a wild justice by terrorism and crime. Secret societies took vengeance on evicting landlords, on their agents, and on peasants who took up holdings from which other peasants had been expelled. But landlords were usually out of reach and their agents were protected by the police; consequently, vengeance often fell on persons who were not responsible for an injustice. Agrarian crime brought terrible evils to Ireland. It challenged the government in a way that could not be ignored, alienated English opinion, prevented the investment of capital and the improvement of agriculture, and poisoned the relations of landlord and tenant. It spread to the towns and retarded industry. Ireland required nothing less than an agricultural revolution which would have been very costly, would have increased temporarily the sufferings of the poor, and would have interfered with the rights of private property. Yet the English cannot be excused for their neglect of Irish wrongs, for the union of the Parliaments carried with it the responsibility of legislating wisely for Ireland.

Wellington and Catholic Emancipation

Catholic emancipation could be granted more easily than most Irish demands because it did not affect property and because it was favored by most Whigs and by some Tories. Yet it would not have been won so soon but for a curious series of circumstances. In 1828 Wellington had accepted a Whig proposal to repeal the Test and Corporation Acts which, since the reign of Charles II, had debarred dissenters from holding national or municipal office. The measure was merely the removal of a formal grievance, for annual indemnity acts had long permitted dissenters to ignore these laws. But political equality for dissenters renewed the question of Catholic emancipation. In 1800, it will be remembered, Pitt had hoped to couple the union of the English and Irish Parliaments with a measure admitting Catholics to membership. Unfortunately the union had been passed without emancipation, and the Irish had believed themselves betrayed.

In the 1820s an Irish patriot, Daniel O'Connell, conducted a great campaign for Catholic emancipation. He was a gifted speaker, a shrewd lawyer, and an able organizer but he was not a revolutionist. He dared to attack agrarian crime, and he proposed to use force but not violence. In 1823 he formed the Catholic Association, which collected a "Catholic rent" of a penny a month from the peasants and organized their voting power under the leadership of their priests. Heretofore the Catholic voter had normally supported his landlord's candidate.

O'Connell ended this practice. In 1828 he stood for election to Parliament from county Clare; headed by the priests, the peasants marched to the polls; O'Connell was returned, though as a Catholic he could not take his seat. He was prepared to employ similar tactics all over Ireland. Wellington and Peel became convinced that they must either grant Catholic emancipation or face an Irish civil war. They decided to yield and passed a bill, over the protests of their own followers, permitting Roman Catholics to sit in Parliament, to hold any office in Great Britain except those of Regent or Lord Chancellor, and any in Ireland except Lord Chancellor and Lord Lieutenant. A Roman Catholic could not act as High Commissioner to the General Assembly of the Church of Scotland.

But Wellington and Peel yielded with a very bad grace. They did not conceal their detestation of what they were doing, they insulted O'Connell by forcing him to be elected over again, and they disfranchised the forty-shilling Irish freeholders and substituted a voting qualification of ownership of land worth £10 a year. This, it was hoped, would prevent O'Connell from controlling the Irish vote, and provision was taken to suppress associations such as O'Connell had employed. Hence the English gained little credit in Ireland. Rather, they taught the lesson that force could bring concessions when right and justice could not. The High Tories were furious with Wellington for granting emancipation. Protestant ascendancy in Ireland had long been a Tory battle cry, and the Tories now were divided not only between Canningites and High Tories, but between High Tories who sought vengeance against Wellington and those who stood by him. He was defeated in 1830 and the Whigs came into office.

FORCES MAKING FOR CHANGE

The years which followed the end of the war in 1815 were, as we know, years of reaction and ultraconservatism among the upper classes. But in the 1830s and 1840s the political atmosphere was much more liberal. What were the forces that brought about this alteration? There are many threads of development, not all of them moving in the same direction, yet most of them preparing men's minds for change. The policies of Canning, Peel, and Huskisson in the period from 1822 to 1828 had shown that moderate and cautious reform was possible without upheaval or danger of revolution, and many sections of the middle classes, growing in prosperity and in their standards of living, saw the desirability of further reform. They were dissatisfied with the old aristocratic world of special privilege and monopoly of political power by the nobility and gentry. Hence the return of more rigid and conservative government under the Duke of Wellington (1828-1830) produced irritation and disappointment.

Jeremy Bentham

An important force making for change during these years was the influence of the gentle lawyer-philosopher Jeremy Bentham, whose excellent health, long life, and private fortune gave him the opportunity to develop his ideas. As early as 1776 he had published his *Fragment on Government,* which challenged the complacent view of the eighteenth century that British society, government, and law had attained as great perfection as could be hoped for. Bentham declared that all law and government were continual experiments in promoting the general welfare—"the greatest good for the greatest number"—

and could never be regarded as final. Every institution, he held, must be subjected to constant investigation and reform and tested by the question, What is the use of it? He supplied a formula which was often followed in the nineteenth century: thorough inquiry by a government commission, corrective legislation by Parliament, careful administration of this legislation by the ministers of state, and official inspection and report.

There was a good deal of pedantry about Bentham, whose view of human nature was much too simple and mechanical. Yet he and his followers, known as philosophical radicals or utilitarians, because they applied the test of utility, did a great service. "They came into a world where medieval prejudice, Tudor law, Stuart economics, and Hanoverian patronage still luxuriated in wild profusion, and by the straight and narrow paths they cut we are walking still."[3] Bentham's spirit, with its emphasis on reason and utility, underlay much of the movement for reform in the nineteenth century. Indeed, his influence was so great that there is danger in making it appear even greater than it was. Many reforms came into existence, not because of any movement or any philosophy, but because officials detected weaknesses in the laws and traditions by which they governed and quietly made improvements.

Bentham was the great foe of special privilege. He saw that antagonisms were certain to exist between those who ruled the state and those who were governed, and he sought a reconciliation by an extension of the franchise. His *Reform Catechism,* published in 1817, advocated the suffrage for all householders. He fully accepted the doctrine of laissez faire as set forth by Adam Smith. He believed that when men promoted their own profit (without doing harm to others) they promoted the general good, and that the state should stand aside in economic matters. There was, however, a contradiction in Bentham's philosophy, a contradiction which ran through much of the political thinking of the nineteenth century. If the state was to investigate, reform, and inspect, it must by necessity invade the sphere of social and economic life and interfere with the rights of private property. If, on the other hand, it followed a policy of laissez faire, no such reform was possible. It became more and more obvious as the century advanced that laissez faire was too negative, that women and children working in factories required protection, that social and economic evils could be removed only by the action of the government, and that interference and control by the state were necessary for progress. In opening the way for greater activity by the government Bentham was a forerunner of modern socialism.

The Evangelical Movement

Alongside the utilitarians, who appealed to reason and were often freethinkers in religion, must be placed the growing evangelical movement. The tremendous impact of evangelical personal religion on Victorian England will be discussed later; here it need only be noted that the evangelical revival prepared men's minds for change. The movement had begun in the eighteenth century and had created the strong and tightly knit organization of the Methodists. In the early nineteenth century various groups of Methodists broke away from the parent body, but nonetheless that body continued to grow and to do a great work among the poor. Methodism in its various branches became the largest religious organization in the country except for the Church of England. Other denominations,

[3] G. M. Young, *Victorian England. Portrait of an Age* (London: Oxford University Press, 1960), p. 10.

such as the Congregationalists and the Baptists, experienced a revival, and the number of nonconformists constantly increased. The influence of these groups on social change was at first rather negative but they made clear their conviction that the methods and morals of the eighteenth century could no longer be regarded as satisfactory; that standards of conduct must be raised; and that new classes, which had counted for little in the past, must now be allowed to express themselves.

Methodism, as we know, had evoked a corresponding movement in the Church of England. The philanthropist William Wilberforce and the writer and schoolteacher Hannah More had brought intelligence, wit, and social standing to the aid of religion. They had labored for a disciplined and industrious working class within the Church of England. Their movement, however, had been conceived in the spirit of the eighteenth century when privilege and social distinctions had been taken for granted. The poor must lead godly, righteous, and sober lives but must not expect improvement in their social or economic lot; there was much truth in Dicken's sneer:

> O let us love our occupations,
> God bless the squire and his relations,
> Live upon our daily rations,
> And always know our proper stations.

The evangelicals in the church fought with success against the grosser forms of vice, against brutal amusements such as bullbaiting, against dueling, and against slavery in the British Empire. For many years they conducted a great campaign against slavery, a campaign in which the nonconformists joined and which showed how moral indignation could be organized politically. The supreme victory of Wilberforce was the abolition of slavery within the empire in 1833. In that very year he died, but something of his spirit was carried on by Lord Ashley, later the Earl of Shaftesbury.

Shaftesbury was an aristocrat who devoted his life to good works: factory legislation, public health, reform of the lunacy laws, improvement in the lot of the agricultural laborer, the protection of the poor little urchins who sometimes were suffocated or burned to death as they cleaned the chimneys of great houses. He taught his fellow peers that they must feel responsibility for the welfare of the poor. But in his mind reform must be the work of the upper classes and he was suspicious of democracy and cold toward any movement of self-help among working people.

The evangelicals and the Benthamite utilitarians did not always see eye to eye. The humanity of the religious bodies, for example, condemned child labor in factories, but utilitarian businessmen wanted labor to be as cheap as possible. Industrialists, however, were also advocates of change. They had to apply reason to the management of their affairs, they were faced with new problems, and they sought new solutions without regard for tradition or inherited beliefs. To them tradition meant the old restrictions of the guilds and the regulations imposed by government. They were rationalists, quite ready to break with the past. They were accustomed to measuring, counting, and observing, and they thought in terms of the present and the future, not of the past.

The Artisan Reformers

Among men of business Robert Owen was unique. He was a manufacturer who combined great executive ability with a deep desire to improve the lot of the working classes. "His mind and character never lost the mark of an upbringing among poor people and among people aspiring earnestly towards an ideal outlook on everyday things."[4] He was naïve and often absurd; yet he taught the great lesson that the new industrialism should not merely be admired or shuddered at but should be controlled by corrective legislation, by cooperation in place of competition, and by a moral approach to social and economic problems. One of the founders of British socialism, he believed that men's characters were formed by heredity and environment and hence that men could be molded by the conditions surrounding them. At the cotton mills at New Lanark in Scotland, of which he became manager and part owner while he was still in his twenties, he conducted a great social experiment. These mills, when he had taken charge of them, were a shocking example of the evils of the factory at its worst. Within a few years he created a model industrial community, with good housing, good pay, and reasonable hours, with care for the education, recreation, and social security of his workpeople, and with the first nursery school in Britain. The resulting high morale among his employees enabled him to make his factory pay a handsome return. He proved that under enlightened management the evils of the factory and the slum could be avoided without impairing efficiency or lessening profits. He made philanthropy pay.

Owen failed to interest his fellow industrialists in copying his ideas, and when he came to London in 1815 and naïvely laid his plans for the welfare of the workers before the Cabinet, ministers were polite but unconvinced. For some years Owen collaborated with the elder Sir Robert Peel in advocating a bill for the protection of children in factories, but the bill as passed in 1819 was easily evaded and did little good. Having failed with the factory owners and with the government, Owen turned in his later years to self-help among the laboring classes—to trade unions, workmen's cooperatives, and utopian schemes for self-governing and cooperative communities such as that at New Harmony, Indiana. He had little interest in the reform of Parliament. Nonetheless, he made a profound impression on the social thinking of the time and set in motion ideas which persisted throughout the century. The success of the mills at New Lanark —philanthropy joined with handsome profits—could not be explained away.

Francis Place, "the radical tailor of Charing Cross," was a workingman who had risen through thrift and business skill to a modest affluence and who sponsored the cause of the laboring classes. "For nearly fifty years he was one of the mainsprings of the democratic movement."[5] He was not an idealist like Owen, but a shrewd and practical man with a rather high opinion of himself and a profound contempt both for other labor leaders and for the "gabbling Whigs" in Parliament. A born manipulator, he employed the art of lobbying to induce Parliament in 1824 to repeal the Combination Acts which formed part of the repressive code enacted in the decade after the French Revolution. These acts prohibited trade unions among workingmen but placed no check on associations of employers. Workers were thus denied the small advantages that might be theirs under the doctrine of laissez faire, although it was common decency to permit them the same rights of combination that were allowed the mill owners. Working through Joseph Hume, a radical member of Parliament, Place brought

---

[4] George Macaulay Trevelyan, *British History in the Nineteenth Century and After 1782–1919* (London: Longmans, 1938), p. 183.
[5] J. R. M. Butler, *A History of England 1815–1918* (London: Oxford University Press, 1960), p. 10.

witnesses from the industrial north to convince a committee of the Commons that the acts were unfair and a cause of bitterness among the poor. Some industrialists regarded the acts as the source of more discontent than they were worth, and their repeal passed through Parliament with surprising ease.

The workers, however, abused their new freedom. After a series of strikes, with some violence and intimidation, the Tories called loudly for restoration of the Combination Acts. But Place obtained a new act in 1825 which permitted trade unions to bargain about wages and hours of labor, though with strict provisions against intimidation. Thus the prohibition of trade unions came to an end; their growth was rapid during the next decade. It is true that the unions committed follies and made false starts. The workers were gullible and followed anybody. Owen and other leaders conceived of vast combinations of workers which would transform all industry into one great cooperative enterprise. The Grand Consolidated Trades Union expanded under Owen's control into an organization of more than half a million workers, but it rested on faulty foundations and collapsed in 1834 when mill owners refused to employ its members and the government conducted some rather cruel prosecutions. Thereafter trade unions began a slower and less ambitious but a more solid and conservative period of growth.

Henry Brougham

The radical demand for change among portions of the middle class may be typified by Henry Brougham. English by ancestry but Scottish by birth and education, Brougham was a lawyer who entered politics and advocated many liberal causes. In a famous speech in Parliament lasting for six hours he exposed the many absurdities of the law. He agitated against slavery, promoted adult education, and denounced sinecures and pensions. But though everyone admitted his brilliant talents, he lacked stability and balance. He could be as embarrassing to his friends as to his foes, and when the Whigs made him Lord Chancellor in 1830, they did so because they believed he would cause less trouble on the woolsack than in the House of Commons.

Romanticism

A movement of a very different kind also swelled the desire for change. This was the romantic movement in literature, which often is said to have begun with the publication in 1789 of William Blake's *Songs of Innocence* and to have ended with the death of Sir Walter Scott in 1832. The romantic writers, revolting from the formal and unsentimental verses of the eighteenth century, relied upon emotion, instinct, and imagination. They wished to escape from what was familiar into a world of their own imagining, into that "serene and blessed mood," as Wordsworth called it, in which the poet, free from earthly contamination, believed he saw into the reality of things. A mystic like Blake was constantly in this visionary ecstasy. But most writers could not sustain the mood for long; when it fled they fell into despondency. Finding their ideals in their own thoughts, they revolted from the restraints of society and from normal rules of social conduct. They asserted their own individuality against the world.

They sought escape from reality in writing about things that were far away, about the marvelous, the abnormal, and the supernatural, about haunted castles, pleasure palaces, and subterranean rivers, demon lovers, and magic casements opening on the foam of perilous seas in fairylands forlorn. Seeking a return to a state of nature, these writers were interested in the life of the savage, the peasant, and the child. There was also an interest in the Middle Ages, as something that was vague, remote, and mysterious. The romanticists were lovers of liberty and haters of oppression in any form.

William Blake, both artist[6] and poet, lived in a world of his own imagination in which vague but mighty forces strove for mastery. The symbolism is confused, but evil forces of disunity, regimentation, and oppression are opposed by freedom, passion, and love, which is identified with imagination, poetry, and art. Some of Blake's poems, such as the *Songs of Innocence,* in which the child represents humanity before it is imprisoned by the world, are filled with joy and laughter; others are peopled by shapeless beings who howl and bellow in the war of light and darkness.

William Wordsworth, the nature poet, rose steadily in poetic power until in the decade from 1797 to 1807 he was writing lofty and majestic verse. Thenceforth his powers declined, though he lived until 1850. At first a young radical, admiring the French Revolution, he became disillusioned with events in France and adopted a philosophy in which patriotism and love of English institutions turned him into a conservative. From a period of deep despondency about 1793 he was rescued largely by contemplating the loveliness of nature. He believed that all sense impressions had their origin in external things but could be molded by the human spirit into lofty ideas. In 1798 he and Samuel Taylor Coleridge published their famous *Lyrical Ballads.* Wordsworth explains that he sought material for this volume in humble and rustic life and employed the language of ordinary men, coloring homely episodes with imagination and seeking insight into the laws of human behavior. A self-centered man, he probed into his own development in an autobiographical poem, *The Prelude.* He recalled the profound impressions made upon him in childhood by the beauties of nature and how these impressions, which had once opened his youthful mind to visions of reality, faded away in middle age. Here perhaps is the secret of his decline.

His intimate friend Coleridge, with whom he published the *Lyrical Ballads,* was a man of great mental powers marred by a disordered private life. Both philosopher and bard, he wrote a handful of great poems but devoted most of his life to philosophical speculation. His role in the *Lyrical Ballads* was to deal with "persons or characters supernatural or at least romantic." The result was *The Rime of the Ancient Mariner.* Other poems—*Christabel* and *Kubla Khan*— were also highly romantic in character.

The most popular of these writers was Sir Walter Scott. He was fascinated by the romance, rapid action, and martial tone of Scottish history, by Scottish ballads and folklore, and by the superstitions, character, and dialect of the Scottish peasant. Scott knew the history of the clans and of noble families; he had an eye for scenery. All these elements were woven together with great skill and imagination in his narrative poems and historical novels. Scott excelled in vivid descriptions of striking scenes and episodes and in fine character sketches; he virtually created the historical novel; and he made a profound impression upon the culture of his age.

A new generation of romantic poets, more rebellious than the old, arose in the early nineteenth century. By far the most famous in his day was George Gordon, Lord Byron, a dissipated young peer who traveled in southern Europe

[6] See page 502.

Coast scene near Naples, by J. M. W. Turner. An example of romanticism in painting; the artist uses light and mystery in combination. (Tate Gallery)

and in the Levant and wrote romantic descriptions of strange lands and tales of amorous adventure in mysterious oriental settings. His *Childe Harold's Pilgrimage* (1812) made him famous. Besieged by women, he began a period of notorious living, which became so scandalous that in 1816 he left England forever. After wanderings chiefly in Italy, he espoused the cause of Greek independence and died in Greece in 1824. His masterpiece was *Don Juan*, the story of a young rake who wandered in many lands and found amours in all of them. The poem is a satire upon the oppressions and hypocrisy of society; it is hostile to war and to the normal conventions of morality. In style Byron vacillates between classical tradition and the newer types of verse. He had moments of grandeur, but today he is rated more highly as a satirist than as a poet.

The conventional and well-to-do background of Percy Bysshe Shelley contrasts strangely with his poetic genius, his radical politics, and his determination to devote his life to a struggle against injustice and oppression. In a similar way his noble ideals contrast with his pathetic incompetence in practical affairs. Thus at the age of eighteen he eloped with a young lady of sixteen whose father had "persecuted her in a most horrible way by endeavoring to compel her to go to school." Shelley's restless wanderings, his financial difficulties, his unconventional relations with women brought disaster upon himself and upon those he loved until he was close to insanity. His poetry is not easy to understand. In his first important poem, *Queen Mab*, a disembodied spirit journeys through space and sees visions of the dreadful state of the world and of happier utopias to come.

God creating Adam, an engraving by William Blake. (Tate Gallery)

Shelley was one of the most erudite of poets; he gave his poems a thoughtful and philosophic content as well as great artistic beauty.

John Keats was the apostle of beauty, as Shelley was of freedom. Springing from humble origins and taken out of school at the age of fifteen, Keats had at least the encouragement of friends who introduced him to other literary people in London. At the age of eighteen he determined to devote himself to writing poetry and applied himself to that art with the greatest earnestness. The rapidity of his development was astonishing. His first long poem, *Endymion*, was flamboyant and undisciplined, but he recognized these faults and set about correcting them. The culmination of his brief career came in 1819, a year in which he produced very great poetry. Two years later, at the age of twenty-six, he died of tuberculosis. Perhaps his greatest gift was his skill in using words to evoke a rich and total image of the mood or object he was describing.

Thus during the 1820s forces of widely different kinds and widely different origins combined to break down the old, irrational dislike of change. New classes were developing that refused to accept the standards of the eighteenth century and that expected more humanity, more justice, and more rationality in government and law. The old regime, with its privileged aristocracy, its corruption, its complacency, its heartlessness must come to an end and make way for a world in which all men had some share in their government. These ideas were fostered by the romantic movement in literature, by the growth of evangelical religion, and by a new faith in progress. It was no longer held that material improvement was rendered doubtful by the growth of population or that the sufferings of the poor were unavoidable. The belief in progress was greatly facilitated by the coming of the railways in the 1830s. Here was a mechanical invention which was not hidden away in the dark mills and factories but was seen and used by all classes. It brought the possibility of enormous growth, it was a perfect example of progress, of applying a new technique to useful ends and of cutting away from old habits and old traditions.

28

REFORM AND DISCONTENT, 1830-1846

The period from 1830 to 1846 was a time of active reform. The men described at the end of the last chapter—moderate Tories, Benthamites, factory owners, evangelicals, middle-class radicals, friends of the workingmen—combined to break down resistance to change and to create a more liberal atmosphere. As a result the Whigs in the 1830s and the Tories in the 1840s enacted a long series of reforms. In view of the conservative character of both parties during these years, their legislation was surprisingly liberal.

And yet, despite these reforms, the period was one of discontent and bitterness. Discontent was due primarily to economic misery, especially in the cruel years of deep depression and unemployment between 1837 and 1843. The lower classes were discontented, as were many middle-class radicals, because the parliamentary Reform Bill of 1832, of which so much was expected, turned out to be a moderate measure which left the nobility and gentry in control of political life. Workingmen were further exasperated by the harshness of a new poor law passed in 1834. They were convinced, moreover, that they were unjustly and needlessly deprived of their share of the nation's wealth. There were two movements of protest. One was Chartism, an interesting though futile attempt of the poor to help themselves; the other was a prolonged and highly emotional agitation by the middle classes against the Corn Laws. Thus during these years the tensions of class hostility, economic distress, and political radicalism continued to plague the nation.

THE WHIGS IN OFFICE

A general election in the summer of 1830, following the unlamented death of George IV, gave to the Whigs thirty additional seats in the House of Commons. Wellington continued as Prime Minister, but after a rash statement in which he opposed parliamentary reform of any kind he fell in November and the Whigs took office. The return to power by the Whigs meant a major shift in politics, for they had not held office since the brief Ministry of All the Talents in 1806 and 1807.

The new Prime Minister, Earl Grey, an elderly and rather austere nobleman and an aristocrat of aristocrats, had all the prejudices of the eighteenth century against any form of democracy. He had not the slightest thought of disturbing the political supremacy of the ruling class, but the Whigs had a tradition of constitutional reform. As a young man in the Commons Grey had advocated reform of the electoral system, and now as an older man in the Lords he was ready to return to his early policy. His Cabinet consisted almost wholly of peers. Its aristocratic nature was really an asset, for if noblemen such as these were willing to reform the House of Commons, then reform could not be very dangerous. By including some of the Canningites, Grey had combined the liberal wings of both the old parties. His Cabinet also contained a few radicals, such as Henry Brougham and Lord Durham, Grey's liberal son-in-law.

Grey assumed office at a moment of dismay and danger. A financial crash in 1825–1826 had caused a return of economic depression. Wages were reduced and there was widespread unemployment, especially among agricultural laborers. Radical societies, including both middle- and lower-class elements, sprang up in various cities. A Reform Association in London collected from its members a "radical rent" of a penny a month, an obvious imitation of O'Connell's methods in Ireland. In Birmingham a local banker of liberal views, Thomas Attwood, founded the Birmingham Political Union to agitate for the reform of Parliament. Grey feared some sort of political upheaval led by portions of the middle class. A revolution of this kind had occurred in France during the summer of 1830, when almost without bloodshed the reactionary Charles X had been driven from the throne, the Citizen King, Louis Philippe, had taken his place, and the supremacy of the middle classes had been established. If such a victory could be won so easily in France, might it not occur in Britain? The parliamentary Reform Bill of 1832 was in a sense an aristocratic appeasement of the middle classes and especially of the numerous shopkeepers. By admitting these classes to the franchise, the nobility and gentry erected a bulwark against the turbulent demands of the classes further down.

The Reform Bill of 1832

The Reform Bill, as first introduced in 1831, swept away about fifty of the smallest boroughs, took one member from some thirty more, all without compensation to the borough owners, and distributed the seats thus released to new industrial towns and to populous county areas. But the extension of the franchise was very small. Grey believed that to pass such a measure was the conservative thing to do, for he thought it would be final and would silence demand for further reform. The bill was introduced in the Commons by Lord John Russell, a younger son of the Duke of Bedford. As he read in his high, thin voice the list of boroughs to be disfranchised, the Tories burst into shouts of derisive laughter. But when the bill was given a second reading three weeks later, members were aware that it had tremendous support throughout the country. The second reading passed by a vote of 302 to 301 in an exciting division vividly described by Macaulay.[1]

---

[1] George Otto Trevelyan, *The Life and Letters of Lord Macaulay* (New York: Longmans, 1876, 2 vols.), I, 186–188.

With so small a majority, Grey knew that the bill could not pass through its later stages, and he persuaded the new King, William IV, a timid, conservative, and slightly ridiculous old sailor, to dissolve Parliament and to hold an election. Such a direct appeal to the people on a single issue, especially one in which the interests of the upper classes were involved, was in itself a novel event. The Whigs were returned with a comfortable majority. Even in the days of an unreformed House of Commons, the nation was able to express its opinion in moments of crisis. The Tories in the Commons, after the election, could do no more than delay the bill during the summer of 1831. On the first of October it was sent to the Lords. A week later, after an all-night session, the Lords threw it out, as well-informed people fully expected they would.

In the eighteenth century, when a defeat in the Lords was as serious as a defeat in the Commons, Grey would doubtless have resigned. But he decided to stay in office because the people were furious with the House of Lords. There was a riot in Bristol, and groups of workingmen were drilling in various places as though they intended to revolt. Grey prorogued Parliament for two months and then reintroduced the bill in December. It passed quickly through the Commons, but the problem of securing its passage through the Lords remained. One method of meeting this difficulty, though a very drastic one, would be the creation of new peers in sufficient quantity to form a majority for the bill in the upper house. The only precedent for such an action had occurred in the reign of Queen Anne, when twelve peers had been created. But sixty new peers might be needed to pass the Reform Bill, and Grey shrank from such a violent remedy. As it happened, there was a group of lords, nicknamed the Waverers, who opposed the bill but dreaded the opprobrium of rejecting it outright. They conceived the idea of allowing it to pass its second reading in order to satisfy the people and then to modify it quietly in committee. The Waverers attempted this strategy in the spring of 1832, but Grey would not permit his bill to be mutilated. He went to the King and demanded the creation of a sufficient number of peers to pass the bill. When the King refused, Grey resigned.

A strange situation thus arose. The nation was greatly excited, the Commons were determined to support Grey and pass the bill but the Lords stood in the way. In May 1832 the King turned to Wellington, asking him to form a Tory Cabinet and to pass a reform bill less drastic than Grey's. But Wellington discovered he could not form a Cabinet. Leading Tories, including Peel, refused to join him. They argued that, having fought the Reform Bill tooth and claw, they could not honestly support a substitute for it. The King was forced to recall Grey's Cabinet, but Grey would not return without a promise that new peers would be created if that became a necessity. When the Tory nobles discovered that Grey possessed this power, they stalked out of the House of Lords in dignified procession, and thus, by absenting themselves, permitted the bill to pass. It became law in June 1832.

The Reform Bill did not alter the total number of seats in the House of Commons. It disfranchised 56 boroughs and took one member from 30 others. Of 143 seats thus released, 65 were given to large towns and cities, 65 were given to newly created rural constituencies in populous counties, and 13 were added to the representation of Ireland and Scotland. In rural areas the forty-shilling freeholders retained the vote, but the franchise was extended to copyholders and to long leaseholders whose lands were worth £10 a year, as well as to short leaseholders and to tenants at will with lands worth £50 a year. In the boroughs the old jungle of voting qualifications was swept away, and one universal rule gave the vote to persons who occupied property either as a residence or as a place of business rated at £10 a year. There was to be a register of voters, the money that could be spent on an election was controlled, the polls were to be open for two days only.

The changes brought about by the Reform Bill were not as great as its terms might imply. "Never," writes G. M. Young, "was a revolution effected with more economy in change."[2] The number of pocket boroughs was reduced, but they continued to exist; it is thought that they could still return about 80 members. The new £50 voters in the counties were certain to be conservative; moreover, the members allotted to industrial towns were balanced rather neatly by new county constituencies in which the landed aristocracy continued to influence elections. Influence in various forms was perhaps even greater after 1832 than before. Both rural and urban voters, in the absence of a secret ballot, were subjected to the scrutiny of their superiors. There was a good deal of rowdyism: "Election day was still a carnival which usually ended in a fight."[3] Dickens' description of an election in *Pickwick Papers* was less of a caricature than one might suppose. The franchise was not extended greatly. The electorate in England and Wales was increased only from 435,000 to 657,000, while that in all of Britain and Ireland rose only from 478,000 to 814,000. The gentry and nobility, who continued to dominate the political life of the nation, were in a stronger position than before, for they had abandoned the absurdities of the old system without losing ultimate control.

The way in which the bill was passed through Parliament strengthened the Cabinet system of government and illustrated its principles. Supported by the House of Commons, the Cabinet had forced its will on the King and the House of Lords. Wellington, without that support, had been unable to form a ministry. Although both parties were conservative by modern standards, the passage of the Reform Bill opened the way for other liberal measures. Under the wise guidance of Sir Robert Peel, the Tories gradually dropped their blind hostility to change and accepted the possibility of cautious, gradual, and judicious reform. The Whigs contained a sprinkling of radicals. Powerful forces in the nation urged further reform, and for a few years the Whigs allowed themselves to become the vehicle of these forces.

The Abolition of Slavery in 1833

The great victory of the evangelicals was the abolition of slavery in 1833. The slave trade had been illegal since 1807, but so long as slavery was permitted in the British colonies there was always a market for Negroes smuggled across the Atlantic; the slave trade, though greatly reduced in volume, continued to exist, often under worse conditions than in the eighteenth century. Severe penalties against slavers made them brutal toward the Negroes; captains of slaving vessels in fear of capture were known to have thrown their Negroes overboard. In 1823 Wilberforce and Thomas Fowell Buxton, a philanthropic member of Parliament, founded an Anti-Slavery Society and began an extensive and well-organized campaign. In 1833 the government passed a measure abolishing slavery in the British empire. The act provided for a period of semiservitude

[2] G. M. Young, *Victorian England. Portrait of an Age* (London: Oxford University Press, 1960), p. 28.
[3] Young, p. 28.

under the guise of apprenticeship, but this arrangement proved unsatisfactory, and by 1838 the slaves had been freed without reservation. A sum of £20,000,000, about half the commercial value of the slaves, was voted as compensation to their former owners.

In only two parts of the empire was slavery deeply entrenched. One was the West Indies. The few British planters, who were usually very wealthy, were violently opposed to emancipation, but their influence at Westminster had declined and they could only submit in helpless rage. Slavery also existed in South Africa, where the Dutch farmers, known as Boers, living in Cape Colony, lost not only their slaves but part of their compensation, for the money was payable only in London. West Indian planters had London agents who collected the money for them, but a simple Boer farmer at the Cape had to sell his claim at a discount. The Boers, however, were not helpless. Hostile to British rule for many reasons, they began in 1837 a mass migration into the interior, where eventually they established two semi-independent republics. This journey, known as the Great Trek, was an unfortunate event, for it scattered a small white population over too large an area and created problems that might have been avoided.

The Factory Act of 1833

In 1833 an important act was passed for the protection of children working in textile factories. As in the campaign to abolish slavery, the drive behind this act was largely humanitarian. When it became known that young children were working for fourteen or sixteen hours a day, the public demanded reform irrespective of party. The movement was led by evangelical Tories who took an understandable delight in exposing the mill owners, largely Whigs and Benthamite radicals, but who, being manufacturers, thought in terms of profits, wanted long working hours, and normally opposed factory legislation. The question of child labor became connected with a demand by workingmen for a ten-hour day. In many factories the work of children was integrated closely with the work of adults, so that if children obtained a ten-hour day adults might hope for it also.

There had been a movement since 1800 for the regulation of child labor, but legislation had not been effective. In 1830 a new agitation was begun by Richard Oastler and Michael Sadler, two evangelical Tories. Sadler, a member of Parliament, secured the appointment of a select committee of investigation. Its report aroused the public and convinced Lord Ashley, later the Earl of Shaftesbury, that legislation was essential. In 1832 he introduced a bill which provided a working day of ten hours for young persons under eighteen. His bill in effect would have established a ten-hour day for all workers. The factory owners, taking alarm, obtained a new inquiry; and on the basis of its findings the Cabinet introduced a bill to take the place of Lord Ashley's. The government bill prohibited the employment of children under nine in textile mills, provided that children under thirteen should work no more than nine hours a day and young persons under eighteen no more than twelve, but permitted children to come to the factories in relays so that the mills could operate for fourteen or sixteen hours daily. Adult workmen, who had hoped for a ten-hour day, were bitterly disappointed. Yet the bill was not a bad bill. One of its principal features was the introduction of government inspectors. This was an important innovation, for the trained inspector, as he gained skill in judging the condition of factories, was later to play a great part in the control of industrial enterprises.

There was further legislation in the 1840s. An act of 1842 prohibited the employment of women and girls and of boys younger than ten underground in coal mines. In 1844 the working day of all children under thirteen was restricted to six and a half hours, and the working day of all women and girls to twelve. An act of 1847 provided a ten-hour day for women and children. This act, however, was modified in 1850 so that factories could remain open for twelve hours a day with an hour and a half for meals. Workingmen again were disappointed, but at least a normal day of ten and a half hours with a half holiday on Saturday had been established. Shorter hours did not decrease production, as employers had feared, for increased efficiency more than made up for a shorter working day.

The Poor Law of 1834

The Poor Law Amendment of 1834 was not passed to assist the poor but to relieve the middle classes of the intolerable burden of the poor rates; both the act and its operation bore the mark of Benthamite utility in a harsh and unpleasant form. There was certainly great need of change. The Elizabethan system, which was administered by the parish vestry and which gave relief only to persons living in the parish workhouse, had broken down in the late eighteenth century. After 1795 relief was given to persons outside the workhouse by supplementing wages from the poor rates. The results were disastrous. Wages declined, the independent poor could not compete with the subsidized laborer, pauperism increased, and the poor rate rose from some £600,000 in 1750 to some £8,000,000 in 1818. The new poor law of 1834 applied a drastic remedy. Its aim was to end outdoor relief for the able-bodied poor and to make the workhouse so unattractive that the poor would resort to it only as a last expedient. In order to spread the burden of the rates more evenly, parishes were combined into larger units, known as unions, administered by locally elected officials. A central commission with great authority supervised the entire system.

The outstanding member of the commission was Edwin Chadwick, a disciple of Jeremy Bentham. Although he was an able and energetic man, he administered the poor law in an unsympathetic way, allowing an element of harshness to dominate poor relief, as though paupers were necessarily idle and vicious and ought to be chastised. "By the workhouse system," he wrote, "is meant having all relief through the workhouse, making this workhouse an uninviting place of wholesome restraint, preventing any of its inmates from going out or receiving visitors without a written order to that effect from one of the overseers, disallowing beer and tobacco, and finding them work according to their ability; thus making the parish fund the last resort of a pauper, and rendering the person who administers the relief the hardest taskmaster and the worst paymaster that the idle and dissolute can apply to." But it was impossible to make the workhouse so unattractive that it frightened away the idler and at the same time make it comfortable and consoling for the aged and infirm. The new bastilles, as the poor called them, became very bleak indeed. Husbands were separated from wives, and children from parents; silence was imposed at meals; paupers were buried at the lowest possible cost without the normal decencies. The poor law, as Disraeli said, outraged the manners of the people. In 1847 the commission was replaced by a central poor law board with less autocratic powers; henceforth the poor were treated with greater humanity.

Chadwick had hoped that the new law would reduce the poor rates and would at the same time induce employers to raise wages. The rates declined, but wages did not increase. Indeed, during the years of depression after 1837, they tended to go down and did not recover until the more prosperous era of the 1850s.

The new poor law established an administrative pattern which was to become familiar: administration in detail by locally elected bodies, local responsibility for finance, but close supervision by the central government. Inevitably the bureaucratic machinery of government was increased and the functions of the state were extended.

The English Municipal Corporations Act, 1835

The English Municipal Corporations Act of 1835 was a direct response to the demand of the middle classes for a drastic reform of local government in the towns. There were nearly 250 incorporated towns in England and Wales, each governed by a corporation consisting of a mayor, aldermen, and common councilors. Over the centuries most of these corporations had become close, exclusive, and self-perpetuating bodies, from which dissenters were excluded by the Corporation Act of 1661. The old town corporations need not be painted too darkly. During the eighteenth century they had governed the towns well enough according to the standards of the time, but hostility mounted against them in the early nineteenth century as the number of dissenters increased and as industrial growth brought wealth into new hands. Their doom was assured when the Corporation Act was repealed in 1828 and when the Reform Bill of 1832 ended their power to manipulate parliamentary elections.

The act of 1835 made sweeping changes. The old corporations were abolished. The government of some 70 of the smallest towns was merged with that of the shire. About 178 towns received new town councils to be elected by all householders who had resided in the town for three years and who paid the local rates. The new councilors served for three-year terms, chose one of their own number as mayor for a term of one year, and selected certain councilors as aldermen for terms of six years. The new corporations expanded their functions rapidly, introduced social services, and became employers on a large scale, but they could not float loans without the consent of the central government, which also audited their books once a year. They had no control over the law courts or over the appointment of judges, nor could they regulate the liquor traffic or license public houses. The Municipal Corporations Act effected a revolution in local government much more complete than did the Reform Bill of 1832 in the structure of Parliament.

Education

In 1833 the Whigs began a modest grant of £20,000 a year for the support of elementary education. The money was shared by two religious societies which sponsored schools for the lower classes: the British and Foreign School Society, which was nonconformist, and the National Society for Promoting the Education of the Poor in the Principles of the Church of England. Their schools were not very good. It was believed at the time that children could be educated in large numbers, several hundred in a room, by the use of child monitors, clever boys or girls who, having learned a short lesson from the master, repeated it over and over to the other children until they learned it by rote. This method could impart very simple ideas, but many of the children never learned to read or write, and the experiment gradually was abandoned. A great step forward was taken in 1839, when the distribution of funds was entrusted to a committee of which Sir James Kay-Shuttleworth was the leading spirit. A man of ability and drive, he established the first training college for teachers. In 1846 a system was begun which consolidated the principles of training colleges, of a teaching certificate, and of additional pay for trained teachers. This was the foundation of the teaching profession. By the middle of the century England had a system of public education, though it was grossly inadequate: half of the children of the poor never went to school at all.

LORD MELBOURNE, 1834–1841

After 1835 the reforming zeal of the Whigs began to slacken. Although they remained in office until 1841 (with two brief Tory intervals), their last years were lethargic and aimless. For this lack of purpose there were three principal causes: the character of the Prime Minister, the problem of Ireland, and weakness in financial management.

Upon Grey's retirement in 1834, the King called upon Lord Melbourne, a conservative Whig, to become Prime Minister. Melbourne was an aristocrat of charm and affability, but he was idle, disillusioned, and contemptuous of vulgarity in any form. He had no great desire for office, he disliked radicals, and he regarded the Benthamites as fools. He had little sympathy for the poor. Indeed, he had no program of any kind save to manage affairs with as little trouble as possible. His greatest service was his influence on Queen Victoria during the first three years of her reign. When William IV died in 1837, his brother, the Duke of Cumberland, became King of Hanover and his niece Victoria became Queen of England. She was only eighteen, the daughter of George III's fourth son, Edward, Duke of Kent, who had been dead for many years. Victoria had been brought up in seclusion by her mother, the German Princess Victoria of Saxe-Coburg, and her education differed little from that of any young woman of the upper classes. She was attractive and virtuous, a little headstrong, with high notions of the powers of the Crown, but with a most sincere desire to do her duty. It was Melbourne's happy function to employ his charm and tact in teaching her those constitutional principles upon which a British sovereign must base his actions. She liked Melbourne personally and profited greatly from his instruction.

During the first years of her reign the fact that she was surrounded by Whigs resulted in a minor constitutional crisis in 1839. In that year Melbourne resigned, and Peel, asked to form a Cabinet, felt that there should be more Tory influences surrounding the Queen. He asked her to remove some of the Whig ladies of her bedchamber and to replace them with Tory ladies. When Victoria refused, Peel abandoned his attempt to construct a ministry, and Melbourne returned for two more meandering years. In 1840 Victoria married her cousin, Prince Albert of Saxe-Coburg-Gotha. A serious young man, he was interested in science, in inventions, in economics, and in the practical problems of government. He exercised a steadying influence on Victoria. Their household was a model of hard work, devotion to duty, and domestic virtue. Victoria created in the public mind a new conception of monarchy. This was of great importance, for the sons of George III, "princes the dregs of their dull race," had brought kingship into such disrepute that it might not have survived another such generation.

Ireland

The problem of Ireland harassed and divided the Whigs. They needed the support of O'Connell, who led an Irish bloc in the Commons; but English and Irish opinion were poles apart on Irish questions, and the Whigs quarreled among themselves. The issue of the moment was that of tithes paid by the Irish peasants for the support of the Anglican Church in Ireland. O'Connell, intent on the repeal of the parliamentary union, wished to leave tithes alone, but the question was forced on him by the Irish Catholic priesthood. Indeed, it was grossly unjust that 6 million Roman Catholic peasants living in great poverty should pay a tenth of their scanty incomes for the support of a church they regarded as heretical and which served only some 850,000 members. In 1832 the Whigs improved the method by which tithes were collected, but the Irish wanted their abolition. Many peasants refused to pay. The resulting disorder was so great that the Whigs had to pass a coercion bill giving the government in Ireland extraordinary powers to cope with Irish crime.

Behind the question of tithes lay the larger question of the Anglican Church in Ireland. Its revenues reached the enormous sum of £800,000 a year, but many Englishmen feared that if this princely income was diminished a precedent would be established for similar encroachment on the revenue of the Church of England. In 1832 the Cabinet introduced some reforms in the finances of the Anglican Church in Ireland, suppressed ten of twenty-two Irish bishoprics, and taxed those that remained for the maintenance of ecclesiastical buildings. But when in 1834 Russell suggested that the revenues of the Anglican Church in Ireland were greater than necessary, he broke up the Cabinet. Peel and the Tories came in for a few weeks; then Melbourne returned with a reconstructed ministry.

Melbourne did his best to conciliate O'Connell. The English poor law was extended to Ireland and Irish municipal corporations were reformed. In 1838 tithes were turned into a tax payable by landowners; the money still came from the peasants but it was collected as part of their rent. More important, the undersecretary in Dublin, Thomas Drummond, governed with a new and admirable impartiality. He divided patronage between Protestants and Catholics, recruited Catholic policemen, permitted Catholics to serve on juries, and astonished landowners by reminding them that property had responsibilities as well as rights. For some years Ireland was quiet, but in 1841 O'Connell began a great agitation for repeal of the parliamentary union. The English, of course, were adamant in refusal, and O'Connell was shortly faced with the dilemma of either dropping his campaign or sanctioning insurrection. He dropped his agitation and thus lost face with his followers. A new group of leaders, very violent and nationalistic, began a movement they termed "Young Ireland." Insurrection would surely have followed, but soon the entire picture in Ireland was altered by the potato blight, to which we will turn presently.

Finance and Depression

A third difficulty of the Whigs concerned finance. Since taking office in 1830 they had never produced a first-class financial minister. Annual deficits followed one another in dreary succession. Not only were the Whigs incompetent in finance; they failed to recognize that the tax system rested on an unsound foundation, being far too dependent on customs and excises which burdened trade and industry. In periods of economic depression, when the yield from customs and excises was small, the revenues of the state declined in a dangerous way. The first five years of Whig rule had been fairly prosperous, but late in 1836 there were signs that a period of depression was approaching. Conditions grew worse until, by 1840, prosperity had disappeared, many manufacturers had been ruined, and the working classes had sunk into a miserable plight. Wages in the factory towns declined to about a third of their former figure, scarcely one man in ten could find employment, a fourth of the houses were empty, with thousands of families living in the workhouse or subsisting on relief administered at the rate of one shilling a head each week.

As the depression deepened, there was naturally much thought concerning the advantages and disadvantages of the Industrial Revolution. Two contrasting points of view were evident. Businessmen stressed the achievements of industry. In their opinion it had brought wealth and opportunity, not only to themselves but to the people as a whole. The depression was merely a pause in industrial growth; if industry could be liberated from the shackles of tariffs, and especially from the Corn Laws, which benefited the landowner at the expense of everyone else, then progress would be resumed and new achievements beneficial to all would follow. The Tory landlord and the workingman regarded the matter quite differently. The Industrial Revolution, they believed, had brought ruin to many independent workers, had exploited women and children, and had unleashed forces which appeared to be reckless, uncontrollable, and destructive of security. Depression, it was held, could not be blamed on the Corn Laws. The fault lay with the manufacturers, who had been guilty of overproduction and speculation until the world was glutted with their goods and no one could make a profit.

THE GROWTH OF POPULATION

Much of the misery of the poor sprang from a deeper cause: the increase of population which began in the eighteenth century and continued throughout the nineteenth at a growing rate. In 1801 the population of England and Wales stood at a little under 9 million; in 1851 it was almost 18 million; in 1871, nearly 23 million; in 1881, almost 26 million. The causes of this tremendous increase are still somewhat obscure. It is no longer believed that it was caused by a decrease in the death rate or by improved medical care, for the growth of population was rapid in an area such as Connaught in Ireland, where medical services were at a minimum. Historians now think that it sprang primarily from altered conditions in rural life which made for earlier marriages and thus increased the span of a woman's childbearing years. Early marriages increased the birth rate, and, as they continued through successive generations, they produced an explosion of population. This was a rural phenomenon, for the cities continued to be unhealthy places and grew largely by immigration. Many people were on the move in England and Scotland in the early nineteenth century—people from crowded rural areas in England, from the Scottish Highlands, and especially from Ireland. After the Irish potato famine in 1845–1847 the number of Irish in Britain became very large.

These wanderers drifted to the towns, for there was no place else to go. But the cities were not prepared to receive such numbers of immigrants. Although we hear of town improvements in the eighteenth century, they were largely in the main streets and not in the slums and alleys. The towns never caught up with the influx of newcomers to which they were subjected. Despite efforts at improvement, most towns in the first half of the nineteenth century reproduced the evils that had existed in London a century earlier. The poor first crowded into old decaying houses which had seen better days. The squalid suburbs arose outside the old center. Speculators ran up flimsy buildings in long continuous rows, each unit attached to others, side to side and back to back, completely hemmed in except in front, without proper light or ventilation and often without water or means of sewage disposal. Dwellings of a similar kind were built in inner courts and in the centers of city blocks until an area was completely choked with housing. Refuse of all kinds, including human excrement, was piled in courts and alleys until it was carted away. Although a practicable water closet had been patented in 1778, sewage flushed away by water was merely deposited in nearby rivers, pools, or open ditches.

It was very difficult to remedy these conditions, for they had become unmanageable before engineers learned how to collect the great quantities of water needed by a modern city, how to pump it to residential areas, or how to build proper sewers. The danger of disease was great, as was apparent in the outbreaks of cholera during the 1830s. The cause of these conditions was not the Industrial Revolution; rather, it was the increase of population and the growth of cities.[4]

CHARTISM

Chartism, a passionate and resentful protest of the poor against the harsh conditions under which they lived, took the form of a working-class demand for the franchise and for a radical reform of Parliament. There was much that was pathetic about it. It called forth bravery and devotion; yet it was so poorly led that it ruined itself. In any case, it could not hope to succeed, for the workingmen were determined to act alone and to repudiate any alliance with the middle classes. Fortunately the movement produced little violence. The Chartists talked in a violent and irresponsible way, but they shrank from insurrection. The government, though it acted firmly, displayed far more good sense and moderation than it had done in the years following the Napoleonic wars.

The movement began in 1836, when William Lovett, a small shopkeeper, an embittered but cautious man, founded the London Working Men's Association composed of upper-class artisans who were intelligent and fairly well paid. The purpose of the association was to draw the working classes together, to inform the public of the conditions in which laborers lived, and to agitate for the political and social rights of all classes. In 1838 Lovett, aided by Francis Place, drew up a program for the reform of Parliament, a program which came to be called the People's Charter. It contained six points: universal manhood suffrage, equal electoral districts, the secret ballot, removal of property qualifications for membership in the House of Commons, payment of members, and annually elected Parliaments.

Unfortunately the movement soon fell into the hands of demagogues. The

[4] See G. Kitson Clark, *The Making of Victorian England* (Cambridge, Mass.: Harvard University Press, 1962), Chap. III.

A slum in London. Wood engraving after Gustave Doré. (The Granger Collection)

Charter was issued at a time when the poor were in great distress, when they were discouraged by their failure to obtain the vote in 1832 and by the collapse of Robert Owen's plan for a gigantic trade union, and when a bitter campaign was in progress in northern England against the new poor law. Workingmen in the north, inclined to physical force, were not likely to be satisfied with Lovett's dignified agitation for the reform of Parliament. They adopted the Charter as a kind of battle cry and found a more congenial leader in Feargus O'Connor, an Irish radical who talked wildly about force without understanding the implications of what he was saying. A large man with a tremendous voice, O'Connor was a powerful public speaker, but his character was low and he was described even by a friend of the people as a "foolish, malignant, and cowardly demagogue." He ruined the Chartist movement. He began a newspaper in Leeds, the *Northern Star,* which fanned discontent and incidentally brought him a good deal of money.

It was now proposed that a petition, signed by millions of people, should be presented to Parliament urging the adoption of the six points of the Charter and that the Chartist leaders should hold a convention in London while the petition was being presented to the House of Commons. About fifty delegates met in London in February 1839. They were earnest but naïve men, vastly impressed with the responsibility entrusted to them. Some of them wrote the letters "M.C." (Member of Convention) after their names, in imitation of the "M.P." used by members of Parliament. Chartist leaders had to consider what the next step would be if Parliament rejected their petition, as it was most likely to do. They were not prepared for insurrection, but they thought that a threat of one might be helpful. They asserted, therefore, that the people had the right to arm, they talked of a refusal to pay rent and taxes, and they considered a general strike. Their petition, presented to Parliament in May, was neglected because of a Cabinet crisis, but was rejected in July.

Meanwhile the country was becoming alarmed. Troops were sent to various points in northern England, though there was no fighting. The convention moved from London to Birmingham, where its coming was the occasion of some ugly riots. After Parliament rejected the petition, the Chartists set a date for a general strike. But they knew that many of their followers had no employer to strike against and that those workpeople who had employment were not likely to leave it. Hence the convention lost its courage, canceled the strike, and dissolved in confused defeat. Talk of an insurrection dwindled away, though there was a small uprising in Monmouthshire which was crushed instantly.

This was the first and most interesting phase of Chartism. Thenceforth it degenerated, falling completely under the sway of O'Connor, who merely led the people astray. In May 1842 a new petition with more than 3 million signatures was presented to Parliament, only to be promptly rejected. Disappointment combined with hard times to produce a number of dangerous strikes. Chartism became connected in the public mind with violence, the strikes failed, some of the Chartist leaders were arrested, and the movement subsided once more.

The final defeat of Chartism occurred in 1848, a year of revolution in Europe. Expectation of change was in the air, and O'Connor, untaught by failure, was ready to play the demagogue again. A monster petition, said to contain 5 million signatures, was prepared to be brought to Parliament by a vast throng assembling at Kennington Common in London. O'Connor appeared at the assembly. The government brought up troops and special constables and informed

O'Connor that the crowd would not be permitted to cross the Thames to the Parliament buildings. At this moment of crisis O'Connor weakly told the crowd to disperse; in place of an overwhelming demonstration of popular strength the petition was carried to Parliament in three hansom cabs. The ignominy of this fiasco was increased when the petition was found to contain many bogus signatures such as Flatnose, No Cheese, and Jack Frost; moreover, the signatures of the Duke of Wellington and of Queen Victoria, which appeared on the list, were not likely to be genuine. Thus the last effort of the Chartists faded away amidst the relief and the ridicule of the upper classes. Yet Chartism must not be dismissed as mere folly. It was a sincere and vigorous effort of the lower classes to help themselves, and the energy it generated passed into other movements. It helped to build the self-respect of workingmen. It called the attention of the nation to the plight of the poor. John Stuart Mill justly named it the victory of the vanquished.

PEEL'S ADMINISTRATION, 1841–1846

Sir Robert Peel became Prime Minister in 1841 after an overwhelming Tory victory at the polls. A contemporary called Peel "the best man of business who was ever Prime Minister." With his great abilities, his tremendous capacity for work, and his high sense of dedication, he brought new order, efficiency, and conscientiousness into government. Perhaps more than any other man in the nineteenth century he raised the standard of public life. He introduced his own budgets, drew up minutes for the Cabinet on all important questions, prepared himself for every debate, and answered in his own hand an enormous number of letters from people of all kinds. His conservatism was not merely that of the landed aristocracy or of the wealthy manufacturers; he wished to support every substantial interest in the country and to draw the middle classes to the new Toryism. At the same time, as we have seen, he felt genuine sympathy for the poor.[5]

Peel's Budgets

Peel's greatest work was in finance. The whole structure of taxation was in need of reform, not merely to balance the budget but to stimulate the lagging tempo of industry and commerce. Four fifths of the government's revenue came from customs and excises and thus placed a heavy burden on industry and foreign trade. Peel discovered that although there were duties on more than a thousand articles, the bulk of the revenue came from very few. If the customs were considered primarily as a source of income, they could be lowered on many articles without great loss. British industry, in fact, was so far ahead of the industry of other countries that it did not require protection; moreover, freer trade would facilitate the entry of British manufactures into foreign markets.

Peel therefore began a series of famous budgets which, greatly reducing customs duties, took England far on the road toward free trade. The budget of 1842 lowered duties on 769 articles, establishing a rate of about 5 percent on imported raw materials, of about 12 percent on semimanufactured articles, and of about 20 percent on fully manufactured goods. Although Peel believed that

[5] E. L. Woodward, *The Age of Reform 1815–1870* (Oxford: Clarendon Press, 1938), p. 106.

Sir Robert Peel, by John Linnell. (National Portrait Gallery, London)

in the long run the income of the government would not suffer, he foresaw a temporary decline. To meet this immediate loss of revenue and to balance the budget, he persuaded Parliament to accept for three years an income tax of 7d. in the pound. By this measure the burden of taxation, which had fallen with unfair severity on the business classes, was distributed more equally over the nation as a whole. The success of the measure was phenomenal. Industry and commerce revived and expanded, employment increased, prosperity began to return.

Lowered duties did not bring serious foreign competition. In the budgets of 1845 and 1846 Peel went further, abolished altogether the customs on 430 articles, lowered the duties on imported raw materials, and allowed most manufactured articles to enter the country with an ad valorem duty of about 10 percent. During his term of office he remitted taxation at the rate of about £2.5 million a year and yet produced a surplus. He repaid £14 million of the national debt, and by establishing confidence in the credit of the government he reduced the interest on the debt that remained, at an annual saving of £1.5 million. But he found that the income tax could not be dropped; it became fundamental for government finance.

The Anti-Corn-Law League

In this general reduction of tariffs there was one great exception. Peel had not touched the Corn Laws save to readjust Wellington's sliding scale. To a large part of the landed aristocracy, and even more to their tenant farmers, the Corn Laws were the very foundation of agricultural prosperity. Yet Peel was gradually converted to free trade in wheat, and in 1845 he broke with his party over this issue.

A campaign had arisen for the repeal of the Corn Laws. It was begun in the autumn of 1838 by a group of Manchester businessmen who, early in the next year, formed the Anti-Corn-Law League. The league found support among large sections of the middle classes. It was an attack upon privilege, and it offered a rallying point for all those who disliked the aristocracy. Like the agitation against slavery, it was nationwide; highly emotional, it appealed to religion—and it was well organized. The league had a clear and simple objective. It made a direct appeal to manufacturers, who regarded the Corn Laws as a tax on the whole community for the enrichment of the landowners; and it also appealed to laborers, who hoped for cheaper bread. The struggle was not merely one between town and country. The aristocracy was supported and even urged forward by the tenant farmers, but agricultural laborers opposed the landlords. A favorite device of the league was to produce a rural laborer who would say at a public meeting, "I be protected and I be starving."

The league possessed two remarkable leaders. One was Richard Cobden, a manufacturer in Manchester. Highly critical of the aristocracy, which he branded as aggressive and warlike, he was nonetheless a cultivated man. He had a fine, reflective mind and a wonderful gift for lucid and forceful exposition of economic questions. The other, John Bright, was also a manufacturer, of Quaker background, who developed into one of the great orators of the age. He could be bitter and vindictive in speaking, but he added liveliness and popular appeal to the arguments of Cobden. The campaign of the league was waged on a tremendous scale. It conducted mass meetings, sent out lecturers, and distributed millions of closely argued tracts which found arguments to appeal to every class except the offending landlords, who cordially hated the league because it held up the aristocracy to the people as a group of knaves and plunderers.[6]

The Irish Potato Famine, 1845–1846

In 1845 Peel became a convert to free trade in wheat. But if he repealed the Corn Laws he could be accused of betraying the interest of the party that

[6] Woodward, p. 118.

had put him in power. Hence he planned to wait until a general election and then to take the issue to the country, when he would offer aid to agriculture to cushion the shock of change. He also believed that he would be supported by the growing Toryism of the middle classes. But his attention was diverted by the Irish famine of 1845-1846. In both these years the Irish potato crop failed completely; some 4 million persons dependent on potatoes for food faced starvation. Cholera and various fevers fastened on the stricken population, and during these tragic years perhaps a million people died in Ireland. The English government did what it could. By 1847 some 700,000 Irishmen were employed on public works; food was distributed to some 2 million more. The Corn Laws did not mean much in Ireland, for the Irish could not afford to buy foreign wheat, but Peel felt that nothing should be done to keep wheat out of Ireland. He saw a lesson for England in the Irish experience: the English peasant must not be forced into dependence on the potato because of the high price of bread.

In December 1845 Peel announced to his Cabinet that the Corn Laws must be repealed. Most of his ministers resisted, the Cabinet broke up, and Peel resigned. Lord John Russell, asked to form a Whig ministry, should have done so, for he had recently declared himself a convert to free trade in wheat. But the Whig aristocrats were landlords no less than the Tories. Russell foresaw a split in his party and an unpleasant struggle in the House of Lords. His efforts to form a Cabinet were halfhearted and he soon abandoned the attempt. Peel was recalled. In June 1846, with the support of a section of the Tories, most of the Whigs, the radicals, and the Irish, he repealed the Corn Laws. Wellington, faithful to a colleague, pushed the measure through the House of Lords. In the case of the Corn Laws, as in the case of Catholic emancipation, Peel and Wellington looked upon themselves as servants of the state who must follow the right or necessary course of action regardless of party or public opinion; but in 1846, in contrast to 1829, the agitation of the league had brought public opinion—though not Tory party opinion—to favor their course of action.

The duty on wheat and other grains was lowered drastically over a period of three years until, in 1849, these grains could enter the country at the nominal rate of one shilling a quarter.

The Results of Repeal

The impact of repeal was greater on politics than on the economic life of the nation. Repeal of the Corn Laws divided the Tory party and ended Peel's career as a great leader. Many Tories had grown restless as Peel had moved toward free trade. Believing that they had been betrayed they turned against him in bitter anger. They found a spokesman in Benjamin Disraeli, a brilliant Jew who had hoped for office in 1841, had been passed over, and had been critical of Peel ever since. Peel, on his side, believed that his party had deserted him. He was always aware to some extent that he was the son of a manufacturer and not an aristocrat. He now denounced the men whom he had been leading. He would not, he said, be the mere tool of a party. "To adopt the opinions of men who have not access to your knowledge, and could not profit from it if they had, who spend their time in eating and drinking, hunting and shooting, gambling, horse racing, and so forth, would be an odious servitude to which I never will submit."[7] The split in the Tory party was irreparable. Those

---

[7] Woodward, pp. 104–105.

Tories who remained faithful to Peel, of whom Gladstone was the greatest, held aloof from both parties for a time but eventually united with the Whigs. Most Cabinets for the next twenty years were Whig Cabinets.

On the other hand, the effect of repeal on the economy was surprisingly small. In good years England could still supply most, though not all, of the wheat she required, English farming methods were as advanced as any in the world, and the vast wheat fields of the American West had not yet been opened by railways and cheap ocean transportation. Hence English agriculture continued to prosper. Indeed, it enjoyed a golden age. The price of wheat held up very well, averaging about fifty-two shillings a quarter, though it would probably have gone higher if the Corn Laws had been retained. It was only in the 1870s that English farming, unable to compete with grain from America, fell from its high position. The repeal of the Corn Laws has sometimes been portrayed as the final victory of the middle classes. But this was not so. Hostility to the landowning aristocracy, as evidenced by Cobden and Bright, was still insufficient to dislodge the old ruling class from its predominant position in politics. That predominance continued for thirty years after the repeal of the Corn Laws.

The potato famine added new bitterness to Anglo-Irish relations. Lord John Russell, who followed Peel as Prime Minister in 1846, did not administer Irish relief skillfully. Nor was the governmental machinery equipped to meet such an emergency. Suffering in Ireland was intense. The population dropped in a few years from 8 million to some 6.5 million. Thousands and thousands of Irishmen left their native land to emigrate to various parts of the empire; even more thousands went to the United States, taking with them a hatred of England intensified by their miseries. This hatred was to make the problem of Ireland much more difficult.

THE COLONIES

Meanwhile important developments were occurring in the British colonies overseas. The highly complicated history of the empire in the nineteenth century is more readily understood if one thinks in terms of three distinct types of expansion. The first was a continuation of the mercantile empire of the seventeenth and eighteenth centuries whose purpose was trade. This mercantile expansion consisted of a series of units each of which served some trading purpose: plantations, commercial centers, naval bases or strategic points from which trade could be controlled and protected. A second kind of expansion was the military conquest and administration of areas in Asia and Africa containing large native populations. An obvious example was British India. A third type of empire consisted of colonies of permanent white settlers, chiefly of British stock, that could grow in wealth and population until they formed new nations. Such colonies arose during the first half of the nineteenth century in Canada, South Africa, Australia, and New Zealand, posing problems quite different from those of trade and conquest, as the North American colonies had done before them. It is about this third kind of empire that a word will now be said.

These colonies did not arouse much interest in England at the beginning of the nineteenth century. They contained few British settlers. In 1815 Canada was strongly French, South Africa was Dutch and Negro, the West Indies contained a small class of white planters and many thousands of Negro slaves, there were even fewer Englishmen in India, Australia was a penal colony. To utilitarians and businessmen in Britain the cost of these colonies seemed greater than their worth. In 1825 an article in the *Edinburgh Review* declared that the British military establishment in the West Indies and in British North America cost the Treasury a million pounds a year, even in time of peace, without any adequate return. Disraeli, the future imperialist, ridiculed the colonies in 1828. In his *Voyage of Captain Popanilla* he describes the discovery of an uninhabited island consisting of bare rock. At once, he says, it is fortified; it is supplied with bishops, judges, and administrators; an agent is appointed to deal with the native inhabitants. This, he adds, is what we call the colonial system. Businessmen pointed out that they sold very little to the colonies, that their trade with the United States was much greater than it was before the American Revolution, that when the world adopted free trade, as they believed it would, colonies would be open to anyone who wished to trade with them. In a word, the colonies were useless and might as well be abandoned. There was also criticism of the Colonial Office, a rather stuffy department with much jobbery and little imagination. Remembering the American Revolution, the Colonial Office was suspicious of white settlements and much preferred a mercantile empire devoted to trade.

Nonetheless, interest in the colonies gradually increased. In South Africa this interest was largely humanitarian. British missionaries, shocked at the way in which the Boers treated the Negroes, worked with evangelicals in England to bring about the abolition of slavery.

Colonization in Australia began very badly. In 1787 Captain Arthur Phillip was sent out with an expedition of some 1100 persons, of whom about 750 were convicts. Early in the following year he founded a penal colony, not at Botany Bay, but at a nearby harbor, which he named Sydney. He annexed the eastern half of Australia, to which the name New South Wales was given. The first free settlers were soldiers who, having served their time with the garrison, later took up land. Although free settlers from Britain came out very slowly, new colonies were gradually formed: Van Diemen's Land (later Tasmania) in 1823, Western Australia in 1829, South Australia in 1834, Victoria in 1850. A colony was founded in New Zealand in 1839. The white population of Australia increased enormously when gold was discovered in Victoria in 1851 so that by 1860 there were 350,000 people in New South Wales and 538,000 in Victoria.

Systematic Colonization

Greater attention in England was directed toward the colonies in the 1830s by a group of men who wished to introduce new methods of colonization. Their leader was Edward Gibbon Wakefield. An original thinker of remarkable ability, Wakefield might have had a great career in politics but for a private scandal. In 1830 he founded the National Colonization Society of which Charles Buller, Sir William Molesworth, and the radical Earl of Durham, Grey's son-in-law, were later members.

Believing that emigration would bring relief to economic misery at home, Wakefield set forth a plan for what he termed "systematic colonization." He saw that throughout the empire there were vast stretches of unoccupied land but a scarcity of capital and labor for their development. His proposal was that the government should not give these lands away but should sell them at reasonable prices. Land would thus pass into the hands of persons with a little capital, and the money obtained by the government could be used to assist the emigration of poorer classes who would serve as laborers until they were able to purchase land of their own. If a supply of labor was thus obtained, men with capital would be more willing to emigrate. The entire process should be supervised by the government in a systematic way. Land should be surveyed and evaluated before it was sold; emigrants should be received at colonial ports and, to discourage them from lingering in the port towns until their money was gone, should be dispatched at once to areas where employment was available.

Wakefield's views were theoretical and never were applied in their entirety. In Canada the public lands had already been given away. Conditions in South Africa were too disturbed for systematic planning. And in Australia Wakefield did not take into account the great size of the sheep ranches on which ex-convicts often lived as squatters. Nevertheless, Wakefield had considerable influence on the colonization of South Australia and New Zealand. His views were provocative. He envisaged the growth of new nations of British emigrants to whom self-government would be given at an early stage and whose ties with the mother country would be economic and sentimental. He strongly opposed the dumping of convicts on unwilling colonists, but he offended the humanitarians at home by disregarding the interests of native populations.

The Durham Report

It was in Canada that colonial self-government first became a reality. The settled parts of the country in the early nineteenth century consisted largely of three areas. The first was the province of Lower Canada (Quebec) along the banks of the St. Lawrence, the home of the French population. The second was Upper Canada (Ontario), a huge western province, in which the early settlements were made in the region between Montreal and the modern city of Detroit. This area, divided from Lower Canada in 1791, had begun to grow when some 10,000 American loyalists had migrated north after the Revolution. The third region, the Maritime Provinces, consisted of Nova Scotia, New Brunswick, Prince Edward Island, and Newfoundland. The government as it existed in 1837 consisted of a Governor General for all the Canadian colonies (except Newfoundland where there was a naval governor), and of a Lieutenant Governor, an appointed council, and a popularly elected assembly in Lower Canada, in Upper Canada, and in each of the Maritime Provinces except Newfoundland. The assemblies had little control of policy, for the Lieutenant Governors were given revenues the assemblies could not touch. There were many causes of friction: French hostility toward the growing British minority in Lower Canada, discord among the provinces, and quarrels in each province between its governor and its assembly.

In 1837 small insurrections took place in both Upper and Lower Canada. It was then that the Prime Minister, Lord Melbourne, sent out Lord Durham to investigate and to propose a solution. Wakefield and Charles Buller accompanied Durham to Canada in 1838, and with their assistance Durham collected the material on which he based his famous *Report on the Affairs of British North America.* Its conclusions were twofold. It proposed, in the first place, that Upper and Lower Canada be thrown together into one province so that a united nation could develop and a British majority could be obtained in a united assembly. But it also proposed that Canada be given responsible government, that is, that the Governor should act only as the King acted in England and that the members of his council should retain office only so long as they were supported by a majority in the Assembly. The power of the assembly should be confined to domestic affairs. The first part of Durham's *Report* concerning the union of the two provinces was adopted at once by the British Parliament. The second part was delayed until 1847, when Lord Elgin, a liberal Governor General and a son-in-law of Lord Durham, began to put its principles into practice. Thenceforth Canada enjoyed self-government. Once granted in Canada, it was quickly extended to other colonies in South Africa, Australia, and New Zealand.

Self-government led to a desire for federation. By the British North America Act of 1867 most of the Canadian provinces united to form the Dominion of Canada, subordinate to Britain in imperial matters but self-governing in domestic affairs. Federation came early to New Zealand, in 1852, and responsible government in 1856. But the union of the Australian colonies was achieved only in 1900, and in South Africa only in 1910.

Despite the problems posed by industrialization, poverty, and the growth of population, and despite the conflicting ideas of Whigs, Tories, Benthamites, evangelicals, businessmen, and landlords, the period from 1830 to 1846 was a time of important and lasting achievement. The parliamentary Reform Bill did away with the absurdities of the old electoral system and opened the way to further change. The impulse for reform, springing from many different origins, brought about the abolition of slavery, the beginnings of effective factory legislation, the reform of the poor law and of municipal government, the advance of public health, the first support of public education by the state, the establishment of self-government in the colonies, and many lesser improvements. More significant than any single reform was a new philosophy of the state in which the government expanded its social and economic functions and developed a bureaucracy to make its control effective. Free trade was a boon to the economy. Though their lot was not greatly improved, the poor asserted themselves in the Chartist movement in a way to bring their plight before the public with a minimum of violence or threat of revolution.

29

the mid-victorians

The years between 1846, when the Corn Laws were repealed, and 1868, when Gladstone formed his first ministry, constitute a distinct period in the history of nineteenth-century Britain. At the beginning of this era a radical such as John Bright believed that the work of fundamental reform would go forward rapidly, that the lower classes would soon obtain the franchise, and that the aristocracy would lose its hold on political life. But these expectations were not fulfilled. In spite of a series of lesser reforms between 1850 and 1854, it is nonetheless true to say that in the middle of the century there came a pause, a time of ineffectiveness in Parliament and of diminished desire for drastic change. The nobility and gentry continued to dominate the political life of the nation.

The most obvious reason for this lull was the remarkable prosperity of the time. Thriving on free trade and untroubled by foreign competition, Britain entered into the full enjoyment of industrial leadership. Not only was she the workshop of the world, she represented a new kind of industrial civilization which other nations envied and sought to emulate. British prosperity was more widely distributed than in the past. Agriculture did well despite the repeal of the Corn Laws. And large sections of the working classes enjoyed higher wages and better food. The healthy state of the economy was reflected in a lessening of class tensions, a pride in the achievements of industry, and a confidence in future progress. In politics this was a time of instability, with no large party majorities in the Commons. Cabinets rose and fell in rapid succession without much alteration in policy.

INDUSTRIAL ACHIEVEMENT

Prosperity was based on solid industrial advance. The cotton industry, which continued to expand, was supplying cotton cloth not only to the home market and to the Continent but to many other parts of the world. In 1815 Britain had imported 82 million pounds of raw cotton; in 1860 that amount had increased to 1000 million. Changes in the woolen industry came more slowly, but the spinning of wool by machinery had advanced rapidly in the first quarter of the century, so that by 1850 most wool was spun and woven in factories, though there was some weaving of fine fabrics by hand. Raw wool was imported from Australia, New Zealand, and the Cape.

Advance in the heavy engineering and metal trades was even more spectacular. The annual production of iron rose tenfold during the first half of the century, the iron industry receiving a tremendous impulse from the building of railways and later of iron ships. The manufacture of iron machinery became a great new industry. Instead of buying wooden machines or iron ones constructed painfully by hand, a manufacturer could now buy iron machines cut to exact specifications and thus increase the durability of his equipment as well as the quality of his product. After restrictions on the exportation of British machinery were removed in 1843, the value of exported machines rose fivefold in the next twenty years. The production of coal more than tripled during the first half of the century, and by 1870 Britain was mining more than 110 million tons a year. A host of inventions—the steam printing press in 1814, the sewing machine invented in France in 1830 and strengthened in the 1850s to pierce leather and thus make shoes, the telegraph in the 1830s—opened new industries; also the use of oil as a lubricant (first developed in Pennsylvania in 1859) was a great improvement over the animal and vegetable fats employed in the past.

The Railways

The early history of railways is the story of bringing rails and the steam engine together. Wooden rails, over which carts were drawn by horses, had been used underground in coal mines since the sixteenth century. By 1800 these rails were made of iron, the flange that kept the wheels in place had been transferred from the rail to the inner side of the wheel, and tracks had been laid above ground to transport coal for short distances from the pit-head, normally to navigable water. Tracks on the surface naturally suggested longer lines. It was proposed in 1799 to build a railway from London to Portsmouth to carry goods; a portion of the line was opened in 1804. The first steam engines, of course, were stationary. Then about 1782 James Watt invented an engine that could turn a wheel; and attempts were soon made to construct a self-propelling engine. In 1801 Richard Trevithick, a mining engineer in Cornwall, built a steam locomotive, known locally as Captain Dick's Puffer, to run on the ordinary roads. In 1804 he constructed a locomotive that operated on rails. About the same time another engineer, William Murdock, was experimenting with engines of the same kind. But none of these locomotives proved successful. A few years later Trevithick opened an amusement park in London in which a small locomotive, the "Catch Me Who Can," pulled a little train around a circular track. But after the engine ran off the track and smashed, Trevithick, not a pratical man, traveled to Peru in the hope of interesting the Peruvians in steam locomotion. A number of other primitive locomotives were built in England before 1825.

The Stockton and Darlington Railway, opened in 1825 in a mining area south of Durham, was built by promoters who rented the tracks to anyone wishing to run his own vehicles over the line. Trucks for coal and lighter carriages for passengers were both to be drawn by horses, but when the line was half built, the promoters decided to use locomotives. A famous inventor, George Stephenson, constructed a steam engine weighing seven tons which could haul a ninety-ton

A coal miner, 1814. Part of the mine appears on a hill in the background. A steam engine, built by Mr. Blenkinsop, draws a train of coal wagons to nearby Leeds. (From Edward Hailstone, ed., *The Costume of Yorkshire*, London, 1885. Historical Pictures Service, Chicago)

train at a speed of four to eight miles an hour. Stephenson's engine, its smoke-stack red hot from its exertions, was the wonder of the countryside. Stationary engines on the tops of hills pulled trains up steep inclines by cables.

The Liverpool and Manchester Railway, which was opened in 1830, was the first modern railway. Stephenson had been conducting experiments which demonstrated the drastic way in which a grade reduces the pulling power of a locomotive. He persuaded the company to abandon stationary engines on the top of hills and to accept the basic principle that tracks must be laid on the level. The company held a competition for the best engine, and Stephenson's locomotive, the *Rocket*, proving far superior to other entrants (two of which would not start), was adopted by the line. The *Rocket* could travel easily at a speed of thirty miles an hour; in one breathless test it covered a distance of four miles in four and a half minutes. Other railways were rapidly constructed in many parts of the country. Such progress was not made without difficulties and mistakes. There were technical problems: boilers burst, trains ran off the tracks, strong resistance to the railways came from the owners of canals and stagecoach lines, from farmers who feared for their local markets, from gentlemen who saw their hunting disturbed, from educators at Eton and Oxford. Rapid construction led to speculation, extravagance, and jobbery. But by the middle of the century Britain was supplied with an excellent network of railways.

The railways exerted a tremendous influence on English life. Quickening all aspects of the economy, they caused a great increase in the production of coal and iron, they became large employers of labor, their influence upon industry was immense. Cheaper and faster transportation increased all production, reduced prices, and attracted foreign buyers. English firms built railways in many parts of the world. Agriculture was scarcely less affected than industry, for perishable goods could be carried long distances, cattle could be brought to market, fertilizers and farm machinery could be more widely distributed. Railways required large capital funds and offered a new form of investment, thus affecting the structure of credit and finance.

Their social effects were no less important. They broke down the isolation of rural areas, enabled city and country folk to visit back and forth, and opened the age of the commuter. The number of passengers was far greater than had been anticipated. An act of 1844, compelling railways to run one train a day on every line at the fare of a penny a mile, made travel possible for the poor. Early railway prints often showed an Irishman wearing a green hat and riding in a roofless box car among the pigs and cattle. The railways forced old-fashioned people into an acceptance of change and encouraged others to think of the future. Brushing prejudice and vested interests aside, they brought obvious advantage to society as a whole. They were also a triumph of private enterprise. The state never built a railway, though it reserved the right to purchase them.

Commerce

The tonnage of British shipping remained fairly constant between 1815 and 1840 but almost doubled in the next twenty years. In the same way the value of British exports, after rising very little between 1815 and 1834, increased rapidly thereafter, from a value of £42 million in 1834 to £199 million in 1870. The total value of imports was much greater: £152 million in 1854 and £303 million in 1870. The difference was made up by earnings in carrying freight by sea and by income from investments abroad. In the middle of the century businessmen obtained better facilities for organizing corporations and for obtaining credit. An act of 1844 made incorporation easier; legislation between 1855 and 1862, limiting the liability of stockholders to the value of their investment, encouraged the public to buy stocks. Before 1850 businessmen had suffered from lack of facilities for borrowing from banks, from unsound banking practices, and from inefficiency in the administration of the Bank of England. Conditions in these matters improved greatly after 1850.[1]

THE IDEA OF PROGRESS

The achievements of industry and the increase of wealth bred a spirit of satisfaction with the present and fervent faith in the idea of progress. Mid-Victorians believed in the worthwhileness of themselves and their world. They had problems, but problems could be solved: the tone of the age was buoyant and

[1] J. R. M. Butler, *A History of England 1815–1918* (London: Oxford University Press, 1960), pp. 31–32.

optimistic. Great opportunities appeared to lie ahead for men who were earnest and industrious. It is also true that the age was materialistic, that great emphasis was placed on the production of wealth, that the aesthetic side of life was neglected.

The pride of the Victorians had finer qualities than vulgar exultation in new riches. Industrial achievement represented a victory over the brute forces of nature, a victory of intelligence over outworn modes of thought. There was pride in man's capacity to strive and to achieve; the smoke hovering over a factory town was sometimes compared with the smoke of a great battle. Material progress was leading to a more civilized life. Cheap cotton cloth increased cleanliness; street lighting reduced crime; safe drinking water and cheaper tea and coffee decreased drunkenness. The speeches of business leaders expressed the hope that expanding commerce would bring peace and unity to all the world. There was belief in the perfectibility of man, in "the creation of certain nobler races, now very dimly imagined."[2] The Great Exhibition of 1851, the first world's fair, caught the imagination of the people and symbolized national pride in the industrial wonders created during the last half century.

Macaulay's *History of England,* of which the first two volumes appeared in 1848, interpreted the past in the spirit of his own generation. He exulted in England's material progress and began with the proud assertion that the history of England since 1688 had been "the history of physical, of moral, and of intellectual improvement." Macaulay's robust and manly style, his cheerful, optimistic, and slightly arrogant assertiveness, his pride in himself and in his country, made his writings immensely popular; his color, vividness, and lucidity, his short, crisp sentences, came as a joy to a generation accustomed to history written in a grandiloquent and heavy style. His interpretation of the past was not entirely sound: he regarded the Whigs as the party of progress and hence normally in the right; the Tories as the party of reaction and hence normally in the wrong; he idealized the Revolution in 1688; and he made the dangerous assumption that if a thing was successful it was also just.

RELIGION

Religion played an enormous part in mid-Victorian England. Some sections of the lower classes, as we shall see, were so neglected and so sunk in ignorance as to be outside the life of the churches. Some skepticism resulted from the advance of science, but most members of the more prosperous classes were Bible-reading, Sabbath-keeping, sincere, and devout Christians. The flocking of earnest men and women to the churches every Sunday, the zeal for missions both at home and abroad, the popularity of hymns and religious verses no matter how dismal, the number of newly built churches, the attack on drunkenness, a more energetic and appealing type of preaching, an increased use of ritual and music by nonconformists, and greater beauty in the services of the Church of England—all offered proof of a deep and widespread interest in religion.

Religion was evangelical. Whether a man attended Wesleyan or other nonconformist chapels or the services of the Established Church, he was taught a personal religion which emphasized conscience and moral conduct. The soul

[2] Butler, p. 153.

must recognize its sinfulness, must seek salvation through Christ, and could thus emerge from a state of wickedness to one of goodness and virtue. Conscience must be an omnipresent guide, sitting in constant judgment over every thought and action. The mid-Victorians were taught a literal interpretation of the Scriptures, an anthropomorphic God, a belief in the Last Judgment, in the joys of Heaven, and in the pangs of Hell.

Some historians have seen in eighteenth-century Methodism the origin of the nineteenth-century revival of religion. But the revival had a broader base. There had been an evangelical movement within the Church of England during the eighteenth century, and some of the older nonconformist sects had become more active. The French Revolution had produced in England by reaction a deep conservatism both in politics and in religious faith, and the victory over Napoleon had added a certain moral vanity and ethical assurance. Thus the evangelical movement, drawing strength from various sources, advanced on a broad front in the nineteenth century until it became almost universal.

The movement hardened into a social code which, with its etiquette, its taboos, and its prudery, divided society sharply into those who were godly and those who were not. Unless a man was respectable, unless his doings would bear investigation, unless he was careful, vigilant, and earnest—unless, in a word, he lived according to the evangelical code—he was looked at askance by his neighbors. Hence the supermorality of the age. In speech and in writing there was an anxious avoidance of anything indelicate and a most guarded reticence toward all matters relating to sex. It was improper to refer to the human body, or to the nasty conditions in the slums, or to that much-maligned plant, the potato (which was commonly called "the root"). The sheltered education of girls made them guardians of the code; and the yards of cotton cloth in which women of the middle classes encased themselves testified both to their inordinate modesty and to their sedentary lives. The social code stressed cleanliness and neatness—a German professor scoffed that the English mistook soap for civilization. There was also an assurance of ethical rectitude, a sense that England, a nation of the elect, was justified in the eyes of the Almighty. The code was probably more rigid in the lower middle classes than elsewhere, which was possibly an indication that new classes were trying to establish themselves and must therefore stress their respectability. The code was also the result of the emergence of society from the brutality of the eighteenth century to a more decent and civilized standard of conduct.[3]

The Growth of Nonconformity

Nonconformity grew enormously during the half century after 1800. Although there was some splintering among the Methodists—we hear of the Primitive Methodists, the Calvinistic Methodists, the Methodists of the New Connection—the parent organization steadily increased its membership and appealed strongly to the working classes. Baptists, Congregationalists, Unitarians, and Quakers also grew in strength and numbers. They tended to attract more middle-class people than did the Methodists, although they made efforts to appeal to the poor. And there were humbler religious bodies of various kinds among the lower classes. A religious census in 1851 disclosed the fact that of all

[3] G. M. Young, *Victorian England. Portrait of an Age* (London: Oxford University Press, 1960), pp. 11–17.

the people who attended a place of worship upon a certain Sunday about fifty-two percent went to services of the Church of England and about forty-eight percent to some sort of dissenting chapel.

The census also revealed that a great many of the poor, especially the unskilled factory workers, did not go to any church. Of a population of 17 million in England and Wales, at least 5 million were outside any religious body. Some of these people had no place of worship near them. Others disliked the way in which the poor were crowded into the free seats at the back or at the sides of the church, or they resented being told that their poverty was the result of idleness and vice, or they had no Sunday clothes. But many others were absent because religion had no meaning for them. Although both the Church of England and the dissenting groups made strenuous efforts to Christianize the mass of heathendom that still remained in Britain, these efforts were only moderately successful.

The Church of England

The Church of England had been subjected to sharp attack in the 1830s because it contained abuses, because the bishops voted against the Reform Bill, and because religious thought at Oxford appeared to be moving toward Catholicism. One cause of criticism was the enormous gap between the incomes of the upper and the lower clergy. A few of the bishops enjoyed princely revenues. The see of Canterbury was worth £30,000 a year, and a few other bishoprics, of which Durham was the richest, brought their incumbents annual incomes of £15,000 to £20,000. On the other hand, there were cases of abject poverty among the lower clergy. Anthony Trollope, in his novels of clerical life, contrasts the affluence of Archdeacon Grantly of Plumstead with the grinding poverty of Rev. Josiah Crawley, Perpetual Curate of Hogglestock.

Absenteeism and pluralities were still serious abuses. In 1827, of 10,500 beneficed clergymen, 4500 were absentees from one of their livings. It should be remembered that there were no pensions for clergymen, so that a priest who was aged or ill could do little but ask permission to be nonresident. Yet there were many cases in which a clergyman simply preferred to live in some other place than in his parish. He was forced by law to supply a curate, but the curate might be given a pitiful stipend. The constitution of the church was cumbersome; bishops often could not discipline their clergy except through action in the ecclesiastical courts. The renting of pews to well-to-do parishioners, so that the poor were crowded into a few free seats, was another unfortunate practice. Many industrial parishes were so thickly populated that clergymen could not hope to administer properly to the people entrusted to them.

During the thirty years between 1830 and 1860 these matters were largely corrected. It was Sir Robert Peel, more than any other man, who saved the Church of England. In 1835 he established the Ecclesiastical Commission to investigate clerical incomes; the salaries of the highly paid clergy were reduced drastically and the number of canons allowed each cathedral was controlled. Peel also facilitated the subdivision of large parishes. Other legislation, passed by the Whigs, forbade clergymen to hold more than two livings simultaneously, created the bishoprics of Ripon and Manchester, and commuted tithes to small money payments. The ecclesiastical courts were reformed. Later, in the 1850s, new central courts of probate and divorce took these areas of jurisdiction away from the courts of the church, leaving them little to do. A charity commission administered nonecclesiastical trusts, that is, money left for educational and charitable purposes but often consumed in sinecures. There was also a great amount of church building; the number of clergymen was increased; and a new spirit of reform, of dedication, and of spiritual earnestness transformed the church with thoroughness and rapidity.[4]

The Oxford Movement

These ecclesiastical reforms were disliked by certain churchmen. In 1833 a group of scholars and clergymen at Oriel College, Oxford, of whom John Henry Newman, John Keble, Edward Pusey, and Hurrell Froude were leaders, formed an Association of Friends of the Church and began to publish pamphlets known as *Tracts for the Times*. This was the origin of the Oxford movement. The writers of these tracts were young men, sincerely religious, but rather given to cleverness and to a subtle type of argument which sometimes appeared sophistic. They were really ignorant of the world to which they addressed their teachings; hence they were impractical and academic. Repelled by the materialism and by the liberalism of the age, they feared that the church was in danger and that those who sought its reform were in reality seeking its destruction. The Tractarians assailed the government for redistributing the revenues of the church. They opposed the admission of nonconformists to Oxford and Cambridge, although in both cases they found themselves on the side of reaction. But they had noble aims. They sought to foster a spiritual conception of the church as a divinely constituted society, above the state's control. They laid stress on ritual, on the church's historic role, and on the doctrine of the apostolic succession which carried the church back without a break to Christ and the apostles.

The thinking of the Tractarians inclined them to Roman Catholicism. In 1841 Newman published Tract No. XC, which argued that the Thirty-nine Articles of Faith of the Church of England contained nothing contrary to the teachings of Rome. W. G. Ward, another Tractarian, declared that the articles could be given a Catholic interpretation and that in subscribing to them he had renounced no Roman doctrine. In 1845 Newman and Ward became members of the Roman Catholic Church. These and other spectacular conversions broke the Oxford movement. A wave of anti-Catholicism swept the country. When in 1850 the papacy established Roman bishops in England, the Prime Minister, Lord John Russell, was applauded for rather foolishly denouncing "papal aggression." The Oxford movement, however, awakened in the clergy a deeper sense of the spiritual significance of the church and of their dedication to a sacred calling, and it made them less inclined to mingle in the work and pleasure of the world. The movement affected the Anglican service, which gradually was made more refined and more beautiful, with greater simplicity and greater reverence.

Later in the century other disputes arose within the Church of England that may be traced to the Oxford movement. A good many of the Anglican clergy, known as Anglo-Catholics, moved toward more elaborate ritual and toward a higher conception of the priesthood. They were opposed, however, by evangelical groups within the church, both lay and clerical, who wished to keep the service simple and distinctly Protestant. So bitter did these disputes become that in 1874 Disraeli passed a Public Worship Act to regulate Anglo-Catholic practices. These divisions also produced the Broad Church Movement, sponsored by liberal

[4] See G. Kitson Clark, *The Making of Victorian England* (Cambridge, Mass.: Harvard University Press, 1962), Chap. VI.

churchmen who wished the church to accept the teachings of science and of biblical criticism but also to stress the broad and unifying essentials of faith on which all Anglicans could agree. The movement has been described as "a disposition to recognize and appreciate that which is true and good under all varieties of forms, and in persons separated from one another by the most conflicting opinions." One of the leaders of the movement was the Reverend Frederick Denison Maurice. He emphasized the unity to be found by Anglicans in the words and services of the Book of Common Prayer. Shunning formal systems of theology, he stressed the means of reconciliation between God and man, such as the incarnation of Christ and the qualities of mercy and forgiveness inherent in God's grace.[5]

Skepticism

Few of the mid-Victorians were disturbed by religious doubt. Yet there were forces at work which challenged religious orthodoxy and fundamentalist belief. The church was not troubled by the advances in astronomy, for as the universe was shown to be ever more vast, the location of Heaven could be projected into space. But geology was another matter. It showed that the earth had not been created in the manner described in Genesis. Biblical scholarship, moreover, was proving that the Scriptures had not been written in the way the churches taught. Most difficult of all was the theory of evolution, set forth in Darwin's *On the Origin of Species by means of Natural Selection* (1859), which undermined the orthodox conception of man's creation. In a word, the religion of the evangelicals could not be reconciled with the teachings of science and scholarship. Men who thought about these things were perplexed and anxious. Some became skeptics who doubted the truth of the Christian religion, or agnostics who held that the nature of God as a first cause was beyond human knowledge and understanding. One reason for the popularity of Tennyson's *In Memoriam* was its recognition of religious doubt and its comforting assurance that somehow all might yet be well.

The physical sciences, with their objective investigations, their organized attack on one problem after another, and their revelation of unalterable laws, led men to apply similar methods to social studies. H. T. Buckle, in his *History of Civilization in England*, tried unsuccessfully to explain man's history in terms of climate and terrain. Walter Bagehot began to apply scientific concepts to politics, Herbert Spencer, to sociology. Historical research, influenced by the German seminar method, became more objective and scientific; similar tendencies appeared in the study of language, as in the great project of the *Oxford English Dictionary*.

LITERATURE

The great variety and fullness of life in mid-Victorian England offered essayists, novelists, and poets ample themes on which to write. The point may be illustrated by glancing at the range and diversity of famous books published in the year 1859. To begin with, John Stuart Mill's essay *On Liberty* carried the conception of personal freedom about as far as it could be carried in an ordered

[5] R. K. Webb, *Modern England* (New York: Dodd, Mead, 1968), pp. 409–411.

society; Samuel Smiles' *Self-Help* set forth in a striking if naïve way the doctrine that hard work and devotion to duty were the keys to material success. Charles Darwin's *Origin of Species* was followed in 1860 by *Essays and Reviews*, in which seven distinguished persons courageously accepted the discoveries of science and of biblical scholarship. The year 1859 also saw the publication of Tennyson's *Idylls of the King* and Dickens' *A Tale of Two Cities*, works that followed literary and Christian tradition; but two novels, George Eliot's *Adam Bede* and George Meredith's *The Ordeal of Richard Feverel*, treated moral issues in an objective, almost pagan, way. Edward Fitzgerald's *Rubáiyát of Omar Khayyám*, in its spirit of resignation and its desire for ease and pleasure, struck a most un-Victorian note.[6]

Despite the individualism of mid-Victorian writers, one can observe certain general characteristics. The mood of social indignation, evident in the period from 1830 to 1850, continued into the middle of the century, but some of the best novels now dealt with the comfortable life of the upper classes. Concern with religious topics persisted; authors appeared as diverse as Thomas Henry Huxley, the champion of science, and Cardinal Newman, who regarded a dogmatic and traditional faith as the only bulwark against irreligion. Although many writers abandoned Christianity, they retained the moral assumptions of an evangelical society. Thomas Carlyle, for example, having rejected Christianity, constructed a new personal faith in which the attributes of Scottish Calvinism played no small part. Indeed, writers were compelled to conform to the conventions of the time if they wished to retain an audience. While some authors followed Macaulay in glorifying material progress, others were convinced that economic success was exacting too high a toll in human misery. Mid-Victorian writers were more concerned with form and craftsmanship than the Romantics had been. A characteristic unpleasant to modern readers was the role of prophet or sage assumed by some popular authors. But the Victorians, earnestly seeking guidance, expected this from literary men. Finally, we must admire the vitality and creative force of Victorian writers.

Authors of nonfictional prose were among the finest thinkers of the age. Thomas Carlyle, historian, biographer, and social critic, was the son of Scottish peasants, from whom he derived a belief in frugality, work, and discipline. He became established in London in the 1830s as a kind of literary sage, who probed into the problems of the time and expressed himself upon them with great vehemence. A blasting social critic, he felt some sympathy with the Chartists and hinted at the inevitability of revolt. His great message was a call to action. "Stop moping," he seemed to be saying, "there is work for all of us to do."[7] Contemptuous of middle-class bungling, he became disillusioned with democracy and turned to the dubious notion of the strong man or hero who would cure social ills by autocratic action. Another prose writer, Matthew Arnold, son of the schoolmaster Dr. Thomas Arnold, was a refined and sensitive critic who wrote with wit and urbanity. He was at first a poet; but his verse was rather melancholy, the broodings of an intellectual disturbed by the ferment around him. He abandoned poetry for prose in a determined effort to be more resolute and active. Turning to literary criticism, he held that literature was a potent force in shaping a civilized society; hence the writer should be highly serious, a thinker who

6 Webb, p. 313.

7 M. H. Abrams, ed., *The Norton Anthology of English Literature* (New York: Norton, 1968), p. 1763.

The Beloved, painting by Dante Gabriel Rossetti. (Tate Gallery)

offered guidance to the world. As social critic Arnold attacked the materialism of the age, its worship of wealth, its crudity in business life, its bad taste in aesthetic values. These faults he attributed to ignorance. He called the aristocrats Barbarians who liked honors, sports, and pleasure; the business classes, Philistines who occupied themselves with fanaticism, moneymaking, and tea meetings; the lower classes, the Populace, of which, he wrote, "the sterner self liked bawling, hustling, and smashing; the lighter self, beer."

Bad taste in art, in architecture, and in domestic furnishings was attacked by John Ruskin, a critic and historian of art, who turned social economist and reformer. A brilliant but erratic man, he wrote with great eloquence and moral intensity. He believed that religious faith and morality formed the basis of aesthetic feeling; that the attributes of God were to be found in things of beauty; that bad art sprang from a decadent society and good art from good social conditions. In the 1860s Ruskin began to express radical opinions upon economics, the condition of the poor, and utopian schemes of reform. Although his views were often eccentric, his attacks upon the cruelty of laissez faire and the social apathy of the well-to-do displayed a nobility of character and a deep sense of social wrong.

Of writers in the field of politics, John Stuart Mill was probably the greatest. An advanced liberal, he held that "genius can only breathe freely in an atmosphere of freedom" and that "the individual is not accountable to society for his actions, in so far as these concern the interests of no person but himself." Mill argued that self-government was more important than efficient government, that the franchise should be extended, that all special privilege should be abolished, that women should have equal rights with men, and that the state should intervene in economic life to protect and to control, even to the point of interference with the rights of property.

A number of famous novelists were writing in the mid-Victorian period. Perhaps the most gifted was Charles Dickens, whose bubbling humor, buoyancy in telling a story, and skill in creating characters placed him in the first rank of novelists. Yet the plots of many of his novels were trite; his pathos approached vulgarity. But he understood the London poor as few writers have ever done. Exposing the evils of society, he taught the moral that poverty was not the result of depravity but of bad social conditions. He portrayed the patience and good nature of the poor. He had no program of reform, however, beyond a larger humanitarianism. Two other novelists, William Makepeace Thackeray and Anthony Trollope, described the life of the upper classes. Thackeray was a disillusioned man, who satirized romantic sentiment and gave his characters reality partly by emphasizing the unpleasant side of human nature. His realism, however, was urbane and was lightened by ironic comedy. His greatest novel, *Vanity Fair,* was a picture of contemporary life, though the story was laid in the early part of the century. Trollope wrote pleasant though unexciting novels of clerical life in the country and of politics in London. There is no better way to become acquainted with the Church of England in the middle of the century than to read his novels of the clergy in the imaginary cathedral city of Barchester. Mary Evans, writing under the pen name of George Eliot, was an agnostic who defied convention in her private life. Yet in her novels she was preoccupied with problems of conscience as it gained in strength or degenerated into weakness.

The most popular of mid-Victorian poets was Alfred Tennyson. His early poems, written in a mood of romantic melancholy, contained no depth of thought but offered promise that the author would become a great master of words. This promise was amply fulfilled. A "lord of language," Tennyson developed a wonderful sense of stately cadence and full-voiced vowel sounds. His mind was somber and ponderous. When he gave himself time for reflection, his ideas were worthwhile. His long elegy, *In Memoriam,* written over a span of seventeen years, dealt gravely with problems of religion and faith and of man's relationship with God and nature. But when he wrote on impulse, he became sentimental and trivial. He wished to deal with contemporary themes; he was fascinated by science and by engineering; he could take pride in England's material progress. But there was always an element of doubt, a fear that an advancing society might end in retrogression. He was essentially a poet of somber introspection, of romantic melancholy, of musical lyrics, a lover of nature who could create scenery appropriate to the mood he wished to portray.

Unlike Tennyson, Robert Browning was a self-confident poet who wrote with great vitality and did not hesitate to break with literary tradition. He was interested in strange and occult tales, in myths of ancient times, in human psychology, especially in the workings of the criminal mind, and in Italian history and social life. His poetry was sometimes obscure. He tended to think that matters clear to him would be clear to his readers, and he often masked his thoughts and opinions in one way or another. This reticence led him to employ the dramatic monologue, a form of poetry in which a speaker in the verse discourses at length, gradually revealing his ideas and indirectly those of the poet. An optimistic man, Browning handled the religious problems of his age with more buoyancy than depth. He implied that the obvious defects of this world would be remedied by the perfection of the world to come, a hope that brought comfort to his more naïve readers. At the same time there was a realism about Browning that is quite modern; he employed colloquial phrases, discordant sounds, and jaw-breaking diction to obtain the effects he desired. Romantic and impulsive, he eloped with the poetess Elizabeth Barrett in order to save her from the domestic tyranny of her father.

Three other important poets should be mentioned: Dante Gabriel Rossetti, both poet and artist, whose polished verses remind one of Tennyson; William Morris, interested at first in poetry and the arts but later in the rise of socialism; and Algernon Charles Swinburne, whose wonderfully musical poetry challenged the moral and intellectual assumptions of the mid-Victorians.

SOCIAL CLASSES

The structure of society continued to be aristocratic. A handful of nobles and gentry owned most of the land; the middle classes were proportionately smaller than they are today; the laboring poor made up the vast bulk of the population. Of this working population, the largest single group of laborers (1,790,000) comprised those connected with agriculture, still the greatest of English industries; the second largest contained the domestic servants (1,039,000). These figures should be compared with 527,000 cotton workers, 284,000 wool workers, 103,000 workers in linen and flax, 133,000 in silk.[8] Thus large numbers of the laboring class were still on the soil or in domestic service; and many thousands of workers—miners, men in the building trades, merchant seamen, blacksmiths, shoemakers, tailors and dressmakers, and those engaged in unspecified labor—although affected indirectly by industrial developments, did not work in factories but used skills which were preindustrial in nature.

The lot of the agricultural laborer was grim. Unless he lived in an area where

---

[8] Figures taken from G. Kitson Clark, *The Making of Victorian England*, pp. 113–114. Based on the census of 1851.

industry competed with agriculture for his services, his wages were low, his housing was bad, his hours of labor were excessive. In the towns the condition of factory workers varied greatly. Abject poverty, ignorance, want, drunkenness, and brutality existed at the bottom of the scale. But there was now an upper crust of skilled or semiskilled workers who received much higher wages than in the past. They formed a class of decent and respectable laboring people who lived in modest comfort, with enough money for a little pleasure and with enough leisure to enjoy it. Parks, free concerts, museums, football matches, and cheap excursions on the railways as well as libraries and institutes for those of a serious turn of mind—these made life more interesting for the respectable poor.

It is not easy to define the middle classes. They contained some business-men of great wealth who for one reason or another, perhaps because they clung to nonconformity, were not considered more than middle class. On the other hand, there were people with very little money who asserted their superiority over workingmen. The ranks of the lower middle class consisted of all kinds of clerks, bookkeepers, and commercial travelers, of an enormous number of small retailers who operated little shops, of saloonkeepers, and of such people as fore-men in factories and in the building trades. The middle classes were pushing men of business, devoted to industry and commerce, often narrow and grasping. In religion they were evangelical, stressing the business virtues of sobriety, in-dustry, and thrift; they were apt to think that the same qualities which brought economic success would also pave the way to Heaven. They had much more money than in the past. They lived in solid comfort, as the growth of suburbs made evident, but in shockingly bad taste. The invention of metal springs began the age of upholstered chairs and sofas, bulbous in form and elephantine in size. Cheap building materials, cheap foreign wood, ugly architecture and furniture, endless knickknacks made in factories, killed the art of local craftsmen and pro-duced a dreary vulgarity in domestic arrangements.

But just as prosperity created an upper crust of laborers, so it also produced an upper middle class of successful business and professional men, a class with wealth, leisure, education, and frequent connections with the aristocracy. New luxuries, new means of enjoyment, new opportunities for thought and culture gave poise and urbanity to this upper middle class and enticed it from the mean-ness and rigidity of middle-class life. The secret of this advance was the reform of the universities and of what the English call the public schools. The mastership of Dr. Thomas Arnold at Rugby from 1828 to 1842 opened a new era for these schools, making them more scholarly and more devoted to the building of charac-ter. Arnold developed the ideal of the Christian gentleman dedicated to public service. Meanwhile, Oxford and Cambridge, under pressure of parliamentary inquiry and legislation, reformed abuses, removed sinecures, broadened curricu-lums, and opened their doors to the upper middle class.

The position of the aristocracy was surprisingly strong. Nobles and gentry, numbering together perhaps 3000 persons, were the great landowners of the country. About a quarter of the land in 1871 was in the hands of 1200 individuals; some years later there were 28 nobles each of whom possessed estates of more than 100,000 acres. Many large estates, which were normally managed well, produced revenue not only from agriculture but also from other sources, such as coal mines or urban property, or from the development of a seaside resort or a port town. Their owners were apt to be sober and practical men who were also putting money into commercial and industrial enterprises. They were by far the wealthiest class in the nation.

Greatly overrepresented in Parliament, the aristocracy continued to dominate politics. The constitutional historian, Walter Bagehot, noted that Parliament had "an undue bias towards the sentiments and views of the landed interest." Cabinet ministers, he added, "present a nearly unbroken rank of persons who either are themselves large landowners, or are connected closely by birth or intermarriage with large landowners." Their influence in borough elections was diminishing, but their hold on the countryside was strong; they could exert many pressures on what Bagehot termed the "deferential" rural electorate. The aristocracy stood at the top of the social scale. Great deference was paid to birth. The pleasures of country life and the possession of landed property fascinated the upper middle classes. The world of the aristocracy, its manners softened and its morals improved, was still an enchanted realm the wealthy businessman admired, imitated, and secretly longed to enter. And yet the rule of the aristocracy, with its inheritance of special privilege, could not continue indefinitely to satisfy the new England of industry and commerce.[9]

LIBERALISM AND POLITICS

Mid-Victorians were liberal in a broad sense. The Tories never had a majority in the Commons during this period, and the Whigs reflected the liberal tone of the country. Even the Whig aristocrats had a liberal tincture, though their liberalism was somewhat tepid. Liberalism meant a belief in reform and progress, a respect for the dignity and worth of the individual, a vague desire to give the lower classes an opportunity for self-improvement, a pride in England's free institutions, a hostility toward autocracies, a sympathy with national aspirations, and a hatred of slavery in any part of the world. There were advanced liberal thinkers, as we know, and also sharp critics of the contemporary scene.

Yet these liberal impulses did not produce a major movement of reform. Not that solicitude for the welfare of the lower classes disappeared. Between 1850 and 1854 a series of acts provided for the safety of miners and merchant seamen; for the regulation in London of burial grounds, lodging houses, and the nuisance of smoke; for an increased number of juvenile reformatories; and for supervision of lighthouses and pilot authorities.[10] On the other hand, moves to widen the franchise came to nothing. This failure was partly due to the fact that intelligent and educated men both in and out of politics, though they might agree with Mill in theory, hesitated to extend the franchise to the lower classes. What they knew of American democracy did not attract them, and they were repelled by the uncultured and sentimental language of nonconformist leaders and businessmen who asked for reform. The constitution, as it stood, was fairly liberal; it provided for government by discussion, though admittedly the role of the aristocracy in politics was far too great.

Nor did the nature of politics in the middle of the century lend itself to the passage of drastic reform. Politics were unstable and confused; Cabinets, without dependable majorities in the Commons, were overthrown on trivial issues. One reason for this instability was the lack of discipline in the Commons. In the eighteenth century members had been controlled by patronage and by the authority of the Crown; later in the nineteenth century they were controlled by party organization. But in the 1850s they did much as they pleased. Without

[9] See Clark, Chap. VII.
[10] David Roberts, *Victorian Origins of the British Welfare State* (New Haven: Yale University Press, 1960), pp. 85–92.

proper discipline, they debated issues in a purposeless way which did not lead to action.

Both Whigs and Tories, moreover, were divided and poorly organized. For some time after 1832 there had been two coherent parties, but the Tory party had been broken by its internal quarrel over the Corn Laws. The free-trade followers of Peel—known as the Peelites—had split from the protectionist Tories who had turned Peel out of office. After the election of 1847 the Peelites numbered about a hundred members and were strong in talent. But they were only a group in the Commons; they refused to work with other Tories and yet would not join the Whigs. The protectionist Tories were better organized but never had a majority. The Whigs as a group were so poorly constructed that they could hardly be called a political party. They were divided between a small radical wing, composed chiefly of businessmen, and a much larger segment of more conservative Whigs. Some of the Irish members, moreover, were inclined to draw together and to vote as an independent bloc. Hence the impossibility of forming a strong majority in the Commons. It is unprofitable to follow in detail the shifts and maneuvers of politics in this period; it is more useful to look at some of the leaders who gave coherence, such as it was, to political life.

Political Leaders

The man of the future among the Peelites was W. E. Gladstone. Trained by Peel in public finance, he made a superb Chancellor of the Exchequer. His budgets completed Peel's work in making England a free-trade country. He moved slowly but steadily from a conservative to a liberal point of view. Already a man of eminence and a giant in debate, he continued to grow in stature, though his greatness belongs to a later period.

The protectionist Tories were headed by the Earl of Derby, with Benjamin Disraeli as leader in the Commons. Derby had been important in politics since 1830. He had served as a cabinet minister under Earl Grey and under Sir Robert Peel, but, essentially conservative in spirit, he had resigned from the first of these Cabinets over Irish policy and from the second over the repeal of the Corn Laws. A skillful debater and parliamentarian, the holder of a great position in fashionable society, he was a man of ability, influence, and solid judgment. He had serious defects, however, as a party leader. His interest in classical studies and also in cards and horse racing frequently appeared to be greater than his interest in politics. Disraeli complained that he did nothing to rally his followers and was bored by the details of party politics. It was only slowly that Disraeli established his leadership of the Tories in the Commons. A Jew by race though an Anglican by conviction, Disraeli did not come from the social class of the men he was leading. The "jockey and the Jew," as a contemporary called them, held office in three short administrations.[11]

Lord John Russell was Prime Minister from 1846 to 1852 and again in 1865–1866. A younger son of the Duke of Bedford, he was the old aristocratic type of Whig. Self-confident, didactic, and egotistic, he permitted personal feelings of pique and vanity to override party loyalty. But he was liberal in policy, a good debater, and a man of courage.

The most prominent statesman of the age was Lord Palmerston. First obtaining office at the age of twenty-three, he served as a Lord of the Admiralty, as

[11] In 1852, 1858–1859, and 1866–1868.

Secretary at War, as Foreign Secretary, as Home Secretary, and finally as Prime Minister from 1855 to 1858 and again from 1859 until his death in 1865. In a span of almost sixty years he was seldom out of office. This remarkable achievement is an indication that below his buoyant and lighthearted manner there was a foundation of hard work and application to the business at hand. His special interest was foreign affairs. He had a knack of explaining his policy to the people and of appealing directly to them for support. In the middle years of the century he was tremendously popular. "His gaiety, his love of horses, his easy-going courage, good temper, and fine bearing, stood in his favor with a high-spirited and over-confident nation."[12]

He followed a liberal foreign policy, looking with favor on the constitutional states of Europe and with disfavor on the despotisms. He saw no reason to conceal his opinions. "England is one of the greatest powers of the world," he wrote to Victoria, "and her right to have and to express opinions on matters . . . bearing on her interests is unquestionable; and she is equally entitled to give upon such matters any advice which she may think useful." Unfortunately Palmerston offered his advice with a bluntness and truculence that were deeply resented abroad. "Generally when Lord Palmerston talks of diplomacy," wrote a contemporary, "he also talks of ships of war." John Bright, who thoroughly distrusted his methods, described him as "meddling everywhere, advising, encouraging, controlling, menacing as he pleases, in every country not of first-class power in Europe." As he grew older he became more rash and bouncy. The people enjoyed his blusterings, but his colleagues did not. Often acting without consulting them, he attempted to make the Foreign Office independent of Cabinet control.

In the middle of the century he was guilty of a number of indiscretions. In 1848 he permitted English arms to be sent to a band of rebels in Sicily because he disliked King Ferdinand of Naples. He defended himself in what an opponent called "a slashing, impudent speech," but was forced to apologize to King Ferdinand. In the same year he delivered a lecture to the Queen of Spain on her illiberalism.

In 1850 occurred the Don Pacifico case. Don Pacifico was a Portuguese moneylender of dubious honesty who claimed to be a British citizen because he had been born in Gibraltar. His house in Athens having been burned by a mob, he made extravagant claims against the Greek government and appealed to Palmerston for help. Palmerston at once sent a gunboat to blockade the coast of Greece. This episode involved a quarrel with France and exposed Palmerston to attack by the opponents of his policy. He defended himself in an able speech ending with the words: "As the Roman, in days of old, held himself free from indignity, when he could say 'Civis Romanus sum,' so also a British subject, in whatever land he may be, shall feel confident that the watchful eye and the strong arm of England will protect him against injustice and wrong." The speech was a popular triumph and made him more than ever the idol of the masses. But shortly he offended again by saying that General Haynau—an Austrian general who had flogged women in Italy—ought to be tossed in a blanket. He also entertained in his house the Hungarian exile Louis Kossuth, contrary to the wish of the Cabinet.

Palmerston's methods infuriated Victoria, who regarded foreign affairs as a sphere in which the sovereign might still participate, and she was far more sym-

[12] E. L. Woodward, *The Age of Reform 1815–1870* (Oxford: Clarendon Press, 1938), p. 212.

pathetic toward German and Austrian autocrats than was Palmerston. After the Don Pacifico episode, she urged Russell, then Prime Minister, to dismiss Palmerston or to shift him from the Foreign Office. She sent Palmerston a memorandum demanding that in submitting dispatches to her he should make his policies perfectly clear so that she would know to what she was giving her consent, and that once she had approved dispatches they should not be altered. Palmerston agreed but went on much as before. In 1851 he expressed to the French Ambassador his personal approval of Louis Napoleon's *coup d'état* in Paris. This angered Russell so much that Palmerston was dismissed. He blithely opposed Russell in the Commons and brought about his defeat in the following year. Thus he had his "tit for tat with John Russell." After a brief interlude of Tory rule under Derby and Disraeli, a coalition of Whigs and Peelites was formed by Lord Aberdeen. Palmerston returned to office as Home Secretary. It was this Cabinet which drifted into the Crimean War.

The Crimean War, 1854–1856

The Crimean War, in which England and France allied with the Turks against Russia, was caused by the decay of Turkey, the aggressiveness of Russia, and the fumbling policies of England and France. Time and again in the nineteenth century the Turkish Empire, its government careless, untrustworthy, and corrupt, appeared to be on the verge of collapse. The Christian peoples over whom it ruled in the Balkans were restless, eager to follow the example of the Greeks who had won their freedom in the 1820s. In the first half of the century Turkey had been menaced also by its overmighty vassal, Mehemet Ali, the Viceroy of Egypt. Above all there was Russia, Turkey's ancient foe, longing for greater influence in the Near East. On several occasions before the Crimean War Czar Nicholas I had approached the British with proposals for dividing the Turkish Empire when the inevitable collapse should take place. Indeed, to use Professor Woodward's phrase, Nicholas suggested immediate vivisection in order to forestall the risks of sudden death.[13] These overtures were received coldly. Suspicion of Russia was strong in England. To prevent Russian encroachment in the Near East was a cardinal principle of British diplomacy, for Britain was a Mediterranean power whose interests would be threatened by Russian advance. It was not forgotten that Napoleon, hoping to strike at India, first made himself master of Egypt. Russia was building a navy and had erected a naval base at Sevastopol in the Crimea. Moreover, the Russians were pushing into central Asia east of the Caspian Sea. This expansion, if continued, would bring them to the northwest frontier of India.

In France Louis Napoleon was desirous of gaining the support of the Catholic party. He attempted to do so in 1852 by reminding the Turks of an old Franco-Turkish treaty of 1740. This treaty provided that the Holy Places in Palestine (shrines connected with the life of Christ) were to be under the jurisdiction of the Roman Catholic Church. But in recent years these Holy Places had been partially controlled by the Greek Orthodox Church, to which Russia adhered.

Russia saw an opportunity to gain advantage over Turkey. Early in 1853 the Czar sent a special envoy, Prince Menshikov, to Constantinople. Menshikov, not a tactful man, demanded not only that the Holy Places remain under the jurisdiction of the Greek Orthodox Church but that Turkey recognize a Russian pro-

---

[13] Woodward, pp. 245–246.

tectorate over the Greek Christians in the Balkans. On the advice of Viscount Stratford de Redcliffe, the English Ambassador at Constantinople, the Turks yielded to Russia's demand concerning the Holy Places but refused the protectorate. There was great indecision in the British Cabinet. Russell thought that the Russians should be resisted; Palmerston was loud for "a bold, firm course." Aberdeen, the Prime Minister, was horrified at the thought of war. Not a strong man, he hesitated, but took steps which brought war closer. In June 1853 he sent a British fleet to Besíka Bay to defend Constantinople if the need arose. The Russians then invaded the Danubian Principalities, the Turks declared war, and British and French warships entered the Black Sea. A demand was made that Russia keep her fleet at Sevastopol. When Russia refused, war began.

An English expeditionary force set sail in February 1854 commanded by Lord Raglan, a keen soldier but a man of only ordinary ability. The troops were sent first to Varna on the Black Sea coast of Bulgaria. The Russians, however, retreated from the Danubian Principalities, the coast at Varna was malarial, and the allies decided to attack the naval base of Sevastopol on the Crimean peninsula. The allied army, which did not reach the Crimea until September, consisted of some 26,000 British, 30,000 French, and 5000 Turkish troops. It is thought that if the allies had stormed Sevastopol at once they might have taken it, but the French commander, St. Arnaud, insisted that the armies move to a plateau south of the fortress and organize a formal siege. This course was followed. Lord Raglan unwisely selected as his base an inlet known as Balaclava, from which only one dirt road ascended a steep hill to the plateau. He neglected to put a hard surface on the road. The British troops, camped on the plateau, were exposed to Russian attack and bore the brunt of two battles, Balaclava and Inkerman, in which the Russians were repulsed. The Battle of Balaclava is famous for the charge of the Light Brigade. Because of a poorly worded order by Raglan, which was misunderstood, 600 British cavalrymen charged up a long valley commanded by Russian guns. The guns were overrun, but few of the Light Brigade survived.

An early blizzard wrecked supply ships in the harbor and rendered the road up the hillside impassable for wagons. The troops on the plateau, though close to the shore, could not be properly supplied. Exposure and disease, combined with lack of food, inadequate clothing, and insufficient medical supplies, all but wiped out the little British army during the winter of 1854–1855. Such miseries had often been the lot of the common soldiers of all nations, but in the Crimean War, for the first time, newspaper correspondents sent home accounts of conditions at the front. The vivid dispatches of William Russell of the *Times* horrified a public unacquainted with war. Accustomed to efficiency in government, the British were indignant at the way in which the war was being mismanaged. A Cabinet crisis caused the resignation of Aberdeen; and Palmerston, to the disgust of many, stepped—or, rather, bounded—into the place of Prime Minister.

Conditions gradually improved at the front during the spring of 1855. Florence Nightingale, a woman of great strength of character, organized a good base hospital staffed with well-trained nurses. Palmerston gave the war effort new vigor. In September the fortress of Sevastopol was finally taken. Peace was signed early in 1856 whereby Russia was forbidden to have warships on the Black Sea or to construct naval installations on its banks; a commission of the states along the Danube was given power to control its navigation; Russia renounced her claim to protect the Christian subjects of the sultan; the independence of Turkey was guaranteed by the powers of Europe; and the Turks promised to reform their government in the Balkans. This treaty stopped the advance of Russia in the Near East for about twenty years, but it did little more. The British were chagrined to discover that Russian expansion, halted at Constantinople, pushed into central Asia more actively than ever. The war shook British confidence in aristocratic rule, hastened the coming of democracy, and produced some reforms in the army, though fundamental changes were not made until 1870.

THE INDIAN MUTINY

Alarming news reached England from India in the summer of 1857. The native troops, or sepoys, in the Bengal army had mutinied; the position of the British in all of northern India appeared to be threatened. Judged from a military point of view, the Mutiny was not as dangerous as it seemed. It was confined, as things turned out, to the Ganges Valley. Its back was broken within four months, and British power was fully restored in seven. Yet the Mutiny had deep and lasting effects on India and on Anglo-Indian relations.

British possessions in India had expanded rapidly during the first half of the nineteenth century. At the time of Pitt's India Act of 1784 those possessions had been confined to Bengal with certain outlying districts, to the Northern Circars and to Madras on the east coast, and to Bombay on the west.[14] Pitt's India Act had forbidden any further extension of British territory, but the attempt to govern British India in isolation from the rest of the country soon broke down. The British possessions were scattered and without natural frontiers. The existence of powerful and lawless native princes, the plunderings of robber bands, the intrigues of the French, the oppressive government of many native rulers—all rendered British intervention inevitable.

The first surge forward was made by Lord Wellesley (Governor General from 1798 to 1805), an elder brother of the Duke of Wellington. An imperious man, Wellesley was angered at the failure of native rulers to honor their treaty obligations and at their cruelty to their people; moreover, he was highly suspicious of French intrigue. By wars, annexations, and treaties he pushed the British frontier far up the Ganges Valley and brought most of southern India under British control. He made treaties, known as subsidiary treaties, with many native princes by which they placed themselves under British protection: the British guaranteed the territories of the native prince against aggression, the prince continued to rule the domestic affairs of his state, but his foreign relations were controlled by the British. Troops of the East India Company were stationed in his territories and gave him protection but they were also a reminder that he would be wise to observe carefully the terms of his subsidiary treaty.

Wellesley acquired territories so rapidly that he was recalled by the frightened authorities at home. But the expansion of British India continued. Lord Hastings (Governor General from 1813 to 1822)[15] fought a number of wars against the powerful Maratha chieftains who occupied central India and whose lands were in a constant state of war and anarchy. Their armies were followed by hordes of robbers, known as Pindaris, who plundered and tortured the hapless

---

[14] See pp. 480–485.
[15] Lord Hastings, a veteran of the Napoleonic Wars, had no connection with Warren Hastings.

peasants. At length the Pindaris encroached on British territory, and Hastings decided they must be crushed, although this involved war with the Maratha chieftains. Between 1816 and 1818, in a series of campaigns on a large scale, the Marathas were defeated and the Pindaris were wiped out. Peace and order of a kind never known before descended on the bulk of India.

Thenceforth wars were confined to the frontiers and to outlying portions of the country. A short war in 1824–1826 drove back the aggressive Burmese. A war against Afghanistan (1836–1841), undertaken by Lord Auckland for fear of Russian infiltration among the Afghans, was unjustifiable and mismanaged, and resulted in a sharp British defeat. It was followed by the even less justifiable conquest of the Amirs of Sind, who lived on the lower reaches of the Indus River. There remained only one strong native power, the Sikhs, who lived in the Punjab, a land of five rivers which flowed together to form the Indus. The Sikhs were excellent soldiers; their great ruler, Ranjit Singh, imported French generals who developed the Sikh army into a magnificent fighting force. So long as Ranjit Singh was alive, the peace was kept with Britain, but after his death in 1839 the

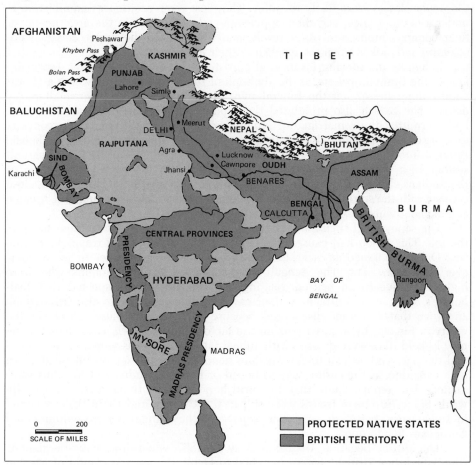

India in 1857

Sikh army got out of control and invaded British territory. In a number of short, fierce wars the Sikhs were defeated after many hard-fought battles. In 1849, as a punishment for a revolt, the British annexed the Punjab.

Such a series of wars and annexations inevitably aroused resentment among the Indians. Under Lord Dalhousie, Governor General from 1848 to 1856, grievances tended to multiply. Some were political. Like Wellesley, Dalhousie was irritated by the inefficiency and despotism of native rulers and sought opportunities to bring native states under British administration. He employed a device known as "the doctrine of lapse" by which, under certain circumstances, a native state lapsed to the British if its ruler died without an heir. It was the custom for native rulers to adopt a son if they did not have one, but Dalhousie held that an adopted heir could not inherit a state without the consent of the paramount power. The princes, believing that they were to be gradually liquidated, were deeply alarmed.

Moreover, there was another difficulty. Whenever an annexation occurred, with its transfer of administration to British officials, the peasants benefited but the upper classes were likely to suffer. They lost their position as administrators under a native prince, and their opportunities to take part in the government of their country diminished. As a result many Indians of the upper classes were resentful and looked upon the English as their enemies.

Religious and social grievances also existed. There was resentment, especially among the Brahmin priests, at the abolition of suttee, a custom by which a Hindu widow flung herself on the funeral pyre of her husband and perished in the flames. The British also prohibited the exposure of unwanted infant girls. New laws permitted the remarriage of Hindu widows and protected Hindu converts to Christianity. Indians also disliked the Western inventions which Dalhousie brought into the country. He built the first railway and set up the first telegraph system. In a word, he moved forward too rapidly for the deep conservatism of the Indians, bringing even the most ignorant and apathetic Hindu into close contact with the spirit of the West. The Mutiny was a military rising, but it came at a moment when there was much civilian discontent.

The sepoys had their own grievances. Their religion forbade them to cross the sea. This taboo had caused such inconvenience in sending troops to Burma that Dalhousie issued an order that all future recruits must agree to serve wherever they were sent. The Bengal army contained many Brahmins who were highly sensitive to all matters relating to caste and who suspected that Dalhousie's order was an attack on their caste position. They were also irritated by an order that a soldier discharged because of ill health must remain in the reserves. Finally, by a grave error in the factory at Woolwich, cartridges for the new Enfield rifles were greased with animal fat. The cow was sacred to the Hindu and the pig was unclean to the Muslim; hence, when the sepoys bit off the cap on a cartridge, as the easiest way to be rid of it, both Hindus and Muslims were defiled. The sepoys knew that the British position in India was momentarily weak. Some European troops were still in the Crimea, and those that remained in India were scattered; moreover, sepoys in the Ganges Valley outnumbered Europeans five to one.

The Mutiny began at Meerut on May 10, 1857, when three native regiments rose, killed their British officers, marched to Delhi, the ancient capital of Muslim India, and massacred the Europeans in that city. A handful of British blew up the magazine, killing themselves and a thousand mutineers. The Mutiny slowly spread down the Ganges Valley to Rohilkhand, to Jhansi, to Oudh, and to western Bengal. This desperate situation called forth heroism on the part of the British forces. An army of some 3500 men under Sir Henry Barnard, coming down from Simla, defeated 30,000 rebels and took up a position on a ridge outside Delhi. Meanwhile there was heavy fighting in Oudh. The mutineers captured Cawnpore after a siege of three weeks and massacred their European prisoners. Cawnpore was retaken in July by Sir Henry Havelock. Lucknow was besieged but did not surrender. In September Havelock was able to fight his way into the city, but the rebels closed behind him, and Lucknow had to be relieved a second time. Meanwhile another British army under John Nicholson, coming from the Punjab by forced marches of twenty-seven miles a day over a period of three weeks, joined the British outside Delhi and took the city by storm in September. With Delhi again in British hands and with the taking of Cawnpore and the strengthening of Lucknow, the tide turned against the mutineers. Strong forces and excellent commanders arrived from England; the last months of the Mutiny consisted of mopping-up operations on a large scale. The rebels degenerated into groups of brigands.

The Mutiny failed because of the devotion of the British on the spot, because the mutineers never developed great leaders, because they never escaped the ancient hostility of Hindu against Muslim, and because the Mutiny was localized. It did not touch the Punjab, Afghanistan, or the bulk of southern India. Many native princes, fearing the anarchy that would follow a British defeat, remained loyal.

The Mutiny brought many changes. An act of 1858 dissolved the East India Company and placed the rule of India entirely in the hands of the government. The change was largely formal, for the company had long since lost its political power. The Board of Control now was abolished, and a Secretary of State for India governed that country from London. In India the Governor General became a Viceroy. Over the years, however, he tended to lose power to the Secretary of State, who could telegraph his instructions to India. The Indian army was reformed, the proportion of European troops was increased, and all artillery units were composed of Europeans. The British renounced the doctrine of lapse and thenceforth fostered the native states with great care. India entered on a period of peace and rapid material progress, but bitterness remained: the memory of atrocities committed by both sides during the Mutiny could not be erased. Hindus turned away from Western ideas and looked to their own civilization and to their own religion as protections against absorption by the West. The gulf between the English and the Indian races tended to widen. British officials in India could visit England more easily than in the past, there were more English women in India, and the British, who lived their own lives instead of adopting native customs, were more aloof and less sympathetic than before.

CHINESE WARS

Two short wars with China were fought during this period. The East India Company had traded at Canton since 1684 and had learned that combination of long-suffering and bribery necessary in dealing with Chinese officials. But in 1833 England ended the company's monopoly and opened the trade at Canton to all British merchants. Without the experience of the company's agents, these merchants were soon in trouble. Moreover, a new difficulty arose. In 1839, when the Chinese Emperor determined to end the importation of opium from India by the British, a high official from Peking seized all the opium in Canton and quarreled with the British over the trial of English nationals in Chinese courts. This led to a short war in which Canton was bombarded. By the Treaty of Nanking in 1842 the Chinese opened Canton, Shanghai, and three other ports to foreign trade, ceded the island of Hong Kong to England, and paid an indemnity to the British merchants at Canton.

Difficulties continued. The Chinese, refusing to admit the equality of foreigners, attempted to curtail the concessions they had made; the British merchants wanted freer access to a rich market. A second war took place between 1856 and 1860 in which British expeditions bombarded Chinese forts near Canton, captured other forts on the Pei-ho River, and burned the Emperor's summer palace at Peking. The Chinese yielded in the Treaty of Peking in 1860, when they opened Tientsin and other ports. They also agreed to the presence of foreign diplomats at Peking and accepted the opium trade on an open and legal basis. There was a strong feeling in England that Palmerston's actions were too highhanded, but he held an election in 1857 and won a majority. In the next year he fell from power though he returned as Prime Minister in 1859 and continued in that office until his death in 1865.

PALMERSTON'S LAST MINISTRY

Palmerston was now an old man who perforce shared power with Russell as Foreign Secretary and with Gladstone as Chancellor of the Exchequer. The period is important for three phases of foreign policy. The first concerned the unification of Italy which culminated in 1859–1860 when Piedmont, under its constitutional King, Victor Emmanuel, and its statesman, Cavour, first secured French assistance in driving the Austrians from northern Italy and then attracted the states of central and southern Italy to join with it in one united kingdom. British policy was constantly on the side of Italian liberty and unification. Palmerston as usual was quite outspoken; Russell talked, quite irrelevantly, about the principles of the English Revolution in 1688; and Gladstone was horrified by what he saw on a visit to Naples. There was also a group of distinguished Italian exiles in England during this period who created an atmosphere of sympathy for the Italian cause. Victoria supported Austria but could not influence Palmerston and Russell, "those two dreadful old men," as she called them. English policy was of great assistance to the Italians and displayed a rare combination of liberalism, detailed knowledge of events in Italy, and enlightened self-interest.

English relations with the United States during the American Civil War, on the other hand, were badly handled. Ministers knew next to nothing about conditions in America. They were strongly opposed to slavery, and Lincoln's first inaugural address was taken to mean that the North accepted slavery in principle. The English sympathized with the right of the South to form a new nation, and it was believed that an independent South would be to England's commercial advantage. Neutrality was proclaimed as soon as the war began, but it was, as Russell admitted, a neutrality hostile to the North. This caused great bitterness in the northern United States.

Two incidents increased ill will. One concerned two southerners, Mason and

Slidell, sent abroad by Jefferson Davis to plead the cause of the South. They boarded a British ship, the *Trent*, at Havana. But an overzealous northern captain, acting without orders, took them off the *Trent* and brought them to the United States. The English were furious. A sharp note demanded an apology and the return of Mason and Slidell. For a short time feeling ran high on both sides of the Atlantic. But Lincoln, with his hands full at home, saw the insanity of a war with Britain. Hence he yielded. The other incident concerned the *Alabama*, a commerce raider built for the South in England. English law forbade British firms to supply equipment to ships of a power at war when England was neutral. But because of Russell's carelessness and official red tape, the *Alabama* left Liverpool on a trial run and did not return. She did a great deal of damage to northern shipping before she was destroyed. This also angered the North, and Russell was careful to see that the incident was not repeated.

A final crisis in foreign relations concerned a short war between Prussia and Denmark over the two duchies of Schleswig and Holstein. There was great sympathy in England for the Danes. Edward, the Prince of Wales, had recently married the Princess Alexandra of Denmark, who was very popular in England. Palmerston indulged in some of his usual saber rattling. If an attempt was made upon the independence of Denmark, he said, those who made the attempt would find that the Danes did not stand alone. But Bismarck continued his plans against Denmark, the English people had no intention of fighting over this issue, and Palmerston suffered the humiliation of seeing his threats ignored. The episode was an indication of the change that was coming over Europe. The military power of Prussia and the statesmanship of Bismarck were not to be deflected by Palmerston's futile blusterings. Forces, more grim and sinister than they had been in the past, were arising in Europe. Italian unification had been based on a broad liberalism, but the German counterpart was to rest on blood and iron.

30

Gladstone and the
Liberal Party 1865-1886

The mid-Victorian interlude described in the last chapter, when politics were confused and reform was of secondary importance, ended about 1867. After that date political life became more stable and effective. By 1867 the Peelites had merged with the Whigs, and Gladstone, the greatest Peelite, had moved to the position of an advanced Liberal. At the same time new forces were emerging in the middle and lower middle classes which added greatly to the strength of the Liberal party, making it truly Liberal rather than Whig. This party won the election in 1868, in 1880, and again in 1885, and formed the dominant fact of political life for twenty years. But in 1886 the Liberals were shattered by Gladstone's Irish policy, the Conservatives gathered strength, and the era of Liberal power came to an end.

The period from 1865 to 1886 had other distinctive features. It was a time of radical reforms which stressed the removal of special privilege and the importance of social questions, such as education. Two parliamentary reform bills brought manhood suffrage and began the era of true political democracy. A new interest in imperialism was to reach its crescendo in the 1890s, but it began in the 1870s encouraged by Disraeli, disliked by Gladstone. Ireland became increasingly difficult, until the Irish problem convulsed and dominated politics. Finally, the two great giants, Gladstone and Disraeli, gave to parliamentary life a fascination unparalleled in English history. Debates in the Commons were reported at length in the newspapers and were followed with zest throughout the country by rich and poor alike.

GLADSTONE AND DISRAELI

Neither Gladstone nor Disraeli sprang from the aristocracy. Gladstone's family, of Scottish origin, had settled in Liverpool and had amassed a fortune in shipping and in the slave trade. Gladstone, who had been educated at Eton and at Christ Church, Oxford, was a very learned man, with a deep interest in theology. A devout member of the Church of England, he had at one time considered becoming a clergyman. He entered Parliament in 1833 as a Conservative. In 1841 Peel had made him Vice-President of the Board of Trade. At first he was slightly mortified. "The science of politics deals with the government of men," he wrote, "but I am set to govern packages." But his training in finance was of the utmost benefit to him, and he became one of the greatest of financial ministers. As we have seen, he broke with the Conservatives in 1846, was a Peelite in the 1850s, and emerged in 1865 as a Liberal, "unmuzzled," as he told his new constituents in South Lancashire. He combined a respect for antiquity with a passion for improvement.

He took politics very seriously, almost with a sense of religious mission, approaching political problems with great moral earnestness. This led him at times to give the impression of a very good man struggling against wicked-minded opponents, but his appeal to morality fitted the temper of the age and pleased the nonconformists. He was rarely ill, could work fourteen hours a day, and could crowd more business into an hour than most men could do in twice that time. For all-round parliamentary ability he has never been surpassed. He acquired great skill in drafting legislation and in guiding it through the Commons. His impressive appearance, fine voice, tremendous vitality, and wonderful power over words made him a superb speaker, a human tornado in debate whom few men could challenge with success. Although he remained in politics too long and developed weaknesses in his old age, in his prime he was a very great man. The statute book is studded with his reforming legislation.

Disraeli was born in London in 1804. His father, Isaac Disraeli, was a wealthy Jew whose family had migrated from Spain to Vienna and then to London in the eighteenth century. The younger Disraeli was educated privately, read widely in his father's library, traveled abroad, and wrote a number of novels. He entered Parliament as a Conservative in 1837. In the struggle over the Corn Laws he made himself the spokesman of the protectionist Tories and did much to destroy Peel's position in the Commons. Disraeli then moved toward the leadership of the Conservatives, but it was an uphill fight. A Jew, a romantic novelist whose rococo effusions showed more than a touch of vulgarity, an upstart whose brilliance often was regarded as impudence, was not a likely leader of the country gentlemen of England. Yet Disraeli, in his own phrase, "climbed to the top of the greasy pole." He did so through ability, audacity, and strength of will. He was a brilliant speaker. There was an imaginative quality in his speeches, a sparkle of wit and humor, a gift for epigram, sarcasm, and irony. But he had more than sparkle. A deadly fighter, he could hit hard and wound deeply. He possessed great courage and a cool and imperturbable solidity. In facing Gladstone he never lost his nerve and always maintained a fighting front.

He had a human quality, a capacity for affection, a gift for managing people which Gladstone lacked. The difference may be seen in their relations with Victoria. Gladstone treated her with great respect and forbearance, but coldly and formally, as though, it was said, she were a public department. She never liked him. Disraeli, on the other hand, gradually overcame her early suspicion; in the end she regarded him as an intimate friend. He had cultivated her carefully and late in life he developed a fantastic attachment to her, thinking of her as a second Gloriana and to his intimates referring to her as "the Fairy."

He is remembered for his ideas rather than for his legislation. He believed in the Church of England, in the monarchy, and in imperialism. He believed in the nobility. Then, passing over the middle classes, he had faith in the British workingman. He stood also for a spirited foreign policy, perhaps because Glad-

W. E. Gladstone, by George Frederick Watts. (National Portrait Gallery, London)

stone could be accused of weakness in this area. But he was not Gladstone's equal. To Disraeli politics was a competitive game, not the means to constructive statesmanship. His measures were largely expedients, or the result of momentary inspiration, or the work of his subordinates.

The Reform Bill of 1867

For the first few years after the death of Palmerston in 1865 neither Gladstone nor Disraeli held the office of Prime Minister. Lord John (now Earl) Russell succeeded Palmerston; Gladstone remained as Chancellor of the Exche-

Benjamin Disraeli, after Sir John Millais. (National Portrait Gallery, London)

quer. Russell considered himself the father of parliamentary reform: he had introduced the bill of 1832 into the Commons, and he had sponsored several measures in the 1850s, though none of them had passed. Now as an old man he wished to try again. At his suggestion Gladstone introduced a reform bill in 1866, a moderate measure which in the boroughs would have lowered the voting qualification for householders from £10 to £7 and in the counties would have created a new class of voters whose premises were worth an annual rent of £14.

There was at first little interest in the bill; then suddenly the issue of parliamentary reform caught fire. The change was due in part to the tactics of a group of conservative Whigs. Led by Robert Lowe, these Whigs attacked the bill on the ground that the lower classes were too ignorant and too vicious to be trusted with the franchise. Lowe and his followers voted with the Conservatives, defeated the bill, and caused Russell to resign. Another Derby-Disraeli Cabinet took office (1866–1868). It did not have a majority because Lowe and his followers returned to the Whig side of the Commons. The country was demanding a reform of Parliament. Lowe's tactics had caused a wave of resentment among the workingmen; the lower middle classes, some of whom were still without the franchise, pressed for reform. In the great surge of liberal sentiment that swept the country there was a slight touch of violence. When the government closed the gates of Hyde Park in order to prevent a demonstration in favor of reform, a crowd pressed gently against the railings, broke them down, entered the park, and held its demonstration. This episode helped Disraeli make up his mind to introduce a bill of his own. He was afraid not to do so, and his belief in the workingman prompted him to act.

The Reform Bill of 1867 was passed so quickly that it was nicknamed the Ten-Minute Bill. Disraeli himself apparently did not fully understand all its clauses. This important bill, which on the surface appeared to be quite radical, gave the vote to all householders in parliamentary boroughs, thus enfranchising large numbers of workingmen; created in the counties a new class of voters whose premises were worth £12 per annum; and took 45 seats from small boroughs. In general, it enfranchised the urban factory worker but the agricultural laborer was still without the vote.

The bill, however, was not as radical as it appeared. Many boroughs now had a greatly enlarged electorate but continued to send two members to Parliament as before; thus their power in the House of Commons was not increased. Of the small boroughs, 87 survived and still returned 105 members. The new £12 qualification in the rural areas continued the exclusion of the agricultural workers. Hence the changes wrought by the bill were not decisive. Although after 1867 the number of businessmen returned by urban constituencies rapidly increased, the ascendancy of the nobility and the gentry in the counties was not fatally impaired. The bill was important in two respects: by doubling the electorate, it was an acceptance of the principle of democracy; and it created new political activity in the boroughs and greatly stimulated the organization of both parties.

THE LIBERAL PARTY

A change came over politics in the years following the Reform Bill of 1867. This change was due less to the bill itself than to the development of the

Liberal party. The general increase in wealth in the middle years of the century had created new forces and new classes in the manufacturing towns. These new forces were welded into a unit by the dynamic personality of Gladstone. To the old aristocratic Whigs new elements were now added: (1) wealthy industrialists, such as Joseph Chamberlain, the mayor of Birmingham, men who wished to be prominent in politics and were ready to take a radical line; (2) the lower middle classes of clerks and shopkeepers; and (3) an upper crust of skilled artisans and craftsmen. Gladstone, who could work with the Whigs, held the key to the situation. But he had become an advanced Liberal, and he had developed a style of speaking which appealed to men outside the educated classes. The sympathy of these audiences affected his thinking and made him more radical.

At the same time the Liberals developed a strong party organization which helped greatly in producing victories at the polls. Local associations were formed of party members, so that for a time it was possible for workingmen to have some share in these associations by attending the meetings in their wards. In 1877 Joseph Chamberlain founded a National Federation of these local groups. The National Federation seemed democratic enough, but in truth it placed control of the party in the hands of wealthy manufacturers. It imposed increasing discipline upon Liberal members of Parliament, and it returned to the Commons a new type of member who was likely to be a businessman, a radical, and a nonconformist. The number of members in the Parliament of 1868 who were willing to disestablish the Church of England was surprisingly large.[1]

GLADSTONE'S FIRST ADMINISTRATION, 1868–1874

The Liberals won an overwhelming victory in the election of 1868, and Gladstone formed his first and greatest ministry. He had a unique opportunity: he was at the height of his mental and physical powers, he had a large majority, and he had been given a popular mandate to press on with the work of reform. It is significant that one of his first measures was the disestablishment of the English church in Ireland, to which we will turn presently.[2] Other reforms came in rapid succession.

One of the most important concerned elementary education. Now that the poor can vote, said a member of the Commons, "we must educate our masters." It was indeed high time to improve the education of the lower classes. In 1833, as we have seen,[3] Parliament had begun to make annual grants for this purpose. These grants had increased to well over half a million pounds a year, but the government's support still went to schools sponsored either by the Church of England or by nonconformist bodies, and almost half the children of school age did not go to school at all. Gladstone found that he could not avoid religious controversy. Both nonconformists and the Church of England insisted upon religious instruction, but the nonconformists wanted a system of secular schools in which there would be no denominational teaching. Such schools, they hoped, would gradually replace the schools of the Church of England. The church

---

[1] G. Kitson Clark, *The Making of Victorian England* (Cambridge, Mass.: Harvard University Press, 1962), pp. 52–58, 230–234, 241.
[2] See page 665. For the sake of clarity, Gladstone's Irish policy will be dealt with as a unit.
[3] See pages 608–609.

defended the denominational principle. In fact, its schools had become so numerous that they would almost certainly be included in any state system.

Gladstone and his minister, William E. Forster, approached the problem from the standpoint of education and not of politics. Their Education Bill of 1870 retained all existing schools with good records and increased the subsidies of the government. This benefited the Church of England because its schools were more numerous than those of the nonconformists. New schools were set up in areas in which the old ones were inadequate. The new schools were known as board schools because they were controlled by locally elected boards of education. They were financed by government grants, local rates, and small student fees, though the boards could excuse the payment of fees by children of the very poor. Religious teaching in the board schools was to be undenominational and was to be given during the first or last hour of the day so that parents could remove their children if they so desired. Gladstone's act placed a school within the reach of every English child. In 1880 attendance was made compulsory and in 1891 all student fees were dropped. But Gladstone was to discover at the next election how deeply he had offended his nonconformist followers.

In 1870 Gladstone improved the civil service by basing appointments on competitive examinations. From the beginning of central civil administration ministers had used patronage in the civil service as a means of keeping their followers in good humor. Persons influential in government circles could obtain places for their friends and relatives, with the inevitable result that there was much laziness and inefficiency in the offices at Whitehall. In 1853 a commission of inquiry had recommended competitive examinations. Examinations began in 1855, but heads of departments were not required to make appointments on the basis of these examinations until Gladstone's act of 1870. Competitive examinations soon proved their worth; thus another blow was struck at the special privileges of the old ruling classes.

The same may be said of a series of reforms in the British army. The Franco-Prussian War of 1870 was a rude shock to England, for it revealed the great inferiority of the British army to Prussia's. Fortunately, Gladstone's Secretary for War, Edward Cardwell, was a man of unusual ability. His first reforms were to abolish flogging in the army in time of peace, to withdraw troops from the self-governing colonies, and to secure a royal order making the commander in chief, the Duke of Cambridge, a cousin of the Queen, subordinate to the Secretary for War.

The measure for which Cardwell is best known was the abolition of promotion in the army by purchase. Prior to this reform a senior officer upon retirement was normally entitled to sell his commission to his successor. This practice, which was deeply rooted, was based on the assumption that officers should be drawn from the upper classes and that their rank in the army was a piece of property which could be sold. The system enabled rich men to buy positions for which they were not trained, and it obstructed, though it did not prevent, promotion by merit. The Crown could, if it wished, deny an officer the right to sell his commission, could dismiss without compensation an officer who had purchased his commission, and could commission an officer who had not the means to purchase one. But the Crown did not normally exercise these rights. A bill in 1871 abolishing purchase passed the Commons with difficulty but was shelved by the Lords. The practice then was abolished by royal warrant. This forced the Lords to pass the bill, for the bill provided compensation to officers who had purchased their commissions whereas the royal warrant did not.

Cardwell also shortened the term of enlistment from twelve years to six with the colors, and six in the reserve. He associated each regiment with a county or with a similar area in Great Britain or Ireland. A regiment was provided with a depot in the county, and, being recruited from this area, could develop local associations. Each regiment contained two battalions, one of which served abroad while the other was training at the depot. Cardwell combined efficiency with economy, which won him Gladstone's confidence. He might have succeeded Gladstone as leader of the Liberal party, but he wore himself out by his work in the army and retired to private life when Gladstone resigned in 1874.

The High Court of Judicature Act of 1873 (as amended in 1876 and 1880) remodeled the central law courts in London and fused the legal systems of common law and equity. In 1873 there were eight central law courts of first instance: the ancient courts of Queen's Bench, Common Pleas, and Exchequer; the Chancery; the High Court of Admiralty, the Court of Probate, the Court for Divorce and Matrimonial Cases, and the London Bankruptcy Court. Procedure differed from court to court, there were various methods of appeal, and there were anomalies and unreasonable practices. The Judicature Act combined these courts into one High Court with three divisions: Queen's Bench, with which Common Pleas, Exchequer, and Bankruptcy were merged; Chancery; and Divorce, Probate, and Admiralty. The rules of common law and of equity were administered concurrently in all these courts, with the rules of equity prevailing in case of conflict. A new Court of Appeal was created to hear appeals from all three divisions. It was at first intended that this appeal should be final, but the House of Lords objected, asserting its ancient role as the highest court in the land. Hence it was made possible to appeal a case from the Court of Appeal to the House of Lords. To handle such appeals four distinguished lawyers were placed in the House of Lords; they held life peerages and were known as law lords. They were also made members of the Judicial Committee of the Privy Council, which heard appeals from courts overseas throughout the empire.

A number of other measures should be mentioned briefly. An act of 1872 introduced the secret ballot. Of considerable importance in England, this act was to bring startling changes in Ireland. A University Tests Act in 1871 opened fellowships and appointments at Oxford and Cambridge to persons of all religious faiths. Another act of 1871 recognized the legal status of trade unions, though it prohibited picketing in any form during industrial disputes; the Licensing Bill of the year following regulated the hours during which public houses could remain open.

The Decline of Gladstone's Ministry

The pace of reform during this famous ministry was strenuous indeed. After 1870 the Cabinet's popularity declined. Gladstone had pushed forward without considering with sufficient care the way in which voters were likely to regard his legislation. He discovered that every measure offended some group or interest: his generosity to the Church of England in his Education Act had been deeply resented by nonconformists; his Irish policy and his curtailment of special privilege had irritated the aristocracy; his bill against picketing had angered the lower classes; his licensing bill cut deeper than anyone would have imagined.[4] The liquor interests turned to the Conservatives; and many pubs became centers

[4] The Licensing Bill of 1872 was a modest measure, but in 1871 another bill (which did not pass) would have permitted magistrates to determine the number of public houses an area required. This proposal alarmed the liquor trade.

of support for the Conservative party. The saloonkeeper emerged as a man who could sway votes as much as the political orator. The Conservatives, it is true, were a little ashamed of their new ally; but the liquor interests made such substantial contributions to the party chest that their help could not be refused. And gradually other businessmen followed the liquor trade into the Conservative camp. Even Gladstone's supporters in the Commons felt they had been driven very hard. There was some justification for Disraeli's gibe in referring to the Liberal ministers on the front bench as a "range of exhausted volcanos."

Another criticism of Gladstone's policy was of a completely different kind. It was felt, not quite fairly, that he permitted England's prestige abroad to suffer loss. During the Franco-Prussian War in 1870 Bismarck made every effort to conciliate Russia, and at his secret suggestion Russia suddenly announced that she would no longer abide by the naval restrictions placed upon her at the end of the Crimean War. There was nothing that England could do but acquiesce, unless she was willing to fight Russia, which she had no intention of doing. This awkward dilemma was no fault of Gladstone's; yet he was blamed for it. Englishmen were angered to think that Britain, with all her wealth and industrial superiority, had suddenly become so impotent in Europe. Gladstone also was accused of weakness in allowing the claims of the United States in the case of the *Alabama* to be settled by arbitration. Gladstone's action was that of a statesman. But arbitration was not popular in England, nor was the payment of an indemnity of £15 million to the United States. Gladstone lost the election of 1874, and Disraeli came to power with a good working majority.

DISRAELI'S MINISTRY, 1874–1880

In view of Disraeli's brilliance and imagination, his ministry was rather disappointing. Its meager achievement can easily be explained. Disraeli had campaigned on a platform of protecting the country from Gladstone's reforming zeal which, he claimed, menaced "every institution and every interest, every class and every calling in the country." England under Disraeli's government may have profited from a period of repose, but repose is scarcely progress. And although Disraeli was a social reformer, desirous of improving the lot of the working classes, he was also the leader of a conservative party containing wealthy men who had little to gain, and possibly much to lose, by a policy of social reform. Moreover, Disraeli's period in office was a time of economic depression. There was a serious slump in trade between 1876 and 1878, the causes of which will be discussed in the next chapter; but here it may be said very generally that England was beginning to feel the competition of goods manufactured in Germany and in the United States. The old unbounded confidence in Britain's industrial future was somewhat shaken. At the same time there was a depression in agriculture. Cheap ocean transportation in iron ships and the extension of American railways to the western prairies made possible the importation of American wheat into England at very low prices. Hence Disraeli had to decide whether he would defend the British farmer by protective tariffs. But any tampering with free trade or any increase in the cost of the poor man's loaf of bread would almost certainly spell disaster for the Conservatives at the next election. Disraeli's decision, therefore, was against protection. Thus the activities of his administration were hampered by depression in trade and agriculture. Disraeli was seventy when he became Prime Minister, he felt very deeply the recent death of his wife, and he suffered severely from gout. It is not unfair to add that he was an opportunist who thought in terms of expedients and devices rather than of constructive statesmanship.

Social Legislation

Disraeli's desire for social reform was reflected in a number of minor measures. A Trade Union Act in 1875 permitted unions more freedom of action in conducting strikes. The act allowed peaceful picketing and declared that actions by a group of persons engaged in a trade dispute were not illegal if the same actions were legal when done by an individual. An Artisans' Dwelling Act passed in the same year empowered municipalities to demolish buildings in slum areas and to erect better housing for the poor. The public was protected by a Food and Drugs Act which prohibited the use of ingredients injurious to health. A Public Health Act, also in 1875 and including provisions from many earlier acts, created a code of sanitation. The Liberals scoffed at this measure as a "policy of sewage," and Disraeli enlivened a dull subject by saying, "Sanitas sanitatum, omnia sanitas"; but the act remained the basis of sanitation law for many years. In 1876, partly because of an unruly outburst in the Commons by Samuel Plimsoll, who was called the "sailor's friend," the Cabinet passed a Merchant Shipping Act which established regulations for the safety of merchant vessels. In 1878 a Factories and Workshops Act codified a large amount of earlier legislation concerning hours and conditions of labor for factory workers. This honest humdrum, as Disraeli called it, benefited the working classes in practical ways without endangering the interests or arousing the opposition of wealthy Conservatives. Disraeli's measures were steps away from laissez faire toward regulation of a mildly socialistic kind by the state.

Imperialism

The drabness of social legislation was offset by the glamour of imperialism and a spirited foreign policy. Although the empire had expanded steadily during the first half of the century, its development had followed unspectacular lines and, as we have seen, had aroused no great interest. But in the 1870s forces were gathering which rendered the idea of empire far more attractive, and Disraeli was shrewd enough to see something of what the future would bring. It was India, that rich jewel in Britain's imperial crown, which stirred his imagination. And it was primarily of India that he was thinking when in 1875 he purchased from the Khedive of Egypt a large bloc of shares in the Suez Canal Company (seven sixteenths of all the shares outstanding).

The canal, built by the French engineer Viscount de Lesseps, had been opened in 1869. Its importance for Britain was obvious. Four fifths of the shipping which passed through it was British. The route through Suez was by far the shortest route from England to India, to Australia and New Zealand, to the Malay Archipelago, and to China and Japan. A sailing ship early in the century, voyaging around Africa, had taken six months to journey from England to India. Now a fast steamship, using the Suez Canal, could reach India in three weeks. Suez altered the shipping lanes of the world. Ships from Europe had formerly sailed due east after rounding South Africa and had then followed a northerly route through the Sunda Strait between Java and Sumatra. The best route was now through Suez to Ceylon and thence through the strait between Sumatra and the Malay Peninsula. This route was dominated by Singapore, which had been acquired by Britain in 1819 on the advice of Sir Stamford Raffles. Parliament had not been sitting when Disraeli learned that the Khedive, who was deeply in debt, wished to sell his shares. Disraeli made the purchase on his own responsibility. This was recognized at once as an act of outstanding wisdom and leadership. Merely as an investment, the purchase price of £4 million brought an eightfold return over the next half century. And the strategic advantage to Britain was enormous.

In 1876 Disraeli proclaimed Victoria Empress of India. The title of Empress recalled to Indians the glories of their past under the Mogul Emperors. Moreover, it gave to India a new status as a country with a ruler of its own who was thus something more than the Queen of a distant power; the concept of an Indian Empire appealed to Indians and strengthened their loyalty to Britain. The new title, however, was criticized by the Liberals with unnecessary sharpness. It was to be used in India, not in England; one peer compared it to a patent medicine, "For external application only." A cartoon represented Disraeli as a Jewish peddler selling new crowns for old. Such criticism was stupid and beside the point. It greatly angered Victoria and increased her bias against the Liberals.

The Congress of Berlin, 1878

Meanwhile, a crisis had arisen in the Near East. Twenty years had elapsed since the Crimean War, and Russia was again on the move. Pan-Slavism, the doctrine that all Slavic peoples should draw together under the aegis of Russia, was prompting her to renew her drive for influence in the Balkans at the expense of Turkey. The Turks were in a desperate strait. Their promises made at the end of the Crimean War to reform their government in the Balkans had not been fulfilled, and Europe was growing weary of Turkish abuses. The Turks also were faced with a growing sense of nationality among the Balkan peoples. The Greeks, independent since 1829, longed to annex various areas inhabited by people of Grecian stock. The Serbs and the Rumanians, though tributary to Turkey, had obtained partial self-government and naturally wanted more. The Bulgars were less developed and were ruled directly by Turkey, but they had secured an ecclesiastical primate, the exarch, a concession which fostered their national aspirations. To the west, moreover, Austria-Hungary entertained hopes of annexing the Turkish provinces of Bosnia and Herzegovina. In the summer of 1875 a revolt broke out in these provinces and spread to Serbia and Bulgaria in the following year. In retaliation the Turks let loose on the Bulgars some irregular troops, the bashi-bazouks, who proceeded to massacre the hapless Bulgarian peasants. To Russia the condition of the Balkans appeared most inviting.

Disraeli was deeply suspicious of Russia. He remembered how Russia in 1870 had repudiated her obligation to have no ships of war on the Black Sea. He believed that if Russia became a power in the eastern Mediterranean through the dismemberment of Turkey she would pose a threat to the Suez Canal. And he was aware that the British Empire contained millions of Muslims who regarded the Sultan as the head of their religion. Hence Disraeli adopted a policy of supporting Turkey against Russia.

To Disraeli's disgust, Gladstone took a different line. Deeply shocked by the massacres in Bulgaria, Gladstone began a famous campaign to incite the English against the Turks. He wrote a pamphlet, *The Bulgarian Horrors and the Question of the East*, which sold 40,000 copies within a few days. "Let the Turks," he wrote, "now carry away their abuses in the only possible manner, namely, by carrying off themselves. Their Zaptiehs and their Mudirs, their Bimbashis and their Zusbashis, their Kaimakams and their Pashas, one and all, bag and baggage, shall I hope clear out from the province they have desolated and profaned." To Disraeli, striving to stand up against the Russians, this seemed foolish and ill-timed. Gladstone knew little about the Balkans and was apparently unaware that massacre in the Balkans was no Turkish monopoly; yet he saw one vital point Disraeli missed: that the nationalism of the Balkan peoples, if strengthened by independence from Turkey, might prove a strong deterrent to Russian expansion.

A conference of the great powers, including England, met at Constantinople in December 1876 and urged the Turks to make reforms. The Turks refused. Thereupon Russia declared war on Turkey early in 1877. Advancing through friendly Rumania, the Russians at first made rapid gains. Then they were held up for months by an able Turkish general, Osman Pasha, who occupied a fortified camp at Plevna. But in December 1877 Osman capitulated; in March 1878 the Russians dictated the Treaty of San Stefano. The most important provision of this treaty created a greatly enlarged Bulgaria, extending from the Danube to the Aegean Sea and from the Black Sea to Albania. Though nominally under Turkish suzerainty, Bulgaria was to become an autonomous principality with a Christian government and a national militia. The Christian government was to be organized by Russia; and if Bulgaria fell eventually into Russian hands, as Disraeli believed it would, the Russians would be on the Mediterranean. Other Balkan nations were given increased independence; though she retained Constantinople, Turkey was almost driven from Europe.

For some months a war fever had been rising in England. She had been neutral in the recent war, but she found it galling to stand by while her old friend Turkey was thus mauled by the Russian bear. A song in the London music halls added a new word, "jingo,"[5] to the English language:

> We don't want to fight, but, by jingo, if we do,
> We've got the ships, we've got the men, we've got the money too.

Disraeli made a number of warlike moves: a British fleet was sent to Constantinople, in a dramatic gesture Indian troops were brought to Malta, Parliament voted a large war credit. Exhausted by the Turkish war, Russia yielded to these threats and agreed to a revision of the terms of the Treaty of San Stefano. The revision was made at the Congress of Berlin (June 13 to July 13, 1878), a glittering assembly of the leading diplomats of Europe. The large Bulgaria set up by the Russians was now divided into three parts. The southern third was handed back to Turkey without safeguards for the welfare of the inhabitants. The central section, known as Eastern Rumelia, was also restored to Turkey, though it became a separate province with a Christian governor appointed by the Sultan. The northern portion was made an autonomous Bulgarian Principality, dependent on Turkey but to be organized by Russia. Bulgaria thus was reduced in size and was excluded from the Aegean; Turkey appeared once more as a European power. Serbia and Montenegro retained the independence given them by the Treaty of San Stefano. But Austria obtained the right to occupy and administer Bosnia and Herzegovina, though the provinces remained nominally Turkish; Disraeli secured the island of Cyprus for England.

Though these arrangements achieved their immediate objective of checking Russia, they created grave problems for the future. Austrian (and later German)

[5] A jingo came to mean an ardent nationalist.

ambitions in the Balkans were greatly encouraged. These ambitions were certain to clash with those of Russia. It was equally certain that there would be friction between Austria and the nationalistic Serbs. Moreover, the area restored to Turkey not only continued to be grossly misgoverned but was to become a bone of contention first between Turkey and the Balkan nations, and then among those countries themselves. But for the time being all was well. Disraeli, returning to England in the summer of 1878 and declaring that he brought "Peace with honor," was hailed with a burst of pride and popularity.

This popularity withered away during his final year and a half in office. The depression in trade lifted somewhat after 1878, but the depression in agriculture did not. Moreover, Disraeli became involved in two small imperial wars, both costly, both unexpectedly difficult, both showing that imperialism had its dark and seamy side.

The first war was in Afghanistan, the small mountainous country just beyond the northwest frontier of India, inhabited by fierce Muslim tribesmen, and of growing strategic importance as the Russians approached it from central Asia. There were two schools of thought in India regarding Afghanistan. One was to keep out of the country and to rely on the Afghans' fanatic spirit of independence to resist any Russian advance. The second, or forward, policy was to push into the wild country between India and Afghanistan and to secure control of the Khyber, Kurram, and Bolan passes through which armies could march from central Asia into northwest India. Disraeli sent out Lord Lytton as Viceroy to pursue the second of these policies. Lord Lytton, who was not fitted for the task, quarreled with Sher Ali, the Amir of Afghanistan, and all but forced him into friendship with the Russians. In 1878, when the Russians sent a military mission to Afghanistan, Lytton acted as though the Amir were to blame; three British armies marched into Afghanistan. The Russians fled, Sher Ali with them. Lytton then arranged for a British agent to reside at Kabul, the Afghan capital, and for British control of the passes. But as soon as the British armies were withdrawn, the tribesmen murdered the British agent, and the war began anew. This was the situation when Disraeli resigned, leaving an awkward problem for his successor.

Policy also was fumbled in South Africa. During the 1830s, as we have seen, a large number of the Boer farmers living in the area of the Cape had become so discontented with British rule that they had migrated into the interior. There they had established two semi-independent republics, the Transvaal and the Orange River Colony. It was the Transvaal which caused difficulty for Disraeli. Its government was extremely weak. The Boers, ranging over an enormous area, administered a crude frontier justice and often refused to pay taxes. In 1877 a British official discovered that the Boer treasury contained 12s. 6d. Moreover, the Boers were frequently at war with the fierce Bantu tribes of the interior. In the 1870s the native danger was especially great. Ketshwayo, the ruler of Zululand, maintained an army of 40,000 young celibate warriors who were as skillful as man has ever been in the use of the spear. Should Ketshwayo invade the Transvaal, he might well wipe out the Boer population. Under these circumstances Lord Carnarvon, Disraeli's Colonial Secretary, wished to annex the Transvaal, not only to strengthen its government but to pave the way for a unification of all the European colonies in South Africa. The annexation was proclaimed in April 1877, but the Boers objected violently. At about the same time a very costly war broke out with the Zulus in which some British troops in an exposed position were massacred in a sudden raid. Eventually Ketshwayo was defeated and his kingdom was divided into a number of smaller units. This war was highly unpopular in England.

The Election of 1880

In the election of 1880 Gladstone exploited the unpopularity of these two wars. He regarded imperialism as both provocative and evil, and he spoke, said a contemporary, as though "the infamy of Disraeli's policy was equalled only by the villainy with which it had been carried out." In a series of flaming speeches known as the Midlothian campaign, since it took place in Scotland, Gladstone stumped the country in a way unknown in English history. Older people were shocked to see a British statesman addressing crowds from the rear platform of a railway carriage. But democracy was bringing new methods of electioneering, and the superior organization and more daring methods of the Liberals gave them an advantage at the polls. The party was more united than it had been in 1874. These factors, together with the depression in agriculture, sufficed to win the election which brought Gladstone back to power.

Disraeli died in 1881. New men were arising in both parties. Among the Conservatives were the Marquis of Salisbury, who was to be Prime Minister three times; his nephew, A. J. Balfour; and Lord Randolph Churchill, father of the great Winston. On the Liberal side there appeared Lord Rosebery and Joseph Chamberlain; and, on a slightly lower plane, Sir Charles Dilke, G. O. Trevelyan, and John Morley. A new Irish leader, Charles Stewart Parnell, was to play a great part.

GLADSTONE'S SECOND MINISTRY, 1880–1885

Gladstone's second ministry was less successful than his first. Although the Liberals had united against Disraeli, there was internal division in the party between its more conservative members, such as Lord Granville and Lord Hartington, and the radicals. Gladstone, though radical himself, had given most of the places in his Cabinet to the conservative wing of the party; indeed, the only effective radical to be admitted was Joseph Chamberlain. There was further division over imperialism. The Liberals as a party were anti-imperialist; yet there were Liberals, such as Chamberlain and Sir Charles Dilke, who were deeply interested in the empire and who saw no reason for allowing the absorbing possibilities of imperialism to become a political monopoly of the Conservatives. They led Gladstone into various imperial ventures which he entered against his will and handled badly. He was much more interested in Ireland. But the problem of Ireland was becoming so extremely difficult that solution appeared all but hopeless. Finally, a minor but irritating problem was posed by Charles Bradlaugh, an atheist member who asked permission to affirm his allegiance instead of taking the parliamentary oath. He should have been allowed to do so. But the Speaker, instead of ruling firmly, allowed the point to be debated. A little group of four Conservatives, nicknamed the Fourth party, of whom Lord Randolph Churchill and A. J. Balfour were members, saw an opportunity to make trouble for Gladstone by rallying Conservatives, Irish members, and nonconformist Liberals against Bradlaugh. Gladstone pleaded nobly for religious toleration but was voted down. This threw discredit upon his ministry. There was a painful scene in which Bradlaugh, a powerful man, was removed from the Commons by ten policemen.

Afghanistan and South Africa

Wishing to reverse the forward policy of Disraeli in Afghanistan and South Africa, Gladstone determined to withdraw all British forces from Afghanistan. Such a move would have been interpreted in Asia as sheer weakness of which the Russians would have taken advantage. Gladstone was saved by the British generals on the spot and by the wisdom of the new Amir, Abdur Rahman. The generals withdrew, but only after marching through Afghanistan in a way that showed their mastery. Abdur Rahman, who was shrewd enough to see the advantages of British friendship, refused to accept a British resident, for he knew that the barbaric customs of his tribesmen would make bad reading abroad, but accepted what was in effect a subsidiary treaty. By this treaty the British were to conduct his foreign affairs, protect him from Russian aggression, and pay him a subsidy. He ruled his country well until his death in 1901. Gladstone was fortunate.

During the electoral campaign of 1880 Gladstone had attacked Disraeli's annexation of the Transvaal and had given the Boers the impression that, should he come to power, the annexation would be annulled. Such was his intention, but on assuming office he was busy with many matters and allowed affairs in South Africa to drift. Suddenly, in December 1880 the Boers in the Transvaal revolted. When a small British force advanced against them they defeated it decisively at Majuba Hill in February 1881. Gladstone was placed in an awkward position. To fight the Boers in the Transvaal was to incur the hostility of all the Boers throughout South Africa and to enforce an annexation of which he disapproved. If, on the other hand, he made concessions, he would be doing so after military defeat and would exalt the self-assurance of the Boers. He decided on the latter course. The Transvaal was granted independence subject to British suzerainty and to British control of its foreign relations. Thus a temporary settlement was made at the cost of future trouble.

Egypt and the Sudan

Gladstone was soon carried into a much larger imperial venture which he disliked and mismanaged—the English occupation of Egypt in 1882. Britain, of course, was deeply interested in the Suez Canal, but the immediate cause of the occupation was financial. The Egyptian Khedive Ismail was an irresponsible spendthrift who had borrowed heavily in Europe and had squandered the money on the toys of Western civilization: palaces, railways, steam yachts, and, for the ladies of his harem, bicycles and player pianos. What Egypt required was reform of a fundamental kind. Its officials were notoriously corrupt and its people downtrodden to the point of serfdom. For many weeks every year the peasants labored without pay cleaning the irrigation canals; they were ruled by the wicked sting of the kurbash, a whip of hippopotamus hide.

For Ismail the reckoning arrived at last. In 1878 the governments of England and France, prompted by the bankers who had loaned money to Ismail, demanded reforms in Egyptian finance and established a Dual Control by which European advisers were installed in Cairo. When Ismail resisted reform the Sultan in Constantinople was persuaded to depose him and to recognize his son Tewfik as Khedive. Meanwhile a dangerous nationalism was rising in Egypt. Led by an army officer, Col. Arabi Pasha, it was aimed indiscriminately at Turks, Christians, and Europeans. Early in 1882 Arabi forced the Khedive to dismiss certain of his ministers and to install Arabi as Minister of War. When it seemed that Arabi's followers might get out of hand a French and British fleet was sent to Alexandria to protect the lives of Europeans. Its presence produced the opposite effect, and in June 1882 a wild riot occurred in Alexandria in which some fifty Europeans were killed and sixty others injured. Gladstone then was persuaded to send a British army to Egypt. He invited French cooperation, but the French declined, and England went into Egypt alone. Arabi's forces were crushed rapidly and Gladstone solemnly declared that the British troops would be withdrawn as soon as order was restored. But it became apparent that the Egyptian government had collapsed. If the British withdrew, some other power would certainly intervene, and this Britain could not permit because of the canal.

Gladstone should have annexed Egypt or declared a protectorate. Instead, he clung to the idea of a temporary occupation. The Khedive retained his throne and his Egyptian ministers, but British advisers, headed by the banker Sir Evelyn Baring, Lord Cromer, were installed throughout the Egyptian administration; their advice could not be disobeyed. This cumbersome arrangement was successful only because of Cromer's outstanding ability. It proved disadvantageous to British diplomacy because the French and Russian members of a Debt Commission for Egypt consistently obstructed British rule. The British had to remain on good terms with Germany in order to get things done in Egypt. Nonetheless, under Cromer's management, the material condition of Egypt greatly improved, her European creditors received their money, and England possessed an area of strategic importance and potential wealth.

Throughout the nineteenth century the rulers of Egypt had made constant efforts to conquer the area south of Egypt known as the Sudan. It was inhabited by a barbarous people, part Negro, part Arab, fanatically Islamic. There were Egyptian garrisons in Khartoum, the principal town, and in other scattered fortresses, but the Egyptian hold on the country was slight; Egyptian government, where it existed, was atrocious. In 1881 a revolt had broken out, led by Mohammed Ahmed, a Sudanese who had proclaimed himself to be the Mahdi, or Muslim Messiah, and had begun a holy war against the Egyptians. Broken as she was, Egypt could not hope to quell the uprising, but Gladstone refused to be drawn into further adventures. To placate Egyptian feeling, however, he agreed to send a British expedition to evacuate the Egyptian garrisons, who would otherwise be slaughtered by the Mahdi's forces. The man selected for this mission was General Charles Gordon, a popular hero in England, a Bible-reading soldier who had fought in the Crimea, China, and the Sudan. Upon reaching Khartoum in February 1884 he should have evacuated at once, for the Mahdi was closing in between him and Egypt. But he did not wish to abandon outlying garrisons, and he devised a plan to set up another Sudanese as a rival to the Mahdi. This proposal was vetoed by the British Cabinet. Meanwhile the Mahdi surrounded Khartoum, and the problem became one of extracating Gordon. Gladstone and his Cabinet delayed. When at last a British expedition fought its way to Khartoum, it arrived too late. Two days earlier, on January 26, 1885, the Mahdi's forces, having stormed Khartoum, massacred every Englishman and Egyptian in the fortress. So great was the popular resentment in England that Gladstone's government never recovered from this blow. The fault had been partly Gordon's, but blame must rest far more on Gladstone and his colleagues for their unaccountable delay and negligence. For the next ten years the Sudan was left to fire and sword; the British did no more than defend the southern frontier of Egypt.

The Reform Bill of 1884–1885

Gladstone's preoccupation with the empire and, as we shall see, with Ireland made it difficult for him to enact important reforms during his second ministry. One of the minor measures permitted the burial of nonconformists in graveyards of the Church of England; another allowed farmers to kill hares and rabbits that destroyed their crops; two acts increased the pay and added to the welfare of seamen in the merchant marine; and married women were given the right to control their own property. A Settled Land Act ended old restrictions on the transfer and sale of land. These restrictions had been imposed in order to hold large estates together; their abolition was another loss of special privilege for the aristocracy. An indication that we are approaching modern times may be seen in the first Electric Lighting Act.

But such measures were a meager return for the majority given to Gladstone in 1880. He therefore pushed forward an important measure of parliamentary reform. It passed easily through the Commons but was bitterly attacked in the Lords and became law only after a series of conferences between Gladstone and Salisbury, the Conservative leader. It was divided into two parts. The first (passed in 1884) extended the franchise to all householders in the counties as the act of 1867 had extended it to all householders in the towns. Some 2 million new voters were thus created in Britain, and about 700,000 in Ireland. The act gave Ireland a larger electorate and a greater representation in Parliament on a basis of population than any other part of the United Kingdom. Parnell, the Irish leader, who knew the power the act would give him, kept very quiet.

The second part of the act abandoned the ancient principle of representation by counties and boroughs and divided most of the country into single-member constituencies of roughly equal population. By this act England became a political democracy in the sense that every man (with a few trifling exceptions) who occupied a permanent home, either as householder or lodger, could vote for a member of Parliament. The act was a severe blow to the political power of the aristocracy. The acts of 1832 and 1867 had protected in various ways the influence of the landed magnates over the rural electorate, but the act of 1884–1885 disregarded the interests of the landlord, destroyed the last of the pocket boroughs, and placed town and country on political equality. It also ended an electoral device of the Liberals, who had often run a Whig and a radical in a two-member constituency in the hope of capturing both seats. After 1885 the radicals tended to crowd out the old aristocratic type of Whig in the new single-member constituencies.[6]

GLADSTONE AND IRELAND

When a message was brought to Gladstone in 1868 indicating that he was about to become Prime Minister he was found engaged in his favorite exercise of cutting down trees on his estate. He leaned on his ax and exclaimed with deep earnestness: "My mission is to pacify Ireland." It is greatly to his credit that he was willing to grasp that bramble and to give to Ireland more intense and sympathetic study than any other Prime Minister of the nineteenth century.

For some years after the potato famine of 1845–1846 Ireland lay prostrate

---

[6] G. Kitson Clark, *The Making of Victorian England,* p. 243.

and subdued. But in the 1860s a new era of violence was opened by the Fenian Brotherhood, an organization of Irish-Americans founded in New York in 1858. The Fenians, Irishmen who had left Ireland after the famine, had carried with them a deadly hatred of England. Hoping to terrorize England into granting independence to Ireland, they perpetrated a series of senseless outrages. They attempted an invasion of Canada from the United States. They attacked police barracks in Ireland. In England they attempted to capture Chester Castle, which was used as an arsenal; to rescue Fenian prisoners from a police van in Manchester (killing a policeman in the process); and to free other Fenians from Clerkenwell Prison in London by blasting an outer wall with a barrel of gunpowder. The explosion, with an impartiality that might have been predicted, killed twelve persons and injured ten times that number. But the Fenians won little support in Ireland either from the Catholic clergy or from the people.

Gladstone hoped—vainly, as it proved—that the redress of religious and economic wrongs might yet reconcile Ireland to English rule. In 1869 he introduced a bill to disestablish the English Church in Ireland. The ease with which this important measure passed through Parliament was an indication of the strong nonconformist element among Gladstone's followers and of the moderation of the House of Lords. The church in Ireland was reduced to a private corporation without connection with the state. Tithes disappeared; so did the Irish church courts and the Irish bishops in the House of Lords. The church in Ireland retained its buildings and some £14 million of its endowment of almost £20 million. The balance was devoted to public purposes in Ireland, such as education and relief work for the unemployed. Thus the religious grievance ended.

An Irish Land Act in 1870 also passed easily because Gladstone aimed to help the Irish peasant without infringing upon the rights of property. The act compelled a landlord to pay compensation to a tenant who was evicted while paying rent and to reimburse him for unexhausted improvements made at the tenant's expense. The act, however, did not forbid evictions, nor did it prevent a landlord from raising the rent; hence it did not reach the heart of the agrarian problem and did little to conciliate Irish opinion. One feature of the act was to be important in the future. A fund was established from which Irish tenants could borrow on easy terms in order to purchase their holdings from the landlord and thus end the contant friction of their relations with him. This principle was to be adopted on a large scale later in the century.

Policy and legislation devised for England but imposed on Ireland in a mechanical way could produce unexpected results in that country. The secret ballot introduced by Gladstone in 1872 had a far greater impact on Ireland than on England. It enabled the Irish peasant to vote independently, free from the scrutiny of his landlord. In a similar way Disraeli's vital decision not to protect British agriculture by a tariff against cheap American wheat was based on conditions in England where the interests of the urban worker were thought to be paramount. But Ireland was a land of farmers. There was little Irish industry except around Belfast. Hence the agricultural depression of the 1870s and 1880s meant widespread ruin to Ireland. Rents that were based on earlier economic conditions simply could not be paid, and an Irish tenant who failed to pay his rent was evicted almost as a matter of course. By 1880, when Gladstone became Prime Minister for a second time, the misery in Ireland was appalling. Some 10,000 persons were evicted in that year. The peasants' answer was agrarian crime; in 1880 there were 2500 such outrages.

Meanwhile a demand was growing in Ireland for an end to the union with England and for the restoration of an Irish Parliament in Dublin. In 1870 an Irish member of the House of Commons, Isaac Butt, had founded the Irish Home Rule Association. He had coined the phrase "Home Rule" because the older word, "Repeal," meaning the repeal of the parliamentary union, was resented in England. Butt's movement made rapid progress; in 1874, thanks to the secret ballot, 59 of the Irish members in the Commons belonged to his party. He was a pleasant, likeable man who presented home rule as a reasonable and moderate proposal which deserved acceptance as a matter of justice. But he was ignored. In 1878, just before Gladstone returned to power, a new Irish leader, Charles Stewart Parnell, became the official head of the Home Rule party.

Parnell was not a typical Irish leader. He was a Protestant, a landlord, an aristocrat, a handsome and fastidious man of fashion. He was also cold, hard, and unemotional, dominating his followers by sheer will and intellectual power. He was a forceful speaker, though not a learned man. On one occasion in the Commons, when Gladstone made an erudite allusion, Parnell showed that he neither knew nor cared what it meant. He had a deep sense of Irish wrongs, a hatred for England—inculcated, it was said, by his mother, who was the daughter of an American admiral—and a contempt for English parliamentary tradition. Butt admitted no force but argument; Parnell, no argument but force.

He developed a fighting front both in the Commons and in Ireland. In Parliament he employed obstruction to disrupt the work of the Commons and to drive the members to a consideration of Irish questions. He once forced the Commons to remain sitting for forty-one hours at a stretch. Filibustering of this kind was quite unheard of and caused a great sensation. Gladstone, after many difficulties, obtained a closure rule by which the Speaker under certain circumstances was empowered to bring a debate to an end. Parnell provoked frequent scenes in the Commons. In a debate on an Irish coercion bill in 1881 most of the Irish members of the Commons were suspended. In Ireland Parnell came to terms with certain Fenians, though he was not a member of the group. He and Michael Davitt, a Fenian who had served seven years in prison, formed the Irish National Land League in 1879, which channeled agrarian crime into an organized reign of terror against evicting landlords and against persons who rented land from which a tenant had been evicted. Barns were burned, cattle mangled, landlords and their agents assaulted and even murdered. A man marked for vengeance might awake in the morning to find a grave dug before his doorstep. Or he might be ostracized by his neighbors, who refused to have contacts with him of any kind. The first victim of this practice was a Captain Boycott whose name added a new word to the language.

Gladstone combined coercion with conciliation. A Coercion Act in 1881 suspended habeas corpus in Ireland, empowering the government to make arrests and to hold prisoners without trial. In the same year Gladstone passed a second Irish Land Act. This act conceded a large part of what the Irish peasants claimed they were fighting for—the three F's: fair rent, fixity of tenure, and free sale of their tenancies. The act set up a Judicial Commission in Ireland with power to determine rents. Upon application by an Irish tenant, the commission could establish what it considered a fair rent for his holding; if he paid that rent he could not be evicted for a period of fifteen years. If he left his holding at the end of that time he could sell unexhausted improvements to his successor.

The weakness of this measure lay in the fact that it conceded to crime and violence what had been refused to justice and reason. The lesson was not lost upon Parnell, who continued his campaign as before. In October 1881 he was arrested under the Coercion Act. He warned that if he was imprisoned "Captain Moonlight" would take his place; this indeed happened, for agrarian crime increased to unbearable proportions. After six months of this war of nerves, Gladstone made a bargain with Parnell in April 1882. Some 100,000 Irish tenants owed large amounts in back rent; they could not appeal to the Judicial Commission until that rent was paid. Gladstone agreed to pass an Arrears Act wiping out this debt and to free Parnell if the latter would use his influence to diminish crime. As a token of good will Gladstone appointed a new Secretary for Ireland, Lord Frederick Cavendish, an able, personable, and popular man who had married a niece of Mrs. Gladstone. Cavendish went to Ireland but within a few hours of his arrival he was assassinated by a murder band known as the Invincibles, who hacked their victim to pieces with long surgical knives. England and Ireland were horrified at this base deed. Parnell himself was unnerved. Believing he was to be the next victim of the Invincibles who opposed his policy, he carried a revolver with him at all times. Yet for the next few years Ireland was quieter. Gladstone fulfilled his pledge of an Arrears Act, and Parnell for various reasons was willing to approve a temporary truce. A Crimes Act gave the government in Ireland extraordinary powers in suppressing disorder.

The Defeat of Home Rule in 1886

The year 1885 and the first half of 1886 formed an exciting period in English politics. During this time the English were called upon to decide whether they would grant home rule to Ireland.

Discredited by Gordon's death at Khartoum, Gladstone resigned in June 1885, though he still commanded a majority in the Commons. There was an element of trickery in his resignation. A general election could not be held for some time because the new voters enfranchised by the act of 1884–1885 had not yet been registered. Hence Gladstone's Conservative successor, the Marquis of Salisbury, would not command a majority in the Commons. The Conservatives, since they were in a minority, began to woo Parnell and his Irish Nationalists. The government of Ireland became more lenient. The Conservatives passed the Ashbourne Act, by which money was loaned to Irish peasants with which to buy out their landlords and thus become the owners of their little holdings. This expedient, first suggested by Gladstone's act of 1870, was now greatly extended and became a permanent policy of the Conservatives. There was also a secret interview between Lord Carnarvon, the new Viceroy in Ireland, and Parnell, in which a mild measure of home rule was discussed in a tentative way.

Parnell believed that he might obtain more from the Conservatives than from the Liberals, and in the election in November 1885 he swung the Irish vote in England to the Conservative side. The result of the election increased his importance. Some of the large cities turned against Gladstone, but the newly enfranchised rural voters gave him a majority of eighty-six over the Conservatives. By a strange coincidence, Parnell, having swept Ireland, returned with a compact Irish party of exactly eighty-six members. He had become the arbiter of governments. If he voted with the Conservatives, he could keep them in office, though he could not give them a majority. If he joined the Liberals, the Irish Nationalists and the Liberals together would command an overwhelming lead.

Meanwhile, some time in the summer of 1885, a momentous decision had been taken. Gladstone had become converted to home rule. His principal reason, apparently, was his conviction that the problems of Ireland could never be solved so long as the two parties in England attempted to make political capital of Irish questions. He wished to take Ireland out of English politics. He would gladly have avoided the thankless task of forcing a measure of Irish home rule through the English Parliament. His own party was divided on this issue. As he saw Parnell and the Conservatives drawing together he hoped that the Conservatives would pass home rule with some Liberal support, as Peel had abolished the Corn Laws in 1846 with Liberal assistance against the protectionist Tories. Gladstone decided to keep his conversion a secret for the moment because, if he supported home rule, the Conservatives might draw away from it. Hence, all through the autumn and through the election in November, he did not commit himself.

Suddenly on December 15 his son, Herbert Gladstone, from pure but mistaken motives, revealed to the press that his father was ready to support home rule. This announcement cause a great sensation. The alliance of Parnell and the Conservatives quickly ended, and Parnell sought Gladstone's support. Gladstone found himself in a most awkward position. The Conservatives, as he had feared, were now ready to fight home rule as a Liberal measure. The Liberals were divided. The Liberal leaders were angry because Gladstone had not confided his change of opinion to them. Joseph Chamberlain, in particular, had been kept in the dark under circumstances which were highly irritating to him. And Gladstone was exposed to the charge that he was adopting home rule just when such action might bring him back to power.

Moreover, new obstacles appeared. Ulster, the northeast province of Ireland, contained many Presbyterians of Scottish ancestry who had no wish to be ruled by a Roman Catholic Parliament in Dublin. As the prospects for home rule brightened, the Ulstermen became more bitter in their opposition; had the measure become law there might well have been an insurrection in Ulster. It also became clear that the British people were more opposed to home rule than was the House of Commons. Lawlessness and crime in Ireland had created the impression that the Irish were not ready for self-government. There was fear that Ireland, in her hostility to England, would use home rule to break the union and would combine with England's foes. And finally, Parnell's tactics in the Commons and his contempt for English tradition had aroused a deep resentment among the English people. This was an aspect of the problem which Parnell had not foreseen.

In view of all these difficulties, Gladstone might well have drawn back from forming a government committed to home rule. Yet he did not hesitate when Salisbury resigned in January 1886. Gladstone was now seventy-six. Old age had a curious effect on him: he retained astonishing physical and mental powers and his speeches continued to be masterly, forceful, and persuasive; but he became less prudent, and he could make serious mistakes of judgment. In April 1886, amid intense excitement, he introduced his home rule bill. It would have created an Irish Parliament and an Irish Cabinet in Dublin, but there were many reserved subjects which the Irish government could not touch: the Crown, the army and navy, foreign relations and the question of peace and war, customs and excises, post office and currency, weights and measures. Irish taxes, moreover, were to be determined in London; some forty percent of the proceeds were to go for imperial defense and for interest on the national debt. The Irish Parliament was not to consist of houses but of two orders which were to sit together though they might vote separately. There were to be no Irish members in the English Parliament. At first this provision was liked but later it was recognized as a weakness because the Irish, if taxed and restricted by an imperial Parliament in which they were not represented, would certainly continue the struggle for greater liberty.

In June the bill was defeated because a large number of dissentient Liberals voted against it. The margin of defeat, however, was not large. Under these circumstances the Cabinet system gave the Prime Minister a choice: he could resign, or he could dissolve Parliament and hold an election on the assumption that the country supported him and would give him a majority in a new House of Commons. But the second of these alternatives was highly dangerous when the party in power was divided against itself. Nonetheless, in a frenzy of mistaken zeal, Gladstone adopted it, although there had been an election only eight months before. He thus shattered the Liberal party. The results at the polls tell the story: 316 Conservatives, 78 dissentient Liberals who came to be called Unionists and eventually merged with the Conservative party, 191 Gladstonian Liberals, 85 Irish Nationalists. Gladstone resigned at once; Salisbury formed his second ministry. With one Liberal interlude the Conservatives governed the country for the next twenty years.

31

salisbury and imperialism

SALISBURY'S SECOND MINISTRY

The Marquis of Salisbury, who formed his second ministry in August 1886, was Prime Minister three times (1885–1886; 1886–1892; 1895–1902), a total of more than thirteen and a half years. He was the last noble to hold that office. A descendant of the Cecils, who had been statesmen under Elizabeth I and James I, Salisbury was a handsome, dignified, impressive man with a great, black beard. His mind was of a somber, aristocratic caste, calm and imperturbable in temper, massive in wisdom and judgment, highly critical, not given to optimism. He was a powerful debater who could expose the weaknesses of his opponents with devastating and sometimes savage force. His gift for epigram was second only to Disraeli's, and there was a sardonic quality about his wit that gave it a cutting edge. His principal interests were foreign and imperial affairs, which he handled with Italian subtlety and admirable judgment. But he did not plan ahead as did Bismarck; he was content to meet problems as they arose. This negative approach was even more evident in his domestic policy. He had little faith in the value of popular reforms. Indeed, he disliked change, was content to leave things much as they were, and had no constructive program. He did not control his colleagues as Disraeli had done but tended to let them alone unless they sought his advice. Always the aristocrat, he had nothing but contempt for the tricks and devices of the low politician; he kept public life on a high and honorable plane.

Politics in 1886

Salisbury was not in a strong position in the early days of his second ministry. He was dependent on the votes of the Liberal Unionists, who had broken with Gladstone over home rule, but the Unionists did not coalesce with the Conservatives until 1895. Salisbury also was troubled by his colleague Lord Randolph Churchill. Churchill had risen to prominence in 1880 when his skill and boldness in debate had enabled him to oppose Gladstone with success. Had he been older and more experienced he might have become the Conservative

Prime Minister after Gladstone's defeat in 1886. He was much closer to Disraeli's tradition of Tory democracy than was Salisbury. Indeed, he was something of a radical. He had fought the more conservative elements of his party and had built up the party machine, much as Joseph Chamberlain had done among the Liberals. In Salisbury's second Cabinet Churchill received the brilliant appointment of Chancellor of the Exchequer and leader of the House of Commons. At the age of thirty-seven he was the youngest man to hold these positions since the younger Pitt.

He began very well, but a quarrel developed in the Cabinet over his first budget. Wishing to make economies, he tried to squeeze the budgets of his colleagues. When they resisted, he wrote to Salisbury that he would resign if they were not overruled. This dangerous and highhanded device was a failure. Salisbury would not overrule other ministers, and Churchill, having published his resignation in the *Times*, had to carry it through. He assumed that he would be recalled to office, but he was not. By a willful and petulant act, which showed him to be impossible as a colleague, he had ruined his political career. Salisbury's position, however, was strengthened.

Moreover, the debacle among the Liberals became more and more obvious. They lost Joseph Chamberlain, their second greatest figure, who took the city of Birmingham with him into the Unionist camp. They lost some of the London radicals who drifted off toward socialism. Almost the entire Whig aristocracy deserted the Liberal party and gave the Conservatives a solid, permanent, and irremovable majority in the House of Lords. Furthermore, there was a fundamental shift of political forces about this time. In the great days of the Liberal party Gladstone had attracted a number of successful businessmen who were willing to take a radical line and welcomed an opportunity to attack the landed aristocracy. But these businessmen had now reached an economic and social position which might well be threatened by radical policies. There was a general movement of business interests from the Liberal to the Conservative side; the Conservative party had become the party of the well-to-do. The Liberals retained the alliance of the Irish Nationalists, but the Nationalists soon were weakened, and the Liberals were thus dependent on the nonconformist Celtic fringe in Wales and Scotland.[1]

Parnellism and Crime

It was also an advantage to Salisbury that Ireland continued to be the center of politics and thus kept alive the issue of home rule. Interest centered in Parnell, the Irish nationalist. In April 1887 the *Times* published some sensational letters, supposedly written by Parnell in 1882, in which he expressed approval of the assassination of Lord Frederick Cavendish by an Irish murder band known as the Invincibles.[2] These letters were the talk of the town. The assassination had horrified England, and Parnell had denounced it in the strongest terms. If, then, he was shown to have approved it in secret, he stood revealed as thoroughly dishonest. With great passion Parnell declared that the letters were forgeries and asked for a parliamentary inquiry. After some delay the government appointed a commission of three eminent judges to conduct an investigation, which was long and thorough. Among the witnesses was a dis-

[1] G. Kitson Clark, *The Making of Victorian England* (Cambridge, Mass.: Harvard University Press, 1962), pp. 230–241.
[2] See page 667.

reputable Irish journalist, Richard Pigott, who did not stand up well under cross-examination. Later he fled the country, mailed a confession to the *Times* acknowledging that he had forged the letters, and committed suicide in Spain. Completely exonerated, Parnell stood at the height of his influence.

Within a year he came crashing down when he was named as corespondent in the divorce case of Captain W. H. O'Shea against his wife. A few people had known for a long time that a liaison existed between Parnell and Mrs. O'Shea, but the news came as a shock to the public, and the story told in court by Captain O'Shea was more damaging to Parnell than the truth would have been. For private reasons Parnell did not contest the case. He believed at first that the scandal would not disturb his position in politics; indeed, most of his Irish followers expressed confidence in him. But the stigma attached to divorce was very great, and the nonconformists in the Liberal party were deeply offended. They intimated to Gladstone that they would not tolerate his continued alliance with Parnell; the Irish must select a new leader. When Parnell refused to give way there followed a long and unseemly wrangle among the Irish members, who split into two groups, one remaining with Parnell, the other seceding from him. He fought fiercely against great odds, but the contest shattered his health and in October 1891 he died. As a parliamentary tactician he has rarely been surpassed. As a patriot fighting for the welfare of his country he must be ranked among the great. The Irish members continued to rend each other, thus greatly weakening the cause of home rule.

Meanwhile, trouble was renewed in Ireland. According to a new device known as the Plan of Campaign the tenants of each Irish estate were encouraged to organize and to decide what a fair rent for their holdings would be. This sum was to be offered to the landlord; if he refused, the money was to be paid into a central fund. The result was a new wave of evictions and an increase in crime. But A. J. Balfour, the Irish Secretary, proved himself a man of force and courage. He secured new coercive legislation and ruled Ireland with a firm hand. At the same time he extended the Ashbourne Act, which gave tenants the opportunity to borrow money and to buy out the landlords. After three tumultuous years Ireland subsided into comparative quiet.

The Local Government Act of 1888

Although the Municipal Corporations Act of 1835 had democratized the government of the towns, rural areas had remained under the ancient jurisdiction of the justices of the peace. A Local Government Act of 1888, which was symbolic of what was happening in the countryside, transferred their administrative and some of their police functions to elected county councils.

The Decline of Aristocratic Control over the Countryside

For many centuries, as we know, the rural areas of Britain had been dominated by the nobility and gentry in both an economic and a political sense. This domination had survived the Reform Bills of 1832 and 1867, the repeal of the Corn Laws, and the disappearance of special privilege. The prints of hunting scenes from the middle of the century, with their robust squires and pretty girls in attractive riding habits, depict a rural aristocracy still firmly entrenched. But in the 1870s and 1880s the hold of the aristocracy over the countryside was undermined by the advance of democracy and by the harsh impact of economic change. The Secret Ballot Act of 1872, the Corrupt Practices Act of 1883, the Reform Bill of 1884–1885 which ended pocket boroughs—all these deprived the landed classes of their old influence over the rural voter.

Of far greater importance than these reforms was the ruin of British agriculture as cheap American wheat began to flood the English market. This wheat, grown on the virgin soil of a new continent, was so low in price that British farmers simply could not compete. It was no fault of theirs that disaster fell on agriculture in Britain, where farming was highly scientific. Her farm animals were carefully bred, her rotation of crops was excellent, her yield per acre was very great. In fact, Britain was leading the world in agriculture almost as much as in industry. Prior to about 1875 British agriculture had maintained a certain supremacy over trade and commerce. The largest single British industry, it employed the greatest number of persons and produced great wealth. But now the railways on the American prairie, the improvement in ocean transportation, and the invention of agricultural machinery for prairie farming brought catastrophic results in Britain. The price of wheat sank from 56s. 9d. a quarter in 1877 to 31s. in 1886; to 26s. 4d. in 1893; and to 19s. 8d. in 1894. Thereafter it rose slightly, though not very much. The acreage under wheat in Britain was cut in half between 1872 and 1900. Rents had to be reduced both in England and in Ireland. In 1888 they stood at about £59 million per annum; in 1901 at about £42 million. Agricultural wages declined, and there was a steady exodus of laborers from the countryside. In 1901 only about one fifth of Britain's total population remained on the land. Britain became increasingly dependent on imported wheat. During the 1890s about sixty-five percent of the wheat she consumed came in from overseas. British agriculture might have been saved by a tariff. Other European nations faced the same problem, and almost all of them protected their farmers with tariff walls. The cost, of course, was high. The factory worker paid more for his loaf of bread; a tariff was a direct subsidy to the farmer which had to be paid in one way or another by the rest of the community. The Continent, believing that farmers made the best soldiers, paid the price. Britain, less preoccupied with war and more highly urbanized, decided not to.[3]

A run of poor harvests between 1874 and 1879—of which the last was especially poor—also contributed to the difficulties of British agriculture. Despite the scarcity of home-grown wheat, prices did not rise because of the wheat that came in from abroad.

And yet the old life of the country gentleman continued, though it was no longer supported by agricultural rents. This was possible because large numbers of the aristocracy now drew their incomes from nonagricultural sources—investments, directorships, the law, political office, a lucrative marriage, perhaps with an American heiress. There was also the ancient process by which old families sold their estates and newly rich ones bought places in the country. By the end of the century the automobile made it possible for a man to live far from the city and yet maintain close connections with it. Country life continued to flourish because wealthy people liked to live in the country, and rural society reshaped itself to cater to their wishes. A number of people whose gentility was derived from past ownership of land now lived in the city, most likely in London, where

[3] R. C. K. Ensor, *England 1870–1914* (Oxford: Clarendon Press, 1936), pp. 115–121, 284–286.

they were courted by other city dwellers who craved a gentility to which they had no pretension.[4]

Meanwhile Salisbury was occupied chiefly with foreign and imperial affairs, to which we will turn presently.

A LIBERAL INTERLUDE, 1892–1895

The two Liberal Cabinets which governed the country between 1892 and 1895 formed no more than an interlude in a long period of Conservative rule. The Liberals were weak and unsuccessful, but their term of power at least kept alive the two-party system and trained a number of able young men who reappeared in 1905 when the Liberals returned to office.

The election of 1892 gave the Liberals and Irish Nationalists a small majority over Conservatives and Unionists. Gladstone at once formed his fourth Cabinet, but his prospects were bleak. He was then almost eighty-three and, though still a formidable debater, he was not the power he had been in his prime. He was burdened by a long list of proposed reforms known as the Newcastle Program to which his party had committed itself. Moreover, he was faced by a hostile and overwhelming opposition in the House of Lords. Indeed, he remained in politics only because of his intense desire to settle the Irish question.

His chief concern was a second home rule bill. Like the bill of 1886, it provided for a Parliament and an executive in Dublin, but with many reserved subjects that could be handled only by the imperial Parliament in London. The new feature of the second bill was a provision for 80 Irish members at Westminster who were to take part in the work of the Commons only when Irish or imperial affairs were under discussion. This provision answered an objection to the first bill that it left the Irish unrepresented in London, but it would have played havoc with the operation of the Cabinet system of government. The bill was defended by Gladstone in a long series of eloquent arguments and was denounced with great power by Chamberlain. It passed through all its stages in the Commons but was thrown out by the Lords in a vote of 419 to 41 and thus came to an end. However, it had made far greater progress than the first bill and its chances of revival were good. Gladstone was keenly aware of the problem created by the Tory majority in the Lords: the Lords defeated the home rule bill, they mangled an important bill on local government (which set up parish councils), and they killed a bill for employers' liability in case of injury to workmen. They created a state of affairs which, Gladstone asserted, could not continue. In March 1894 he resigned, sixty-one years after he had first spoken in the Commons.

The Liberal government limped along for another sixteen months under the premiership of Lord Rosebery. Its position was weaker than ever. Rosebery was a personable man—young, handsome, rich, and eloquent—but he was not an adroit politician, and he never aroused the loyalty of his followers. Many of them thought that Sir William Harcourt, the Chancellor of the Exchequer, should have been Gladstone's successor. The nonconformists were suspicious of Rosebery, not only because he was a Whig aristocrat and an imperialist, but because he was a great patron of the turf. Twice while he was Prime Minister his horses won the Derby. He had few other successes. The House of Lords was adamant in its

---

[4] G. Kitson Clark, *The Making of Victorian England*, pp. 242–274.

opposition to all Liberal measures. Cabinet ministers were furious and sent up measure after measure which they knew would be defeated. They thought that "filling up the cup" of the Lords' iniquities would turn the nation against the upper chamber. But to the people such a policy appeared weak and ineffective. Although the Lords had their way and practically drove Rosebery from office, in the long run they were digging their own grave.

The Lords did not dare touch the budget. Harcourt's important budget of 1894 increased death duties by taking all the assets of an estate, landed and otherwise, and taxing them as a unit instead of taxing the several fractions that went to various beneficiaries. This was a new form of direct taxation which later Chancellors of the Exchequer were not likely to forget. Its drawbacks were that it could be increased easily and that the government was taking capital and spending it as income.

Rosebery resigned in June 1895, an election gave the Conservatives a good majority, and Salisbury formed his third Cabinet. It contained five Unionists, including Chamberlain, who took the post of Colonial Secretary and was so powerful that he was almost copremier. Chamberlain's attention now shifted from Ireland and from radical reform to questions concerning the empire.

THE NEW IMPERIALISM

British interest in the empire increased during the last quarter of the nineteenth century until imperial expansion became a dominant theme in British thought and policy. The desire for empire and for the acquisition of colonies was not confined to England. Between 1870 and 1900 the nations of Europe divided almost the whole of Africa among themselves, acquired large sections of Asia, and annexed hundreds of islands throughout the Pacific Ocean. The British added some 5 million square miles to their empire until by 1900 it included a fifth of all the land on the face of the globe. So eager were the nations for colonies and spheres of influence that competition brought dangerous international crises. This competition sounds very old-fashioned today, for Europe is now in retreat from Asia and Africa and is being excluded from its former influence there. We are now feeling what may be called the backlash of nineteenth-century imperialism.

The most fundamental reason for imperialism was economic. England's position is highly instructive. The wonderful prosperity she had enjoyed in the middle years of the century reached a climax about 1870, when British foreign trade was greater in value than the combined foreign trade of France, Germany, and Italy. England's production of pig iron—the basis of both puddled iron and steel—was larger than the production of all the rest of the world. She was mining almost half the world's coal, her shipbuilding industry reached outstanding pre-eminence, she was selling vast quantities of textiles in Europe, America, and the East. But after 1874 came a period of industrial and commercial depression, falling prices, and increased foreign competition. During a serious depression in the years 1876–1878 about ten percent of the working population was unemployed; a second depression quickly followed between 1883 and 1886. These two slumps, coming in rapid succession, ended the buoyant optimism of the mid-Victorians. Indeed, England was never again quite the same. In absolute terms her wealth continued to increase, her population to grow, and her foreign trade to expand, but the pace was slower than in the past, much slower than the rate of increase

Joseph Chamberlain, by Frank Hall. (National Portrait Gallery, London)

in Germany or in the United States. In brief, Britain was no longer the only workshop in the world. Germany, the United States, Belgium, and, to a lesser extent, France, Japan, and portions of the British Empire were becoming industrial nations. They protected their industries by tariff walls against British goods. Total exports of British iron and steel increased, but the amounts sold to countries with high tariffs declined. By 1900 Germany produced more steel than Britain did, and the United States produced twice as much. British exports of cotton goods, which declined slightly, were sold for the most part in India, China, and the Near East; they were almost excluded from Europe and the United States.

The articles of British export which showed an increase were indicative of changed conditions. One was machinery. The value of exported machinery more than doubled between 1880 and 1900. But exported machines increased the industrial potential of foreign countries and reduced their demand for British goods. Britain also built many ships for foreign customers. But as the world's greatest carrier of goods by sea, she was making other nations less dependent on her by selling them ships. Finally, the export of British coal greatly increased. It was admirably suited for use by steamships and was mined close to the sea, but coal was an irreplaceable national asset which should have been saved for the industrial needs of the future. The picture must not be made too dark, for Great Britain was still a very wealthy country with enormous resources at home and abroad.[5]

These developments made the empire appear more attractive than in the past. It was a market for British goods. The quantity of cotton cloth sent to India, for instance, was enormous; British iron and steel and countless other manufactured articles were sold in the empire all over the world. The empire was a source of raw materials—cotton, wool, oil, rubber, lumber, jute, palm oil for soap, sugar, tobacco, tea, and coffee. Improvement of transportation by sea enabled ships to carry larger cargoes at greatly reduced freight rates. The change from wooden sailing ships to iron and steel ships propelled by steam had been very slow. It was only in the 1860s that iron largely replaced wood and only in the 1880s that steel replaced iron. Many iron ships (including the composites with wooden walls over an iron frame) were propelled by sail, for the early steamers consumed such quantities of coal that little space was left for cargo. But after compound engines, introduced about 1863, cut in half the amount of coal required, the number of steamships increased rapidly. And once the change was made, it brought enormous advantages. Iron and steel ships could be many times the size of wooden ones; they were safer than wood, lighter, and less costly in repairs. Independent of the wind, steamers could run on regular schedules and could make many more voyages than sailing ships in a given time. They could penetrate easily in areas where sailing ships had trouble, such as the rivers of China or the coast of West Africa near the equator. The speed of steamers was increased greatly in 1881 by the introduction of triple-expansion engines. Three years later the Cunarder *Umbria* (not, of course, a freighter) crossed the Atlantic westward in five days and twenty-two hours.

The empire also provided opportunities for the investment of surplus capital. Many enterprises at home had reached a point at which increased investment did not produce great profit, perhaps bringing a return of only two or three percent. On the other hand, an investment in some undeveloped area might offer dividends of fifteen or twenty percent, though the risk was greater. In the last quarter of the nineteenth century between one half and two thirds of surplus British capital was going abroad; by 1914 the British had invested some £4 billion in enterprises overseas. If she was no longer the workshop of the world, she was the world's capitalist, its landlord, its banker, and its bond and mortgage holder.

[5] R. C. K. Ensor, *England 1870–1914*, pp. 102–115, 269–284.

The stocks of hundreds of companies throughout the empire were bought and sold on the London Stock Exchange.

There were other motives for imperialism. The possession of colonies was the symbol of a great power. Nations with colonies took pride in them; nations without them, such as Italy, struggled to obtain them and cast envious eyes at the huge British Empire. The acquisition of colonies became a game at which a nation must not be outdone by its neighbors. Imperialism was popular with both rich and poor. One can understand why manufacturers, merchants, shipowners, bankers, and diplomats favored it. What is surprising, the English lower classes also liked it. Empire meant employment. Moreover, it offered the thrill and excitement of international conflict as well as an opportunity for chauvinistic excesses. This taste was catered to by a cheap sensational press that appeared in England toward the end of the century and by a literature of adventure and stories of the sea, spiced with depictions of brutality and of life in the raw. The public, it was said, wanted more chops—bloody ones with gristle. Meanwhile, the upper classes were influenced by such misunderstood phrases from Darwinian evolution as "the survival of the fittest" and "the struggle for existence," which appeared to justify the conquest of weaker peoples by the imperialists of Europe. It is only fair to add, however, that imperialism also carried a sense of mission. Europe must assume "the white man's burden" and must take civilization to the backward peoples of the world.

The Partition of Africa

The scramble for Africa was precipitated by three events. The first was the achievement of the explorer H. M. Stanley in crossing tropical Africa. In 1874 he plunged into the wilderness on the east coast with three other white men (who died on the way) and with a little band of Arab guides and Negro porters. Pushing through prairies, swamps, and jungles, braving wild beasts, savages, and tropical fevers, he made his way to the upper stretches of the Congo River and followed that great stream to the Atlantic. He attempted in vain to interest the British government in the Congo Basin and then reluctantly entered the service of King Leopold of Belgium, who eventually created the Congo Free State and became its ruler. A second development was the action of the French, who pushed inland from their settlements on the Senegal River, crossed to the upper reaches of the Niger, consolidated this inland empire, and began to connect it with their stations along the western coast. And in 1882 Bismarck annexed the territory known as German Southwest Africa, which up to that time the British might have had for the taking.

Salisbury's diplomacy obtained a great deal of African territory for England without causing a war with other powers, but the initial effort came from a remarkable group of lesser men—explorers, merchants, and shipowners—who penetrated or sent agents into the wilds of Africa and made treaties with native chiefs on which British diplomacy could base its claims. In West Africa Sir George Taubman Goldie united into the Royal Niger Company (1886) a number of British firms trading on the Niger and pushed northward along the river, making treaties until he met the French. He thus acquired modern Nigeria for Britain. How these treaties were made is described vividly by the explorer Sir Harry Johnston, who tells how he ascended a river in West Africa, the only white man in a large canoe with forty native paddlers. He landed at a small village and for a time was lodged in a hut around the roof of which he saw a frieze of human skulls. Hanging from the ceiling was a smoked human ham. When the chief appeared, Johnston told him that he had come from a great white Queen who wished to make a book of friendship with him. Johnston then was taken back to the canoe, where he produced a treaty blank on which the chieftain scratched an X. This agreement was solemnly ratified in London, and the chief discovered later, and to his surprise, that he had placed his lands under the protection of the British Crown.

In East Africa Sir William Mackinnon and Sir John Kirk became advisers of the Sultan of Zanzibar and employed Stanley and Johnston to make treaties with the chiefs on the mainland. The British East Africa Company, chartered in 1888, obtained for Britain what is now Kenya and Uganda. Expansion in South Africa was the work of Cecil Rhodes. The son of an English clergyman, he went to South Africa in 1870 just as diamonds were discovered in the vicinity of Kimberley. Rhodes, who made a great fortune in diamonds and later in gold, became

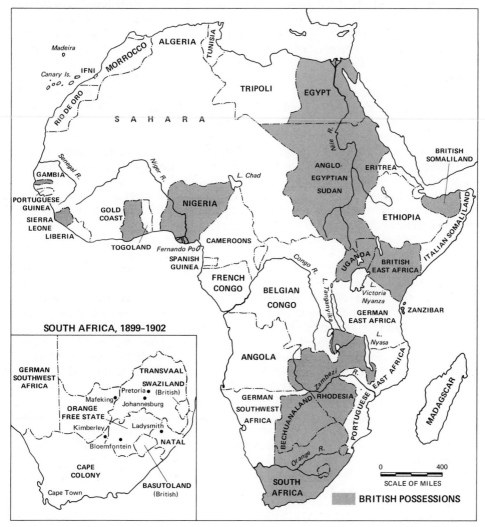

Africa in 1914

Prime Minister of Cape Colony in 1890. A year earlier he had obtained a charter for the British South Africa Company, which, pushing northward, claimed for England the territories known as Northern and Southern Rhodesia.

But local agreements with African chiefs meant nothing unless they were backed by diplomacy in London and resulted in international treaties. In 1890 three important treaties concluded with Germany, France, and Portugal delineated African boundaries and went far toward easing tension among the great powers. "Taken together they form the most positive achievement of Lord Salisbury's diplomacy."[6]

A sharp clash with France in 1898–1899 was known as the Fashoda incident. It concerned the Sudan, the area south of Egypt from which the British had been driven in 1885 when Gordon had been slain at Khartoum.[7] The Sudan was important because it controlled the Nile, the key to the control of Egypt. The British, therefore, determined upon its reconquest. In 1896 the Sudan was invaded from the north by Sir Herbert Kitchener, the commander of the British army in Egypt. He moved slowly, consolidating his conquest and building a railway as he advanced. In September 1898 he defeated a large army of dervishes at the Battle of Omdurman and entered nearby Khartoum, thus avenging the death of Gordon. Suddenly he heard that a French expedition had appeared at Fashoda 500 miles farther up the Nile. This expedition was commanded by Captain Marchand, a gallant French officer who had made his way across Africa from the French Congo. Kitchener quickly reached Fashoda, where a dramatic meeting took place between the two commanders. Kitchener was in superior force, but any violence might have caused war with France. Kitchener therefore handed Marchand a written protest, hoisted the English and Egyptian flags, and referred the matter to London. The French could hardly have hoped to acquire the Sudan although they may have thought they could obtain a corridor from French West Africa to the Nile. But Salisbury was absolutely firm, and after several months of great tension the French gave way and Marchand was recalled. Thus the English were entrenched firmly throughout the entire Valley of the Nile.

The Boer War

Meanwhile events were approaching a crisis in South Africa. When the Cape had been acquired by the British in 1815 it had contained about 25,000 Boer farmers, about 30,000 Negro slaves, and perhaps another 20,000 free Negroes. The Boers had never been handled properly. As we have seen, they resented British rule and hated British missionaries. After the abolition of slavery in 1833 a large number of Boers, perhaps as many as 10,000, had sought to escape from British control by moving into new territory to the north and east. A small white population thus was scattered over an enormous area. By the middle of the century there were four separate colonies in South Africa: the Orange Free State and the Transvaal, which were entirely Boer; and Cape Colony and Natal, which contained both Boers and British settlers. The Boer governments were weak, unstable, and primitive; relations among the four colonies were far from satisfactory. Disraeli, as we have seen, annexed the Transvaal in 1877, but Gladstone reversed this action.

The normal development of the area was disturbed further by the discovery

[6] Ensor, pp. 187–194.
[7] See page 663.

of great mineral wealth. In 1870 a Boer farmer found his children playing with a bright little stone which turned out to be a diamond worth $25,000. The mines at Kimberley soon were producing most of the world's diamonds. When, in 1886, rich deposits of gold were discovered on the Witwatersrand in the Transvaal, foreigners came rushing in to exploit the gold mines. Johannesburg, the capital of the Transvaal, became a large city, but trouble was certain to arise between the foreigners, or Uitlanders, and the Boers. The newcomers, pushing and aggressive, determined to make money quickly, and intolerant of the Boers, were far from ideal settlers. Most of them, though by no means all, were British. The Boers, on the other hand, were frontiersmen whose ancestors had lived for centuries in great isolation from the rest of the world. They were independent and courageous, but stubborn, ignorant, unprogressive, religious in a narrow sense, deeply suspicious, thoroughly exasperating.

It was the policy of Paul Kruger, the President of the Transvaal and the very incarnation of the Boer character, to make the Uitlanders pay heavily for the privilege of exploiting the mines. Some ninety percent of the taxes came from the miners. Kruger also obstructed trade between the Transvaal and the Cape. He began to buy armaments from Europe, he employed Dutch civil servants who were very anti-British, and he sought support from continental powers, especially Germany.

The Uitlanders organized and plotted insurrection. Most unfortunately, Rhodes, although he was Prime Minister of Cape Colony, allowed himself to be drawn into these conspiracies. A revolt was planned for 1895. Part of the plan was to collect on the western frontier of the Transvaal a force of mounted police who would make a dash for Johannesburg at the moment of the revolt, but for various reasons the uprising was postponed. Nonetheless, Dr. Jameson, the commander of the mounted police, who had not been properly warned, invaded the Transvaal with his little force on December 29, 1895. Four days later he fell into an ambush and surrendered.

The Jameson Raid completely altered the situation in South Africa. The raid was utterly unjustifiable; it ruined Rhodes, who resigned as Prime Minister; it caused an outburst of anti-British feeling in Germany; and it united all the Boers in South Africa against Britain. The Kaiser sent Kruger a telegram congratulating him on his success in repelling invasion. Joseph Chamberlain, who was Colonial Secretary, had no foreknowledge of the raid, but he did know of the impending revolt, and the suppression of some of his messages to Rhodes made the Boers suspicious. Thenceforth Kruger openly prepared for war. Negotiations between him and Sir Alfred Milner, the British High Commissioner at the Cape, were fruitless. During these negotiations the British Cabinet was not bellicose, but there was a swaggering aggressiveness among the people in London. The Boers were also very truculent.

The war may be divided into three well-defined stages. The first (October 1899 to February 1900) was one of Boer aggression and success. The British had only some 15,000 regulars in South Africa to oppose 50,000 Boers, who were greatly superior in artillery. There were a number of British defeats, and the Boers besieged the British towns of Ladysmith, Kimberley, and Mafeking. These sieges were strategic errors: had the Boers made straight for Cape Town they might have overrun the country and been in a very strong position. Their delays gave the British time to send strong reinforcements under their best generals. The arrival of Lord Roberts and Lord Kitchener opened the second phase of the war (February to September 1900), in which the British took the offensive and defeated the Boer armies. Roberts invaded and annexed both the Orange Free State and the Transvaal. When organized resistance came to an end, the British thought they had won the war.

But the third and longest period was to come (September 1900 to May 1902). This consisted of prolonged guerrilla warfare by mobile bands of Boer commandos who harassed the British armies and inflicted serious local reverses upon them. The Boers did not wear uniforms, so that a Boer could be a dangerous sharpshooter one moment and a peaceful farmer the next; indeed, every farmhouse was a base of operations. Kitchener divided the whole country into compartments surrounded by heavy wire fences and swept every person in one compartment after another into concentration camps. The result was unavoidable suffering, with high mortality among the children. Peace was signed in May 1902. The British insisted on complete sovereignty, but once that point was settled they gave very generous terms. Representative government was to be established at once and self-government was to follow shortly; a free gift of £3 million to restore agriculture was supplemented by loans; the Dutch language was safeguarded, though the official language was English. The Boers never had more than 60,000 men in the field; the English sent 450,000 at a cost of £222 million. The war showed clearly the great need for a British general staff and for better military intelligence service. Most of the English generals had done their previous fighting in India. Having painfully learned to fight on the African veld they had to unlearn these lessons in 1914.

THE CONTINENTAL SYSTEM OF ALLIANCES

During the Boer War England felt very much alone in a hostile world. She had no ally, no friendly nation to give her moral and diplomatic support, and it was obvious that profound changes had taken place on the Continent. The fundamental cause of these changes was the sudden rise of Germany in 1870 to a position of great military strength with which England could not hope to compete. England had a large navy but a small army, for the people would not have tolerated conscription, though it became the norm on the Continent. The consequence was that England no longer enjoyed the place of pre-eminence she had formerly occupied in the affairs of Europe. She had, for example, played an important part in the unification of Italy before the Franco-Prussian War but had exerted no influence whatever on the unification of Germany which followed that war. Moreover, a system of alliances had grown up in Europe in which England had no part. For a time this did not seem to matter. England exulted in her "splendid isolation" which gave her freedom to determine her policy solely on the basis of her own interests. But the Boer War brought doubts and questionings.

To understand the European system of alliances one must begin with Bismarck. His policy after the Franco-Prussian War was twofold: to isolate France so that she could never wage a war of revenge, and to maintain friendly relations with both Austria and Russia. In 1872 Bismarck arranged a meeting in Berlin of Kaiser William I of Germany, Emperor Francis Joseph of Austria, and Czar Alexander II of Russia. This meeting, though it concluded no formal treaty, proclaimed the friendship of the three powers. They held other conferences, and their informal alliance was called the League of the Three Emperors. But concord was threatened by clashes in the Balkans between Austria and Russia. Bismarck recognized that if he had to choose between these two allies, his choice by necessity would be Austria. In 1879 he concluded with Austria a secret defensive alliance which remained the cornerstone of German policy. It was joined in 1882 by Italy, thus becoming the Triple Alliance. But Bismarck also made treaties with Russia. In 1881 he managed to revive for a time the League of the Three Emperors; and later in 1887 he arranged secret conventions with Russia by which both parties promised a friendly neutrality in case of attack. As Bismarck hoped, these treaties isolated France, but they had to be handled with great skill. Kaiser William II did not renew the convention with Russia, a coolness ensued between the two countries, Russia drifted first into isolation and then into friendship with France. France and Russia concluded a general entente in 1891 and a formal alliance in 1894.

Thus England, faced with two alliances, found it more difficult than ever to obtain friendly cooperation. Her sprawling empire made her vulnerable. Other powers were building navies, and the invention of the torpedo and the submarine created the danger that small ships could attack large ones and that a sudden knockout blow could destroy British naval supremacy. Under these circumstances British statesmen, regarding isolation as no longer possible, began a search for allies.

The Search for Allies

The two powers with whom Britain had been clashing over imperial questions were Russia and France. At the Congress of Berlin in 1878 Disraeli had suspected Russian designs not only in the Balkans but also in the Persian Gulf, in Egypt, and in Suez. Russian expansion into central Asia led her toward Persia and the northwest frontier of India. There had been a period of tension in 1885 when the Russians captured the village of Penjdeh on the northern frontier of Afghanistan. In the 1890s Anglo-Russian rivalry shifted to China. Taking advantage of Chinese weakness after her defeat by Japan in 1894–1895, various European powers encroached on Chinese territory. The British acquired Weihaiwei in 1898, but strongly resented Russian expansion into Manchuria and the Liaotung Peninsula and the obvious Russian interest in Korea. Meanwhile the French, smarting under their defeat by Prussia, set out to find compensation in an empire. This led to friction with Britain in West Africa, in Indochina, and in the Sudan. In 1887 England concluded a secret treaty with Italy and Austria to maintain the status quo in the Mediterranean, a treaty aimed at Russia and France. An alliance with either of these powers seemed quite out of the question.

England's relations with Germany were friendly as long as Bismarck was Chancellor. In the late 1880s Bismarck had played with the idea of an Anglo-German alliance, and though this had not developed, the two countries had reached a comprehensive adjustment of their African disputes in 1890. But Germany under William II became more difficult. The Kaiser, desiring colonies in Africa and elsewhere, pushed his policy with vigor. He fell into an irritating habit of demanding compensation whenever any other power made acquisitions. There was a brusqueness about German diplomacy that angered the English. The Kaiser's telegram to Kruger in 1896, for example, was a gratuitous insult. And shortly thereafter Germany began in earnest to build a navy.

Nonetheless the British Cabinet preferred to try for an agreement with Germany rather than for one with France and Russia. In 1898 Chamberlain obtained permission to suggest an alliance to Germany. It was to be a defensive alliance based on settlement of differences in China and elsewhere, but Germany declined the British offer. The Germans feared that an alliance with Britain might lead to war with Russia. They assumed that England would never settle her disputes with either Russia or France and that Germany could probably obtain better terms from Britain some time in the future. The possibility of an alliance was discussed once more in 1901. But the Germans, thinking again that they could afford to wait, asked that Britain make commitments to both Austria and Italy. This the British declined to do. When these negotiations, which might have altered the course of history, came to an end, Britain turned elsewhere for allies.

To the astonishment of the world, Britain concluded an alliance with Japan in 1902. It was a defensive alliance against Russia. Japan was determined to fight if Russia attempted to acquire Korea; England wanted protection for her commercial interests in China. Both feared that, if events in the Far East brought war with Russia, the French would come to Russia's assistance. The agreement provided that if either of the contracting powers, because of their interests in China or Korea, were attacked by a third power, the other party would remain neutral. If either of the contracting parties were attacked by two powers, the other party would come to its assistance. This was England's first major break from her old policy of splendid isolation. In 1904 she concluded an even more surprising agreement with France, to which we will turn in the next chapter.

THE END OF THE CENTURY

The death of Queen Victoria in 1901, after the longest reign in English history, and the retirement of Salisbury in 1902 underlined the fact that an era of history had ended. It is worthwhile to pause for a moment to contrast the England of 1900 with the England of the mid-Victorians. Many of the social and moral characteristics of the middle of the century had begun to disappear around 1890. The old taboos relaxed, the passion for respectability subsided, there was far greater latitude in thought and conduct. In short, it was a freer age. But there was more diversity, more uncertainty, more doubt and apprehension about the future.

A marked decline took place in religious belief and in the observance of the Sabbath. Evangelical religion was losing its hold on the educated classes. The number of brilliant young men at the universities who took Anglican orders greatly diminished. Many other careers were now open to them, but there was also the fact that they no longer regarded religion as the central theme of life. The difficulty of recruiting men for the ministry was also felt by the nonconformists, for able young men of the lower middle classes could now find places in the world of business or in the labor movement. One factor in the decline of the Anglican clergy was the unprofitableness of agriculture, which had supported rural livings. These livings were now greatly impoverished. An urge toward ritualism and Anglo-Catholic practices among the clergy disturbed and alienated many of their parishioners. Church attendance fell off greatly, especially in the cities. Family prayers and teaching in Sunday schools declined. Since Sunday was no longer a day devoted to religion, the necessity arose to provide other means of spending it profitably. Museums and art galleries were opened on

Sunday afternoons, there were public concerts and cheap excursions on the railways. The weekend in the country, leaving the cities strangely deserted on Sundays, became a national institution.

There was also a revolution in the press. The newspapers of the mid-Victorians had been dignified and responsible but dull and stuffy, appealing only to intelligent readers. They were now driven out by a cheap, sensational press that put everything in the form of a story, used short sentences and short paragraphs with glaring headlines, and served up the news in chatty and spicy tidbits for uneducated minds. The new journalism did not aim to inform; it aimed to amuse, to pander to low taste, and to make money. "Written by office-boys for office-boys," was Salisbury's acid comment. This revolution was the work of Alfred Harmsworth, later Lord Northcliffe, who founded the *Daily Mail* in 1896. He ran competitions and offered a trifling form of insurance in order to increase his circulation and he was immensely successful. His paper was read by thousands who considered themselves far above the working class.

The 1890s were years of increased comfort and general well-being in spite of trade depressions. They were also years of technological advance. Electric lights, telephones, cables, the wireless, electric trolleys and underground railways, the internal combustion engine that opened the way for automobiles and airplanes, finer and stronger steel that could be used for a thousand purposes, industrial chemistry, new drugs and better medical research, the adding machine, the cash register, and the dictaphone, faster transportation by sea, and, unfortunately, vastly improved armaments—all made this period one of unprecedented progress.

The problem of the poor remained. A large proportion of the people lived in extreme poverty and miserable slums and tenements, where they easily fell into vice and depravity. The collapse of agriculture had caused a new migration into the towns. To many thinking people the great problem of the age was to probe the causes of poverty and to apply what remedies were possible. This is the background of English socialism and the rise of the Labor party.

THE RISE OF SOCIALISM

Socialism in Britain was in part a product of the Victorian conscience. Perhaps the most important of the new social service agencies was the Salvation Army, founded in 1878 by William Booth and his devoted wife. It was intended to be a purely religious movement, revivalist in nature, but it was soon a center of social service. Booth's book, *In Darkest England and the Way Out* (1890), was a description of urban poverty that shocked the world. Booth was interested in the fate of the agricultural laborers who had drifted to the towns, and he advocated a program of training that would fit them for emigration. Toynbee Hall, founded in 1884, was the first of many settlement houses in East London. Many nonconformist churches preached a social gospel of aiding the poor. Two strikes caught the attention of the public. One, in 1888, was a strike of 700 girls employed in making lucifer matches in London. Public support enabled this defenseless group in a badly sweated industry to win. Another strike that aroused much sympathy was that of the London dock workers in 1889. Miserably paid, they had only casual employment and lived in chronic poverty. They struck for a wage of 6*d.* an hour and for four consecutive hours of employment at a time.

They obtained most of their demands. In 1889 Charles Booth, a wealthy man not related to William Booth, began to publish a series of studies of the London poor. His conclusion was that thirty percent of Londoners lived in abject poverty, often below the subsistence level. He also was interested in the problem of the aged poor.

Meanwhile there was a growth of socialist ideas. Although Karl Marx wrote his explosive book, *Das Kapital,* in England, English socialism did not adopt his doctrine of the war of classes or of the violent overthrow of capitalism. For the most part English socialism has been idealistic, utopian, and good natured. It was strongly influenced by an American book, Henry George's *Progress and Poverty* (1879), which advocated the nationalization of land. George's phrase "the unearned increment," referring to a rise in the value of land due to the progress of society and not to any effort by the owner, became widely current in England. Edward Bellamy, in *Looking Backward* (1887), and William Morris, in *News from Nowhere* (1891), sketched impossible utopias. Much more influential among the lower classes was *Merrie England* (1894) by Robert Blatchford, who also published a weekly, the *Clarion,* which caught the fancy of young people by its sprightly articles about cycling, music, arts and crafts, feminism, and other timely topics. High spirits, fun, happiness, courtship, and socialism were all jumbled together. Blatchford had no program but his writings stressed the injustice of the economic system.[8]

The Fabian Society, founded in 1884, achieved a fame out of proportion to its size because of its distinguished members George Bernard Shaw and Beatrice and Sidney Webb. The Fabians, as their name implies, suggested that socialistic change must come gradually and gently without revolutionary upheaval. They combined a strong desire to improve the lot of the individual with a deep respect for existing institutions of law and government. Rejecting the violence of Marx and the emotional approach of men like Blatchford and William Morris, the Fabians held that socialistic objectives could be attained through the normal processes of parliamentary legislation and that the state could thus be molded into an agent for the promotion of the general good. Socialism, said Webb, was merely the economic side of democracy. The Fabians sought practical legislation on both the national and the local levels. They worked, for example, for the municipal ownership of public utilities, whence they derived the nickname of the "gas and water socialists."

Socialism could not go far in politics without the financial support of the trade unions, but for a long time the older unions were not interested either in politics or in socialism. In 1875 they had obtained the right of collective bargaining; they had a central agency, the Trades Union Congress; they represented a small aristocracy of skilled labor; and they had placed a few workingmen in Parliament who voted with the Liberals and were known as Lib-Labs. The old trade unions had no wish to experiment. But a new unionism composed of unskilled workers appeared in the 1890s. Led by socialists, it wanted a party organization separate from that of the Liberals. One of its great personalities, Keir Hardie, who had gone to work in Glasgow at the age of seven and had become a miner at the age of ten, broke with the Liberals and formed a Scottish Labor party. In 1892 this party placed three members in the House of Commons of whom Keir Hardie was one. He came to the opening of Parliament wearing

[8] Alfred F. Havighurst, *Twentieth Century Britain* (New York: Harper & Row, 1962), pp. 25–30.

his miner's costume and preceded by a man blowing a horn. Other members in the customary morning dress must have lifted their eyebrows.

Shaw and Webb also supported a separate party for labor. In 1893 a conference of socialists of many shades of opinion and some trade-union leaders was held at Bradford and founded the Independent Labor party, an event of great significance. There was now a popular socialist party devoted to the interests of labor. Its object was the "collective ownership of all means of production, distribution, and exchange"; its method was to work through Parliament. Associated with it were many persons famous in the history of the labor movement: Hardie, Blatchford, Shaw, the Webbs, Ben Tillett, and Tom Mann, who had organized the dock workers' strike in 1889, G. N. Barnes, and later Philip Snowden and James Ramsay MacDonald.

By 1900 the Trades Union Congress, feeling less secure than of old, was also ready for parliamentary action. It summoned a congress of cooperative, socialist, trade-union, and other working-class organizations which set up a labor representation committee to secure the election of laboring men to Parliament. The secretary of that committee was Ramsay MacDonald. It did not aim to form a party; it merely hoped to establish a labor group in the Commons which would cooperate with any party whose program favored labor. In the election of 1900 it contested only fifteen seats and won only two. In the election of 1906, however, it won twenty-nine seats, and these members formed the parliamentary Labor party, which is the party that we know today.[9]

THE BALFOUR MINISTRY, 1902–1905

In 1902 Salisbury was followed as Conservative Prime Minister by his nephew, A. J. Balfour. The new administration lasted for a little more than three years and then ended in disaster. Proposals to abandon free trade and to adopt tariffs that would give the colonies a favorable position in the British market divided the Conservatives, united the Liberals in opposition, and brought about a Liberal victory at the polls in 1906. The consequent stigma of failure attached to Balfour's ministry is not fair, for although Balfour committed blunders and found it difficult to make up his mind about tariff reform, he was placed in an almost impossible position. His legislation contained wise and useful measures, and vital decisions were made in foreign affairs, but he aroused strong opposition. The Conservative party, after its long tenure of office, had grown blind to the wishes of the nation as a whole.

The Education Act of 1902 was a statesmanlike measure. Prior to its passage the control of elementary education was vested in the school boards set up in 1870; but plans for secondary and technical education were being developed both by the school boards and by the county councils established in 1888. It was felt, however, that the plans of the school boards for secondary education contained serious defects. Hence the act of 1902 abolished the school boards and gave control of elementary, secondary, and technical education to the county councils, except in large urban areas which were to have authority over their own ele-

[9] In addition to these twenty-nine members, twenty-four other Labor members were elected in 1906. Of the additional twenty-four, a few were Lib-Labs of the ordinary kind, but most of them were officials of miners' unions. Thus in 1906 the Commons contained a total of fifty-three Labor members.

mentary schools. In a complicated arrangement the county councils were also to control the schools that had been managed for almost a century by the Church of England or by nonconformist bodies. These schools were now to be supported by public funds. The arrangement pleased the church because the burden of supporting its schools had become intolerable but the nonconformists, who had hoped that the church schools would disappear through lack of funds, were furious. The act continued the church schools and supported them by taxation which must be paid in part by the nonconformists.

An Irish Land Purchase Act of 1903 facilitated the Conservative policy of lending money to Irish peasants to buy out their landlords. The new act enabled Irish peasants on an estate to purchase the entire estate as a unit rather than to buy it piecemeal in small parcels. A Licensing Act of 1904 was another wise though controversial measure. The country contained far too many saloons or public houses, and there was pressure, especially from nonconformist bodies, to reduce the number of licenses. But if a publican lost his license, not as a punishment for disorder but as a result of general policy, he had a grievance. Balfour's act gave him compensation from a levy on the whole liquor industry. But the nonconformists opposed compensation in any form. In foreign affairs there were momentous events: the conclusion of the Boer War, the alliance with Japan, an entente with France, a crisis over Morocco in 1905.[10]

Imperial Federation and Tariff Reform

To understand the division among the Conservatives over tariff policy we must return for a moment to one aspect of imperialism in the nineteenth century.

In the 1880s and 1890s there was a movement in England for some kind of federation between Britain and the self-governing colonies. The purpose was to bind the colonies closer to the mother country and to devise some kind of imperial council by which the empire could act as a whole. The Imperial Federation League was founded in 1884, though it never formulated its rather vague proposals. The idea of federation also was furthered by the stirring and elaborate jubilees of 1887 and 1897 commemorating the fiftieth and sixtieth anniversaries of the Queen's accession. Since the prime ministers of all the self-governing colonies were present in 1887, it was suggested that a conference be held between them and the ministers in Britain. The first in a long and important line of colonial conferences, it was addressed by Salisbury, who took as his theme the necessity of united action for self-defense. But the conference came to no conclusions. A second conference in 1894, held in Ottawa, Canada, was a rather small affair. It had been summoned to discuss oceanic cables and faster mail service. The Canadians introduced the subject of preferential tariffs, that is, tariffs by which one colony could trade with another or with Great Britain at lower rates than those charged to the rest of the world.

A third colonial conference in 1897 dealt with imperial federation, naval and military cooperation, and preferential tariffs. But again the results were rather disappointing. Chamberlain, now Colonial Secretary, urged federation. He asked for a central imperial council which, he hoped, would develop into a federal body to determine common policy. The colonies did not respond to this suggestion. Above all else they cherished their right of self-government and they feared that

[10] See pages 682, 684, 701–702.

a federal council might encroach on it. They knew that by necessity the final decisions on high policy would be made by Britain. If their representatives in London consented to these decisions, the colonists at home could hardly impose a veto. Disregarding Chamberlain's plea, they passed a resolution declaring that existing relations between them and Britain were satisfactory. This resolution ended for all time the hope of federation.

There were also differences concerning imperial defense. The British naturally thought in terms of high strategy for the defense of the empire as a whole. A colony, for example, might be protected by warships that were thousands of miles away. But the colonial prime ministers were laymen who did not understand grand naval strategy: they wanted battleships in their own waters. They were far more interested in preferential tariffs, for such tariffs would be greatly in their favor. But the position of England was very different. Her tradition was one of free trade and in order to give preference to the colonies she would have to erect tariffs against the rest of the world. Only a fraction of her trade was colonial, and it was by no means certain that British industry as a whole would benefit from tariffs. There was danger that tariffs would cause a general rise of prices at home, especially a rise in the cost of bread. There was also the danger that the colonies might erect tariffs against British goods. Chamberlain, who had always been a free trader, decided in 1897 that England must remain a free-trading nation.

In 1902, however, Chamberlain changed his mind. At a fourth colonial conference, which met in that year, the colonies pressed again for preferential tariffs. And Canada, which had given British goods a preference and had been punished by German tariffs for doing so, declared that if Canadian goods received no preference in England Canada would act as her interests demanded. This conference convinced Chamberlain that England should grant colonial preferences. A tariff, he came to believe, not only would help the colonies but would protect British industry and could be used as a weapon against the world at large. What was needed, he said, was not free trade but fair trade. At once there was opposition in the Cabinet. Balfour should have made up his mind one way or the other. Instead, he offered compromises and said that the matter should be discussed. Few Prime Ministers have had such a dangerous issue raised by a friendly colleague. The Cabinet began to break up. Chamberlain resigned and made a series of speeches which moved closer and closer to a purely protective tariff policy. The free traders in the Cabinet also resigned, and in 1905 Balfour followed their example. The election of 1906 was a Liberal landslide. Tariffs as yet made no appeal in either agricultural or industrial constituencies.

Chamberlain's campaign had a number of results. It gave a bad fright to the Germans, who profited greatly from British free trade. It also gave the Liberals an issue on which they could unite. They had been badly split over the Boer War, but they could now re-form their ranks in defense of free trade. They became more radical. When they were again in office they had to find new sources of revenue; having rejected tariffs they had to turn to new methods of raising taxes. Finally, Chamberlain had turned the thoughts of Englishmen toward colonial problems in a new way.

Before the Conservatives left office they thoroughly alienated the laboring classes. One issue was the importation of Chinese coolies to South Africa to work in the mines. The coolies were housed in compounds they were not permitted to leave, and they were not accorded the normal rights of free men. There was also a legal decision which caused great alarm in labor circles. During a strike against the Taff Vale Railway in Wales the railway had suffered some injury to its property. It sued the railway union and obtained damages. But if a union could be sued for damage done by its members during a strike, the labor movement was in great peril.

In a word, Balfour was blind to the feelings and convictions of labor. The Conservative party, leaving Tory democracy far behind, had become the party of the upper classes and was too exclusively concerned with the interests of its own members. It paid the penalty at the polls in 1906.

32

SOCIALISM AND WAR

The Liberal victory early in 1906 was one of the most sweeping on record. The Liberals won 337 seats, the Conservatives only 157; there were 83 Irish Nationalists and 53 Labor members who were certain to vote with the Liberals, giving that party a very large majority. The composition of the Commons was more varied than in the nineteenth century. Although country gentlemen were still to be found in Parliament, members were also drawn from many other classes and occupations—from the law, from business, from journalism, and from labor. That the urge toward social democracy ran very deep was made clear by this election. It was not nineteenth-century Liberalism that won the victory in 1906; rather, it was the electoral power of the laboring classes demanding a higher standard of living, more equality of opportunity, and greater protection against such causes of poverty as sickness, unemployment, and old age. Many Liberals, as well as Labor members, were ready to vote for advanced legislation of this kind.

The desire of the working classes for radical social reform was not the result of acute suffering. The national economy between 1900 and 1914 was fairly prosperous, with employment at a higher level than in the 1890s. There was, it is true, a certain stagnation in industry; as a result of a lack of capital investment it did not expand, nor did it take full advantage of new techniques. Opportunities for investment abroad, in the Dominions and elsewhere, were so attractive that too much money was going overseas and industry at home was starved for capital.

SIR HENRY CAMPBELL-BANNERMAN, 1905–1908

The new Prime Minister, Sir Henry Campbell-Bannerman, was quite ready to adopt a program of social reform. A shrewd and wealthy Scot, he had become leader of the Liberals in 1898, when their prospects were dim. He had shown ability, steadfastness, and devotion during long years in opposition, and he proved even more effective in office. Though not a brilliant speaker, he could succinctly express the sentiment of the Commons, as on the famous occasion when he reproved Balfour for making politics a kind of sport for gentlemen rather than a serious task for dedicated men. Like Gladstone, he moved to the left with advancing years. And in his kindly and generous old age[1] he proved an excellent leader for a Commons containing many idealistic but inexperienced members. His Cabinet was rich in talent. It contained three Liberal imperialists from Rosebery's ministry: Herbert Asquith, Sir Edward Grey, and R. B. Haldane. Other members of unusual ability were John Morley, James Bryce, Augustine Birrell, and David Lloyd George; younger men outside the Cabinet included Reginald McKenna, Winston Churchill, Herbert Samuel, and Walter Runciman. This was a very unusual group.

The Cabinet had a clear mandate from the people to enact a program of social reform. Yet the House of Lords contained a large and permanent majority of Conservative peers. When Rosebery had been Prime Minister, these peers, as we have seen, had voted along strict party lines and had wrecked legislation merely because it came from a Liberal House of Commons. In the years after 1906 the Lords were not as intransigent as this. They believed that in opposing the measures of the Cabinet they were acting as the wise amenders of hasty and ill-advised legislation, yet they often voted as members of a Conservative party ready to employ the power of the upper chamber under the constitution to decide which of the measures proposed by a Liberal government should be allowed to pass.

Moreover, they could not forget that they were aristocrats who belonged to a class that had governed the country from time immemorial. They assumed they had a right to rule and that England's greatness was the result of their past guidance. The function of the electorate, they would have said, was not to send workingmen to Parliament but to decide whether it wished to be governed by Liberal or Conservative aristocrats. Hence the Lords looked with distrust on the House of Commons elected in 1906. It contained men from the working classes and many others of humble origin and slender means. Lloyd George, brought up by his uncle, a village cobbler, was a member of the Cabinet. Could people like this be trusted to govern the country properly? What the Lords forgot was that although Rosebery's position in the Commons and in the country had been weak and crumbling, Campbell-Bannerman's was strong.

Social Legislation

A clash between the two houses was thus inevitable. It forms an important and dramatic part of the history of the time, but social legislation, though less spectacular, was really more important. The Lords allowed a good deal of it to become law. For this there were a number of reasons. Old-age pensions, for example, had been accepted in principle by both parties, and could be considered as part of a Conservative program. In other matters, even in some rather radical ones, the Lords hesitated to incur the antagonism of the working classes. And certain measures could be regarded as nonpartisan.

In 1906 they passed three pieces of social legislation. One, a measure for workmen's compensation, extended the principle that employers must compensate laborers for injuries suffered during hours of employment; some 13 million

---

[1] The phrase is that of R. C. K. Ensor, *England 1870–1914* (Oxford: Clarendon Press, 1936), p. 391.

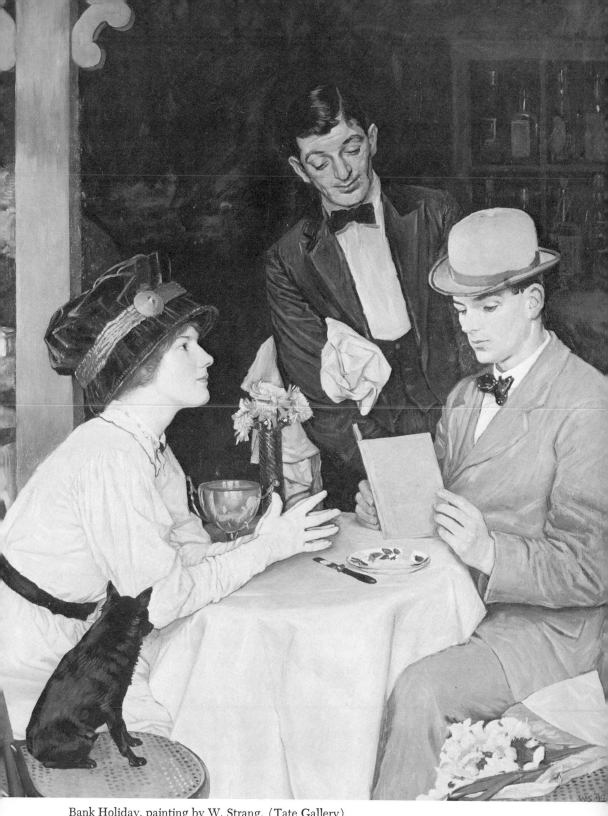

Bank Holiday, painting by W. Strang. (Tate Gallery)

workers, including domestic servants, now were protected in this way. Another bill provided free or cheap meals for children who were sent to school in the morning without any breakfast. A more controversial measure was a Trade Disputes Act. Labor had been greatly alarmed by a legal decision in 1901 awarding damages to the Taff Vale Railway when it had sued a union for injuries suffered during a strike. A Trade Disputes Act now declared that unions could not be so sued. Indeed, it gave them a broad immunity from legal actions. So radical a measure might well have been questioned by the Lords but they allowed it to pass.

An Old Age Pensions Bill sponsored by Lloyd George in 1908 was important. Old age was an obvious cause of extreme poverty, for a workingman could not normally hope to accumulate savings for himself and his wife in their old age. The pension provided by the bill was modest enough: to qualify for it a person must be seventy and must have an income of no more than 10*s.* a week. His pension was to be a weekly sum of 5*s.*; the pension of an elderly couple living together was frugally reduced to 7*s.* 6*d.* Yet even this slender sum might suffice to keep a man or woman from the stigma of the poorhouse. The Lords began to tamper with the bill, but they were outmaneuvered because it was attached to the budget and so they let it through. Another measure limited the working day of miners to eight hours.

In 1909 a royal commission appointed by Balfour in 1905 to study the operation of the Poor Law published its conclusions, which included a minority report. Both majority and minority reports proposed to abolish the local guardians of the poor established by the act of 1834 and to entrust poor relief to the county councils. The minority report—the work of Sidney and Beatrice Webb—suggested that poor relief as such be ended altogether and that various welfare services be extended to provide a minimum standard of life for everyone. The Cabinet failed to act on these proposals, but certain bills were passed as an indirect result of the Poor Law reports. Winston Churchill sponsored the Labor Exchange Bill through which unemployed laborers could obtain information about jobs in various parts of the country. Churchill was also responsible for the Act for the Establishment of Trade Boards in certain industries. Under this act a board appointed to examine a sweated industry could establish a minimum wage in that trade. These measures were passed by the House of Lords. The Lords also passed, though with great reluctance, the National Insurance Act of 1911, to which we will turn presently.

Bills Rejected by the House of Lords

There were other measures, however, which the Commons sent up to the Lords, only to have them rejected. The most important of these in the session of 1906 was an education bill. On this bill the Liberals had set their hearts, for they regarded Balfour's Education Act of 1902 as far too generous to the Church of England. The Cabinet clearly had a mandate to enact a new bill, but the Lords destroyed the education bill of 1906 by hostile amendments. They also threw out a plural voting bill which would have restricted every voter to one vote although he qualified in several constituencies. In 1907 four measures concerning land were either rejected or mutilated by the House of Lords.

As a result of these rejections an important debate took place in the House of Commons concerning its relations with the House of Lords. Campbell-Bannerman declared that "in order to give effect to the will of the people, it is necessary that the power of the other House to alter or reject bills passed by this House should be so restricted by law as to secure that within the limits of a single Parliament [a period of seven years] the final decision of the Commons should prevail." In the debate that followed, Lloyd George remarked that the House of Lords was not the watchdog of the constitution: it was merely Mr. Balfour's poodle. Churchill referred to the Lords as unrepresentative and irresponsible.

HERBERT ASQUITH

Early in 1908 Campbell-Bannerman died and was succeeded as Prime Minister by Herbert Asquith. A Yorkshireman of nonconformist stock, Asquith was a lawyer whose strength lay in the admirable precision and lucidity with which he could present complicated matters to the Commons. He never lacked for cogent arguments in defense of Liberal measures. He had a clear head for business, and he employed tact and moderation in keeping the strong-willed members of his Cabinet working together. He gave his colleagues loyal support but he was not a crusader. He was perhaps somewhat lacking in imagination, and after the war began in 1914 he did not develop into a great war leader. He had entered Parliament in 1886 as something of a radical and had been a member of Gladstone's Cabinet in 1892. After 1895, when his party was out of power, he had become less influential in politics. His marriage to Margot Tennant took him into high society, which he enjoyed but which weakened his Liberal connections. He returned to office as Campbell-Bannerman's Chancellor of the Exchequer and then succeeded him as Prime Minister.

In 1908 the Lords rejected an important licensing bill, a temperance measure that was well thought out and well framed. It was greatly needed, for the amount of drinking in the early twentieth century was excessive and the number of pubs enormous. The bill would have gradually reduced them by about one third (some 30,000) over a period of fourteen years; compensation would have been given for licenses revoked. King Edward VII and a few of the moderate peers urged the House of Lords to pass this measure, but at a Conservative party meeting it was decided to reject it.

The outlook for the Cabinet seemed bleak: it could not get its most desired bills through the Lords, trade was depressed in 1908, and by-elections were going against the government. In 1909 a naval scare resulted in a decision to lay down eight battleships in one year, a most costly undertaking. The old-age pensions plan was also proving expensive. Lloyd George, now Chancellor of the Exchequer, would have to find £15 million in new taxation.

The Budget of 1909 and the Parliament Act of 1911

This was the background of Lloyd George's budget in 1909. The Conservatives later regarded this budget as a cunning trap set for the downfall of the House of Lords, but one cannot tell how much Lloyd George was thinking in terms of strategy and how much he was trying to provide for necessary expenditures. Certainly the budget was aimed at the rich. Death duties were increased sharply, so that estates could be taxed up to twenty-five percent of their total value. The income tax also was increased, with surtaxes on incomes above £5000 and with heavier duties on incomes derived from stocks and bonds than on those derived from salaries. Heavy duties also were laid on automobiles, furs, tobacco, liquor, and other luxuries. There were two new taxes: one a twenty percent tax on the unearned increment of land whenever it changed hands, the other a small tax on the capital value of undeveloped land and minerals. Conservative hostility to the budget was intense. Not only would it tax the wealthy very heavily; its enactment would eliminate all hope of tariff reform and it might well be the opening wedge for a much more radical program of socialism. The Harmsworth press, delighting in the sensational, played up the budget as very radical indeed.

If Lloyd George had laid a trap for the Lords, they fell into it promptly. Conservative opposition to the budget was uncompromising in the Commons; the Lords pledged themselves to fight it in their own chamber. Lloyd George began a series of speeches in which he denounced the peers as rich and selfish men who cherished special privilege and sought to escape their share of taxation. And the more violently the Lords replied, the more certain the public became that their motives were sinister. In the Cabinet some members wished to draw back, but Asquith supported Lloyd George. The Lords then rejected the budget. This was clearly unconstitutional, for if any principle of the constitution had been steadily maintained since 1688 it was that the Commons had complete control of finance. Asquith at once carried a resolution in the Commons that "the action of the House of Lords in refusing to pass into law the financial provisions made by this House for the service of the year is a breach of the constitution and a usurpation of the rights of the Commons."

An election was fought in January 1910 on the merits of Lloyd George's budget and on the larger question of the veto power of the House of Lords. As a result of the election the Liberals came back with 275 seats, the Conservatives with 273, the Irish with 82, and Labor with 40. The Liberal victory was greater than the figures seem to imply. The Liberals had been losing ground; hence it was thought that the Conservatives would be the victors. But in fact the Conservatives lost about 100 seats they were considered likely to win, Labor and Irish members were solidly behind a reform of the House of Lords—Labor in the hope of further social legislation, the Irish in the hope of home rule. The budget was now accepted by the Lords. But the larger question of curbing the power of the upper chamber remained.

The Cabinet was preparing its campaign when it was interrupted in May 1910 by the death of King Edward VII.[2] His successor, George V, hoped for a compromise. In the long series of conferences between committees of the two houses, nothing was accomplished. A second election held in December 1910 did not materially alter the party figures in the Commons. It then became known that Asquith had the King's permission to announce the creation of a great number of new peers unless the House of Lords gave way. Although a group of diehard Conservatives wished to force this creation, it was avoided because the more moderate peers abstained from voting and allowed the bill to pass.

There were three essential provisions. Money bills were to become law one month after passage by the Commons even if the Lords had not passed them. Should there be a question about whether a certain bill was a money bill, the issue was to be decided by the Speaker of the House of Commons. Bills that were not money bills might become law without the consent of the House of Lords if the Commons passed them in three successive sessions. This provision enabled the Lords to delay a bill for two years but not to block it permanently.

---

[2] See below.

Thus the Lords could no longer challenge the supremacy of the Commons. Finally, the legal life of a Parliament was reduced from seven to five years.

THE MONARCHY

When Edward VII came to the throne at the death of Victoria in 1901 he was almost sixty. A brilliant man of the world had succeeded a recluse.[3] After Albert's death in 1861 Victoria had retired for many years from almost all public activities, and though she emerged from her seclusion about 1874, her court was never lively. Edward referred to Buckingham Palace in her reign as a sepulcher. But when he became King it was a sepulcher no longer. Edward liked high society, he was fond of shows and displays, he delighted in uniforms and decorations, and he played the host in a truly regal fashion. Balls and dinner parties attracted the fashionable world to Buckingham Palace. Edward was widely traveled, was personally acquainted with most of the important people in Europe and in the empire, and possessed a knowledge of the world through contacts with all kinds of people. As a symbol of empire he was valuable to the state. Yet his influence over its affairs was much less than Victoria's. Victoria had been willing to spend her days laboriously reading dispatches. Edward occupied his time more pleasantly; there was a general impression that he was fond of good cheer, of race horses, and of pretty women. Early in life he had rebelled against the strictness with which he was being educated. He turned away from books. As a man he never read anything except the newspapers and an occasional novel. Victoria had excluded him from the business of the state. He was fifty before she allowed him to see the reports of Cabinet meetings. But if he lacked industry, he had his gifts: he could be both dignified and charming; he could handle people with great tact; he was a good linguist and possessed an excellent memory.

In 1910 Edward was succeeded by a very different kind of person. George V, resembling Victoria, was grave and serious, with a high sense of duty. Like her, he disliked society. He was very conventional and rather distrusted intellectual people. So far as possible he wished to live the life of a simple country gentleman. During World War I he displayed an impressive spirit of dedication and self-sacrifice, and he was truly beloved. He was an ideal sovereign in an age when the King must maintain the dignity of kingship but must not aspire to influence in the affairs of the state.

DOMESTIC ANARCHY

The years from 1910 to 1914 were disturbing ones for moderate and sensible Englishmen. Not only was the international horizon more threatening; unrest, disunity, and violence were chronic in domestic affairs. The Liberal alliance with Labor and with the Irish Nationalists weakened. There was also much labor disquiet. Home rule for Ireland again convulsed the nation. The Conservatives continued the bitter and uncompromising tone they had adopted during the curbing of the House of Lords. Many people set forth their principles in a militant way without respect for the principles of others, for violence seemed to

[3] The phrase is that of R. C. K. Ensor, *England 1870–1914*, p. 342.

obtain better results than patient and orderly conduct. Men might well feel that their world was getting out of hand.

Labor Unrest

The strength of the Labor movement throughout the country was greater than the number of Labor members in the Commons would indicate, and the Labor party believed that it did not carry the weight in Parliament to which it was entitled. Labor also felt its defeat in the Osborne Case, a court decision declaring that unions could not impose compulsory levies on their members in order to raise funds for political purposes. The decision was a blow to some Labor members who had no income beyond the support they received from their unions. To meet this grievance the government in 1911 secured a financial resolution in the House of Commons providing a salary of £400 a year for each member. Nonetheless, the Labor party was dissatisfied. Growing cool toward the Liberals, it fostered a socialist program of its own.

There was a corresponding change in the thinking of Labor leaders, who turned away from Parliament toward syndicalism, that is, toward the notion that the union and not the state was the center of democratic action. Labor leaders should influence Parliament, not by becoming members, but by direct action outside politics, by the sympathy strike, by the general strike, and even by sabotage. Similar ideas appeared in other countries, for there was labor unrest in most industrialized nations at this time. A number of strikes took place in Britain during the years from 1910 to 1912. The most important were a railway strike in 1911 and a strike of coal miners in 1912. The strike on the railways lasted only two days, but it paralyzed the nation during that period. The miners' strike continued for five weeks, affecting 850,000 miners and 1,250,000 workers in other industries. Strikes tapered off with better times in 1913–1914. But three of the most aggressive unions—those of the railway men, the miners, and the transport workers—formed an industrial alliance in 1913. If the 2 million workers in these trades all struck at the same time they could cripple industry as well as prevent the distribution of food.

In 1911 the Cabinet secured the passage of a National Insurance Act which protected almost the entire working population in case of sickness. It was true insurance in that the worker, the employer, and the government each contributed a few pennies a week to a central fund. Benefits included medical care and small money payments, varying according to circumstances over a period no longer than twenty-six weeks. An attempt made to insure workers in certain trades against unemployment was admittedly experimental. Contributions were arranged as in sickness insurance; benefits were payable over a period of fifteen weeks, during which time it was assumed that a laborer could normally find new employment. The Conservative party was furious. The measure would never have become law if the Lords had possessed the power to stop it. The contributions made by laborers (normally 4*d*. a week) were denounced as robbery of the poor, noble ladies exhorted workingmen to resist such tyranny, the medical profession was urged to refuse the government its cooperation. Lloyd George answered in rather demagogic fashion; altogether the controversy greatly debased the currency of politics.

Violence of another kind arose from the woman-suffrage movement. An agitation for woman suffrage had been conducted for some time in an orderly fashion. But in 1903 Mrs. Emmeline Pankhurst organized the Woman's Social and Political Union, which resorted to violence in order to promote its cause. Public meetings were disrupted, pictures were slashed in art galleries, fires were set, acid was poured into mail boxes, women chained themselves to the galleries of the House of Commons so that they could not be easily removed. A woman threw herself before the horses as they ran in the Derby. In prison the suffragists resorted to hunger strikes. A "Cat and Mouse" Act was passed by which prisoners could be released when ill and arrested again when they had recovered. The public turned against the "suffragettes" and for the time the movement produced no results.

Home Rule

In 1912 the government introduced a Home Rule Bill for Ireland. This bill was certain to be controversial; it increased the bitterness of political life and inflamed the tendency toward violent action regardless of the law. It was based upon a federal concept. Ireland was to be autonomous in domestic affairs, with a Parliament and a responsible government in Dublin, but the imperial Parliament in London was to remain supreme and was to handle many matters of wider importance in Anglo-Irish government. Forty-two Irish members were to sit in the English House of Commons. Conditions in Ireland had altered greatly since Gladstone's first home rule bill in 1886. The Irish land problem had been solved. Irish peasants, thanks to loans from the English government, had largely bought out their landlords and had become prosperous and self-respecting small farmers. Through a system of county and district councils introduced in 1898 they had become accustomed to self-government in local affairs. Moreover, John Redmond, the Irish Nationalist leader, had none of Parnell's hatred of England. Unfortunately a problem arose in the area of Ulster, where the population, largely of Scottish ancestry, was Protestant and industrial in contrast to the Roman Catholic and agricultural society of southern Ireland. Ulstermen were determined not to be placed under the domination of a Catholic Parliament in Dublin. The Conservatives in England, in their furious opposition to home rule, fostered a spirit of revolt in Ulster. Sir Edward Carson, an Irish member of Parliament, and Bonar Law, the official leader of the Conservative party, gave full support to preparations in Ulster to resist home rule by force. As volunteer armies organized both in Ulster and in southern Ireland, the country was headed for civil war.

Asquith handled the situation badly. He might have known that Ulster could not be forced to accept home rule and he should certainly have taken vigorous steps to suppress the private armies springing up in Ireland. Instead, he permitted matters to drift and remained committed to a bill which placed all Ireland under a Parliament at Dublin. Meanwhile Carson and Law were making speeches calculated to induce the British army to refuse to coerce the Ulstermen. Such open defiance of law and order was highly scandalous and most unsettling for the nation as a whole. When the bill became law, after the Lords had delayed it for two years, World War I had begun. The operation of the act was deferred for the duration of hostilities.

The dangerous division and violence of this period ended with the coming of war. In facing the challenge from Germany the British people—though not the people of southern Ireland—closed their ranks and achieved a new unity and a new faith in themselves.

THE EMPIRE

Between 1906 and 1914 the Liberals took important steps toward the extension of self-government within the empire. They were generous to the Boers. The treaty at the end of the war in 1902 had promised the Boers representative government in the near future and responsible government at a later time. Balfour's ministry had been preparing to meet the first of these promises when it fell from office. Campbell-Bannerman decided to skip the representative stage and to grant responsible government at once. This move was strongly denounced by the Conservatives, but it could be carried into effect through letters patent and did not have to be placed before the House of Lords. Self-government was granted to the Transvaal in 1906 and to the Orange River Colony (formerly the Orange Free State) in 1907. The result was highly satisfactory. General Botha, who was elected Prime Minister of the Transvaal, with General Smuts as his principal colleague, cooperated fully with the British to make the new government a success. Events moved rapidly toward the unification of the four states of South Africa into one dominion. This came in 1910. The new dominion was not a federation, as were Canada and Australia, but a unified state, a form adopted because South Africa was faced with such serious problems that a highly centralized government seemed most suitable.

The Liberals also took a tentative step toward self-government in India. A nationalist movement had arisen in India during the second half of the nineteenth century. In 1885 it had taken shape in the establishment of the Indian National Congress, a body composed largely of Hindu intellectuals educated in the Western tradition. They were moderate, they recognized the benefits of British rule, and they requested that representative institutions be introduced into India as rapidly as possible.

Gradually, however, the Congress came to be dominated by extremists who assumed a more violent tone. There were many reasons for this increased aggressiveness. The 1890s were a difficult time for India. The country was visited by both plague and famine, and it suffered economically because its standard of value was silver whereas the standard in England was gold. As the price of silver declined in terms of gold, Indian payments in London required nearly twice the number of rupees that would have discharged an equal obligation twenty years before. The Indian Mutiny, as we have seen, left a legacy of bitterness. Indians turned to their own religion and to their own civilization as a bulwark against Westernization, which many of them regarded as essentially evil. And those Indians who understood the West had been educated through reading the liberal writings of the nineteenth century, which made them realize how autocratic their government was. Many local grievances further increased discontent.

Anti-British feeling rose to new heights in the years between 1898 and 1905 when Lord Curzon was Viceroy. An extremely able but a rather autocratic ruler, he was eager to introduce reforms and was rather impatient of criticism from Hindu sources. A violent campaign in Bengal against many of his policies led to assassinations, bomb throwing, and constant disturbance of the peace.

India was governed by a Secretary of State in London and by a Viceroy in India. A small executive council, whose members for the most part were the heads of large departments, assisted the Viceroy. There was also a legislative council composed of a much larger group of lesser officials. Both councils were almost exclusively British. The country was divided into eleven provinces under governors and lieutenant governors, each with his own executive and legislative councils. The Indian civil service, a body of about 1200 British officials of very high quality, was responsible for all kinds of administration and often governed small areas within the provinces. In addition, in some 500 native states, internal affairs were administered by native princes, but foreign relations were conducted through the British government.

In 1909 the Liberals passed the Morley-Minto reforms, John Morley being Secretary for India and Lord Minto being the Viceroy. The reforms included the appointment of an occasional Indian to the executive councils. The legislative councils were greatly enlarged to include many Indians who were elected by constituencies representing various classes, interests, and religions. Members of the legislative councils could criticize the proposals of the government, including financial proposals, but the executive could disregard these criticisms. Thus India received representative government of a restricted kind, with responsibility remaining in British hands. This halfway house on the road to self-government could be no more than a temporary measure.

THE APPROACH OF WAR

The Entente with France

About the turn of the century, as we have seen, Britain had abandoned her traditional isolation and had begun a search for allies. Her first approach had been to Germany, but she had been repulsed; in 1902 she had announced her alliance with Japan. In 1904 she concluded a much more important agreement with France. This was not an alliance but an entente, an understanding, an attempt to end the constant friction over colonies and empire that poisoned relations between the two countries. Disagreements were seen to fall into two categories. The first was a long series of local irritations and minor disputes which were ironed out in hard bargaining. They dealt with Newfoundland, West Africa, Siam, Madagascar, and the New Hebrides.

The second category was a matter of high policy. Ever since the English had occupied Egypt, the French had used their treaty rights in that country to obstruct British administration. England had been forced to seek the support of Germany in Egyptian affairs. Now, however, the French were interested in Morocco, where the government of the Sultan was slowly disintegrating. Possession of Morocco would connect Algeria with French West Africa and would strengthen French naval power. Thus a bargain was possible. France agreed to give England a free hand in Egypt, and the English recognized French interest in Morocco. Success in these negotiations was the result of good will on both sides of the Channel. The British Foreign Minister, Lord Lansdowne, was quite pro-French, and he was assisted in winning French approval by a visit of Edward VII to Paris in 1903. Delcassé, the French Foreign Minister, perhaps did not love the British, but he was convinced that France could never sustain a war with Germany without more assistance than she was likely to obtain from the Russians.

Thus from the beginning the entente may have been anti-German in the minds of the French, but there is no evidence that this was so in England. It was later developments that turned the entente into an anti-German alliance of France and Britain. One of these was the steady increase in the size of the German navy. Even in the days before the entente the British had been strengthening their naval bases in Scotland and had begun to assemble naval units in home waters. British naval power in the Mediterranean had been reduced. This policy was gradually expanded until, in 1914, the British fleet was concentrated in Scottish bases facing Germany across the North Sea, while the French fleet was concentrated in the Mediterranean. No such close cooperation had been foreseen in 1904.

A second influence drawing England and France together was the Russo-Japanese War, which weakened Russia and thereby increased the relative strength of Germany. There was also the first Moroccan crisis in 1905–1906. As French ambitions in Morocco became clearer, the Kaiser suddenly visited Tangier in March 1905, where he asserted that Morocco was an independent country in which Germany and other nations had interests. The German move was a challenge to the entente and an attempt to weaken it, but the result was quite the opposite. At an international conference at Algeciras in Spain in 1906 English diplomacy supported France, and Germany obtained nothing. The entente had been greatly strengthened.

Meanwhile Lord Lansdowne had been succeeded by Sir Edward Grey as British Foreign Secretary. A Liberal imperialist, Grey saw no reason to alter the policy of his predecessor. Grey was an aristocrat, a Northumberland country gentleman, not an ambitious politician. Although his idealism and his good will fitted him for his task, he knew little about the rest of the world, including the Continent. He spoke no other language than English.

As the Algeciras conference was about to begin, Paul Cambon, the French Ambassador in London, told Grey that France greatly feared a sudden attack by Germany. Cambon asked whether England would assist France in resisting such an attack and whether she would permit military conversations between the two powers concerning possible cooperation. Without such conversations, Cambon argued, British assistance would be futile. Grey replied that he could not commit his country in advance; but after consultation with Campbell-Bannerman, Asquith, and Haldane (the Secretary for War), though not with the whole Cabinet, he permitted the conversations to begin. They continued for many years. They included arrangements for rushing the British army to France within a period of a few days. The nature of the entente thus was transformed. Grey might insist that England was not bound by treaty to come to the aid of France if France was attacked by Germany. Nonetheless, the military conversations implied a moral obligation, for how could England make detailed plans to assist the French and then not do so when the crisis came? There were also naval conversations leading, as we have seen, to French concentration in the Mediterranean and to British concentration in the North Sea. But if, while this arrangement continued, the German fleet should attack the northern coast of France, how could the British escape the moral duty of intervention?

In 1907 a treaty was signed with Russia. It, too, was an entente, similar to the agreement with France, for it did no more than settle imperial differences between Russia and Britain. Friction between the two countries had lessened in both the Near and the Far East, and it was only in the Middle East that serious difficulties remained. They concerned Persia, Afghanistan, and Tibet. Each of these countries was treated differently. Persia was divided into three zones: a northern one in which the Russians might seek concessions, a southern one in which the British might do the same, and a central one in which both countries might be active. The Russians recognized the special interest of Britain in

Afghanistan and agreed to have no dealings with the Afghans except through British sources. Both countries agreed to stay out of Tibet. By 1909 Europe thought in terms of the Triple Entente as a counterbalance to the Triple Alliance.

Armaments and Crises

Britain continued to be preoccupied with the problem of defense. In 1906 she completed a new battleship, the *Dreadnought*, the first all-big-gun ship, which revolutionized naval design. Earlier battleships had normally carried four heavy guns with a number of medium guns and light, quick-firing ordnance. The designers of the *Dreadnought* swept aside all secondary armaments and equipped the vessel with eight of the heaviest guns then made. The *Dreadnought* rendered all other battleships obsolete. As Admiral Fisher boasted, it could sink the whole German navy. The Germans agreed. They laid down four such ships in 1908, whereas the British only laid down two. Admiral von Tirpitz planned four more in 1909, and by accumulating guns and equipment well in advance he greatly shortened the time required for construction. In the ensuing naval scare in Britain Asquith suggested that four battleships be built in 1909, with four later if the need arose. The public was not satisfied. "We want eight and we won't wait," was the theme of the music halls. The government then yielded to pressure and laid down eight dreadnoughts in one year.

Meanwhile the Secretary for War, R. B. Haldane, took in hand the reorganization of the army. Knowing that English opinion would not tolerate conscription, upon which the huge armies of the Continent were based, he kept the regular army small (160,000 men) but made it very good. This army, with its transport, artillery, and medical services, could be sent to France within a few days. Haldane also created a second army, known as the Territorial Force. Composed of volunteers, it stood between the regular army on one hand and the militia on the other; by 1910 it numbered 276,000 men. A general staff was now established for the first time; a war council, which did not amount to a general staff but made an advance in that direction, also was created for the navy.

Between 1908 and 1914 a series of international crises brought Europe closer to war. The Bosnian crisis of 1908 arose from the rivalry of Austria and Russia in the Balkans. Taking advantage of difficulties in Turkey, Austria suddenly announced the annexation of the provinces of Bosnia and Herzegovina, which she had administered since 1878. The Kaiser disliked this move, but he supported Austria by suggesting that the annexation be approved in an exchange of notes among the great powers. When the Russians delayed their answer, Germany demanded a reply in peremptory terms. Russia gave way but was deeply humiliated. The Agadir crisis of 1911 concerned Morocco once more. Since 1906 the French had been continuing their penetration of that country. In 1911 they dispatched a small army to quell some rebellious tribesmen. Germany at once sent a gunboat to Agadir, a port on the Atlantic coast of Morocco. Her purpose was to secure some compensation to balance Morocco's absorption by France, but Grey thought that she planned to seize Agadir as a naval base. Thereupon Lloyd George made a militant speech, warning that when Britain's interests were involved she was not to be treated "as if she were of no account in the cabinet of nations." Tension eased when it became clear that Germany sought only compensation. Ultimately she obtained a slice of the French Congo, a poor return for the dangerous risks that she had taken.

In 1912 interest shifted once more to the Balkans. Serbia, Bulgaria, Greece, and Montenegro won surprising victories in a war against the Turks. In the next year, however, they fell out among themselves and waged war on each other. The final result was that Bulgaria, Austria's friend, was weakened, whereas Serbia, Austria's enemy, was strengthened and rendered more ambitious. Relations between Austria and Serbia remained tense and hostile.

The Outbreak of War

On June 28, 1914, the Archduke Francis Ferdinand, heir to the Austro-Hungarian throne, and his wife were assassinated at Sarajevo, the capital of Bosnia. The deed was done by Bosnian nationalists who had received inspiration and guns from Serbians. The Austrian government, though it could not trace the assassination to the government of Serbia, determined to use the incident to deal with Serbia once and for all. The Kaiser gave his approval for strong action. On July 23 Austria sent Serbia a very stiff ultimatum which was meant to bring about war. The Serbs, however, gave way on almost every point. Nonetheless, the Austrians declared war on Serbia July 28. At the last minute the Germans tried to restrain their aggressive ally, but it was too late. The Russians began to mobilize first against Austria and then against Germany. Hence the Germans also began to mobilize. On August 1 Germany declared war against Russia and on August 3 against France.

The rapidity of these events astonished both the British Cabinet and the British people. Grey's proposal of a conference in London of the ambassadors of the great powers was accepted by France but refused by Germany. Thereafter the question was not whether England could prevent the war but whether she should enter it. Russia and France pressed desperately for a commitment. But the British Cabinet was divided, and Grey had to reply that he could give no pledge. He obtained permission to inform Germany that Britain would not tolerate a German naval attack on the northern coast of France. France and Germany were asked whether they would respect Belgian neutrality. The French reply was satisfactory; the German reply was not.

On the afternoon of August 3 Grey presented his case in the Commons. He argued that although the military conversations with France did not bind England to come to her support, there was a moral obligation to do so. He pointed out that if France were crushed, the British Empire would be in jeopardy. He reported the Cabinet's decision to defend the northern coast of France. Then he came to Belgium. On the previous day the Germans had demanded from Belgium the right to send troops through that country; the violation of Belgium was certain to follow. It had long been British policy to prevent the occupation of Belgium by any great power. The Commons strongly supported Grey. Next day an ultimatum was sent to Germany threatening war if Belgium was invaded. The ultimatum expired at 11 P.M. on August 4. Thereafter Britain and Germany were at war.

THE FIRST WORLD WAR, 1914–1918

The master plan of the Germans, which led them to violate Belgian neutrality, was to make a great, semicircular sweep into northern France, to roll up the French against other German armies on the Franco-German frontier, and to crush France within six weeks. Holding the Channel ports, such as Calais and

Boulogne, the Germans could then fend off any English attack while they turned their full strength on Russia, bringing about her speedy collapse. The war was to be quickly over. This plan was frustrated at the Battle of the Marne in September 1914, when the Germans were stopped by the French and British armies. Instead of lasting a few weeks the war dragged on for fifty-two months. It destroyed the German, Austrian, and Turkish empires, it precipitated the Russian Revolution, and it brought about profound changes in England and the British Empire.

British strategy remained essentially the same as it had been in other great wars, such as those against Louis XIV and Napoleon. In each case a dominant continental power controlled the land mass of Europe. British strategy was two-fold. It consisted, in the first place, of a naval blockade to halt the flow of raw materials to the enemy and to deny him access to world markets. In the second place, Britain sought allies along the periphery of the continental power, assisting them with men, money, and munitions. Thus the British began at the circumference and worked toward the center.

But the First World War differed greatly from earlier wars because of the development of weapons. Artillery was vastly more effective than in the past. Machine guns, barbed wire, and grenades gave great defensive strength to trench warfare. Zeppelins, airplanes, poison gas, and wireless added new dimensions to war; torpedoes, mines, and submarines altered the conditions of blockade and revolutionized naval combat. The British navy carried on under the new conditions. German merchantmen disappeared at once from the oceans; a few German warships in scattered parts of the world were soon run down and destroyed. The British Grand Fleet at Scapa Flow in the Orkneys, with light craft at Harwich, and the second Fleet at Sheerness in the mouth of the Thames, maintained a remote blockade of the German High Seas Fleet in its fortified harbors in northern Germany. Vast numbers of soldiers were taken across the Channel, or brought from the Dominions, or later from the United States with very little loss. Food and war materials flowed into Britain. The blockade was effective, though it caused the usual friction with neutral nations. In spite of a large ship-building program carried on in Britain her navy was under great strain.

Britain continued to search for allies. Belgium was perforce one from the beginning. So was Serbia, at war with the Austrians. Japan quickly pounced on German possessions in the Far East. But although every effort was made to conciliate Turkey, she threw in her lot with the Central Powers. This was of vital concern. Surrounded by enemies in Europe, Germany possessed no outlets save those of the Balkans, Turkey, and Asia Minor. Moreover, Turkey blocked communications between the western Allies and Russia as well as threatened British power in both the Near and the Middle East. After some hesitation Bulgaria also sided with the Central Powers. Rumania remained neutral until 1916, then joined the Allies, only to be quickly crushed. Italy also joined the Allies. Her entrance into the war was not impressive, for she sold to the highest bidder. Desirous of lands held by Austria, Italy was offered a little by Austria and a great deal more by the Allies, who could be generous with another people's territory. Italy's entrance into the war opened a new front which engaged large numbers of Austrian troops.

A British army of some 100,000 men, placed in France within a few days, was too late to help the Belgians but gave great assistance to the French. It fought delaying actions against the advancing Germans at Mons and at Le

Cateau; it took part in the Battle of the Marne, which stopped the Germans and forced them back to the Aisne; it defended a forward salient at Ypres in desperate fighting to save the Channel ports of Calais and Boulogne. Had these ports been captured by the Germans, British communications with France would have been much more difficult. As a result of these battles, the British Expeditionary Force was reduced to a small fraction of its original size. But it was able to give time for new armies to be recruited at home. Lord Kitchener, the popular hero of many imperial campaigns and now Secretary for War, called initially for 100,000 volunteers, who were quickly sent to France, along with the Territorial Force and troops from the Dominions. The Western Front was already stabilized in a line of trenches extending 600 miles from the Channel to the Swiss frontier. This front swayed back and forth over small distances in an agony of shells, machine guns, barbed wire, and mud, with frightful casualties on both sides.

Stalemate came quickly in the west; hence the Allies pinned their hopes on Russia, who began offensives from Russian Poland to the north into East Prussia and to the south into Austrian Galicia. But in East Prussia the Russians suffered a rout at Tannenberg (August 26–29, 1914), where a quarter of a million were captured. The Russians did much better against the Austrians, until a German counteroffensive into Poland forced them to withdraw. Early in 1915 they were driven far back into Russia in one of the great disasters of the war.

There were various schools of high strategy among the Allies. To the French, fighting on their own soil, with their iron- and coal-producing areas in enemy hands, the Western Front seemed all-important. Many British soldiers agreed with them. Admiral Fisher, on the other hand, advocated an attack on the Baltic in an attempt to break through to Russia. This plan was abandoned as too dangerous. Lloyd George believed that a landing in the Balkans would gain allies and open a way into Austria. Winston Churchill, First Lord of the Admiralty, urged a drive through the Dardanelles to Constantinople, thus knocking Turkey out of the war and gaining access to the Black Sea. When this was attempted in 1915 it began as a naval operation; but the Turks had German advisers, the forts on the Dardanelles were strongly held, the Straits were mined, and the naval attack was a failure. A month later troops were landed on the Gallipoli Peninsula. With the element of surprise lost, only exposed beach heads could be occupied. The troops were withdrawn at the end of the year. Another defeat fell on the British in Mesopotamia. A British expedition moved from Basra on the Persian Gulf up the Tigris and Euphrates Valley and captured Kut-al-Imara, 300 miles above Basra. But an advance toward Baghdad was repulsed and Kut-al-Imara was besieged. After enduring many privations the British forces there surrendered to the Turks in 1916.

Meanwhile the Western Front in 1915 was the scene of heavy fighting and severe British losses. British offensives at Neuve-Chapelle and at Festubert in March and in May, another battle at Ypres, and an offensive known as the Battle of Loos in September all resulted in more and more casualties without an appreciable gain against the German lines. Sir John French was replaced by Sir Douglas Haig as supreme commander. An obvious cause of British failures was a shortage of shells and other types of arms. The number of shells required was fantastic: in one battle the British used more than were used in the whole South African war. These reverses caused a Cabinet crisis in May 1915 to which we will turn presently. Asquith remained in power but formed a coalition Cabinet which included a number of Conservatives and one member of the Labor party.

A Ministry of Munitions was created and placed in the vigorous hands of Lloyd George. Production of shells increased greatly, though it hardly affected the fighting in 1915.

The year 1916 brought new reverses. The Germans, deciding that Russia could be ignored, concentrated their power against the French lines at Verdun. France had already suffered 2 million casualties, and the Germans thought that she could now be crushed or at least bled white. For almost half a year the Battle of Verdun engaged the entire French army at a cost of some 350,000 casualties, but when the fighting slackened, Verdun was still in French possession. The British were naturally expected to relieve the pressure by opening an offensive on the western section of the front. This offensive, known as the Battle of the Somme, was thus a political necessity though a bad military risk because the Germans were well prepared to meet it. Still short of artillery, the British lost 60,000 men on the first day and some 410,000 before the offensive was abandoned. In return for this heavy loss of life they could show only an advance of six or seven miles along a thirty-mile front.

The one naval engagement on a grand scale between the British and the German fleets was the Battle of Jutland in the North Sea in May 1916. This battle has been the subject of a great amount of controversy. There was natural disappointment that although the British superiority was very great (twenty-eight battleships and nine battle cruisers against sixteen battleships and five battle cruisers), the Germans not only escaped destruction but inflicted more damage than they received. But many answers can be given. The British losses occurred before the two main fleets were engaged; during their brief encounter the Germans were worsted and never tried again. They stayed in port for the remainder of the war, except for one brief sortie, yielding to Britain the fruits of victory.

It is true that at Jutland the British Admiral Sir John Jellicoe was very cautious. He felt strongly that he was the one man in the world who could lose the war in an afternoon. Upon sighting the British Grand Fleet, Admiral Scheer, the German commander, knew that he was in great danger and turned away to avoid combat. Then he returned to fight, but finding his position even worse than before, he devoted all his efforts to escaping. That he was able to do so was due to three things. The first was poor visibility, which prevented Jellicoe from knowing that Scheer had turned away upon the first encounter. The second was Jellicoe's turn under torpedo attack. A fleet attacked by torpedoes turns parallel to the course of the oncoming missles, thus reducing the target area. But a fleet can turn either toward the torpedoes or away from them. Jellicoe turned away, and only one of his battleships was hit. Had he turned the other way, more ships would have been torpedoed, but he would have drawn closer to Scheer. The third reason for Scheer's escape was the gathering darkness, for Jellicoe declined a night action, which would have favored the Germans. The net result of the battle was that the British hold on the North Sea was left intact though the Grand Fleet had to maintain its vigil and the British navy could continue its countless tasks. But the Germans lost hope of defeating the British Grand Fleet.

The year 1917 brought tremendous developments and offered hope for the future, though the present was grim. In March the Revolution began in Russia, overthrowing the Czar and demoralizing the Russian armies. Their disintegration exposed the Allies to new dangers, for the Austrians were then able to send large numbers of troops to Italy. At Caporetto in October the Italians were defeated disastrously. They rallied on the Piave River, a few miles north of Venice, where

The Imperial War Cabinet and Conference, 1917. Left to right (seated): A. Henderson, Lord Milner, Lord Curzon, Bonar Law, Lloyd George, Sir Robert Borden, William Ferguson Massey, and General J. C. Smuts. Standing (in middle): Sir Satyendra Sinha, the Maharajah of Bikanir, Sir James Meston, Austen Chamberlain, Lord Robert Cecil, Walter Long, Sir Joseph Ward, Sir George Perley, Robert Rogers and John Douglas Hazen. Standing (back row): Captain Amery, Admiral Jellicoe, Sir Edward Carson, Lord Derby, General Morris, Sir M. Hankey, Henry Charles Miller Lambert, and Major Storr. (Historical Pictures Service, Chicago)

they were stiffened by French and British troops sent from the Western Front.

As Russia was leaving the war, the United States was entering it because of a change in German policy in the use of the submarine. During the first two years of the war the depredations of German submarines had not been great, nor did submarines normally sink vessels without warning. Yet the practice of sinking without warning tended to increase because it facilitated the escape of the submarine. The sinking of the Cunard liner *Lusitania* in May 1915, with the loss of 100 American lives, brought a sharp protest from President Wilson, and the Germans agreed not to sink ships without warning. But at the beginning of 1917 the morale of the Germans was low. They had been fighting on many different fronts; their standard of living was declining under the impact of the British blockade. In February 1917, therefore, the Germans decided to disregard neutral nations and to embark on unrestricted submarine warfare. It was more important, they thought, to strike fiercely at Britain than to keep the United States out of the war. Losses of British shipping rose ominously. In April these losses reached 875,000 tons, a rate that would soon have reduced England to starvation. Unrestricted submarine warfare, however, brought the United States into the war in April.

The Allies gradually learned how to fight submarines. So novel was the problem that at the beginning of the war the British had tried to train sea lions to detect submarines; but the sea lions, finding submarines inedible, were indifferent to them. Submarines could be destroyed by nets, mines, depth charges, and gunfire. The best protection for shipping was the convoy; the best method of detection was constant scouting by surface craft. The hydrophone was developed to pick up underwater sounds.[4] Toward the end of the war submarines were destroyed so rapidly that they averaged only about six trips each, a mortality which had a numbing effect on the crews. Nonetheless, submarines demanded a far greater effort on the part of the Allies in combating them than on the part of Germany in building them.

The year 1917 was a tragic one for the Allies in France. The Germans retired a short distance to new defenses, the Siegfried—or Hindenburg—line, which greatly strengthened their position. An overoptimistic offensive by the French General Nivelle ended in collapse. Nivelle was superseded by General Pétain, the commander at Verdun. Later in the year Haig launched an offensive at Passchendaele toward the coast of Flanders. This also bogged down.

British arms met better fortune in fighting the Turks. A new push up the Tigris and Euphrates Valley captured Baghdad; and an invasion of the Holy Land from Egypt resulted in the capture of Jerusalem.

Early in 1918 the Germans opened a great offensive. Staking all on one desperate thrust, they gambled on cracking the Allies before the strength of America could be brought fully into play. The Treaty of Brest-Litovsk with the Bolsheviks not only ceded large sections of Russian territory to Germany but also liberated German troops to fight on the Western Front. The full fury of this offensive fell first on the British under Haig, who had his back to the wall but held on. In May the offensive shifted to the French, who retreated. Now was fought the second Battle of the Marne. Regarding Pétain as too pessimistic, Haig accepted General Foch as the supreme commander of all the forces on the Western Front. The German offensive came to a halt.

Thereafter the Germans were on the verge of defeat. Bulgaria collapsed, Turkey surrendered, Austria capitulated after a defeat of her armies in Italy. A mutiny broke out among the seamen in the German fleet. The armistice signed on November 11 brought the war to an end.

The Home Front

Criticism of the government was regarded as unpatriotic in the early days of the war. The leadership of Asquith's Cabinet—in which the war effort was directed by the Prime Minister, by Kitchener, and by Winston Churchill—was accepted loyally by all parties. But difficulties arose in May 1915 as a result of reverses in France. Kitchener came under criticism. A thorough soldier, accustomed to lonely command in faraway places, he found it difficult to cooperate with civilians either at the War Office or in the Cabinet. His dual position as Commander in Chief and as Secretary for War made for overcentralization. The shortage of shells and the quarrel between Churchill and Admiral Fisher over the Dardanelles campaign also caused adverse comment. The Conservatives under Bonar Law thereupon informed the Prime Minister that they would oppose the government unless Churchill and Haldane (who was thought to be sympathetic toward the Germans) were removed from office.

---

[4] An even better sonar device, known as Asdic, was not invented until after the war was over.

It was then that Asquith constructed the coalition Cabinet mentioned earlier. Grey and Kitchener retained their places, but Haldane was dropped and Churchill was relegated to minor office, while four Conservatives—Bonar Law, Carson, Balfour, and Lord Curzon—were brought into the Cabinet, as was also Arthur Henderson, the leader of the Labor party. Lloyd George was placed in charge of a new Ministry of Munitions to end the shortage of shells, a task in which he succeeded admirably. Hailed as the one man who could win the war, he found his prestige rising rapidly. When Kitchener was drowned at sea in June 1916, his place as Secretary for War was given to Lloyd George.

But the coalition was not working smoothly. The Conservatives thought that the Liberals still held the key positions and that Liberal reluctance to interfere with the rights of private citizens hindered the war effort. The Liberals, for instance, opposed conscription. But voluntary enlistment no longer supplied the number of soldiers required; it had drained away the most idealistic young men and had sacrificed them in the first years of the war. In January 1916 a Military Service Act, supported by the Conservatives as well as by Lloyd George, made all men under forty-one liable for service. An unexpected consequence of the act was the magnificent way in which British women stepped forward to perform all kinds of work formerly done by men, who now went to the front.

New criticism of the government arose in the autumn of 1916. It was directed at Asquith, who was thought to lack vigor and decisiveness. Lloyd George complained that the Prime Minister came to Cabinet meetings without a policy, listened to what was said, summed up the debate with admirable clarity, and then postponed decision. Some of the newspapers began to attack Asquith; Bonar Law joined the opposition. It was suggested to Asquith that he remain as Prime Minister but that the direction of the war be placed in the hands of a War Council headed by Lloyd George. After several days of confused intrigue Asquith resigned, convinced that Lloyd George had betrayed him. The result was a split in the Liberal party, some members following Asquith, some Lloyd George who, despite his arguments with Asquith, quickly combined the office of Prime Minister with the direction of the war effort.

Lloyd George created a small War Cabinet of five men—he himself (the only Liberal), Bonar Law, Milner, Curzon, and Arthur Henderson. Largely free from departmental duties, the Cabinet could devote itself almost entirely to the larger issues of the war. It was assisted by a Cabinet secretariat and by the innovation of keeping minutes of Cabinet meetings. The new Prime Minister was a remarkable man, combining resourcefulness, vigor, decision, and imagination with unusual administrative ability and great oratorical power. More than anyone else he was the organizer of victory. But he displayed a ruthlessness and a lack of loyalty to his colleagues which made him the object of distrust and suspicion.

At the beginning of the war the Cabinet encouraged the impression that business and ordinary civilian life should continue as usual. The war was to be conducted with as little interference as possible with private enterprise and personal liberty. But it became evident, as the war continued, that the state must exercise firm controls and that the war required a total mobilization of the country's resources, both human and material. The powers of the government over the economy steadily increased. A series of Defense of the Realm Acts (nicknamed DORA) gave the Cabinet power to issue general regulations for the public safety and to exercise broad controls over economic life. Lloyd George's vigorous administration of the Ministry of Munitions discarded trade-union rules, diluted skilled labor with unskilled and women workers, limited war profits, out-lawed strikes, curtailed excessive drinking. Before the war was over the government was managing coal mines and all means of transport, determining the hours and wages of labor, and settling industrial disputes. The number of civil servants expanded into a large bureaucracy. As the submarine menace grew more dangerous, Lloyd George created new ministries of Food, of Blockade, of Pensions, and of Labor. The rationing of food was introduced early in 1918.

Because goods and services were in short supply, inflation could not be avoided. It is thought that up to the end of 1917 prices rose at a rate of about 27 percent each year, though after that date further increases were slowed by controls of prices and wages and by heavy taxation. Even so, wholesale prices at the end of the war were about 140 percent above their prewar level; the pound had shrunk to about 8*s*. 3*d*. in purchasing power. The national debt rose to the astonishing figure of some £7 billion. Yet England paid the cost of the war more fully by current taxation than did most other nations. The income of the Exchequer was four times as high at the end of the war as at its beginning; large incomes were taxed at the rate of 6*s*. in the pound.[5]

The war was a profound emotional experience for every Briton. It began with a mood of exultation and idealism, shortly followed by bewilderment, and then by grim determination and dogged resolve. As the war continued month after month with little change in position on the Western Front there was a declining interest in following its details and a growing sense of agony at the appalling casualty lists. In many cases this agony was followed by bitterness and cynicism and by an utter loathing of that horrible thing called war. In the end there was exhaustion. Yet the British also had hope for better things; in Lloyd George's phrase, they longed for "a country fit for heroes to live in."

[5] These figures are taken from Henry Pelling, *Modern Britain 1885–1955* (Edinburgh: T. Nelson, 1960), pp. 81–82.

33

politics and depression, 1918-1931

The First World War was followed by a period of very difficult readjustment for Britain. More shattering than at first imagined, the war had disrupted Britain's foreign trade and had shaken her position as a world power. It was followed by depression and unemployment and by difficulties in foreign and imperial affairs. But though problems appeared to grow more and more complex, the men who controlled the government did not grow in stature. They handled routine business with competence, but their aim was to return to prewar conditions, they looked to the past, and hence they applied remedies that were out of date. Economic recovery was therefore very slow. At the end of the war the Labor party and large numbers of the working classes hoped for an advance toward socialistic goals. These hopes were disappointed; yet by an interesting paradox, the Conservatives, who were in power most of the time, were forced by economic necessity to do a number of things that looked toward socialism. Twice during this period the Labor party was in power. It was unable to accomplish much, but the fact that it held office was significant for the future and was a unique experiment in British democracy.

LLOYD GEORGE AND POSTWAR PROBLEMS

The Peace Treaties

Much of the government's time in 1919 was occupied by the Peace Conference at Paris, in which Lloyd George, assisted by British experts, played a major role. His mandate from the British electorate was to impose a harsh peace on the Germans, but he found himself mediating between the idealism of President Wilson, who stood for self-determination of peoples and for no annexations, and the realism of the French leader Clemenceau, who was interested primarily in the subjugation of Germany and the exaction of heavy reparations. In return for a number of concessions, Wilson obtained the League of Nations—an idea which owed much to British opinion. Germany was disarmed. Her army was limited to a force of 100,000 enlisted men; she was to have no military aircraft, no submarines, and no battleships of more than 10,000 tons. The map of Europe was drawn anew. France received Alsace-Lorraine and semipermanent possession of the Saar. A number of new states appeared—Czechoslovakia, Yugoslavia, and Poland, with a corridor of land extending to the Baltic and separating East Prussia from the rest of Germany. Rumania, Greece, and Italy obtained additional territory; Bulgaria, Austria, and Hungary were greatly reduced; the Turks lost their empire.

Britain's share, as usual, was colonial. Colonies were not given to her in complete ownership, however, but at mandates under the League of Nations. The idea of a mandate had been developed by various writers in the Labor party. Its principle was that the League should assume responsibility for the welfare of colonial peoples, but that the administration of colonies should be entrusted to individual powers under the supervision of the League. By the end of the war a number of former German colonies were in the possession of the British Dominions. The South Africans held German Southwest Africa; the Australians, North-East New Guinea; the New Zealanders, Samoa. The Dominions were permitted to keep these areas as mandates and to administer them as integral parts of their own territories. Great Britain obtained a mandate over German East Africa (renamed Tanganyika) and over the former Turkish possessions of Mesopotamia and Palestine.

The treaties concluded in Paris left many questions unsettled, and there followed a long series of international conferences in which Lloyd George took a leading part. Yet in the end he failed to achieve a stable European settlement. A major difficulty was that the Senate of the United States refused to ratify the treaty with Germany and thus withdrew from all responsibility for the affairs of the Continent. This action increased the desire of the British to withdraw also, but it intensified the determination of the French to obtain some sort of security against future German attack. France made alliances with the newly created states of Europe as a protection against Germany.

Security was connected closely with reparations and war debts. It became evident very quickly that the Germans would have to pay reparation in goods and not in money. But German goods as reparations—German coal, for example —destroyed the British market on the Continent and delayed Britain's economic recovery. Hence Lloyd George began to urge a more lenient tone toward Germany. The French, however, were adamant in demanding reparations. A serious rift appeared between England and France, and the two countries ceased to cooperate in European policy. France was interested in reparations partly because of her war debts to Britain and to the United States. Britain could not afford to be generous. Of the £1740 million she had loaned to her allies, £568 million loaned to czarist Russia were completely lost, and she owed £842 million to the United States.[1] The United States insisted on repayment. Under these circumstances Lloyd George struggled against increasing difficulties, his prestige diminished, and his fall from power in 1922 was in the making.

A conference on disarmament called by the United States and held in Washington, D.C., in 1921–1922 had some success. Clashes between the British and the French prevented any reduction in land forces. However, the United States

---

[1] These figures are taken from Henry Pelling, *Modern Britain 1885–1955* (Edinburgh: T. Nelson, 1960), pp. 88–89.

proposed that all naval tonnage under construction be scrapped, that a naval holiday be established for the next ten years, and that the existing ratio between the five naval powers be kept at 5–5–3–1.75–1.75. This arrangement provided for parity between the United States and Britain, for a ratio of about 60 percent for Japan, and of about 35 percent for Italy and France. The proposal was accepted by Britain, whose former naval supremacy thus was reduced to parity with that of the United States. The latter also persuaded Britain to abandon her alliance with Japan and to substitute for it a four-power treaty between the United States, Britain, France, and Japan to guarantee existing conditions in the Pacific.

Ireland

Soon after the end of the war Lloyd George had to face a new crisis in Ireland. An Irish Home Rule Bill, introduced by the Liberals in 1912, had become law in 1914, though its operation had been deferred until the end of hostilities.[2] It was soon quite out of date. The Home Rule party of Parnell and John Redmond declined and was superseded by a much more radical movement known as Sinn Fein (We Ourselves), which demanded an independent Irish republic extending over the whole island. An army formed in southern Ireland was known as the Irish Volunteers. In 1916 the Sinn Feiners and the Volunteers rose in rebellion against English rule. This revolt was quickly suppressed, but it threw the movement for independence into the hands of extremists. When Lloyd George held a general election in 1918, the Sinn Fein party swept Ireland, returning seventy-three members. These members refused to come to London. Instead, they met at Dublin (that is, twenty-six of them did; most of the others were in jail) and formed their own Parliament, the Dail Eireann. This body proclaimed the independence of Ireland and the establishment of an Irish republic. The Volunteers, organized by Michael Collins, became the Irish Republican Army. Other Irish leaders were Arthur Griffith, the founder of Sinn Fein; Cathal Brugha, a man who lived for fighting; and Eamon de Valera, the only one of the four to survive these desperate times.

Soon a state of war existed between the Irish Republican Army and the Royal Irish Constabulary, a government police force hastily strengthened by new recruits who wore khaki uniforms and black helmets and who were nick-named the Black and Tans. They lacked the discipline of trained police. Both sides soon were committing barbarities—assassinations, ambushes, tortures, and kidnapings—which shocked the Anglo-Saxon world. A turn for the better came in 1921, when King George V in a speech at Belfast pleaded for an end of hostilities and for a negotiated settlement. In a prolonged series of conferences between Lloyd George and the Irish leaders, Lloyd George offered southern Ireland the status of a dominion (the Irish Free State) whose only link with England would be an oath of allegiance to the Crown. This arrangement was accepted by Collins and Griffith. De Valera, on the other hand, demanded a republic, denounced allegiance to the Crown, and approved only of some vague external connection with the empire. A new civil war broke out between the two wings of the Sinn Fein party. Having recognized the Irish Free State in 1922, England left the Irish to fight among themselves. In the following year De Valera decided to resist no longer, though he did not abandon his ideas. In 1949 southern

[2] See page 699.

Ireland became a republic. Ulster remained a part of the United Kingdom of Great Britain and Northern Ireland.

The Election of 1918

Meanwhile, in December 1918, a few weeks after the ending of the war, Lloyd George held an election. Wishing to remain in office, he proposed a continuation of the coalition which had brought the war to a successful close. The Labor party, however, withdrew from the coalition, and Lloyd George was unable to make peace with the official Liberal party under Asquith. He therefore sought the support of the Conservatives and of those Liberals who had continued to follow him. His colleagues in the War Cabinet were Conservatives; he had no party machinery of his own. As a result, some 400 Conservative candidates stood for election, but only about 140 Lloyd George Liberals. All coalition candidates were given a written endorsement signed both by Lloyd George and by Bonar Law, the leader of the Conservative party. Asquith contemptuously called this endorsement a "coupon" or ration ticket, and the election became known as the "coupon" election. Lloyd George offered an attractive program of reconstruction, but the election was fought in an emotional atmosphere in which revenge on Germany was the dominant note. The result was a sweeping victory for the coalition. It was returned with 484 seats in the Commons, of which 338 were held by Conservatives and 136 by Lloyd George Liberals. Labor won 59 seats, the Asquith Liberals only 26. The 73 Irish members, as we have seen, refused to come to London.

There were many important aspects of this election. One was the shattering of the Liberal party. It had been weakened before the war by the violence connected with Ulster and with other issues, and the split between Lloyd George and Asquith in 1916 weakened it further. In 1918 the continuation of that split was fatal. The Liberals came back with less than half their former strength, and that half was itself divided. Moreover, the rise of the Labor party deprived them of radical support. As their position as a middle party became less and less tenable, they gradually sank to a position of insignificance. Although Labor increased its strength only from forty-two to fifty-nine members, its gain in popular votes was far greater than these figures suggest. The Conservatives, of course, came back in great numbers. They were to be the dominant party for the next twenty years. Their victory placed Lloyd George in a dangerous position, for they could dispense with him at any time and form a Conservative government with a majority in the Commons. His actions henceforth often reflected his captivity.

The election, however, had a deeper meaning: it emphasized a new alignment in political life. In the nineteenth and early twentieth centuries Liberals and Conservatives had been largely drawn from the same social classes. They looked alike and fundamentally they thought alike. But now at the end of the war there was a marked distinction between Conservative and Labor members. It was the difference between the right and the left, based on economics and on class distinctions. The Conservatives in the new House of Commons contained many successful businessmen, directors of corporations, and leaders in commerce and finance. The remark that they were "hard-faced men who looked as if they had done well out of the war" was unjust but contained an element of truth. They thought in terms of capitalism and private enterprise, of the maintenance of the gold standard, of tariffs for the protection of British industry. Proud of the empire, distrusting the masses and distrusting the Labor party, they wished a minimum of state control. In foreign policy they wished to withdraw from continental commitments, to give the League of Nations only limited support, and to stabilize Europe in order to increase trade. Naturally, they were deeply suspicious of Russia and hostile to communism.

The left, on the other hand, drew its strength from the great mass of workingmen, from trade unions and socialistic societies, and from dissatisfied Liberals, who now joined the Labor party. The left was composed of men of various shades of socialism. In 1918 the Labor party drew up a new constitution which committed its members to socialistic objectives, though in moderate form. Its aims were

> to secure for the producers by hand and by brain the full fruits of their industry, and the most equitable distribution thereof that may be possible, upon the basis of the common ownership of the means of production and the best obtainable system of popular administration and control of each industry and service.[3]

The left thus registered its opposition to capitalism. It wished to nationalize key industries, it opposed the gold standard, and it advocated an ambitious housing program and an extension of old-age pensions and national insurance. In foreign affairs the left supported the League of Nations and the concept of collective security; it also stood for disarmament. Toward Russia its tone was friendly though cautious. Hostile to imperialism, it sympathized with India's national aspirations. This moderate socialism should not be regarded as revolutionary, for the vast majority of the members of the Labor party assumed that their objectives would be attained through the normal process of parliamentary legislation. There was an element that favored direct action in the form of a general strike, but the party as a whole was moderate; it rejected affiliation with the small group of British Communists.[4]

Nonetheless, to many workingmen the time seemed ripe for an advance toward socialistic goals. The war had given workingmen a new confidence in themselves and in their unions. Labor leaders had gained political experience both as members of the War Cabinet and as spokesmen for the opposition. After the war the Trades Union Congress, which met only once a year, established a general council to direct policy between the annual meetings; the party's new constitution, drawn up in 1918, made it a national party that might in time attract middle-class support. Though Labor leaders might already regard the Russians with some skepticism, the Russian Revolution was still an inspiration to the rank and file. The war, moreover, had seen a vast extension of government controls. New ministries had been established; the civil service had greatly expanded; a Ministry of Reconstruction, created in 1917, had made voluminous reports. Thus the machinery of the state was fully adequate for an extension of a socialistic or collectivist program.

Lloyd George and Labor

Lloyd George, however, though he had once been a radical, was now surrounded by Conservative colleagues who opposed an extension of the activities

---

[3] Quoted in Charles Loch Mowat, *Britain between the Wars 1918–1940* (Chicago: University of Chicago Press, 1955), p. 18.
[4] Alfred F. Havighurst, *Twentieth Century Britain* (New York: Harper & Row, 1966), pp. 165–169.

of the state or any move toward nationalization. On the contrary, they wanted decontrol, and Lloyd George yielded to this demand. Wartime restrictions were permitted to lapse, factories and surplus commodities were sold, and rationing was ended. The production of electric power, which might well have been nationalized, was placed under the loose supervision of a government board. The railways were returned to private companies, though now combined into four great systems. In dealing with labor unrest Lloyd George appeared to be playing for time. In February 1919 he summoned a National Industrial Conference attended by employers and trade-union representatives. Lloyd George sent a message saying that he would listen sympathetically to labor's grievances, and there was high hope that the conference would open a new chapter in the relations of labor and management. But once the conference ended, nothing more was done.

Lloyd George's greatest difficulty was with the coal miners, who expected that after the war the coal industry would be nationalized and that their working conditions would be improved. When the government took no action, they threatened to strike in 1919. Thereupon Lloyd George persuaded the labor leaders to postpone the strike while a royal commission—the Sankey Commission —investigated the industry. The commission recommended nationalization, but the government, rejecting this solution, kept the industry under temporary control and appeased the miners by wage increases. Trouble was merely postponed until 1921, when the situation had altered completely. A short business boom following the war had ended during 1920, after which date the continental market for British coal collapsed and the industry was in a serious depression. With heavy losses imminent, the Cabinet hurried coal mining back to private operators, who could not make ends meet without a reduction in wages. In their strike in 1921 the miners called on their allies, the railway and transport unions, to support them by a sympathy strike, but these unions refused. The miners, thus left alone, went down to bitter defeat and were forced to accept lower wages.

Lloyd George's government extended the social services in two directions. The first was housing. There had been very little building during the war, and it was estimated that 800,000 new houses were required. An act of 1919 provided subsidies through which some 200,000 houses were built in the next four years, and though this was far from adequate, the principle was established that housing was a concern of the state. An Unemployment Insurance Act of 1920 extended benefits to some 12 million workers, whereas the former law had covered only about 4 million. Small contributions, as before, were made by the worker, the employer, and the government; benefits covered fifteen weeks of continuous unemployment in any one year.

Losses in Foreign Trade

After the collapse of the boom in 1920, a long depression settled on Britain. Even before the war, as we have seen, her share of world trade had been diminishing; the war accelerated this tendency. While Britain was intent on war production, foreign competitors, especially the neutral nations, pressed into her old markets. Backward countries, unable to buy goods from Britain as they had formerly done, began to develop their own manufactures. In the years after the war, Britain found that she was selling much less to Russia than before 1914 and that the important German market had all but collapsed because of Germany's poverty. Italy, developing her hydroelectric potential, ceased to import large quantities of British coal. The newly created countries of Europe eagerly expanded their industries; the United States, a great exporting nation, not only competed with Britain but raised tariffs against her. Moreover, the staple British exports—coal, textiles, iron, and steel—were losing their former position in international trade. British exports of coal declined from 82 million tons in 1907 to 70 million in 1930; her exports of cotton cloth from an annual value of £105 million to £86 million. Her foreign trade in the 1920s was no more than 80 percent of its former value.

The result was widespread unemployment. It was worst in the shipbuilding industry along the Clyde, in the area of Newcastle, in Lancashire, and in the coal fields of South Wales. During the decade before the war, unemployment had averaged 4.5 percent of the labor force; in 1921, when 2 million persons were unemployed, the figure reached 22.4 percent; for the next ten years it averaged 10 to 12 percent.[5]

The sudden slump in 1920 caused a great outcry for economy in the expenditures of the government and for a reduction of taxation. To answer these demands the Cabinet in 1921 appointed a committee of business leaders to suggest economies; but the committee, headed by Sir Eric Geddes, recommended such drastic reductions that the government itself was aghast. The "Geddes ax" would have crippled the normal functioning of the state. Its suggested economies were only partially carried out, though even so there were sharp reductions in expenditures. At the same time the government raised interest rates. The result was a deflation which discouraged business and depressed the entire economy. Nor did a few cautious moves toward a protective tariff or a slight reduction of taxation make matters better.

It is easy to look back at these measures and to criticize them as inadequate. The Cabinet would have been wiser to have stimulated new industries, to have modernized the equipment of British factories, to have increased purchasing power, and to have sought a more flexible foreign exchange than the rigid gold standard. Without these remedies, recovery was slow and painful, with much poverty and unemployment, a low gross national product, and a decline in the standard of living. Indeed, Britain would have faced an impossible situation if certain things had not helped her. She enjoyed what are called favorable terms of trade. This meant that agricultural products and other raw materials were cheap in the years following the war, while manufactured articles were expensive, so that British exports of manufactured goods brought a high price in relation to the cost of imported raw materials. Britain also possessed certain invisible exports. She retained about three fourths of her prewar investments overseas, and although she was unable to increase them, they brought her handsome dividends. London continued to be a world center of insurance, shipping, and international exchange. The City could still perform many services for foreign customers. It was to retain these customers that Britain clung to the gold standard, although the gold standard kept her exports high in price and low in volume.

The Fall of Lloyd George
The fall of Lloyd George in 1922 was partly the result of a revolt against him by the rank and file of Conservative members and partly the result of the

[5] Henry Pelling, *Modern Britain 1885–1955*, pp. 89–90; Alfred F. Havighurst, *Twentieth Century Britain*, pp. 161–162.

Chanak crisis. Lloyd George was a man who was either admired or detested. His extraordinary cleverness, his promptness in decision and action, his occasional ruthlessness, and his lack of loyalty to his colleagues inspired some men and alienated others. He was supported by the leaders of the coalition—by Austen Chamberlain, Arthur Balfour, Lord Birkenhead, Winston Churchill, and, for a long time, Bonar Law. On the other hand, most of the Conservatives disliked him intensely. He was so clever that he was not trusted. He was accused of minor corruption in bestowing honors on wealthy men who contributed to his Liberal party chest.[6] His solution of the Irish question irritated Conservatives, who had fought home rule all their lives. They wanted a protective tariff, which Lloyd George opposed for fear of losing Liberal support.

The Chanak crisis in 1922, which might have led to a war with Turkey, further alienated Conservatives. A portion of Turkish Anatolia had been awarded to the Greeks after the war; but the Turks, under their nationalist leader Mustapha Kemal, turned on the Greeks and drove them out. In this affair the Conservatives were pro-Turkish; Lloyd George, pro-Greek. It was said that Lloyd George would destroy the Conservative party as he had destroyed the Liberals. This fear turned Bonar Law against him. At a famous meeting of the Conservative parliamentary party at the Carlton Club in October 1922—despite the pleadings of Austen Chamberlain and Arthur Balfour—the Conservatives voted to withdraw from the coalition; Lloyd George resigned that afternoon. After his interview with George V the King remarked, "He will be Prime Minister again." But he never was. He remained in the Commons for many years, admired but out of office. The men who succeeded him as Prime Minister were less likely to inspire hostility, but they were far less vigorous and far less able to get things done. The days of the giants were over; ministers of second-rate capacity fumbled for solutions of Britain's complex problems.

THE CONSERVATIVES IN POWER, 1922–1924

The fall of the coalition restored the pattern of three political parties functioning independently. But divisions and anomalies remained, and it was several years before any one strong and united party held a long tenure of office. Bonar Law formed a Conservative Cabinet, but some of the ministers of the late coalition—Lord Birkenhead, Austen Chamberlain, and Arthur Balfour—angry at the way in which the coalition had been dissolved, refused to join the new government. Thus Conservative leadership was divided; and a number of younger and lesser men, such as Stanley Baldwin, secured high office and established themselves so firmly in the party hierarchy that they never were dislodged. Bonar Law held an election in November 1922. The Conservatives won 347 seats in the Commons, the Asquith Liberals 60, the Lloyd George Liberals 57, Labor 142. The Liberals remained divided, while Labor, increasing its strength from 59 to 142 members, became the second largest party in the Commons.

Bonar Law's Cabinet, with Lord Curzon as Foreign Secretary, was more concerned with foreign than with domestic problems. At a conference at Lausanne, Curzon secured a new treaty with the Turks following the Chanak crisis. He also had to deal with Germany and France during the French occupa-

[6] Charles Loch Mowat, *Britain between the Wars 1918–1940*, pp. 10, 133–135.

tion of the Ruhr—the desperate effort of the French to secure payment of reparations after the Germans defaulted. The French were met by the passive resistance of German workers and officials; financial chaos and wild inflation soon followed in Germany. The French occupation of the Ruhr revealed a sharp division of policy: France was determined to obtain reparations; Britain wanted to restore the German economy in the hope of creating a better market for her exports. Curzon's attempted mediation led in time to a new approach to the problem of reparations, a new plan of payment (the Dawes Plan), and an American loan to Germany. Reparations were closely linked with war debts. In 1923 Baldwin, then Chancellor of the Exchequer, and Montagu Norman, the Governor of the Bank of England, visited the United States to negotiate a settlement of Britain's enormous debt. The best they could obtain was an arrangement for payment over a period of sixty-one years at interest of 3 percent for the first ten years and 3.5 percent thereafter. The attitude of the United States was neither generous nor wise.

In May 1923 Bonar Law resigned because of ill health. He died in October. A man of integrity and with a high sense of duty, he was narrow, uninterested in ideas, and unable to inspire devotion. His opponents thought that he worshiped nothing but success. The selection of the next Prime Minister lay between Stanley Baldwin and Lord Curzon. Baldwin, a wealthy industrialist and country gentleman, was a newcomer to high office whose character was as yet obscure, though he was obviously conciliatory, friendly, and moderate. Curzon, on the other hand, was a brilliant man who had had a brilliant career. He had been Viceroy of India, he had been a member of the War Cabinet, he was now Foreign Secretary, deputy Prime Minister, and Conservative leader in the House of Lords. He had every reason to assume that he would be Bonar Law's successor. However, he was a peer. Leading Conservatives advised the King that the Prime Minister must be in the Commons; hence the King sent for Baldwin and not for Curzon. Curzon was stunned. He praised Baldwin in public, saying that he possessed many merits, among them the "supreme and indispensable qualification of not being a peer."

Baldwin remained in office only from May 1923 to January 1924. His principal aim was to unite the Conservative party. To appease Austen Chamberlain he appointed Austen's younger brother, Neville Chamberlain, as Chancellor of the Exchequer. When Baldwin announced his conversion to a protective tariff the country was taken by surprise. The Conservatives united and rallied behind their leader, but Liberal and Labor members joined in strong opposition. Controversy became so heated that Baldwin held an election in December 1923. The Conservatives came back with 258 seats in the Commons (as opposed to 346 before the election); the two wings of Liberals, with 158; Labor, with a great advance to 191. Baldwin's strategy was to be triumphant in the end, but it began with an electoral defeat.

THE FIRST LABOR GOVERNMENT, JANUARY TO NOVEMBER 1924

It was not at first clear what kind of government would follow the election of 1923. The Conservatives were the largest single party in the Commons. But the country had rejected protection; Labor was the strongest antiprotection

Ramsay MacDonald. (National Portrait Gallery, London)

party and with Liberal support could outvote the Conservatives. Hence the possibility arose of the formation of a Labor cabinet. Some politicians wished to exclude Labor at all costs. The City of London professed great alarm at the prospect of a socialist government. Wild predictions were made of the dire results of Labor rule; it was suggested that Labor might break down the bonds of marriage and give official sanction to free love. Calmer men, however, saw clearly that Labor could never assume office under safer conditions than those which then existed. Labor would be helpless without Liberal support. It would be too weak to do much harm, as Neville Chamberlain remarked, but not too weak to be discredited. Asquith decided that the Liberals would support a Labor government and thus give it a temporary majority. The Labor leaders, for their part, felt that to refuse office would be to acknowledge incompetence. Hence, when Baldwin was defeated by a combination of Labor and Liberal votes, he resigned, and the King called upon Ramsay MacDonald to form a Cabinet. The King noted in his diary: "Today 23 years ago dear Grandmama died. I wonder what she would have thought of a Labor government."[7]

As an experiment in politics, Labor's first tenure of power was highly interesting. MacDonald had some difficulty in forming his Cabinet. His initial choice of J. H. Thomas, a former locomotive engineer, genial, easygoing, and somewhat given to profanity, as Foreign Secretary was killed by the ridicule of the press. MacDonald became his own Foreign Secretary; Thomas accepted the Colonial Office. Philip Snowden, a weaver's son, a keen debater with a very sharp tongue, was made Chancellor of the Exchequer. Other ministers included Arthur Henderson, the son of a Glasgow cotton spinner; J. R. Clynes, who once worked in a cotton mill; and the radicals John Wheatley and F. W. Jowett. MacDonald brought in two men from outside the party, Lord Haldane as Lord Chancellor, and Lord Chelmsford, once Viceroy of India, as First Lord of the Admiralty. On the whole, it was a moderate Cabinet, which reassured the country.

A Labor member remarked, "At any rate we have the handsomest of all Prime Ministers." MacDonald's fine face, brilliant eye, and noble presence gave him an aristocratic appearance. His pride and courage confirmed the impression. He was master of an emotional, poetic eloquence. But his weaknesses were obvious. "Gentleman Mac" was never popular with the rank and file of his party, toward whom he was rather distant. Far too sensitive to criticism, jealous, given to intrigue, under heavy pressure he was prone to make sudden decisions that were too drastic and were often irrevocable. Very much the moderate, he was determined to tame the wild men of his party and to make the party respectable. Hence he was deeply angered when radical left-wingers on the benches behind him assailed rich "nincompoops" who were said to spend their lives in idleness and feasting. MacDonald believed that socialism could come only through evolution and only with the consent of the majority of the people.[8]

The atmosphere of the House of Commons tamed the wild men quickly. The first visit of the ministers to Buckingham Palace to receive their seals of office was a unique occasion. The King was genial and friendly and put the ministers at their ease. Some Labor members were astonished that "Wheatley—the revolutionary—went down on both knees and actually kissed the King's hand,"[9] but the majority of workingmen took pride in seeing their own people moving in such exalted circles. Despite some snobbery, many members of the Commons were friendly and conciliatory toward the new ministers, who were invited to social functions. The "aristocratic embrace," the willingness of politicians to accept the Labor Cabinet, was much in evidence, and Labor members liked it.

The achievements of the first Labor government were necessarily limited. Most of the new ministers were without experience in office and had much to learn. It was obvious they dared not offend the Liberals. An unexpected bar to

[7] Quoted in Alfred F. Havighurst, *Twentieth Century Britain*, p. 183.
[8] Charles Loch Mowat, *Britain between the Wars 1918–1940*, pp. 148–149, 186, 397.
[9] Quoted in Alfred F. Havighurst, *Twentieth Century Britain*, p. 183.

socialistic experiment was the rigid orthodoxy of Philip Snowden's budget, which provided no surplus funds to spend on public works in an effort to relieve unemployment. Labor, like the Conservatives before them, failed to solve the problem posed by the unemployed. But the Cabinet improved the social services, liberalized unemployment insurance, and passed an excellent housing bill which provided houses that were within the means of the working classes.

The government was also successful in foreign policy. MacDonald helped to initiate the Dawes Plan for the payment of German reparations, improved Franco-German relations, and arranged for the French withdrawal from the Ruhr. At the League of Nations, Labor ministers supported the Geneva Protocol, which provided for the compulsory arbitration of international disputes. Wishing to draw closer to Russia, the Cabinet recognized the Soviet Union, concluded a commercial treaty with Russia, and provided the Russians with a British loan. These actions were bitterly opposed by the Conservatives, who raised a furor over the case of a British Communist, J. R. Campbell, the author of an article that appeared to incite mutiny in the army. The Conservatives, accusing the government of leniency toward communism, called for a vote of censure. Rather surprisingly, MacDonald announced that he would regard the vote as a vote of confidence. He was demanding all or nothing. He was defeated and thereupon dissolved Parliament in October 1924. A few days before the election the *Times* published a letter supposedly from a Russian leader, Zinoviev, to the British Communist party outlining a plan for revolution. This letter counted heavily against Labor in the election. The Conservatives returned with an enormous majority, winning 414 seats, whereas Labor won only 151 and the Liberals only 42. For the first time since the war a political party came into power with the overwhelming support of the people. The defeat of Labor was temporary, but the Liberals were shattered beyond repair.

BALDWIN'S SECOND MINISTRY, 1924–1929

Baldwin's second ministry lasted from 1924 to 1929, the full five years permitted by law without an election. During these years his prestige was high. He created an image of himself as a plain, sensible man who expressed simple ideas in simple words that everyone could understand, an honest country gentleman who loved rural life and enjoyed nothing better than gazing fondly at his pigs. This image was a pose, for he was an able politician who healed the divisions in his party, handled crises well, won the confidence of the nation, and showed that on occasion he could fight. His success in the 1920s was in marked contrast to his failure in foreign policy a decade later. But even in the 1920s he exposed his weaknesses. He had no policy beyond moderation and good will. He wished to soften the clash of capital and labor and to maintain a balanced and harmonious society; he sought stability and repose. But he was really a lazy man who disliked business, who hated to make decisions, who could fight in a crisis but delayed fighting as long as possible. He followed events and was not their master. He must be judged as a statesman of mediocre stature.[10]

Baldwin's Cabinet included Austen Chamberlain, Lord Birkenhead, and later Arthur Balfour. Their presence in the Cabinet healed the breach in Con-

[10] See Charles Loch Mowat, *Britain between the Wars 1918–1940*, pp. 195–197.

servative ranks and strengthened the party. Baldwin also induced Winston Churchill to become Chancellor of the Exchequer.

In foreign affairs, with Austen Chamberlain as Foreign Secretary, the Conservatives undid much of the work of the Labor government. The treaties with Russia were abandoned; in 1927 diplomatic relations with Russia were broken off. The Geneva Protocol was rejected, though Chamberlain pursued an alternate policy of bringing Germany into the orbit of nations without disturbing the French insistence on security. Chamberlain secured the Locarno Pact of 1925

Stanley Baldwin. (National Portrait Gallery, London)

which guaranteed the Franco-German frontier. The Rhineland was demilitarized; Germany and France agreed not to make war on each other but to settle their differences through arbitration; and Germany was admitted to the League of Nations. A better spirit prevailed for a time in international affairs.

In 1925 Britain returned to the gold standard at prewar parity, which meant that the pound was raised to its old value of $4.86.[11] This action represented the climax of Britain's attempt to return to conditions existing before the war. The hope was to enhance the position of London as a financial and commercial center and to increase its business with foreign customers, but the result was disappointing: the price of British exports was pitched too high for the world market. As a result of the world depression, Britain abandoned gold in 1931.

The General Strike

The most dramatic event of these years was the general strike in 1926. This strike, though often described as the climax of labor unrest following the war, in reality took place after the crisis was over. By 1926 labor was moving away from the militant socialism of the first postwar years. The leaders of the Labor movement—MacDonald, Henderson, J. H. Thomas, and Ernest Bevin— were moderate men who wished to quell the zeal of left-wing elements. These elements, however, remained among the rank and file. For a moment in 1926 they gained the upper hand and precipitated the general strike. Once the strike was over, the Labor movement as a whole returned to a moderate course. The strike was really a sympathy strike in support of the coal miners, though it was organized on so extensive a scale as to be called a general strike.

The coal-mining industry, as we have seen, had been depressed since the end of the war. It fell into new difficulties when the French evacuated the Ruhr, thus increasing the continental output of coal, and when Britain returned to the prewar gold standard. The operators declared that a slight increase in wages since 1921 would have to be abandoned. The miners threatened to strike and were strongly supported by the powerful general council of the Trades Union Congress. A widespread strike, involving many workers besides the miners, seemed likely. In order to gain time, as Lloyd George had done, Baldwin appointed a new commission, headed by Sir Herbert Samuel, to investigate the coal industry. Reporting in March 1926, this commission accepted a number of reforms suggested by the miners but rejected a policy of government subsidies to keep the industry afloat. This meant that either wages would have to be temporarily reduced or the working day made longer. The miners stood firm: "Not a penny off the pay, not a minute on the day." The strike began on May 4, 1926. Some 3 million workers—miners; railway men; transport workers; dockers; printers; workmen in steel, chemical, and power plants; and men in the building industries —went on strike.

Very few had revolution in mind, but the government assumed they did. Police and soldiers were used to protect volunteer workers, to convoy food, and to keep essential services in operation. Baldwin declared that the strike was unconstitutional. He was supported by Sir John Simon, a distinguished lawyer who asserted in the Commons that the strike was illegal and that its leaders were liable for damages. These statements frightened the general council of the Trades

---

[11] An act of 1920, which had prohibited the export of gold, was now allowed to lapse. Mowat, pp. 199–200.

Union Congress. The council, already nervous lest the strike get out of control, began to seek an excuse for bringing it to an end. When Sir Herbert Samuel suggested that reduction of miners' wages be postponed until the recommendations of his commission had been put into effect, the council grasped at the proposal and ended the strike after nine days, though no agreement with the Cabinet had been reached. In a word, the council surrendered. Many workers felt they had been betrayed. The coal strike ended in total defeat, with lowered wages and much unemployment.

The collapse of the strike was a personal triumph for Baldwin, but in the years that followed he did very little either to relieve the miners, many of whom fell into a wretched state, or to attack the broader problem of unemployment. Perhaps he thought that the workers should be taught a lesson—or perhaps the strike gave him a welcome excuse for inaction.

There was some advance in the social services during this period, thanks to Neville Chamberlain, Minister of Health, and to Winston Churchill, Chancellor of the Exchequer. An act in 1925 provided allowances for widows and orphaned children and enabled a workingman who made contributions to obtain a pension at sixty-five instead of at seventy. In 1927 a new act for insurance against unemployment lowered both contributions and benefits in an effort to extend the length of time during which benefits could be paid. The act was a move away from insurance to a policy of assistance based on need, for widespread and continuous unemployment was undermining the principle of true insurance. A Local Government Act in 1929 abolished the system of local guardians of the poor and transferred their powers to the county councils.

The Election of 1929

Baldwin held an election in 1929. His prestige was now somewhat tarnished because of his failure to improve the economy, though he seemed to believe that the Conservatives were assured of victory. Both the Liberals and the Labor party made strenuous preparations for the electoral campaign. Lloyd George, with the aid of an able economist, J. M. Keynes, set forth a broad program of public works and economic planning to relieve unemployment and to make better use of surplus capital. The Labor party proposed to increase unemployment benefits, extend other social services, nationalize a number of industries, and lessen British imperial commitments. In the election that followed, Labor won 289 seats, the Conservatives 260, and the Liberals only 58. Labor, for the first time, was the strongest party in the Commons. The Conservatives suffered a severe though not a crushing defeat. On the other hand, the slight gain made by the Liberals was in reality a reverse in view of the efforts Lloyd George had been making: his attempt to revive the Liberal party had failed.

THE GREAT DEPRESSION

Ramsay MacDonald, now Prime Minister for the second time, formed a Cabinet which remained in office from June 1929 to August 1931. Of the nineteen ministers who had served in his first government, twelve reappeared in his second, with most of the radicals excluded. Snowden returned as Chancellor of the Exchequer, Arthur Henderson became Foreign Secretary, J. H. Thomas was assigned the task of dealing with unemployment. Among the newcomers was Miss Margaret Bondfield, Minister of Labor, the first woman to be a member of a British Cabinet.

The government announced a broad and attractive program of legislation to relieve unemployment and to improve other aspects of the economy. Unhappily, Britain was shortly engulfed in a world depression touched off by a crash on the New York Stock Exchange in the autumn of 1929. Trouble spread quickly from the United States to the Continent and thence to Britain. Foreign trade declined and unemployment mounted. The figures of unemployment, which had stood at 1,200,000 when MacDonald assumed office, rose to 1,600,000 in March 1930 and to the staggering figure of 2,500,000 by December of that year. The Cabinet appeared to be paralyzed by this disaster. It took no decisive action, nor did it carry through the program it had announced when it came into power. MacDonald, whose enthusiasm for socialism had long since waned, made his weak position in the Commons an excuse for doing nothing. Snowden's finance remained rigidly orthodox, avoiding all heroic measures. J. H. Thomas failed miserably in dealing with unemployment. Meanwhile, the funds available for the relief of unemployment were exhausted, so that the Cabinet was faced with a large deficit.

A crisis arose in August 1931. As the financial position of the government steadily worsened, Snowden had appointed a committee in March under Sir George May, a businessman prominent in insurance, to suggest economies. His report, issued on July 31, called for drastic reductions in expenditures, including smaller benefits for the unemployed. This report precipitated a run on sterling by Britain's foreign creditors. To meet the emergency, Britain would have to borrow heavily in New York and Paris. Foreign bankers, however, hesitated to lend money until they were assured that the recommendations of May's committee would be carried out. Their hesitation caused a crisis in the Cabinet. A number of ministers refused to sanction cuts in unemployment benefits, and MacDonald warned the King that unless the Cabinet could agree he would have to resign.

Faced with the possibility of MacDonald's resignation, the King consulted with the leaders of other parties: with Baldwin for the Conservatives, and with Sir Herbert Samuel, who spoke for the Liberals during an illness of Lloyd George. They made various suggestions, but both agreed to serve in a coalition or National Cabinet under MacDonald. The King then summoned MacDonald, Baldwin, and Samuel; the resolution was taken to form such a government. Returning to an awkward interview with the Labor ministers, MacDonald informed them that the Labor Cabinet was at an end, that they were no longer in office, but that he was to remain as the head of a National government. He asked them whether they would follow him into a coalition with Conservatives and Liberals. Only three agreed to do so. The Labor party, astounded at these events, repudiated MacDonald and went into opposition.

Much controversy has raged around this crisis. Labor members have regarded it as a plot to drive them from power. This belief appears to be unfounded; yet it seems that MacDonald had been considering for some time the possibility of a National government, so that when the moment came he allowed himself to be persuaded. Nevertheless, he should have consulted his Labor colleagues before consenting to form a new Cabinet; certainly he did not treat them with frankness. The question has also been raised as to whether King George, impelled by a sense of urgency, was more active than a constitutional monarch should have been in promoting the formation of a National government. One should add that these events were infinitely more complex than any brief sketch can indicate. The secret motives of public men acting under great pressure can only be guessed at.[12]

Credits were obtained in New York and Paris, and the financial crisis passed, but Britain was forced to abandon the gold standard in September. The pound sank to a dollar value of about $3.40.

Thus the second Labor government ended in frustration and financial collapse. For the moment the Labor party was routed, but it had come a long way since the war and in due time it would return to power. Meanwhile, even under Conservative rule, the welfare state was developing.

SOCIETY IN THE 1920s

Social conditions in the 1920s were naturally very different from those before the war. Indeed, the danger is that one may see nothing but change and may miss the evidence of continuity from an earlier period and the stability of an older social order. Many of the changes in the 1920s were in manners and fashions and in the uses of a new technology rather than in the basic structure of English society.

The population of Great Britain increased slowly from 40,831,000 in 1911 to 44,795,000 in 1931. The greatest growth was in London and in the counties of southeastern England. Since many of the newer industries were located in this area, it attracted population from other parts of the country, from the northern and eastern counties, from the Midlands, and from Wales. This was a process that has continued to the present day and will probably continue in the future. Britain was more urban than ever. In 1931 only about one fifth of the people lived in the country. The number of women in the population was greater than that of men, though the ratio was closer than it had been at the end of the war. Due to a declining birth rate, the proportion of persons over sixty-five years of age had increased. The sufferings and the awful wastage of war were keenly felt in the years following the peace. Men who had been maimed or crippled, widows left to rear fatherless children, young women who had lost their fiancés, shortages, rationing, and restraints, industrial unrest—all underlined the price that had been paid for victory. Within a few years these tragedies were more or less accepted and permanent patterns began to emerge.

The upper and middle classes, of course, continued to dominate politics and to fill the higher positions in the civil service, in business, and in the professions. Although fashionable society was not as glittering as before the war, its gatherings in London and at sporting events began to be chronicled by the press once more. The nobility, which numbered 708 persons in 1923, had been recruited by 176 creations since 1910. It was true that after the war a good many country houses were sold and large estates broken up; taxes and death duties redistributed wealth and property. Nonetheless, the aristocracy remained a wealthy class, and a new plutocracy, often enriched by the war, was seeking admission to society. A similar story can be told of the middle classes. Prices had risen much faster than salaries and inflation had sharply diminished the value of prewar savings.

---

[12] The crisis can be followed in Mowat, pp. 379–399.

Some members of the middle classes called themselves the new poor. But this was an exaggeration. The middle classes continued to send their children to expensive public schools. There was no great change in the percentage of the national income that went to various classes of society.

Class distinctions and inequality of opportunity were perpetuated by the educational system. The upper and middle classes sent their children to the public schools; these were boarding schools and were in fact very private, exclusive, and costly. Attendance at a public school, followed by a university education, was the first and essential step in a career of importance. The education of the working classes in the publicly supported elementary and secondary schools was quite another matter. In the early 1920s, despite hope from an education act of 1918, only some 12 percent of the children leaving the elementary schools continued full time in secondary education, and only a few more than 4 in every 1000 attended a university. Attendance in school was compulsory until the age of fourteen. An important step was taken, as the result of the Hadow Report, in 1926. Children were sorted out according to their skills and abilities at the age of eleven and were placed in one of three types of secondary schools: grammar schools that prepared them for university work; technical schools; or so-called modern schools that gave a rounded education, combining features of the other two. But the government provided so few university scholarships that the number of ex-elementary school children who obtained a university education was microscopic. By 1931 some 30,000 students were attending British universities.

A generation gap existed in the 1920s. The older generation, still very much in control, was followed by an appalling gap among the men who had done the fighting. The next generation, which came of age after 1918, was inclined to go its own way and to set its own standards of thought and conduct. Typical of this set was the emancipated young woman—the bright young thing or flapper—who supported herself in London as a secretary or a salesgirl and who attended gay parties, smoked cigarettes and drank cocktails, and talked about sex with some freedom. Dancing to jazz music from America was popular. These uninhibited young people gave an impression of reckless gaiety that did not represent society as a whole.

The flapper was a step in the emancipation of women. The movement for woman suffrage before the war had grown so militant that the public had turned against it. But the response of women to the call of duty during the war years had been so magnificent that in 1918 they were given the vote almost as a matter of course. The act enfranchised all men over twenty-one and all women over thirty who qualified, or whose husbands qualified, for the franchise in local government. The act redrew the boundaries of constituencies with the aim of creating single member units each representing 70,000 people. Plural voting was restricted, though not abolished, all elections were to be held on one day, a candidate must post a bond of £150 which was forfeited if he did not obtain one eighth of the votes cast. By this act 2 million men and 6 million women were added to the franchise. In 1928 women were given the vote on the same terms as men; this act increased the number of women voters by another 6 million. In 1920 Oxford University admitted women both as students and as candidates for degrees, though Cambridge did not follow for another quarter of a century. The emancipation of women and doubtless the excess of women over men led to fashions in dress which minimized femininity and gave women a curveless schoolboy shape, though before the end of the decade short skirts and curves began to reveal the female figure more gracefully. Men's clothes tended toward informality, comfort, and brighter colors.

Wages, which had risen during the war, remained at a level about eleven percent higher than before 1914. Thus a workingman's position was improved unless he was swept up in the dreadful wave of unemployment. Even if unemployed, he benefited from extended social services including unemployment insurance. A good deal of new housing was built for the working classes. In the inner cities, after a slum area had been cleared, there was not much to be done except to construct apartments which the poor could afford to rent. However, municipalities also built housing estates on the outskirts of the city. These consisted of enormous numbers of two story semidetached houses built in units of two or four dwellings on curving streets with a yard for each family. The housing estates gave the working classes better quarters than they had ever had before. Unfortunately, as things turned out, they were too expensive for most of the workers; only the upper crust of artisans, who merged with the lower middle classes, could afford them. They were often a long journey from a man's place of employment. And while they were bright and fresh, they were sometimes bleak, lacking trees and amenities such as churches and town halls.

Like all suburbs, they were dependent upon transportation to the city. In London some of the Underground lines were extended on the surface into the country and the railways provided suburban service, which was gradually electrified. But the great development was the bus. The number of buses increased enormously, not only in the city and its suburbs but also in rural areas. Motor trucks or lorries carried all kinds of goods. Long-distance motor coaches competed successfully with the railways, for they could pick up passengers in out of the way places. As for the railways, they improved in speed and safety without startling innovations; they were slipping in their ability to produce good profits. The commercial use of the airplane did not develop as rapidly as had been anticipated. The first companies, offering flights to the Continent, were failures. Imperial Airways, however, founded in 1924 with a government subsidy, consolidated earlier lines and opened service to distant parts of the empire. The number of privately owned automobiles increased threefold, reaching the million mark in 1930.

The changes of the era naturally were reflected in literature and art. Some of the older writers—G. B. Shaw, W. B. Yeats, and John Galsworthy—retained their popularity. Galsworthy's *Forsyte Saga*, a picture of Victorian life, was widely read. On the whole, however, literature was dominated by a younger generation who turned against what it regarded as ornate and artificial writing. Ready to experiment and strongly influenced by Sigmund Freud, the younger writers were interested in the psychology of sex, in the impact of a changing world upon the individual, in scenes and thoughts of violence. D. H. Lawrence glorified sexual love; Evelyn Waugh satirized the smart young set in London. A more versatile writer was the younger Aldous Huxley, whose *Point Counter Point* was much admired. A new type of poetry—learned, symbolic, highly intellectual—appeared in the writings of T. S. Eliot. *The Waste Land*, expressing the dreariness of a great modern city, appealed to those who regarded the era as one of disintegration. Writers who employed a stream-of-consciousness technique were Virginia Woolf and, in a different way, James Joyce. In painting a struggle arose between traditional artists and more radical painters who preferred works of abstraction. The Royal Academy sponsored exhibits of traditional art, while an exhibit arranged by Osbert and Sacheverell Sitwell in 1919 stirred interest in modern art in France. The Tate Gallery, aided by a generous gift, purchased excellent examples of modern abstraction; gradually the public was won over to this kind of painting. In sculpture the work of Jacob Epstein, which was very modernistic, aroused the wrath of conventional people. Architecture, on the other hand, remained largely traditional, condemned by moderns as lacking in originality and imagination. In the 1930s it grew more adventurous. The love of good music rapidly increased. It was stimulated by excellent orchestral conductors such as Sir Thomas Beecham and Sir Henry Wood, by broadcasting, by phonograph records, and by the establishment in 1930 of the orchestra of the British Broadcasting Corporation.

Many new forms of amusement—in which the lower classes largely joined—came into existence after the war. One was the motion picture or cinema. The production of motion pictures had been begun in England before the war but had faded away in the war years. The American industry, on the other hand,

Recumbent Figure, by Henry Moore. (Tate Gallery)

had grown enormously; it dominated the British market in the postwar period. By 1930, however, four important British corporations produced films and operated chains of theaters where the films were shown. Talking pictures, which appeared in the United States in 1926, were not at first taken seriously in England.

Broadcasting began in England on an experimental basis in 1922. A good many companies, seeing the broadcasting boom in the United States, wished to broadcast programs in the hope of selling receiving sets. But the Post Office, which controlled wireless under an act of 1904, eventually decided in favor of a monopoly; the British Broadcasting Corporation, therefore, came into existence in 1926 as a monopoly controlled by the government. Its policy was influenced strongly by its director, J. C. W. Reith, a Scot who insisted that broadcasting should be used for instruction as well as entertainment and that it should preserve a high moral tone as a matter of paramount importance. Thus the character of the BBC was set in its infancy. Its news bulletins may have weakened the power of the press but they did not diminish the enormous circulation of the cheaper daily papers, whose ownership became concentrated in a few large combinations.

Great sporting events, at which huge crowds watched contests between professional teams, became extremely popular. Cricket matches, soccer, and rugby football games, as well as horse racing and racing by greyhounds after a mechanical hare were attended by millions of people. Betting, of course, added zest to these sports. It increased at such an enormous pace that it may be called a national vice, though close supervision kept it from becoming corrupt. These sports had their drawbacks, but at least they provided rivals to the pub; convictions for drunkenness steadily decreased.

The years following the war were difficult ones for the British farmer. Due to the decline of agriculture in the last quarter of the nineteenth century, Britain was growing only about a fifth of the wheat it consumed when the war broke out in 1914. The war brought about a determined effort to increase production: 3 million acres of pasture were ploughed and planted; farmers were guaranteed against loss on wheat and oats; a minimum wage was established for agricultural laborers. But after the war there came a slump: the world market was glutted with agricultural produce and prices fell sharply. Faced with large payments to honor its pledges, the government abandoned the farmer and the farm laborer. Hence wages fell and agriculture began to decline once more. In 1931 the acreage under wheat was smaller than before the war, though the yield per acre was large. The food produced in Britain was only about forty percent of what was needed.[13]

[13] Mowat, pp. 201–258; Henry Pelling, *Modern Britain 1885–1955*, pp. 104–110.

34

the second world war,
1939-1945

The years covered by this chapter fall into two distinct periods: the somber decade that preceded the Second World War, and the period of the war itself. In 1931 the country was in the depths of the depression with a shocking amount of unemployment and much economic distress. The power of Hitler and Mussolini threatened the peace of Europe. The Conservatives, who were in office, had some success in combating the depression, but in foreign affairs they fell into the weak and humiliating policy of appeasing the dictators. It is not surprising that the British people, confused by mediocre leadership, pinched by economic depression, and fearful of a new war, were momentarily unnerved. But when the storm finally broke in 1940 and when they were led by a courageous war minister, Winston Churchill, they found themselves once more after years of indecision. United in firm resolve, they fought a grim war against great odds and emerged victorious.

THE NATIONAL GOVERNMENT, 1931–1940

As a result of the events described in the last chapter, Ramsay MacDonald formed a National Cabinet which came into office late in August 1931. It was supported by the Conservatives, who were strong in the Commons; by the Liberals, who were weak; and by a handful of Labor members who adhered to MacDonald. The bulk of the Labor party, still the largest single party in the Commons, was in angry opposition. Soon there was talk of an election. It was urged by the Conservatives, who saw an opportunity to appeal to the country on patriotic grounds for support of the National government (in which they would predominate), and at the same time to denounce the Labor party as the source of the nation's ills and to push for a protective tariff. The Labor and the Liberal members of the Cabinet opposed an election but yielded to Conservative pressure. They refused to support a tariff; hence it was decided that the ministers should agree to disagree. MacDonald should ask the electors for a vote of confidence without committing himself on tariff policy; other ministers could advocate what they pleased—they could at least agree in attacking Labor. The result was a confusing, vindictive, and rather fraudulent election in which ministers contradicted each other and in which the Labor party was denounced in violent terms. The National government won by a landslide. Its supporters consisted of 472 Conservatives, 68 Liberals, and 13 National Labor members. The Labor party in opposition won only 46 seats.

The results of this election were highly important. For the next nine years the Conservatives enjoyed an overwhelming supremacy in the Commons. Behind the façade of a National government they wielded a power they could not have obtained through their own electoral strength. MacDonald might be Prime Minister, but the key men in the Cabinet were Baldwin and Neville Chamberlain. There was no need to pay attention to the wishes of the opposition nor to bring in new blood. Neither Lloyd George nor Winston Churchill was a member of the coalition. "It was no 'National' government," wrote a contemporary. "It was simply a get-together on the part of the Boys of the Old Brigade, who climbed on the Bandwagon and sat there, rain or shine, until they brought the British Empire to the verge of destruction."[1]

MacDonald's captivity was soon evident, for Neville Chamberlain, Chancellor of the Exchequer, pressed for tariff reform. He was strong enough to have his way, though Labor and Liberal ministers protested and some of them later resigned. A tariff, established early in 1932, imposed general duties of 10 percent on imports (with certain exceptions); and an advisory board was empowered to fix additional duties up to 33⅓ percent. Shortly after the tariff became law, an imperial economic conference was held in Ottawa for the purpose of concluding preferential agreements with the Dominions. The result was disappointing. Britain had no intention of sacrificing her farmers, and the Dominions were determined to protect their growing industries. British trade with the Dominions increased to some extent. But it was the Dominions, not Britain, that profited, for increased imperial trade disturbed old links with other markets; British exports made only a slight recovery after 1932.

Ministers and Kings

MacDonald remained Prime Minister until June 1935. He became a rather tragic figure. He was of great use to the Conservatives, for he enabled them to maintain the fiction of a National government. However, his effectiveness declined, his speeches were evasive and confused, and there was less and less reason for his remaining in office. In 1935 he and Stanley Baldwin, who was Lord President of the Council, exchanged places; in 1937 MacDonald retired and died shortly thereafter. Although he had done much to build the Labor movement, Labor never forgave him for his desertion of the party in 1931.

Baldwin held office as Prime Minister for two years. It was his misfortune that these were years of crisis in foreign affairs about which he cared very little. Meanwhile a domestic problem of a most unusual character arose. King Edward VIII, who had succeeded to the throne in January 1936, had little sympathy with the symbolic duties of a British monarch. Moreover, he became interested in an American divorcée, Mrs. Wallis Warfield Simpson, and was constantly in her

[1] R. Boothby, *I Fight to Live* (London: Gollancz, 1947), p. 93, quoted in Charles Loch Mowat, *Britain between the Wars 1918–1940* (Chicago: University of Chicago Press, 1955), p. 400.

company. When it was indicated to him that Mrs. Simpson should leave the country, he angrily told the Prime Minister, "I mean to marry her and I am prepared to go." The country, at least the country outside London, was solidly against the marriage. Baldwin confronted Edward with the alternative of either renouncing Mrs. Simpson or abdicating the throne. Baldwin's speech of explanation in the House of Commons was plausible. An abdication bill was passed, Edward went into exile with the title of Duke of Windsor, and his brother, the Duke of York, became George VI. Many people felt that Edward had been hustled along rather brusquely. Shortly after this crisis Baldwin retired. The final word concerning him is yet to be written. It is evident, however, that behind his pose of being a simple country gentleman there was more cleverness and less frankness than appeared on the surface.

Society in the 1930s

The problems facing the nation in the 1930s were very difficult indeed: continued depression; appalling unemployment; the rise of Hitler and Mussolini; the Spanish Civil War which sharply divided British sympathies. Hence the prevailing mood in this period was serious and somber, without the buoyancy of the 1920s. The sad plight of the depressed areas and the glaring inequalities between rich and poor led to introspection and self-criticism; the nation was more inclined to look inward at its domestic problems than outward toward the rest of the world. Much thought was given to social and economic questions. The era was one of awakened social conscience, of surveys, of apprehension about the nation's future.

The hard core of unemployment centered in the areas that depended upon the staple industries of the nineteenth century—coal, textiles, shipbuilding, iron and steel. These areas included most of northern England, almost all of industrial Scotland, all of South Wales, and parts of North Wales. At the beginning of 1933 the unemployed reached the dreadful figure of 3 million persons. The distress in Wales and Lancashire was acute; half of Glasgow was unemployed; in the shipbuilding town of Jarrow on the Tyne two thirds of the workers were without jobs. A number of books, such as J. B. Priestley's *English Journey* (1934), described the derelict towns. They were all much alike—the shops closed, the houses in need of repairs, the men standing idly at the street corners with their hands in their pockets. The unemployed fell into three categories. The first contained those who were temporarily out of work or were working part time. Then came the young men who had never had employment. Finally there were the long-term unemployed who had not had jobs for years. They included the older men who would probably never find employment. The evils of unemployment were obvious: the hopelessness of continual idleness, the loss of self-respect, the frustrations of chilling poverty. For many families a major problem was to keep warm; the easiest solution was to go to bed early and get up late. Little luxuries —the cinema and small bets—offered some diversion. Moreover, a great many agencies sprang up to keep the men occupied and physically fit. The government sponsored training centers of various kinds. Much more, however, was done by voluntary bodies who helped workmen form clubs, some for amusement, some for training, some for education, some for work on farms or in workshops or in the operation of abandoned coal mines. The government did not offer employment on public works; indeed, it cut the amount of the dole in 1931; but it attempted to relieve distress. The machinery for the administration of relief was

Unemployed men eating in a three penny dinner kitchen. (Wide World Photos)

improved, although an attempt to gauge the means of each family as a whole (the "means" test) was resented. It penalized thrift, invaded privacy, and led to petty gossip.

These sad conditions in unemployed Britain were only dimly understood by the more prosperous areas in the south. As a matter of fact, a significant economic revival occurred in Britain during the second half of the 1930s. It was due very largely to the cheapness of imported raw materials, which kept down the cost of living and provided some money for increased investment at home. Manufacturers gave greater attention to production for the home market. Profits were less than those in foreign trade, but real wages were increasing and with them the purchasing power of the middle and lower classes. Neville Chamberlain encouraged business by forcing down the rates of interest. A notable increase occurred in the building of houses. Some recovery took place in steel, china, and railways; and the new industries, such as chemicals, rayon, electrical goods, motor cars, packaged and prepared foods, expanded. These new industries centered in the southeast of England, especially in the London area, and to some extent in the western midlands around Birmingham. It was natural that young men and women from the depressed areas in the north migrated to localities that offered greater hope of employment. Population, which had shifted northward more than a century earlier, began to turn south again. In southeastern England large numbers of modest families enjoyed higher standards of living than they had known before.

Many persons outside of politics were giving serious thought to social and economic problems. The quest for new solutions was evident in the work of the economist J. M. Keynes. His important book, *General Theory of Employment, Interest, and Money* (1936), developed the doctrine that governments should combat, and might prevent, depressions by adjustments of credit and investment, by reducing interest rates, by deficit spending for public works to relieve unemployment and to increase the purchasing power of the people. Within a decade this book revolutionized government policy toward economic questions. A belief in the value of economic planning by the state steadily grew. It was noticed that Russia had escaped the impact of the world depression; hence much of the economic thinking and writing of the time contained admiration for Russian communism. Communism undoubtedly had attractions for some professional men, for scientists and other intellectuals, for undergraduates in the universities. When the civil war in Spain developed into a struggle between communist and fascist Europe, the Communist Party in Britain sent volunteers as well as munitions and medical supplies. Young people, especially students, regarding the Labor Party as out of date, were prepared to join communists and other elements in a popular front against fascism. A *Left Book Club,* managed by Victor Gollancz, issued books in rather uncritical support of Russia. Poetry with a socialist or communist slant was published by a *Left Review.*

Behind this furor, social changes begun in the previous decade continued to develop. Road transport of all kinds grew steadily; the city dweller enjoyed rides in the country in his car. There was a great increase in hiking, fostered by Youth Hostels and by campaigns to keep physically fit. Facilities developed for indoor ice skating, for lawn tennis in the public parks, for swimming and sun bathing, which led to abbreviated swim suits. The cinema was popular. Newspapers, partly because of their keen competition, held contests for readers and printed tidbits about such matters as the rector of Stiffkey, an ex-clergyman who appeared on the vaudeville stage clad in a barrel, or the most recent antics of the Loch Ness monster.

The public also desired matter for serious reading; this accounts for the popularity of the Penguin paperbacks, some of them selling for as little as 6*d.*, of the *Listener,* a magazine issued by the BBC, and of popular accounts of mathematics, science, and philosophy. Good taste in music continued to improve. The other arts, unfortunately, became rather highbrow and experimental. Painters and sculptors produced abstractions that were difficult to understand. Architecture grew more imaginative but did not win popular approval.[2]

Britain and the Dictators

The softness and appeasement of British policy toward Hitler and Mussolini during the 1930s are invariably associated with Neville Chamberlain, who became Prime Minister in 1937. But this policy began under MacDonald and Baldwin; Chamberlain merely carried it forward with disastrous ineptness. The

[2] Mowat, pp. 432–437, 480–531.

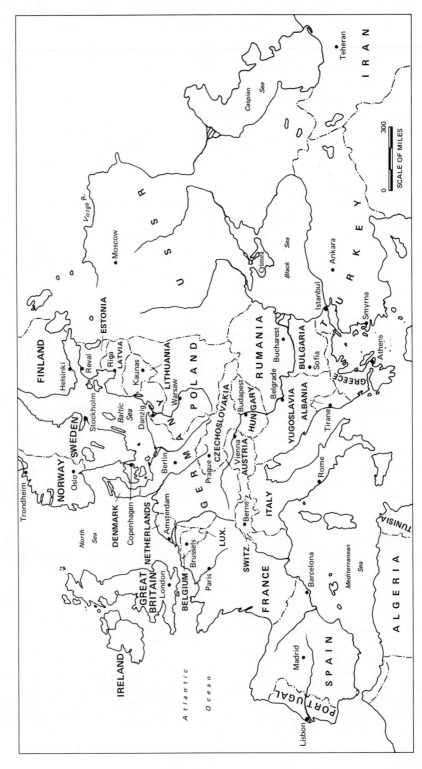

Europe in 1930

world depression and the bitter discontent of certain nations led to an era in which force and threats of force took the place of negotiation. In 1931, when the depression was at its worst, Japan made war on China in Manchuria and then created the satellite state of Manchukuo. In 1932 the weakness of the Weimar Republic in Germany enabled Hitler to rise to power. Becoming Chancellor in January 1933, he withdrew Germany from the League of Nations and began to rearm. In 1935 he announced the existence of the German air force; in violation of the Treaty of Versailles he introduced conscription for his army. In the same year Mussolini attacked Ethiopia in eastern Africa. It is easy to see, as we look back, that Britain should have taken an early stand against these violations of international law, but it is also easy to understand why she did not.

Britain had suffered terribly from the First World War. The filthy war in the trenches, the frightful casualties, and the sufferings of the bereaved made many people in Britain regard another war as unthinkable. No international problem, it was held, could justify another carnage. Every crisis brought the longing that it would pass without a war or at least without a war involving Britain. Great faith was placed in the League of Nations as a means of achieving collective security. Opposition to rearmament was widespread. Such thinking was confused, for if Britain did not arm and if other nations followed her example, the League would not be strong enough to resist aggressors.

Constant clashes with France in the 1920s made British sentiment rather pro-German. Germany, it was felt, had been badly treated at Versailles. The danger to Europe lay in communism, not in fascism, and so the Nazis could be regarded as a bulwark against Russia. With such ideas current in Britain, statesmen faced the duty of educating the public to the need for rearmament and for a tougher policy toward the dictators. But MacDonald and Baldwin were not energetic, Chamberlain believed in appeasement, and Labor opposed rearmament; moreover, ministers were carefully attuned to the wishes of the voters. Hence it was easy to believe that when Hitler spoke of peace he could be trusted and that when he threatened war he could be contained by negotiation. In 1935 the Cabinet announced its intention to rearm and to strengthen the Royal Air Force, but little was done. In an election in the same year (won by the National government) Baldwin told the people what they wanted to hear: that Britain would make the League of Nations the keystone of her policy and would take her stand on collective security.

Unfortunately the League was showing that it could not stop aggression. When Mussolini attacked Ethiopia in 1935 the British public assumed that the League would assert its authority and would apply sanctions against Italy, but Baldwin's policy was to stay out of the Italian-Ethiopian crisis. An agreement was made with the French by which Mussolini would be allowed to seize about half of Ethiopia. In this instance British statesmen were softer than was the British public. A storm of protest arose over the action of the government; Baldwin thereupon dropped his Foreign Secretary, Sir Samuel Hoare, and annulled the agreement, but in the meantime Mussolini had completed his conquest.

In the same year Baldwin concluded a treaty with Germany permitting Hitler to increase his naval strength to thirty-five percent of that of Britain. British policy was to play off one dictator against the other so that she would not be quarreling with both of them at the same time. But Hitler was insatiable. In 1936 he sent his troops into the Rhineland although the Rhineland had been demilitarized by treaty. Baldwin accepted this coup without demur and caught at German proposals to secure the future peace of Europe. The people as a whole agreed. Hugh Dalton, a Labor member, remarked in the Commons: "It is only right to say bluntly and flatly that public opinion in this country would not support and certainly the Labor party would not support the taking of military sanctions or even economic sanctions against Germany at this time in order to put German troops out of the German Rhineland." One of the few voices of protest was that of Winston Churchill, who attacked the Cabinet's slowness in rearmament. The government, he declared, "simply cannot make up their minds, or they cannot get the Prime Minister to make up his mind. So they go on in strange paradox, decided only to be undecided, resolved to be irresolute, adamant for drift, solid for fluidity, all-powerful to be impotent."[3]

The Spanish Civil War

The Spanish Civil War, which broke out in July 1936, influenced Britain profoundly and proved to be the first step in awakening the people to the dangers of appeasement. A Republican government, supported by liberals and by various left-wing parties, had been established in Spain in 1931. In 1936, however, a revolt against this government was begun by the fascist General Francisco Franco. The Spanish were not allowed to fight out the quarrel among themselves. Franco at once received aid from Hitler and Mussolini, who saw in the revolt a pattern of fascist intervention and a dress rehearsal for a larger war to come. The Republican government was aided by volunteers from many lands and by tanks and planes from Russia. The British government announced its neutrality. At first this policy won general support, and the Cabinet accepted a French proposal that the major powers not intervene in Spain. But nonintervention soon proved to be an error. Hitler and Mussolini, under thin disguises, continued to send aid to Franco. In practice, nonintervention was a farce that played into Franco's hands. It denied assistance to the Republicans, undermined the doctrine of collective security, bypassed the League, exalted the dictators, and increased the bitterness of liberals everywhere at the savage brutality of Franco's campaign.

There were sharp attacks on the government in England. The Labor party, forgetting its pacifism, denounced nonintervention. Opposition arose from such totally different persons as Winston Churchill and Clement Attlee, the leader of the Labor party. Churchill attacked the Cabinet for its neglect of imperial interests, for a victory by Franco would endanger Gibraltar. Attlee charged that the Cabinet was motivated by upper-class sympathy for Franco, by concern for business, and by a fondness for the dictators. To the average Englishman the war symbolized the clash of communism and fascism, and there was general sympathy with the former. But the more the people protested, the more tenaciously the Cabinet clung to the fiction of nonintervention, ignored its infringement by the dictators, and seemed determined on peace at any price. Meanwhile, Franco won the war.[4]

Neville Chamberlain and Appeasement

In May 1937 Baldwin was followed as Prime Minister by Neville Chamberlain, in many ways a much stronger man. Honest, industrious, patient, and

---

[3] These attitudes and events are well summarized in Alfred F. Havighurst, *Twentieth Century Britain* (New York: Harper & Row, 1966), pp. 540–554.

[4] Charles Loch Mowat, *Britain between the Wars 1918–1940*, pp. 572–582.

Neville Chamberlain. (National Portrait Gallery, London)

methodical, he was essentially the efficient civil servant who handled administrative problems with careful skill, but he was narrow, cold, and overconfident. He was scornful of the Labor members, one of whom remarked that he must have been "weaned on a pickle." Toward Conservatives he was a disciplinarian. He was inclined to follow his own ideas without seeking proper advice and resented criticism even from his friends.

Although his training and experience lay in domestic affairs, he made foreign relations the principal sphere of his activity. He expected the Foreign Office and the Foreign Secretary (Anthony Eden) to follow the lead he gave them; yet he did not hesitate to by-pass them and to deal directly with Hitler and Mussolini. He believed that the League of Nations had failed, that collective security had failed with it, that no reliance could be placed on the United States, and that direct negotiations with the dictators could lead to compromise. He let Hitler know that Britain would not oppose changes in central Europe provided those changes came about through peaceful agreement. This policy was interpreted in Germany as meaning that Britain would offer no serious objection to Hitler's plans. The Germans saw that the pretense of negotiations must be maintained. Ribbentrop, the German Ambassador in London, wrote to his master, "We must continue to foster England's belief that a settlement and an understanding between Germany and England are still possible."[5] But in the meantime German plans for aggression must not be interrupted. And thus, while Chamberlain strove to remove tensions through negotiation, the Nazis were preparing for military conquest. Chamberlain hoped to strengthen his hand against Hitler by agreements with Mussolini. His softness toward Italy caused the resignation of Anthony Eden in February 1938. Unfortunately, Eden had just been criticized by Hitler, so that his resignation looked like another humiliation for the democratic powers. In the following month Hitler sent his troops into Austria and absorbed that country into the Reich. Britain protested but made no other move.

Attention turned quickly to the more vital question of Czechoslovakia, an important country with an army of thirty divisions, with strong defensive fortifications, and with the Skoda munition works. She was the ally of France and she might well have received assistance from Russia. But after Austria's incorporation into the Reich, Czechoslovakia was ringed by German territory. Moreover, there were some 3,500,000 Germans in an area vaguely called the Sudetenland. Hitler determined upon Czechoslovakia's destruction. He protested violently against the supposed ill treatment of the Sudeten Germans, and events moved swiftly to a crisis.

Chamberlain hoped that the Sudeten question could be settled without undermining the independence of Czechoslovakia. Rejecting French and Russian moves to organize resistance, he assumed full control of British policy and engaged in direct talks with Hitler to prevent German military action against the Czechs. He talked with Hitler twice in September 1938. In the first interview he agreed that the Sudetenland should be surrendered to Germany after a plebiscite. In the second Hitler demanded immediate occupation before the plebiscite was held. This Chamberlain refused. War now appeared inevitable, and Britain made hasty preparations for the safety of the people.

Then suddenly Hitler asked for a conference at Munich to which he invited Chamberlain, Mussolini, and Premier Daladier of France. Here it was agreed to

[5] Quoted in Alfred F. Havighurst, *Twentieth Century Britain,* pp. 267–268.

permit Hitler to occupy the Sudetenland on his own terms without a plebiscite. Hitler guaranteed the integrity of what remained of Czechoslovakia and signed an innocuous agreement suggested by Chamberlain promising to negotiate any new difference that might arise between England and Germany. The immediate reaction in England was one of profound relief. Chamberlain was hailed with enthusiasm as he proclaimed, "I believe it is peace in our time." However, he met sharp attacks in the House of Commons. Churchill called Munich "a total and unmitigated defeat." It was soon clear that Hitler had every intention of taking the rest of Czechoslovakia. The blow fell in March 1939, when Hitler sent troops into Bohemia and Moravia. Czechoslovakia disappeared.

The reaction in Britain was violent. Even Chamberlain was convinced at last that he had been wrong and that appeasement had failed. A revolution took place in British policy. The production of military aircraft was stepped up. The navy was empowered to build its strength to a level equal to that of the German and Japanese navies combined. Conscription was introduced to raise an army quickly. Moreover, Chamberlain pledged British support to various nations—Poland, Rumania, Greece, and Turkey. An attempt was made, though rather feebly, to reach an agreement with Russia.

Events now rushed to a climax. Hitler determined to attack Poland. He also made secret approaches to Russia; a sure indication of impending war was the announcement on August 23 of a German-Russian nonaggression pact. As everyone suspected, it contained secret clauses for the partition of eastern Europe between the two powers. Russia had found she had more to gain from Germany than from England; and Hitler, facing war in the west, wished to protect his eastern frontier. On September 1 German troops invaded Poland. Britain honored her pledges, and war began on September 3.

It would be unfair to place all the blame for the humiliating era of appeasement upon Chamberlain's shoulders. The policy began before he became Prime Minister, and to the end he received strong support from many quarters in Britain. The Labor party long opposed rearmament in a blind and doctrinaire way. Men in public life felt the shame and humiliation of Munich but secretly hoped that Hitler could be bought off by acquiesence in his villainies toward smaller nations. The people as a whole during this era were listless, frightened, and confused. One cannot blame them for dreading war, but they could have been heartened by a bolder government. Criticism must fall on the leaders—Baldwin, Simon, Hoare, and Halifax, as well as Chamberlain—who permitted their country to drift into such weak and disastrous policies.

THE SECOND WORLD WAR

The Twilight War

The Second World War began with Hitler's smashing assault on Poland, which broke that country in seventeen days. England and France could not aid the Poles. France, it is true, might have attacked Germany along the Rhine, but the French were dominated by a strategic concept of static defense. They occupied their magnificent fortifications known as the Maginot Line and felt secure, though the Maginot Line faced eastward and did not extend along the frontier between France and Belgium. A British army under Lord Gort was sent to northwestern France but it was not in contact with the enemy. Land operations, therefore, were at a standstill in western Europe during the winter of 1939–1940, and there ensued the strange period that Churchill dubbed the twilight war (Americans called it the phony war) in which very little happened.

There was some activity at sea. A German submarine sank the British aircraft carrier *Courageous;* a second submarine daringly penetrated the defenses of the British naval base at Scapa Flow in the Orkneys and sank the battleship *Royal Oak.* These were serious losses. On the other hand, the German pocket battleship *Admiral Graf von Spee,* which had been raiding British commerce, was cornered by British cruisers off Montevideo in Uruguay and scuttled by her crew. The British began a naval blockade they believed was having some effect. An element of unreality about the war persisted during the first winter, and there was a natural decline in the morale of the people. Air-raid precautions, rationing, and evacuation from large cities began to be considered annoyances; many evacuated persons drifted back to their homes. The sense of unreality was intensified when Hitler declared that he would welcome peace. Having crushed the Poles and divided their country with Russia, he asked blandly, "Why should the war in the west be fought?" Although Chamberlain insisted in public that the German proposals were worthless, he hoped in secret that war might be avoided in western Europe.

Such dreams were rudely shattered by events in Scandinavia. In November 1939 the Russians had attacked Finland in order to secure a stronger western frontier, and this led to a British decision to assist the Finns. A British force was to have driven across northern Norway, but Hitler acted first. In a lightning attack on April 9, 1940, he overwhelmed Denmark in a few hours and Norway in a few days, though not without serious naval losses from Norwegian and British resistance. The British landed troops near Trondheim on the Atlantic coast of Norway and later at Narvik farther to the north. But the Trondheim campaign was abandoned because of fear of German air power; and by the time the Germans were pushed out of Narvik their invasion of France had reduced the operations in Norway to small importance.

The campaign in Scandinavia ended Chamberlain's government. At the beginning of the war he sought to broaden his ministry by bringing in a number of new men, including Churchill at his old post at the Admiralty and Anthony Eden as Secretary for the Dominions. But neither the Labor nor the Liberal party would form a coalition with Chamberlain. When he announced the withdrawal of British forces from the area of Trondheim, the demand arose that he resign. He fought to retain his leadership but could not do so. He resigned in favor of Winston Churchill on May 10, 1940.

Arms and the Man[6]

On the very day that Churchill became Prime Minister of Britain, Hitler's forces invaded Holland and Belgium on their way to attack the French. Churchill's supreme opportunity had come. He had been one of the few who denounced appeasement during Chamberlain's ministry and he had had no part in that policy. Now, at a moment of grave national peril, he came into office with great power and prestige. By daily contact with the Chiefs of Staff he directed the entire war effort. He evoked a new spirit in the British people. He never

[6] This is the title of a chapter in D. C. Somervell, *British Politics Since 1900* (London: Dakers, 1950).

minimized difficulties and hardships; yet he called forth courage, determination, unity, and sacrifice. In his first speech in the House of Commons as Prime Minister he declared that he could offer nothing but

> blood, toil, tears, and sweat. . . . You ask, what is our policy? I will say: It is to wage war, by sea, land, and air with all our might and with all the strength that God can give us. . . .What is our aim? . . . Victory—victory at all costs, victory in spite of all terror; victory, however long and hard the road may be.

A deep and emotional patriotism transformed the nation as it prepared for the battle for survival. Pacificism vanished. Leaders of all parties accepted places in Churchill's War Cabinet or in ministries outside it. Within a month the number of airplanes produced by British factories greatly increased. An astonishing piece of legislation placed all persons and all property at the disposal of the government to be employed in the best interests of the nation.

This steadfast, determined, and unified spirit was indeed necessary in the days that followed. On May 13–14 the Germans broke through the French lines at Sedan in the Ardennes sector west and north of the Maginot Line. Within ten days they had swept westward to the Channel, dividing the British and some French units from the main French armies. The British Expeditionary Force was in great danger of annihilation, but a corridor was kept open to Dunkirk, German naval units were held at bay, the Royal Air Force gave adequate protection, and some 338,000 troops (about two thirds of them British) were evacuated from the beaches at Dunkirk to England, most of them by the navy but many in small boats of all kinds that crossed and recrossed the Channel. Dunkirk was a triumph of British valor and determination, but the equipment of the troops was lost and a front on the Continent became impossible. On June 21 the new French Premier, General Pétain, signed an armistice with Germany. Its terms gave Hitler possession of the northern half of France, including Paris, and the entire French Atlantic coast. An inland, unoccupied zone was left to the Pétain government with a captial at the obscure town of Vichy.

The Battle of Britain

The fall of France left Britain exposed to immediate invasion, and the summer and autumn of 1940 formed the most dangerous period of the war. There was scarcely enough equipment in Britain to arm two divisions, but Churchill's fighting spirit never wavered. "We shall defend our Island," he declared, "whatever the cost may be, we shall fight on the beaches, we shall fight on the landing grounds, we shall fight in the fields and in the streets, we shall fight in the hills; we shall never surrender." Home defenses were hastily prepared, the coastal areas strengthened, obstructions set up to prevent the landing of enemy planes. The Local Defense Volunteers, later known as the Home Guard, swelled to half a million men.

It was assumed that Hitler had a master plan for invasion but he did not. In fact, he had hardly looked beyond the defeat of France; he had assumed that once France was knocked out of the war the British would recognize the folly of further resistance. It was apparently not until May that he contemplated invasion and not until the middle of July that he began determined preparations for a landing in Britain. Such an operation required both naval power and command of the air. After long debate with his advisers, Churchill came to the "hateful decision" that the French fleet could not be allowed to fall into German hands.

Superiority at sea was the one advantage left in British hands and it could not be threatened. British warships thereupon bombarded and put out of action French naval units at Oran in Algeria and at Dakar in French West Africa.

Meanwhile the German air raids against Britain increased in intensity. On August 1 Hitler issued instructions for an all-out campaign to destroy the Royal Air Force and the British aircraft industry. For three weeks in late August and early September an average of a thousand German planes was over Britain daily, attacking airfields, factories, radar stations, and the docks of East London. The Blitz was on. Fire fighting in London and elsewhere became a major concern of the government. Many Londoners slept in the stations of the Underground, or in "Andersons"—small shelters accommodating four or six people and protecting them from flying glass and splinters though not from direct hits—or trickled into the countryside at night. But in defiant London there was a high degree of discipline and order, and essential services continued. During the last week of August and the first week of September the issue of the battle in the air was doubtful. Thereafter the Royal Air Force grew in strength and effectiveness; by the middle of September it was downing two German planes for every British one lost. The German effort to gain control of the air over Britain was a failure. Hitler postponed and then canceled the invasion, the shipping assembled for the descent on Britain was dispersed, and by the end of September the British knew there would be no invasion in 1940. But heavy air raids on Britain continued at night when darkness made defense more difficult. Hitler then began a systematic attempt to destroy British centers of industry. Throughout the winter of 1940–1941 there were constant raids on London. On the night of December 8–9, 400 German bombers swept over the city, inflicting heavy damage. Other cities—Coventry, Birmingham, Plymouth, Liverpool—were also under heavy attack. It was not until June 1941, when Hitler turned on Russia, that the pressure on Britain from the air diminished.

North Africa and the Mediterranean

Very heavy fighting also developed in the Mediterranean. Mussolini, who entered the war as France was falling, had visions of conquering Greece as well as securing Egypt as a connecting link between Libya and the Italian possessions in East Africa. Both efforts met with failure. In September 1940 the Italians invaded Egypt from Cyrenaica, but soon came to a halt because of lack of transport and were pushed back into their own territories by a British counterattack from Egypt. Another British force drove from Kenya into Italian Somaliland and Ethiopia, forcing the Italians from those areas. A pro-German regime in Iraq quickly was smashed; British and Free French forces occupied Syria and Lebanon. Mussolini also failed in his war against Greece; and in two fierce assaults the British defeated the Italian navy at its base in Taranto in southern Italy and in a battle at sea off Cape Matapan in Greece.

The situation altered early in 1941, when the Germans decided to intervene. Hitler sent General Rommel to stiffen the Italians in North Africa; a powerful German offensive was launched in the Balkans against Yugoslavia and Greece. To meet this danger, some 58,000 British troops were brought to Greece from Egypt. But the Greeks did not cooperate properly, Yugoslavia was quickly overrun by the Germans, and it soon became necessary to evacuate the British forces, first to Crete, and then, after a brilliant assault on Crete by German airborne troops, from Crete back to Egypt. The whole campaign in Greece and Crete was a sharp reverse for Britain. Rommel, opposed by weaker British forces, made alarming progress in North Africa.

Aid from the United States

Meanwhile the United States was moving closer to all-out aid to Britain. At the beginning of the war, when American sentiment was overwhelmingly against involvement, Congress would do no more than permit the sale of war materials to Britain on a cash-and-carry basis. This meant that goods must be picked up by British ships in American ports and must be paid for at once. But the fall of France drove home the fact that Britain might be overwhelmed and that all of Europe might soon be under the domination of the Nazis. Keenly aware of this, President Roosevelt pledged in June 1940 that the United States would supply material assistance to "the opponents of force." Late in the summer he transferred to Britain fifty overage American destroyers in exchange for air and naval bases in British America, chiefly in the West Indies. Then in December he announced his policy of lend-lease, an arrangement by which the United States might sell, exchange, lend, or lease materials of war to any nation whose defense was deemed essential to American security. Becoming law in March 1941, lend-lease made vast quantities of war materials available to Britain, though it would be some time before their impact was felt on the battle fronts.

Too large an amount of these supplies was being lost at sea. German submarines could operate from any port along the western seaboard of the Continent north of Spain, while Irish neutrality denied to Britain the use of ports in southwestern Ireland which would have been of great value. In April 1941—when Hitler intensified the submarine war—Britain lost 195 ships, totaling some 700,000 tons. So great was the pressure on the British navy that, whereas in the First World War a convoy had often been protected by eight or ten destroyers, it was now escorted by two or three or sometimes by only one. Roosevelt did what he could. He began an American patrol in the western North Atlantic which broadcast the whereabouts of German ships and aircraft. He occupied Greenland and assisted in the defense of Iceland. More decisive steps were taken in the autumn of 1941, when American naval units began to escort British convoys in the North Atlantic and armed American merchantmen carried goods directly to Britain. A vast program of shipbuilding was begun in the United States. Yet the Battle of the Atlantic was far from won.

Attacks on Russia and on the United States

Hitler's massive invasion of Russia along a broad front in June 1941 and the Japanese air attack on the American fleet at Pearl Harbor in December drew these countries into the war and altered the entire complexion of the conflict. Hitler apparently believed that the Russian army, which had been purged in 1937, could be conquered in a single campaign and that the wheat of the Ukraine and the oil of the Caucasus could be won before the coming of winter. The Germans met with initial success, especially in the south. But in the north neither Leningrad nor Moscow was captured, and with the arrival of winter and with a Russian counteroffensive in December the Germans suffered great hardships and heavy losses.

Relations between Japan and the United States had become very strained as the Japanese had extended their power in China and in Southeast Asia while Europe was engulfed in war. In 1940 Japan had concluded a military alliance with Germany and Italy directed primarily against the United States. Hence the attack on Pearl Harbor brought America into the war not only against Japan but also against Germany and Italy. Although Pearl Harbor was a heavy blow, it united all classes of Americans as nothing else could have done. In an address before Congress Churchill aptly posed the question, "What kind of people do they think we are?"

Britain was no longer alone. Russia and the United States proved to be far more formidable military powers than Hitler had imagined. Yet their entry into the war was followed by a long series of disasters. For the first year, as Churchill remarked, Russia was a positive obstacle to Allied success, for she was sent large quantities of supplies badly needed elsewhere. Stalin made insistent and embarrassing demands for a second front in western Europe, though an Allied invasion of the Continent would be impossible for a long time to come. In June 1942 the Germans began a new and dangerous offensive in southern Russia. Sevastopol and Rostov fell in rapid succession; a series of great battles was fought in the vicinity of Stalingrad for the control of the Volga Basin.

The attack on Pearl Harbor also was followed by shattering losses in the Far East. The Japanese, knowing that success depended on speed, began a series of lightning strokes against American, British, and Dutch possessions. Hong Kong fell on Christmas Day, 1941. The Japanese pushed south along the Malay Peninsula, destroyed by air attack two British warships, the *Repulse* and the *Prince of Wales,* and captured Singapore along with 100,000 prisoners. The Americans were driven from the Philippines in April 1942; by May the Dutch East Indies were in Japanese hands and Burma was overrun. The Japanese were in a position to harass British and Indian commerce in the Bay of Bengal, to cut off Allied aid to China over the Burma Road, and to invade both India and Australia. In North Africa Rommel began a new offensive in June 1942. Defeating British tanks, he captured Tobruk, which had withstood his earlier attacks, and pushed on to El Alamein in Egypt, only seventy-five miles from Alexandria. Meanwhile the Battle of the Atlantic seemed to be going in favor of the Germans. German submarines began to operate off the eastern coast of the United States, and for a time the American navy, lacking small craft for patrol, was unable to cope with this danger. Submarines and airplanes also took a heavy toll of British convoys sailing north of Scandinavia to Russia or fighting their way through the Mediterranean to bring supplies to Malta.

The Turning of the Tide

It was in the last months of 1942 and in the first half of 1943 that the tide of victory began to turn in favor of the Allies. In Russia the Germans were stopped at Stalingrad on the Volga. As the winter of 1942–1943 approached, they should have retreated, but Hitler ordered them to hold their ground. Bogged down by snow and frigid weather and pounded without mercy by Russian artillery, the German army at Stalingrad suffered enormous casualties and surrendered in February 1943, a signal defeat. Thenceforth the Russians were able to take the offensive and to push the Germans back. As Churchill acknowledged later, it was the Russians who did "the main work of tearing the guts out of the German army."

In the Pacific the United States reacted quickly despite the disaster at Pearl Harbor. In two remarkable naval engagements, fought almost entirely by airplanes from rival carriers, the Japanese navy was severely damaged. The first, the

Battle of the Coral Sea in May 1942, stopped a sea-borne attempt to invade Australia. The second, the Battle of Midway in June, was a decisive victory over the Japanese fleet. Australia, however, was not out of danger. The Japanese were moving south through New Guinea and were attempting to cut the supply line from the United States to Australia by attacks on the Solomon Islands. In the severe fighting that took place in both areas the Japanese were turned back and the foundations were laid for American counterattacks from New Guinea toward the Philippines and across the Pacific from Hawaii toward Japan. It was some time before the British could do more than defend India against the Japanese in Burma. Nevertheless, the tide of Japanese conquest had been turned and would soon begin to ebb.

In North Africa, as the flow of Allied supplies around the Cape of Good Hope became established and as new generals, Sir Harold Alexander and Sir Bernard Montgomery, assumed command, the British inflicted an important defeat on Rommel. In a tremendous battle lasting twelve days in October 1942 Rommel's defenses at El Alamein were broken and he was driven westward. He continued to retreat for more than a thousand miles. Meanwhile in November a powerful Anglo-American army landed in Algeria and in Morocco and began to move eastward toward Rommel in a vast pincers movement. The German game in Africa appeared to be over. But Hitler, who hated above all things to relinquish ground that he had conquered, sent strong reinforcements to Tunisia and ordered Rommel to turn on his pursuers. The fighting in North Africa thus was prolonged for six months. In May 1943, however, the Allies closed in on Tunisia, capturing more than a quarter of a million Germans and Italians. This ended the fighting in North Africa. It was the best the Allies could do at the time to satisfy Stalin's constant demand for a second front in Europe.

The battle against the submarine became much more successful during 1943. Air patrols based in Newfoundland and Iceland, together with small escort carriers from which planes could fight submarines in mid-ocean, now gave air protection to convoys all the way across the Atlantic. During the second half of 1943 the rate of destruction of submarines greatly increased while that of transport and merchant vessels greatly declined. The U-boat all but disappeared from the Mediterranean, and convoys sailing north of Scandinavia slowly were freed from attack by German warships. But the strategic bombing of Germany was only beginning to gather strength during this year.

The Invasion of Europe

Ever since the American entry into the war there had been frequent meetings between Churchill and Roosevelt and their chiefs of staff. Hopeful communiqués were issued after each of these conferences, but a good deal of disagreement existed below the surface. Where should the war effort be concentrated and how should vital supplies be apportioned among the various fronts? Some American officers thought that the United States should put its main strength in the war against Japan, but Roosevelt supported Churchill in believing that the European theater must take precedence over the Far East. Americans wished an offensive in northern Burma to reopen the Burma Road to China, but the British wished to concentrate on the defense of India. Above all, the Americans urged an invasion of France at the earliest possible moment. The prolonged fighting in North Africa, however, made such a plan impossible for 1943; in any case, Churchill preferred an offensive in the Mediterranean, perhaps in the

Balkans, to strike "at the soft underbelly of the Axis." A strong believer in strategic bombing, he hoped to secure bases in the Mediterranean from which to destroy the German war machine.

Amid these conflicting proposals a compromise was found in an invasion of Sicily and Italy from North Africa. In July 1943 the Allies moved into Sicily and shortly cleared the Germans from that island. At this point Mussolini fell from power and a new Italian government was formed by Marshal Badoglio, who concluded an armistice with the Allies. But the Germans quickly seized control of Italian affairs, so that when the Allies pushed into Italy in September they found themselves opposed by strong German forces who took advantage of the mountainous terrain and fought with skill and determination. Progress was therefore very slow, the Allies were halted south of Rome during the winter of 1943–1944, and it was not until June 1944 that Rome was occupied. Thereafter the Italian front became less important because of the invasion of France, although the fighting in Italy pinned down large numbers of German troops to the very end of the war.

The great assault on the fortress of Europe was now in the making. It required elaborate planning and a gigantic build-up of American forces in Britain. It was preceded by massive air attacks on Germany which, although they did not cripple German industry, went far toward destroying the German air force. The invasion began on June 6, 1944, when a vast fleet assembled south of the Isle of Wight. Thence, wrote Churchill,

> in an endless stream, led by the mine-sweepers on a wide front and protected on all sides by the might of the Allied navies and air forces, the greatest armada that ever left our shores set out for the coast of France.

The British General Montgomery was in charge of field operations, though the supreme commander was the American General Eisenhower. The plan was to seize the coast of Normandy, the British on the left flank holding back the Germans while the Americans on the right broke through to the south and then turned east.

This plan succeeded, though there were initial setbacks. It was not until late in July that the American General Patton broke out into Brittany at St.-Lô. The Germans held for some time at Caen, but in August they retreated and large numbers of them were captured after complicated flanking movements by the Allies at Falaise. Meanwhile another Allied invasion from the French Mediterranean coast pushed up the valley of the Rhone. The Germans were now in full flight from France. By September the Allies held a very large area, their lines extending from Antwerp southward to Namur and Metz and then west to Orléans and Nantes. The end of the war appeared to be in sight. But Germany did not collapse. On the contrary, Hitler launched a counteroffensive in December which drove a large salient into the American lines north of Luxembourg and threatened Liège and Namur. These attacks in the Battle of the Bulge were contained, but the hope of ending the war in 1944 disappeared.

Meanwhile, new problems arose concerning the future of eastern Europe and the Balkans as the Russian armies pushed westward. It had been partly to preserve some British influence in these areas that Churchill had advocated an Allied front in the Balkans. In October he flew to Moscow in the hope of striking a bargain with Stalin, and some arrangements were made, though the Russians disregarded them later. In February 1945, Churchill, Roosevelt, and Stalin met for a conference at Yalta in the Crimea. Here, with considerable misgivings,

Churchill and Roosevelt made concessions to Russia both in the Far East and in eastern Europe in order to maintain the alliance, to bring Russia into the war against Japan, and to induce Stalin to cooperate in forming the United Nations. These concessions were unfortunate, for they opened the way for Russian predominance throughout eastern Europe. But there was not much that the British and the Americans could do. "What would have happened," Churchill asked later, "if we had quarrelled with Russia while the Germans still had three or four hundred divisions on the fighting front?"

It was February 1945 that the final thrusts at Germany began. They were accompanied by massive air raids on German industry, oil refineries, and railway connections. British and American armies pushed to the Rhine and then across it. By the end of April the Russians had surrounded Berlin. Early in May the Germans surrendered, first in Italy and then in Germany to Montgomery, to Eisenhower, and to the Russians in Berlin.[7]

The war against Japan was not yet won, but the Allies were closing in from various directions. Lord Louis Mountbatten, the head of the British Southeast Asia command, was instructed to begin an invasion of Burma early in 1945, a tremendous undertaking. A number of armies commanded by General Slim converged from India on Mandalay in Upper Burma and captured that city, along with many Japanese prisoners. Slim then raced south to Rangoon, which he also captured, taking it just before the coming of the monsoon rains. Thus Burma was cleared of the Japanese.

Two other movements were converging on them. One was led by General MacArthur, who moved north from New Guinea to the Philippines, where there was severe fighting for six months. Meanwhile the United States navy was pushing westward from Hawaii toward Japan. The Mariana Islands were taken in 1944, Iwo Jima in March 1945, and Okinawa in May. The Americans were now close to the Japanese home islands. Elaborate plans were evolved for an invasion of Japan which, it was feared, would be very costly in human lives. But with the dropping of the first atomic bombs on Hiroshima (August 6) and on Nagasaki (August 9) and with a Russian declaration of war against Japan, the Japanese had had enough. They surrendered unconditionally on August 14; the formal document was signed on September 2. This ended the Second World War.

THE HOME FRONT DURING THE WAR

As the danger from Hitler unfolded in May 1940, Churchill was able to form a truly national government. He established a War Cabinet of five men. He himself took the post of Minister of Defense; Lord Halifax, a veteran Conservative politician, remained as Foreign Secretary; Chamberlain agreed to serve as Lord President of the Council. His loyalty to Churchill in the Cabinet preserved the unity of the Conservative party and rendered a service to the country. Clement Attlee, the leader of the Labor party, became Lord Privy Seal and deputy leader of the Commons; Arthur Greenwood, another Labor member, served at first without portfolio and later was placed in charge of postwar reconstruction. Members of all three parties served as ministers outside the Cabinet. Two of the most important were Ernest Bevin, the secretary of the Transport and General Workers Union, who became Minister of Labor and

[7] Alfred F. Havighurst, *Twentieth Century Britain*, pp. 335–356.

National Service, and Lord Beaverbrook, a newspaper magnate of drive and energy, who was appointed Minister of Aircraft Production. They were shortly brought into the Cabinet. Sir John Anderson, an eminent civil servant, was added in 1941, and Anthony Eden replaced Halifax. Beaverbrook later was replaced by Oliver Lyttelton, a Conservative; and Greenwood first by Sir Stafford Cripps and then by Herbert Morrison, both Labor members. These men conducted the war for several years. The Cabinet concentrated on major decisions, leaving details to powerful committees.

Most ministers had had experience in administration during the First World War and had also had time during Chamberlain's regime to consider what should be done in another conflict. Hence they were able to avoid earlier mistakes and to establish at once the full control that had come only in the later stages of the First World War. The country was governed during the Second World War with admirable firmness and judgment. Its entire resources of human and material power were channeled into the war effort with completeness and success.

The process began in September 1939 while Chamberlain was still Prime Minister. The Cabinet assumed wide powers. New ministries were created for Economic Warfare, Information, Food, and Shipping. A national registration was carried through and identity cards were issued to everyone. Much more drastic measures were taken after Churchill assumed office. As mentioned earlier, an unprecedented law passed in June 1940 placed all persons and all property at the disposal of the government. An Essential Work Order of March 1941 enabled the Cabinet to place workers in occupations in which their skills would be most beneficial to the war effort. By the summer of 1941 about 8 million men and women were in the armed forces, in home defense, or in factories producing war materials. It was estimated then that about 2 million more would be required by the summer of 1942 and that the army would have to be enlarged, although a high percentage of skilled labor would have to be retained in war factories, especially in plants producing aircraft. These objectives were achieved only by the strictest budgeting of human resources and by the use of women and of men over military age in all sorts of employment. Nonessential industry was curtailed, utility standards were introduced for consumer goods, rationing was intensified, all persons between the ages of eighteen and fifty were made eligible for national service. A number of young men—the Bevin Boys, as they were called—were detailed to work in the mines. Of every nine men in Britain's labor force in 1944, two were in the armed services and three were in war production.

There was comparatively little unrest in the factories because labor strongly supported the war and because labor leaders, such as Bevin and Morrison, were given authority to deal with labor problems. Bevin pleased labor by forcing employers to provide social services, such as nursery schools for the children of women workers. Even the Communists were willing to cooperate after Russia entered the war. Taxation was very high. The income tax was imposed on incomes that had not been taxed before the war and was made to increase more rapidly on incomes in the higher brackets. At the same time the government held down the cost of living by price controls and by subsidies to farmers.

Plans for Reconstruction

Thus the life of the nation was carefully planned during the war and the economy was closely controlled. Why should not the same process be applied to the problems of reconstruction? Reconstruction was very much in the public mind, even at times when the outcome of the war seemed doubtful. The devastated areas of London and other cities were obviously in need of new building and offered opportunities for town planning. Many unofficial bodies developed plans concerning economic policy, land, agriculture, town and country planning, education, public health, and similar topics. The war inspired ideals of social and economic equality. Despite the austerity of wartime conditions, many laboring men were economically better off than ever before, whereas the middle and upper classes found their standard of life reduced by scarcities and by heavy taxation. Some of the officials in the Treasury, such as the economist J. M. Keynes, were quite willing to use the budget to redistribute wealth and to encourage planning. A pamphlet by the historian R. H. Tawney, *Why Britain Fights,* set forth ideals of social justice and of opportunity for all to enjoy the fruits of civilization.

Churchill was not greatly interested in planning: his mind was on the war. He disliked anything that might detract from the war effort and he feared that plans for reconstruction might become so ambitious as to be unattainable and thus an ultimate disappointment. But he could not ignore the national urge to look toward the future. As we have seen, he asked Arthur Greenwood to study the problems of reconstruction. A number of committees of investigation were appointed. One such committee, headed by Sir Montague Barlow, dealt with the relocation of industries and of factory workers in areas away from congested urban districts. Its aim was to spread employment more evenly throughout the country. A Location of Industries Act was passed in 1945. The Scott Committee, concerned with the utilization of land, stressed the need to foster agriculture, to preserve places of natural beauty, and to induce industry to use old sites in decaying towns in order to restore their prosperity. The Uthwatt Report recommended that the state purchase land both in towns and in the country so as to control the course of future building. Some of these recommendations were contained in a Town and Country Planning Act of 1944.

The most ambitious and controversial of these reports was that of Sir William Beveridge, which dealt with social insurance and which proposed that social insurance be made a part of a larger plan of social security. All the social services, Beveridge believed, should be united under the control of a new ministry. He advocated compulsory insurance for everyone under a uniform system of payments and benefits. A minimum income at the subsistence level should be guaranteed to all, and there should be special benefits to cover the expenses of marriage, childbirth, and death. His report, said Beveridge, was a statement of the uses to which the nation could apply its victory when victory had been achieved.

The Beveridge Report was received with enthusiasm by the Labor party and by the public as a whole, but the government, intent on the war, did not wish to commit itself to such far-reaching proposals, and only tentative steps were taken to implement the report. Churchill appointed as the Minister of Reconstruction, Lord Woolton, who issued a number of white papers on social insurance, national health, and full employment. One of these papers contained a pledge that the government would use its financial power to ensure full employment after the war. Thus the social legislation of the postwar era, to which we shall turn in the next chapter, was clearly foreshadowed during the war period.[8]

[8] Henry Pelling, *Modern Britain 1885–1955* (Edinburgh: T. Nelson, 1960), pp. 148–159; Alfred F. Havighurst, *Twentieth Century Britain,* pp. 321–331.

35

contemporary Britain

After the Second World War, as after the first one, Britain faced many problems of readjustment. Fundamentally these problems were much the same, but the intensity of Britain's difficulties in 1945 and the emergence of the United States and Russia as the two world giants forced Britain to recognize, as she had not done in 1918, that her old predominance as a great power had ended. She was left with a certain moral grandeur, but she had sacrificed much of her economic strength to obtain the victory. During the first five years of peace, as she passed through bleak austerity in the struggle to restore her economy and to regain her foreign trade, the margin between economic survival and disaster was often very small. Britain's weakened position was quickly evident, for example, in her relations with her empire. Yet it was during this time that the Labor party, with a large majority in the Commons, established the welfare state with its welcome but costly increase in social security. After 1951, when the temper of the people had become less radical, the Conservatives obtained a long lease of power. The economy remained a matter of delicate balance, but conditions greatly improved. Britain enjoyed a modest prosperity. Prices rose, but so did wages, and the Conservatives could boast that they had handled economic problems well. Although the task was much less difficult than it had been in the years of Labor rule, their boast was justified. Unfortunately, affluence brought other economic problems, of which the worst was inflation.

THE ELECTION OF 1945

In the spring of 1945, when Allied success over the Axis Powers was assured, there was talk in Britain of an early election. Churchill, who assumed that his great prestige as the architect of victory would bring the Conservatives success at the polls, set July 5 as the day of the election. Actually, the Labor party was much better prepared to fight an election than were the Conservatives. Determined to end the political truce after the war was won, Labor had kept its views before the public through a series of pamphlets dealing with such matters as housing, full employment, public health, and the nationalization of industry. Labor's electoral manifesto, *Let Us Face the Future*, set forth in clear and temperate language a program of expanded social services, limited nationalization, and continued controls to ease the transition to a peacetime economy.

The Conservatives, with no such clear-cut program, declared that after the peace they would examine each industry in turn and would do what seemed best in individual cases. Churchill clearly favored an abandonment of government controls and the encouragement of private enterprise. He launched an attack on socialism, comparing it with the totalitarian regimes of the fascists. The reaction of the people was one of amused skepticism. A Labor leader remarked that "Winston was having a night out." This "moth-eaten debate on socialism vs. free enterprise"—as one newspaper put it—left the people cold.[1] Unafraid of economic planning, the people were thinking of housing, employment, and social security; their mood for the moment was rather radical. They did not regard the winning of the war as the achievement of any one party. Many voters recalled the Conservative policy of appeasement during the 1930s and were determined to throw out the "men of Munich." Hence the Labor party won by a landslide in the election of 1945. The new House of Commons contained 393 Labor members and only 189 Conservatives. The nation was rather astonished at what it had done. So was Churchill. He wrote later that he had exercised power during more than five years of war, "at the end of which time, all our enemies having surrendered unconditionally or being about to do so, I was immediately dismissed by the British electorate from all further conduct of their affairs."

LABOR AND THE WELFARE STATE

The Labor Cabinet of 1945

Clement Attlee, the Labor Prime Minister, was a moderate man, cool in temperament, and persuasive in maintaining harmony within his Cabinet. An able debater, with long experience in the Commons, he was industrious, honest, and loyal. But he lacked Churchill's glamour and oratorical power. As he drove to Buckingham Palace in his small family car to kiss the royal hand as Prime Minister, he was a symbol of postwar Britain—sensible, practical, and patient, but a little drab. His most important colleague in the new Cabinet was Ernest Bevin, the Foreign Secretary. Other Cabinet ministers included Hugh Dalton, the sharp-tongued Chancellor of the Exchequer; Herbert Morrison, leader of the House of Commons; Sir Stafford Cripps, President of the Board of Trade; and Aneurin Bevan, the radical and controversial Minister of Health.

For the first time in history the Labor party commanded a large majority in the Commons. It could claim a mandate to move ahead with a program of expanded social services and nationalization. About half the Labor members were in the Commons for the first time. Like the Liberals in 1906, they were inexperienced yet zealous. They pushed their program with rapidity, but they were harassed and hampered by the desperate economic plight in which Britain found herself.

[1] Quoted in Alfred F. Havighurst, *Twentieth Century Britain* (New York: Harper & Row, 1966), p. 366.

The Economic Problem

Although the loss of life in the British armed forces during the Second World War was much less than during the earlier war, the material damage at home was much greater. Sections of London and of other cities had been leveled to the ground, some 5 million houses had been destroyed or rendered unsafe for habitation, 18 million tons of shipping had been lost. British railways, factories, and power plants had been subjected to constant and grueling use in war production without normal maintenance and modernization. The cost of rebuilding and replacement was greater than Britain could afford, for she had liquidated about a third of her foreign securities and had lost many of her invisible exports.

It was essential for Britain to restore her factories, regain some portion of her foreign trade, and expand her shrunken exports until they balanced the cost of imported goods and raw materials. It was hoped that American assistance in the form of lend-lease would be continued after the war, but the United States brought lend-lease to a rather abrupt termination in September 1945, following the surrender of Japan. To meet this crisis Britain obtained from the United States a loan of $3750 million, which was to carry interest of two percent and was to be repaid in fifty annual installments beginning in 1951. A loan of $1250 million was secured from Canada on somewhat more generous terms. These credits, it was hoped, would carry Britain over the first years of reconstruction. Unfortunately, the cost of raw materials was high in 1945 and the money was spent more quickly than had been anticipated.

The Labor government, in handling economic problems, relied on strict controls. This seemed the natural thing to do: controls had been successful during the war, and economic planning was in fashion. Wartime restrictions were therefore continued into the peace. Through an elaborate system of licenses and allocations the government regulated the importation of raw materials and their distribution to British manufacturers, favoring those industries which fed the export trades. Steel, machine tools, and other necessities also were allotted carefully among industrialists. To conserve the supply of machines and raw materials required by industry, the government established a system of licenses for exports as well as imports. Expansion by industry was regulated, prices were fixed, and foreign exchange was carefully controlled. The government, though retaining ample powers of coercion, preferred to employ persuasion and consultation in dealing with labor and management; many of these controls were exercised by industrial magnates who worked closely with the Board of Trade and with other ministries. At the same time domestic consumption and private building were curtailed through rationing, price controls, taxation, and building permits.

The price of food was held at a low level. The Ministry of Food bought agricultural products from British farmers and sold them to the public at substantially lower prices; imported food often was bought in bulk in order to obtain it at a cheap rate. The result was that even persons with very low incomes could obtain a nutritious diet, though there were many complaints about its monotony.

The effect of this control of industry was disappointing. Strict regulation, which had achieved its purpose during the war, failed to produce the desired results in time of peace. One difficulty was that the workers no longer felt the stimulus of war conditions; many years of tension and struggle now were followed by a natural decline in morale. Although the demand for labor was high and there was full employment, productivity did not rise in proportion to the number of men at work. There were stoppages and evidence of slackness. Diminished incentive affected manufacturers, for excessive controls hampered private enterprise. Rising wages and cheap interest rates increased purchasing power, but rationing and restrictions severely limited what people were permitted to buy. Manufacturers saw no reason to produce articles the public was not allowed to purchase.

The economy improved very slowly. It was stronger in 1946 than it had been in 1945, but a severe slump occurred in 1947, a year that began badly with an unusually severe winter, during which snow and ice blocked roads and railways. As reserves of coal shrank, factories closed for lack of fuel, and some 2 million men were temporarily idle. British exports declined during the first half of 1947, just as the American and Canadian credits were running out. A new austerity program was announced by the government, and a new drive for greater productivity was begun.

It was fortunate for Britain that late in 1947 the American government decided to give economic aid to Europe under the Marshall Plan. The Americans feared very rightly that if Europe did not develop economically the way would lie open for an advance of communism. Hence the Organization for European Economic Cooperation was established early in 1948 to place large American credits at the disposal of European countries and to induce them to cooperate in removing tariff barriers. Marshall Plan aid helped to improve the British economy in 1948. There were other reasons for the advance: several of the controls over British industry were now relaxed, industry throve under less rigid supervision, and both labor and management made a greater effort to increase productivity. The year 1949 was rather disappointing. A slight depression in the United States caused a decline in American imports from Britain, and so precarious was the basis of the British economy, that this moderate drop was sufficient to force a devaluation of the pound, which fell from $4.03 to $2.80 in September. Conditions improved once more in 1950.

Nationalization

A time of such uncertain economic conditions as the period following a war might well appear inappropriate for socialistic experiment. Yet the Labor party, from the moment it came into office, followed a policy of partial nationalization of industry. A nationalized industry was one whose total assets had been purchased by the state. Private owners received a fair price for their property, all nationalization being based on acts of Parliament. The industries thus acquired were operated by public corporations responsible to various ministries for general policy but not for the details of management. In some cases the business executives who had managed industries before nationalization were employed to continue their direction. The position of labor was unaffected. Without participating in the guidance of nationalized industry, labor continued to deal with management through collective bargaining and through the right to strike.

The Cabinet began by nationalizing the Bank of England in 1946. Stockholders received government stock in place of their old certificates; the directors of the bank were to be appointed by the Cabinet. The relations of the bank and the Treasury, however, had been so close before nationalization that they were changed very little. A member of Parliament dubbed the entire proceeding "an elaborate game of make-believe." The government acted partly because it regarded nationalization as a kind of retribution for the role the bank was supposed to have played in overthrowing the Labor Cabinet in 1931.

A Coal Industry Nationalization Act also was passed in 1946. Although the Conservatives criticized the details of this measure, its principles were accepted by both parties. There was an obvious need to bring the independent mining companies—some 800 in all—under central regulation; the state of the industry was most unsatisfactory, with low productivity, low morale among the miners, bad blood between labor and management, and poor living conditions in mining areas. The act established a national coal board to control the industry under the general supervision of the Minister of Fuel and Power. Nationalization also was applied to civil aviation, to cables and wireless, and to electricity and gas. A drastic, complicated, and far-reaching measure dealt with inland transport— railways, canals, docks and harbors, buses, and road haulage.

Controversy arose over Labor's desire to nationalize iron and steel, an industry which could claim that it was efficient and productive and that it had established effective controls over itself, with machinery for fixing prices and for allocating production quotas. On the other hand, the Cabinet asserted that the industry was semimonopolistic and that, intent upon profits, it did not attempt to meet the nation's demand for steel or the laborer's need for full employment. The nationalization of iron and steel became a symbol of the success or failure of Labor's program. The Conservatives feared that, if this industry was nationalized, the way would be opened for the nationalization of many others. Labor believed that failure in this case might jeopardize all its efforts. A division arose over this measure between the doctrinaire socialists and the more practical politicians in the Labor party. Further, it became obvious that because of opposition in the House of Lords the legislation on iron and steel would be a lengthy business. Hence in 1949 Labor passed an act which limited to one year instead of two the power of the Lords to delay legislation. The iron and steel bill passed through Parliament in 1949, but it was not to become effective until 1951, before which date there would be a general election.

Labor pressed forward with its program of nationalization in a spirit of idealism and crusading zeal, but the results were disappointing. Socialists had hoped that workers in nationalized industries would develop a sense of indirect ownership, would take pride in their participation in public enterprises, and would acquire some influence through consultation with management. Few of these expectations were fulfilled. Public ownership failed to stir the imagination of workingmen. In their view, conditions remained as they had always been, and the boss was still the boss. Socialists had also hoped that public ownership would result in lowered salaries for business managers and would thus advance equalization of income. Nationalized industries, however, had to compete with private enterprise for able executives and had to pay them roughly comparable salaries. Nor was public ownership a cure for the ills of industry, though it is true that conditions were sometimes improved. The coal-mining industry, for example, was in a more satisfactory state following nationalization. Yet the production of coal was less than the goals that were set, and the morale of the men was low despite high wages and fringe benefits. Having paid a fair price for the industries it acquired, the state expected them to show a profit. But profits did not necessarily follow. The railways, now feeling the full competition of airplanes and motor cars, have been operated at enormous loss. The nationalization of iron and steel became a political liability. Public ownership was neither a cure for economic ills nor a factor in reshaping society.[2]

The Extension of the Social Services

Another portion of Labor's program dealt with the extension of the social services. Several acts, closely following the recommendations of the Beveridge Report, were passed between 1946 and 1948. The most comprehensive was the National Insurance Act, by which older legislation dealing with old-age pensions and with insurance against illness and unemployment was consolidated into one vast insurance plan for the entire population. Almost every adult now paid small weekly sums to the government, and employers made similar payments for each employee. These contributions amounted to about thirty percent of the cost of the insurance plan; the remainder was met by general taxation. Benefits included weekly payments during periods of illness and unemployment, old-age pensions, and supplementary sums to meet emergencies, such as pregnancy, childbirth, widowhood, and death.

Industrial injuries also were placed on an insurance basis. Each workman paid a few pennies a week (matched by his employer) into a central fund from which benefits were drawn. A Family Allowances Act, passed by Churchill's government in 1945, provided small sums to every family for each child (except the first) until that child reached fifteen. A National Assistance Act abolished the old poor laws, offered the minimum cost of food and shelter to every applicant, and provided for half a million persons who because of age or infirmity required special care.

The most popular item in the extension of the social services was the National Health Service Act of 1946. This act had a longer history than is often supposed: for many years the medical profession, the public, and various governments had considered plans for the improvement of medical services, but a white paper issued by the Cabinet in 1944 alarmed the doctors. They were afraid that a national service would undermine the freedom of their profession and that bureaucrats at the local level would mismanage hospitals. Aneurin Bevan, the Minister of Health, who piloted the bill through Parliament, was roundly abused. The bill had a stormy passage but once it became law it was received gratefully by the people. It provided free medical and dental service, free glasses, dentures, and prescriptions for medicine, and free hospitalization for the entire population. It called for clinics and health centers, though these were too costly to be introduced at once. The plan retained as much flexibility as possible. Physicians could continue in private practice if they wished; patients could select their doctors. There can be little doubt that the health service has improved the health of the nation. Persons who had gone to doctors only in emergencies, or who could not afford specialists, now received adequate attention. Used far more than had been anticipated, the health service became very costly. Yet so great was its popularity, that the Conservatives campaigning in 1950 promised to continue it if they were returned to power.

A number of other measures should be mentioned, including two important housing acts. The first, in 1946, curtailed private building and aimed at the construction of low-priced houses the state could rent for as little as 10s. a week. Rising costs soon made this figure unrealistic, but rents were kept very low. A

[2] See Havighurst, pp. 369–372, 409–414.

second act, passed in 1949, encouraged local authorities to improve large city houses which had degenerated through subdivision into apartments and cheap lodgings. The housing program, supervised by Aneurin Bevan, was subjected to severe criticism because of the acute shortage, the high cost, the arbitrary fixing of rents, and some unavoidable waste. Nonetheless, within five years Bevan built 806,000 permanent houses and apartments and 157,000 temporary houses; he also created 333,000 new units through the conversion of older dwellings.[3]

The government hoped to implement an ambitious Education Act passed in 1944, but was badly hampered by a shortage of trained teachers and of school buildings. Some progress was made, especially in training teachers; the school-leaving age was raised to fifteen. The state began to give greatly increased assistance to universities and to university students. A New Towns Act in 1946 empowered the government to build new industrial and residential towns on the outskirts of large cities, thus drawing industry and population away from congested urban centers. An Atomic Energy Act authorized experiments in the uses of atomic energy for peaceful purposes. Two measures dealt with the constitution. The first abolished the last vestiges of plural voting. The universities lost their representation in the Commons; businessmen who had voted both in the constituencies in which they resided and also in those in which they occupied business premises were allowed to vote only in the first. In 1949, as we have seen, the power of the House of Lords to delay legislation was reduced from two years to one.[4]

Relations with Russia

In conducting foreign affairs the Labor government experienced the disillusionment of worsening relations with Russia. The radicals of the party believed that if her policy were truly socialistic Britain should be able to get on with the Russians. But it was quickly evident that Russian aims were incompatible with British interests. British influence disappeared in most of eastern Europe as the countries of that area were reduced to Russian satellites. The Russian *coup d'état* in Czechoslovakia in 1948 was as ruthless as Hitler's nine years before. Russian efforts to obtain one of the former Italian colonies in North Africa, as well as Russian intrigues in Greece, threatened the British position in the eastern Mediterranean. Moreover, Russia refused to participate in the Marshall Plan and prevented her satellites from doing so. Finally, in Germany, where lay the central problem, Russia's attitude was distinctly hostile. In 1948 she attempted to block the access of the Western Powers to their sectors of Berlin, a move adroitly countered by a massive airlift to Berlin from the West. Meanwhile there was constant vilification of the West by Russian propaganda.

Ernest Bevin, Foreign Secretary in the Labor Cabinet, a trade-union man rather than a doctrinaire socialist, followed tradition by defending British interests as best he could. He thought in terms of a defensive alliance of western European nations to fill the power vacuum created by Germany's defeat. In 1947 he concluded such an alliance with France; in the next year he brought in Holland, Belgium, and Luxembourg. The culmination of this policy was the North Atlantic Treaty Organization (NATO) established in 1949. This organization included the powers along the western seaboard of Europe (except for Spain

---

[3] Havighurst, pp. 416–417.
[4] Henry Pelling, *Modern Britain 1885–1955* (Edinburgh: T. Nelson, 1960), pp. 174–175.

and Ireland), together with the United States, Canada, Iceland, and Italy. Greece and Turkey entered NATO in 1951. It was a military alliance aimed at keeping the Russians at bay.

Evaluation of Labor's Tenure of Power

What had the Labor government accomplished during its five years of power? Britain's position in international affairs, after the establishment of NATO, was more secure and influential than it had been at the end of the war. Labor's principal achievement at home was not nationalization, of which the benefits were doubtful, but, rather, the establishment of the welfare state. By 1950 the social services were expanded greatly, unemployment scarcely existed, income sufficient to meet the minimal cost of food and shelter was guaranteed to all, and a free medical service was available. The housing problem was being attacked with vigor, and educational policy, though not achieving all that had been hoped, was set on a more democratic course. There were fair shares for all. This advance had come, not as the result of a sudden revolution in thought or action, but through an evolutionary trend toward greater concern for the welfare of the population as a whole. An all-important question remained: could the welfare state become an affluent state with a rising standard of living for all classes, or must the wealth of the country remain static and the condition of the poor improved solely by taxing away the resources of the well-to-do? This was the question posed through the 1950s.

THE TRANSITION TO CONSERVATIVE GOVERNMENT

The Labor party, after its strenuous five years of advanced legislation, could hardly hope for another great victory at the polls. The bulk of its proposed reforms had been enacted; it could offer the public only a continuation of the same bill of fare. Its time in office had been marked by high taxation and by irksome shortages and controls. The economic crisis of 1947 had brought great discomfort and unwelcome austerity. Labor, moreover, was threatened by a revolt of its radical wing in opposition to Bevin's foreign policy. The party program in 1950, therefore, was moderate. Ministers proposed to extend the welfare state but would act with caution. They affirmed their faith in nationalization, but they had little to say about economic planning and they recognized the role of private enterprise in industry. As Mr. Attlee toured the country in his small automobile with his wife at the wheel, he presented an image of sensible economy and disarming moderation.

The Conservatives, despite a good deal of frustration, had been growing in strength, had improved their party organization, and had acquired an adequate party chest. Their problem was whether to accept the welfare state. Although there were many things about it they did not like, they knew that it had the backing of the majority of voters and hence they wisely regarded it as something which had come to stay. They claimed they could improve its administration and reduce its cost. They opposed nationalization. But, with the exceptions of iron and steel and road haulage, they agreed not to disturb those industries already nationalized. The two parties were closer together in 1950 than might be supposed.

The election in February 1950 proved to be a stalemate. Labor lost its large majority, though with 315 seats it remained the strongest party in the Commons. The Conservatives, with 298, were not far behind; Labor's majority over all other parties combined was only 6. Attlee remained as Prime Minister. Unable to press contentious measures, he offered only a limited program of legislation in the speech from the throne which opened the new Parliament. Churchill declared in the Commons that the speech should have read: "My government will not introduce legislation in fulfillment of their election program because the only mandate they have received from the country is not to do it."[5] The fear of defeat in a snap vote forced Labor members to be diligent in their attendance in the Commons.

Although the Labor party remained in office for about a year and a half, it was beset with many difficulties, barely escaping defeat when it gave effect to the act of 1949 nationalizing iron and steel. The act had provided that nationalization should take place in 1951, but the Conservatives, pointing to Labor losses in the recent election, now pressed for further delay, which the government refused. Other problems arose from the conflict in Korea. This broke out in June 1950 when the United States, acting under a resolution of the Security Council of the United Nations, defended South Korea against Communist attack from the north. The Cabinet approved this action and sent naval units to Korea. But Britain did not wish to lose her trade with China; moreover, she feared that the United States would broaden the war into a general conflict, and she felt the necessity of increasing her armaments. Rearmament, which caused new division between the moderate and radical wings of the Labor party, was denounced by Aneurin Bevan, who declared that its cost would take money away from the social services. In April 1951 he resigned from the Cabinet. Other resignations, coming at a time when several key ministers were ill, reduced the drive and momentum of the government. The national economy, having done very well in 1950, sagged in 1951, so that a new balance-of-payments crisis was in the making. Under these circumstances Attlee held an election in October 1951.

The trend away from Labor continued in this election, though the Commons remained very evenly divided between the two major parties. The Conservatives won 321 seats whereas Labor won 295. Over all other parties combined the Conservative majority was only 17. Yet this shift in strength, though small, was sufficient to bring in the Conservatives and to end Labor's term of office. The election was more decisive than was imagined at the time, for the Conservatives were to remain in power for the next thirteen years.

THE CONSERVATIVES IN POWER, 1951–1963

Churchill's Cabinet, 1951–1955

Winston Churchill, still surprisingly vigorous at seventy-seven, immediately formed a Conservative government. He assumed his old post of Minister of Defense and brought into the Cabinet several elder statesmen with whom he had worked during the war. One was Lord Woolton, who became a coordinating Minister for Food and Agriculture. Another was Lord Cherwell, a physicist who was placed in control of atomic energy and research. Younger ministers included Sir Anthony Eden as Foreign Secretary, R. A. Butler as Chancellor of the Exchequer, and Harold Macmillan as Minister of Housing.

[5] Quoted in Alfred F. Havighurst, *Twentieth Century Britain*, p. 428.

Churchill's majority was so small that he acted cautiously. He dropped his idea of restoring to the universities their former seats in the Commons. He left the nationalized industries as they were, with two exceptions. One was iron and steel, which was returned to private ownership, though an iron and steel board supervised the industry, determined prices, and directed capital investment. The nationalized transport industry also was altered so as to permit haulage by road in privately owned trucks. Again, the supervision of the government by no means disappeared. Churchill faced a balance-of-payments crisis. Rearmament, the high cost of raw materials, and the constant tendency to increase imports had caused a heavy drain on the pound and on dollar reserves. Churchill curtailed imports, raised the bank rate, discouraged capital investment, and retarded the accumulation of inventories. Fortunately the balance of payments soon improved. Between 1952 and 1954 manufactured articles rose in price in the world market while the cost of raw materials declined. These favorable trends were accompanied by an increase in British productivity. It was possible to end the rationing of food in 1954, and Butler reduced taxation slightly, though this advantage was offset by his discontinuance of food subsidies. Hence the price of food rose somewhat. Macmillan won praise by building over 300,000 new houses a year.

In April 1955 Sir Winston Churchill at eighty stepped down from his office of Prime Minister. With his lion's heart, his magnificent confidence in himself and in his country, his ability to inspire others, his capacity for prompt decision, his power over words, he was one of England's greatest warrior-statesmen. His life was an epitome of British history for almost sixty years. He was succeeded as Prime Minister by his Foreign Secretary, Sir Anthony Eden, who at once dissolved Parliament.

The Election of 1955

The election of 1955, coming in the middle of the decade, illustrates a number of trends and developments. There was, in the first place, a continued swing to the right. Having increased their strength in the elections of 1950 and 1951, the Conservatives now further improved their position by winning a comfortable majority of 58 seats over all other parties combined. This was an unusual occurrence. It is normal for a party, once in power, to enact its program and then decline in popularity until it grows weak and tired. The Conservatives, reversing this pattern, were making the 1950s a Conservative decade.

Their success was due in large measure to the improved condition of the economy. They had been fortunate in coming to power at a time when world economic conditions were moving forward; they had made the most of their opportunity. The working classes, with full employment and good wages, were tasting an increased prosperity. With many of the old controls now lifted, industry was thriving and was pushing new techniques and new products. The great success story was that of the automobile. The production of motor cars was four times as large in 1955 as it had been in 1946. Everybody wanted a car. Automobiles became an important article of export. There was, of course, a price to be paid, for Britain is a small and crowded island whose country lanes, blind corners, and crooked city streets are ill adapted to motor traffic. Nonetheless, the manufacture of automobiles was giving an important stimulus to the economy. Other industries, such as the production of aircraft, radios, chemicals, electrical goods, and new machines of all kinds, were doing well—appealing to the home market and competing successfully in world trade. There was also a great amount of building.

The election appeared to indicate that some people were turning away from socialism. The welfare state, now accepted by both parties, was rather taken for granted. Labor did not offer much that was new, and many working people probably wondered what socialism could offer which they did not already possess. Economic planning, with its depressing controls, seemed less attractive than in the past. It was not the nationalized industries that were advancing in prosperity but rather that segment of the economy which remained in private hands. There was a shift in emphasis away from the socialistic goals of full employment and social justice to the importance of increased productivity and to the hope for greater wealth. In 1954, R. A. Butler, the Chancellor of the Exchequer, asked: "Why should we not aim to double our standard of living in the next twenty-five years, and still have our money as valuable then as now?" Although the question was premature, for the economy declined in 1955–1956, Butler expressed the general hope for a society which could provide social security and also attain greater affluence.

The election of 1955 indicated a certain apathy toward politics. The number of persons who voted was less in 1955 than in 1951, a decline more harmful to the Labor party than to the Conservatives. Apathy was due perhaps in part to a feeling that the destiny of the world was no longer controlled by Britain, but rather by Russia and the United States. It was due in part to greater contentment with conditions as they were and to a belief that policy would be much the same no matter which party was in power.

Apathy also sprang from certain changes in the functioning of the constitution. The late nineteenth and the early twentieth centuries had seen an increase in the power of both the Cabinet and the Prime Minister at the expense of the House of Commons. This increase was the result of strict party discipline. When a division was about to take place in the Commons, the whips rounded up the members of the majority party, the voting followed party lines, and the will of the Cabinet was enforced with the impact and precision of a steam roller. The results were that the Cabinet dictated policy, that legislation sometimes passed in the Commons with little discussion, that oratory had small effect on voting, and that there was perhaps some decline in the caliber of members. Candidates for election could hardly hope for success without the endorsement of a major political party. The Cabinet, of course, remained highly sensitive to public opinion, which could express itself in many ways—in newspapers, in periodicals, in demonstrations, in public meetings. The Cabinet tended to respond quickly and directly, without waiting for opinion to find a voice in the House of Commons. The Commons were by-passed. They seemed no longer the master of the Cabinet; rather, the Cabinet, supported by the electorate, was becoming the master of the Commons. The influence of the Commons also was diminished by the growing importance of the permanent civil service, to which large powers often were delegated by legislation.

Cabinets, of course, were not omnipotent, for their followers in the Commons could revolt. One aspect of politics in the 1950s was the Labor party's difficulty in maintaining discipline within its ranks. Aneurin Bevan was often at

Bertrand Russell climbing onto the base of the Nelson Monument in Trafalgar Square, London, to address a Peace Rally. (Photo by Christopher Angeloglov. Pix, Inc.)

the bottom of the trouble; on one occasion he was expelled temporarily from the parliamentary Labor party. In December 1955, when Clement Attlee resigned as leader of the party, Bevan was passed over, and the leadership went to Hugh Gaitskell, an economist of high integrity and of moderate socialistic views. Bevan became more temperate. As we have seen, there were differences between the moderate and radical wings of the party. The radicals urged a further nationalization of industry, the disestablishment of the Church of England, withdrawal of Britain from imperial commitments, reduction in the size of the army, and abandonment of close relations with capitalistic America. They opposed nuclear defense because they held that Britain, whether prepared or not, would be destroyed in the course of a war involving nuclear weapons.

Sir Anthony Eden, 1955–1957

Sir Anthony Eden remained as Prime Minister only from April 1955 to January 1957. A handsome man, attractive in manners and appearance, as Foreign Secretary under Neville Chamberlain he had resisted the policy of appeasement toward Hitler and Mussolini. He had long enjoyed the confidence of Churchill, who thought of him as his successor both during the war and during Churchill's last premiership. As Prime Minister Eden was a disappointment. It was a great disadvantage to him—or to anyone—to follow such an outstanding figure as Churchill. Eden did not arouse enthusiasm among the rank and file of the party, nor did he appear to give the full commitment to his office that was necessary for success. He had to deal with a serious crisis in 1956 when Britain and France intervened in a war between Egypt and Israel, sent troops into the Suez Canal zone, and then, under strong pressure both from Russia and the United States, agreed to withdraw their forces. This episode greatly weakened Eden's government. He resigned as Prime Minister in January 1957, though his party remained in power.

Harold Macmillan, 1957–1963

It was thought that Eden's successor as Conservative Prime Minister would be R. A. Butler, who had been Chancellor of the Exchequer in Churchill's last Cabinet. Butler, however, was passed over, perhaps because he had privately expressed his opposition to the venture in Suez; the premiership went to Harold Macmillan. A member of the Commons for many years, Macmillan had first held office in 1951 as Churchill's Minister of Housing, when he had been a brilliant success and had served as Foreign Minister and later as Chancellor of the Exchequer under Eden. His position as Prime Minister was at first precarious: his party was divided by the Suez crisis, and the public was critical of it. Had Labor been stronger and more united it might have overthrown the Conservatives and formed a Labor government.

But Macmillan quickly proved his ability. He established his leadership among the Conservatives. His economic policy was successful. The Suez crisis, which had been very costly, forced Britain to purchase oil from the United States at a time when the balance of payments was already unfavorable. To meet this crisis, Macmillan resorted to the usual methods of checking capital expenditures and curtailing imports. His principal weapon was an extremely high bank rate of seven percent, which held borrowing to a minimum. The balance of payments righted itself, foreign trade increased, and soon the economy again was permitted to expand. The year 1959 was an excellent one and the government was able to reduce taxes. It is not surprising, therefore, that when the Conservatives held an election in October they won a handsome victory, increasing their majority in the Commons to 100.

In the early 1960s, however, the Conservatives found themselves in difficulties of various kinds. Weaknesses appeared in the economy. Hoping to expand trade with the Continent, Macmillan applied in 1961 for admission to the European Economic Community, known as the Common Market, an economic association of six countries (France, West Germany, Italy, Holland, Belgium, and Luxembourg) among whom tariff barriers had been substantially reduced. The economies of these countries were developing at a faster rate than was that of Britain. Membership in the Common Market would expand British exports and would assist her in maintaining sterling as an international currency as well as in developing backward areas in the Commonwealth. Negotiations continued for more than a year. But in January 1963 the French President, Charles de Gaulle, who did not wish to admit a rival to French leadership in the Common Market, managed to close the door against British participation. He contended that British membership and the changes Britain proposed would alter the nature of the Common Market. His action was a rebuff to Macmillan, who had been basing his economic and political policy on the assumption that Britain would be admitted.

Macmillan was further embarrassed by decisions in the United States which showed that Britain was depending on America for missiles to carry her nuclear weapons. The winter of 1962–1963 was a severe one, with a power shortage and with a greater amount of unemployment than had existed since before the war. Then came the Profumo scandal, in which the Secretary for War was involved with a woman who might have been a security risk. On October 1963 Macmillan resigned as Prime Minister. After a rather bitter intraparty contest, he was succeeded by the Earl of Home who, renouncing his peerage, took his seat in the Commons as Sir Alec Douglas-Home.[6]

An aristocrat of charm and intelligence, Sir Alec had a quiet manner which was effective over television and in the House of Commons. He had done well as Foreign Secretary under Macmillan. On the other hand, some people considered him too old (he was sixty) and too conservative; they doubted whether he would prove a dynamic leader.[7] He came to power at a time when an election was approaching and when the Conservatives were thought to be heading for a severe defeat. During the year of Sir Alec's ministry, however, their chances improved. Forecasts indicated that the country was again very evenly divided between the two major parties; the election, held on October 15, 1964, resulted in a narrow victory for Labor with 317 seats, as against 304 for the Conservatives and 9 for the Liberal party. If Conservatives and Liberals voted together, Labor's majority would be only 4.

[6] A Peerage Act of July 1963 gave all existing peers the right to renounce their peerages within the next six months. Persons succeeding to peerages subsequent to the act were allowed a year in which they might do the same. Another change in the law of the peerage had been made in 1958 when life peerages were created. In 1965 the House of Lords, with a membership of about 900, contained 99 life peers, several of whom were women.

[7] Thomas P. Peardon, "Politics in Britain," *Current History,* XLVI (May 1964), pp. 282–286.

LABOR AGAIN IN POWER

After the election of October 1964, the Labor party came into office, for the first time in thirteen years. Its Party Manifesto issued before the election was a vigorous document promising new ministries for economic affairs and for technology, greater scope and expansion for the nationalized industries, and the nationalization of iron and steel. Harold Wilson, the Labor Prime Minister, who had become leader of the party in 1963 at the death of Hugh Gaitskell, was regarded, if not as a radical, at least as a man around whom radicals gathered. A politician of vigor, perseverance, and skill, he echoed the tone of the Party Manifesto, declaring that despite his small majority he intended to govern with decisiveness.

During his five and a half years in office, however, he was not in a position to push controversial legislation. His majority, as we have seen, was very small, sometimes shrinking to the vanishing point, until in March 1966, sensing a favorable moment, he called an unexpected election and won a handsome majority of ninety-seven seats. A far greater cause for moderation was the fact that throughout his premiership he was faced with serious economic problems: inflation, demands for higher wages, crises in the balance of payments. Unfortunately in Britain, when the economy is booming and wages and profits are high, as was the case under Macmillan, inflationary pressures begin to mount. The demand for goods and services increases, imports multiply, foreign holders of sterling sell short in hope of devaluation, and a balance-of-payments crisis is shortly at hand. This was the situation when Wilson took office, and similar problems plagued him year after year.

To maintain the parity of the pound and to reverse the unfavorable balance of payments, Wilson employed the same tactics that the Conservatives had used in the past: surtaxes on many imports, tax relief to exporters, emergency budgets increasing general taxation, tight money, discouragement of economic expansion, an attempt to find "an incomes policy," that is, to regulate wage increases (even by legislation) and to retain a correlation between them and increased productivity. Britain reduced her military budget, curtailed her imperial commitments, and increased the payments by employers and employees to support the social services. Even so, Wilson was forced to devalue the pound from about $2.80 to about $2.40 in November 1967. He also turned toward the Conservative policy of seeking English membership in the European Economic Community or Common Market.

Thus Wilson's radicalism disappeared. He defended his moderate policies by saying that the two parties were moving toward a consensus; in the election of 1966 he referred to his government as a national government. But many of his followers were unhappy with his measures. He felt great pressure from trade unions demanding wage increases. Indeed, the whole field of labor relations was in ferment, with many work stoppages and with orderly bargaining disturbed by wildcat strikes. Wilson also was under attack from Labor members who wanted lower interest rates and greater economic expansion and disliked British support of the United States in Vietnam.

The economic situation improved in 1969. In June 1970, again believing that the moment was opportune, Wilson dissolved Parliament and held an election. To the consternation of the Labor party, the Conservatives won by some thirty seats, Wilson resigned, and Edward Heath, who had succeeded Sir Alec Douglas-

Home as Conservative leader, formed a Cabinet. It is likely that Heath will assert Britain's position in the world more clearly than did the Labor party. At home he has promised higher productivity, more stable prices, and greater wealth. Whether he can fulfill these pledges remains to be seen.

THE EMPIRE SINCE 1918

Changes of a fundamental nature have taken place in the British Empire since the end of the First World War. The maturing of the older Dominions into sovereign states, the insistent nationalism among the peoples of Asia and Africa, the grant of independence to many of these peoples, and the evolution of what is sometimes called the Second Commonwealth have transformed the empire into something very different from what it once was. The crucial points, as we shall see, were the granting of independence to India and to Pakistan in 1947 and their desire to become republics, though within the Commonwealth. It was fortunate that the Labor party, with its liberal approach to colonial questions, was the party in power at that time. For the truth was that Britain lacked the resources to continue her former imperial commitments and could not hope either to check the tide of nationalism or to defend and develop the empire as she had done in the past. It was possible for Labor to give independence to India, Pakistan, Burma, and Ceylon quickly and easily. The Conservatives, on the other hand, when in power during the 1950s reverted for a moment to older concepts in dealing with Egypt and the Suez Canal. This policy proved a failure. Thereafter, the Conservatives accepted the new order, which called for liberation of the colonies at a very rapid pace.

India

Nationalism in India, the origins of which we have traced,[8] increased greatly in intensity during the years following the First World War. When hostilities began in 1914 there had been a burst of loyalty and enthusiasm in India for the British cause. India had offered generous assistance, and many Indians had been brought into the civil service to take the place of British officials called to war duties in other areas. But as the war dragged on year after year, enthusiasm gave way to disillusionment. Muslims disliked fighting against their coreligionists, the Turks, and resented the harsh terms of peace imposed on Turkey. British officials, returning to positions in India after the war, displaced the Indians who had been doing their work. A new constitution granted to India in 1919 was regarded as disappointing, for it did little more than make Indian ministers responsible for the less important parts of local government. Public opinion, already irritable, was alienated by two other events. One was a series of statutes enlarging the powers of the government to suppress plots and conspiracies. These statutes were regarded as oppressive. The other was the Amritsar incident, a most unfortunate episode in which a British commander opened fire on an unarmed crowd that had assumed a threatening tone.

These were the circumstances which brought Mohandas K. Gandhi to the fore as the leader of the nationalist movement. Gandhi was a strange combination of saint and revolutionist, of holy man and cunning politician, modest yet dicta-

[8] See pages 700–701.

torial, gentle yet wholly unreasonable. He soon produced great changes. The nationalist movement had been largely confined to the educated classes, but he turned it into a movement of the people. He transformed the Congress party into a revolutionary body, pledged to overthrow the existing government by all peaceful means. The Congress became a kind of rival government to that of the British. Gandhi refused self-government by installments; he demanded it at once. It must be immediate, and it must be complete.

In 1919 Gandhi began the first of his disobedience campaigns. The people were instructed not to buy British goods and not to cooperate with the British government in any way. When in 1922 disobedience reached the stage of refusal to pay taxes, Gandhi was arrested, and his campaign temporarily subsided.

A new wave of nationalist revolt swept over India in 1927. The report of a British commission headed by Sir John Simon which recommended an extension of self-government on the local level was ignored, and in 1930 Gandhi launched a new disobedience campaign. He soon was arrested. Meanwhile, the Prime Minister, Ramsay MacDonald, who sympathized with Indian aspirations, held a series of round-table conferences between British ministers and Indian leaders. Very little was accomplished, but MacDonald, with Baldwin's support, obtained the passage of a new India Act in 1935. This act entrusted the whole field of local government to Indian ministers responsible to the provincial legislatures. It also envisaged a federal framework at the center, with a legislature and a Cabinet responsible to it, though the Viceroy still retained control of defense, foreign affairs, and religious policy. The portion of the act concerning provincial government went into effect in 1937 and made a fair beginning. The formation of the federal framework at the center was deferred, pending negotiations with the native princes, and was still in abeyance at the beginning of the Second World War.

Meanwhile, the Congress party was becoming more and more autocratic. It claimed to represent all India, to be the one true party of Indian nationalism, the sole heir of British power. No other party and no other leadership were to count in the India of the future. When the Congress party won elections to the provincial legislatures it refused to share power with any other party, and Congress members conducted themselves as the future rulers of India. This attitude greatly alarmed the Muslims. If the Congress was to dominate the government after independence was won, the Muslim position would be hopeless. Hence the Muslims drew together and improved the strength of their organization, the Muslim League. They found an able leader in the fiery and impressive Mr. Jinnah. Forming the Muslim League into a compact fighting party, Jinnah declared that the Muslims would accept no constitution of either Hindu or British manufacture but would achieve their own destiny in their own way. The Muslims, he asserted, were not an Indian minority but a separate nation. Those parts of the country with a clear Muslim majority of population should be formed into a separate state cut off from the rest of the country. Thus the policy of partition, which resulted later in the creation of Pakistan, came into existence.

During the Second World War the Congress party, refusing to fight for Britain until India was free, demanded immediate independence. The Muslim League, taking a middle course, did not tell its members to stay out of the war effort but refused to cooperate officially unless its policy of partition was accepted. The British made many efforts to win over the major parties. At one point Sir Stafford Cripps flew to India and offered complete independence after the war, with a settlement to be devised by the Indians, if only they would cooperate in the war effort. His offer was rejected. In 1942 Gandhi prepared for a new disobedience campaign, though the Japanese army was now on India's eastern frontier. He was arrested, and the British remained in full control of the country. Many thousands of Indians, it should be added, played their part in the war as soldiers and civilians.

The Labor party, which came to power at the end of the war, was prepared to grant India its independence. By a strange paradox, the problem now was to bring Hindus and Muslims together in some sort of government which both would accept. Negotiations continued with no end in sight. In February 1947, in the midst of Britain's coal shortage, Mr. Attlee declared that Britain would withdraw from India, whatever the situation might be in that country, at a date no later than June 1948. Even so, Hindus and Muslims could not agree. To Lord Mountbatten, the last British Viceroy, partition appeared the only possible solution. It was, moreover, a solution that must come quickly in order to prevent a civil war. With great skill Mountbatten won both the Hindu Congress and the Muslim League to accept his proposals. On August 15, 1947, India was divided into the two independent states of India and Pakistan. They agreed to remain within the Commonwealth with Dominion status. India became a republic in 1950; Pakistan, in 1956.

Egypt

Although Britain recognized with promptness and decision that independence for India was inevitable, she was slower to see the necessity for a comparable change of policy toward the Middle East. Britain was, of course, intensely aware of the importance of the Suez Canal; having controlled the Arab world during the war and having defended Egypt against Mussolini and Hitler, she was inclined to think of the Middle East in the old imperial terms. In the Suez crisis of October-November 1956 she acted as she might have done in the late nineteenth century. The result was a sharp reminder that times had changed.

Part of the background of this crisis lay in the violence of Egyptian nationalism, which rose to white heat at the end of the First World War. Negotiations for some kind of settlement came to nothing. Thereupon in 1922 Britain took the unusual course of declaring unilaterally that Egypt was an independent country, though with certain reservations: Britain insisted that the passage of shipping through the canal must be secure; she reserved the right to defend Egypt against aggression, thus warning other powers to keep away; and the administration of the Anglo-Egyptian Sudan was to remain in her hands. Egypt refused these terms. But in 1936, alarmed at Mussolini's attack on Ethiopia, the Egyptians concluded a treaty with Britain. Egyptian independence was confirmed; relations were thrown into the form of a military alliance by which Britain might use Egyptian airfields and the naval base at Alexandria and might occupy the canal zone.

This alliance was in operation during the Second World War. But once the war was ended, a new wave of nationalism arose in Egypt and riots and demonstrations against the presence of British troops became commonplace as the Egyptians sought to modify the treaty of 1936. The Labor government, hoping to preserve the military alliance, agreed to withdraw British troops from Cairo and from the Nile Delta, though not from the canal zone. But the Egyptians became more and more hostile and terrorists harassed the British troops remaining along the canal. After a number of military *coup d'états* in Egypt, the dominant power in 1954 was the Premier, Lieutenant Colonel Nasser, a fiery army officer and ardent nationalist, bold, shrewd, and cunning. Britain now agreed, very reluctantly, to withdraw her troops within the next two years. By June of 1956 British soldiers had evacuated the canal zone, leaving one of the world's largest military bases in the hands of civilian caretakers.

Palestine

Events in Palestine also formed part of the background of the Suez crisis. Unfortunately for the British, their mandate in Palestine, begun in 1920, was an impossible one that contained a basic contradiction. Britain undertook to build a Jewish national state in Palestine and at the same time to foster the free development of the Arabs, who hated the Jewish immigrants. Hostility between the two peoples became uncontrollable after the Second World War. Various plans for a binational state, for partition, and for cooperation with the United States in finding a solution came to nothing, and in 1948 Britain brought her mandate to an inglorious end by withdrawing her forces and leaving Jews and Arabs to fight out the issue among themselves. A number of Arab countries, including Egypt, made war on the Jews. But the Jews proved to be surprisingly tough; they pushed the Arabs back and established the independent state of Israel. The Arabs smarted under this defeat, and Nasser, when he came to power, made the destruction of Israel one of his prime objectives. In 1955, by a sudden deal wtih Russia, he obtained a large quantity of armaments from Czechoslovakia; he then stepped up Egyptian raids into Israeli territory. A new war appeared most likely.

The Suez Crisis

The United States and Britain, alarmed at Nasser's action in obtaining Russian arms, agreed to help Egypt build a dam at Aswan on the Nile. When the United States suddenly withdrew her offer, Nasser reacted with furious violence. On July 26, 1956, only a few weeks after British forces had evacuated the canal zone, Nasser proclaimed that Egypt would nationalize the Suez Canal, that it would be operated by Egypt, and that the tolls would be used to build the Aswan Dam. There was great alarm in London and Paris and great pressure to intervene. Suddenly Israel determined to attack the Egyptians before they learned to use their Russian arms. On October 29, Israeli troops pushed toward the canal, easily routing the Egyptians.

The next day England and France issued an ultimatum to both parties demanding that they cease hostilities and withdraw ten miles from each side of the canal. Egypt was asked to allow Anglo-French forces to protect the canal by occupying key points in the canal zone. Israel agreed to these demands but Egypt rejected them. Britain and France then bombarded Egyptian airfields and sent troops into the canal zone on November 5. World opinion was hostile, Russia threatened to intervene, and the United States, angry because she had not been consulted, denounced the action of her allies. British opinion was divided. Under enormous pressure, Eden decided on November 6 to withdraw British forces if troops were sent by the United Nations to protect the peace in Egypt. To this all parties eventually agreed, and the crisis subsided. The episode was most unfortunate for Britain. It damaged her prestige among the Arabs, it exalted Nasser as an Arab hero when his weakness might well have been exposed by Israel, it left bitterness between England and America, and it showed beyond question that imperialism of the old kind was not only out of date but dangerous.

FROM EMPIRE TO COMMONWEALTH

Changes of a fundamental character have taken place in the structure of the British Empire during the twentieth century. The major units of the old empire, both the Dominions and many former dependencies, have become sovereign states, loosely associated together as a Commonwealth of Nations. Since 1947 the term "Dominion" has fallen into disuse. All sovereign states are known as "Members of the Commonwealth" and include many Asiatic and African peoples as well as those of European stock. There are, of course, a large number of British dependencies, but these are so rapidly achieving their independence that the empire is in a state of swift and basic transition. The word "Commonwealth" is now used as a comprehensive term to include all British territories, whatever their status.

Development of the Dominions

At the beginning of the century the empire was divided sharply into two parts. The first consisted of the Dominions of Canada, Newfoundland, Australia, New Zealand, and South Africa. Except for Newfoundland, where there were few inhabitants,[9] the Dominions contained large permanent populations predominantly of British origin, though there were many French Canadians and the Boers in South Africa outnumbered the British. The Dominions were self-governing in their domestic affairs. The other portion of the empire was composed of a large number of dependencies inhabited by non-European peoples. In general, the dependencies were not considered as candidates for self-government. India was perhaps an exception, for the British talked as if India might one day become self-governing, though the British timetable, if left to itself, would have been a slow one.

But though the Dominions had achieved self-government in their internal affairs, they had not done so in their foreign policy. Diplomatically the empire functioned as a unit, with policy formulated in London. The Dominions, for example, were automatically at war in 1914 when Great Britain declared war on Germany. This conflict, in which they played so notable a part, increased their sense of independence and nationhood; the time had come when they must either be allowed to cooperate in constructing a common foreign policy or be permitted to develop foreign policies of their own. The second alternative took place. The Dominions secured separate representation at the Peace Conference at Paris, they were entrusted with the administration of mandated territories, and they became members of the League of Nations. Ireland, a dominion since 1922, wished to become a republic. During the 1920s Canada developed her own diplomatic service and sent an ambassador to Washington in 1927. When the Dominions obtained control of their foreign policy, they became sovereign states. Their position was clearly phrased in a famous resolution drafted by Lord Balfour at the Imperial Conference in 1926. The Dominions, this statement read,

> are autonomous communities within the British Empire, equal in status, in no way subordinate one to another in any aspect of their domestic or external affairs, though united by a common allegiance to the Crown, and freely associated as members of the British Commonwealth of Nations.

[9] Newfoundland ceased to be a dominion in 1934 and reverted to the status of a Crown colony. In 1949 it became a Canadian province.

The Statute of Westminster in 1931 gave parliamentary sanction to this statement and spelled out some of its implications by repealing certain laws infringing on the sovereignty of the Dominions. No British statute was applicable to a dominion without its consent, any alteration in the succession to the Crown must be approved by the Dominions, a dominion might withdraw from the Commonwealth if it so desired. The new diversity in foreign policy was clearly evident when war again broke out in 1939. Australia and New Zealand considered themselves automatically at war with Germany after the British ultimatum to Hitler. But the decision to enter the war was taken in Canada and in South Africa only after a vote in their parliaments; and in South Africa, where the Prime Minister was opposed to war, he resigned and was succeeded by one in favor of it. Ireland remained neutral, and in 1949 left the Commonwealth and became a republic.

The Commonwealth of Nations

The grant of independence to India and Pakistan in 1947 proved to be a new departure in the history of the Commonwealth. In the first place, the decision was taken to offer these countries the status of dominions, which they decided to accept. This meant that Britain would treat them as she treated the older Dominions; thus a pattern was set for dealing with other non-European nations within the empire as they received their independence from it. Few persons realized in 1947 how numerous the new independent nations were to be. Secondly, India expressed her desire to become a republic and yet remain within the Commonwealth. Such an arrangement was possible only by abandoning the common allegiance to the Crown which had hitherto been regarded as essential to membership in the Commonwealth. A meeting of Commonwealth prime ministers in 1949, recognizing that India was to become a sovereign, independent republic, noted:

> The government of India have declared and affirmed India's desire to continue her full membership of the Commonwealth of Nations and her acceptance of the King as the symbol of the free association of its independent member nations and as such the Head of the Commonwealth.
>
> The governments of the other countries of the Commonwealth, the basis of whose membership of the Commonwealth is not hereby changed, accept and recognize India's continuing membership in accordance with the terms of this declaration.[10]

Thus the King became a symbol of the free association of member nations; he held the title of Head of the Commonwealth, the title assumed by Queen Elizabeth II when she succeeded to the throne in 1952. In that year it was decided that each nation might use a form of title suitable to its own circumstances.

Following the Indian pattern, other portions of the empire, as they became independent, sovereign states, could, if they so desired, remain within the Commonwealth whether they were monarchies or republics. Some have declined membership—Burma in 1948, Ireland in 1949, the Sudan in 1956—but most of them have not done so. Their numbers have been very large. Ceylon became independent and a member of the Commonwealth in 1948. Then, after a lapse

[10] Quoted in Arthur C. Turner, "The Commonwealth: Evolution or Dissolution?" *Current History*, XLVI (May 1964), p. 260.

of some years, others followed in rapid succession: Ghana (Gold Coast; 1957), the first Negro member; the Federation of Malaya (1957); the Federation of Nigeria (1960); Cyprus (1960); Sierra Leone (1961); Tanganyika (1961); Jamaica (1962); Trinidad and Tobago (1962); Uganda (1962); Zanzibar (1963); Kenya (1963); Malawi (Nyasaland; 1964); Zambia (Northern Rhodesia; 1964); the State of Malta (1964); Gambia (1965); Botswana (Bechuanaland; 1966); Lesotho (Basutoland; 1966); Guyana (1966); and Barbados (1966). The nations that were once the older Dominions are far outnumbered by the newcomers.

The Future of the Commonwealth

The question arises whether the Commonwealth is merely a step in the dissolution of the empire and will grow weak and meaningless in the future, or whether, as a kind of smaller United Nations, it will increase in influence and effectiveness as a force in world affairs. One must confess that the future of the Commonwealth does not appear as bright today as it did some years ago.

The Commonwealth displays both strength and weakness. The ties of kindly sentiment toward Britain among overseas populations of British origin are a potent force. The voluntary nature of the Commonwealth promotes good will. Anglo-Indian relations have greatly improved since India received her independence. And if sentimental attachment can hardly be expected of nations like Tanzania[11] and Malawi, these countries have acquired habits of cooperating with Britain and of looking to her for leadership.

Economic bonds are also strong. Almost half of British foreign trade, import and export, is with the nations of the Commonwealth. The sale of raw materials to Britain is vital to some Commonwealth countries. On the other hand, although Britain can help with planning and technology, the day is past when she can send large sums of money overseas for investment in colonial enterprises. Moreover, economic ties with the Commonwealth have been placed under strain in recent years as Britain has looked toward Europe and toward the Common Market for new trading opportunities. This is a development which has caused alarm in the Commonwealth as well as in Britain. Yet Britain must seek economic advantage where she can find it, a policy followed consistently in the past by most of the colonies.

Political ties among the nations of the Commonwealth have been strengthened by the desire for union in a world dominated by the United States and Russia. But in the event of a third world war, Britain could not defend the Commonwealth in any adequate way. Indeed, some of the most important Commonwealth countries—Canada, Australia, and New Zealand—are linked to some extent with the United States for purposes of defense. Despite efforts at equality all round, Britain cannot in practice treat all the members of the Commonwealth alike. Secret information sent to Canada, her NATO ally, can hardly be imparted to Gambia, one of the newest and smallest of the Commonwealth nations. It may be that eventually an inner and an outer circle of Commonwealth nations will emerge, though Britain does not desire such a development.

The gravest danger to the cohesion of the Commonwealth at the present time appears to be the racial conflict between whites and blacks in Africa. Sentimental bonds as well as economic and political considerations are lost in this

[11] Tanganyika and Zanzibar united under the name of Tanzania in April 1964.

fierce struggle. South Africa, where the whites are following a policy of domination over the blacks, left the Commonwealth in 1961—or, rather, was virtually expelled from it—over this issue. The same problem troubled the central African countries of Nyasaland and Northern and Southern Rhodesia. These lands were united into a federation in 1953 in order to promote their economic development, but the racial issue has torn the federation apart. Nyasaland, almost wholly African in population, dreaded domination by the whites in Rhodesia, whose ideas are similar to those of the whites in South Africa. A strong African party in Nyasaland demanded separation from the federation, and the country became independent (as Malawi) in 1964. In Southern Rhodesia, on the other hand, some 224,000 whites are determined to maintain supremacy over about 3,750,000 blacks. Friction between Southern Rhodesia and the Cabinet in London over racial policy became so serious in 1965 that on November 11 Southern Rhodesia severed connection with the empire and declared herself to be an independent nation. The result of this unilateral action is as yet uncertain, though it clearly arouses apprehensions concerning the future of the Commonwealth. Harold Wilson, who had to deal with the problem, refused to use force. When the concessions he offered were rejected, he secured the application of economic sanctions. But the revolutionary regime in Rhodesia is still intact. Further negotiations will undoubtedly be attempted by the Conservative Prime Minister, Edward Heath. Northern Rhodesia (Zambia) contains about 76,000 whites, who can hardly hope to avoid subjection in a nation with a population of 3,500,000 Negroes.

The prospects for the Commonwealth have also been clouded by other developments: the bitter quarrel between India and Pakistan over the possession of Kashmir; the danger that nations controlled by Africans will unite against South Africa and Southern Rhodesia; the military *coups* in several African states and the dreadful civil war in Nigeria.

The Commonwealth of Nations is a unique experiment in combining liberty with voluntary cooperation among peoples of very different kinds. It is based on noble and generous instincts as well as on necessity and the hope of profit. Yet, after a period of prestige and influence, it faces a doubtful future.

SOCIETY IN CONTEMPORARY BRITAIN

For almost a decade after the end of the war in 1945 life was dull and depressing to many Englishmen. The demobilized soldier or sailor came home to austerity, to an acute housing shortage, to more meager rations than he had had in the armed forces. The winter of 1946–1947, as we have seen, was so severe that it brought new hardships. Despite cold weather, the domestic use of electricity was forbidden during the working day in factories; the ration of gasoline for private automobiles was suspended. Later in the year a crisis in foreign exchange brought a ban on travel abroad. Although the government was forever urging greater productivity, the more attractive articles produced were reserved for export and could not be bought by the British public. So severe was the shortage in housing that for a time almost all building was forbidden except the construction of schools, factories, and houses for the working classes. Local authorities, attempting to provide these houses, built ugly prefabricated dwellings that were not intended to last more than ten years. Permanent houses met higher standards, but style and embellishments were sacrificed to utility. It is small wonder that such austerity, after the strain of a great war, dampened the spirits of the people.

Nonetheless the working classes were far better off than before the war. Wages, which had been rising rapidly during the war years, continued to improve after the peace. Moreover, unskilled laborers were now better paid, so that their wages drew closer to those of skilled artisans. The welfare state brought many benefits, especially in medical attention. Yet by far the most important cause of growing prosperity among the lower classes was full employment. After the peace in 1919, as we know, the economy had slumped and the result had been widespread unemployment. But in 1945 the situation was entirely different. At the end of World War II a tremendous amount of building was essential, city planning was in the air, manufacturers were urged to produce exportable goods at top speed, the demand for coal was enormous, and both political parties—following Keynesian economics—were committed to full employment as a policy of state. Nor were labor-saving devices widely available. Thus the working classes—backed by strong trade unions—stood to gain greatly in the postwar period. Seebohm Rowntree, who conducted inquiries into poverty in the city of York over a period of many years, had found in 1936 that 31 percent of the working population was below a given poverty line; in 1950 he found a mere 2.77 percent.

Fashionable society did not emerge as quickly as it had done in the 1920s, partly because the royal family discouraged ostentation and partly because social functions could hardly be held at hotels while the price of a dinner was restricted to 5s. The aristocracy, as well as the working classes, faced a housing problem. Country houses, some of them enormous, were taxed heavily, required an army of servants, and produced little or no income. The only way that many owners could maintain them was to open them to the public and charge a small admission fee. Or they could be sold to schools or nursing homes or given to the nation, in which case they were administered by the National Trust, a public body that cares for ancient monuments. Many upper-class families were now content with handsome London flats.

Foreign travel, stimulated by the automobile and improved roads on the Continent, became popular as soon as it was permitted; vacationers favored Italy, Spain, and Yugoslavia. British films were superior to those before the war. Some notable films were based upon the novels of Charles Dickens and upon Shakespeare's plays. The annual Edinburgh Festival of Music and Drama, which drew talent from all over the world, began in 1947. Two public celebrations, the Festival of Britain, a world's fair held in 1951, and the coronation of Queen Elizabeth II in the year following, may be taken to mark the transition from postwar austerity to a happier and more affluent period.

The population of Great Britain in 1961 was 51,283,892, a figure indicating only moderate growth but laying to rest the fear of a sharp decline, which had often been predicted in the 1930s. At that time the birth rate was decreasing; but it shot forward in the years after the war, though it was leveling off by 1960. A notable feature of the postwar period was the influx into Britain of colored immigrants from the British West Indies, West Africa, India, and Pakistan until they numbered some 800,000 persons in 1965; the highly controversial question arose as to whether some bar should be erected against a further increase in their number. The proportion of the people living in cities remained steady since 1931 at about eighty percent of the population; this fact would indicate a slight absolute increase in those living in rural areas.

Development of Urban Areas

A striking feature of contemporary Britain has been the development of the conurbation, which is the urban area formed when a number of neighboring towns expand toward each other until they become one continuous city. The term conurbation is used for seven areas: Greater London, West Midlands (Birmingham), Southeast Lancashire (Manchester), Merseyside (Liverpool), West Yorkshire (Leeds), Tyneside (Newcastle), and Clydeside (Glasgow). Greater London, containing over 8 million persons in 1961, is, of course, unique. New office buildings of streamlined glass and modern design have made their appearance, as have also skyscrapers such as the Shell Building, the Hilton Hotel, and Vickers House. A telecommunications tower 580 feet in height has been erected by the General Post Office. The parks have not been disturbed; Kew Gardens and the Royal Park at Windsor have been enlarged.

City planning became an absolute necessity. It was essential in bombed-out cities such as Coventry and Plymouth and even more essential in London. The first plan for Greater London, prepared by Patrick Abercrombie in 1944, was conceived in terms of four concentric circles. The first was inner London, from which some factories and many factory workers were to be removed; the second a ring of old suburbs, to be left much as it was; the third a green belt ring of small towns and villages in rural settings; the fourth an outer circle of existing towns and of new towns to be built under an act of 1946. This plan was only partially fulfilled. A million factory workers were removed from the inner ring, but for the most part they settled in the outer rings and their places were quickly taken by people working in offices. A more recent plan called for an extension of the green belt ring to restrict the growth of the metropolis, more new towns, and an even more distant circle of large new cities. This plan was really a regional one for southeast England.

In the new towns, which are perhaps twenty-five miles from the center of the city, an effort has been made not only to build houses, schools, and shopping centers, but also to locate factories. Some sixteen of these new towns are now in existence, eight of them around London. They are attractive communities, fresh, neat, and well planned; the factories are built in good modern designs; there is a picturesque blending of old and new—one may find an Anglo-Saxon church around the corner from an electronics factory. Another aspect of city planning is an attack on the problems of modern traffic. Anyone who has seen the congestion in Oxford Street in London knows what these problems can be. The solution lies in the establishment of shopping centers from which automobiles are excluded, of easier access to these centers, and of outer roads for trucks or lorries. Raised streets with parking facilities below are possible in hilly cities such as Edinburgh. There has also been regional planning for large areas.

Opportunity and the Quality of Life

The lower classes continued to improve their economic and social status during the 1950s and 1960s. Some of the figures are startling. Real wages rose some sixteen percent in the 1950s, so that in 1959 the average male worker was earning over £13 a week and almost half of the working families enjoyed a yearly income of £850. In 1964 the average wage for men was £18 2s. 2d. per week and for women £8 19s. 1d. There is evidence, however, that these figures give a false impression. A high income for working families almost always meant that two or even three members of the family were gainfully employed, often making extra money by overtime. While the average was high, some forty-two percent of families had an annual income of less than £500. Working people, of course, had very little capital, though the government fostered home owner-ship by loans and subsidies. In the early 1960s some two percent of the people owned nearly half the wealth of the country. Nonetheless, the dreadful London slums of the nineteenth century and the degradation of the lowest elements of society in that age were now things of the past.

Few features of modern society in Britain have contributed more to the general welfare than has the National Health Service. It has been hailed as a notable achievement. Although it was denounced at first by the medical pro-fession, official inquiries into its functioning and costs have concluded that it has not been widely abused and, considering its accomplishments, has not been unreasonably expensive. The income of the doctors who work in it has been a serious difficulty. Speaking very broadly, doctors have not been well paid in England, but under the Health Service many have felt that they were more poorly paid than ever. The problem has been investigated a good deal and has been the subject of many negotiations between the government and the British Medical Association. But although the income of physicians has been increased, the problem is far from solution. A massive program of building new hospitals and new clinics was announced by the Health Service in 1962.

The changes in English education have been tremendous, though this has not been true of elementary education, where the problems were largely those of coping with a growing number of children. Issues in secondary education have been more controversial. The system in operation before the war sorted out the children at the age of eleven and placed them according to their abilities and interests in grammar schools, or technical schools, or so-called modern schools which combined characteristics of the other two. This system was criti-cized on the ground that a child's capabilities could not be judged accurately when the child was only eleven years of age. An answer has been found in the establishment of comprehensive schools which offer all types of education and permit children to pass from one type to another as their abilities appear to warrant. A great deal of discretion is allowed the local authorities in determining policy. The school-leaving age has been raised to fifteen by an act of 1944; a further rise to sixteen, recommended in 1959, is now about to go into effect.

It is at the university level, however, that an educational explosion has taken place. In 1961 more than 100,000 students were registered in British universities, twice the number of those before the war. Moreover, four fifths of these postwar students were receiving aid from the government; indeed, the government was paying more than half the cost of all university education. A large number of new universities have been founded since the war, including those at Keele, Southampton, Hull, Exeter, Leicester, Brighton, York, Norwich, Lancaster, Colchester, Canterbury, and Coventry. These often take their name from the county in which they are located. Together with Oxford and Cambridge and with a number of universities founded in the nineteenth and early twentieth centuries, they provide Great Britain with a superior system of higher education. Moreover, the children of working-class parents now have an opportunity for university training equal to that of children from wealthy and influential homes.

Such fundamental and far-reaching changes leave the future of the public schools in some doubt. In 1964 the Labor Party daringly proposed to absorb them into the national system.

Leisure and Entertainment

The growing affluence of Britain has created a greater amount of leisure for all classes and also new ways in which that leisure can be used. In the suburban areas around the large towns one finds a lively set of well-to-do business people who live in fine houses with extensive grounds; they form what has been called the cocktail belt. Social life, as with the same set in America, centers in golf and country clubs; weekend guests devote their time to golf, tennis, picnics, and parties. Some of the wealthier suburbanites belong to fox hunts; there is much riding, with ponies for the children. Thus country life persists, though it is jazzier than of old.

Middle- and lower-class families must live more frugally than this, but here also old forms of entertainment are giving way to new. The interest in cricket matches and football games has somewhat abated; attendance at the cinema has declined. The reason for this change is the television, which was introduced in the 1950s and has become so popular that nine out of every ten families are said to possess a set. Until 1955 broadcasting of this type was a monopoly of the BBC. In that year, after violent debate, the decision was taken to permit commercial television, though the programs were to be carefully supervised by an Independent Television Authority.

Older forms of amusement have other rivals. Automobile racing, both by professionals and by amateurs who do such things as race up high hills, is popular. These meets are not the fastidious gatherings that attend horse races at Ascot or Goodwood. The crowd is noisy, the air foul with gasoline fumes, the audience composed to a considerable extent of young men in sweaters and girls in pants. Another sport is bowling, which can be made a family affair and offers a hilarious evening at low cost. Gambling laws have been modified to permit bingo, a game that supplies a small thrill without danger of great loss. Sailing has also grown popular. There are numerous yacht clubs; a growing problem is reminiscent of the automobile—where does one park one's yacht?

Foreign travel has grown enormously, for rich and poor alike. An American staying in a London hotel is surprised when the chambermaid tells him that she and her husband are about to take a holiday in Spain. To rent a foreign villa for a few weeks is quite the vogue. Travels in southern Europe have produced an interest in wine, in sidewalk cafes, in foreign restaurants, and in foreign clothes such as Italian shoes and Paris fashions. In fact, London has become a center for designers of women's clothes, which are far more stylish than they used to be. Dancing is very popular. Like other amusements, it lends itself to the formation of clubs.

As in other countries, the young people show tastes that their elders find difficult to understand. The craving for popular music, the Mods, Rockers, Teddy Boys, and Beatniks, the worshipers of the Beatles, the fashion of mini skirts for girls and of long hair for young men—attest to the determination of youth to go its own way. The moral code is more permissive than in the past.

Intellectual entertainment is also available. The London theaters present good drama and are well attended. Of special note are the National Theatre Company which puts on good drama at the Old Vic, the Royal Shakespeare

Company playing both at Stratford on Avon and at the Aldwych Theatre in London, and the Sadler's Wells Ballet, incorporated in the Royal Ballet in 1957. London has become a great musical center. Orchestral concerts, recitals by outstanding artists, and a full season of opera attract large crowds. The University of London, by far the largest university in Britain, adds to the intellectual climate of the city, as do famous libraries, museums, and art galleries. One should also mention the Third Program of the BBC, which broadcasts literary and dramatic performances of high merit. Although much of the press is sensational, many newspapers, as well as weeklies and quarterlies, contain material for the serious reader.[12]

Who can deny that Great Britain has met with marked success in solving the tremendous problems of the twentieth century and in creating a more humane, enlightened, and equalitarian society than it could boast a century ago? England also is producing a new type of Englishman, less conventional and less inhibited than of old.

[12] Alfred F. Havighurst, *Twentieth Century Britain,* pp. 491–533; Henry Pelling, *Modern Britain 1885–1955,* pp. 180–193; David Thomson, *England in the Twentieth Century 1914–1963* (London: J. Cape, 1964), pp. 214–239; Anthony Sampson, *Anatomy of Britain* (New York: Harper & Row, 1962).

BOOKS FOR FURTHER READING

The purpose of this list of books is not to supply a bibliography of English history or even to point out the most important contributions to scholarship in various fields. My purpose is merely to indicate a number of books that would be useful to the undergraduate who wishes to continue his reading beyond the narrow limits of the text. Each section begins with a number of surveys and then proceeds to books on various topics and books that are more advanced, though I have excluded many important works that seemed too technical or too specialized for my purpose. An attempt has been made to mention recent books, for books on English history become out of date much more quickly than they did half a century ago. Most books cover a longer period than do the individual chapters of the text, and hence the bibliographical essay has been divided into sections, each covering the material in a group of chapters.

BIBLIOGRAPHIES AND BOOKS OF REFERENCE

The standard bibliography for medieval England is still Charles Gross, *The Sources and Literature of English History* (New York: McKay, 1915). It is a critical and comprehensive guide, though in need of being brought up to date. A *Bibliography of British History: Tudor Period 1485–1603* by Conyers Read (Oxford: Clarendon Press, 1959) is a model bibliography—extensive, well arranged, and easy to use. A companion volume, Godfrey Davies, *Bibliography of British History: Stuart Period 1603–1714* (Oxford: Clarendon Press, 1928), is scholarly but less practical. A second edition, revised by Mary Freer Keeler, appeared in 1970. This series is continued by Stanley Pargellis and D. J. Medley, *Bibliography of British History: The Eighteenth Century 1714–1789* (Oxford: Clarendon Press, 1951). Two English scholars are preparing volumes dealing with the nineteenth century.

The Conference on British Studies, a group of scholars centered in New York City, is sponsoring a series of short bibliographical handbooks, of which two have appeared: Mortimer Levine, *Tudor England 1485–1603* (Cambridge: Cambridge University Press, 1968), and Josef L. Altholz, *Victorian England 1837–1901* (Cambridge: Cambridge University Press, 1970). These excellent little volumes are useful and practical.

Three bibliographies dealing with the seventeenth century are: James Thayer Gerould, *Sources of English History of the Seventeenth Century, 1603–1689, in the University of Minnesota Library* (Minneapolis: University of Minnesota Press, 1921);

Wilbur Cortez Abbott, *A Bibliography of Oliver Cromwell* (Cambridge, Mass.: Harvard University Press, 1929); and Clyde Leclare Grosse, *A Bibliography of British History, 1660–1760* (Chicago: University of Chicago Press, 1939).

Annual Bulletins of Historical Literature and short bibliographies on special topics, such as Charles Loch Mowat, *British History Since 1926: A Select Bibliography* (London, 1960), are published by the Historical Association, a British society of teachers of history. The Royal Historical Society in London publishes an annual volume of *Writings on British History* compiled by A. Taylor Milne and published by Jonathan Cape. The best way to keep abreast of current publications is to follow the book reviews, book lists, and occasional bibliographical articles in such journals as the *English Historical Review, History,* the *Historical Journal* (formerly the *Cambridge Historical Journal*), the *Economic History Review,* the *American Historical Review,* and the *Journal of Modern History.*

An indispensable aid to students of English history is the *Dictionary of National Biography* which contains short biographies of persons important in British history. The articles vary in quality and there are a good many errors. A new edition is now proposed. The *Oxford English Dictionary* is also indispensable. A *Handbook of British Chronology* edited by Sir Maurice Powicke (London: Royal Historical Society, 1961) contains useful lists of rulers, high officials, bishops, peers, and parliaments. Vicary Gibbs, ed., G. E. Cokayne, *The Complete Peerage* (London: St. Catherine Press, 1910–1959, 13 vols.), provides biographical sketches of members of the nobility; for the gentry see G. E. Cokayne, *The Complete Baronetage* (Exeter: W. Pollard, 1900–1906, 5 vols.), and W. Shaw, *The Knights of England* (London: Sherratt and Hughes, 1906, 2 vols.). W. R. Shepherd, *Historical Atlas* (New York: Barnes & Noble, 1964), is a standard work.

There is no history of England in a single volume that can be called satisfactory. The most readable is George Macaulay Trevelyan, *A History of England* (New York: McKay, 1937), a sound and workmanlike volume suggesting many interesting lines of thought.

THE PERIOD BEFORE 1066

PREHISTORY

Jacquetta and Christopher Hawkes, *Prehistoric Britain* (London: Chatto & Windus, 1942), is a fascinating survey of early man in Britain. It is based upon wide research and yet is free from technical terminology. Other interesting books dealing with this theme are Grahame Clark, *Prehistoric Britain* (London: Batsford, 1962), R. C. J. Atkinson, *Stonehenge* (London: H. Hamilton, 1956), K. P. Oakley, *Man the Tool-maker* (London: British Museum, 1949), T. G. E. Powell, *The Celts* (London: Thames and Hudson, 1958), and several books by Sir Cyril Fred Fox, *Pattern and Purpose: Early Celtic Art in Britain* (Cardiff, Wales: National Museum, 1958), *Life and Death in the Bronze Age: An Archaeologist's Fieldwork* (London: Routledge, 1959), and *The Personality of Britain: Its Influence on Inhabitant and Invader in Prehistoric and Early Historic Times* (Cardiff, Wales: National Museum, 1947).

ROMAN BRITAIN

Peter Hunter Blair, *Roman Britain and Early England 55* B.C.–A.D. *871* (Edinburgh: T. Nelson, 1963), an excellent introduction, is the first volume of a new series which when complete will cover all English history. A. L. F. Rivet, *Town and Country in Roman Britain* (London: Hutchinson's University Library, 1958), and I. A. Richmond, *Roman Britain* (Harmondsworth, Middlesex: Penguin Books, 1955), are interesting books. A. R. Burn, *Agricola and Roman Britain* (London: English Universities Press, 1953), and J. Collingwood Bruce, *Handbook to the Roman Wall* (London: Longmans, 1947), deal with special topics. A longer and more detailed work is R. G. Collingwood and J. N. L. Myres, *Roman Britain and the English Settlements* (Oxford: Clarendon Press, 1937). This is the first volume of the Oxford History of England, the best modern series dealing at length with English history. Individual volumes are cited in the appropriate sections below. All are provided with elaborate bibliographies.

ANGLO-SAXON ENGLAND

Good introductions to the history of the Anglo-Saxon period may be found in the later chapters of Peter Hunter Blair, *Roman Britain and Early England*, cited above, in Christopher Brooke, *From Alfred to Henry III 871–1272* (Edinburgh: T. Nelson, 1961), in Helen Cam, *England before Elizabeth* (London: Hutchinson's University Library, 1950), and in Peter Hunter Blair, *An Introduction to Anglo-Saxon England* (Cambridge: Cambridge University Press, 1956). A work of high quality, G. O. Sayles, *The Medieval Foundations of England* (London: Methuen, 1950), begins with chapters on the government, the agriculture, and the social structure of the Anglo-Saxons. The later chapters in R. G. Collingwood and J. N. L. Myres, *Roman Britain and the English Settlements*, cited above, are important. Of fundamental value is the excellent volume by Sir Frank Stenton, *Anglo-Saxon England* (Oxford: Clarendon Press, 1947). This is not an easy book to read, but it is one that repays study.

Social and economic conditions are well described in Dorothy Whitelock, *The Beginnings of English Society* (Harmondsworth, Middlesex: Penguin Books, 1952), in H. R. Loyn, *Anglo-Saxon England and the Norman Conquest* (New York: St. Martin's, 1963), and in C. S. and C. S. Orwin, *The Open Fields* (Oxford: Clarendon Press, 1954). The last of these books is important for all of medieval agriculture. Bryce Lyon, *A Constitutional and Legal History of Medieval England* (New York: Harper & Row, 1960), and J. E. A. Jolliffe, *The Constitutional History of Medieval England* (London: A. & C. Black, 1961), deal with Anglo-Saxon government. Documents are found in Carl Stephenson and Frederick George Marcham, *Sources of English Constitutional History* (New York: Harper & Row, 1937). For the church, see E. S. Duckett, *Anglo-Saxon Saints and Scholars* (New York: Macmillan, 1948), and John Godfrey, *The Church in Anglo-Saxon England* (Cambridge: Cambridge University Press, 1962).

1066 TO 1307

SURVEYS AND POLITICAL HISTORIES

An excellent survey both of political narrative and of social life and institutions is provided by Christopher Brooke, *From Alfred to Henry III 871–1272*, cited above. Other surveys include Charles Homer Haskins, *The Normans in European History* (Boston: Houghton Mifflin, 1915), a famous series of lectures, H. R. Loyn, *The Norman Conquest* (London: Hutchinson's University Library, 1965), Frank Barlow, *The Feudal Kingdom of England 1042–1216* (New York: McKay, 1955), and G. W. S. Barrow, *Feudal Britain: The Completion of the Medieval Kingdoms 1066–1314* (London: E. Arnold, 1956). The last of these volumes includes a discussion of the Celtic borderlands. Longer accounts are found in three volumes of the Oxford History: Sir Frank Stenton, *Anglo-Saxon England*, cited above, which concludes with a section on the Conquest; Austin Lane Poole, *From Domesday Book to Magna Carta 1087–1216* (Oxford: Clarendon Press, 1955), a lucid and valuable account; and Sir Maurice Powicke, *The Thirteenth Century 1216–1307* (Oxford: Clarendon Press, 1962), a brilliant book, though not one for the beginner.

David C. Douglas, *William the Conqueror: The Norman Impact upon England* (Berkeley: University of California Press, 1964), is the standard biography, superseding F. M. Stenton, *William the Conqueror and the Rule of the Normans* (New York: Putnam, 1908). Frank Barlow, *William I and the Norman Conquest* (New York: Macmillan, 1965), is a short, readable life. There are two lives of Henry II, both written some time ago, Mrs. J. R. Green, *Henry II* (London: Macmillan, 1905), and L. F. Salzman, *Henry II* (Boston: Houghton Mifflin, 1914). Two excellent lives of Henry's wife supplement each other: Amy Kelly, *Eleanor of Aquitaine and the Four Kings* (Cambridge, Mass.: Harvard University Press, 1950; New York: Knopf, 1958), and Curtis Howe Walker, *Eleanor of Aquitaine* (Chapel Hill: University of North Carolina Press, 1950). Useful also for political history are J. E. A. Jolliffe, *Angevin Kingship* (London: A. & C. Black, 1963), Sidney Painter, *The Reign of King John* (Baltimore: The Johns Hopkins Press, 1949), R. F. Treharne, *The Baronial Plan of Reform 1258–1263* (Manchester: University of Manchester Press, 1932), and C. Bémont, *Simon de Montfort* (trans. by E. F. Jacob. Oxford: Clarendon Press, 1930). The continental background of events in England may be followed in R. W. Southern, *The Making of the Middle Ages* (London: Hutchinson's University Library, 1953; New Haven: Yale University Press, 1959), and in Z. N. Brooke, *History of Europe 911–1198* (London: Methuen, 1951).

FEUDALISM

Feudalism and the feudal structure of society may be studied in Carl Stephenson, *Mediæval Feudalism* (Ithaca, N. Y.: Cornell University Press, 1942), F. L. Ganshof, *Feudalism* (New York: Harper & Row, 1961), and Sidney Painter, *French Chivalry: Chivalric Ideas and Practices in Medieval France* (Ithaca, N. Y.: Great Seal Books, 1957). More specialized accounts are Sir Frank Stenton's excellent *First Century of English Feudalism 1066–1166* (Oxford: Clarendon Press, 1961), and Sidney Painter, *Studies in the History of the English Feudal Barony* (Baltimore: The Johns Hopkins Press, 1943). For the political theories lying behind feudalism, see C. H. McIlwain, *Growth of Political Thought in the West* (New York: Macmillan, 1964), and Fritz Kern, *Kingship and Law in the Middle Ages* (trans. by S. B. Chrimes. Oxford: B. Blackwell, 1939).

CONSTITUTIONAL HISTORY

One can hardly speak of constitutional and legal history in this period without mentioning two elderly classics which have formed the starting point for modern research: William Stubbs, *The Constitutional History of England* (Oxford: Clarendon Press, 1897, 3 vols.), and Frederick Pollock and Frederick William Maitland, *History of English Law before the Time of Edward I* (Cambridge: Cambridge University Press, 1898, 2 vols.). Bryce Lyon, *A Constitutional and Legal History of Medieval England*, J. E. A. Jolliffe, *The Constitutional History of Medieval England*, and G. O. Sayles, *The Medieval Foundations of England*, of which the last is excellent for the Norman period, have been cited above. Other constitutional histories are H. G. Richardson and G. O. Sayles, *The Governance of Medieval England from the Conquest to Magna Carta* (Edinburgh: University of Edinburgh Press, 1963), Bertie Wilkinson, *Constitutional History of England 1216–1399* (New York: McKay, 1948–1963, 3 vols.), T. F. T. Plucknett, *A Concise History of the Common Law* (London: Butterworth, 1956), and W. S. McKechnie, *Magna Carta: A Commentary on the Great Charter of King John* (Glasgow: J. Maclehose, 1914). The last is the standard description of the charter.

SOCIAL AND ECONOMIC HISTORY

An excellent introduction to the social history of this period is Doris Mary Stenton, *English Society in the Early Middle Ages 1066–1307* (Harmondsworth, Middlesex: Penguin Books, 1952), which deals with social classes, the rural scene, the towns, and the position of the church. Sir Frank Stenton, Simone Bertrand, *et al.*, eds., *The Bayeux Tapestry: A Comprehensive Survey* (London: Phaidon, 1957), supplies a detailed description of this famous source. Many aspects of medieval life, such as monasteries, warfare, castles, cathedrals, costume, and handwriting, are described in Austin Lane Poole, ed., *Medieval England* (Oxford: Clarendon Press, 1958, 2 vols.). Other useful books are Sidney Painter, *Medieval Society* (Ithaca, N.Y.: Cornell University Press,

1951), H. R. Loyn, *Anglo-Saxon England and the Norman Conquest* (London: Longmans, 1963), P. Boissonade, *Life and Work in Medieval Europe* (trans. by E. Power, New York: Knopf, 1927), U. T. Holmes, *Daily Living in the Twelfth Century* (Madison, Wisconsin: University of Wisconsin Press, 1952), a book based on the observations of Alexander Neckam in London and Paris, and G. C. Homans, *English Villagers of the Thirteenth Century* (Cambridge, Mass.: Harvard University Press, 1941).

H. Pirenne, *Economic and Social History of Medieval Europe* (trans. by I. E. Clegg. London: Routledge, 1936), is a good modern economic survey. Nellie Neilson, *Medieval Agrarian Economy* (New York: Holt, Rinehart and Winston, 1936), serves as an introduction to agriculture, while C. S. and C. S. Orwin, *The Open Fields*, cited above, remains of fundamental importance. Summerfield Baldwin, *Business in the Middle Ages* (New York: Holt, Rinehart and Winston, 1937), Sir William Savage, *The Making of Our Towns* (London: Eyre and Spottiswoode, 1952), and H. Pirenne, *Medieval Cities* (trans. by Frank D. Halsey. Princeton: Princeton University Press, 1925), are useful. R. A. Newhall, *The Crusades* (New York: Holt, Rinehart and Winston, 1927), is a brief sketch; the standard history is S. Runciman, *A History of the Crusades* (Cambridge: Cambridge University Press, 1951–1954, 3 vols.).

THE CHURCH

Brief introductions are Summerfield Baldwin, *The Organization of Medieval Christianity* (New York: Holt, Rinehart and Winston, 1929), and S. R. Packard, *Europe and the Church under Innocent III* (New York: Holt, Rinehart and Winston, 1927). Longer works include Z. N. Brooke, *The English Church and the Papacy from the Conquest to the Reign of John* (Cambridge: Cambridge University Press, 1931), Dom David Knowles, *The Monastic Order in England 943–1216* (Cambridge: Cambridge University Press, 1940), the same author's *Religious Orders in England 1216–c.1340* (Cambridge: Cambridge University Press, 1948, vol. 1), J. R. H. Moorman, *Church Life in England in the Thirteenth Century* (Cambridge: Cambridge University Press, 1946), and the same author's *History of the Church in England* (London: A. & C. Black, 1953). C. C. Crump and E. F. Jacob, eds., *The Legacy of the Middle Ages* (Oxford: Clarendon Press, 1932), contains valuable chapters on religion, literature, and thought in the Middle Ages. Charles Homer Haskins, *The Rise of Universities* (New York: Holt, Rinehart and Winston, 1923), is a good introduction. The standard work is F. M. Powicke and A. B. Emden, eds., H. Rashdall, *The Universities of Europe in the Middle Ages* (Oxford: Clarendon Press, 1936, 3 vols.).

1307 TO 1485

SURVEYS AND POLITICAL HISTORIES

There are two excellent surveys, George Holmes, *The Later Middle Ages 1272–1485* (Edinburgh: T. Nelson, 1962), and A. R. Myers, *England in the Late Middle Ages* (Harmondsworth, Middlesex: Penguin Books, 1952). Longer accounts are V. H. H. Green, *The Later Plantagenets 1307–1485* (London: E. Arnold, 1955), and two volumes in the Oxford History, May McKisack, *The Fourteenth Century 1307–1399* (Oxford: Clarendon Press, 1959), a thorough and workmanlike account, and E. F. Jacob, *The Fifteenth Century 1399–1485* (Oxford: Clarendon Press, 1961), which is scholarly but rather specialized. Some of the older histories are also useful: T. F. Tout, *The History of England from the Accession of Henry III to the Death of Edward III* (London: Longmans, 1905), C. W. C. Oman, *The History of England from the Accession of Richard II to the Death of Richard III* (London: Longmans, 1918), and K. H. Vickers, *England in the Later Middle Ages* (London: Methuen, 1930). A more attractive and more readable book is George Macaulay Trevelyan, *England in the Age of Wycliffe* (London: Longmans, 1929).

Political events may also be followed in Sydney Armitage-Smith, *John of Gaunt* (Westminster: Constable, 1904), in J. E. Lloyd, *Owen Glendower* (Oxford: Clarendon

Press, 1931), in R. A. Newhall, *The English Conquest of Normandy 1416–1424* (New Haven: Yale University Press, 1924), in E. F. Jacob, *Henry V and the Invasion of France* (London: English Universities Press, 1947), in K. H. Vickers, *Humphrey, Duke of Gloucester* (London: Constable, 1907), in P. M. Kendall, *Richard the Third* (New York: Norton, 1957), and in the same author's *Warwick the Kingmaker* (New York: Norton, 1957).

CONSTITUTIONAL HISTORY

Some of the constitutional histories mentioned in the section above continue into the later Middle Ages. A work of great importance for constitutional as well as legal history is Sir William Holdsworth, *History of English Law* (London: Methuen, 1903–1909, 3 vols.; 1903–1952, 13 vols.). This work is so broadly conceived that it can be used as a book of reference for many aspects of constitutional history. Faith Thompson, *A Short History of Parliament 1295–1642* (Minneapolis: University of Minnesota Press, 1953), is a good introduction to the history of Parliament in the Middle Ages. For those who wish to follow it further, a useful guide is G. Templeman, "The History of Parliament in the Light of Modern Research," *University of Birmingham Historical Journal*, I (1948), 202–231.

THE NOBILITY AND WAR

The warlike life of the nobility and the system of indentured retainers may be studied in the following: Édouard Perroy, *The Hundred Years' War* (trans. by W. B. Wells. London: Eyre and Spottiswoode, 1951), J. H. Beeler, ed., C. W. C. Oman, *A History of the Art of War in the Middle Ages* (Princeton: Princeton University Press, 1953), F. M. Stenton, *The Development of the Castle in England and Wales* (London: Historical Association, 1910), R. Allen Brown, *English Medieval Castles* (London: Batsford, 1954), William H. Dunham, *Lord Hastings' Indentured Retainers 1461–1483* (New Haven: Yale University Press, 1955), and G. A. Holmes, *The Estates of the Higher Nobility in Fourteenth-Century England* (Cambridge: Cambridge University Press, 1957). Important articles include F. M. Stenton, "The Changing Feudalism of the Middle Ages," *History*, XIX (1935), K. B. McFarlane, "Bastard Feudalism," *Bulletin of the Institute of Historical Research*, XX (1943–1945), the same author's "Parliament and 'Bastard Feudalism,'" *Transactions of the Royal Historical Society*, 4th ser., XXVI (1944), and his "Investment of Sir John Fastolf's Profits of War," *ibid.*, 5th ser., VII (1957), N. B. Lewis, "The Organization of Indentured Retainers in Fourteenth-century England," *ibid.*, 4th ser., XXVII (1945), A. E. Prince, "The Indenture System under Edward III," in J. G. Edwards, V. H. Galbraith, and E. F. Jacob, eds., *Essays in Honour of James Tait* (Manchester, printed for the subscribers, 1933), and B. P. Wolffe, "The Management of English Royal Estates under the Yorkist Kings," *English Historical Review*, LXXI (1935).

SOCIAL AND ECONOMIC HISTORY

Medieval People, by Eileen Power (New York: Doubleday, 1955), is a fascinating volume based upon wide research. There are also some fine chapters on this period in George Macaulay Trevelyan, *English Social History* (New York: McKay, 1942). Many other books deal with aspects of social life: Dorothy Margaret Stuart, *Men and Women of Plantagenet England* (London: Harrap, 1932), Annie Abram, *English Life and Manners in the Later Middle Ages* (London: Routledge; New York: Dutton, 1913), L. F. Salzman, *English Life in the Middle Ages* (London: Oxford University Press, 1926), Ruth Bird, *The Turbulent London of Richard II* (New York: McKay, 1949), C. W. C. Oman, *The Great Revolt of 1381* (Oxford: Clarendon Press, 1906), G. G. Coulton, *Chaucer and his England* (London: Methuen, 1946), the same author's *Medieval Panorama* (Cambridge: Cambridge University Press; New York: Macmillan, 1938), H. S. Bennett, *The Pastons and their England* (Cambridge: Cambridge University Press,

1922), and A. W. Parry, *Education in England in the Middle Ages* (London: W. B. Clive, 1920). "The Fifteenth Century," *Economic History Review,* IX (1939), and "Some Economic Evidence of Declining Population in the Later Middle Ages," *Economic History Review,* second series, II (1950), are important articles by M. M. Postan.

Economic histories include Eileen Power, *The Paycockes of Coggeshall,* (London: Methuen, 1920), and *The Wool Trade in English Medieval History* (New York: Oxford University Press, 1955), E. M. Carus-Wilson, *Medieval Merchant Venturers* (London: Methuen, 1954), L. F. Salzman, *English Industries of the Middle Ages* (Oxford: Clarendon Press, 1923), the same author's *Building in England Down to 1540* (Oxford: Clarendon Press, 1952), J. W. F. Hill, *Medieval Lincoln* (Cambridge: Cambridge University Press, 1948), and Sylvia L. Thrupp, *The Merchant Class of Medieval London 1300–1500* (Chicago: University of Chicago Press, 1948).

THE CHURCH

The history of the church may be studied in the following books: J. R. H. Moorman, *Church Life in England in the Thirteenth Century* (Cambridge: Cambridge University Press, 1946), and his more general *History of the Church in England* (London: A. & C. Black, 1953), Kathleen L. Wood-Legh, *Studies in Church Life in England under Edward III* (Cambridge: Cambridge University Press, 1934), Eileen Power, *Medieval English Nunneries, c. 1275 to 1535* (Cambridge: Cambridge University Press, 1922), K. B. McFarlane, *John Wycliffe and the Beginnings of English Nonconformity* (London: English Universities Press, 1952), A. Hamilton Thompson, *The English Clergy and their Organization in the Later Middle Ages* (Oxford: Clarendon Press, 1947), John Harvey, *Gothic England: A Survey of National Culture 1300–1550* (London: Batsford, 1947), and several books by G. H. Cook, *The English Mediaeval Parish Church* (London: Phoenix House, 1954), *The English Cathedral through the Ages* (London: Phoenix House, 1957), and *English Monasteries in the Middle Ages* (London: Phoenix House, 1961).

THE TUDOR PERIOD

SURVEYS AND POLITICAL HISTORIES

S. T. Bindoff, *Tudor England* (Harmondsworth, Middlesex: Penguin Books, 1950), is an excellent introduction to the history of the Tudor age. It is especially concerned with economic developments. Another survey, more strictly political, is Conyers Read, *The Tudors: Personalities and Practical Politics in Sixteenth Century England* (New York: Holt, Rinehart and Winston, 1936). This volume devotes a chapter to each of the Tudor rulers. Two other short surveys are James A. Williamson, *The Tudor Age* (London: Longmans, 1957), and Christopher Morris, *The Tudors* (London: Batsford, 1955). Of longer works, by far the best single volume history is G. R. Elton, *England under the Tudors* (London: Methuen, 1955), a brilliant book which sets forth new interpretations. The two volumes of the Oxford History are J. D. Mackie, *The Earlier Tudors 1485–1558* (Oxford: Clarendon Press, 1952), a learned book though not easy to read, and J. B. Black, *The Reign of Elizabeth 1558–1603* (Oxford: Clarendon Press, 1959), a sound, judicious, and most useful volume. Two older accounts, H. A. L. Fisher, *From the Accession of Henry VII to the Death of Henry VIII* (London: Longmans, 1913), and A. F. Pollard, *From the Accession of Edward VI to the Death of Elizabeth* (London, Longmans, 1910), are still useful, though subject to revision. Roger Lockyer's *Tudor and Stuart Britain 1471–1714* (New York: St. Martin's, 1964), based upon the research done in the Tudor and Stuart periods during the last twenty-five years, contains a useful bibliography but loses much of its effect because it includes very few footnotes.

Tudor politics may also be followed in a number of biographies: James Gairdner, *Henry VII* (London: Macmillan, 1889); A. F. Pollard, *Henry VIII* (London: Longmans, 1905); J. J. Scarisbrick, *Henry VIII* (Berkeley: University of California Press, 1968), a new and important book; Garrett Mattingly, *Catherine of Aragon* (Boston: Little, Brown, 1941); A. F. Pollard, *Wolsey* (London: Longmans, 1929); R. W. Chambers, *Thomas More* (New York: Harcourt, 1935), the best life; A. F. Pollard, *England under the Protector Somerset* (London: Routledge, 1900), too favorable to Somerset; Hester Chapman, *The Last Tudor King* (London: J. Cape, 1958); H. F. M. Prescott, *Mary Tudor* (London: Eyre and Spottiswoode, 1952); and J. E. Neale, *Queen Elizabeth I* (New York: Harcourt, 1934). The last of these biographies, now in paperback (New York: Doubleday, 1957), has been translated into many languages and has become a classic. Scholarly articles on Henry VII by G. R. Elton and J. P. Cooper appear in the *Historical Journal*, I (1958), II (1959), IV (1961); and on Henry VIII by G. R. Elton, *Henry VIII: an Essay in Revision* (London: Historical Association, 1962).

GOVERNMENT

D. L. Keir deals with Tudor government in an excellent textbook, *The Constitutional History of Modern Britain* (New York: Van Nostrand, 1961). Documents are found in J. R. Tanner, *Tudor Constitutional Documents* (Cambridge: Cambridge University Press, 1930), and in G. R. Elton, *The Tudor Constitution: Documents and Commentary* (Cambridge: Cambridge University Press, 1960); the commentary in the first of these volumes is superseded by that in the second. Excellent accounts of the courts, of Tudor law, and other aspects of the constitution are contained in Sir William Holdsworth, *History of English Law*, vols. I, IV, and V, cited above. Of two volumes by K. Pickthorn, *Early Tudor Government* (Cambridge: Cambridge University Press, 1934), the first, on Henry VII, is useful; the second, on Henry VIII, tends to become a general history of the reign. G. R. Elton, *The Tudor Revolution in Government* (Cambridge: Cambridge University Press, 1953), is a study of administrative changes under Henry VIII, with special emphasis on the work of Thomas Cromwell. F. G. Emmison, *Tudor Secretary: Sir William Petre at Court and Home* (Cambridge, Mass.: Harvard University Press, 1961), traces the career of a high-ranking civil servant and includes a good deal of social history. An important addition to Tudor parliamentary history is Stanford E. Lehmberg's scholarly study, *The Reformation Parliament 1529–1536* (Cambridge: Cambridge University Press, 1970).

Turning to the constitution under Queen Elizabeth, one finds sound but unexciting descriptions of various parts of the government in Edward P. Cheyney, *History of England from the Defeat of the Armada to the Death of Elizabeth* (New York: McKay, 1914, 1926, 2 vols.). Special studies include H. E. Bell, *An Introduction to the History and Records of the Court of Wards and Liveries* (Cambridge: Cambridge University Press, 1953), Joel Hurstfield, *The Queen's Wards* (London: Longmans, 1958), Penry Williams, *The Council in the Marches of Wales under Elizabeth I* (Aberystwyth: University of Wales Press, 1958), F. W. Brooks, *The Council of the North* (London: Historical Association, 1953), Conyers Read, *Mr. Secretary Walsingham and the Policy of Queen Elizabeth* (Cambridge, Mass.: Harvard University Press, 1925, 3 vols.), the most comprehensive study of foreign policy, the same author's *Mr. Secretary Cecil and Queen Elizabeth* (London: J. Cape, 1955), his *Lord Burghley and Queen Elizabeth* (London: J. Cape, 1960), important but overloaded with quotations from the sources, and Gladys Scott Thomson, *Lords Lieutenants in the Sixteenth Century* (London: Longmans, 1923).

J. E. Neale's volumes on the House of Commons form the most important contribution of recent years to the history of the Tudor constitution: *The Elizabethan House of Commons* (London: J. Cape, 1949), *Elizabeth I and her Parliaments 1559–1581* (London: J. Cape, 1953), and *Elizabeth I and her Parliaments 1584–1601* (London: J. Cape, 1957). The first volume is descriptive; the second and third chronological. They are indispensable for the political, constitutional, and ecclesiastical history of the reign.

RELIGIOUS HISTORY

Short surveys, not above criticism, include T. M. Parker, *The English Reformation to 1558* (London: Oxford University Press, Home University Library, 1950), H. Maynard Smith, *Pre-Reformation England* (London: Macmillan, 1938), and the same author's *Henry VIII and the Reformation* (London: Macmillan, 1948). Longer accounts include Dom David Knowles, *The Religious Orders in England. vol. III. The Tudor Age* (Cambridge: Cambridge University Press, 1959), an important book; A. Savine, *English Monasteries on the Eve of the Dissolution* (Oxford: Clarendon Press, 1909), severely technical; G. Baskerville, *English Monks and the Suppression of the Monasteries* (New Haven: Yale University Press, 1937), hostile to the monks; Philip Hughes, *The Reformation in England* (London: Hollis and Carter, 1950–1954, 3 vols.), an excellent Catholic history; A. F. Pollard, *Thomas Cranmer and the English Reformation* (London: Longmans, 1905); H. Darby, *Hugh Latimer* (London: Epworth, 1953); C. H. Garret, *The Marian Exiles* (Cambridge: Cambridge University Press, 1938). The religious settlement at the accession of Elizabeth may be studied in the second volume of Neale's trilogy; a chapter by Frederick William Maitland in the old *Cambridge Modern History* (vol. II) is still important. For the Church of England see V. J. K. Brook, *A Life of Archbishop Parker* (London: Oxford University Press, 1962), and W. H. Frere, *The English Church in the Reigns of Elizabeth and James I* (London: Macmillan, 1904). The best history of the Catholics is A. O. Meyer, *England and the Catholic Church under Elizabeth* (London: Routledge, 1916); there is also a brief survey, E. I. Watkin, *Roman Catholicism in England from the Reformation to 1950* (London: Oxford University Press, Home University Library, 1957). For the Puritans, see M. M. Knappen, *Tudor Puritanism* (Chicago: University of Chicago Press, 1939), the standard work, A. F. Scott Pearson, *Thomas Cartwright and Elizabethan Puritanism* (Cambridge: Cambridge University Press, 1925), and William Haller, *The Elect Nation. The Meaning and Relevance of Foxe's Book of Martyrs* (New York: Harper & Row, 1963).

SOCIAL AND ECONOMIC HISTORY

There are excellent chapters on social life in George Macaulay Trevelyan, *English Social History*, and in Sir Sidney Lee, ed., *Shakespeare's England. An Account of the Life and Manners of His Age* (Oxford: Clarendon Press, 1916, 2 vols.). An indispensable book, and a most enjoyable one, which discusses the social structure in great detail is A. L. Rowse, *The England of Elizabeth* (London: Macmillan, 1950, paperback New York: Macmillan, 1961). Of many other books, one may mention F. P. Wilson, *The Plague in Shakespeare's London* (Oxford: Clarendon Press, 1927), L. F. Salzman, *England in Tudor Times* (Cambridge: Cambridge University Press, 1926), M. St. C. Byrne, *Elizabethan Life in Town and Country* (London: Methuen, 1954), A. H. Dodd, *Life in Elizabethan England* (New York: Putnam, 1962), Frank Aydelotte, *Elizabethan Rogues and Vagabonds* (Oxford: Clarendon Press, 1933), Mildred Campbell, *The English Yeoman under Elizabeth and the Early Stuarts* (New Haven: Yale University Press, 1942), W. K. Jordan, *Philanthropy in England 1480–1660* (London: G. Allen, 1959), *The Charities of London 1480–1660* (New York: Russell Sage, 1960), and *The Charities of Rural England 1480–1660* (London: G. Allen, 1961). A controversy among historians concerning the gentry is noted in the list of books dealing with the early Stuart period.

Economic affairs are discussed to some extent in Bindoff, Black, and Elton, *England under the Tudors*, mentioned above. Sir John Clapham, *Concise Economic History of Britain* (Cambridge: Cambridge University Press, 1949), is a good introduction; longer accounts are found in E. Lipson, *The Economic History of England* (New York: Macmillan, 1929–1931, 3 vols.), and in E. F. Heckscher, *Mercantilism* (New York: Macmillan, 1955, 2 vols.). See also Peter Ramsey, *Tudor Economic Problems* (London: Gollancz, 1963), F. J. Fisher, "Economic Trends and Policy in the Sixteenth Century," *Economic History Review*, X (1940), P. J. Bowden, *The Wool Trade in Tudor and*

Stuart England (London: Macmillan, 1962), G. D. Ramsay, *English Overseas Trade during the Centuries of Emergence* (London: Macmillan, 1957), and Joan Thirsk, *Tudor Enclosures* (London: Historical Association, 1959). R. H. Tawney, *Religion and the Rise of Capitalism* (New York: Harcourt, 1926), is the most important work on economic thought.

Of the many books dealing with Elizabethan voyages and sea power, the following are important and usually very good reading: James A. Williamson, *A Short History of British Expansion* (New York: Macmillan, 1945, 2 vols.), a good introduction; the same author's *Age of Drake* (London: A. & C. Black, 1938), an excellent survey of Elizabeth's reign; A. L. Rowse, *The Expansion of England* (New York: St. Martin's, 1955), a fascinating book that deals also with English influence in the Celtic parts of Britain; James A. Williamson, *Sir John Hawkins* (Oxford: Clarendon Press, 1927); Sir William Foster, *England's Quest of Eastern Trade* (London: A. & C. Black, 1933); Michael Lewis, *The History of the British Navy* (Harmondsworth, Middlesex: Penguin Books, 1957); Garrett Mattingly, *The Armada* (Boston: Houghton Mifflin, 1959), a remarkably well-written book; A. L. Rowse, *Sir Richard Grenville of the Revenge* (Boston: Houghton Mifflin, 1937); the same author's, *The Elizabethans and America* (London: Macmillan, 1959); D. B. Quinn, *Raleigh and the British Empire* (London: English Universities Press, 1947); and James A. Williamson, *The Ocean in English History* (Oxford: Clarendon Press, 1941), which deals with Tudor propaganda for exploration.

IRELAND AND SCOTLAND

The standard history of Ireland for this period is R. Bagwell, *Ireland under the Tudors* (London: Longmans, 1885–1890, 3 vols.). See also E. Curtis, *History of Ireland* (London: Methuen, 1950), Cyril Falls, *Elizabeth's Irish Wars* (London: Methuen, 1950), E. W. (later Lord) Hamilton, *Elizabethan Ulster* (London: Hurst and Blackett, 1919), C. G. Cruickshank, *Elizabeth's Army* (Oxford: Clarendon Press, 1946), and chapters in Rowse, *Expansion of England*, mentioned above.

For Scotland see William Croft Dickinson, *Scotland from the Earliest Times to 1603* (Edinburgh, T. Nelson, 1961), P. Hume Brown, *History of Scotland* (Cambridge: Cambridge University Press, 1900–1909, 3 vols.), and T. F. Henderson, *Life of Mary Queen of Scots* (New York: Scribner, 1905, 2 vols.).

THE STUART PERIOD

SURVEYS AND POLITICAL HISTORIES

Maurice Ashley, *England in the Seventeenth Century* (Baltimore: Penguin, 1962), provides a good introduction to the Stuart period. The first half of the book is less penetrating than the second, a deficiency remedied by J. D. Mackie, *Cavalier and Puritan* (London and Edinburgh: T. Nelson, 1930), an able survey that deals with basic issues. George Macaulay Trevelyan, *England under the Stuarts* (New York: Putnam, 1949), may be described as an elderly classic. The volumes in the Oxford History are Godfrey Davies, *The Early Stuarts 1603–1660* (Oxford: Clarendon Press, 1959), a sound, judicious, and cautious book, and Sir George Clark, *The Later Stuarts 1660–1714* (Oxford: Clarendon Press, 1956), an excellent work. The seventeenth century is well provided with long continuous narrative histories. One of the greatest achievements of English historical writing is the work of Samuel Rawson Gardiner, *History of England from the Accession of James I to the Outbreak of the Civil War 1603–1642* (London: Longmans, 1883–1884, 10 vols.), followed by *The History of the Great Civil War 1642–1649* (London: Longmans, 1893, 4 vols.), and *The History of the Commonwealth and Protectorate 1649–1656* (London: Longmans, 1903, 4 vols.). These volumes are surprisingly accurate and form the starting point for modern research in political, constitutional, and diplomatic history, to which they are largely devoted. The story is continued on the same scale by Charles Harding Firth, *The Last Years of the Protectorate 1656–1658* (London: Longmans, 1909, 2 vols.), and by Godfrey Davies, *The Restoration of Charles II* (San Marino, Calif.: Huntington Library, 1955). The period after 1660 is covered by David Ogg, *England in the Reign of Charles II* (Oxford: Clarendon Press, 1956, 2 vols.), *England in the Reigns of James II and William III* (Oxford: Clarendon Press, 1963), *William III* (London: Collins, 1956), and by Thomas Babington Macaulay's famous *History of England from the Accession of James II* (London: Longmans, 1849–1861, 5 vols.). Though pro-Whig and robustly patriotic, Macaulay's volumes are excellent reading and not bad history. Chapter III on the life of the times is excellent. G. M. Trevelyan's little book, *The English Revolution 1688–1689* (New York: Oxford University Press, 1965), and his important work, *England under Queen Anne* (London: Longmans, 1930–1934, 3 vols.), enrich the historiography of a century done in the grand manner.

Various aspects of the continental background may be followed in Garrett Mattingly, *Renaissance Diplomacy* (London: J. Cape, 1955), in C. V. Wedgwood, *The Thirty Years War* (New York: Doubleday, 1949), and in G. N. Clark, *The Seventeenth Century* (Oxford: Clarendon Press, 1931; New York: Oxford University Press, 1961).

Politics may be followed further in David Harris Willson, *King James VI and I* (London: J. Cape, 1956, paperback, 1963), which deals with the major events of the reign, and in the books of Miss C. V. Wedgwood, *The King's Peace, 1637–1641* (London: Collins, 1955), *The King's War, 1641–1647* (London: Collins, 1958), *The Trial of Charles I* (London: Collins, 1964), and *Thomas Wentworth, First Earl of Strafford: A Revaluation* (London: J. Cape, 1961). Jack H. Hexter, *The Reign of King Pym* (Cambridge, Mass.: Harvard University Press, 1941), A. H. Burne and Peter Young, *The Great Civil War* (London: Eyre and Spottiswoode, 1959), Leo F. Solt, *Saints in Arms* (Stanford: Stanford University Press, 1959), and Austin Woolrych, *Battles of the English Civil War* (London: Batsford, 1961), are useful. The best short life of Cromwell is Charles Harding Firth, *Oliver Cromwell and the Rule of the Puritans in England* (London: Putnam, 1901), a clear and understandable study. A good account of Cromwell's religious life is found in Maurice Ashley, *The Greatness of Oliver Cromwell* (New York: Macmillan, 1958). For the period after 1660, see Robert S. Bosher, *The Making of the Restoration Settlement 1649–1662* (London: A. & C. Black, 1951), Osmund Airy, *Charles II* (London: Longmans, 1904), and F. C. Turner, *James II* (London: Eyre and Spottiswoode, 1950).

CONSTITUTIONAL HISTORY

Constitutional history may be followed in D. L. Keir and in volumes IV and VI of Sir William Holdsworth, *History of English Law*, cited above. Important aspects are discussed in J. N. Figgis, *The Divine Right of Kings* (Cambridge: Cambridge University Press, 1914), in Wallace Notestein, *The Winning of the Initiative by the House of Commons* (London: Proceedings of the British Academy, 1925), in David Harris Willson, *The Privy Councillors in the House of Commons 1604–1629* (Minneapolis: University of Minnesota Press, 1940), in G. E. Aylmer, *The King's Servants: The Civil Service of Charles I 1625–1642* (New York: Columbia University Press, 1961), in the same author's *The Struggle for the Constitution 1603–1689* (London: Blandford, 1963), in H. F. Kearney, *The Eleven Years Tyranny of Charles I* (London: Historical Association, 1962), and in M. A. Judson, *The Crisis of the Constitution* (New Brunswick: Rutgers University Press, 1949).

SOCIAL AND ECONOMIC HISTORY

Most of the books dealing with society in the Elizabethan period apply also to the first half of the seventeenth century. There is, however, an excellent book, Wallace Notestein, *The English People on the Eve of Colonization 1603–1630* (New York: Harper & Row, 1962), devoted to the reign of James I. An older book, Eleanor Trotter,

Seventeenth Century Life in the Country Parish (Cambridge: Cambridge University Press, 1919), is useful for local government and administration.

A long and sometimes violent discussion has arisen among historians concerning the gentry and the aristocracy during the century before the Civil War, and this discussion has broadened into a debate as to why the war took place. The material is found in articles of which the following are the most important: R. H. Tawney, "The Rise of the Gentry, 1558–1640," *Economic History Review*, XI (1941); Lawrence Stone, "The Anatomy of the Elizabethan Aristocracy," *ibid.*, XVIII (1948); H. R. Trevor-Roper, "The Gentry, 1540–1640," *ibid.*, *Supplements*, I (1953), "The Country House Radicals" and "The Social Causes of the Great Rebellion," *Historical Essays* (London: Macmillan, 1957), and "Oliver Cromwell and His Parliaments," in Richard Pares and A. J. P. Taylor, eds., *Essays Presented to Sir Lewis Namier* (London: Macmillan, 1956); Christopher Hill, "Recent Interpretations of the Civil War," in his *Puritanism and Revolution* (London: Secker, 1958); J. H. Hexter, "Storm over the Gentry," *Reappraisals in History* (London: Longmans, 1961); Perez Zagorin, "The Social Interpretation of the English Revolution," *Journal of Economic History*, XIX (1959); and Willson H. Coates, "An Analysis of Major Conflicts in Seventeenth-Century England," in W. A. Aiken and Basil Duke Henning, eds., *Conflict in Stuart England* (London: J. Cape, 1960). Tawney's original thesis, that the rise in economic power of the gentry was a major cause of the civil war, though corrected in detail, seems to this writer to remain intact. A large and important book, Lawrence Stone, *The Crisis of the Aristocracy 1558–1641* (Oxford: Clarendon Press, 1965), throws light on many aspects of this controversy.

Most of the books cited as economic histories of the Tudor period are useful also for the early Stuarts. Much of the new work is severely technical. Two recent books, however, contain a good deal of economic history without becoming too specialized: Christopher Hill, *The Century of Revolution 1603–1714* (Edinburgh: T. Nelson, 1961), and Charles Wilson, *England's Apprenticeship 1603–1763* (New York: St. Martin's, 1965). An important book is R. H. Tawney, *Business and Politics under James I. Lionel Cranfield as Merchant and Minister* (Cambridge: Cambridge University Press, 1958). B. E. Supple, *Commercial Crisis and Change in England 1600–1642* (Cambridge: Cambridge University Press, 1959), Maurice Ashley, *Financial and Commercial Policy under the Cromwellian Protectorate* (London: F. Cass, 1962), Charles Wilson, *Mercantilism* (London: Historical Association, 1958), Sir George Clark, *War and Society in the Seventeenth Century* (Cambridge: Cambridge University Press, 1958), are helpful.

James A. Williamson, *A Short History of British Expansion*, continues to be an excellent guide. Two interesting books are Arthur Percival Newton, *The European Nations in the West Indies 1493–1688* (London: A. & C. Black, 1933), and K. G. Davies, *The Royal African Company* (London: Longmans, 1958).

RELIGIOUS HISTORY

Some recent books and pamphlets on the religious history of the seventeenth century include S. B. Babbage, *Puritanism and Richard Bancroft* (London: SPCK, 1962), Paul A. Welsby, *George Abbot, the Unwanted Archbishop 1562–1633* (London: SPCK, 1962), H. R. Trevor-Roper, *Archbishop Laud* (London: Macmillan, 1962), Christopher Hill, *Economic Problems of the Church from Archbishop Whitgift to the Long Parliament* (London: Oxford University Press, 1956), William Haller, *The Rise of Puritanism 1570–1643* (New York: Columbia University Press, 1938), and his *Liberty and Reformation in the Puritan Revolution* (New York: Columbia University Press, 1955), G. Yule, *The Independents in the English Civil War* (Cambridge: Cambridge University Press, 1958), H. G. Plum, *Restoration Puritanism* (Chapel Hill: University of North Carolina Press, 1943), G. R. Cragg, *Puritanism in the Period of the Great Persecution 1660–1688* (Cambridge: Cambridge University Press, 1957), and G. Every, *The High Church Party 1688–1718* (London: SPCK, 1956).

THE EIGHTEENTH CENTURY

SURVEYS AND POLITICAL HISTORIES

The bibliography of English history in the eighteenth century has unique characteristics. There is a great abundance of original material—letters, diaries, journals, memoirs—though some of this is buried in old-fashioned biographies that are useless save for the sources printed in them. But one finds very few sustained chronological narratives of the period. J. H. Plumb, *England in the Eighteenth Century 1714–1815* (Baltimore: Penguin, 1964), is a useful introductory survey; a brief summary of eighteenth-century history is found in volume X of Sir William Holdsworth's *History of English Law* (London: Methuen, 1938). Of the two volumes in the Oxford History, one, Basil Williams, *The Whig Supremacy 1714–1760*, has been revised by C. H. Stuart (Oxford: Clarendon Press, 1962), the other, J. Steven Watson, *The Reign of George III 1760–1815* (Oxford: Clarendon Press, 1960), is an excellent history, full, compact, critical, and abreast of modern research. A famous work, William Edward Hartpole Lecky, *A History of England in the Eighteenth Century* (New York: Appleton, 1879–1890, 8 vols.), must be classed as Whiggish and out of date. Yet Lecky's volumes contain fine chapters on social conditions and are written in a most engaging style. Sir Charles Grant Robertson, *England under the Hanoverians* (New York: Putnam, 1930), follows Lecky closely.

The interpretation of politics has been deeply affected by two books of Sir Lewis Namier, *The Structure of Politics at the Accession of George III* (New York: St. Martin's, 1957, 2 vols.), and *England in the Age of the American Revolution* (New York: St. Martin's, 1962). Important essays by Namier have appeared in *Monarchy and the Party System* (Oxford: Clarendon Press, 1952) and in *Personalities and Powers* (London: H. Hamilton, 1955). These volumes have challenged old ideas about eighteenth-century politics and have introduced many new interpretations. They represent research in depth, and Namier's students have tended to write very detailed studies of short periods, such as John Brooke, *The Chatham Administration 1766–1768* (New York: St. Martin's, 1956), and Ian R. Christie, *The End of North's Ministry 1780–1782* (New York: St. Martin's, 1958). John B. Owen, in his *Rise of the Pelhams* (London: Methuen, 1957), ably applies the methods of Namier to the last years of Walpole's ministry and to the period of the Pelhams. Many aspects of politics are discussed in Richard Pares, *King George III and the Politicians* (Oxford: Clarendon Press, 1953). Certain features of Namier's work have been criticized by H. Butterfield, *George III and the Historians* (New York: Macmillan, 1959).

Sir Lewis Namier and John Brooke have edited three volumes of a new and highly important history of Parliament containing biographical sketches of members, *The House of Commons 1754–1790* (New York: Oxford University Press for the History of Parliament Trust, 1964, 3 vols.).

Political events may also be followed in: Basil Williams, *Stanhope, a Study in Eighteenth-century War and Diplomacy* (Oxford: Clarendon Press, 1932), J. H. Plumb, *Sir Robert Walpole* (London: Cresset Press, 1956, 1960, 2 vols.), Basil Williams, *Carteret and Newcastle: A Contrast in Contemporaries* (Cambridge: Cambridge University Press, 1943), the same author's rather too favorable life of *William Pitt, Earl of Chatham* (New York: McKay, 1913, 2 vols.), Sir Philip Magnus, *Edmund Burke* (London: J. Murray, 1939), H. Butterfield, *George III, Lord North and the People 1779–1800* (London: G. Bell, 1949), Raymond Postgate, *That Devil Wilkes* (New York: Vanguard, 1930), J. Holland Rose, *William Pitt* (London: G. Bell, 1911, 1912, 3 vols.), Donald Grove Barnes, *George III and William Pitt 1783–1806* (Stanford: Stanford University Press, 1939), Holden Furber, *Dundas* (London: Oxford University Press, 1931), Philip Anthony Brown, *The French Revolution in English History* (London: Lockwood, 1918), G. S. Veitch, *The Genesis of Parliamentary Reform* (London: Constable, 1913), Michael Roberts, *The Whig Party 1807–1812* (London: Macmillan,

1939), and Betty Kemp, *King and Commons 1660–1832* (New York: St. Martin's, 1957). Two short readable books are J. H. Plumb, *Chatham* (London: Collins, 1953), and J. Holland Rose, *A Short Life of William Pitt* (London: G. Bell, 1925).

ECONOMIC HISTORY

The best book is T. S. Ashton, *An Economic History of England. The Eighteenth Century* (New York: Barnes & Noble, 1955), a masterly survey. Two shorter accounts are W. H. B. Court, *A Concise Economic History of Britain from 1750 to Recent Times* (Cambridge: Cambridge University Press, 1954), and C. R. Fay, *Great Britain from Adam Smith to the Present Day* (New York: McKay, 1928). The first half of the century is well portrayed in M. Dorothy George, *England in Transition. Life and Work in the Eighteenth Century* (Baltimore: Penguin, 1962), and in Charles Wilson, *England's Apprenticeship 1603–1763* (New York: St. Martin's, 1965), a volume in a new social and economic historical series edited by Asa Briggs.

A great amount of learning is behind T. S. Ashton's short *Industrial Revolution 1760–1830* (London: Oxford University Press, 1948); two other interpretations are Hugh Lancelot Beales, *The Industrial Revolution 1750–1850* (London: F. Cass, 1958), and Arthur Redford, *The Economic History of England 1760–1860* (London: Longmans, 1960). There are many studies of special places and industries, such as J. David Chambers, *Nottinghamshire in the Eighteenth Century* (London: P. S. King, 1932), W. H. B. Court, *The Rise of Midland Industries 1600–1838* (London: Oxford University Press, 1938), and T. S. Ashton, *The Coal Industry in the Eighteenth Century* (Manchester: University of Manchester Press, 1964). Agriculture is dealt with in Roland Prothero, Lord Ernle, *English Farming Past and Present*. This book, though criticized, has gone through many editions; the sixth is Chicago: Quadrangle, 1962. See also J. L. and Barbara Hammond, *The Town Labourer 1760–1832* (New York: McKay, 1925), and the same authors' *The Village Labourer* (New York: McKay, 1920), which present a very gloomy picture; W. G. Hoskins, *The Midland Peasant. The Economic and Social History of a Leicestershire Village* (New York: St. Martin's, 1957); and A. H. Johnson, *The Disappearance of the Small Landowner* (Oxford: Clarendon Press, 1909).

SOCIAL HISTORY

An excellent introduction is A. S. Turberville, *English Men and Manners in the Eighteenth Century* (Oxford: Clarendon Press, 1929; New York: Oxford University Press, 1957). There are also fine chapters in George Macaulay Trevelyan, *English Social History* (New York: McKay, 1942). Many aspects of social life are described in: A. S. Turberville, ed., *Johnson's England. An Account of the Life and Manners of His Age* (Oxford: Clarendon Press, 1952, 2 vols.), Brian Connell, *The Portrait of a Whig Peer, Compiled from the Papers of the 2nd Viscount Palmerston* (London: A. Deutsch, 1957), R. B. Mowat, *England in the Eighteenth Century* (New York: McBride, n.d.), A. E. Richardson, *Georgian England* (London: Batsford, 1931), E. Neville Williams, *Life in Georgian England* (London: Batsford, 1962), Lewis Melville, *Bath under Beau Nash* (London: Hutchinson, 1907), and C. Van Muyden, ed., *César de Saussure, A Foreign View of England in the Reigns of George I and George II* (New York: Dutton, 1902). Among famous contemporary lives and memoirs are G. Birkbeck Hill, ed., James Boswell, *Life of Johnson* (Oxford: Clarendon Press, 1934–1950, 6 vols.), Romney Sedgwick, ed., Lord Hervey, *Memoirs of the Reign of King George II* (London: Eyre and Spottiswoode, 1931, 3 vols.), and the works of Horace Walpole: Mrs. Paget Toynbee, ed., *Letters of Horace Walpole* (Oxford: Clarendon Press, 1903–1905, 16 vols.), George F. R. Barker, ed., *Memoirs of the Reign of King George III* (New York: Putnam, 1894, 4 vols.), and A. F. Steuart, ed., *Last Journals* (New York: J. Love, 1910, 2 vols.). R. W. Ketton-Cremer, *Horace Walpole* (London: Methuen, 1964), is a satisfactory life.

The life of the lower classes is depicted in G. D. H. Cole and Raymond Postgate, *The British Common People 1746–1938* (New York: Knopf, 1939), in Dorothy Marshall, *The English Poor in the Eighteenth Century* (London: Routledge, 1926), and in M. Dorothy George, *London Life in the Eighteenth Century* (New York: Knopf, 1925).

A recent book, Peter Laslett, *The World We Have Lost* (New York: Scribner, 1965), offers some new approaches to the study of English society before the industrial age.

RELIGIOUS HISTORY

The standard work on the Church of England is Norman Sykes, *Church and State in England in the Eighteenth Century* (Cambridge: Cambridge University Press, 1934). It can be supplemented by a famous diary, J. Beresford, ed., *The Diary of a Country Parson 1758–1802: the Reverend James Woodforde* (London: Oxford University Press, 1924–1931, 5 vols.). For the evangelical movement within the church one should consult E. M. Howse, *Saints in Politics* (Toronto: University of Toronto Press, 1952), W. K. Lowther Clarke, *Eighteenth Century Piety* (New York: Macmillan, 1944), Sir Reginald Coupland, *Wilberforce* (Oxford: Clarendon Press, 1923), Mary Gwladys Jones, *Hannah More* (Cambridge: Cambridge University Press, 1952), and the same author's *The Charity School Movement in the Eighteenth Century: a Study of Eighteenth Century Puritanism in Action* (Cambridge: Cambridge University Press, 1938). Methodism and its influence may be studied in Maldwyn L. Edwards, *John Wesley and the Eighteenth Century* (London: G. Allen, 1933), in William Joel Warner, *The Wesleyan Movement in the Industrial Revolution* (New York: McKay, 1930), and in Evelyn Douglas Bebb, *Nonconformity and Social and Economic Life 1660–1800* (London: Epworth, 1935). Elsie Harrison, *Son to Susannah* (London: Penguin Books, 1945), is a psychological study of Wesley in the light of his mother's influence on him. Eric Williams, *Capitalism and Slavery* (Chapel Hill: University of North Carolina Press, 1944), deals with the beginnings of the movement against slavery and the slave trade.

THE EMPIRE AND THE AMERICAN REVOLUTION

James A. Williamson, *A Short History of British Expansion*, cited above, continues to be a useful guide. Longer accounts, apart from the American colonies, are found in: V. T. Harlow, *The Founding of the Second British Empire 1763–1793* (New York: McKay, 1952, 1964, 2 vols.), J. C. Beaglehole, *The Exploration of the Pacific* (London: A. & C. Black, 1934), the same author's *Discovery of New Zealand* (London: Oxford University Press, 1961), James A. Williamson's little book, *Cook and the Opening of the Pacific* (London: English Universities Press, 1946), Lowell Joseph Ragatz, *The Fall of the Planter Class in the British Caribbean 1763–1833* (New York: Appleton, 1928), Richard Pares, *War and Trade in the West Indies 1739–1763* (Oxford: Clarendon Press, 1936; London: F. Cass, 1963), and his *A West Indian Fortune* (New York: McKay, 1950).

For the American Revolution C. M. Andrews, *The Colonial Background of the American Revolution* (New Haven: Yale University Press, 1931), John Chester Miller, *Origins of the American Revolution* (Boston: Little, Brown, 1943; Stanford: Stanford University Press, 1959), the same author's *Sam Adams: Pioneer in Propaganda* (Boston: Little, Brown, 1936), Oliver M. Dickerson, *The Navigation Acts and the American Revolution* (Philadelphia: University of Pennsylvania Press, 1951), Robert E. Brown, *Middle-class Democracy and the Revolution in Massachusetts 1691–1780* (Ithaca: Cornell University Press, 1955), Edmund S. and Helen M. Morgan, *The Stamp Act Crisis: Prologue to Revolution* (Chapel Hill: University of North Carolina Press, 1953), Edmund S. Morgan, *The Birth of the Republic 1763–1789* (Chicago: University of Chicago Press, 1965, paperback), his *American Revolution. A Review of Changing Interpretations* (Washington: American Historical Association, 1958), and Eric Robson,

The American Revolution in its Political and Military Aspects 1763–1783 (London: Batchworth, 1955), serve to open the subject.

Of the many books on India during the eighteenth century, the following may be selected: Edward Thompson and G. T. Garrett, *The Rise and Fulfilment of British Rule in India* (London: Macmillan, 1934), a competent textbook; P. E. Roberts, *History of British India under the Company and under the Crown* (Oxford: Clarendon Press, 1923), a survey of political events; C. Northcote Parkinson, *Trade in the Eastern Seas 1793–1813* (Cambridge: Cambridge University Press, 1937); Edward Penderel Moon, *Warren Hastings and British India* (New York: Macmillan, 1949); Cyril H. Philips, *The East India Company 1784–1834* (Manchester: University of Manchester Press, 1940); Lucy S. Sunderland, *The East India Company in Eighteenth-century Politics* (Oxford: Clarendon Press, 1952), a definitive study of a complicated subject; and P. E. Roberts, *India under Wellesley* (London: G. Bell, 1929). Two interesting books deal with the life of the English in the East: Alfred Spencer, ed., *Memoirs of William Hickey 1749–1809* (New York: Knopf, 1921–1925, 4 vols.), and Percival Spear, *The Nabobs* (London: Oxford University Press, 1963, paperback).

THE NINETEENTH CENTURY

GENERAL

The literature dealing with the history of Great Britain in the nineteenth century is overwhelming in bulk, and it is possible to mention only a few books that are useful or important. Brief surveys are to be found in J. R. M. Butler, *A History of England 1815–1918* (New York: Oxford University Press, 1960), and David Thomson, *England in the Nineteenth Century 1815–1914* (London: Penguin Books, 1950). A number of single-volume histories should be mentioned. George Macaulay Trevelyan, *British History in the Nineteenth Century and After 1782–1919* (New York: McKay, 1938), was famous in its day. Information about politics without much analysis may be found in J. A. R. Marriott, *England Since Waterloo* (New York: Putnam, 1916). Anthony Wood, *Nineteenth Century Britain 1815–1914* (London: Longmans, 1960), is a British textbook. By far the best single-volume political history, however, is R. K. Webb, *Modern England from the Eighteenth Century to the Present* (New York: Dodd, Mead, 1968), a book that illustrates the modern approach to religious, social, and economic history. The Oxford History supplies two authoritative and well-written volumes: Sir Llewellyn Woodward, *The Age of Reform 1815–1870* (Oxford: Clarendon Press, 1962), and Sir Robert Ensor, *England 1870–1914* (Oxford: Clarendon Press, 1936). Élie Halévy, *History of the British People in the Nineteenth Century* (London: Benn, 1961, paperback, 6 vols.), has become a classic due to its keen analysis of political, religious, and cultural developments. Halévy carries the story to 1852, then takes it up once more at 1895 and continues to 1914; the intervening years are covered briefly by R. B. McCallum. Two older writers, Sir Spencer Walpole, whose *History of England from the Conclusion of the Great War in 1815* (London: Longmans, 1890, 6 vols.), and *History of Twenty-five Years* (New York: McKay, 1904–1908, 4 vols.), are still good surveys of political events, and Herbert Paul, *A History of Modern England* (London: Macmillan, 1904–1906, 5 vols.), together cover most of the century. Walpole's volumes are much better balanced and less partisan than those of Paul.

POLITICAL HISTORY

There are many other books on political history. Many of the older biographies were written at the request of friends and relatives and are too favorable to the men with whom they deal. It is best, therefore, to use recent books. Among these the following may be listed: A. Aspinall, *Lord Brougham and the Whig Party* (Manchester: University of Manchester Press, 1927), J. R. M. Butler, *The Passing of the Great Reform Bill* (New York: McKay, 1914), George Macaulay Trevelyan, *Lord Grey of the Reform*

Bill (New York: McKay, 1920), H. W. C. Davis, *The Age of Grey and Peel* (Oxford: Clarendon Press, 1929), Lord David Cecil, *Lord M: or the Later Life of Lord Melbourne* (London: Constable, 1954), Chester W. New, *Lord Durham* (Oxford: Clarendon Press, 1929), Norman Gash, *Politics in the Age of Peel* (New York: McKay, 1953), George Kitson Clark, *Peel and the Conservative Party* (London: F. Cass, 1964), Philip Guedalla, *Palmerston* (New York: Putnam, 1927), and the same author's *Gladstone and Palmerston* (London: Gollancz, 1928), which contains correspondence between the two men.

Gladstone and Disraeli have been provided with full-length biographies: John Morley, *The Life of William Ewart Gladstone* (London: Macmillan, 1903, 3 vols.), and W. F. Moneypenny and G. E. Buckle, *The Life of Benjamin Disraeli, Earl of Beaconsfield* (London: J. Murray, 1929, 2 vols.). Morley's volumes are artistic though inclined to assume the virtue of the Liberal party; Moneypenny and Buckle contain a fuller discussion of politics. These works have been cleverly condensed and telescoped in D. C. Somervell, *Disraeli and Gladstone* (New York: Doubleday, 1926).

For politics in the later part of the century one may also consult Sir Philip Magnus, *Gladstone* (London: J. Murray, 1954), Hector Bolitho, *The Reign of Queen Victoria* (New York: Macmillan, 1948), C. C. O'Brien, *Parnell and his Party* (Oxford: Clarendon Press, 1957), Winston S. Churchill, *Lord Randolph Churchill* (London: Odhams, 1952, 2 vols.), and J. L. Garvin and Julian Amery, *Life of Joseph Chamberlain* (London: Macmillan, 1932–1951, 4 vols.).

ECONOMIC AND SOCIAL HISTORY

Sir John Clapham's *Concise Economic History of Britain from the Earliest Times to 1870* (Cambridge: Cambridge University Press, 1949), is useful; his *Economic History of Modern Britain: vol. I. The Early Railway Age, vol. II. Free Trade and Steel, vol. III. Machines and National Rivalries* (Cambridge: Cambridge University Press, 1926–1938), is of fundamental importance. Though very detailed, it is not as difficult to read as it appears. Shorter economic histories are S. G. Checkland, *The Rise of Industrial Society in England 1815–1885* (New York: St. Martin's, 1964), C. R. Fay, *Great Britain from Adam Smith to the Present Day* (New York: McKay, 1928), Gilbert Slater, *The Growth of Modern England* (Boston: Houghton Mifflin, 1932), and T. K. Derry and T. L. Jarman, *The Making of Modern Britain: Life and Work from George III to Elizabeth II* (New York: New York University Press, 1956). W. T. Jackman, *The Development of Transportation in Modern England* (London: F. Cass, 1962, 2 vols.), is a standard work.

The condition of the people in the first half of the century is described in F. O. Darvall, *Popular Disturbances and Public Order in Regency England* (London: Oxford University Press, 1934), in G. D. H. Cole and Raymond Postgate, *The British Common People 1746–1938* (cited above), in G. D. H. Cole, *Life of William Cobbett* (London: Collins, 1925), in Graham Wallas, *Life of Francis Place* (New York: Knopf, 1919), in J. L. and Barbara Hammond, *The Bleak Age* (West Drayton, Middlesex: Penguin Books, 1947), which presents a very gloomy view, and in the same authors' *Lord Shaftesbury* (London: Constable, 1936). Sidney and Beatrice Webb, *History of Trade Unionism* (New York: McKay, 1920), is a standard work; and Frank Podmore, *Robert Owen: A Biography* (New York: Appleton, 1924), Ford K. Brown, *Fathers of the Victorians: The Age of Wilberforce* (Cambridge: Cambridge University Press, 1961), are interesting books. Among the best works dealing with the Chartists are Mark Hovell, *The Chartist Movement* (Manchester: University of Manchester Press; New York: McKay, 1918), G. D. H. Cole, *Chartist Portraits* (London: Macmillan, 1941), and Asa Briggs, *Chartist Studies* (New York: St. Martin's, 1959).

Many aspects of social life during the middle portion of the century are ably described in G. M. Young, ed., *Early Victorian England 1830–1865* (London: Oxford University Press, 1934, 2 vols.), of which one chapter printed separately, G. M. Young,

Victorian England. Portrait of an Age (London: Oxford University Press, 1960, paperback), is a brilliant survey of the era, though not easy for the beginner to follow. George Macaulay Trevelyan, *English Social History*, cited above, contains good chapters on the nineteenth century. A book of fundamental importance is G. Kitson Clark, *The Making of Victorian England* (Cambridge, Mass.: Harvard University Press, 1962), which describes the social forces at work and explains how they formed the background for political change. The works of Asa Briggs, *Victorian People: Some Reassessments of People, Institutions, Ideas, and Events 1851–1867* (London: Odhams, 1954), *The Age of Improvement* (New York: McKay, 1959), *1851* (London: Historical Association, 1951), and *Victorian Cities* (London: Odhams, 1964) are important. J. W. Dodds, *The Age of Paradox: A Biography of England 1841–1851* (New York: Holt, Rinehart and Winston, 1952), W. E. Houghton, *The Victorian Frame of Mind 1830–1870* (New Haven: Yale University Press, 1957), and two older books, George Macaulay Trevelyan, *Life of John Bright* (London: Constable, 1913), and John McCunn, *Six Radical Thinkers* (London: E. Arnold, 1907), add to the picture in various ways. An important book dealing with administration and legislation is David Roberts, *Victorian Origins of the British Welfare State* (New Haven: Yale University Press, 1960).

Of a host of works dealing with the latter part of the century, one might mention H. M. Lynd, *England in the 1880's* (New York: Oxford University Press, 1945), H. Wickham Steed, *The Press* (Harmondsworth, Middlesex: Penguin Books, 1938), Sir Edward Cook, *Delane of the Times* (London: Constable, 1916), Holbrook Jackson, *The Eighteen Nineties* (New York: Knopf, 1922), Herman Ausubel, *In Hard Times. Reformers among the Late Victorians* (New York: Columbia University Press, 1960), M. I. Cole, *The Story of Fabian Socialism* (Stanford: Stanford University Press, 1961), A. M. MacBriar, *Fabian Socialism and English Politics 1884–1918* (Cambridge: Cambridge University Press, 1962), and D. C. Somervell, *British Thought in the Nineteenth Century* (London: Methuen, 1929).

FOREIGN AFFAIRS

A good short survey, embodying the results of modern research, is R. W. Seton-Watson, *Britain in Europe 1789–1914: A Survey of Foreign Policy* (New York: Macmillan, 1937). A. Cecil, *British Foreign Secretaries 1807–1916* (London: G. Bell, 1927), is a more popular account. Special studies include C. K. Webster, *The Foreign Policy of Castlereagh 1815–1822* (London: G. Bell, 1925), H. W. V. Temperley, *The Foreign Policy of Canning 1822–1827* (London: G. Bell, 1925), H. C. F. Bell, *Life of Palmerston* (New York: McKay, 1936, 2 vols.), Lady Gwendolen Cecil, *Life of Robert, Marquess of Salisbury* (London: Hodder and Stoughton, 1921–1932, 4 vols.), A. F. Pribram, *England and the International Policy of the European Great Powers* (Oxford: Clarendon Press, 1931), and A. J. P. Taylor, *Struggle for Mastery in Europe 1848–1918* (Oxford: Clarendon Press, 1954).

THE EMPIRE

James A. Williamson, *A Short History of British Expansion*, cited above, remains a good guide; other surveys include Paul Knaplund, *The British Empire 1815–1939* (New York: Harper & Row, 1941), Eric A. Walker, *The British Empire: Its Structure and Spirit 1497–1953* (Cambridge: Bowes and Bowes, 1953), and Hector Bolitho, *The British Empire* (London: Batsford, 1948). In addition to P. E. Roberts and to Edward Thompson and G. T. Garrett, cited above, a useful book is Henry Dodwell, *A Sketch of the History of India from 1858 to 1918* (London: Longmans, 1925). South Africa may be studied in Eric A. Walker, *The Great Trek* (London: A. & C. Black, 1934), in the same author's *History of South Africa* (New York: McKay, 1957), in C. W. de Kiewiet, *A History of South Africa, Social and Economic* (Oxford: Clarendon Press, 1941), in Basil Williams, *Cecil Rhodes* (New York: Constable, 1921), and in W. K. Hancock, *Smuts: The Sanguine Years 1870–1919* (Cambridge: Cambridge University

Press, 1962). See further Lord Cromer, *Modern Egypt* (London: Macmillan, 1908, 2 vols.), George Young, *Egypt* (London: Benn, 1927), B. M. Allen, *Gordon and the Sudan* (London: Macmillan, 1931), Lord Elton, *General Gordon* (London: Collins, 1954). A modern interpretation is Ronald Robinson and John Gallagher with Alice Denny, *Africa and the Victorians. The Climax of Imperialism* (New York: St. Martin's, 1961). For other aspects of the empire, see Carl F. Wittke, *History of Canada* (New York: Appleton, 1941), George M. Wrong, *The Canadians: The Story of a People* (New York: Macmillan, 1938), and Ernest Scott, *Short History of Australia* (London: Oxford University Press, 1916).

CONTEMPORARY WRITINGS

Much about English history in the nineteenth century may be gathered from the novels of Charles Dickens, Anthony Trollope, and George Eliot, from the poems of Tennyson, from S. Smiles, *Self-Help* (1859), J. S. Mill, *On Liberty* (1859), *Representative Government* (1861), *Autobiography* (1873), Matthew Arnold, *Culture and Anarchy* (1869), Walter Baghot, *The English Constitution* (1867), and from the political memoirs of Charles Greville. The fullest edition is Lytton Strachey and Roger Fulford, eds., *The Greville Memoirs 1814–1860* (London: Macmillan, 1938, 8 vols.).

THE TWENTIETH CENTURY

SURVEYS

The best and indeed the only survey of the entire period is Alfred F. Havighurst, *Twentieth Century Britain* (New York: Harper & Row, 1966, paperback). Detailed and well informed, this is an excellent account of politics and of the thinking of the time. It deals only briefly with military and naval operations. Another useful book, though even more of a survey, is Henry Pelling, *Modern Britain 1885–1955* (Edinburgh: T. Nelson, 1960). David Thomson, *England in the Twentieth Century 1914–1963* (London: Penguin Books, 1965), covers a great deal of ground rather lightly. An older book, J. A. R. Marriott, *Modern England 1885–1945* (London: Methuen, 1948), contains a great deal of information for the earlier period but becomes thin as it approaches its conclusion.

Two outstanding books cover large portions of the period. One is *Britain between the Wars 1918–1940* by Charles Loch Mowat (Chicago: University of Chicago Press, 1955), excellent for political, for social and economic history, and for bibliographical information. The other is the last volume of the Oxford History, A. J. P. Taylor, *English History 1914–1945* (New York: Oxford University Press, 1965). This admirable volume contains a wealth of information, is well written, provides an excellent bibliography, and approaches its subject in a spirit of keen and penetrating analysis.

1900–1914

The period before the war is covered by Robert Rhodes James, *Rosebery* (London: Weidenfield and Nicolson, 1963), Kenneth Young, *Arthur James Balfour* (London: G. Bell, 1963), J. A. Spender, *The Life of the Right Hon. Sir Henry Campbell-Bannerman* (London: Holden and Stoughton, 1923, 2 vols.), Roy Jenkins, *Asquith* (London: Collins, 1964), J. A. Spender and Cyril Asquith, *Life of Lord Oxford and Asquith* (London: Hutchinson, 1932, 2 vols.), Sir Philip Magnus, *King Edward the Seventh* (London: J. Murray, 1964), Simon Nowell-Smith, ed., *Edwardian England 1901–1914* (London, New York: Oxford University Press, 1964), W. S. Adams, *Edwardian Heritage. A Study in British History 1901–1906* (London: F. Muller, 1949), and F. J. C. Hearnshaw, ed., *Edwardian England, A. D. 1901–1910* (London: Benn, 1933). Special topics are discussed in Emily Allyn, *Lords Versus Commons: A Century of Conflict and Compromise 1830–1930* (New York: Appleton, 1931), Roy Jenkins, *Mr. Balfour's Poodle* (London: Heinemann, 1954), George Dangerfield, *The Strange Death of Liberal England* (New York: Capricorn, 1961), Roger Fulford, *Votes for Women. The*

Story of a Struggle (London: Faber, 1957), George M. Monger, *The End of Isolation: British Foreign Policy 1900–1907* (Camden, N.J.: Nelson, 1963), Lord Newton, *Lord Lansdowne* (London: Macmillan, 1929), and E. L. Woodward, *Great Britain and the German Navy* (Oxford: Clarendon Press, 1935).

THE FIRST WORLD WAR

The military aspects of the war are covered briefly in Cyril Falls, *The First World War* (London: Longmans, 1960), C. R. M. F. Cruttwell, *A History of the Great War* (Oxford: Clarendon Press, 1934), and Sir James Edmonds, *A Short History of World War I* (New York: Oxford University Press, 1951).

Politics in England during the war may be studied in Sir Harold Nicolson, *King George the Fifth: His Life and Reign* (London: Constable, 1952), A. J. P. Taylor, *Politics in Wartime* (London: H. Hamilton, 1964), Thomas Jones, *Lloyd George* (Cambridge, Mass.: Harvard University Press, 1951), Sir Philip Magnus, *Kitchener: Portrait of an Imperialist* (New York: Duton, 1959), Sir Evelyn Wrench, *Alfred Lord Milner* (London: Eyre and Spottiswoode, 1958), Alfred M. Gollin, *Proconsul in Politics: A Study of Lord Milner in Opposition and in Power* (London: A. Bland, 1964), Lord Beaverbrook, *Politicians and the War* (New York: Doubleday, 1928), and the same author's *Men and Power* (London: Hutchinson, 1956).

The increasing powers of the state are illustrated by Sir William Beveridge, *British Food Control* (London: Oxford University Press; New Haven: Yale University Press, 1928), Lord Hankey, *Government Control in War* (Cambridge: Cambridge University Press, 1945), and Samuel J. Hurwitz, *State Intervention in Great Britain 1914–1919* (Cambridge: Cambridge University Press, 1949). The effect of the war upon society is described in Caroline E. Playne, *Society at War 1914–1916* (Boston: Houghton Mifflin, 1931).

BETWEEN THE WARS, 1918–1939

The literature dealing with this period is very large. Two able books cited above, Charles Loch Mowat, *Britain between the Wars,* and A. J. P. Taylor, *English History 1914–1945,* supply a comprehensive narrative of events. D. C. Somervell, *Between the Wars* (London: Methuen, 1948), is a lively but much slighter volume. One may follow politics and diplomacy during the post-war years in Harold Nicolson, *Peacemaking, 1919* (New York: Harcourt, 1939), in the same author's *Curzon: The Last Phase 1919–1925* (London: Constable, 1934), in Lord Beaverbrook's dramatic *Decline and Fall of Lloyd George* (New York: Duell, Sloan & Pearce, 1963), in Robert Blake, *The Unknown Prime Minister: The Life and Times of Andrew Bonar Law 1858–1923* (London: Eyre and Spottiswoode, 1955), in John Raymond, ed., *The Baldwin Age* (London: Eyre and Spottiswoode, 1960), in Julian Symons, *The General Strike* (London: Cresset, 1957), and in John Montgomery, *The Twenties* (New York: Macmillan, 1957).

For the rise of the Labor party to power and its collapse in 1931, see Henry Pelling, *Short History of the Labour Party* (London: Macmillan; New York: St. Martin's, 1965), Carl F. Brand, *The British Labour Party: A Short History* (Stanford: Stanford University Press, 1964), Philip P. Poirier, *The Advent of the British Labour Party* (New York: Columbia University Press, 1958), Richard W. Lynam, *The First Labour Government, 1924* (London: Chapman and Hall, 1957), Reginald Bassett, *Nineteen Thirty-One: Political Crisis* (London, New York: Macmillan, 1958), and Dean Eugene McHenry, *The Labour Party in Transition 1931–1938* (London: Routledge, 1938).

Social changes may be followed in David C. Marsh, *The Changing Social Structure of England and Wales 1871–1951* (New York: Humanities Press, 1958), in Robert Graves and Alan Hodge, *The Long Week-End: A Social History of Great Britain 1918–1939* (New York: Norton, 1963), in J. B. Priestley, *English Journey* (New York: Harper & Row, 1934), and in Malcolm Muggeridge, *The Thirties, 1930–1940, in Great Britain* (London: H. Hamilton, 1940).

For diplomacy in the years of appeasement see P. A. Reynolds, *British Foreign Policy in the Inter-War Years* (New York: McKay, 1954), Keith Feiling, *Life of Neville Chamberlain* (London: Macmillan, 1946), Thomas Jones, *Diary with Letters, 1931–1950* (New York: Oxford University Press, 1954), K. W. Watkins, *Britain Divided. The Effect of the Spanish Civil War on British Political Opinion* (Camden, N.J.: Nelson, 1963), R. W. Seton-Watson, *Britain and the Dictators. A Survey of Post-War British Policy* (New York: Macmillan; Cambridge: Cambridge University Press, 1938), and A. J. P. Taylor, *The Origins of the Second World War* (London: H. Hamilton, 1961).

THE SECOND WORLD WAR

Two brief histories of the war are Cyril Falls, *The Second World War: A Short History* (London: Methuen, 1950), and Louis L. Snyder, *The War. A Concise History 1939–1945* (New York: Messner, 1960). Winston Churchill deals with the war in the grand manner, *The Second World War* (Boston: Houghton Mifflin, 1948–1954, 6 vols.). The early years of the war are described in Basil Collier, *The Battle of Britain* (New York: Macmillan, 1962), and in Ronald Wheatley, *Operation Sea Lion* (Oxford: Clarendon Press, 1958), which deals with Hitler's invasion plans.

ENGLAND SINCE THE SECOND WORLD WAR

Labor's period of power from 1945 to 1951 is described in Maurice Bruce, *The Coming of the Welfare State* (London: Batsford, 1961), Robert A. Brady, *Crisis in Britain: Plans and Achievements of the Labour Government* (University of California Press, 1950), Richard Titmuss, *Income Distribution and Social Change* (London: G. Allen, 1962), M. Penelope Hall, *Social Services of Modern Britain* (London: Routledge, 1963), Benjamin W. Lewis, *British Planning and Nationalization* (New York: Twentieth Century Fund, 1952), and Emanuel Shinwell, *The Labour Story* (London: Macdonald, 1963).

Social changes are described in Anthony Sampson, *Anatomy of Britain* (New York: Harper & Row, 1962), Anthony Hartley, *A State of Britain* (London: Hutchinson, 1963), and Arthur Marwick, *The Explosion of British Society 1914–1962* (London: Pan Books, 1963).

EMPIRE AND COMMONWEALTH

Paul Knaplund, *Britain, Commonwealth and Empire* (New York: Harper & Row, 1955), is a workmanlike textbook covering the first half of the century. *The Indian Problem*, by R. Coupland (New York: Oxford University Press, 1944), is an elaborate analysis of Indian affairs before partition and suggests various solutions that disappeared in the rush of events. Nicholas Mansergh, an authority on the contemporary history of the Commonwealth, is the author of *South Africa 1906–1961: The Price of Magnanimity* (New York: Praeger, 1962), *The Irish Free State, Its Government and Politics* (New York: Macmillan, 1934), and *Survey of British Commonwealth Affairs* (New York: Oxford University Press, 1958, 2 vols.). A. J. Barker, *Suez: The Seven Day War* (New York: Praeger, 1965), Leon D. Epstein, *British Policies in the Suez Crisis* (Urbana: University of Illinois Press, 1964), and William F. Longgood, *Suez Story: Key to the Middle East* (New York: Greenberg, 1957), deal with a famous episode. Two recent books are Frank H. Underhill, *The British Commonwealth: An Experiment in Cooperation among Nations* (Durham, N. C.: Duke University Press, 1956), and Kenneth Bradley, ed., *The Living Commonwealth* (London: Hutchinson, 1961). An excellent article by Arthur C. Turner, "The Commonwealth: Evolution or Dissolution?" is to be found in *Current History*, XLVI (May 1964).

HEADS OF CABINETS AND PRIME MINISTERS
With Dates of Taking Office

April 1721	(Sir) Robert Walpole	Whig
February 1742	{ Earl of Wilmington John Lord Carteret (Earl Granville)	Whig
August 1743	Hon. Henry Pelham	Whig
February 1746	Earl of Bath	Whig
February 1746	Hon. Henry Pelham	Whig
March 1754 (Resigned November 1756)	Duke of Newcastle	Whig
June 1757	{ Duke of Newcastle William Pitt	Whig
March 1761	{ Duke of Newcastle Earl of Bute	Whig
May 1762	Earl of Bute	Whig
April 1763	George Grenville	Whig
July 1765	Marquis of Rockingham	Whig
July 1766 August 1766	{ William Pitt, Earl of Chatham Duke of Grafton	Whig
November 1768	Duke of Grafton	Whig
February 1770	Lord North	Whig
March 1782	{ Marquis of Rockingham Earl of Shelburne	Whig
July 1782	Earl of Shelburne	Whig
April 1783	{ Duke of Portland Lord North Charles James Fox	Whig
December 1783	William Pitt, the Younger	Whig
March 1801	Henry Addington	Whig
May 1804	William Pitt, the Younger	Whig
January 1806	{ Lord Grenville Charles James Fox Henry Addington, Lord Sidmouth (The Ministry of All the Talents)	Coalition
March 1807	Duke of Portland	Tory
September 1809	Spencer Perceval	Tory
June 1812	Earl of Liverpool	Tory
April 1827	George Canning	Tory
September 1827	Viscount Goderich	Tory
January 1828	Duke of Wellington	Tory
November 1830	Earl Grey	Whig
July 1834	Viscount Melbourne	Whig
December 1834	Sir Robert Peel	Conservative
April 1835	Viscount Melbourne	Whig
September 1841	Sir Robert Peel	Conservative
July 1846	Lord John Russell	Whig
February 1852	Earl of Derby	Conservative

December 1852	Earl of Aberdeen	Coalition
February 1855	Viscount Palmerston	Whig
February 1858	Earl of Derby	Conservative
June 1859	Viscount Palmerston	Whig
October 1865	Earl Russell	Whig
June 1866	Earl of Derby	Conservative
February 1868	Benjamin Disraeli	Conservative
December 1868	W. E. Gladstone	Liberal
February 1874	Benjamin Disraeli	Conservative
April 1880	W. E. Gladstone	Liberal
June 1885	Marquess of Salisbury	Conservative
February 1886	W. E. Gladstone	Liberal
August 1886	Marquess of Salisbury	Conservative
August 1892	W. E. Gladstone	Liberal
March 1894	Earl of Rosebery	Liberal
June 1895	Marquess of Salisbury	Conservative
July 1902	A. J. Balfour	Conservative
December 1905	Sir Henry Campbell-Bannerman	Liberal
April 1908	H. H. Asquith	Liberal
May 1915	H. H. Asquith	Coalition
December 1916	David Lloyd George	Coalition
January 1919 (formed) October 1919 (operative)	David Lloyd George	Coalition
October 1922	A. Bonar Law	Conservative
May 1923	Stanley Baldwin	Conservative
January 1924	J. Ramsay MacDonald	Labor
November 1924	Stanley Baldwin	Conservative
June 1929	J. Ramsay MacDonald	Labor
August 1931	J. Ramsay MacDonald	National
November 1931	J. Ramsay MacDonald	National
June 1935	Stanley Baldwin	National
May 1937	Neville Chamberlain	National
May 1940	Winston S. Churchill	Coalition
May 1945	Winston S. Churchill	Conservative
July 1945	Clement R. Atlee	Labor
October 1951	Winstin S. Churchill	Conservative
April 1955	Sir Anthony Eden	Conservative
January 1957	Harold Macmillan	Conservative
October 1963	Sir Alec Douglas-Home	Conservative
October 1964	Harold Wilson	Labor
June 1970	Edward Heath	Conservative

index

Abbott, George, archbishop of Canterbury, 350

Abdur Rahman, Amir of Afghanistan, 662

Abelard, 116, 118, 121

Abercrombie, Patrick, 778

Abercromby, James, general, 478

Aberdeen, 371

Aberdeen, George Hamilton-Gordon, Earl of: and Crimean War (1854–1856), 640–641; forms Cabinet, 640

Aboukir Bay (Egypt), 571

Acadia. *See* Nova Scotia

Achin, 312, 402

Acre, 88

Act of Settlement, 423–424, 443

Acton Burnell, burgesses meet at, 149

Acts of Trade, 431, 456, 572, 581; as a cause of the American Revolution, 523–525

Addington, Henry (Lord Sidmouth), 574–575, 576, 585

Addison, Joseph, writer, 436, 499

Adela, mother of Stephen of Blois, 72

Adelard of Bath, 119

Adolf of Nassau, King of Germany, 145

Adrian IV, Pope, 116

Afghanistan, 660–662, 683, 702, 703; Gladstone's handling of, 660–662; war against (1836–1841), 643; war with (1878), 660

Africa, 431, 675, 683, 739, 746–750, 775–776; partition of, 678–680. *See also by colony, by country,* East Africa, North Africa, South Africa, West Africa

Agadir, crisis over (1911), 295, 703

Agincourt, Battle of, 155, 188

Agra, 482

Agreement of the People, 387, 389, 390

Agricola, Roman governor, 11

Agriculture, 152, 206; Anglo-Saxon, 17, 33–36; effect of Black Death on, 162–163, 165; effect of Norman Conquest on, 61–62; in eighteenth century, 446, 491–492, 542–544; and enclosures, 263–264, 544; in fifteenth century, shrinks/expands, 194, 198; medieval, 122–126; in nineteenth century, 580, 581–582, 591–592, 619, 623, 626, 656, 660, 664, 665, 672–674, 684; prehistoric, 4–5, 6, 8, 9; in Roman Britain, 12; and sale of Crown lands, 264; in seventeenth century, 377–378, 403–404; in Tudor period, 262–265; in twentieth century, 699, 732, 755, 756

Aidan, Celtic monk, 19

Aids, feudal, 53, 57

Aix-la-Chapelle, Peace of, 468–469, 471

Alamein, El, 748; Battle of, 749

Albert of Saxe-Coburg-Gotha, Prince: death of, 697; marries Queen Victoria, 609

Alexander III, King of Scots, 141

Alexander I, Czar of Russia, 576, 578, 586

Alexander II, Czar of Russia, 682

Alexander, Sir Harold, general, 749

Alexandra of Denmark, Princess, 647

Alexius Comnenus, Eastern Roman Emperor, 87

Alfred, King of Wessex, 14, 23, 24, 31, 36, 38, 45, 47; character of, 27–30; and Danes, 27–29; and reconstruction of society, 29

Algeciras conference, 702

Ali Vardi Khan, Nabob of Bengal, 484

Allegiance, Oath of, 343

Allen, William, founds Catholic college at Douai, 283